CME PROJECT
Algebra 1
COMMON CORE

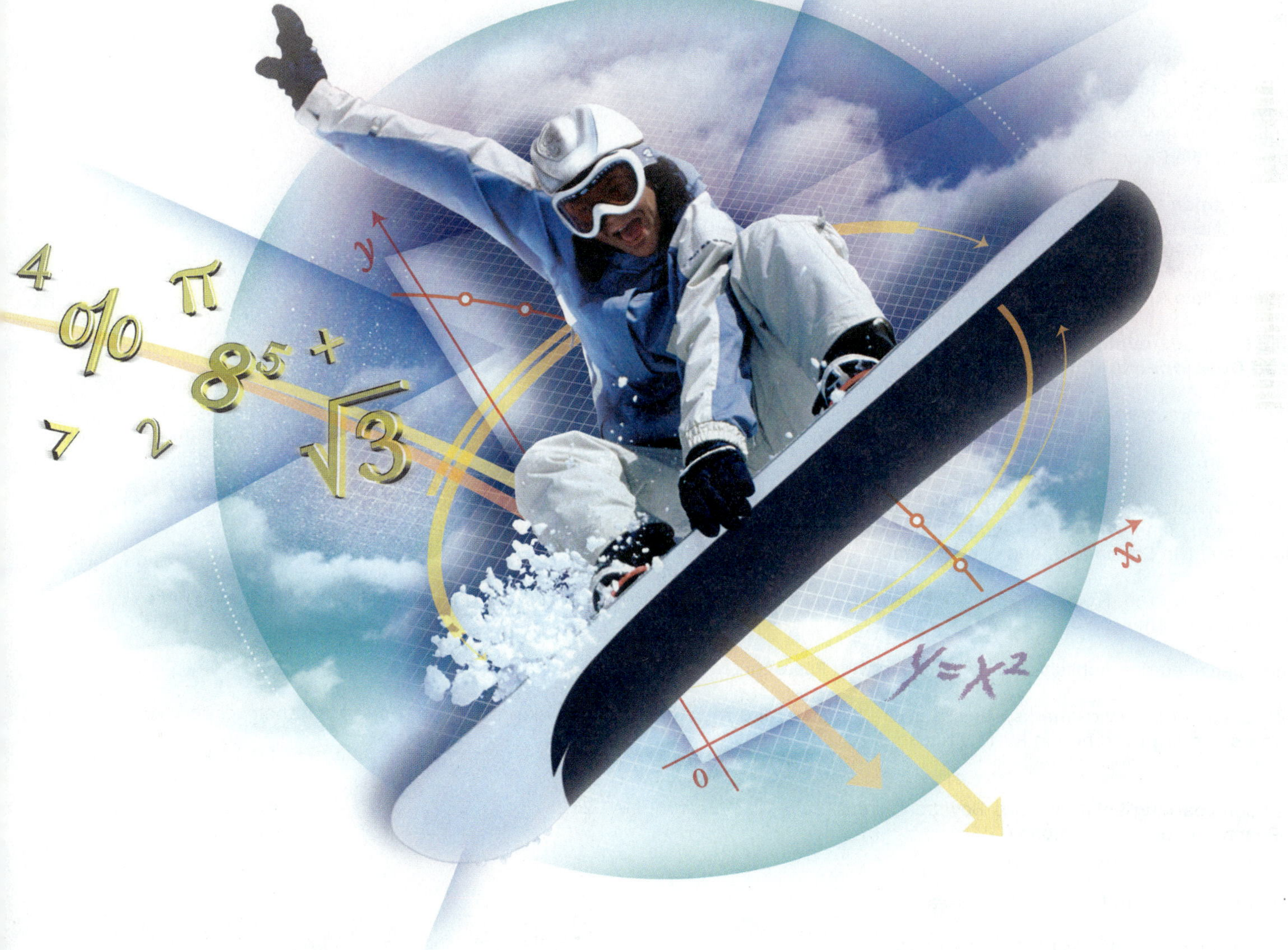

PEARSON

The Center for Mathematics Education Project was developed at Education Development Center, Inc. (EDC) within the Center for Mathematics Education (CME), with partial support from the National Science Foundation.

Education Development Center, Inc.
Center for Mathematics Education
Newton, Massachusetts

This material is based upon work supported by the National Science Foundation under Grant No. ESI-0242476, Grant No. MDR-9252952, and Grant No. ESI-9617369. Any opinions, findings, and conclusions or recommendations expressed in this material are those of the author(s) and do not necessarily reflect the views of the National Science Foundation.

Cover Art: 9 Surf Studios; Mike Chew/Corbis; Ajosch/AFP/Getty Images

Taken from:

CME Project: Algebra 1
By the CME Project Development Team
Copyright ©2009 by Educational Development Center, Inc.
Published by Pearson Education, Inc.
Upper Saddle River, New Jersey 07458

CME Common Core Additional Lessons: Algebra 1
By the CME Project Development Team
Copyright ©2012 by Educational Development Center, Inc.
Published by Pearson Education, Inc.
Upper Saddle River, New Jersey 07458

CME Project Development Team
Lead Developer: Al Cuoco

Core Development Team: Anna Baccaglini-Frank, Jean Benson, Nancy Antonellis D'Amato, Daniel Erman, Brian Harvey, Wayne Harvey, Bowen Kerins, Doreen Kilday, Ryota Matsuura, Stephen Maurer, Sarah Sword, Audrey Ting, and Kevin Waterman

Others who contributed include Steve Benson, Paul D'Amato, Robert Devaney, Andrew Golay, Paul Goldenberg, Jane Gorman, C. Jud Hill, Eric Karnowski, Helen Lebowitz, Joseph Leverich, Melanie Palma, Mark Saul, Nin Shteingold, and Brett Thomas.

All rights reserved. No part of this book may be reproduced, in any form or by any means, without permission in writing from the publisher.

This special edition published in cooperation with Pearson Learning Solutions.

All trademarks, service marks, registered trademarks, and registered service marks are the property of their respective owners and are used herein for identification purposes only.

Pearson Learning Solutions, 501 Boylston Street, Suite 900, Boston, MA 02116
A Pearson Education Company
www.pearsoned.com

Printed in the United States of America

1 2 3 4 5 6 7 8 9 10 V011 17 16 15 14 13 12

0002000102716610 95

MD

ISBN 10: 1-256-74146-9
ISBN 13: 978-1-256-74146-6

Contents in Brief

Introduction to the CME Project iv
Contributors v
CME Project Student Handbook xiv
Go Online xxi

Chapter 1 Arithmetic to Algebra 2
Chapter 2 Expressions and Equations 88
Chapter 3 Graphs 186
Chapter 4 Lines 320
Chapter 5 Introduction to Functions 422
Chapter 6 Exponents and Radicals 514
Chapter 7 Polynomials 606
Chapter 8 Quadratics 694

TI-Nspire™ Technology Handbook 790
Tables
    Math Symbols 800
    Measures 801
    Formulas From Geometry 802
Properties and Theorems 803
Glossary 806
Selected Answers 814
Index 846
Acknowledgments 853

Introduction to the CME Project

The CME Project, developed by EDC's Center for Mathematics Education, is a new NSF-funded high school program, organized around the familiar courses of algebra 1, geometry, algebra 2, and precalculus. The CME Project provides teachers and schools with a third alternative to the choice between traditional texts driven by basic skill development and more progressive texts that have unfamiliar organizations. This program gives teachers the option of a problem-based, student-centered program, organized around the mathematical themes with which teachers and parents are familiar. Furthermore, the tremendous success of NSF-funded middle school programs has left a need for a high school program with similar rigor and pedagogy. The CME Project fills this need.

The goal of the CME Project is to help students acquire a deep understanding of mathematics. Therefore, the mathematics here is rigorous. We took great care to create lesson plans that, while challenging, will capture and engage students of all abilities and improve their mathematical achievement.

The Program's Approach

The organization of the CME Project provides students the time and focus they need to develop fundamental mathematical ways of thinking. Its primary goal is to develop in students robust mathematical proficiency.

- The program employs innovative instructional methods, developed over decades of classroom experience and informed by research, that help students master mathematical topics.

- One of the core tenets of the CME Project is to focus on developing students' Habits of Mind, or ways in which students approach and solve mathematical challenges.

- The program builds on lessons learned from high-performing countries: develop an idea thoroughly and then revisit it only to deepen it; organize ideas in a way that is faithful to how they are organized in mathematics; and reduce clutter and extraneous topics.

- It also employs the best American models that call for grappling with ideas and problems as preparation for instruction, moving from concrete problems to abstractions and general theories, and situating mathematics in engaging contexts.

- The CME Project is a comprehensive curriculum that meets the dual goals of mathematical rigor and accessibility for a broad range of students.

About CME

EDC's Center for Mathematics Education, led by mathematician and teacher **Al Cuoco**, brings together an eclectic staff of mathematicians, teachers, cognitive scientists, education researchers, curriculum developers, specialists in educational technology, and teacher educators, internationally known for leadership across the entire range of K–16 mathematics education. We aim to help students and teachers in this country experience the thrill of solving problems and building theories, understand the history of ideas behind the evolution of mathematical disciplines, and appreciate the standards of rigor that are central to mathematical culture.

Contributors to the CME Project

National Advisory Board The National Advisory Board met early in the project, providing critical feedback on the instructional design and the overall organization. Members include

Richard Askey, University of Wisconsin
Edward Barbeau, University of Toronto
Hyman Bass, University of Michigan
Carol Findell, Boston University
Arthur Heinricher, Worcester Polytechnic Institute
Roger Howe, Yale University
Barbara Janson, Janson Associates
Kenneth Levasseur, University of Massachusetts, Lowell
James Madden, Louisiana State University, Baton Rouge
Jacqueline Miller, Education Development Center
James Newton, University of Maryland
Robert Segall, Greater Hartford Academy of Mathematics and Science
Glenn Stevens, Boston University
Herbert Wilf, University of Pennsylvania
Hung-Hsi Wu, University of California, Berkeley

Core Mathematical Consultants **Dick Askey**, **Ed Barbeau**, and **Roger Howe** have been involved in an even more substantial way, reviewing chapters and providing detailed and critical advice on every aspect of the program. Dick and Roger spent many hours reading and criticizing drafts, brainstorming with the writing team, and offering advice on everything from the logical organization to the actual numbers used in problems. We can't thank them enough.

Teacher Advisory Board The Teacher Advisory Board for the CME Project was essential in helping us create an effective format for our lessons that embodies the philosophy and goals of the program. Their debates about pedagogical issues and how to develop mathematical topics helped to shape the distinguishing features of the curriculum so that our lessons work effectively in the classroom. The advisory board includes

> Jayne Abbas, Richard Coffey, Charles Garabedian, Dennis Geller, Eileen Herlihy, Doreen Kilday, Gayle Masse, Hugh McLaughlin, Nancy McLaughlin, Allen Olsen, Kimberly Osborne, Brian Shoemaker, and Benjamin Sinwell

Field-Test Teachers Our field-test teachers gave us the benefit of their classroom experience by teaching from our draft lessons and giving us extensive, critical feedback that shaped the drafts into realistic, teachable lessons. They shared their concerns, questions, challenges, and successes and kept us focused on the real world. Some of them even welcomed us into their classrooms as co-teachers to give us the direct experience with students that we needed to hone our lessons. Working with these expert professionals has been one of the most gratifying parts of the development—they are "highly qualified" in the most profound sense.

California **Barney Martinez,** Jefferson High School, Daly City; **Calvin Baylon** and **Jaime Lao,** Bell Junior High School, San Diego; **Colorado** **Rocky Cundiff,** Ignacio High School, Ignacio; **Illinois** **Jeremy Kahan, Tammy Nguyen,** and **Stephanie Pederson,** Ida Crown Jewish Academy, Chicago; **Massachusetts** **Carol Martignette, Chris Martino** and **Kent Werst,** Arlington High School, Arlington, **Larry Davidson,** Boston University Academy, Boston; **Joe Bishop** and **Carol Rosen,** Lawrence High School, Lawrence; **Maureen Mulryan,** Lowell High School, Lowell; **Felisa Honeyman,** Newton South High School, Newton Centre; **Jim Barnes** and **Carol Haney,** Revere High School, Revere; **New Hampshire** **Jayne Abbas** and **Terin Voisine,** Cawley Middle School, Hooksett; **New Mexico** **Mary Andrews,** Las Cruces High School, Las Cruces; **Ohio** **James Stallworth,** Hughes Center, Cincinnati; **Texas** **Arnell Crayton,** Bellaire High School, Bellaire; **Utah** **Troy Jones,** Waterford School, Sandy; **Washington** **Dale Erz, Kathy Greer, Karena Hanscom,** and **John Henry,** Port Angeles High School, Port Angeles; **Wisconsin** **Annette Roskam,** Rice Lake High School, Rice Lake.

Special thanks go to our colleagues at Pearson, most notably Elizabeth Lehnertz, Joe Will, and Stewart Wood. The program benefits from their expertise in every way, from the actual mathematics to the design of the printed page.

1 Arithmetic to Algebra

Chapter Opener 2

Investigation 1A

    1.0 Habits of Mind 4

  The Tables of Arithmetic 8

    1.01 Getting Started 9
    1.02 Thinking About Negative Numbers 12
    1.03 Extending the Addition Table 17
    1.04 Extending the Multiplication Table 23
    1.05 The Basic Rules of Arithmetic—Properties of Operations 28
    Mathematical Reflections 33

Investigation 1B

  The Number Line 34

    1.06 Getting Started 35
    1.07 Numbers Besides the Integers—Fractions 37
    1.08 Decimals—Addresses on the Number Line 41
    1.09 Number Line Addition 46
    1.10 Number Line Multiplication 51
    Mathematical Reflections 56

Mid-Chapter Test 57

Investigation 1C

  The Algorithms of Arithmetic 58

    1.11 Getting Started 59
    1.12 Addition and Subtraction Algorithms 61
    1.13 Adding and Subtracting Fractions 67
    1.14 Multiplication Algorithms 71
    1.15 Multiplying and Dividing Fractions 77
    Mathematical Reflections 81

Project: Using Mathematical Habits

    Lo . . . ong Division 82

Chapter Review 84

Chapter Test 86

2 Expressions and Equations

Chapter Opener 88

Investigation 2A — Expressions 90
2.01 Getting Started 91
2.02 Modeling General Situations—Writing Expressions 93
2.03 Evaluating Expressions 98
2.04 Simplifying Expressions 103
2.05 Rephrasing the Basic Rules 110
Mathematical Reflections 115

Investigation 2B — Equations 116
2.06 Getting Started 117
2.07 Reversing Operations 120
2.08 Solving Equations by Backtracking 126
Mathematical Reflections 132

Mid-Chapter Test 133

Investigation 2C — Solving Linear Equations 134
2.09 Getting Started 135
2.10 When Backtracking Does Not Work 138
2.11 The Basic Moves for Solving Equations 143
2.12 Solutions of Linear Equations 148
2.13 Focus on the Distributive Property 153
Mathematical Reflections 157

Investigation 2D — Word Problems 158
2.14 Getting Started 159
2.15 Building Equations 162
2.16 Solving Word Problems 167
2.17 More Than One Variable—
    Solving in Terms of Each Other 172
Mathematical Reflections 178

Project: Using Mathematical Habits
Good Questions About Perfect Squares 179

Chapter Review 180

Chapter Test 182

Cumulative Review 184

3 Graphs

Chapter Opener **186**

Investigation 3A — Introduction to Coordinates 188
- 3.01 Getting Started 189
- 3.02 Transformations 196
- 3.03 Distance and Absolute Value 202
- 3.04 Graphing Related Quantities 210
- Mathematical Reflections 217

Investigation 3B — Statistical Data 218
- 3.05 Getting Started 219
- 3.06 Mean, Median, and Mode 223
- 3.07 Data Displays 230
- 3.08 Paired Comparisons— Box-and-Whisker Plots 237
- 3.09 Catogorical Data 245
- 3.10 Two-Variable Data—Scatter Plots 253
- Mathematical Reflections 262

Mid-Chapter Test **263**

Investigation 3C — Equations and Their Graphs 264
- 3.11 Getting Started 265
- 3.12 Equations as Point-Testers 267
- 3.13 Graphing by Plotting 272
- 3.14 Intersection of Graphs 279
- Mathematical Reflections 283

Investigation 3D — Basic Graphs and Translations 284
- 3.15 Getting Started 285
- 3.16 Two Basic Graphs: $y = cx$, $y = \frac{c}{x}$— Direct and Inverse Variation 289
- 3.17 Four More Basic Graphs: $y = x^2$, $y = x^3$, $y = \sqrt{x}$, $y = |x|$ 298
- 3.18 Translating Graphs 305
- Mathematical Reflections 314

Project: Using Mathematical Habits
Drawing With Graphs 315

Chapter Review 316

Chapter Test 318

4 Lines

Chapter Opener 320

4A All About Slope 322
4.01 Getting Started 323
4.02 Pitch and Slope 327
4.03 Rates of Change 333
4.04 Collinearity 348
Mathematical Reflections 347

4B Linear Equations and Graphs 348
4.05 Getting Started 349
4.06 Equations of Lines 353
4.07 Jiffy Graphs: Lines 358
4.08 Overtaking—Slope in Distance-Time Graphs ... 363
Mathematical Reflections 368

Mid-Chapter Test 369

4C Intersections 370
4.09 Getting Started 371
4.10 Solving Systems: Substitution 374
4.11 Slope and Parallel Lines 382
4.12 Solving Systems: Elimination 387
Mathematical Reflections 393

4D Applications of Lines 394
4.13 Getting Started 395
4.14 Inequalities With One Variable 398
4.15 Linear Trends in Data 406
Mathematical Reflections 414

Project: Using Mathematical Habits
Wireless Phone Plans 415

Chapter Review 416

Chapter Test 418

Cumulative Review 420

5 Introduction to Functions

Chapter Opener 422

Investigation 5A
Functions—The Basics 424
- 5.01 Getting Started 425
- 5.02 Building Functions 428
- 5.03 Is It a Function? 434
- 5.04 Naming Functions 440
- 5.05 Function Inputs and Outputs 445
- 5.06 Graphing Functions 449
- Mathematical Reflections 458

Mid-Chapter Test 459

Investigation 5B
Functions, Graphs, and Tables 460
- 5.07 Getting Started 461
- 5.08 Constant Differences 465
- 5.09 Recursive Rules 474
- Mathematical Reflections 481

Investigation 5C
Functions and Situations 482
- 5.10 Getting Started 483
- 5.11 From Situations to Equations 487
- 5.12 From Situations to Recursive Rules 496
- Mathematical Reflections 507

Project: Using Mathematical Habits
Managing Money 508

Chapter Review 510

Chapter Test 512

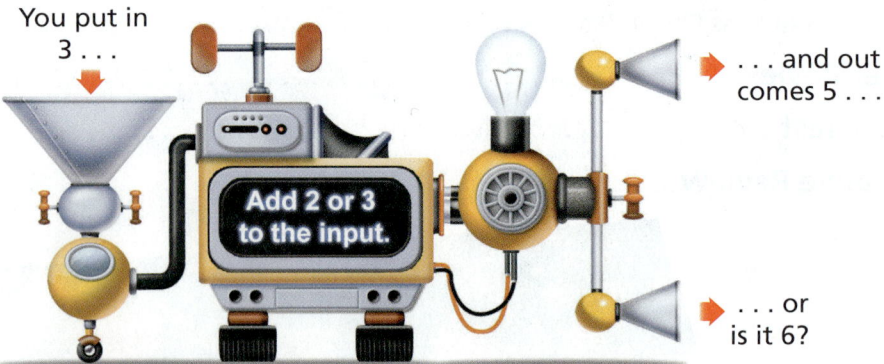

You put in 3 . . .

Add 2 or 3 to the input.

. . . and out comes 5 . . .

. . . or is it 6?

Algebra 1

6 Exponents and Radicals

Chapter Opener **514**

Investigation 6A
Exponents **516**
6.01 Getting Started 517
6.02 Squares, Cubes, and Beyond—
      Some Basic Rules of Exponents 520
6.03 More Basic Rules of Exponents 526
6.04 Zero and Negative Exponents 531
6.05 Scientific Notation 537
Mathematical Reflections 542

Mid-Chapter Test **543**

Investigation 6B
Radicals **544**
6.06 Getting Started 545
6.07 Defining Square Roots 547
6.08 Arithmetic With Square Roots 552
6.09 Conventions for Roots—
      Simplified Forms for Radicals 556
6.10 Rational and Irrational Numbers 561
6.11 Roots, Radicals, and the *n*th Root 568
Mathematical Reflections 573

Investigation 6C
Exponential Expressions and Functions **574**
6.12 Getting Started 575
6.13 Compound Interest 578
6.14 Graphs of Exponential Functions 584
6.15 Constant Ratios 589
Mathematical Reflections 597

Project: Using Mathematical Habits
   Calculating Square Roots 598

Chapter Review 600

Chapter Test 602

Cumulative Review 604

Contents   xi

7 Polynomials

Chapter Opener 606

Investigation 7A

The Need for Identities—Equivalent Expressions 608
- 7.01 Getting Started 609
- 7.02 Form and Function—
  Showing Expressions Are Equivalent 612
- 7.03 The Zero-Product Property—
  $ab = 0 \Rightarrow a = 0$ or $b = 0$ 619
- 7.04 Transforming Expressions—
  Introduction to Polynomial Factoring 625
- Mathematical Reflections 631

Investigation 7B

Polynomials and Their Arithmetic 632
- 7.05 Getting Started 633
- 7.06 Anatomy of a Polynomial 636
- 7.07 Normal Form—Standard Representation of a Polynomial 643
- 7.08 Arithmetic With Polynomials. 649
- Mathematical Reflections 654

Mid-Chapter Test. 655

Investigation 7C

Factoring to Solve: Quadratics. 656
- 7.09 Getting Started 657
- 7.10 Factoring a Difference of Squares 661
- 7.11 Factoring Monic Quadratics—
  When $a = 1$ in $ax^2 + bx + c$ 669
- 7.12 Factoring by Completing the Square 677
- Mathematical Reflections 687

Project: Using Mathematical Habits
  Differences of Squares. 688

Chapter Review 690

Chapter Test 692

8 Quadratics

Chapter Opener 694

Investigation 8A — The Quadratic Formula 696
8.01 Getting Started 697
8.02 Making It Formal—
  Deriving the Quadratic Formula 699
8.03 Going the Other Way—
  Building a Quadratic Equation From Its Roots 706
8.04 Factoring Nonmonic Quadratics—
  When $a \neq 1$ in $ax^2 + bx + c$ 711
Mathematical Reflections 716

Mid-Chapter Test 717

Investigation 8B — Quadratic Graphs and Applications 718
8.05 Getting Started 719
8.06 Optimization—Finding Maximums and Minimums 721
8.07 Graphing Quadratic Equations 727
8.08 Jiffy Graphs: Parabolas 736
Mathematical Reflections 745

Investigation 8C — Working With Quadratics 746
8.09 Getting Started 747
8.10 Solving by Graphing 750
8.11 Inequalities With Two Variables 755
8.12 Graphing Linear Inequalties 763
8.13 Difference Tables of Quadratics 773
Mathematical Reflections 781

Project: Using Mathematical Habits
  Iteration and Fixed Points 782

Chapter Review 784

Chapter Test 786

Cumulative Review 788

CME Project
Student Handbook

What Makes CME Different

Welcome to the CME Project! The goal of this program is to help you develop a deep understanding of mathematics. Throughout this book, you will engage in many different activities to help you develop that deep understanding. Some of these instructional activities may be different from ones you are used to. Below is an overview of some of these elements and why they are an important part of the CME Project.

The Habits of Mind Experience

Mathematical Habits of Mind are the foundation for serious questioning, solid thinking, good problem solving, and critical analysis. These Habits of Mind are what will help you become a mathematical thinker. Throughout the CME Project, you will focus on developing and refining these Habits of Mind.

Lesson 1.0 is an introduction to Habits of Mind. This lesson consists of experiments that allow you to tinker with the mathematical ideas that you will formalize throughout the course.

Developing Habits of Mind

Develop thinking skills. This feature provides you with various methods and approaches to solving problems.

You will develop, use, and revisit specific Habits of Mind throughout the course. These include

- **Process** (how you work through problems)
- **Visualization** (how you "picture" problems)
- **Representation** (what you write down)
- **Patterns** (what you find)
- **Relationships** (what you find or use)

Developing good habits will help you as problems become more complicated.

Habits of Mind

Think. These special margin notes highlight key thinking skills and prompt you to apply your developing Habits of Mind.

You can find **Developing Habits of Mind** **on pages** 20, 29, 38, 42, 47, 52, 72, 77, 105, 120, 122, 153, 173, 203, 204, 223, 225, 237, 269, 274, 280, 290, 294, 300, 307, 310, 328, 335, 378, 401, 409, 419, 441, 446, 475, 489, 523, 615, 622, 626, 645, 661, 681, 700, 712, 723, 728, 729, 731, and 752.

Minds in Action

Discussion of mathematical ideas is an effective method of learning. The Minds in Action feature exposes you to ways of communicating about mathematics.

Join Sasha, Tony, Derman, and others as they think, calculate, predict, and discuss their way towards understanding.

Minds in Action   prologue

Sasha, Tony, and Derman have just skimmed through their CME Project Algebra 1 book.

Sasha Did you notice the student dialogs throughout the book?

Derman Sure did!

Tony They talk and think just the way we do.

Sasha I know! And they even make mistakes sometimes, the way we do.

Tony But I like how they help each other to learn from those mistakes. I bet they use the Habits of Mind I saw all over the book, too.

Sasha That's great! They should help a lot.

You can find **Minds in Action** on pages 17, 67, 99, 103, 121, 143, 197, 206, 240, 272, 292 305, 353, 363, 364, 398, 428, 449, 451, 489, 494, 531, 532, 547, 579, 589, 612, 643, 649, 663, 670, 679, 680, 706, 707, 711, 712, 721, 723, 736, 738, 750, 756, and 776.

Exploring Mathematics

Throughout the CME Project, you will engage in activities that extend your learning and allow you to explore the concepts you learn in greater depth. Two of these activities are In-Class Experiments and Chapter Projects.

In-Class Experiment

In-Class Experiments allow you to explore new concepts and apply the Habits of Mind.

You will explore math as mathematicians do. You start with a question and develop answers through experimentation.

You can find In-Class Experiments on pages 5, 6, 7, 110, 441, 502, 589, 640, and 699.

Chapter Projects

Chapter Projects allow you to apply your Habits of Mind to the content of the chapter. These projects cover many different topics and allow you to explore and engage in greater depth.

Chapter Projects
Using Mathematical Habits

Here is a list of the Chapter Projects and page numbers.

Chapter 1	Lo . . . ong Division	82
Chapter 2	Good Questions About Perfect Squares	179
Chapter 3	Drawing With Graphs	315
Chapter 4	Wireless Phone Plans	415
Chapter 5	Managing Money	508
Chapter 6	Calculating Square Roots	598
Chapter 7	Differences of Squares	688
Chapter 8	Iteration and Fixed Points	782

Using your CME Book

To help you make the most of your CME experience, we are providing the following overview of the organization of your book.

Focusing your Learning

In *Algebra 1*, there are 8 chapters, with each chapter devoted to a mathematical concept. With only 8 chapters, your class will be able to focus on these core concepts and develop a deep understanding of them.

Within each chapter, you will explore a series of Investigations. Each Investigation focuses on an important aspect of the mathematical concept for that chapter.

Student Handbook

The CME Investigation

The goal of each mathematical Investigation is for you to formalize your understanding of the mathematics being taught. There are some common instructional features in each Investigation.

Getting Started

You will launch into each Investigation with a Getting Started lesson that activates prior knowledge and explores new ideas. This lesson provides you the opportunity to grapple with ideas and problems. The goal of these lessons is for you to explore—not all your questions will be answered in these lessons.

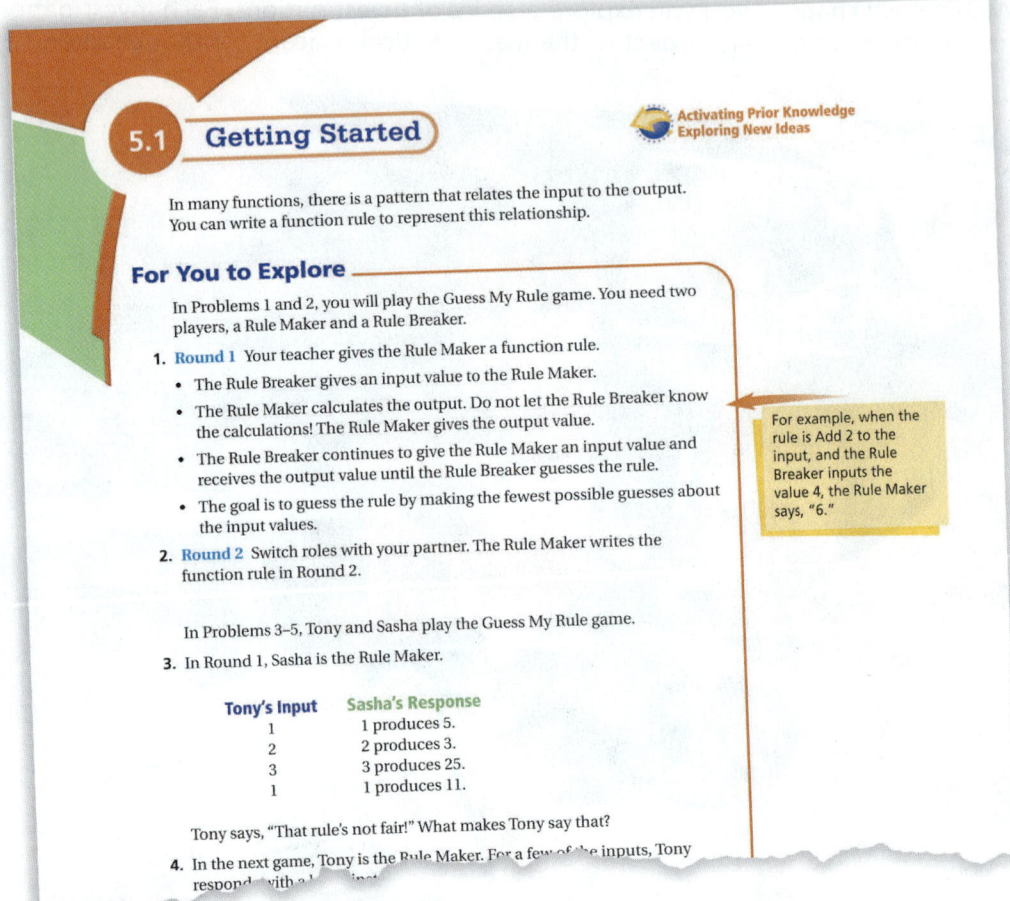

Learning the Mathematics

You will engage in, learn, and practice the mathematics in a variety of ways. The types of learning elements you will find throughout this course include

- **Worked-Out Examples** that model how to solve problems
- **Definitions and Theorems** to summarize key concepts
- **In-Class Experiments** to explore the concepts
- **For You to Do** assignments to check your understanding
- **For Discussion** questions to encourage communication
- **Minds in Action** to model mathematical discussion

Communicating the Mathematics

Minds in Action

Student dialogs
By featuring dialogs between characters, the CME Project exposes you to a way of communicating about mathematics. These dialogs will then become a real part of your classroom!

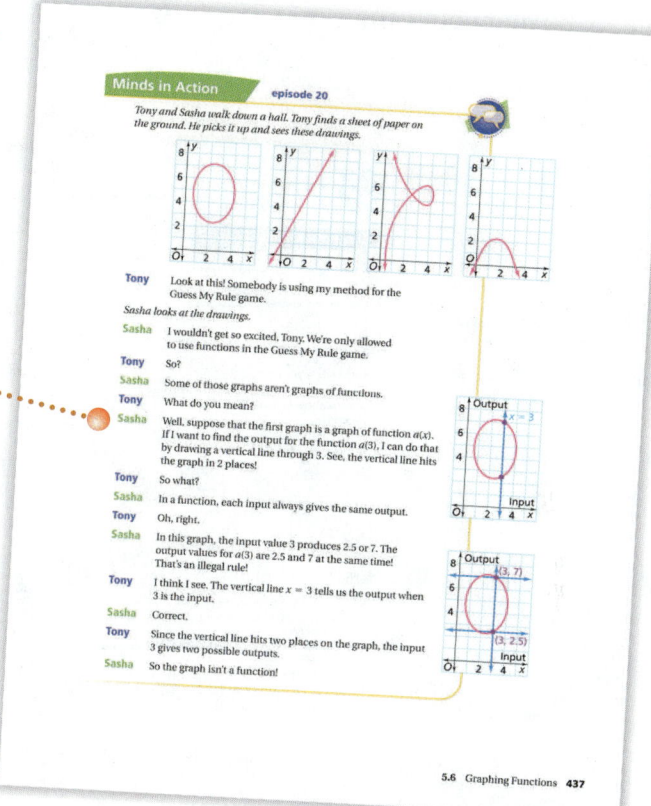

Reflecting on the Mathematics

At the end of each Investigation, Mathematical Reflections give you an opportunity to put ideas together. This feature allows you to demonstrate your understanding of the Investigation and reflect on what you learn.

Student Handbook   xix

Practice

The CME Project views extensive practice as a critical component of a mathematics curriculum. You will have daily opportunities to practice what you learn.

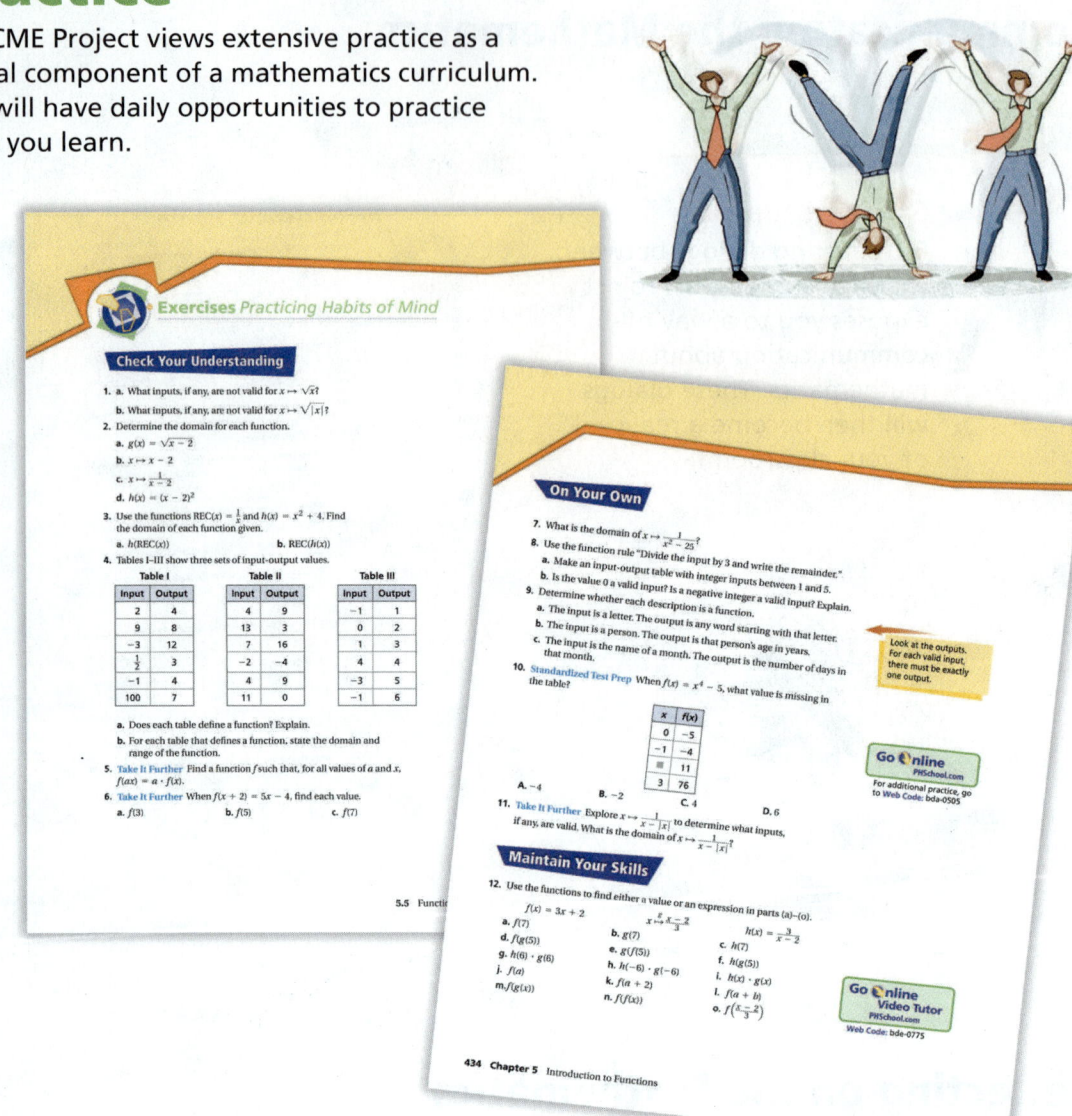

Check Your Understanding
Assess your readiness for independent practice by working through these problems in class.

On Your Own
Practice and continue developing the mathematical understanding you learn in each lesson.

Maintain Your Skills
Review and reinforce skills from previous lessons.

Also Available
An additional Practice Workbook is available separately.

Go Online

With PearsonSuccessNet your teachers have selected the best tools and features to help you succeed in your classes.

Log-in to www.pearsonsuccessnet.com to find:

- **an online Pearson eText version of your textbook**
- **extra practice and assessments**
- **worksheets and activities**
- **multimedia**

Check out **PearsonSuccessNet**

Student Handbook

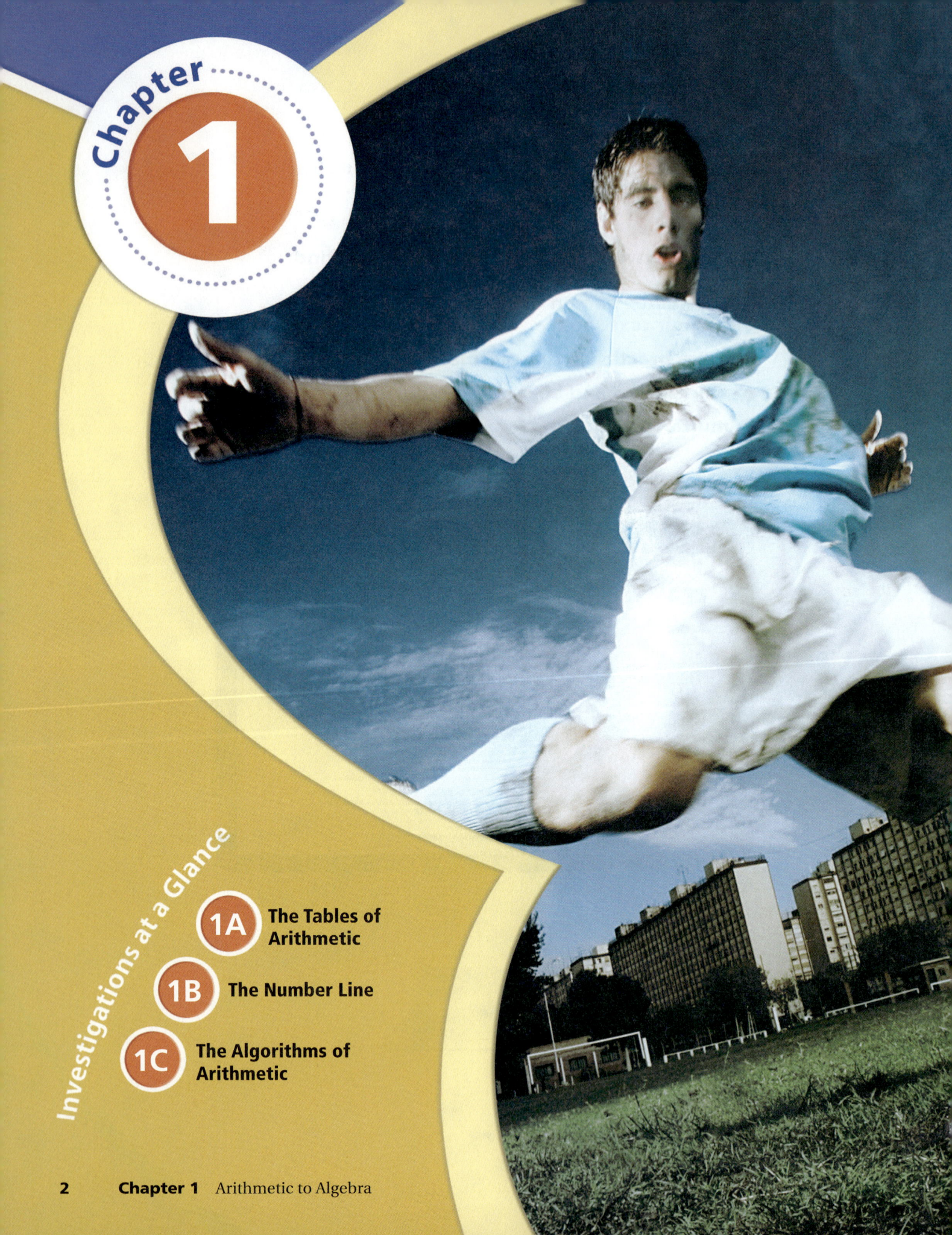

Arithmetic to Algebra

Most sports have very complicated rules. Soccer, for instance, seems like a simple game of kicking the ball into the goal. However, there are many rules.

Who developed the rules of soccer? In the 1600s, schools in England started making soccer rules. Today, an international organization maintains soccer rules so that teams around the world can use the same rules.

Mathematicians have agreed on a common set of rules and symbols. They have extended the rules and made guesses about the way numbers work. Finally, mathematicians have proved their guesses based on rules that they already knew.

Vocabulary and Notation

- additive identity
- additive inverse
- algorithm
- axiom
- basic rules of arithmetic
- decimal expansion
- decimal representation
- equivalent fractions
- expansion box
- extension of a rule
- integers
- least common denominator
- lowest terms
- multiplicative identity
- negative number
- number line
- opposites
- place-value part
- reciprocal
- square root
- · (multiplication)

1.0 Habits of Mind

Mathematical habits of mind are the most fundamental concepts and applications that you will take away from your mathematics courses. These habits are the bedrock for serious questioning, good problem solving, and critical analysis.

Mathematical Habits of Mind

Performing thought experiments Proof and justification are ways to establish results, communicate ideas, and discover new conjectures. In the CME Project textbooks, you will learn to read and understand logical arguments, and learn to construct such arguments yourself.

Finding and explaining patterns Being able to articulate what you see in precise language and, of course, explaining why things happen, is at the heart of doing mathematics.

Using precise language To express your understanding in mathematics, you will be asked to articulate your insights in precise mathematical language.

Creating and using representations The mathematical habit of representing—mapping a new situation into one that is better understood—is ubiquitous in mathematics and is a focus of the CME Project.

Generalizing from examples Sometimes you may look at a problem and have no idea how to start. General results in mathematics often spring from trying examples, looking for regularity, and seeking what seem to be general trends.

Expecting mathematics to make sense The "experience before formality" principle in the CME Project has sense-making as one of its main goals. For example, in these textbooks, you will see algebraic expressions purposefully transformed to reveal where an expression is zero or where it is optimized.

Algebraic Habits of Mind

Seeking and expressing regularity in repeated calculations This habit arises when you are performing the same calculation over and over and begin to notice the "rhythm" in the operations.

"Delayed evaluation"—Seeking form in calculations Often in algebra, if you delay numerical evaluation until the end of a process, you will see how operations are sequenced. Then the structure of the calculation (rather than its value) becomes more apparent.

"Chunking"—Changing variables in order to hide complexity Often in algebra, you may treat a whole expression as a single object. For example, if you cover up parts of an equation with a hand and ask yourself "what's under the hand" as a single thing, you can easily identify a numerical value for that quantity.

Reasoning about and picturing calculations and operations A key habit of mind in algebra involves predicting how a calculation "will go" without having to carry it out.

Extending operations to preserve rules for calculating This habit of extending to preserve rules is a key algebraic habit of mind, found throughout the CME Project. Extensions of algebraic operations are not arbitrary—they are forced on us by the desire to maintain the basic rules of arithmetic.

Purposefully transforming and interpreting expressions The phrase "mindful manipulation" refers to the habit of transforming algebraic expressions in order to reveal hidden meaning.

Seeking and specifying structural similarities You will look for regularity and structure in almost every lesson of the CME Project. From looking for hidden structure in the tables of arithmetic, to our approach to completing the square, to "chunking" to remove terms in the factoring lessons, CME Project is devoted to seeing and making use of structure in algebraic expressions.

Can you think of any other mathematical habits?

Try some of the following activities. As you proceed through the course, think about how you are thinking. Pay attention to your habits of mind!

In-Class Experiment

Finding and Explaining Patterns
Performing Thought Experiments

You have developed the mathematical habits of mind you need to play Sudoku already. These habits are second nature.

1. Copy and play the easy game. Complete the table so that each row, column, and 3-by-3 square contains the numbers 1–9 with no repetition.

Easy

4	7	8			2	6	3	
2	3	6	4	7			5	8
9	1						7	
3		2	1	6	5	4		
	6						2	
			8		9	3	1	
	5	9		1		7		3
		4	9			8		5
				5		1		2

Difficult

			B		G		A	
			H	D	F			C
D							G	
								D
C			D	A	E			I
B								
	F							H
A			G	I	C			
	E		A		H			

2. Copy and play the difficult game above. Explain how using letters instead of numbers changes how you play the game.

In-Class Experiment

Generalizing from Examples
Reasoning about and Picturing Calculations and Operations

Here is an equation that you solve by moving the given number of toothpicks to make a true equation. You do not remove toothpicks from the equation.

3. $VII + V = X$; one toothpick
4. $IX + I = VII$; one toothpick
5. $IV - II = V$; two toothpicks
6. a. Remove two toothpicks from the pattern of squares and leave two squares.

   b. Remove two toothpicks from the original pattern and leave three squares.

   Use the figure in Problem 6. You may cross the toothpicks to make squares.

Remember...

Roman and Arabic Numerals

I	1	VI	6
II	2	VII	7
III	3	VIII	8
IV	4	IX	9
V	5	X	10

7.

Number of Toothpicks to Move	2	2	3	4	4	4
Number of Squares to Make	6	7	3	2	3	10

1.0 Habits of Mind

In-Class Experiment

Expecting Mathematics to Make Sense
Seeking and Specifying Structural Similarities

In the early grades, you developed habits and skills with number operations.

8. Copy and complete the cross-sums table using the following rules. Pay attention to how you think about solving the puzzle. The first row and column are complete.

    - The unshaded numbers in each row or partial row add up to the shaded number at the left of the row.
    - The unshaded numbers in each column or partial column add up to the shaded number above the column.
    - The addends for each sum are numbers from 1 to 9 without any repeated numbers.

9. Copy the blank cross-sums game. Make a cross-sums game to give to a classmate. Make an answer grid.

In-Class Experiment

Performing Thought Experiments
Generalizing from Examples

In this game of "Dodgeball," you may combine the habits of mind by thinking ahead and considering the possibilities. If you do this, you know exactly what to expect.

10. Players A and B copy a table. Use these rules.

    - Each player gets 6 turns. The symbols are always visible to both players.
    - Player A fills Row 1 with X's and O's. Player B writes X or O in Cell 1.
    - On each turn, Player A completes a row and Player B completes a cell.
    - Player A wins if any of Player A's rows matches Player B's row. Otherwise, Player B wins.

11. Decide which player, A or B, has an advantage in this game. Explain.

In-Class Experiment

Finding and Explaining Patterns
Using Precise Language

Important habits of mind include looking for, finding, extending, and asking questions about patterns that you observe. Work in small groups. Study the look-and-say sequence at the right.

1
11
21
1211
111221
312211
13112221
1113213211
31131211131221
13211311123113112211

Habits of Mind

Experiment. Why do you sometimes read vehicle license plate characters aloud?

You can say this is a look-and-say license plate.

12. Find a pattern and write the next three strings of numbers. (*Hint:* To help find the pattern, try reading the numbers in each string aloud. As you read, look also at the preceding string.)

13. What other patterns can you find in the strings of numbers?

14. What questions can you ask about the number strings not yet listed?

In-Class Experiment

Creating and Using Representations
Reasoning about and Picturing Calculations and Operations

In a row of six houses, each house is a different color. The house colors are blue, purple, red, white, green, and yellow. Pets live in five of the six houses. The pets are a dog, a cat, a bird, a fish, and a hamster.

- The blue house is fourth from the left.
- The cat lives in the white house.
- The yellow house is next to the white house.
- The blue house is between the yellow house and the green house.
- The cat does not live next to the dog, the bird, or the house with no pet.
- The hamster lives in the first (left-most) house.
- The white house is not next to the red house.
- The bird lives next to the house with no pet.

15. Which colors of houses could be second in the row?

16. Which colors of houses could be fifth in the row?

17. Which color of house does the fish live in?

18. Which pets could live in the blue house?

19. Also suppose the red house is first, the dog lives in the purple house, and the blue house has no pet. What is the order of the houses and pets?

Investigation 1A

The Tables of Arithmetic

In *The Tables of Arithmetic,* you will learn about adding and multiplying integers using addition and multiplication tables. You will also learn about the basic rules of arithmetic.

By the end of this investigation, you will be able to answer questions like these.

1. How can you illustrate the properties of addition by using an addition table?

2. How can you illustrate the properties of multiplication by using a multiplication table?

3. Why is the sum of two negative numbers negative, and the product of two negative numbers positive?

You will learn how to
- identify, describe, and justify patterns in addition and multiplication tables
- perform integer addition and multiplication
- explain the rules for multiplying and adding negative integers
- subtract using integers, which is the same as to add the integer's opposite
- apply the basic rules of arithmetic to integers

You will develop these habits and skills:
- Identify, describe, and explain patterns.
- Gain a sense of how a mathematician works.
- Extend concepts and patterns to build mathematical knowledge.

Whether you are solving a maze or a mathematics problem, you use similar habits and skills.

1.01 Getting Started

Activating Prior Knowledge
Exploring New Ideas

In multiplication and addition tables, you can find many number patterns.

For You to Explore

These parts of an addition table and a multiplication table may differ from tables you have seen, because they start in the lower left corner.

> Usually, addition and multiplication tables show smaller numbers in the upper left corner.

Addition Table

+	0	1	2	3	4	5	6	7	8	9	10	11	12
12	12	13	14		16	17	18	19	20	21	22	23	24
11	11	12	13			16	17	18	19	20	21	22	23
10	10	11	12		14		16	17	18	19	20	21	22
9	9	10	11		13	14		16	17	18	19	20	21
8	8	9	10		12	13	14		16	17	18	19	20
7	7	8	9		11	12	13	14		16	17	18	19
6	6	7	8		10	11	12	13	14		16	17	18
5	5	6	7		9	10	11	12	13	14		16	17
4	4	5	6		8	9	10	11	12	13	14		16
3	3	4	5		7	8	9	10	11	12	13	14	
2	2	3	4		6	7	8	9	10	11	12		14
1	1	2	3		5	6	7	8	9	10		12	13
0	0	1	2	3	4	5	6	7	8	9	10	11	12

Multiplication Table

×	0	1	2	3	4	5	6	7	8	9	10	11	12
12	0	12	24	36	48	60	72		96	108	120	132	144
11	0		22	33	44	55		77	88	99	110	121	132
10	0	10		30			60	70	80	90	100	110	120
9	0	9	18			45	54	63	72	81	90	99	108
8	0	8	16			40	48	56	64	72	80	88	96
7	0	7		21	28		42	49	56	63	70	77	84
6	0		12	18	24	30		42	48	54	60	66	72
5	0	5	10	15	20	25	30		40	45	50	55	60
4	0	4	8	12	16	20	24	28		36	40	44	48
3	0	3	6	9	12	15	18	21	24		30	33	36
2	0	2	4	6	8	10	12	14	16	18		22	24
1	0	1	2	3	4	5	6	7	8	9	10		12
0	0	0	0	0	0	0	0	0	0	0	0	0	0

Use the addition and multiplication tables.

1. What are the missing numbers in each table?
2. Find and explain several patterns in the addition table.
3. Find and explain several patterns in the multiplication table.
4. Explain how values in the addition table change when you move in a direction given.
   a. up 1 row
   b. down 1 row
   c. right 1 column
   d. left 1 column
5. a. Copy a part of the multiplication table. Label each axis with factors from 0 to 7. Circle the even products. Describe the pattern.
   b. When you choose at random a product in the table, what is the probability that the product is even? Explain.
   c. **Take It Further** Does your result in Problem 5b change when you use a table with factors from 0 to 12? Explain.

Exercise 1 gives you a few patterns.

Remember...
The number 0 is an even number.

Exercises Practicing Habits of Mind

On Your Own

6. How does each value in the addition table change when you move up one row and right one column? Explain.
7. Explain how each value in the addition table changes when you move up 5 rows and left 3 columns.
8. Illustrate the following arithmetic fact using an addition table. When you choose a number, add 5 and subtract 9 from the result, the result is 4 less than the number you chose.

10 Chapter 1 Arithmetic to Algebra

9. **a.** Make a part of the addition table. Label each axis with summands from 0 to 7. Circle the even sums. Describe the pattern.

   b. When you choose at random a sum in the table, what is the probability that the number is even? Explain.

   c. **Take It Further** Does your result in Exercise 9b change when you use a table of summands from 0 to 12? Explain.

> **Remember...**
> A summand is either one of the two numbers that you add. For example, 5 and 8 are summands in $5 + 8 = 13$.

Maintain Your Skills

10. Find each sum.
    a. $0 + 1 + 2 + 3 + 4$
    b. $1 + 2 + 3 + 4 + 5$
    c. $2 + 3 + 4 + 5 + 6$
    d. $3 + 4 + 5 + 6 + 7$
    e. $4 + 5 + 6 + 7 + 8$
    f. What pattern in the sums do you find?

11. Find each sum.
    a. $1 + 2 + 3 + 4 + 5 + 6 + 7 + 8$
    b. $2 + 3 + 4 + 5 + 6 + 7 + 8 + 9$
    c. $3 + 4 + 5 + 6 + 7 + 8 + 9 + 10$
    d. $4 + 5 + 6 + 7 + 8 + 9 + 10 + 11$
    e. $5 + 6 + 7 + 8 + 9 + 10 + 11 + 12$
    f. What pattern in the sums do you find?

1.01 Getting Started

1.02 Thinking About Negative Numbers

The first number system you learned was the whole number system, {0, 1, 2, ... }. The addition and multiplication tables in Lesson 1.01 use only the whole numbers.

When you first saw the subtraction 12 − 17, you probably started using **negative numbers.** Here are just a few ways that you can illustrate negative and positive numbers.

Temperature Whether you use a Fahrenheit or Celsius scale, thermometers measure temperatures "below zero." On the Celsius scale, water freezes at 0°. A negative Celsius temperature means that the temperature is below freezing. On the Fahrenheit scale, water freezes at 32°F.

For You to Do

1. Use the photo. Find the temperature, in degrees Celsius, that is the same as −13°F.

What determines the point you choose for 0 on a thermometer's Celsius number line?

Number Line A **number line** is like a scale on a thermometer. To make a number line, choose two points and label them 0 and 1. Then mark equal lengths in both directions. Label the marks with positive and negative numbers. The number line continues forever in both directions.

For You to Do

2. Suppose you start at 5 on the number line and move left 4 units. You will land on 1. So, moving left is similar to subtracting. Start at 5 on the number line below. Move left 4 units, right 1 unit, left 4 units, left 3 units, and right 2 units. On what number do you land?

$$\longleftarrow \;-6\;-5\;-4\;-3\;-2\;-1\;\;0\;\;1\;\;2\;\;3\;\;4\;\;5\;\;6\;\longrightarrow$$

Money Balances When you have a checking account, you can get into trouble if you write checks for more money than you have, or overdraw your account. Many banks allow you to overdraw your account, leaving a negative balance in your account. For instance, suppose you have $45 in your account and you withdraw $145. Then your balance is −$100.

When keeping track of money, bookkeepers write profits in black ink and losses in red ink. The phrase *$100 in the red* means a balance of −$100.

For You to Do

3. Your checking account balance is −$100 and you deposit $85. What is your new balance? How much more do you need to deposit to have a balance of $75?

Subtraction Results When you first learned to subtract, you only subtracted a smaller number from a larger one. How do you evaluate an expression such as $15 - 17$?

Suppose $15 - 17$ represents a value. You know that subtracting 17 is the same as subtracting 15 and then subtracting 2. You can represent this idea using math symbols.

$$15 - 17 = 15 - 15 - 2$$

Since $15 - 15 = 0$, you can write $15 - 17$ this way.

$$15 - 15 - 2 = 0 - 2$$

What value does $0 - 2$ represent? It is the value that is 2 less than 0. The value must be -2.

For You to Do

4. What value do you find for $243 - 569$ by using the method described above? Is there a quicker way to find the difference?

Opposite of a Number The number 0 is special. When you add it to any number, you get the number itself. For example, $5 + 0 = 5$, $6 + 0 = 6$, and $0 + 0 = 0$.

To solve equations in algebra, you may need to add a value to another value to get 0. What value do you add to 5 to get 0? Since $5 + (-5) = 0$, you can think of -5 and 5 as **opposites.**

You can also use opposites to find the difference in subtraction. Suppose you think that $15 - 17$ equals -2. How do you explain your result? When you add 2 to $15 - 17$, the result is 0.

$$15 - 17 + 2 = 17 - 17 = 0$$

Since adding 2 to $15 - 17$ gives 0, then $15 - 17$ must be the opposite of 2. The opposite of 2 is -2.

So, $15 - 17 = -2$, just as you suspected.

For You to Do

5. Use opposites to calculate $115 - 300$. How does the subtraction $300 - 115$ help you find the difference $115 - 300$?

> **Remember...**
> Subtraction is the same as adding the opposite of a number. So, $5 + (-5)$ is the same as $5 - 5$.

> **Habits of Mind**
> **Represent a number using words.** Some mathematicians use *negative of a number,* instead of *opposite of a number.* So, the *negative* of 5 is -5. The *negative* of -3 is 3.

1.02 Thinking About Negative Numbers

Exercises Practicing Habits of Mind

Check Your Understanding

1. Derman opens a checking account on June 14. He records his check withdrawals and deposits, but he does not calculate his balance for a week. On June 20, the bank tells Derman that he has overdrawn his account.

Number	Date	Purpose	Payment	✓	Deposit	Balance
	6/14	Deposit			$100	
001	6/16	Mulberry Comics	$40			
002	6/18	Jake's Joke Shop	$50			
003	6/18	Spica's Sports Equipment	$120			
004	6/19	On the Edge Books	$50			

   a. When did Derman first overdraw his account?

   b. How much money does he need to deposit to reach a positive balance?

   c. How could Derman have avoided overdrawing his account?

   > Derman overdrew his account when he wrote a check for more than his bank balance. Banks do not like a checking account to have a negative balance.

2. In Detroit, Michigan, at 10 A.M., the temperature is 28°F. It drops 14°F by 2 P.M. Then suddenly, a cold front causes the temperature to drop 50°F in an hour. By 4 P.M., the temperature increases 25°F and stays the same for the rest of the day.

   a. What is the coldest temperature during the day?

   b. What is the temperature at the end of the day?

3. Start with each number given. Add 2, subtract 7, add 11, and subtract 15. Write each ending number.

	Starting Number	Ending Number
a.	12	■
b.	23	■
c.	6	■
d.	8	■

   e. Write a simple recipe explaining how to get from the starting number to the ending number.

   f. If the ending number is −4, what was the starting number?

   > In this situation, a recipe gives directions for finding a result.

14 Chapter 1 Arithmetic to Algebra

On Your Own

4. Start with the number given. For each number, subtract 1, add 5, add 2, and subtract 13. Write each ending number.

   a. 10   b. 6   c. 22   d. 2

   e. Write a simpler recipe explaining how to get from the starting number to the ending number.

5. **Standardized Test Prep** Maria plays a board game. On each turn, she moves her game piece forward or backward a number of spaces. In her first four moves, she moves forward 2 spaces, backward 3 spaces, backward 2 spaces, and forward 4 spaces. What is the ending position of Maria's game piece in relation to its starting position after all four moves?

   A. ahead 1 space   B. ahead 2 spaces

   C. back 1 space   D. back 2 spaces

6. **Write About It** Sasha says, "When I draw two diagonals in the addition table, I notice something interesting. On the first line, all the sums are 8. On the second line, all the sums are 17. It seems that on any diagonal line, the sums are the same. I can't explain why." Explain the pattern that Sasha notices.

Addition Table

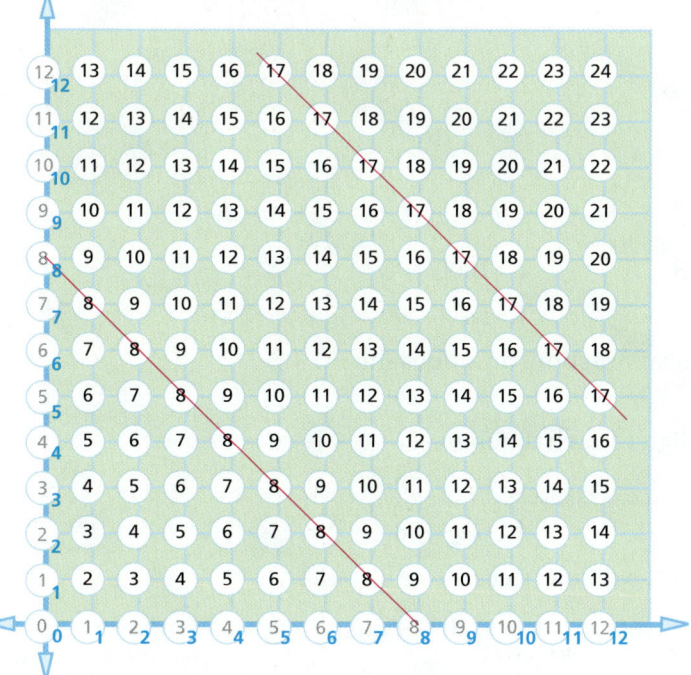

7. **Write About It** Derman explains, "Draw a line through a row of numbers in the addition table. When you move up 1 row and left 1 column, you find the same row of numbers." Describe the pattern that Derman notices.

Addition Table

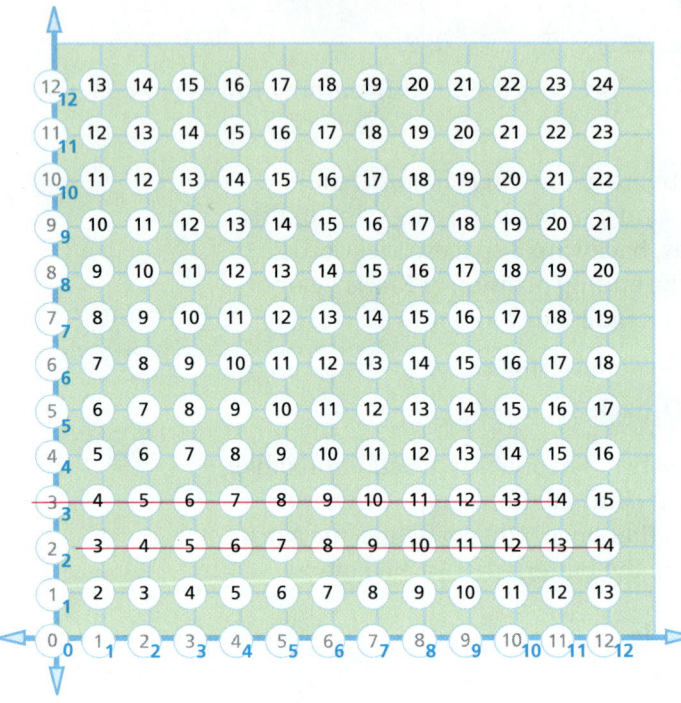

Maintain Your Skills

8. Find each difference.
   - a. $313 - 189$
   - b. $189 - 313$
   - c. $1000 - 5$
   - d. $5 - 1000$
   - e. $760 - 88$
   - f. $88 - 760$
   - g. When you reverse the summands in subtraction, how does the result change?

9. Find each difference. Record the last digit of each difference.
   - a. $62 - 38$
   - b. $62 - 48$
   - c. $62 - 58$
   - d. $62 - 68$
   - e. $62 - 78$
   - f. $62 - 88$
   - g. Identify a pattern in the last digits of the differences.

1.03 Extending the Addition Table

You may already know how to add and subtract negative numbers. In this lesson, you will learn why the rules of addition for negative numbers make sense.

Minds in Action episode 1

Tony and Sasha think about how to add negative and positive numbers.

Tony What we need to do is extend the addition table to the left and below each axis.

Addition Table

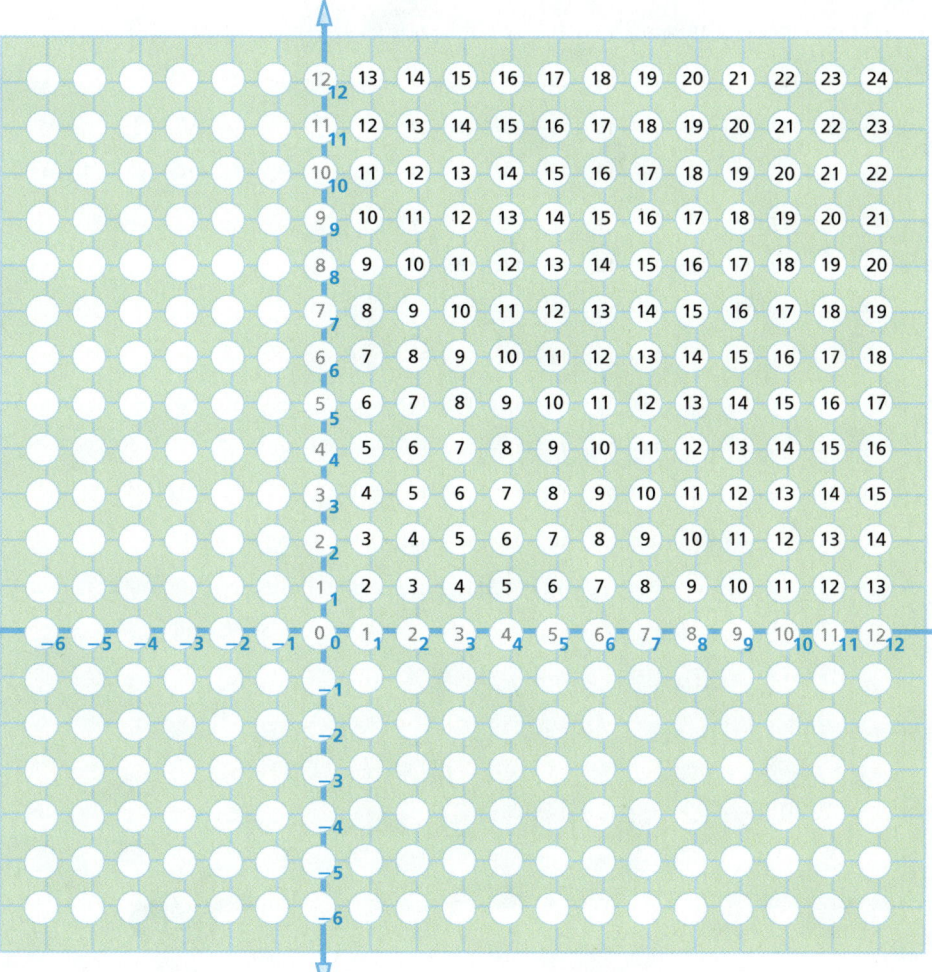

Sasha I want to figure out what to write in all the blanks.

Tony and Sasha think for a moment.

Tony It seems to me that we can fill in the blanks in any way that we want to. Let's just write a 5 in every blank. That's easy. What's wrong with that?

Sasha Well, when you do that, you get things you don't want. You get $-3 + 3 = 5$. Don't you want $-3 + 3$ to equal 0? Why do we have $-2 + 1 = 5$ in the table? It doesn't make any sense. I think it's better if we try to extend some of the patterns in the table.

Tony and Sasha quietly think for a few moments.

Tony I have an idea. Look at the row starting with 3.

Tony draws a line through the row starting with 3.

Why does $(-3) + 3$ equal 0?

Addition Table

Tony Sasha, in Lesson 1.01, you noticed that moving 1 entry to the left was the same as subtracting 1. Maybe we can use that idea to fill in the blanks in the third row. We just need to keep moving to the left.

Sasha So, let's keep subtracting 1. We'll get something like this.

18   Chapter 1 Arithmetic to Algebra

Addition Table

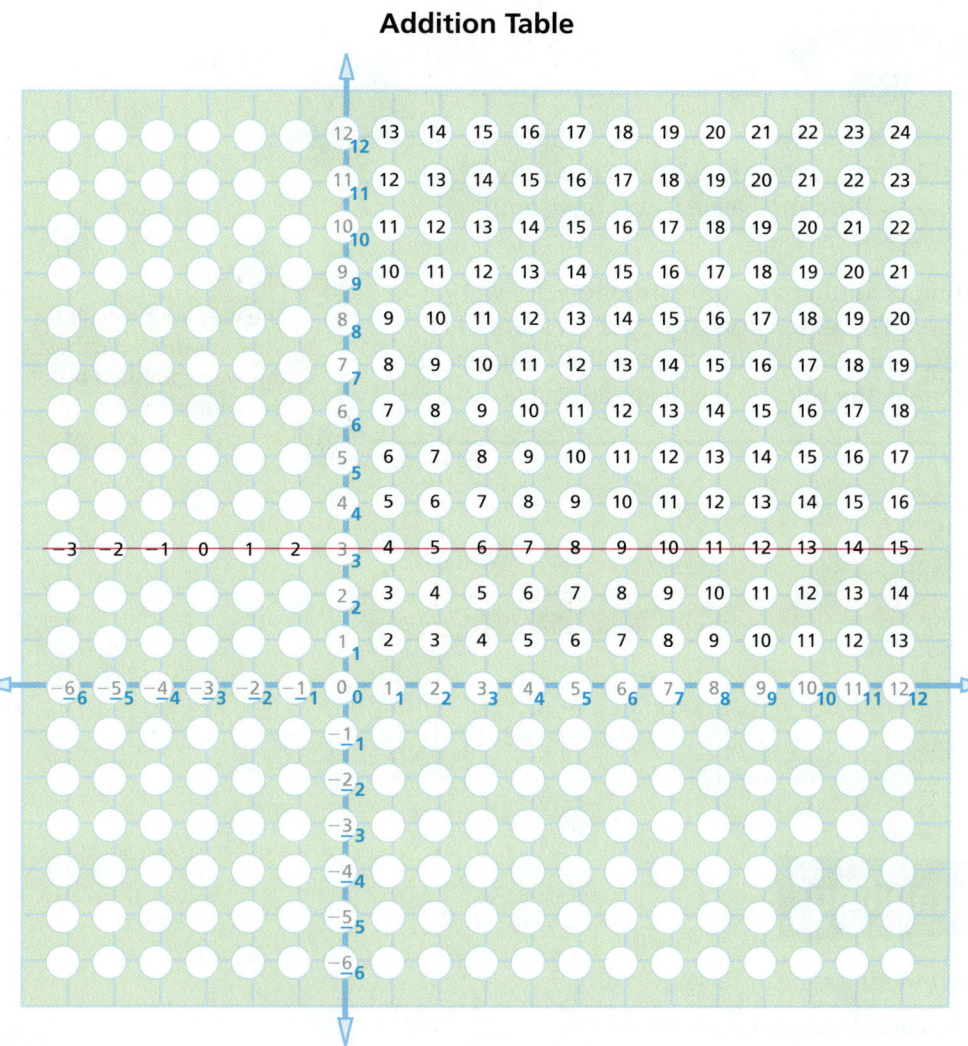

Tony   Wait, where did you get that −1 in the first entry to the left of zero on the horizontal axis?

Sasha   I just subtracted 1 from 0, or $0 - 1 = -1$.

Tony   Okay.

Sasha   This looks really good. We get $-3 + 3 = 0$, just as we want. The other entries make sense, too. Okay. Let's complete the table by extending the patterns in each row.

> What does Sasha mean by saying, "The other entries make sense, too"?

For You to Do

1. On a copy of Tony and Sasha's table, fill in the missing numbers.

For Discussion

2. In the completed table, do all the patterns for positive numbers work?

1.03 Extending the Addition Table

Developing Habits of Mind

Maintain a consistent process. The way you completed the table matches the way scientists and mathematicians add and multiply. Is this a coincidence? No, because Tony and Sasha were consistent and careful.

As they extended the operation of addition to more numbers, they made sure the rules still worked. The **extension of a rule** is essential in mathematics. In this case, you extended the rules from whole numbers to integers. You do not want to break the rules that you already have.

The way your calculator does addition matches the way you filled out the addition table.

Exercises Practicing Habits of Mind

Check Your Understanding

1. Determine whether each statement is true or false. Explain.
   a. The sum of two positive integers is always positive.
   b. The sum of two negative integers is always negative.
   c. The sum of a negative integer and a positive integer is always negative.
   d. The sum of a negative integer and a positive integer is always positive.

2. Match each sum in column 1 with an equal sum in column 2.

Column 1	Column 2
$3 + (-11)$	$2 + 8$
$(-23) + 13$	$(-4) + (-4)$
$20 + (-10)$	$16 + (-2)$
$32 + (-18)$	$1 + (-11)$

3. Suppose you do not know the value of the subtraction $11 - 5$. How can you use the addition table to find the difference?

4. Explain how you can use the addition table to find a difference.

5. Which of the following equations are true?

   a. $166 + (-117) \stackrel{?}{=} 166 - 117$

   b. $421 - (-29) \stackrel{?}{=} 421 - 29$

   c. $300 - (-92) \stackrel{?}{=} 300 + 92$

   d. $166 - (5 + 13) \stackrel{?}{=} 166 - 5 + 13$

   e. $421 - (17 + 43) \stackrel{?}{=} 421 - 17 - 43$

6. How many times does the number 143 appear in the entire addition table? Describe the location of each number 143 in the table.

On Your Own

7. Calculate each sum. Use the addition table.

   a. $9 + (-3)$
   b. $7 + (-3)$
   c. $(-4) + (-3)$
   d. $1 + (-4)$
   e. $4 + (-4)$
   f. $(-2) + (-4)$
   g. $(-9) + (-8)$
   h. $6 + (-11)$

8. Complete the part of an addition table shown below.

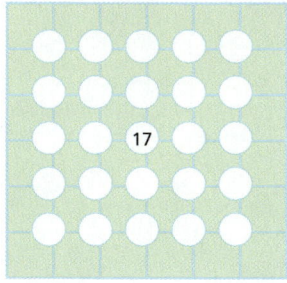

1.03 Extending the Addition Table

9. Find the product of each pair of numbers.

   a. a number and 0

   b. a number and 1

   c. How can you illustrate your results from parts (a) and (b) by using the multiplication table?

For Exercises 10–12, use an addition table. Describe the location of the given number, or set of numbers, in the table. For each number, or set of numbers, describe the pattern in the table. (*Hint:* Zero is neither a positive nor a negative number.)

Addition Table

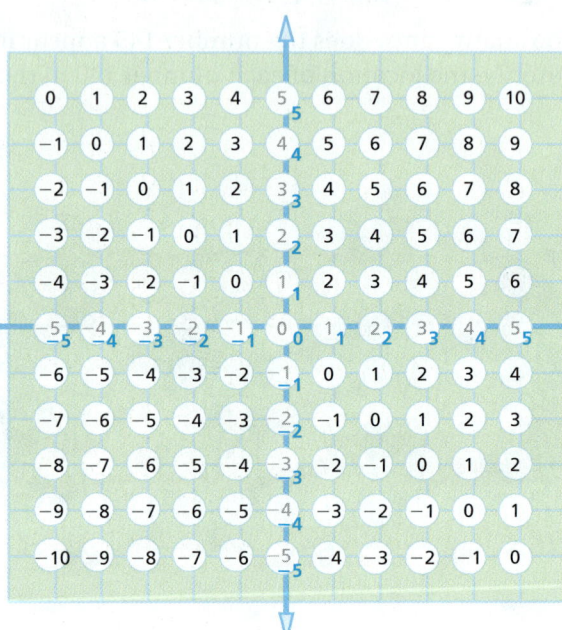

10. zeros

11. positive numbers

12. negative numbers

13. **Standardized Test Prep** In Calgary, Alberta, on Sunday, the low temperature forecast is 3°C. The low temperature will drop 4°C on Monday, 6°C on Tuesday, and 5°C on Wednesday. The low temperature will increase 2°C on Thursday and 1°C on Friday. What is the lowest temperature forecast?

    A. −18°C

    B. −15°C

    C. −12°C

    D. −9°C

Maintain Your Skills

For Exercises 14 and 15, find each sum.

14. a. $3 + 7 + 3 + 8 + 3 + (-8) + 3 + (-7)$

    b. $3 + 27 + 3 + 28 + 3 + (-28) + 3 + (-27)$

    c. $3 + 247 + 3 + 248 + 3 + (-248) + 3 + (-247)$

    d. What pattern can you use to find each sum?

15. a. $1 + 2 + 2 + 1$

    b. $1 + 2 + 3 + 3 + 2 + 1$

    c. $1 + 2 + 3 + 4 + 4 + 3 + 2 + 1$

    d. $1 + 2 + 3 + 4 + 5 + 5 + 4 + 3 + 2 + 1$

    e. $1 + 2 + 3 + 4 + 5 + 6 + 7 + 8 + 9 + 9 + 8 + 7 + 6 + 5 + 4 + 3 + 2 + 1$

    f. What pattern can you use to find each sum?

1.04 Extending the Multiplication Table

You can extend the multiplication table in the same way that Sasha and Tony extended the addition table. Then check that the extension is correct.

For You to Do

Explain how each value in the multiplication table changes when you move in each direction.

1. up 1 row
2. down 1 row
3. right 1 column
4. left 1 column

Using the multiplication table may help.

The multiplication table below is partially complete. You can complete the table by extending patterns. You can start by extending the patterns for multiplying a negative number by 0 or 1.

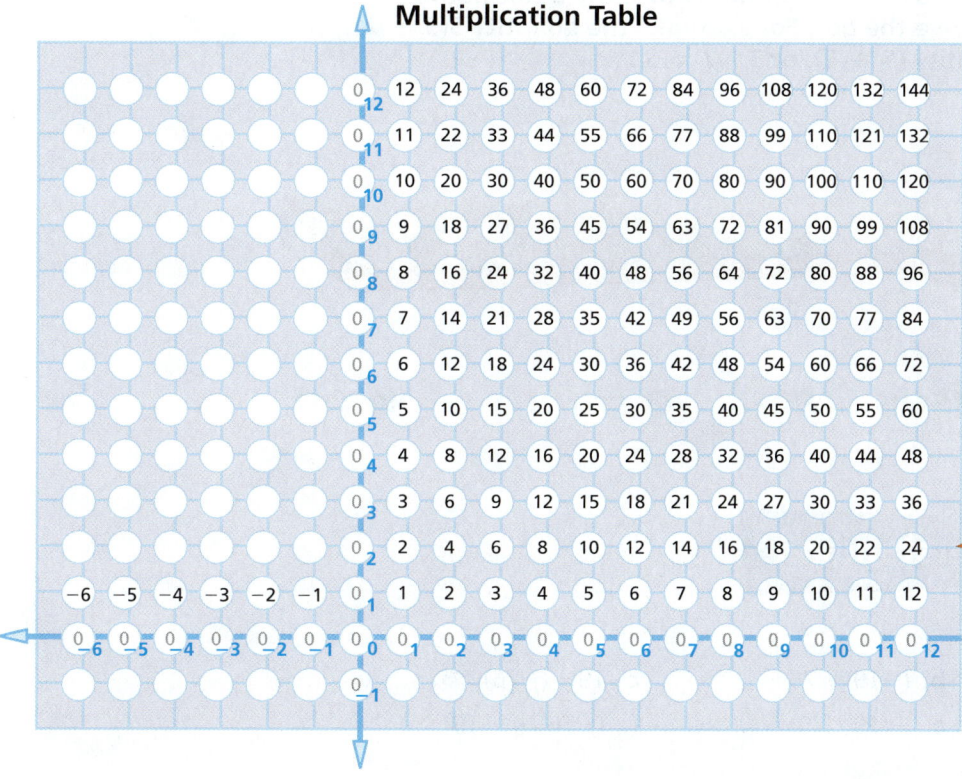

Why does each entry in this row increase by 2 from left to right?

Look at the row starting with the number 2. As you move one entry to the right, you add 2 each time. As you move one entry to the left, you subtract 2 each time.

A similar pattern works for the row starting with 3. You add 3 for each move to the right, and you subtract 3 for each move to the left. You can find similar patterns in the columns, too. Using patterns, you can extend the table in all directions.

For You to Do

5. On a copy of an incomplete multiplication table, complete the table.

For Discussion

6. Sasha and Tony check their multiplication table by looking for more patterns. Tony says that 4×3 is the same as $4 + 4 + 4$. He thinks that $(-4) \times 3$ is the same as $(-4) + (-4) + (-4)$. Does your multiplication table show this result?

Facts and Notation

In algebra, you can use a dot, $\cdot$, to show multiplication, instead of the $\times$ used in arithmetic. Instead of writing $(-3) \times 7 = -21$, you can write $(-3) \cdot 7 = -21$. When you need parentheses to show a calculation, you can sometimes remove the dot. For example, the quantity $3(5 + 2)$ means 3 times the quantity $(5 + 2)$, or $3 \cdot 7 = 21$.

Exercises Practicing Habits of Mind

Check Your Understanding

1. Find each product.
   - a. $19 \cdot 76$
   - b. $(-19) \cdot 76$
   - c. $19 \cdot (-76)$
   - d. $(-19) \cdot (-76)$
   - e. $-(19 \cdot 76)$
   - f. $(-76) \cdot (-19)$

2. Find each quotient.
   - a. $76 \div 19$
   - b. $(-76) \div (-19)$
   - c. $(-76) \div 19$
   - d. $76 \div (-19)$
   - e. $19 \div 76$
   - f. $19 \div (-76)$

3. What pair of numbers with sum 18 has the largest product?

4. Use the multiplication table. Explain why each fact is true.

   a. $4 \cdot (-3) = -12$

   b. $-4 \cdot (-3) = 12$

5. How many times does the number 10 appear as an entry in the multiplication table? Explain.

6. Does 17, 24, 19, or 72 appear most frequently as an entry in the entire multiplication table?

7. **Take It Further** Use the multiplication table.

   a. Which numbers from 0 to 150 appear most frequently as entries in the multiplication table?

   b. Which numbers from 0 to 150 appear least frequently as entries in the multiplication table?

On Your Own

8. Determine whether each statement is true or false. Use examples to support your claim.

   a. The product of two positive integers is always positive.

   b. The product of two negative integers is always negative.

   c. The product of two negative integers is always positive.

   d. The product of a negative integer and a positive integer is always negative.

   e. The product of a negative integer and a positive integer is always positive.

9. Which pair of numbers with sum 8 has the largest product?

10. **Standardized Test Prep** A store displays watermelons in a rectangular space. Mrs. Burres wants the space to be 5 fence sections long and 4 fence sections wide. Mr. Chang prefers a length of 7 sections and a width of 2 sections. How much less storage area will there be in the 7 section-by-2 section space than in the 5 section-by-4 section space?

    A. 2 square sections

    B. 3 square sections

    C. 6 square sections

    D. 9 square sections

In a rectangular space, it is easier to display square watermelons than round watermelons.

1.04 Extending the Multiplication Table

For Exercises 11–13, use a multiplication table. Describe the location of the given number, or set of numbers, in the table. For each number, or set of numbers, describe the pattern in the table.

11. zeros
12. positive numbers
13. negative numbers

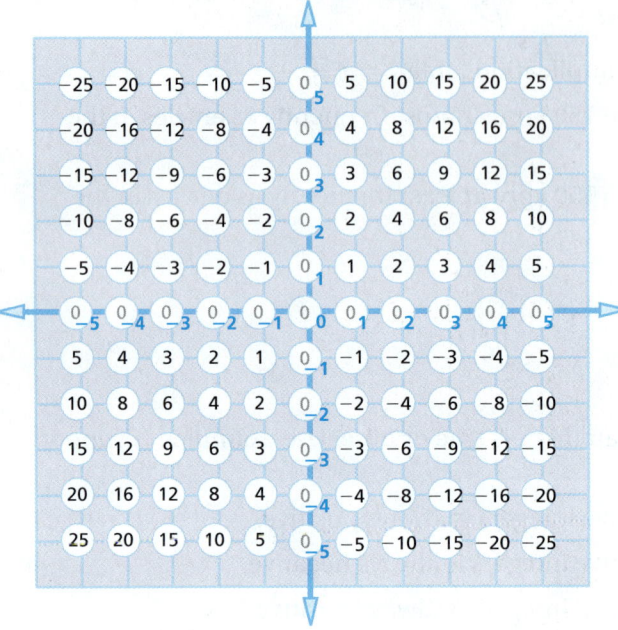

Remember...
Zero is neither a positive nor a negative number.

14. Find and describe patterns on the diagonal shown.

Maintain Your Skills

For Exercises 15 and 16, evaluate each expression or pair of expressions.

15. **a.** $(-1)^2$
    b. $(-1)^3$
    c. $(-1)^4$
    d. $(-1)^5$
    e. $(-1)^{347}$
    f. What pattern do you find in the exponents and the results?

16. **a.** $5(3 + 7)$ and $5 \cdot 3 + 5 \cdot 7$
    b. $(-5)(3 + 7)$ and $(-5) \cdot 3 + (-5) \cdot 7$
    c. $5(3 + (-7))$ and $5 \cdot 3 + 5(-7)$
    d. $5((-3) + (-7))$ and $5(-3) + 5(-7)$
    e. $(-5)((-3) + (-7))$ and $(-5)(-3) + (-5)(-7)$
    f. Make a conjecture about the values in each pair of calculations.

17. Given the fact that $1 + 2 + 3 + 4 + 5 + 6 + 7 + 8 + 9 + 10 = 55$, find each sum.
    a. $2 + 4 + 6 + 8 + 10 + 12 + 14 + 16 + 18 + 20$
    b. $3 + 6 + 9 + 12 + 15 + 18 + 21 + 24 + 27 + 30$
    c. $7 + 14 + 21 + 28 + 35 + 42 + 49 + 56 + 63 + 70$
    d. $11 + 22 + 33 + 44 + 55 + 66 + 77 + 88 + 99 + 110$
    e. $12 + 24 + 36 + 48 + 60 + 72 + 84 + 96 + 108 + 120$
    f. What shortcut can you use?

> A conjecture is what you believe is a true statement in general, based on specific examples.

Habits of Mind

Speed up your process. You can save time if you do not use a calculator and you look for shortcuts.

1.05 The Basic Rules of Arithmetic

The **basic rules of arithmetic** govern how addition and multiplication work for the set of integers. Studying the basic rules of arithmetic, or the properties of operations, is an important way that algebra differs from arithmetic. Studying number systems is another difference.

Facts and Notation

The capital letter $\mathbb{Z}$ stands for the set of **integers**,

$$\{\ldots -5, -4, -3, -2, -1, 0, 1, 2, 3, 4, 5, 6, 7 \ldots\}$$

Zahl means "number" in German.

What are the basic rules, or properties, for $\mathbb{Z}$? Roughly speaking, order does not matter when you add or multiply.

Properties Any-Order, Any-Grouping in $\mathbb{Z}$

Addition

- The order in which you add two numbers in a sum does not affect the result.

    $5 + 3 = 8$ $\qquad\qquad$ $3 + 5 = 8$

- When you add more than two numbers, the way you group them does not matter.

    $5 + (3 + 7) = 15$ $\qquad\qquad$ $(5 + 3) + 7 = 15$

Multiplication

- The order in which you multiply two numbers in a product does not affect the result.

    $5 \cdot (-3) = -15$ $\qquad\qquad$ $-3 \cdot (5) = -15$

- When you multiply more than two numbers, the way you group them does not matter.

    $4 \cdot (3 \cdot 5) = 60$ $\qquad\qquad$ $(4 \cdot 3) \cdot 5 = 60$

You call the first and third rules the commutative properties of addition and multiplication. You call the second and fourth rules the associative properties of addition and multiplication.

In this book, the letters AOAG stand for the any-order, any-grouping properties.

Developing Habits of Mind

Understand the process. You have probably used AOAG before. You can just accept the properties as  or basic facts, requiring no justification. Also, you can recall some processes you've seen before. If you insist on knowing why these properties are true, start thinking about the way you use positive integers to count. For example, suppose you line up some 5's in an array.

5 5 5 5
5 5 5 5
5 5 5 5

What sum do you find when you add the 5's? There are three processes you can use.

Habits of Mind

Understand the process. If you multiply 479 and 21 using paper and pencil, which number do you write first? Explain. Why can you choose which number to write first?

Process 1 There are three rows and four columns in the array, so there are $4 \cdot 3$, or twelve, 5's. The sum is the same as $12 \cdot 5 = 60$. You calculate the result to the following multiplication.

$(4 \cdot 3) \cdot 5 = 60$

Process 2 Each row contains four 5's, so the sum in each row is $4 \cdot 5 = 20$.

5 5 5 5 = 20
5 5 5 5 = 20
5 5 5 5 = 20

There are three rows, so the sum of the 5's is $3 \cdot 20$. You calculate the result by multiplying.

$3 \cdot (4 \cdot 5) = 60$

Process 3 Each column contains three 5's, so the sum in each column is $3 \cdot 5 = 15$.

$$\begin{array}{cccc} 5 & 5 & 5 & 5 \\ 5 & 5 & 5 & 5 \\ \underline{5} & \underline{5} & \underline{5} & \underline{5} \\ 15 & 15 & 15 & 15 \end{array}$$

There are four columns, so the sum of all the 5's is $4 \cdot 15$. You evaluate the following multiplication.

$4 \cdot (3 \cdot 5) = 60$

The product is 60, no matter what order you multiply the numbers.

$(4 \cdot 3) \cdot 5 = 3 \cdot (4 \cdot 5) = 4 \cdot (3 \cdot 5) = 60$

Rafts carrying 5 riders each can go through the rapids in any order. No matter what the order is, 12 of them will carry 60 people in all.

The next three basic rules for $\mathbb{Z}$ are about the special numbers 0 and 1.

Properties Identities and Inverses in $\mathbb{Z}$

- When you add 0 to any number, the result is the number itself. The number 0 is the **additive identity.**
- When you multiply 1 by any number, the result is the number itself. The number 1 is the **multiplicative identity.**
- When you add any number to its opposite, the result is 0. If the sum of two numbers is 0, each number is the opposite of the other. Every integer has a unique additive inverse. **Additive inverse** is another name for opposite.

Why do you use the word *the* in *the identity*? Is there a number besides 0 that you can add to another number that gives the second number as a result?

For You to Do

1. What is the result when you add 17, −5, 0, 5, 12, and −17? Find a shortcut to simplify your work. Explain.

Remember...
What is the opposite of 0?

Another basic rule of arithmetic summarizes how multiplication and addition work together. This is one of the most useful rules in algebra.

Property Distributive Property

Multiplying a number by a sum is the same as multiplying the number by each term in the sum and then adding the results.

An example of the Distributive Property follows.

$$4 \cdot (50 + 3) = 4 \cdot 50 + 4 \cdot 3$$
$$= 200 + 12$$
$$= 212$$

How can you use this property to calculate $5 \cdot 99$? You can rewrite 99 as $100 + (-1)$. Then you apply the Distributive Property.

$$5 \cdot (99) = 5 \cdot (100 + (-1))$$
$$= 5 \cdot 100 + 5 \cdot (-1)$$
$$= 500 + (-5)$$
$$= 495$$

Mentally, you can just multiply 5 times 100 and then add 5 times (-1). Many tricks for doing mental calculations rely on the Distributive Property.

For You to Do

2. Calculate 27 · 102 without using a calculator, or paper.

For Discussion

3. Use this array to show that 4 · (50 + 3) = 4 · 50 + 4 · 3.

   50   50   50   50
   3   3   3   3

Exercises Practicing Habits of Mind

Check Your Understanding

1. Use the multiplication table to show that order does not matter in multiplication. For example, 5 × 3 is the same as 3 × 5.

2. Use the multiplication table to show that when you multiply a number by 1, you get the number itself. For example, 5 × 1 = 5.

3. What is the opposite of −5? Explain.

4. **Take It Further** Which of the basic rules of arithmetic are true when you restrict the number system to the positive integers?

On Your Own

5. Use the basic rules of arithmetic to rewrite each calculation more simply.

   a. 2 · (473 · 5)   b. 12 · 199
   c. 42 · 203   d. 4 · 27 · 5 · 3

6. Find each result.

   a. 15 · 3 + (−6)   b. 15(3 + (−6))   c. 15 + 3(−6)
   d. 15 + (−6)3   e. 15 + (−6)3 + (−15)

Go Online
pearsonsuccessnet.com

1.05   The Basic Rules of Arithmetic

7. **Standardized Test Prep** Rosa finds the product of 32 and 96. She rewrites 96 as a sum or difference of two numbers and uses the Distributive Property. Which of the following could be a step in her computations?

    A. $32 \cdot 95 + 31$

    B. $30 \cdot 98$

    C. $2700 + 12$

    D. $3200 - 128$

8. **Take It Further** Use the basic rules of arithmetic to show that each statement is true.

    a. $(5 + 3)(5 - 3) = 5 \cdot 5 - 3 \cdot 3$

    b. $(4 + 5)(4 - 5) = 4 \cdot 4 - 5 \cdot 5$

Maintain Your Skills

For Exercises 9 and 10, find each result.

9. a. $10 \cdot 3 + 5$

    b. $10(10 \cdot 3 + 5) + 6$

    c. $10(10(10 \cdot 3 + 5) + 6) + 2$

    d. $10(10(10(10 \cdot 3 + 5) + 6) + 2) + 9$

    e. Find a pattern that you used to find each result.

10. a. $6 - 1 + 6 - 2 + 6 - 3 + 6 - 4$

    b. $5 - 1 + 5 - 2 + 5 - 3 + 5 - 4$

    c. $4 - 1 + 4 - 2 + 4 - 3 + 4 - 4$

    d. $3 - 1 + 3 - 2 + 3 - 3 + 3 - 4$

    e. $2 - 1 + 2 - 2 + 2 - 3 + 2 - 4$

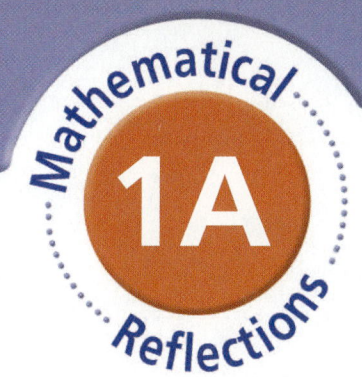

Mathematical Reflections 1A

In this investigation, you learned to add and multiply integers. You also learned the basic rules of arithmetic. These questions will help you summarize what you have learned.

1. In an addition table, what is the total change in the values when you move as follows?

    a. up 2 rows and left 1 column   **b.** up 1 row and left 2 columns

2. Choose a number between 1 and 20. Add 3, subtract 4, and add 1. How is your result related to your starting number? Explain.

    Calculate each sum or product.

3. **a.** $8 + (-1)$ **b.** $(-8) + 5$ **c.** $(-8) + (-2)$ **d.** $8 + (-8)$

4. **a.** $4(5)$ **b.** $4(-5)$ **c.** $(-4)(5)$ **d.** $(-4)(-5)$

5. Tony asks Sasha to multiply 15 times 98. She calculates $1500 - 30 = 1470$. Is Sasha correct? Explain. What basic rule of arithmetic did she use?

6. How can you illustrate the properties of addition by using an addition table?

7. How can you illustrate the properties of multiplication by using a multiplication table?

8. Why is the sum of two negative numbers negative, and the product of two negative numbers positive?

Vocabulary and Notation

In this investigation, you learned these terms and symbols. Make sure you understand what each one means and how to use it.

- additive identity
- additive inverse
- axiom
- basic rules of arithmetic
- extension of a rule
- integers, $\mathbb{Z}$
- multiplicative identity
- negative number
- number line
- opposites
- · (multiplication)

Taking a different point of view can help you find a solution.

Investigation 1B

The Number Line

In *The Number Line*, you will order fractions and decimals on the number line. You will extend the basic rules of arithmetic to the set of real numbers.

By the end of this investigation, you will be able to answer questions like these.

1. How can you tell whether two fractions that look different represent the same number?

2. How do you add numbers on the number line?

3. Where is $\sqrt{2}$ located on the number line?

You will learn how to

- draw line segments with different endpoints and different scales
- represent fractions and real numbers as points on a number line
- represent a rational number in many different ways
- extend the basic rules of addition and multiplication from the integers to the real numbers

You will develop these habits and skills:

- Think of decimal representations as tools for locating points on the number line with any degree of precision.
- Choose the best representation of a number to solve a problem efficiently.
- Use the number line to visualize numbers and operations, such as addition and multiplication.
- Extend the basic rules to the set of real numbers.

This unusual-looking vertical number line has marks for 0 and one other number.

1.06 Getting Started

In Getting Started, you will review fractions on the number line.

For You to Explore

On graph paper, draw seven horizontal line segments that are 24 units in length. Label the endpoints 0 and 1.

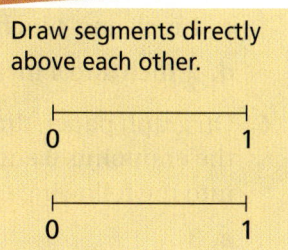

Draw segments directly above each other.

1. For parts (a)–(e), divide one segment into the given number of equal parts. Label each dividing point. Explain why the labels are appropriate.

   a. 2 b. 3 c. 4 d. 5 e. 6

   f. Which segment is the most difficult to divide equally? Explain why.

2. a. On the sixth line segment, label points for halves, thirds, fourths, and sixths. Which points have multiple labels? Explain.

   b. Using this line segment, order the following numbers from least to greatest: $\frac{1}{3}, \frac{4}{6}, \frac{3}{5}, \frac{1}{2}, \frac{1}{4}, \frac{5}{6}, \frac{2}{5}$.

3. a. Place each number on the seventh line segment.

   $\frac{1}{12}, \frac{2}{12}, \frac{6}{24}, \frac{1}{8}, \frac{4}{8}, \frac{25}{100}, \frac{2}{10}, \frac{5}{10}, \frac{10}{60}, \frac{6}{12}, \frac{5}{8}, \frac{0}{13}, \frac{11}{11}, \frac{1,000,000}{2,000,000}$

   b. Explain why some points have more than one label.

Exercises Practicing Habits of Mind

On Your Own

For Exercises 4 and 5, place a piece of paper next to this ruler. Copy the ruler's markings along one edge of the paper.

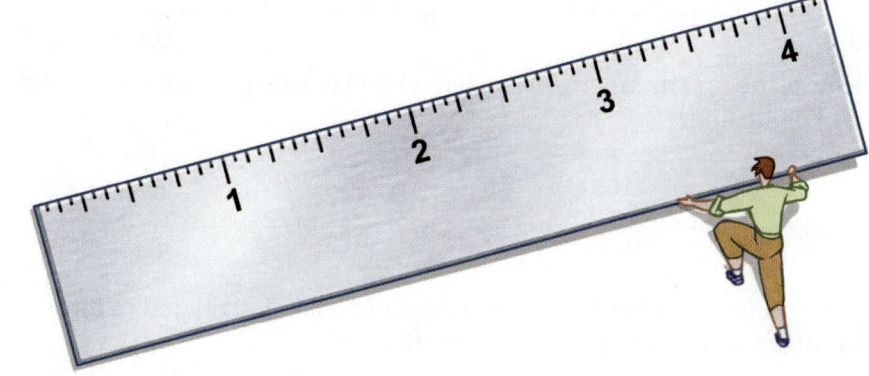

4. Label the ruler for each point given.

   a. $\frac{1}{2}$ inch b. $\frac{1}{4}$ inch c. $\frac{1}{8}$ inch

   d. $1\frac{1}{2}$ inches e. $3\frac{1}{4}$ inches f. $\frac{1}{3}$ foot

5. Mark a point on the ruler that is halfway between the two numbers in each pair below.

   a. 3 inches and 4 inches

   b. 2 inches and 4 inches

   c. 1 inch and 4 inches

   d. $\frac{1}{2}$ inch and 4 inches

6. On graph paper, draw a horizontal line segment that is 24 units long. Label the endpoints 0 and 72. Mark and label the points that divide the segment into the following equal parts.

   a. 3

   b. 8

Maintain Your Skills

7. In each list, the numbers increase by the same amount. Fill in the missing values.

   a. 0, 3, ■, ■, 12, ■

   b. 0, ■, 20, ■, 40, ■

   c. 0, ■, ■, ■, 160, 200

   d. 0, ■, ■, ■, ■, 35

   e. How does the second number in each list relate to the last number in each list?

For Exercises 8 and 9, points divide each line segment into five equal parts. Use the numbers shown for the first and sixth points. Label each of the remaining four points.

Each line segment shows a different scale.

8. a.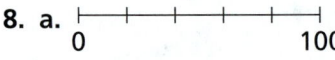
   0   100

   b.
   0   35

   c.
   0   0.5

   d.
   0   0.1

   e. How is the first number you labeled related to the number at the right end of the line?

9. a.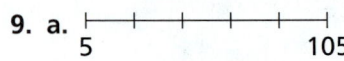
   5   105

   b.
   5   40

   c.
   5   5.5

   d.
   5   5.1

   e. **Take It Further** How is the first number you labeled related to the numbers at both ends of the segment?

36 Chapter 1 Arithmetic to Algebra

1.07 Numbers Besides the Integers

A number line labeled with only integers has gaps between the integers.

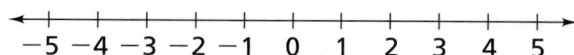

In each gap between two integers, there are many more numbers. In Lesson 1.06, you located some numbers on the number line.

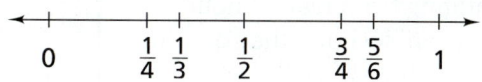

Fractions are numbers, just like integers, so they follow the basic rules of arithmetic. In this investigation, you will use the number line to extend arithmetic to fractions.

For You to Do

1. Plot each number on a number line.

   $\frac{1}{4}$, 0, −1, −$\frac{2}{4}$, $\frac{6}{4}$, $\frac{3}{4}$, −$\frac{6}{4}$, $\frac{5}{4}$

In Lesson 1.06, you learned that different fractions can refer to the same location on a number line. For example, $\frac{1}{2}$, $\frac{2}{4}$, and $\frac{3}{6}$ name the same point, because they represent the same number.

Enter 1 ÷ 2 in a calculator. What is the result? What is the result when you enter 2 ÷ 4, or 3 ÷ 6?

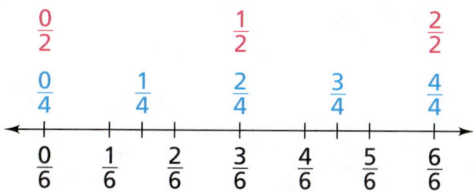

$\frac{1}{2} = \frac{2}{4} = \frac{3}{6}$

For You to Do

2. Find an equivalent fraction for $\frac{1}{3}$.

You can use the number line to define **equivalent fractions**. You can say that two fractions are equivalent when they refer to the same location on the number line.

Developing Habits of Mind

Visualize fractions. Fractions with different denominators represent different units. A fraction with a denominator of 6 measures in sixths. *Measures in sixths* means divides the interval from 0 to 1 into six equal parts. A fraction with a denominator of 2 measures in halves.

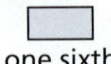   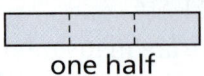
one sixth   one half

Changing from halves to sixths is similar to changing from feet to inches. You are converting from one unit to another. You can describe the equation $\frac{1}{2} = \frac{3}{6}$ by saying, "There are 3 sixths in 1 half."

You can draw a picture to visualize the equation $\frac{2}{3} = \frac{4}{6}$.

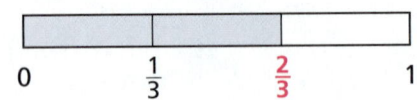   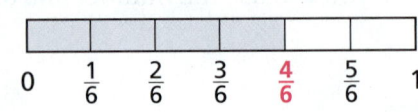

For Discussion

3. There is an arithmetic method for changing the denominator of a fraction. Suppose you want to find the number of sixths in $\frac{2}{3}$. You multiply the numerator and denominator of the fraction by 2.

$$\frac{2}{3} = \frac{2 \cdot 2}{3 \cdot 2} = \frac{4}{6}$$

Since $\frac{2}{3} = \frac{4}{6}$, $\frac{2}{3}$ and $\frac{4}{6}$ are equivalent fractions. Explain.

> What do *numerator* and *denominator* mean? Why did you multiply by 2?

Some important skills for working with fractions include

- finding equivalent fractions, especially for adding fractions
- writing fractions in lowest terms

You can say that $\frac{2}{3} + \frac{1}{12} = \frac{24}{36} + \frac{3}{36} = \frac{27}{36}$, but most of the time, $\frac{3}{4}$ is clearer than $\frac{27}{36}$. To write $\frac{27}{36}$ in **lowest terms,** you can write $\frac{(27 \div 3) \div 3}{(36 \div 3) \div 3} = \frac{3}{4}$, or $\frac{27 \div 9}{36 \div 9} = \frac{3}{4}$.

> A fraction is in lowest terms when the numerator and denominator do not have any common factor except 1. The fraction $\frac{84}{147}$ is not in lowest terms, because both 84 and 147 are divisible by 21.

For You to Do

Write each fraction in lowest terms.

4. $\frac{15}{20}$ 5. $\frac{72}{14}$ 6. $\frac{-5}{-15}$ 7. $\frac{3}{6}$ 8. $\frac{7}{31}$

38   Chapter 1   Arithmetic to Algebra

Exercises Practicing Habits of Mind

Check Your Understanding

For Exercises 1–3, copy each number line on graph paper. Label the missing points.

1.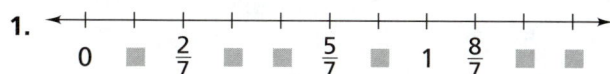
2.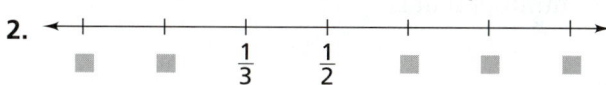
3.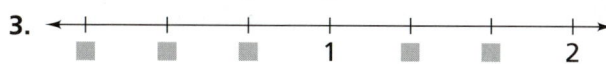

4. How many thirds are in each number?
   a. $\frac{8}{3}$
   b. $\frac{25}{3}$
   c. 3
   d. $\frac{14}{3}$
   e. 17
   f. $\frac{12}{6}$
   g. $\frac{5}{6}$
   h. $\frac{60}{30}$
   i. 11

5. **What's Wrong Here?** Rosa draws this number line incorrectly. Explain why this is not an accurate number line. Correct the number line.

   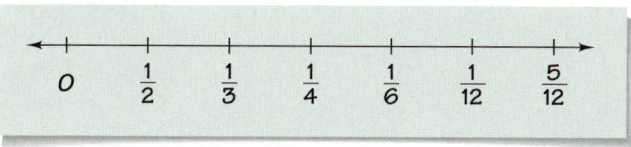

6. Place the following numbers on a number line.

   $$\frac{3}{2}, \frac{4}{3}, \frac{5}{3}, \frac{5}{4}, \frac{6}{4}, \frac{7}{4}, \frac{7}{6}, \frac{8}{6}, \frac{9}{6}, \frac{10}{6}, \frac{11}{6}$$

   a. Which fractions represent the same number, or are equivalent?
   b. What is the least number in this list?

7. Draw a picture that illustrates the equivalence $\frac{2}{5} = \frac{4}{10}$.

The vertical number line shows the height of the tide.

On Your Own

8. Find four different fractions equivalent to $\frac{7}{3}$.

9. A $\frac{3}{8}$-inch wrench is slightly too small to fit a bolt on your lawn mower. You have three more wrenches that measure $\frac{7}{16}$, $\frac{11}{16}$, and $\frac{5}{16}$ inches. Which wrench should you try next? Explain.

1.07 Numbers Besides the Integers 39

10. **Write About It** Travis says, "The number 12 is greater than 3. The number 17 is greater than 4. So, $\frac{12}{17} > \frac{3}{4}$." Explain to someone who knows nothing about fractions why Travis is wrong.

11. Match each number to a point on the number line.

    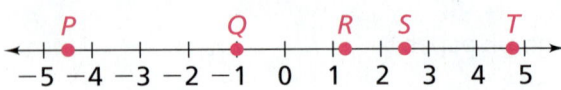

    a. -1 b. $\frac{5}{2}$ c. $-\frac{9}{2}$ d. $\frac{19}{4}$ e. $1\frac{1}{4}$

12. Plot each pair of numbers on a number line. Name a third number that is located between the pair of numbers.

    a. $\frac{7}{2}$ and $\frac{9}{2}$ b. $-\frac{5}{2}$ and 0

    c. $\frac{7}{9}$ and 1 d. $-\frac{8}{11}$ and $-\frac{9}{11}$

13. **Standardized Test Prep** Which number is between $\frac{27}{7}$ and $\frac{31}{8}$?

    A. $\frac{215}{56}$ B. $\frac{35}{36}$

    C. $\frac{217}{56}$ D. $\frac{433}{112}$

14. Use equivalent fractions. How many of each fractional part are in $\frac{1}{2}$?

    a. fourths b. eighths

    c. tenths d. hundredths

Maintain Your Skills

15. Identify the fractions equivalent to 7.

    a. $\frac{35}{5}$ b. $\frac{42}{7}$ c. $\frac{-42}{-6}$

    d. $\frac{17}{10}$ e. $\frac{7}{49}$ f. $\frac{81}{13}$

    g. Explain how you can decide whether a fraction is equivalent to 7.

16. Identify the fractions equivalent to -2.

    a. $\frac{8}{-4}$ b. $\frac{-6}{2}$

    c. $\frac{-20}{10}$ d. $\frac{-100}{20}$

    e. $\frac{-18}{-9}$ f. $\frac{12}{-6}$

    g. Explain how you can decide whether a fraction is equivalent to -2.

17. Identify the fractions equivalent to $\frac{3}{4}$.

    a. $\frac{6}{-8}$ b. $\frac{300}{400}$ c. $\frac{75}{200}$

    d. $\frac{-3}{-4}$ e. $\frac{60}{80}$ f. $\frac{36}{60}$

    g. Explain how you can decide whether a fraction is equivalent to $\frac{3}{4}$.

1.08 Decimals

The decimal system locates numbers on a number line. The **decimal expansion** of a number is its address on the number line. For example, the decimal expansion for 1.63 is 1 unit + 6 tenths + 3 hundredths.

Example

Problem Locate 1.63 on a number line.

Solution $1.63 = 1 + 0.6 + 0.03$

$\qquad = 1 + 6 \text{ tenths} + 3 \text{ hundredths}$

The decimal expansion 1 + 6 tenths + 3 hundredths leads to the following recipe for locating 1.63 on a number line.

Step 1 Find the number 1.

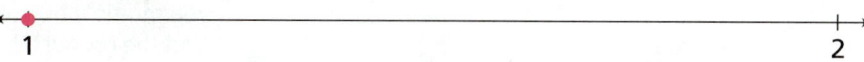

Step 2 Add an additional 6 tenths to the number 1.

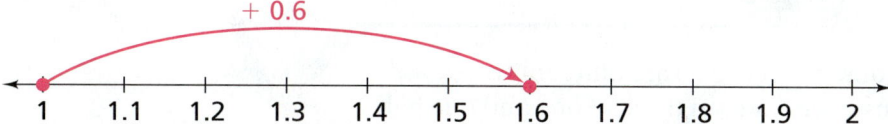

Step 3 Add an additional 3 hundredths to 1 and 6 tenths.

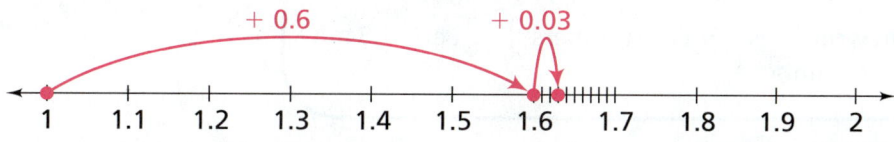

Decimal notation also provides the basis for a similar recipe for locating any number on a number line. The decimal expansion for 287.5 is as follows.

$$287.5 = 200 + 80 + 7 + 0.5$$

Here is a recipe for locating 287.5 on a number line.

Step 1 Locate 200 on a number line.

Step 2 Add an additional 80, or 8 tens.

Step 3 Add an additional 7, or 7 ones.

Step 4 Add an additional 0.5, or 5 tenths.

Sometimes it is useful to convert a fraction to a decimal. A fraction is just another way to write division. For example, $\frac{8}{2} = 8 \div 2$, $\frac{18}{3} = 18 \div 3$, and $\frac{3}{4} = 3 \div 4$.

$$\frac{3}{4} = 3 \div 4 = \begin{array}{r} 0.75 \\ 4\overline{)3.00} \\ -2.8 \\ \hline 0.20 \\ -0.20 \\ \hline 0 \end{array}$$

To convert the fraction $\frac{3}{4}$ into decimal notation, you perform long division as shown. The decimal representation of $\frac{3}{4}$ is 0.75.

Sometimes the long division does not end. Not every fraction has a simple **decimal representation,** because some decimals continue forever. A decimal representation can be useful for approximating the value of a number.

> The decimal representation of $\frac{1}{3}$ is 0.333 . . . The 3's repeat forever.

For You to Do

Label each number on a number line.

1. 1.81
2. $\frac{7}{4}$
3. $\frac{5}{3}$

4. Use your calculator to estimate $\sqrt{2}$ to 2 decimal places.

> The **square root** of 2, or $\sqrt{2}$, is the number that you multiply by itself to find the product 2. So, $\sqrt{2} \cdot \sqrt{2} = 2$.

Developing Habits of Mind

Represent a number. Fractions and decimals are different ways to represent a number. For instance, you can think of one and one half as 1.5, 1.50, $\frac{3}{2}$, or $\frac{9}{6}$.

What is the sum $\frac{3}{2} + \frac{1}{6}$? To find the sum, you can rewrite $\frac{3}{2}$ as $\frac{9}{6}$.

Is $\frac{3}{2}$ greater than 1.4? You can write $\frac{3}{2}$ as 1.5. The numbers $\frac{3}{2}$, $\frac{9}{6}$, and 1.5 are all representations of the same number.

For You to Do

Here are four different ways to represent the number $\frac{16}{25}$.

$\frac{16}{25}$ 0.64 $\frac{32}{50}$ $\left(\frac{4}{5}\right)^2$

For Problems 5–7, choose a representation above to help you find the answer. Explain each choice.

5. What is the sum $\frac{16}{25} + \frac{17}{50}$?

6. Is $\frac{16}{25}$ greater than 0.65?

7. Is there any number that you can multiply by itself to get $\frac{16}{25}$?

Exercises Practicing Habits of Mind

Check Your Understanding

1. Convert each fraction to a decimal with at most five decimal places. If the decimal repeats, write *repeating decimal*.
   a. $\frac{2}{5}$
   b. $\frac{2}{3}$
   c. $\frac{7}{8}$
   d. $\frac{9}{4}$
   e. $\frac{5}{9}$
   f. $\frac{7}{11}$

2. Convert each decimal to a fraction in lowest terms.
   a. 0.48
   b. 2.47
   c. 0.2
   d. 3.333
   e. 3.8
   f. −13.69
   g. **Take It Further** 0.88888 . . .
   h. **Take It Further** 0.414141 . . .

3. Dana tells Andrew that, no matter what two points he names, she can always find a third point on the number line between those two points.

   Andrew replies, "I'm thinking of 0.99 and 1."

   Dana says, "That's easy! 0.997 is between those two numbers."

   Andrew says, "Okay, try 0.9999 and 1."

   Dana answers, "0.9999314 is between those two numbers."

   Is Dana correct? Can she always find a third point between any two points? Explain.

4. Hideki hears Dana tell Andrew that she can always find a number between two given numbers.

   Hideki says, "That's nothing, Dana. No matter what points you name, I can find *two* new points between your points."

   Show how Hideki can do this. Find two points between the two given numbers.
   a. 0.99 and 1
   b. 0.9999 and 1
   c. 0.999999 and 1
   d. Is Hideki correct? Can you always find two new points between any two points? Explain.

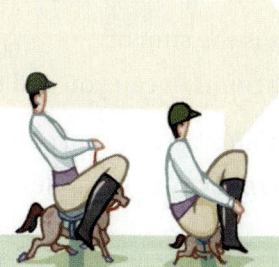

5. Draw a number line from 0 to 4. Plot each number.
   a. $\sqrt{2}$ b. $\frac{3}{2}$ c. $\sqrt{7}$ d. 2.3   e. $\sqrt{16}$
   f. 1.3   g. $\sqrt{3}$ h. 3.75   i. $\sqrt{8}$

   You can use a calculator to approximate the value of a square root.

6. **What's Wrong Here?** Derman labels a number line incorrectly.

   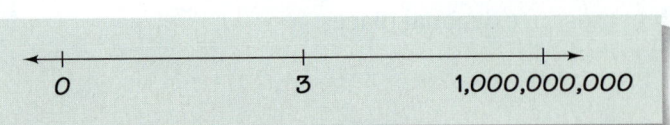

   a. Explain what is wrong with Derman's labels.
   b. Using graph paper, why is it difficult to draw a number line including 0, 3, and 1,000,000,000?

On Your Own

For Exercises 7 and 8, use graph paper. Copy each number line. Write the missing numbers.

7.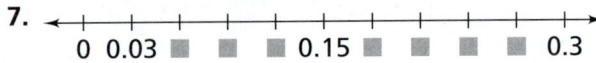

8.
   8.75 9   10.5   11

9. Convert each decimal to a fraction in lowest terms.
   a. 1.63   b. 0.711   c. 14.75
   d. -11.5 e. -0.125 f. -0.001

10. **Standardized Test Prep** Choose the pair of numbers that makes the inequality ■ < $\sqrt{14}$ < ■ true.
    A. 2.5 and 3.0   B. 3.0 and 3.5
    C. 3.5 and 4.0   D. 4.0 and 4.5

11. Here are four representations of the number $\frac{7}{4}$.

    $\frac{7}{4}$ 1.75 $\frac{175}{100}$ $\frac{21}{12}$

    For parts (a)–(d), choose one of the representations above to help you find the answer. Explain each choice.

    a. What is the sum of $\frac{7}{4} + \frac{3}{100}$?
    b. What number can you add to $\frac{7}{4}$ to get 3.86?
    c. What number can you add to $\frac{7}{4}$ to get $\frac{23}{12}$?
    d. **Take It Further** What number can you add to $\frac{7}{4}$ to get $\frac{7}{3}$?

Chapter 1 Arithmetic to Algebra

12. Order the numbers from least to greatest:

    3.009   3.08   3.7   3.18   3.5999

13. Which point is closest to −2 on the number line?

    a. $-\frac{1}{2}$ b. 2.3   c. $\frac{9}{2}$ d. −3   e. $-\frac{7}{2}$

Maintain Your Skills

14. Which numbers are between 1 and 2 on the number line?

    a. $\frac{7}{4}$ b. $\frac{5}{4}$ c. $\frac{7}{3}$ d. $\frac{5}{3}$ e. $\frac{13}{11}$

    f. $\frac{13}{17}$ g. $\frac{101}{121}$ h. $\frac{121}{101}$ i. $\frac{221}{101}$

    j. Explain how you can decide whether a fraction is between 1 and 2.

15. Find the number that is halfway between each pair of numbers.

    a. 2 and 8

    b. −3 and −6

    c. 3.2 and 3.8

    d. −2.3 and −2.34

    e. 0.5 and −2

    f. Sasha says, "I can find the number halfway between any two numbers by adding them together and then dividing by two." Does Sasha's method work? Explain.

    g. At about what time in the video clip below does Tara pick up her dog, Scruffy?

> The number 3.5 is halfway between 3 and 4.

1.09 Number Line Addition

In Investigation 1A, you added integers using the addition table and learned the basic rules of arithmetic. You cannot use the addition table to add fractions. Instead, you can use the number line. To add using the number line, think about numbers as lengths that point in either a positive or negative direction.

Example 1

Problem Illustrate $4.5 + 3.5$ on the number line.

Solution First, illustrate both 4.5 and 3.5 as lengths on the number line.

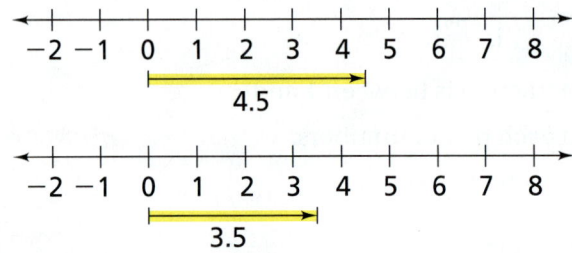

To add the lengths, line up the tail of the second arrow with the tip of the first arrow on a single number line. You can see that $4.5 + 3.5 = 8$.

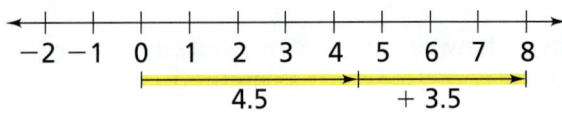

Example 2

Problem Illustrate $7 + (-2)$ on the number line.

Solution Use the solution method in Example 1. Note that (-2) points in a negative direction.

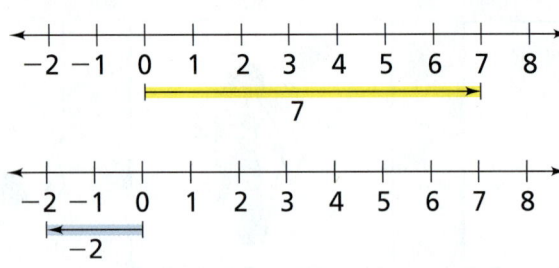

46 Chapter 1 Arithmetic to Algebra

Line up the tail of the second arrow with the tip of the first arrow on the same number line. The sum of 7 + (−2) is 5.

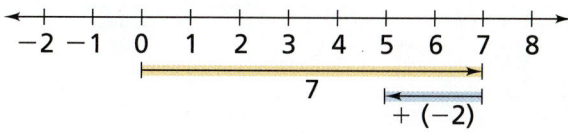

Why do you need to think about addition using the number line? You can add any two real numbers on the number line. For instance, you can add $\frac{31}{7}$ and $\sqrt{5}$.

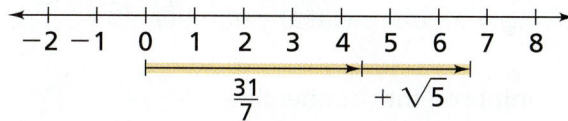

By using the number line, you preserve the rules of addition in Investigation 1A. Do you remember the following rule?

> The order in which you add two numbers in a sum does not affect the result.

This rule is still true when you think about addition on the number line. The number lines show that $\frac{31}{7} + \sqrt{5} = \sqrt{5} + \frac{31}{7}$.

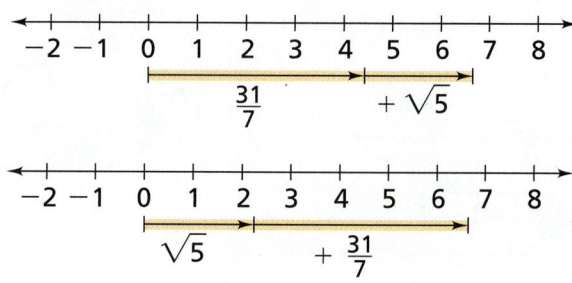

For Discussion

1. Illustrate the following rule using the number line: If you add 0 to any number, the result is the number itself.

Developing Habits of Mind

Recognize a similar process. The rules for adding real numbers on the number line are the same as the rules of addition that you learned for integers.

- You can add any two real numbers.
- You can extend the basic rules of addition that held for $\mathbb{Z}$.

1.09 Number Line Addition

Exercises Practicing Habits of Mind

Check Your Understanding

1. Illustrate each sum on a number line.
   a. $6 + (-3)$
   b. $\frac{1}{2} + \frac{5}{2}$
   c. $(-2) + \left(-\frac{3}{4}\right)$
   d. $0 + 4$

2. Use the number line to illustrate the following addition rule: If any number is added to its opposite, the result is 0.

3. Copy the number line. A and B are the two points on the number line represented by open dots. Match each of the solid dots with one of the following labels.

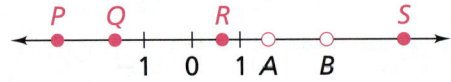

   a. $-A$
   b. $A + B$
   c. $-B$
   d. $\frac{1}{A}$

4. **What's Wrong Here?** Tony says, "Here's how I illustrated $5 + (-3)$ on the number line. The answer I got was 8 and not 2, so I know I did something wrong." What did Tony do wrong?

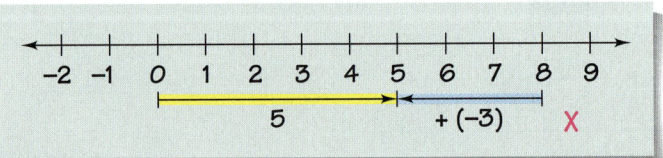

5. Find each sum.
   a. $\frac{1}{3} + \frac{7}{3}$
   b. $\frac{1}{3} + \frac{1}{6}$
   c. $\frac{11}{6} + \left(-\frac{3}{2}\right)$
   d. $\frac{3}{7} + \left(-\frac{4}{11}\right)$
   e. $\frac{33}{11} + \left(-\frac{18}{6}\right)$

6. In each list, the numbers increase by the same amount each time. Fill in the blanks.

   Sample

   Fill in the blanks. $0, \frac{1}{3}, \blacksquare, \blacksquare, \blacksquare, \blacksquare$

   Solution $0, \frac{1}{3}, \frac{2}{3}, 1, \frac{4}{3}, \frac{5}{3}$

   a. $0, \frac{1}{2}, \blacksquare, \blacksquare, \blacksquare, \blacksquare, \blacksquare$
   b. $0, \blacksquare, \frac{1}{2}, \blacksquare, \blacksquare, \blacksquare, \blacksquare$
   c. $0, \blacksquare, \frac{1}{4}, \blacksquare, \blacksquare, \blacksquare, \blacksquare$
   d. $0, \blacksquare, \blacksquare, \blacksquare, \blacksquare, \blacksquare, \frac{2}{3}$

On Your Own

7 Copy the number line. Locate each point on the number line.

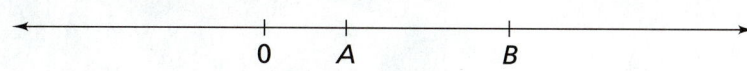

a. $-A$
b. $A + B$
c. $B - A$
d. $B + B$

8. What's Wrong Here? Calvin draws the picture below to find $\frac{1}{2} + \frac{1}{4}$ on a number line.

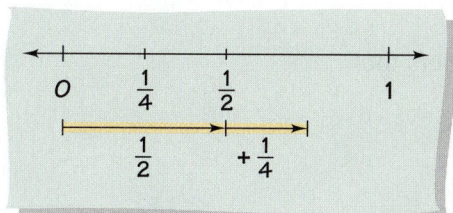

He explains, "To label the point $\frac{1}{2} + \frac{1}{4}$, I'll just add across the top and the bottom. So, $\frac{1}{2} + \frac{1}{4} = \frac{2}{6}$, which is the same as $\frac{1}{3}$." What is wrong with Calvin's reasoning?

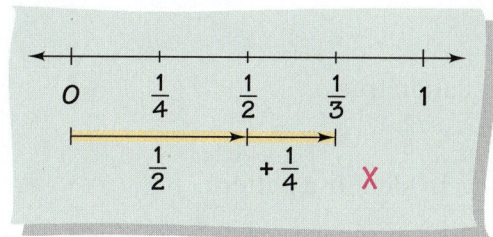

9. In each list, the numbers increase by the same amount each time. Fill in the blanks.

a. 0, 0.2, ■, ■, ■, ■, ■

b. 0, ■, 0.6, ■, ■, ■, ■,

c. 0, ■, 2.2, ■, ■, ■, ■

d. 0, ■, ■, ■, ■, ■, 3.6

1.09 Number Line Addition 49

10. Use a number line. Find the starting or ending number. Start at the number given. Move three units to the right, five units to the left, three units to the right, and four units to the left.

	Starting Number	Ending Number
a.	3	■
b.	−7	■
c.	11	■
d.	■	5
e.	■	0

11. **Standardized Test Prep** Choose the pair of numbers that makes the inequality ■ $< (\sqrt{2} + \sqrt{3}) <$ ■ true.

    A. 1.5 and 2.0
    B. 2.0 and 2.5
    C. 2.5 and 3.0
    D. 3.0 and 3.5

Maintain Your Skills

12. Fill in the blank with a number that makes the equation true.

    a. $\frac{1}{3} +$ ■ $= 1$ b. $\frac{1}{4} +$ ■ $= 1$ c. $\frac{2}{5} +$ ■ $= 1$
    d. $\frac{4}{3} +$ ■ $= 1$ e. $\frac{-3}{11} +$ ■ $= 1$ f. Identify a pattern.

13. For each value of point B on the number line, find the distance from point B to 10.

    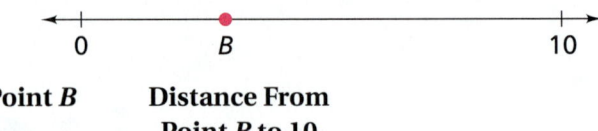

	Point B	Distance From Point B to 10
a.	2	■
b.	3	■
c.	4	■
d.	7.3	■
e.	$\frac{11}{3}$	■

    f. In general, how is the distance from point B to 10 related to the value at point B?

1.10 Number Line Multiplication

In this lesson, you will use number lines to extend multiplication to all numbers. To show how to multiply 7 times 2, find 7 on the vertical number line and 2 on the horizontal number line. The product of 7 and 2 is the area of this rectangle.

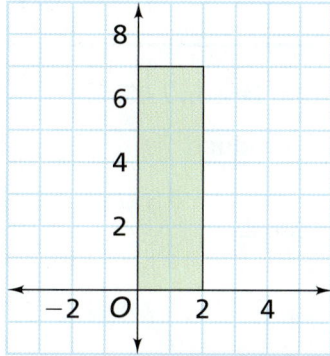

Using this method, you can show how to multiply *any* two positive numbers on the number lines. For instance, what is $\frac{7}{3}$ times $\sqrt{2}$? The number lines below illustrate the product.

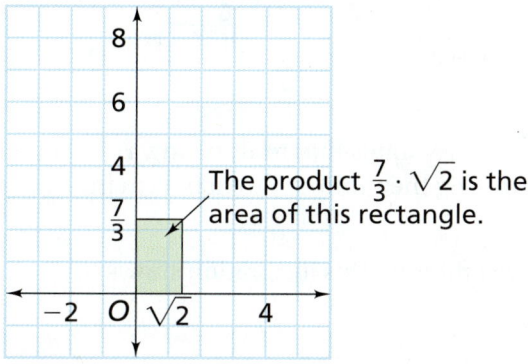

The product $\frac{7}{3} \cdot \sqrt{2}$ is the area of this rectangle.

You can extend the multiplication rules from Investigation 1A using the diagrams below. If you multiply a negative number and a positive number, the product is negative. If you multiply two negative numbers, the product is positive.

Multiplying Two Numbers With Different Signs

Multiplying Two Numbers With Same Signs

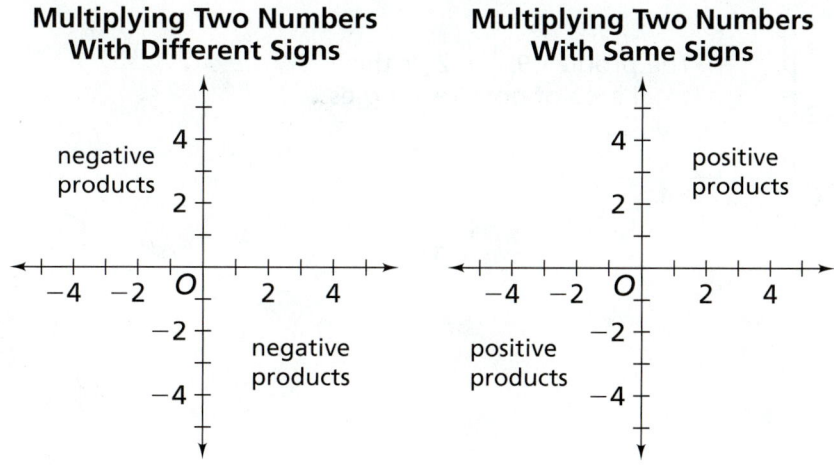

Developing Habits of Mind

Visualize multiplication in a different way. It is impractical to draw two number lines every time you multiply. However, looking at a familiar process in a different way is sometimes helpful. When you use two number lines to multiply, you can understand why the basic rules for multiplication extend to all numbers.

Recall one of the any-order, any-grouping properties from Lesson 1.05.

> The order in which you multiply two numbers in a product does not affect the result.

← This is the Commutative Property of Multiplication.

Here is how to use number lines to show $\frac{31}{7} \cdot \sqrt{5} = \sqrt{5} \cdot \frac{31}{7}$.

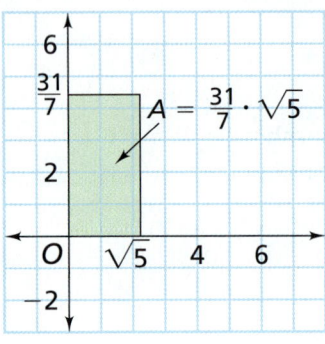 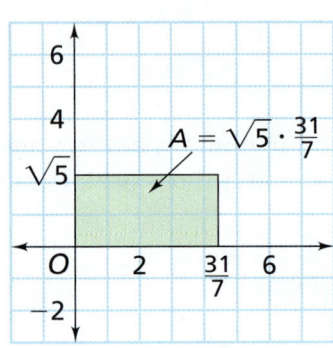

The Distributive Property in Investigation 1A states that multiplying a number by a sum is the same as multiplying the number by each term in the sum and then adding the results.

Here is an illustration of the Distributive Property. This illustration shows that $9 \cdot \left(\frac{1}{3} + 2\right) = 9 \cdot \frac{1}{3} + 9 \cdot 2$.

The product $9 \cdot \frac{1}{3}$ is the area of the shaded rectangle.

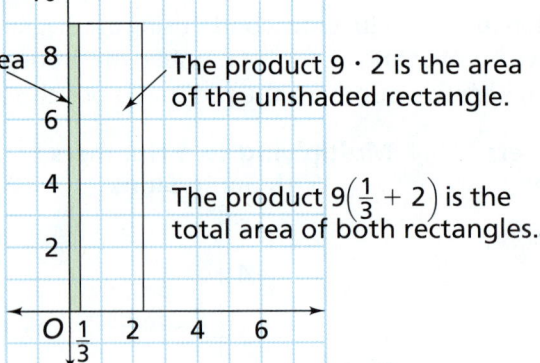

The product $9 \cdot 2$ is the area of the unshaded rectangle.

The product $9\left(\frac{1}{3} + 2\right)$ is the total area of both rectangles.

For You to Do

Find each product using the Distributive Property.

1. $9 \cdot \left(\frac{1}{3} + 2\right)$
2. $12 \cdot \left(5 + \frac{1}{4}\right)$
3. $10 \cdot \left(5 - \frac{1}{10}\right)$

For Discussion

4. Using number lines and multiplication, explain why the following basic rule is true: If you multiply any number by 0, then the product is 0.

Exercises Practicing Habits of Mind

Check Your Understanding

1. Find each product using the Distributive Property.
   a. $15 \cdot \left(\frac{1}{3} + \frac{1}{5}\right)$
   b. $10 \cdot \left(\frac{1}{2} + \frac{1}{5}\right)$
   c. $25 \cdot \left(\frac{1}{5} + \frac{7}{25}\right)$
   d. $\frac{9}{4} \cdot \left(\frac{4}{3} + \frac{8}{9}\right)$

2. Sasha notices that if you move the negative sign in a multiplication problem, the change doesn't affect the product. For instance, $(-2) \cdot 5$ and $2 \cdot (-5)$ both equal -10. Using number line multiplication, explain Sasha's observation.

3. Every number except 0 has an inverse for multiplication. Why doesn't 0 have a multiplicative inverse?

4. Copy the number line. Points A and B are numbers represented by the open dots. Match each of the solid dots with one of the following labels.

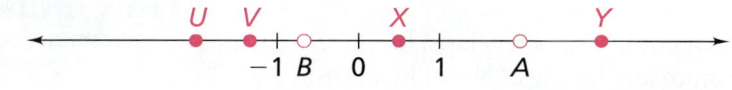

a. $A \cdot B$ b. $\frac{3}{2}A$ c. $3B$ d. $\frac{1}{A}$

1.10 Number Line Multiplication

5. Fill in each blank with a number that makes the equation true.

   a. $4 \cdot \left(\frac{1}{2} + \blacksquare\right) = 3$

   b. $-\frac{1}{3} \cdot (8 + \blacksquare) = -\frac{10}{3}$

   c. $\frac{1}{7} \cdot (18 + \blacksquare) = \frac{22}{7}$

   d. $14 \cdot \left(\frac{3}{2} + \blacksquare\right) = 28$

   e. $-5 \cdot \left(\frac{1}{9} + \blacksquare\right) = 0$

   f. $24 \cdot \left(\frac{1}{2} + \blacksquare\right) = 4$

   g. How did you find each missing number?

On Your Own

6. Find each product using the Distributive Property.

   a. $20 \cdot \left(\frac{1}{10} + \frac{1}{5}\right)$

   b. $12 \cdot \left(\frac{1}{2} + \frac{1}{3}\right)$

   c. $35 \cdot \left(\frac{1}{5} + \frac{1}{7}\right)$

   d. $\frac{1}{4} \cdot \left(\frac{4}{3} + \frac{4}{5}\right)$

7. **Standardized Test Prep** Evaluate $6 \cdot \left(\frac{5}{7} + \frac{4}{63}\right)$.

   A. $\frac{54}{70}$

   B. $\frac{14}{3}$

   C. $\frac{4}{1}$

   D. $\frac{49}{21}$

8. Copy the number line. Points A and B are numbers represented by the open dots. Match each of the solid dots with one of the following labels.

   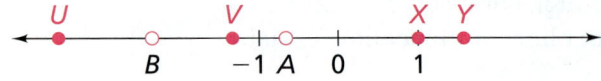

   a. $2A$

   b. $\frac{3}{2}B$

   c. AB

   d. $B \cdot \frac{1}{B}$

9. **Take It Further** Derman swims laps in a pool. After a few laps, he says, "I'm a quarter of the way there." After one more lap, he says, "Now I'm a third of the way there." How many laps does Derman intend to swim?

54   Chapter 1   Arithmetic to Algebra

Maintain Your Skills

For Exercises 10–12, fill in the missing number to make each equation true.

10. a. $3 \cdot \blacksquare = 12$
    b. $3 \cdot \blacksquare = 7$
    c. $3 \cdot \blacksquare = -11$
    d. $3 \cdot \blacksquare = 4$
    e. $3 \cdot \blacksquare = -5$
    f. How did you determine each missing number?

11. a. $7 \cdot \blacksquare = 1$
    b. $\frac{2}{5} \cdot \blacksquare = 1$
    c. $-\frac{5}{19} \cdot \blacksquare = 1$
    d. $-3 \cdot \blacksquare = 1$
    e. $\frac{22}{5} \cdot \blacksquare = 1$
    f. $\frac{1}{7} \cdot \blacksquare = 1$
    g. $\frac{88}{7} \cdot \blacksquare = 1$
    h. How did you determine each missing number?

12. a. $7 \cdot \left(\frac{1}{7} + \blacksquare \right) = 3$ b. $\frac{1}{5} \cdot (11 + \blacksquare) = \frac{14}{5}$
    c. $\frac{1}{3} \cdot (8 + \blacksquare) = \frac{7}{3}$ d. $-5 \cdot \left(\frac{1}{2} + \blacksquare \right) = -5$
    e. $6 \cdot \left(\frac{1}{2} + \blacksquare \right) = 5$ f. $-10 \cdot \left(\frac{1}{2} + \blacksquare \right) = 1$
    g. How did you determine each missing number?

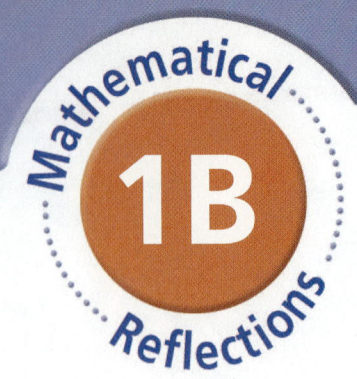

Mathematical Reflections 1B

In this investigation, you learned to locate fractions and decimals on the number line. You also used the number line to add and multiply real numbers. These questions will help you summarize what you have learned.

1. Draw a horizontal line segment about 2 inches long. Label the endpoints 0 and 1. Label points for $\frac{1}{2}, \frac{7}{8}, \frac{1}{4}$, and $\frac{3}{8}$. Which fraction is larger, $\frac{1}{4}$ or $\frac{1}{8}$? Explain.

2. Which of these fractions is NOT equal to the other fractions?

   A. $\frac{2}{3}$ B. $\frac{8}{12}$ C. $\frac{4}{5}$ D. $\frac{10}{15}$

3. Find the sum $1.25 + \frac{1}{2}$ in the following two ways.

   a. Change $\frac{1}{2}$ to a decimal.

   b. Change 1.25 to a fraction.

4. Illustrate each sum using a number line.

   a. $6 + (-2)$ b. $(-2) + 6$

   c. $(-3) + (-4)$ d. $(-2) + 2$

5. Draw a number line. Label the number halfway between -1 and 0 point A. Point B is a number between 2 and 3. Mark the approximate location of each expression.

   a. point A b. point B c. $A \cdot B$ d. $A + B$

6. How can you tell whether two fractions that look different represent the same number?

7. How do you add numbers on the number line?

8. Where is $\sqrt{2}$ located on the number line?

Vocabulary

In this investigation, you learned these terms. Make sure you understand what each one means and how to use it.

- decimal expansion
- decimal representation
- equivalent fractions
- lowest terms
- square root

Which girl can ride on the carnival attraction?

Chapter 1 Mid-Chapter Test

Do not use a calculator.

Multiple Choice

1. How many entries in the following part of a multiplication table are incorrect?

    A. 1   B. 2   C. 3   D. 4

    Multiplication Table

    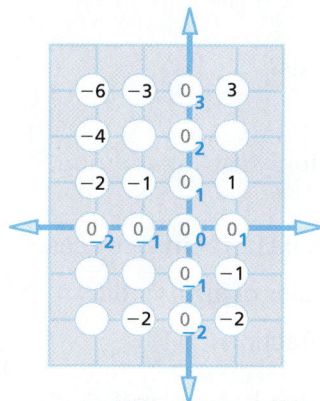

2. Which of these fractions is NOT equal to the other fractions?

    A. $\frac{6}{9}$ B. $\frac{3}{4}$

    C. $\frac{9}{12}$ D. $\frac{30}{40}$

3. Which expression gives the same result as $89 + (-144)$?

    A. $-(89 - 144)$

    B. $144 - 89$

    C. $-144 - 89$

    D. $-(144 - 89)$

4. Which expression is NOT equal to the other expressions?

    A. $57 \times (136 + 41)$

    B. $57 \times 136 + 41$

    C. $(41 + 136) \times 57$

    D. $57 \times 136 + 57 \times 41$

5. Suppose that this part of an addition table is complete. What is the sum of the numbers that will be in the four circles?

    Addition Table

    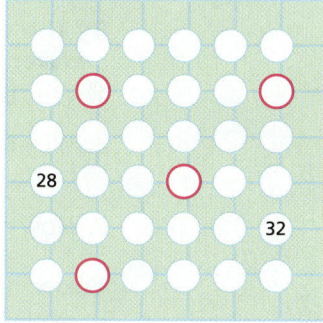

    A. 120   B. 122

    C. 124   D. none of the above

Open Response

6. Kelley picks a spot in the addition table. Then he repeatedly moves up 2 rows and right 1 column. He finds numbers that always increase by the same amount. Is Kelley correct? Explain.

7. Eileen does exactly what Kelley does in Exercise 6, except she uses a multiplication table. Does she always find numbers that increase by the same amount? Explain.

8. Explain each sentence. Use a number line illustration or a numerical example.

    a. Any number plus its opposite equals 0.

    b. If you change the order of numbers in a product, you find the same result.

9. Why is it true that the sum of two negative numbers is negative, while the product of two negative numbers is positive?

Challenge Problem

10. Find a number that is an entry in the entire multiplication table exactly 18 times.

Investigation 1C

The Algorithms of Arithmetic

In *The Algorithms of Arithmetic,* you will learn why traditional methods work for the four operations.

By the end of this investigation, you will be able to answer questions like these.

1. Why do traditional ways to add and multiply numbers work?
2. Why do people say that dividing is the same as multiplying by the reciprocal?
3. How many weeks are in 1 billion seconds?

You will learn how to
- explain why the algorithms you commonly use for addition, subtraction, and multiplication work
- use nontraditional algorithms that can be faster in some cases
- become more familiar with the basic rules of arithmetic
- perform arithmetic with integers and fractions

You will develop these habits and skills:
- Find and justify new shortcuts for doing arithmetic.
- View algorithms and other mathematical processes not just as shortcuts for answering math questions, but also as ideas that mathematicians study.

1.11 Getting Started

**Activating Prior Knowledge
Exploring New Ideas**

In Getting Started, you will use the four operations and rational numbers. Unless stated otherwise, complete the exercises in this investigation without using a calculator.

For You to Explore

1. Perform each operation. Find shortcuts to simplify your work. Keep track of your steps.

   a. 48×5

   b. $2 + 55 + 31 + 45 + 98 + 9$

   c. $125 \cdot 13 \cdot 80$

   d. 2×98

   e. $\frac{1}{10} + \frac{37}{100} + \frac{243}{1000}$

   f. 0.1
      0.37
      $+0.243$

   g. $641 - 244$

   h. $\frac{1}{2} + \frac{3}{4} + \frac{5}{8}$

   i. $\frac{1}{2} \cdot \frac{2}{3} \cdot \frac{3}{4} \cdot \frac{4}{5}$

   j. $\frac{21}{83} \cdot \frac{77}{19} \cdot \frac{31}{21} \cdot \frac{19}{31} \cdot \frac{83}{77}$

   k. $\frac{14}{15} \cdot \frac{50}{28} \cdot \frac{11}{20} \cdot \frac{16}{22}$

   l. $\dfrac{\frac{10}{13}}{\frac{5}{13}}$

   m. $148 + 93 - 74 + 107 - 53 - 11$

   n. $81 - 72 + 63 - 54 + 45 - 36 + 27 - 18 + 9$

2. Explain any shortcuts you used in Problem 1.

Exercises Practicing Habits of Mind

On Your Own

For Exercises 3 and 4, each letter represents a single digit from 0 to 9. Find all possible values of each digit that make the arithmetic exercise true.

3. Find all possible values for A, B, and C.

    ```
       AB
       AB
       AB
     + AB
     ----
       CA
    ```

4. Find all possible values for A, B, and C.

    ```
       ABA
     + BAB
     -----
       CCC
    ```

5. At a sports store, a water bottle cost $7.99, a pair of shorts costs $24.99, and a pair of shoes costs $61.99.

    a. Without using a calculator, find the total cost of these items.

    b. **Write About It** Describe how to find the sum.

Maintain Your Skills

6. Find each sum.

    a. $1 + \frac{1}{2}$
    b. $1 + \frac{1}{2} + \frac{1}{4}$
    c. $1 + \frac{1}{2} + \frac{1}{4} + \frac{1}{8}$
    d. $1 + \frac{1}{2} + \frac{1}{4} + \frac{1}{8} + \frac{1}{16}$
    e. $1 + \frac{1}{2} + \frac{1}{4} + \frac{1}{8} + \frac{1}{16} + \frac{1}{32}$
    f. Describe a pattern that you can use to find the sum.

7. Find each result.

    a. $1 - \frac{1}{2}$
    b. $1 - \frac{1}{2} + \frac{1}{4}$
    c. $1 - \frac{1}{2} + \frac{1}{4} - \frac{1}{8}$
    d. $1 - \frac{1}{2} + \frac{1}{4} - \frac{1}{8} + \frac{1}{16}$
    e. $1 - \frac{1}{2} + \frac{1}{4} - \frac{1}{8} + \frac{1}{16} - \frac{1}{32}$
    f. Describe a pattern that you can use to find the result.

1.12 Addition and Subtraction Algorithms

This lesson focuses on addition and subtraction **algorithms.** An algorithm is a set of ordered steps for solving a problem. You will examine the algorithms to find why they work. Many of these algorithms are based on breaking up a number into place-value parts. In this lesson, you will review a number's place-value parts.

Facts and Notation

A **place-value part** is a number, such as 6000, 20, or 5 that has a single leading digit followed by some number of zeros. The number 270 is not a place-value part but is the sum of two place-value parts, 200 + 70.

For You to Do

Write each number as the sum of place-value parts.

1. 1982 **2.** 305 **3.** 39,150

Addition Using Columns The traditional addition algorithm follows these steps.

Step 1 Start with the column farthest to the right and add each number in the column.

Step 2 Write the sum of the ones digit column below the column.

Step 3 If the sum is 10 or greater, carry the tens to the top of the next column.

Step 4 Repeat a similar process with the next column, moving from right to left.

Here is an example.

$$
\begin{array}{r}413\\254\\+\ 91\\\hline\end{array}\ \rightarrow\ \begin{array}{r}413\\254\\+\ 91\\\hline 8\end{array}\ \rightarrow\ \begin{array}{r}\overset{1}{4}13\\254\\+\ 91\\\hline 58\end{array}\ \rightarrow\ \begin{array}{r}\overset{1}{4}13\\254\\+\ 91\\\hline 758\end{array}
$$

   Step 1   Step 2   Step 3

Here are the steps you follow to find the sum above.

Step 1 Find the sum of 3, 4, and 1. Write the sum 8 below the ones column.

Step 2 Add 1, 5, and 9. The sum is 15. Write the digit 5 below the tens column. Write the other digits at the top of the next column.

Step 3 Add the carried digit 1 to 4 and 2. The sum is 7. The sum of 413 + 254 + 91 is 758.

Millions of people trust this algorithm. It gives the correct answer, but not many people ask why it works.

Example

Problem

a. Explain why addition using columns works.

b. When is this algorithm useful?

Solution

a. The algorithm uses the any-order, any-grouping properties of addition. To understand why this is true, look at the place-value parts in the addition algorithm.

$$413 + 254 + 91$$

Break each number into place-value parts. Then rearrange the place-value parts. Group the ones, tens, and hundreds together.

$$413 + 254 + 91 = (400 + 10 + 3) + (200 + 50 + 4) + (90 + 1)$$
$$= (400 + 200) + (10 + 50 + 90) + (3 + 4 + 1)$$

You can rearrange the numbers because the AOAG properties state that the order you use to add the numbers does not affect the result.

Adding by columns is the same as adding the place-value parts separately. First, add the ones digits. Next, add the tens digits. Finally, add the hundreds digits.

$$= (400 + 200) + (10 + 50 + 90) + 8$$
$$= (400 + 200) + 150 + 8$$
$$= 600 + 150 + 8$$

When you add $1 + 5 + 9$ in the tens column to get 15, you are actually adding $10 + 50 + 90$ to get 150. You need to carry, because 150 is not a place-value part. You need to split 150 into two place-value parts, $150 = 100 + 50$. You combine the number 100 with the other numbers in the next place value to the left.

$$(400 + 200) + 150 + 8 = (400 + 200) + (100 + 50) + 8$$
$$= (400 + 200 + 100) + 50 + 8$$
$$= 700 + 50 + 8$$
$$= 758$$

You can perform addition in any order and use any grouping, so $(400 + 200) + (100 + 50)$ is the same as $(400 + 200 + 100) + 50$, or $(50 + 400) + (100 + 200)$.

b. You can use this algorithm to add any numbers, so it is very useful. The only time that it is not useful is when you add larger numbers and do not have a pencil or paper.

> Can a decimal such as 2.853 be broken up into place-value parts? Explain.

For Discussion

4. When adding by columns, you add the ones column before you add the digit in the tens column. Why do you add by columns moving from right to left?

Exercises Practicing Habits of Mind

Check Your Understanding

In a small group, you will discuss one or more algorithms and understand why each algorithm works.

For Exercises 1–7, answer these questions using sentences.

- How and why does the technique or algorithm work? Include the basic rules of arithmetic in your explanation, if possible.
- When is the technique or algorithm useful?

1. Add more and then subtract. Find the sum.

$$\begin{array}{r} \$17.99 \\ +\$19.99 \\ \hline \end{array}$$

Think about $17.99 as $18 − $.01, and $19.99 as $20 − $.01. Then, add $18 and $20 and subtract $.02.

Here is how the calculation works.

$$\begin{aligned} \$17.99 + \$19.99 &= (\$18 - \$.01) + (\$20 - \$.01) \\ &= (\$18 + \$20) - \$.01 - \$.01 \\ &= \$38 - \$.02 \\ &= \$37.98 \end{aligned}$$

1.12 Addition and Subtraction Algorithms

2. **Reorder the terms.** When you add many numbers, changing the order of the numbers can make finding a sum easier. How can you make this addition easier?

   $$\begin{array}{r} 148 \\ 3 \\ 60 \\ 37 \\ +\ 152 \\ \hline \end{array}$$

   Adding is easier if you can find numbers with a sum that equals a multiple of ten. For example, $3 + 37 = 40$, and adding 60 more equals 100. The other sum, $152 + 148$, equals 300. Finally, $100 + 300 = 400$.

3. **Subtract using columns.** The traditional subtraction algorithm uses columns. Instead of carrying, you "borrow" a unit. You borrow when a column shows a subtraction, such as $3 - 4$, that does not give a positive result.

   For the subtraction $3 - 4$ in Step 2, you borrow 1 from the column at the left. You change 5 to 4 (column at the left) and 3 to 13 (Step 2). Then you find the difference $13 - 4$ in the second column. The last step is to subtract 3 from 5 in the column at the left.

   $$\begin{array}{r} 537 \\ \underline{341} \\ \end{array} \quad \rightarrow \quad \begin{array}{r} 537 \\ -\ 341 \\ \hline 6 \end{array} \quad \rightarrow \quad \begin{array}{r} {}^{4\ 13}\!\!\!\!\!\!\!\!\!\!\! 537 \\ -\ 341 \\ \hline 6 \end{array} \quad \rightarrow \quad \begin{array}{r} {}^{4\ 13}\!\!\!\!\!\!\!\!\!\!\! 537 \\ -\ 341 \\ \hline 96 \end{array} \quad \rightarrow \quad \begin{array}{r} {}^{4\ 13}\!\!\!\!\!\!\!\!\!\!\! 537 \\ -\ 341 \\ \hline 196 \end{array}$$

   Step 1   **Step 2**   **Step 3**   **Step 4**

4. **Subtract some more.** Suppose you want to subtract 341 from 537. You can break up the number 341 into 337 and 4. Then you can subtract: $537 - 337 = 200$ and $200 - 4 = 196$.

   $$\begin{array}{r} 537 \\ -\ 337 \\ -\ \ \ \ 4 \\ \hline \end{array}$$

5. **Add from left to right.** Tyler has a method for adding numbers mentally. He explains his method this way.

   "Look at the sum $42 + 37 + 55 + 96$.

   Start with the largest place value. These are all 2-digit numbers, so the largest place value is the tens place. First, you add just the tens.

   $$\underbrace{\underbrace{\underbrace{42 + 3}_{70}7 + 5}_{120}5 + 9}_{210}6$$

   40 plus 30 is 70, 70 plus 50 is 120, and 120 plus 90 is 210. Next, take 210 and add the ones.

   $$\underbrace{\underbrace{\underbrace{42 + 3}_{70}7 + 5}_{120}5 + 9}_{210}6$$
   $$\ \ \ 212\ \ \ \ \ \ 219\ \ \ \ \ \ 224\ \ \ \ \ \ 230$$

   210 plus 2 is 212, 212 plus 7 is 219, 219 plus 5 is 224, and 224 plus 6 is 230. This is much easier!"

6. **Subtract by counting up.** To find the difference 1017 − 345, start with 345 and add numbers until you reach 1017. Here is one way to do this.

   $$345 + 600 = 945$$
   $$945 + 60 = 1005$$
   $$1005 + 10 = 1015$$
   $$1015 + 2 = 1017$$

   Because 345 + (600 + 60 + 10 + 2) = 1017, (600 + 60 + 10 + 2) is the difference 1017 − 345 = 672.

   > Since the result is the sum of 600 + 60 + 10 + 2, it is generally simpler to add place-value parts when you can.

7. **Add consecutive integers.** Here is a trick for adding a list of consecutive integers. Add the integers from 1 to 9. Then regroup the numbers so that many sums are the same.

   $$1 + 2 + 3 + 4 + 5 + 6 + 7 + 8 + 9 = (1 + 9) + (2 + 8) + (3 + 7) + (4 + 6) + 5$$
   $$= 10 + 10 + 10 + 10 + 5$$
   $$= 45$$

On Your Own

Unless stated otherwise, complete Exercises 8–15 without using a calculator.

8. Kye invents a subtraction method. Here is an example.

   ```
     73
   − 48
   ─────
     −5
     30
   ─────
     25
   ```

   Kye reasons that 3 − 8 is −5, 70 − 40 is 30, and 30 − 5 is 25. Use Kye's method. Find the difference 47 − 59.

9. **Write About It** Does Kye's method in Exercise 8 always work? Explain.

10. Find the sum 6312 + 2483.

1.12 Addition and Subtraction Algorithms

11. **Standardized Test Prep** Jason has his own method for subtraction. He rewrites $A - B = C$ as $B + C = A$. Then he starts at the left-most digit in the number B. He finds the greatest place-value part that he can add to B. He makes sure that this sum is no greater than the number A. Then Jason moves from left to right across B. He adds place-value parts until the sum of the place-value parts is the number A. Which of the following shows his method for finding $3964 - 2587$?

    A. $2587 + 7 = 2594$
        $2594 + 70 = 2664$
        $2664 + 300 = 2964$
        $2964 + 1000 = 3964$
        $2587 + 1377 = 3964$

    B. $2587 + 1400 = 3987$
        $3987 - 30 = 3957$
        $3987 + 7 = 3964$
        $2587 + 1407 - 30 = 1377$

    C. $2587 + 1000 = 3587$
        $3587 + 300 = 3887$
        $3887 + 70 = 3957$
        $3957 + 7 = 3964$
        $2587 + 1377 = 3964$

    D. $3964 - 2587 = 300 + 7 + 1000 + 70$
        $300 + 7 + 1000 + 70 = 1377$

12. Without adding, explain how you know that both sums are the same.

    ```
       413            294
       254            451
    +   91         +   13
    ```

13. A standard football field is 100 yards long from end zone to end zone. Vince measures a field and finds that it is five feet shorter than a standard field. How long is the shorter field?

14. A professional football field is 100 yards long from end zone to end zone and 160 feet wide.

    a. If you want to find the field's area, can you multiply 100 by 160?
    b. Find the area of the field in square feet.
    c. Find the area of the field in square yards.
    d. How many square feet are in a square yard?

Maintain Your Skills

15. a. How many $\frac{1}{6}$'s are in $\frac{1}{2}$?
    b. How many $\frac{1}{6}$'s are in $\frac{2}{3}$?
    c. How many $\frac{1}{4}$'s are in $2\frac{1}{2}$?
    d. How many 5's are in 37?
    e. Make a conjecture about the general rule that you can use to find each result.

1.13 Adding and Subtracting Fractions

In this lesson, you will learn to add and subtract fractions with like and unlike denominators.

Minds in Action   episode 2

Tony and Sasha work on Exercise 13 from Lesson 1.12.

A standard football field is 100 yards long from end zone to end zone. Vince measures a field and finds that it is five feet shorter than a standard field. How long is the shorter field?

Tony I've got the answer. It's 295 feet.

Sasha Two hundred ninety-five? I got 95. That seems fine to me.

Tony No, the answer is definitely 295 feet.

Sasha How can the field be 295 feet long? The regular field is 100 yards. Oh, I see. You got 295 feet. Now I see what I did wrong.

To find the length of the shorter field, you can write this subtraction. When Sasha subtracts the numbers, the calculation does not make sense. The units are not the same!

```
  100 yards
−   5 feet
  ─────────
     ■
```

There are two ways to change the units. You can convert 100 yards to feet, or convert 5 feet to yards. Converting yards to feet gives you this subtraction problem.

```
  300 feet
−   5 feet
  ─────────
     ■ feet
```

There are three feet in a yard, so 100 yards equal 300 feet. You can also convert 5 feet to $\frac{5}{3}$ yards. Then subtract that amount from 100 yards. The result is in yards, instead of feet.

You can use this method to add and subtract fractions. For example, you can write the sum $\frac{2}{3} + \frac{1}{5}$ like this. You need to convert the denominators of both fractions to a common unit.

```
  2 thirds
+ 1 fifth
  ─────────
     ■
```

Here are some ways to write $\frac{2}{3}$ as an equivalent fraction.

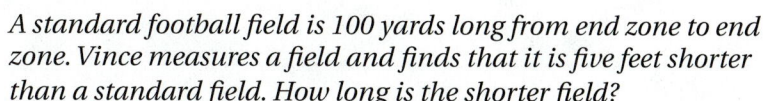

Here are some equivalent fractions for $\frac{1}{5}$.

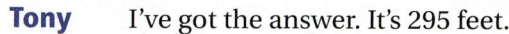

In the list below there is a matching unit, fifteenths. Two thirds is equivalent to ten fifteenths, and one fifth is equivalent to three fifteenths. Now that you have a common unit, you can find the sum.

Fifteenths is the lowest possible match. So 15 is the least common denominator. What other matches are possible?

```
  10 fifteenths
+  3 fifteenths
  ─────────────
  13 fifteenths
```

$$\frac{2}{3} + \frac{1}{5} = \frac{10}{15} + \frac{3}{15}$$
$$= \frac{13}{15}$$

1.13 Adding and Subtracting Fractions   67

There is always a choice of common denominators for any two fractions. Using the lowest, or **least common denominator,** as the common unit is the most efficient. You can use the same idea when you subtract fractions. Since $\frac{5}{6}$ is equal to $\frac{10}{12}$, the result is $\frac{10}{12} - \frac{7}{12} = \frac{3}{12}$.

```
  5 sixths
- 7 twelfths
```

Even if you use the least common denominator, you can sometimes simplify the result of a calculation further.

$$\frac{3 \div 3}{12 \div 3} = \frac{1}{4}$$

The fraction $\frac{1}{4}$ is in lowest terms, which means that the numerator and denominator do not share a common factor greater than 1.

For You to Do

1. Find $\frac{11}{24} + \frac{3}{8}$ and $\frac{11}{24} - \frac{3}{8}$. Write each result in lowest terms.

For Discussion

2. Suppose you add $\frac{2}{3} + \frac{1}{5}$. How is the common denominator, 15, related to thirds and fifths? Is this always true?

Exercises Practicing Habits of Mind

Check Your Understanding

1. Find the sum of $\frac{1}{3} + \frac{1}{4} + \frac{1}{5} + \frac{1}{20} + \frac{1}{6}$ without a calculator.

   You can find this sum quickly and simply by adding the terms in a certain order.

2. The least common denominator for $\frac{2}{3}$ and $\frac{1}{5}$ is 15, and 15 is the product of 3 and 5.

   a. Find the least common denominator for each pair of fractions.

   $\frac{1}{3}$ and $\frac{1}{5}$ $\qquad$ $\frac{2}{3}$ and $\frac{4}{5}$

   b. Find the least common denominator for each pair of fractions.

   $\frac{3}{8}$ and $\frac{5}{16}$ $\qquad$ $\frac{3}{8}$ and $\frac{5}{7}$ $\qquad$ $\frac{3}{10}$ and $\frac{1}{12}$

68 Chapter 1 Arithmetic to Algebra

c. When is the least common denominator of two fractions the product of the denominators?

d. **Take It Further** Is it possible for the least common denominator of two fractions to be greater than the product of the two denominators? Explain using examples.

3. Jill explains how she learned to add fractions using a crisscross style. She says, "You have $\frac{3}{5} + \frac{4}{7}$. I know the common denominator is 5 times 7, or 35, so I write that. The numerator, though, I get by doing a crisscross. I know that 3 times 7 is 21, and 5 times 4 is 20. I add those to get 41. The result of the addition is $\frac{41}{35}$. It works every time."

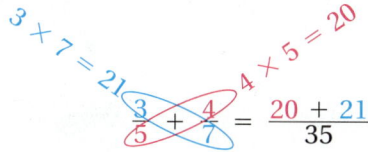

Use Jill's method to find each sum.

a. $\frac{3}{11} + \frac{1}{4}$ **b.** $\frac{1}{5} + \frac{3}{5}$

c. **Take It Further** Explain why Jill's method works.

d. **Take It Further** Can you apply Jill's method to subtracting fractions?

On Your Own

4. Find the product $24 \cdot \left(\frac{1}{3} + \frac{1}{4} + \frac{1}{8} + \frac{1}{6}\right)$ without using a calculator.

5. Find each sum or difference.

a. $\frac{1}{3} + \left(\frac{1}{11} - \frac{1}{3}\right)$ **b.** $-\frac{3}{7} + \left(\frac{1}{10} + \frac{3}{7}\right)$

c. $\left(\frac{1}{2} - \frac{7}{19}\right) + \left(\frac{7}{19} - \frac{1}{4}\right)$ **d.** $\left(\frac{2}{3} - \frac{1}{8}\right) - \left(\frac{1}{6} - \frac{1}{8}\right)$

6. **Standardized Test Prep** What is the sum $\frac{2}{9} + \frac{3}{18} + \frac{3}{27}$?

A. 1 **B.** $\frac{8}{27}$

C. $\frac{13}{27}$ **D.** $\frac{1}{2}$

7. **Write About It** Write a step-by-step procedure for adding any two fractions for someone who does not know how to add fractions.

8. Find three distinct fractions having a sum that equals each number given.

   a. 1   **b.** −2   **c.** $\frac{1}{4}$

9. Fill in each missing number.

   a. $\frac{1}{3} + \blacksquare = 2$ **b.** $\frac{1}{5} + \blacksquare = \frac{7}{10}$

   c. $\frac{1}{2} + \blacksquare = \frac{5}{4}$ **d.** $\frac{3}{2} - \blacksquare = \frac{13}{14}$

Maintain Your Skills

10. Find each sum. Write the result in lowest terms.

    a. $\frac{1}{3} + \frac{1}{6} + \frac{1}{9} + \frac{1}{18}$

    b. $\frac{1}{4} + \frac{1}{8} + \frac{1}{12} + \frac{1}{24}$

    c. $\frac{1}{10} + \frac{1}{20} + \frac{1}{30} + \frac{1}{60}$

    d. $\frac{1}{101} + \frac{1}{202} + \frac{1}{303} + \frac{1}{606}$

    e. Describe the pattern that you used to find each result.

11. Find each sum.

    a. $1 + \frac{1}{3}$

    b. $1 + \frac{1}{3} + \frac{1}{9}$

    c. $1 + \frac{1}{3} + \frac{1}{9} + \frac{1}{27}$

    d. $1 + \frac{1}{3} + \frac{1}{9} + \frac{1}{27} + \frac{1}{81}$

    e. $1 + \frac{1}{3} + \frac{1}{9} + \frac{1}{27} + \frac{1}{81} + \frac{1}{243}$

    f. Describe the pattern you used to find each result.

12. Find each result.

    a. $1 - \frac{1}{3}$

    b. $1 - \frac{1}{3} + \frac{1}{9}$

    c. $1 - \frac{1}{3} + \frac{1}{9} - \frac{1}{27}$

    d. $1 - \frac{1}{3} + \frac{1}{9} - \frac{1}{27} + \frac{1}{81}$

    e. $1 - \frac{1}{3} + \frac{1}{9} - \frac{1}{27} + \frac{1}{81} - \frac{1}{243}$

    f. Describe the pattern that you used to find each result.

Go Online
pearsonsuccessnet.com

1.14 Multiplication Algorithms

In this lesson, you will look at *why* multiplication algorithms work. You may already know a multiplication algorithm, but you may not know why it works.

In the traditional multiplication algorithm, you first place the greater number above the lesser number. Next, you multiply the number on top by the ones digit of the number on the bottom. Then, you multiply the number on top by the tens digit of the number on the bottom, and so on. Finally, you add these numbers in a column form, using the addition algorithm.

You can find the product 327 × 6 using these steps.

$$\begin{array}{r}327\\\times\;\;6\\\hline\end{array} \rightarrow \begin{array}{r}\overset{4}{3}2\overset{}{7}\\\times\;\;\;\;6\\\hline 2\end{array} \rightarrow \begin{array}{r}\overset{1\;4}{3}27\\\times\;\;\;\;6\\\hline 62\end{array} \rightarrow \begin{array}{r}\overset{1\;4}{3}27\\\times\;\;\;\;\;6\\\hline 1962\end{array}$$

                  Step 1   **Step 2**   **Step 3**

Step 1 Multiply 6 × 7. The product equals 42. Write 2 below the line and carry 4.

Step 2 Multiply 6 × 2. The product equals 12. Add the 4 that you carried to get 16. Write 6 below the line. Carry 1.

Step 3 Multiply 6 × 3 and add 1 to get 19. Since you are done multiplying, you do not carry any more, and you write 19 below the line.

Look closely at what you are doing. As you did with addition, break down the greater number into its place-value parts.

    327 = 300 + 20 + 7

You can rewrite the problem using place-value parts.

    327 × 6 = (300 + 20 + 7) × 6

Then you can perform separate multiplications on each digit, starting with the ones digit and moving left. Remember that when you multiply 6 × 2 in the algorithm above, you are really multiplying 6 × 20.

    6 × 7 = 42

    6 × 20 = 120

    6 × 300 = 1800

                  1800   120   42
    327 × 6 = (300 × 6) + (20 × 6) + (7 × 6)

Then add the products. The product of 327 and 6 is 1962.

    1800 + 120 + 42 = 1962

You can estimate the height of the Bank of China Tower when you know a few facts about the tower. It is 70 stories high, each story is 3 windows high, and each window is about 1.33 meters high.

Developing Habits of Mind

Represent the multiplication process. You can use an **expansion box** to represent the equation $327 \times 6 = 1962$.

Write the place-value parts for 327 in the first column. Write the place-value parts for 6 in the first row. Each entry in the table is the product of its row and column. For example, $300 \times 6 = 1800$. The product 327 times 6 equals the sum of the numbers inside the box.

	6
300	1800
20	120
7	42

> You can add the numbers in any order using any grouping. How can you add them to model the usual multiplication algorithm?

You can find some shorter ways of multiplying other numbers using an expansion box. For example, you can represent 98 using place-value parts $90 + 8$. However, if you are multiplying a number by 98, a simpler representation might be $98 = (100 - 2)$. Compare the following expansion boxes. Which expansion box makes the calculations quicker?

	90	8
2	180	16

	100	−2
2	200	−4

You get the same result using either box: $180 + 16 = 196$ and $200 - 4 = 196$.

Exercises *Practicing Habits of Mind*

Check Your Understanding

1. **Traditional algorithm** In this lesson, you used the traditional algorithm to multiply a three-digit number (327) by a one-digit number (6). The Distributive Property is important in understanding why the algorithm works.

   a. Explain how to use the standard algorithm to multiply a three-digit number by a two-digit number.

   b. Using the Distributive Property, explain how the algorithm works.

   c. When is this algorithm useful?

2. **Multiply by 5.** To multiply a number by 5, halve the number. Then multiply by 10. For instance, to multiply 48 × 5, halve 48 to get 24. Then multiply by 10 to get 240.

   a. Using the basic rules of arithmetic, explain why this algorithm works.

   b. When is this algorithm useful?

   c. Invent a similar algorithm for multiplying by 25.

3. **Multiply by closest place-value.** You want to multiply a number by 99. For this algorithm, use the place-value amount closest to 99, which is 100, and the fact that 99 = 100 − 1. For example, to evaluate 8 · 99, start with the product of 100 that is closer to 8 · 99, which is 800. Then subtract 8 from 800 to get 792.

   a. Using the basic rules of arithmetic, explain why this algorithm works.

   b. Can you think of a situation in which this algorithm will be useful?

   c. Invent a similar algorithm for multiplying by 98.

4. **Russian method** Here is an alternative algorithm for multiplying numbers. To find 21 × 5, make a table. Then you successively take half of one factor (throwing away any remainder) and double the other.

   Multiplication Algorithm

Half	Double	Save
21	5	*
10	10	
5	20	*
2	40	
1	80	*

   > Half of 21 is not really 10. It is 10 with $\frac{1}{2}$ left over. So, you put a 10 under 21 and a * in the Save column to show that there is a remainder.

   There is a * in each row where an odd number is in the Half column. Add the numbers in the Double column that have a * to their right: 5 + 20 + 80 = 105. The product 21 × 5 is 105.

   a. Using the basic rules of arithmetic, explain why this algorithm works. (*Hint:* You can write every even number as a sum of powers of 2. You can write every odd number as a sum of 1 and powers of 2.)

   b. Can you think of a situation in which this algorithm will be useful?

5. **Multiplication and division using lines** To find a product or quotient, use graph paper and a slanted "multiplication line." Draw horizontal and vertical number lines. Label them using integers. At 1 on the vertical number line, draw a heavy horizontal line.

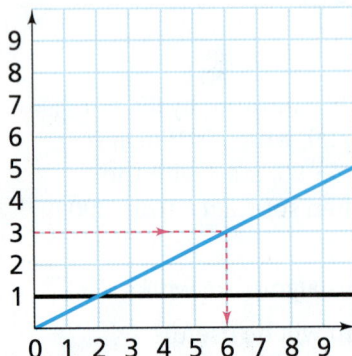

To multiply 2 and 3, draw a slanted multiplication line that starts at 0. The slanted line crosses the horizontal line at 2, since 2 is a factor. Draw a horizontal line at 3, since 3 is the other factor. Then move down to the horizontal number line to find the product 6.

   a. Use the basic rules of arithmetic. Explain why this algorithm works.

   b. When is this algorithm useful?

   c. Make a grid on graph paper to find each product.

   4×3 2×7 $6 \times \frac{1}{2}$

   d. Describe a "division using lines" algorithm.

On Your Own

6. How many of each unit are in 1 million seconds? Use a calculator.

   a. minutes

   b. hours

   c. days to the nearest day

7. **Take It Further** You can measure speed in feet per second, in miles per hour, or in many other ways. A pitcher throws a baseball at 92 miles per hour. How many feet per second does the baseball travel? (*Hint*: There are 5280 feet in a mile.)

You can use radar to find the speed of a pitch in miles per hour.

8. Use expansion boxes. Find each product.

   a. 89×42

   b. 101×99

   c. 1989×37

   d. $4\frac{2}{3} \times 3\frac{1}{4}$

There is more than one way to set up an expansion box. Are some boxes easier to use than others?

9. Each letter represents a single digit from 0 to 9. Find all possible values for A, B, C, D, and E. The digits 3 and 1 are given.

$$\begin{array}{r} 1ABCDE \\ \times 3 \\ \hline ABCDE1 \end{array}$$

10. Each letter represents a single digit from 0 to 9. Some digits are given.

$$\begin{array}{r} 2B3 \\ \times 327 \\ \hline 6CD5A \end{array}$$

What digit multiplied by 3 gives a product ending in 1? When you know the value of E, use it to find the value of D.

   a. What is the value of A? Explain.

   b. **Take It Further** Find the values of B, C, and D.

11. **Standardized Test Prep** Teresa makes a puzzle by assigning the letters A–E to the even-number digits. When she multiplies each number by each of the other numbers, she finds that she needs two more letters, J and K. They represent the tens place in the product. Here are Teresa's product pairs.

$A \cdot A = JA$	$A \cdot B = DB$	$A \cdot C = C$	$A \cdot D = KD$	$A \cdot E = BE$
	$B \cdot B = KA$	$B \cdot C = C$	$B \cdot D = E$	$B \cdot E = JD$
		$C \cdot C = C$	$C \cdot D = C$	$C \cdot E = C$
			$D \cdot D = B$	$D \cdot E = KA$
				$E \cdot E = AB$

Which of the following shows how Teresa assigned the letters?

A. $A = 6$, $B = 4$, $C = 0$, $D = 2$, $E = 8$, $J = 1$, $K = 3$

B. $A = 2$, $B = 4$, $C = 0$, $D = 6$, $E = 8$, $J = 3$, $K = 1$

C. $A = 4$, $B = 2$, $C = 0$, $D = 8$, $E = 6$, $J = 1$, $K = 3$

D. $A = 6$, $B = 4$, $C = 0$, $D = 2$, $E = 8$, $J = 3$, $K = 1$

Go Online
pearsonsuccessnet.com

12. Use expansion boxes to find each product. Find more than one way to set up each expansion box.

    a. 103×97
    b. $3\frac{1}{3} \times 2\frac{2}{5}$
    c. 2.9×0.99
    d. 995×1.2

Maintain Your Skills

Find each product.

13. a. 107×109
    b. 1007×1009
    c. $10{,}007 \times 10{,}009$
    d. What is 17×19? How is this product related to the other products?

14. a. 17×102
    b. 18×102
    c. 42×102
    d. 35×102
    e. Describe the pattern that you used to find each product.

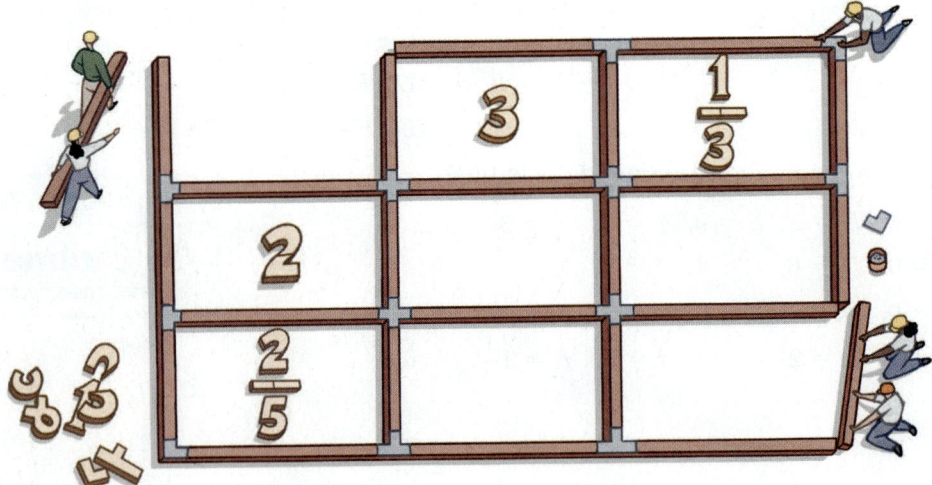

76   Chapter 1   Arithmetic to Algebra

1.15 Multiplying and Dividing Fractions

Multiplying fractions is usually simpler than adding fractions. To find the product, you just multiply the numerators and multiply the denominators.

Developing Habits of Mind

Find relationships. To find the product $\frac{2}{3} \cdot \frac{5}{7}$, why do you multiply numerators and multiply denominators? This is not an easy question to answer. For now, you can use the following ideas and assumptions to understand why.

You can think of multiplication as repeated addition.

$$\frac{1}{3} \cdot 3 = \frac{1}{3} + \frac{1}{3} + \frac{1}{3} = \frac{3}{3} = 1$$

When you multiply $\frac{1}{3}$ by 3, you get 1. Is there any other number you can multiply by 3 to get 1? No, you can assume for now that the only number you can multiply by 3 to get 1 is $\frac{1}{3}$.

Because $\frac{2}{3} \cdot 3 = 2$, you can also assume that if you multiply a mystery number by 3 and get 2, then the mystery number is $\frac{2}{3}$.

You can assume that the any-order, any-grouping properties work for multiplication of real numbers, including fractions.

Why is $\frac{2}{3} \cdot \frac{5}{7} = \frac{10}{21}$? One way to explain this result is to multiply $\frac{2}{3} \cdot \frac{5}{7}$ by 21 and find whether the product is 10. To do that, rearrange the order of the calculations and use the assumptions above.

$$\left(\frac{2}{3} \cdot \frac{5}{7}\right) \cdot 21 = \left(\frac{2}{3} \cdot \frac{5}{7}\right) \cdot 7 \cdot 3$$
$$= \left(\frac{2}{3} \cdot 3\right) \cdot \left(\frac{5}{7} \cdot 7\right)$$
$$= 2 \cdot 5 = 10$$

Multiplying $\frac{2}{3} \cdot \frac{5}{7}$ by 21 gives a product 10. So, $\frac{2}{3} \cdot \frac{5}{7}$ is $\frac{10}{21}$.

> A common mistake is to apply the process for multiplication to addition of fractions. It is not true that $\frac{2}{3} + \frac{4}{5} = \frac{2+4}{3+5}$. Adding fractions usually involves converting to a common denominator.

To divide by a fraction, you can multiply by the reciprocal. What is a reciprocal? The reciprocal of 13 is a unit fraction, such as $\frac{1}{13}$. The reciprocal of $\frac{5}{3}$ is $\frac{3}{5}$. The **reciprocal** of a fraction is the result you get by flipping the numerator and denominator.

Notice something that both cases have in common. When you multiply a number by its reciprocal, the product is 1. For instance, $13 \cdot \frac{1}{13} = \frac{13}{13}$, or 1 and $\frac{5}{3} \cdot \frac{3}{5} = \frac{15}{15}$, or 1.

Mathematicians use this property to write a more precise definition of a reciprocal. When you find the reciprocal of any number, you find another number that you can multiply times that number to get a product 1.

> The number 0 does not have a reciprocal. Explain.

1.15 **Multiplying and Dividing Fractions** 77

For You to Do

Find each reciprocal.

1. 99
2. $\frac{3}{11}$
3. $-\frac{8}{101}$
4. -5
5. -1

Dividing by a number is the same as multiplying by the number's reciprocal.

$$\frac{5}{3} \div \frac{5}{3} \stackrel{?}{=} \frac{5}{3} \cdot \frac{3}{5}$$

- You know from the rules of division that any number divided by itself equals 1. So, $\frac{5}{3} \div \frac{5}{3}$ equals 1.
- You also know about reciprocals. So, $\frac{5}{3} \cdot \frac{3}{5} = \frac{15}{15}$, or 1.
- Therefore, dividing by $\frac{5}{3}$ is the same as multiplying by $\frac{3}{5}$. The reciprocal of $\frac{5}{3}$ is $\frac{3}{5}$.

Exercises Practicing Habits of Mind

Check Your Understanding

Describe an actual situation in which the given number is the practical result of dividing 17 by 4. For example, when you divide 17 soccer balls equally among 4 teams, each team gets 4 balls.

1. 5
2. 4.25

3. Sasha knows a trick for multiplying fractions. "Sometimes a number is in the numerator of one fraction and in the denominator of another fraction. So, the numbers cancel each other. Look at this example. The 21 is in the numerator and denominator. So, I can cancel the 21's. I can also cancel the 83's, 19's, and 77's."

$$\frac{\cancel{21}}{83} \cdot \frac{77}{19} \cdot \frac{31}{\cancel{21}} \cdot \frac{19}{31} \cdot \frac{83}{77}$$

Using Sasha's cancelling method, find each product.

a. $\frac{3}{8} \cdot \frac{7}{3} \cdot \frac{8}{10}$

b. $\frac{-2}{15} \cdot \frac{15}{3} \cdot \frac{9}{-2}$

c. $\frac{21}{83} \cdot \frac{77}{19} \cdot \frac{31}{21} \cdot \frac{19}{31} \cdot \frac{83}{77}$

d. $\frac{4}{5} \cdot \frac{25}{3} \cdot \frac{9}{40}$

e. Why does Sasha's cancelling method work?

4. Jill says that she can divide fractions using a method similar to the crisscross method in Lesson 1.13.

   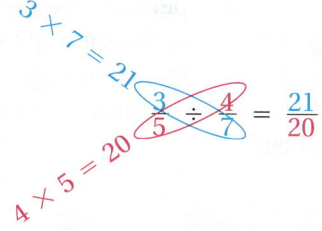

   Jill explains, "I multiply the two numbers from the upper left, and that's the numerator. I multiply the two numbers from the lower left, and that's the denominator." Here is an example.

   Use Jill's method to find each quotient.

   a. $\frac{2}{3} \div \frac{4}{5}$ **b.** $\frac{10}{13} \div \frac{5}{13}$

   c. Explain how Jill's method relates to multiplying by the reciprocal.

5. You can think of division as a way of measuring. When you divide 35 by 5, you find how many 5 unit lengths are in 35. You can count seven 5's in 35.

   $$5 + 5 + 5 + 5 + 5 + 5 + 5 = 35$$

   This idea applies to fractions, too.

   a. How many 5's are in 105? **b.** How many $\frac{1}{2}$'s are in 23?

   c. How many $\frac{1}{4}$'s are in $\frac{11}{2}$? **d.** How many $\frac{1}{100}$'s are in $\frac{1}{4}$?

   e. Take It Further How many $\frac{1}{7}$'s are in $\frac{1}{4}$?

On Your Own

6. Explain to someone who knows how to multiply fractions but doesn't know why the algorithm works, why $\frac{3}{5} \times \frac{4}{9} = \frac{12}{45}$.

7. Derman has a different way to divide fractions. He explains, "To divide fractions, I get a common denominator, just as when I add them. Then, I just divide the numerators.

   $$\frac{\frac{5}{6}}{\frac{7}{8}} = \frac{5}{6} \div \frac{7}{8}$$

   I get a common denominator for 6 and 8. It's 24. So

   $$\frac{\frac{5}{6}}{\frac{7}{8}} = \frac{\frac{20}{24}}{\frac{21}{24}}$$

   $$= \frac{20}{21}$$

   I never use another method." Does Derman's method always work? Explain.

8. **a.** How many 9's are in 720? **b.** How many $\frac{1}{3}$'s are in $\frac{22}{3}$?

   c. How many $\frac{1}{3}$'s are in 25? **d.** How many $\frac{1}{3}$'s are in $\frac{1}{6}$?

9. **Standardized Test Prep** Fifty-four percent of a high school senior class will attend a four-year college. Of the students going to a four-year college, two thirds have taken three or more years of a foreign language. What percent of the senior class have taken three or more years of a foreign language and will attend a four-year college?

   A. 81%

   B. 72%

   C. 40%

   D. 36%

Remember...
You can write 54% as the fraction $\frac{54}{100}$.

10. Fill in each missing number.

    a. ■ · (11) = $\frac{11}{5}$

    b. ■ · $\frac{100}{7}$ = 1

    c. ■ · $\frac{4}{5}$ = 2

    d. ■ · $\frac{7}{9}$ = −2

Maintain Your Skills

11. Find each product.

    a. $\frac{1}{2} \times \frac{2}{3}$

    b. $\frac{1}{2} \times \frac{2}{3} \times \frac{3}{4}$

    c. $\frac{1}{2} \times \frac{2}{3} \times \frac{3}{4} \times \frac{4}{5}$

    d. $\frac{1}{2} \times \frac{2}{3} \times \frac{3}{4} \times \frac{4}{5} \times \frac{5}{6}$

    e. $\frac{1}{2} \times \frac{2}{3} \times \cdots \times \frac{8}{9} \times \frac{9}{10}$

    f. Describe the pattern that you used to find these products.

12. Write each fraction in lowest terms.

    a. $\dfrac{\frac{5}{13}}{\frac{10}{13}}$ **b.** $\dfrac{\frac{5}{19}}{\frac{10}{19}}$ **c.** $\dfrac{\frac{3}{4}}{\frac{7}{4}}$ **d.** $\dfrac{\frac{11}{3}}{\frac{7}{3}}$ **e.** $\dfrac{\frac{11}{100}}{\frac{43}{100}}$

    f. Describe the pattern that you used to write these fractions in lowest terms.

Mathematical Reflections 1C

In this investigation, you learned why addition, subtraction, and multiplication algorithms work. You applied each operation to fractions. These questions will help you summarize what you have learned.

1. Sasha buys a paperback novel for $6.99, a magazine for $1.99, and a cookbook for $22.99. Without using a calculator, find the total cost of these items.

2. You can add quickly $42 + 26 + 33 + 64 + 58 + 47$ without using a calculator by reordering the numbers. Find the sum. Explain how you reordered the numbers.

3. Find each sum. Write your result in lowest terms.
   a. $\frac{1}{3} + \frac{1}{8}$
   b. $\frac{2}{3} + \frac{1}{8}$
   c. $\frac{1}{2} + \left(\frac{2}{3} + \frac{5}{6}\right)$

4. Make two different expansion boxes to multiply $197 \cdot 3$.

5. Without using a calculator, find each product or quotient.
   a. $\frac{2}{5} \cdot \frac{3}{7}$
   b. $\frac{2}{5} \div \frac{3}{7}$
   c. $\frac{3}{5} \cdot 5$
   d. $\frac{3}{5} \div 5$
   e. $\frac{3}{4} \cdot \frac{2}{5} \cdot \frac{5}{9}$

6. Why do traditional ways to add and multiply numbers work?

7. Why do some people say that dividing is the same as multiplying by the reciprocal?

8. How many weeks are in 1 billion seconds?

Vocabulary

In this investigation, you learned these terms. Make sure you understand what each one means and how to use it.

- algorithm
- expansion box
- least common denominator
- place-value part
- reciprocal

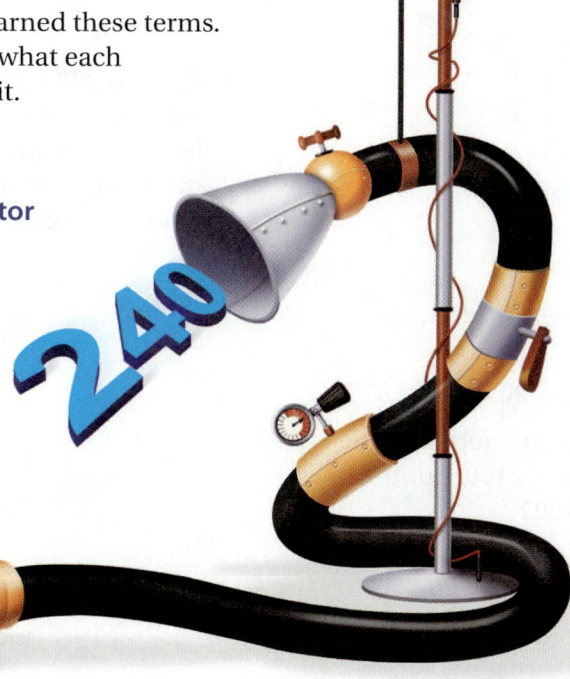

Project Using Mathematical Habits

Lo . . . ong Division

Division algorithms are some of the most complicated algorithms. In different parts of the world and at different times in history, people have used various methods for long division. In this project, you will learn how and why some different division algorithms work.

Traditional Division

1. Explain the steps you can use to perform this long division.

$$
\begin{array}{r}
14 \\
216\overline{)3162} \\
\underline{216} \\
1002 \\
\underline{864} \\
138
\end{array}
$$

Ladder Division

2. Some people arrange long division like this.

$$
\begin{array}{r}
4 \\
10 \\
216\overline{)3162} \\
\underline{2160} \\
1002 \\
\underline{864} \\
138
\end{array}
$$

They say,

- There are between 10 and 20 216's in 3162.
- Write 10 in the space for the quotient and then multiply: $10 \times 216 = 2160$. Subtract 2160 from 3162 to get 1002.
- There are between 4 and 5 216's in 1002.

- Write 4 in the space for the quotient (above the 10) and then multiply: $4 \times 216 = 864$. Subtract 864 from 1002 to get 138.
- 138 is smaller than 216, so 138 is the remainder.
- Find the quotient by adding: $10 + 4 = 14$.

a. Does this method always work?

b. Is it easier or harder than the traditional method?

For Exercises 3–6, find each quotient using ladder division. Check your work using traditional division.

3. $6\overline{)2112}$

4. $27\overline{)1998}$

5. $41\overline{)2296}$

6. $113\overline{)6215}$

Division Using Subtraction

7. Around 300 B.C., Greek mathematicians counted how many of one length fit into a greater length. The number of the smaller lengths is the quotient, and any leftover part of the greater length is the remainder.

In modern notation, you repeatedly subtract the smaller length from the greater length to find the quotient.

In this algorithm, you subtract 216 a total of 14 times. You can count them! You can say, "216 goes into 3162 fourteen times with 138 left over." In other words, the quotient is 14, and the remainder is 138.

a. Does this method always work?

b. Is it easier or more difficult than the traditional method?

c. Why does the number 1002 appear in this algorithm and in Exercises 1 and 2?

For Exercises 8–10, divide using subtraction.

8. $54\overline{)650}$

9. $89\overline{)1224}$

10. $186\overline{)2215}$

11. **Write About It** Write a detailed explanation, including examples, to show why the method in Exercise 1 gives the correct answer.

```
  3162
−  216
  ————
  2946
−  216
  ————
  2730
−  216
  ————
  2514
−  216
  ————
  2298
−  216
  ————
  2082
−  216
  ————
  1866
−  216
  ————
  1650
−  216
  ————
  1434
−  216
  ————
  1218
−  216
  ————
  1002
−  216
  ————
   786
−  216
  ————
   570
−  216
  ————
   354
−  216
  ————
   138
```

Use any method to find each quotient.

12. $3372 \div 67$

13. $59\overline{)4165}$

14. $2488 \div 31$

15. $1005 \div 5$

16. $3872 \div 17$

As volunteers fill the sandbags, they subtract the same amount again and again from the pile of sand.

Chapter 1 Review

In **Investigation 1A,** you learned how to
- identify, describe, and justify patterns in arithmetic and in multiplication tables
- perform integer addition and multiplication
- explain the rules for multiplying and adding negative integers
- subtract using an integer, which is the same as using the integer's opposite to add
- apply the basic rules of arithmetic to whole numbers

The following questions will help you check your understanding.

1. In this part of the addition table, the number -4 is circled.

   Addition Table

   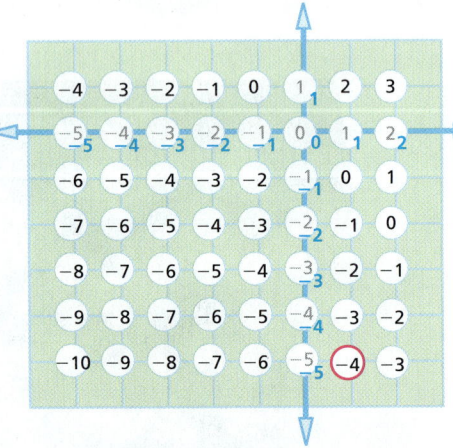

   a. Write the addition problem that the table shows.
   b. Find another entry of -4 and write the addition problem.

2. Use the multiplication table to find each product.

   Multiplication Table

   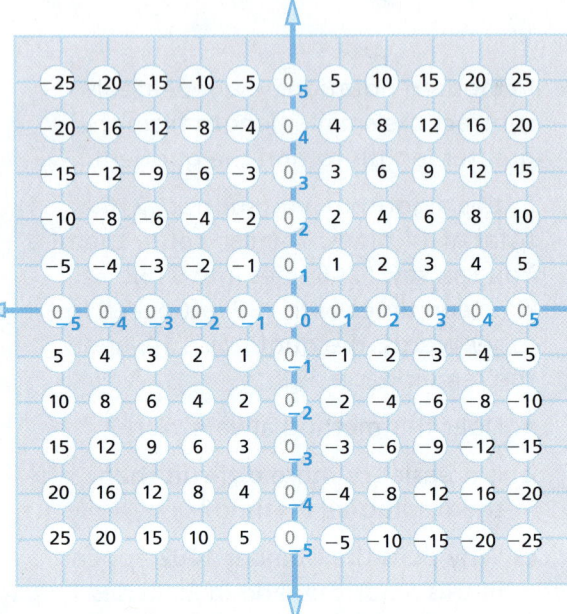

   a. $(4)(-2)$
   b. $(-4)(-2)$
   c. $(-4)(0)$
   d. $(-4)(2)$
   e. Is it true that a negative number times a positive number is a negative number? Explain by using the table.

3. Use the basic rules of arithmetic to rewrite each calculation as an easier one. Find each product.

   a. $8 \cdot 99$ b. $20 \cdot 18 \cdot 5$

In **Investigation 1B,** you learned how to
- draw line segments with different endpoints and scales
- think of fractions and real numbers as points on a number line
- represent a rational number in many different ways
- extend the basic rules of addition and multiplication from the integers to the real numbers

The following questions will help you check your understanding.

4. Place the numbers 2, $\frac{1}{3}$, $\frac{4}{5}$, $-\frac{4}{5}$, -1.1, and $\frac{8}{10}$ on a number line.

    a. Are any of these numbers equivalent? If so, which numbers are equivalent?

    b. Which positive number in the list is least?

5. Sasha starts at 0 on the number line. She moves 3 units to the right, 5 units to the left, 4 more units to the left, and 1 unit to the right.

    a. On what number on the number line does Sasha land?

    b. Write an addition problem to model Sasha's moves.

6. Find each product.

    a. $20 \cdot \left(\frac{1}{2} + \frac{4}{5}\right)$

    b. $\frac{1}{2} \cdot \left(\frac{2}{7} + \frac{4}{7}\right)$

    c. $\frac{2}{3} \cdot \left(\frac{3}{8} + \frac{3}{4}\right)$

In **Investigation 1C,** you learned how to
- explain why the algorithms you commonly use for addition, subtraction, and multiplication work
- use nontraditional algorithms that can be faster in some cases
- become more familiar with the basic rules of arithmetic
- perform arithmetic with integers and fractions

The following questions will help you check your understanding.

7. Without actually adding, explain how you know that both sums give the same answer.

    a. $212 + 18 + 35$

    b. $235 + 12 + 18$

8. What fraction do you add to each of the following to get a sum of 1?

    a. $\frac{2}{3}$

    b. $\frac{5}{8}$

    c. $\frac{1}{4} + \frac{1}{2}$

    d. $\frac{3}{4} + \frac{5}{8}$

9. Make an expansion box to find each product.

    a. $28 \cdot 31$

    b. $2\frac{2}{3} \cdot 3\frac{1}{4}$

Chapter 1 Test

Do not use a calculator.

Multiple Choice

1. How many tenths are in two fifths?
   A. $\frac{1}{2}$
   B. 1
   C. 4
   D. 100

2. Point X on the number line is between 1 and 2. Point Y on the number line is between -1 and 0. Which point could represent the product of X and Y?

   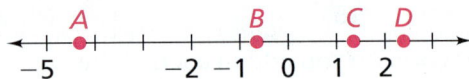

   A. point A
   B. point B
   C. point C
   D. point D

3. Which point is closest to -3 on the number line?
   A. $\frac{-20}{2}$
   B. $\frac{-20}{-2}$
   C. $\frac{-2}{-20}$
   D. $\frac{-2}{20}$

4. What is the opposite of $-\left(-\frac{4}{7}\right)$?
   A. $-\frac{7}{4}$
   B. $-\frac{4}{7}$
   C. $\frac{4}{7}$
   D. $\frac{7}{4}$

5. Which fraction is NOT equal to $\frac{8}{7}$?
   A. $\frac{16}{14}$
   B. $\frac{64}{49}$
   C. $\frac{32}{28}$
   D. $\frac{72}{63}$

6. Let $a = \frac{49}{54}$, $b = \frac{74}{81}$, and $c = \frac{11}{12}$. Which of the following is true?
   A. b is closer to a than it is to c.
   B. b is closer to c than it is to a.
   C. b is equally close to a and c.
   D. none of the above

7. Which of the following is NOT a valid way to compute $a \cdot b$ using a multiplication table? Assume $a < 0 < b$.
   A. Move down $-a$ spaces and then right b spaces.
   B. Move left $-a$ spaces and then up b spaces.
   C. Move right b spaces and then down $-a$ spaces.
   D. Move left $-a$ spaces and then down b spaces.

Open Response

8. Write an addition problem and two subtraction problems that you can illustrate using the addition table below.

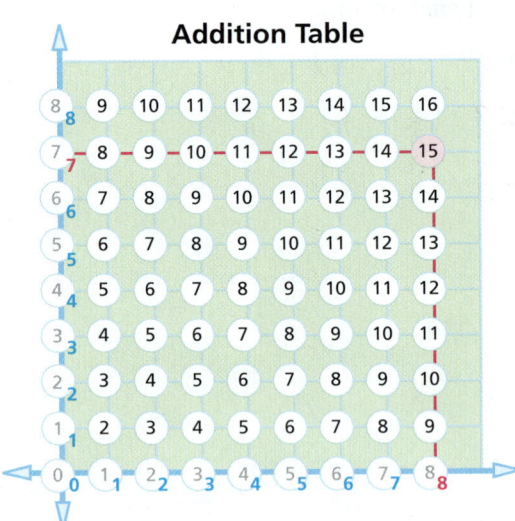

9. Write a multiplication problem and two division problems that you can illustrate using the multiplication table below.

Multiplication Table

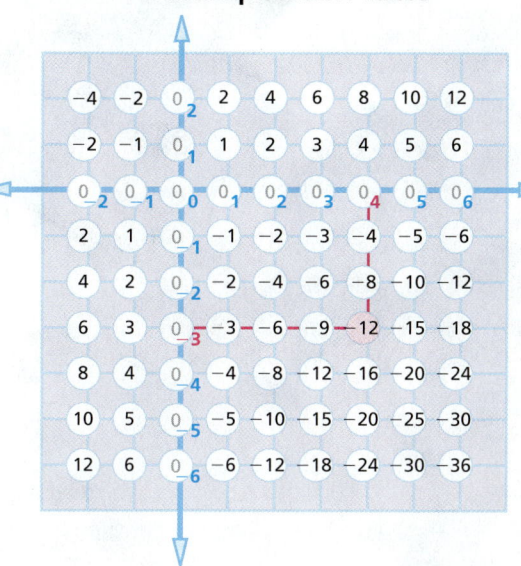

Use any method (except a calculator) to solve Exercises 10–23. Show your work.

10. $1 + 2 + 3 + \cdots + 48 + 49 + 50$
11. $2 + 4 + 6 + \cdots + 96 + 98 + 100$
12. $2 + 4 + 6 + \cdots + 86 + 88 + 90$
13. $-41 \cdot (152)$
14. $-105 \cdot (-112)$
15. $\frac{5}{6} + \frac{1}{8} + \frac{1}{6} + \frac{3}{8}$
16. $\frac{4}{9} \div \frac{8}{15}$
17. $\frac{4}{5} \cdot \left(\frac{3}{4} - \frac{5}{8}\right)$
18. $81 - 36 + 19 - 21 + 31 - 14$
19. $107 + 56 + 27 + 14 + 83$
20. $7 \div \frac{1}{5}$
21. $\frac{\frac{3}{4}}{2}$
22. $-\frac{1}{5} \cdot (-3) \cdot 4 \cdot \frac{3}{4} \cdot (-5)$
23. $\frac{5}{6} \div \frac{7}{9}$

24. Draw a number line from 0 to 1. Label $\frac{2}{8}, \frac{3}{5}, \frac{1}{3}$, and $\frac{3}{6}$ on the number line.

25. Draw a number line from -1 to 1. Label $\frac{1}{4}, -\frac{1}{4}, -\frac{3}{4}$, and $-\frac{7}{8}$ on the number line.

26. Draw a number line from 0 to 4. Label 1, 2, 3, $\sqrt{3}$, $\sqrt{8}$, and $\sqrt{11}$ on the number line.

27. Make a 2-by-2 expansion box to find the product $203 \cdot 197$.

28. Make a 2-by-2 expansion box to find the product of $2\frac{3}{4}$ and $-1\frac{1}{8}$.

29. Convert $\frac{5}{6}$ to a decimal.

For Exercises 30 and 31, convert each decimal to a fraction.

30. 0.8

31. 0.125

32. Explain why dividing a positive number by one half gives a result that is greater than the original number. For example, $6 \div \frac{1}{2} = 12$, and 12 is greater than 6.

Challenge Problem

33. A number plus its reciprocal equals $\frac{29}{10}$. Find both possible values for this number.

Chapter 2

Investigations at a Glance

- **2A** Expressions
- **2B** Equations
- **2C** Solving Linear Equations
- **2D** Word Problems

Expressions and Equations

Both dancers and mathematicians use symbolic language. Dancers read dance notation to learn their parts. Mathematicians use algebraic symbols to solve problems.

When you follow steps in mathematics, science, or the arts, you may find intriguing patterns. Here are some simple mathematical steps to follow.

- Choose a number.
- Add 4 to your number.
- Multiply the result by 2.
- Subtract 6.
- Find half of the result.
- Subtract your starting number.
- Add 3.
- Find half of the result.

Why is the result 2? To find out, you can represent each step using algebraic symbols and the basic rules of arithmetic.

You can also follow steps to solve word problems. You can represent a situation using algebraic symbols and the basic rules. In the last step, you will find the solution.

Vocabulary

- backtracking
- basic moves for solving equations
- evaluate
- expression
- guess-check-generalize method
- like terms
- linear equation
- reversible operation
- solution
- theorem
- variable

Chapter 2 Expressions and Equations

Investigation 2A

Expressions

In *Expressions*, you will invent and perform number tricks. Using variable expressions, you will learn to describe a situation algebraically. Then, you will apply the basic rules of arithmetic to variable expressions.

By the end of this investigation, you will be able to answer questions like these.

1. Why are variables useful?

2. How can you invent a number trick that always gives the same ending number?

3. Use the following steps. Choose a number. Multiply by 5. Add 2. Multiply by 3. Subtract 8.

    a. Choose the number 4. What ending number do you get?

    b. Choose the variable x. What ending expression do you get?

You will learn how to
- state the need for variables and expressions
- determine the appropriate order for evaluating a numerical expression and explain why the order works
- express word problems using variables and mathematical notation
- evaluate numerical expressions involving parentheses, powers, and fraction bars
- write formulas using two or more variables

You will develop these habits and skills:
- Evaluate expressions using a variety of numbers such as integers, fractions, and decimals.
- Generalize patterns using words and algebraic methods.
- Consider the difference between evidence and proof and use variables to prove conjectures.

You can understand x, $5x$, $5x + 2$, ..., regardless of the language you speak.

2.01 Getting Started

Activating Prior Knowledge
Exploring New Ideas

When you understand how a number trick works, you can have fun writing and performing your own. In this lesson, you will learn from Spiro the Spectacular and Maya the Magnificent, who specialize in number tricks.

For You to Explore

1. Here is one of Spiro the Spectacular's favorite number tricks.
   - Choose a number.
   - Add 6.
   - Multiply by 3.
   - Subtract 10.
   - Multiply by 2.
   - Add 50.
   - Divide by 6.

   Spiro says, "Now, tell me the result."
   Georgia replies, "17."
   Spiro exclaims, "Your starting number was 6!"
   Georgia replies, "You're right! How did you know that?"

   a. How did Spiro find Georgia's number?

   b. If Georgia's ending number is 13, what was her starting number?

   c. If Georgia's ending number is 6, what was her starting number?

2. Maya the Magnificent also does number tricks. Here is one of her favorites.
   - Choose a number.
   - Multiply by 3.
   - Subtract 4.
   - Multiply by 2.
   - Add 20.
   - Divide by 6.
   - Subtract your starting number.

   a. What is the trick?

   b. Explain why the trick always works.

3. **a.** Make up your own number trick.

   b. Find a partner. Perform your number tricks for each other. Try different starting numbers until you find how your partner's trick works.

Habits of Mind

Look for a pattern. Try it with numbers! Pick a number and see what you get. Do this a few times.

Exercises Practicing Habits of Mind

On Your Own

Do the number tricks in Exercises 4 and 5 work for all numbers? Explain.

4. Choose a number. Add 5. Multiply by 2. Subtract 7. Add 1. Divide by 2. Subtract 2. You get your starting number!

5. Choose a number. Add 3. Multiply by 2. Add 7. Subtract 15. Add 2. What is the result of the trick?

6. Ask someone you know who is older than you the following question: When you think about algebra, what do you think? Record the response.

7. Evaluate $\dfrac{17 \cdot 4 + 17 \cdot 3 + 17 \cdot 2 + 17 \cdot 1}{17}$.

> What happens if you label the starting number x? After the first step, you will have $x + 5$, then $2 \cdot (x + 5)$, and so on.

Maintain Your Skills

In Exercises 8 and 9, use the given number trick. Find the missing numbers.

8. Choose a number. Add 5. Subtract 3. Multiply by 2. Subtract 4.

	Starting Number	Ending Number
a.	2	■
b.	3	■
c.	7	■
d.	−2	■

   e. Is there a simpler way to get from the starting number to the ending number than by following each step?

9. Choose a number. Add 3. Multiply by 3. Subtract 3. Divide by 3.

	Starting Number	Ending Number
a.	2	■
b.	3	■
c.	7	■
d.	−2	■

   e. Is there a simpler way to get from the starting number to the ending number than by following each step?

2.02 Modeling General Situations

You may hear that algebra is "full of *x*'s and *y*'s." Using letters to represent numbers lets you describe a general situation easily.

Example 1

Problem During a natural disaster, such as an earthquake or flood, many people must leave their homes and go to shelters. The table gives three situations. It shows how much food and how many beds a disaster relief group must provide.

Relief Camp Supplies

Number of People	Number of Beds	Amount of Food (lb)
1,000	1,010	3,000
5,000	5,010	15,000
10,000	10,010	30,000

The ten extra beds are for the relief workers.

Write expressions for how much food and how many beds you will need for any number of people.

Solution A disaster relief group can describe the general situation this way.

- (the number of people) + 10 beds
- 3 pounds of food per day · (the number of people)

There is a simper way to describe the situation. Let the **variable** x stand for the number of people needing food and shelter at a relief camp. Here is what the camp needs for x people.

- $(x + 10)$ beds
- $(3 \cdot x)$ pounds of food per day

The variable x stands for an unknown number. When the relief group knows the number of people at the camp, they can replace x with that number.

*The letter x is a **variable**, or a placeholder for a number that you do not know. Mathematical phrases, such as $x + 10$ and $3 \cdot x$, are **expressions** that use operations to combine numbers and variables.*

For Discussion

For each number of people, how many beds and how much food per day will a relief group need?

1. 15,000
2. 500
3. 8200

Example 2

Problem Ricardo has 3 fewer apples than Jeremy. Let j stand for the number of apples that Jeremy has. Write an expression for the number of apples that Ricardo has.

Solution Think about the steps you take to find how many apples Ricardo has.

Suppose Jeremy has 10 apples. Ricardo has 3 fewer apples than Jeremy, or $10 - 3$ equals 7 apples.

Suppose Jeremy has 15 apples. Ricardo has 3 fewer apples than Jeremy, and $15 - 3$ equals 12 apples.

Use j for the number of apples that Jeremy has. Suppose Jeremy has j apples. Ricardo has 3 fewer apples than Jeremy. The expression $j - 3$ equals the number of apples that Ricardo has.

Habits of Mind

Establish a process. Keeping track of your steps is a very useful habit in algebra.

For Discussion

4. Hideki says, "I chose a number. I multiplied it by 7. Then I subtracted 4." Let h stand for Hideki's starting number. Write an expression for Hideki's ending number.

Exercises Practicing Habits of Mind

Check Your Understanding

1. Mary was born one year before Barbara. No matter how old they are, Mary will always be one year older than Barbara. Find the missing ages in years.

	Mary's Age	Barbara's Age
a.	11	
b.	7	
c.	53	
d.	65	
e.	m	
f.		n

94 Chapter 2 Expressions and Equations

2. A relief group can use expressions to plan for disasters. At a relief camp, you need many kinds of supplies.

   - For each adult, the camp needs 10 gallons of water per week.
   - For every 10 adults, the camp needs one medical kit.
   - The camp needs 30 more blankets than the number of adults.
   - For every 100 adults, the camp needs one doctor.
   - The camp needs 100 more pillows than the number of adults.

   Let a equal the number of adults in the camp.
   Match each expression to one of the five items above.
   Explain your answers.

   a. $\frac{a}{100}$ **b.** $10 \cdot a$ **c.** $\frac{a}{10}$

   d. $a + 100$ **e.** $a + 30$

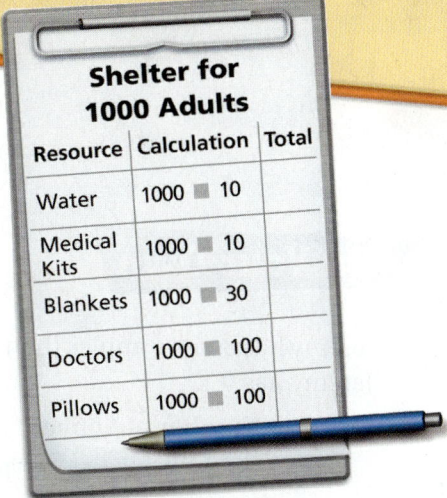

3. Match each expression below to a set of steps I–V.

   a. $2 \cdot x - 2$ **b.** $3 \cdot (x + 5)$ **c.** $2 \cdot (x - 2)$

   d. $5 \cdot (x + 3)$ **e.** $3x + 5$

   I. Choose any number.
   Subtract 2.
   Multiply it by 2.

   II. Choose any number.
   Multiply it by 2.
   Subtract 2.

   III. Choose any number.
   Add 3.
   Multiply it by 5.

   IV. Choose any number.
   Add 5.
   Multiply it by 3.

   V. Choose any number.
   Multiply it by 3.
   Add 5.

4. For each expression, write a number trick.

   a. $2 \cdot x + 1$ **b.** $-2 \cdot (x - 1)$

   c. $5 \cdot (x + 2) - 2$ **d.** $7 \cdot (3 \cdot (x + 1) - 2) - 9$

5. Use the number x as your starting number. Write the expression resulting from following the steps.

   - Choose a number.
   - Add 5.
   - Subtract 11.
   - Multiply by 2.
   - Add 3.

On Your Own

6. Jeremy has 3 more apples than Ricardo. Find the number of apples Jeremy has.

   Number of Apples

	Ricardo	Jeremy
a.	2	▪
b.	13	▪
c.	107	▪
d.	r	▪

7. Match each expression below to a set of steps I–IV.

   a. $-7 \cdot x + 5$ b. $5 \cdot (x - 7)$

   c. $7 \cdot (x - 5)$ d. $7 \cdot x - 5$

   I. Choose any number.   II. Choose any number.
   Subtract 5.   Multiply by -7.
   Multiply by 7.   Add 5.

   III. Choose any number.   IV. Choose any number.
   Subtract 7.   Multiply by 7.
   Multiply by 5.   Subtract 5.

8. **What's Wrong Here?** Travis writes an expression using the following steps.
   - Start with x.
   - Subtract 3.
   - Multiply by 10.
   - Subtract 13.

   He writes the final expression $10x - 3 - 13$. Explain what he did wrong. Then find the correct expression.

9. **Standardized Test Prep** David counts the quarters in his change jar. He has 24 more quarters than his brother Rob. If r is the number of quarters Rob has, which expression represents the number of quarters that David and Rob have in all?

   A. $r + 24$ B. $2r - 24$ C. $2r$ D. none of these

10. A rectangle has length ℓ and width w. For a rectangle, write an expression for each of the following.
    a. area
    b. perimeter

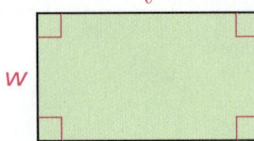

11. You overhear Mrs. Antonellis say, "During fifth period, I teach math. There are four other classes that meet during that period: computer, gym, history, and art. I notice some interesting things about the class sizes.

    - For every two students in my math class, there is one student in computer class.
    - For each student in math class, there are two students in gym class.
    - There are two more students in my math class than in the history class.
    - There are two more students in the art class than in my math class."

    Let x equal the number of students in Mrs. Antonellis' math class. Using x, write an expression for the number of students in each class.

    a. computer   b. gym   c. history   d. art

    e. Write an expression for the total number of students in the math, computer, gym, and history classes.

Maintain Your Skills

12. While in office, President Dwight D. Eisenhower standardized the proportions of United States flags. For every ten units of width, the flag must have nineteen units of length.

    Find a flag's length, in inches, for each given width.

    a. 20 inches   b. 5 inches
    c. 1 inch   d. x inches

13. A computer company wants to make computers with rectangular cases. The length of the longer side is four times the length of the shorter side.

    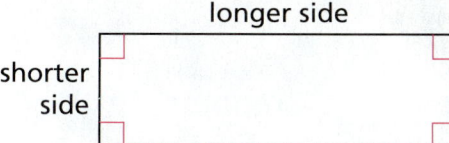

    Find the length of the longer side, in centimeters, for each given length of the shorter side.

    a. 20 cm   b. 25 cm   c. x cm

2.02 Modeling General Situations

2.03 Evaluating Expressions

One type of expression that you will often use is a scientific formula. Using a formula to make calculations is an important skill.

Example

Problem If you drop an object, the object's speed after t seconds is $32t$ feet per second.

Suppose you drop a coin from a hot-air balloon over the desert. What is its speed after 1, 2, 3, 4, and 5 seconds?

Solution After 1 second, $t = 1$. To calculate the speed of the coin after 1 second, you substitute $t = 1$ into the expression $32t = 32 \cdot (1) = 32$.

You can use a table to arrange your answers.

Speed of a Coin

Time t (s)	Speed (ft/s)
1	$32 \cdot 1 = 32$
2	$32 \cdot 2 = 64$
3	$32 \cdot 3 = 96$
4	$32 \cdot 4 = 128$
5	$32 \cdot 5 = 160$

To **evaluate** an expression, replace the variable with the given number. Do the math to get a single number for your result. In this example, you evaluate $32t$ if $t = 1$ and get 32. If $t = 2$, you get 64, and so on.

For You to Do

1. How fast does the coin travel after 5.5 seconds? After $\frac{1}{8}$ of a second?

How does the height of the balloon affect the speed of an object that you drop from it?

Minds in Action   episode 3

Sasha thinks she has discovered one of Spiro the Spectacular's many secrets.

Sasha I can perform one of your tricks.

Spiro Show me.

Sasha Okay. Choose a number. Add 6. Multiply by 3. Subtract 10. What's your ending number?

Spiro 23.

Sasha turns away for a moment. She does some calculations on paper. After thirty seconds, she turns around.

Sasha Your starting number was 5!

Spiro That's right. How did you do it?

Sasha Well, I called your starting number x. Then I wrote an expression for the ending number.

Choose a number.	x
Add 6.	$x + 6$
Multiply by 3.	$3 \cdot (x + 6)$
Subtract 10.	$3 \cdot (x + 6) - 10$

Spiro Then what did you do?

Sasha Then I substituted different numbers for x until I found your ending number. I kept track of the answers in a table.

Starting Number	Add 6	Multiply by 3	Subtract 10
1	7	21	11
2	8	24	14
3	9	27	17
4	10	30	20
5	11	33	**23**

Your ending number was 23, so your starting number was 5.

For Discussion

2. If Spiro chooses -2 as his starting number, what will his ending number be?

Exercises Practicing Habits of Mind

Check Your Understanding

1. A disaster relief group must provide beds, food, and water for a camp. It uses the following expressions for the quantities it needs. The expressions depend on two variables, the number of adults and the number of children. Let a = the number of adults. Let c = the number of children.
   - $a + c + 10$ beds
   - $5a + 2c$ pounds of food
   - $9a + 5c$ gallons of water

   How many beds and how much food and water are needed for 500 adults and 100 children? For 1000 adults and 300 children?

2. Evaluate $\frac{4x + 3x + 2x + x}{x}$ for each value of x.

   a. 3   b. 17   c. −2   d. 11

3. Maya says, "Choose a number. Subtract 1. Multiply by 3. Add 5."
   For each starting number given, what is your ending number?

   a. n b. 11   c. 1

4. Spiro says, "Choose a number. Multiply by 3. Subtract 2. Multiply by 5."
   For each starting number given, what is your ending number?

   a. n b. 4   c. $\frac{4}{3}$

5. A trapezoid is a shape with four sides that has one pair of parallel sides.

   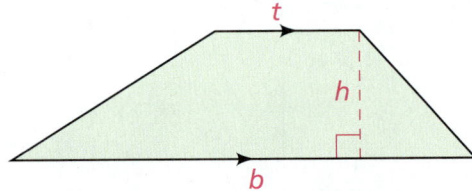

   You can find the area of a trapezoid using the three dimensions of the trapezoid labeled b, t, and h in the diagram. The expression for the area of a trapezoid is $\frac{(b + t)}{2} \cdot h$.

   Find the area of each trapezoid with the given dimensions.

   a. $b = 5, t = 3, h = 6$
   b. $b = 2, t = 3, h = 7$
   c. $b = \frac{3}{2}, t = \frac{1}{2}, h = \frac{7}{4}$
   d. $b = 8, t = 6, h = \frac{1}{4}$

   The variables b and t represent the lengths of the bottom and top parallel sides, respectively. The variable h represents the height of the trapezoid.

6. Insert parentheses to make each equation true.

   Sample $2 + 3 \cdot 7 \stackrel{?}{=} 35$
   Solution $(2 + 3) \cdot 7 = 35$

   a. $3 \cdot 7 + 3 \stackrel{?}{=} 30$
   b. $-3 + 3 \cdot 5 + 11 \stackrel{?}{=} 11$
   c. $-3 + 3 \cdot 5 + 11 \stackrel{?}{=} 45$
   d. $25 - 5 + 4 \cdot 5 \stackrel{?}{=} 0$
   e. $25 - 5 + 4 \cdot 5 \stackrel{?}{=} -20$

On Your Own

7. Boyle's Law in chemistry states that when temperature is constant, the pressure of a gas is inversely proportional to its volume. Let p represent the pressure, and let V represent the volume of the gas. At a certain temperature, $V = \frac{\text{constant}}{p}$. By what factor does the volume of the gas change if the pressure changes by each given factor?

   a. 2
   b. 3
   c. 4
   d. 5

8. **What's Wrong Here?** Linda evaluates the expression $7 + 5x$ for $x = 3$ and $x = \frac{4}{5}$. When $x = 3$, she gets $7 + 5x = 7 + 5 \cdot (3) = 12 \cdot (3) = 36$.
   When $x = \frac{4}{5}$, she gets $7 + 5x = 7 + 5 \cdot \left(\frac{4}{5}\right) = 12 \cdot \left(\frac{4}{5}\right) = \frac{48}{5}$.

   What does Linda do wrong?

9. Evaluate the expression $5 + 3x$ for each value of x.

   a. 3
   b. -1
   c. -5
   d. 0
   e. -11
   f. -3

10. Evaluate the expression $(z + 3)^2 - 4$ for each value of z.

    a. 3
    b. -1
    c. -5
    d. 0
    e. -11
    f. -3

When you squeeze a balloon in one place, the increased pressure will force a bulge in another.

2.03 Evaluating Expressions

11. You can find a person's speed by dividing how far the person travels by the time spent traveling. The equation $r = \frac{d}{t}$ shows this relationship, where r is the rate (or speed), d is the distance, and t is the time.

    a. Anh jogs 100 meters in 40 seconds. What is his rate in meters per second?

    b. Isabel runs 50 yards in 25 seconds. What is her rate in yards per second?

    c. Rosario jogs at a rate of 6 miles per hour. How far does she run in 30 minutes?

12. **Standardized Test Prep** Evaluate $14 - 6 + 32 \div 8 \cdot 2$.

    A. 10

    B. 6

    C. 16

    D. 12

Maintain Your Skills

13. Evaluate the expression $(x - 1) \cdot (x - 2) \cdot (x - 3) \cdot (x - 4) \cdot (x - 5)$ for each x value.

    a. 1

    b. 2

    c. 3

    d. 4

    e. 5

    f. What is similar about these five cases? Is there a sixth similar case? Explain.

14. Here are a complicated expression and a simple expression.

    - $3x + (x - 1) \cdot (x - 2) \cdot (x - 3) \cdot (x - 4) \cdot (x - 5)$
    - $3x$

    Evaluate both expressions above for each x value.

    a. 1

    b. 2

    c. 4

    d. What are the x values that produce the same result in both expressions?

102 Chapter 2 Expressions and Equations

2.04 Simplifying Expressions

You can take an expression that looks complicated and make it simpler to use.

Minds in Action   episode 4

Tony I think I know your secret, Maya. The key is to use variables.

Maya Show me what you mean.

Tony Well, look at this trick. Choose a number. Add 3. Multiply by 2. Subtract 6.

The ending number will always be twice as large as the starting number.

Maya How do you know that?

Tony Watch. If I start with x, I can follow these steps.

Choose a number.	x
Add 3.	$x + 3$
Multiply by 2.	$2 \cdot (x + 3)$
Subtract 6.	$2(x + 3) - 6$

Now watch this. You can simplify $2(x + 3)$. Use the Distributive Property and multiply: $2 \cdot (x + 3) = 2 \cdot x + 2 \cdot 3 = 2x + 6$.

Since $2(x + 3) = 2x + 6$, $2(x + 3) - 6 = 2x + 6 - 6 = 2x$. So the ending number is $2x$.

Maya Very good, Tony. Now can you figure out my other tricks?

For Discussion

1. Here is a number trick.
   - Choose any number.
   - Multiply by 2.
   - Add 7.
   - Multiply by 5.
   - Add 25.
   - Divide by 10.
   - Subtract 6.

   What is the trick? Use expressions to show that it always works.

In Lesson 1.05, you learned the basic rules of arithmetic. You can apply the rules to expressions and numbers. For instance, you can change the order of numbers and variables in a sum.

$$x + 7 = 7 + x$$

You can regroup the numbers and variables in a sum.

$$(a + 8) + z = a + (8 + z)$$

You can use the Distributive Property.

$$2(x + 3) = 2 \cdot (x + 3)$$
$$= 2 \cdot x + 2 \cdot 3$$
$$= 2x + 6$$

The identities are still true.

$$x \cdot 1 = x \text{ and } x + 0 = x$$

You can also use the Distributive Property *backward*. For instance, you can simplify $2x + 3x$ using the Distributive Property.

$$2x + 3x = 2 \cdot x + 3 \cdot x$$
$$= (2 + 3)x$$
$$= 5x$$

The expression $2x + 3x$ has two terms connected by the plus (+) sign. A term is an expression that only uses multiplication or division. When the variables are the same in both terms, you call them **like terms.** Grouping parts of an expression such as $2 + 3$ is called **combining like terms.**

Example

Problem Find a simpler way to write $3x + 7y + 8 + 4x + 2y - 10$.

Solution Rewrite the expression. Group the x terms together and the y terms together. Then group the numbers together.

$$3x + 4x + 7y + 2y + 8 - 10$$

Combine the like terms. Group the $3x$ and the $4x$ together to get $7x$ by using the Distributive Property backward.

$$3x + 4x = (3 + 4)x = x \cdot 7 = 7x$$

You can combine the y terms the same way. There are two terms with y, $7y$ and $2y$, that you can combine.

$$7y + 2y = (7 + 2) \cdot y = 9y$$

You can transform the expression this way.

$$3x + 7y + 8 + 4x + 2y - 10 = 3x + 4x + 7y + 2y + 8 - 10$$
$$= 7x + 9y + (-2)$$
$$= 7x + 9y - 2$$

You can simplify this expression using the any-order, any-grouping properties, but be careful of subtraction!

For Discussion

2. Use the Distributive Property to explain why $3x + 5x = 8x$. Then explain why $7y + (-2y) = 5y$.

Developing Habits of Mind

Visualize combining like terms. You can think about combining like terms using either math symbols or a length model. Using symbols, you can simplify $(2x + y) + (3x + 2y)$ by grouping the x terms.

$$2x + 3x = 5x$$

Then you can group the y terms.

$$y + 2y = 3y$$

The simplified expression looks like this.

$$(2x + y) + (3x + 2y) = (2x + 3x) + (y + 2y)$$
$$= 5x + 3y$$

You cannot combine $5x$ and $3y$, because they are not like terms.

You can use the Distributive Property to show why you can combine like terms. For instance, $2x + 3x = (2 + 3)x = 5x$, and $y + 2y = (1 + 2)y = 3y$. You cannot use the Distributive Property to combine unlike terms such as $5x$ and $3y$.

By using a model to visualize combining like terms, you can think of x and y as lengths.

Here is a model of $2x + y + 3x + 2y$ using lengths for x and y.

You can arrange the lengths by grouping the x terms and the y terms. You can count the total number of x's and the total number of y's.

Since x and y are different lengths, you cannot combine them.

For You to Do

Simplify each expression.

3. $3(x + 2) + 5x$
4. $2z + 7z - z + 5$
5. $3a + 4b + 5a + 6$
6. $4(x - 1) - 3(x + 2)$

Exercises *Practicing Habits of Mind*

Check Your Understanding

1. Here is a number trick similar to the trick in For Discussion Problem 1.
   - Choose any number.
   - Multiply by 2.
   - Add 7.
   - Multiply by 5.
   - Add 25.
   - Divide by 10.
   - Subtract your starting number.

   What is the trick? Will it work for any number? Explain by using expressions.

2. Here is a number trick with one missing step.
   - Choose any number.
   - Multiply by 2.
   - Add 7.
   - Multiply by 5.
   - ?
   - Divide by 10.
   - Subtract your starting number.
   - Your ending number is 7.

   What is the missing step?

3. Here is a number trick with the last step missing.
   - Choose any number.
   - Multiply by 3.
   - Add 5.
   - Multiply by 4.
   - Add 16.
   - Divide by 12.
   - ?

   For each result given below, what is the last step in the number trick?

   a. The ending number is the same as the starting number.
   b. The ending number is 3.

106 Chapter 2 Expressions and Equations

4. Evaluate the expression $\frac{x + 2x + 3x + 4x + 5x}{x}$ for each x value given.

   a. 1 b. 2 c. 3 d. -3
   e. -11 f. $\frac{1}{2}$ g. 197

   h. Use the Distributive Property to simplify the expression.

5. The lengths and widths of four rectangles are given below. For each rectangle, find an expression for the area and an expression for the perimeter.

   a. length: $4x + 2$ width: 3

   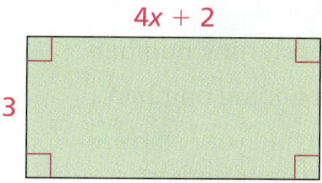

   b. length: 7 width: $x - 4$
   c. length: $6x - 8$ width: $\frac{1}{2}$
   d. length: $10 - 2x$ width: 9

On Your Own

6. Use the basic rules of arithmetic and what you know about like terms. Decide which expressions equal the expression $4x + 2y$. If an expression does not equal $4x + 2y$, explain why it does not.

   a. $4x + 6y + (-4y)$
   b. $4(x + y) - 2y$
   c. $6xy$
   d. $(4x)(2y)$
   e. $x + x + x + x + x + x - y - y - y - y + 2(3y - x)$

7. The lengths and widths of four rectangles are given below. For each rectangle, find an expression for the area and an expression for the perimeter.

   a. length: $5x + 9$ width: 2

   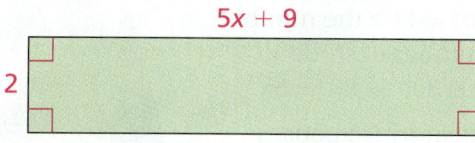

   b. length: 11 width: $x - 3$
   c. length: $2x + 9$ width: 2
   d. length: $8 - 3x$ width: 5

2.04 Simplifying Expressions 107

8. Use the two number tricks.

   Trick 1
   - Choose a number.
   - Add 6.
   - Multiply by 3.
   - Subtract 4.
   - Multiply by 2.
   - Add 2.
   - Divide by 6.
   - What is your ending number?

   Trick 2
   - Choose a number.
   - Multiply by 2.
   - Subtract 6.
   - Multiply by 5.
   - Add 50.
   - Divide by 10.
   - Subtract your starting number.
   - What is your ending number?

   a. Using one of these tricks, Spiro the Spectacular can find your starting number. Which trick can he use? How does he find your number?

   b. Even Spiro the Spectacular cannot find your starting number using the other trick. Explain why not.

9. Evaluate the expression $2(3m + 5) - 5(m + 1) - 4$ for each value of m.

   a. 3
   b. 17
   c. -2
   d. 4
   e. $\frac{1}{3}$
   f. $-\frac{4}{11}$

   g. Simplify the expression.

10. **Standardized Test Prep** Simplify the expression $7(6t + 2) + 3 - 5(t + 1)$.

    A. 49
    B. $37t + 12$
    C. $42t + 17$
    D. $47t + 22$

11. When Derman shops, he tries to buy all his clothes at the same store. Derman explains, "A store charges 6% sales tax on each purchase. Suppose you buy a shirt that costs s dollars at one store and a pair of pants that costs p dollars at another store. You pay $0.06 \cdot s$ in taxes for the shirt and $0.06 \cdot p$ in taxes for the pants. So you're paying taxes *twice*. If you buy them at the same store, you only pay the 6% once. So you're saving money."

    Is Derman correct? Using expressions, explain.

12. Jabari's art club raises $300 to pay for a trip to a local museum. The bus costs $90, and admission is $6 per student. Jabari writes an expression for the amount the club has left based on the number of students who go to the museum. If x is the number of students who go to the museum, the amount remaining is $300 - 90 - 6x$.

    a. What is the amount remaining after paying field trip expenses for 28 students? For 29 students? For 30 students?

    b. What is the greatest number of students who can go on the field trip for $300?

In Exercise 12, suppose the student admission price changed to $8. How would this affect the expression $300 - 90 - 6x$?

108   Chapter 2   Expressions and Equations

Maintain Your Skills

13. Evaluate the expression $x \cdot (x + 1)$ for each value of x.
   - **a.** 1
   - **b.** 2
   - **c.** 3
   - **d.** 4
   - **e.** 11
   - **f.** −3
   - **g.** −7
   - **h.** Explain why $x \cdot (x + 1)$ is always even if x is an integer.

14. Evaluate the expression $2 \cdot (x + 1)$ for each value of x.
   - **a.** 1
   - **b.** 2
   - **c.** 3
   - **d.** 4
   - **e.** 11
   - **f.** −3
   - **g.** −7
   - **h.** Explain why $2 \cdot (x + 1)$ is always even if x is an integer.
   - **i.** Explain why $2 \cdot x + 1$ is always odd if x is an integer.

15. Simplify each expression.
   - **a.** $x + 2x + 3x + 4x + 5x - 12x$
   - **b.** $x + 2x + 3x + 4x + 5x - 13x$
   - **c.** $x + 2x + 3x + 4x + 5x - 14x$
   - **d.** $x + 2x + 3x + 4x + 5x - 15x$
   - **e.** $x + 2x + 3x + 4x + 5x - 16x$
   - **f.** $x + 2x + 3x + 4x + 5x - 17x$

16. Evaluate the expression $\frac{1 - x^2}{1 - x}$ for each value of x.
   - **a.** 2
   - **b.** 3
   - **c.** −3
   - **d.** −11
   - **e.** $\frac{1}{2}$
   - **f.** 197
   - **g.** Identify a pattern in the results.

17. Evaluate the expression $(x + 1)^2 - x^2$ for each value of x.
   - **a.** 2
   - **b.** 3
   - **c.** −3
   - **d.** −11
   - **e.** $\frac{1}{2}$
   - **f.** 197
   - **g.** Identify a pattern in the results.

2.05 Rephrasing the Basic Rules

You have applied the basic rules of arithmetic to expressions. Now you can use these expressions to write the basic rules concisely.

In-Class Experiment

Match each statement in List 1 with a statement in List 2 that has the same meaning.

List 1 Basic Rules of Arithmetic Using Words

1. The order in which you add numbers in a sum does not affect the result.
2. If you add more than two numbers, the order in which you group them does not matter.
3. The order in which you multiply two numbers in a product does not affect the result.
4. If you multiply more than two numbers, the order in which you group them does not matter.
5. Multiplying a number by a sum is the same as multiplying the number by each term in the sum and then adding the results.
6. When you add 0 to any number, the result is the number itself.
7. When you multiply 1 by any number, the result is the number itself.
8. When you add any number to its opposite, the result is 0. When the sum of two numbers is 0, each number is the opposite of the other.
9. When you multiply a nonzero number by its reciprocal, the result is 1. When the product of two numbers is 1, each number is the reciprocal of the other number.

List 2 Basic Rules of Arithmetic Using Symbols

A. For any three numbers a, b, and c, $a + (b + c) = (a + b) + c$.
B. For any two numbers a and b, $ab = ba$.
C. For any three numbers a, b, and c, $a(b + c) = ab + ac$.
D. For any number a, $a + 0 = a$.
E. For any three numbers a, b, and c, $a(bc) = (ab)c$.
F. For any two nonzero numbers a and b, $a \cdot \frac{1}{a} = 1$, and if $ab = 1$, $b = \frac{1}{a}$.
G. For any two numbers a and b, $a + b = b + a$.
H. For any number a, $a \cdot 1 = a = 1 \cdot a$.
I. For any two numbers a and b, $a + (-a) = 0$, and if $a + b = 0$, $b = -a$.

Facts and Notation

The list below gives four properties of arithmetic with names you will see in other math books. This book refers to these as the any-order, any-grouping properties.

- **Commutative Property of Addition** For any numbers a and b,

    $a + b = b + a$

- **Associative Property of Addition** For any numbers a, b, and c,

    $a + (b + c) = (a + b) + c$

- **Commutative Property of Multiplication** For any numbers a and b,

    $ab = ba$

- **Associative Property of Multiplication** For any numbers a, b, and c,

    $a(bc) = (ab)c$

You will also see the following names for the properties about identities and inverses.

- **Additive Identity** For any number a,

    $a + 0 = a$

- **Additive Inverse** For any number a,

    $a + (-a) = 0$

    If $a + b = 0$, then $b = -a$.

- **Multiplicative Identity** For any number a,

    $a \cdot 1 = a$

- **Multiplicative Inverse** For any nonzero number a,

    $a \cdot \frac{1}{a} = 1$

    If $ab = 1$, then $b = \frac{1}{a}$.

Finally, the Distributive Property relates addition and multiplication.

- **Distributive Property** For any numbers a, b, and c,

    $a(b + c) = ab + ac$

Exercises *Practicing Habits of Mind*

Check Your Understanding

1. Express each sentence using variables.
   a. Dividing is the same as multiplying by the reciprocal.
   b. Subtracting is the same as adding the opposite.
   c. If you have a product of two numbers, and you find the products of the opposites of the numbers, you get the same result.
   d. If you multiply two numbers together and the result is 1, then the numbers are reciprocals.

2. The Zero-Product Property states that if the product of two numbers is zero, then one of the numbers equals zero. You can write the property using symbols this way.

   If $ab = 0$, then $a = 0$ or $b = 0$.

   The steps show you a proof of this property. Start with the equation $ab = 0$.

   a. If $a = 0$, then you can stop doing the proof. Explain.
   b. Assume $a \neq 0$. Then a has a reciprocal. Explain.
   c. Since a has a reciprocal $\left(\frac{1}{a}\right)$, you can use a basic rule and multiply both sides of the equation by this reciprocal. What effect does this have on the left side of the equation? On the right side of the equation?
   d. Explain why these steps prove the Zero-Product Property.

Remember...
Sometimes you will see the term *negative* or *additive inverse* instead of *opposite*. They all mean the same thing.

On Your Own

3. The binary operation ♥ is defined by the following rule.

   $x ♥ y = 3x + y$

   a. Explain how to find $4 ♥ 6 = 18$.
   b. Evaluate $6 ♥ 4$.
   c. Is ♥ commutative? In other words, does ♥ have an any-order property?

4. The binary operation ♠ is defined by the rule $x ♠ y = -3(x + y)$.
   a. Is ♠ commutative? In other words, does ♠ have an any-order property? Explain.
   b. Is ♠ associative? In other words, does ♠ have an any-grouping property? Explain.

The prefix *bi-* means "two." A **binary operation** takes two numbers and produces one number.

112 Chapter 2 Expressions and Equations

5. Simplify.

   a. $2(x + 2) - (x + 2)$

   b. $2(x + 2) - (x + 2) + 4(x + 2) - 3(x + 2)$

   c. $2(x + 2) - (x + 2) + 4(x + 2) - 3(x + 2) + 6(x + 2) - 5(x + 2)$

   d. $2(x + 2) - (x + 2) + 4(x + 2) - 3(x + 2) + 6(x + 2) - 5(x + 2) + 8(x + 2) - 7(x + 2)$

   e. $2(x + 2) - (x + 2) + 4(x + 2) - 3(x + 2) + 6(x + 2) - 5(x + 2) + 8(x + 2) - 7(x + 2) + 10(x + 2) - 9(x + 2)$

   f. Evaluate each simplified expression for $x = -2$. What is the pattern in your results? Explain.

For Exercises 6 and 7, use the any-order, any-grouping properties and the Distributive Property to simplify each expression. Remember to combine like terms.

6. a. $4(x + 2) + 11$ b. $x + 2(5 + 2x)$

   c. $9(2x - 5) - 3$ d. $5(x - 1) + 8(x + 1)$

   e. $7(x + 1) + (7x + 7)$ f. $7(x + 1) + (-1)(7x + 7)$

7. a. $2(x + 4) + 7$ b. $13 + 3(1 + 2x)$

   c. $3(2x - 5) - 8$ d. $4(x + 3) + 7(x + 3)$

   e. $6(3 - 2x) - 3(x + 1)$ f. $4(x - 7) - 2(2 - 3x)$

8. Here is one of Maya the Magnificent's number tricks.

   - Choose a number.
   - Add 6.
   - Multiply by 3.
   - Subtract 10.
   - Multiply by 2.
   - Add 50.
   - Divide by 6.

   Maya says, "I take the ending number and subtract 11. That's your starting number."

   a. Let the starting number equal x. Write the result after each step. Simplify each expression after each step.

   b. Identify four places where you used a basic rule to simplify an expression.

   c. Explain why Maya only needs to subtract 11 to get the starting number.

2.05 Rephrasing the Basic Rules

9. **Standardized Test Prep** Define the binary operation ⊗ with the rule

    $a \otimes b = ab + a$.

    Which of the following statements is true?

    A. The binary operation ⊗ is associative but not commutative.

    B. The binary operation ⊗ is commutative but not associative.

    C. The binary operation ⊗ is both associative and commutative.

    D. The binary operation ⊗ is neither associative nor commutative.

10. **Take It Further** Tony buys CDs at a music store Web site. He says, "You get a great deal. You get 20% off the price of a CD. You still have to add 5% sales tax. But you find the sales tax after the discount. So you save money on taxes, too."

    How much money does Tony save by getting the discount *before* adding the sales tax? Explain by using expressions.

    > Start by writing an expression for the cost of a CD in which you calculate the sales tax after the discount.

Maintain Your Skills

Find each product. Look for patterns.

11. **a.** $(5 \times 4) \times 2$
    b. $(5 \times 213) \times 2$
    c. $(5 \times 91{,}827) \times 2$
    d. Describe a pattern.

12. **a.** $(25 \times 17) \times 4$
    b. $(25 \times 22) \times 4$
    c. $(25 \times 197) \times 4$
    d. Describe the pattern.

13. **a.** $\left(\frac{10}{13} \times 54\right) \times 13$
    b. $\left(\frac{10}{13} \times 81\right) \times 13$
    c. $\left(\frac{10}{13} \times 1113\right) \times 13$
    d. Describe a pattern.

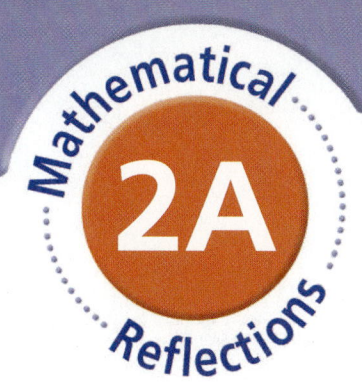

Mathematical Reflections 2A

In this investigation, you used and invented number tricks. You learned to write a variable expression to model a situation. Using the basic rules of arithmetic, you evaluated and simplified expressions. These questions will help you summarize what you have learned.

1. To build a rectangular dog pen, Cheng uses a wall of his house for one of the long sides. Let ℓ equal the length of the longer side. Let w equal the length of the shorter side.

    a. Write an expression for the amount of fencing Cheng needs to build the pen.

    b. How much fencing does Cheng need if he wants a width of 8 feet and a length of 12 feet?

    c. How much fencing does Cheng need if he wants a width of 5 feet and a length of 20 feet?

    d. Suppose the length is 9 feet more than the width. Use only *one* variable to write an expression for the amount of fencing Cheng needs.

2. Evaluate the expression $4(2x + 3) + 2(x + 1) - 7$ for each value of x.

    a. 1   b. 6   c. -2 d. $\frac{1}{2}$

    e. Simplify the expression. When you evaluate the simplified expression for $x = 1$ and $x = 6$, do you get the same results as in part (a) and part (b)? Do you get the same result for every value of x?

3. Why are variables useful?

4. How can you invent a number trick that always gives the same ending number?

5. Use the following steps.

    - Choose a number.
    - Multiply by 5.
    - Add 2.
    - Multiply by 3.
    - Subtract 8.

    a. Choose the number 4. What ending number do you get?

    b. Choose the variable x. What ending expression do you get?

Puedes comprender x, $5x$, $5x + 2$, . . . , sin importar la lengua que hables.

Vocabulary

In this investigation, you saw these terms. Make sure you understand what each one means and how to use it.

- **binary operation**
- **combining like terms**
- **evaluate**
- **expression**
- **like terms**
- **variable**

Investigation 2B

Equations

In *Equations*, you will develop techniques for solving equations using the language of algebra. To solve equations, you will learn how to reverse, or undo, an operation.

By the end of this investigation, you will be able to answer questions like these.

1. What is an equation?

2. What are some ways to solve an equation?

3. Breanna chooses a number, multiplies it by 3, and subtracts 8. The ending number is 7. What is Breanna's starting number?

You will learn how to
- reverse, or undo, a series of steps
- understand the relationship between an equation and its solutions
- use backtracking to solve a problem

You will develop these habits and skills:
- Find the reverse operation that undoes a particular operation.
- Use equations to solve a complex problem.
- Apply a standard formula, such as temperature conversion or velocity of falling objects, to solve a problem.

To reassemble the bike, recall the steps you took to disassemble it. Then backtrack.

2.06 Getting Started

Activating Prior Knowledge
Exploring New Ideas

You know the directions from your home to school. To go from school to your home, it may be possible to simply reverse the directions. Such a "backtracking" skill will be useful for solving equations.

For You to Explore

Kelly gives directions for walking from Cambridge, Massachusetts, to the Thomas P. O'Neill Federal Building in Boston.

- Walk across the Longfellow Bridge from Cambridge to Boston on Cambridge Street. Stay on the right side of Cambridge Street to avoid the construction.
- When you reach Staniford Street, turn left. Walk down the hill. Staniford Street becomes Causeway Street. You should see the O'Neill Federal Building on your left—it's gigantic! You can't miss it.

When you arrive at the O'Neill Federal Building, you see Justin. He asks you for directions to return to Cambridge.

1. Work in a group. Write directions for Justin.

2. Compare the directions you write to Kelly's directions. How do your directions differ from Kelly's? How are your directions the same as Kelly's?

3. Spiro the Spectacular asks you to choose a number, multiply it by 5, and then subtract 10. When you tell Spiro the ending number, which of the following methods can he use to find your starting number?

    a. Multiply the ending number by 5 and then subtract 10.
    b. Divide the ending number by 5 and then subtract 10.
    c. Divide the ending number by 5 and then add 10.
    d. Add 10 to the ending number and then divide by 5.
    e. Add 10 to the ending number, double it, and then divide by 10.
    f. Drop the last digit of the ending number and then add 10.
    g. Divide the ending number by 5 and then add 2.

   More than one of these methods will work. Find them all.

4. Maya wants to be absolutely sure that she can undo any step, so that she can find the starting number without guessing. For each step, describe how to undo it, or explain why you cannot undo it.

    a. Add 5.
    b. Divide by 10.
    c. Multiply by 0.
    d. Multiply by 3 and then subtract 28.
    e. Find the sum of the digits of a number.
    f. Subtract 11 from a number six times in a row.

5. Spiro tells you to start with the number 3 and then add 5 as many times as you want. You tell him your ending number. Spiro tells you how many times you added 5. Explain.

Exercises Practicing Habits of Mind

On Your Own

6. Dae gives directions from the baseball field to her house.
   - You should be on Clark right now, heading south.
   - Turn right on Addison.
   - After about 4 blocks, turn left on Western.
   - At the next street, turn right on Belmont.
   - When you see a police station on the corner, turn right.
   - My house is the fourth building on the left.

   Write directions to return to the baseball field from Dae's house.

7. Use the Internet to find driving direction between two cities or towns. Record the directions. Then, write directions for the return trip. How do the directions compare?

   Sometimes, you cannot simply backtrack. Explain.

8. Jamal describes the steps he uses to get each ending number. Find each starting number. If you cannot, explain why.

		Ending Number
a.	Multiply by 4.	36
b.	Subtract 18.	−14
c.	Double the number 3 times.	−48
d.	Divide the number by itself.	1
e.	Divide by 23 and then multiply by a favorite number.	12
f.	Subtract 4 and then multiply by a favorite number.	100
g.	Add 7, divide by 10, subtract 3, multiply by 4, and add 13.	37

   The operation in part (b) looks like this picture.

9. Maya starts with a number and repeats an operation several times. Find the number of times she repeats the operation to get each ending number. If you cannot, explain why.

	Starting Number	Repeated Operation	Ending Number
a.	8	Add 5.	93
b.	1	Multiply by 10.	1,000,000
c.	30	Subtract 2.	−100
d.	0	Multiply by 5.	0
e.	100	Divide by 2.	$3\frac{1}{8}$
f.	5	Multiply by −1.	−5
g.	10	Add 7.	more than 1000

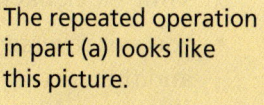

The repeated operation in part (a) looks like this picture.

10. **Write About It** Spiro asks you to choose a number, add 10, and then find the remainder when you divide by 7. When you tell him the ending number, can Spiro always find your starting number? Explain.

Maintain Your Skills

11. List the six sets of steps below in pairs. The steps in each pair must produce the same ending number when you use the same starting number.

  I. Divide a number by three and then multiply by twelve.

  II. Add three to a number and then add the original number.

  III. Multiply a number by four.

  IV. Divide a number by three, multiply by four, and then divide by eight.

  V. Divide a number by six.

  VI. Double a number and then add three.

2.07 Reversing Operations

You can reverse some actions. You cannot reverse others. Here are some reversible actions.

- You can reverse opening a window by closing the same window.
- To reverse setting a 12-hour clock forward by one hour, you can set the same clock back one hour, or set the clock forward another 11 hours.
- You can reverse putting on socks and then shoes by taking off the shoes and then taking off the socks.

Some examples of irreversible actions include sending an e-mail, compacting trash, and skydiving.

> *Reverse* in this lesson has the same meaning as *undo* in Lesson 2.06.

In mathematics, you can reverse some operations on a number and not others. An operation is a **reversible operation** if there is a second operation that always brings you back to the situation before the first operation. For example,

- You can reverse adding 5 to a number by subtracting 5 from the result.
- You can reverse multiplying a number by 3 by dividing the result by 3.
- You can reverse adding seven hours to the current time on a 12-hour clock by adding five more hours to the resulting time.

> If the starting number is n, you can write this expression as $n + 5$. Reversing the operation looks like $(n + 5) - 5$.

You cannot reverse other operations. For example,

- When you multiply a number by 0, it is impossible to find your starting number. Explain.
- You can't reverse adding the digits of a number together. Explain.

Developing Habits of Mind

Prove by counterexample. Here is one way to show that you cannot reverse a particular operation. Find *two* different starting numbers that produce the same ending number. There is no way to know from the ending number what the starting number was.

For example, think about the operation of adding the digits together. The starting numbers 17 and 26 both have a digit sum of 8. If you only know 8 is the digit sum, it is impossible to tell what the starting number was.

Minds in Action   episode 5

Takashi guesses what number Tom chose.

Tom   Hey, I'll bet you can't guess my number!

Takashi   Guessing again? Okay. Is it 246.3?

Tom   No.

Takashi   What about 137 and a quarter?

Tom   No. I'll give you a big hint, but then you get only one guess. When you square my number, you get 169. Alright, so, what's my number?

Takashi gets out a calculator and fiddles with it for a moment.

Takashi   I got it. It's 13.

Tom   No! I fooled you.

For Discussion

1. What did Takashi do wrong? What number do you think Tom chose?

One way Takashi can be sure what number Tom chose is not to allow him to choose a negative number. Some operations are only reversible when the set of starting values does not include all numbers.

Now, you will learn a method called **backtracking,** which means reversing operations. Spiro and Maya use backtracking in their number tricks.

Example

Problem   Find the value of x that solves the equation $3x - 14 = 37$.

Solution   Use backtracking to solve $3x - 14 = 37$.

Step 1   Write the steps, in order, that show how to get from the input variable x to the output value 37.

- Multiply by 3.
- Subtract 14.

Here is a machine diagram showing the steps.

input x

output 37

> You read the equation as, "Three times some starting number, minus 14, is equal to 37." The equation is like one of Spiro's number tricks.

2.07   Reversing Operations   **121**

Step 2 Make a list that reverses the order of the first list and shows how to undo each operation.

- Add 14.
- Divide by 3.

Here is a machine diagram showing these steps.

> Why is it important to keep track of the steps?

Step 3 Start with the output. Perform each step on the list of reverse steps to find the value of the input variable x. Start with output 37.

$37 + 14 = 51$ Add 14 to the output 37.

$51 \div 3 = 17$ Divide by 3 to find the value of the input variable, x.

$x = 17$

> This process is the same as following 37 through the machine diagram above.

Developing Habits of Mind

Establish a process. Here is a method for performing good backtracking steps.

Step 1 Make a list of steps, in order, that show how to get from the input variable to the output. You can build a machine diagram or a flowchart to show your steps.

Step 2 Make a list that reverses the order of the steps in the first list and shows how to undo each operation.

Step 3 Start with the output. Perform each step on the list of reverse steps to find the value of the input variable.

For Discussion

2. Derman solves an equation such as $3x - 14 = 37$ by making a guess, checking it, and then making a better guess until he finds the solution. Compare Derman's method with the backtracking method. What advantages does backtracking have? Are there any disadvantages to backtracking?

Exercises Practicing Habits of Mind

Check Your Understanding

1. Getting into a car involves these steps.
   - Open the car door.
   - Sit down.
   - Close the car door.
   - Buckle the seat belt.

   Describe the steps you take in getting out of a car. How are they related to the steps involved in getting into a car?

2. Find a partner. Each person thinks of a number. Take your number and follow these steps.
   - Add 6.
   - Divide by 4.
   - Multiply by 8.
   - Add 7.
   - Multiply by 10.

   Take your partner's result and find the starting number. Describe your process.

   Remember... You perform each step starting with the result that you got from the step before it.

3. Write each algebraic expression as a statement of one or more operations. For each operation that is reversible, describe the operation that reverses it.

   a. $n + 13$
   b. $\dfrac{b}{-2}$
   c. $3(5m - 12)$
   d. $15m - 36$

   Describe, in words, what each of these expressions tells you to do with the number.

4. Dana says, "I take a number, multiply it by 2, add 7, and then subtract 5. My final result is 22." What is Dana's starting number?

5. Hideki says, "I take a number, multiply it by 12, and then subtract 9. My final result is -5." What is Hideki's starting number?

6. Here is a table for the input and output of $y = x^2$, where x has integer values from -4 to 4. Some values of x^2 are missing.

Input, x	Output, x^2
-4	16
-3	■
-2	■
-1	■
0	■
1	■
2	■
3	9
4	■

   a. Copy and complete the table.

   b. From this table, how do you know that squaring is not a reversible operation?

   c. Make a similar table for cubing the input. This means that if the input is x, the output is x^3. Use inputs from -4 to 4. Is this operation reversible?

   d. Make tables for the outputs x^4, x^5, x^6, and x^7. Which powers produce reversible operations?

   e. Why is the result $(-3)^4$ positive? What powers of -3 produce negative numbers?

A sky diver's jump from an airplane is not a reversible step.

On Your Own

7. Write each algebraic expression as a statement of one or more operations. For each operation that is reversible, describe the operation that reverses it.

   a. $y^2 + 6$

   b. $3x - 28$

   c. $\dfrac{j - 8}{4}$

   d. $3x - 33 + 5$

   Describe, in words, what each of these expressions tells you to do with the number.

8. Marty says, "I take a number, add 5, and then multiply by 8. My final result is 24." What is Marty's starting number?

9. Bianca says, "I take a number, multiply it by 4, and then add 11. My final result is 39." What is Bianca's starting number?

10. **Write About It** Describe how you can use backtracking to solve the equation $179x + 318 = 1429$. Describe your steps without solving the equation.

11. Suppose each table represents the entire chart for an input-output operation. Which tables show a reversible operation?

Table A

Input	Output
−2	−3
−1	−3
0	−3
1	−3
2	7

Table B

Input	Output
0	1
1	3
2	5
3	7
4	9

Table C

Input	Output
1	4
2	0
3	0
4	0
5	12

Table D

Input	Output
0	1
1	2
2	4
3	8
4	16

12. **Standardized Test Prep** Which step can you use to undo the operation in the equation $\frac{5}{3}x = 10$? Give the most complete answer.

   I. Multiply by $\frac{3}{5}$.
   II. Multiply by $\frac{5}{3}$.
   III. Divide by $\frac{3}{5}$.
   IV. Divide by $\frac{5}{3}$.

   A. I only   **B.** III only   **C.** II or III   **D.** I or IV

13. **Take It Further** For each operation below, can you restrict the types of numbers you use as the input so that the operation is reversible? Explain.

    a. Multiply your number by zero.
    b. Find the sum of the digits of your number.

14. For each operation, find a number that produces itself as the output. This number is a fixed point for the operation. If you cannot find a fixed point, explain.

    a. Take the average of your number and the number 5.
    b. Add 6 to your number.
    c. Take the square root of your number.
    d. Multiply your number by 3 and then add 12.
    e. **Take It Further** Square your number and then subtract 6.

Habits of Mind

Represent words with an expression. For part (a), if n is the input, then the output for the first operation is $\frac{n+5}{2}$. Can the input equal the output?

Maintain Your Skills

Choose any number and perform the operations. Then take the result and repeat the operations. Repeat this process many times. Explain how the results change.

15. Add 3 and then divide that sum by 2.
16. Add 5 and divide by 2.
17. Add 1 and divide by 2.

2.08 Solving Equations by Backtracking

In Lesson 2.07, you learned the technique called backtracking. You can also use that technique to solve equations. You have seen arithmetic equations, such as $3 + 4 = 7$. In algebra, equations can include variables and complex expressions, but the idea of what an equation is remains essentially the same as in arithmetic.

Definition

An **equation** is a mathematical sentence that states that two quantities are equal.

The quantities can be any mathematical expression such as 12, $42x + 10$, or $3a^2b + 2ab^2 + 7c$.

The definition does not state that an equation must be true. It only states that it is a complete thought about numbers. The equation $3 + 4 = 7$ happens to be true. The statement $2 + 1 = 9$ is also an equation. It just happens to be false.

Here are some more examples of equations.

$2 + 5 = 7$	true
$3 + 8 = 10$	false
$x + y = y + x$	true
$x^2 = x \cdot x$	true
$x = x + 1$	false

Things can get a tricky when you start looking at equations with variables. You do not know what the values of the variables are. How do you know if the equation is true or false?

For Discussion

1. How do you know that $x + y = y + x$ is always true?
2. How do you know that $x^2 = x \cdot x$ is always true?
3. How do you know that $x = x + 1$ is always false?

Most of the time, an equation containing one or more variables is only true when those variables have certain values. For example, $x + 1 = 8$ is true only when x has a value of 7.

Definition

The values of the variables that make an equation true are **solutions** of the equation.

Example 1

Problem Why is the value 3 a solution to the equation $x + 4 = 7$?

Solution The value 3 is a solution to the equation $x + 4 = 7$, since 3 makes the equation true.

$$x + 4 = 7$$
$$3 + 4 = 7 \quad \checkmark \text{ true}$$

Any other value of x makes the equation false, so 3 is the only solution.

Habits of Mind

Represent x with a number. Try replacing x with a number different from 3. What is your result?

Some equations have more than one solution. For instance, $x^2 = 9$ has two solutions, 3 and -3, since both numbers make it true. You use the term **solution set** for the collection of all solutions of an equation. The expression $x^2 = 9$ has the solution set $\{-3, 3\}$.

When an equation is always false, it has no solutions. For instance, the equation $x = x + 1$ has no solutions, so its solution set is the **empty set,** or the **null set.**

You can write the empty set as two braces with nothing inside { } or the null symbol Ø.

To find out if a number is a solution to an equation, just test it out! A variable such as x represents a number, so every time you see an x in an equation, replace it with the same number. If you get a true statement, that number is a solution.

Example 2

Problem Is the number 7 a solution to the equation $3x - 28 = 46$?

Solution No. Replace x with 7 and find whether the result is true.

$$3x - 28 = 46$$
$$3 \cdot 7 - 28 \stackrel{?}{=} 46$$
$$-7 \neq 46 \quad \textbf{X} \text{ false}$$

For Discussion

4. Suppose you want to find the solution to $3x - 28 = 46$ by guessing. How can you do it?

5. Can you solve the equation $3x - 28 = 46$ by backtracking? Explain.

6. Suppose you want to find both solutions to $x^2 - x - 2 = 0$. How can you do this?

Example 3

Problem Solve the equation $81 = \frac{q}{3} + 76$ to find the value of q.

Solution Suppose you divide the starting number q by 3 and then add 76. Backtrack by reversing each step in the opposite order. To find q, start with the ending number, 81, and follow these steps.

- Subtract 76. $81 - 76 = 5$
- Multiply by 3. $5 \cdot 3 = 15$

> Think: I have a number, add 76, and get 81. My number is $81 - 76$, or 5.

The starting value of q is 15. After the first backtracking step, what remains is $5 = \frac{q}{3}$. You find the value of q by multiplying.

Verify that $q = 15$ is a solution by replacing q with 15.

$$81 = \frac{q}{3} + 76$$
$$81 \stackrel{?}{=} \frac{15}{3} + 76$$
$$81 \stackrel{?}{=} 5 + 76$$
$$81 = 81 \quad \checkmark \text{ true}$$

> Think: I have a number, divide it by 3, and get 5. My number is $3 \cdot 5$, or 15.

For Discussion

7. Solve the equation $3(a - 1) - 5 = 34$.

8. Explain *why* backtracking helps you solve the equation in Problem 7. Use the phrase "reversible operations."

Exercises Practicing Habits of Mind

Check Your Understanding

Use backtracking to find the solution of each equation in Exercises 1–6.

1. $7 + y = 3$

2. $2x - 7 = 110$

3. $10 = \frac{z}{12}$

128   Chapter 2   Expressions and Equations

4. $15 - 2w = 31$

5. $\frac{n - 13}{12} = 3.5$

6. $38 = 5n - 1$

7. The equation $3a + 6b = 75$ gives a relationship between the variables a and b.

    a. If the value of a is 11, find the value of b.
    b. If the value of b is 12, find the value of a.
    c. Copy and complete this table relating a and b for different values of a.
    d. Describe the relationship in the table between a and b.

a	b
0	■
1	■
2	■
3	■
4	■
5	■

8. a. Show that $x = 1$ and $x = 8$ are solutions to the equation $x^3 + 26x = 11x^2 + 16$.

    b. Find two numbers that are *not* solutions.

    c. **Take It Further** Find another number, besides 1 and 8, that is a solution.

Another way to write the equation in Exercise 4 is $15 + (-2) \cdot w = 31$.

Using a truck 11 ft high is not a solution for passing under this bridge.

On Your Own

9. Tony and Sasha are trying to solve the equation $3(x + 2) - 11 = 26$.

    Tony explains, "First I write the steps to get from the starting number to 26. Then I make a list of how to undo each operation in reverse order. Here is my list.

    - Add 11.
    - Divide by 3.
    - Subtract 2.

    Then I use those steps to find the starting number."

    Sasha says, "I do it differently, Tony. First I simplify the expression on the left side of the equation.

    $$3(x + 2) - 11 = 3x + 6 - 11$$
    $$= 3x - 5$$

    Then I have the equation $3x - 5 = 26$. To backtrack this equation, I follow the following steps.

    - Add 5.
    - Divide by 3."

    Do both methods work?

10. a. Write the expression $3(a + 2) - 1$ as a set of steps describing the operations.

  b. Write the steps to reverse the operations.

11. Use your result from Exercise 10. Solve each equation.

  a. $3(a + 2) - 1 = 17$
  b. $3(a + 2) - 1 = 8$
  c. $3(a + 2) - 1 = -19$
  d. $3(a + 2) - 1 = 0$

12. Andrew explains, "I choose a number. I add 1 and multiply by -4. Then I add 2. My ending number is 22." What is Andrew's starting number?

13. Standardized Test Prep Joya adds 8 to her starting number and then multiplies by 3. She subtracts 15 from the result and multiplies by 2. The ending number is 6. What is Joya's starting number?

  A. -2
  B. 2
  C. 10
  D. none of these

14. In Exercise 8f from Lesson 2.06, Jamal chose a starting number, subtracted 4, and multiplied by his favorite number. His ending number was 100. Parts (a)–(d) refer to n as Jamal's starting number and f as Jamal's favorite number.

  a. Suppose Jamal's favorite number is 25. Find the starting number.

  b. Suppose Jamal's favorite number is 10. Find the starting number.

  c. Write an equation that tells you the starting number n in terms of Jamal's favorite number f.

  d. Are there any numbers Jamal cannot use as his favorite number in this situation?

> The right side of the equation needs to have an f in it.

Maintain Your Skills

15. Solve each equation using backtracking.

  a. $-5x + 13 = 93$
  b. $13 - 5x = 93$
  c. $-7x + 12 = -45$
  d. $12 - 7x = -45$
  e. $-3x - 17 = 4$
  f. $-17 - 3x = 4$

Go Online
pearsonsuccessnet.com

16. Use backtracking to solve these equations. Write the steps in the correct order.

    a. $10(x + 3) = 73$

    b. $10x + 3 = 73$

    c. $73 = 10(x + 3)$

    d. $73 = 10x + 3$

    e. $\dfrac{x + 3}{10} = 73$

    f. $\dfrac{x}{10} + 3 = 73$

    g. $73 = \dfrac{x - 3}{10}$

    h. $73(3x) = 10$

Historical Perspective
Temperature Scales

In the 1600s and early 1700s, scientists devised as many as 35 different temperature scales. The Fahrenheit and Celsius scales have survived as standard scales today.

In 1714, a German scientist, Daniel Fahrenheit, developed a more accurate thermometer than what existed. He used mercury encased in glass. The advantage of using mercury is that it expands at a nearly constant rate. This means that you can mark a scale on a thermometer similar to the way that you mark a scale on a ruler. In the Fahrenheit temperature scale, 32° is the freezing point of water and 212° is the boiling point of water.

Anders Celsius, a Swedish astronomer, developed the Celsius scale in 1742. He chose 0° as the boiling point of water and 100° as the freezing point of water. After Celsius died, 0°C became the freezing point, and 100°C became the boiling point.

The Celsius temperature scale (sometimes called centigrade) is the standard scale in most of the world outside the United States. *Centigrade,* derived from Latin, means "100 steps." It refers to dividing the interval between the freezing point and the boiling point of water into 100 equal parts. When you travel, you may want to convert between Celsius and Fahrenheit temperatures. You can use the conversion formula

$$F = \tfrac{9}{5} C + 32$$

where C is temperature in degrees Celsius (°C), and F is temperature in degrees Fahrenheit (°F).

Daniel Fahrenheit designed his thermometer at age 28.

Twenty-eight years after Fahrenheit designed his thermometer, Anders Celsius (above) described the scale that now uses his name.

Mathematical Reflections 2B

In this investigation, you learned to reverse arithmetic operations. You defined an equation and its solutions. Using the backtracking method, you found the solution to an equation. These questions will help you summarize what you have learned.

1. Scientists often use the Kelvin temperature scale. You call the temperature 0 kelvins absolute zero. The formula for converting from degrees Celsius to kelvins is $K = C + 273.15$.

   You name units in the Kelvin scale kelvins, *not degrees Kelvin.*

   a. Write a formula to convert kelvins to degrees Celsius.
   b. What is absolute zero in degrees Celsius?
   c. What is absolute zero in degrees Fahrenheit?
   d. **Take It Further** Write a formula to convert kelvins to degrees Fahrenheit.

2. For each set of steps, describe how to undo the steps.
   a. Add 3 to your number.
   b. Subtract 6 from your number.
   c. Multiply your number by 2 and add 5.
   d. Add 2 to your number and divide by 3.

3. Use backtracking to find the solution to each equation.
   a. $2x + 5 = 11$
   b. $3m - 4 = -7$
   c. $\frac{y}{3} + 1 = 5$
   d. $\frac{y + 1}{3} = 5$

4. a. Show that $w = 8$ is a solution to the equation $18 = 3(w - 2)$.
   b. Show that $x = 3$ and $x = -2$ are solutions to the equation $x^2 = x + 6$.

5. Show that $n = -4$ is not a solution to the equation $2(3n + 1) = 22$.

6. What is an equation?

7. What are some ways to solve an equation?

8. Breanna chooses a number, multiplies it by 3, and subtracts 8. The ending number is 7. What is Breanna's starting number?

If the trail fails on a bike trip, you can backtrack.

Vocabulary

In this investigation, you saw these terms. Make sure you understand what each one means and how to use it.

- backtracking
- empty set
- equation
- null set
- reversible operation
- solution
- solution set

Chapter 2 Mid-Chapter Test

Multiple Choice

1. An expression for the perimeter of a rectangle with length ℓ and width w is $2\ell + 2w$.

   Which of these pairs gives a perimeter of 100?

   A. $\ell = 25$ and $w = 4$
   B. $\ell = 50$ and $w = 50$
   C. $\ell = 30$ and $w = 20$
   D. $\ell = 40$ and $w = 20$

2. Which of these values for x make the value of the expression $(x - 5)(x + 7)$ the greatest?

   A. -9 B. -4
   C. 0 D. 5

3. When r is -19, find the value of $\frac{r + 2r + 3r + 4r}{r}$.

   A. -118
   B. -110
   C. -10
   D. none of the above

4. Which of these operations can you NOT backtrack?

   A. Multiply a number by 17 and then subtract 3.
   B. Square a number and then subtract 3.
   C. Cube a number and then subtract 3.
   D. Divide a number by 17 and then subtract 3.

5. Which of these sequences of steps can you use to solve the equation $5(t - 4) = 65$?

   A. Multiply by 5 and then subtract 4.
   B. Subtract 4 and then multiply by 5.
   C. Add 4 and then divide by 5.
   D. Divide by 5 and then add 4.

6. Which of these equations has exactly one solution?

   A. $3n + 5 = 17$
   B. $3 + 5 = 17$
   C. $12 + 5 = 17$
   D. $3n + 5 = 5 + 3n$

Open Response

7. Maria has two coupons for pizza. Coupon A offers 15% off a pizza. Coupon B offers $2 off a pizza.

   a. If a pizza originally costs $10, how much will it cost when Maria uses Coupon A?
   b. If a pizza originally costs $10, how much will it cost when Maria uses Coupon B?
   c. If Maria wants to buy an extra large pizza that costs $18, which coupon offers the better deal?
   d. Suppose the pizza originally costs x dollars. Write an expression for the pizza's cost using Coupon A. Write another expression for using Coupon B.

8. Maya the Magnificent chooses a number, and then performs these three steps, in order.

   - Subtract 7.
   - Multiply by 5.
   - Add 6.

   a. If Maya starts with 4, what is her ending number?
   b. Maya says, "It's amazing. My ending number is 0!" Use backtracking to find her starting number.
   c. If Maya's starting number is s, write an expression for her ending number.

9. Solve the equation $13 - 5x = 48$ using backtracking. Show your work.

10. Invent a number trick with at least four steps that always returns the same number. Use at least three different operations (addition, subtraction, multiplication, division, or others). Explain why your number trick always works.

Challenge Problem

11. Find both solutions to the equation $n^2 + 12n = 28$.

Investigation 2C: Solving Linear Equations

In *Solving Linear Equations*, you will evaluate and simplify an expression using the basic rules of arithmetic. Using basic moves, you will solve an equation that may have one solution, more than one solution, or even no solution.

By the end of this investigation, you will be able to answer questions like these.

1. How can you solve an equation for which backtracking does not work?
2. How can you visualize an equation using the number line?
3. Solve the equation $5x = x + 24$.

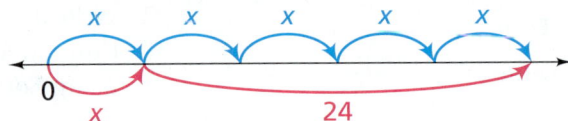

You will learn how to
- evaluate and simplify expressions using the basic rules
- solve equations using the basic moves
- understand that equations can have multiple solutions or no solutions
- solve an equation involving many variations of the Distributive Property

You will develop these habits and skills:
- Visualize solving an equation in a variety of ways.
- Understand why the basic moves do not change the solutions of an equation.
- Quickly solve linear equations.
- Check results to ensure that your algebraic steps are correct.
- Use expansion boxes to distribute expressions.

When an equation is true, the amounts on both sides of the = sign are the same.

2.09 Getting Started

**Activating Prior Knowledge
Exploring New Ideas**

In Lesson 2.08, you used backtracking to find the starting number in a number trick. Can you always use backtracking to find your starting number? Here are some number tricks for you to explore.

For You to Explore

1. Sasha says, "I pick a number.
   - I multiply my number by 2.
   - I add 3.
   - I subtract 8.
   - My final result is 13."

   What is Sasha's starting number?

2. Tony says, "I pick a number.
   - I subtract 11 from my number.
   - I multiply by $\frac{1}{2}$.
   - I add 3.
   - My final result is 8."

   What is Tony's starting number?

3. Derman says, "I pick a number.
   - I add 4 to my number.
   - I multiply by -2.
   - I subtract 19.
   - My final result is -9."

   What is Derman's starting number?

4. Casey says, "I pick a number.
   - I multiply my number by 7.
   - I add 18.
   - My final result is ten times my starting number."

   What is Casey's starting number?

5. Anna says, "I pick a number.
   - I multiply my number by 3.
   - I subtract 4.
   - I subtract 3.
   - My final result is two times my starting number."

   What is Anna's starting number?

6. Sophie says, "I pick a number.
   - I multiply my number by 5.
   - I add 6.
   - My final result is my starting number times 3 plus 12."

   What is Sophie's starting number?

7. James says, "I pick a number.
   - I add 1 to my number.
   - I multiply by 4.
   - I subtract 11.
   - My final result is two times my starting number."

   What is James's number?

8. Emma says, "I pick a number.
   - I add 1 to my number.
   - I multiply by 6.
   - I add 1.
   - My final result is 18 more than my starting number."

   What is Emma's starting number?

9. Here is an arrangement of two rectangles placed side by side to form a larger rectangle. The smaller rectangles have the same width. Find an expression for the area of each of the two smaller rectangles. Find two expressions for the area of the larger rectangle.

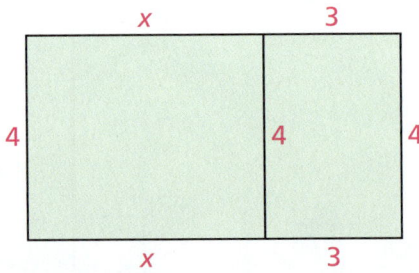

You can combine two photos that have the same height to make a panoramic scene.

Exercises Practicing Habits of Mind

On Your Own

10. Solve each equation using backtracking.

  a. $3a + 11 = 29$ **b.** $-2(p - 15) + 5 = -15$

11. **Write About It** You cannot solve the equation $3t + 12 = 5t + 6$ by using backtracking. Explain why.

12. **Take It Further** Solve the equation $3t + 12 = 5t + 6$. Explain your steps.

13. For each equation, determine whether $r = -2$ is a solution.

  a. $6r + 2 = 12 + r$ **b.** $3r + 2 + 10r = 7 + 7r + (-17)$

  c. $r + 11 - 3r = 15 + 2r$ **d.** $7(r + 2) + 8 = 4r + 16$

14. For each equation, determine whether $s = \frac{4}{3}$ is a solution.

  a. $4s = s + 4$ **b.** $9s - 2 = 5s + \frac{10}{3}$

  c. $5(s - 1) - 1 = 2s - \frac{2}{3}$ **d.** $2(s + 1) + 5 = 7s + \frac{1}{3}$

15. Colleen works on a number game. She says, "I'm thinking of a number. I do some things to it, and I end up with 27. The last step in my game is to add -7."

What is Colleen's ending number if she changes the last step of her game to each of the following?

  a. add 8   **b.** multiply by 2   **c.** subtract 7

16. Here is an arrangement of two small squares and two rectangles that form a large square. Find an expression for the area of each of the four smaller regions. Find *two* expressions for the area of the large square.

Maintain Your Skills

17. For each equation, find a value of x that makes the equation true.

  a. $8 \cdot x = 1$ **b.** $-19 \cdot x = 1$ **c.** $\frac{11}{13} \cdot x = 1$

  d. $\frac{10}{11} \cdot \frac{11}{13} \cdot x = 1$ **e.** $\frac{5}{7} \cdot \frac{11}{12} \cdot x = 1$

2.10 When Backtracking Does Not Work

As you saw in Lesson 2.09, you cannot solve all equations using backtracking. For instance, you cannot solve the equation $3t + 12 = 5t + 6$ from Exercise 6 by using backtracking because there is a t on both sides of the equation. You cannot write the equation as a process. Instead, you can look at this kind of equation in different ways.

Equality on the Number Line

To illustrate the equation $3t + 12 = 5t + 6$, you can draw t as an unknown length. Whatever length you choose for t, you cannot compare it to the length of 6 or 12, because you do not yet know the value of t. You do know that every t has the same length.

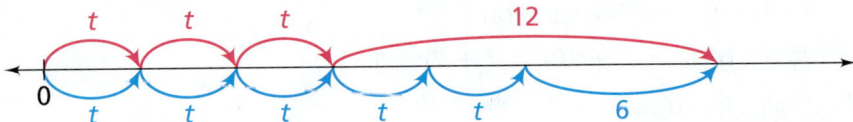

The symbols above the number line show $3t + 12$. The symbols below the number line show $5t + 6$. The equation $3t + 12 = 5t + 6$ tells you that the two expressions are equal. So, when you draw the two expressions, they can start and end at the same point on the number line.

Look at the $3t$'s on the left above and below the line.

$3t$ is in each expression.

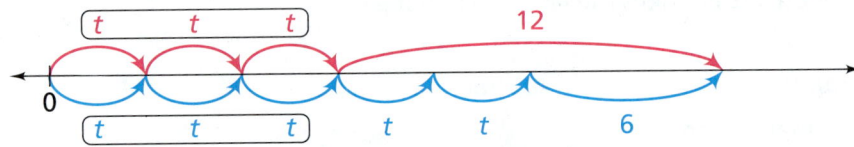

Suppose you ignore the $3t$'s on both the top and bottom. The 12 above the line and the $2t + 6$ below the line start and end at the same point on the number line. So they must be equal.

Ignoring the $3t$'s above and below the line is the same as subtracting $3t$ from both sides of the equation. Above the line, 12 units are left over, and below the line $2t + 6$ units are left over. Now you have an equation, $12 = 2t + 6$, that you can solve using bactracking.

For You to Do

1. Solve the equation $12 = 2t + 6$.

For Discussion

2. Solve the equation $7w + 8 = 4w + 23$.

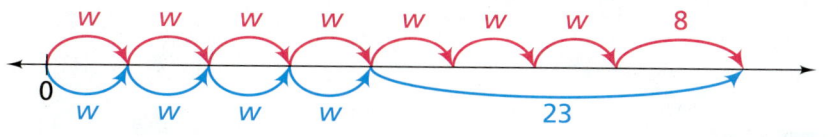

Keeping it Equal

You can represent equations by illustrating each number and variable. Each triangle represents a 1, and each square represents a t.

$$3t + 12 = 5t + 6$$

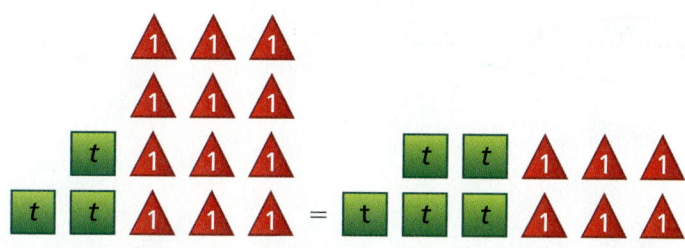

If you remove the same number from each side of the equation, the equation is still true. To begin, you can remove $3t$'s from each side.

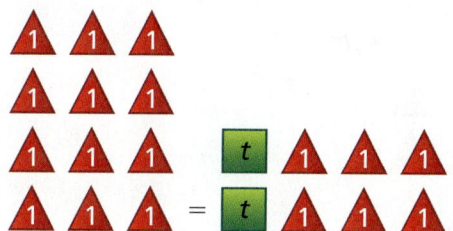

Again, you get a simpler equation, $12 = 2t + 6$.

To finish solving the equation, you can remove 6 triangles from each side.

For Discussion

3. Solve the equation $2x + 4 = x + 8$.

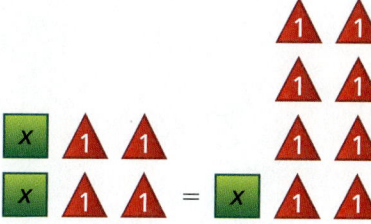

2.10 When Backtracking Does Not Work

Exercises Practicing Habits of Mind

Check Your Understanding

Solve each equation.

1. $2\ell + 5 = 35$

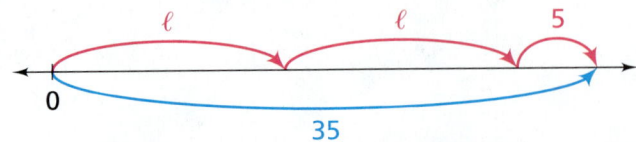

2. $7j = 5j + 10$

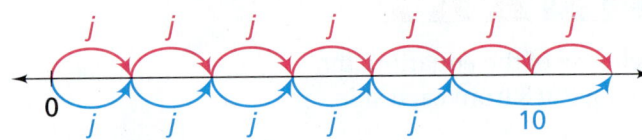

3. $4n + 7 = 2n + 10$

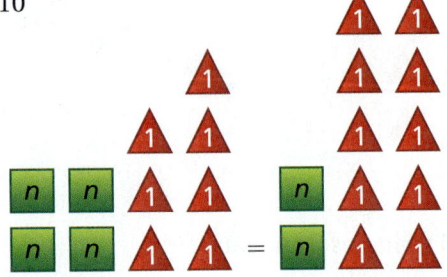

4. $6x + 2 = x + 10$

5. $3x = -15$
6. $2y + 11 = 27$
7. $2a + 5 = a + 8$
8. $4u - 5 = u + 16$
9. $11m + 1 = 8m + 28$

10. Each expression is the left side of an equation. Write an expression for the right side so that $x = 3$ is a solution of the equation.

    a. $2(x + 1)$ b. $3x - 1$ c. $7x + 5 + 2(x - 1)$

    d. 6 e. any expression

11. Solve each equation.

    a. $5r + 11 = 95 - r$

    b. $14 - 23x = 60x + 180$

    c. $37a + 12 + 14a - 9 = 6a + 11 - 14 + 5a$

    d. $s - 2s + 3s - 4s + 5s = s + 100$

On Your Own

Solve each equation.

12. $6r + 2 = r + 12$

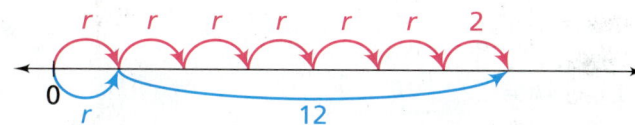

13. $2d + 10 = 5d + 4$

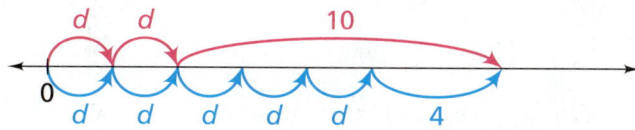

14. $3p = 36$

15. Solve the equation $7x - 8 = x + 16$.

16. Solve each equation.

    a. $3x + 5 = 26$ b. $26 = 3(x - 1) + 5$

    c. $26 = 3(x + 3) + 5$ d. $3(x - 7) + 5 = 26$

    e. $26 = 3(2x + 1) + 5$ f. $3(5 - 2y) + 5 = 26$

17. James says to his sister Emma, "I'm six years older than you. Two years from now, I'll be twice as old as you." Since you don't know Emma's or James's age, you can let x stand for Emma's age today.

    a. Write an expression for James's age today.

    b. Write an expression for Emma's age in two years.

    c. Write an expression for James's age in two years.

    d. In two years, James will be twice as old as Emma. Explain why the equation $x + 8 = 2(x + 2)$ represents this fact.

    e. Solve the equation in part (d). How old is James today? How old is Emma today?

18. **Standardized Test Prep** Shantell and Yahaira have the same amount of money to spend on shoes. Shantell purchases 7 pairs of shoes and has $17 left. Yahaira purchases 4 pairs of shoes and has $71 left. Each pair costs the same amount and there is no sales tax. What is the cost of a pair of shoes?

    A. $8 **B.** $17 **C.** $18 **D.** $22

19. Solve each equation.

    a. $5x - 7 = 2x + 2$

    b. $3g - 8 = 5g - 20$

    c. $1 - 3b = 2b - 8$

    d. $15 - 4k = 12 - 7k$

20. **Take It Further** Find all the solutions to the equation $5x^2 - 27 = 2x^2 + 48$.

Maintain Your Skills

21. Solve each equation.

    a. $3x + 1 = 19 + x$
    b. $4x + 1 = 19 + x$
    c. $5x + 1 = 19 + x$
    d. $6x + 1 = 19 + x$
    e. $7x + 1 = 19 + x$

    f. Which steps are the same for solving each of the equations in parts (a)–(e)? Which steps are different?

22. Solve each equation.

    a. $3(x - 1) = 2(x + 1)$
    b. $4(x - 1) = 2(x + 1)$
    c. $5(x - 1) = 2(x + 1)$
    d. $6(x - 1) = 2(x + 1)$
    e. $7(x - 1) = 2(x + 1)$
    f. $8(x - 1) = 2(x + 1)$

    g. Which steps are the same for solving each of the equations in parts (a)–(f)? Which steps are different?

2.11 The Basic Moves for Solving Equations

In this lesson, you will solve a one-variable equation using two basic moves for solving equations.

Minds in Action — episode 6

Tony and Sasha solve the equation $7x - 8 = x + 16$.

Tony To solve this problem, I'd start by drawing a number line, and and then . . .

Sasha Don't bother with all of that, Tony. I've got a shortcut.

Tony Show me.

Sasha Well, whenever I solve an equation, the solution ends up being $x =$ some number. So, I make the equation look like that.

Tony How?

Sasha First I get rid of the x term on one side of the equation. To do that, I subtract x from each side of the equation.

$$\begin{array}{rl} 7x - 8 = & x + 16 \\ -x & -x \\ \hline 6x - 8 = & 16 \end{array}$$

See, no x term on the right. I'm almost done.

Tony This equation is like the ones we've solved before.

Sasha Exactly. Then, add 8 to each side.

$$\begin{array}{rl} 6x - 8 = & +16 \\ +8 & +8 \\ \hline 6x = & 24 \end{array}$$

Now we have $6x = 24$. Finally, I divide each side by 6 to get the answer.

$$\frac{6x}{6} = \frac{24}{6}$$

$$x = 4$$

Tony Are you sure that's the correct answer?

Sasha Let's check it.

Tony substitutes $x = 4$ into the equation $7x - 8 = x + 16$.

$$7x - 8 = x + 16$$
$$7(4) - 8 = (4) + 16$$
$$28 - 8 = 20$$
$$20 = 20 \quad \checkmark \text{ true}$$

Tony $x = 4$ works. Each side of the equation is 20.

Sasha I use that method to solve all sorts of equations.

For Discussion

1. Use Sasha's method to solve the equation $3x - 5 = x + 7$.
2. Why does Sasha's method work?

Sasha's method will help you solve many equations. She adds the same value to each side of the equation, or she subtracts the same value from each side of the equation. Then, she does not change the solutions of the equation. There is a special name for moves that never change the solutions of an equation—the **basic moves for solving equations.**

Assumption   The Basic Moves for Solving Equations

1. If you start with an equation and add the same number to each side, you do not change the solutions of that equation.

    In symbols, for any three numbers a, b, and c,
    $a = b$ if, and only if, $a + c = b + c$.

2. If you start with an equation and multiply each side of the equation by the same nonzero number, you do not change the solutions of that equation.

    In symbols, for any three numbers a, b, and c, where $c \neq 0$,
    $a = b$ if, and only if, $ac = bc$.

Habits of Mind

Represent a variable with a number. Why is $c \neq 0$? Try replacing the variables a and b with different numbers.

For Discussion

3. You can also use the following two basic moves.
   - If you start with an equation and subtract the same number from each side, you do not change the solutions of that equation.
   - If you start with an equation and divide each side of the equation by the same number (unless that number is zero), you do not change the solutions of that equation.

   These rules are both correct, but they are not in the list of basic moves. Why do you think these rules are not in the list of basic moves?

For You to Do

4. Use the basic moves to solve the equation $3s - 5 = s + 7$.
5. Explain which basic move you used at each step.

Example

Problem Solve $4x + 3 = 7x + 15$.

Solution First, subtract $4x$ from each side of the equation. This step removes $4x$ from the left side, leaving only one side with an x variable.

$$\begin{array}{rl} 4x + 3 = & 7x + 15 \\ -4x & -4x \\ \hline 3 = & 3x + 15 \end{array}$$

Next, subtract 15 from each side.

$$\begin{array}{rl} 3 = & 3x + 15 \\ -15 & -15 \\ \hline -12 = & 3x \end{array}$$

By subtracting, you isolate $3x$ on the right side. To make the equation look like "some number $= x$," divide each side by 3.

$$\frac{-12}{3} = \frac{3x}{3}$$
$$-4 = x$$

The result is $x = -4$. Finally, check your result by plugging it into the starting equation.

$$\begin{aligned} 4x + 3 &= 7x + 15 \\ 4(-4) + 3 &= 7(-4) + 15 \\ -16 + 3 &= -28 + 15 \\ -13 &= -13 \quad \checkmark \text{ true} \end{aligned}$$

The correct solution is $x = -4$.

Habits of Mind

Look for relationships. Subtract 15. Then divide by 3. These steps look a lot like backtracking.

Exercises Practicing Habits of Mind

Check Your Understanding

1. Solve each equation.

   a. $6x + 12 = 11x - 33$
   b. $8x + 13 = -4x + 11$
   c. $13 + 8x = 11 - 4x$
   d. $6(a + 2) = 11(a - 3)$
   e. $2z + 9z = 4z + 45 + 2z$
   f. $3n + 13 = 3n + 13$

   > Something is different about the equation in part (f).

2. Suppose that you teach a robot to do your algebra homework. Give the steps for solving the equation $73x - 15 = 48x + 99$.

3. Sasha says, "I'm thinking of a number. I do some things to it, and I end up with 13. The last step is adding 10. What will I get if everything stays the same except for the last step, which becomes adding 8?"

4. Describe one basic move you can use to transform the equation $3t + 13 = 5t + 6$ into each equation.

   a. $3t + 7 = 5t$
   b. $2t + 13 = 4t + 6$
   c. $3t + 113 = 5t + 106$
   d. $13 = 2t + 6$
   e. $-2t + 13 = 6$
   f. $15t + 65 = 25t + 30$

5. Choose three equations from Exercise 4. Solve each equation. Explain your results.

6. a. Solve the equation $4(x - 7) + 13 = 27$ using backtracking. Show all your steps.

   b. Solve the equation $4(x - 7) + 13 = 27$ using basic moves.

   c. In parts (a) and (b), how are the steps similar? How are they different?

7. So far, most equations you have solved have only one solution. However, not all equations have exactly one solution. Match one equation to each number of solutions. Explain.

   $3s + 12 = 3(s + 3) + 3 \qquad 2x + 2 = 2x + 7 \qquad 4z + 2 = z - 4$

   a. one solution
   b. no solutions
   c. infinitely many solutions

On Your Own

For Exercises 8–10, solve each equation.

8. $7f - 19 = 4f + 41$
9. $4r + 6 = 2r - 17$
10. $4a + 1 = 11a + 8$

11. Describe the one basic move you need to change the equation $2x + 17 = 36$ into each equation.

    a. $2x + 13 = 32$
    b. $2x - 12 = 7$
    c. $2x = 19$
    d. $6x + 51 = 108$
    e. $x + 8.5 = 18$
    f. $5x + 17 = 3x + 36$
    g. $2x - 19 = 0$
    h. $x + 17 = 36 - x$

12. Choose three of the equations in Exercise 11. Solve for x. Explain your results.

13. Here is one of Maya the Magnificent's number tricks.

    Choose any number. Multiply by 3. Add 5. Multiply by 4. Add 16. Divide by 12. Subtract your starting number.

    Maya says, "I know what your final answer is!"

    a. Let your starting number equal x. Record the result and simplify the expression after each step.
    b. Does Maya know for sure what your final answer is? Explain.

14. a. For which numbers n is $(5n + 12)$ equal to $(5n + 13)$? Explain.
    b. Solve the equation $5x + 12 = 5x + 13$. What are your results? What does the resulting equation tell you about the solutions to the starting equation?

15. **Standardized Test Prep** Solve the equation $17 - (5 - p) = 2(5p - 16)$. What is the value of p?

    A. $\frac{28}{11}$
    B. 4
    C. $\frac{44}{9}$
    D. 5

16. a. For which numbers n is $(3n - 7)$ equal to $(3n - 7)$?
    b. Try to solve the equation $3x - 7 = 3x - 7$. What are your results? What does the resulting equation tell you about the solutions to the starting equation?

Maintain Your Skills

17. Solve each equation.

    a. $3x + 2 = 22 - x$
    b. $(3x + 2) + 1 = (22 - x) + 1$
    c. $(3x + 2) + 2 = (22 - x) + 2$
    d. $(3x + 2) + 5 = (22 - x) + 5$
    e. $(3x + 2) - 11 = (22 - x) - 11$
    f. $(3x + 2) + \frac{99}{7} = (22 - x) + \frac{99}{7}$
    g. What do these equations have in common? Explain.

2.11 The Basic Moves for Solving Equations

2.12 Solutions of Linear Equations

You have already extended the basic rules of arithmetic to include numbers and variables. You can also use the basic rules as a starting point for deriving new rules. Then you can use derived rules in the same way that you use basic rules.

The difference between basic rules and derived rules is that derived rules are not assumptions. You call derived rules of mathematics *theorems*. Later, you will prove many theorems starting from basic assumptions. The first few theorems below are concepts that you may already accept. However, now you can use the basic rules to make certain that the theorems are true.

> A **theorem** is a fact that follows logically from other known facts. For example, you know that San Diego is in California, and that Tony lives in San Diego. Based on these assumptions, you can derive and prove the theorem that Tony lives in California.

Theorem 2.1

If a is any real number, then $a \cdot 0 = 0 \cdot a = 0$.

Theorem 2.2

The number 0 does not have a reciprocal.

Theorem 2.3

For all real numbers a and b, $a - b = a + (-b)$.

> **Remember...**
> You can define the expression $a - b$ as the number that, if you add it to b, you get a.

For Discussion

1. How can you use the basic rules and Theorem 2.1 to derive Theorem 2.2?
2. **Take It Further** How can you use just the basic rules to derive Theorem 2.1?
3. **Take It Further** How can you use the basic rules and the definition of subtraction to derive Theorem 2.3?

The real power of Theorem 2.3 is that now you have a way to apply the any-order, any-grouping properties to subtraction. For example, you know that

$$5 - 3 \neq 3 - 5$$

because you cannot subtract in any order. If you change the statement using Theorem 2.3, you get a true statement.

$$5 + (-3) = (-3) + 5$$

You will use this theorem over and over again when simplifying and solving equations.

For Discussion

4. Sasha tried solving the equation $3x + 2 = 2x + x + 7$ using the basic moves.

$$3x + 2 = 2x + x + 7$$
$$3x + 2 = 3x + 7$$
$$3x + 2 - 3x = 3x + 7 - 3x$$
$$2 \stackrel{?}{=} 7$$

Did Sasha do something incorrectly? Why did Sasha get $2 \stackrel{?}{=} 7$ on the last line?

For You to Do

5. What results do you get when you try to solve the equation $4(x + 1) = 4x + 4$?

In this lesson, you are using linear equations. A **linear equation** is any equation in which the variable terms are not raised to a power. For example,

- $3t + 2 = 4t - 1$ is a linear equation.
- $3t^2 + 5t = 9$ is not a linear equation because it has a t^2 term.

There are only three possibilities for the solutions of a linear equation.

- A linear equation can have no solutions. For example,
    $3x + 2 = 3x + 7$
- A linear equation can have one solution. For example,
    $6x - 3 = 4x + 13$
- Every real number can be a solution to the linear equation. For example,
    $4(x + 1) = 4x + 4$

    is true for every real number x.

For You to Do

Determine whether each equation has no solutions, one solution, or every real number as a solution.

6. $10a - 2 = 10(a + 1) - 8$

7. $7 - 2z = 5 - 2z$

8. $2p + 3p = p + 6$

9. $-5k + 10 = 5(2 - k)$

10. $3(j + 2) = 3j + 2$

For Discussion

11. Write 5 equations that have no solutions.

12. Write 5 equations that have one solution.

13. Write 5 equations that have every real number as a solution.

2.12 Solutions of Linear Equations

Exercises Practicing Habits of Mind

Check Your Understanding

Solve each equation. (*Hint:* Some equations may not have a solution. Others may have infinitely many solutions.)

1. $2r + 1 = 5r - 11$
2. $4 - w = 3w + 1$
3. $16t + 9 = 2(8t + 1)$
4. $5u + 8 = 40 - 2u$
5. $\frac{3}{2}r + 4 = 10$
6. $4 + 11e = 2 + 5e + (2 + 6e)$
7. **a.** Write an equation that has $x = 3$ as a solution.
   b. Write an equation that has a variable on both sides and $x = 5$ as a solution.
   c. Write an equation that has a variable on both sides and $x = -11$ as a solution.
   d. Write an equation that has a variable on both sides and $x = \frac{5}{3}$ as a solution.
   e. Write an equation that has a variable on both sides but does not have any solutions.
8. Explain how you can use the basic moves to transform the equation $6x + 2y = 15$ into each of the following equations.
   a. $6x + 2y - 15 = 0$
   b. $0 = 15 - 6x - 2y$
   c. $2y = 15 - 6x$
   d. $y = \frac{15}{2} - 3x$
9. If $10(7a + 5) = 90$, what is $(7a + 15)$?

10. Tony says, "I'm thinking of a number. I do some things to it, and I end up with 36. The last two steps are add 11 and then multiply by 3. What do I get if the last two steps change to each of the following, and everything else stays the same?"

    a. Add 8 and then multiply by 8.
    b. Multiply by 5 and then subtract 20.
    c. Add 19 and then multiply by 5.

11. Suppose you know that the equation $x + y = 7$ is true. Which of these must be true also? Which must be false? Which might be true or false?

    a. $x + y + 6 = 12$
    b. $x + y - 4 = 3$
    c. $3(x + y) = 28$
    d. $xy = 12$
    e. $\frac{x + y}{7} = 1$
    f. $7 = x + y$
    g. $x - y = 3$
    h. $y = 7 - x$
    i. $x < 7$

On Your Own

Solve each equation. (*Hint:* Some equations may not have a solution. Some equations may have infinitely many solutions.)

12. $2a + 1 = 6a + 11$
13. $11 - 2(d - 1) = -2d + 13$
14. $4(n - 1) = 6n - 12$

15. Solve each equation.

    a. $25 = 3x + 5$
    b. $3(x - 1) + 5 = 25$
    c. $3(x + 3) + 5 = 25$
    d. $25 = 3(x - 7) + 5$
    e. $3(2x + 1) + 5 = 25$
    f. $25 = 3(5 - 2y) + 5$

16. If you know that $3r + 2 = 9$, which of these must also be true? Which must be false? Which might be true or false?

    a. $2(3r + 2) = 18$
    b. $3r + 22 = 20$
    c. $3r + 22 = 29$
    d. $-9 = -2 - 3r$
    e. $3r - 9 = 0$
    f. $6r + 4 = 18$
    g. $3r = 7$
    h. $r = -4$

17. **Standardized Test Prep** What is the number of solutions for each of the following equations?

   I. $4s - 4 = 3(s - 3) + 5 + s$

   II. $-3(t + 2) = 8(t + 1) - 11(t - 2)$

   III. $5(t - 1) = -5(t + 4) + 15$

   A. I has 0 solutions.
      II has 1 solution.
      III has more than 1 solution.

   B. I has more than 1 solution.
      II has 1 solution.
      III has 1 solution.

   C. I has 1 solution.
      II has more than 1 solution.
      III has 0 solutions.

   D. I has more than 1 solution.
      II has 0 solutions.
      III has 1 solution.

Maintain Your Skills

18. Solve each equation.

   a. $5d - 2 = 2d + 10$

   b. $5d - 2 = 3d + 10$

   c. $5d - 2 = 4d + 10$

   d. $5d - 2 = 5d + 10$

   e. $5d - 2 = 6d + 10$

   f. $5d - 2 = 7d + 10$

   g. $5d - 2 = 8d + 10$

   h. Which equation has a different number of solutions than the other equations? Explain.

   i. Describe another pattern in the solutions.

19. Solve each equation.

   a. $4c + 2 = 4c - 1$

   b. $4c + 2 = 4c$

   c. $4c + 2 = 4c + 1$

   d. $4c + 2 = 4c + 2$

   e. $4c + 2 = 4c + 3$

   f. Which equation has a different number of solutions than the other equations? Explain.

2.13 Focus on the Distributive Property

Learning to use the Distributive Property is especially important when solving equations. It helps you avoid losing a negative sign somewhere and finding an incorrect result.

For You to Do

1. **What's Wrong Here?** Rebecca, Anna, and Jenna tried to solve the equation $40 - 4(x + 3) = 7x - 5$. They got three different results.

Rebecca

$40 - 4(x + 3) = 7x - 5$
$40 - 4x + 12 = 7x - 5$
$52 - 4x = 7x - 5$
$52 - 4x + 5 = 7x - 5 + 5$
$57 - 4x = 7x$
$57 - 4x + 4x = 7x + 4x$
$57 = 11x$
$\frac{57}{11} = x$

Anna

$40 - 4(x + 3) = 7x - 5$
$40 - 4x + 3 = 7x - 5$
$43 - 4x = 7x - 5$
$39x = 7x - 5$
$39x - 7x = 7x - 5 - 7x$
$32x = -5$
$x = -\frac{5}{32}$

Jenna

$40 - 4(x + 3) = 7x - 5$
$40 - 4x - 12 = 7x - 5$
$28 - 4x = 7x - 5$
$28 - 4x + 4x = 7x - 5 + 4x$
$28 = 11x - 5$
$28 + 5 = 11x - 5 + 5$
$33 = 11x$
$3 = x$

Who has the correct result? What mistakes did each of the others make?

Developing Habits of Mind

Repeat a familiar process. In Investigation 1C, you used an expansion box for multiplying numbers. Recall that to multiply $327 \cdot 6$, you made an expansion box similar to the one below.

	300	20	7
6	1800	120	42

Then you added all the numbers inside the box to get the product.

You can use an expansion box to apply the Distributive Property to expressions, too. Use an expansion box to multiply $7(3x - 4)$.

	$3x$	-4
7	$21x$	-28

So $7(3x - 4) = 21x + (-28) = 21x - 28$.

For You to Do

Expand each expression. It may be useful to use expansion boxes.

2. $3(16 - 2x)$
3. $7 - 5(y - 11)$
4. $2(3z + 1) - (z - 6)$
5. $11(a + 5b - 3c)$

As you get more comfortable with distributing expressions, it might seem unnecessary to set up expansion boxes every time you distribute an expression. They are a useful technique when you deal with more complicated expressions.

Exercises Practicing Habits of Mind

Check Your Understanding

For Exercises 1–10, solve each equation.

1. $2(x + 3) = 15$
2. $5(j - 3) = 10(j - 2)$
3. $3(k - 4) + 6 = 2$
4. $-(x + 3) = 7$
5. $-(s + 2) = 4(s + 1)$
6. $-2(2w + 3) = 10$
7. $-(-3 - q) = -\frac{1}{2}(6q - 26)$
8. $4(e + 4) = 2(17 - 2e)$
9. $2(2x + 1) - 3(x - 5) = 18$
10. $-\left(z + \frac{2}{3}\right) = z$

11. **What's Wrong Here?** Using expansion boxes or some other method, show that $(a + b)^2$ does not necessarily equal $a^2 + b^2$.

12. Use this array to show that $4(a + b) = 4a + 4b$.

    $a\ a\ a\ a$
    $b\ b\ b\ b$

13. Use this array to show that $4(a + b + c) = 4a + 4b + 4c$.

    $a\ a\ a\ a$
    $b\ b\ b\ b$
    $c\ c\ c\ c$

14. Look at the arrays in Exercises 12 and 13. Make an array that illustrates this fact.

    $7(x + y + z) = 7x + 7y + 7z$

> The expression $(a + b)^2$ is equal to $(a + b)(a + b)$, since *squaring* means to multiply the expression by itself.

On Your Own

For Exercises 15–21, solve each equation.

15. $5(2a - 1) = 60$
16. $-(d - 4) = 13$
17. $15 = -5(x - 4)$
18. $3(x - 2) + 2(x - 2) = 40$
19. $28 = -7(2x - 3)$
20. $-4(p + 2) + 8 = 2(p - 1) - 7p + 15$
21. $2(5 - n) = 6 + 6n$

$5(4 + 5) = 5 \cdot 4 + 5 \cdot 5$

22. Use expansion boxes or another method to write each expression without parentheses.

    a. $12(2x - 7)$
    b. $3(4 - x)$
    c. $x(2x + 5)$
    d. $\frac{2}{3}(3x - 18)$
    e. $\frac{4}{7}(14x - 3)$
    f. $(-4)(3x - 6)$
    g. $(-3)(x^2 + 7x - 14)$
    h. $\left(-\frac{5}{6}\right)(12x + 18)$
    i. $\left(-\frac{1}{2}x\right)(7x^2 - 22)$

23. **Standardized Test Prep** Which expression equals $4z - 2az$?

    A. $-2z(2a - 2)$
    B. $-2(2z - az)$
    C. $-z(2a - 4)$
    D. $-z(-2a + 4)$

2.13 Focus on the Distributive Property

24. **What's Wrong Here?** Decide whether Jade solved each equation correctly. If Jade made a mistake, find the correct result. Explain her mistake.

   a. **Problem** $-(x - 3) = 13$

   Jade's Solution
   $$-(x - 3) = 13$$
   $$-x - 3 = 13$$
   $$-x = 16$$
   $$x = -16$$

   b. **Problem** $-\left(\frac{1}{4} - u\right) = 3u - \frac{17}{4}$

   Jade's Solution
   $$-\left(\frac{1}{4} - u\right) = 3u - \frac{17}{4}$$
   $$-\frac{1}{4} + u = 3u - \frac{17}{4}$$
   $$-\frac{1}{4} = 2u - \frac{17}{4}$$
   $$-\frac{1}{4} + \frac{17}{4} = 2u$$
   $$\frac{16}{4} = 2u$$
   $$4 = 2u$$
   $$2 = u$$

   c. **Problem** $-3(v - 8) = 5(v + 1)$

   Jade's Solution
   $$-3(v - 8) = 5(v + 1)$$
   $$-3v - 24 = 5v + 5$$
   $$-24 = 8v + 5$$
   $$-29 = 8v$$
   $$-\frac{29}{8} = v$$

Maintain Your Skills

25. Solve each equation.

   a. $5x = 2x + 21$

   b. $5(x - 100) = 2(x - 100) + 21$

   c. $5(x - 40) = 2(x - 40) + 21$

   d. $5(x - 90) = 2(x - 90) + 21$

   e. $5(x - 8) = 2(x - 8) + 21$

   f. $5(x + 100) = 2(x + 100) + 21$

   g. Find a pattern in the relationship between the calculations and the result.

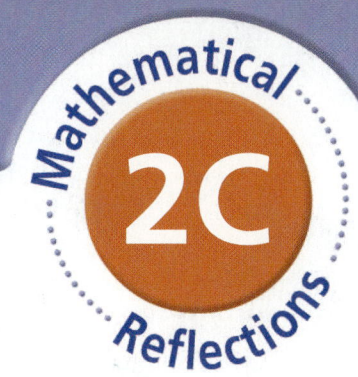

Mathematical 2C Reflections

In this investigation, you learned the basic moves for solving an equation. An equation may have only one solution, more than one solution, or no solution. These questions will help you summarize what you have learned.

1. Give an example of an equation that has no solution. Give an example of an equation that has infinitely many solutions.

2. For each equation, determine whether $x = -3$ is a solution.

   a. $4x + 1 = 2x - 5$
   b. $x - 4 = -2x$
   c. $2(x + 1) + 5 = x + 2$
   d. $2x + 3 - 4x = -3x$

3. Solve each equation.

   a. $6x + 3 = 2x + 7$
   b. $4m - 3 = m + 12$

4. Solve each equation. (*Hint:* Some equations may not have a solution. Other equations may have infinitely many solutions.)

   a. $5x - 6 = 3x + 4$
   b. $x + 2 + 3x = 4(x - 1)$
   c. $2(3x + 4) + 2 = 6x + 10$
   d. $3 - x = 2x + 9$

5. Solve the equation $2(m + 3) - 4(2m + 1) = m - 3(2 + m)$.

6. How can you solve an equation for which backtracking does not work?

7. How can you visualize an equation using the number line?

8. Solve the equation $5x = x + 24$.

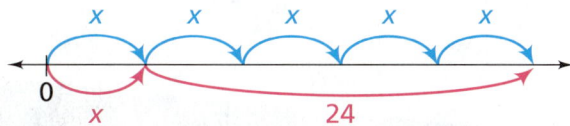

When you add to one side of an equation, you must add the same amount to the other side, or the solutions will change.

Vocabulary

In this investigation, you saw these terms. Make sure you understand what each one means and how to use it.

- basic moves for solving equations
- linear equation
- theorem

Investigation 2D

Word Problems

In *Word Problems,* you will learn to write an equation to represent a situation. Then you will use the basic moves to solve the equation, and thus solve the word problem.

By the end of this investigation, you will be able to answer questions like these.

1. How can you use the guess-check-generalize method to solve a word problem?

2. How do you solve for y in a two-variable equation?

3. What number plus one fourth of itself equals 560?

You will learn how to
- use the guess-check-generalize method for solving word problems
- solve a two-variable equation
- build an equation from a mathematical situation

You will develop these habits and skills:
- Use the guess-check-generalize method to solve a mathematical problem.
- Interpret a situation and represent it mathematically.

Diagrams and symbols can help you solve a problem.

2.14 Getting Started

Activating Prior Knowledge
Exploring New Ideas

You can solve a number puzzle using any method that works. Later in this investigation, you will learn a systematic method that you can use with any puzzle.

For You to Explore

1. Chiko says, "There's an amazing fact about the number I'm thinking of. I call this fact the four 4's. Using my number, you can get four different answers if you add 4, subtract 4, multiply by 4, or divide by 4. That's not impressive, but if you add all the answers, you get 60."

   a. Is Chiko's number 12?

   b. Is Chiko's number 8?

   c. Find Chiko's number. Describe how to find it.

2. Find the number with four 5's (add 5, subtract 5, multiply by 5, and divide by 5) that have a sum of 144.

3. This problem is from a collection of puzzles made around A.D. 500. The puzzle is about the Greek mathematician Diophantus, who lived around A.D. 250.

   > His childhood lasted one sixth of his life; he grew a beard after one twelfth more; one seventh later, he was married. Five years later, he had a son. The son lived exactly half as long as his father. Four years later, Diophantus died. How old was he?

   a. Guess how old Diophantus was when he died. Check your guess. Do not worry about making a good guess!

   b. Make another guess. Write the steps you use to find whether your guess is correct.

   c. Suppose your guess is a number n. How can you check whether n is the correct result?

   d. Find the correct result without guessing.

4. Cameron tells about his trip to the Big Books store. "How awful! They want me to join their club to get 10% off. It costs $15 to join the club. It costs $8 more to buy my books if I join the club than if I don't!" How much do Cameron's books cost without joining the club?

> Diophantus' age is an integer.

Habits of Mind

Look for a relationship. These steps are the same ones you follow in checking numerical guesses.

Exercises Practicing Habits of Mind

On Your Own

5. Is each statement true for all, some, or no numbers? If it is true for all or no numbers, explain.

   a. Adding 6 to a number gives the same result as multiplying that number by 3.

   b. $n + 6 = 3n$

   c. Subtracting 3 from a number gives the same result as adding 3 to that number.

   d. $5n - 6 = 3n + 34$

   e. $2n - 6 = 34$

   f. Doubling a number and then adding 6 gives the same result as adding 3 to a number and then doubling the result.

   g. $n - 3 = n + 3$

   h. $2n + 6 = 2(n + 3)$

   i. Subtracting 5 from a number and then squaring the result gives the result 16.

   > Equations are statements about numbers. They can be true for all, some, or no numbers.

6. Vanessa works 32 hours per week at her job. Her boss offers her a full-time position (40 hours per week) and a $2-per-hour raise. She says, "This is great! Now I'll make $200 more per week!" What is Vanessa's hourly wage before the raise?

In Exercise 6, you can guess Vanessa's pre-raise wage and then check your guess. An easy wage to begin with is $10 per hour.

7. For each statement in Exercise 5 that is true for some numbers, find what numbers make the statement true.

8. **a. Write About It** Explain why the equation $5n + 8 = 3n + 22$ has the same solution as the equation $5n + 8 - 3n = 22$.

   b. Solve the equation $7n - 13 = 4n + 35$ by using basic moves.

   c. Solve the equation $13(n - 1) = 5(2n + 7)$ by using the Distributive Property and basic moves.

Maintain Your Skills

9. Solve each equation.

   a. $3x - 7 = 13 - x$

   b. $3(a + 2) - 7 = 13 - (a + 2)$

   c. $3(5b) - 7 = 13 - (5b)$

   d. $3(8 - c) - 7 = 13 - (8 - c)$

   e. $3(12 + 2d) - 7 = 13 - (12 + 2d)$

   f. How can you solve each equation without using the Distributive Property?

Habits of Mind
Look for relationships. Does your solution to part (a) help you solve parts (b)–(f)? Explain.

10. Solve each equation.

    a. $5x - 3 = x + 14$

    b. $7a - 3 = 3a + 14$

    c. $5m - 19 = m - 2$

    d. $-2q - 6 = -6q + 11$

    e. What pattern do you find when you solve these equations? How does the pattern relate to Exercise 9?

    f. Write another equation that fits the pattern in this exercise.

2.15 Building Equations

Many students are good equation solvers. Sometimes the hardest part is setting up the equation when you are solving a word problem. In this lesson, you will learn the **guess-check-generalize method** to find an equation for a word problem.

Remember...
To *solve* an equation, you find all the numbers that make the equation true.

Example

Problem Vanessa works 32 hours per week at her job. Her boss offers her a full-time position (40 hours per week) and a $2-per-hour raise. She says, "This is great! Now I'll make $200 more per week!" What is Vanessa's hourly wage before the raise?

Solution Use the guess-check-generalize method to write an equation. Here is how the method works.

First, guess what Vanessa's hourly wage was before the raise. The point of this method is not to guess the correct answer, but to learn how to check a guess. Suppose you guess $10 per hour.

Next, check your guess. It is important to keep track of the steps.

	Check	Step
1	If Vanessa made $10 per hour before her raise, she makes $10 + $2, or $12, per hour after her raise.	Add $2 to her wage before the raise.
2	Before her raise, she made $320 per week.	Multiply her wage before her raise by 32.
3	After her raise, she makes $480 per week.	Multiply her wage after her raise by 40.
4	If the guess $10 is correct, she makes $320 plus $200, or $520, after her raise.	Add 200 to the result of step 2.
5	This $520 should equal the amount in step 3. It doesn't, so $10 is incorrect. That's okay.	Compare this sum to the result in step 3.

You can draw lines between each step in the check to help you keep track of the steps.

Repeat the process until the steps become automatic. The crucial point is that you understand how you can check whether any guess is correct. Suppose your second guess is that Vanessa's wage before her raise was $13 per hour.

	Check	Step
1	Now Vanessa makes $13 + $2, or $15, per hour.	Add $2 to her wage before the raise.
2	Before, she made 32 • $13 = $416 per week.	Multiply her wage before her raise by 32.
3	Today, she makes 40 • $15 = $600 per week.	Multiply her wage after her raise by 40.
4	If the guess $13 is correct, then she makes $416 plus $200, or $616, after her raise.	Add 200 to the result of step 2.
5	This $616 should equal the $600 in step 3. It doesn't, so $13 is incorrect.	Compare this sum to the result in step 3.

Finally, generalize by making your guess a variable. Let w equal Vanessa's wage before the raise. Apply the same steps shown above to w:

	Check	Step
1	Now Vanessa makes $w + 2$ dollars per hour.	Add $2 to her wage before the raise.
2	Before, she made $32 \cdot w = 32w$ dollars per week.	Multiply her wage before her raise by 32.
3	Today, she makes $40 \cdot (w + 2) = 40(w + 2)$ dollars per week.	Multiply her wage after her raise by 40.
4	The sum $32w + 200$ should equal $40(w + 2)$. The correct equation is $32w + 200 = 40(w + 2)$.	Add 200 to the result of step 2. The sum should equal the product in step 3.

The last line of the check gives you the equation $32w + 200 = 40(w + 2)$. Many algebra students like this method. Try it!

For You to Do

1. Solve the equation $32w + 200 = 40(w + 2)$.
2. What is Vanessa's wage before her raise? After her raise?
3. Recheck your result.

Exercises Practicing Habits of Mind

Check Your Understanding

1. Ancient Egyptian mathematicians used the concept of *false position* to solve equations. You guess a convenient answer and then adjust it to find the correct answer. Here's an example.

    A number plus one fourth of itself equals 210. What is the number?

    a. A convenient guess is 4. Why is 4 a convenient guess?

    b. Suppose you guess 4. What is the result of the calculation a number plus one fourth of itself?

    c. Suppose you guess 12. What is the result of the calculation a number plus one fourth of itself? How is that result related to the result of guessing 4?

    d. Use the guess-check-generalize method to solve this exercise.

    > You call this method *false position* since you assume an incorrect answer is correct. You check the incorrect result to find the correct one.

2. Last summer, Katie mowed lawns to earn money. She mowed 35 lawns per week and charged $6 per lawn. This summer, Katie wants to earn an additional $150 per week. She will raise her price to $8 and find more customers.

    a. If Katie finds 4 new customers and still keeps her former customers, will she earn an additional $150 per week?

    b. If Katie finds 13 new customers, will she earn an additional $150 per week?

    c. If Katie finds 8 new customers, will she earn an additional $150 per week?

    d. Use the guess-check-generalize method to build an equation for finding the number of new customers Katie needs to earn an additional $150.

    e. Solve your equation.

3. Suppose Katie charges $9 per lawn. How many new customers will she need to find to earn an additional $150 per week?

   Katie hopes all her customers still want to hire her after she raises the price.

4. Tony has a $100 gift certificate at a music store Web site. The store offers a 15% discount off the retail price of CDs. Tony must also pay $12 for shipping per order. Find whether Tony can buy each order given.

   a. 6 CDs for $15.99 each

   b. 7 CDs for $15.99 each

   c. 2 CDs for $15.99 each and 5 CDs for $11.99 each

   d. Tony wants to spend exactly $100 including the discount and shipping cost. What is the greatest total retail price he can afford?

5. In 36 years, Anna will be five times as old as she is today. How old is Anna? Use the guess-check-generalize method.

On Your Own

6. Derman says, "I'm halfway through reading my book. If I read another 84 pages, I'll be two thirds of the way through my book." How many pages are in Derman's book?

7. Seventeen years ago, Arnold was $\frac{2}{3}$ as old as he is now. How old is Arnold?

   Start by making a guess.

8. **Standardized Test Prep** Use a calculator. Five years ago, Allen was two years older than $\frac{5}{6}$ of his age today. What is his age today?

   A. 35

   B. 37

   C. 42

   D. cannot be determined

9. If Cameron pays $15 to join the Big Books club, he gets 10% off the price of each book. He wants to decide whether to join the club. For each amount given that he spends on books, will he save money by joining the club?

   a. $70

   b. $250

   c. $100

   d. How much money does Cameron need to spend so that the cost of his books is the same whether he joins the club or not?

10. **What's Wrong Here?** Travis solved the equation below incorrectly. Here are his steps.

$$x + 5 - \tfrac{1}{10}x = 12 + \tfrac{1}{2}x$$

$$\tfrac{11}{10}x + 5 = 12 + \tfrac{1}{2}x$$

$$\tfrac{11}{10}x + 5 - \tfrac{1}{2}x = 12 + \tfrac{1}{2}x - \tfrac{1}{2}x$$

$$\tfrac{6}{10}x + 5 - 5 = 12 - 5$$

$$\tfrac{6}{10}x = 7$$

$$x = \tfrac{70}{6}$$

$$= \tfrac{35}{3}$$

   a. Show that Travis found the incorrect result.
   b. Explain what Travis did wrong.
   c. Solve the equation correctly.

11. Mr. Rodriquez comments on a recent test. "Well, the class average on that test is exactly 83. If I take away the best score, the average is exactly 82. Fine work, Anya." If there are 16 students in the class, what is the best score?

12. Taylor gets a $100 gift certificate to a music store for her birthday. She buys seven CDs and has $16 left on her gift certificate. The CDs cost the same amount of money. How much does each CD cost?

Maintain Your Skills

13. Find the value of x that makes each equation true.
    a. $5x - 3 = x + 15$
    b. $6x - 3 = x + 15$
    c. $10x - 3 = x + 15$
    d. $99x - 3 = x + 15$
    e. $181x - 3 = x + 15$
    f. These equations have the form $Ax - 3 = x + 15$. How does the solution x change as A increases?
    g. **Take It Further** Solve $Ax - 3 = x + 15$ to find an expression in terms of A.

To solve *in terms of* A means to find the solution in which x equals some expression that may have A in it.

2.16 Solving Word Problems

In this lesson, you will solve more advanced word problems. You will combine an ability to set up equations and an ability to work with percentages or fractions. The guess-check-generalize method can help you find the correct equation.

For You to Do

1. **What's Wrong Here?** Tony solved the following problem incorrectly using the guess-check-generalize method.

   Mr. Corrado buys 60 bagels. He gets a 25% discount on bagels. The total cost of the bagels with the discount is $24.75. How much does a bagel cost without the discount?

   Tony explains, "First, I guess that a bagel costs $1. I check this guess and keep track of my steps in this table."

	Check	Step
1	If a bagel costs $1, then 60 bagels cost 60 · 1 = 60.	Multiply the cost of a bagel by 60.
2	Next I find the discount. It's a 25% discount, so that's 60 · (0.25) = 15.	Multiply the cost of the bagels by 0.25.
3	I check whether this is the correct cost: $15 \stackrel{?}{=} 24.75$.	Compare with 24.75.
4	It's not correct, so I'll make another guess.	

   "For my second guess, I try $2 and apply the same steps."

	Check	Step
1	60 · 2 = 120	Multiply the cost of a bagel by 60.
2	120 · (0.25) = 30	Multiply the cost of the bagels by 0.25.
3	$30 \stackrel{?}{=} 24.75$	Compare with 24.75.
4	It's not correct.	

"I know what the steps are, so I try using a variable *b* to stand for the cost of the bagels."

	Check	Step
1	$60 \cdot b = 60b$	Multiply the cost of a bagel by 60.
2	$60b \cdot (0.25) = 15b$	Multiply the cost of the bagels by 0.25.
3	I check whether this is the correct cost: $15b \stackrel{?}{=} 24.75$.	Compare with 24.75.
4	That's my equation.	

"Finally, I solve that equation."

$$15b = 24.75$$
$$b = 1.65$$

"So, one bagel costs $1.65."

What is wrong with Tony's steps? Find the correct result.

For Discussion

2. Use the guess-check-generalize method to write an equation for this situation.

   Al drives from Boston to Washington, D.C., and then returns. On his trip to Washington, he travels 60 miles per hour. On his return trip, he travels 50 miles per hour. His trip to Boston takes an hour and a half longer than his trip to Washington. How far apart are Washington and Boston?

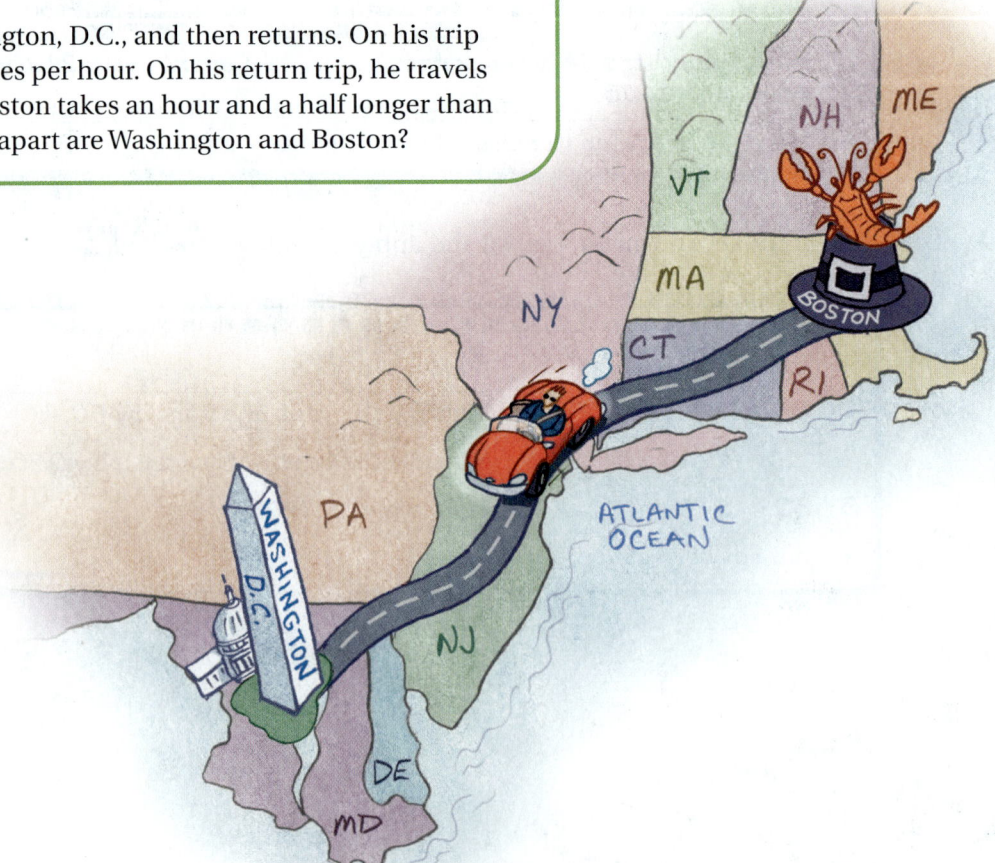

Exercises Practicing Habits of Mind

Check Your Understanding

1. Ms. Ramirez buys school supplies for her students. She gets a $12 bulk discount. The new cost of supplies is 80% of the original cost.

   a. If d is the cost of the school supplies, explain why you can use the equation $\frac{d - 12}{d} = \frac{8}{10}$ to represent Ms. Ramirez's purchase. What is the significance of $\frac{8}{10}$ in this equation?

   b. Explain why the value of d cannot be zero in the equation given.

   c. Multiply each side of the equation by d (a basic move). Write the resulting equation.

   d. Multiply each side by 10 (another basic move) to remove all fractions from the equation.

   e. Find the value of d by solving the equation.

> You can multiply by d, because you know that d is not zero. The supplies are not free!

For Exercises 2–4, find each probability. **Probability** describes the likelihood that a specific event will happen. For example, the probability that today is Thursday is $\frac{1}{7}$, since there are 7 days in each week, and only 1 day is Thursday. You can represent a probability as a fraction or a decimal. 100% becomes 1 when written as a decimal, and 50% becomes 0.5.

2. a. On Monday, a meteorologist says that there is 30% chance of rain. What is the probability that it will rain on Monday?

   b. What is the probability that it will not rain on Monday?

   c. On Tuesday, the meteorologist says that there is 0.1 probability that it will rain. What is the probability that it will not rain on Tuesday?

   d. Suppose the probability that it will rain today is p. Find the probability that it will not rain today, in terms of p.

3. A meteorologist says that there is a 50% greater chance of rain than no rain on Wednesday. What is the probability that it will rain on Wednesday?

4. A meteorologist says that there is a 50% chance of rain on Saturday and a 50% chance of rain on Sunday. He concludes that it will definitely rain at least once next weekend. Does his conclusion sound reasonable?

2.16 Solving Word Problems

5. Heidi tries to qualify for a gymnastics team. Qualifying is based on the average of six event scores. Heidi knows she needs at least a 7.5 average in the six events to make the team. Her scores for the first five events are 6.4, 8.0, 8.1, 6.5, and 8.2.

   Average in the events refers to the mean, not the median.

   a. What is Heidi's mean event score for five events? What is her median score?

   b. Suppose Heidi scores a 7.6 in the final event. Will she make the team? Show your steps.

   c. Make another guess about the minimum score Heidi needs to make the team. Check your guess. Keep track of your steps.

   d. Use the guess-check-generalize method to find an equation for the minimum score Heidi needs to make the team.

   e. Solve your equation.

6. **Take it Further** Use Exercise 5.

   a. The rules change so that you exclude the highest and lowest scores before finding the average. What score does Heidi now need to make the team?

   b. Suppose you exclude the highest and lowest scores. What is the highest possible average Heidi can get? What is the lowest possible average?

On Your Own

7. Ms. Meyer remarks, "Isn't it great? This theater usually charges $9 per student. On Student Night, I can bring 47 more students for the same cost!" How many students can Ms. Meyer bring to the theater in the photo on the right?

8. Chi has a big pile of nickels. He says, "Even if I use 100 of these nickels, I'll still have 95% of my original pile." How many nickels does Chi have?

9. Eight years from now, Bianca will be 50% older than she is now. How old is Bianca?

10. A round trip from Seattle, Washington, to Orlando, Florida, is one of the longest flight paths in the continental United States. The jet stream that blows from west to east affects the flight's average speed. A plane flying nonstop from Seattle to Orlando can fly at an average speed of 523 miles per hour. The same plane flying from Orlando to Seattle travels at an average speed of 415 miles per hour. The full round trip takes exactly 11 hours. To the nearest mile, how far is Seattle from Orlando?

11. **Standardized Test Prep** Eduardo goes to a restaurant for lunch. He orders a turkey sandwich for $6.75 and a fruit smoothie for $3.95. Eduardo must also pay a sales tax and a tip. The sales tax is 8%. The tip is 15% of the pretax cost of the meal. Which expression shows how Eduardo computes his final bill?

   A. $6.75 + 3.95(0.23)$

   B. $(6.75 + 3.95)(0.23)$

   C. $6.75 + 3.95 + (6.75 + 3.95)(0.23)$

   D. $6.75 + 3.95 + (6.75 + 3.95)(0.08) + (6.75 + 3.95)(0.08)(0.15)$

12. **What's Wrong Here?** Derman tried to solve the equation $20 - 3(x - 2) = 9x - 4$.

$$20 - 3(x - 2) = 9x - 4$$
$$20 - 3x - 6 = 9x - 4$$
$$14 - 3x = 9x - 4$$
$$14 - 3x + 4 = 9x - 4 + 4$$
$$18 - 3x + 3x = 9x + 3x$$
$$18 = 12x$$
$$\frac{18}{12} = x$$
$$\frac{3}{2} = x$$

   a. Show that Derman found the incorrect result.

   b. Explain what Derman did wrong.

   c. Solve the equation correctly.

Maintain Your Skills

For Exercises 13 and 14, you do not need to solve the equations. Determine which equation in each set of three equations has no solution. Explain.

13. $2x + 5 = 3x + 11$
    $2x + 5 = 19x + 11$
    $2x + 5 = 2x + 11$

14. $-11k + 14 = -3k - 25$
    $-11k + 14 = -11k - 25$
    $-11k + 14 = 14k - 11$

2.17 More Than One Variable

Many equations relate variables to each other. Equations with more than one variable, such as $3x + 4y = 12$, often have more than one solution.

Example 1

Problem High-definition television screens are different sizes. However, they all have the same proportions. If you divide the width of an HDTV screen by its height, the result is $\frac{16}{9}$. If you label the height h and the width w, then every HDTV screen satisfies the two-variable equation.

$$\frac{w}{h} = \frac{16}{9}$$

Find the width of each HDTV screen for the height given in inches.

a. 18

b. 36

c. 30

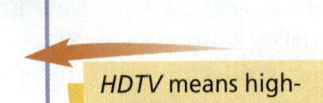

HDTV means high-definition television.

Solution For parts (a)–(c), use a single equation, $\frac{w}{h} = \frac{16}{9}$, instead of setting up three separate equations.

Use the basic move of multiplying each side by the same quantity. Multiply each side by h.

$$\frac{w}{h} \cdot h = \frac{16}{9} \cdot h$$
$$w = \frac{16h}{9}$$

What is the importance of this? You have solved the equation for w. For any value of h, you can find w. Here are the results for each problem using the equation solved for w.

You can "eyeball" different-sized HDTV screens and see that they are all proportional.

a. Find w. Let height h equal 18.
$$w = \frac{16 \cdot 18}{9}$$
$$= 32$$

b. Find w. Let height h equal 36.
$$w = \frac{16 \cdot 36}{9}$$
$$= 64$$

c. Find w. Let height h equal 30.
$$w = \frac{16 \cdot 30}{9}$$
$$= \frac{480}{9}$$
$$= \frac{160}{3}$$

Chapter 2 Expressions and Equations

Developing Habits of Mind

Represent the solution with a variable. The previous example illustrates solving for one variable. When you solve for w, you get w on one side of the equation by itself. The equation $w = \frac{16h}{9}$ is correctly solved for w, but the equation $w = \frac{16h}{9} + 3w$ is not solved for w, since there is a w term on both sides.

One way to think about these equations is to treat any variable you are not solving for as a number that you cannot combine with other numbers. Solving $3x + 4y = 12$ is just like solving $3(176) + 4y = 12$. You follow the same steps. However, you will not get an equation like this.

$y =$ some number

Instead, you will get an equation like this.

$y =$ some expression involving x

Example 2

Problem Solve the equation $7y - 13 = 2x + 3y$ for y.

Solution To solve for y, use basic moves to get the variable y by itself on the left side of the equation. Since there are y terms on each side of the equation, you can subtract $3y$ from each side.

$$7y - 13 = 2x + 3y$$
$$7y - 13 - 3y = 2x + 3y - 3y$$
$$4y - 13 = 2x$$

You want only y on the left side. So you add 13 to each side.

$$4y - 13 = 2x$$
$$4y - 13 + 13 = 2x + 13$$
$$4y = 2x + 13$$

Finally, divide each side by 4.

$$4y = 2x + 13$$
$$\frac{4y}{4} = \frac{2x + 13}{4}$$
$$y = \frac{2x + 13}{4}$$

To check this equation, you can try an "easy" value of x, such as 10, in the final equation and find y. Do these values work in the original equation?

Remember...
Solve for y means that the final equation must have the variable y by itself on one side of the equation, and no y's are on the other side!

You can say that you solved the equation $y = \frac{2x + 13}{4}$ for y in terms of x. The phrase *in terms of x* means the solution may have x in it.

For Discussion

1. Solve the equation $3x + y + 15 = 2(x + 1) - 5$ for y.

2.17 More Than One Variable

Exercises Practicing Habits of Mind

Check Your Understanding

1. Solve the equation $6x + 3y = 5x - 13 + 2y$ for y.

2. Example 2 shows that the equation $7y - 13 = 2x + 3y$ is equivalent to the equation $y = \frac{2x + 13}{4}$.

   > The first basic move is to subtract $3y$ from each side of the equation.

   a. Suppose x is 0. Use either equation to find the value of y. Think about which equation might be easier to use.

   b. Suppose x is 10. Use either equation to find the value of y.

   c. Suppose y is 0. Use either equation to find the value of x.

   d. Is the pair (20, 13) a solution to the equation $2x + 3y = 7y - 13$? Explain.

   e. Is the pair (20, 13) a solution to the equation $y = \frac{1}{2}x + 3\frac{1}{4}$? Explain.

   > **Remember...**
   > The notation (20, 13) means that $x = 20$ and $y = 13$.

3. If w is the width of a standard television set, and h is the height, then w and h satisfy the equation $\frac{w}{h} = \frac{4}{3}$.

   a. Solve for w.

   b. Solve for h.

   c. What is the height of a standard TV set that is 15 inches wide?

   d. How wide is a standard TV set that is 21 inches high?

   e. Stores advertise TV sizes by giving the corner-to-corner diagonal length of the screen. If a TV screen is 21 inches high, how long is its diagonal?

4. The equation $5x + 6y = 90$ relates x and y.

   a. Suppose x is 10 and y is 6. Do these values make the equation true? Explain.

   b. Suppose x is 9. Find a value of y that makes the equation true. Find two values of y that make it false.

   c. Find four pairs of points (x, y) that make the equation true.

   d. **Take It Further** Locate the points you found in part (c) on a coordinate grid. Are they related?

174 Chapter 2 Expressions and Equations

5. In the Range Game, a player guesses the price of an object. The player wins the object if the guess is no more than $75 from the actual value.

   a. If you win with a guess of $2599, what is the range of the actual price?

   b. If the actual price is $4599, what is the range of possible guesses that allows you to win?

   c. If g is the amount you guess, and p is the actual price of the object, describe the situation in terms of g and p.

6. **Take It Further** Javan manages a picture framing shop. When he frames a photograph, he mats it on a piece of cardboard. He allows 2 inches of cardboard on each side of the photo.

   Javan realizes that he can use an equation to determine whether a piece of cardboard is the appropriate size for matting a photograph. He says, "If h is the height of the cardboard, and w is the width, then a piece of cardboard will be the right size if it satisfies the equation $\frac{w-4}{h-4} = \frac{4}{3}$."

   > Javan typically trims the photographs so that the ratio of the width to height is 4 : 3.

   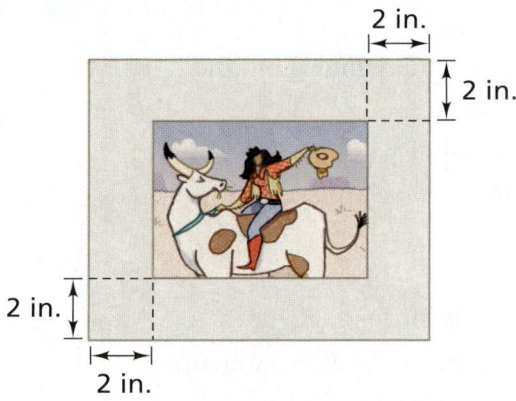

   a. Explain how Javan found the equation.

   b. Solve the equation for w.

   c. If the piece of cardboard is 12 inches high, how wide is it?

   d. If the piece of cardboard is 15 inches high, how wide is it?

   e. If the piece of cardboard is 20 inches high, how wide is it?

7. Chi has nickels and dimes. He has a total of 90 cents. Let n stand for the number of nickels that Chi has. Let d stand for the number of dimes that Chi has.

   a. Can Chi have 4 nickels and 8 dimes? Explain.

   b. Can Chi have 6 nickels and 4 dimes? Explain.

   c. Write an equation using n and d to find how much money Chi has.

   d. Solve your equation for d.

   e. **Take It Further** Can Chi have an odd number of nickels? Explain.

On Your Own

8. Which of these statements are true for all numbers? Not true for all numbers? If a statement is not true for all numbers, change the statement to make it true for all numbers.

   a. If $y = 2x + 4$, then $5y = 5(2x + 4) = 10x + 4$.
   b. 25% of a number n is $0.25n$.
   c. For any numbers a and b, $3a + 4b$ is the same as $7(a + b)$.
   d. For any numbers a and b, $3a \cdot 4b$ is the same as $12ab$.
   e. For any number m, $0.9m - 2m$ is the same as $-2.9m$.
   f. The expression $-4(d + 6)$ means the same as the expression $-4d + 24$.
   g. The fraction $\frac{10x}{10y}$ has the same value as the fraction $\frac{x}{y}$.
   h. The fraction $\frac{x + 3}{3}$ is the same as x.

9. The perimeter of a rectangle is 10 centimeters more than four times the difference between its length and width.

   a. If the rectangle's length is ℓ and its width is w, what is its perimeter?
   b. Explain why the equation $2\ell + 2w = 10 + 4(\ell - w)$ is true for the rectangle.
   c. Solve the equation in part (b) for the variable ℓ.
   d. If the rectangle's width is 10 centimeters, what is the length?

10. **Standardized Test Prep** Nathan wants to buy snow globes and key chains for his friends. A snow globe costs $3, and a key chain costs $2. He has a total of $15 to spend. If Nathan wants to buy two snow globes, what is the greatest number of key chains he can buy?

    A. 3   B. 4   C. 5   D. 6

For Exercises 11 and 12, use the following information. Corey needs at least $2.10 in postage. She has $.41 letter stamps and $.26 postcard stamps. Let ℓ equal the number of letter stamps and p equal the number of postcard stamps. The amount of postage is exact when $41\ell + 26p = 210$.

11. a. If Corey has 3 letter stamps, can she make exactly $2.10 in postage by adding postcard stamps?
    b. If Corey has 3 letter stamps, what is the least number of postcard stamps she needs?
    c. If $\ell = 3$, find the value of p that makes the equation $41\ell + 26p = 210$ true. How can you use this equation for part (b)?

176 Chapter 2 Expressions and Equations

12. **a.** Solve the equation $41\ell + 26p = 210$ for the variable p. Write the equation in the form $p =$ an expression.

b. Copy and complete the table to show the minimum number of postcard stamps Corey needs when she has different numbers of letter stamps.

Even though the equation gives a decimal answer, Corey cannot split up the postcard stamps. How can she round the answer correctly? What is the result when there is enough postage using only the letter stamps?

Number of Stamps

Letter Stamps	Postcard Stamps
0	■
1	■
2	■
3	■
4	■
5	■
6	■
7	■

c. Take It Further What is the least expensive choice Corey can make using letter and postcard stamps?

Maintain Your Skills

13. Solve for y in each equation. Write the equation in the form y equals an expression. Then solve for x.

    a. $5x + 6y = 90$

    b. $11x + 13y = 150$

14. Solve for each variable in the equation $5x + 6y + 7z = 90$.

    a. x

    b. y

    c. z

    d. How are the results in parts (a)–(c) related?

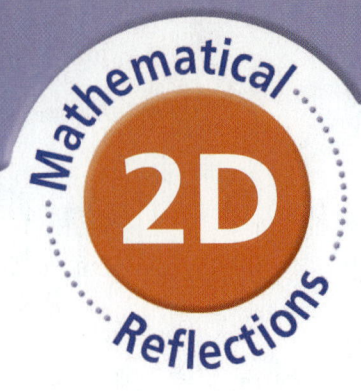

Mathematical Reflections 2D

In this investigation, you learned to the use the guess-check-generalize method to solve word problems. For two-variable equations, you learned to solve for either variable. These questions will help you summarize what you have learned.

1. Adding 5 to a number and then multiplying the number by 2 gives the same result as multiplying the number by 5 and then adding 1. What is the number?

2. Use the guess-check-generalize method. Six years ago, Bill was $\frac{1}{4}$ as old as he is now. How old is Bill?

3. Jim raises money for his summer vacation by walking his neighbors' dogs. He charges $8 a week for each dog. He walks 10 dogs each week.
   a. If he wants to make $96 each week, how many additional dogs does he need to walk?
   b. If Jim decides to raise his price instead of finding new customers, how much should he increase his price to make his goal of $96 each week?

4. Solve the equation $2x + 3y = x - 4y + 10$ for y.

5. How can you use the guess-check-generalize method to solve a word problem?

6. How do you solve for y in a two-variable equation?

7. What number plus one fourth of itself equals 560?

Vocabulary

In this investigation, you saw these terms. Make sure you understand what each one means and how to use it.

- **guess-check-generalize method**
- **probability**

She scores a goal! Her team solved a problem.

Project: Using Mathematical Habits

Good Questions About Perfect Squares

Mathematicians ask questions about numbers to understand the underlying structure of numbers. In this project, you will answer some questions about the sums of perfect squares. A perfect square is an integer that is the square of another integer. For example, each of the following numbers is a perfect square.

$$1 = 1^2 \quad 4 = 2^2 \quad 9 = 3^2$$

Finding Perfect-Square Sums

Paulo writes a few sums of two perfect squares.

$$1^2 + 1^2 = 2$$
$$1^2 + 2^2 = 5$$

Based on these examples, he asks this good question about positive integers. Is every integer the sum of two nonzero perfect squares?

1. Can you write every integer as the sum of two nonzero perfect squares? If you can, tell how to find the two perfect squares for a given integer. If not, find an integer that cannot be written as the sum of two nonzero perfect squares.

   A table similar to an addition table can help you find all possible sums of two perfect squares. Use an addition table with the squares 1, 4, 9, 16, 25, 36, 49, 64, 81, and 100 along each axis to answer Exercises 2 and 3.

2. Find two perfect squares that are both the sum of two perfect squares.

3. Are there any integers you can write as the sum of two nonzero squares in two different ways? Explain. Note that

   $$5 = 1^2 + 2^2 \text{ and } 5 = 2^2 + 1^2$$

   do *not* represent two different ways to write 5 as the sum of two perfect squares.

Asking Good Questions

An important habit is asking a good question. Paulo based his question on two examples. The following exercises show three more ways to come up with good questions.

For Exercises 4–6, start with each question given. Replace each italicized word with another word. Do you think your question is a good one? Explain.

4. Is every integer the sum of two nonzero perfect *squares*?

5. Is every integer the *sum* of two nonzero perfect squares?

6. Is every integer the sum of *two* nonzero perfect squares? Write a question different from any you wrote in Exercises 4 and 5.

7. You can ask a good question by extending an idea. Paulo's question is about positive integers only. Does it suggest a good question you could ask about negative integers? Explain.

8. Good answers to good questions can lead to more good questions. Write a good question that Exercise 2 suggests. Do you already know the answer to your question?

Chapter 2 Review

In **Investigation 2A,** you learned how to
- state the need for variables and expressions
- determine the appropriate order for evaluating a numerical expression and explain why the order works
- express word problems using variables and mathematical notation
- write formulas using two or more variables

The following questions will help you check your understanding.

1. Use the variable x as your starting number. Write the expression you get by following the steps. Simplify the expression.
   - Choose a number.
   - Multiply by 3.
   - Add 4.
   - Multiply by 5.
   - Subtract 2.

2. Evaluate $2(3x + 5) + x$ for each value of x.
   a. 2
   b. 5
   c. -3
   d. Simplify the expression. Then evaluate the expression for $x = 2$.

3. Name the property that each equation illustrates.
   a. $5 + 4 = 4 + 5$
   b. $(c \cdot 7) \cdot 8 = c \cdot (7 \cdot 8)$
   c. $w = w + 0$
   d. $9 \cdot \frac{1}{9} = 1$
   e. $2(8 + 3) = 2(8) + 2(3)$

4. Use the any-order, any-grouping properties and the Distributive Property. Simplify each expression. Remember to combine like terms.
   a. $3(x + 5) + 8$
   b. $2(4x - 3) + 7(x + 2)$
   c. $3(2x - 8) - 4(x - 5)$
   d. $2(3x - 4) - (2x - 1)$

In **Investigation 2B,** you learned how to
- reverse, or undo, a series of steps
- understand the relationship between an equation and its solutions
- use backtracking to solve a problem

The following questions will help you check your understanding.

5. Describe how to undo each instruction, if possible. If not possible, explain.
   a. Add 3.
   b. Multiply by 5.
   c. Find the sum of the digits.
   d. Divide by 10.

6. Write each algebraic expression as a statement of an operation.
   a. $x^2 + 15$
   b. $\frac{y + 9}{7}$
   c. $5(8b + 2)$
   d. $7a - 12 + 4$

7. Use backtracking to find the solution to each equation.
   a. $2x + 4 = 10$
   b. $3x - 2 = 8$
   c. $\frac{x}{4} + 1 = 7$
   d. $\frac{x + 2}{5} = -1$

180 Chapter 2 Expressions and Equations

In **Investigation 2C,** you learned how to
- evaluate and simplify expressions using the basic rules
- solve equations using the basic moves
- understand that equations can have multiple solutions or no solutions
- solve an equation involving many variations of the Distributive Property

The following questions will help you check your understanding.

8. For each equation, determine whether $x = -3$ is a solution.
   a. $2x + 7 = x + 2$
   b. $x - 4 + 3x = 8 - x$
   c. $2(x - 1) = x - 5$
   d. $(x - 4) - (3 - x) = 5x + 2$

9. What equation does each model represent?
   a.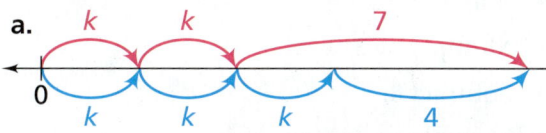
   b.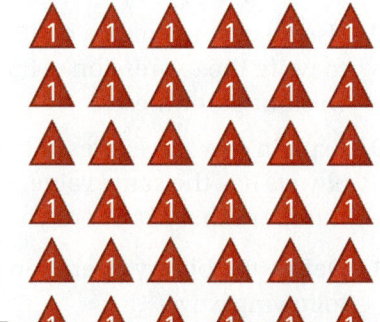

10. Solve each equation.
    a. $3x + 2 = x - 12$
    b. $x + 2(3x - 5) = 5x - 6$
    c. $2(x + 1) + 3(2x - 5) = 4(2x + 3)$

11. Determine whether each equation has no solutions, one solution, or every real number as a solution.
    a. $7(a + 2) - 5 = 7a + 9$
    b. $11 - 3t = 8 - 3t$
    c. $6(x + 7) = 6x + 7$
    d. $7q + 8q = q + 12$

In **Investigation 2D,** you learned how to
- use the guess-check-generalize method to solve word problems
- solve a two-variable equation
- build an equation from a mathematical situation

The following questions will help you check your understanding.

12. Solve each equation for x.
    a. $y = 8x$
    b. $y = 8x - 3$
    c. $y = 8(x - 3)$
    d. $y = 8(x - 3) + 7$

13. Sue scores 90, 85, and 83 on her first three math tests.
    a. What is Sue's average?
    b. If Sue scores 90 on the fourth test, what will her average be?
    c. If Sue wants an average of 90, what score does she need on the fourth test?

14. Henry shoveled snow during the last snowstorm. He charged $5 for a sidewalk and $12 for a driveway. He earned $80. Let x equal the number of sidewalks and y equal the number of driveways.
    a. Write an equation to model the situation.
    b. Solve for y.

Chapter 2 Test

Multiple Choice

1. Which number is NOT a solution to the equation $(x - 3)(x - 5)(x + 7) = 0$?
   - **A.** -7
   - **B.** 3
   - **C.** 5
   - **D.** 7

2. Which expression is NOT equal to the other expressions?
   - **A.** $-5(t + 4)$
   - **B.** $-5(t - 4)$
   - **C.** $5(4 - t)$
   - **D.** $-(5t - 20)$

3. Which expression is a simplified version of the expression $3(2x - 4) - 2(5x - 1)$?
   - **A.** $16x - 14$
   - **B.** $-4x - 14$
   - **C.** $-4x - 10$
   - **D.** $-4x - 5$

4. Which equation can you NOT solve by backtracking?
   - **A.** $28 = \frac{t}{6} + 4$
   - **B.** $5(b - 3) + 4 = 39$
   - **C.** $7x + 2 = 5x - 8$
   - **D.** $12 = \frac{p}{3}$

5. Which equation can you use to represent the following model?

   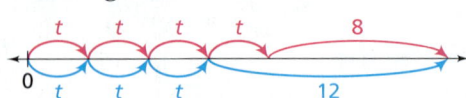

   - **A.** $7t = 20$
   - **B.** $4t + 8 = 3t + 12$
   - **C.** $t = 4$
   - **D.** cannot be determined

6. Find the solution of the equation $3(b - 2) = 2(b + 1)$.
   - **A.** 3
   - **B.** 4
   - **C.** 7
   - **D.** 8

7. Which equation is $2x + 3y = 5x + 6$ correctly solved for x?
   - **A.** $x = \frac{5x - 3y + 6}{2}$
   - **B.** $x = 3$
   - **C.** $x = y - 2$
   - **D.** $x = \frac{3x - 6}{7}$

Open Response

8. Use the number y as your starting number. Write the expression you get by following the steps. Simplify the expression.
   - Choose a number.
   - Add 7.
   - Multiply by 3.
   - Subtract 8.
   - Multiply by 2.

9. Use an expansion box or another method to write the expression $-4(3x + 2y - 6)$ without parentheses.

10. Explain why the expression $\frac{r + 2r + 3r + 4r}{r}$ always has the same value, no matter what number other than zero you choose for r.

11. Define the binary operation ♣ in the following way.
    $$x \clubsuit y = 5(x - y)$$
    a. Find $5 \clubsuit 15$.
    b. Find x if $x \clubsuit 3 = 20$.
    c. Find y if $3 \clubsuit y = 20$.
    d. Is the ♣ operation commutative? Explain.

12. For each equation, determine whether $x = 4$ is a solution.
    a. $2x + 7 = x + 11$
    b. $x - 4 + 3x = 8 + x$
    c. $x^2 = 36$
    d. $3(x - 2) = x + 7$

13. Use the basic rules and moves to solve the equation $5(2x - 3) - 6x = 0.5(4x - 10)$. Show your work.

14. Sarah has two coupons for pizza. Coupon A offers the pizza at 15% off. Coupon B offers the pizza for $2 off.

    a. If the pizza without the discount costs x dollars, write an expression for the pizza's cost with each coupon.

    b. What price of a pizza makes Coupon A and Coupon B worth the same amount? Build and solve an equation to find the price to the nearest cent.

15. Find three ways to rewrite the expression $4(2z - 12)$ without changing its value. For example, rewriting the expression as $8z - 12$ is incorrect, since $8z - 12$ is not equal to $4(2z - 12)$.

16. Write a number trick that results in each of the following expressions.

    a. $3 \cdot x - 5$
    b. $3 \cdot (x - 5)$
    c. $2 \cdot (x + 1) + 6$
    d. $4 \cdot (2 \cdot (3 \cdot x + 6) - 7)$

17. Use the any-order, any-grouping properties and the Distributive Property to simplify each expression. Remember to combine like terms.

    a. $5(2x - 1) - 9$
    b. $4(3x + 1) + 2x$
    c. $3(2x - 5) + 2(5x + 8)$
    d. $3 + 2(4x - 5)$
    e. $2(x - 3) - (x + 4)$
    f. $5x - 3(2x - 6)$

18. Here is a number trick with the final step missing.
    - Choose any number.
    - Add 10.
    - Multiply by 4.
    - Subtract 8.
    - Divide by 2.
    - Subtract 2.
    - Divide by 2.
    - ?

    a. What is the final step if you want the ending number to be the same as the starting number?

    b. What is the final step if you want to end with the same number, no matter what the starting number is?

19. Use the conversion formula $F = \frac{9}{5}C + 32$, where F is a temperature in degrees Fahrenheit and C is a temperature in degrees Celsius.

    a. Convert $100°C$ to degrees Fahrenheit.

    b. The temperature of a healthy human body is $98.6°F$. Use backtracking to find this temperature in degrees Celsius.

    c. Solve the equation $F = \frac{9}{5}C + 32$ for C.

    d. Use the equation you found in part (c) to convert $68°F$ to degrees Celsius.

20. Ashlee makes beaded jewelry. She charges $6 for a bracelet and $12 for a necklace. She earned $168. Let a equal the number of bracelets and b equal the number of necklaces.

    a. Write an equation to model the situation.

    b. Solve for b.

Challenge Problem

21. Write an equation that has $x = 3$ and $x = 7$ as its only solutions.

Chapter 2 Cumulative Review

These questions will help you summarize what you have learned in Chapters 1 and 2.

1. Start with any number. Subtract 4, then add 2, and finally subtract 6.
   a. Find the ending number if you start with 3.
   b. Find the starting number if you end with -6.

2. Find each product or quotient mentally.
   a. $36 \cdot (-4)$
   b. $(-36) \div (-4)$
   c. $36 \div (-4)$
   d. $(-36) \cdot 4$
   e. $13 \cdot 299$
   f. $5 \cdot 17 \cdot 2$
   g. $23 \cdot 302$

3. Use a number line.
   a. Place the following fractions, in order, on the number line.
   $$\frac{3}{5}, \frac{2}{3}, \frac{7}{5}, \frac{5}{3}, \frac{8}{15}, \frac{9}{15}, \frac{21}{15}$$
   b. Which fractions represent the same number?
   c. What is the smallest number in the list?
   d. Which of the fractions in the list is closest to 0.5 on the number line?
   e. Illustrate the sum $\frac{4}{3} + \frac{5}{3}$ on a number line.
   f. Illustrate the sum $-5 + 8$ on a number line.

4. Calculate.
   a. $\frac{1}{8} \cdot \left(\frac{8}{5} + \frac{8}{9}\right)$
   b. $40 \cdot \left(\frac{1}{20} + \frac{1}{10}\right)$
   c. $5735 + 3142$
   d. $\frac{1}{5} + \frac{1}{15} + \frac{1}{30}$
   e. $\frac{5}{27} \cdot \frac{14}{10} \cdot \frac{9}{7}$
   f. $\frac{-3}{25} \cdot \frac{8}{21} \cdot \frac{5}{-4}$
   g. $\frac{1}{8} \cdot \left(\frac{8}{5} + \frac{9}{8}\right)$

5. Match each expression to a set of steps.
   I. $(x + 3) \cdot 7$
   II. $(x + 7) \cdot 3$
   III. $3x + 7$

   a. Choose any number, add 7, and then multiply the result by 3.
   b. Choose any number, multiply it by 3, and then add 7 to the result.
   c. Choose any number, add 3, and then multiply the result by 7.

In Exercises 6 and 7, evaluate the expression for each value of x given.

6. $7x - 8$
   a. 2
   b. 3
   c. 10

7. $4(x + 3)$
   a. 8
   b. 4
   c. 0
   d. -3

184 Chapter 2 Expressions and Equations

8. Use properties to simplify each expression and combine like terms.

   a. $5(3x + 4) - 8$

   b. $2(5 + 3x) - 2(6 - x)$

   c. $15 + 4(3 + 4x)$

   d. $11 - 2(4a - 2)$

   e. $-8(c - 1) + 8$

   f. $\frac{2}{3}n + \frac{3}{8}n$

9. Describe the operations that reverse the operations in each expression.

   a. $5m - 14$

   b. $\frac{n}{-5}$

   c. $2(3m + 6)$

   d. $5\left(\frac{x}{-6}\right)$

   e. $-13 + 3x$

   f. $3 + 2(x - 4)$

10. Solve each equation.

    a. $-4x + 10 = -2$

    b. $7x + 8 = 1$

    c. $\frac{x}{100} = 8$

    d. $5p + 7 = 7p - 1$

    e. $5q + 3 = 3q + 1$

    f. $5(c - 3) = 7(6 - 2c)$

11. Explain how you can transform the equation $3x + 7y = 42$ into each equation.

    a. $3x + 7y - 42 = 0$

    b. $3x = 42 - 7y$

    c. $x = \frac{42 - 7y}{3}$

12. Last year the price of a computer was $150 more than it is this year. This year's price is three fourths of last year's price. What is this year's price for the computer?

13. During a cat food sale, a pet store sold 220 cans of cat food. At the end of the sale, the store still had 80% of the original number of cans of cat food. How many cans of cat food did the store have at the end of the sale?

14. Suppose x equals 9.

    a. What value of y makes $7x - 3y = 42$ true?

    b. Find three other pairs of coordinates (x, y) that make the equation true.

Chapter 3

Investigations at a Glance

- **3A** Introduction to Coordinates
- **3B** Statistical Data
- **3C** Equations and Their Graphs
- **3D** Basic Graphs and Translations

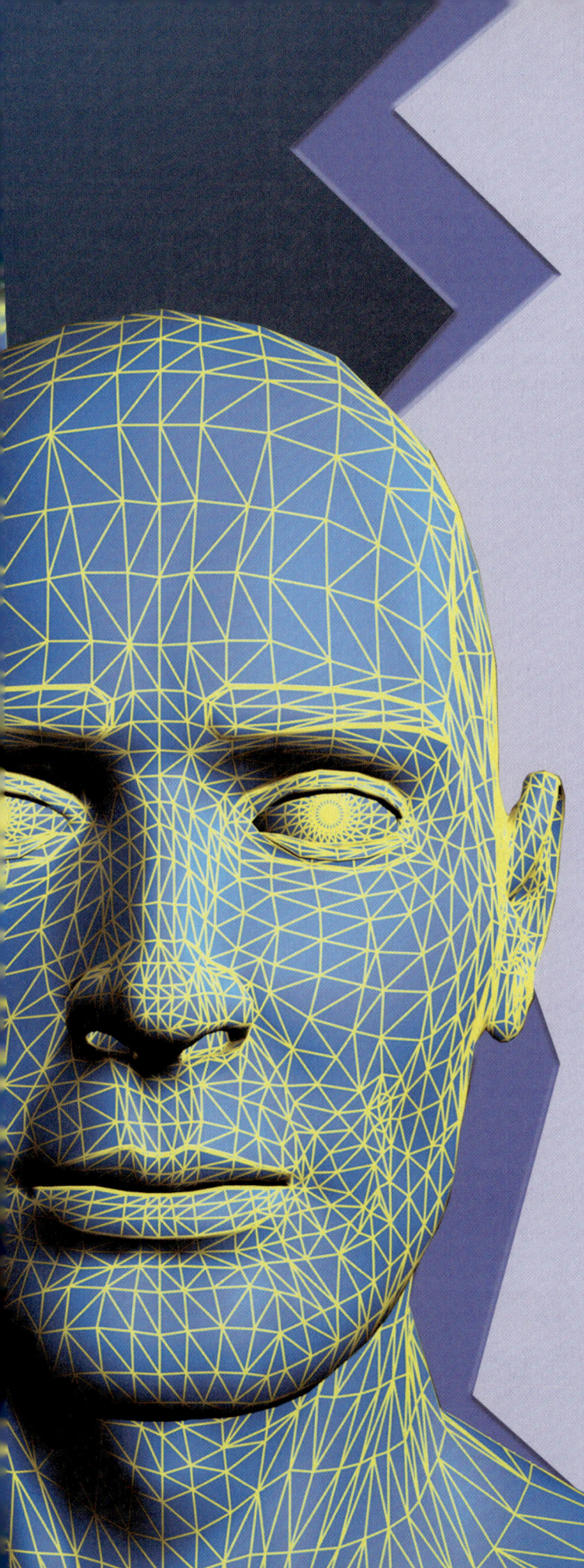

Graphs

Both video games and movies rely on amazing graphic images that computers produce. Animators make these images by representing the desired shape as a collection of polygons. A polygon is a closed shape with edges that are line segments, such as a square, a rectangle, a triangle, or a hexagon. The computer draws line segments connecting the polygons' corners to form a "wire frame" version of the shape.

Various mathematical techniques bring the images to life. They describe movement and color and simulate light that shines on the image.

You are not going to make computer animations yet, but you will explore the idea at the heart of computer graphics. You will connect algebraic ideas about numbers with the geometric representation of those ideas in visual form.

Vocabulary and Notation

- **absolute value,** $|x - y|$
- **association**
- **box-and-whisker plot**
- **coordinate**
- **coordinate plane**
- **correlation coefficient**
- **direct variation**
- **dot plot**
- **first quartile**
- **five-number summary**
- **frequency table**
- **graph of an equation**
- **histogram**
- **independent**
- **interquartile range**
- **intersection point**
- **inverse variation**
- **maximum**
- **mean**
- **median**
- **minimum**
- **mode**
- **negatively associated**
- **ordered pair**
- **origin**
- **outlier**
- **point-tester**
- **positively associated**
- **quadrant**
- **range**
- **scatter plot**
- **stem-and-leaf display**
- **third quartile**
- **transformation**
- **two-way frequency table**
- **x-axis**
- **x-coordinate**
- **y-axis**
- **y-coordinate**
- **$\mapsto$ (maps to)**
- **$\pm$ (plus or minus)**

Investigation 3A: Introduction to Coordinates

In *Introduction to Coordinates*, you will use the coordinate plane to represent equations. You will plot points, sketch the graph of an equation, and graph data in different ways.

By the end of this investigation, you will be able to answer questions like these.

1. How can you locate a point on a coordinate plane using the point's coordinates?

2. You have a picture in the coordinate plane. What is the effect of changing all x-coordinates or all y-coordinates of the points in the picture by the same amount?

3. According to the graph, who won the race, the tortoise or the hare? How can you tell? What else does the graph tell you about the race?

Tortoise and Hare Race

You will learn how to
- plot points and read coordinates on a graph
- describe how transformations operate on ordered pairs
- use absolute value and relate it to distance
- connect graphs to sets of data

You will develop these habits and skills:
- Identify patterns among coordinates of collinear points.
- Estimate coordinates of points, using fractions, decimals, and negative numbers.
- Calculate distance between points on a number line or in a coordinate plane.
- Generalize patterns with equations or rules.
- Read and interpret line graphs and scatter plots.

Archaeologists use a coordinate grid to map the locations of artifacts.

3.01 Getting Started

Activating Prior Knowledge
Exploring New Ideas

In Chapter 1, you used the number line as a system for describing locations. Each point on the number line corresponds to a unique number, which is the point's **coordinate.** You call each point the number's **graph.**

The point on the line corresponds to the number, 2.5.

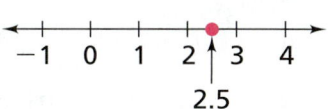

The point in the plane corresponds to two numbers, 2 and 4.

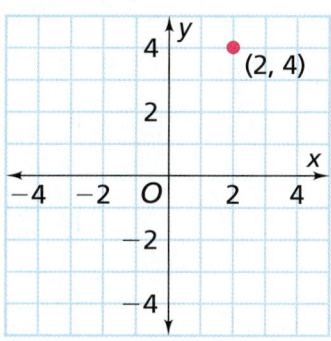

You can extend this idea from one dimension to two dimensions by developing a system for describing locations in the plane. A common way to assign coordinates to points in the plane uses two number lines that are perpendicular to each other. The **coordinate plane,** or Cartesian plane, is the name of this system.

In the coordinate plane, a horizontal number line, the **x-axis,** and a vertical number line, the **y-axis,** intersect. The **origin** is the point where the axes intersect.

Coordinate Plane

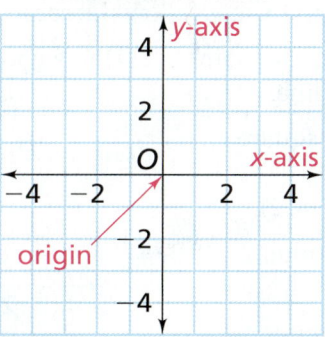

Each point in the plane corresponds to two numbers that you write as an **ordered pair,** (x, y). An ordered pair describes the location of a point in the coordinate plane.

The first number in the ordered pair, the **x-coordinate,** tells how far the point is to the right or left of the origin measuring along the x-axis. The second number, the **y-coordinate,** tells how far the point is above or below the origin measuring along the y-axis.

Remember...
In an ordered pair, order is important.

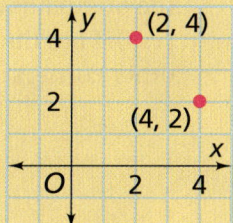

The point with coordinates (2, 4) is not the same as the point with coordinates (4, 2).

For You to Explore

1. **a.** Match each coordinate pair with its graph.

   I. (1, 2)   **II.** (−1, 2)

   III. (1, −2)   **IV.** (0, 0)

   b. Find the coordinates for the remaining labeled points.

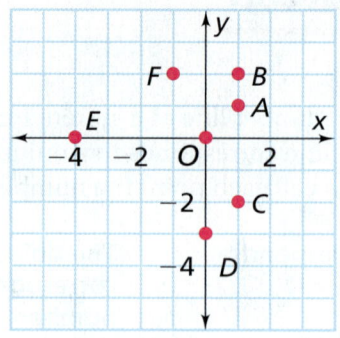

2. Line ℓ is vertical and passes through (3, 7).

   a. Find the coordinates of six points on ℓ.

   b. Find the coordinates of six points not on ℓ.

   c. How can you tell whether a point is on ℓ just by looking at its coordinates?

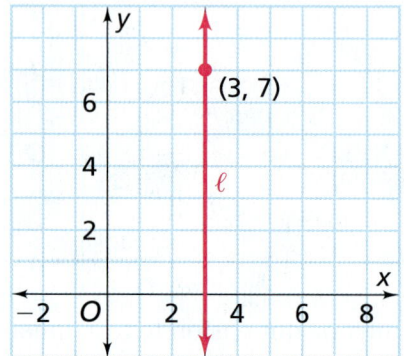

3. The y-axis is the only vertical line that passes through the point (0, 0). What do the coordinates of the points on the y-axis have in common? How can you tell whether a point is on the y-axis just by looking at its coordinates? Do the points on the x-axis follow the same rules? Explain.

4. Graph a horizontal line through the point (−2, 1) in a coordinate plane. Name two other points on the line.

5. The diagram shows a nonlevel square with its center on the origin. The coordinates of point A are (4, 2).

   a. Find the coordinates of the other three corners.

   b. A different square with its center on the origin has corners at (−3, 1) and (1, 3). Find the coordinates of the two other corners of the square.

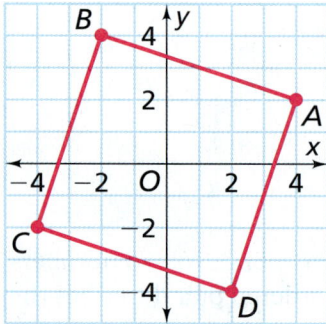

190   Chapter 3   Graphs

6. Use your results from Problem 5.
   a. Make a nonlevel square with its center on the origin but with different corners than the nonlevel squares from Problem 5. Name the coordinates of the square's corners.
   b. Describe the pattern in the coordinates of the corners of nonlevel squares.

7. Suppose you want to find the point (a, b) on the coordinate plane, but you do not know the exact values of a or b. (It is possible that a and b are not integers.) Shade the region or set of points on a coordinate plane where you find (a, b) in each of the following cases.
   a. $3 \leq a \leq 4$ and $0 \leq b \leq 1$
   b. $2 \leq a \leq 5$ and $0 \leq b \leq 1$
   c. $\frac{1}{2} \leq a \leq \frac{5}{3}$ and $-2 \leq b \leq \frac{1}{2}$
   d. $a = 3$ and $4 \leq b \leq 7$
   e. $a = 2$ or $a = 4$, and $b = -1$ or $b = 1$

8. You can draw the tree below by connecting, in order, the following points.

   (1, 1)   (2.5, 3)   (2, 3)   (3.5, 5)   (3, 5)   (4, 7)
   (5, 5)   (4.5, 5)   (6, 3)   (5.5, 3)   (7, 1)   (1, 1)

   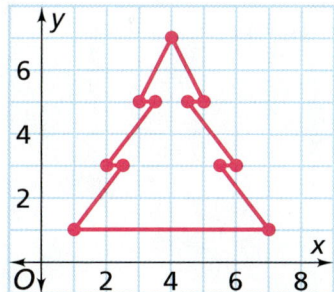

   a. For each point in the tree, add 2 to the x-coordinate. For instance, (1, 1) becomes (3, 1). Connect the resulting points to draw another picture.
   b. Describe the similarities and differences between the first picture and the second picture.

Exercises Practicing Habits of Mind

On Your Own

9. a. Copy and complete the missing point names or coordinate pairs in the table below, using the graph of labeled points. Estimate, if necessary.

Point	Coordinates
E	■
O	■
■	(0, 1)
C	(3, 2)
J	■
■	(2.5, −2.5)
M	■
■	(−2.5, ■)
D	■
B	■
G	$\left(-\frac{1}{2}, -3\right)$
■	(1, 0)
A	■
F	■

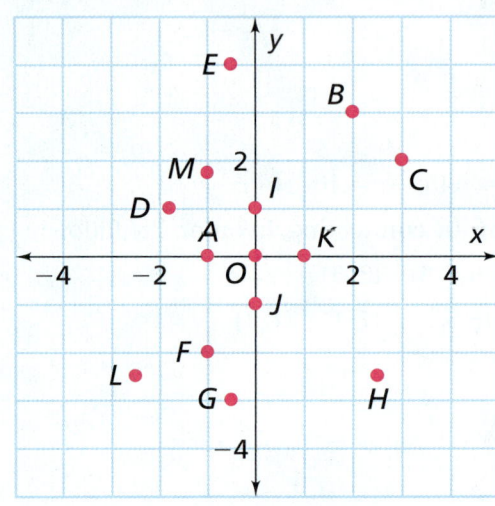

b. Plot point N at (3, −3). Is point N to the left or right of point H? Is point N above or below point H?

10. When you follow the recipe below, what picture in the coordinate plane do you draw?

Draw a line segment connecting each pair of points.

- (−2, −3) and (0, 3)
- (0, 3) and (2, −3)
- (−3, 1) and (3, 1)
- (3, 1) and (−2, −3)
- (−3, 1) and (2, −3)

A move from D5 to C5 takes the opponent's piece. Is this a wise move?

192   Chapter 3   Graphs

11. **a.** Plot each point and connect the points in the order given.

   (1, 0) (1, 1) (3, 1) (3, 0) (4, 0) (4, 1) (6, 1) (6, 0) (7, 0)

   b. Describe a pattern in the points. Extend your pattern in both directions by naming at least two coordinate pairs that come before (1, 0) and two pairs that come after (7, 0).

12. Use coordinates to write a recipe for drawing each letter in the coordinate plane.

   a. N

   b. W

   c. block letter T

13. What are the coordinates of the origin? Why do you think mathematicians use the name *origin*?

14. Use the rectangle below. For each description, find the coordinates of four points that are in the location given.

   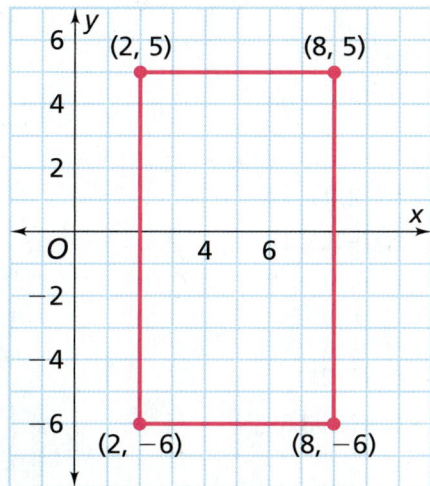

   a. inside the rectangle

   b. outside the rectangle

   c. on the rectangle but not on a corner point

   d. How can you tell whether a point is inside the rectangle just by looking at its coordinates?

15. The figure shows horizontal lines ℓ and m in the coordinate plane.

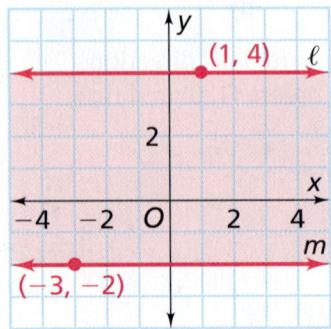

   a. Find the coordinates of six points between ℓ and m.

   b. Find the coordinates of six points that are not between ℓ and m.

   c. How can you tell whether a point is between ℓ and m just by looking at its coordinates?

16. A rectangle in the coordinate plane has one corner with coordinates $(-2, -2)$. One of its sides has a length of 5. Give some possible coordinates for the other three corners.

Maintain Your Skills

For Exercises 17 and 18, plot each point.

17. a. $(0, 1)$ b. $(1, 1)$ c. $(2, 1)$
    d. $(6, 1)$ e. $(-2, 1)$ f. $(-3.5, 1)$
    g. $\left(\frac{1}{3}, 1\right)$
    h. How are the locations of these points related?

18. a. $(1, 0)$ b. $(1, 1)$ c. $(1, 2)$
    d. $(1, 6)$ e. $(1, -2)$ f. $(1, -3.5)$
    g. $\left(1, \frac{1}{3}\right)$
    h. How are the locations of these points related?

19. Plot each point. The x- and y-coordinates are the same.

    a. $(0, 0)$ b. $(1, 1)$ c. $(2, 2)$
    d. $(6, 6)$ e. $(-2, -2)$ f. $(-3.5, -3.5)$
    g. $\left(\frac{1}{3}, \frac{1}{3}\right)$
    h. How are the locations of these points related?

Habits of Mind

Look for relationships. What is the difference between Exercises 17 and 18?

20. Plot each point. Each *x*-coordinate is the opposite of the *y*-coordinate.
    a. (0, 0)
    b. (1, −1)
    c. (2, −2)
    d. (6, −6)
    e. (−2, 2)
    f. (−3.5, 3.5)
    g. $\left(\frac{1}{3}, -\frac{1}{3}\right)$
    h. How are the locations of these points related?

21. Here are some points for which the sum of the *x*- and *y*-coordinates is 5. Plot each point.
    a. (3, 2)
    b. (2, 3)
    c. (−2, 7)
    d. (6, −1)
    e. (0, 5)
    f. (1.5, 3.5)
    g. (−1, 6)
    h. How are the locations of these points related?

You can say *negative* instead of *opposite*.

Go Online
pearsonsuccessnet.com

Historical Perspective
Describing Geometric Ideas With Algebraic Language

Mapmakers, such as Ptolemy, an Egyptian astronomer, mathematician, and geographer, used grids as early as about A.D. 150. In China, mapmakers began using coordinates for mapmaking around the same time.

However, René Descartes (1596–1650) usually receives credit for developing the systematic use of coordinates to describe geometric figures. Mathematicians named the coordinate system the Cartesian coordinate system in honor of Descartes.

In his well-known book *La Géométrie*, published in 1637, Descartes described how to use coordinates to translate geometry problems into algebra, and algebra into geometry. About the same time, another Frenchman, Pierre Fermat (1601–1665), independently had similar thoughts. Fermat's article on coordinates was not published until 1679. Coordinate, or analytic geometry, is what mathematicians call this blending of algebra and geometry.

The word *Cartesian* comes from the Latin version of René Descartes's name, Renatus Cartesius. In the 1600s, it was the custom for scholars and scientists to take Latin names.

3.02 Transformations

In Lesson 3.01, you found the coordinates for the graph of this pine tree shape by adding 2 to each *x*-coordinate. You drew a tree that looked like this.

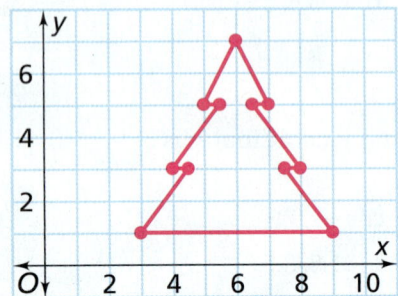

A rule that takes a set of points and produces another set of points is a **transformation**. The rule tells you to take every point (x, y) and replace it with $(x + 2, y)$. The result of applying the rule is a set of points. When you connect the points, you draw a tree with the same shape and size as the tree above, but your tree is 2 units to the right of the tree shown here. You transform the tree by shifting it 2 units to the right.

For You to Do

1. How does the picture of the tree above change when you subtract 4 from each *y*-coordinate?

Facts and Notation

Sometimes a transformation uses a combination of operations (addition, subtraction, multiplication, or division) that you perform on each point. A transformation transforms, or maps, the original point to another point.

You use the symbol $\mapsto$ to describe a transformation. The symbol means "maps to." When you read the transformation $(x, y) \mapsto (x + 3, y)$, you say, "$(x, y)$ maps to $(x + 3, y)$." The rule tells you to add three to the *x*-coordinate of each point and leave the *y*-coordinate of each point unchanged.

For example, if you perform the transformation $(x, y) \mapsto (x + 3, y)$ on the point $(5, 12)$, the result is $(8, 12)$. You say, "$(5, 12)$ maps to $(8, 12)$." You can also say, "$(5, 12)$ is transformed to $(8, 12)$."

What do you see from the stands when all the band members march 10 yards to the left?

Minds in Action episode 7

Sasha and Tony plot three points on a coordinate plane and connect them to form a triangle.

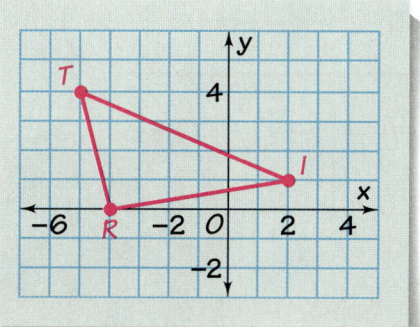

Sasha Let's apply a rule to the coordinates of the triangle and see what happens to it.

Tony Okay! How about if we use $(x, y) \mapsto (x + 3, y)$?

Sasha Well, that means that we add 3 to the *x*-coordinates. The *y*-coordinates stay the same.

Tony Wait! I need some way to label the new points. Then I can remember whether points are old or new.

Sasha I've seen it done like this.

T (−5, 4)	T′ (−2, 4)
R (−4, 0)	R′ (−1, 0)
I (2, 1)	I′ (5, 1)

When you read *T′*, you say "T prime."

Tony Good idea, Sasha! That little mark after the letter means the point is a transformed point. Let's plot the new points so we can see what happens to the triangle.

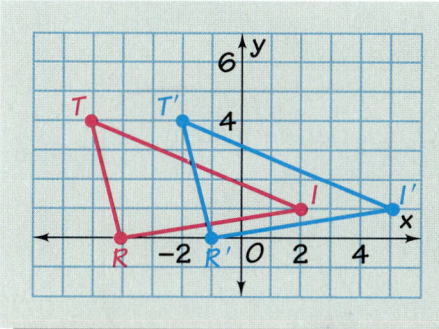

3.02 Transformations

For You to Do

Describe the relationship between the original triangle *TRI* and the triangle that each transformation produces.

2. $(x, y) \mapsto (x - 3, y)$

3. $(x, y) \mapsto (2x, y)$

4. $(x, y) \mapsto (2x, 2y)$

5. $(x, y) \mapsto (-x, y)$

The *x*- and *y*-axes divide the coordinate plane into four parts, or **quadrants.**

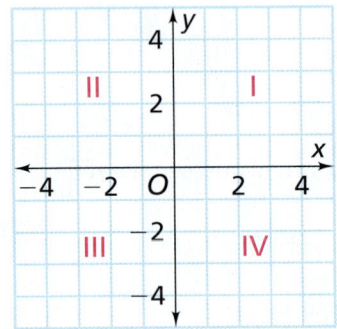

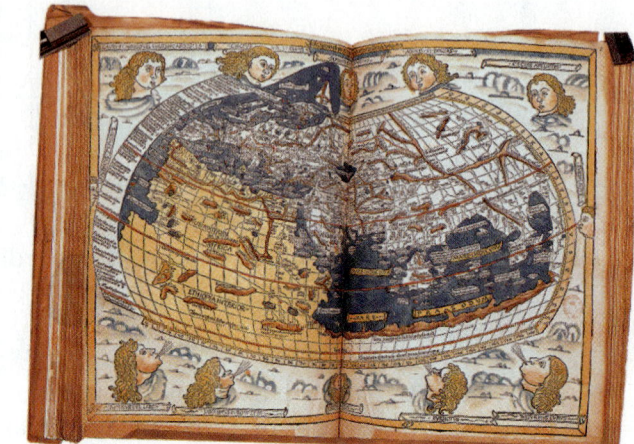

Ptolemy made maps with grids and quadrants about A.D. 150.

Here are some examples of points in each quadrant.

Quadrant I	(1, 1)	(3, 2)	$\left(\frac{1}{12}, \frac{1}{17}\right)$	(200, 468)
Quadrant II	(−1, 1)	$\left(-1.8, \frac{4}{3}\right)$	$\left(-7, \frac{3}{2}\right)$	(−4, 1003)
Quadrant III	(−1, −1)	(−3, −2)	$\left(-\frac{1}{12}, -\frac{1}{17}\right)$	(−200, −468)
Quadrant IV	(3, −2)	(6, −5)	(9.3, −1)	(0.07, −0.001)

For Discussion

6. How can you tell what quadrant a point is in just by looking at its coordinates?

7. In what direction are the quadrants numbered?

For You to Do

The tree in Lesson 3.01 is in the first quadrant. Describe a transformation that places the tree entirely in each quadrant given.

8. second quadrant

9. third quadrant

10. fourth quadrant

Exercises Practicing Habits of Mind

Check Your Understanding

1. Describe how a point's location changes after each transformation.

    a. Add a positive value to the *x*-coordinate of an ordered pair and leave the *y*-coordinate the same.

    b. Add a positive value to the *y*-coordinate of an ordered pair and leave the *x*-coordinate the same.

    c. Add a negative value to the *x*-coordinate and leave the *y*-coordinate the same.

2. Draw the square with corners $A(1, 3)$, $B(-3, 1)$, $C(-1, -3)$, and $D(3, -1)$. Transform all four points using each rule given. Describe the effect of the transformation on each point and on each square.

    a. $(x, y) \mapsto (x + 1, y)$

    b. $(x, y) \mapsto (x + 5, y + 2)$

    c. $(x, y) \mapsto (x - 2, y + 1)$

3. a. Is there a transformation that locates square *ABCD* from Exercise 2 entirely in the first quadrant? If so, describe the transformation.

    b. **Take It Further** Is there a transformation that locates three corners of square *ABCD* in the fourth quadrant and one corner in the first quadrant? If so, describe the transformation.

4. Draw a square with corners $S(1, 1)$, $T(-1, 1)$, $U(-1, -1)$, and $V(1, -1)$. Transform each point using the rule given. Describe the effect of the transformation on each point and on the square.

    a. $(x, y) \mapsto (x, 2y)$

    b. $(x, y) \mapsto (2x, y)$

    c. $(x, y) \mapsto (2x, 2y)$

    d. **Take It Further** $(x, y) \mapsto (-y, x)$

5. **Take It Further** Sometimes a transformation rearranges the points in a figure but leaves the overall figure looking the same. Find at least two transformations that leave the square in Exercise 4 looking the same.

> A transformation like this "fixes" the figure.

3.02 Transformations

6. Apply each transformation to the number 23 in the coordinate plane. Make a sketch of each result.

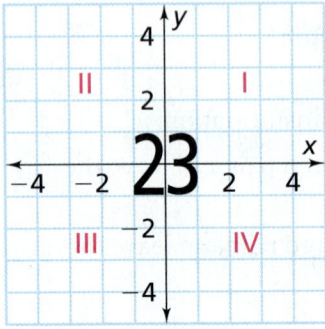

   a. $(x, y) \mapsto (x, 2y)$ b. $(x, y) \mapsto (2x, y)$ c. $(x, y) \mapsto (2x, 2y)$

7. **Write About It** Is there any slanted line that passes through only two quadrants and does not pass through the origin? Explain.

On Your Own

8. Describe how the position of a point changes with each transformation given.

   a. Change the sign of its x-coordinate, but keep the sign of the y-coordinate the same.

   b. Change the sign of its y-coordinate, but keep the sign of the x-coordinate the same.

   c. Change the sign of both coordinates.

9. For each part, draw a set of coordinate axes. Shade the quadrants with points that match each description.

   a. negative x-coordinates

   b. positive y-coordinates

   c. negative x-coordinates and positive y-coordinates

10. On graph paper, draw a set of coordinate axes.

    a. Shade the region where $5 \leq x \leq 8$.

    b. Shade the region where $-3 \leq y \leq 6$.

    c. Is there any overlap of the shaded regions? If so, what shape is the intersection of the shaded regions? What is its area in square units?

    d. Rewrite the instructions in parts (a) and (b) to make the shaded intersection in the shape of a square. What is the area of your square?

Habits of Mind

Experiment. Try it with points! Choose points from different quadrants.

There is more than one possible result.

11. **Write About It** Is it possible for a line to pass through only one quadrant? To pass through all four quadrants? Explain.

12. **Standardized Test Prep** The transformation
$$(x, y) \mapsto (-x, y)$$
maps points in the second quadrant to points in another quadrant. To which quadrant does the transformation map points of the second quadrant?

   A. first

   B. second

   C. third

   D. fourth

13. Follow the recipe for drawing a picture.
    - Draw a square with corners (1, 1), (4, 1), (1, 4), and (4, 4).
    - Transform this square using the rule $(x, y) \mapsto (x + 2, y + 2)$. Draw the resulting square on the same coordinate plane as the starting square.
    - Connect each corner of the original square to its matching corner in the transformed square. What does your picture look like?

> The *matching corner* means the location of the corner point after the transformation. Another name for the matching corner is the *image* of the corner.

Maintain Your Skills

For Exercises 14–16, apply the transformation to each shape given. Draw a sketch for each transformation.

- triangle A with corners (−4, 2), (0, 2), and (−3, 4)
- triangle B with corners (1, 1), (6, 1), and (1, 3)
- a rectangle with corners (5, 3), (7, 3), (5, 7), and (7, 7)

14. $(x, y) \mapsto (x - 4, y + 2)$

   a. triangle A   b. triangle B   c. rectangle

   d. Describe how far and in what direction the transformation moves each point.

15. $(x, y) \mapsto (2x, y)$

   a. triangle A   b. triangle B   c. rectangle

   d. Describe how the transformation changes each shape.

16. $(x, y) \mapsto (y, -x)$

   a. triangle A   b. triangle B   c. rectangle

   d. Describe how the transformation moves each shape.

3.03 Distance and Absolute Value

In Lesson 3.01, you learned that points have no size, only location. Shapes, such as a triangle, a square, or even the pine tree in Lesson 3.02, do have size. You can make these shapes from line segments. One way to measure these shapes is to find the lengths of these segments.

For You to Do

Find the distance between each pair of points.

1. $(-1, -3)$ and $(4, -3)$
2. $(-1, -3)$ and $(-1, 9)$
3. $(2, 1)$ and $(-3, 1)$
4. $(2, 1)$ and $(2, -16)$

When you measure a side of a triangle or a square, the side length is always positive. The distance between two points is also always positive. When you say that the distance on the number line between 1 and 4 is 3, it does not matter if you start measuring from 1 or 4—the distance is the same.

The easiest way to calculate the distance between two numbers on a number line is to subtract the smaller number from the greater one. You do not always know which number is greater, especially if you are using variables, such as a and b. You can say, "If a is greater than b, then the distance from a to b is $a - b$, or if a is less than b, then the distance from a to b is $b - a$." Luckily, there is an easier way to say that.

> The number that you find when you measure distance is undirected. It indicates size, but not direction. By convention, distance between two points is the length of the line segment connecting the points.

Definition

If x and y are two numbers, then the **absolute value** of $(x - y)$, written as $|x - y|$, is the distance between the numbers x and y on a number line.

For example,

- $|8 - 3| = 5$, since 5 units is the distance between 8 and 3 on the number line.

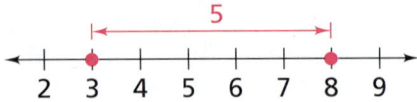

- $|3 - 8| = 5$, which has the same value as $|8 - 3|$ above.

> Here, distance is the length of the segment with endpoints located at x and y.

202 Chapter 3 Graphs

- $|1 - (-5)| = 6$, since 6 units is the distance between 1 and -5 on the number line.

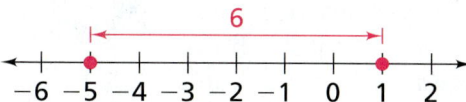

- $|-6 - 0| = 6$, since 6 units is the distance between -6 and 0.

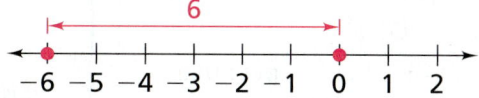

For You to Do

Evaluate each expression.

5. $|(-2) - 6|$ **6.** $|4 - 10|$ **7.** $|(-3) - (-5)|$

Developing Habits of Mind

Find a representation. $|8 + 10|$ does not have the form $|x - y|$, so does $|8 + 10|$ represent a distance? You can rewrite $|8 + 10|$ as $|8 - (-10)|$, which is the distance between -10 and 8. The distance between -10 and 8 on the number line is $|8 - (-10)| = |8 + 10| = 18$.

In each example above, your first instinct may be to simplify the expression inside the absolute value bars as shown below.

- $|8 - 3| = |5| = 5$
- $|3 - 8| = |-5| = 5$
- $|1 - (-5)| = |6| = 6$
- $|-6 - 0| = |-6| = 6$
- $|8 + 10| = |18| = 18$

The following theorem states a very simple pattern that emerges.

Theorem 3.1

The absolute value of a number x is its distance from 0 on the number line.

> You can also use a more familiar rule: Take what you have and make it positive.

Proof

By the definition, the distance between 0 and a point x on the number line is given by $|x - 0|$.

The examples above show that you can simplify the expression inside the absolute value symbols. Since $x - 0 = x$, then $|x - 0| = |x|$.

3.03 Distance and Absolute Value

Developing Habits of Mind

Represent absolute value. There is an algebraic way to describe the absolute value of a number. If x is not negative, then $|x|$ is just x. If x is negative, then $|x|$ is the opposite of x. Here is how to write these words using algebraic symbols.

$$|x| = \begin{cases} x, & \text{if } x \geq 0 \\ -x, & \text{if } x < 0 \end{cases}$$

Note that $-x$ on the preceding line does not mean that $|x|$ is a negative number. The condition is "if $x < 0$." This means that x itself is negative, so its opposite, $-x$, must be positive.

> It is easy to forget that $-x$ does not mean "make it negative."

Here are two examples showing absolute value.

Evaluate $|13|$. Since $13 \geq 0$, then $|13| = 13$.

Evaluate $|-2|$. Since $-2 < 0$, then $|-2| = -(-2) = 2$. The answer is still a positive value!

The definition of absolute value and Theorem 3.1 can help you solve equations that use absolute value.

Example

Problem Solve $|x - 3| = 5$.

Solution You can think about an equation such as $|x - 3| = 5$ in two ways.

You can ask, "For what values of x is the distance from x to 3 equal to 5 units?" In other words, "What numbers are 5 units away from 3?" There are two possible results, $x = 8$ or $x = -2$. Both are correct, so the equation has two solutions.

There is another way to look at solving $|x - 3| = 5$. If $|x - 3| = 5$, then $x - 3$ equals either 5 or -5 (since 5 and -5 are the two numbers that have an absolute value equal to 5). Solving this equation looks like this.

$$|x - 3| = 5$$
$$x - 3 = 5 \quad \text{or} \quad x - 3 = -5$$
$$x = 5 + 3 \quad \text{or} \quad x = -5 + 3$$
$$x = 8 \quad \text{or} \quad x = -2$$

For You to Do

Find the solutions, if any, to each equation.

8. $|x + 7| = 10$

9. $|x + 7| = -10$

Facts and Notation

You can read the symbol ± as "plus or minus." Often you use this symbol to represent two possible solutions to an equation that uses absolute value. In the previous Example, you can write the solution as $x = 3 \pm 5$ since the solutions are $x = 3 + 5 = 8$ and $x = 3 - 5 = -2$.

Compare this solution to the one in the last Example.

The symbol ± shortens the notation you use in solving equations. Instead of breaking an absolute value equation into two equations, you can use the notation for both 5 and −5.

$$|x - 3| = 5$$
$$x - 3 = \pm 5$$
$$x - 3 + 3 = \pm 5 + 3$$
$$x = 3 \pm 5$$
$$x = 8 \text{ or } x = -2$$

You cannot add or subtract directly when you work with a quantity marked with ±, but you can multiply or divide a quantity marked with ±.

Habits of Mind

Experiment. Add $\pm 18 + 3$. The sum is 21 or −15. Divide ± 18 by 3. The quotient is ± 6.

You can extend this idea of measuring distance between two points on a number line to measuring the distance between two points on the coordinate plane. Finding the distance between two points on the coordinate plane when they have the same *x*- or *y*-coordinate is easy.

For two points with the same *y*-coordinate, such as (3, 2) and (5, 2), think of the horizontal segment connecting the points. Then, use the *x*-axis to find the distance between 3 and 5. For the same *x*-coordinate, such as (1, 3) and (1, −2), use the *y*-axis to find the distance between 3 and −2.

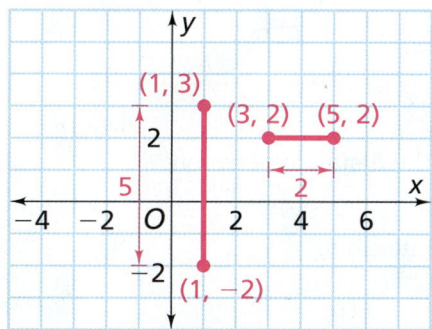

But how do you find the distance between two points, such as (1, 3) and (5, 2), when they have neither an *x*- nor a *y*-coordinate in common?

Minds in Action   episode 8

Derman and Sasha measure the distance between points A(−1, 1) and B(3, −2).

Derman The segment connecting the points isn't horizontal or vertical. See, I drew a horizontal line and a vertical line through the point A, but neither hits B, so the absolute value trick won't work.

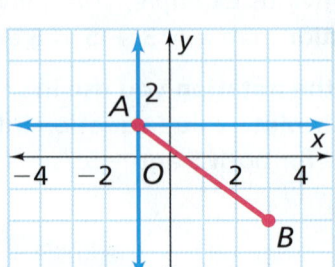

Sasha I know, but look, Derman, you're brilliant! If I draw a horizontal line through B, it hits the vertical line through A.

Derman Yes, so? What does that do for us?

Sasha Horizontal lines are perpendicular to vertical lines, don't you see? So the horizonal and the vertical intersect at (−1, −2), forming a right angle. Let's call that point C.

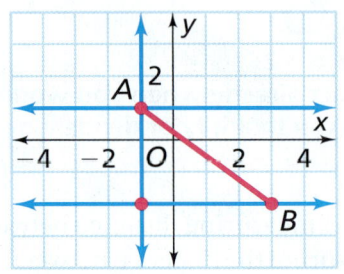

Derman Okay.

Sasha So, now we have a right triangle. We can find the lengths of the two legs.

Derman With the Pythagorean Theorem, we can find the length of the hypotenuse.

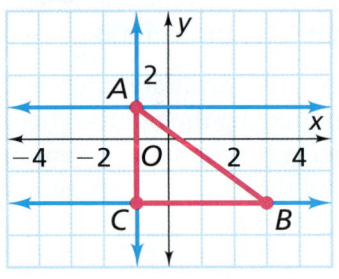

You can use Sasha and Derman's method to find the distance between any two points in the coordinate plane.

Here is the theorem that Derman was trying to remember.

Theorem 3.2 Pythagorean Theorem

In a right triangle in which the lengths of the legs are *a* and *b*, and the length of the hypotenuse is *c*, the side lengths have the relationship $a^2 + b^2 = c^2$.

The distance between bases is 90 ft. The distance from home plate to second base is $\sqrt{90^2 + 90^2}$ ft.

For You to Do

10. Use the Pythagorean Theorem to help Derman find the distance between (−1, 1) and (3, −2).

Exercises Practicing Habits of Mind

Check Your Understanding

1. Find the distance between each pair of points.
   a. $(5, 3)$ and $(5, -3)$
   b. $(-2, 6)$ and $(98, 6)$
   c. $(3, 4)$ and $(4, 5)$
   d. $(1, 2)$ and $(-3, -1)$
   e. $(0, 3)$ and $(b, 3)$

2. **Write About It** Explain why the expression $\pm a + b$ does not represent the same value as $\pm(a + b)$.

3. a. Write a sentence about distance that restates the equation $|x - 5| = 7$. Then find two numbers that make the equation true.
   b. Solve $|x + 7| = 4$.

4. Solve each absolute value equation.
   a. $|x - 5| = 3$
   b. $|3x - 7| = 16$
   c. $|-4x + 10| = 0$
   d. $|2x - 5| = -5$
   e. $|2x - 5| - 12 = -5$
   f. $|8 - 3x| = 2$

5. Write an expression for the result that uses the symbol $\pm$. Then find both possible results.

   a. In 2007, the average of the minimum and maximum distances from Earth to the moon was about 381,500 kilometers. Due to the moon's elliptical orbit, the moon was as much as 25,000 kilometers closer to or farther from Earth. What were the maximum and minimum distances between Earth and the moon in 2007?

   b. Christine and her sister were born four years apart. When Christine is 29 years old, how old is her sister?

   c. Keith estimates the cost of a week-long trip to Hawaii. His estimate is within 5% of the actual cost of $4500. Find the lowest and highest possible estimates.

6. Find an equation using absolute values that has the solutions given.
   a. two solutions, 11 and -11
   b. two solutions, 5 and 29
   c. two solutions, -15 and 3
   d. no solutions
   e. one solution, 4
   f. two solutions, 6 and 11

Habits of Mind

Experiment. Try Exercise 2 with positive and negative numbers. Use your examples to explain.

On Your Own

7. A pollster took an opinion poll of eligible voters 10 weeks before the 2000 election. The table shows the results. The poll reported a ±3.8% margin of error. According to this poll and its margin of error, was Gore clearly favored by voters?

Election Opinion Poll

Candidate	Vote (%)
George W. Bush	40
Al Gore	46
Other	8
Undecided	5

SOURCE: International Communications Research

> The margin of error suggests how accurate a measurement is. The ±3.8% margin of error in the election poll means that the percent of voters in favor of George W. Bush was likely between 36.2% and 43.8%.

8. Find the distance between the origin (0, 0) and each point given.

  a. (3, 4)

  b. (−4, −5)

  c. Write About It Describe how to find the distance between any point (x, y) and the origin (0, 0).

9. What's Wrong Here? Henry says that the equation $|z + 10| = |z| + 10$ is always true.

He says, "I think it works. I replaced z with 3. The equation was true! I plugged in 5 for z. The equation was true again."

What is wrong with Henry's reasoning?

10. In the statements below, each variable represents any number. Decide whether each statement is true for all, some, or no values of the variables. If the statement is true for all or no values, explain. If the statement is true for some values, give one example of a value for which it is true and two examples of values for which it is false.

  a. $|a + b| = |a| + |b|$

  b. $|a - b| = |a| - |b|$

  c. $|ab| = |a| \cdot |b|$

  d. $\left|\frac{p}{q}\right| = \frac{|p|}{|q|}$

  e. $|x + y| > |x| + |y|$

The margin of error in fingerprint measurements is near zero.

11. Solve each equation or inequality.
    a. $|x + 142| = 81$
    b. $|2x - 6| = 81$
    c. $|5x + 12| = -81$
    d. $|5x + 12| + 81 = 0$
    e. $|13x - 8| = 0$
    f. $|x - 7| < 2$

12. **Standardized Test Prep** Which of the following shows the solution(s) to the equation $|x + 2| = 6$?
    A. $x = 4$
    B. $x = 4$ or $x = -2$
    C. $x = 4$ or $x = -4$
    D. $x = 4$ or $x = -8$

13. **Take It Further** Find the solutions, if any, to $|(|(|x - 2| - 16)| - 10)| = 5$.

14. Find the solutions, if any, to $|(|(|x - 2| - 16)| - 10)| = -5$.

Habits of Mind
Establish a process. You can use backtracking to solve Exercise 13. Keep track of your steps carefully.

Maintain Your Skills

15. Find the solutions, if any, to each equation.
    a. $|x| = 11$
    b. $|2y| = 11$
    c. $|3z| = 11$
    d. $|10a| = 11$
    e. What is the pattern to the solutions?

16. Find the solutions, if any, to each equation.
    a. $|x - 5| = 11$
    b. $|2y - 3| = 11$
    c. $|3z + 7| = 11$
    d. $|10a - 17| = 11$
    e. How do these solutions relate to the solutions in Exercise 15?

3.04 Graphing Related Quantities

You can use *x*- and *y*-coordinate axes to represent a variety of numerical relationships. For instance, let the horizontal axis represent free throws attempted in a basketball game. Let the vertical axis represent free throws made. Look at the following points.

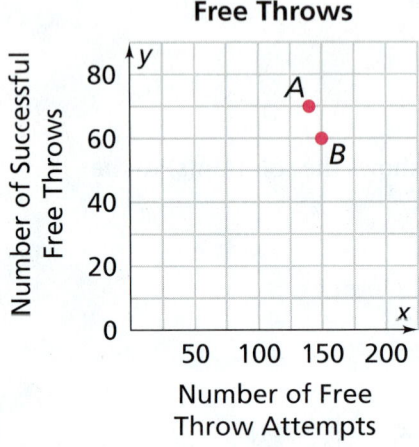

Point A (140, 70) represents a person who attempts 140 free throws and makes 70 of them. Point B (150, 60) represents a person who attempts 150 free throws and makes 60 of them.

Habits of Mind

Visualize. Which person has a better free-throw percentage?

Now, change the meaning of the axes. Let the horizontal axis represent the weight in pounds of a person. Let the vertical axis represent the person's height in inches.

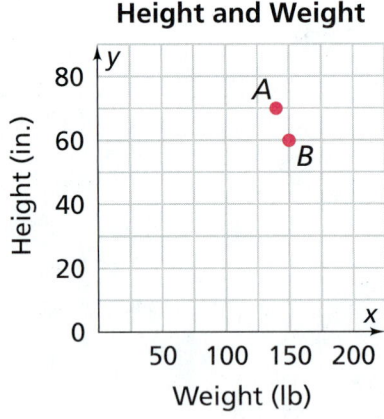

Point A (140, 70) represents a person who weighs 140 pounds and is 70 inches tall. Point B (150, 60) represents a person who weighs 150 pounds and is 60 inches tall. Person B is shorter and heavier than Person A.

The numerical values of points A and B stay the same. However, the axes represent entirely different quantities. The first graph shows free throws made against free throws attempted. The second graph shows height against weight.

In general, you can graph any numerical value against any other numerical value.

Example

Problem Invent a story that the graph illustrates.

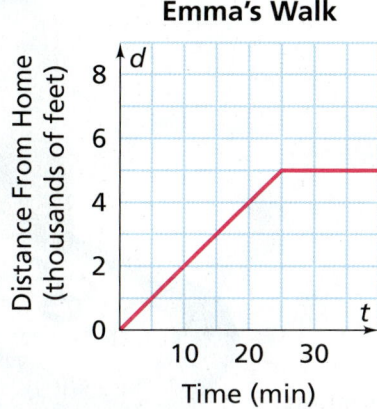

Solution In the graph, the horizontal axis represents time. The vertical axis represents distance from home. Time and distance increase as you move to the right from the origin. After 25 minutes, time increases, but distance from home stays the same.

You can use this information to write a story about Emma.

Emma leaves home at the point (0, 0). While she walks at a constant rate to the basketball court, the graph slants upward. After 25 minutes, she arrives at the basketball court, at the point (25, 5000).

When she gets to the court, Emma plays basketball for 15 minutes. During the time she plays, the *y*-coordinate, or her distance from home, remains the same. So the graph is flat from (25, 5000) to (40, 5000).

For Discussion

Emma's story is unfinished. For each ending, draw a graph of the complete story.

1. Emma walks home at the same speed as she walked to the basketball court. She arrives home in 25 minutes.
2. Emma realizes she will be late for dinner, so she runs home. She takes 10 minutes to get home.
3. Emma gets a ride home from a friend. She takes 5 minutes to get home.

3.04 Graphing Related Quantities

For You to Do

What's Wrong Here? Adam makes a graph to represent the following situation. Jen walks to school. When she is halfway to school, Jen realizes that she has forgotten her lunch. She turns around and walks home. Jen realizes she will be late, so she runs to school.

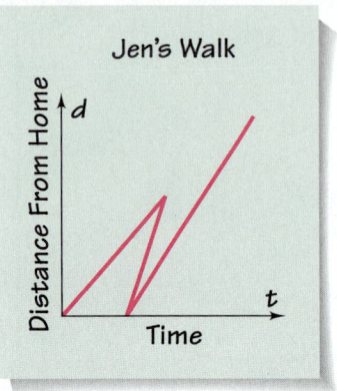

A pedometer counts your strides. Stride length is about 0.4 times your height. Distance you walk = stride count × stride length.

4. Explain what is wrong with Adam's graph.
5. Make a graph that more accurately represents the situation.

Exercises Practicing Habits of Mind

Check Your Understanding

1. Write a sentence that can explain this graph when the axes have the following labels.

Horizontal Axis	Vertical Axis
a. Time	Distance From Home
b. Price of Movie Tickets	Number of Tickets Sold
c. Distance Driven	Amount of Gas in Tank

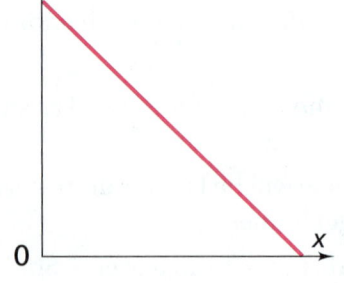

212 Chapter 3 Graphs

2. George and Martha leave their house in Washington at the same time in separate cars. The graph represents their trips.

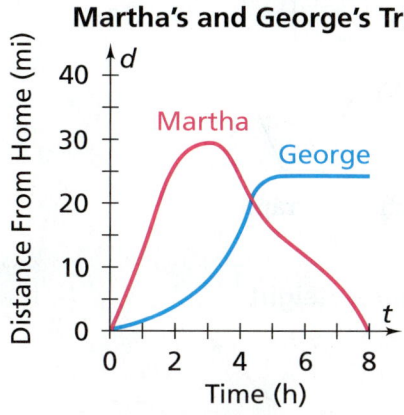

> Assume they travel a straight road from their house.

a. Write a story about George's trip that matches the graph.
b. Write a story about Martha's trip that matches the graph.
c. What happens in each trip at the point where the graphs cross?
d. What does the horizontal part of George's graph represent?
e. About how many miles does Martha travel during her trip?
f. About how many miles does George travel during his trip?

3. **Write About It** Suppose you have an empty bucket. The cross section of the bucket is in the shape of a rectangle. You fill the bucket with water that runs at a constant rate from a faucet. The height of the water in the bucket rises at a constant rate. Explain why the graph represents this situation.

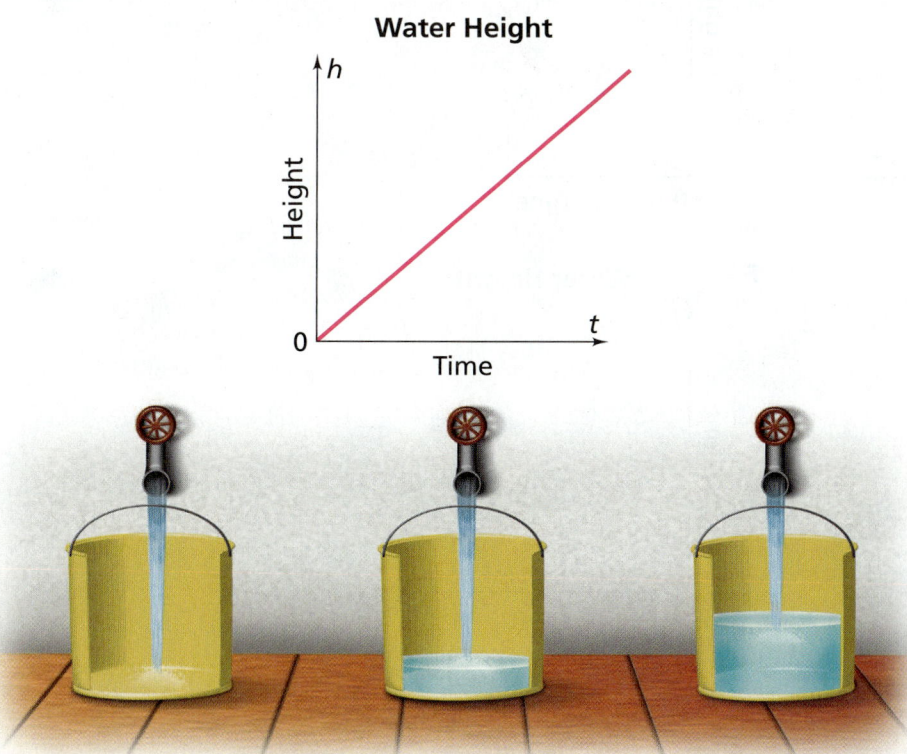

3.04   Graphing Related Quantities   **213**

4. Each diagram represents a cross section of a bucket.

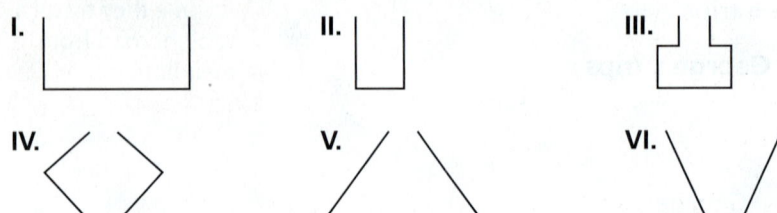

Water flows into the bucket at a constant rate. Match each graph to the corresponding bucket. Explain each choice.

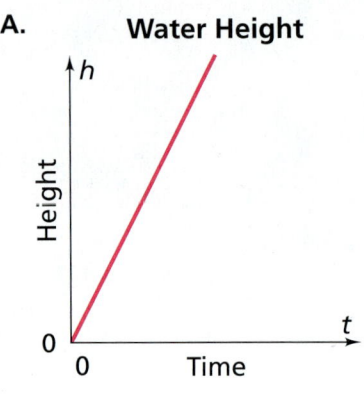

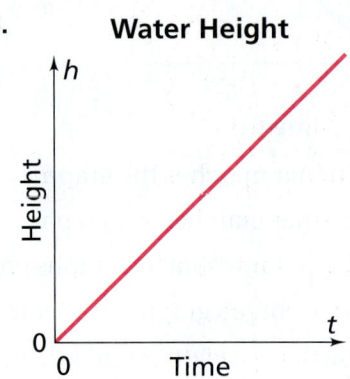

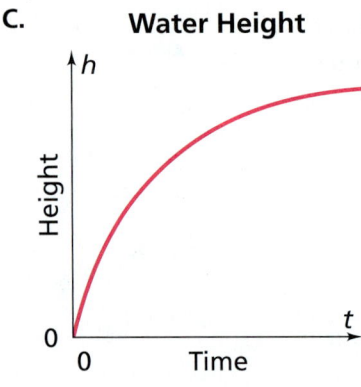

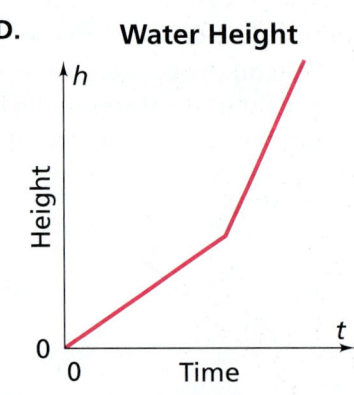

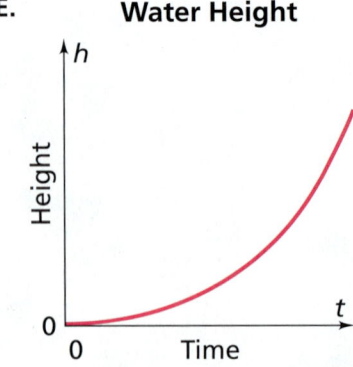

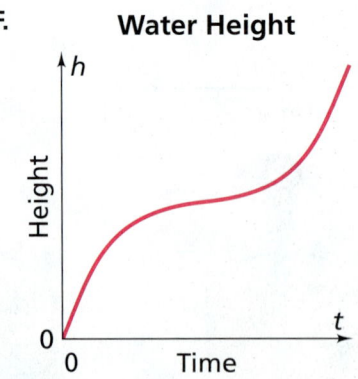

On Your Own

5. Every day, Mr. Hayashi walks his dog. This graph illustrates his walk.
   a. Which two points on the graph show Mr. Hayashi at his house?
   b. In the middle of the graph, there is a sharp angle. What does Mr. Hayashi do at this point in his walk?

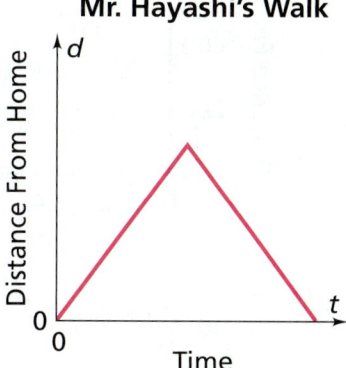

Mr. Hayashi's Walk

6. Francesca and Demitri run a race. Francesca is faster than Demitri, so she reaches the finish line first. Make a graph that illustrates this situation by graphing distance against time.

   > There is not enough information in Exercise 6 to draw a precise graph. You can draw a graph that illustrates the basic idea.

7. Draw a graph of each situation.
   a. To make the race more even, Demitri starts the race 10 feet closer to the finish line. Francesca catches up to him and still reaches the finish line first.
   b. Francesca gives Demitri a 5-second head start. Francesca never catches up, and Demitri wins the race.

8. Ruth runs a 100-meter race. For parts (a)–(c), make a graph that illustrates each situation.
   a. Ruth's official time is 14 seconds.
   b. Ruth trips and falls at the beginning of the race. She loses five seconds, so her official time is 19 seconds.
   c. Ruth starts running two seconds before the starting gun. Nobody notices, and her official time is 12 seconds.
   d. Fill in the blank. To get from the graph in part (a) to the graph in part (b), you can apply the rule $(x, y) \mapsto (x + \blacksquare, y)$.
   e. Fill in the blank. To get from the graph in part (a) to the graph in part (c), you can apply the transformation $(x, y) \mapsto (x + \blacksquare, y)$.

3.04 Graphing Related Quantities

9. **Standardized Test Prep** Jamar walks quickly to the store, buys a newspaper, and then walks slowly home. Which graph best describes his walk?

A.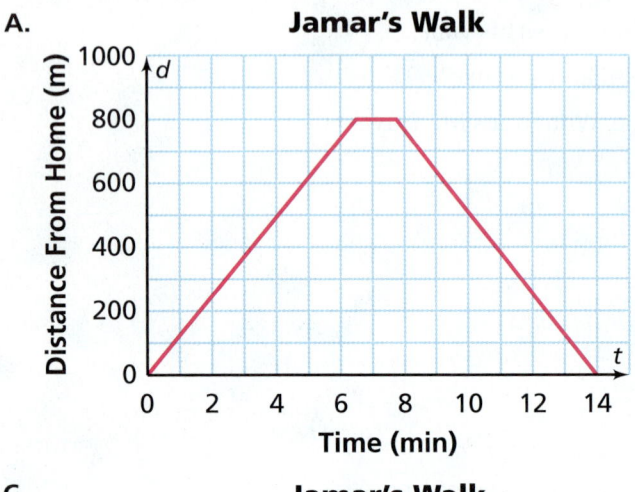
B.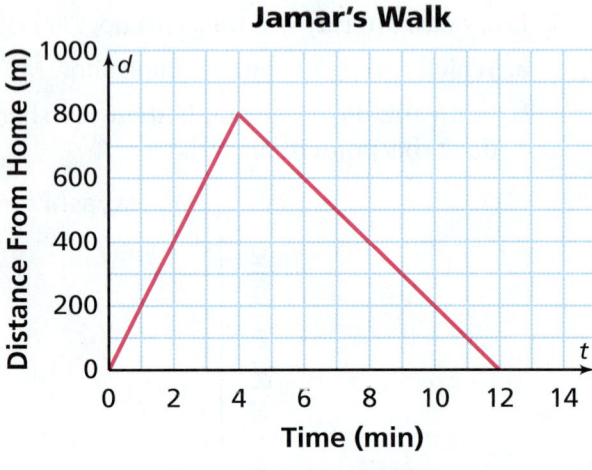
C.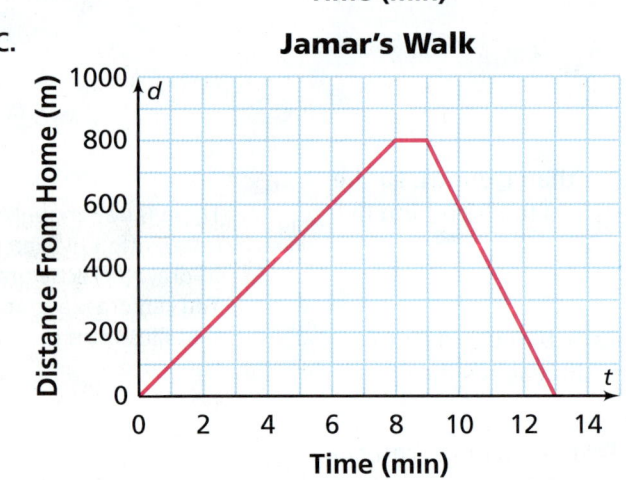
D.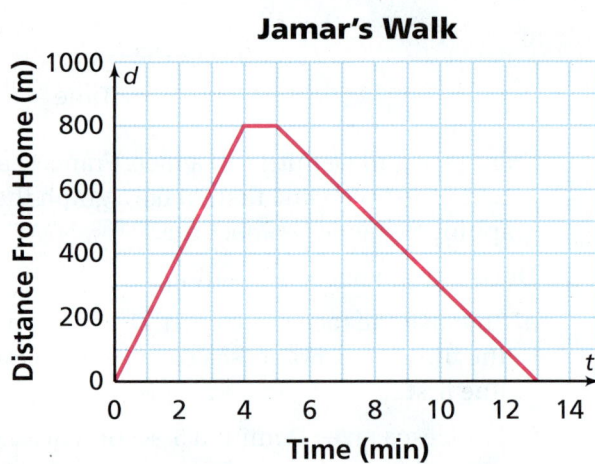

Maintain Your Skills

10. Adam makes a table showing the number of factors the number n has. Adam writes the number of factors in the second column. Adam says, "The number 6 has four factors: 1, 2, 3, and 6. I write 6 in the first column and 4 in the second column."

    a. Make a graph of the number of factors of n against the number n. Label the horizontal axis n. Label the vertical axis Number of Factors of n. For instance, (6, 4) is a point on this graph because the number 6 has 4 factors. Does it make sense to connect the dots on this graph?

    b. What do the points on the horizontal line passing through (3, 2) have in common?

Adam's Table

n	Number of Factors
1	1
2	2
3	2
4	3
5	2
6	4
7	2

216   Chapter 3   Graphs

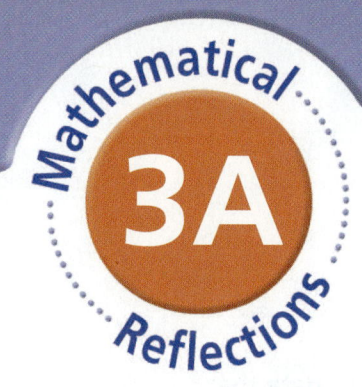

Mathematical Reflections 3A

In this investigation, you learned to transform points and shapes in the coordinate plane by applying rules to coordinates. You also learned the meaning of a graph for a given situation. These questions will help you summarize what you have learned.

1. Suppose line ℓ is horizontal and passes through $(13, -2)$.
   a. Sketch a graph of ℓ.
   b. Find the coordinates of six points on ℓ.
   c. Find the coordinates of six points not on ℓ.
   d. How can you tell whether a point is on ℓ just by looking at its coordinates?

2. Find the distance between each pair of points.
   a. $(12, 5)$ and the origin
   b. $(-12, 5)$ and the origin
   c. $(9, 7)$ and $(-3, 2)$

3. How can you locate a point on a coordinate plane using the point's coordinates?

4. You have a picture in the coordinate plane. What is the effect of changing all x-coordinates or all y-coordinates of the points in the picture by the same amount?

5. According to the graph, who won the race, the tortoise or the hare? How can you tell? What else does the graph tell you about the race?

Vocabulary and Notation

In this investigation, you learned these terms and symbols. Make sure you understand what each one means and how to use it.

- absolute value, $|x - y|$
- coordinate
- coordinate plane
- graph of a number
- ordered pair
- origin
- quadrant
- transformation
- x-axis
- x-coordinate
- y-axis
- y-coordinate
- $\mapsto$ (maps to)
- $\pm$ (plus or minus)

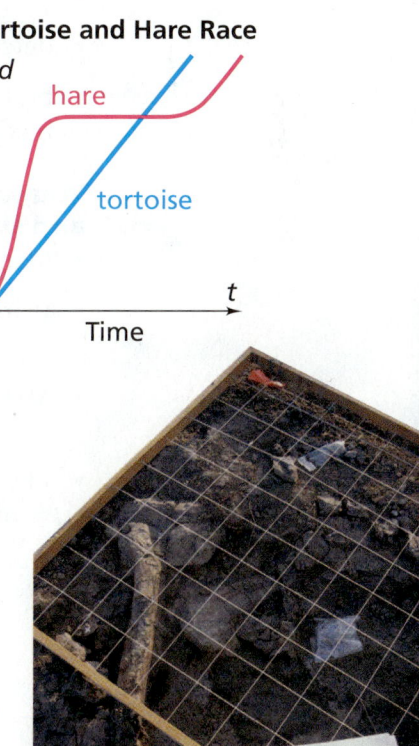

For accuracy, an archaeologist fits a smaller grid inside a larger grid system.

Investigation 3B

Statistical Data

In *Statistical Data*, you will explore ways to represent data that will help you find trends and patterns. Graphs and tables are powerful visual tools for summarizing and understanding large amounts of data.

By the end of this investigation, you will be able to answer questions like these.

1. How can you use graphs, charts, and tables to understand data?

2. How can you make informed conclusions about data?

3. Mr. Siddiqui tells his students about a correction for a test. He says, "It turns out that one problem didn't have a solution. To make up for my mistake, I gave everyone an extra 5 points credit for that problem. That changes the class average from 83 to 87 points." Is this possible? Explain.

You will learn how to

- determine the mean, median, and mode for a set of data, and decide how meaningful they are in specific situations

- interpret data lists, frequency tables, and stem-and-leaf displays

- determine the five-number summary for a set of data

- build data graphs such as histograms, box-and-whisker plots, and scatter plots

You will develop these habits and skills:

- Identify trends in data.

- Work with a variety of types of numbers in a variety of forms.

- Make and interpret visual and tabular representations of data.

- Identify limitations, or misuses, of visual representations of data.

Some visual information may not be what it seems. What you see depends on how you look at it.

218 Chapter 3 Graphs

3.05 Getting Started

Activating Prior Knowledge
Exploring New Ideas

You can use measures such as mean, median, and mode to interpret data such as test scores and sports averages. Workers in business, health care, and many other areas use these measures to help them make decisions.

For You to Explore

1. Work in pairs to gather data for this experiment. Each pair has a stopwatch.

   - The first person holds the stopwatch so that the second person cannot see it.
   - The first person says "Go" and starts the stopwatch.
   - The second person guesses when 30 seconds have elapsed and says "Stop."
   - The first person stops the watch.
   - The first person announces the actual time that elapsed and records that time. Round to the nearest second.
   - The first person times the second person once more. The first person reports and records the time for the second try.
   - The first and second person reverse roles. The second person has the stopwatch. The first person guesses when 30 seconds have elapsed.

   When you finish the experiment, you will have two recorded times for each person. What observations can you make about your data?

2. The table lists the ages of the winners of the Academy Awards Best Actor and Best Actress in a Leading Role awards, at the start of the year of their film achievements, from 1986 through 2006.

Winners Best Actor and Best Actress Awards

Year	Actor	Age	Actress	Age
1986	Paul Newman	61	Marlee Matlin	21
1987	Michael Douglas	43	Cher	41
1988	Dustin Hoffman	51	Jodie Foster	26
1989	Daniel Day-Lewis	32	Jessica Tandy	80
1990	Jeremy Irons	42	Kathy Bates	42
1991	Anthony Hopkins	54	Jodie Foster	29
1992	Al Pacino	52	Emma Thompson	33
1993	Tom Hanks	37	Holly Hunter	35
1994	Tom Hanks	38	Jessica Lange	45
1995	Nicolas Cage	31	Susan Sarandon	49
1996	Geoffrey Rush	45	Frances McDormand	39
1997	Jack Nicholson	60	Helen Hunt	34
1998	Roberto Benigni	46	Gwyneth Paltrow	26
1999	Kevin Spacey	40	Hilary Swank	25
2000	Russell Crowe	36	Julia Roberts	33
2001	Denzel Washington	47	Halle Berry	35
2002	Adrien Brody	29	Nicole Kidman	35
2003	Sean Penn	43	Charlize Theron	28
2004	Jamie Foxx	37	Hilary Swank	30
2005	Philip Seymour Hoffman	38	Reese Witherspoon	29
2006	Forest Whitaker	45	Helen Mirren	61

Source: Academy of Motion Picture Arts and Sciences

Sophia claims that the typical winner of the Best Actor award is much older than the typical winner of the Best Actress award. Make some arguments that support or oppose Sophia's claim.

Exercises Practicing Habits of Mind

On Your Own

3. Describe how to find each measure for seven test scores. What does each measure tell you?

   a. mean

   b. median

   c. mode

   Habits of Mind

   Experiment. Try it with numbers! Calculate each measure using a set of seven scores.

4. Milo sits next to a tollbooth and counts the number of people in each of 50 cars. He records his findings in the table. Then Milo calculates the mean number of people in each car.

   Car Survey

Number of People in Car	Number of Cars
1	31
2	12
3	3
4	2
5	2

   a. **What's Wrong Here?** On his first try, Milo finds the mean of the five numbers, 31, 12, 3, 2, and 2, to be 10. Explain why this cannot be the mean number of people in each car.

   b. Find the correct mean number of people in each car.

   Find the total number of people Milo counted in 50 cars.

5. **Write About It** Describe at least three situations in which you can use each measure.

   a. mean

   b. median

   c. mode

6. This table lists the salaries for the 25 players on a professional baseball team.

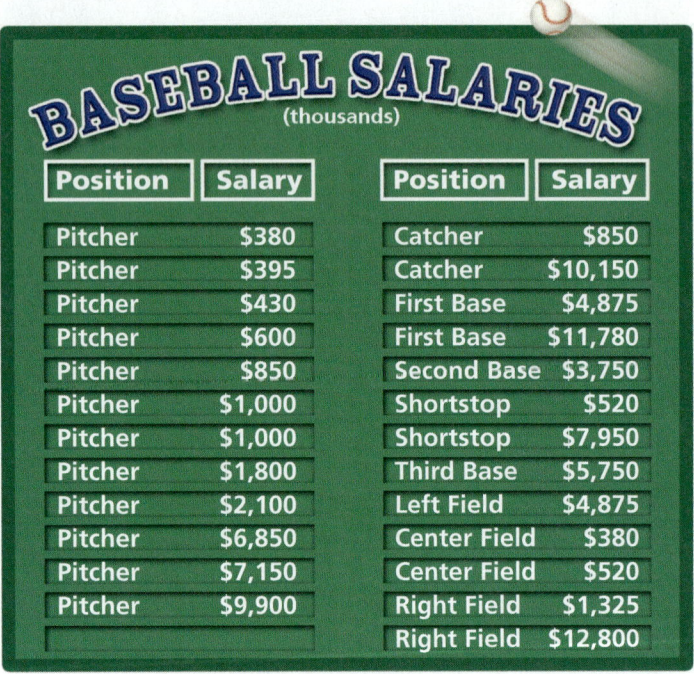

   a. Calculate the mean salary and the median salary.
   b. Why is it not useful to calculate the mode?

7. A player representing the players' union argues that the players should make more money.
   a. Which measure, the mean or the median, supports more convincingly the case for raising salaries? Explain.
   b. What makes the mean and median so different for this data set?
   c. A salary cap limits the total amount a team can spend on players' salaries. If this team has reached its salary cap, what salary adjustments would increase the mean salary? The median salary?

Maintain Your Skills

8. Describe how you obtain the data set {22, 58, 47, 62, 79, 84, 34} from {20, 56, 45, 60, 77, 82, 32}. How do the mean and the median change?

3.06 Mean, Median, and Mode

Patterns in data may not be obvious. You have to see a regularity, search for a pattern, and then be able to describe and explain the pattern you find. Sometimes you may find and describe a pattern that gives no useful results.

The best techniques for studying data may not be obvious, either. Meanings that you find may depend as much on your choice of technique as on the data.

Suppose a student collects data through an online survey of United States residents using the survey question "What generic word do you use to describe a carbonated soft drink?"

A **frequency table** is a list of categories that classifies the number of occurrences in each category. The frequency table below shows soft-drink response data from four states. Each state represents a different region of the country.

What Do You Call Carbonated Drinks?

State	"Pop"	"Soda"	"Coke"	Other
Minnesota	4265	630	39	92
New York	3321	7364	262	200
Georgia	49	346	2196	149
Washington	2678	714	105	98

SOURCE: Alan McConchie's Survey

The other choices included cola, soda pop, tonic, and many more!

The table shows that 630 Minnesotans call soft drinks *soda* while 2678 people in Washington call soft drinks *pop*.

For Discussion

1. If someone asks you what a New Yorker most likely calls a carbonated soft drink, how would you decide?

Developing Habits of Mind

Represent an average. The word *average* has many meanings in everyday language. In statistics, there are three common ways to find an average.

- **Mean**   Add the values and divide by the number of values.
- **Median**   Arrange the values in order. Then, find the middle value. If there are two middle values, find the mean of the two middle values.
- **Mode**   Find the data value that occurs most often.

3.06 Mean, Median, and Mode   223

The descriptions above tell you how to find each average. None of them tells you what each average is good for. The average you use depends on the situation. For example, the soft drink survey data are a collection of preferred words, not numbers. The only sensible average is the mode.

For You to Do

2. In the soft drink survey, what is the mode for each state? For all four states combined?

Example

A class of 20 students takes a 5-question multiple choice test. Each question is worth 20 points. The table shows the scores.

Test Scores

Score	Frequency
0	1
20	0
40	2
60	5
80	5
100	7

Notice that the sum of the frequencies, 20, is the number of students in the class.

Problem Find the mean, median, and mode.

Solution To find the mean, add the data values. Then divide by the number of values. To find the sum of the data, add the scores.

You can use the basic rules and calculate the mean using the table.

Test Scores

Score	Frequency		number of students	×	score	=	total of scores
0	1		1	×	0	=	0
20	0		0	×	20	=	0
40	2		2	×	40	=	80
60	5		5	×	60	=	300
80	5		5	×	80	=	400
100	7		7	×	100	=	700
							1480

The sum of the scores is $0 + 2(40) + 5(60) + 5(80) + 7(100) = 1480$.
The mean score is $1480 \div 20 = 74$.

To find the median, sort the data. Then find the middle value in the sorted list. Since there are 20 scores, the median breaks the scores into the top 10 scores and the bottom 10 scores. To find the median using the list below, start from the beginning of the list and count the number of scores until you count 10 scores.

$$\underbrace{0, 40, 40, 60, 60, 60, 60, 60, 80, 80,}_{\text{bottom 10}} \underbrace{80, 80, 80, 100, 100, 100, 100, 100, 100, 100}_{\text{top 10}}$$

Again, you can use a frequency table to shorten your work when you find the median.

Test Scores

Score	Frequency
0	1
20	0
40	2
60	5
80	5
100	7

score	number of students
0	1
0–20	$1 + 0 = 1$
0–40	$1 + 0 + 2 = 3$
0–60	$1 + 0 + 2 + 5 = 8$
0–80	$1 + 0 + 2 + 5 + 5 = 13$
0–100	$1 + 0 + 2 + 5 + 5 + 7 = 20$

If there are 20 scores, the median is a number between the 10th score and the 11th score. You can add the number of students in each category in the table until you reach the median score. When you start with the lowest score and reach the 10th score and 11th score, you will find that they are both 80. So the median is 80.

> Can you find the median by starting with the highest score?

To find the mode, identify the score with the highest frequency. The mode is 100, since there are 7 scores of 100, more than any other score.

Just because you can calculate each average, you cannot assume that it has any significance. The next step, interpreting what the averages mean in relation to the data set, is more important.

> You can usually decide which values will be meaningful before calculating them.

Developing Habits of Mind

Represent an average in three ways. Here are some ways to interpret the statistical test results in the previous example.

- The mode tells you the most "popular" score. The mode is most meaningful when used with data from polls, such as one taken before an election or the soft drink poll. The mode tells you who or what item is most popular.

It is not clear what the mode tells you about the data in the Example, though. The most frequently occuring test score doesn't really mean much. You might think that a mode of 100 means that the class is doing well, but the mode gives you no idea about the other grades. The remaining scores might have been failing grades, and the mode might still be 100.

- The median shows the midpoint for the number of scores. A teacher might feel good about a class median test score of 80. At least half the students scored 80 or better.

> Why does a teacher say "at least half"?

Similar to the mode, the median tells you where a particular score is. A set of data in which the first nine scores are 20 or below and the last 11 scores are 80 or above still has a median of 80. This respectable median masks the fact that too many students did not understand the test material.

- The mean gives a midpoint for the scores. If you subtract the mean from each number in the data set, and then add the differences, the sum is 0.

A mean of 74 may be a good performance on a test, but not necessarily. If 10 people score 48 and 10 people score 100, the mean is still 74.

Usually you cannot make informed decisions about data by looking at just one average. It may help to compare two averages, such as the mean and the median, to each other. You need to know more about the context of any statistics for them to be meaningful.

Exercises Practicing Habits of Mind

Check Your Understanding

1. Look at the lesson's Example about test scores. Verify that the mean is the balancing point by finding the sum of the differences between the scores and 74.

   > If you have exactly two scores, the balancing point is at the midpoint of their graphs on the number line. Using 20 scores, the balancing point is harder to see.

   a. How can you change these scores so that the mean score is 5 points higher?

   b. How can you change these scores so that the median score is 100?

2. **Standardized Test Prep** What statistical measure does a store manager use to determine the best-selling item in the store?

   A. mean   B. mode   C. range   D. median

226 Chapter 3 Graphs

3. Find the median of these five numbers.

3×10^4 5×10^3 6.02×10^{23} 8.7×10^5 62

4. Describe how you obtain each data set below from the following data set. Then describe how the mean and median change.

{20, 56, 45, 60, 77, 82, 32}

a. {19, 55, 44, 59, 76, 81, 31}

b. {30, 66, 55, 70, 87, 92, 42}

On Your Own

5. Find the mean of each pair of numbers. Graph the numbers and the mean on a number line.

a. 5 and 15

b. −5 and 15

c. −5 and −15

d. 137 and 441

6. **Standardized Test Prep** Each of 50 people bowls one game in a charity event. The table shows the results of the games.

Bowlers' Scores

Score Range	Number of Bowlers
0–50	9
51–100	12
101–150	10
151–200	13
201–250	4
251–300	2

Based on the table, which statement about the bowlers' scores is true?

A. 6% of the bowlers score more than 200.

B. 52% of the bowlers score no more than 100.

C. The median score is between 51 and 100.

D. The median score is between 101 and 150.

7. A spinner has eight zones. Each zone shows the number of coins you win for landing in that zone.

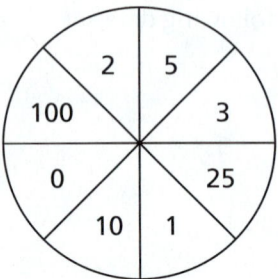

a. This game costs 4 coins for one spin. If each of the eight zones has the same probability of winning, is this a good game to play? Explain.

b. **Take It Further** A computer simulates the spinner and is programmed so that the eight zones are not equally likely. This table shows the probability of landing in each of the eight zones. What is the mean number of coins you expect to win in a single spin in this game?

Spinner Game

Zone	Probability (%)
0	17
1	40
2	15
3	10
5	10
10	5
25	2
100	1

c. **Take It Further** This game costs 4 coins for one spin, and you know the probabilities. Is this a good game to play? Explain.

Even though the balloons seem to fill the wall, the area for direct hits may be less than half the wall area.

8. Kay explains an unusual way of finding the mean of the data set {82, 68, 50, 100}.

   She says, "First I guess a mean; say it's 80. Then I find that the differences from 80 of the data values are $+2$, -12, -30, and $+20$, or a total of -20. On average, the data values are $\frac{-20}{4}$, or -5, from my guess. That means that the real mean must be $80 - 5$, or 75. Check this out. It really works!"

   a. Use Kay's method to find the mean of the set {13, 29, 19, 15, 24, 26}.

   b. **Take It Further** Explain why Kay's method works.

   c. Can you use Kay's method to find the mean of the data in Exercise 4, Lesson 3.05? Explain.

9. **Take It Further** Use the basic rules of algebra to simplify each expression.

   a. $\left(\frac{a+b}{2} - a\right) + \left(\frac{a+b}{2} - b\right)$

   b. $\left(\frac{a+b+c}{3} - a\right) + \left(\frac{a+b+c}{3} - b\right) + \left(\frac{a+b+c}{3} - c\right)$

   c. How does this exercise relate to the topic of this lesson?

10. Derman looks at his five algebra test grades for the past two months.

    Derman's Test Scores

Month	Test 1	Test 2	Test 3	Average Score
September	80	96	100	92
October	80	96		88

    He says, "I can find my average test score for September and October by taking the average of 92 and 88." Is Derman correct?

11. **Standardized Test Prep** The mean of Ampara's first five quiz scores is 77. What score does she need on the sixth quiz to raise her average to 80?

    A. 80   **B.** 83   **C.** 92   **D.** 95

Maintain Your Skills

12. a. Find the mean and median of the data set {100, -25, 3, 7, 23, 17, 15}.

    b. Add six to each data value from part (a). Find the mean and median of the resulting data set.

    c. Double each data value from part (a). Find the mean and median of the resulting data set.

    d. How do the changes in the data set relate to the changes in the mean and median?

3.07 Data Displays

In Lesson 3.06 you learned some measures of the *center of data*, including the mean and median. Knowing the center of data is important, but it is part of a larger framework, including these questions:

- How widely *spread* are the data?
- What is the rough *shape* of the data?
- Are there individual *outliers*, elements of data that are not close to the rest of the data?

Visual representations of data make it easier to answer these important questions. One simple representation is the **dot plot**. Here is a dot plot for the ages of the 21 winners of Best Actor in a Leading Role from Lesson 3.05.

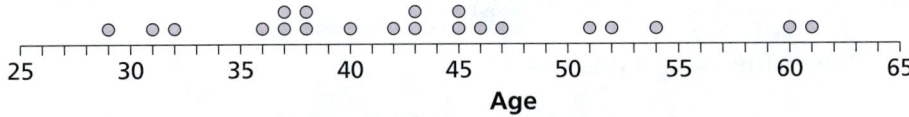

Source: Academy of Motion Picture Arts and Sciences

> Each dot is one award winner, so two people won the Best Actor award at age 37 and no one won at age 57.

A dot plot can make some observations easier, especially gaps and outliers, and gives an overall sense of the data's center, spread, and shape.

For You to Do

1. Build a dot plot for the ages of the 21 winners of Best Actress in a Leading Role from Lesson 3.05.
2. Identify any significant gaps and outliers in the data.

A similar representation is the **histogram**, which shows frequencies as bars. Unlike dot plots, which display single values, the bars of a histogram (sometimes called *bins*) may have any fixed width. Here are two histograms for the Best Actor data:

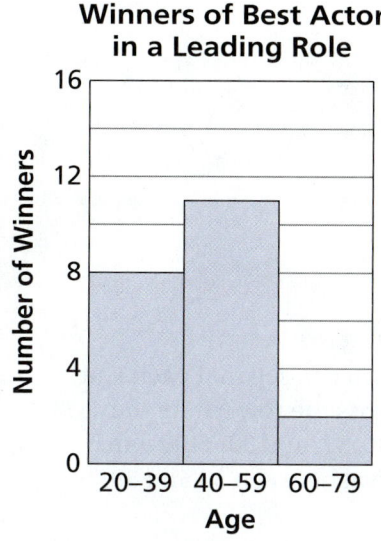

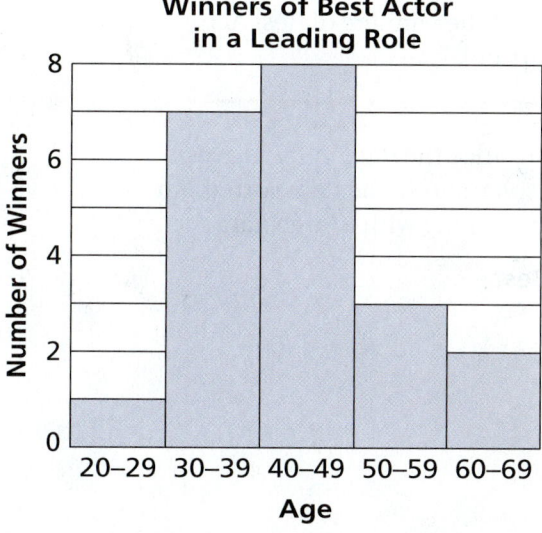

The bars of the histogram show intervals of data. The second bar tells you that seven people who won the Best Actor award were from 30 to 39 years old, since the next bar starts at 40.

Both histograms display the same data, but they have different shapes. The width of a histogram's bins can affect how well it shows the center, spread, shape, and outliers of the corresponding data. There is no single "correct" bin width for a histogram.

For Discussion

3. For the Best Actor data, describe or draw a histogram with bin width 1.
4. How can you use a histogram to estimate the mean and median of data?

You can also use a stem-and-leaf display to show data that are divided into intervals. A **stem-and-leaf display** is a graph that organizes the leading digits of data as stems. The remaining digits become leaves. Each stem typically has more than one leaf. For example, here is an unordered stem-and-leaf display for the Best Actor data from Lesson 3.05.

When you turn the stem-and-leaf display on its side, it looks similar to the histogram in this lesson with bin width 10.

Ages of Winners of Best Actor in a Leading Role

```
2 | 9
3 | 2 7 8 1 6 7 8
4 | 3 2 5 6 0 7 3 5
5 | 1 4 2
6 | 1 0
```

If you think of connecting the stem and the leaf, you can see that each leaf corresponds to a piece of data. When you read across the row where the stem is 3, you read the data values 32, 37, 38, 31, 36, 37, and 38. There are 7 data values corresponding to stem 3 in the interval between 30 and 39.

For You to Do

5. Use the stem-and-leaf display to find the ages of the winners of Best Actor in a Leading Role who were more than 50 years old.

The stem-and-leaf display above is unordered since the data in the leaves are not sorted. The ordered stem-and-leaf display shows the data sorted. An ordered stem-and-leaf display is useful when working with a large data set.

Ages of Winners of Best Actor in a Leading Role

```
2 | 9
3 | 1 2 6 7 7 8 8
4 | 0 2 3 3 5 5 6 7
5 | 1 2 4
6 | 0 1
```

For You to Do

6. Find the median age of the 21 Best Actor winners using an ordered stem-and-leaf display.

232 Chapter 3 Graphs

Exercises Practicing Habits of Mind

Check Your Understanding

1. Make a histogram for the Best Actor data in this lesson. Use bin widths of 5 years, such as 20–24 years, 25–29 years, and so on.

   For help making a histogram, see the TI-Nspire™ Handbook, p. 790.

2. In 2001, the mean family income in the United States was $66,863. The median family income was $51,407. What could account for such a wide difference between these two measures?

3. The table lists how many prime numbers exist among the first 800 positive integers.

   Prime Numbers

Interval	Number of Prime Numbers
1–100	25
101–200	21
201–300	16
301–400	16
401–500	17
501–600	14
601–700	16
701–800	14

   Remember... A prime number is a number with exactly two positive factors, 1 and itself. The number 1 is not prime, since it has only one positive factor.

   a. Make a histogram for the data.
   b. How does the number of primes change from the first interval to the last?

On Your Own

4. Use the dot plot you made of the ages of the Best Actress winners from the *For You To Do* on page 1.

   a. Determine the median age for all Best Actress winners.
   b. Estimate the mean age for all Best Actress winners.
   c. Make an ordered stem-and-leaf display.
   d. Make a histogram, and clearly mark the bin width you used.

   If a stem between the least and the greatest values has no leaves, you still include the stem in the list of values.

3.07 Data Displays 233

5. **Standardized Test Prep** The stem-and-leaf display shows the ages of 50 teachers. Based on the stem-and-leaf display, which percent of the teachers are more than 50 years old?

   Teachers' Ages

2	1 2 3 5 7
3	1 2 3 5 5 7 7 8
4	2 3 3 3 4 4 5 6 6 7 8
5	1 2 3 4 4 4 6 7 8 9 9 9
6	1 1 1 2 2 3 4 4 4 5 5 6 7 7

   A. 26%

   B. 47%

   C. 51%

   D. 52%

6. Draw a histogram for the teachers' ages in Exercise 5. Use five bins of width 10 years.

   Use this stem-and-leaf display below for Exercises 7 and 8. To decide what items to stock, a store keeps track of the ages of customers who come into the store. This stem-and-leaf display shows the data for a 15-minute period.

   Customers' Ages

0	6 7 8
1	0 1 1 1 2 2 3 4 4
2	5 8 8 8 8 8 9 9 9
3	3 4 8 9

7. **a.** Make a dot plot for the data.

   b. How many people enter the store during the 15-minute period?

   c. Using the dot plot, what do you notice as the most important feature of the data?

   d. What is the mode of the data? Explain how you can use the dot plot to find this information.

   e. The mean age in this group of customers is 21. Would you consider this a "typical" or "likely" age for a customer? Explain.

   f. How would you describe a "typical" or "likely" age for a customer in this group?

8. Plot the data in Exercise 7 using two different histograms. In one histogram, use bins of width 10 years: 0–9 years, 10–19 years, and so on. In the other histogram, use bins of width 10 years: 5–14 years, 15–24 years, and so on.

   a. What patterns of customers' ages do you find in your two histograms? What inference can you draw about the customers based on each pattern?

   b. Which of your histograms corresponds to the stem-and-leaf display?

   c. Is there anything you notice about the data that might help you decide which histogram better reflects the ages of the store's customers?

234 Chapter 3 Graphs

9. **Standardized Test Prep** The histogram shows a swim team's membership by age. How many swim team members are age 14 or older?

   A. 2
   B. 8
   C. 12
   D. 14

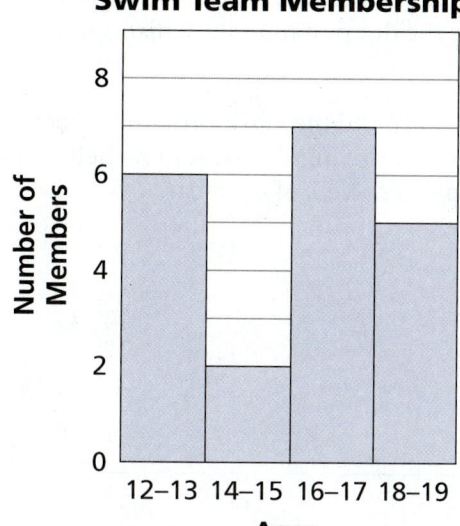

10. Gather at least 20 pennies. Find the age of each penny.
    a. Make a dot plot of the data.
    b. Make a histogram of the data using 5-year bins.

11. A histogram of the salaries for players on a professional baseball team is displayed below. The mean salary and median salary are also marked.

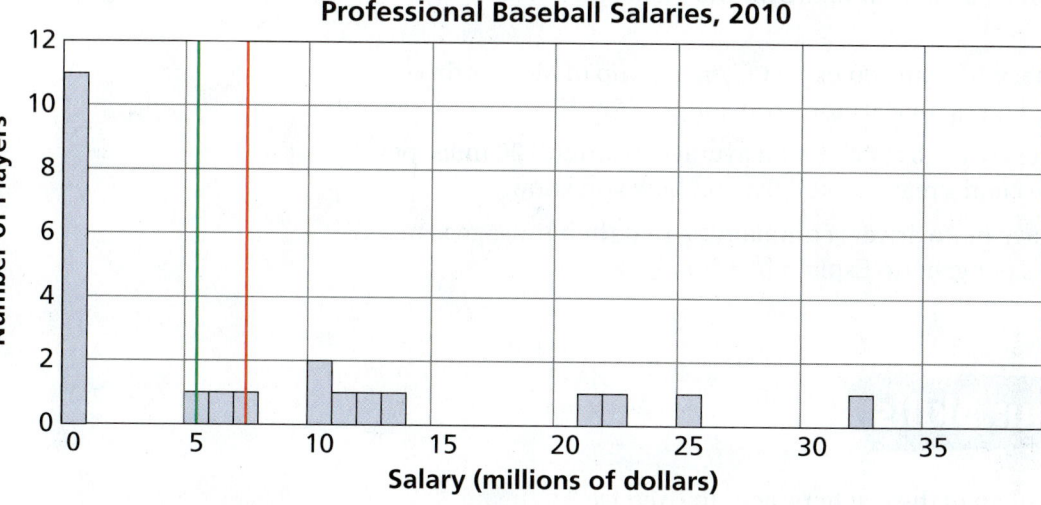

   a. Which marking is the median? Which one is the mean? How do you know?
   b. Based on the histogram, describe the overall shape of the data. Are the data clustered, symmetrical, or skewed?
   c. Identify any outliers in the data. Justify your reasoning.
   d. Explain the meaning of *median salary* to a person who doesn't understand the meaning of the term *median*.

   > What range of salaries is represented by the bin that starts at 0 and ends at 1?

3.07 Data Displays 235

12. Research the ages at inauguration of all U.S. Presidents and make a dot plot of the data. Then use the dot plot to make a histogram of the data using 5-year bins.

13. Two new cars, the Melody and the Harmony, are expected to get about 26 miles per gallon in city driving. The dot plots below show the miles per gallon for a sample of drivers of each car.

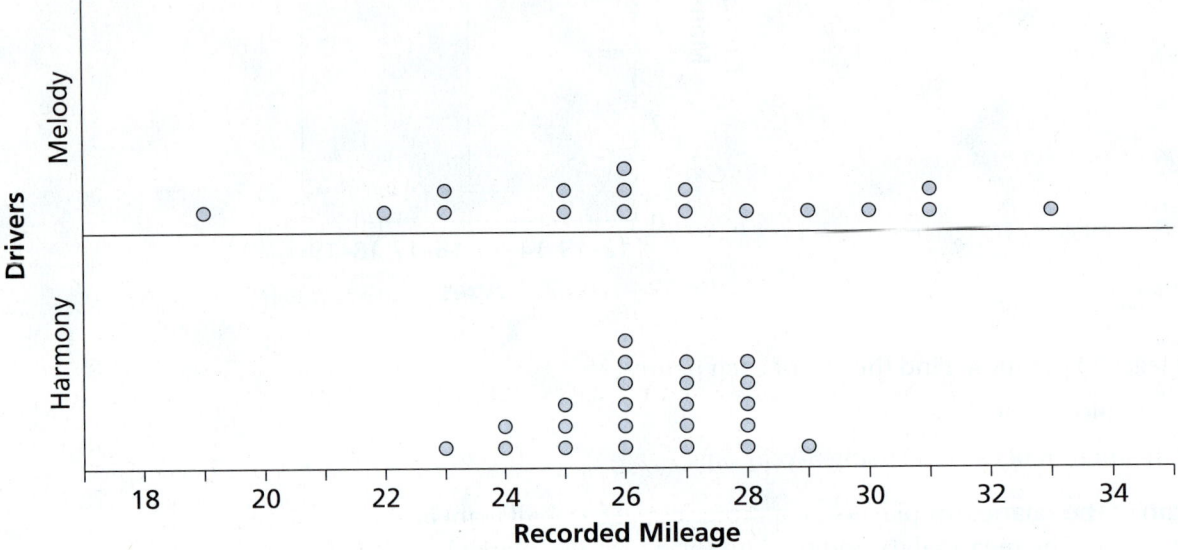

   a. How does the spread of data compare for the Melody and Harmony drivers?

   b. Based on the data, what can you expect from a group of Melody drivers that differs from a group of Harmony drivers?

   c. The manufacturers of each car claim an average of around 26 miles per gallon. Are these claims reasonable? Explain how you know.

   d. Which car will have more drivers complaining that their mileage is much less than 26 miles per gallon? Explain how you know.

Maintain Your Skills

14. a. Calculate the median of the teachers' ages in Exercise 5.

    b. Where on the histogram do you find the median for the teachers' ages? What is the relationship between the median and the pattern of the data in the histogram?

3.08 Paired Comparisons

The statistics you have learned can be very helpful when you work with two sets of comparable data. You might have sets of scores in two different classes, or the life expectancies of men and women. Paired comparisons give you powerful visual representations of data that you can use to make at-a-glance comparisons and interpretations of two data sets.

You can display and compare the results from two data sets using a **box-and-whisker plot.** Before you make the plot, you analyze the data using the five-number summary. The **five-number summary** is an overview of a sorted set of data that uses five numbers.

- The **minimum** is the least value.
- The **first quartile** is the data value that is greater than or equal to the lowest 25% of the data values.
- The **median** is the middle value of the sorted data set.
- The **third quartile** is the data value that is greater than or equal to the lowest 75% of the data values.
- The **maximum** is the greatest value.

These five numbers give the overall shape of a data set, since they split the data into four equal parts. Equal numbers of elements from the data set are in all of the four intervals between the summary numbers.

> Why do you think that you call this the third quartile? Is there a second quartile?

Developing Habits of Mind

Establish a process. To find the median, sort the data. The process depends on whether you have an odd or even number of elements.

- If an odd number of elements are in the data set, the median is the single value in the middle of the sorted list.
- If an even number of elements are in the data set, two elements are in the middle of the sorted list. The mean of those two numbers is the median.

The median splits the data set into two sets, the upper half and the lower half of the set. If the number of data points in the original set of data is odd, then the median is not in either set. In each data set, take the data above or below the median, even if some of the data points have the same value as the median. You can determine each quartile by finding the median of each of the two sets.

- To find the first quartile, find the median of the lower half of the data.
- To find the third quartile, find the median of the upper half of the data.

> **Remember...**
> You need to sort the data before calculating the median and quartiles!

Example

The table shows the life expectancies at birth for males and females in 14 countries having names that start with the letter A. Ages are rounded to the nearest year.

Life Expectancy at Birth

Country	Male	Female
Afghanistan	43	43
Albania	75	80
Algeria	72	75
American Samoa	72	80
Andorra	81	87
Angola	37	40
Anguilla	74	80
Antigua and Barbuda	70	75
Argentina	72	80
Armenia	68	76
Aruba	76	83
Australia	78	84
Austria	76	82
Azerbaijan	60	68

SOURCE: *The World Fact Book*, 2007

Problem Find the five-number summary for the life expectancy of females in these 14 countries.

Solution Sort the 14 data values from lowest to highest. The median is between the seventh and eighth values.

40, 43, 68, 75, 75, 76, 80, 80, 80, 80, 82, 83, 84, 87

Another way to find the two middle values is to cross out values at alternating ends of the list until only two are left.

~~40~~ 43 68 75 75 76 80 80 80 80 82 83 84 ~~87~~
~~40~~ ~~43~~ 68 75 75 76 80 80 80 80 82 83 ~~84~~ ~~87~~

⋮

~~40~~ ~~43~~ ~~68~~ ~~75~~ ~~75~~ 76 80 80 80 ~~80~~ ~~82~~ ~~83~~ ~~84~~ ~~87~~
~~40~~ ~~43~~ ~~68~~ ~~75~~ ~~75~~ ~~76~~ 80 80 ~~80~~ ~~80~~ ~~82~~ ~~83~~ ~~84~~ ~~87~~

The two middle numbers are 80 and 80. The median is their average, 80.

The first quartile is the middle value in the list below the median. The third quartile is the middle value in the list above the median.

40 43 68 75 75 76 80   80 80 80 82 83 84 87

The first quartile is 75. The third quartile is 82.

The maximum and minimum values are the first and last numbers in the sorted list. The five-number summary is below.
- minimum   40
- first quartile (Q_1)   75
- median   80
- third quartile (Q_3)   82
- maximum   87

> **Remember...**
> The symbols Q_1 and Q_3 stand for the first and third quartiles.

For Discussion

1. Without calculating, can you tell whether the mean age for the 14 female life expectancies is greater than or less than 80? Explain.

You can find two basic measures of the spread of data using the five-number summary. One measure is the **range,** which is the difference between the maximum and minimum of the data. The other measure is the **interquartile range** (IQR), which is the difference between the third quartile (Q_3) and first quartile (Q_1). The range covers 100 percent of the data. The interquartile range covers the middle 50 percent.

You can present the five-number summary graphically using a box-and-whisker plot. This plot gives you some control over larger data sets. Here is a box-and-whisker plot for the data from the Example with directions for making the plot.

> For help drawing a box-and-whisker plot, see the TI-Nspire Handbook, p. 790.

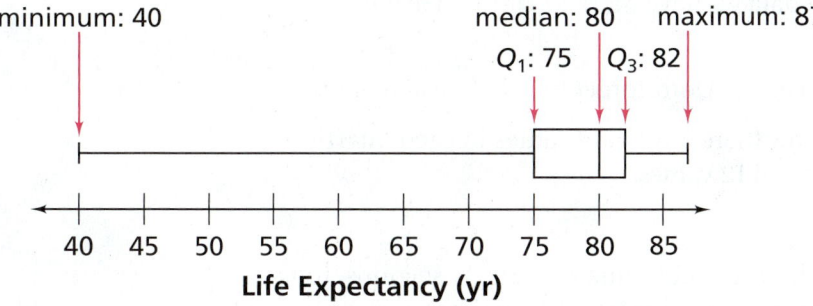

- Find the five-number summary.
- At each of the five numbers, draw a short vertical segment above a number line.
- Draw a box from the first to the third quartile representing the interquartile range. The vertical segment for the median is inside the box.
- Draw segments (whiskers) to connect the box to the minimum and maximum values.

A box-and-whisker plot gives additional information about the five-number summary. For example, the plot shows that there is a wide range of data between the minimum and the first quartile. The range of data is less between the first and third quartiles.

Minds in Action episode 9

Sasha and Tony talk about the stopwatch experiment in Lesson 3.05.

Sasha So, we had 12 people try the experiment.

Tony Is there a table of how everyone did?

Sasha Sure, here are the two tries for each person.

Elapsed Time Estimates

Time 1	Time 2	Time 1	Time 2
28	36	29	31
26	35	24	27
7	27	23	32
24	28	29	26
26	37	31	34
14	30	24	31

Tony Wow, only one person hit 30 seconds exactly.

Sasha Right, it seems that most people counted 30 seconds too quickly the first time.

Tony Some counted way too quickly! Okay, I'll make a box-and-whisker plot for the data we have marked Time 1. We'll see what it looks like.

Sasha I'll do the same for Time 2. Don't forget to sort everything first.

Tony Sure thing. I also know there are 3 data values in each quartile, since there are a total of 12 values.

They work for awhile.

Sasha Okay, I think we're done. I'll add a line to mark 30 seconds, too, since that's the time everyone was trying to estimate.

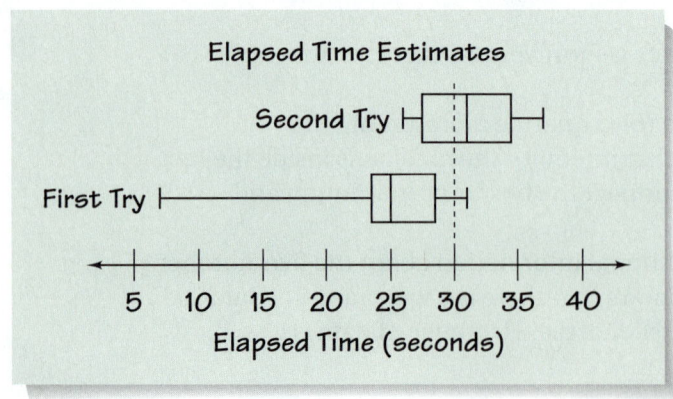

Why might it be difficult to tell how many seconds have elapsed with a 30-second timer?

Tony The plots really show the differences between the first try and the second try. Almost no one counted a full 30 seconds on the first try, but the median is more than 30 seconds on the second try!

Sasha I think it's interesting that the middle half of the data is still about as wide as it was before. I was expecting it to be more narrow.

Tony Yes, but overall, the spread is narrower. The second try doesn't show any crazy points that are far away from the rest.

Sasha That's true. In any case, putting the plots next to each other helps make these comparisons easy.

For Discussion

2. Using Sasha and Tony's box-and-whisker plot, which set of data has a wider interquartile range?

Since box-and-whisker plots provide a quick look at the shape of a data set, they are particularly well suited for paired comparison. Using these plots, you can quickly demonstrate that one data set is significantly different from another data set.

Exercises Practicing Habits of Mind

Check Your Understanding

1. **Standardized Test Prep** Which statement best interprets the data set {20, 15, 10, 20, 15, 10, 20, 20, 50}?

   A. Only the mean is 20.

   B. The range of the set of data is 20.

   C. The mean, median, and mode are all 20.

   D. The mode and median are not the same.

3.08 Paired Comparisons

2. Using the data from the stopwatch experiment in Lesson 3.05, calculate the five-number summary for two data sets. The data sets are the first try and the second try at estimating 30 seconds.

3. Use the five-number summaries from Exercise 2 to make a paired box-and-whisker plot of the two data sets. Describe at least two differences between the data sets that the box-and-whisker plots show.

4. Each of two data sets has a median of 80. Set A has twice the interquartile range of Set B.

   a. Draw a possible paired box-and-whisker plot for Set A and Set B.

   b. Is it possible for the maximum value in Set A to be less than the maximum value in Set B, even though Set A has a greater interquartile range? Explain.

5. **Take It Further** The data set {61, 67, 70, 70, 76, 79, 80, 82, 84, 88, 91, 92, 95} has a median of 80.

   Describe a rule that makes a different data set that doubles the interquartile range but leaves the median, 80, unchanged.

   An example of a rule that makes a different data set: Add 5 to each data value and then double the sum.

On Your Own

6. Can you find each measure below using only a box-and-whisker plot? Explain.

   a. mean b. median c. mode d. range

7. **Standardized Test Prep** The box-and-whisker plot below shows the heights of 20 players on a school soccer team.

   Players' Heights

   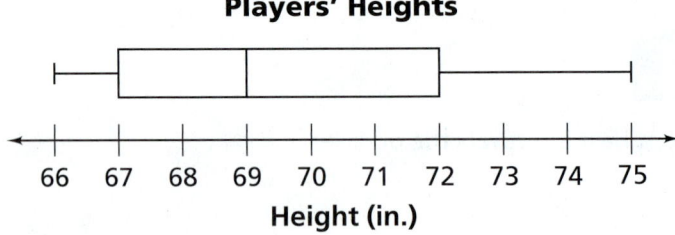

   Height (in.)

   Based on the information in the box-and-whisker plot, which of the following statements must be true?

   A. The mean height of the team is 69 inches.

   B. Half of the players' heights are between 67 and 72 inches.

   C. The height of the shortest player on the team is 67 inches.

   D. The range of players' heights is 5 inches.

8. **Write About It** Describe the steps you use to calculate the five-number summary for the 14 male life expectancies on page 238.

9. Here is the five-number summary for the 14 male life expectancies on page 238.
   - Minimum   37
   - First quartile (Q_1)   68
   - Median   72
   - Third quartile (Q_3)   76
   - Maximum   81

   Make paired box-and-whisker plots for the male and female life expectancies in the 14 countries. Describe what the plots show about the data sets.

   > The five-number summary for female life expectancies is on page 239.

10. **Standardized Test Prep** Felipe made this box-and-whisker plot using the heights of 40 baseball players.

    Heights of Baseball Players

    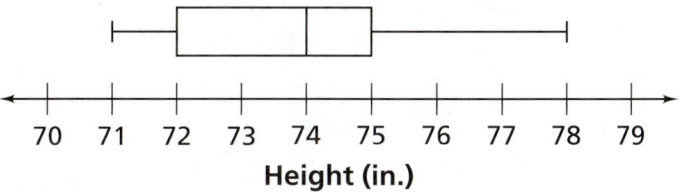

    Height (in.)

    Which of the following conclusions can you NOT draw from the box-and-whisker plot?

    A. The range of players' heights is 7 inches.

    B. At least 30 players are six feet tall or taller.

    C. The mean height of the 40 players is 74 inches.

    D. One quarter of the players are at least 6 feet 3 inches tall.

The median height of the nine players is the height of the fifth-tallest (or fifth-shortest) player.

11. **Write About It** The paired box-and-whisker plots show the test scores from two different classes on the same test.

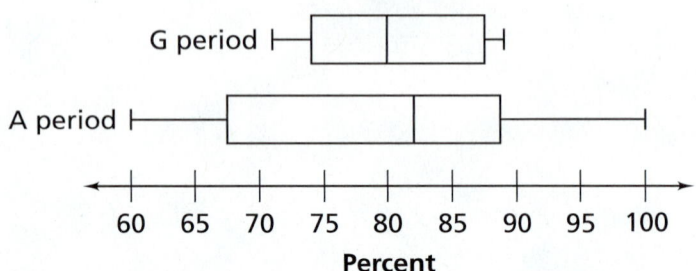

Based on the data, in which class would you prefer to be? Explain.

12. **Take It Further** Five numbers are in the data set {16, 4, 6, 2, x}. The mean and median are the same number. What are the possible values of x?

Maintain Your Skills

What is the mean of each data set?

13. {1, 2, 3}
14. {1, 2, 3, 4}
15. {1, 2, 3, 4, 5}
16. {1, 2, 3, 4, 5, . . . , n}
17. {2, 4, 6, 8, 10, . . . , 2n}

3.09 Categorical Data

So far, you have used number lines as tools to organize quantitative data, such as with dot plots and box-and-whisker plots. But *categorical data*, like yes-or-no answers to a survey, are not organized this way. In this lesson, you will learn some ways to deal with data organized into categories and some concepts that apply when more than one data variable is present.

In-Class Experiment

At a school, administrators are thinking about starting and ending the school day one hour later. A teacher was concerned that athletes may feel differently about this possibility than non-athletes. She conducted a survey of students in her class. She recorded whether or not they played a sport, and their response (*agree* or *disagree*) to the statement "Classes should start and end one hour later." Here are the responses from this study:

Study on School Start and End Times

Athlete or Non-Athlete?	Agree or Disagree?	Athlete or Non-Athlete?	Agree or Disagree?
Athlete	Agree	Athlete	Agree
Athlete	Disagree	Non-Athlete	Disagree
Non-Athlete	Agree	Athlete	Disagree
Non-Athlete	Disagree	Non-Athlete	Agree
Athlete	Agree	Non-Athlete	Agree
Athlete	Agree	Athlete	Agree
Non-Athlete	Disagree	Athlete	Disagree
Non-Athlete	Agree	Athlete	Disagree
Athlete	Disagree	Non-Athlete	Agree
Athlete	Disagree	Athlete	Disagree
Athlete	Agree	Non-Athlete	Disagree
Athlete	Agree	Athlete	Agree

1. Find a way to organize the responses numerically. Describe what you did.

2. Write a ratio of the number of athletes who agree with the statement to the total number of athletes.

3. Write a ratio of the number of athletes who agree with the statement to the total number of students who agree with the statement.

For the survey, there are two *categorical variables:*

- Are you an athlete or a non-athlete?
- Do you agree or disagree with the statement?

A **two-way frequency table** displays the distribution for two categorical variables. The frequency of responses for another group is displayed below.

	Athlete	Non-Athlete
Agree	10	5
Disagree	6	3

Each entry of this two-way table is the number (frequency) of students in a specific category for each variable. The table indicates that 10 of the 24 students in this group are athletes *and* agree with the statement.

Example

The frequency table below includes the results for a larger sample of students than the one in the In-Class Experiment.

	Athlete	Non-Athlete
Agree	31	23
Disagree	44	19

Problem

a. Write a ratio of the number of athletes who agree with the statement "Classes should start and end one hour later" to the total number of athletes.

b. Write a ratio of the number of students surveyed who agree with the statement to the total number of students surveyed.

Solution

a. 31 athletes agree, and 44 athletes disagree: there are 75 total athletes. The ratio of athletes who agree to all athletes is $\frac{31}{75}$, or about 41.3%.

b. For a complete count it makes sense to extend the table by adding totals.

The 42 responses from non-athletes *do not matter* in this part of the problem.

	Athlete	Non-Athlete	Total
Agree	31	23	54
Disagree	44	19	63
Total	75	42	117

Habits of Mind

Read tables carefully. Sometimes, entries may be totaled in one direction but not the other.

54 students agree, and 63 students disagree: there are 117 total responses. The ratio of students who agree to all students is $\frac{54}{117}$, or about 46.2%.

For You to Do

4. What percent of non-athletes agreed with the statement?

5. What percent of those who agreed with the statement were non-athletes?

In the survey, non-athletes were more likely than athletes to agree with the statement. For this reason, you can say there is an **association** between the two types of students and their responses to the statement.

> Association is also known as a *correlation*.

Often, variables have no association. If the percents of athletes and non-athletes who agreed with the statement were not significantly different, you could say the two variables are *not associated*, or **independent**.

To determine whether two categorical variables have an association, look at the distribution of one variable for each outcome of the second variable. Consider these two questions:

- What percent of athletes agree with the statement?
- What percent of non-athletes agree with the statement?

If the answers to these two questions are significantly different, then whether or not a student is an athlete is *associated* with whether or not the student agrees with the change. If the answers to these two questions are not significantly different, then the two categorical variables are independent. Two-way frequency tables help answer these questions quickly.

Habits of Mind

Use precise language. For now, there is no precise way to say what is a *significant* difference and what isn't. Essentially, a difference is significant if it is too rare to occur by chance. You'll revisit this concept in a later course, along with a more detailed definition of *independent*.

For Discussion

6. Think of two categorical variables you might expect to be independent. How would you determine if the variables are actually independent?

Developing Habits of Mind

Connect data and probability. Two-way frequency tables isolate data by category, and make it easier to answer *conditional* questions, such as "If you look only at athletes, what fraction agree with the statement?" Each row or column in a two-way frequency table is a *conditional distribution* made from a part of the original data.

The same concept also applies in probability. Consider a deck of cards, and the question "If a drawn card is not a jack, what is the probability that it is a face card?" A two-way frequency table can help you to analyze this question by listing the number of outcomes in each category:

3.09 Categorical Data

	Jack	Not a Jack	Total
Face Card	4	8	12
Not a Face Card	0	40	40
Total	4	48	52

Remember...
There are 52 cards in a standard deck. The deck has 12 face cards: 4 jacks, 4 queens, 4 kings. The other 40 cards have 4 of each number from ace (one) through ten.

According to the two-way frequency table, there are 48 cards that are not jacks, and 8 of those are face cards. If a drawn card is not a jack, the probability that it is a face card is $\frac{8}{48}$, or $\frac{1}{6}$.

If a card *is* a jack, the probability that it is a face card is $\frac{4}{4} = 1$, a certainty. The probability of drawing a face card changes, depending on whether it is or isn't a jack. These conditional probabilities are different, and the two events (drawing a jack, drawing a face card) are not independent.

In this example, you can calculate exact probabilities, but a lot of data come from samples, studies, and surveys. The percentages reported by data can be used to estimate long-term probabilities. Keep in mind that estimates can change or improve with more data.

For You to Do

7. If a drawn card is a face card, what is the probability that it is a jack?

8. If a drawn card is *not* a face card, what is the probability that it is a jack?

Exercises Practicing Habits of Mind

Check Your Understanding

1. Refer to the survey from the Example on page 9. What does each of the following fractions tell you in the context of the survey?

a. $\frac{54}{117}$ b. $\frac{42}{117}$ c. $\frac{23}{42}$ d. $\frac{23}{54}$ e. $\frac{23}{117}$

2. Tess claims that athletes are more likely than non-athletes to agree with the statement from the Example on page 9.

Tess: 31 athletes agreed with the idea, but only 23 non-athletes agreed. It looks like athletes are more likely to agree, which surprises me.

Give an argument supporting or rejecting Tess's claim. Are athletes actually more likely to agree than non-athletes?

3. A teacher recorded the gender of 100 students, and whether or not they were wearing a watch. This two-way frequency table shows the results.

	Wearing Watch	No Watch
Male	13	44
Female	9	34
Total	22	78

> Why is it not enough to say that more males wore watches?

Which gender was more likely to wear a watch, males or females? Explain how you know.

4. In a study on a flu vaccine, of the 1000 people who received the flu vaccine, 149 still developed the flu. Of the 402 people who did not get the flu vaccine, 68 got the flu.

   a. Create a frequency table to summarize the results of this study.

   b. Do you think the vaccine helped reduce the occurrence of the flu? Provide evidence for your conclusions.

> The two variables are the vaccine and the flu, and there are four possible situations.

5. Here is a two-way frequency table with variables where values should be:

	Left-Handed	Right-Handed
Male	a	c
Female	b	d

   a. Fill in the values of a, b, c, and d in a way that makes the two categorical variables independent. Explain how you know they are independent.

   b. In terms of the variables given, write a ratio of the number of left-handed people who are male to the number of males.

   c. In terms of the variables given, write a ratio of the number of right-handed people who are male to the number of males.

   d. In terms of the variables given, write a ratio of the number of males to the total number of people.

6. **Take It Further** For the two-way frequency table in Exercise 5, show that if the ratio of left-handed males to males equals the ratio of right-handed males to males, then the number of males who are left-handed equals the number of males who are right-handed.

7. Complete the two-way frequency table below for integers n from 1 to 100, and determine if the categorical variables are associated.

	Prime	Not Prime
$1 \leq n < 25$	■	■
$25 \leq n \leq 100$	■	■

> **Remember...**
> 1 is not a prime number, but 2 and 3 are. Prime numbers have exactly two factors.

On Your Own

For Exercises 8–12, use the table below. It shows the results of a survey of students that was conducted to learn more about whether eye dominance is associated with other traits, such as handedness, gender, or being an athlete.

Survey Results

Name	Location	Eyedness	Handedness	Athlete	Gender
Elham Y	Connecticut	Right	Right	Yes	Female
Michael B	Connecticut	Right	Right	Yes	Male
Danielle S	L. A.	Right	Right	Yes	Female
Frederic P	Connecticut	Right	Left	Yes	Male
Jessica Y	L. A.	Left	Right	No	Female
Kaily W	Connecticut	Right	Left	Yes	Female
Anmol A	L. A.	Right	Right	Yes	Male
Aaron B	Connecticut	Right	Right	Yes	Male
Sahar B	L. A.	Right	Left	Yes	Female
Sam S	L. A.	Right	Right	No	Male
Alex S	L. A.	Right	Right	Yes	Male
Mitchell O	L. A.	Left	Right	Yes	Male
Alex L	L. A.	Left	Right	No	Male
Christian K	Connecticut	Left	Right	Yes	Male
Mariana B	L. A.	Right	Right	Yes	Female
Anna R	L. A.	Left	Right	No	Female
Nicolai S	L. A.	Right	Right	No	Male
Olivia A	Connecticut	Left	Right	Yes	Female
Matt W	L. A.	Left	Right	Yes	Male
Ben S	L. A.	Left	Right	Yes	Male
James C	Connecticut	Left	Left	No	Male
Susannah W	Connecticut	Right	Right	No	Female
Rae W	L. A.	Left	Left	Yes	Female
Will D	L. A.	Left	Right	Yes	Male

Most people are either left-eyed or right-eyed. You can find out which you are by holding your hands in front of you while looking at an object 10 to 15 feet away. Make a small space between your hands to see through to the object, and then close your right eye. If you can still see the object, you are left-eyed. If the object is hidden, open your right eye and close your left eye. If you can see the object now, you are right-eyed.

There are five categorical variables in this survey:
- Do you live in Los Angeles or Connecticut?
- Are you left-eyed or right-eyed?
- Are you left-handed or right-handed?
- Do you play a sport (yes or no)?
- Are you male or female?

8. Build a two-way frequency table to determine whether there is an association between location and eye dominance.

9. Build a two-way frequency table to determine whether there is an association between eye dominance and being an athlete.

10. Choose any two categorical variables and build a two-way frequency table to determine whether there is an association between them.

11. The following two-way frequency table came from a larger survey than the one on page 13.

	Athlete	Non-Athlete	Total
Left-Eyed	11	16	27
Right-Eyed	41	17	58
Total	52	33	85

    a. In this survey, which group of students was more likely to be left-eyed: athletes or non-athletes? Describe the calculations you used.

    b. Are the categorical variables of eye dominance and athletic status associated? Explain how you know.

12. Katrina noticed something unusual about the data.

    Katrina: It looks like there might be an association between being left-handed and being from Connecticut! That's very strange.

    a. What fraction of students from Connecticut were left-handed?
    b. What fraction of students from Los Angeles were left-handed?
    c. **Reflect and Write** Do you think there is an association between handedness and location? What might you do to investigate this further?

13. Suggest two categorical variables you expect to be associated, and explain why you expect this.

14. Suggest two categorical variables you expect to be independent, and explain why you expect this.

15. Conduct a survey of at least 25 people on your categorical variables from Exercise 13 or 14. Then decide whether the categorical variables are associated or independent.

Maintain Your Skills

Exercises 16–18 use the life expectancy data from Lesson 3.08.

16. For the 14 countries, determine the mean life expectancy for:
    a. men
    b. women

17. Complete this two-way frequency table.

	Male Expectancy Below Mean	Male Expectancy Above Mean	Total
Female Expectancy Above Mean	■	■	■
Female Expectancy Below Mean	■	■	■
Total	■	■	■

18. Do you think there is an association between male and female life expectancy? Explain.

3.10 Two-Variable Data

In Lesson 3.08, Sasha and Tony made two box-and-whisker plots for the stopwatch experiment. Each plot represents a single set of data, either the times for the first try or the times for the second try.

You can think of the two times for each person as a coordinate pair: (time 1, time 2). Then, you can represent the two data sets together as a **scatter plot**, a graph showing each pair of related data as a point in the coordinate plane.

A scatter plot can be used to identify trends and *outliers*, data points that are significantly different from the rest of the data. An outlier could occur for many reasons, such as an inaccurate measurement or an unusual situation.

Habits of Mind

Use precise language. Deciding which points are *significantly* different from the rest is a challenge. For now, use your best judgment to decide.

Minds in Action   episode 10

Sasha and Tony continue talking about the stopwatch experiment in Lesson 3.05.

Sasha Let's try a scatter plot. I'll draw a blank coordinate grid. We can draw a point for each person.

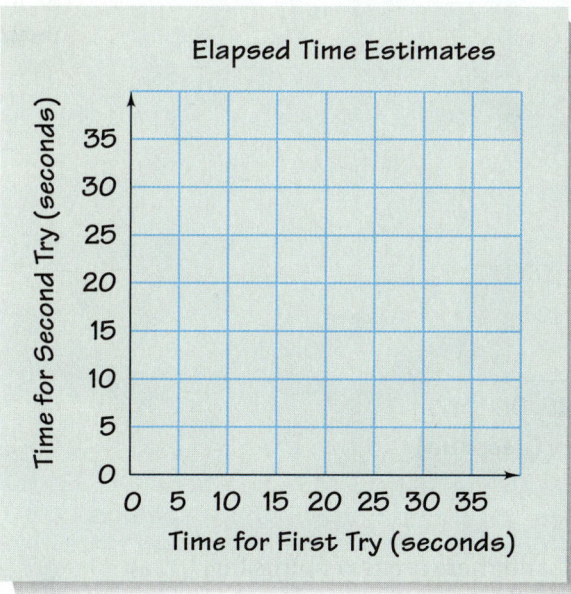

Tony The data are positive for both variables, so we really only need the first quadrant.

Sasha The first person estimates 28 seconds the first time and 36 seconds the second time. We'll draw the first point at (28, 36).

3.10 Two-Variable Data 253

Tony Does this look right?

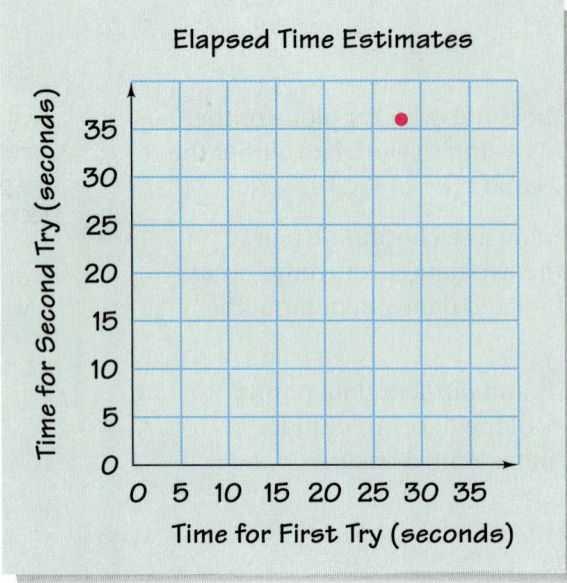

Sasha Yes. Find 28 seconds on the horizontal axis and 36 seconds on the vertical axis. Let's do the rest to get the final scatter plot.

They plot all 12 points.

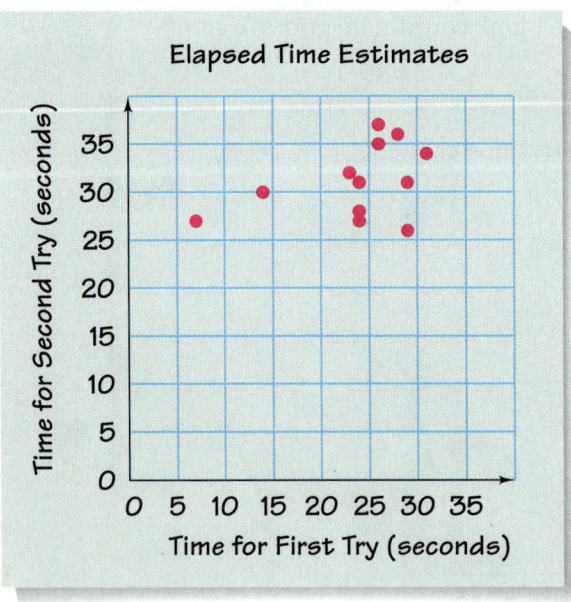

> Sasha and Tony are plotting time on the second try against time on the first try. Should they connect the dots?

Tony Most of the data seem clumped, and there are two points far to the left. I guess those are the outliers.

Sasha I agree. Those two were way too fast their first time. Actually, I think almost everyone was faster on their first try.

Tony Oh, and we could see that on the graph, by drawing a diagonal line through (0, 0) and (30, 30)!

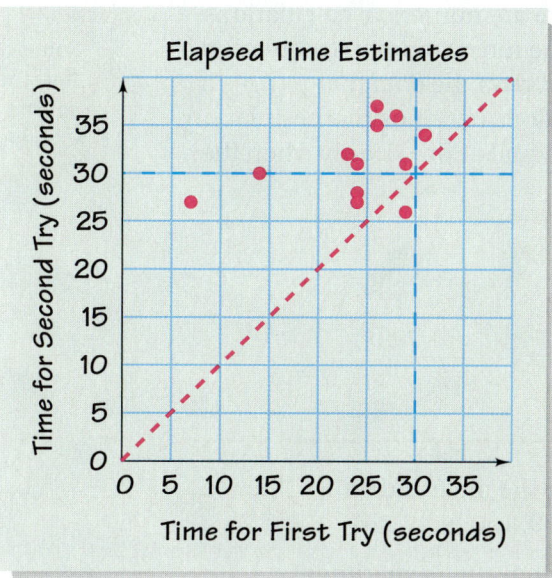

Sasha Great job, Tony. Scatter plots seem pretty useful for analysis. And all we're doing is plotting one variable against another.

For You to Do

1. Build a scatter plot for the 14 countries' life expectancy data from Lesson 3.08. Each point's coordinates are the life expectancies for men and women in a particular country.

2. Describe any pattern you see in the scatter plot.

When you can see patterns in a scatter plot, there is an **association** between the two variables. Most associations can be described as *positive* or *negative*.

Definition

Two variables are **positively associated** when large values of the first variable tend to occur with large values of the second, and small values of the first variable tend to occur with small values of the second.

Two variables are **negatively associated** when large values of the first variable tend to occur with small values of the second, and small values of the first variable tend to occur with large values of the second.

For Discussion

3. Explain why there is a positive association for life expectancies for the 14 countries in the scatter plot from the *For You to Do*.

4. Consider the data for the stopwatch experiment. Is there a positive association between the two variables, a negative association, or neither? Explain how you know.

Associations can be strong or weak, and there are numerical calculations that measure the strength of associations. The most common calculation is the **correlation coefficient**, a calculation based on the data that returns a number between −1 and 1. Positive associations have positive correlation coefficients, and the correlation coefficient equals 1 or −1 only when the entire scatter plot lies on a straight line.

> Some calculators can find the correlation coefficient for two variables.

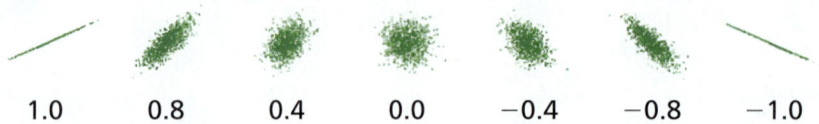

1.0   0.8   0.4   0.0   −0.4   −0.8   −1.0

For You to Do

5. One of these is the correlation coefficient for the male and female life expectancy data: −1, −0.99, −0.4, 0, 0.4, 0.99, 1. Which is it?

6. Estimate the correlation coefficient for the stopwatch experiment.

Developing Habits of Mind

Reason about calculations. Here are two common pitfalls to avoid when thinking about association and correlation:

- When the correlation coefficient is very close to 1 or −1, it suggests a strong linear association between the two variables. However, the correlation coefficient does not detect nonlinear associations. Consider the following data:

x	−3	−2	−1	0	1	2	3
y	9	4	1	0	1	4	9

Plotting these points shows a clear association: all the points make the equation $y = x^2$ true.

The correlation coefficient for these 7 data points is exactly zero! There is no *linear* association between these variables, but there is still an association.

- When two variables have an association, it does not mean that a change in one *causes* a change in the other. For example, life expectancies for men and women are positively associated, but this does not mean that male life expectancy is high *because* female life expectancy is high!

> What are some possible causes of higher or lower life expectancy in different countries?

This is a very common fallacy in statistics. **Correlation does not imply causation.** For an example, see Exercise 6.

Some of the work in an advanced statistics class involves learning how to properly determine causation. It involves eliminating other possible causes for the association.

Exercises Practicing Habits of Mind

Check Your Understanding

1. Use the data from your stopwatch experiment in Lesson 3.05. Make a scatter plot similar to the plot shown in episode 10.

2. Use the scatter plot in Exercise 1. Find the percent of students in your class who are too fast the first time and too slow the second time.

   For help drawing a scatter plot, see the TI-Nspire Handbook, p. 790.

3. Here is a table showing the horsepower of several cars, as well as their fuel efficiency in miles per gallon.

Horsepower	110	255	198	173	292	197	155	202	209	210	332	210	194	200	266	170
Miles per Gallon	40	15	35	16	22	16	34	15	27	13	20	14	16	13	17	17

   Make a scatter plot showing the horsepower on the horizontal axis and the fuel efficiency on the vertical axis.

   a. Is there a positive association between these two variables? A negative association?

   b. Estimate the correlation coefficient for these variables.

4. Here is a table of the results of the United States Census for the years 1900 through 1990.

   a. Make a scatter plot. Show the years from 1900 to 2000 on the horizontal axis. Show the population from 0 to 300 million people on the vertical axis.

   b. Based on the scatter plot, guess the U.S. population in the years 1890 and 2000.

United States Population

Year	Population (millions)
1900	76.2
1910	92.2
1920	106.0
1930	123.2
1940	132.2
1950	151.3
1960	179.3
1970	203.3
1980	226.5
1990	248.7

SOURCE: United States Census Bureau

The United States Census Bureau conducts a census every ten years, as required by the United States Constitution. The first census occurred in 1790.

5. A person's *arm span* is the distance between their fingertips when their arms are at their widest.

   a. Estimate the correlation coefficient between *height* and *arm span*. Explain your estimate.

   b. Measure the heights and arm spans of at least 10 people. Make a scatter plot showing the data.

   c. Estimate the correlation coefficient for the data. How does this compare with your estimate from part (a)?

   d. In your sample, which was more likely, being taller or shorter than your arm span? Explain how you know.

3.10 Two-Variable Data 257

6. Here is a table of several countries' life expectancies, along with the number of televisions per 1000 people in those countries.

Country	Life Expectancy	TVs per 1000 People
Argentina	75.3	201.1
Australia	81.2	505.2
Bermuda	80.7	1009.7
Brazil	72.4	196.1
Canada	80.7	655.4
China	73.0	306.2
Egypt	71.3	99.3
Ethiopia	52.9	9.3
France	80.7	573.7
Germany	79.4	623.6
Hong Kong	82.2	266.7
Iceland	81.8	330.3
India	64.7	58.3
Italy	80.5	521.5
Japan	82.6	678.9
Malta	79.4	702.5
Mexico	76.2	241.0
Spain	80.9	401.6
Sweden	80.9	511.0
Switzerland	81.7	442.0
United Kingdom	79.4	504.6
United States	78.3	740.5

Make a scatter plot showing the life expectancy on the horizontal axis and the number of televisions per 1000 people on the vertical axis.

   a. Is there a positive association between these two variables? A negative association?

   b. **Write About It** Derman says the data make it clear that television helps people live longer. What would you say to him?

On Your Own

Another measure of association is called the Quadrant Count Ratio, or QCR. On a scatter plot, draw vertical and horizontal lines at the mean of each variable. This scatter plot shows the 14 countries' life expectancy data from Lesson 3.08, along with lines marking the means:

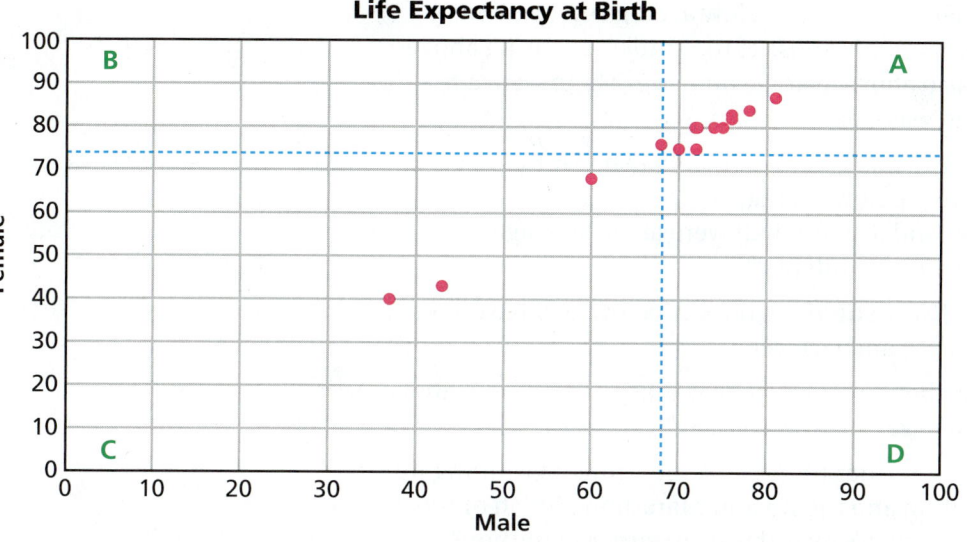

There are two points at (72, 80), but you can only see one.

The QCR counts the difference between the number of data points with positive and negative associations, and then divides by the total:

$$\text{QCR} = \frac{(\text{number of points in A and C}) - (\text{number of points in B and D})}{(\text{number of points})}$$

7. Determine the QCR for the life expectancy data.

8. **a.** What are the maximum and minimum possible values for QCR? Explain.

   b. Draw two scatter plots, one in which QCR is very close to zero, and one in which QCR is as negative as possible.

Remember...
While the name of QCR includes *quadrant* because of the four zones, *quadrant* normally refers to the four parts of the coordinate plane.

9. **a.** Copy and complete this two-way table for the data from Exercise 3:

	Horsepower Below Mean	Horsepower Above Mean
Miles per Gallon Above Mean	▪	▪
Miles per Gallon Below Mean	▪	▪

You will need to compute the mean of each variable. How does the two-way table compare to the scatter plot from Exercise 3?

   b. Use the two-way table to compute the QCR for these variables.

10. Match each verbal statement with the value of QCR it best matches. Drawing sample scatter plots might help you decide.

    QCR values: −1   0   0.33   0.81   1

    a. Mrs. A: "Every student who was below average on test 1 was also below average on test 2. Every student who was above average on test 1 was also above average on test 2."

    b. Ms. B: "Most of the students who were below average on test 1 were below average on test 2. Similarly, most of the students scoring above average on test 1 were also above average on test 2. There were a few exceptions, but the trend was clear."

    c. Mr. C: "Wow, there was really no correlation between test 1 and test 2! Half the students who were below average on the first test were also below average on the second test, but half were above average! The same was true for the above average students!"

    d. Mr. D: "This is so weird. Every student who was below average on test 1 was above average on test 2, and vice versa."

    e. Mr. E: "Of those scoring above average on test 1, about 60% were above average on test 2, but 40% were below average."

11. **Standardized Test Prep** The scatter plot shows the women's winning times in the New York City Marathon and the Boston Marathon. Which of the following is true about the women's record time in either marathon?

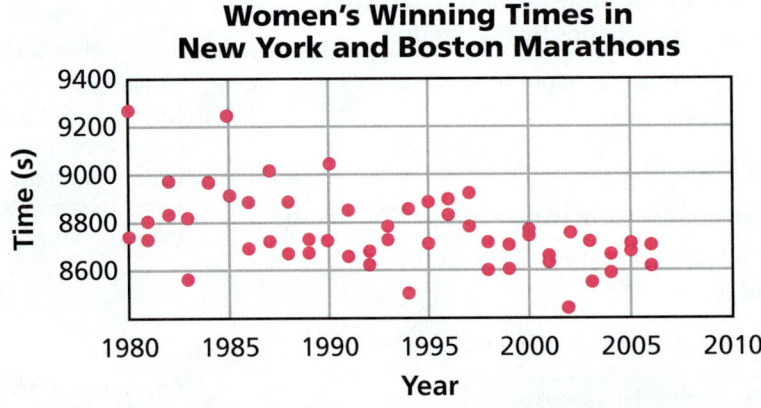

SOURCE: Boston Marathon official Web site and New York City Marathon official Web site

In 1984, the winning times were only 2 seconds apart!

A. The women's record time occurred in 2002.

B. The women's record time occurred in 1985.

C. The women's record time occurred in 2006.

D. You cannot tell from the scatter plot in which year the women's record time occurred.

12. **Write About It** A class performed the stopwatch experiment from Lesson 3.05. Elyse calculated the correlation coefficient between the first and second tries and found it was about -0.95. Does this mean that students' guesses got *worse* between their first and second tries? If not, what does a strong negative correlation mean?

13. **Take it Further**
    a. Consider the data set of points $(1, 35)$, $(2, 44)$, $(3, 52)$, $(4, 63)$, and $(5, 71)$. Show that the mean $\bar{x}$ of the x-coordinates is 3 and the mean of the squares of the x-coordiantes $\overline{x^2}$ is 11.
    b. Find the values $\bar{y}$ and $\overline{y^2}$.
    c. To find the value of the expression $\overline{xy}$, find product of the coordinates for each point. Then find the mean of those products.
    d. Determine the two variables' correlation coefficient r by the following calculation.

    $$r = \frac{\overline{xy} - \bar{x} \cdot \bar{y}}{\sqrt{\overline{x^2} - (\bar{x})^2} \cdot \sqrt{\overline{y^2} - (\bar{y})^2}}$$

    Be careful! Each piece of this calculation is different.

Maintain Your Skills

For Exercises 14 and 15, use the Best Actor and Best Actress age data in Lesson 3.05. Make each plot and describe your findings.

14. paired box-and-whisker plot
15. scatter plot
16. Find the mean of each data set.
    a. 4, 3, 9, 7, 7, 4, 8
    b. 14, 13, 19, 17, 17, 14, 18
    c. 1004, 1003, 1009, 1007, 1007, 1004, 1008
    d. $(n + 4)$, $(n + 3)$, $(n + 9)$, $(n + 7)$, $(n + 7)$, $(n + 4)$, $(n + 8)$

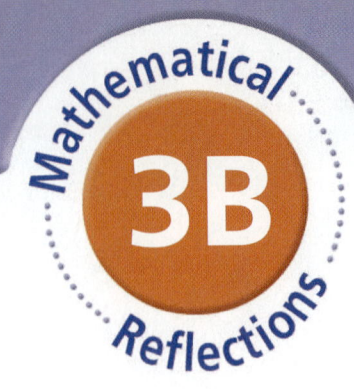

Mathematical Reflections 3B

In this investigation, you represented data using data lists, frequency tables, stem-and-leaf displays, dot plots, histograms, box-and-whisker plots, two-way frequency tables and scatter plots. These questions will help you summarize what you have learned.

1. The list shows the number of glasses of lemonade Annette sold each day from July 13 to August 1.

   2   7   11   15   21   28   33   38   35   51   36   25   24   3   14
   16   20   22   31   26

   a. Use Annette's daily sales data to make a stem-and-leaf display.

   b. Make two histograms of Annette's sales data. On one histogram, use 5-unit intervals. On the other histogram, use 10-unit intervals.

   c. Based on the histograms, about how many glasses of lemonade did Annette sell on each day?

2. Which measure for average (mean, median, or mode) can you use to determine the winner of an election? Explain.

3. Make a box-and-whisker plot for the baseball salary information in Lesson 3.05.

4. How can you use graphs, charts, and tables to understand data?

5. How can you use a two-way frequency table to determine it data is associated or independent?

6. Mr. Siddiqui tells his students about a correction for a test. He says, "It turns out that one problem didn't have a solution. To make up for my mistake, I gave everyone an extra 5 points credit for that problem. That changes the class average from 83 to 87 points." Is this possible? Explain.

What does this butterfly look like if you view it from the curb at the upper left?

Vocabulary

In this investigation, you learned these terms. Make sure you understand what each one means and how to use it.

- association
- box-and-whisker plot
- correlation coefficient
- dot plot
- first quartile
- five-number summary
- frequency table
- histogram
- independent
- interquartile range
- maximum
- mean
- median
- minimum
- mode
- negatively associated
- outlier
- positively associated
- range
- scatter plot
- stem-and-leaf display
- third quartile
- two-way frequency table

Chapter 3 Mid-Chapter Test

Multiple Choice

1. Which of the following points is farthest from the origin?
   A. (3, 4)
   B. (2, 5)
   C. (2, 6)
   D. (0, 7)

2. The paired box-and-whisker plots show the scores for 26 students on two tests. According to the graph, which of these statements must be true?

   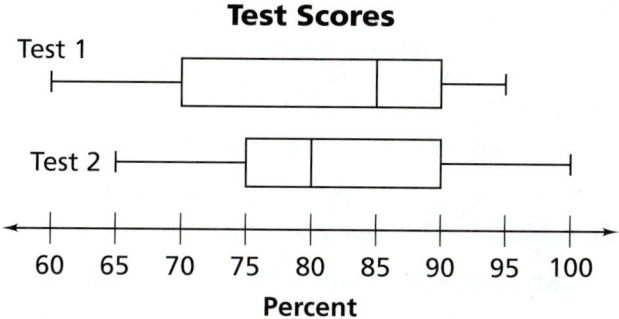

   A. The maximum score on Test 1 is higher than the maximum score on Test 2.
   B. The minimum score on Test 1 is higher than the minimum score on Test 2.
   C. The mean score on Test 1 is higher than the mean score on Test 2.
   D. The median score on Test 1 is higher than the median score on Test 2.

3. Find the resulting point when you transform (3, −4) according to the rule $(x, y) \mapsto (2x, -y)$.
   A. (1.5, 4)
   B. (6, 4)
   C. (6, −4)
   D. (−6, −4)

Open Response

4. Give a rule in the form $(x, y) \mapsto (\blacksquare, \blacksquare)$ for transforming point (3, 6) to the point (−3, 6). Then use the rule to transform (−3, −7).

5. Describe a sequence of events that corresponds to this graph.

   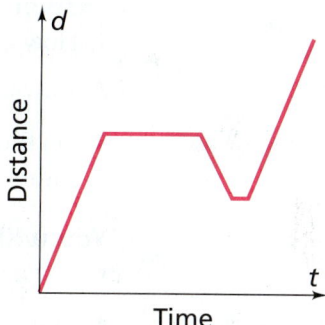

6. Build a five-number summary with a median exactly 10 units larger than the mean. Calculate the mean and median to check your data set.

7. Solve each equation.
   a. $|-3x + 7| = 8$
   b. $21 - |2x - 4| = 13$

8. Build an ordered stem-and-leaf plot that has at least ten data values and this five-number summary.
   - Minimum   19
   - First quartile (Q_1)   33
   - Median   40
   - Third quartile (Q_3)   44
   - Maximum   63

9. What is the effect on a picture in the coordinate plane of changing the x-coordinate? The y-coordinate? Both coordinates? Give an example illustrating each effect.

Investigation 3C: Equations and Their Graphs

In *Equations and Their Graphs,* you will focus on graphs of algebraic equations. You will use graphs to represent data and to draw pictures. Graphs can help you understand complicated data.

By the end of this investigation, you will be able to answer questions like these.

1. How are equations and graphs related?

2. How can you tell if a point is on a graph?

3. Do the graphs of $4y = (x - 3)^2$ and $3x - y = 14$ intersect at (5, 1)? Explain.

You will learn how to
- test a point to determine whether it is on the graph of an equation
- graph an equation by plotting points
- write the equation of a vertical or horizontal line given its graph or a point on its graph
- read a graph to identify points that are solutions to an equation
- find the intersection point of two graphs and understand its meaning

You will develop these habits and skills:
- Substitute values for variables.
- Write an equation that corresponds to a graph.
- Identify different graphs as belonging to the same family of graphs.

Security compares eye-scan data against a database in order to grant access.

3.11 Getting Started

Activating Prior Knowledge
Exploring New Ideas

In this lesson, you will explore some properties of graphs in the coordinate plane.

For You to Explore

1. Each point in the following table satisfies the equation $x + y = 5$.

   a. Complete the table.

   b. Graph the (x, y) coordinates that satisfy the equation $x + y = 5$.

   c. What shape is the graph?

x	y	(x, y)
1	4	(1, 4)
2	■	■
−3	■	■
■	0	■
$\frac{1}{2}$	■	■
■	−2	■
■	$-\frac{11}{3}$	■

Remember...
If a point's coordinates make an equation true, the point "satisfies the equation."

2. On a coordinate plane, draw a vertical line that passes through (5, 3).

   a. List six points that are on your line.

   b. List six points that are not on your line.

   c. How do you tell whether a point is on your line by looking at its coordinates?

3. The graph of the equation $y = x^2 - 3x + 2$ follows.

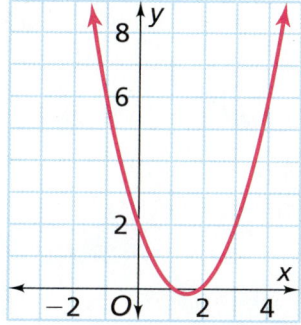

   a. Use a graphing calculator to generate this graph.

   b. What values of x make $y = 0$ in this equation? Explain.

   c. Apply the transformation $(x, y) \mapsto (x + 5, y)$ to each point on the graph of $y = x^2 - 3x + 2$. Sketch the resulting graph. What is the equation of the new graph?

4. Use the equation $2x + 3y = 12$.

   a. Find five points that satisfy the equation.

   b. Find five points that do not satisfy the equation.

5. Sketch a graph of all the (x, y) coordinates that satisfy the equation $y - x^2 = -1$. What shape is the graph?

Habits of Mind
Experiment. Choose values for x and find the y values. Then plot those points.

Exercises Practicing Habits of Mind

On Your Own

For Exercises 6 and 7, sketch a graph of the (x, y) coordinates that satisfy the equation. Describe the shape of each graph.

6. $(y - 3) = -1(x - 2)$

7. $y = |x|$

8. On a coordinate plane, draw a horizontal line that passes through (5, 3). List six points that fit each description.

  a. on the line

  b. not on the line

  c. How can you tell whether a point is on the line by looking at its coordinates?

9. Use the graph of $y = x^2 - 13x + 42$.

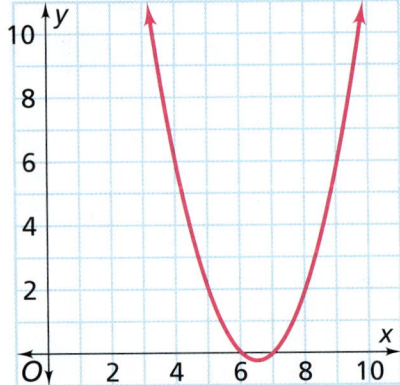

  a. Use a graphing calculator to generate this graph.

  b. What values of x make $y = 0$ in this equation? Explain.

  c. Apply the transformation $(x, y) \mapsto (x + 5, y)$ to each point on this graph. Sketch the graph. What is the equation of the graph?

Maintain Your Skills

For Exercises 10–12, sketch a graph of the (x, y) coordinates that satisfy the equation. What shape is each graph?

10. $x + y = 0$

11. $x + y = 1$

12. $x + y = 2$

13. How are the graphs in Exercises 10–12 similar?

3.12 Equations as Point-Testers

In Lesson 3.11, you sketched graphs of equations. For each equation, some (x, y) pairs make the equation true. If you plot on a coordinate plane each pair that satisfies the equation, the result is a graph of the equation.

You can test whether a coordinate pair is part of the graph of an equation by plugging the coordinates into the equation. For instance, suppose you want to find whether the point $(6, 0)$ is part of the graph of the equation $2x + 3y = 12$. You can just plug $x = 6$ and $y = 0$ into the equation.

$$2x + 3y = 12$$
$$2 \cdot (6) + 3 \cdot (0) \stackrel{?}{=} 12$$
$$12 + 0 \stackrel{?}{=} 12$$
$$12 = 12 \checkmark$$

Since $12 = 12$ is true, the point $(6, 0)$ satisfies the equation.

There are (x, y) pairs that do not satisfy the equation. For instance, test the point $(-1, 8)$. You plug $x = -1$ and $y = 8$ into the equation.

$$2x + 3y = 12$$
$$2 \cdot (-1) + 3 \cdot (8) \stackrel{?}{=} 12$$
$$-2 + 24 \stackrel{?}{=} 12$$
$$22 \neq 12 \text{✗}$$

Since $22 = 12$ is false, the point $(-1, 8)$ does not satisfy the equation.

In fact, there are many more pairs that do not satisfy the equation.

For You to Do

1. Find two additional points that make the equation $2x + 3y = 12$ true. Then find two additional points that make the equation false.

The graph of the equation $2x + 3y = 12$ is a line.

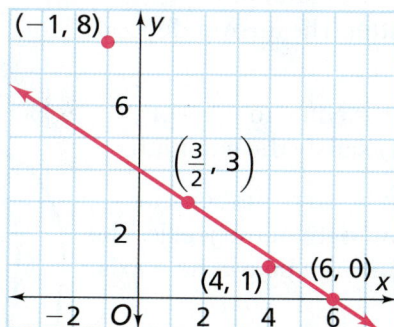

Each point that makes the equation true is on this line. Each point on the line makes the equation true. Notice that $(6, 0)$ is on the line, but $(-1, 8)$ is not on the line.

Does $\left(\frac{3}{2}, 3\right)$ satisfy the equation? Does $(4, 1)$ satisfy the equation?

You can use the equation $2x + 3y = 12$ as a **point-tester.** Some points, such as $(6, 0)$, pass the test. Other points, such as $(-1, 8)$, fail. Points that pass the test are part of the graph. Points that fail are not part of the graph. Using this method, you can draw a graph of all points that satisfy an equation.

A recurring theme in algebra is that equations are point-testers.

- Any point that is on the graph of the equation makes the equation true.
- Any point that makes the equation true is part of the graph of the equation.

> A point satisfies an equation if its coordinates make the equation true.

Definition

The **graph of an equation** is the collection of all points with coordinates that make the equation true.

Example

Problem In the coordinate plane, draw the graph of the equation $y = -1$.

Solution To find the graph of the equation $y = -1$, you need to determine *every* point that makes the equation true. Test any point by plugging it into the equation. Find out whether the equation is true. For instance, does the point $(2, 5)$ make the equation true? Since the y-coordinate is 5, you plug 5 into the equation: $5 \stackrel{?}{=} -1$.

The equation is false, so $(2, 5)$ is *not* on the graph.

Does the point $(2, -1)$ make the equation true? Plug the y-coordinate -1 into the equation: $-1 \stackrel{?}{=} -1$.

The equation is true, so $(2, -1)$ is on the graph of the equation $y = -1$.

What other points make the equation true? Usually, when you test a point, you substitute two numbers (x-coordinate and y-coordinate) into an equation. In this case, the x-coordinate doesn't matter. The answer depends only on the y-coordinate.

A point makes the equation true if the y-coordinate is equal to -1. For example, points such as $(1, -1)$, $(5, -1)$, and $(0, -1)$ satisfy the equation.

If the y-coordinate equals -1, the x-coordinate can be any number. The graph of the equation $y = -1$ extends to the left and right of the y-axis. The graph of the equation $y = -1$ is a horizontal line one unit below the x-axis.

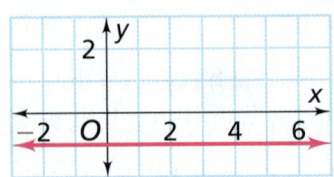

Developing Habits of Mind

Represent a solution. Equations can have different types of solutions, depending on the context. If the equation has one variable, a solution is a number that satisfies the equation when you use it in place of the variable. $x = 2$ is a solution of $3x + 7 = 13$.

In this chapter, you will look for points (pairs of numbers) that satisfy an equation with two variables. The solutions to the equation $3x + 7y = 13$ are a collection of points that include $(2, 1)$ and $(-5, 4)$. There are infinitely many other points that satisfy $3x + 7y = 13$. You cannot list them all. Instead, you can represent the solutions as a graph in the coordinate plane.

Exercises Practicing Habits of Mind

Check Your Understanding

1. **a.** Name and plot six points that are on the graph of $y = 4$.
   b. Describe the graph of $y = 4$. Draw the graph.

2. Line m is horizontal and passes through $(3, 7)$.
   a. Draw a graph of m.
   b. Find the coordinates of six points that are on m.
   c. Find the coordinates of six points that are *not* on m.
   d. How can you tell whether a point is on m by looking at its coordinates?
   e. Write an equation for m.

3. Line ℓ is vertical and passes through $(3, 7)$.
   a. Draw a graph of ℓ.
   b. Find the coordinates of six points that are on ℓ.
   c. Find the coordinates of six points that are *not* on ℓ.
   d. How can you tell whether a point is on ℓ by looking at its coordinates?
   e. Write an equation for ℓ.

4. Some graphs have more complicated equations. The graph of the equation $x^2 + y^2 = 25$ is a circle.

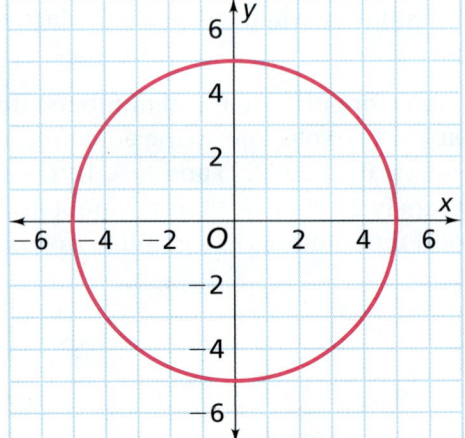

   a. Determine whether $(5, 0)$, $(-3, 0)$, and $(-3, 4)$ are on the graph.

   b. Find four more points that are on the circle. (Or, find four more points that satisfy the equation.)

5. a. Find five points that are on the graph of the equation $y = x$.

   b. Find five points that are not on the graph of the equation $y = x$.

   c. What does the graph of the equation look like? Draw the graph and explain why the graph is correct.

6. Draw a coordinate plane.

   a. Name and plot six points with a first coordinate that is the opposite of the second coordinate.

   b. A graph shows every point with a first coordinate that is the opposite of the second. What shape is the graph?

   c. Which of the following equations describes this graph? Explain.

   A. $y = x$ **B.** $x + y = 5$ **C.** $|x| = y$ **D.** $y = -x$

On Your Own

7. Let $P = (-2, 4)$.

   a. Line r is horizontal and passes through P. Write an equation for r.

   b. Line s is vertical and passes through P. Write an equation for s.

8. Use your equations from Exercise 7 to determine whether each of the following points is on r, s, neither r nor s, or on both r and s.

   a. $(1, 1)$ b. $(-2, 1)$ c. $(4, -2)$ d. $(4, 4)$

   e. $(-2, -2)$ f. $(3, -2)$ g. $(1, 4)$ h. $(-1, -3)$

9. Apply the transformation $(x, y) \mapsto (x + 3, y - 2)$ to the graph in Exercise 4.

   a. Sketch the resulting graph.

   b. **Take It Further** Find the equation of the resulting graph.

10. Line h is horizontal and passes through (5, 2).

    a. Find four points on h.

    b. Write a point-tester equation for h.

    c. Draw a graph of h.

11. Line v is vertical and passes through $(-4, 3)$.

    a. Find four points on v.

    b. Write a point-tester equation for v.

    c. Draw a graph of v.

12. Find the point that is on both lines h and v from Exercises 10 and 11. Explain.

13. **Write About It** Is there any vertical line that contains both (0, 2) and (2, 0)? Explain.

All points of a horizontal line are the same distance above the horizontal floor.

14. a. Find five points that satisfy the equation $2y - 4x = 24$.

    b. Find five points that do not satisfy the equation $2y - 4x = 24$.

15. Add $4x$ to both sides of the equation $2y - 4x = 24$. Divide both sides by 2.

    $$2y - 4x = 24$$
    $$2y - 4x + 4x = 24 + 4x$$
    $$2y = 24 + 4x$$
    $$y = 12 + 2x$$

    The result is the equation $y = 12 + 2x$.

    a. Find five points that satisfy this equation.

    b. Find five points that do not satisfy this equation.

    c. Compare your points in this exercise with the points in Exercise 14. How are they similar? Explain.

16. **Standardized Test Prep** Which point is NOT on the graph of $5x + 6y = -42$?

    A. $(6, -12)$ B. $(-12, 3)$ C. $(-9, 0.5)$ D. $(4, -10)$

Maintain Your Skills

17. Graph each equation.

    a. $y = x$
    b. $(y - 1) = x$
    c. $(y - 2) = x$
    d. $(y - 3) = x$
    e. $(y - 4) = x$
    f. $(y - 5) = x$

    g. Describe the pattern. How do the equations change? How does the change affect the graphs?

3.12 Equations as Point-Testers 271

3.13 Graphing by Plotting

To draw a graph, you might start by plotting several points.

Minds in Action   episode 11

Sasha is working through her algebra homework. Tony walks over to ask for some help.

Tony   How do you find the graph of this equation?

Tony points to the equation $y = x^2 - 4x + 3$.

Sasha   Plug in different values of x. Try $x = 0$.

$$y = x^2 - 4x + 3$$
$$y = (0)^2 - 4 \cdot (0) + 3$$

> When Sasha says *plug in*, she means "substitute."

Tony   0 is a good one to start with. All those zeros go away, since $(0)^2 = 0$, and $-4 \cdot (0) = 0$.

Sasha   Right, and we get this.

$$y = (0)^2 - 4 \cdot (0) + 3$$
$$y = 0 - 0 + 3$$
$$y = 3$$

Tony $y = 3$? Now what do I do with the 3?

Sasha   Remember, we started by saying $x = 0$ and found that if $x = 0$, then $y = 3$. The point $(0, 3)$ is on our graph.

Sasha plots the point $(0, 3)$ on a coordinate plane.

Sasha   Now you try one.

Tony   Okay, so if $x = -1$, then we get this.

$$y = x^2 - 4x + 3$$
$$y = (-1)^2 - 4 \cdot (-1) + 3$$
$$y = 1 - (-4) + 3$$
$$y = 8$$

> $(-1)^2 = 1$, not -1.
> $1 - (-4) = 1 + 4$.

Tony   We now know that the point $(-1, 8)$ satisfies our equation. It's also on our graph.

Sasha   Exactly.

Sasha draws the point (−1, 8) on the coordinate plane.

Sasha   Let's find some more points on the graph. We can figure out what the whole graph looks like. Here, you try $x = 1$, $x = 2$, and $x = 3$. I'll try $x = 4$ and $x = 5$.

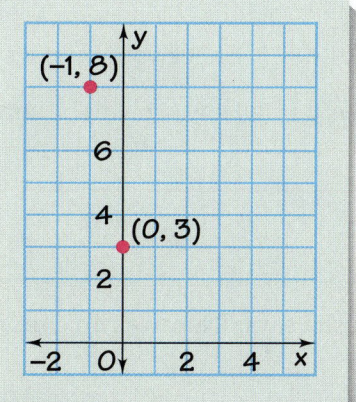

Sasha and Tony both start working on their points.

Tony   Okay, I've found the points (1, 0), (2, −1) and (3, 0).

Sasha   I've found the points (4, 3) and (5, 8).

Sasha plots all of the points on a coordinate plane.

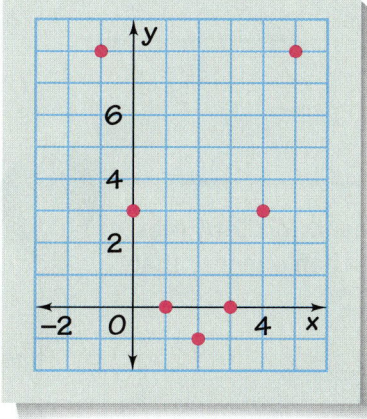

Tony   Oh, I can tell the shape of the graph. It looks like a big smile.

Sasha   That seems right. Now we can connect the dots, and that's our graph.

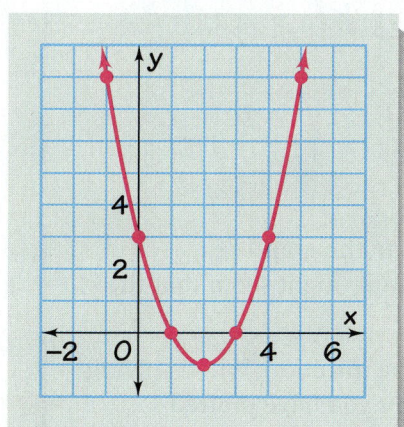

3.13   Graphing by Plotting

For You to Do

Use the graph from episode 11.

1. Guess what values of x make $y = 0$. Check your guesses in the equation.

2. Guess what values of x make $y = 3$. How can you be sure that your guesses are correct?

For Discussion

3. At the end of episode 11, Sasha says, "Now we can connect the dots." Do you agree? Explain.

4. If you plug $x = 2.5$ into the equation $y = x^2 - 4x + 3$, what is the result? Can you use Sasha's graph to approximate this result?

5. Give an equation with a graph that has the shape of a big frown.

Developing Habits of Mind

Consider more than one strategy. In the Example, Sasha and Tony plot five points. Then they connect the dots. There is more than one way that they can connect the dots.

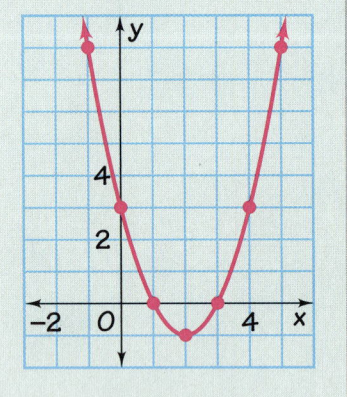 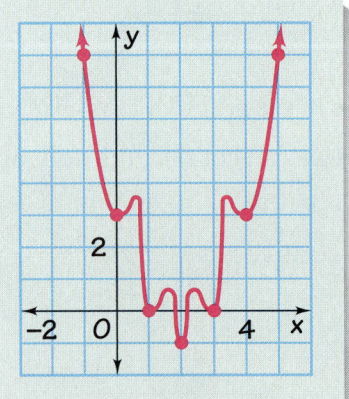

Is it possible that Sasha and Tony are incorrect? Can the graph of $y = x^2 - 4x + 3$ be the bumpy graph on the right? It might seem that the correct graph is on the left, but can you be sure?

For now, graphing by plotting points involves some intuition. When solving an unfamiliar equation, you need to judge whether you have plotted enough points. For the exercises that follow, you will rely on your own judgment to solve each equation.

There is never any harm in plotting a few additional points.

Exercises Practicing Habits of Mind

Check Your Understanding

1. These four equations may look different, but three of them have the same graph. Which graph is different? Explain.

   A. $y = \frac{3}{2}x + 2$

   B. $2y + 3x = 4$

   C. $(y - 5) = \frac{3}{2}(x - 2)$

   D. $2y - 3x = 4$

2. Use the equation $2y + 5x = 10$. For each point, find the value of k that satisfies the equation. Then plot the point.

   a. $(0, k)$ **b.** $(1, k)$

   c. $(-3, k)$ **d.** $\left(\frac{1}{5}, k\right)$

   e. $(3, k)$ **f.** $(-4, k)$

   g. Using the plotted points, draw the graph of the equation $2y + 5x = 10$.

3. Look at the graphs of the equations $y = |x - 3|$ and $(y - 3) = |x|$. Which graph corresponds to each equation? Explain.

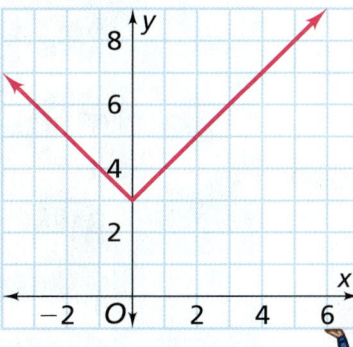 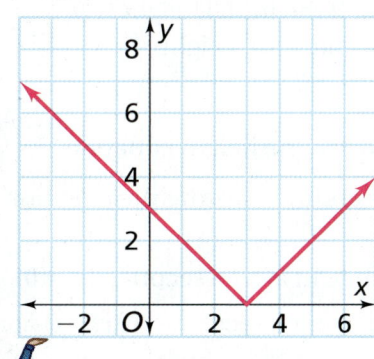

3.13 Graphing by Plotting

4. Match each equation with a graph. Explain each choice.
   a. $2x - y = -1$
   b. $x = 2$
   c. $y = x^2 + 1$
   d. $(y - 1) = 2(x - 3)$

I.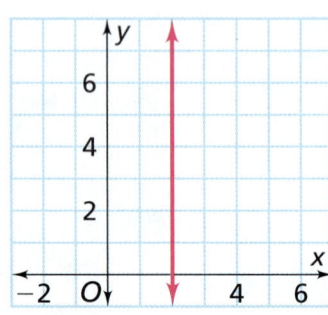

II.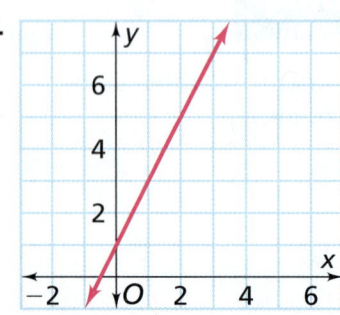

III.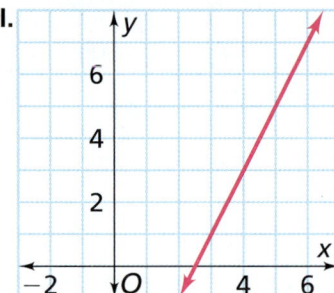

IV.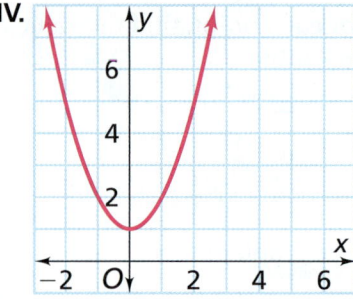

The Leaning Tower of Pisa stands about 183 ft high. Since $0 = 183 - 16(3.38)^2$, it takes about 3 s for a grape to reach the ground from the top of the tower.

For Exercises 5 and 6, use what Molly has learned in science about calculating the height of a falling object. If the initial height is h_0, then after t seconds, the object is at the following height.

$$h = h_0 - 16t^2$$

5. Molly drops grapes from her balcony to test the height equation.
   a. Molly's balcony is 160 feet above the ground. Rewrite the equation using 160 feet as the initial height.
   b. Use the equation to find the grape's height after 0 seconds ($t = 0$).
   c. How high is the grape after 1 second? After 2 seconds? After 3 seconds?
   d. How long does it take the grape to reach the ground? Round your result to the nearest tenth of a second.
   e. Use the points you have calculated. Sketch a graph by hand or with a calculator. Plot the grape's height against time.
   f. Sketch a picture of the grape's path.

6. Molly's friend Aya lives on a floor that is 320 feet above the ground. Molly goes to Aya's balcony to test the height equation using a different initial height.
   a. Rewrite the height equation using 320 feet for the initial height.
   b. According to the equation, how high is the grape after 0 seconds ($t = 0$)?

276 Chapter 3 Graphs

c. How high is the grape after 1 second? After 2 seconds? After 3 seconds? After 4 seconds?

d. Molly says, "I'm dropping the grape from 320 feet. It should take twice as long to hit the ground as it does if I drop it from 160 feet." Is she correct? Explain.

e. Sketch a graph of the grape's height against time.

This graph is not a picture of the path of the grape.

On Your Own

7. Use the equation $\frac{2}{3}y - x = 2$. For each point, find the value of h so that the point satisfies the equation. Plot the point.

a. $(h, 3)$ **b.** $(h, -3)$ **c.** $(h, 0)$

d. $(h, 1)$ **e.** $(h, 9)$ **f.** $(h, -2)$

g. Using the plotted points, draw the graph of $\frac{2}{3}y - x = 2$.

8. Match each equation with a graph. Explain your choice.

a. $y = -2$ **b.** $x + y = -2$

c. $y = (x + 1)^2$ **d.** $x = -2$

I.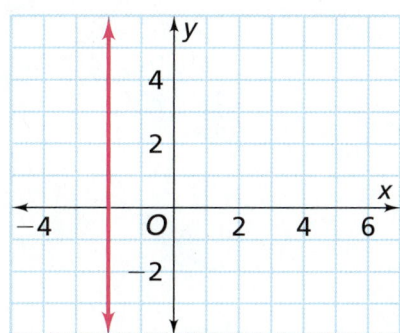

II.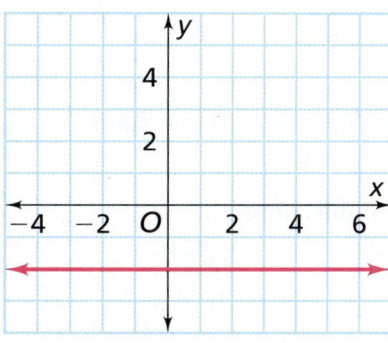

III.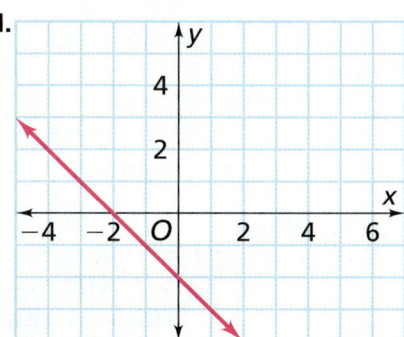

IV.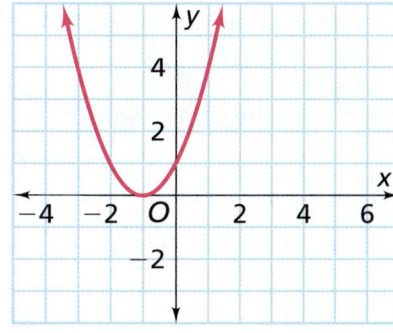

Go Online
pearsonsuccessnet.com

3.13 Graphing by Plotting

For Exercises 9 and 10, graph the equation.

9. $(y - 1) = 2x$

10. $(y - 4) = 2(x - 2)$

11. **Take It Further** Use the equation $x^2 - xy + y^2 = 1$.

    a. Find four points on the graph of the equation.

    b. Show that if (a, b) is on the graph, then $(-a, -b)$ is also on the graph.

    c. Sketch the graph.

12. **Standardized Test Prep** Which point is NOT on the graph of $y = x^2 - 5x + 4$?

    A. (0, 4)   **B.** (4, 0)

    C. (3, 2)   **D.** (1, 0)

Maintain Your Skills

13. Graph each equation on the same coordinate plane.

    a. $y = x$ b. $y = 2x$

    c. $y = 3x$ d. $y = 4x$

    e. $y = 5x$

    f. Describe the pattern. How do the equations change? How does the change affect the graphs?

14. Graph each equation on the same coordinate plane.

    a. $y = x$ b. $2y = x$

    c. $3y = x$ d. $4y = x$

    e. $5y = x$

    f. Describe the pattern. How do the equations change? How does this change affect the graphs?

15. Plot points to graph each equation on the same coordinate plane.

    a. $y = x^2$

    b. $(y - 1) = x^2$

    c. $(y - 2) = x^2$

    d. $(y - 3) = x^2$

    e. Describe the pattern. How do the equations change? How does this change affect the graphs?

3.14 Intersection of Graphs

Look at the graphs of the equations $y = x^2 - 1$ and $y = 3$ on two different coordinate planes.

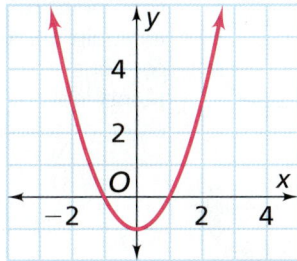 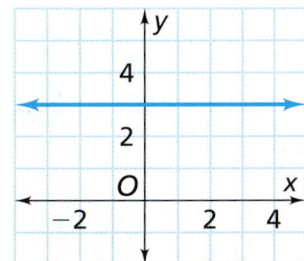

Each point on this graph satisfies the equation $y = x^2 - 1$.

Each point on this graph satisfies the equation $y = 3$.

Notice the result when you draw both graphs on the same coordinate plane.

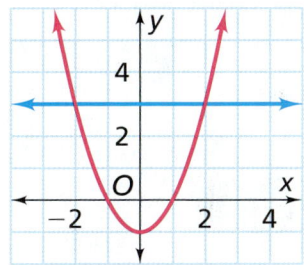

The graphs intersect at two points, $(2, 3)$ and $(-2, 3)$.

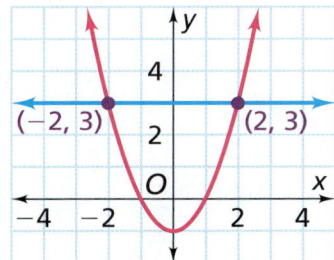

The points where two graphs cross are **intersection points.** Since the intersection points are on both graphs, they must satisfy both equations.

Can you describe six intersections suggested by this picture?

For Discussion

1. Use the equations of the two graphs above. Show that the graphs intersect at $(2, 3)$ and $(-2, 3)$.

Developing Habits of Mind

Find a relationship. There is a relationship between an intersection point of two graphs and the corresponding equations.

- An intersection point of two graphs satisfies both of the corresponding equations.
- If a point makes two equations true, then it is an intersection point of the corresponding graphs.

For a point to satisfy an equation, the coordinates of the points must make the equation true.

Exercises Practicing Habits of Mind

Check Your Understanding

1. Use the graphs of the equations $y = x$ and $y = 1000 - x$. These graphs intersect at one point. Explain why each point is not the intersection of the two graphs.

   a. $(100, 25)$

   b. $(-25, -25)$

   c. $(1000, 1000)$

   d. $(1000, 500)$

   e. Explain why the point $(500, 500)$ is an intersection of the two graphs.

2. Find two equations with graphs that intersect at $(3, -1)$. Show that $(3, -1)$ makes both equations true.

3. a. Does the graph of the equation $y = 3x - 2$ intersect the graph of the equation $y = 3x + 2$? Explain.

   b. Describe the result you find when you solve the equation $3x - 2 = 3x + 2$.

4. a. Find two equations with graphs that never intersect.

   b. **Take It Further** Explain why the graphs of the equations in part (a) do not intersect. In addition to drawing the graphs, explain how you can be certain that the graphs do not intersect.

280 Chapter 3 Graphs

5. The graphs of the equations $x^2 + y^2 = 25$ and $16x^2 + 9y^2 = 288$ are on the same coordinate plane.

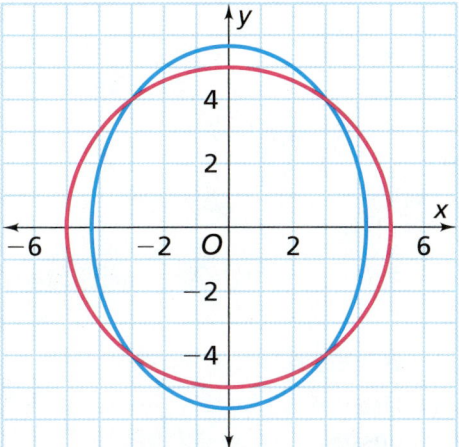

> The shapes are a circle and an ellipse. An ellipse is an oval shape that has some unique properties.

a. Match each graph with its equation.

b. Use the graphs to estimate the points where the graphs intersect. Use the equations to show that your guesses are correct or to find better guesses.

On Your Own

6. Graph the equations $y = x^2$ and $y = 3x - 2$. Where do these graphs intersect?

7. Find two equations with graphs that intersect at the point $(-5, 4)$. Show that the point $(-5, 4)$ makes both equations true.

8. **Standardized Test Prep** Which point is the intersection of the graphs of $y = 3$ and $y = -2x + 5$?

   A. $(0, 3)$
   B. $(4, 3)$
   C. $(3, 4)$
   D. $(1, 3)$

The paths of the planets are ellipses.

9. Look at the graphs of the equations
$x^2 + 16y^2 = 25$ and $y = \frac{1}{4}(x + 5)$.

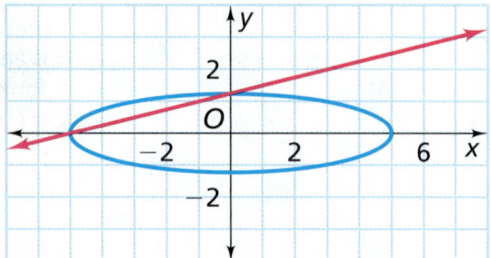

   a. Match each graph with its equation.

   b. Use the graphs to estimate the points where the graphs intersect. Use the equations to show that your guesses are correct or to find better guesses.

Maintain Your Skills

10. Find the intersection of the graph of $y = -2$ and the graph of each equation.

    a. $x = 0$

    b. $x = 1$

    c. $x = 2$

    d. $x = 3$

    e. $x = 4$

    f. What is the pattern of the graphs?

11. Find the intersection of the graph of $x = -1$ and the graph of each equation.

    a. $(y - 3) = 2(x + 1)$

    b. $(y - 3) = 13(x + 1)$

    c. $(y - 3) = -4(x + 1)$

    d. $(y - 3) = \frac{(x + 1)}{5}$

    e. $(y - 3) = -99(x + 1)$

    f. What is the pattern of the graphs?

282   Chapter 3   Graphs

Mathematical 3C Reflections

In this investigation, you related an equation to a graph. You learned to find an intersection point of two equations. These questions will help you summarize what you have learned.

1. **a.** Find five points that satisfy the equation $5y + 3x = -13$.
   b. Find five points that do not satisfy the equation $5y + 3x = -13$.

2. Match each equation with a graph. Explain each choice.
   a. $y = 3$
   b. $y + 3 = x$
   c. $y = x + 3$
   d. $y + 3 = x^2$

   I. 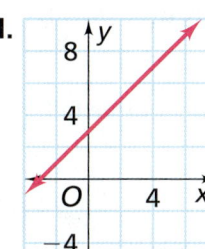   II. 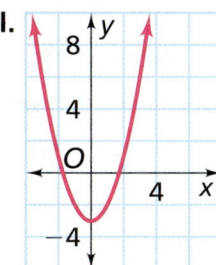   III. 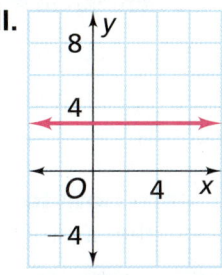   IV.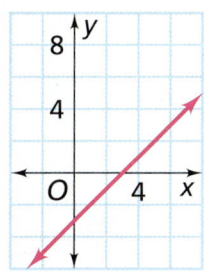

3. Graph the equations $y + 2x = 0$ and $x + 2y = 0$. Where do these graphs intersect?

4. For each point, find the value of h such that the point satisfies the equation $y^2 = x + 4$.
   a. $(h, 0)$
   b. $(h, 1)$
   c. $(h, 2)$
   d. $(h, 3)$
   e. $(h, -1)$
   f. $(h, -2)$
   g. Draw the graph of the equation $y^2 = x + 4$ by plotting the points in parts (a)–(f).

5. How are equations and graphs related?

6. How can you tell if a point is on a graph?

7. Do the graphs of $4y = (x - 3)^2$ and $3x - y = 14$ intersect at $(5, 1)$? Explain.

Access granted.

Vocabulary

In this investigation, you learned these terms. Make sure you understand what each one means and how to use it.

- graph of an equation
- intersection point
- point-tester

Investigation 3D

Basic Graphs and Translations

In *Basic Graphs and Translations*, you will look at six basic graph shapes for common equations. Knowing the key features of each shape will enable you to sketch many graphs quickly and easily.

By the end of the investigation, you will be able to answer questions like these.

1. What does it mean to say two variables vary directly or inversely?

2. What are the six basic graphs? Sketch each graph.

3. If you free fall 4.9 meters in one second, how far do you free fall in four seconds?

You will learn how to

- decide whether a situation represents direct or inverse variation

- sketch the graphs of the equations
  $y = x$, $xy = 1$, $y = x^2$, $y = x^3$, $y = \sqrt{x}$, $y = |x|$,
  and variations of these equations

- recognize the distinguishing features of the basic graphs, such as their general shape, and the points and quadrants that they pass through

- describe the rules for translating graphs of equations vertically or horizontally

You will develop these habits and skills:

- Use an equation as a point-tester for a graph.
- Quickly sketch the graph of a basic equation.
- Recognize proportionality in direct and inverse variation.
- Find similarities and differences between scatter plots and continuous graphs.

The transformation $(x, y) \mapsto (x, y + 10)$ takes you up 10 floors.

284 Chapter 3 Graphs

3.15 Getting Started

*Activating Prior Knowledge
Exploring New Ideas*

In this lesson, you will relate some simple equations to basic graph shapes. You will also observe how changing an equation changes a graph.

For You to Explore

In this experiment, you will build patterns using tiles and cubes.

1. Start building larger squares using smaller square tiles.

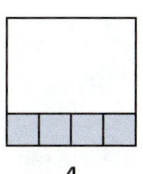
4

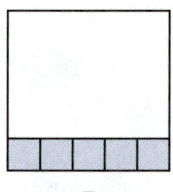
5

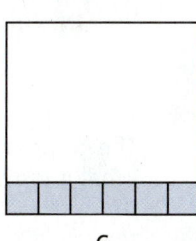
6

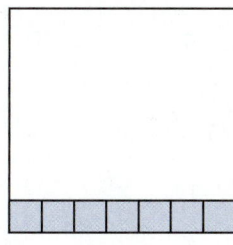
7

> Suppppose the number of tiles you need for a square is *n,* and the number of tiles in the bottom row is *t.* Write an equation that relates *n* and *t.*

Graph the number of tiles you need to complete each larger square against the number of tiles in the bottom row. If you continue to build larger squares, what will be the next five points on the graph?

2. Build larger cubes using smaller cubes. Record the *width* of each larger cube.

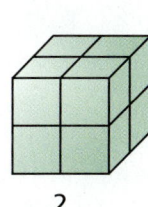
2

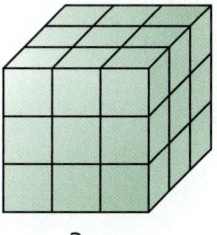
3

> Suppose the number of smaller cubes you need for a larger cube is *n,* and the width is *w.* Write an equation that relates *n* and *w.*

Graph the number of smaller cubes that you need to complete the larger cubes against the width of the bottom row. If you continue to build larger cubes, what are the next five points on the graph?

3. Graph the number of smaller cubes you need to complete the larger cubes against the number of smaller cubes in the bottom layer of each cube. If you continue to build larger cubes, what will be the next five points on the graph?

Exercises Practicing Habits of Mind

On Your Own

4. For each equation, find at least seven ordered pairs (x, y) that make the equation true.

   a. $y = x^2$
   b. $y = (x - 5)^2$
   c. $y = (x + 3)^2$
   d. $(y - 6) = x^2$
   e. $(y + 4) = x^2$
   f. $(y - 8) = (x - 7)^2$

5. Use the points you found in Exercise 4, and additional points if needed, to graph each equation in Exercise 4. Draw the graphs in separate coordinate planes.

   Use the same scale on the x- and y-axes for all the graphs.

6. Describe how each graph you drew for Exercise 5, parts (b)–(f), is related to the graph of the equation $y = x^2$ that you drew for part (a).

7. Look at the graph of the equation $x^2 + y^2 = 25$.

   The graph is a circle. What is the center of the circle? What is the radius?

   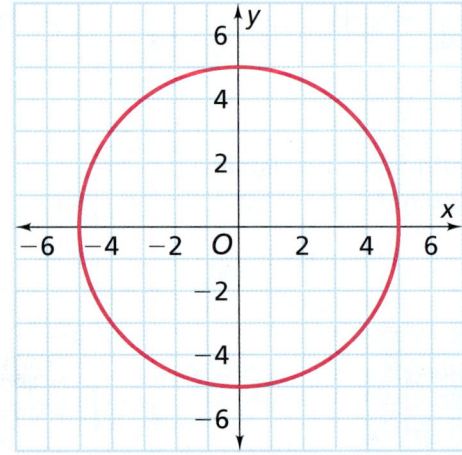

   Decide whether each point is on the graph.

   a. $(3, 4)$
   b. $(-3, -4)$
   c. $(4.9, 1)$
   d. $(-5, 0)$
   e. $(0, 0)$
   f. $(-2, -4.5)$

8. Look at the graph of the equation $x^2 + (y - 2)^2 = 25$.
   Decide whether each point is on the graph.
   a. (3, 6)
   b. (−3, −6)
   c. (3, −2)
   d. (5, 4)
   e. (0, −2)
   f. (−5, 2)

> How can you get this graph from the graph in Exercise 7?

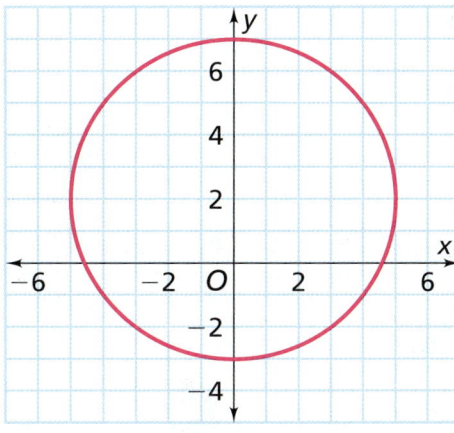

9. Suppose an object is in free fall, being pulled to the ground by Earth's gravity. The equation $v = 9.8t$ shows the relationship between the velocity v of the object, in meters per second, and the time t, in seconds, that it has been falling.

   a. If t is 0, what is v?
   b. Find v when t is 4, 8 and 16.
   c. If t doubles, how does v change?
   d. What is t if v is 100? If v is 300?
      Round to the nearest hundredth.
   e. If v triples, how must t have changed?

Habits of Mind

Establish a process. You may find it useful to make a table to keep track of your results.

You are in free fall for much of the time you spend jumping on a trampoline.

10. Katie earns $1000 by mowing lawns during the summer.

    a. If Katie charges $4 per lawn, how many lawns does she need to mow to earn $1000?
    b. If Katie charges $10 per lawn, how many lawns does she need to mow to earn $1000?
    c. If Katie can only mow 50 lawns during the summer, how much does she need to charge per lawn to earn $1000?
    d. Katie decides to double what she charged last year. If she wants to earn the same amount of money as last year, how does the number of lawns she needs to mow change?
    e. Write an equation that relates the amount c Katie charges per lawn and the number of lawns n she needs to mow to reach $1000.

3.15 Getting Started

11. A rectangular piece of paper has an area of 80 square inches. Draw a graph that shows the possible lengths and widths of the paper.

> Graph length against width, or width against length. Why don't you get much information if you graph area against width?

Maintain Your Skills

12. Find the solutions to each equation.

    a. $7x - 3 = 2x + 17$

    b. $7(x - 4) - 3 = 2(x - 4) + 17$

    c. $7(x - 8) - 3 = 2(x - 8) + 17$

    d. $7(x - 83) - 3 = 2(x - 83) + 17$

    e. $7(x + 9) - 3 = 2(x + 9) + 17$

    f. $7(x + 1) - 3 = 2(x + 1) + 17$

    g. **Write About It** Explain in detail the relationship among the solutions in parts (a)–(f).

    h. Without using any basic moves, find the solution to the equation $7(x - 13) - 3 = 2(x - 13) + 17$.

    i. Without using any basic moves, find the solution to the equation $7(x + 13) - 3 = 2(x + 13) + 17$.

13. Find the number of intersections of the graphs for each pair of equations.

    a. $y = 2x$ and $y = 10 - 3x$

    b. $y = 2(x + 3)$ and $y = 10 - 3(x + 3)$

    c. $y = 2(x - 5)$ and $y = 10 - 3(x - 5)$

    d. $y = x^2$ and $y = 10 - 3x$

    e. $y = (x - 5)^2$ and $y = 10 - 3(x - 5)$

    f. $(y + 6) = x^2$ and $(y + 6) = 10 - 3x$

3.16 Two Basic Graphs: $y = cx$, $y = \frac{c}{x}$

In Investigation 3C, you learned to sketch graphs by using equations as point testers.

There are several basic shapes for graphs. Knowing these basic shapes can help you sketch graphs more quickly than you can using the point-tester method.

For You to Do

1. A ride on a carousel costs $3 per person. Using at least six points, draw a scatter plot with the number of riders on the horizontal axis and the total cost for the riders on the vertical axis.

Direct Variation

A **direct variation** is the relation of two variables that are in a constant ratio. For example, you find the number of days in a given number of weeks by multiplying by 7. If d is the number of days and w is the number of weeks, then the equation

$$d = 7w$$

expresses the relationship between d and w. The ratio between the number of days and number of weeks is always 7. If the value of w doubles, then the value of d also doubles. If the value of d doubles, then the value of w doubles.

For You to Do

2. There are 98 days in 14 weeks. How many days are there in 140 weeks? In 42 weeks?

Habits of Mind

Check your equation. You may expect the equation to be $7d = w$, because you are thinking that there are 7 days in 1 week. When there is any doubt, you can check your equation by substituting. If you use 7 for d and 1 for w, which equation is true, $7d = w$ or $d = 7w$?

Example

Problem A ride on a carousel costs $3. Let the variable r stand for the number of rides. Let c stand for the cost of the rides. Then $c = 3r$, and c and r vary directly.

Draw a graph of the direct variation $c = 3r$ for all values of r from 0 to 8, including noninteger values. Label the horizontal axis r and the vertical axis c.

Solution The table shows some points of the graph. The relationship between c and r is almost the same as the relationship between the number of riders on the carousel and the total cost for the riders. But the graph below shows the difference. The graph of the direct variation $c = 3r$ is a continuous line instead of distinct points.

Direct Variation

r	c
0	0
0.5	1.5
1	3
2	6
3	9
6	18

> When you plot cost c against the number of riders r, the values of r and c are nonnegative integers. In the complete graph of $c = 3r$, both r and c represent all real numbers. When r can have both positive and negative values, what quadrants would contain the complete graph?

Developing Habits of Mind

Represent a direct variation. In direct variation, an increase in one variable means a proportional increase in the other variable. The ratio of the two numbers stays constant.

$$\frac{y}{x} = c$$

The standard equation for direct variation looks like this.

$$y = cx$$

The graph of the equation $y = cx$ is always a line that passes through the origin (0, 0) and the point (1, c). Here is the graph when $c = \frac{1}{2}$, along with a table of values for the graph.

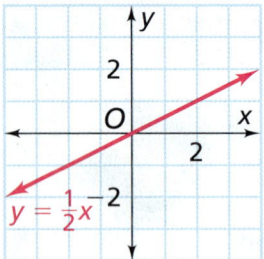

x	y
-2	-1
-1	$-\frac{1}{2}$
$-\frac{1}{2}$	$-\frac{1}{4}$
0	0
$\frac{1}{2}$	$\frac{1}{4}$
1	$\frac{1}{2}$
2	1

> The variable c is a number (a constant), while x and y are variables, each representing any number. So $y = 5x$ is a direct variation equation in which $c = 5$.

The location of the graph depends on whether c is positive, negative, or zero. If c is positive, the graph passes through Quadrants I and III. If c is negative, the graph passes through Quadrants II and IV.

For Discussion

3. How do you know that the graph of $y = cx$ goes through $(0, 0)$, no matter what number c is?

4. What is the difference between the graph of $y = 3x$ and the graph of the carousel riders in this lesson?

Inverse Variation

An **inverse variation** is the relation between two variables that have a constant product.

What does the word *inverse* mean in everyday language?

Suppose, for example, that you have 100 grapes to share equally among your friends. Here are some ways that you can do this.

- 25 grapes to each of 4 friends
- 10 grapes to each of 10 friends
- 2 grapes to each of 50 friends

If g is the number of grapes that you give to each of f friends, the product of g and f must be 100.

$$g \cdot f = 100$$

The product of g and f is a constant. When the value of f doubles, the value of g is halved. When the value of g doubles, the value of f is halved. You can say that g and f vary inversely.

For You to Do

5. Give an example using numbers for f and g to illustrate the sentence "When the value of f doubles, the value of g is halved."

Minds in Action episode 12

Sasha and Tony work on Exercise 11 from Lesson 3.15.

11. *A rectangular piece of paper has an area of 80 square inches. Draw a graph that shows all the possible lengths and widths of the paper.*

Sasha We need some points to graph. The paper could be 8 inches by 10 inches, so we should plot (8, 10). That area is 8 × 10, or 80 square inches.

Tony So can we use any two numbers that multiply to 80? Okay. The paper could be 4 inches by 20 inches. It could be 5 inches by 16 inches. I'm just finding any number that divides 80 evenly.

Sasha I'll graph these three points. They're all in the first quadrant.

Tony That looks good, but I can't complete the graph from 3 points. It's not a line through the origin. We need more points. I can think of (1, 80) and (2, 40).

Sasha Those help a little. We need to know what the graph is when the length is more than 8. What happens if the length is 10 inches?

Tony Then the width is 8 inches! All the points show up again, reversed. That gives us a ton of points.

They plot all the points that fit and draw this graph.

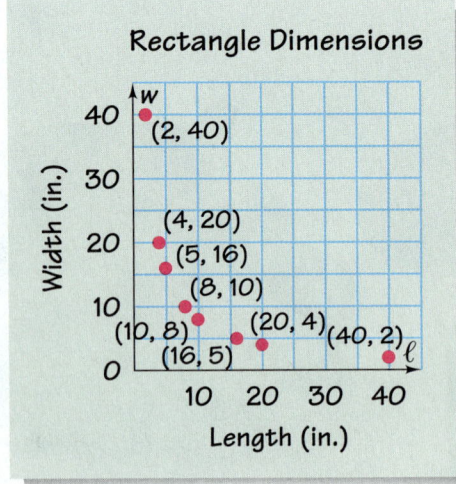

Tony So, is that all? Did we get all the points?

Sasha I'm not sure, but I think there might be more. This graph paper is $8\frac{1}{2}$ inches by 11 inches. Can we have a length of $8\frac{1}{2}$ inches and still get an area of 80 square inches?

Tony Sure, that's like solving an equation. What number times $8\frac{1}{2}$ makes 80? I don't know exactly what it is, but I know there is one.

Sasha What does that mean for our graph?

Tony I think it means we need more points.

Sasha A lot more! The length could be anything! We'll be plotting points forever.

Tony Ah. It's not going to be a scatter plot, then. It's going to be like a line. I'll draw a curved line instead of a bunch of dots. I'll connect the points as smoothly as I can.

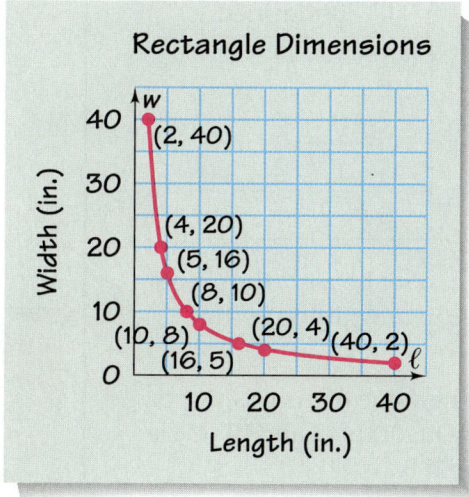

How are the points that correspond to (4, 20) and (20, 4) related?

Sasha That looks great! I think it's perfect. Is there an equation for this thing?

For You to Do

6. Find an equation for Sasha and Tony's graph.

For Discussion

7. The point (800, 0.1) is not visible in the graph that Tony draws, but is the point part of the graph? Explain.

Developing Habits of Mind

Represent an inverse variation. In an equation representing inverse variation, the product of x and y is constant, or $xy = c$. You can also write the equation $xy = c$ as $y = \frac{c}{x}$. The equation shows that an increase in one variable means a proportional decrease in the other variable.

The graph of $y = \frac{c}{x}$ passes through $(1, c)$ and $(c, 1)$. This graph is the second basic graph shape. Here are the graph and a table of values for $c = 6$.

> The variable c is a number (a constant), while x and y are both variables that represent a number. So $xy = -5$ is an inverse variation equation, in which $c = -5$.

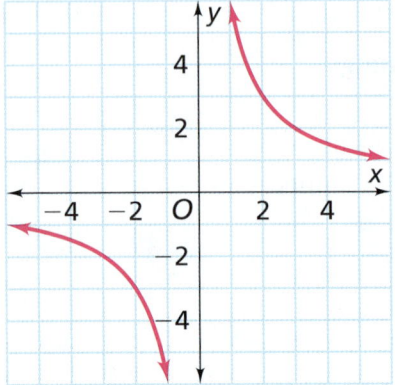

x	y
-6	-1
-3	-2
-1	-6
$-\frac{1}{2}$	-12
0	undefined
$\frac{1}{2}$	12
1	6
3	2
6	1

This graph is in two pieces! Since the value of x cannot be zero, the graph cannot cross the y-axis. If x is near zero, y is large in magnitude for both positive and negative values of x.

The location of the graph depends on whether the value of c is positive or negative. If c is positive, the graph goes through Quadrants I and III. If c is negative, the graph goes through Quadrants II and IV.

> Another term for *magnitude* is *absolute value*. The number -1000 is greater in magnitude than 16, although $-1000 < 16$.

San Francisco, 1906

San Francisco, 2006

The greater magnitudes possible for sway in modern structures make them less likely to be damaged in earthquakes. If you stand relaxed on a bumpy bus ride, it is easier to stay upright than if you rigidly brace yourself.

Exercises Practicing Habits of Mind

Check Your Understanding

1. Suppose a TV show offers a $1 million grand prize for a contest. If more than one person wins the contest, the winners split the prize.

    a. If five people win, how much money does each winner receive?

    b. Heidi wins and finds it shocking that her share of the grand prize is less than $50,000. Suppose each person receives less than $50,000. What is the least number of people who can split $1 million?

    c. Is this a case of direct variation or inverse variation? Explain.

    d. Describe this situation by defining variables and writing an equation.

2. Here is a graph for a direct variation situation.

    a. Is the point (16, 4) on the graph? Explain.

    b. The equation for direct variation is $y = cx$. Find c.

    c. **Write About It** Describe a situation that this graph represents. Define the variables x and y in the situation.

3. Decide whether each point is on the graph of $y = 3x$.

    a. $(-2, 6)$ b. $(3, 1)$ c. $(-2, -6)$

    d. $(2, 6)$ e. $(-4, -3)$ f. $(0, 0)$

4. Decide whether each point in Exercise 3 is on the graph of $xy = 12$.

5. As the value of x increases in the equation $xy = 6$, how does the value of y change? Can y equal zero?

6. What symmetries does the graph of $xy = 6$ have?

7. a. Find at least six ordered pairs (x, y) that are on the graph of $xy = -12$.

    b. What quadrants does the graph of $xy = -12$ pass through? Explain.

    c. Sketch the graph of the equation $xy = -12$, including the points you found in part (a).

8. How many points of intersection are on the graphs of $y = 3x$ and $xy = -12$?

9. **Take It Further** Suppose (a, b) is on the graph of $xy = 100$.

   a. Show that $(-a, -b)$ and (b, a) are also on the graph.

   b. What other points are on this graph?

On Your Own

10. A supermarket sells two cartons of milk for a total of $5.00.

    a. How much do you pay for 10 cartons?

    b. How much do you pay for one carton if each carton costs the same amount?

    c. Write a rule relating the number n of cartons to the total cost c.

    d. Is this situation an example of direct variation or inverse variation? Explain.

11. The distance a car travels at a constant speed varies directly with time. Suppose the car travels at 55 miles per hour.

    a. Find the amount of time it takes to travel 330 miles.

    b. How many miles does the car travel in 20 minutes?

    c. How many miles does the car travel in 40 minutes?

    d. Draw a graph of the number of miles traveled against the number of hours traveled.

    e. Find an equation relating distance d to time t.

12. Find a direct variation equation with a graph that contains each given point.

    a. $(3, 21)$

    b. $(21, 3)$

    c. $(-3, 21)$

    d. Find an inverse variation equation with a graph that contains the points $(3, 21)$ and $(21, 3)$.

13. The graphs of $y = 3x$ and $xy = 12$ intersect at two points.

    a. Explain why $(2, 6)$ and $(-2, -6)$ are intersection points.

    b. Sketch the graphs on graph paper. Show the location of the intersections.

Your distance from the lightning and the time it takes to hear the thunder are in direct variation.

14. **Standardized Test Prep** Which of the following points is an intersection point of the graphs of $y = x$ and $y = \frac{16}{x}$?

    A. (16, 1)

    B. (−4, −4)

    C. (−2, 8)

    D. (2, 2)

15. **a.** Plot points and sketch the graph of $(x - 4) \cdot y = 12$.

    b. How does the graph in part (a) relate to the graph of $xy = 12$ in Exercise 13?

16. Suppose the equation $y = \frac{6}{x}$ is true.

    a. Are there any values that x cannot equal? Explain.

    b. Are there any values that y cannot equal? Explain.

Habits of Mind

Experiment. Try replacing x with numbers near 4. What pattern do you find in your results?

Maintain Your Skills

17. Graph each equation on the same coordinate plane.

    a. $y = x$

    b. $y = 2x$

    c. $y = 3x$

    d. $y = 4x$

    e. $y = 5x$

    f. Describe the pattern. How do the equations change? How does this change affect the graphs?

18. Graph each equation on the same coordinate plane.

    a. $y = x$

    b. $y = \frac{1}{2}x$

    c. $y = \frac{1}{3}x$

    d. $y = \frac{1}{4}x$

    e. $y = \frac{1}{5}x$

    f. Describe the pattern. How do the equations change? How does this change affect the graphs?

3.17 Four More Basic Graphs

The two basic graphs in Lesson 3.16 are graphs of the simple equations $y = cx$ and $xy = c$. You can represent the remaining four graphs using simple equations also. Becoming familiar with the location and shape of each graph is your goal for now.

The Equation $y = x^2$

In Lesson 3.15, you graphed the relationship between the side length and the area of a square. You can represent this relationship with the equation $y = x^2$, where x is the side length and y is the area.

The graph of this relationship is almost the same as the graph in Lesson 3.15 that relates the total number of tiles and the number of tiles in each row. The difference is that the area graph (at the right) is a smooth continuous curve that allows for all possible side lengths.

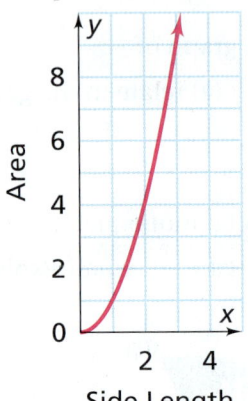

Quadratic Growth

Even this graph is not the complete graph of $y = x^2$, because the side lengths include only positive numbers. The complete graph of $y = x^2$ allows for all real-number values of x. The complete graph lies in Quadrants I and II.

$y = x^2$

x	y
-2	4
-1	1
$-\frac{1}{2}$	$\frac{1}{4}$
0	0
$\frac{1}{2}$	$\frac{1}{4}$
1	1
2	4

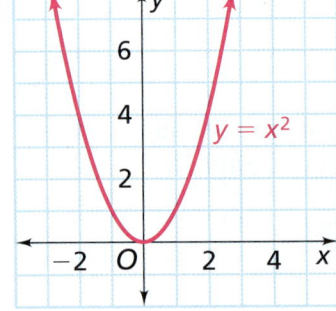

Habits of Mind

Experiment. To find points on the graph, substitute a value for x in the equation $y = x^2$. Then find y. Equations are point-testers, so if the value makes the equation true, the value is on the graph!

No matter what real number you choose for x, the value of x^2 is never negative. There are no negative y values on the graph.

Cross sections of these solar panels are quadratic curves.

For Discussion

1. According to the graph of the equation $y = x^2$, how many values of x make $y = 9$?
2. Use only the graph of $y = x^2$ to find a close approximation of $\sqrt{5}$.

The Equation $y = x^3$

In Lesson 3.15, you graphed the relationship between the width of a cube on an edge and the number of smaller cubes in a larger cube. You used the equation

$$y = x^3$$

where x is the length of an edge and y is the volume of the cube. The graph of this relationship is the same as the graph in Lesson 3.15, showing the number of smaller cubes in a larger cube against the number of smaller cubes on an edge. The difference is that this graph is a smooth graph that includes all possible values of the side lengths.

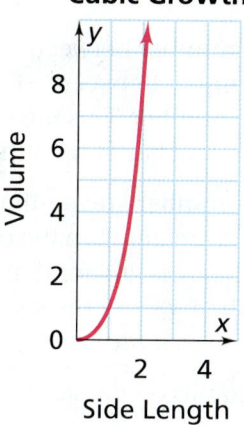

Cubic Growth

The complete graph of $y = x^3$ includes all the points on the above graph and the points where x is negative. When you cube a negative number, the result is also a negative number. For instance,

$$(-2)^3 = (-2) \cdot (-2) \cdot (-2) = -8$$

Unlike the graph of $y = x^2$, the other half of the graph of $y = x^3$ passes through Quadrant III.

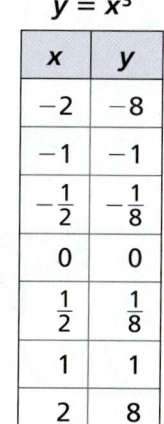
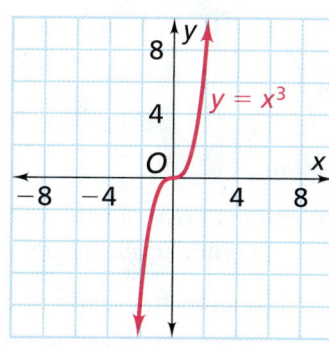

$y = x^3$

x	y
-2	-8
-1	-1
$-\frac{1}{2}$	$-\frac{1}{8}$
0	0
$\frac{1}{2}$	$\frac{1}{8}$
1	1
2	8

As the graph above shows, both x and y can be positive, negative, or zero.

For You to Do

3. According to the graph, between which two integers is the value of x for which $x^3 = -5$?

Developing Habits of Mind

Look for a relationship. The graph of $y = x^2$ and the graph of $y = x^3$ can look the same near the origin. Both graphs are nearly flat close to the origin, pass through the point (1, 1), and increase rapidly after that. Now, take a closer look.

When you square or cube a number between −1 and 1, the result is close to 0. However, the cube of a number between −1 and 1 is smaller in absolute value than the square of the number. This means that near zero the graph of $y = x^3$ is closer to the x-axis and flatter than the graph of $y = x^2$.

When you square or cube a number greater than 1 or less than −1, the absolute value of the result is greater than the original number. The cube of a positive number greater than 1 is greater than the square of the number. This means that in the graph of $y = x^3$ the values of y to the right of the intersection point (1, 1) increase more quickly than in the graph of $y = x^2$.

This sketch shows the two graphs on the same axes, when x is between −2 and 2.

Habits of Mind

Experiment. Replace x in $y = x^2$ with numbers between −1 and 1. Then, replace x with numbers greater than 1 or less than −1. Compare how far the y-values are from 0. Repeat the experiment for $y = x^3$.

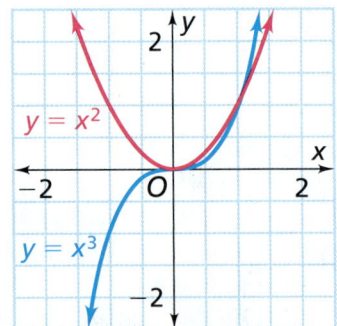

Notice that the two graphs intersect at two points, (0, 0) and (1, 1). These points of intersection occur since 0^3 equals 0^2, and 1^3 equals 1^2.

Notice that the graph of $y = x^3$ is below the graph of $y = x^2$ when x is between 0 and 1.

Equations are point-testers. Points (0, 0) and (1, 1) are on the graph of $y = x^2$, because $0^2 = 0$ and $1^2 = 1$. Also, (0, 0) and (1, 1) are on the graph of $y = x^3$ because $0^3 = 0$ and $1^3 = 1$. Why are there no other intersections?

The Equation $y = \sqrt{x}$

In Lesson 3.15, you graphed the relationship $y = x^2$ between a square's side length x and the square's area y.

You can look at the relationship between side length and area in another way. Suppose you need to change the area of a square and want to know the effect this would have on side length. You can represent the relationship with the equation $y = \sqrt{x}$, where x is the area and y is the side length.

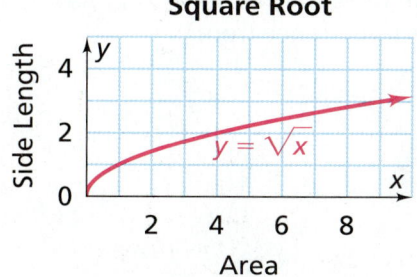

The graph of $y = \sqrt{x}$ looks like the graph of $y = x^2$, except the axes are reversed. There is, however, a big difference between the graphs of $y = x^2$ and $y = \sqrt{x}$. Part of the graph of $y = x^2$ lies in Quadrant II where the values of x are negative. For the equation $y = \sqrt{x}$, the value of x cannot be negative.

> Turn your book **90°** counterclockwise. Does this graph now look like the graph of $y = x^2$?

By convention, the square root of a number is always nonnegative, so the value of y cannot be negative, either. Since both x and y cannot be negative, the graph of $y = \sqrt{x}$ lies only in Quadrant I.

$y = \sqrt{x}$

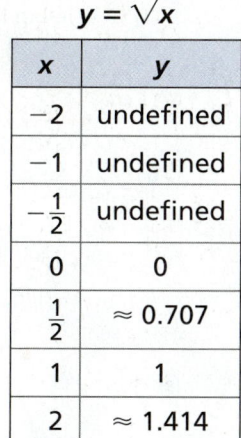

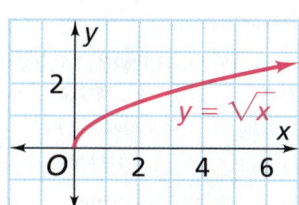

For You to Do

4. Is there a value for x that makes y greater than 100 on the graph of $y = \sqrt{x}$? Find a value if you can. If you cannot, explain.

The Equation $y = |x|$

Suppose you want to graph the relationship between a number and its distance from 0 on the number line. In Lesson 3.03, you learned that the absolute value of a number represents a number's distance from 0 on a number line. You can express this relationship with the equation $y = |x|$, where x is the number on the number line and y is its distance from 0. The graph below shows this relationship.

Absolute Value

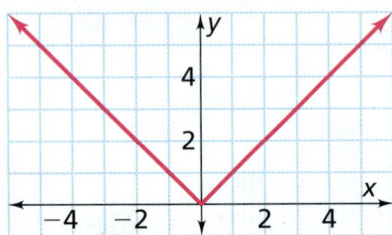

This graph resembles the graph of $y = x^2$ but has a sharp corner at the origin. Also, its sides are straight, not curved.

If you look at the graph as two pieces, each piece is a straight line, much like the direct-variation graphs. When x is positive, the graph looks just like the graph for the equation $y = x$. When x is negative, y is still positive since the absolute value of a number is never negative. The graph looks just like the graph of $y = -x$.

> Breaking the graph into two pieces relates to the meaning of absolute value in Lesson 3.03.
> $$|x| = \begin{cases} x, & \text{if } x \geq 0 \\ -x, & \text{if } x < 0 \end{cases}$$

The complete graph lies in Quadrants I and II, with a sharp corner at (0, 0).

$y = |x|$

x	y
−2	2
−1	1
$-\frac{1}{2}$	$\frac{1}{2}$
0	0
$\frac{1}{2}$	$\frac{1}{2}$
1	1
2	2

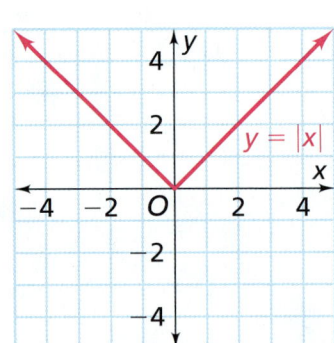

For Discussion

5. How does the graph change if y is the distance of x from 3 on the number line instead of from zero?

Exercises Practicing Habits of Mind

Check Your Understanding

Exercises 1–5 use the graphs of these six equations.

- $y = x$
- $y = x^2$
- $y = \sqrt{x}$
- $y = \frac{1}{x}$
- $y = x^3$
- $y = |x|$

1. Which of the six graphs pass through $(1, 1)$?

2. Which of the six graphs pass through $(-1, 1)$?

3. Which of the six graphs pass through Quadrant IV?

4. Each set of axes shows three (I–III) of the six graphs. Write the equation for each graph.

a.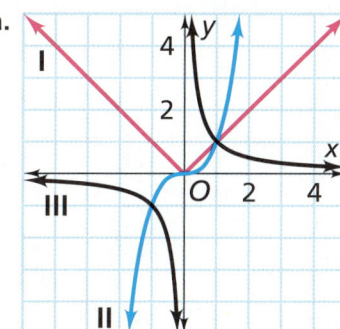

b.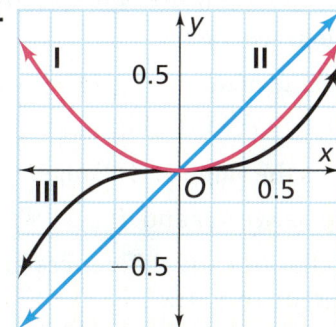

As the number of painters increases, the time that it takes to paint a mural decreases. Which basic graph does this suggest?

5. Name all of the six graphs that pass through each point.

   a. $(9, 3)$
   b. $(-2, -8)$
   c. $(-4, 4)$
   d. $(-10, -10)$
   e. $(10, 10^2)$
   f. $(-10, -0.1)$
   g. $(10^2, 10^6)$
   h. $(10^2, 10)$

6. Suppose x is a number greater than 1000. Order the values $|x|, \frac{1}{x}, x^3, x^2,$ and $\sqrt{x}$ from least to greatest.

7. Sketch a graph of each equation. What are the possible values of x and y?
   a. $y = \sqrt{x - 4}$
   b. **Take It Further** $y = \sqrt{-x}$

On Your Own

8. Suppose x is a positive number less than 1 and close to 0. Order the values $|x|, \frac{1}{x}, x^3, x^2,$ and $\sqrt{x}$ from least to greatest.

9. Suppose x is a small-magnitude negative number greater than -1. Order the values $|x|, \frac{1}{x}, x^3, x^2,$ and x from least to greatest.

3.17 Four More Basic Graphs

10. Suppose x is a large-magnitude negative number less than -1000. Order the values $|x|, \frac{1}{x}, x^3, x^2,$ and x from least to greatest.

11. **Standardized Test Prep** Choose the rule that shows the relationship between x and y in the table.

    A. $y = -3x + 4$ B. $y = 4x$

    C. $y = \sqrt{x}$ D. $y = x^2$

x	y
−4	16
−1	1
0	0
3	9
7	49

12. Find the number of points of intersection for the graph of each pair of equations.

    a. $y = x^2$ and $y = x^3$ b. $y = x$ and $y = x^3$

    c. $y = |x|$ and $y = \frac{1}{x}$ d. $y = x^2$ and $y = |x|$

13. **Take It Further** Recall the six equations listed before Exercise 1. Which two of these equations have graphs with more than three intersection points? How many intersection points do the two graphs have?

14. You can represent the relationship between time and distance for an object in free fall in Earth's gravity with the equation $d = 4.9t^2$. Here, d is the distance in meters and t is the time in seconds.

    a. If the value of t is 0, what is the value of d?

    b. Find the value of d when the value of t is 4, 8, and 16.

    c. If the value of t doubles, how does the value of d change?

    d. Draw a graph of the relationship between t and d.

    e. **Write About It** Describe the similarities and differences between the graph in part (d) and the basic graph of $y = x^2$.

15. **Take It Further** Use the equation $d = 4.9t^2$.

    a. What is the value of t when d is 100? When d is 300? Round to the nearest hundredth.

    b. If the value of d triples, how does the value of t change?

Maintain Your Skills

16. Sketch the graph of each equation.

    a. $y = (x + 3)^2$ b. $y = (x + 3)^3$ c. $y = |x + 3|$

    d. $y = \sqrt{x + 3}$ e. $(y - 6) = x^2$ f. $(y - 6) = x^3$

    g. $(y - 6) = |x|$ h. $(y - 6) = \sqrt{x}$ i. $(y - 6) = (x + 3)^2$

    j. $(y - 6) = (x + 3)^3$ k. $(y - 6) = |x + 3|$ l. $(y - 6) = \sqrt{x + 3}$

    m. How are the graphs in parts (a)–(l) related to the basic graphs?

Habits of Mind

Look for a pattern. If you can find the pattern, you can sketch these graphs more quickly.

3.18 Translating Graphs

In this lesson, you will learn how a change in an equation results in a graph moving to the left, to the right, upward, or downward. Conversely, you will learn how such a translation of a graph affects the equation.

Minds in Action   episode 13

Tony and Sasha work on Exercise 16 in Lesson 3.17.

Tony This first one tells you to graph $y = (x + 3)^2$.

Sasha Okay, let's plot some points. When x is zero, I add 0 plus 3, and then square the answer. That's 9.

Tony I'll make a table and keep trying numbers, like 1, 2, and 3.

Tony's First Table

x	y
0	9
1	16
2	25
3	36
4	49

Sasha This is getting us nowhere. I'm going to need a bigger graph to plot those numbers.

Tony Maybe we should try some negative numbers for x, since the equation tells us to add 3 every time.

Sasha Okay, so if x is -3, we add 3 to make 0 and then square that. We still get 0.

Tony Let's find some more points.

Sasha Look at the numbers for y. They're the same numbers you use for $y = x^2$.

Tony Yes, but they don't line up right. They're all three rows off. For $y = x^2$, the 0 for y is next to the 0 for x. Here, it's next to the -3.

Tony's Second Table

x	y
−4	1
−3	0
−2	1
−1	4
0	9
1	16
2	25
3	36
4	49

3.18 Translating Graphs **305**

Sasha Sure, that makes sense. It's $(x + 3)$ instead of x, so if you want the equation to behave the way it did at 0, you've got to start with -3 instead.

Tony Okay, let's graph that. I'm not going any higher than 20 on the y-axis.

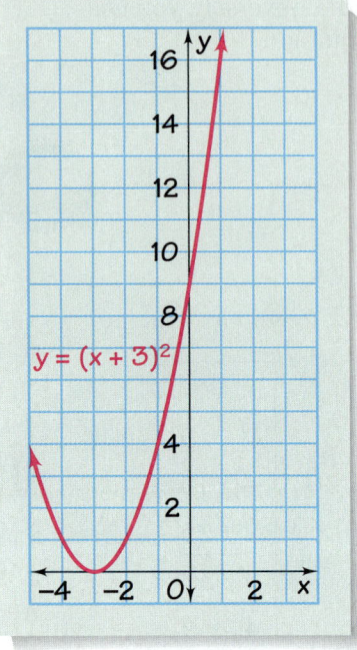

Sasha So the graph is the same as $y = x^2$, except it is three units to the left.

Tony That's because of what you said. When the equation has $(x + 3)$ in it and you want the numbers to behave the way they did before, you've got to make them three less.

Sasha Well, this should make the next three graphs in Exercise 16 a lot easier. They all use $(x + 3)$, too.

For Discussion

1. What does the graph of $y = (x - 9)^2$ look like? Explain.

Developing Habits of Mind

Look for a relationship. You can find a relationship between the equations $7x - 3 = 2x + 17$ and $7(x - 4) - 3 = 2(x - 4) + 17$.

In Lesson 3.15, you solved the equation

$$7x - 3 = 2x + 17$$

and found $x = 4$. Then you solved the equation

$$7(x - 4) - 3 = 2(x - 4) + 17$$

and found $x = 8$.

Notice that when you replace the variable x with $(x - 4)$, the solution of the equation increases by 4. When you replace x with $(x - 6)$, the solution increases by 6.

Here's how you can explain this pattern. In the second equation, suppose that you replace $(x - 4)$ with M. The resulting equation, $7M - 3 = 2M + 17$, looks just like the first equation! Since $x = 4$ is a solution to the first equation, $M = 4$ is a solution to this equation. Thus, $(x - 4) = 4$, or $x = 8$.

To summarize, suppose you have an equation in x and the solution is $x = c$. If you replace x with $(x - 4)$ in the equation, the solution becomes $(x - 4) = c$, or $x = c + 4$. Replacing x with $x - 4$ increases the solution by 4.

How do these steps relate to Lesson 3.02?

For Discussion

2. When you replace x with $2x$ in an equation, how does the solution change?

The rules for a two-variable equation are similar to the rules for a one-variable equation. But there is one important difference. If you replace x with $x - 3$, for example, then you have to add 3 to the x-values of *all* the ordered pair solutions of the first equation. The resulting graph is 3 units to the right of the original graph.

The graph of the equation

$$y = (x - 3)^2$$

has the same shape as the graph of $y = x^2$. All of the points that are solutions to $y = x^2$ have matching points in the graph of $y = (x - 3)^2$, but the values of x that make the equation $y = (x - 3)^2$ true increase by 3. The point (2, 4) on the graph of $y = x^2$ matches up with the point (5, 4) on the graph of $y = (x - 3)^2$. Similarly, (0, 0) matches up with (3, 0), and (1, 1) matches up with (4, 1). The graph of $y = (x - 3)^2$ is 3 units to the right of the graph of $y = x^2$.

You can use this powerful concept just described to sketch a family of graphs related to the six basic graphs.

Habits of Mind

Look for relationships. Following the rule that you just learned, if you know what the graph of $x^2 + y^2 = 25$ looks like, you can quickly graph $(x - 3)^2 + y^2 = 25$.

Example

Problem Sketch the graph of each equation.

a. $(y + 7) = x^2$ **b.** $y = \sqrt{x + 5} - 4$

Solution

a. The equation $(y + 7) = x^2$ is based on the equation $y = x^2$, in which you replace y with $(y + 7)$. The graph of $(y + 7) = x^2$ is seven units below the graph of $y = x^2$. Here are some values that make $y = x^2$ true and some that make $(y + 7) = x^2$ true.

$y = x^2$

x	y
−3	9
−2	4
−1	1
0	0
1	1
2	4
3	9

$(y + 7) = x^2$

x	y
−3	2
−2	−3
−1	−6
0	−7
1	−6
2	−3
3	2

There is a match between the two sets of points. You can use the y values of the equation $y = x^2$ and subtract 7. The graph of $(y + 7) = x^2$ is at the right.

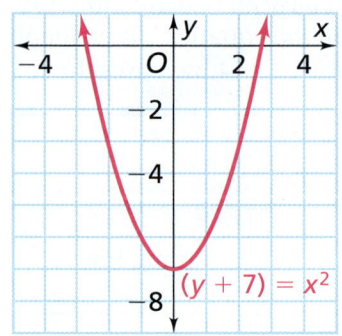

You can also think of $(y + 7) = x^2$ as $y = x^2 - 7$. The y-values on this graph are 7 less than the y-values on the graph of $y = x^2$.

b. You need to change the equation $y = \sqrt{x + 5} - 4$ slightly, since the corresponding basic graph is of the equation $y = \sqrt{x}$ and not of the equation $y = \sqrt{x} - 4$. You can make the equation fit the rule by adding 4 to both sides.

$$y = \sqrt{x + 5} - 4$$
$$y + 4 = \sqrt{x + 5} - 4 + 4$$
$$(y + 4) = \sqrt{x + 5}$$

Now you can apply the translation rules. The graph of $y + 4 = \sqrt{x + 5}$ is the basic graph of $y = \sqrt{x}$ translated five units to the left and four units down.

Another way to think about the graph of $y = \sqrt{x + 5} - 4$ is to ask, "What effect does the −4 in the equation have on the graph?" Remove −4 from the equation, and the graph of $y = \sqrt{x + 5}$ is the basic graph of $y = \sqrt{x}$ translated five units to the left. The equation $y = \sqrt{x + 5} - 4$ tells you to subtract 4, or move the graph four units down. Either way of thinking about the graph of $y = \sqrt{x + 5} - 4$ is useful.

Here are two tables, showing the basic graph of $y = \sqrt{x}$ and the related graph $y = \sqrt{x + 5} - 4$.

$y = \sqrt{x}$

x	y
0	0
1	1
2	≈ 1.414
3	≈ 1.732
4	2
5	≈ 2.236
6	≈ 2.449

$y = \sqrt{x + 5} - 4$

x	y
−5	−4
−4	−3
−3	≈ −2.586
−2	≈ −2.268
−1	−2
0	≈ −1.764
1	≈ −1.551

To build the second table, take the x values from the first table and subtract 5. Then take the y values from the first table and subtract 4. Here is the graph of $y = \sqrt{x + 5} - 4$.

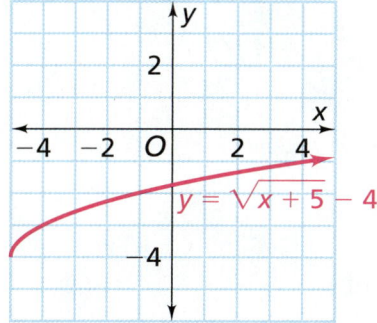

For You to Do

3. Write an equation with a graph that looks like $y = |x|$, with the point of the V-shaped graph at $(3, -7)$.

For Discussion

4. Use the equation of the circle in Lesson 3.16 to graph the equation $(x - 3)^2 + (y + 2)^2 = 25$.

5. Is the graph of $y = x^2 - 7$ translated horizontally or vertically, compared to the basic graph $y = x^2$? Explain.

Developing Habits of Mind

Represent an equation. When you use a graphing calculator or some types of computer software, you can only enter an equation after you solve for *y* in the equation. For example, you need to write the equation

$$(y - 1) = 3(x + 3)$$

in the following form:

$$y = 3(x + 3) + 1$$

For each of the six basic graphs, you can simply use a single backtracking step to solve for *y*. In this case, you add 1 to both sides of the equation.

Exercises Practicing Habits of Mind

Check Your Understanding

1. Write an equation with a graph that is the same shape as the graph of $y = \frac{1}{2}x$ but that passes through the point (3, 7).

2. **What's Wrong Here?** Sasha uses a calculator to draw this graph of $y = x^2 + 2x - 8$.

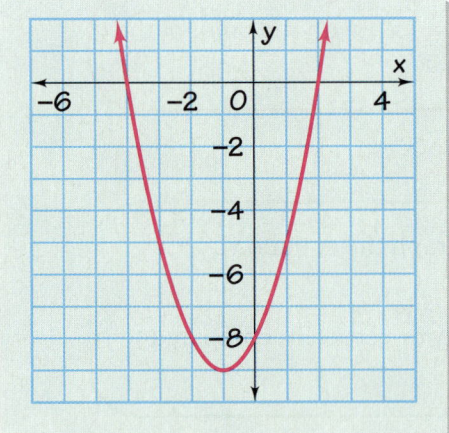

Then her teacher asks her to write an equation for this graph.

Sasha says, "The graph is three units to the right of the original, so that means the equation should be $y = (x - 3)^2 + 2x - 8$." When she tries to graph this on a calculator, her graph is not correct. What is she doing wrong?

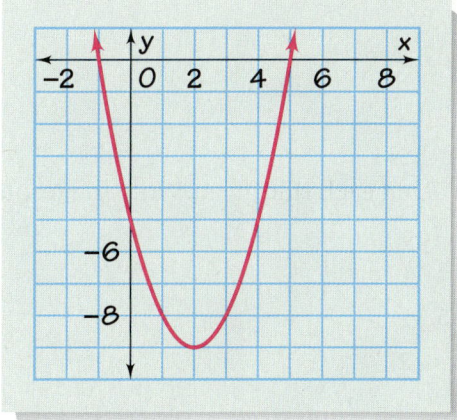

You call the shape of this graph a "Folium of Descartes." This particular graph is a graph of the equation $x^3 + y^3 = 10xy$.

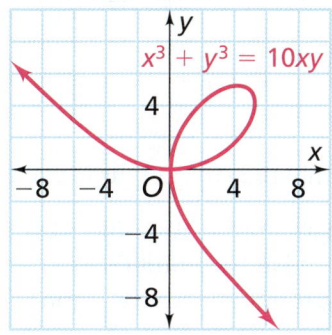

3. **a.** Which two of the following points are on the graph of the folium?
   $(0, 0)$ $(-3, 1)$ $(5, 5)$ $(5, -8)$

   b. Which graph below is the graph of $x^3 + (y + 4)^3 = 10x(y + 4)$?

   I.
   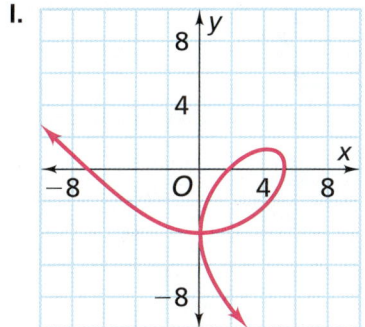

   II.
   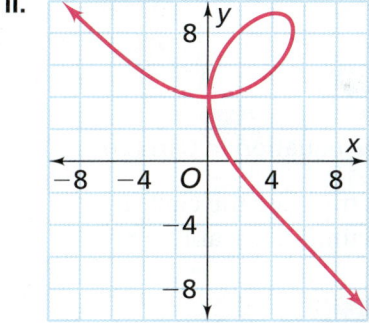

   III.
   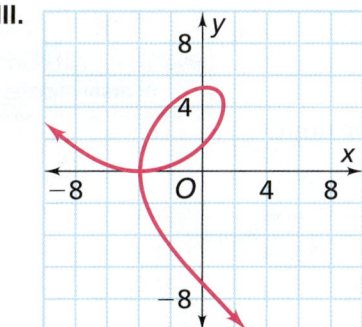

4. Write an equation for all three graphs in Exercise 3b. Recall that the original graph's equation is $x^3 + y^3 = 10xy$.

A diver's path follows a parabolic curve.

3.18 Translating Graphs 311

On Your Own

5. Transform each equation using each rule given. Write the resulting equation and sketch its graph.

  a. $y = x^2$, $(x, y) \mapsto (x + 5, y)$

  b. $y = x^2$, $(x, y) \mapsto (x - 5, y)$

  c. $y = |x|$, $(x, y) \mapsto (x, y - 2)$

  d. $y = |x|$, $(x, y) \mapsto (x - 5, y + 2)$

6. Sketch the graph of each equation on the same coordinate plane.

  a. $y - 2 = (x + 1)^2$

  b. $y - 2 = (x + 1)^3$

  c. $y - 2 = x + 1$

  d. How do these graphs compare to the graphs in Exercise 4b in Lesson 3.17?

7. The graph of the equation $x^2 + y^2 = 6x + 8y - 24$ is a circle of radius 1 centered at the point (3, 4). Use a translation to write the equation for a graph that is a circle of radius 1 with the given center.

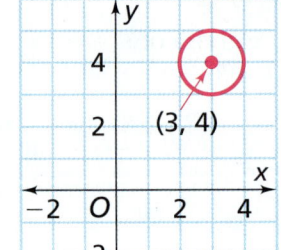

This graph is not a basic graph, but all the rules still apply.

  a. center $(3, -1)$

  b. center $(-10, 4)$

  c. center $(0, 0)$

  d. Expand and simplify the equation in part (c).

8. Write About It When you translate the circle in Exercise 7, how do the circumference and area change? Explain.

9. a. Draw a graph of the equation $y = 3x$.

  b. Write three different equations that translate the graph of $y = 3x$ so that it passes through the point $(5, -2)$.

10. The graph of the equation $(y - 4) = (x - 3)^2 + N$ passes through the point $(5, 2)$. Find the value of N.

11. Decide whether each point is on the graph of the equation $x^2 - xy + y^2 = 27$.
    a. (2, 0)   b. (3, −3)
    c. (4, −2) d. (−3, 3)
    e. (8, −9) f. (−3, −6)

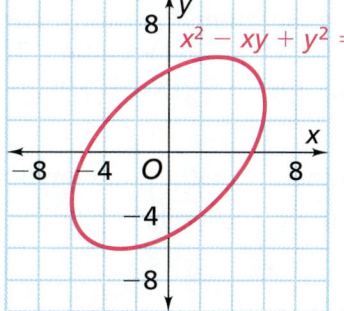

12. Use the graph of $x^2 - xy + y^2 = 27$, shown at the right, to sketch the graph of $(x + 3)^2 - (x + 3)(y - 4) + (y - 4)^2 = 27$.

Sketch means to draw a rough picture. Do not worry about making an exact graph.

13. **Standardized Test Prep** Which graph is the graph of $y = |x - 2| + 3$?

A.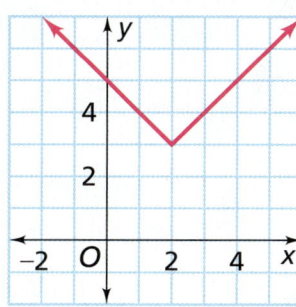

B.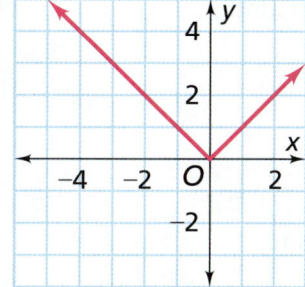

C.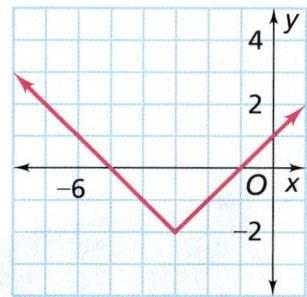

D.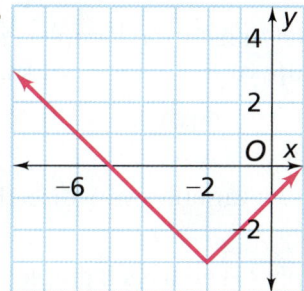

14. **Take It Further** Find an equation of a graph that is the same size and shape as the graph of $x^2 - xy + y^2 = 27$, but that passes through the point (0, 4).

If you know a point on the original graph, you can use a translation.

15. **Take It Further** Sketch the graph of $x^2 - xy + y^2 = 108$.

Maintain Your Skills

16. Sketch the graph of each equation.
    a. $(y - 5) = 3(x - 1)$
    b. $(y + 4) = 3(x + 2)$
    c. $(y + 7) = 3(x + 3)$
    d. $y = \frac{1}{2}(x - 6)$
    e. $(y + 3) = \frac{1}{2}x$
    f. $(y + 2) = \frac{1}{2}(x - 2)$
    g. What pattern do you find?

17. Use the graphs from Exercise 16. Find an ordered pair (x, y) that makes all the equations in Exercise 16 parts (a)–(f) true.

3.18 Translating Graphs 313

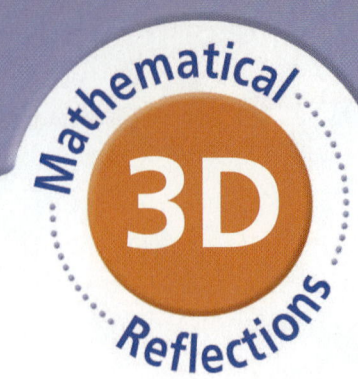

Mathematical Reflections 3D

In this investigation, you learned about six basic graphs and their equations. Two of the basic graphs show direct and inverse variation. These questions will help you summarize what you have learned.

1. Show that the points are on the graph of the given equation.
   a. $(6, 13)$ and $(-6, -13)$, $xy = 78$
   b. $(12, 3)$ and $(3, 12)$, $xy = 36$

2. Describe the relationship between the graphs of $y = x^2$ and $y + 4 = (x - 5)^2$.

3. What is the point that all six basic graphs pass through?

4. Sketch a graph of each equation.
   a. $y = (x + 2)^2$
   b. $y - 3 = x^3$
   c. $y + 4 = |x - 2|$
   d. $y = 5x$
   e. $xy = 5$
   f. $y = 5x^2$

5. a. Sketch the basic graph of $y = x^2$.
   b. Transform the graph using the rule $(x, y) \mapsto (x + 3, y)$.
   c. The points $(0, 0)$ and $(2, 4)$ are on the graph of $y = x^2$. What are the corresponding points on the transformed graph from part (b)?
   d. Write an equation for the transformed graph. Test your points from part (c) to make sure your equation works.
   e. **Write About It** How does the equation relate to the transformation rule?

6. What does it mean to say two variables vary directly or inversely?

7. What are the six basic graphs? Sketch each graph.

8. If you free fall 4.9 meters in one second, how far do you free fall in four seconds?

Vocabulary

In this investigation, you learned these terms. Make sure you understand what each one means and how to use it.

- direct variation
- inverse variation

The transformation $(x, y) \mapsto (x, y - 10)$ takes you down 10 floors.

Project Using Mathematical Habits

Drawing with Graphs

In this project, you will learn to write directions for a computer to make an image using graphs. You can draw lines and curves using this method.

Below are the steps for drawing this square.

Graph each equation.

- $y = \frac{3}{4}x + \frac{17}{4}$ for x values between 1 and 5
- $y = \frac{3}{4}x - 2$ for x values between 4 and 8
- $y = -\frac{4}{3}x + \frac{19}{3}$ for x values between 1 and 5
- $y = -\frac{4}{3}x + \frac{44}{3}$ for x values between 5 and 8

Drawing Shapes

1. Write a series of equations with the ranges you need to draw this figure.

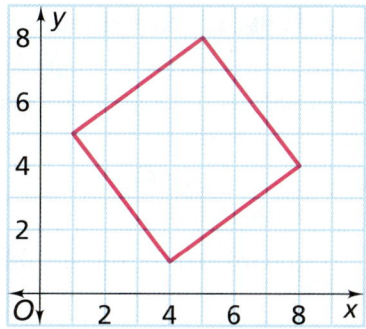

2. Graph each equation. Draw and name the shape.
   - $y = 3$ for x values between -1 and 5
   - $x = -1$ for y values between -3 and 3
   - $y = x - 2$ for x values between -1 and 5

3. Change the steps in Exercise 1 so that the resulting arrow fits each description given.

   a. 3 units left of the original arrow

   b. points left and is anywhere on the graph

   c. points up

4. Graph each equation. Draw and name the shape.
   - $x = 0$ for y values between 2 and 3
   - $y = \frac{9}{4}\left(x - \frac{3}{2}\right) + 3$ for x values between 1 and $\frac{3}{2}$
   - $y = -\frac{9}{4}\left(x + \frac{3}{2}\right) + 3$ for x values between -1 and $\frac{3}{2}$
   - $y = \frac{3}{2}(x - 2) + \frac{3}{2}$ for x values between 2 and $\frac{8}{3}$
   - $y = -\frac{3}{2}(x + 2) + \frac{3}{2}$ for x values between -2 and $\frac{8}{3}$
   - $y = (x - 3) + \frac{7}{8}$ for x values between 3 and $\frac{23}{6}$
   - $y = -(x + 3) + \frac{7}{8}$ for x values between 3 and $\frac{23}{6}$
   - $y = -\frac{x^2}{8} + 2$ for x values between -4 and 4
   - $y = \frac{x^2}{8} - 2$ for x values between -4 and 4
   - $x^2 + y^2 = 1$ for all x values
   - $x^2 + y^2 = 4$ for all x values

5. Write a series of equations for drawing a shape. Use at least one curved graph.

Chapter 3 Project

Chapter 3 Review

In **Investigation 3A,** you learned how to

- plot points and read coordinates on a graph
- describe how transformations operate on ordered pairs
- use absolute value and relate it to distance
- connect graphs to sets of data

The following questions will help you check your understanding.

1. Use the points on this coordinate plane.

   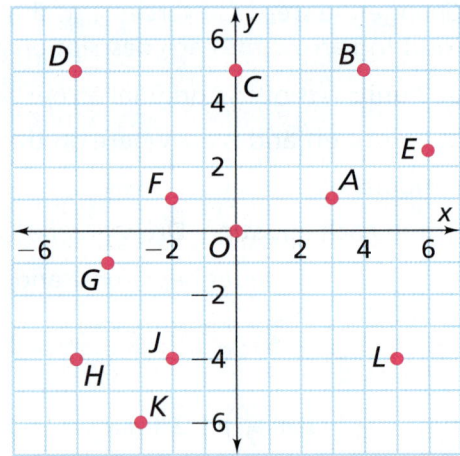

   a. How many labeled points are completely in Quadrant IV?
   b. Name two labeled points that have the same *x*-coordinate.
   c. Write a rule that transforms point *E* to point *G*.

2. Solve each equation.
   a. $7 = |x + 2|$
   b. $|2x - 3| = 9$
   c. $|7 - x| = 6$
   d. $|3x + 4| = -1$

3. Josh keeps track of how much he spends on salads at four different salad bars. Which labeled point on the graph represents the salad bar with the lowest price per ounce?

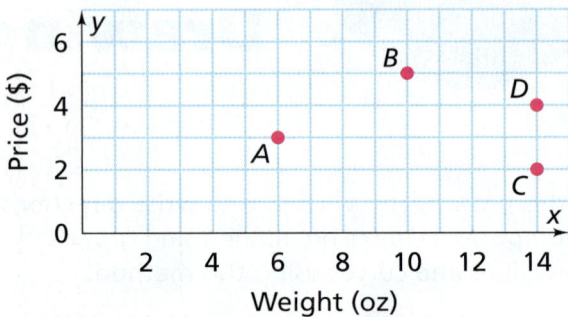

In **Investigation 3B,** you learned how to

- determine the mean, median, and mode for a set of data and decide how meaningful they are in specific situations
- interpret data lists, frequency tables, and stem-and-leaf displays
- determine the five-number summary for a set of data
- build dot plots, histograms, box-and-whisker plots, and scatter plots
- use two-way tables to organize and display categorical data.

The following questions will help you check your understanding.

For Exercises 4–6, use the stem-and-leaf display that shows the ages of the women's singles winners in the United States Open Tennis Championship.

United States Open Women's Singles Tennis Championship 1993–2007

```
1 | 6 7 9 9
2 | 0 0 1 1 2 2 2 4 5 6 7
```

4. Find the mean and mode.
5. Find the five-number summary.
6. Sketch a box-and-whisker plot.

In **Investigation 3C,** you learned how to

- test a point to determine whether it is on the graph of an equation
- graph equations by plotting points
- write the equation of a vertical or horizontal line given its graph or a point on its graph
- read a graph to identify points that are solutions to an equation
- find the intersection point of two graphs and understand its meaning

The following questions will help you check your understanding.

7. The graph of $(x - 3)^2 + (y - 4)^2 = 25$ is a circle. Determine whether each point is on the circle. Explain.

   a. $A = (0, 8)$
   b. $B = (7, 7)$
   c. $C = (7.5, 2)$
   d. $D = (3, -1)$

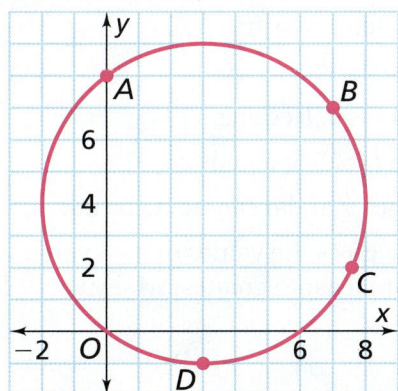

8. Graph the equations $y = (x - 3)^2$ and $x + y = 5$. What are the intersection points?

In **Investigation 3D,** you learned how to

- decide whether a situation represents a direct or inverse variation
- sketch the graphs of the equations $y = x$, $xy = 1$, $y = x^2$, $y = x^3$, $y = \sqrt{x}$, $y = |x|$, and variations of these equations
- recognize the distinguishing features of the basic graphs, such as their general shape, and the points and quadrants that they pass through
- describe the rules for translating graphs of equations vertically or horizontally

The following questions will help you check your understanding.

9. Sketch each graph.

   a. $y + 4 = |x - 3|$
   b. $y = \sqrt{x - 7}$
   c. $y = \frac{1}{3}x$
   d. $y - 3 = (x + 2)^3$
   e. $y = \frac{15}{x}$
   f. $y - 1 = -x^2$

10. The figure shows parts of four basic graphs.

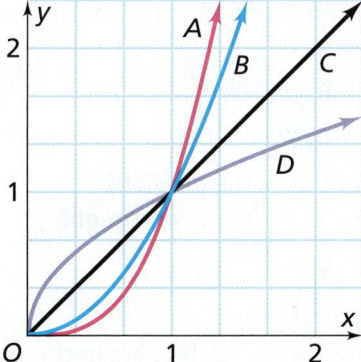

   a. Identify each graph.
   b. Which graph is part of two different basic graphs? Identify the two basic graphs.
   c. For each graph, name the quadrant that is not shown that the graph passes through.

Chapter 3 Test

Go Online
pearsonsuccessnet.com

Multiple Choice

1. Which equation has a graph that goes through points (2, 3) and (−1, −5)?

   A. $3x - 4y = -6$
   B. $y = 3x^2 - 9$
   C. $8x - 3y = 7$
   D. $x^2 + y^2 = 26$

2. Which point is on the graph of $x^2 - 2y^2 = 1$?

   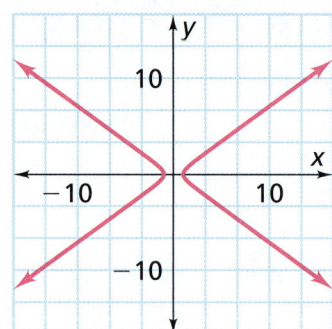

   A. (7, 5) B. (0, 0)
   C. (10, −7) D. (−17, −12)

3. Which is an intersection point of the graphs of $y = 4$ and $y = \sqrt{x}$?

   A. (16, 4) B. (4, 16)
   C. (4, 2) D. (2, 4)

4. Which quadrant does the graph of $(y + 3) = (x - 4)^2$ NOT pass through?

   A. I B. II
   C. III D. IV

5. How many intersection points are in the graphs of the equations $(y + 4) = |x|$ and $(y - 2) = \sqrt{x + 1}$?

   A. 0 B. 1
   C. 2 D. 3

6. Based solely on this stem-and-leaf display of the ages of the 43 United States presidents at their first inauguration, which statement is true?

   Ages of United States Presidents at First Inauguration

   ```
   4 | 3 6 6 6 7 8 9 9
   5 | 0 1 1 1 2 2 2 2 4 4 4 4 4 5 5 5 6 6 6 6 7 7 7 7 8
   6 | 1 1 1 2 4 4 4 5 8 9
   ```

   A. None of the presidents were inaugurated at age 58.
   B. The first quartile age at inauguration is 51 years.
   C. The range of ages is 42 years.
   D. The median age at inauguration is 54 years.

7. The relationship between variables a and b is an inverse variation. When a equals 100, b equals 6. Which statement is true?

   A. If a equals 200, b equals 12.
   B. If a equals 5, b equals 120.
   C. If a equals 25, b equals 25.
   D. Variables a and b can never be equal.

8. Which list gives the values of the expressions, in order, from least to greatest when $x = -2$?

   A. $|x|, 1, x^2, x^3$
   B. $1, |x|, x^2, x^3$
   C. $x^3, 1, |x|, x^2$
   D. $x^3, x^2, 1, |x|$

Open Response

9. Write three different equations with graphs that contain the point (3, 7). Explain how you know that each graph contains (3, 7).

10. Sketch the graph of $y = x^2 - 5x + 6$.

4.01 Getting Started

**Activating Prior Knowledge
Exploring New Ideas**

You can describe the steepness of a line by comparing rise to run. Carpenters calculate the steepness of roofs and ramps. Mathematicians calculate the steepness of lines.

For You to Explore

1. Which roof is the steepest?

   a.

   b.

   c.

   d.

   > Explain how you decided which roof is the steepest to a person who does not understand the word *steep*.

2. The gable end of a roof is the triangular part of the wall. It supports the peak of the roof at each end of the house. When building a gable end, a builder supports the roof with vertical boards. The builder spaces the boards 16 inches apart.

   Diagram of a Gable End

4.01 Getting Started 323

The diagram shows half of the gable end of a house.

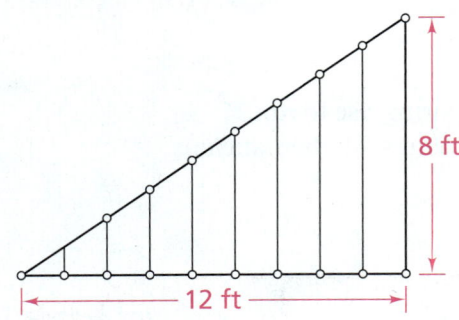

a. What are the rise and run of the gable end?
b. How many vertical boards are there? How are the vertical boards spaced?
c. How long is each of the vertical boards?

3. Tony makes a distance-time graph for a bike trip he took with Sasha.

   a. Who rode faster, Tony or Sasha? Explain.
   b. What does the intersection of the lines represent?
   c. How many miles did Sasha travel in an hour?
   d. How many miles did Tony travel in an hour?

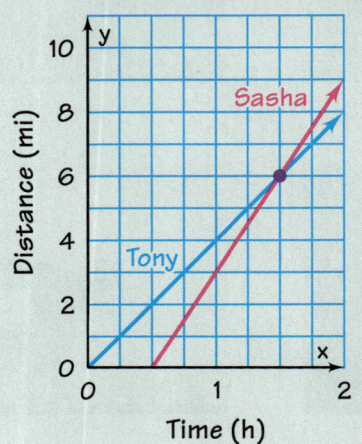

4. Use your graphing calculator. Which equations have a graph that is a line? What do the equations with graphs that are lines have in common?

   a. $y = x$
   b. $y = x^2$
   c. $y = 5x + 2$
   d. $y = \frac{1}{x}$
   e. $y = x^3 - x^2 + 5$
   f. $y = 4x - 13 + 2x - 7$
   g. $y = x + 1$
   h. $y = \sqrt{x} + 1$
   i. $y = x^3 + 1$
   j. $y = 2(13 - 7x)$

> **Rise** is the difference between the starting and ending points on a vertical number line.
> **Run** is the difference between the starting and ending points on a horizontal number line.

For Problems 5 and 6, plot the points given. Draw a straight line through them. Name three points that are on the same line as each given pair of points.

5. (3, 1) and (7, 3)
6. (7, 1) and (12, −3)

> Points that lie on the same line are **collinear**.

324 Chapter 4 Lines

Exercises Practicing Habits of Mind

On Your Own

7. Manny uses an extension ladder to paint the window shutters on his house. A safety label on the ladder states that you need to place the base of the ladder 1 foot from the wall for every 4 feet the ladder reaches up the wall. The diagram shows a ladder that reaches 8 feet up the wall. The base of the ladder is 2 feet from the wall.

   An extension ladder is a ladder with a length you can change.

   a. How far away from the wall should Manny place the base of the ladder if he needs to paint window shutters 12 feet up the wall?

   b. How far away from the wall should Manny place the base of the ladder if he needs to paint window shutters 10 feet up the wall?

   c. How can Manny determine the ladder's safe distance from a wall if he knows how high he wants the top of the ladder?

   d. Manny needs to get to the roof of a two-story building. Each story is 9 feet. The ladder should extend 1 foot above the wall for him to get on the roof safely. How long does he need to make the ladder to get to the roof safely?

8. a. What is an equation of the vertical line that contains the point $(5, 7)$?

   b. What is an equation of the horizontal line that contains the point $(2, -1)$?

   c. At what point do the two lines intersect?

9. Determine whether the three points are collinear. Explain.

   Remember... Points are collinear if they lie on the same straight line.

   a. $X(-3, 3)$, $Y(4, 3)$, $Z(100, 3)$

   b. $P(-3, 8)$, $Q(-3, 2)$, $R(-3, -4)$

   c. $A(-1, 3)$, $B(4, 15)$, $C(14, 39)$

   d. $E(3, 5)$, $F(4, 6)$, $G(10, 13)$

10. Maria rode her bike 8 miles in 1 hour. How fast did she travel in miles per hour?

11. **Write About It** The graph shows the distance Maria travels against the time she bikes.

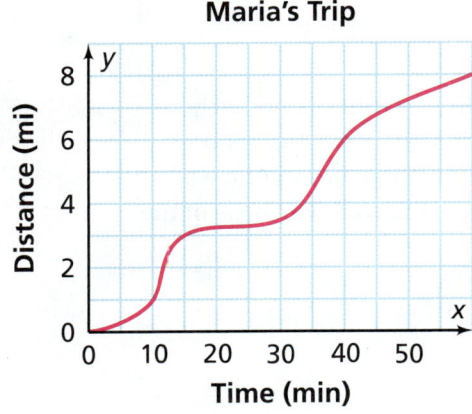

Maria's Trip

> The vertical axis on this graph represents the actual distance Maria travels on her bike. It does not necessarily represent the exact distance she is from her starting point.

   a. Why is this graph a better representation of Maria's trip than the description in Exercise 10?

   b. Does Maria travel at a constant pace? Explain.

   c. How does the pace you calculated in Exercise 10 relate to the graph?

Maintain Your Skills

12. Use graph paper. Sketch each pair of equations.

   a. $y = x$ and $y = -x$

   b. $y = 2x$ and $y = -2x$

   c. $y = \frac{1}{2}x$ and $y = -\frac{1}{2}x$

   d. What do you notice about the pairs of graphs?

For Exercises 13 and 14, graph each equation on graph paper. Look for a pattern.

13. a. $y = x$ b. $y = 2x$ c. $y = 3x$
    d. $y = 4x$ e. $y = 15x$ f. $y = 1000x$
    g. Describe the pattern.

14. a. $y = \frac{1}{2}x$ b. $y = \frac{1}{3}x$ c. $y = \frac{1}{4}x$
    d. $y = \frac{1}{5}x$ e. $y = \frac{1}{15}x$ f. $y = \frac{1}{1000}x$
    g. Describe the pattern.

Go Online
pearsonsuccessnet.com

326 Chapter 4 Lines

4.02 Pitch and Slope

Builders describe the steepness of a roof using a number that they call the *pitch*. The pitch tells how many inches the roof rises vertically for every 12 inches of horizontal run.

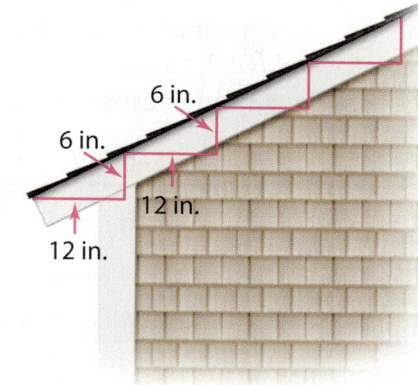

Suppose a roof rises 6 inches for every 12 inches of horizontal run. You can say that the roof has a "6 in 12 pitch," "6–12 pitch," or "6 pitch."

In mathematics, you use a number, or *slope*, to describe the steepness of a line between one point and another point in the Cartesian plane. Suppose the vertical rise from one point to another on a line is 6 units, and the horizontal run is 12 units. You can say that the line has a slope of $\frac{6}{12}$, or $\frac{1}{2}$.

> In carpentry, the custom is to write pitch as a number related to 12, because there are 12 inches in a foot. There is no such custom for slope. You can express slope as a fraction in simplest form.

Example 1

Problem Suppose a line connects points $A(5, 6)$ and $B(9, 13)$. Find the slope of the line between the points.

Solution $m(A, B) = \frac{\text{rise}}{\text{run}} = \frac{13 - 6}{9 - 5} = \frac{7}{4}$. The slope is $\frac{7}{4}$.

> It is common to use m to denote slope. The expression $m(A, B)$ represents the slope of a line between points A and B.

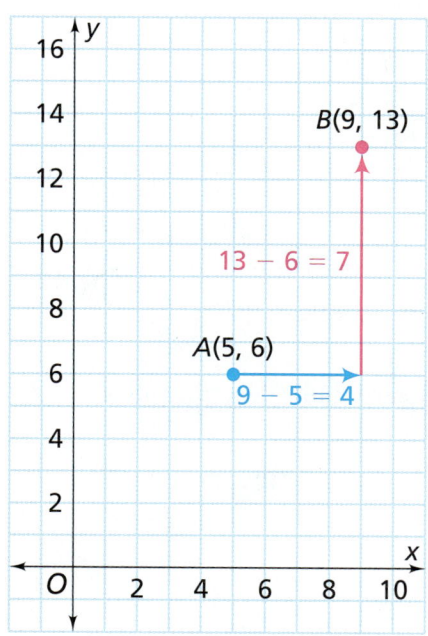

Developing Habits of Mind

Represent slope. You can represent slope in different ways. For example, the slope between points A and B in Example 1 is $\frac{7}{4}$. You can also write $\frac{7}{4}$ as $1\frac{3}{4}$, $\frac{14}{8}$, 1.75, or any other expression that represents the same number as $\frac{7}{4}$.

For You to Do

Graph points A and B from Example 1.

1. Find two other points, S and T, such that $m(S, T) = \frac{7}{4}$ also.

2. Does $m(S, T) = m(T, S)$?

3. Given point $M(3, 15)$, plot 6 other points such that the slope from each of the points to M is $\frac{4}{3}$.

Draw lines through points A and B and through points S and T.

Example 2

Problem Find the slope between the points $R(7, 2)$ and $S(10, 0)$.

Solution $m(R, S) = \frac{0 - 2}{10 - 7} = \frac{-2}{3} = -\frac{2}{3}$. The slope is $-\frac{2}{3}$.

Is $m(S, R)$ also negative?

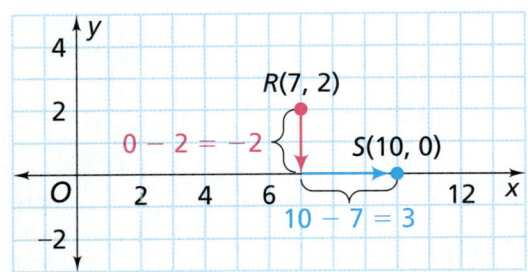

For Discussion

4. How can you calculate the slope between two points? Explain, using an example.

5. What are some differences between the ways that carpenters describe pitch and mathematicians describe slope?

Definition

In the Cartesian plane, the **slope** between two points with different x-coordinates is the change in their y-coordinates divided by the change in their x-coordinates.

For any two points $A(x_1, y_1)$ and $B(x_2, y_2)$,

$$m(A, B) = \frac{\text{rise}}{\text{run}} = \frac{\text{change in the } y\text{-coordinates}}{\text{change in the } x\text{-coordinates}} = \frac{\Delta y}{\Delta x} = \frac{y_2 - y_1}{x_2 - x_1}.$$

> If the x-coordinates are the same, slope is undefined. This happens when the two points are in line vertically.

Facts and Notation

- The Greek letter Δ, delta, means *change in*.
- The "1" and "2" in x_1 and x_2 are **subscripts.** The subscripts indicate that x_1 and x_2 represent different variables. Likewise, y_1 and y_2 are different variables.

> You can use different letters to represent the coordinates. However, using x_1 and x_2 makes it clear that they both represent x-coordinates. Similarly, y_1 and y_2 are both y-coordinates. The subscripts also help you keep track of relationships among variables.

For You to Do

6. **What's Wrong Here?** Sasha calculates the slope from $P(3, 4)$ to $Q(2, 6)$.

    The change in the y-coordinates is $4 - 6 = -2$.
    The change in the x-coordinates is $2 - 3 = -1$.
    The slope is $\frac{-2}{-1} = 2$.

    Tony calculates the slope differently.

    The change in the y-coordinates is $6 - 4 = 2$.
    The change in the x-coordinates is $2 - 3 = -1$.
    The slope is $\frac{2}{-1} = -2$.

    a. Who found the correct slope?

    b. What can you say to help the person with the incorrect slope?

Exercises Practicing Habits of Mind

Check Your Understanding

1. Find the slope between each pair of points.
   a. (2, 1) and (6, 8)
   b. (6, 8) and (2, 1)
   c. (3, 10) and (12, 2)
   d. (3, 10) and $\left(\frac{15}{2}, 6\right)$
   e. $\left(\frac{15}{2}, 6\right)$ and (12, 2)
   f. (−4, 5) and (0, 0)
   g. (5, 4) and (0, 0)
   h. (−8, 10) and (0, 0)
   i. (−4, 5) and (12, 5)
   j. (5, 4) and (−20, 4)
   k. (3, 3) and (25, 25)
   l. (4, 5) and (4, −7)

2. For each of the following, graph points A and B. Find another point C such that $m(A, B) = m(A, C)$.

   Remember...
   The slope is the rise over the run.

   a. $A(-2, 4), B(-1, 5)$
   b. $A(3, 4), B(-1, 5)$
   c. $A(0, 0), B(4, -12)$
   d. $A(-3, 1), B(0, 0)$
   e. What can you conclude about points A, B, and C when $m(A, B) = m(A, C)$?

3. Find two points A and B that will make each statement true, if possible.
   a. $m(A, B) > 0$
   b. $m(A, B) < 0$
   c. $m(A, B) = 0$
   d. $m(A, B)$ does not exist.

4. Use tables to graph each equation. Choose three points on each graph to test for a constant slope. How do the graphs that have a constant slope differ from those that do not?

   Constant slope means that the slope between any two points on the graph is the same.

   a. $y = \frac{1}{2}x - 4$
   b. $y = x^2$
   c. $y = 5x$
   d. $y + 3 = 2(x - 4)$
   e. $y = 2^x$
   f. $y = 2x^2 + 1$

If the rise is the same and the runs are opposites, then the slopes are opposites.

5. **Write About It** What are some other situations in which you can describe and compare steepness?

6. **Take It Further** The slope between points $J(9, r)$ and $K(6, 3)$ is $-\frac{1}{3}$. What is the value of r?

On Your Own

7. Find the slope between each pair of points.

   a. $(-6, 4)$ and $(0, 0)$
   b. $(4, 6)$ and $(0, 0)$
   c. $\left(\frac{1}{2}, 13\right)$ and $\left(-2\frac{2}{3}, 13\right)$
   d. $(27, -7.1)$ and $(27, 5.2)$
   e. $(-6, -1)$ and $(-1, 8)$
   f. $(-6, -1)$ and $(4, 17)$
   g. $(4, 17)$ and $(-1, 8)$
   h. $(3, 4)$ and $(5, 1)$
   i. $(5, 1)$ and $(3, 4)$

   Again, plot the points to find the slope.

8. Given $A(5, 3)$ and $O(0, 0)$, find a point B that makes the following true.

   a. $m(A, B) = 3$
   b. $m(A, B) = -3$
   c. $m(A, B) = -\frac{1}{3}$
   d. $m(A, B) = 0$
   e. $m(A, B) = m(O, B)$
   f. $m(A, B) = \frac{3}{4}$ and the distance between points A and B is 5.

9. How can you describe the relative positions of A and B in each situation?

   a. $m(A, B) > 0$
   b. $m(A, B) < 0$
   c. $m(A, B) = 0$
   d. $m(A, B)$ does not exist.

10. a. What is $m(T, J)$?
    b. Choose another point P on $\overleftrightarrow{TJ}$. Calculate $m(T, P)$ and $m(P, J)$.

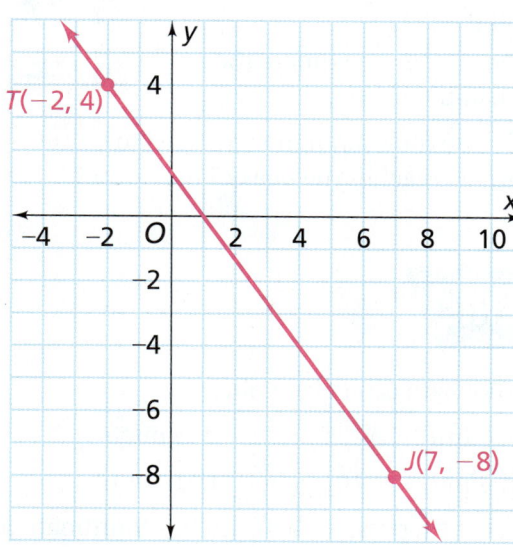

Go Online
pearsonsuccessnet.com

11. Jenna tests whether points $A(3, 4)$, $B(5, 7)$, and $C(9, 13)$ are on the same line. She plots the points. Then she draws triangles with sides parallel to the x- and y-axes.

    She explains her test. "To go from A to B, I go over 2 and up 3. To go from B to C, I go over exactly twice as far and up exactly twice as far."

    Try Jenna's test on Exercise 10. Does her method work? Explain. Use the word *slope* in your explanation.

12. **Standardized Test Prep** Lorna writes a computer game on a coordinate grid. The frog in her game can jump from one pair of integer coordinates to another pair. Point A is at $(4, 5)$ and $m(A, B) = -\frac{2}{3}$. Which of the following cannot be the coordinates of point B?

    A. $(10, 1)$ **B.** $(7, 3)$ **C.** $(1, 7)$ **D.** $(2, 8)$

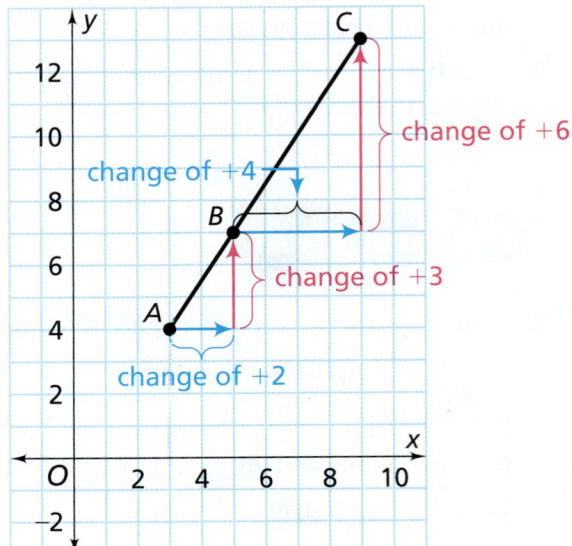

13. **Take It Further** The roof pitch for the house at the right is 6–12. The house is 28 feet wide.

    a. What is the attic roof height h?

    b. Steps are usually 8 inches high. The treads you step on are usually 12 inches from the front to the back of the tread. About how high above the ground is the front porch?

    c. About how far from the porch foundation is the front of the bottom step?

    d. About how high is the house? (*Hint*: Estimate the height between the porch and the attic.)

    e. About how far from the house foundation do you need to place a ladder so that it safely reaches the peak of the house?

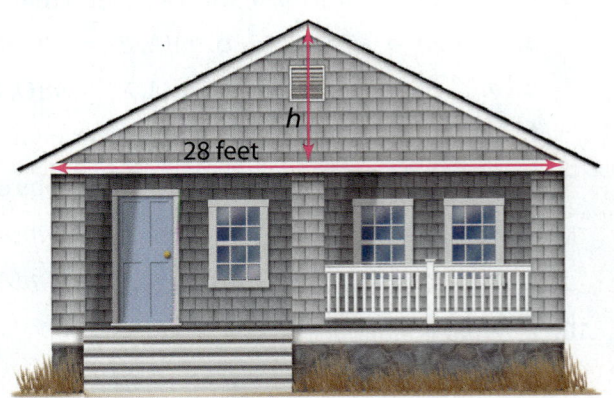

For safety, a ladder's base must be 1 foot from the wall for every 4 feet it extends up the wall.

Maintain Your Skills

14. Use graph paper. Sketch a roof with each given pitch.

    a. 1–12 b. 3 in 12 c. 6 pitch
    d. 2 in 12 e. 4 pitch f. 12 in 12

15. Suppose each roof in Exercise 14 represents a line in the coordinate plane.

    a. Write the pitch of each line as a fraction in lowest terms.

    b. How does each fraction relate to the steepness of each roof?

4.03 Rates of Change

In Lesson 3.04, you graphed one set of data against another. For instance, you used this graph to illustrate Emma walking to a basketball court.

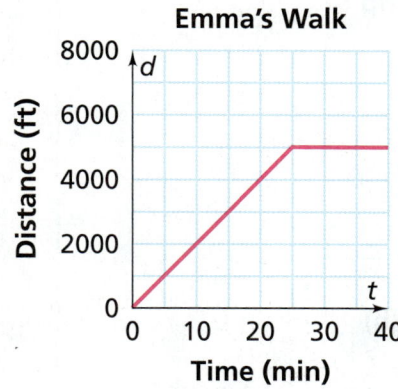

In that example, you focused on describing her distance from home at particular times. You can also use the graph to determine her average speed between two points on the graph.

Speed is the rate at which distance traveled changes. For example, Emma travels 5000 feet in 25 minutes. You can find her average speed using this formula.

$$\text{average speed} = \frac{\Delta \text{distance}}{\Delta \text{time}}$$
$$= \frac{5000 \text{ ft}}{25 \text{ min}}$$
$$= \frac{200 \text{ ft}}{1 \text{ min}}$$

Emma travels at 200 feet per minute (ft/min).

You can also calculate her speed by finding the slope between the two points $A(10, 2000)$ and $B(25, 5000)$.

$$m(A, B) = \frac{5000 \text{ ft} - 2000 \text{ ft}}{25 \text{ min} - 10 \text{ min}}$$
$$= \frac{3000 \text{ ft}}{15 \text{ min}}$$
$$= \frac{200 \text{ ft}}{1 \text{ min}}$$

Per implies division. *Percent* means "part of one hundred."

If Emma is not traveling at a constant speed, you can still calculate her average speed by finding the slope between two points.

Example

Problem The graph represents a trip Tia took. The labeled points on the graph have the coordinates $O(0, 0)$, $A(1, 75)$, $B(1.5, 7.5)$, and $C(2, 100)$.

What is Tia's average speed between the following points?

a. O and A

b. B and C

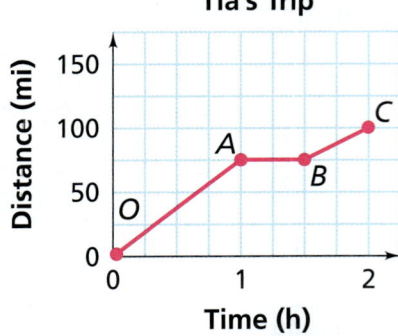

> The distance on this graph is the actual distance the car traveled. It is not necessarily the exact distance Tia is from home.

Solution The average speed between two points on a distance-time graph is the change in distance divided by the change in time. As you saw in Tia's case, the slope between these two points is the same as her average speed between the two points.

a. Calculate Tia's average speed from point O to point A.

$$m(O, A) = \frac{75 \text{ mi} - 0 \text{ mi}}{1 \text{ h} - 0 \text{ h}} = \frac{75 \text{ mi}}{1 \text{ h}} = 75 \text{ mi per hour}$$

Her average speed is 75 miles per hour.

b. Calculate Tia's average speed from point B to point C.

$$m(B, C) = \frac{100 \text{ mi} - 75 \text{ mi}}{2 \text{ h} - 1.5 \text{ h}} = \frac{25 \text{ mi}}{0.5 \text{ h}} = 50 \text{ mph}$$

Her average speed is 50 miles per hour.

> You can write abbreviations, such as mi for miles and h for hours. You can also write mph, or mi/h, for miles per hour.

For You to Do

1. What is Tia's average speed between point A and point B?

If you pick any two points on a distance-time graph, the slope between the two points is the same as the average speed of travel between those points. This statement is true because of the facts below.

- On a graph, you calculate the slope between two points as the vertical change divided by the horizontal change.
- On a distance-time graph, vertical change represents the distance traveled.
- On a distance-time graph, horizontal change represents the elapsed time.
- Therefore, the slope between two points on a distance-time graph is distance traveled divided by elapsed time. You can calculate average speed the same way.

Theorem 4.1

The slope between two points on a distance-time graph is the average speed of travel between those points.

For You to Do

2. Explain the theorem in your own words. Give an example.

Developing Habits of Mind

Visualize relationships. You can compute the average speed if you know the total change in position divided by the change in time. In these graphs, the total change in distance is 100 miles. The total change in time is 2 hours.

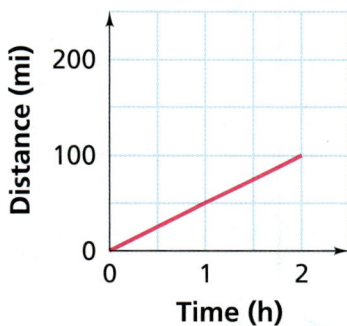

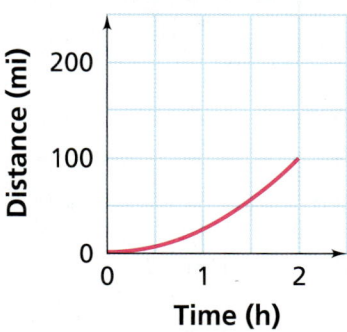

The Moving Steadily graph is a line because the slope between any two points is the same.

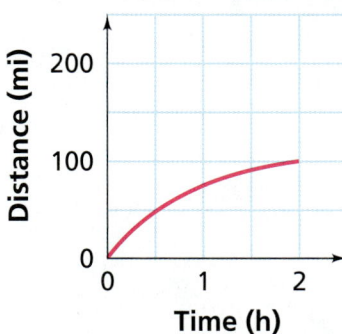

In each case, the overall rate of change is 50 miles per hour. Remember that the average speed is the slope between the start and end points on a graph.

4.03 Rates of Change 335

The graphs below show speed against time instead of distance against time for the same situations. In speed-time graphs, you view speed differently than in distance-time graphs. In distance-time graphs, you think of average speed as the change in distance over a large interval of time. In speed-time graphs, you can think of speed as the change in distance over a very small amount of time.

A car's speedometer shows average speed for a very small interval using this method.

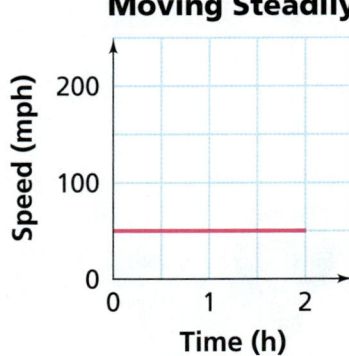

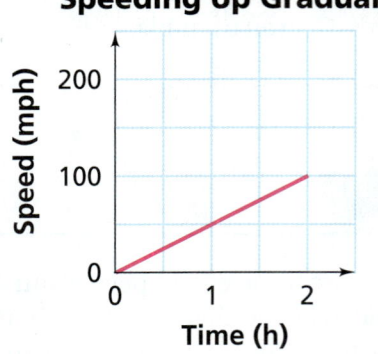

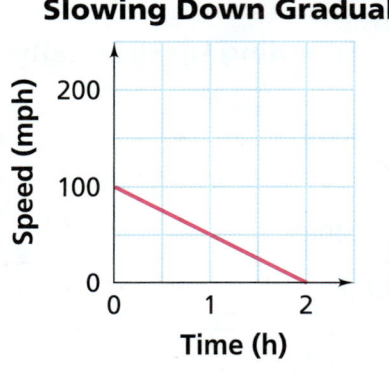

In a speed-time graph at $t = 1$, the plotted value of speed is approximately the change in distance from $t = 1$ to $t = 1.0001$ hours. The ratio may involve very small numbers, such as 0.005 mi/0.0001 h, or 50 mi/h. You can think of travelling 50 mi/h for a very short time interval.

336 Chapter 4 Lines

For You to Do

3. Write a story for another trip with an average rate of change of 50 mph. Illustrate this story with a graph different from the graphs above. Draw a distance-time graph and a speed-time graph for your story.

4. Explain how each of the speed graphs relates to the corresponding distance graph.

You have seen examples of rate of change that compare distance over time. In fact, rate of change problems can compare any two numerical quantities. For example, accountants measure rate of change by tracking money over time. Electric companies track the amount of electricity a customer uses over time. Exercise physiologists calculate the Calories a person burns for each minute of exercise.

Rates of change do not always involve time. The nutrition labels on food show the number of Calories per serving. Fabric shops and carpet stores charge for their goods by the square yard.

Exercises Practicing Habits of Mind

Check Your Understanding

1. The graph shows additional details of Tia's trip. As in the Example, the points on the graph are $O(0, 0)$, $A(1, 75)$, $B(1.5, 75)$, and $C(2, 100)$. The coordinates for points D and E are unknown.

   a. Compute the average speed between points D and A.

   b. Compute the average speed between points A and E.

   c. Estimate the coordinates of points D and E. Approximate the average speed between points D and E.

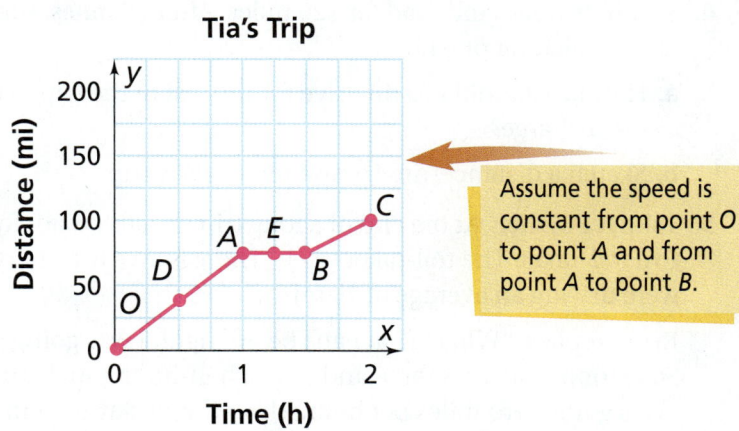

Assume the speed is constant from point O to point A and from point A to point B.

4.03 Rates of Change

When entering a toll road, you take a ticket that shows your location. When leaving the toll road, you give the ticket to a toll-taker. The toll-taker reads the ticket to tell how far you have traveled and collects the correct toll.

Some toll road systems also time-stamp a ticket when you take it. A toll-taker can then tell how far you have traveled and the time you have taken. Using these two numbers, the toll-taker can calculate your average speed.

For Exercises 2–5, make the following assumptions.

- A toll ticket shows your location and the time that you entered a toll road.
- The toll is 3¢ per mile.
- A toll-taker charges an extra $100 if your average speed is between 65 mi/h and 80 mi/h.
- A toll-taker charges an extra $200 if your average speed is more than 80 mi/h.

2. Tanner enters a toll road at 3 P.M. He leaves the toll road at 6:30 P.M. He travels 200 miles.

   a. What is the toll for the distance he travels?

   b. What is his average speed? Is there an extra charge?

3. Tanner travels home on a toll road from 10 A.M. to 1 P.M. He travels 200 miles.

   a. What is the toll for the distance he travels?

   b. What is his average speed? Is there an extra charge?

   c. Tanner does not want to pay an extra charge. What is the shortest time that he could travel on a toll road home?

4. Kristin travels a toll road for 120 miles. After 70 miles, she notices that she has traveled for one hour.

   a. How fast should Kristin drive for the rest of the trip to avoid an extra charge?

   b. Sketch a distance-time graph for Kristin's trip.

5. **Take It Further** At the end of a long trip on a toll road, Ryota gives his ticket to a toll-taker. The toll-taker says, "There is an extra charge of $100. You were driving an average of 70 mi/h."

   Ryota replies, "What? That can't be. All right, I was going a little too fast. So I stopped at a rest area and took a half-hour nap. During that time, I was going zero miles per hour. Also, when I started out, I was going 0. And now I'm going 0 again. So, how could I average 70 mi/h?"

The astute toll-taker responds, "Well, take out the nap time and you averaged 80 mi/h."

Catching the drift, Ryota murmurs, "OK, so maybe I didn't take a nap."

a. How many miles was Ryota's trip? How long did it take, including the alleged nap?

b. Sketch two possible distance-time graphs for Ryota's trip. Include his nap in one graph but not in the other.

On Your Own

6. You can measure a car's fuel efficiency in miles per gallon. Compare the number of miles driven to the number of gallons of gasoline used. The graph shows examples of distance against gas used in highway driving for three car models.

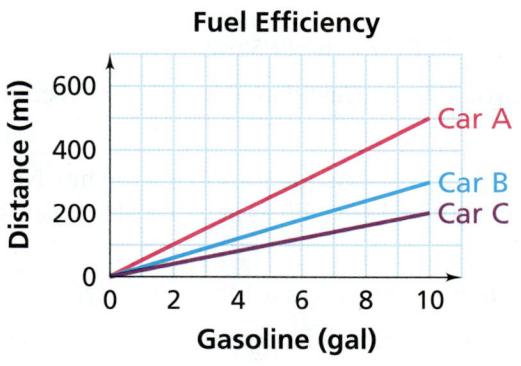

SUV

Sedan

Hybrid

a. Based on the type of car at the right, which graph do you think represents the fuel used by each car?

b. Find each car's rate of change in miles per gallon.

7. The time it takes to download files from the Internet varies depending on the type of connection. The rate of transfer is measured in kilobits per second (kbps).

A trailer for a new video game is available online. It is 6 megabytes, which is about 49,000 kilobits. How long does it take to download the trailer with the following connections?

a. cable modem running at 1200 kbps

b. DSL line running at 384 kbps

c. 56-kbps modem

d. 2400-baud modem (2.4 kbps)

> The first modems transferred data at a rate of 300 baud, or about 0.3 kbps. Today's modems are nearly 200 times as fast!

8. An advertisement claims a car can go from zero to 60 in five seconds.

a. What unit of measure is implied by 60?

b. Is it impressive that a car can go 60? Are there any cars that cannot go 60?

c. Draw a speed-time graph for a car that travels from zero to 60 in five seconds.

4.03 Rates of Change

9. **Take It Further** Refer to Exercise 8.
   a. What is the rate of change of the car's speed?
   b. What word usually describes the rate of change of speed?
   c. Draw a distance-time graph for a car traveling from 0 to 60 in 5 seconds. How far does the car travel during those 5 seconds?

For Exercises 10 and 11, assume Katie bikes at a rate of 230 yards per minute.

10. a. How far will she bike in 5 minutes?
    b. How long will it take her to bike the length of a football field? A football field is 100 yards long.
    c. Draw a distance-time graph of Katie biking for 5 minutes.
    d. Choose any two points on your graph. Calculate the slope between those two points.

11. One minute after Katie starts biking, two friends start following her. Nick bikes at a rate of 200 yards per minute. Lance bikes at a rate of 300 yards per minute.
    a. Will Nick catch Katie? If so, how long will it take him?
    b. Will Lance catch Katie? If so, how long will it take him?

12. **Standardized Test Prep** Tamara travels 1 mile at 60 miles per hour. She travels the next 1 mile at 30 miles per hour. How long is her trip, in minutes? What is her average speed, in miles per hour?

    A. 2 min; 45 mi/h
    B. 2 min; 40 mi/h
    C. 3 min; 40 mi/h
    D. 3 min; 45 mi/h

Competitive racers can travel at the rate of 900 yards per minute.

13. **a.** Between which pairs of points is the speed constant?
    b. Between which pair of points is the speed 0?

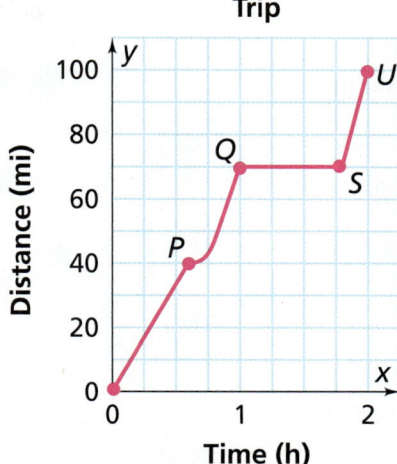

14. **Take It Further** Tony tosses a ball straight up. Sasha records its flight with a video camera. Later they graph the ball's height against time. Graph the ball's speed against time.

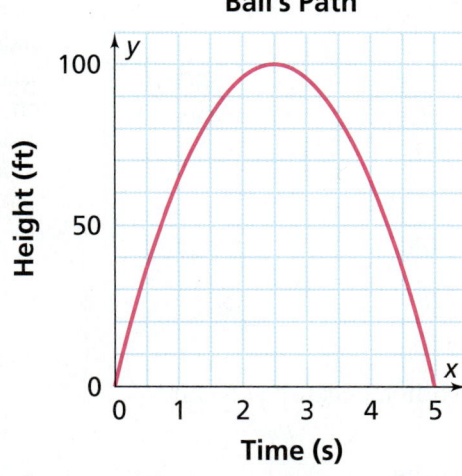

If the ball travels straight up, why does the graph move up and across?

15. **Write About It** Kwata says, "I can use a car's speedometer to figure out my average speed between any two points. I note my speed at each point. Then I find the average of the speeds." Is Kwata correct? Explain.

Maintain Your Skills

16. Draw a distance-time graph for a three-hour trip at these steady speeds.
    a. 30 mph **b.** 40 mph **c.** 45 mph
    d. 50 mph **e.** 60 mph

4.04 Collinearity

You can always draw a line that includes any two given points. However, you cannot always draw a single line that includes three or more points.

> Sometimes, the three points form a triangle.

Definition

Points in a set are collinear if they all lie on the same line.

These points appear to form a triangle. They are not collinear.

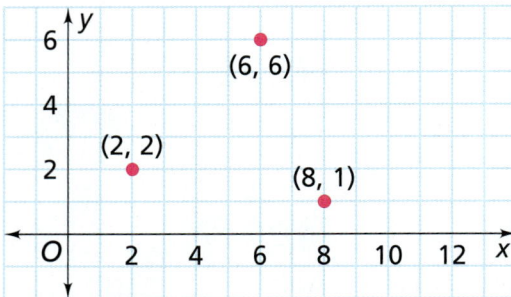

These points lie on a horizontal line. They are collinear.

> How can you tell whether points are on a horizontal line by looking at their coordinates?

Here are a few facts about points and collinearity:

- Any two points are always collinear with each other, because you can draw a line that contains them both.
- All the points on a line are collinear with each other.
- A point that is not on a line cannot be collinear with any pair of points on the line.

For Discussion

1. What are some possible ways to determine whether three points are collinear by looking at their coordinates? How can you tell if three points lie on a horizontal line? On a vertical line? On any line?

Chapter 4 Lines

You can use slope between points to test for collinearity. In this lesson, you may already have made conjectures about pairs of points that have the same slope. As you work with equations of lines, these conjectures will be very important.

Assumption

Three points, A, B, and C, are collinear if and only if the slope between A and B is the same as the slope between B and C. That is,

A, B, and C are collinear $\Leftrightarrow$ $m(A, B) = m(B, C)$

Read the symbol $\Leftrightarrow$ as *if and only if*.

In this diagram, $m(A, B) = m(B, C)$ so A, B, and C are collinear.

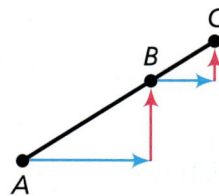

However, in this diagram, $m(A, B) \neq m(B, C)$ so A, B, and C are not collinear.

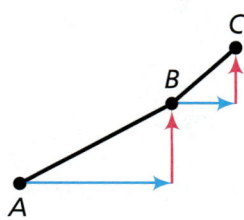

For You to Do

Suppose line ℓ contains the points $(1, -2)$ and $(7, 1)$.

2. What is the slope between the points given?
3. Explain why the point $(5, 0)$ is collinear with these two points.
4. Explain why the point $(13, 5)$ is not collinear with these two points.
5. Explain why the following fact proves that the point $(11, 3)$ is on the line ℓ.
$$\frac{3-1}{11-7} = \frac{1}{2}$$
6. **Take It Further** Suppose point (x, y), different from $(7, 1)$, is a point in the same plane as line ℓ.
Explain why the equation $\frac{y-1}{x-7} = \frac{1}{2}$ is true if and only if (x, y) is on line ℓ.

Exercises Practicing Habits of Mind

Check Your Understanding

1. Are the three points collinear?

   a. $A(-1, 3)$, $B(4, 15)$, $C(14, 39)$

   b. $X(-3, 3)$, $Y(4, 3)$, $Z(100, 3)$

   c. $P(-3, 8)$, $D(0, 2)$, $Q(3, -4)$

   d. $N(3, 5)$, $M(4, 6)$, $D(10, 13)$

2. Which three points lie on the same line? Explain.

   $A(-4, -1)$ $B(-1, 2)$ $C(2, 4)$ $D(3, 6)$

3. Derman is wondering about the assumption in this lesson. He says, "Why do they use $m(A, B) = m(B, C)$? Why not use $m(B, A) = m(A, C)$ or $m(A, C) = m(C, B)$?" How would you explain to Derman that these all work as well?

4. Name another point on the line containing X and Y.

   a. $X(3, -4)$, $Y(0, -4)$

   b. $X(-4, 2)$, $Y(-4, 8)$

   c. $X(0, 0)$, $Y(1, 2)$

5. Describe a point-tester to determine whether a point is on the line that contains $(2, 3)$ and $(12, -4)$.

You can use words or write an equation.

On Your Own

6. Find three points on the graphs of each equation. Are they collinear?

   a. $y - 5 = 4(x - 2)$

   b. $3x + 2y = 4$

   c. $y = x^2$

   d. $y = -4x - 3$

   e. $y = 2^x + 1$

7. **Standardized Test Prep** In the morning, the temperature at the top of Mt. Washington in New Hampshire was $-10°$ Fahrenheit. Use the conversion formula $C = \frac{5}{9}(F - 32)$ to find the temperature to the nearest Celsius degree.

   A. $-48°$ B. $-28°$ C. $-23°$ D. $-12°$

For Exercises 8–10, suppose ℓ is the line that contains the points $R(-2, 4)$ and $S(6, 2)$.

8. Which of the following points are on ℓ? Explain.
   a. $(1, 3)$
   b. $\left(1, \frac{13}{4}\right)$
   c. $\left(1, \frac{14}{3}\right)$
   d. $\left(2, \frac{13}{4}\right)$
   e. $(2, 3)$
   f. $\left(2, \frac{14}{3}\right)$
   g. $\left(4, \frac{13}{4}\right)$
   h. $(4, 2.6)$
   i. $\left(4, \frac{5}{2}\right)$

9. Find the missing numbers if these points are on ℓ.
   a. $(3, a)$
   b. $(5, b)$
   c. $(c, 8)$
   d. $(7, d)$
   e. $(13, e)$
   f. $(120, f)$
   g. $(x, -2)$
   h. $(y, -5)$
   i. $(z, 12)$
   j. $(v, v + 1)$
   k. $(w, 1.5w)$
   l. $(u, u + 14)$

10. What is an equation that you can use to determine whether a point is on line ℓ?

11. **Standardized Test Prep** Which equation describes the relationship between x and y in the table?

    A. $x + y = -2$
    B. $2x - 3y = -9$
    C. $2x + 3y = -3$
    D. $x + 3y = 0$

x	y
-3	1
-1	$2\frac{1}{3}$
1	$3\frac{2}{3}$
3	5
5	$6\frac{1}{3}$

12. Recall the house with a roof pitch of 6–12 from Lesson 4.02. Use graph paper. Draw the pitch on a Cartesian plane. The origin is in the lower left corner. Find each slope.

    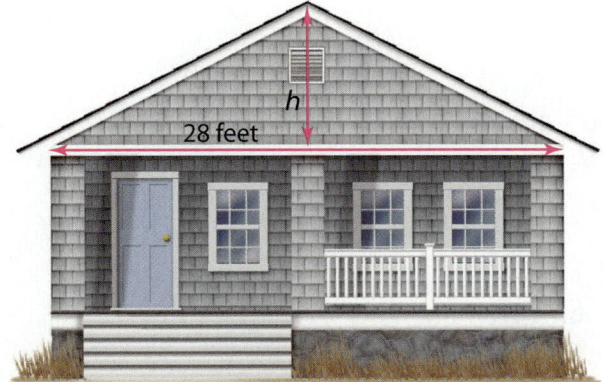

    a. left half of the roof
    b. right half of the roof

4.04   Collinearity

13. **Take It Further** Here is a picture of a castle. The attached building in front is a carriage house.

> A shipbuilder designed this copper roof. Do you see any connection between the roof design and the builder's experience?

   a. Where on the left side of the carriage house roof is the slope least?
   b. Where is the slope greatest?

Maintain Your Skills

As you do these exercises, you may find a fast way to determine collinear points. Find a pattern and you may not need to find the slope between every pair of points.

> When you are in doubt, calculate each slope.

For Exercises 14–16, points A, B, and C are collinear. Is point X collinear with points A, B, and C? Look for a pattern.

14. a. $A(7, 0)$, $B(2, 0)$, $C(-5, 0)$, $X\left(\frac{14}{9}, 0\right)$
    b. $A(3, 3)$, $B(-8, 3)$, $C(7, 3)$, $X(-2, -3)$
    c. $A(5, -2)$, $B\left(\frac{3}{7}, -2\right)$, $C(-\sqrt{3}, -2)$, $X(2, 3)$
    d. $A\left(17, \frac{14}{9}\right)$, $B\left(21, \frac{14}{9}\right)$, $C\left(2.4, \frac{14}{9}\right)$, $X\left(\frac{17}{9}, \frac{14}{9}\right)$
    e. Describe a pattern.

15. a. $A(4, 3)$, $B(4, 9)$, $C\left(4, -\frac{2}{3}\right)$, $X(4, 0)$
    b. $A(-\sqrt{7}, 7)$, $B(-\sqrt{7}, 5)$, $C(-\sqrt{7}, 3)$, $X(-\sqrt{7}, 0)$
    c. $A(0, 1)$, $B(0, 2)$, $C(0, 3)$, $X(4, 0)$
    d. $A\left(-\frac{14\pi}{23}, \pi\right)$, $B\left(-\frac{14\pi}{23}, -2.9801\right)$, $C\left(-\frac{14\pi}{23}, -1383\right)$, $X\left(-\frac{14\pi}{23}, 3\pi\sqrt{5}\right)$
    e. Describe a pattern.

16. a. $A(1, 2)$, $B(2, 4)$, $C(3, 6)$, $X(4, 8)$ b. $A(1, 3)$, $B(2, 6)$, $C(3, 9)$, $X(-4, -12)$
    c. $A(8, -1)$, $B(16, -2)$, $C(-24, 3)$, $X(64, 8)$ d. $A(-6, 2)$, $B(9, -3)$, $C(0, 0)$, $X(-3\sqrt{2}, \sqrt{2})$
    e. Describe a pattern.

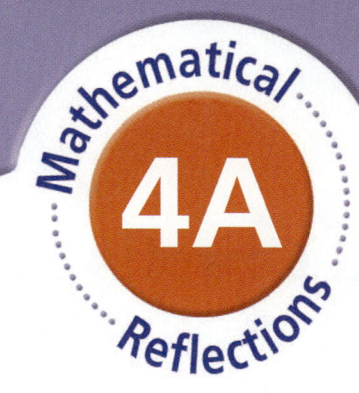

Mathematical Reflections 4A

In this investigation, you found the slope between two points. You also studied the similarity between pitch and slope. You have also learned how to determine if three or more points are collinear. These questions will help you summarize what you have learned.

1. How can you find the average speed of a car from its distance-time graph?

2. Are the three points collinear? Explain.
   a. $P(-1, 2)$, $Q(3, 2)$, $R(11, 2)$
   b. $D(4, 6)$, $E(3, 8)$, $F(5, 12)$
   c. $G(0, 3)$, $H(-1, 2)$, $I(2, 7)$
   d. $J(-5, 1)$, $K(-5, 5)$, $L(-5, -1)$

3. Given points $A(-4, 1)$ and $B(2, y)$, find the value of y such that the following are true.
   a. $m(A, B) = 2$
   b. $m(A, B) = -1$
   c. $m(A, B) = 0$
   d. $m(A, B)$ does not exist.

4. Chan leaves his house at 8:00 A.M. to walk $\frac{1}{2}$ mile to his grandmother's house. He arrives there at 8:15 A.M. He stays for 1 hour. Then he walks 3 miles to the park to meet his friends at 10:15 A.M. He stays there until noon.
   a. Draw a distance-time graph to represent this situation.
   b. Find Chan's average speed walking from his home to his grandmother's house.
   c. Find Chan's average speed walking from his grandmother's house to the park.
   d. Find Chan's average speed from 8:00 A.M. to 10:15 A.M.

5. Find three points on the graph of each equation. Are they collinear?
   a. $y = 3x - 2$
   b. $2x - y = 5$
   c. $y = 3x^2 + 1$
   d. $y - 2 = -(x + 1)$

6. How do people use linear equations and slope in different fields of work such as carpentry, engineering, and mathematics?

7. How can you use slopes to tell whether three points are collinear?

8. How can you use a point-tester to tell whether the point $(3, -2)$ is on the line through $A(2, -5)$ and $B(4, 3)$?

Slope between points can be a negative number close to zero.

Vocabulary

In this investigation, you learned these terms. Make sure you understand what each one means and how to use it.

- collinear points
- rise
- run
- slope
- speed
- subscript

Investigation 4B

Linear Equations and Graphs

In *Linear Equations and Graphs*, you will find the relationship between a linear equation and its graph. To make this connection, you will use what you know about slope and point-testers. You will also look at distance-time graphs again.

By the end of this investigation, you will be able to answer questions like these.

1. How can you determine whether the graph of an equation is a line?

2. How can you use a distance-time graph to tell when one runner overtakes another in a race?

3. How can you write an equation of the line that connects points $(-3, 7)$ and $(4, 2)$?

You will learn how to

- write linear equations
- sketch graphs of linear equations
- determine the slope from its equation
- determine whether a runner will overtake another runner

You will develop these habits and skills:

- Use a point-tester to write a linear equation.
- Understand various ways of a constructing an equation, using the most efficient method based on the information given.
- Realize that you can use any two points on a line to graph the line.
- Calculate intersections in distance-time graphs.

After the first lap, a Nordic skier's distance-time graph can suggest a linear function.

4.05 Getting Started

**Activating Prior Knowledge
Exploring New Ideas**

In Investigation 4A, you found the slope between points. In this investigation, you will learn how to find the slope of a line. You will also use slope to write equations of lines.

For You to Explore

In Investigation 3D, you studied several basic graphs, such as $y = x$, $y = \frac{1}{x}$, $y = |x|$, and $y = x^2$. For Problems 1–4, you will calculate slopes between points on each graph.

1. The figure below shows a graph of the direct variation equation $y = 3x$.

   a. Choose two points on the graph. Calculate the slope between them.

   b. Choose two other points on the graph. Calculate the slope between them.

   c. How do the two slopes compare?

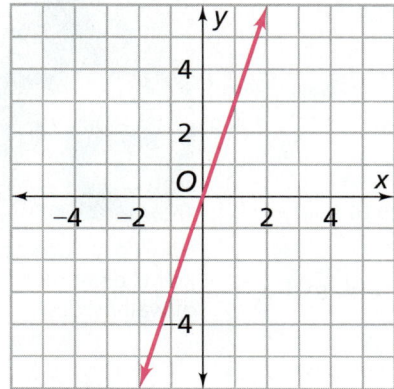

For Problems 2 and 3, answer parts (a)–(c) in Problem 1.

2. $y = \frac{5}{x}$

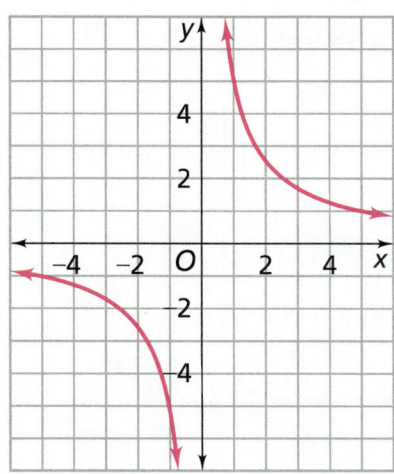

4.05 Getting Started 349

3. $y = 2x^2$

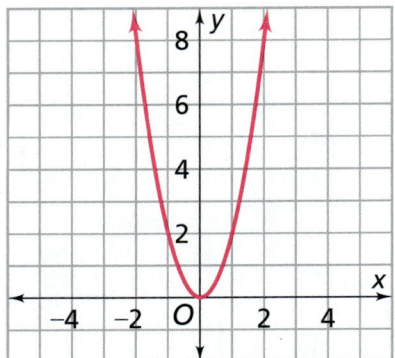

4. The figure below shows a graph of the equation $y = |4x|$.

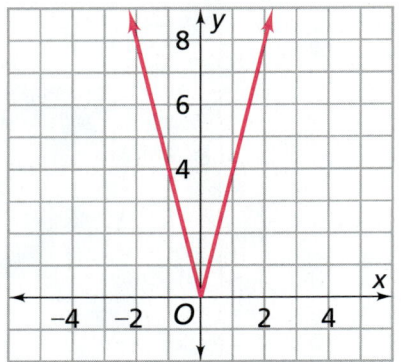

   a. Choose two points in the first quadrant on the graph. Calculate the slope between them.
   b. Choose two other points in the first quadrant on the graph. Calculate the slope between them.
   c. How do the two slopes compare?
   d. Choose two points in the second quadrant on the graph. Calculate the slope between them.
   e. How does this slope compare to the slope between points in the first quadrant?

5. For each pair of points, find three other points that are collinear. Sketch all five points on the same graph.

   a. (5, 7) and (1, 8)
   b. (7, 0) and (0, 5)
   c. (−2, 3) and (−3, −5)
   d. (1, −8) and (4, 6)

6. For each part in Problem 5, use a point-tester to see whether the points you chose are collinear with the two given points.

How does slope between points differ for the two types of water slides?

Exercises Practicing Habits of Mind

On Your Own

7. John leaves his house at 8:00 A.M. He rides his bike to school. He pedals at a constant rate of 15 ft/sec. How far has John biked at each of the following times?

   a. 8:10 A.M.

   b. 8:20 A.M.

   c. 8:45 A.M.

   d. t minutes after 8:00 A.M.

8. Pete, John's older brother, leaves their house 10 minutes after John. He rides at 20 ft/sec to the same school. At the times shown in parts (a)–(c), how far has Pete biked? Has he caught up with John?

   a. 8:10 A.M.

   b. 8:20 A.M.

   c. 8:45 A.M.

   d. At t minutes after 8:00 A.M., write an expression for how far Pete has ridden.

   e. How can you find the exact time when Pete catches up with John?

9. **What's Wrong Here?** Derman tests whether four points, $E(2, 4)$, $F(5, 6)$, $G(6, 7)$, and $H(9, 9)$, are collinear.

   Derman says, "To test whether points are collinear, I should find the slope between them and compare. The slope between E and F is $m(E, F) = \frac{6-4}{5-2} = \frac{2}{3}$. The slope between G and H is $m(G, H) = \frac{9-7}{9-6} = \frac{2}{3}$. The two slopes are equal, so all four points must be collinear."

   a. Sketch the four points to show they are not collinear.

   b. What is wrong with Derman's reasoning?

   c. What can you say about the line that contains E and F and the line that contains G and H?

10. Find three points such that the slope between each point and the given point is the given slope. Sketch all four points.

    a. point $(5, 0)$, slope $\frac{1}{2}$

    b. point $(0, 6)$, slope $\frac{3}{8}$

    c. point $(-1, 4)$, slope $\frac{9}{7}$

    d. point $(1, 4)$, slope $-\frac{3}{5}$

11. For each part in Exercise 10, use a point-tester. Determine whether the slope between the given point and some point $P(x, y)$ is the given slope.

4.05 Getting Started

12. Solve each equation for y. Simplify.

    a. $y + 3 = 2(x - 5)$
    b. $y - 2 = -\frac{1}{3}(x + 3)$
    c. $4x - 5y = 7$
    d. $\frac{y - 8}{x} = -3$
    e. $y + 6 = 2x + 1$
    f. $\frac{y - 2}{x - 1} = 5$
    g. $\frac{y + 7}{x - 3} = -\frac{11}{3}$
    h. $xy = 9$

Remember...

Solve for y means use the basic rules and moves to get *y* alone on one side of the equation. The other side of the equation will be an expression that does not include *y*.

Simplify means to combine or multiply terms where you can.

Maintain Your Skills

For Exercises 13 and 14, parts (a)–(f), find the slope between each pair of points. Sketch the two points and the line containing them. Then complete parts (g)–(i).

13. a. (1, 2) and (3, 3)
    b. (2, 3) and (4, 4)
    c. (3, 4) and (5, 5)
    d. (4, 5) and (6, 6)
    e. (5, 6) and (7, 7)
    f. (6, 7) and (8, 8)
    g. Is there a pattern among the lines? Describe.
    h. What is the slope between $(1 + a, 2 + a)$ and $(3 + a, 3 + a)$? How does it relate to the slope in part (a)?
    i. Given $A(1, 2)$ and $B(3, 3)$, transform the points using the rule $(x, y) \mapsto (x + a, y + b)$, where *a* and *b* are any numbers. You will get two new points, A' and B'. How does $m(A', B')$ relate to $m(A, B)$?

14. a. (1, 2) and (3, 3)
    b. (2, 4) and (6, 6)
    c. (3, 6) and (9, 9)
    d. (4, 8) and (12, 12)
    e. (5, 10) and (15, 15)
    f. (6, 12) and (18, 18)
    g. Is there a pattern among the lines? Describe.
    h. What is the slope between $(a, 2a)$ and $(3a, 3a)$? How does it relate to the slope in part (a)?
    i. Given $A(1, 2)$ and $B(3, 3)$, transform the points using the rule $(x, y) \mapsto (ax, by)$, where *a* and *b* are any numbers. You will get two new points, A' and B'. How does $m(A', B')$ relate to $m(A, B)$?

Go Online
pearsonsuccessnet.com

4.06 Equations of Lines

The Assumption in Lesson 4.04 is essential in developing a way to write the equation of a line. From that assumption comes the following theorem.

Theorem 4.2

The slope between any two points on a line is constant.

In other words, if the slope between two points on a line is m, then the slope between any two points on that line must be m.

For Discussion

1. Prove Theorem 4.2.

Remember...
By definition, all points on a line are collinear.

In the previous lessons, you defined slope as a measurement between two points. With Theorem 4.02, you can now describe the slope of a line.

Definition

The **slope** of a line is the slope between any two points on the line.

To find the equation of a line, you only need to know one point on the line and the slope of the line. Once you know these, the equation of the line is just a point-tester. You can verify that the slope between some arbitrary point on the line and the fixed point matches the slope of the line.

Minds in Action — episode 14

Sasha and Tony are trying to find the equation of the line ℓ that goes through points $R(-2, 4)$ and $S(6, 2)$.

Sasha To use a point-tester, we first need to find the slope between R and S.

Tony goes to the board and writes

$$m(R, S) = \frac{2 - 4}{6 - (-2)} = \frac{-2}{8} = -\frac{1}{4}.$$

Tony It's $-\frac{1}{4}$.

Sasha Okay. Now, we want to test some point, say P. We want to see whether the slope between that point and one of the first two, say R, is equal to $-\frac{1}{4}$. If it is, that point is on ℓ. So our test is $m(P, R) \stackrel{?}{=} -\frac{1}{4}$.

It doesn't matter which point you choose as the base point. Either point R or point S will work.

Tony Let's guess and check a point first, like $P(7, 2)$. Tell me everything you do so I can keep track of the steps.

Sasha Well, the slope between $P(7, 2)$ and $R(-2, 4)$ is $m(P, R) = \frac{2-4}{7-(-2)} = \frac{-2}{9} = -\frac{2}{9}$. This slope is different, so P isn't on ℓ. Maybe we should use a variable point.

Tony How do we do that?

Sasha A point has two coordinates, right? So use two variables. Say P is (x, y).

Tony Then the slope from P to R is $m(P, R) = \frac{y-4}{x-(-2)} = \frac{y-4}{x+2}$. The test is $\frac{y-4}{x+2} = -\frac{1}{4}$.

So, that must be the equation of the line ℓ.

Notice how Sasha switches to letters. She uses x for point P's x-coordinate. She uses y for point P's y-coordinate.

Example 1

Problem *What's Wrong Here?* Tony and Sasha go back to check their work. They want to make sure both R and S work in their point-tester equation.

Sasha says, "Okay, let's try R."

Sasha writes the following on the board.

$$\frac{y-4}{x+2} = -\frac{1}{4}$$
$$\frac{4-4}{-2+2} \stackrel{?}{=} -\frac{1}{4}$$
$$\frac{0}{0} \stackrel{?}{=} -\frac{1}{4}$$

Tony states, "We can't divide by 0. Now what?" Why doesn't the point tester equation work for the point R?

Solution Sasha knows she has a problem, because she cannot divide by 0. The easiest way to eliminate that problem is to multiply the variable x out of the denominator. You can do this by multiplying each side by the denominator, $(x + 2)$.

$$\frac{y-4}{x+2} \cdot (x+2) = -\frac{1}{4} \cdot (x+2)$$
$$y - 4 = -\frac{1}{4}(x+2)$$

Multiplying each side of an equation by an expression containing a variable is not a basic move. The resulting equation may have more or fewer solutions than the original equation. Here, the resulting equation gains a solution, (−2, 4). This is exactly the solution you were missing.

For You to Do

2. Test whether the points R and S satisfy the equation $y - 4 = -\frac{1}{4}(x+2)$.

You can simplify and change the equation $y - 4 = -\frac{1}{4}(x + 2)$ with basic rules and moves. The different forms the equation can take highlight different information about the line. You will work with the different forms throughout the rest of this investigation.

You can use the basic rules and moves to change any form of an equation of a line to the form $ax + by = c$, where a, b, and c are constants.

Any such equation is a linear equation.

> It works the other way, too. The graph of any equation in the form $ax + by = c$ is a line.

Example 2

Problem Find the slope of the line with the equation $2x + y = 5$.

Solution Find two points on the line.

If $x = 0$, then $2(0) + y = 5$. So $y = 5$, and $(0, 5)$ is on the line.

If $x = 1$, then $2(1) + y = 5$. So $y = 3$, and $(1, 3)$ is on the line.

The slope between the points $(0, 5)$ and $(1, 3)$ is $\frac{5 - 3}{0 - 1} = \frac{2}{-1} = -2$.
The slope of the line is -2.

Exercises Practicing Habits of Mind

Check Your Understanding

1. Use Sasha and Tony's method to find an equation for line ℓ. This time, use point S as the base point. Do you get the same equation? Explain.

2. Try Sasha and Tony's method with two points of your own. Use your equation. Test some points to see if they are on your line.

For Exercises 3 and 4, write an equation for each line.

3. **a.** through $A(6, 7)$ and $B(12, 1)$ **b.** through $(5, 4)$ and $(-3, -4)$
   c. through the origin and $(9, 3)$
   d. through $(0, 10)$ and parallel to the line in part (c)
   e. through the origin and parallel to the line in part (a)

> Two lines in the same plane are **parallel** if they do not intersect.

4. **a.** a horizontal line that passes through (6, 7)

   b. through (5, 4) and (5, −4)

   c. through the origin that splits the first and third quadrants in half

   d. line through the origin and parallel to the line in part (a)

5. For each part:
   - Decide whether the graph is a line. Explain.
   - If the equation represents a line, find the slope and the points where the line crosses the x- and y-axes.

   a. $y - 3 = \frac{3}{4}(x - 8)$ **b.** $xy = 12$ **c.** $y = \frac{3}{4}x - 3$

   d. $y = 5x - 7$ **e.** $3x - 4y = 12$ **f.** $y = -\frac{5}{3}x - 9$

   g. $x^2 + y^2 = 1$ **h.** $3x - 4y = 9$ **i.** $y = -\frac{5}{3}x + 8$

6. Prove that the slope between any two points on the line $3x - y = 7$ is 3.

> You can use these hints to help you.
> - Test a few points.
> - Keep track of your steps!
> - Develop a point-tester.
> - Translate your point-tester into an equation.

On Your Own

7. **Write About It** Explain Sasha and Tony's method for finding the equation of a line as an algorithm. Be sure to include precise instructions and steps.

8. Write the equation of the line that includes each pair of points or matches each description. Write the equation in $y = ax + b$ form.

   a. (5, 2) and (−3, −4)

   b. (5, 4) and the origin

   c. (5, 5) and (7, 7)

   d. includes (5, 4) and has slope $\frac{2}{3}$

   e. passes through the origin and is parallel to the line in part (a)

   f. passes through the origin and is parallel to the line in part (d)

9. What is the slope of each line that has the description or equation given?

   a. through (−5, 6) and (−3, −4)

   b. $y = \frac{3}{4}x + 7$

   c. $2x + 4y = 8$

   d. $2x + 4y = 15$

   e. $5.1476x + 5.1476y = 15$

   f. $y - 3 = \frac{7}{13}(x - 4)$

   g. $y - 7.3591 = \frac{7}{13}(x - 4.0856)$

   h. through the origin and parallel to the line in part (d)

> What do the lines in parts (c) and (d) have in common?

10. **a.** What is the equation for the line containing points $J(3, -6)$ and $K(8, 4)$? Use J as the base point.

    b. What is the equation through $J(3, -6)$ and $K(8, 4)$ if you use K as the base point?

    c. Prove that the two equations in parts (a) and (b) describe the same graph. Use basic rules and moves.

11. Alejandra is selling candy bars for $.85 each.
    a. If she sells 20 candy bars, how much does she make?
    b. If she sells 50 candy bars, how much does she make?
    c. Let c be the number of candy bars Alejandra sells. Let s be her sales in dollars. Which equation represents the relationship between c and s?
        A. $c = 0.85(s)$
        B. $s = 0.85(c)$
        C. $s = c + 0.85$
        D. $s = c + 85$

12. **Standardized Test Prep** What is the slope of the line with equation $5x + 2y = 10$?
    A. $-\frac{2}{5}$
    B. $-\frac{5}{2}$
    C. $\frac{5}{2}$
    D. $\frac{2}{5}$

13. **Write About It** Find an equation of the line that contains $(5, 3)$ and has a slope of -4. Can you find a point that satisfies your equation but is not on the line? Explain.

    > How many lines pass through (5, 3) and have a slope of −4?

14. **Take It Further** Explain why the slope between any two points on the line $ax + y = b$ is constant.

15. **Take It Further** Given $A(5, 2)$, $B(3, 7)$, and $C(10, 4)$, find equations for the lines that form the sides of $\triangle ABC$.

Maintain Your Skills

16. Sketch each pair of equations. Do the lines intersect?
    a. $y - 2 = 2(x - 7)$ and $y - 2 = 5(x - 7)$
    b. $y + 4 = \frac{2}{3}(x - 1)$ and $y + 4 = \frac{3}{2}(x - 1)$
    c. $y - \frac{14}{23} = \frac{1}{7}\left(x + \frac{13}{23}\right)$ and $y - \frac{14}{23} = \frac{1}{6}\left(x + \frac{13}{23}\right)$
    d. $y - 5 = x - 10$ and $y - 5 = 3(x - 10)$
    e. What pattern do you notice in the line intersections?

17. a. Graph the family of equations.
    $2x - 3y = 0$
    $2x - 3y = 1$ $2x - 3y = -1$
    $2x - 3y = 2$ $2x - 3y = -2$
    b. What pattern do you notice among the graphs?

    > You can use the term family to describe a collection, or a set. This family is the set of equations in the form $2x - 3y = k$, where k is any number.

18. a. Find equations for five distinct lines that include the point $(5, 1)$.
    b. Is there a pattern among the equations? Explain.

4.07 Jiffy Graphs: Lines

You can write the equation of a line in many different ways, and the equations are still equivalent. No matter what form of equation you use, you only need to find two points to graph a line. However, it may be very time-consuming to work with a linear equation like this one.

$$6x + 3(x + 2y) - 5y + 18 = 4(2y + 3) + 5(x + 3) - 4\left(y - \frac{1}{2}\right)$$

You can transform such an equation into a simpler form. You can use the simpler equation to find points and sketch a graph. Each of the following equations is equivalent to the equation above.

$$y - 3 = \frac{4}{3}(x - 5) \qquad 4x - 3y = 11 \qquad y = \frac{4}{3}x - \frac{11}{3}$$

Remember...
Two equations are equivalent if you can use the basic rules and moves to change one to the other.

For You to Do

1. Show that $y - 3 = \frac{4}{3}(x - 5)$, $4x - 3y = 11$, and $y = \frac{4}{3}x - \frac{11}{3}$ are equivalent.

Example

Problem Sketch the graph of the line whose equation is $4x - 3y = 11$.

Solution In Chapter 3, you sketched a graph by finding enough points to determine the basic pattern. In this case, you know the graph is a line, so you only need to find two points on the graph. Then you can draw the line that goes through them both.

To find two points, choose numbers that make the calculations as easy as possible. When you have an equation such as $4x - 3y = 11$, you can find one point easily by plugging in 0 for x and solving for y. Then you can plug in 0 for y and solve for x.

$$4x - 3y = 11 \qquad\qquad 4x - 3y = 11$$
$$4(0) - 3y = 11 \qquad\qquad 4x - 3(0) = 11$$
$$-3y = 11 \qquad\qquad 4x = 11$$
$$y = -\frac{11}{3} \qquad\qquad x = \frac{11}{4}$$

When you plug in 0 for x, you find the point where the line crosses the y-axis. That point is called the **y-intercept**. The point where a line crosses the x-axis is called the **x-intercept**.

The points $\left(0, -\frac{11}{3}\right)$ and $\left(\frac{11}{4}, 0\right)$ will both be on the graph. Draw the points and the line that contains them.

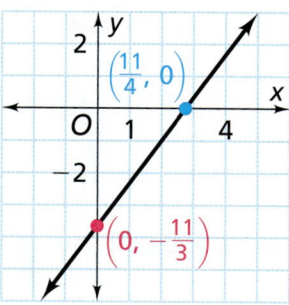

For Discussion

2. What numbers can you use to find points on the graph of $y = \frac{4}{3}x - \frac{11}{3}$? On the graph of $y - 3 = \frac{4}{3}(x - 5)$? Choose points that are easy to use.

3. How do you know the graphs of the equations $y = \frac{4}{3}x - \frac{11}{3}$ and $y - 3 = \frac{4}{3}(x - 5)$ will be the same as the graph of $4x - 3y = 11$?

Some equations have specific names. You can determine certain pieces of information just by looking at certain equations. Recognizing these forms helps you graph lines or write linear equations more quickly. If you forget how to work with these forms, remember that you can always rely on the point-tester to write an equation, and you need only two points to graph a line.

For You to Do

Let ℓ be the line with the equations $y = \frac{4}{3}x - \frac{11}{3}$, $4x - 3y = 11$, and $y - 3 = \frac{4}{3}(x - 5)$.

4. What is the slope of line ℓ?

5. Where does ℓ cross the y-axis? The x-axis?

6. Which equation for ℓ makes it easiest to see that the point $(5, 3)$ is on the line? Explain.

For Discussion

7. Does the slope of line ℓ appear in any of its equations? Do the x- and y-intercepts appear?

4.07 Jiffy Graphs: Lines

Exercises Practicing Habits of Mind

Check Your Understanding

1. Write an equation for each line that contains the given point and that has the given slope m.

   a. $(4, 3)$; $m = -1$
   b. $(-2, 5)$; $m = \frac{1}{3}$
   c. $(7, -3)$; $m = \frac{4}{5}$
   d. $(-1, -5)$; $m = -\frac{11}{7}$
   e. $\left(-\frac{3}{2}, -\frac{1}{2}\right)$; $m = 2$
   f. $(14.6, -9.8)$; $m = -4.38$
   g. $(0, 12)$; $m = \frac{5}{6}$
   h. $(0, -3)$; $m = -\frac{2}{3}$
   i. $\left(0, -\frac{8}{5}\right)$; $m = \frac{5}{16}$
   j. $(0, 5)$; $m = \frac{21}{13}$
   k. $(3, 9)$; $m = 0$
   l. $(-8, 7)$; slope is undefined

Try to find the quickest way to write an equation. You might decide it is easier to work with one particular form.

For Exercises 2 and 3, graph each equation.

2. a. $y - 2 = \frac{1}{2}(x + 4)$
   b. $y + 3 = -4(x + 1)$
   c. $y + 7 = \frac{5}{4}(x - 2)$
   d. $y - \frac{1}{2} = -\frac{9}{7}\left(x + \frac{2}{3}\right)$
   e. $y = -\frac{2}{3}(x - 6) + 6$
   f. $y = 18(x - 27) - 38$
   g. $y = -\frac{7}{5}\left(x - \frac{5}{7}\right) + 3$
   h. $y = \frac{4}{13}\left(x + \frac{1}{4}\right) - \frac{7}{4}$

3. a. $y = 4x - 3$
   b. $y = -2x + 1$
   c. $y = 7x + 5$
   d. $y = -4x - 6$
   e. $y = -\frac{1}{2}x + 4$
   f. $y = \frac{3}{7}x - 2$
   g. $y = -\frac{15}{4}x + \frac{9}{2}$
   h. $y = \frac{21}{17}x + \frac{5}{8}$

On Your Own

4. Use any of the three equations from For You To Do. Find the value of k such that $(100, k)$ is on line ℓ.

5. **Write About It** Use Exercises 1–3.

   a. Does it matter which form of an equation you use to graph a line? Explain.

   b. Do you prefer one form of an equation over another form? If so, which form do you prefer? Explain.

Which equation makes your work easiest?

6. Alejandra is selling candy bars for $.85 each. She buys a box of 100 candy bars for $20.00. Let m be the amount of money she makes. Let c be the number of candy bars she sells. Notice that if Alejandra does not sell any candy bars ($c = 0$), then she will lose $20.00 ($m = -20$).

   > You answered a similar question about Alejandra in Lesson 4.06.

   a. Which equation represents the relationship between the amount of money Alejandra makes and the number of candy bars she sells?

   A. $c = 0.85(m) + 20$ **B.** $m = 0.85(c) - 20$

   C. $c = 0.85(m) - 20$ **D.** $m = 0.85(c) + 20$

   b. How many candy bars must Alejandra sell to break even?

7. **Standardized Test Prep** In which case is it possible to graph a linear equation by finding both its x- and y-intercepts?

   A. The graph goes through the origin.

   B. The graph has an undefined slope.

   C. The graph has a slope of zero.

   D. The coordinates of the x- and y-intercepts of the graph are all negative.

For Exercises 8–27, write an equation for the line through the given points or having the given slope and through the given point.

8. $(-3, -5)$ and $(1, 11)$
9. $(6, -7)$ with slope $\frac{7}{5}$
10. $(-5, 13)$ and $(4, -23)$
11. $(0, 13)$ with slope $\frac{11}{3}$
12. $\left(-\frac{1}{2}, -\frac{3}{2}\right)$ with slope $-\frac{2}{3}$
13. $(14, -1)$ with slope 3
14. $(0, 7)$ and $(-4, 9)$
15. $(4, 7)$ and $(4, -2)$
16. $(-6, 0)$ and $(2, -15)$
17. $(0, -2)$ with slope 5
18. $(-3, 0)$ and $(0, 11)$
19. $\left(0, -\frac{1}{2}\right)$ with slope $\frac{5}{4}$
20. $(-2, -4)$ with slope $3\frac{1}{3}$
21. $(8, -2)$ and $(2, -8)$
22. $(-7.5, 3.6)$ with slope -4.8
23. $(-5, 3)$ with slope $-\frac{7}{6}$
24. $(0, 2)$ and $(-4, 0)$
25. $(0, 0)$ and $(15, -12)$
26. $(5, 0)$ and $(-3, -1)$
27. $(10, -3)$ with slope 7

For Exercises 28–39, graph each equation.

28. $x + y = 3$
29. $y = \frac{1}{3}x + 3$
30. $x - 4y = 8$
31. $y - 7 = \frac{2}{3}(x - 9)$
32. $-5x + 3y = 15$
33. $y - 2 = -\frac{9}{4}(x - 3)$
34. $3(y - 3) = x$
35. $y = -\frac{2}{5}x - 4$
36. $y + 2 = -3(x + 1)$
37. $-2x - 3y = 6$
38. $-y = \frac{2}{3}x - 7$
39. $2(y - 4) = -\frac{2}{5}(x + 6)$

For Exercises 40–49, solve each equation for y.

40. $-6x + y = -1$
41. $9x + y = 4$
42. $2x - 3y = 15$
43. $-x - 4y = -20$
44. $3y + 7 = 4x - 7y + 9$
45. $\frac{1}{2}x + \frac{2}{3}y - \frac{11}{4} = \frac{1}{3}y - \frac{9}{2} - \frac{3}{8}x$
46. $4x - 3(y - 4) + 6 = 2x - y$
47. $y - (x - y) = 5$
48. $2(x + y) - 4(x + y) = 8(x + 2) - 8(y + 2)$
49. $2x + 3y - 4(x + 2y) = 13 - 2(3y - x) + y$

Maintain Your Skills

50. Write an equation of a line that contains each pair of points. Use the form $ax + by = c$.

    a. $(4, 0)$ and $(0, 5)$
    b. $(1, 0)$ and $(0, -2)$
    c. $(-15, 0)$ and $(0, -7)$
    d. $(-6, 0)$ and $(0, 4)$
    e. How do integers a, b, and c relate to the coordinates given?

51. **Take It Further** Write an equation of a line that passes through each pair of points in the form $ax + by = c$.

    a. $\left(\frac{1}{2}, 0\right)$ and $\left(0, -\frac{2}{3}\right)$
    b. $\left(-\frac{11}{7}, 0\right)$ and $\left(0, \frac{17}{4}\right)$
    c. $\left(\frac{5}{9}, 0\right)$ and $\left(0, \frac{10}{9}\right)$
    d. $\left(-\frac{3}{8}, 0\right)$ and $\left(0, \frac{1}{2}\right)$
    e. How do integers a, b, and c relate to the coordinates of the two points? How is this relationship different from Exercise 50?

52. For each linear equation, find the slope.

    a. $3x + y = 7$
    b. $3x + y = -3$
    c. $3x + 7y = \frac{42}{13}$
    d. $2x - 7y = 9$
    e. $2x - 7y = -11$
    f. $5x - 4y = 20$
    g. $3x - 4y = 15$
    h. $2x - 4y = 19$
    i. How is slope related to the coefficients of x and y?

4.08 Overtaking

Tony and Sasha bike from their school to a nearby lake. Tony leaves at 2:00 P.M. He travels at 4 miles per hour. Sasha leaves at 2:30 P.M. She travels on the same bike path at 6 miles per hour. When she catches up with Tony, she waves and yells, "Too late to stop now," and continues to the lake. Later they meet at the lake and talk about what happened.

Minds in Action   episode 15

Tony   You were really moving!

Sasha   I had to go faster than you to catch up.

Tony   What time did you pass me? Around 3:00?

Sasha   I'm not sure. Let's figure it out. Let's assume I passed you at 3:00. At 3:00, I had been riding for half an hour, so I'd biked 3 miles.

Tony   I had been on the road for an hour, so I'd gone 4 miles. That means I was still ahead of you.

Sasha   Maybe I passed you at 4:00. At 4:00, I'd biked for an hour and a half. So, I had ridden 9 miles. You were biking for 2 hours, so you had gone 8 miles. I was ahead of you at that point.

Tony   I think an equation will help. If you biked for t hours when you passed me, you'd gone $6t$ miles. I biked 4 miles per hour, but for how many hours?

Sasha   You started half an hour before me, so t plus a half.

Tony   Nice. That means I biked for $4\left(t + \frac{1}{2}\right)$ hours, which is the same as $4t + 2$ hours.

Sasha   Now, when I passed you, we'd gone the same distance. We need to solve the equation $6t = 4t + 2$.

Tony   That's not very hard, it's $t = 1$. What time is that?

Sasha   What did t represent? My time or yours?

> Sasha bikes at 6 miles per hour, so in a half hour, she travels 3 miles.

Habits of Mind

Represent a variable. Tony uses t instead of x, to remind himself that the time is unknown.

For You to Do

1. How did Tony get $t = 1$? What does t represent? At what time did Sasha pass Tony?

Minds in Action episode 16

Tony made a distance-time graph for their trip.

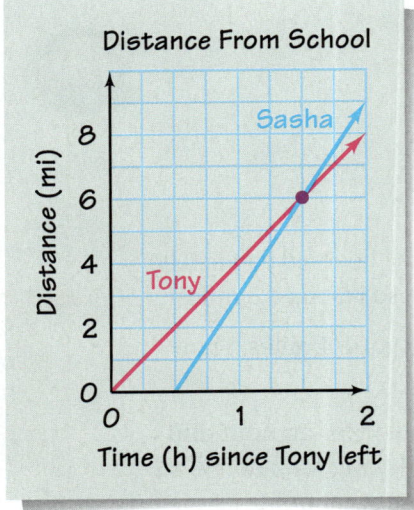

Sasha How did you draw this graph?

Tony On a distance-time graph, speed is the same as slope. Each of our graphs has a constant slope, which means they're lines. Your line has a slope of 6. My line has a slope of 4.

Sasha I understand. Also, since I started half an hour later than you, my graph doesn't start until time $\frac{1}{2}$.

Tony There is one thing I don't understand. We traveled on exactly the same bike path, but it looks like you went up a steeper hill than I did.

Sasha The graph isn't a picture of our trip. That would look like this.

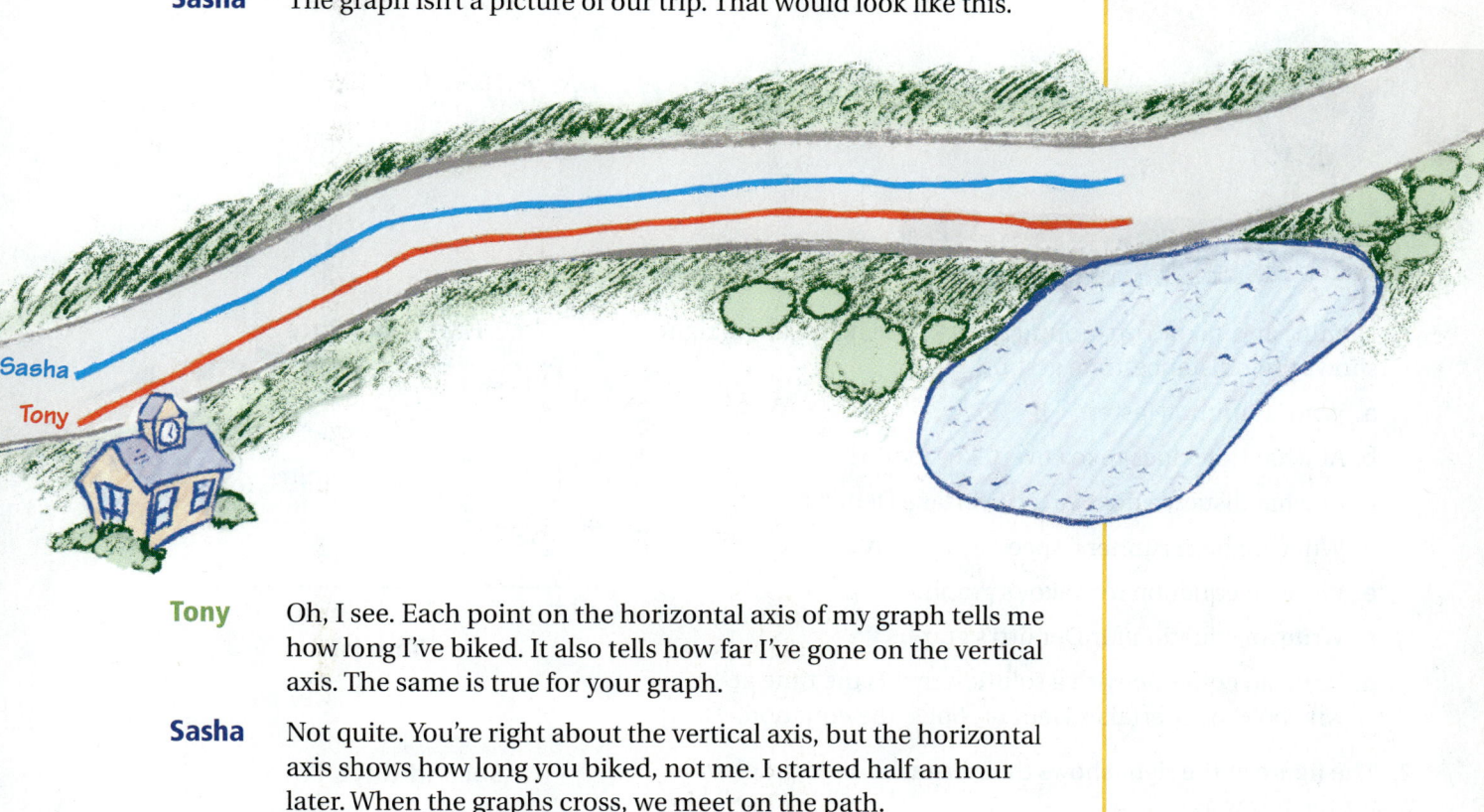

Tony Oh, I see. Each point on the horizontal axis of my graph tells me how long I've biked. It also tells how far I've gone on the vertical axis. The same is true for your graph.

Sasha Not quite. You're right about the vertical axis, but the horizontal axis shows how long you biked, not me. I started half an hour later. When the graphs cross, we meet on the path.

Tony That's because we are the same distance from school, even though our times are different.

For You to Do

2. Write equations for Tony's line and for Sasha's line.

3. At what point do the lines intersect?

4. If the lake is 8 miles from school, what time did Sasha arrive? When did Tony arrive?

Recall that Tony started biking at 2 P.M.

In Lesson 3.13, you learned that the point where two graphs intersect must satisfy the equations for both of the graphs. Similarly, the intersection point, where Sasha passed Tony, must satisfy both of the equations you found. In the next investigation, you will learn some algebraic strategies for finding the intersection points of lines without graphing.

Exercises Practicing Habits of Mind

Check Your Understanding

1. Demitri and Yakov run around a track. The figure at the right shows their distance-time graphs.

   a. Who is running faster?
   b. At what time does Yakov overtake Demitri?
   c. At what distance does Yakov overtake Demitri?
   d. What are both runners' speeds?
   e. Write an equation for Yakov's graph.
   f. Write an equation for Demitri's graph.
   g. Write an equation with a solution that is the time at which Yakov overtakes Demitri. Solve the equation.

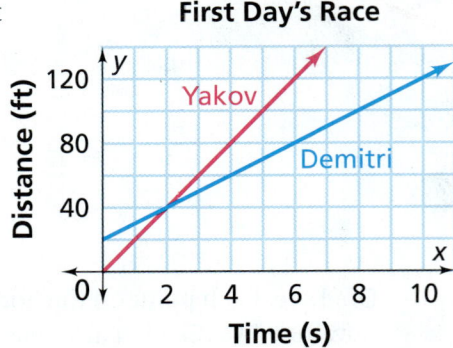

First Day's Race

2. The figure at the right shows their distance-time graphs for the next day.

   a. Who is running faster?
   b. When does Yakov overtake Demitri?
   c. What are the runners' speeds?
   d. Write an equation for Yakov's graph.
   e. Write an equation for Demitri's graph.
   f. Write and solve an equation with a solution that is the time at which Yakov overtakes Demitri.

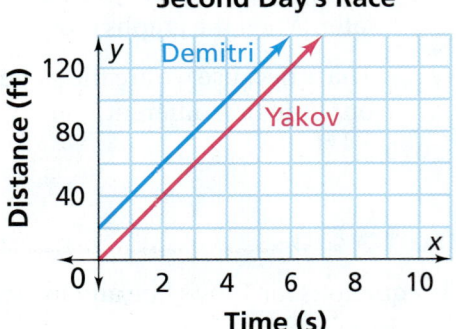

Second Day's Race

3. The runners practice again on a third day.

   a. When does Yakov overtake Demitri in the race?
   b. Do the two graphs intersect? Explain.
   c. Approximately where would the lines of the two graphs intersect?
   d. Can two different lines intersect at more than one point?

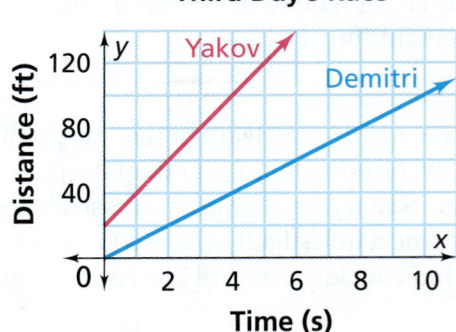

Third Day's Race

On Your Own

4. **Write About It** The next day, Demitri runs 500 feet per minute. Yakov runs 501 feet per minute. Demitri gets a 50-foot head start. Will Yakov eventually catch and pass Demitri? Explain.

5. Tony and Derman often run quarter-mile races. A quarter mile is about 440 yards. Derman's best time in the race is $1\frac{3}{8}$ minutes. Tony's best time is $1\frac{1}{2}$ minutes. Who has the best time?

Exercises 6–8 are about a quarter-mile race that Derman and Tony ran. In this race, Tony had a 20-yard head start. Assume that both matched the speed of their best times given in Exercise 5.

6. Sketch a distance-time graph that shows Tony's and Derman's run on the same axes.

    It may be helpful to use yards for distance and seconds for time.

7. Will Derman overtake Tony? If so, when? If not, why not?

8. How long does each runner take to run the race?

9. **Write About It** As you walk down the sidewalk, you see someone walking ahead of you. Although you do not know how fast either of you is walking, you realize that you are walking faster than the other person. If you both keep walking at the same speed, will you eventually catch up? Explain.

10. **Write About It** You see someone walking ahead of you on the sidewalk. This time, you are walking at exactly the same speed as the other person. If you both keep walking at the same speed, will you eventually catch up? Explain.

11. **Standardized Test Prep** Mrs. Merrill drives from Dallas to St. Louis. The length of the trip is 650 miles. She travels at 50 miles per hour. Her husband leaves two hours later and travels at 62.5 miles per hour. At what distance from Dallas will Mr. Merrill catch up with his wife?

    A. 500 miles **B.** 600 miles **C.** 625 miles

    D. Mrs. Merrill arrives in St. Louis before her husband.

Maintain Your Skills

12. For each equation, find the points that lie on both graphs.

    a. $y = 2x$ and $y = 3x$
    b. $y = 2x + 1$ and $y = 3x + 1$
    c. $y = 2x - 1$ and $y = 3x - 1$
    d. $y + 1 = 2x$ and $y + 1 = 3x$
    e. $y - 2 = 2x$ and $y - 2 = 3x$
    f. $y - 2x = 2$ and $y - 3x = 2$

Mathematical Reflections 4B

In this investigation, you learned to find the slope of a line. You also wrote equations given a slope and a point. These questions will help you summarize what you have learned.

1. Name three points collinear with each pair. Sketch all five points.

   a. (2, 5) and (6, 13)

   b. (−1, 3) and (5, 3)

   c. (1, −4) and (3, −5)

   d. (−6, 7) and (−6, 0)

2. What is the equation of the line through each point and with the given slope? Write in $y = ax + b$ form.

   a. $A(1, 4)$ with slope = $\frac{1}{2}$

   b. $Q(1, -4)$ and $R = (0, 2)$

   c. $B(-2, 5)$ with slope = 0

   d. $B(-2, 5)$ with an undefined slope

   e. $B(-2, 5)$ and parallel to the line with equation $2x - 3y = 8$

3. Sketch the graph of each equation. Is the point (4, 5) on the line?

   a. $y = 2x - 3$

   b. $y - 1 = \frac{1}{2}(x + 4)$

   c. $2x + 3y = 6$

   d. $3x - y = 7$

4. Solve each equation for y.

   a. $2x + y = 5$

   b. $3x - y = 4$

   c. $x + 2y = -6$

   d. $y - 4 = 3(x - 2)$

5. After soccer practice, Ling runs home at the rate of 6 miles per hour. Her sister, Akira, left soccer practice one half hour before Ling. She is walking the 4 miles home at 3 miles per hour.

   a. Sketch a distance-time graph that shows Ling's and Akira's walk home.

   b. When will Ling overtake Akira?

6. How can you determine whether the graph of an equation is a line?

7. How can you use a distance-time graph to tell when one runner overtakes another in a race?

8. How can you write an equation of the line that connects points (−3, 7) and (4, 2)?

The slope of a Nordic skier's distance-time graph increases near the end of a race. Explain.

Vocabulary

In this investigation, you learned these terms. Make sure you understand what each one means and how to use it.

- **parallel lines**
- **slope of a line**
- **x-intercept**
- **y-intercept**

Chapter 4 Mid-Chapter Test

Multiple Choice

1. The graphs of these equations are lines. Which line has a negative slope?
   A. $y = 2x - 6$
   B. $y = 4$
   C. $y - x = 5$
   D. $2x + y = 10$

2. What is the slope between the points $A(-3, 5)$ and $B(2, 1)$?
   A. $-\frac{4}{5}$
   B. $\frac{4}{5}$
   C. -4
   D. 4

3. Which linear equation has a graph that passes through the point $(10, -7)$?
   A. $(y + 7) = 3(x + 10)$
   B. $(y + 7) = 3(x - 10)$
   C. $(y - 7) = 3(x - 10)$
   D. $(y - 7) = 3(x + 10)$

4. Point A is at $(4, 5)$, and $m(A, B) = -\frac{2}{3}$. Which of the following CANNOT be the coordinates of point B?
   A. $(10, 1)$
   B. $(7, 3)$
   C. $(1, 7)$
   D. $(2, 8)$

For Exercises 5 and 6, use this distance-time graph for Dario's trip.

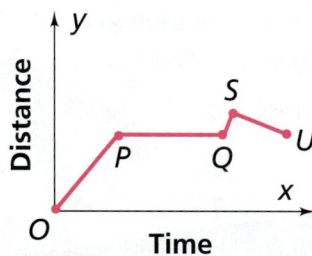

5. Between which two points does Dario travel the farthest?
   A. O and P
   B. P and Q
   C. Q and S
   D. S and U

6. Between which two points does Dario travel the fastest?
   A. O and P
   B. P and Q
   C. Q and S
   D. S and U

7. Which of the following could be an equation for this line?
   A. $y = -3x - 6$
   B. $y = 2x + 6$
   C. $y = 3x - 6$
   D. $y = -3x + 6$

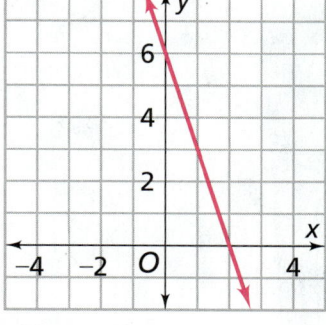

Open Response

8. a. Write an equation for a nonvertical line that contains the point $(2, -4)$. Explain your steps.
   b. Use your equation from part (a). What is the value of y when $x = -20$?

9. Points A, B, and C lie in the coordinate plane. The slope between points A and B is 2. The slope between points B and C is 6.

   Sean says the slope between A and C is 4, the average of 6 and 2. Is Sean correct? Explain.

10. Suppose ℓ is the line through $R(-2, 4)$ and $S(6, 2)$. Find three other points on this line. Prove that each point is on the line.

11. On a turnpike, if you have an average speed over 65 miles per hour, you will get a speeding ticket. The average speed is determined when you exit the turnpike. Caleb gets on the turnpike at 4:00 p.m. At 6:00 p.m., he has traveled 150 miles.
    a. Was Caleb speeding? Explain.
    b. What is the highest average speed Caleb can go for the next 100 miles of the turnpike without getting a ticket? Round to the nearest mile per hour.

Chapter 4 Mid-Chapter Test 369

Investigation 4C

Intersections

In *Intersections*, you will interpret the meaning of the intersection of two lines in the coordinate plane. You will use algebra to find this point of intersection. You will also explore characteristics of parallel lines.

By the end of this investigation, you will be able to answer questions like these.

1. How can you find the intersection of two lines?

2. How can you determine from their equations whether two lines will intersect?

3. Are the graphs of $3x - 4y = 16$ and $y = \frac{3}{4}x - 1$ parallel? Explain.

You will learn how to
- solve systems of linear equations with two variables using substitution and elimination
- determine whether two lines are parallel or intersecting using the slope of each line
- write and solve word problems for systems of equations

You will develop these habits and skills:
- Understand the relationship between systems of equations and intersections of graphs.
- Interpret the intersection of two graphs as a solution to the corresponding system of equations, and vice versa.
- Use basic moves to build new problem solving techniques.

The ball and a teammate should meet where their paths intersect.

4.09 Getting Started

**Activating Prior Knowledge
Exploring New Ideas**

Knowing the slope of a line can help you solve many problems. You can use the slope of two lines to find where they intersect. Likewise, you can find the slope of two lines to find their common solution.

For You to Explore

1. Tuan wants to sell printed shirts to raise money for the school band. He spends $72.00 to buy a silk-screen machine and ink. He buys each shirt for $1.25. Tuan sells each printed shirt for $5.75. How many shirts does Tuan need to sell to break even?

2. What is the intersection point of the graphs of $y = 72 + 1.25x$ and $y = 5.75x$?

3. Tuan decides to buy a high-quality silk-screen machine and long-lasting inks, making his starting costs for printing shirts $130.00. The cost of the shirts and his selling price remain the same. How many shirts does Tuan need to sell to make a profit?

4. Nicole and Katy ride their bicycles. Nicole rides at 300 yards per minute. Katy rides at 375 yards per minute. Since Katy is a faster rider, she gives Nicole a head start of 125 yards.

   In the graph, the horizontal axis represents the time in minutes since Katy started. The vertical axis represents the distance in yards from where they start. The two lines show each rider's distance d against time t.

   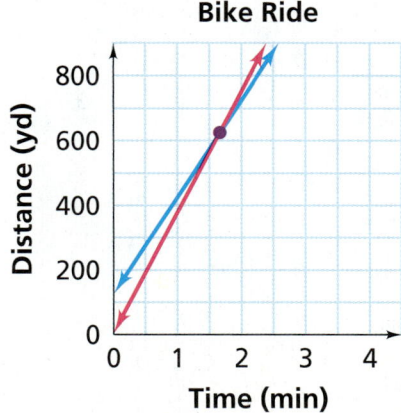

   a. Which line corresponds to Nicole's ride? To Katy's ride?

   b. Write an equation for Katy's graph.

   c. Write an equation for Nicole's graph.

   d. In Lesson 3.13, you learned that the intersection point of two graphs satisfies both equations. In the distance-time graph, the two lines intersect. This shows that Katy catches up to Nicole. At what time and distance does this happen?

5. Conan waits at the train station for Courtney. Courtney gets off the train 217 feet away from where Conan is waiting on the platform. They start running toward each other. Conan runs 11 feet per second. Courtney runs 10 feet per second.

   a. How long will it take for them to meet?

   b. How far will Conan have run when they meet?

   c. Write an equation that can be used to find how long it will take for Conan and Courtney to meet.

   d. Suppose they had started 350 feet apart. Calculate how long it would take them to meet in this situation.

On Your Own

6. Write a problem similar to Problem 4. Decide the distance of the head start and the speed of each rider. Draw graphs that represent each bicyclist.

7. Graph ℓ and m. Are the given points on ℓ, m, both, or neither?

   a. $\ell: y = 2x + 1$ and $m: y + 3x = 1$

   points: $A(0, 0)$, $B(0, 1)$, and $C\left(1, \frac{1}{3}\right)$

   b. $\ell: y = x^2$ and $m: \frac{1}{2}y + x = 4$

   points: $A(-2, 4)$, $B(2, 4)$, and $C(0, 0)$

   c. $\ell: y = \frac{1}{5}x - 1$ and $m: x = 5$

   points: $A(5, 0)$, $B(5, 3)$, and $C(-5, 2)$

   d. $\ell: y = 2x$ and $m: y = \frac{3}{2}x + 1$

   points: $A(1, 2)$, $B(6, 10)$, and $C(2, 4)$

8. For each pair of lines, find each of the following:

   - a point on neither line
   - a point on one line but not the other
   - a point on both lines

   a. $p: y + 3 = x$ and $q: x + y = 3$

   b. $p: y = \frac{3}{5}x + 2$ and $q: y = -\frac{5}{3}x + 2$

   c. $p: 2y + 10x = -8$ and $q: y - \frac{1}{5}x = -4$

9. Find the equations of two lines that intersect at (2, −4). Check that the point (2, −4) satisfies both equations.

10. In 2002, Town X had a population of 7250, and Town Y had a population of 9000. Since 1990, the population of Town X has been steadily decreasing by 120 people per year. The population of Town Y has been steadily increasing by 300 people per year. In what year did Town X and Town Y have the same population?

Maintain Your Skills

11. Graph each pair of linear equations. Name any points they have in common.

    a. $y = 2x + 1$ and $y + 3x = 1$

    b. $(y - 0) = \frac{1}{2}(x - 3)$ and $(y - 0) = -3(x - 3)$

    c. $(y + 1) = 2(x - 3)$ and $3y - 6x = 9$

    d. $y = \frac{5}{2}x - 1$ and $2\left(y - \frac{5}{2}\right) = 5(x + 1)$

    e. $y = \frac{3}{5}x + 1$ and $y = -\frac{5}{3}x + 1$

    f. When do the graphs of two lines intersect at one point?

    g. When do the graphs of two lines have no intersection points?

Use slope for Exercises 11f and 11g.

4.09 Getting Started

4.10 Solving Systems: Substitution

In Lesson 4.08, you compared the graphs of two different lines. When the slopes, or rates of change, of the two graphs were different, the graphs eventually intersected. How can you find the intersection point directly from the equations?

Consider this pair of equations.

$d = 375t$

$d = 300t + 125$

These equations describe Katy's and Nicole's bike ride in Lesson 4.09.

If you graph the equations, the intersection point is at approximately $t = 1.5$.

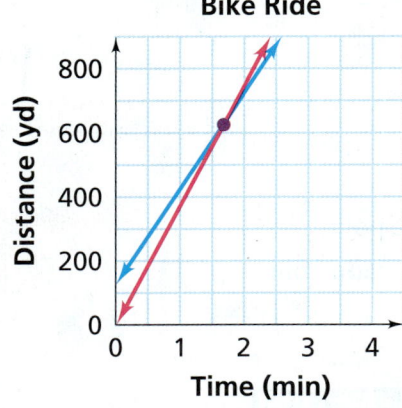

Test whether $t = 1.5$ gives the same value for d in each equation.

Substitute $t = 1.5$ into the first equation.

$d = 375t$

$d = 375(1.5)$

$d = 562.5$

Substitute $t = 1.5$ into the second equation.

$d = 300t + 125$

$d = 300(1.5) + 125$

$d = 575$

The values of d are different, so $t = 1.5$ does not give the intersection point. But it is close. You could refine your guess, trying a value of t that is slightly greater.

If $t = 1.5$, Nicole has biked 575 yards and Katy has biked 562.5 yards. Since Katy bikes faster, she still has not passed Nicole. So the value of t must be greater than 1.5.

The guess-and-check process will eventually give you the answer. However, there is a way to calculate the intersection exactly. Wherever the graphs cross, both variables must have the same values in the two equations. In other words, the values of both t and d are the same in both equations.

You are given the two equations $d = 375t$ and $d = 300t + 125$.
If the values of d have to equal each other, then these expressions are also equivalent.

$$d = 375t$$
$$d = 300t + 125$$
$$375t = d = 300t + 125$$
$$375t = 300t + 125$$

You can use this equation to find the exact value of t at the intersection. Solve with the basic moves.

$$375t = 300t + 125$$
$$75t = 125$$
$$t = \frac{125}{75}$$
$$t = \frac{5}{3}$$

To find the d-value, substitute $t = \frac{5}{3}$ into either of the two original equations. The first equation seems simpler.

$$d = 375t$$
$$d = 375\left(\frac{5}{3}\right)$$
$$d = 625$$

Habits of Mind

Experiment. Try the same value of t in the other equation. If your result is the same, you have found the correct point of intersection.

The intersection point is $\left(\frac{5}{3}, 625\right)$. You can also write the coordinates as mixed numbers, $\left(1\frac{2}{3}, 625\right)$.

For You to Do

1. For what value of t is Katy leading the ride?
2. For what values of t is Nicole leading?
3. Who rides 1 mile first?

It is not a coincidence that both equations are in "$d =$" form. Situations often suggest describing one variable in terms of operations on another variable. It is less common for a situation to yield an equation like $2x + 3y = 87$.

Sometimes, you are given two equations that are in different forms, for example, $ax + by = c$ or $y - b = m(x - a)$. There are several ways you can find the intersection points of these lines. You can solve both equations for the same variable and then set the other sides equal to each other. You can also use the **substitution method.** First solve one of the equations for any variable. Then substitute this result for the variable in the other equation.

4.10 Solving Systems: Substitution

Example

Problem Find an ordered pair (x, y) that makes both equations true.

$$2x + 5y = 20$$
$$x - y = 3$$

Solution First solve one equation for a variable in terms of the other. Either variable in either equation can be selected. Typically, you want to select the one that requires the least work. In this example, it is easiest to solve the second equation for x.

$x - y = 3$ Add y to both sides.

$x - y + y = 3 + y$ Simplify.

$x = 3 + y$

Next you want to substitute the expression $3 + y$ for every x in the first equation.

$2x + 5y = 20$ Substitute $3 + y$ for x.

$2(3 + y) + 5y = 20$

Don't forget the parentheses!

You now have an equation with only one variable. Solve using the basic moves.

$2(3 + y) + 5y = 20$

$6 + 2y + 5y = 20$

$6 + 7y = 20$

$7y = 14$

$y = 2$

The y-coordinate of the intersection point is 2. Substitute 2 for y in either equation to find the corresponding x-coordinate.

$x - y = 3$

$x - (2) = 3$

$x = 5$

The intersection point is $(5, 2)$. Check your work by substituting $x = 5$ and $y = 2$ into each equation.

$2x + 5y = 20$ $x - y = 3$

$2(5) + 5(2) = 20$ ✓ $5 - 2 = 3$ ✓

The point $(5, 2)$ makes both equations true. It is the intersection point for the graphs of $2x + 5y = 20$ and $x - y = 3$.

For Discussion

4. The point (5, 2) is an intersection of the graphs of $2x + 5y = 20$ and $x - y = 3$. Are there any others? Explain.

For You to Do

5. Find an ordered pair (a, b) that solves the equations $a = 15 - 2b$ and $3a - 5b = 15 - 2a$.

6. What's Wrong Here? Tony needs to find the intersection point of the graphs of $2x + 5y = 20$ and $y = x - 3$. He says, "Since the second equation is solved for y, I can substitute into the first equation. I just need to replace y with $x - 3$.

$$2x + 5y = 20$$
$$2x + 5x - 3 = 20$$
$$7x = 23$$
$$x = \frac{23}{7}$$

Now I plug this value of x in to find y in either equation. I'll pick the second one.

$$y = x - 3$$
$$y = \frac{23}{7} - 3$$
$$y = \frac{2}{7}$$

Let me check my work. I'll plug the point $\left(\frac{23}{7}, \frac{2}{7}\right)$ into the first equation.

$$2x + 5y = 20$$
$$2\left(\frac{23}{7}\right) + 5\left(\frac{2}{7}\right) \stackrel{?}{=} 20$$
$$\frac{46}{7} + \frac{10}{7} \stackrel{?}{=} 20$$
$$\frac{56}{7} \stackrel{?}{=} 20$$
$$8 \neq 20 \text{ ✗}$$

I must have done something wrong. I'm glad I checked the result. Now I know to look for a mistake."

What was Tony's mistake?

4.10 Solving Systems: Substitution

Developing Habits of Mind

Use a different process to find the same result. As you have seen in this lesson, you can find the intersection of the graphs of two equations without sketching the graphs. You can find the points algebraically by solving a system of equations. A **system of equations** is a group of equations with the same variables. When you solve the system, you find a common solution to all the equations at once.

Exercises Practicing Habits of Mind

Check Your Understanding

1. At a lunch shop, Aisha buys 2 veggie wraps, 3 apples, and a drink. Her bill is $6.24. Jaime buys 3 veggie wraps, 2 apples, and a drink. His bill is $6.64. If drinks cost $.99, how much does a veggie wrap cost?

2. What is the intersection point of the graphs of these linear equations?

$$2v + 3a + 0.99 = 6.24$$
$$3v + 2a + 0.99 = 6.64$$

3. Many phone companies offer a "10-10" number that you can dial before a long-distance call to save money. If you dial 10-10 with BigPhone Company, you pay $.39 for the connection and $.03 per minute. If you dial 10-10 with LittlePhone Company, you pay $.25 for the connection and $.07 per minute. Assume you are charged for the exact time you use.

   a. How much does a 6-minute call cost with each company?

   b. For how much time do the two companies charge the same amount?

   c. Which company's plan is less expensive for a 10-minute call?

4. For each pair of equations, find any common solutions. Check that your result satisfies both equations.

   a. $y = 6x - 7$
      $y = -2x - 9$

   b. $m = 8n - 3$
      $m = -4n + 6$

   c. $y = 3x$
      $3x - 2y = 12$

   d. $(y - 5) = 3(x + 2)$
      $(y - 5) = 6(x + 2)$

   e. $y = 9x + 4$
      $y = 9x - \frac{2}{3}$

   f. $(y - 1) = \frac{2}{3}(x + 1)$
      $(y - 1) = 4\left(x - \frac{1}{4}\right)$

5. The Walton Taxi Company charges $2.25 for each trip plus $.19 for every $\frac{1}{10}$ mile. The Newtham Taxi Company charges $1.50 for each trip plus $.25 for each $\frac{1}{10}$ mile.

   a. How much will a $\frac{3}{10}$-mile ride cost with each company?

   b. How much will a 1-mile ride cost with each company?

   c. Use t for the total cost of the ride and m for each $\frac{1}{10}$ mile. Write an equation to describe each taxi company's fee schedule. Graph the two equations on the same set of axes.

   d. For what distance do the taxi companies charge the same amount?

   e. Which company charges less if you need to travel 6 miles?

   f. When is it less expensive to use the Walton Taxi Company?

Is this a Walton or a Newtham taxi meter?

4.10 Solving Systems: Substitution

6. What is the intersection point for each pair of lines?

a.

b.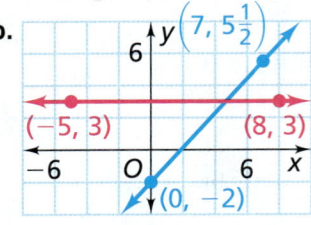

c.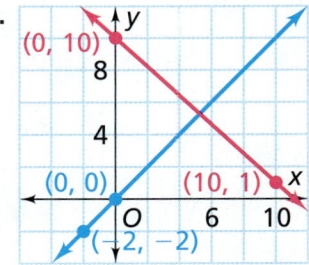

Write About It Describe a situation that could make use of each given system.

7. system of two equations in two variables

8. system of three equations in two variables

On Your Own

9. Tyrell needs to call a plumber. RotoPlumb charges $75 for the first half hour of work and $30 for each additional half hour. Just Plumbing charges $45 for every half hour of work. Which plumbing company should Tyrell choose if the job takes the given amount of time?

   a. 1 hour
   b. 6 hours
   c. For what time will both companies charge the same amount?

10. **Standardized Test Prep** Each DVD club offers some DVDs for free and then charges a fixed price for other DVDs. If you join Club 1, you receive 4 free DVDs. You must purchase at least 4 DVDs at the club price. The club price for each DVD is $11.99. If you join Club 2, you receive 5 free DVDs. You must purchase at least 4 DVDs at the club price. The club price for each DVD is $13.99.

Total Number of DVDs	Total Cost	
	Club 1	Club 2
9	■	■
10	■	■
11	■	■
12	■	■

   a. You plan to get a total of nine DVDs including the free DVDs. What will be the total cost with Club 1? With Club 2?
   b. Copy and complete the table.
   c. Use the data from your completed table to draw a graph.
   d. Compare the two offers. Explain which is the most economical.

11. **a.** Use substitution to find the intersection point of the graphs of $y = 5 - 3x$ and $y + 3x = 1$. Explain what happens.

    b. Graph each equation. What do the graphs suggest about the solution to the system of equations?

12. **Take It Further** Suppose k and ℓ are fixed numbers. Since the following are lines with different slopes, the graphs of the two lines $y = 18x + k$ and $y = 5x + \ell$ must always intersect somewhere. Find a formula, using k and ℓ, for the intersection point.

13. What is the solution to each system of equations? If there is not any solution, explain.

    a. $y = 18x - 30$ and $y = 17.5x + 12$

    b. $y = 18x - 30$ and $y = 18x + 12$

Maintain Your Skills

14. Write equations for lines ℓ and m. Tell whether ℓ and m are parallel.

    a. ℓ passes through $(-1, 5)$ and $(-3, 1)$; m passes through $(2, -2)$ and $(5, 4)$.

    b. ℓ passes through $(10, 4)$ and $(-5, 1)$; m passes through $(5, 0)$ and $(15, 2)$.

    c. ℓ passes through $\left(0, \frac{1}{2}\right)$ and $(3, -4)$; m passes through $(0, 5)$ with slope 2.

    d. ℓ passes through $(7, 7)$ and $(-1, -1)$; m passes through $(0, -7)$ and $(7, 0)$.

    e. ℓ passes through $(3, 7)$ and $(9, 11)$; m passes through $(3, 1)$ and $(-6, -4)$.

    f. ℓ passes through $(-3, 12)$ and $(4, 5)$; m passes through $\left(\frac{1}{2}, 4\right)$ and $\left(\frac{3}{2}, 3\right)$.

    g. ℓ passes through $(0, -9)$ and $(2, -1)$; m passes through $(0, 0)$ and $(4, 4)$.

    h. How can you tell from the equations whether lines ℓ and m are parallel?

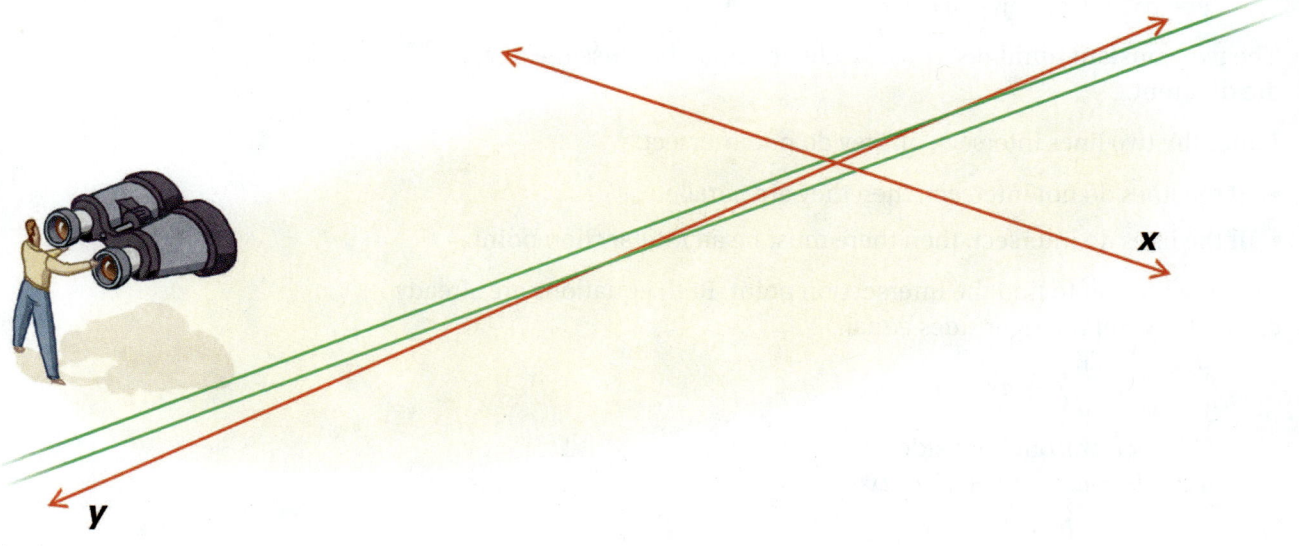

4.11 Slope and Parallel Lines

Slope is an important concept in understanding lines that do not intersect. You can determine if lines intersect by finding their slopes.

For You to Do

What is the slope of each line?

1. $3x - 2y = 7$
2. $y = 5x - 3$
3. $x = 3y + 2$
4. $(y - 4) = 7(x + 5)$

How are parallel runways used?

Throughout this chapter, you have encountered graphs of two lines that do not intersect. For example, when you sketch the distance-time graphs of two objects traveling at the same constant speed, the two lines never cross. Two lines that do not intersect are parallel.

Definition

Two lines in the same plane are parallel if they have no points in common.

You may have noticed in this investigation that if two different lines have the same slope, they are parallel. You can prove that this conjecture is true.

Theorem 4.3

If two distinct lines have the same slope, then they are parallel.

Distinct means "different." Distinct lines will not have the same graph.

Proof Consider two different lines with the same slope. Let a be the slope of the lines. Write equations for these lines.

$$y = ax + b \text{ and } y = ax + d$$

The two constant numbers, b and d, are not equal because the lines are different.

Either the two lines intersect, or they do not intersect.

- If the lines do not intersect, then they are parallel.
- If the lines do intersect, then there must be an intersection point.

Use substitution to find the intersection point. Both equations are already solved for y. Set the right sides equal.

$$\left.\begin{array}{l} y = ax + b \\ y = ax + d \end{array}\right\} \rightarrow ax + b = ax + d$$

Subtract ax from both sides.

$$ax + b - ax = ax + d - ax$$
$$b = d$$

But this contradicts the fact that $b \neq d$. Therefore, the two lines cannot intersect.

Thus, if two distinct lines have the same slope, then they are parallel.

For Discussion

Explain why the following sentences from the proof are true.

5. If the lines do not intersect, then they are parallel.
6. If $b = d$, then the two lines, $y = ax + b$ and $y = ax + d$ must be the same.

Different lines with the same slope are parallel. Can lines that do not have the same slope also be parallel? The next theorem states that they cannot.

Theorem 4.4

If two lines have different slopes, then they must intersect in exactly one point.

Proof Consider two lines, as in the previous proof. Let a be the slope of the first line and let c be the slope of the second line. Write equations for these lines where $a \neq c$, and b and d are two constant numbers that may or may not be equal.

$$y = ax + b \text{ and } y = cx + d$$

If there is a point of intersection, then the lines cannot be parallel. Use substitution to find the intersection.

$$\left. \begin{array}{l} y = ax + b \\ y = cx + d \end{array} \right\} \rightarrow ax + b = cx + d$$

Solve this equation for x.

$ax + b = cx + d$	Subtract cx from each side.
$ax - cx + b = d$	Subtract b from each side.
$ax - cx = d - b$	"Undistribute" the x.
$(a - c)x = d - b$	Divide each side by $a - c$.
$x = \frac{d - b}{a - c}$	

You also can find out that $y = \frac{ad - bc}{a - c}$. The intersection point is $\left(\frac{d - b}{a - c}, \frac{ad - bc}{a - c} \right)$.

> The fact that $a \neq c$ is important. If $a = c$, then $a - c$ equals 0, and you cannot divide by 0.

For Discussion

Complete the proof by answering these questions.

7. You found an expression for the intersection point. How does this fact prove the theorem?
8. Can there be more than one intersection point?

You proved that parallel lines have the same slope and intersecting lines do not have the same slope. Therefore, the statements "two distinct lines are parallel" and "two distinct lines have the same slope" are equivalent. Logicians write equivalence statements such as the following:

Two different lines are parallel if and only if they have the same slope.

Exercises Practicing Habits of Mind

Check Your Understanding

1. Identify the graphs of each pair of equations as *parallel*, *intersecting*, or *identical*. Explain.

    a. $4x - y = 12$ and $y = 4x + 7$
    b. $y = \frac{5}{3}x + 9$ and $y = -\frac{3}{5}x + 200$
    c. $y = \frac{4}{12}x + 9$ and $y = \frac{1}{3}x - 3.7$
    d. $6x + 9y = 1$ and $9y - 1 = -6x$
    e. $x - 4y = 13$ and $2x + \frac{1}{2}y = \frac{3}{4}$
    f. $y - 5 = -2x - 6$ and $y - 2 = -x + 1$

2. In Lesson 4.10, you worked with BigPhone's plan. If you dial "10-10-B-I-G," you pay $.39 as a connection fee and $.03 per minute. Huge Phone offers a plan that has a connection fee of $10, but only charges $.01 per minute. Sasha thinks that Huge Phone will always be more expensive than BigPhone. Tony thinks that if you talk for a very long time, Huge Phone might be less expensive. Who is correct?

3. Describe a calling plan that is always more expensive than BigPhone's plan from Exercise 2. Justify your example.

4. Sasha graphs a line with the equation $2x + 3y = 7$. Then she multiplies both sides by 4 to get $8x + 12y = 28$. She graphs this equation. The graph is not another line. Explain.

On Your Own

For Exercises 5–9, write an equation of the line that contains the given point and is parallel to the line with the given equation.

You may want to develop a point-tester.

5. $(10, 15)$; $y = -\frac{1}{5}x + 4$

6. $(-4, 3)$; $2x - 4y = 7$

7. $\left(13, -\frac{22}{7}\right)$; $y - 5 = \frac{22}{7}(x - 8)$

8. $(0, 0)$; $y = ax + b$ (a and b are constant numbers, and $b \neq 0$.)

9. a. $(5, -3)$; $y = 7$
   b. $(5, -3)$; $x = 7$

10. **Write About It** Meredith describes to Liza two purchases she made. "On Monday, I bought 39 books and 21 CDs for $396. On Tuesday, at the same prices, I bought 52 books and 28 CDs for $518."

    Liza thought about the numbers and said, "That's impossible!" Is Liza correct? Assume that all books cost the same amount and all CDs cost the same amount. Explain.

11. **Write About It** Tim tries to solve a system of two linear equations. He concludes that there is no solution. Explain what this means about the graphs.

    When you solve a system of linear equations, you find the point where the graphs of the lines intersect.

12. **Standardized Test Prep** Julia and Marcia buy identically priced cans of chili and identically priced jars of salsa.
    - Julia buys 3 cans of chili and 2 jars of salsa for $10.07.
    - Marcia buys 2 cans of chili and 4 jars of salsa for $12.98.

    Which system of equations can be used to find x, the cost of 1 can of chili, and y, the cost of 1 jar of salsa?

    A. $x + y = 10.07$
       $x + y = 12.98$

    B. $10.07x + 12.98y = 11$
       $x + y = 11$

    C. $2x + 4y = 10.07$
       $2x + 3y = 12.98$

    D. $3x + 2y = 10.07$
       $2x + 4y = 12.98$

13. **Write About It** Diego needs to solve this system.

    $2x + 3y = 7$

    $4x - 3y = 5$

    He graphs each line to get an estimate of the solution. Next, he adds the equations. His result is $6x = 12$. Diego says, "What a great way to solve systems! I hope that adding the equations is a legal move."

    > What does the graph of $6x = 12$ look like on the Cartesian plane?

    a. If you use the equation $6x = 12$, what is the solution to the system?

    b. Is Diego's move legal? Explain.

Maintain Your Skills

14. What is the value of k such that the graph of the equation will pass through $(0, -5)$?

    a. $y = 2x + k$

    b. $y = 3x + k$

    c. $y = 4x + k$

    d. $y = 99x + k$

    e. What pattern do you notice about the values of k?

15. What is the value of k such that the graph of the equation will pass through $(-5, 0)$?

    a. $y = 2x + k$

    b. $y = 3x + k$

    c. $y = 4x + k$

    d. $y = 99x + k$

    e. What do you notice about the relationship between k and the slope?

4.12 Solving Systems: Elimination

Recall the following basic move:

> If you start with any equation and add the same number to each side, you will not change the solutions to the equation.

For example, suppose $x = 5$ and $y = 6$. What is true about $x + y$? You can easily decide that $x + y$ is 11. You can also get this result using basic moves. Start with $x = 5$ and add 6 to each side.

$$x = 5$$
$$x + 6 = 5 + 6$$

Since $y = 6$, substitute y for 6 on the left side of the equation.

$$x + 6 = 5 + 6$$
$$x + y = 5 + 6$$

This is a great deal of work for such a simple problem. You can extend the basic rules so that you can say, "Add the same value (instead of number) to each side of an equation." *Value* can mean a variable, number, or any mathematical expression.

Theorem 4.5 Additive Property of Equality

If $X = A$ and $Y = B$, then $X + Y = A + B$, where A, B, X, and Y can be any mathematical expressions.

The proof of this theorem is exactly like the example above.

This theorem explains why Diego's idea in Lesson 4.11 works. It also points to another method for solving systems of equations. You can combine equations in ways that eliminate one of the variables. When you reduce the system to a simpler one, you can find the solution easily.

Example 1

Problem Find the intersection of the graphs of $x + y = 10$ and $x - y = 3$.

Solution Use the Additive Property of Equality. If $x + y$ is 10 and $x - y$ is 3, then their sum must be 13.

$$
\begin{array}{r}
x + y = 10 \\
(+) \quad x - y = 3 \\
\hline
(x + y) + (x - y) = 13
\end{array}
$$

Habits of Mind

Use a different process to get the same result. Draw the graph to estimate the solution.

When you use the **elimination method**, you use either addition or subtraction to remove a variable. For example, the result of adding $(x + y) + (x - y)$ is $2x$. You have eliminated the variable y.

In general, it is faster to add each variable separately. Write the two equations one under the other so that matching variables line up. Then, add each column. First add the x values. Then add the y values. Add the numbers last.

$$\begin{aligned} x + y &= 10 \\ (+)x - y &= 3 \\ \hline 2x - 0y &= 13 \end{aligned}$$

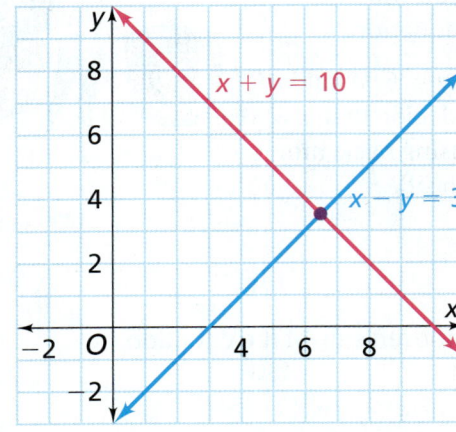

You can write the plus sign + in parentheses to indicate that it applies to all of the terms on both sides of the second equation.

The result is $2x = 13$, so x is $6\frac{1}{2}$.

Substitute the x value, $6\frac{1}{2}$, into one of the equations to find that $y = 3\frac{1}{2}$. The graphs of the equations intersect at $\left(6\frac{1}{2}, 3\frac{1}{2}\right)$.

For You to Do

1. Use the Additive Property of Equality. Solve the system of equations.

    $6y - 4x = 3$

    $4x + 2y = 1$

For Discussion

2. When you add these equations, you will not eliminate any variables.

    $3x + 2y = 11$

    $3x - 5y = 25$

    Is it a legal move to subtract equations the same way you add them? If $X = A$ and $Y = B$, is it always true that $X - Y = A - B$? What is the solution to this system?

Try replacing A and B with numbers. Is the equation always true?

388 Chapter 4 Lines

Elimination by adding or subtracting works whenever the coefficients of one variable are the opposite or the same, respectively, for both equations. Some systems of equations, like the one below, do not have a variable with the same coefficient.

$$5y - 2x = -15$$
$$12y + 3x = 3$$

You can still use elimination to solve these equations, but you will need some extra steps.

Example 2

Problem What is the intersection of the graphs of $5y - 2x = -15$ and $12y + 3x = 3$?

Solution Remember this basic move of equations.

If you multiply both sides of an equation by the same nonzero number, you will not change the solutions of that equation.

- Multiply both sides of the first equation by 3 to get $15y - 6x = -45$. The coefficient of x is now -6.
- Multiply both sides of the second equation by 2 to get $24y + 6x = 6$. The coefficient of x is now 6.

Now when you add the equations together, you eliminate the x term.

$$
\begin{array}{r}
15y - 6x = -45 \\
(+)\ 24y + 6x = 6 \\
\hline
39y = -39
\end{array}
$$

Divide both sides by 39 to solve the equation and get $y = -1$.

Plug this y value into either of the original equations. Find x at the intersection.

$$5y - 2x = -15$$
$$5(-1) - 2x = -15$$
$$-5 - 2x = -15$$
$$10 = 2x$$
$$5 = x$$

The intersection point is $(5, -1)$.

For Discussion

3. Why did you change both x coefficients to 6?
4. Can you solve this system by eliminating y instead? Explain.

Exercises Practicing Habits of Mind

Check Your Understanding

1. Use elimination. Solve each system of equations. Check that your solution satisfies both equations.

    a. $x + y = 30$ and $x - y = 6$

    b. $-10a + 6b = 25$ and $10a + 5b = 30$

    c. $2x + y = 4$ and $x - y = 2$

    d. $2x - 3y = 17$ and $2x - 3y = 1$

    e. $4z - 5w = 15$ and $2w + 4z = -6$

    f. $y = 7x + 1$ and $y = 15$

2. At a snack bar, 2 granola bars and 2 drinks cost $3.50. Two granola bars and 4 drinks cost $6.00. What is the cost of each item? Assume items at the snack bar are tax-free.

3. Isabel solves the system of equations below. Explain each step.

    $10x + 3y = 34$
    $5x + 4y = 37$

    $10x + 3y = 34$
    $(+) -10x + -8y = -74$
    _____
    $-5y = -40$
    $y = 8$

    $5x + 4(8) = 37$
    $5x + 32 = 37$
    $5x = 5$
    $x = 1$

    $10(1) + 3(8) = 34$ ✔
    $5(1) + 4(8) = 37$ ✔

4. a. Write the equation of the horizontal line that passes through the intersection of the graphs of $2x + 5y = 17$ and $3x - 2y = 16$.

    b. Write the equation of the vertical line that passes through the intersection in part (a).

    c. The sum of the equations in part (a) is $5x + 3y = 33$. How is the graph of this equation related to the graphs of the equations in part (a)?

390 Chapter 4 Lines

5. **Take It Further** Solve this system of equations.

$$2x + 3y + 5z = 11$$
$$x - y + z = 1$$
$$3x - 4y - 5z = 16$$

6. **Take It Further** Prove that Theorem 4.6 gives the solution of any system of linear equations in two variables.

Theorem 4.6

Given the system $ax + by = e$ and $cx + dy = f$, where a, b, c, d, e, and f are known constants, the unique solution is $(x, y) = \left(\dfrac{de - bf}{ad - bc}, \dfrac{af - ce}{ad - bc}\right)$ when $ad - bc \neq 0$. If $ad - bc = 0$, the graphs of the two equations have the same slope, so they are either parallel (the system has no solutions) or the same (the system has infinitely many solutions).

On Your Own

7. a. Write the equations of two lines that do not intersect.

   b. Write the equations of two lines that intersect at $(1, -2)$.

8. Kenji bought 2 hats and an umbrella for $22.00. The next day, he bought 2 hats and 3 umbrellas for $33.00. The hats are identical, as are the umbrellas.

   a. What is the price of 2 umbrellas?

   b. What is the price of 1 umbrella?

   c. What is the price of 1 hat?

   d. What combination of hats and umbrellas, if any, would cost $77.00?

9. **Standardized Test Prep** Jeremy helps Madeline build a rectangular pen with a perimeter of 86 feet. Twice the pen's width is one more than three times its length. What is the width of the pen?

   A. $8\frac{3}{5}$ feet

   B. 17 feet

   C. 26 feet

   D. $33\frac{2}{5}$ feet

You can find the cost of two umbrellas in one step.

10. What is the point of intersection of each pair of graphs? Check that this point satisfies both equations.

    a. $y = -5x + 30$
       $3x - 4y = 41$

    b. $y = 2x - 1$
       $y = 9x + 6$

    c. $3x + 2y = 7$
       $-2x + 2y = -2$

    d. $5e - 2f = 30$
       $9e - 2f = 54$

    e. $27x + 5y = 30$
       $-3x - 2y = 1$

    f. $5j - 4k = 19$
       $-7j - 3k = 22$

11. Solve each system.

    a. $2x + 3y = 5$
       $3x - 2y = 14$

    b. $2x + 3y = 5$
       $6x - 4y = 28$

    c. $2x - 3y = 5$
       $3x + 2y = 14$

    d. $2x + 3y = 5$
       $6x + 9y = 18$

12. **Take It Further** Solve each system.

    a. $3x - 2y = 10$
       $4x + y = 5$
       $x + 3y = -7$

    b. $3x - 2y = 10$
       $4x + y = 5$
       $x + 3y = -6$

13. You can use graphs of the following equations to draw a triangle.

    $y = \frac{3}{2}x$

    $y = -\frac{9}{4}x + \frac{15}{2}$

    $y = -\frac{3}{8}x - \frac{15}{4}$

    Draw the graph of the triangle and list its vertices.

Maintain Your Skills

14. Which pairs of equations in the following list form a system with a solution that is (1, 1)? Justify your answer.

    $x + y = 2$

    $x + 2y = 3$

    $x + 3y = 4$

    $x + 4y = 5$

    $\vdots$

    $x + (n - 1)y = n$

    $x + ny = n + 1$

392 Chapter 4 Lines

Mathematical 4C Reflections

In this investigation, you used slope to find the intersection of two lines. You also used slope to determine whether two lines were parallel. These questions will help you summarize what you have learned.

1. Graph the equations $y = 2x - 3$ and $x - y = 3$. Name a point that satisfies each description.

   a. on neither line
   b. on only one line
   c. on both lines

2. What are the equations of two lines that intersect at $(1, -3)$? Check that $(1, -3)$ satisfies both equations.

3. What is the intersection of each pair of linear equations? Sketch the graphs.

   a. $2x + 3y = 2$
      $y = x - 1$

   b. $y - 2 = 3(x + 1)$
      $x + y = 3$

   c. $y = 2x$
      $y = -x - 3$

4. Write an equation for each description.

   a. line parallel to $2x - y = 4$

   b. line intersecting $2x - y = 4$ at $(1, -2)$

5. Solve each system.

   a. $x - 2y = 5$
      $3x + 2y = -1$

   b. $2x - 3y = 15$
      $x + y = 10$

   c. $4x + 3y = 12$
      $8x + 6y = 8$

   d. $2x + 3y = 1$
      $4x - 2y = 10$

6. How can you find the intersection of two lines?

7. How can you determine from their equations whether two lines will intersect?

8. Are the graphs of $3x - 4y = 16$ and $y = \frac{3}{4}x - 1$ parallel? Explain.

Vocabulary

In this investigation, you learned these terms. Make sure you understand what each one means and how to use it.

- **elimination method**
- **substitution method**
- **system of equations**

An opponent anticipates where the ball and the receiver's paths should intersect.

Investigation 4D

Applications of Lines

In *Applications of Lines*, you will solve inequalities in one variable using graphs. You will also find linear trends in data. Using a scatter plot, you can identify linear trends easily.

By the end of this investigation, you will be able to answer questions like these.

1. How do the solutions of inequalities relate to the solutions of equations?
2. How can you approximate data using a line of best fit?
3. One taxi charges $1.10 for the first mile and $1 for each additional mile. Another taxi charges $2.30 for the first mile and $.60 for each additional mile. For what distances will the first taxi be less expensive than the second?

You will learn how to
- solve inequalities algebraically and by using graphs
- graph the solution set of an inequality
- find the balance point of a data set and estimate the line of best fit

You will develop these habits and skills:
- Use an equation as a point-tester for a graph.
- Graph lines and inequalities.
- Identify graphs, such as those for $y = x^2$ and $y = |x|$, by their shape.
- Estimate the intersection points of graphs.
- Check that the difference between actual data and your prediction is low.

Some shapes occur commonly and are easy to identify.

4.13 Getting Started

**Activating Prior Knowledge
Exploring New Ideas**

In this investigation, you will solve and graph inequalities with one variable. You will also determine fitting lines for scatter plots of data.

For You to Explore

1. Consider the equation $4x - 7 = -2x + 9$.
   a. Is the equation true or false when $x = 5$?
   b. What are the values of x that make the equation true?
   c. Describe the values of x that make the equation false.
   d. List five values of x that make $4x - 7 < -2x + 9$ true.
   e. List five values of x that make $4x - 7 > -2x + 9$ true.
   f. Write a rule that states whether a value of x makes $4x - 7 < -2x + 9$ or $4x - 7 > -2x + 9$ true. Test more values if necessary.

2. The local Big Games store is offering a special trade-in deal. When you buy a new game, Flat Tire Racing, you receive $6 for each used game you trade in. The game costs $49.99, plus 5% tax.
   a. How much does the game cost, including tax? Round to the nearest cent.
   b. Justin has $10 and 7 used games to trade. Can he afford the game?
   c. Jason has $20 and 15 used games to trade. Can he afford the game?
   d. If Jason has $20, what is the minimum number of used games he needs to trade to get the new game? Explain.
   e. How many different options does Jason have if he has $20? Explain.

3. Sketch the graphs of the equations $y = 4x - 7$ and $y = -2x + 9$. Find their intersection point.

4. Use the graph of $y = x^2 - 5$ and $y = x + 1$ at the right.
   a. Name all the solutions to the equation $x^2 - 5 = x + 1$.
   b. Draw a number line. Shade it with all the solutions of $x^2 - 5 > x + 1$.

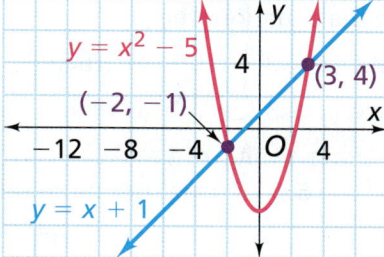

For part (a), find each x value for which $y = x^2 - 5$ and $y = x + 1$ have the same y value. Where do you see this on the graph?

5. Consider the equations $y = (x - 11)^2 - 5$ and $y = (x - 11) + 1$.

   a. List the solutions to $(x - 11)^2 - 5 = (x - 11) + 1$.

   b. Draw a number line. Shade it with all the solutions of $(x - 11)^2 - 5 < (x - 11) + 1$.

6. a. Find seven points that make the inequality $y > 2x - 5$ true. Plot them on a coordinate plane.

   b. Graph the points in the coordinate plane that make the inequality $y > 2x - 5$ true.

7. **Take It Further** Graph the points in the coordinate plane that make the inequality $y \leq x^2$ true.

Exercises Practicing Habits of Mind

On Your Own

8. Consider the equation $(x - 3)^2 + 5 = 41$.

   a. Is the equation *true* or *false* when $x = 7$?

   b. Test whether -3 makes the equation true.

   c. What other number(s) make the equation true?

   d. Find five values of x that make $(x - 3)^2 + 5 < 41$ true.

   e. Find five values of x that make $(x - 3)^2 + 5 > 41$ true.

   f. Write a rule to determine whether a value of x makes $(x - 3)^2 + 5 < 41$ or $(x - 3)^2 + 5 > 41$ true. Test more values if necessary.

9. Draw a number line. Mark it with all the values of x that satisfy each inequality.

   a. $5x + 14 < 2x - 12$

   b. $5x + 14 \leq 2x - 12$

   c. $(x - 3)^2 + 5 > 41$

396 Chapter 4 Lines

10. Use the graph of $y = x^3 - 3x$ and $y = x$.

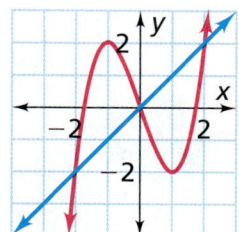

   a. At how many points do the graphs intersect?
   b. What are the exact coordinates of the intersection point(s)?
   c. What are the solutions to the equation $x^3 - 3x = x$?
   d. Describe the values of x that make $x^3 - 3x < x$ true.

11. Describe the numbers that make each statement true.
   a. $3a - 16 > 23$
   b. $3b - 16 \geq 23$
   c. $|d - 4| < 3$
   d. $|h - 4| \leq 3$
   e. $(d - 4)^2 < 9$

Maintain Your Skills

12. Suppose n is a number greater than 10. What do you know about the value of each of the following?
   a. $2n$
   b. $n - 20$
   c. $-n$
   d. $\frac{n}{2}$
   e. $-3n + 7$

13. What is the intersection point for each pair of lines?
   a. $y = 3x - 5$ and $y = -2x + 10$
   b. $y = 3x - 8$ and $y = -2x + 7$
   c. $y = 3x + 5$ and $y = -2x + 20$
   d. $y = 3(x - 4) - 5$ and $y = -2(x - 4) + 10$
   e. What patterns do you notice in the graphs?

4.14 Inequalities With One Variable

Tony's parents are choosing a new long-distance phone plan. Tony and Sasha try to determine which one is cheaper.

Minds in Action — episode 17

Tony The phone company offers two plans. With Plan 1, a long-distance call costs 43 cents plus 2 cents per minute. With Plan 2, a long-distance call costs 25 cents plus 4 cents per minute. My mom makes a lot of long calls, so she wants to know which plan is cheaper for longer calls.

Sasha Let's write expressions for each plan first. If m is the number of minutes, then the cost for a phone call with Plan 1 is $43 + 2m$. A call with Plan 2 is $25 + 4m$. Let's try to figure out when Plan 1 is less than Plan 2. We can use the statement $43 + 2m < 25 + 4m$.

Tony That's an inequality. I've seen those before, but I don't remember what to do with them.

> An **inequality** is a statement that compares two expressions. It is similar to an equation, but, rather than an equal sign, it has $<$ (less than), $\leq$ (less than or equal to), $>$ (greater than), or $\geq$ (greater than or equal to).

Sasha We can write each of the two plans as a separate equation. Let's pick c for the cost of the call. The equation for Plan 1 is $c = 43 + 2m$. The equation for Plan 2 is $c = 25 + 4m$.

Tony That looks like a system of equations. We know how to solve that.

Sasha We do, but does that help with the inequality? What if we graph the two equations first?

Sasha graphs the two equations on her calculator.

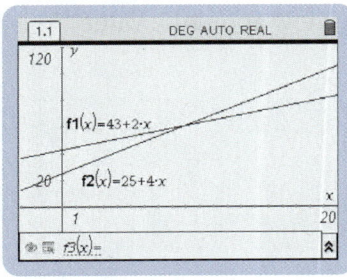

> Show the graph on the coordinate plane. See the TI-Nspire™ Handbook, p. 790.

Sasha Judging by the graphs, the line $c = 25 + 4m$ is above the line $c = 43 + 2m$ to the right of the intersection point.

Tony I see. We want to find where the Plan 2 line is higher than the Plan 1 line, for instance, where $m = 15$.

Sasha So when m is greater than the m-value at the intersection, the call is cheaper using Plan 1.

398 Chapter 4 Lines

Tony The intersection looks like it's at about 9 minutes. We could estimate, but my mom likes me to be precise. Actually, where the two graphs intersect, it's the solution to the system of equations! I told you we should have solved that system.

Sasha You're right, Tony. We also could just solve the equation $43 + 2m = 25 + 4m$. That's the inequality written as an equation.

$43 + 2m = 25 + 4m$ Subtract 25 from both sides.
$18 + 2m = 4m$ Subtract $2m$ from both sides.
$18 = 2m$ Divide both sides by 2.
$m = 9$

Tony The result is 9. Plan 1 is less expensive for any call longer than 9 minutes. Plan 1 is a better choice since my mom talks with business clients on the phone for hours.

Tony and Sasha found that the solution to the inequality $43 + 2m < 25 + 4m$ is $m > 9$. Sometimes, when the inequality you start with has a less than sign, the result has a greater than sign. If you check the two graphs, the result is clear.

You can also express the solution set of an inequality by sketching a graph of the solutions on a number line. There is a conventional notation that indicates the differences in inequalities, such as $m > 9$ and $m \geq 9$.

Facts and Notation

On a number line, solutions to inequalities are displayed as shaded rays on intervals. A closed circle includes an endpoint. An open circle excludes it. The inequality $3 < x \leq 6$ would look like this.

0 1 2 3 4 5 6

Notice the circle at $x = 3$ is not filled in, while the circle at $x = 6$ is filled in.

> The notation $3 < x \leq 6$ means that x is greater than 3 and less than or equal to 6.

For You to Do

1. Use a number line. Show the solution to $43 + 2m < 25 + 4m$.

You can also solve and graph more complicated inequalities.

Example

Problem Draw a number line. Show the solutions to $|2x - 7| \leq \frac{1}{2}x + 2$.

Solution Graph the two equations $y = |2x - 7|$ and $y = \frac{1}{2}x + 2$ to estimate the solution set.

Notice that the y-values on the graph of $y = |2x - 7|$ are below the y-values on the graph of $y = \frac{1}{2}x + 2$ in the region between the two intersection points.

Find the intersection points. If $|2x - 7|$ equals $\frac{1}{2}x + 2$, then $2x - 7$ must be $\frac{1}{2}x + 2$ or $-\left(\frac{1}{2}x + 2\right)$.

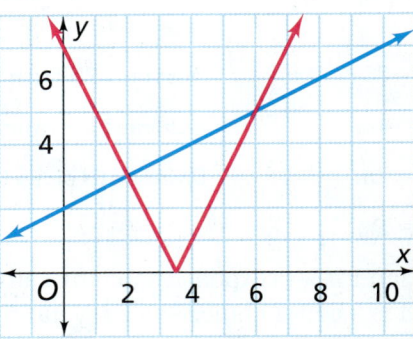

For help finding the intersection point(s) of two graphs, see the TI-Nspire Handbook, p. 790.

$$2x - 7 = \tfrac{1}{2}x + 2 \qquad\qquad 2x - 7 = -\tfrac{1}{2}x - 2$$
$$2x - 7 + 7 = \tfrac{1}{2}x + 2 + 7 \qquad\qquad 2x - 7 + 7 = -\tfrac{1}{2}x - 2 + 7$$
$$2x = \tfrac{1}{2}x + 9 \qquad\qquad 2x = -\tfrac{1}{2}x + 5$$
$$2x - \tfrac{1}{2}x = \tfrac{1}{2}x - \tfrac{1}{2}x + 9 \qquad\qquad 2x + \tfrac{1}{2}x = \tfrac{1}{2}x - \tfrac{1}{2}x + 5$$
$$\tfrac{3}{2}x = 9 \qquad\qquad \tfrac{5}{2}x = 5$$
$$\tfrac{2}{3}\left(\tfrac{3}{2}x\right) = \tfrac{2}{3}(9) \qquad\qquad \tfrac{2}{5}\left(\tfrac{5}{2}x\right) = \tfrac{2}{5}(5)$$
$$x = 6 \qquad\qquad x = 2$$

When $x = 2$ and $x = 6$, the inequality is true. Draw closed circles at 2 and 6 on a number line.

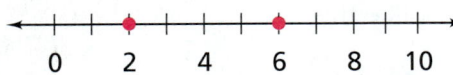

The two intersections divide the number line into three regions. Compare your number line with the original graph. Notice that the number line lines up exactly with the graph.

Shade the region on the number line that corresponds to where the graph of the line is above the absolute value graph.

The number line gives you the solution to the inequality. You can also write it as $2 \leq x \leq 6$.

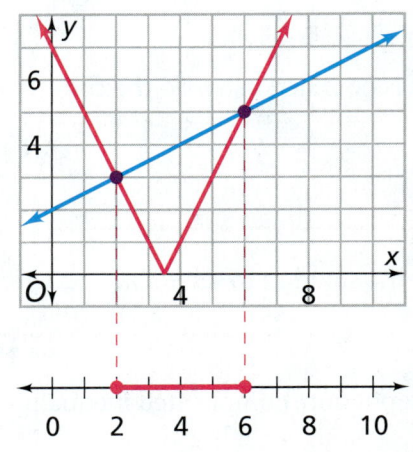

400   Chapter 4   Lines

Developing Habits of Mind

Use a different process to get the same result. The intersections of the graphs act as **cutoff points**. The x-coordinates of the cutoff points split the number line into regions to check.

If you do not have your calculator or you cannot picture the graphs in your head, you can check one point from each region to see which graph is above the other. If one point from a region is above, then the whole region is above. Likewise, if one point from a region is below, then the whole region is below.

For You to Do

2. Use the graphs of $y = x^2 - 5$ and $y = x + 1$. On a number line, draw the solution to the inequality $x^2 - 5 > x + 1$.

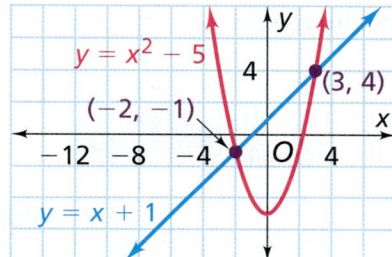

Exercises Practicing Habits of Mind

Check Your Understanding

1. For each inequality, graph the solution on a number line.

   a. $5x < 25$

   b. $3x + 7 \geq 19$

   c. $4x - 9 > 2x + 3$

   d. $14x + 13 \leq 6(2x + 4)$

4.14 Inequalities With One Variable

2. Use algebra and a graphing calculator. Solve each inequality.

   a. $5x - 23 > -2x + 50$
   b. $|x - 4| < 3$
   c. $3(x + 3)^2 > 192$
   d. $(x - 3)^2 \leq 0.01$
   e. $(x + 5)^2 \leq -0.01$
   f. $7x - 23 > 50$
   g. $x^2 \geq |x|$

   For instructions on adjusting the window settings, see the TI-Inspire Handbook, p. 790.

3. a. Use algebra and testing intervals. Solve the inequality $-27.4x + 13 > -27.2x + 12$.

   b. Use a graphing calculator. Plot $y = -27.4x + 13$ and $y = -27.2x + 12$ on the same axes. Is it more difficult or less difficult to use a graphing calculator to solve this exercise? Explain.

4. a. What is the solution set to the inequality $5x - 17 > 2x - 6$?

   b. How can you most easily find the solution set to the inequality $5x - 17 < 2x - 6$?

   c. What is the solution set to the inequality $5(x - 3) - 17 > 2(x - 3) - 6$?

   d. Graph the solutions to parts (a) and (c) on number lines. Compare the solutions to the two parts.

   e. Predict the solution set to $5(x - 11) - 17 > 2(x - 11) - 6$. Check your result.

   f. Predict the solution set to $5(x + 8) - 17 > 2(x + 8) - 6$. Check your result.

5. Use a graphing calculator. Draw the graphs of $y = \frac{x + 4}{2}$ and $y = \sqrt{4x}$ on the same axes. Use the graphs to solve the inequality $\frac{x + 4}{2} > \sqrt{4x}$.

6. **Take It Further** Answer each question to solve the inequality $\frac{x - 5}{x + 3} \leq 2$.

   Note that ">" does not include equality.

   a. What value of x makes the equation undefined?

   b. What is the solution of the corresponding equation?

   c. Draw the two values for x from parts (a) and (b) on a number line. Remember to use a filled circle if the number is part of the solution to the inequality. Use an open circle if it is not.

   d. Test a value in each chunk defined by these points. Solve the inequality.

   e. Use a graphing calculator or computer software. Draw a graph of the equation $y = \frac{x - 5}{x + 3}$. How can you use this graph to solve the inequality?

402 Chapter 4 Lines

On Your Own

7. Solve each inequality. Graph your solution on a number line.

   a. $2x > 18$

   b. $9x \leq 27$

   c. $-4x + 11 \geq 43$

   d. $17 - 9x > 2x - 16$

   e. $2(3x + 1) < x + 6$

   f. $4x - 5 \leq 23$

   g. $13 + x > 13 - x$

   h. $-2(3 - 2x) \geq 4x + 7$

8. **Write About It** Explain how you can use this graph to draw a number-line graph for the solutions to $x^2 - 3x - 4 > 0$.

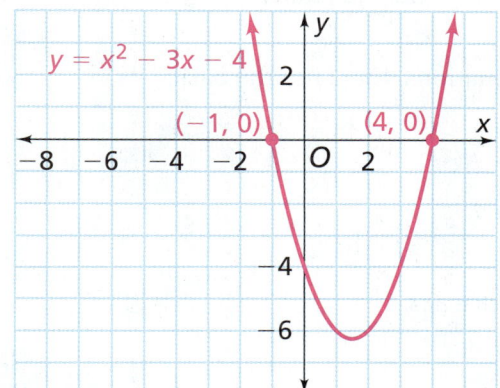

   What are the cutoff points for this inequality?

9. Use different methods to find all the values of x such that $x^3 > x$. Draw your solution set on a number line.

10. The equation $x^3 + 28x = 10x^2 + 24$ has two solutions, $x = 2$ and $x = 6$. Answer each question to find the graph of the solution set for $x^3 + 28x < 10x^2 + 24$ without graphing either side.

    a. Does the number 2.5 make $x^3 + 28x < 10x^2 + 24$ *true* or *false*?

    b. Try again with 3, 3.5, and 5. Do they make $x^3 + 28x < 10x^2 + 24$ *true* or *false*?

    c. Your answers to parts (a) and (b) should be the same. Explain why this would happen.

    d. The solutions $x = 2$ and $x = 6$ separate the number line into three parts. Test a value in each part. Draw the solution on a number line.

11. a. Draw a number line to represent $x > 3$.

    b. Draw a number line to represent $x \leq 10$.

    c. How can the number lines from parts (a) and (b) be combined to show a number line for $3 < x \leq 10$?

    d. What x values make $x > 3$, $x \leq 10$, or both true? How does that look on a number line?

4.14 Inequalities With One Variable

12. **Take It Further** Consider the equation $\frac{6}{x-4} = 2$.

    a. Is the equation true or false when $x = 7$?

    b. Are there any values x cannot be? If so, what are they?

    c. What values of x make the equation true?

    d. Find the values of x that make the equation false.

    e. List five x values that make $\frac{6}{x-4} < 2$ true.

    f. List five x values that make $\frac{6}{x-4} > 2$ true.

    g. Graph the solution to $\frac{6}{x-4} \leq 2$ on a number line.

13. **What's Wrong Here?** Tony and Derman try to solve the inequality $2x - 4 \geq 3x + 11$.

    Derman says, "Inequalities look almost like equations. Can I use the basic moves to solve them like equations?"

    Tony replies, "I don't know. Let's try it out."

    Tony writes the following:

    | $2x - 4 \geq 3x + 11$ | Add 4 to both sides. |
    | $2x \geq 3x + 15$ | Subtract 3x from both sides. |
    | $-x \geq 15$ | Divide both sides by -1. |
    | $x \geq -15$ | |

    Derman says, "That looks like a fine result."

    Tony suggests, "We should make sure it's correct. Let's try $x = 0$."

    Derman replies, "Zero is greater than -15, so it's in the solution set."

    Tony argues, "But does $2(0) - 4 = 3(0) + 11$? Since -4 is not greater than or equal to 11, zero makes the first inequality false. Did we do something wrong? What happened?"

    a. Each step in Tony and Derman's solution shows a different inequality. Substitute 0 in each step. What are true inequalities?

    b. What basic move caused the result to be false? Explain.

14. In Chapter 2, you learned the two basic moves for equations. Determine whether each statement is *always true*, *sometimes true*, or *never true*. If your result is sometimes true, add a condition that makes the statement always true.

    a. For all real numbers a, b, and c, $a < b$ if and only if $a + c < b + c$.

    b. For all real numbers a, b, and c, $a < b$ if and only if $ac < bc$.

Habits of Mind

Check your work. Do not just assume your conjectures work. Derman has the right idea to try extending the basic moves to cover inequalities. However, always make sure you test your conjecture with numbers.

The basic moves for equations:
For all real numbers a, b and c,
- $a = b$ if and only if $a + c = b + c$
- $a = b$ if and only if $ac = bc$ and $c \neq 0$

15. **Standardized Test Prep** Which inequality does the graph represent?

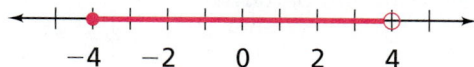

A. $2 < n + 6 \leq 10$ **B.** $-12 \leq -3n < 12$
C. $-4 \leq 2n < 4$ **D.** $6 \geq 2 - n > -2$

Maintain Your Skills

16. For each inequality, graph the solution on a number line.
    a. $x > 6$ **b.** $(x - 5) > 6$
    c. $(x + 3) > 6$ **d.** $2x + 12 \leq 4$
    e. $2(x - 1) + 12 \leq 4$ **f.** $2(x + 6) + 12 \leq 4$

17. For each inequality, graph the solution on a number line.
    a. $x > 3$ **b.** $x > -3$
    c. $-x > 3$ **d.** $-x > -3$
    e. $2x < 9$ **f.** $-2x < 9$
    g. $-x - 1 \geq 2$ **h.** $x + 1 \geq 2$

4.15 Linear Trends in Data

Scientists perform experiments to collect data. Retailers keep track of sales figures and costs. Many professionals analyze data. They try to find patterns and relationships to make predictions.

As you saw in Chapter 3, there are many ways to represent data. You can use the scatter plot to spot trends in data.

These data points show a linear trend.

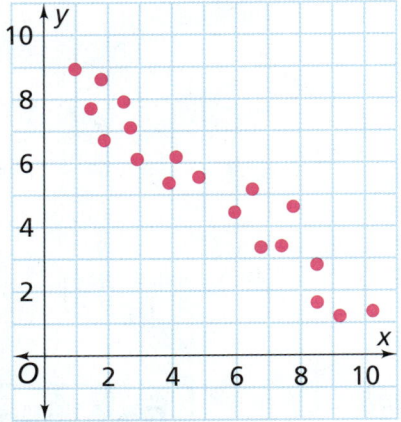

Bar codes and scanners simplify data gathering.

These data points do not show a linear trend.

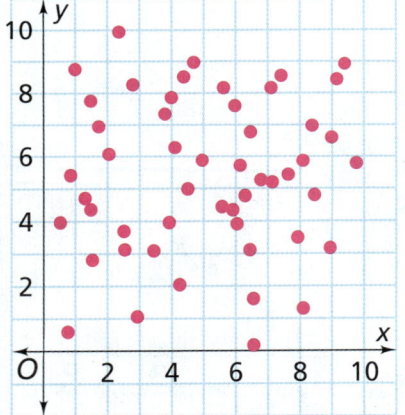

The trend of the data in the first scatter plot is linear. All the data points seem to follow a straight line. However, an entire set of data points is rarely collinear. You can find a **fitting line** that comes "close" to the data points. The equation of this fitting line helps you predict other data points.

406 Chapter 4 Lines

Example

Problem Mark Green is the manager of concessions at Down the Chute Water Park. He wants to be able to estimate the amount of food he needs each day. Last summer, he collected data. He recorded the weather, the high temperature of the day, and the number of visitors to the park. This table shows the data for fourteen sunny days last summer.

Water Park Attendance

Temperature (°F)	Number of Visitors (thousands)	Temperature (°F)	Number of Visitors (thousands)
62	36.8	80	45.4
67	40.9	83	48.4
69	36.9	85	51.5
70	37.1	88	57.7
72	44.3	94	57.3
77	42.3	96	56.1
79	45.8	98	58.9

Write an equation that Mr. Green can use to estimate the number of visitors for any sunny day.

Solution Draw a scatter plot to see if there is a linear trend to the data.

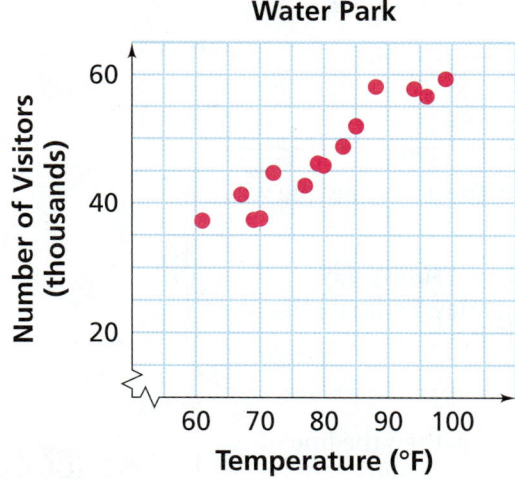

This scatter plot shows a general upward trend in data. You want to find the equation of a line that approximates the data. Remember, to find the equation of a line, you need a point on the line and the line's slope.

4.15 Linear Trends in Data

In Chapter 3, you saw that the mean of a set of numerical data is the balance point of those numbers on a number line. Similarly, the mean of the data points is the balance point of those points on the coordinate plane. The x-coordinate of the balance point is the mean of the x-coordinates of the data, about 80°F. The mean of the y-coordinates is around 47,100 people. The fitting line should go through the point (80, 47.1).

> You can write the balance point as $(\bar{x}, \bar{y})$.

Substitute these values into the general form of an equation.

$$y - 47.1 = m(x - 80)$$

What slope should you use? Make a guess at a reasonable slope. Draw a line that looks like it fits the data. Then determine the slope of that line. The slope is about $\frac{2}{3}$. The equation of a fitting line might be $y - 47.1 = \frac{2}{3}(x - 80)$.

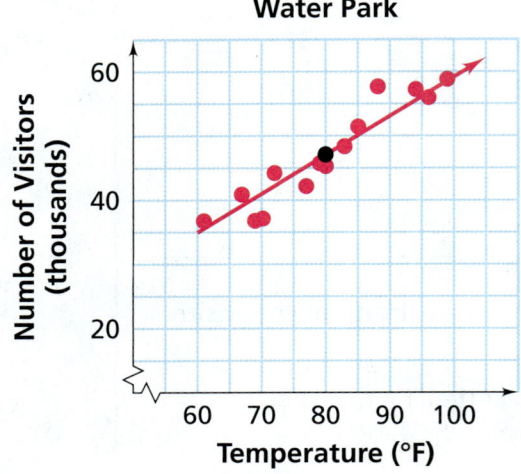

For You to Do

1. The forecast is for sun, with a high of 75°F. Estimate how many people will visit the park.
2. Mr. Green knows that 57,500 people visited the park one sunny day. He forgot to write down the high temperature for that day. Estimate that day's temperature.

For any data set, if $(\bar{x}, \bar{y})$ is the balance point of the data, then the line of best fit is in the form $y - \bar{y} = m(x - \bar{x})$.

You might wonder how to decide whether one line is a better fit than another. Calculators use the balance point and a formula to find the best possible slope for the fitting line. This formula comes from minimizing the difference between the actual data and the results predicted by the fitting line.

> **Remember...**
> This equation comes from the point-tester $\frac{y - \bar{y}}{x - \bar{x}} = m$, since the line goes through the point $(\bar{x}, \bar{y})$.

Developing Habits of Mind

Check your work. When you find the equation of a fitting line, very few data points will actually satisfy the equation. You can determine how far off each data point is by comparing the actual data with the prediction.

Test Mr. Green's equation by plugging in each temperature to find the predicted number of visitors. Then compare the actual number of visitors to the predicted number according to the fitting-line equation.

Data vs. Line Fit

Temperature (°F)	$y - 47.1 = \frac{2}{3}(x - 80)$ Number of Visitors (thousands)		Error (Actual − Predicted)
	Actual	Predicted	
62	36.8	35.1	1.7
67	40.9	38.4	2.5
69	36.9	39.8	−2.9
70	37.1	40.4	−3.3
72	44.3	41.8	2.5
77	42.3	45.1	−2.8
79	45.8	46.4	−0.6
80	45.4	47.1	−1.7
83	48.4	49.1	−0.7
85	51.5	50.4	1.1
88	57.7	52.4	5.3
94	57.3	56.4	0.9
96	56.1	57.8	−1.7
98	58.9	59.1	−0.2

The goal of finding the best fit is to make the numbers in the Error column as small as possible. Since some sets of data can contain hundreds of points, you need a single number that represents the error for the entire data set. Adding the individual errors does not really help. One prediction that is 10,000 too high offsets a prediction that is 10,000 too low.

A **line of best fit** is the graph of the linear equation that shows the relationship between two sets of data most accurately.

> If you add all the errors in the table, what is your result?

Exercises Practicing Habits of Mind

Check Your Understanding

1. Your graphing calculator can find a linear regression of data. Consider the attendance data from Down the Chute Water Park. Enter the attendance data as thousands. Use 36.7 for 36,700 as in the table. The result is approximately $y = 0.678x - 7.1$.

   The method for finding the line of best fit is **linear regression**. For help with linear regression, see the TI-Nspire Handbook, p. 790.

   a. What do x and y represent in the calculator output?

   b. Plot the balance point (80, 47.1). Is it approximately on this line?

2. a. Where is the balance point on a ruler?

   b. Where is the balance point on a coin?

   c. **Write About It** Can an object have a balance point that is not part of the object? Explain and give an example.

3. Which equation best represents the data in the graph?

   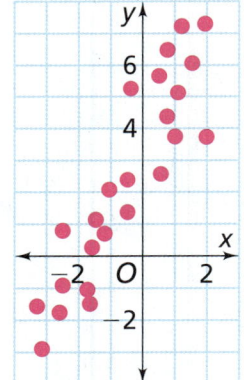

   A. $y = 2x + 3$
   B. $y = 2x - 3$
   C. $y = \frac{1}{2}x + 3$
   D. $y = -2x + 3$

The gymnast's balance point is along the vertical line that passes through her right hand.

4. Use the table.

   a. Are all the points in the table on a line?
   b. Plot the data points. Is there a linear trend?
   c. Find and plot the balance point. Is the balance point along the trend?

   United States Population

Year	Population (millions)
1900	76.0
1910	92.0
1920	105.7
1930	122.8
1940	131.7
1950	150.7
1960	179.3
1970	203.2
1980	226.5
1990	248.7
2000	281.4

   SOURCE: United States Census Bureau

On Your Own

5. Plot each data set. Is there is a linear trend to the data?

   a. **Table 1**

Input	Output
1	2
2	4
3	7
4	9
5	12

   b. **Table 2**

Input	Output
2	1
5	3
7	4
10	6
13	8

   c. **Table 3**

Input	Output
2	0
3	6
4	8
5	6
6	0
7	−10

   d. **Table 4**

Input	Output
1	−5
2	−1
2	2
3	4
4	9

4.15 Linear Trends in Data

6. For each table in Exercise 5, calculate the balance point $(\bar{x}, \bar{y})$. Plot it along with the data.

7. For each table with a linear trend in Exercise 5, estimate the slope of the trend. Use the balance point you found in Exercise 6 to write a trend line equation. Graph each trend line on the same plot as your data.

8. These data follow a somewhat linear trend.

Input	Output
1	1.8
2	1.7
3	3.6
5	5.4
6	7.3
7	7.2

   Plot the points. Then graph each line below on the same axes. Which line do you think fits the data best?

   A. $y = x + 1$
   B. $y = 0.5x + 2.5$
   C. $y = 0.9x + 0.9$
   D. $y = x + 0.5$

9. This table shows an analysis of the line with equation $y = x + 1$ from Exercise 8.

   Data vs. Line Fit

Input, x	Actual, y	Predicted, $y = x + 1$	Error (Actual − Predicted)
1	1.8	2	−0.2
2	1.7	3	−1.3
3	3.6	4	−0.4
5	5.4	6	−0.6
6	7.3	7	0.3
7	7.2	8	−0.8

   a. What do the negative values in the Error column suggest about this line as a line of best fit?

   b. Perform the same analysis for the other lines in Exercise 8. Which line has the fewest errors? Which line has the smallest errors?

10. **Standardized Test Prep** The graph shows the total federal debt at the end of each year from 2001 through 2006. Use the line of best fit to predict the federal debt at the end of 2010.

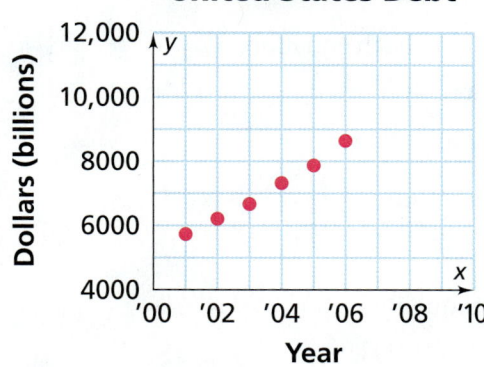

Source: US Census Bureau

A. $570 billion

B. $9100 billion

C. $10,900 billion

D. $12,000 billion

Maintain Your Skills

11. The balance point of the data from Exercise 8 is (4, 4.5). The line of best fit passes through that point. Consider these fitting lines.

    $y - 4.5 = x - 4$

    $y - 4.5 = 2(x - 4)$

    $y - 4.5 = 3(x - 4)$

    a. For each fitting line, make a table like the one in Exercise 9.

    b. Add the values in the error column for each table. What pattern do the sums have?

    c. What is the sum of the errors if the slope is $\frac{1}{2}$? If the slope is -18? If the slope is m? Explain.

> Notice that each line passes through the balance point (4, 4.5).

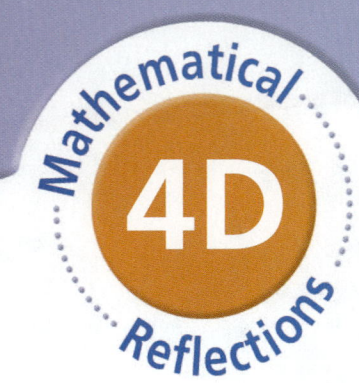

Mathematical Reflections 4D

In this investigation, you solved and graphed inequalities with one variable. You drew scatter plots and found trends to predict unknown data. These questions will help you summarize what you have learned.

1. Use a graphing calculator. Find the number of solutions to each equation.
   a. $3x + 7 = 5 - x$
   b. $3x + 7 = x^2$
   c. $3x + 7 = 3x - 2$
   d. $3x + 7 = -x^2$

2. Solve each inequality. Graph your solution on a number line.
   a. $3x - 5 > 1$
   b. $x - 8 \geq 2x - 5$
   c. $|x - 2| < 7$

3. Use algebra and a graphing calculator. Solve each inequality.
   a. $4x + 2 > 5x - 3$
   b. $2x + 3 \leq 48$
   c. $|2x + 1| < 5$

4. Consider the table of data points.
   a. Find the balance point.
   b. Graph the points and the balance point. Draw a line that best fits the data. Estimate the slope.
   c. Write an equation for your line of best fit.

Input	Output
−1	3.5
1	4
4	5.5
5	4
0	2
−3	−1

5. How do the solutions of inequalities relate to the solutions of equations?

6. How can you approximate data using a line of best fit?

7. One taxi charges $1.10 for the first mile and $1 for each additional mile. Another taxi charges $2.30 for the first mile and $.60 for each additional mile. For what distances will the first taxi be less expensive than the second?

A parabola is the graph of an equation containing x^2.

Vocabulary and Notation

In this investigation, you learned these terms and symbols. Make sure you understand what each one means and how to use it.

- balance point, $(\bar{x}, \bar{y})$
- cutoff point
- fitting line
- inequality
- line of best fit
- linear regression

Project Using Mathematical Habits

Wireless Phone Plans

Wireless phone companies charge monthly for the number of minutes that you use for incoming and outgoing calls. Some plans offer unlimited minutes for night and weekend calls.

In a contract with a phone company, you agree to pay an amount for a limited number of minutes each month. When you exceed the limited number of minutes, you pay for each minute. The charge for extra minutes can be very high.

Comparing Phone Plans

Here are four different wireless phone plans.

Cell Phone Plans

Plan	Monthly Charge	Number of Minutes Included	Cost per Minute Over Limit
A	$35.95	300	$.35
B	$39.95	350	$.30
C	$39.95	400	$.38
D	$49.95	2000	$.45

1. If you choose Plan A, what is the monthly cost for 250 minutes? For 300 minutes? For 350 minutes?

2. Graph the monthly cost for Plan A against the number of minutes. The graph you draw has two segments, a segment representing the cost for 300 minutes or less and a segment representing the cost for more than 300 minutes.

3. On the same graph, show the monthly cost for Plans B, C, and D against the number of minutes. Use a calculator. Adjust the axes in the calculator window to show the complete graphs.

4. What are the break-even points for each pair of plans?

5. Under what circumstances would it be better to use Plan A? Plan B? Plan C? Plan D?

6. **Write About It** Which plan would be best for you?

Phone plans also include fees for messaging, ring tones, video clips, and Internet access.

Chapter 4 Review

In **Investigation 4A,** you learned how to
- calculate the slope between two points
- calculate the average speed between two points on a distance-time graph
- find other points on a line when given a slope and a point

The following questions will help you check your understanding.

1. Graph points A and B. Find another point C such that $m(A, B) = m(A, C)$.
   a. $A(0, -2)$ and $B(3, 1)$
   b. $A(4, 2)$ and $B(6, -2)$
   c. $A(-5, -1)$ and $B(-8, 3)$
   d. $A(-2, 3)$ and $B(5, 3)$
   e. What can you say about points A, B, and C?

2. On a recent car trip, Lily drove 180 miles on the highway in 3 hours. She stopped for $\frac{1}{2}$ hour to have lunch. She continued her trip on two-lane roads, traveling 60 miles in $1\frac{1}{2}$ hours.
   a. Draw a distance-time graph to represent Lily's trip.
   b. What was Lily's average speed on the highway?
   c. What was Lily's average speed on the two-lane roads?
   d. What was Lily's average speed for the entire trip?

3. Let ℓ be the line that passes through $P(4, -1)$ and $Q(6, 5)$.
   a. Is the point $R(5, 2)$ on ℓ?
   b. Find a if the point $A(-2, a)$ is on ℓ.
   c. Write an equation that can be used to test whether points are on ℓ.

In **Investigation 4B,** you learned how to
- write linear equations
- sketch graphs of linear equations
- determine the slope of a line from its equation
- determine whether a runner will overtake another runner

The following questions will help you check your understanding.

4. Write an equation for each line that passes through the given point and has the given slope.
   a. $(3, 7)$ with slope 2
   b. $(2, -4)$ and $(-1, 0)$
   c. $(-6, 4)$ with slope 0
   d. $(-6, 4)$ with undefined slope

5. Let ℓ be the line with equation $3x + 5y = -15$.
   a. What is the slope of line ℓ?
   b. Sketch the graph of line ℓ.
   c. Solve the equation for y.

6. Scott leaves home and walks 1.5 miles to school at a rate of 3 miles per hour. Fifteen minutes later, his brother leaves for school. He is riding his bike at a rate of 9 miles per hour.
   a. Draw a distance-time graph to represent this situation.
   b. When will Scott's brother overtake him?
   c. How far from home will they be when they meet?

In **Investigation 4C,** you learned how to
- solve systems of linear equations with two variables using substitution and elimination
- determine whether two lines are parallel or intersecting using the slope of each line
- write and solve word problems for systems of equations

The following questions will help you check your understanding.

7. Write the equations of two lines that intersect at the point $(-2, 3)$. Check that $(-2, 3)$ satisfies both equations.

8. Solve each system.
   a. $4x + y = 3$
   $3x - 2y = 5$
   b. $x - 3y = 11$
   $2x + y = 1$

9. Write an equation of the line through $(-1, -2)$ that is parallel to the line with equation $3x - 2y = 8$.

In **Investigation 4D,** you learned how to
- solve inequalities algebraically and by using graphs
- graph the solution set of an inequality
- find the balance point of a data set and estimate the line of best fit

The following questions will help you check your understanding.

10. Solve each inequality. Graph your solution on a number line.
   a. $8x \leq 24$
   b. $3(x - 1) > 2x - 5$
   c. $4x - 3 < 7x + 9$
   d. $|x + 3| \geq 5$

11. Consider the following set of data points.
$(-2, 6)$, $(-1, 4.5)$, $(0, 5)$, $(1.5, 4)$, $(4.5, 3)$, $(5, 2.5)$, (a, b)

   a. Find a and b such that the balance point is $(2, 4)$.
   b. Graph the data points and the balance point.
   c. Will the slope of the line of best fit be positive or negative? Explain.

Chapter 4 Test

Multiple Choice

1. Consider these lines.

   $\ell : y = 2x - 1$

   $m : 5x - 3y = -30$

   What is true about point $(-3, -5)$?
   - **A.** It is on both lines.
   - **B.** It is not on either line.
   - **C.** It is on line ℓ only.
   - **D.** It is on line m only.

2. The intersection of the two lines $y = 5x + 10$ and $y = 6x - 3$ is in which quadrant?
   - **A.** I
   - **B.** II
   - **C.** III
   - **D.** IV

3. Which pair of lines does NOT intersect?
   - **A.** $y = 3x - 5$ and $y = -3x + 5$
   - **B.** $(y + 7) = 2(x - 3)$ and $(y - 4) = 2(x + 5)$
   - **C.** $2x - 3y = 12$ and $y = 4$
   - **D.** $y = 2x - 1$ and $5x - 3y = -30$

4. Which equation best represents the data in the graph?

   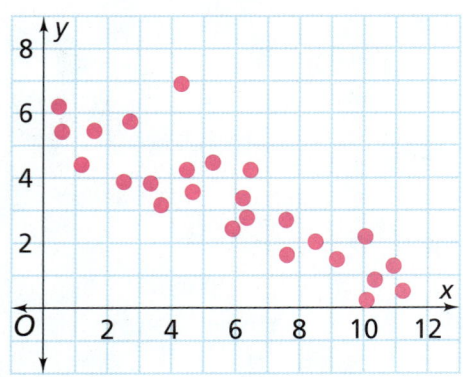

   - **A.** $y = -x + 9$
   - **B.** $y = -\frac{1}{4}x + \frac{9}{2}$
   - **C.** $y = -\frac{1}{2}x + 6$
   - **D.** $y = -\frac{1}{2}x + 5$

5. Use the graphs of $y = 3 - x^2$ and $y = \frac{1}{2}x$.

   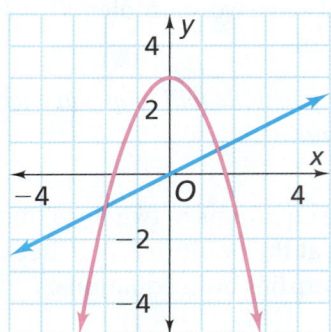

   What is the solution to the inequality $\frac{1}{2}x > 3 - x^2$?
   - **A.** $-2 \leq x \leq 1.5$
   - **B.** $x \leq -2$ or $x \geq 1.5$
   - **C.** $-2 < x < 1.5$
   - **D.** $x < -2$ or $x > 1.5$

6. Suppose a is less than 10. Which of these must be true?
   - **A.** $-a > 10$
   - **B.** $a \leq 9$
   - **C.** $3a + 7 < 40$
   - **D.** $|a| < 10$

Open Response

7. Solve this system of equations. Show your work.

   $$x + 2y = 17$$
   $$5x - 2y = 16$$

8. At a store, six bottles of juice and two bags of nuts cost $11.50. Three bottles of juice and four bags of nuts cost $11.75. What is the cost of a single bottle of juice? Show your work.

9. Graph the two lines. Find the exact coordinates of their point of intersection.

   $$5x - 3y = -30$$
   $$y = -4x$$

10. Graph the solution set to the inequality $-3a + 15 > -3$.

11. How can you tell by their equations whether two lines will intersect?

12. Consider the following data table.

Input	Output
1	20
2	26
3	35
4	41
5	37
6	52
7	55

    a. Find the balance point of the data.

    b. Use your balance point from part (a) and a slope of 5 to write the equation of a fitting line. Test the fitting line using an error table like the one below. The Error column is the value in the Actual column minus the value in the Predicted column.

Input	Actual	Predicted	Error
1	20	■	■
2	26	■	■
3	35	■	■
4	41	■	■
5	37	■	■
6	52	■	■
7	55	■	■

    c. Make an error table as you did in part (b) to test the fitting line passing through the balance point and having slope 6.

    d. Which line is a better fit? Explain.

Challenge Problem

13. Find three points M, N, and P such that $m(M, N) = \frac{1}{2}$, $m(M, P) = 5$, and $m(N, P) = -\frac{2}{3}$.

Chapter 4 Cumulative Review

1. Without paper and pencil or a calculator, find each result.
   a. $27 \cdot (-3)$
   b. $27 \div (-3)$
   c. $-27 \cdot (-3)$
   d. $-27 \div 3$

2. Use the following rule for parts (a) and (b). Start with any number. Add 6. Subtract 2. Multiply by 3 and add -5.
   a. Find the starting number if the ending number is 10.
   b. Find the ending number if the starting number is -5.

3. a. Restate the equation $|x - 7| = 10$ by writing a sentence about distance.
   b. Find all values that make the equation true.

4. Match each expression to a set of steps.
   a. $(x - 5) \cdot 2$ b. $5(x - 2)$ c. $2x - 5$
   I. Choose any number, subtract 5, and then multiply the result by 2.
   II. Choose any number, multiply by 2, and then subtract 5 from the result.
   III. Choose any number, subtract 2, and then multiply the result by 5.

5. Describe a situation that the graph below could represent.

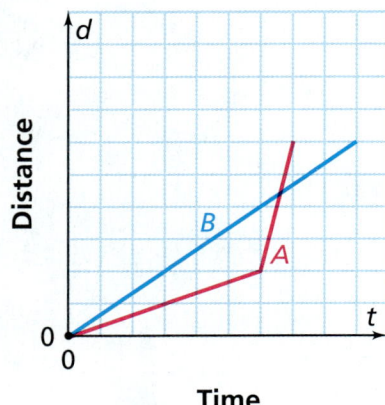

6. a. Make a scatter plot for the ordered pairs.
      (4, 5), (6, 6), (10, 8), (14, 10), (16, 11)
   b. Use your scatter plot to predict the corresponding values of y for x values 2, 8, and 18.

7. Use the stem-and-leaf display. What percent of the coaches have more than 23 years of experience?

   Coaches' Years of Experience

0	6 7 7 8
1	0 1 3 3 5 5 9
2	1 1 2 2 4
3	0 0 2 3

8. a. Explain how to find the median and range of the data in the box-and-whisker plot.

   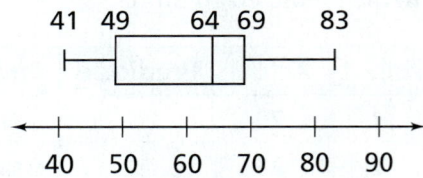

   b. Determine the five-number summary for the data.

Use the following data sets for Exercises 9 and 10.
   Set I {14, 21, 23, 31, 38, 42}
   Set II {19, 26, 28, 36, 43, 47}

9. Describe the relationship between Sets I and II.

10. Describe the relationships among the mean, median, and range of the data sets.

11. On graph paper, draw a square with vertices at $(-1, 2)$, $(4, 2)$, $(4, -3)$, and $(-1, -3)$. Transform the square using each rule. Describe each resulting shape.
    a. $(x, y) \rightarrow (x, 3y)$
    b. $(x, y) \rightarrow (-2x, y)$
    c. $(x, y) \rightarrow (3x, 3y)$

For Exercises 12 and 13, use the equation $3x - 5y = 45$.

12. Find five points that satisfy the equation.

13. Find five points that do NOT satisfy the equation.

14. Points $(h, -5)$, $(k, -13)$, and $(m, 15)$ are on the graph of $\frac{1}{4}y + x = 3$. Find the values of h, k, and m.

15. Use the equation $xy = -24$.
    a. Find at least six ordered pairs (x, y) that are on the graph of the equation.
    b. Through which quadrants will the graph $xy = -24$ pass? Explain.
    c. Sketch the graph of the equation. Include the six points from part (a).

16. Suppose x is a large-magnitude negative number less than -1000. Place the following values, in order, from least to greatest.
    $|x|, \frac{1}{x}, x^3, x^2,$ and x

17. Graph the equations $y = x^2 + 2$ and $y = x + 4$. Where do the graphs intersect?

18. Transform $y = x^2$ using each rule given. Find each resulting equation.
    a. $(x, y) \to (x + 3, y)$
    b. $(x, y) \to (x - 2, y)$
    c. $(x, y) \to (x + 3, y - 2)$

19. Mr. Ortiz traveled 145 miles from 11:00 A.M. to 1:30 P.M. What was his average speed?

20. Find the slope of the line that passes through $A(-3, 6)$ and $B(5, -2)$.

21. A line passes through points $(-3, 1)$ and $(1, -7)$. Explain how you know whether $(2, -1)$, $(-4, 3)$, and $(0, 5)$ are on the line.

22. Find an equation of the line passing through $(3, -11)$ with slope -4.

23. Write an equation of the line that passes through $(12, -11)$ and is parallel to the graph of $y = -\frac{1}{3}x + 5$.

24. For each equation, explain whether the equation's graph is a line. If it is a line, find the slope and the points where the line crosses the axes.
    a. $y = 5 + \frac{1}{5}x$
    b. $y = x^2 - 5x$
    c. $y = 5\left(1 + \frac{1}{5}\right)x$

25. Use substitution to find a common solution to the equations $b = 3$ and $2a - b = -5$.

26. Jason bought four soups and one salad for $8.50. Jill bought four salads for $10. What is the cost of one salad? Of four soups? Of one soup?

27. a. Place the following numbers on a number line.
    $\frac{1}{3}, \frac{2}{3}, 1\frac{5}{12}, \frac{7}{12}, 1\frac{1}{6}, \frac{8}{12}$
    b. Are any pairs of the numbers equivalent?
    c. What is the least number in the list?
    d. What is the greatest number?

28. Describe the operations that reverse the operations in each expression.
    a. $2m - 5$ b. $7 - 4p$ c. $\frac{q+3}{6}$

29. Explain how to transform $5x - 6y = 94$ into each of the following equations.
    a. $5x - 6y - 94 = 0$
    b. $5x = 94 + 6y$
    c. $y = \frac{94 - 5x}{-6}$
    d. $x = \frac{94 + 6y}{5}$

For Exercises 30–32, solve each equation.

30. $2m - 5 = 3$ 31. $7 - 4p = 3$
32. $\frac{q+3}{6} = 3$

33. Last year the price of a television was $100 more than this year's price. This year's price is 80% of last year's price. What was last year's price for the television?

34. Find three solutions for the equation $(x - 7)(x + 8)(x - 4) = 0$.

Chapter 5

Investigations at a Glance

- **5A** Functions—The Basics
- **5B** Functions, Graphs, and Tables
- **5C** Functions and Situations

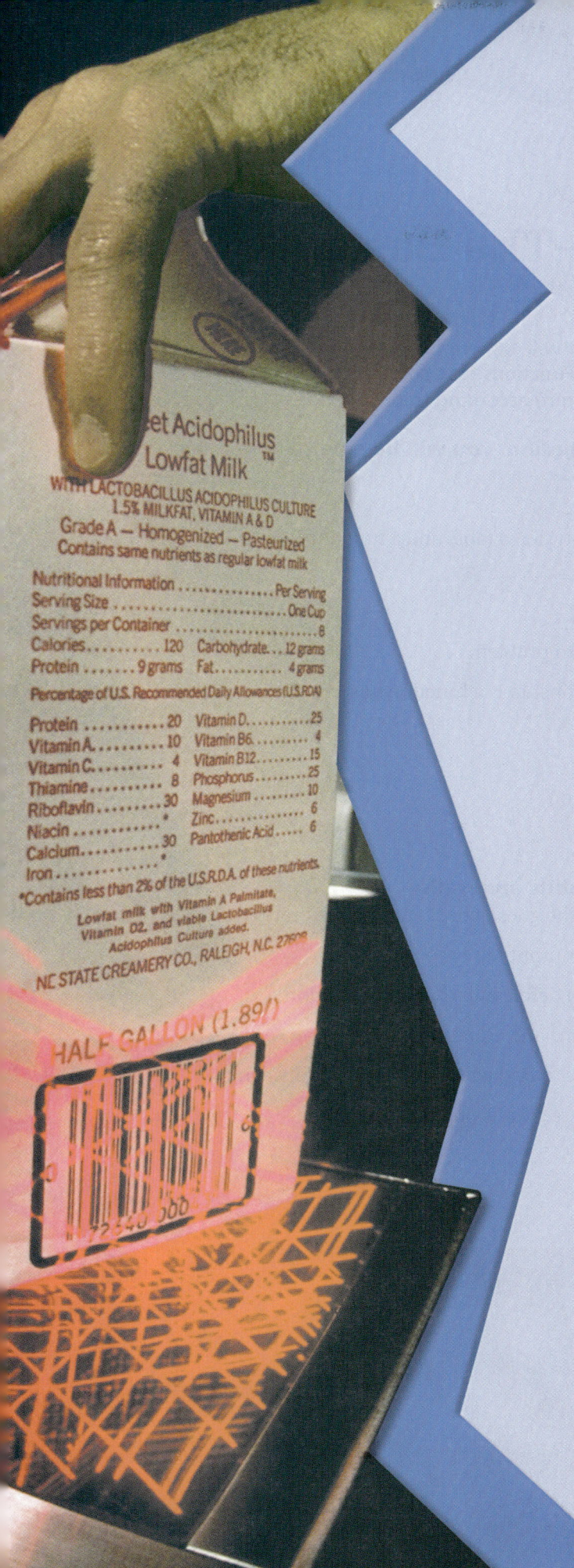

Introduction to Functions

Until the 1980s, most cash registers were simply adding machines. A cashier entered the prices into a register that added the prices. Cashiers had to use their heads to figure out how much change to make and the amount of tax!

Today a computer scans the bar code on a product and finds its price. The computer adds the prices of the taxable items and calculates the tax. Then it sums the non taxable prices, the taxable prices, and the tax before displaying the total sale price.

A central computer connects the cash registers and supplies the bar code information that uniquely identifies each product. The product name, cost, and tax status are functions of the bar code. The total tax on a sale is a function of the total price of the taxable items.

Functions are a part of everyday life. Your weekly pay is a function of your hourly pay and the number of hours worked. The distance you travel using a tank of gas is a function of the capacity of the gas tank and the car's efficiency. In this chapter, you will explore some important features of functions.

Vocabulary and Notation

- base case
- closed form
- composition
- domain
- exponential function
- fixed point
- function, $f(x)$
- graph of a function
- Koch snowflake
- linear function
- period
- periodic function
- range
- recursive rule

Investigation 5A

Functions—The Basics

In *Functions—The Basics,* you will explore function rules. Functions are like machines. Functions take something in (input) and give something out (output) according to certain rules.

By the end of this investigation, you will be able to answer questions like these.

1. What is a function?
2. What is the relationship between a table and a function?
3. What is the domain of $f(x) = \dfrac{\sqrt{x}}{x-9}$?

You will learn how to
- build a function from a word problem
- determine whether a relationship is a function based on its description or graph
- make input-output tables
- find the domain of a function
- graph a function

You will develop these habits and skills:
- Find a function rule using the guess-check-generalize strategy.
- Look for patterns in input-output tables.
- Recognize different ways to define and express a function.
- Compare graphs of functions and equations.
- Simplify and compare rules to find whether they are equivalent.
- Build functions and generate graphs on your calculator.

Like a function, a camera takes input—the image of your face, for example—and gives output—a photo.

5.01 Getting Started

**Activating Prior Knowledge
Exploring New Ideas**

In many functions, there is a pattern that relates the input to the output. You can write a function rule to represent this relationship.

For You to Explore

In Problems 1 and 2, you will play the Guess My Rule game. You need two players, a Rule Maker and a Rule Breaker.

1. **Round 1** Your teacher gives the Rule Maker a function rule.
   - The Rule Breaker gives an input value to the Rule Maker.
   - The Rule Maker calculates the output. Do not let the Rule Breaker know the calculations! The Rule Maker gives the output value.
   - The Rule Breaker continues to give the Rule Maker an input value and receives the output value until the Rule Breaker guesses the rule.
   - The goal is to guess the rule by making the fewest possible guesses about the input values.

   > For example, when the rule is Add 2 to the input, and the Rule Breaker inputs the value 4, the Rule Maker says, "6."

2. **Round 2** Switch roles with your partner. The Rule Maker writes the function rule in Round 2.

In Problems 3–5, Tony and Sasha play the Guess My Rule game.

3. In Round 1, Sasha is the Rule Maker.

Tony's Input	Sasha's Response
1	1 produces 5.
2	2 produces 3.
3	3 produces 25.
1	1 produces 11.

   Tony says, "That rule's not fair!" What makes Tony say that?

4. In the next game, Tony is the Rule Maker. For a few of the inputs, Tony responds with a letter instead of a number.

Sasha's Input	Tony's Response
1	1 returns a.
2	2 returns 7.
5	5 returns 11.
1	1 returns b.
2	2 returns c.

   > Tony uses the word *returns* instead of *produces* just for variety.

   a. When Tony uses a fair rule, what is the value of c?
   b. How are the variables a and b related?
   c. Do you have enough information to find the value of a? Explain.

5. Sasha uses the rule "After each input, I flip a coin. When it shows heads, I write, 'x produces x + 2.' When it shows tails, I write, 'x produces x + 3.'" Sasha's responses are left blank below.

Tony's Input	Sasha's Response
1	1 produces ■.
3	3 produces ■.
−3	−3 produces ■.
7	7 produces ■.
1	1 produces ■.

a. Can you know for certain Sasha's responses? Explain.
b. Will Tony complain that Sasha's rule isn't fair? Explain.

Exercises Practicing Habits of Mind

On Your Own

6. Tony and Sasha play the Guess My Rule game. What is Sasha's rule?

Tony's Input	Sasha's Response
0	0 returns 3.
2	2 returns 5.
3	3 returns 6.
8	8 returns 11.

7. Sasha uses the rule "x produces $x^2 + 1$." Use this rule to fill in the blanks.

Tony's Input	Sasha's Response
1	1 produces ■.
■	■ produces 5.
5	5 produces ■.
■	■ produces 2.
■	■ produces 1.

a. Is there more than one correct value that you can use to fill in any one of the blanks? Explain.
b. Using Sasha's rule, how many input values produce the output value 2? How many output values does the input value 2 produce?

8. Tony and Sasha play the game with a new rule. Based on Sasha's responses below, what is the output for the input $\frac{1}{2}$? For the input $\frac{3}{5}$? For Tony's input of 0, explain why Sasha does not respond. Is Sasha's rule fair?

Tony's Input	Sasha's Response
5	5 produces $\frac{1}{5}$.
2	2 produces $\frac{1}{2}$.
-3	-3 produces $-\frac{1}{3}$.
113	113 produces $\frac{1}{113}$.
0	0 produces . . .

9. Tony and Derman guess a new rule of Sasha's. Tony says, "The rule is 'x produces $3 - x$.'" Derman replies, "No, the rule is 'x produces $|x - 3|$.'" Is there any number that will help determine the correct rule? Explain.

Tony and Derman's Input	Sasha's Response
0	0 produces 3.
1	1 produces 2.
2	2 produces 1.
3	3 produces 0.

10. Tony and Derman guess another new rule. Tony says, "The rule is to multiply x by itself and then add x." Derman replies, "No, the rule is to multiply x by $x + 1$." Is there any number that will help decide the correct rule? Explain.

Tony and Derman's Input	Sasha's Response
0	0 produces 0.
1	1 produces 2.
2	2 produces 6.
3	3 produces 12.

Maintain Your Skills

Sasha and Tony play the game. Sasha's rule is pick a number, add $\frac{1}{2}$, double your answer, subtract 3, and find half of the result.

11. For each of Tony's inputs below, what output does Sasha's rule produce?
    a. 4   b. 5   c. 6   d. -4 e. -5
    f. -6 g. $\frac{1}{4}$ h. $\frac{3}{4}$ i. $6\frac{1}{4}$

12. For each of Sasha's responses below, what input did Tony give?
    a. 4   b. 5   c. 6   d. -4 e. -5
    f. -6 g. $\frac{1}{4}$ h. $\frac{3}{4}$ i. $6\frac{1}{4}$

13. Find a simpler rule that does the same thing as Sasha's rule.

5.02 Building Functions

You can build a function to calculate total cost.

Minds in Action   episode 18

Sasha and Tony look at the deals on CDs at a music store Web site.

Sasha Look, at the bottom of the page are all these CDs for 28% off.

Tony Yes, but by the time you add in sales tax and shipping, you'd be better off going to the mall to get them.

Sasha Are you sure? We'd better try pricing some. I'll choose a bunch, but I won't order them until we see how much they really cost.

They pick out six CDs and add them to the shopping cart. Then they click on the checkout button.

> Businesses charge sales tax at the mall, too. What is Tony's logic here?

For You to Do

Sasha and Tony's checkout page looks like this table.

Items to Purchase Now

Item	Price Original	Price Discounted	Tax (5%)	Shipping Cost	Total Cost
Ultimate Broadway	$12.98	■	■	$2.00	■
Greatest Movie Songs	$14.99	■	■	$2.00	■
Patriotic Medley	$11.98	■	■	$2.00	■
Top Country Hits	$16.98	■	■	$2.00	■
A History of Soul	$18.98	■	■	$2.00	■
90s Favorites	$ 5.89	■	■	$2.00	■

1. Copy and complete the table.

> **Habits of Mind**
>
> **Establish a process.** As you calculate the costs, keep track of your steps. Find and repeat the pattern in your steps. For example, multiply, subtract, multiply, add, and add again.

Sasha and Tony check some of the prices in the table.

Sasha Let's try the first price, $12.98. To get the discount, I multiply the price by 0.28 to get 3.6344, or just $3.63. Then I subtract that from $12.98 to get the total cost. That gives $9.35.

Tony Now let's figure the tax and shipping.

Sasha A 5% tax on $9.35 equals 0.05 × 9.35, or 0.4675. Round that to $.47. Now we're back up to $9.82.

Tony And shipping adds $2.00, so the total cost will be $11.82.

428 Chapter 5 Introduction to Functions

Sasha and Tony look at the checkout page, and the totals agree with their calculations.

Sasha   It's pretty mechanical. Look, for the next one, I write this.

Sasha writes on a piece of paper.

$$14.99 \times 0.28 = 4.1972$$
$$14.99 - 4.1972 = 10.7928$$
$$10.7928 \times 0.05 = 0.53964$$
$$10.7928 + 0.53964 = 11.33244$$
$$11.33244 + 2 = 13.33244$$

So, the total cost is $13.33. And that's what it is in the table!

Tony   Look, the calculations are even more mechanical if you keep track of the steps. They go this way. Suppose the cost is some number C.

Now Tony writes on a piece of paper.

$0.28C$	Discount
$C - 0.28C$	
$(C - 0.28C) \times 0.05$	Tax
$(C - 0.28C) + (C - 0.28C) \times 0.05$	Cost with tax
$(C - 0.28C) + (C - 0.28C) \times 0.05 + 2$	Total cost

Sasha   Good job! The last line is like a machine that does it all.

$$(C - 0.28C) + (C - 0.28C) \times 0.05 + 2$$

This rule calculates the total cost of any CD during the sale.

For You to Do

2. Use Sasha and Tony's machine to calculate the total cost of each CD in their list. Check your results against the total costs that you found on the checkout page.

Developing Habits of Mind

Establish a process. Sasha and Tony build a function machine that calculates the total cost of a CD given its list price. The rule they use is

$$(C - 0.28C) + (C - 0.28C) \times 0.05 + 2$$

Other people may write different rules to do the same thing.

When you establish a process for repeated calculations, you can find a general rule that works for any input x. You can use the rule to program your calculator, so that it becomes a function machine that does the calculations.

For You to Do

Use Sasha and Tony's rule from the preceding page. Find the total costs of CDs priced between $15 and $20. Use price increments of $1.

3. Describe any patterns in the table.
4. Find a simpler rule than Tony and Sasha's rule that agrees with the table.
5. Tony and Sasha pay 5% tax whether they buy CDs at the mall or the music store Web site. Assume that the nondiscounted price of each CD is exactly the same at the mall and at the music store Web site.
   a. At what price is it a better deal to buy a CD at the music store Web site? At the mall? (*Hint:* Make a table comparing final costs.)
   b. At what price is the final cost of a CD the same at the music store Web site and at the mall?

For Discussion

Function machines are all around you. Some examples include a(n)
- toaster
- TV remote control
- light switch
- ice maker

Each device takes an input (from you or a machine) and produces an output (toast, for example) in a predictable way.

6. What are the inputs and outputs for each function?
7. Describe the inputs and outputs of other devices that are functions.

Each machine calculates the output from the input using a rule such as Tony and Sasha's CD rule. Often, only the people who built the machine know the rule.

Exercises Practicing Habits of Mind

Check Your Understanding

Changing units of time is sometimes necessary. To find miles traveled in an hour, you may need to change minutes to hours. To find time needed to stop a car quickly, you may need to change minutes to seconds.

1. Convert minutes to seconds.
   a. 9 min
   b. 3.5 min
   c. 4.1 min
   d. 1.35 min
   e. 2.43 min
   f. Find a rule for converting minutes to seconds.

430 Chapter 5 Introduction to Functions

2. Convert minutes to hours.

   a. 9 min   b. 35 min   c. 41 min   d. 135 min   e. 243 min

   f. Find a rule for converting minutes to hours.

3. For lunch at Steve's Diner, Alan has a hamburger and iced tea. Lou has a Caesar salad, a cup of chili, and a cola. Katie has a grilled cheese sandwich, French fries, and a ginger ale. The waiter hands them the check.

   a. Calculate the total amount each person owes including a 5% tax and an 18% tip on the pretax total.

   b. Write a rule that gives the total amount each person owes when you know the pretax cost of each person's food.

Steve's Diner

Item	Cost
Hamburger	$4.95
Caesar salad	$6.95
Cup of chili	$1.96
Grilled cheese	$4.50
French fries	$1.75
Cola	$.99
Iced tea	$.99
Ginger ale	$.99
Subtotal	$23.08
Tax (5%)	$1.15
Total	$24.23

4. Antonio signs up for a charity run. His sponsors can donate either a fixed amount or an amount of money based on the number of miles that he runs. The table shows the amount that each of Antonio's sponsors will donate.

Sponsors

	Fixed Donation	Donation per Mile
Mom	$ 0	$3.50
Uncle	$ 0	$2.75
Teacher	$10	$0
Coach	$ 0	$2.50
Agustina	$ 5	$0

To calculate how much money he will raise, Antonio makes this table.

Charity Run Donations

Number of Miles	Mom	Uncle	Teacher	Coach	Agustina	Total Donation
1	■	■	$10.00	■	$5.00	■
2	■	■	$10.00	■	$5.00	■
3	■	■	$10.00	■	$5.00	■
4	■	■	$10.00	■	$5.00	■
5	■	■	$10.00	■	$5.00	■

   a. Copy and complete the table.

   b. Write a rule that tells the total amount of money Antonio will raise based on how many miles he will run.

   c. If he runs 7 miles, how much money will Antonio make?

   d. How many miles must Antonio run to raise $50? To raise $100? Round up your answer to the nearest mile.

Show the total on a spreadsheet. See the TI-Nspire™ Handbook, p. 778.

5. Antonio's brother, Carlos, agrees to donate $1.50 for each mile. His grandmother agrees to donate $7.75 no matter how far Antonio runs. How does the rule in Exercise 4 change?

On Your Own

Exercises 6 and 7 are similar to Exercises 1 and 2. Your formulas will convert time measurements from larger to smaller units.

6. Convert hours to minutes. Round each answer to the nearest tenth of a minute.

   a. 3 h   b. 3.05 h   c. 4.1 h   d. 1.35 h   e. 2.43 h

   f. Find a rule for converting hours to minutes.

7. Convert seconds to minutes.

   a. 9 s   b. 37 s   c. 71 s   d. 105 s   e. 279 s

   f. Find a rule for converting seconds to minutes.

8. Filmmakers photograph movies on very long pieces of 35-mm film. Movie projectors play film at the rate of 90 feet per minute. A one-minute movie is 90 feet long. This list shows the running times of some popular movies.

   - *Finding Nemo*   1 hour, 41 minutes
   - *The Fellowship of the Ring* 2 hours, 58 minutes
   - *Beauty and the Beast*   1 hour, 24 minutes
   - *Field of Dreams*   1 hour, 46 minutes

   a. Calculate how many feet of film you need for each movie.

   b. A movie is m minutes long. Find a rule to calculate how many feet of film you need for the movie.

   c. How many feet of film do you need for a movie that is 4 hours long?

9. Sofia's car gets an average of 24 miles per gallon. Gas costs $2.11 per gallon.

   a. How much does it cost to travel 200 miles? To travel 400 miles?

   b. Write a rule that gives the cost of the trip when you know how many miles the trip is.

Gas prices change often. This price may not be realistic.

10. Suppose that the price of gasoline drops to $1.95. How does the price drop change the rule? Using the new price of gasoline, how far can Sofia travel for $20.00?

pearsonsuccessnet.com

432 Chapter 5 Introduction to Functions

11. Jody saves her money to buy a used car. The price of the car is $4000. The car dealer reduces the price by $125 for each month that the car remains unsold. Jody has $2500 in savings. She can save an additional $250 each month.

    a. Write an algebraic expression to represent each of the following.
       - price of the car in n months
       - amount of money Jody has saved after n months

    b. Determine the number of months until Jody can purchase the car. Show your work.

12. **Standardized Test Prep** Kai's car uses a gallon of gas to travel 28 to 32 miles. Gas prices range from $2.80 to $3.10 per gallon. Which amount is the best estimate of how much Kai spends on gas for a 1200-mile road trip?

    A. $91   B. $105
    C. $119   D. $133

13. **Take It Further** Everyone in a room shakes hands with everyone else exactly once.

    a. How many handshakes occur among 6 people? Among n people?

    b. Find a rule that computes the number of handshakes that occur.

Suppose your car gets 28 to 32 miles per gallon of gas. What value would *you* use to estimate how far your car will go on a full tank?

Maintain Your Skills

14. A store offers a holiday discount of 10% on everything in the store. The state sales tax is 5%, and the city tax is 3%. You apply each tax to the actual cost of items after the discount. What does it cost Derman to buy the following items when he applies the discount?

    a. A coat costs $49.99, and a belt costs $12.95.

    b. A CD player costs $49.99, and a CD costs $12.95.

    c. An air conditioner costs $499.90, and a fan costs $129.50.

5.02 Building Functions 433

5.03 Is It a Function?

The diagram illustrates how a function is like a machine. You supply the machine with an input. Then the machine follows a rule and gives back an output.

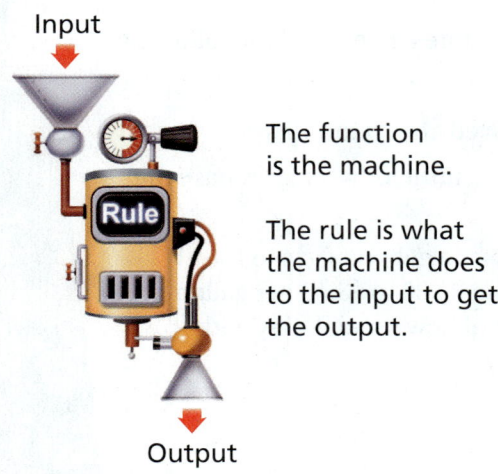

The function is the machine.

The rule is what the machine does to the input to get the output.

For example, Add 2 to the input is a rule that defines a function.

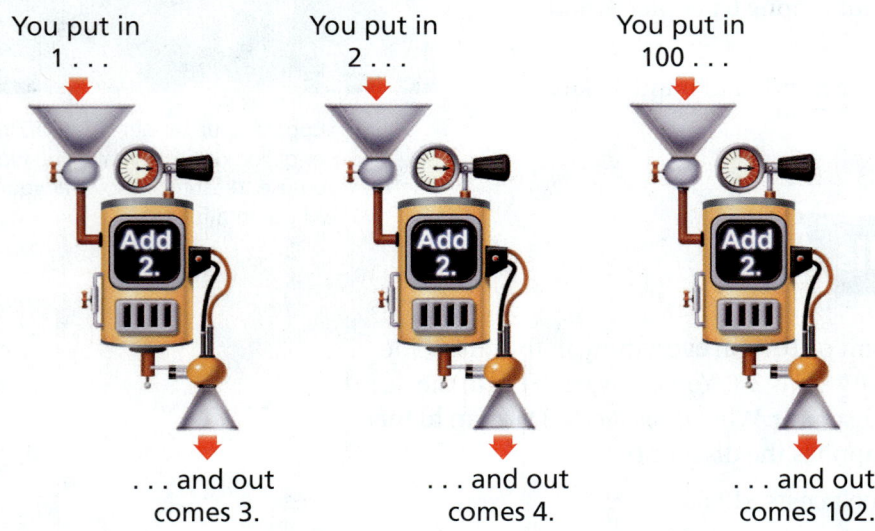

You put in 1 . . . and out comes 3.

You put in 2 . . . and out comes 4.

You put in 100 . . . and out comes 102.

There are many examples of rules that define functions. For example,

- Multiply the input by 3.
- Square the input.
- Take the number's absolute value and then add 5.

Only special kinds of rules, however, define functions.

In Lesson 5.01, Tony complains that some of Sasha's rules are illegal when the function gives two different outputs for the same input. One of Sasha's illegal rules is "x produces $x + 2$ or $x + 3$," depending on a coin flip.

You put in 3 . . .

Add 2 or 3 to the input.

. . . and out comes 5 . . .

. . . or is it 6?

Mathematicians define functions as "predictable rules." In other words, each input must produce the same output every time it goes through the machine.

Definition

A **function** is a rule that assigns each element from the set of inputs to exactly one element from the set of outputs.

Sasha's illegal rule does not define a function, because the rule does not always give the same output. When 3 is the input, there are two possible outputs, 5 and 6.

Example

Problem Does the rule "Add 4 to the input and square the result" define a function?

Solution Yes, because each input gives precisely one output.

$$1 \text{ returns } (1 + 4)^2 = 5^2 = 25.$$
$$2 \text{ returns } (2 + 4)^2 = 6^2 = 36.$$
$$-1 \text{ returns } (-1 + 4)^2 = 3^2 = 9.$$
$$x \text{ returns } (x + 4)^2.$$

There are other rules that look different from $(x + 4)^2$ that you can find in the example, but they define the same function. For example, for any real number x, you can apply the basic rules of arithmetic to write a rule that looks different.

$$(x + 4)^2 = x^2 + 8x + 16$$

In words, the rule tells you to square the input, add the result to 8 times the input, and then add 16.

5.03 Is It a Function?

Example

Problem Does the rule "Find a number that is less than the input" define a function?

Solution No, it does not, because this rule gives many different outputs for the same input. For instance, when 5 is your input, the output can be 3, 2, $\frac{3}{7}$, -6, -100, or any other number less than 5.

For Discussion

1. Give three examples of rules that define functions and three examples of rules that do not define functions.

What happens when you put a variable such as x into the function machine instead of a particular number?

You put in x . . .

. . . and out comes $x + 2$.

Functions are often expressions like the expressions in Chapter 2. You can define functions in other ways, also. For example, you can give a set of instructions like the instructions in the Guess My Rule game in this chapter.

For Discussion

2. Tony suggests that $x \mapsto 3$ is not a function of x, because the rule does not actually use x. Is he correct?

3. Sasha suggests that $x \mapsto x$ is not a function, because the rule does not transform its input. Is she correct?

> You read the symbol $\mapsto$ as "maps to." For example, you can read $x \mapsto x + 2$ as "x maps to x plus 2." This means add 2 to the input to get the output.

Exercises Practicing Habits of Mind

Check Your Understanding

1. Determine whether each rule defines a function. If it does, make a table of output values. Use integer inputs from -3 to 3. If the rule is not a function, explain.

   a. Multiply the input by 5 and then add 2.

   b. Square the input.

   c. When x is the input, the output is a fraction larger than x.

   d. Take the absolute value of the input and then subtract 7.

   e. $x \mapsto \pm x$

2. For each rule in Exercise 1 that is a function, write the rule in "$x \mapsto$" form.

3. You can link function machines to make more complex functions. The diagram illustrates an example.

   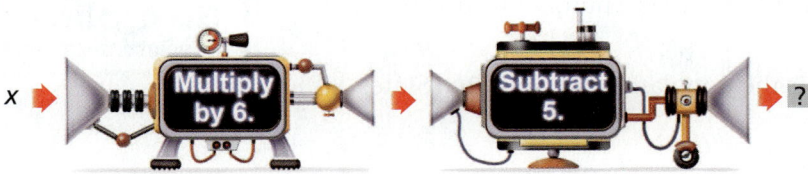

   Make sure you can use what comes out of the first machine in the second machine.

   a. Copy the table at the right. Use this machine network to complete the table.

   b. What is the output when you put x into the network?

4. When you switch the order of the two machines, you get another function.

   a. Copy the table at the right. Use this machine network to complete the table.

   b. What is the output when you put x into the network?

   c. Is this function the same function you found in Exercise 3?

Input	Output
0	■
1	■
-2	■
5	■
■	7

Input	Output
0	■
1	■
-2	■
5	■
■	7

On Your Own

5. Determine whether each rule defines a function. If it does, make a table of output values using integer inputs from 0 to 4. If it does not, explain.

   a. Take the opposite of the input and then add 2.

   b. Square the input and then subtract 4.

   c. $x \mapsto \dfrac{x^2 + 3x}{x - x}$

   d. x produces a number that is 4 units to the left of x on the number line.

   e. x produces a number that is 4 units away from x on the number line.

6. Modeling situations as functions is common. Decide whether each description represents a function. Explain.

   a. The input is a day of the year. The output is the average temperature in Barcelona on that day.

   b. The input is the speed of a car. The output is the time it takes for a car moving constantly at that speed to travel 100 miles.

   c. The input is a positive number. The output is a number whose absolute value is the input.

   d. The input is a year. The output is the population of the United States during that year.

Population of the United States

1800s

Present Day

7. For each description in Exercise 6, reverse the descriptions for input and output. Which new descriptions result in functions? Explain.

8. **Write About It** Why do some people refer to the input of a function as the independent variable and the output as the dependent variable?

9. Dana's favorite number is 5. She invents five different rules shown below.

    $x \mapsto \frac{x}{5} + 4$

    $x \mapsto 10(x - 5) + 5$

    $x \mapsto 5^{x-4}$

    $x \mapsto \frac{x^2}{5}$

    $x \mapsto (x - 5)^2 + x$

    a. Show that each rule fixes 5. In other words, show that when the number 5 is the input, the number 5 is also the output.

    b. Pick any whole number between 2 and 10 (except 5). Change Dana's rules so that the new rules fix the number you choose.

    c. Show that your five new rules fix the number you choose.

10. **Standardized Test Prep** Which statement is true about the rule "Subtract 4 from the input and divide by 2"?

    A. The rule is a function, because each input gives exactly one output.

    B. The rule is not a function, because some inputs have fraction outputs.

    C. The rule is a function, because each input gives a positive number output.

    D. The rule is *not* a function, because the input 2 produces the values 1 and -1.

Maintain Your Skills

11. Tony plays with his calculator's square root key. He picks a large number such as 123 and finds its square root. Then he finds the square root of the result. Next he finds the square root of that result. He continues in this way 20 or 30 times. What does Tony get as a final output?

12. Try Tony's experiment in Exercise 11 with any integer greater than 1. Explain your results.

For Exercises 13–15, choose a value for x and apply the given rule. Use the output as the next input, and apply the rule again. Repeat the process several times. Explain your results.

13. $x \mapsto \frac{1}{x}$

14. $x \mapsto x^2$

15. $x \mapsto \frac{x+3}{2}$

5.04 Naming Functions

Often you can more easily examine and ask questions about a function by giving it a name. You can often use a single letter, such as f, to name a function. You write the output of function f as $f(x)$ and say "f of x."

$f(x) = 2x^3 - 1$

> Computer programmers often use a term such as *cube* to name a function.

You can define a function using the "maps to" notation and name the function at the same time.

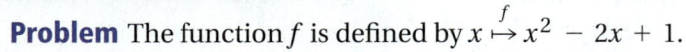

$x \xmapsto{f} 2x^3 - 1$ means the same as $f(x) = 2x^3 - 1$.

Example

Problem The function f is defined by 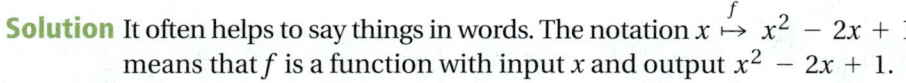 $x \xmapsto{f} x^2 - 2x + 1$.

What is each of the following?

$f(1)$ $\quad\quad$ $f(3)$ $\quad\quad$ $f(\pi)$

$f(a + 7)$ $\quad\quad$ $f(a) + f(7)$

What is $f(x)$?

Solution It often helps to say things in words. The notation $x \xmapsto{f} x^2 - 2x + 1$ means that f is a function with input x and output $x^2 - 2x + 1$.

$f(1)$ is the output of the function when $x = 1$. The notation looks like $1 \xmapsto{f} 1^2 - 2 \cdot 1 + 1 = 0$, or $f(1) = 0$.

Similarly, for each of the remaining inputs, replace x with the given input.

$f(3) = (3)^2 - 2(3) + 1 = 4$

$f(\pi) = (\pi)^2 - 2(\pi) + 1$

$f(a + 7) = (a + 7)^2 - 2(a + 7) + 1$

$f(a) + f(7) = [(a)^2 - 2(a) + 1] + [(7)^2 - 2(7) + 1]$

The function $f(x)$ is just $x^2 - 2x + 1$.

> Why is the following statement true?
> $f(a + 7) \ne f(a) + f(7)$?

Developing Habits of Mind

Represent a function. You can write function notation in two ways. Each way emphasizes a different part of the function.

The $\mapsto$ notation highlights what the function does. The function $x \mapsto 7x^3 - 1$ transforms any input (x) into an output $(7x^3 - 1)$. The $f(\ )$ notation highlights the output of a function. When you write $f(x) = 7x^3 - 1$, x is the input, f is the function, and $7x^3 - 1$ is the output. In both cases, you define the function with the expression $7x^3 - 1$.

> You name the function f. Its output for a given input x is $f(x)$.

You can give a function any name. Sometimes you use a letter such as g or h. On a calculator or a computer, you may name functions using a few letters.

Transformation Notation	Function Name	Function Notation
$x \mapsto 4x^2$	g	$g(x) = 4x^2$
$x \mapsto 3x - 7$	h	$h(x) = 3x - 7$
$x \mapsto \lvert x \rvert$	ABS	$\text{ABS}(x) = \lvert x \rvert$
$x \mapsto \sqrt{x}$	SQRT	$\text{SQRT}(x) = \sqrt{x}$

You can build combinations of function machines such as $\text{ABS}(g(x))$.

In goes x . . . out comes $g(x)$.   In goes $g(x)$ . . . out comes $\text{ABS}(g(x))$.

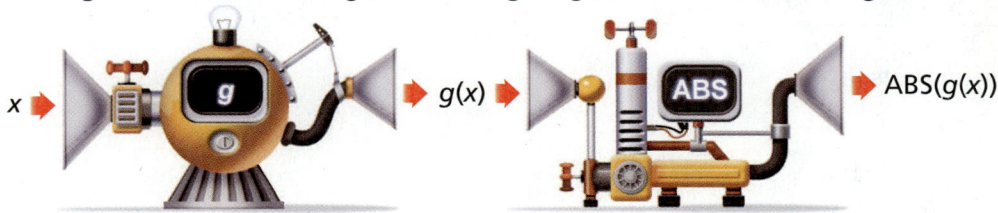

> You usually call combinations of function machines such as $\text{ABS}(g(x))$ **compositions**.

For Discussion

1. Draw a function machine illustrating $x \mapsto \text{ABS}(h(x))$. Then draw a function machine illustrating $x \mapsto h(\text{ABS}(x))$.
2. Is $\text{ABS}(h(x)) = h(\text{ABS}(x))$?
3. What is the value of $\text{SQRT}(h(3))$? The value of $\text{SQRT}(h(1))$?

In-Class Experiment

Use your calculator to discover the keys that are functions. Press each of the following keys.

4. ABS
5. SIN
6. RAND
7. 10^x

Experiment with different inputs and make conjectures about which keys are functions. Record your observations. Then choose any other keys on the calculator. Which of these keys are functions?

Exercises Practicing Habits of Mind

Check Your Understanding

1. Copy the table. Use the function $f(x) = -2x + 5$ to complete the table.

Input, x	Output, f(x)
0	■
1	3
2	■
3	■
4	-3
5	■

2. Use the functions below for parts (a)–(e).
   $$\text{REC}(x) = \frac{1}{x}$$
   $$h(x) = x^2 + 4$$

   a. What is $h(2)$? $\text{REC}(2)$?

   b. Draw a function machine that illustrates $\text{REC}(h(1))$. Then calculate $\text{REC}(h(1))$.

   c. Draw a function machine that illustrates $\text{REC}(h(x))$. Then calculate $\text{REC}(h(5))$.

   d. Draw a function machine that illustrates $h(\text{REC}(x))$. Then calculate $h(\text{REC}(1))$ and $h(\text{REC}(5))$. Does $h(\text{REC}(x)) = \text{REC}(h(x))$?

   e. What result do you get when you calculate $\text{REC}(0)$?

3. Find two functions f and g such that $f(g(x)) = g(f(x))$.

4. Find at least two functions f such that $f(f(x)) = x$ for any value of x.

5. Some functions take multiple inputs, but these functions must always give back only one output. For instance, addition is a function that takes two inputs and gives back only one output.

   ADD(a, b) = $a + b$

   Use each multi-input function for parts (a) and (b).

   Addition   ADD(a, b) = $a + b$
   Multiplication   MULT(a, b) = ab

   > Another way to write ADD(a, b) is (a, b) $\mapsto a + b$.

   a. What is the value of ADD(1, 1)? The value of MULT(2, 3)?
   b. Is ADD(a, b) = ADD(b, a)?
   c. What is the value of MULT(a, ADD(b, c)) − ADD(MULT(a, b), MULT(a, c))?
   d. Is MULT(3, ADD(x, 4)) = ADD(MULT(3, x), MULT(3, 4))?
   e. What is the value of MULT(b, ADD(a, $-a$))?

On Your Own

6. Use these four functions for parts (a) and (b).

   $f(x) = 3x + 1$ $x \stackrel{h}{\mapsto} x^2 + 1$
   $x \stackrel{g}{\mapsto} 3x - 1$ $j(x) = 2x + 5$

   a. Hideki chooses one of these functions. When he uses the number 5 as the input, the output is 14. Can you tell which function he is using?
   b. Hideki puts in a 0 and gets back a 1. Can you tell which function he is using?
   c. Hideki says, "The input I chose this time gives the same output for function f and function j." What input did he choose?
   d. What input(s), if any, give the same outputs for function g and for function j?
   e. What input(s), if any, give the same outputs for function f and for function g?

   > For help defining functions, see the TI-Nspire Handbook, p. 778.

7. Suppose you drive on a straight road at 30 miles per hour. Model this situation using a function that converts driving time into distance traveled.

8. Dorothy describes the following number trick. Pick a number. Multiply it by 3. Add 5. Double it. Add 8. Divide by 6. Subtract the original number. Dorothy always tells your ending number.

    a. Choose at least 5 different numbers as inputs for Dorothy's function. Write the input-output pairs in a table.

    b. Input x into Dorothy's rule. Apply each step in Dorothy's rule to x and record each step. What is the final result?

    > First, you multiply x by 3 to get $3x$. Then, use $3x$ as the input for the second step, adding 5, and so on.

9. Use the functions $g(x) = x^2 - 5$ and $h(x) = |3x + 1|$. Evaluate each function.

    a. $g(0), g(1),$ and $g(-1)$
    b. $h(0), h(1),$ and $h(-1)$
    c. $g(3) + 5$
    d. $g(4) + h(4)$

10. Let m represent a function that uses two points as inputs and gives back a number as an output. The two input points are $P(x_1, y_1)$ and $Q(x_2, y_2)$.

    $$m(P, Q) = \frac{y_2 - y_1}{x_2 - x_1}$$

    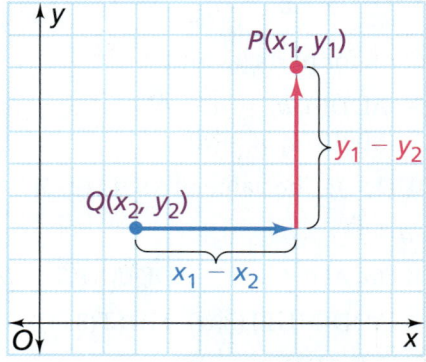

    a. What does the output $m(P, Q)$ represent?

    b. Calculate $m(P, Q)$ when P is $(-1, 2)$ and Q is $(2, 6)$.

11. **Standardized Test Prep** When t is 2.5, what is the value of $h(t)$ in the equation $h(t) = -16t^2 + 8t + 6$?

    A. -74 B. -54 C. -14 D. 126

Maintain Your Skills

12. Use these two functions to evaluate each function in parts (a)–(j).

    $$f(x) = 3x + 1 \qquad g(x) = \frac{x - 1}{3}$$

    a. $f(2)$
    b. $f(f(2))$
    c. $f(f(f(2)))$
    d. $g(2)$
    e. $g(g(2))$
    f. $f(g(2))$
    g. $g(f(2))$
    h. $f(g(f(2)))$
    i. $g(f(g(f(2))))$
    j. $f(f(g(g(2))))$

444 Chapter 5 Introduction to Functions

5.05 Function Inputs and Outputs

The definition of a function describes mapping as a set of inputs corresponding to a set of outputs. Each set has a special name.

Definition

The set of inputs is called the domain of the function.

The set of outputs that a function produces is called the range of the function.

The set of outputs is sometimes called the image of the function.

The definitions of function, domain, and range do not mention any numbers. You can design functions that use any kind of input, as long as each input always gives only one output. For example,

- A juicer is a function. The input is a piece of fruit. The output is the fruit juice.

- Your library's computer catalog system is a function. The input is the book's title. The output is the call number that tells you where to find the book.

The call number is a function of the book.

For Discussion

Identify each domain and range.

1. The salary of a worker is a function of his or her skill level.
2. The price of an advertisement during a television show is a function of the number of viewers.
3. The magnitude of a sonic boom is a function of an airplane's weight and fuselage length.

Defining the domain of a function is just as important as writing the function rule. You can restrict the domain to a specific set of numbers even though your function rule works for other sets of numbers. For example, when your function maps time traveled against distance, you can define the domain values for time as the set of positive numbers.

Some functions break down with certain inputs. For example, a juicer can juice oranges, apples, and even carrots, but not shoes. Some function rules cannot use certain inputs either. You can exclude the numbers that do not work when you define the function domain.

For Discussion

4. What inputs do not work in the function $x \mapsto \frac{1}{x}$?

Example

Problem What is the domain of the function $x \mapsto \frac{1}{x - 7}$?

Solution This function takes numbers for input. You must decide what numbers make sense, or are valid, for the function.

Look at the function. Is there any number x for which $\frac{1}{x - 7}$ does not make sense? Since $x - 7$ is in the denominator, make sure that $x - 7$ never has the value of 0. To find when $x - 7$ equals 0, solve the equation below.

$$x - 7 = 0$$
$$x - 7 + 7 = 0 + 7$$
$$x = 7$$

When x equals 7, the function does not work. The domain is all real numbers except 7.

For You to Do

Find the domain of each function.

5. $x \mapsto \frac{1}{x + 2}$

6. $x \mapsto \frac{13x + 5}{2x + 1}$

7. $x \mapsto \frac{6x^2 + 52x - 37}{x^2 - 4}$

8. $x \mapsto x$th prime number

You can define some functions on a much smaller scale. For instance, the table at the right defines a perfectly good function. The domain of this function is $\{1, 2, 3, 4\}$ and the range is $\{-3, 3, 4, 9\}$.

In the next investigation, you will look at tables in a different way. Tables provide a snapshot of a function with domain and range that are larger than what is in the table. Make sure you understand the context of any problem so you can decide whether the table is the entire function or just a snapshot.

Input	Output
1	3
2	4
3	9
4	−3

446 Chapter 5 Introduction to Functions

Exercises Practicing Habits of Mind

Check Your Understanding

1. **a.** What inputs, if any, are not valid for $x \mapsto \sqrt{x}$?
   b. What inputs, if any, are not valid for $x \mapsto \sqrt{|x|}$?

2. Determine the domain for each function.
   a. $g(x) = \sqrt{x - 2}$
   b. $x \mapsto x - 2$
   c. $x \mapsto \frac{1}{x - 2}$
   d. $h(x) = (x - 2)^2$

3. Use the functions $\text{REC}(x) = \frac{1}{x}$ and $h(x) = x^2 + 4$. Find the domain of each function given.
   a. $h(\text{REC}(x))$
   b. $\text{REC}(h(x))$

4. Tables I–III show three sets of input-output values.

   Table I

Input	Output
2	4
9	8
−3	12
$\frac{1}{2}$	3
−1	4
100	7

   Table II

Input	Output
4	9
13	3
7	16
−2	−4
4	9
11	0

   Table III

Input	Output
−1	1
0	2
1	3
4	4
−3	5
−1	6

   a. Does each table define a function? Explain.
   b. For each table that defines a function, state the domain and range of the function.

5. **Take It Further** Find a function f such that, for all values of a and x, $f(ax) = a \cdot f(x)$.

6. **Take It Further** When $f(x + 2) = 5x - 4$, find each value.
   a. $f(3)$
   b. $f(5)$
   c. $f(7)$

On Your Own

7. What is the domain of $x \mapsto \dfrac{1}{x^2 - 25}$?

8. Use the function rule "Divide the input by 3 and write the remainder."

   a. Make an input-output table with integer inputs between 1 and 5.

   b. Is the value 0 a valid input? Is a negative integer a valid input? Explain.

9. Determine whether each description is a function.

   a. The input is a letter. The output is any word starting with that letter.

   b. The input is a person. The output is that person's age in years.

   c. The input is the name of a month. The output is the number of days in that month.

> Look at the outputs. For each valid input, there must be exactly one output.

10. Standardized Test Prep When $f(x) = x^4 - 5$, which of the four values is missing in the table?

x	f(x)
0	−5
−1	−4
■	11
3	76

   A. −4   **B.** −2   **C.** 4   **D.** 6

11. Take It Further Explore $x \mapsto \dfrac{1}{x - |x|}$ to determine what inputs, if any, are valid. What is the domain of $x \mapsto \dfrac{1}{x - |x|}$?

Maintain Your Skills

12. Use the functions to find either a value or an expression in parts (a)–(o).

$$f(x) = 3x + 2 \qquad x \xmapsto{g} \dfrac{x-2}{3} \qquad h(x) = \dfrac{3}{x-2}$$

   a. $f(7)$ **b.** $g(7)$ **c.** $h(7)$

   d. $f(g(5))$ **e.** $g(f(5))$ **f.** $h(g(5))$

   g. $h(6) \cdot g(6)$ **h.** $h(-6) \cdot g(-6)$ **i.** $h(x) \cdot g(x)$

   j. $f(a)$ **k.** $f(a + 2)$ **l.** $f(a + b)$

   m. $f(g(x))$ **n.** $f(f(x))$ **o.** $f\left(\dfrac{x-2}{3}\right)$

5.06 Graphing Functions

You can represent functions in many ways. You have already used three ways: machines, expressions, and tables. Graphs provide another useful way to represent many functions.

Minds in Action episode 19

Tony plots outputs f(x) against inputs x.

Sasha Let's play the Guess My Rule game again.

Tony Okay, but please promise not to do any more crazy functions like $f(x) = \frac{3x^2 + 7x - 19}{x + 11}$.

Sasha Fine.

Sasha thinks for a moment and then writes $x \mapsto 4x - 3$.

Tony's Input	Sasha's Response
2	2 produces 5.
0	0 produces -3.
1	1 produces 1.
$\frac{1}{2}$	$\frac{1}{2}$ produces -1.

Tony I think your rule is "x produces $4x - 3$."

Sasha You're right! That was fast. What's your strategy?

Tony I turn your responses into a graph.

Sasha What do you mean?

Tony Each time you give me a response, I write my input and your response as a point. Then I plot that point. Since 2 produces 5, I plot (2, 5).

Sasha Okay. Since the value 0 produces -3, you plot (0, -3).

Tony Exactly. I do that for all points and look at the graph. It looks like all points fall on a line.

Sasha It does.

Tony I try to find an equation of a line that passes through these points.

First, I calculate the slope between (0, -3) and (1, 1).

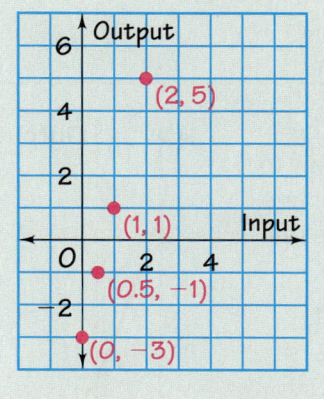

Tony plots outputs f(x) against inputs x.

Tony scribbles some calculations on his paper.

Tony   The slope is 4. Then I write the equation as a point tester.

Sasha How do you do that when there's no variable y?

Tony   It's just like before, except we use $f(x)$ instead of y. Since the number 4 is the slope, and $(1, 1)$ is on the line, we can test any point $(x, f(x))$. The point is on the line when $\frac{f(x) - 1}{x - 1} = 4$.

Sasha When you clean that up, you get $f(x) - 1 = 4(x - 1)$.

Tony   That simplifies to $f(x) - 1 = 4x - 4$.

Sasha Or $f(x) = 4x - 3$. That was my rule!

For You to Do

1. Tony and Sasha play the Guess My Rule game.

Tony's Input	Sasha's Response
1	1 produces $-\frac{1}{6}$.
3	3 produces $2\frac{1}{2}$.
0	0 produces $-\frac{3}{2}$.
−1	−1 produces $-2\frac{5}{6}$.

   Use Tony's graphing method described above to find Sasha's rule.

Definition

When g is a function, the **graph of g** is the graph of the equation $y = g(x)$.

> Graphing the equation $y = g(x)$ is the same as graphing $g(x)$ against x.

For Discussion

2. The coordinate plane shows the graph of function f. Explain how to use this graph and the vertical line $x = -2$ to estimate $f(-2)$. Use the same method to estimate $f(0)$.

3. Give the approximate value(s) of x when $f(x) = 2$.

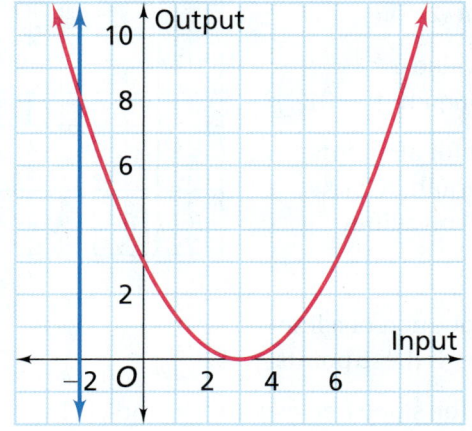

450 Chapter 5 Introduction to Functions

Minds in Action
episode 20

Tony and Sasha walk down a hall. Tony finds a sheet of paper on the ground. He picks it up and sees these drawings.

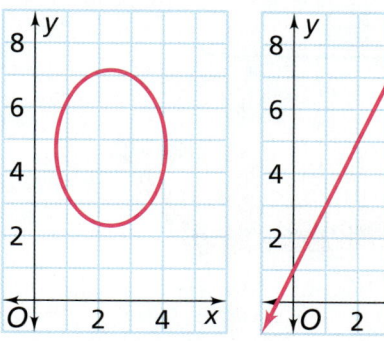
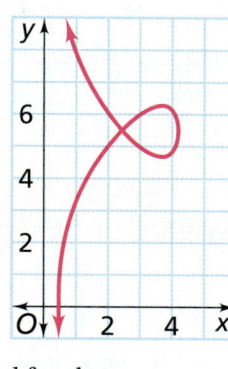
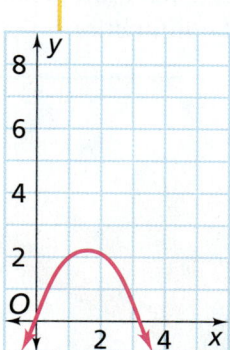

Tony Look at this! Somebody is using my method for the Guess My Rule game.

Sasha looks at the drawings.

Sasha I wouldn't get so excited, Tony. We're only allowed to use functions in the Guess My Rule game.

Tony So?

Sasha Some of those graphs aren't graphs of functions.

Tony What do you mean?

Sasha Well, suppose that the first graph is a graph of function $a(x)$. If I want to find the output for the function $a(3)$, I can do that by drawing a vertical line through 3. See, the vertical line hits the graph in 2 places!

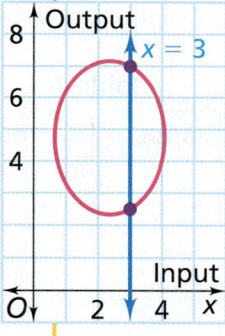

Tony So what?

Sasha In a function, each input always gives the same output.

Tony Oh, right.

Sasha In this graph, the input value 3 produces 2.5 or 7. The output values for $a(3)$ are 2.5 and 7 at the same time! That's an illegal rule!

Tony I think I see. The vertical line $x = 3$ tells us the output when 3 is the input.

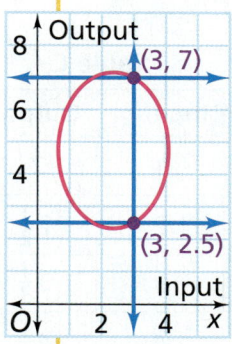

Sasha Correct.

Tony Since the vertical line hits two places on the graph, the input 3 gives two possible outputs.

Sasha So the graph isn't a function!

5.06 Graphing Functions

For Discussion

4. Use Sasha's method to determine whether each of the other three graphs Tony found is a graph of a function. Explain how to use Sasha's method for any graph. Then draw at least three new graphs of functions and three new graphs of nonfunctions.

Exercises Practicing Habits of Mind

Check Your Understanding

1. Find a function that produces each table. You can write your rule in $f(x)$ form, $x \mapsto$ form, or in words.

Habits of Mind

Visualize. Plot the points and see if you recognize the shape of the graph.

Table A

Input, n	Output
0	9
1	7
2	5
3	3
4	1

Table B

Input, s	Output
0	−1
1	0
2	3
3	8
4	15

Table C

Input, n	Output
1	2
2	$2\frac{1}{2}$
3	$3\frac{1}{3}$
4	$4\frac{1}{4}$
5	$5\frac{1}{5}$

Table D

Input, x	Output
0	12.875
1	13
2	13.125
3	13.25
4	13.375

2. Decide whether each graph is the graph of a function.

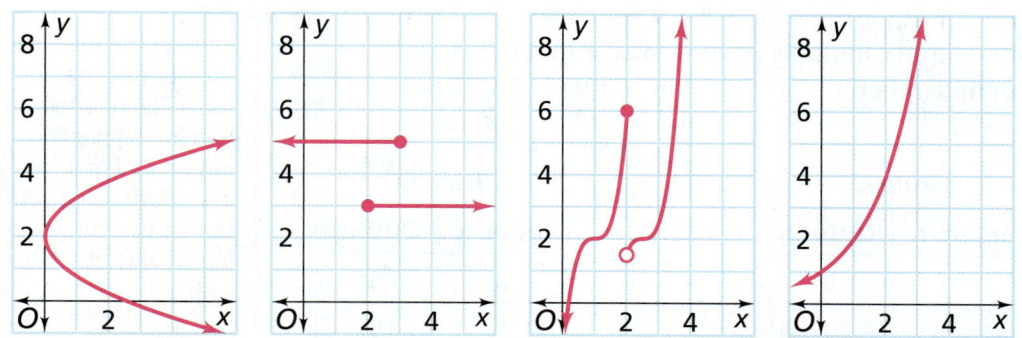

3. Suppose that you switch the axes in the coordinate planes in Exercise 2. In other words, let the *x*-axis represent the outputs and the *y*-axis represent the inputs. Which graphs are the graphs of functions in this case?

4. Tony and Sasha play the Guess My Rule game. After three inputs, Tony guesses the rule.

   Tony says, "I think your rule is '$x \mapsto 2 - 5x$.'"

   Sasha replies, "No, my rule is '$x \mapsto -5(x + 1) + 7$.'"

   Tony says, "That's the same!"

   a. Are the valid inputs for each rule the same?

   b. Make an input-output table for each rule. Use at least five inputs. Are the tables the same?

   c. Graph each rule. Are the graphs the same?

   d. Are the rules the same? If not, explain when they are the same.

5. Travis compares two functions.

   $$s(x) = (x - 1)^2 \qquad t(x) = x^2 - 1.99x + 1$$

   Travis says, "When $x = 0$, both functions have an output value of 1. Then I graph them on a calculator. They look the same." Travis concludes that functions s and t are equal. Is Travis correct?

   For help graphing a function on the coordinate plane, see the TI-Nspire Handbook, p. 778.

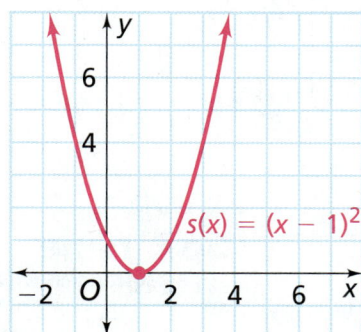 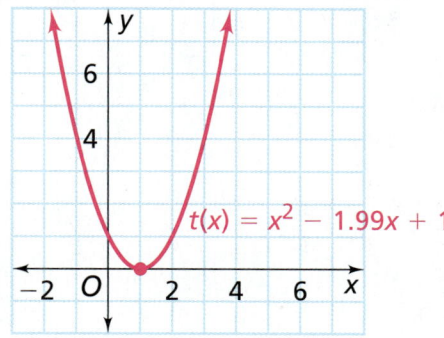

5.06 Graphing Functions 453

6. Copy the tables. Use rules C and D to complete the tables.

    Rule C When the input value is 0, the output value is 5. For the other inputs, multiply the previous output by 2. For example, when 1 is an input, the output is 2 × 5, or 10.

    Rule D $x \mapsto 5(2^x)$

    > You can use the output for 0 to find the output for 1. The rule tells you to take the previous output and multiply that by 2. Notice that you cannot use this rule for inputs between 0 and 1, such as 0.5.

    Rule C

Input, n	Output
0	5
1	10
2	■
3	■
4	■
5	■

    Rule D

Input, x	Output
0	5
1	10
2	■
3	■
4	■
5	■

    Look at the tables above. Consider both the set of valid inputs and the graph for each function. Compare and contrast the functions.

7. Function v uses positive integers for inputs and returns the number of positive factors that the input has.

    Extend the table for whole number inputs up to 24. Make several conjectures about the function. Explain any shortcuts for calculating an output.

Input, n	Output, v(n)
1	1
2	2
3	2
4	3
5	2
6	4
7	2
8	4
9	3

On Your Own

8. Graph each function.

    a. $x \mapsto 4x + 9$

    b. $x \mapsto \frac{x^2}{5}$

    c. $x \mapsto \frac{x}{2} + 4$

    d. $x \mapsto x + 1$

9. Which graph of a function has a maximum value of 10?

A.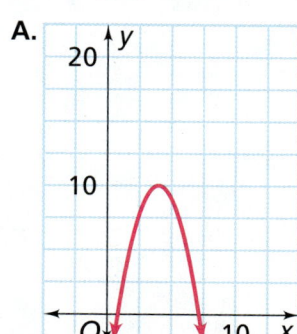

B.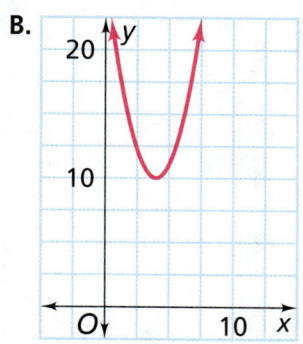

C.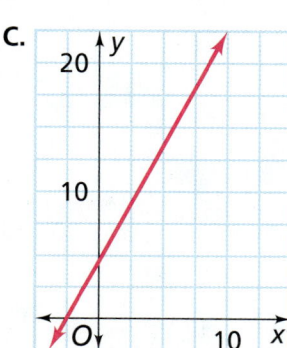

D.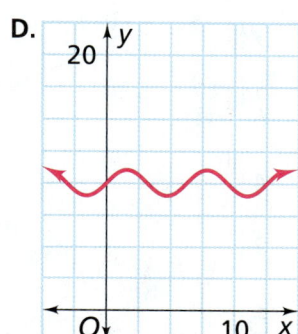

10. Elaine explains how she finds fixed inputs, or inputs that remain unchanged by a function. "Let's say you want to find a value fixed by the rule $x \mapsto 4x - 9$. First, graph $y = 4x - 9$. Then, graph $y = x$. The graphs intersect at (3, 3). See! The rule $x \mapsto 4x - 9$ fixes the value 3."

    Use Elaine's method to find fixed inputs for each function in Exercise 8. Does her method work?

    For other ways to graph on the coordinate plane, see the TI-Nspire Handbook, p. 778.

11. **Take It Further** The floor function takes any real number x as input and returns the greatest integer less than or equal to x. A common symbol for the floor function is $\lfloor \ \rfloor$.

    a. Write a rule for $\lfloor x \rfloor$ on a number line.

    b. Draw the graph of $x \mapsto \lfloor x \rfloor$.

x	$\lfloor x \rfloor$
3	3
3.5	3
3.9	3
3.99	3
4	4

12. Use the functions p and q given below.

    $$p(x) = x - 2 \qquad q(x) = \frac{x^2 - 4}{x + 2}$$

    a. Make an input-output table for each function. Use at least five inputs. Are the tables the same?

    b. Are the valid inputs for each rule the same?

    c. Graph each function. Illustrate your answers for parts (a) and (b) on your graphs.

5.06 Graphing Functions

13. Decide whether each graph is the graph of a function.

   a.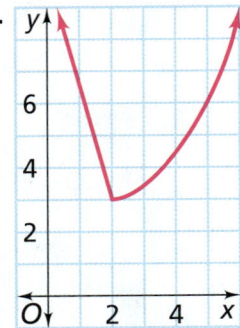

   b.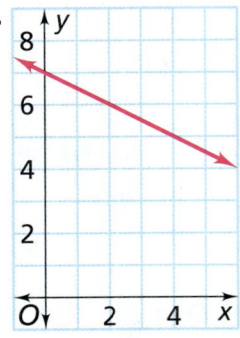

   c.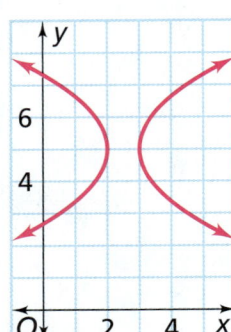

   d.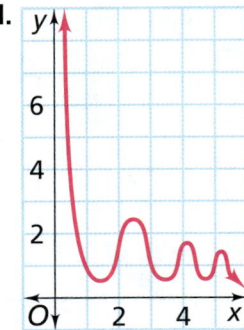

14. Use Rules 1 and 2 given below.

    Rule 1 $x \mapsto 4x + 1$

    Rule 2 $x \mapsto 4x + 1 + x(x - 1)(x - 2)$

    a. Without calculating any values, determine whether the two rules define the same function.

    b. Make an input-output table for each rule. Use whole-number inputs 0, 1, and 2. Are the tables the same?

    c. Can you find an input value for which the outputs for the two rules differ?

15. Use the rules in Exercise 14 and Rules 3 and 4 given below.

    Rule 3 $x \mapsto 4x + 1 + x(x - 1)(x - 2)(x - 3)(x - 4)$

    Rule 4 $x \mapsto 4x + 1 + x(x - 1)(x - 2)(x - 3)(x - 4)(x - 5)$

    a. Make an input-output table for Rules 1 and 3 using whole-number inputs from 0 to 4. Are the outputs the same?

    b. Is Rule 3 the same function as Rule 1 or Rule 2? Explain.

    c. Without calculating actual values, how do the outputs using Rule 1 and Rule 4 compare? Use whole-number inputs from 0 to 5. Explain.

    d. Is it possible to write a rule that gives the same outputs as $x \mapsto 4x + 1$ and defines a different function? Use whole-number input values from 0 to 6. Then extend the input values to 100. Explain.

16. **Standardized Test Prep** Larissa selects mobile phone service. Each company charges a fixed monthly fee plus an additional charge for each minute in excess of the free time allowance.

Mobile Phone Service Plans

Company	Monthly Fee	Free Minutes per Month	Cost per Additional Minute
A	$35	300	$.08
B	$22	400	$.15

Larissa plans to use her mobile phone as her only phone. She predicts that she will use it between 600 and 900 minutes per month. To find t, the total monthly charge for each company based on m minutes of phone use, Larissa writes the equations below.

Company A $t = 35 + (m - 300)(0.08)$ when $m \geq 300$
Company B $t = 22 + (m - 400)(0.15)$ when $m \geq 400$

Which is the less expensive plan for 600 minutes of phone use per month?

A. Company A

B. Company B

C. Both plans cost the same amount for 600 minutes.

D. cannot be determined

> When Larissa talks for only 200 minutes per month, why don't her equations work?

Maintain Your Skills

Use the functions f and g for Exercises 17 and 18.

$$f(x) = 3x + 2 \qquad x \overset{g}{\mapsto} \frac{x-2}{3}$$

17. Sketch the graph of each function.

    a. f

    b. $r(x) = f(x - 1)$

    c. $s(x) = f(x + 1)$

18. Sketch the graph of each function.

    a. g

    b. $t(x) = f(g(x))$

    c. $s(x) = g(f(x))$

Mathematical Reflections 5A

In this investigation, you learned how to write function rules, make input-output tables, and graph functions. These questions will help you summarize what you have learned.

1. Use $x \xmapsto{f} -2x + 3$ and $x \xmapsto{g} x^2 - 1$.

   a. Graph each function.
   b. Use your graphs to estimate $f(0.25)$ and $g(0.5)$.
   c. Use each function rule to find $f(0.25)$ and $g(0.5)$.
   d. Use your graph to approximate all values of x such that $g(x) = 2$.

2. Decide whether each statement defines a function. For each function, make a table using integer values from -2 to 2. Write the function in $x \mapsto$ form.

   a. Multiply the input by 2 and subtract 3.
   b. Multiply the input by a value that is one more than the input.
   c. When x is the input, the output is a value not equal to x.
   d. Take the opposite of the input and add 3. Then square the result.

3. Use $f(x) = 3x + 5$ and $g(x) = 3x^2$.

   a. $f(2)$
   b. $g(2)$
   c. $g(22)$
   d. $f(12)$
   e. $f(g(2))$
   f. $g(f(2))$

4. Determine the domain for each function.

   a. $f(x) = 2x - 7$
   b. $g(x) = x^2 + 1$
   c. $x \xmapsto{h} \sqrt{x - 1}$
   d. $A(x) = \dfrac{2}{x + 5}$

5. What is a function?

6. What is the relationship between a table and a function?

7. What is the domain of $f(x) = \dfrac{\sqrt{x}}{x - 9}$?

Vocabulary and Notation

In this investigation you learned these terms and symbols. Make sure you understand what each one means and how to use it.

- composition
- domain
- function, f(x)
- graph of a function
- range

The input could be two images and the output one photo.

Chapter 5 Mid-Chapter Test

Multiple Choice

1. Which function includes $f(3) = 5$ and $f(-3) = 23$?

   A. $f(x) = 3x - 4$

   B. $f(x) = x^2 - 4$

   C. $f(x) = -3x + 14$

   D. $f(x) = -x^3 - 4$

2. Which rule does NOT describe a function?

   A. Take an input and square it. Then subtract 4.

   B. Take an input and multiply it by any number between 5 and 10. Then subtract 100.

   C. Take an input and divide it by 100. Then multiply by 100.

   D. $x \mapsto |x - 5|$

3. Which tables define a function?

   Table I

Input	Output
6	−3
9	9
−1	−3
−7	3
4	8
−1	−3

   Table II

Input	Output
1	1
0	2
1	3
0	4
1	5
0	6

   Table III

Input	Output
1	0
2	1
3	0
4	1
5	0
6	1

   A. table I only

   B. table II only

   C. table I and table III

   D. table I, table II, and table III

4. Which graph is the graph of a function?

   A.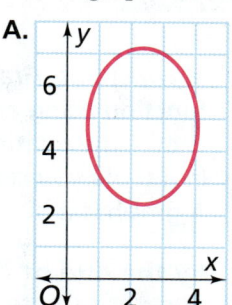

   B.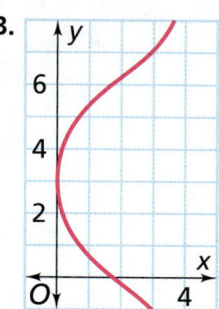

   C.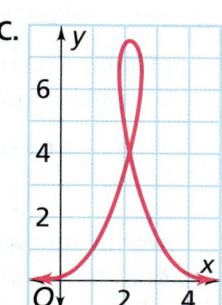

   D.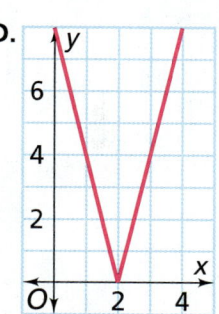

Open Response

5. Find an input that gives the same output for $x \stackrel{k}{\mapsto} 7x - 3$ and $x \stackrel{m}{\mapsto} x + 16$. Show your work.

6. Find the domain for each function.

   a. $f(x) = \sqrt{x + 1}$ **b.** $x \mapsto x + 1$

   c. $x \mapsto \dfrac{1}{x + 1}$ **d.** $g(x) = \dfrac{1}{\sqrt{x + 1}}$

   e. $h(x) = \dfrac{1}{(x - 3)(x + 1)}$

7. Graph function p for which $p(-2) = 0$ and every other x value makes $p(x)$ positive.

8. Function $N(d)$ tells you the number of candles you can buy with d dollars. Each candle costs $3.

   a. Calculate $N\left(25\frac{1}{2}\right)$ and $N(308)$.

   b. Find two values of d such that $N(d) = 70$.

   c. Graph $N(d)$ for inputs of d between 0 and 10.

9. Make a table for $f(x) = 4x - 3$, $g(x) = 7 - x$, and $h(x) = x^2 - 5$. Use integer inputs from −2 to 3.

10. Find each value using the functions in Exercise 9.

    a. $f(g(3))$ **b.** $g(f(3))$ **c.** $f(h(-1))$ **d.** $h(g(f(0)))$

Investigation 5B

Functions, Graphs, and Tables

In *Functions, Graphs, and Tables* you will learn to model a function using an equation, a graph, or a table. A function shows the relationship between input and output values. In a table you can see specific input and output values. A graph is a picture of the function.

By the end of this investigation, you will be able to answer questions like these.

1. How do you find a function that matches a table?

2. What is a recursive rule? How can you use recursion to define functions?

3. What is a recursive rule for the values in the table?

Input	Output
−1	6
0	5
1	4
2	3
3	2

You will learn how to

- determine whether a table represents a linear function
- fit a linear function to a table where possible
- calculate the outputs of a recursive rule
- describe a recursive rule
- find a recursive rule to match a table

You will develop these habits and skills:

- Use a Δ column to find whether a table represents a linear function.
- Use tables to answer questions involving recursive rules.

The position of the spring toy on each step depends on its position on the previous step.

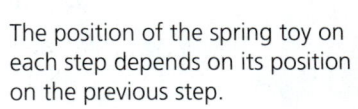

5.07 Getting Started

Activating Prior Knowledge
Exploring New Ideas

Function tables can represent different types of functions. You can identify tables that represent linear functions by using an efficient method for finding the output values.

A **linear function** is a function with a graph that is a line. In For You to Explore, you will identify tables that represent linear functions.

For You to Explore

Determine whether each table represents a linear function. Plot the points on a graph to find collinear points.

1. Table A

x	A(x)
0	2
1	4
2	6
3	8
4	10

2. Table B

k	B(k)
0	1
1	4
2	7
3	10
4	13

3. Table C

a	C(a)
0	0
1	1
2	4
3	9
4	16

4. Table D

n	D(n)
0	−7
1	−4
2	−1
3	2
4	5

5. Table E

p	E(p)
0	−1
1	0
2	3
3	8
4	15

6. Table F

x	F(x)
0	4
1	2
2	1
3	$\frac{1}{2}$
4	$\frac{1}{4}$

7. Table G

x	G(x)
0	7
1	1
2	−5
3	−11
4	−17

8. Table H

n	H(n)
0	$\frac{4}{5}$
1	1
2	$1\frac{1}{5}$
3	$1\frac{2}{5}$
4	$1\frac{3}{5}$

9. Table I

x	I(x)
0	1
1	2
2	5
3	10
4	17

10. The table showing grain needed assumes that each person needs 323 kilograms of grain per year.

World Population
SOURCE: United Nations Secretariat

Year	Population (billions)
1975	4.08
1980	4.45
1985	4.86
1990	5.29
1995	5.72
2000	6.12

World Grain Production
SOURCE: United Nations Secretariat

Year	Grain Production (MMT)
1975	1237
1980	1429
1985	1647
1990	1768
1995	1708
2000	1842

World Grain Needed

Population (billions)	Grain Needed (MMT)
1	323
2	646
3	969
4	1292
5	1615

Millet is a grain that farmers grow extensively in Africa and Asia. Farmers in India (photo below) use the wind to separate millet seeds from chaff.

MMT stands for million metric tons. A metric ton is about 2205 pounds.

a. Use the tables to make predictions. Will there be enough grain to feed the world in 2020? In 2030?

b. What kinds of factors could change your predictions?

Exercises Practicing Habits of Mind

On Your Own

11. Use Tables A and B.

    Table A

Input	Output
0	2
1	4
2	6
3	8
4	10

    Table B

Input	Output
0	$\frac{2}{3}$
1	2
2	6
3	18
4	54

    a. Graph the data.

    b. Based on your graphs, are the points collinear in Table A? In Table B?

12. You need to cut five 2 × 6's for the vertical roof supports shown in the diagram at the right. The boards are 16 inches apart. (The symbol ″ in the diagram stands for inches.) The length of the first board is 5 inches.

    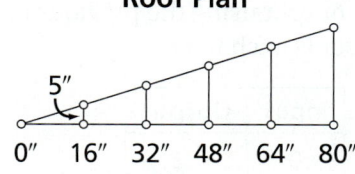

    Roof Plan

    a. Calculate the lengths of the other four boards. Copy and complete the table.

Distance From End (in.)	Length of Board (in.)
16	5
32	■
48	■
64	■
80	■

    b. How do you calculate the length at 32 inches? At 48 inches?

    c. What pattern do you find in the table?

    d. What is the slope of the roof?

5.07 Getting Started 463

13. **Standardized Test Prep** This table shows the water temperature in an industrial water heater. What is the rate of temperature increase in degrees per hour?

Industrial Water Heater

Time (h)	Water Temperature (°F)
0	72
3	87
6	102
9	117

A. 5 degrees per hour
B. 12.2 degrees per hour
C. 12.5 degrees per hour
D. 15 degrees per hour

Maintain Your Skills

Describe how to find each output using the previous output. Find a function that represents each table.

14.
Input	Output
0	0
1	3
2	6
3	9
4	12

15.
Input	Output
0	2
1	5
2	8
3	11
4	14

16.
Input	Output
0	−3
1	0
2	3
3	6
4	9

17.
Input	Output
0	−3
1	1
2	5
3	9
4	13

Chapter 5 Introduction to Functions

5.08 Constant Differences

When you make a table using a function, each input-output pair in the table represents a point on the graph of a function. For instance, the point (0, 1) is on the graph of the function that generates this table. The first row shows an input of 0 and an output of 1.

Input	Output	Δ
0	1	3
1	4	3
2	7	3
3	10	3
4	13	3
5	16	

> When you use integer inputs that increase by the same amount, you can spot patterns more easily.

To be certain that a table represents a linear function, you need to find the slope between all points in the table. That can take you a long time!

To make that work easier, you can add a third column to your table. Then you can keep track of the differences between **consecutive outputs** for evenly spaced inputs. You can record this difference in the Δ (delta) column in a table.

To find a Δ value, subtract the output in the given row from the output in the next row. For instance, in the highlighted portion of the table shown, 3 is in the Δ column next to 13, because $13 - 10 = 3$.

For You to Do

1. Copy and complete the Δ column in each table.

Table A

Input	Output	Δ
0	0	
1	1	
2	4	5
3	9	
4	16	
5	25	

Table B

Input	Output	Δ
0	2	
1	6	
2	10	
3	14	
4	18	
5	22	

In Table A, notice that the sum of the numbers highlighted in one row equals the number highlighted in the next row: $4 + 5 = 9$. When the inputs are evenly spaced, this pattern occurs in every row of the table.

> This property is sometimes called the "up-and-over" property in tables with a Δ column.

In Lesson 5.07, you explored tables and their graphs. You learned that a table's graph lies on a line when the difference between consecutive outputs is the same.

Developing Habits of Mind

Look for a pattern. Patterns can help you solve problems. In this table each output is 5 more than the previous output.

Input	Output	Δ
0	3	5
1	8	5
2	13	5
3	18	5
4	23	5
5	28	5
6	33	

Based on problems in Lesson 5.07, you might guess that the points with coordinates that are the input-output pairs in the table above are collinear. Graphing the points seems to confirm this fact.

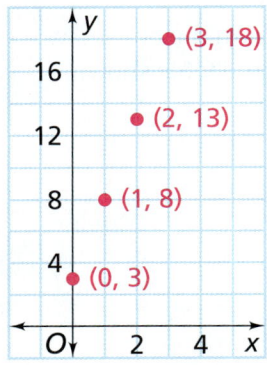

How do you know that the points in the graph fall on a line? The slope between any two points must be constant. To find the slope between the first two points (0, 3) and (1, 8), you can use the slope formula.

$$\text{slope} = \frac{y_2 - y_1}{x_2 - x_1} = \frac{8 - 3}{1 - 0} = \frac{5}{1} = 5$$

You can find the slope between the second and third points, (1, 8) and (2, 13), also.

$$\text{slope} = \frac{y_2 - y_1}{x_2 - x_1} = \frac{13 - 8}{2 - 1} = \frac{5}{1} = 5$$

The slopes are the same. You do not have to do all this work! The table has a difference column, so the value in the Δ column already shows the calculation for $y_2 - y_1$ for consecutive rows. The value equals 5. Since the input column increases by 1 from row to row, you know that $x_2 - x_1$ is always 1 for consecutive rows. The slope between any two points is 5.

What is the difference between rows that are not consecutive? Find the slope between (1, 8) and (4, 23). Explain.

466 Chapter 5 Introduction to Functions

To find a function that represents the values in the table below, look at how to find each output using the previous output. You can find the output 8 by adding 5 to the previous output, 3. The next output, 13, is the result of adding $8 + 5$, or $(3 + 5) + 5$. The calculations below show how to find the output 33.

Input	Output	Δ
0	3	5
1	8	5
2	13	5
3	18	5
4	23	5
5	28	5
6	33	

$33 = 28 + 5$
$ = (23 + 5) + 5 \qquad = 23 + 2 \cdot 5$
$ = (18 + 5) + 2 \cdot 5 = 18 + 3 \cdot 5$
$ = (13 + 5) + 3 \cdot 5 = 13 + 4 \cdot 5$
$ = (8 + 5) + 4 \cdot 5 = 8 + 5 \cdot 5$
$ = (3 + 5) + 5 \cdot 5 = 3 + 6 \cdot 5$

In general, to find the output for input value n, start with 3 and add n 5's. The formula you write is $3 + 5n$. A function that agrees with the table is $f(n) = 3 + 5n$.

In fact, the graph of $f(n) = 3 + 5n$ is the same as the graph of $y = 3 + 5x$. They are both lines.

For You to Do

2. Explain how to find the number 28 in the table using the reasoning described above.

The tables below illustrate the "hockey stick method" for finding an output in any row. First, choose the row with the output you want to find. Next, add the first output and all Δ values in the rows above your chosen row. The sum equals the output for your chosen row.

Input	Output	Δ
0	1	3
1	4	3
2	7	3
3	10	3
4	13	3
5	16	

Input	Output	Δ
0	1	3
1	4	3
2	7	3
3	10	3
4	13	3
5	16	

Input	Output	Δ
0	1	3
1	4	3
2	7	3
3	10	3
4	13	3
5	16	

You can use the hockey stick method to find the output in a table. The output equals the sum of the numbers on the handle plus the number on the blade.

5.08 Constant Differences

The number of times you add 3 to get the output is the same number as the input value.

Input	Output
2	$7 = 1 + 3 + 3 = 1 + 3(2)$
3	$10 = 1 + 3 + 3 + 3 = 1 + 3(3)$
4	$13 = 1 + 3 + 3 + 3 + 3 = 1 + 3(4)$
10	$1 + 3 + 3 + 3 + 3 + 3 + 3 + 3 + 3 + 3 + 3 = 1 + 3(10)$

In general, the output for input value n is $1 + 3n$, or $f(n) = 3n + 1$. The graph shows all the points on the same line, since the difference between outputs is 3. You can summarize these findings in a theorem.

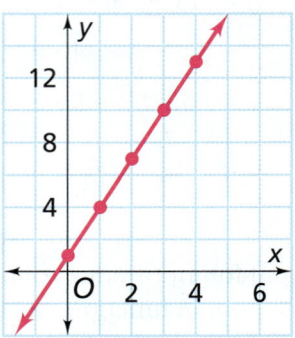

Theorem 5.1

When the differences between consecutive outputs in a table are the same, and the differences between consecutive inputs are the same, you can write a linear function for the table.

Habits of Mind

Detect patterns. When inputs increase by 1, the slope of the graph of the function is the same as the constant number in the difference column.

Exercises *Practicing Habits of Mind*

Check Your Understanding

1. Copy and complete the table for each rule.
   a. To find an output, multiply the input by 7. Then add 1.
   b. $x \mapsto x^2 - x - 4$
   c. $f(x) = -3x + 1$
   d. When 0 is the input, the output is 4. To find a new output, add 6 to the previous output.

Input	Output	Δ
0	■	■
1	■	■
2	■	■
3	■	■
4	■	■
5	■	

2. Find a linear function that matches each table. If not possible, explain.

a. **Table L**

Input, x	Output, L(x)
0	1
−1	−1
−2	−3
1	3
2	5

b. **Table M**

Input, x	Output, M(x)
0	0
1	3
2	12
3	27
4	48

c. **Table N**

Input, x	Output, N(x)
0	3
1	3
2	3
3	3
4	3

d. **Table O**

Input, x	Output, O(x)
0	$-\frac{1}{3}$
1	0
2	$\frac{1}{3}$
3	$\frac{2}{3}$
4	1

Habits of Mind

Look for relationships. When a linear function such as $f(x) = ax + b$ matches a table, what is the relationship between a and b and the values in the table?

3. In the table the variable a represents an arbitrary number.

Input	Output	Δ
0	3	a
1	▪	a
2	▪	a
3	▪	a
4	4a + 3	a
5	▪	

a. Copy and complete the table by finding the missing outputs in terms of a.

b. Find a linear function that matches the table.

How can you know that there is such a linear function?

5.08 Constant Differences

4. In the table, variables *a* and *b* represent arbitrary numbers.

Input	Output	Δ
0	b	a
1	■	a
2	■	a
3	■	a
4	4a + b	a
5	■	

   a. Copy and complete the table in terms of *a* and *b*.
   b. Find a linear function that matches the table.
   c. You just proved Theorem 5.1 in parts (a) and (b). Explain.

5. Matt asks Emily for help in finding a function for Table P.

   Matt says, "The difference between consecutive rows is always two, but I can't make any linear function work."

   Emily replies, "That's because there is no linear function that works."

   Table P

Input, n	Output, P(n)
0	1
1	−1
2	1
3	−1
4	1

   a. Does this table represent a linear function? If so, what is it? If not, does this table of values contradict Theorem 5.1? Explain, using a graph or a diagram.
   b. Describe the pattern in this table using words. Then write the pattern in $x \mapsto$ form.

On Your Own

6. **What's Wrong Here?** Matt decides whether a linear function generated Table D. Matt reasons, "Each output is two more than the previous output, so the function must be linear, but I can't make any rule work. For instance, $f(x) = 2x + 1$ works for the first few inputs, but it doesn't work for inputs 4 or 7."

Table D

Input, x	Output, f(x)
0	1
1	3
2	5
4	7
7	9

   a. What is Matt doing wrong? Explain.

   b. Use plotted points or a diagram to show that the table does not match a linear function.

7. When a diver goes under water, the weight of the water exerts pressure on the diver. The table shows how the water pressure on the diver increases as the diver's depth increases.

Water Pressure on a Diver

Diver's Depth (ft)	Water Pressure (lb/in.²)
10	4.4
20	8.8
30	13.2
40	17.6
50	22.0

   a. What is the water pressure on a diver at a depth of 60 feet? At a depth of 100 feet? Explain.

   b. Write an equation describing the relationship between the depth D and the pressure P.

   c. Use your equation in part (b) to determine the depth of the diver, assuming the water pressure on the diver is 46.2 pounds per square inch. Explain.

8. Copy and complete each table.

a.
Input	Output	Δ
0		6
1		6
2		6
3		6
4	13	6
5		

b.
Input	Output	Δ
0	1	
1	3	
2	9	
3	27	
4	81	
5	243	

c.
Input	Output	Δ
0	−2	
1	−$\frac{6}{5}$	
2	−$\frac{2}{5}$	
3	$\frac{2}{5}$	$\frac{4}{5}$
4	$\frac{6}{5}$	
5	2	

d.
Input	Output	Δ
0		−2
1		−2
2	5	−2
3		−2
4		−2
5		

e. Which tables can you generate using a linear function?

f. Write a function for each table.

9. Emma cannot remember a linear function rule. She does remember that when 2 is the input, 3 is the output. When 4 is the input, 11 is the output. Does Emma remember enough to find a linear function rule? Explain.

10. **Standardized Test Prep** The table shows the annual salaries of company employees based on the number of years of employment. What is the annual salary of an employee who has just completed 10 years of service?

    A. $46,500 B. $45,000
    C. $43,500 D. $40,000

Annual Salary

Years of Employment	Salary
0	$30,000
1	$31,500
2	$33,000
3	$34,500
4	$36,000

11. Find a linear function for each situation.
    a. Every even input gives an even output, and every odd input gives an odd output.
    b. Every even input gives an odd output, and every odd input gives an even output.
    c. Both even and odd inputs give odd outputs.

12. Without graphing, decide whether each table matches a linear function. For each table, graph the data and write a linear function, if possible.

a. **Table H**

Input	Output
0	12
1	9
2	6
3	3
4	0

b. **Table I**

Input	Output
0	11
1	3
2	2
3	1
4	−7

c. **Table J**

Input	Output
0	12
1	6
2	3
3	$\frac{3}{2}$
4	$\frac{3}{4}$

d. **Table K**

Input	Output
0	$\frac{1}{2}$
1	$1\frac{2}{3}$
2	$2\frac{5}{6}$
3	4
4	$5\frac{1}{6}$

Maintain Your Skills

13. Copy and complete each table. Find a linear function that gives the outputs.

a.

Input	Output	Δ
0	5	■
1	8	■
2	11	■
3	14	■
4	17	

b.

Input	Output	Δ
0	−7	■
1	−4	■
2	−1	■
3	2	■
4	5	

c.

Input	Output	Δ
0	12	■
1	9	■
2	6	■
3	3	■
4	0	

d.

Input	Output	Δ
0	r	s
1	■	s
2	■	s
3	■	s
4	■	

5.09 Recursive Rules

In Lesson 5.08 you used the hockey stick method to find a linear function, $x \mapsto 3 + 5x$, that matches this table.

Input	Output	Δ
0	3	5
1	8	5
2	13	5
3	18	5
4	23	5
5	28	5
6	33	

There is another way to describe this function rule. You can say, "The output for 0 is 3. For integer inputs that increase by 1, each output after the first one is 5 more than the previous output." This description of a function is an example of a **recursive rule**, an idea that is very useful in mathematics and science.

The first row in the table shows the starting number, or **base case,** 3. You can determine each row after the first row by looking at the row directly above it. Then follow the recursive rule of adding 5 to the previous output. The first several outputs are as follows.

$$f(0) = 3$$
$$f(1) = f(0) + 5 = 3 + 5 = 8$$
$$f(2) = f(1) + 5 = 8 + 5 = 13$$

> You can think of recursive rules as descriptions that tell how to get an output from previous outputs.

For You to Do

1. Describe a recursive rule that agrees with the table.

Input	Output
0	3
1	7
2	11
3	15
4	19
5	23
6	27

Developing Habits of Mind

Find associations. Often you can associate what you learn in mathematics to things you see in everyday life. For example, a recursive rule produces patterns similar to patterns you see in nature.

Plants and trees often look as if they consist of smaller copies of themselves. A pine tree branch looks like the whole pine tree. A broccoli floret looks like a smaller version of the whole broccoli head. A recursive rule is similar, because the rule $f(n)$ contains a copy of itself, $f(n-1)$.

When you write a recursive rule, you tell how to get the next output from the previous output. For example, suppose you have a function f that matches the table shown. Instead of writing "The output for input 6 is the output for input 5 plus the difference 5," you can write the following equation.

$$f(6) = f(5) + 5$$

This reasoning works for other inputs, such as

$$f(5) = f(4) + 5$$
$$f(4) = f(3) + 5$$

n	f(n)	Δ
0	3	5
1	8	5
2	13	5
3	18	5
4	23	5
5	28	5
6	33	

The "backing up" method described here to find outputs does not work for the input 0. For 0, you need to find the output using the function equation. This statement of output is called the base case.

As the pattern continues, you get, for example,

$$f(127) = f(126) + 5$$

In general, $f(n) = f(n-1) + 5$. To calculate any output for function f, you need to use the function f itself. Suppose you have a function machine for f. If you open it, you would find another copy of the machine for function f.

To summarize the function using the recursive rule and base case, you write the following equation.

$$f(n) = \begin{cases} 3 & \text{if } n = 0 \\ f(n-1) + 5 & \text{if } n > 0 \end{cases}$$

For help defining a function recursively, see the TI-Nspire Handbook, p. 778.

For Discussion

2. Tony thinks that the recursive rule above defines a function that is the same as the linear function $x \mapsto 3 + 5x$. Is he correct? Test your answer with an input of $\frac{1}{2}$.

Example

Problem James saves $85. He wants to put it in a savings account so it will gain interest. Bank L makes the following offer: "If you keep your money with us, at the end of every year we'll give you $5." How much money will James have after 5 years if he invests in Bank L? Write a recursive rule that tells the amount of money James will have after n years.

Solution You can use a calculator to find the totals for the first few years. Enter the outputs in a table.

Bank L

Year	James's Savings	Interest
0	$ 85	$5
1	$ 90	$5
2	$ 95	$5
3	$100	$5
4	$105	$5
5	$110	

> For help showing the totals on a spreadsheet, see the TI-Nspire Handbook, p. 778.

At this point you can graph the results, or you can take a shortcut. Notice that the difference between consecutive outputs in the table is always $5. You can generate the table using a linear function. Since 5 is the value in the column, you know that the graph has a slope of 5. Since the output for 0 is 85, $f(n) = 85 + 5n$.

For Discussion

3. Across the street from Bank L is Bank E. It offers James the following investment plan: "Every year, we'll add 5% of the money you had the previous year to your account." James sets up this table to explore Bank E's plan.

   Copy and complete the table, rounding to the nearest cent. Which bank offers the greater return on James's money in the short run? In the long run?

Bank E

Year	James's Savings	Interest
0	$85	$4.25
1	▪	▪
2	▪	▪
3	▪	▪
4	▪	▪
5	▪	

> This rule is recursive, but it is different from the previous one. The resulting table does not have constant differences, so it cannot be matched with a linear function. However, can you still find a pattern?

Exercises Practicing Habits of Mind

Check Your Understanding

1. Copy and complete Table 1 using each of the following rules.

   a. To get a new output, add 4 to the previous output.

   b. To get a new output, multiply the previous output by 3.

   c. To get a new output, multiply the previous output by 2 and then add 2.

   d. To get a new output, multiply the input by 4 and then add 2.

   Table 1

Input	Output
0	2
1	6
2	■
3	■
4	■
5	■

2. Which of the tables generates a linear function? Find a linear function for each table if possible.

   a. Table 2

Input	Output
0	8
1	4
2	2
3	1
4	$\frac{1}{2}$

   b. Table 3

Input	Output
0	5
1	7
2	9
3	11
4	13

   c. Table 4

Input	Output
0	−3
1	−1
2	1
3	3
4	5

   d. Table 5

Input	Output
0	3.4
1	34
2	340
3	3,400
4	34,000

3. Write a recursive rule for each table in Exercise 2.

5.09 Recursive Rules

4. Adam proposes that his mother changes his allowance according to the following rule: "The first week, you'll only give me $.02. Then each week after the first week, you'll pay twice what you paid the week before." He explains that even though this is less than the $5 per week he gets now, he will feel better because he will always get more than he got the previous week.

   a. If Adam's mother agrees with him, how much will Adam receive in the fifth week?

   b. How much will his allowance be in the tenth week? In the fifteenth week?

5. In Exercise 4, Adam tries to convince his mother to change his allowance. Adam's mother offers the following plan instead: "The first week you get $.16. Then each week after the first week you get $1.00 plus 75% of the previous week's allowance."

   a. Make a table that shows how much Adam will get for each of the first five weeks.

   b. How much will he get in the tenth week? In the fifteenth week?

   c. Is his mother's plan a better deal for Adam than his plan?

6. Adam makes a last attempt to outsmart his mother. He explains, "We'll use the same plan you proposed, except instead of starting with $.16, I'll start with $10."

   a. Make a table that shows how much Adam will get each of the first five weeks.

   b. How much will he get in the tenth week? In the fifteenth week?

   c. Is Adam's new plan a good deal for Adam in the short run? In the long run?

Adam used to get $5 per week for allowance.

7. Maria knows a mystery function g. She says, "First of all, $g(0) = 1$. Next, to get any output, multiply the input by the previous output. For example,

   $g(5) = 5 \cdot g(4)$
   $g(6) = 6 \cdot g(5)$
   $g(15) = 15 \cdot g(14)$

   and so on."

   Make a table showing the first six entries for Maria's function. Can you find a simple rule that matches the table?

On Your Own

8. Do these two functions produce the same output for every nonnegative integer input? Make a table for each rule.

   $f: x \mapsto \frac{x}{3} - \frac{2}{3}$

   $g:$ When the input is 0, the output is $-\frac{2}{3}$. To get each new output, add $\frac{1}{3}$ to the previous output.

9. Dana's parents start saving money for her college education. They deposit $5000 in a fund that earns 10% interest at the end of each year. Write a recursive rule that describes how the amount of money increases over time. How much money will Dana's parents have after 3 years?

10. **Standardized Test Prep** Zack charges $2.50 per hour for baby-sitting one child. He charges $.75 per hour for each additional child. Which table shows Zack's hourly charges for baby-sitting?

    A.
Number of Children	Hourly Charge
1	$2.50
2	$3.25
3	$3.25

    B.
Number of Children	Hourly Charge
1	$3.25
2	$4.00
3	$4.75

    C.
Number of Children	Hourly Charge
1	$2.50
2	$3.25
3	$4.00

    D.
Number of Children	Hourly Charge
1	$3.25
2	$4.00
3	$4.00

11. Anna earns money by raking leaves. She buys a rake that costs $20. For each lawn she rakes, she earns $6.

    a. Make a table using the number of lawns as the input. The amount of money she makes is the output. Calculate how much money Anna earns when she rakes 0 to 5 lawns.

    b. Describe the pattern in the output values. Can a linear function generate this table?

    c. Anna wants to buy a video game that costs $54.99. How many lawns will she need to rake to earn that amount?

    Anna will lose money when she does not rake any lawns.

12. Dana's grandparents invest $5500 in an educational fund. The fund earns 6% interest at the end of each year. Write a recursive rule that describes how the amount of money will grow over time. How much money will Dana's grandparents have after 3 years? Round to the nearest penny.

13. You can make patterns of shapes by connecting matchsticks. Stage 1 is one square. You can obtain each consecutive stage by adding a square to the side of the previous stage. Draw a diagram showing Stages 4 and 5. Copy and complete the table. Write a recursive rule that describes this pattern.

Matchsticks Table

Stage	Number of Matchsticks
1	4
2	7
3	■
4	■
5	■

Maintain Your Skills

Make a table for each recursive rule. Use the integers 0 to 4 for input values. If possible, find a linear function that generates each table.

Inputs   Output

14. a. Rule A $\begin{cases} 0 \\ 1 \text{ to } 4 \end{cases}$ 3
 6 more than the previous output

   b. Rule B $\begin{cases} 0 \\ 1 \text{ to } 4 \end{cases}$ -4
 6 more than the previous output

   c. Rule C $\begin{cases} 0 \\ 1 \text{ to } 4 \end{cases}$ $\frac{1}{2}$
 6 more than the previous output

   d. Rule D $\begin{cases} 0 \\ 1 \text{ to } 4 \end{cases}$ 3
 6 times the previous output

Inputs   Output

15. a. Rule 1 $\begin{cases} 0 \\ 1 \text{ to } 4 \end{cases}$ 3
 3 more than the previous output

   b. Rule 2 $\begin{cases} 0 \\ 1 \text{ to } 4 \end{cases}$ 3
 6 less than the previous output

   c. Rule 3 $\begin{cases} 0 \\ 1 \text{ to } 4 \end{cases}$ 3
 $\frac{1}{2}$ more than the previous output

   d. Rule 4 $\begin{cases} 0 \\ 1 \text{ to } 4 \end{cases}$ 3
 $\frac{1}{2}$ times the previous output

Mathematical Reflections 5B

In this investigation, you explored linear functions and learned how to write recursive rules using data in a table. These questions will help you summarize what you have learned.

1. Copy and complete each table. Find a function that produces each table.

   a.
Input	Output	Δ
0	■	3
1	■	3
2	■	3
3	■	3
4	14	3
5	■	3

   b.
Input	Output	Δ
0	5	■
1	2	■
2	−1	■
3	−4	■
4	−7	■
5	−10	

2. Make a table for each recursive rule. Use the integer inputs from 0 to 5. Which tables can you generate using a linear function?

   a. If 0 is the input, the output is 3. To get a new output, take the previous output and subtract 2.

   b. If 0 is the input, the output is 8. To get a new output, multiply the previous output by $\frac{1}{2}$.

3. How do you find a function that matches a table?

4. What is a recursive rule? How can you use recursion to define functions?

5. What is a recursive rule for the values in the table?

Input	Output
−1	6
0	5
1	4
2	3
3	2

Vocabulary

In this investigation, you learned these terms. Make sure you understand what each one means and how to use it.

- base case
- linear function
- recursive rule

Recursion ends when there is no more input.

Investigation 5C

Functions and Situations

In *Functions and Situations*, you will build function-machine networks and write recursive functions. Then you will learn how you can use these networks to understand banking situations.

By the end of this investigation, you will be able to answer questions like these.

1. How can you use functions to solve problems?

2. When do you use a recursively defined function?

3. What is the monthly payment on a 48-month car loan at 7.9% APR if the car costs $12,000?

You will learn how to
- translate a word problem into an equation
- build and understand a function-machine network
- find a recursive function that models a word problem
- write a rule for a recursive function
- work with recursive functions

You will develop these habits and skills:
- Build function-machine networks.
- Use the guess-check-generalize strategy to solve more advanced word problems.
- Use tables to answer questions about recursive functions.

The input is a dollar bill.

5.10 Getting Started

Using the guess-check-generalize strategy, you can sometimes find the rule for a function. A more efficient way to find a function rule is to build a function-machine network that shows your calculations. Then you can write the rule without guessing.

For You to Explore

For Problems 1 and 2, use this function machine network. Both inputs and outputs are single numbers.

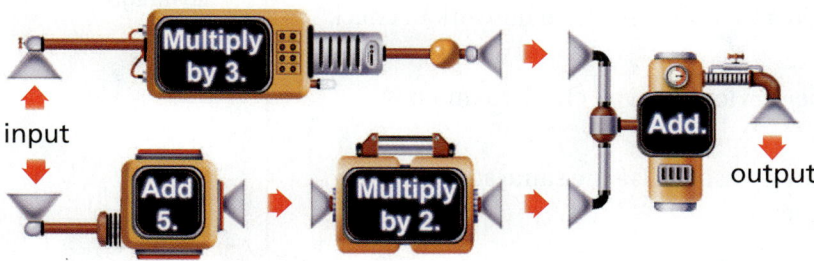

1. **a.** If the input is 6, what is the output?
    b. If the input is -6, what is the output?
    c. If the input increases by 1, how does output change?
    d. Write a rule for the output of this network using function notation, $f(n)$, where n is the input to the network.

2. **a.** If the input is 15, what is the output?
    b. If the output is 15, what is the input?
    c. If the output is 16, what is the input?
    d. If the output is y, find the input in terms of y.

Problems 3 and 4 are similar to problems in Lesson 2.14, except now you will use function-machine networks.

3. Ben chooses a certain number. He says, "There's an amazing fact about my number. First you need to know about something I call the four 4's. You can get four different answers when you add 4 to my number, subtract 4 from my number, multiply my number by 4, or divide my number by 4. That's not impressive, but when you add all those answers, you get exactly 60."

    a. Build a function-machine network that represents all the calculations Ben does to get 60.
    b. Use the function-machine network to find whether Ben's number is 12.
    c. Use a function network to find Ben's number. Describe how you found it.
    d. Use a function network to find the number whose four 5's (add 5, subtract 5, multiply by 5, and divide by 5) have a sum of 144.

Habits of Mind

Experiment. Choose a reasonable maximum for Ben's number. Then test each number using Ben's conditions. When you find Ben's number, the output of the network is 60.

4. About A.D. 500, a collection of puzzles included a problem about the Greek mathematician Diophantus, who lived around A.D. 250. Here is another way to state the problem.

He was a child one sixth of his life.
He grew a beard after one twelfth more.
One seventh later, he took a wife.
Five years later, a son his wife bore.
Exactly half as long as he did, lived his son.
Four years later, over Diophantus death won.

How old was he?

a. Guess how old Diophantus was when he died. Then check your guess. Do not worry about making a good guess!

→ Diophantus's age is an integer.

b. Make another guess. Then build a function-machine network to check your guess.

c. Suppose your guess is a number n. How can you check to find out whether n is the correct answer?

d. Find the correct answer without guessing. Use the same steps you followed to check numerical guesses.

5. Consider the function $f(a) = a^3 + 7$.

→ The expression $a^3 + 7$ tells you to cube the input and then add 7. The variable a is a placeholder. You can replace a using numbers and expressions.

a. Write an expression for $f(1003)$. Without calculating, how many digits does this number have?

b. Write an expression for $f(7 + 5)$ without calculating anything (not even $7 + 5$). Why does this expression include parentheses? Then calculate the entire result.

c. When $n = 7$, find the value of $f(n) + f(n - 1) + f(n - 2)$.

d. **Take It Further** Find a value for n that makes $f(n) - f(n - 1) = 1261$.

6. Veronica has a BigBank credit card that has an annual percentage rate (APR) of 18%. The APR is the rate of change for the balance each year. Each month, she gets a statement with the current balance for her credit card.

a. BigBank charges 1.5% interest per month. Explain how this figure relates to the 18% APR.

b. When Veronica owes $2000 on her credit card, how much is her monthly interest charge?

c. BigBank expects a minimum payment of 2.5% on the current balance. When Veronica owes $2000 on her credit card, how much is her minimum payment?

d. Veronica's balance at the end of the month is the starting balance for the month, plus the interest owed, and minus the monthly payment. When Veronica owes $1200 on the credit card, what is her balance at the end of the month?

e. Build a function-machine network using the balance at the start of a month as the input. The output is the balance at the end of that month.

Exercises Practicing Habits of Mind

On Your Own

7. Veronica's BigBank credit card balance reaches her credit limit at $2000. BigBank charges 18% annual interest, which it divides into 12 payments. (In other words, BigBank charges 1.5% interest per month.) The bank expects a minimum monthly payment of 2.5% of the balance.

   a. How much does Veronica still owe at the end of the first month, after making the minimum payment and paying the 1.5% interest?

   b. Based on the new balance at the end of the first month, recalculate Veronica's next minimum monthly payment (2.5% of the new balance) and her next interest payment (1.5% of the new balance).

   c. Find Veronica's balance at the end of one year (12 months) when she continues to make only the minimum monthly payment.

   d. **Take It Further** After how many months will Veronica owe less than $1000?

8. Ancient Egyptian mathematicians used the concept of *false position* to solve equations. They guessed a convenient answer and then adjusted to find the correct answer. The false position method assumes that an incorrect result is correct. Then when you check the incorrect result, you find the correct result.

   Consider this problem. A number plus one fourth of itself equals 210. What is the number?

   a. What result do you get when you guess 4? Why is 4 a convenient guess?

   b. What result do you get when you guess 12? How does this result relate to the result in part (a)?

   c. Use the relationship between the results of your guesses to solve the exercise.

   d. When your guess is n, find a function $f(n)$ relating the guess to the result. Use the function to solve the exercise.

9. A certificate of deposit carries an annual interest rate of 4.5%. This means you earn $4.50 in interest in one year for every $100 you invest.

   a. You invest d dollars. Explain why you will have $d + 0.045d$ at the end of one year.

   b. If you invest $1000, how much money will you have at the end of 15 years?

   c. If you invest $4000, how much money will you have at the end of 15 years? How is the amount of money related to investing $1000?

   d. How much do you need to invest to have $10,000 at the end of 15 years?

> Actually, most credit card companies split the monthly interest charge into daily charges.

> **Habits of Mind**
> **Make a guess.** Before you solve Exercise 7d, guess the result. Then check your guess by solving the exercise.

5.10 Getting Started **485**

10. Derek is trying to qualify for a figure skating team. Qualification is based on the mean of six performance scores using the 6.0 judging system. Derek knows that he needs at least a 4.7 mean score in the six events to qualify. His scores for the first five events are 5.5, 4.6, 3.9, 5.2, and 4.1.

    a. For the first five events, what is Derek's mean event score? Derek's median event score?

    b. Derek scores a 4.8 in the final event. Will he make the team? Show your work.

    c. Build a function-machine network in which the input is Derek's last event score. The output is his mean score for all six events.

    d. Use the function-machine network to find the minimum score Derek needs to make the team.

11. a. **Take It Further** The rules change so that the mean score does not include the highest and lowest scores. What score does Derek now need to make the team?

    b. When Derek excludes the highest and lowest scores, what is the highest possible mean score he can get? What is the lowest possible mean score?

Maintain Your Skills

Use the function $f(x) = \frac{1}{2}x - 7$.

12. Calculate each value.

    a. $f(2)$
    b. $f(-6)$
    c. $f(-10)$
    d. $f(f(2))$
    e. $f(f(f(2)))$

13. Find the value of x.

    a. $f(x) = 3$
    b. $f(x) = -10$
    c. $f(x) = x$
    d. $f(x) = \frac{1}{2}x + 3$

5.11 From Situations To Equations

In Lesson 5.02, you built a function to calculate the total cost of items at a music store. Using the guess-check-generalize strategy, you can build a detailed function network that makes it easier to write equations and solve problems.

Example

Problem At a music store Web site, CDs cost 28% off the original price. After that discount, you add a 5% sales tax and a $2 shipping charge.

a. Build a function-machine network using the original price of a CD as the input. The output is the cost on the music store Web site.

b. If a CD costs $15 on the music store Web site, what was its original price?

Solution

a. To build the function-machine network, test an input value. Keep track of your steps. The steps below show the results when the price is $20.

Step 1 Calculate the discount: 28% of $20 is $0.28 \cdot \$20 = \$5.60$.

Step 2 Subtract the discount from $20 to get the cost of the CD: $\$20 - \$5.60 = \$14.40$.

Step 3 Calculate the tax: 5% of $\$14.40 = 0.05 \cdot \$14.40 = \$.72$.

Step 4 Add the tax to the cost of the CD: $\$14.40 + \$.72 = \$15.12$.

Step 5 Add a $2 shipping charge to the total cost of the CD: $\$15.12 + \$2.00 = \$17.12$.

Record each step. Draw a function machine for these steps.

> You can test any value. Your goal is to find the steps to build the correct function. You are not trying to choose the correct input that produces $15.

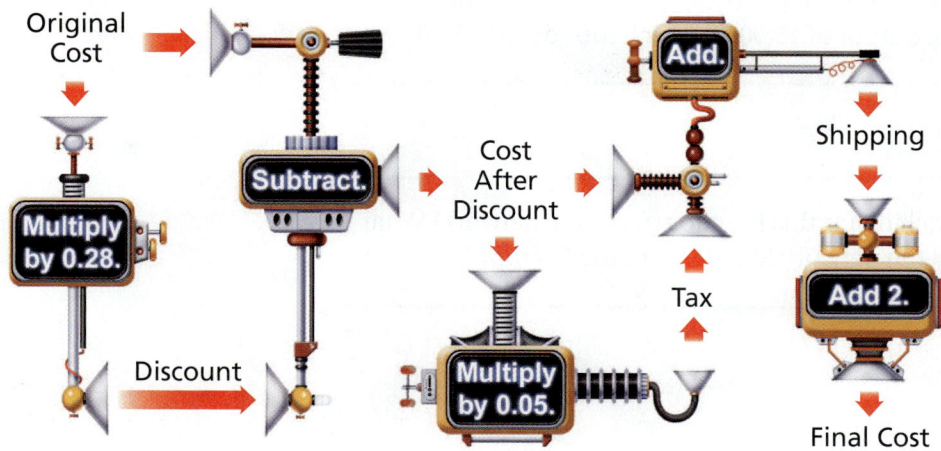

b. You know that the total cost of the CD is $15, which means the output value is 15. You want to find the original price of the CD, or the input value. To do this, use the function-machine network from part (a) to build an equation. Then solve the equation.

Suppose you drop the variable x into the machine. What is the output?

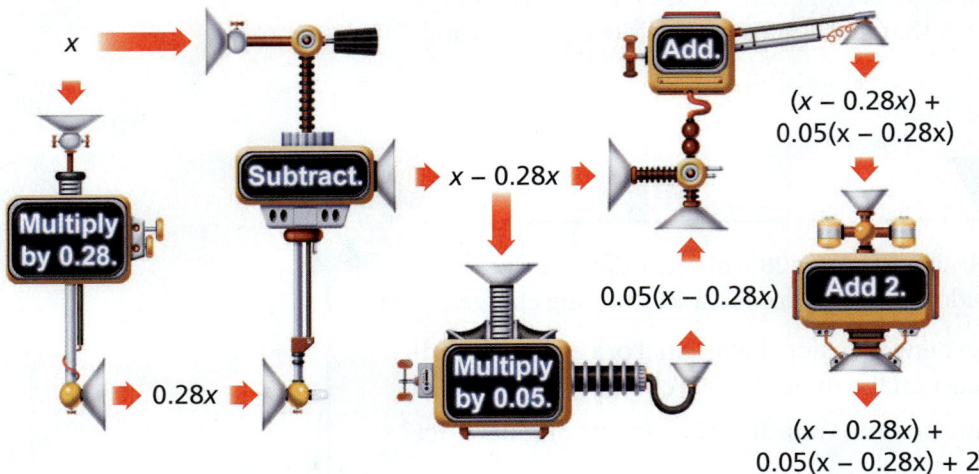

When the variable x is input, the expression $(x - 0.28x) + 0.05(x - 0.28x) + 2$ is output. If you want to find the input when the output is 15, write an equation. Set the output expression equal to the output value 15. Then you can solve for x using the basic moves.

$$(x - 0.28x) + 0.05(x - 0.28x) + 2 = 15$$
$$0.72x + 0.05(0.72x) + 2 = 15$$
$$0.72x + 0.036x + 2 = 15$$
$$0.756x + 2 = 15$$
$$0.756x = 13$$
$$x = \frac{13}{0.756} \approx 17.20$$

$x - 0.28x = 0.72x$

The original price was $17.20. Running this value through the function machine network gives an output of 15.0032, which rounds to $15.00.

For Discussion

1. Why can't you use backtracking for this function-machine network? What are some ways to simplify the network in part (b) of the Example?

Developing Habits of Mind

Look for a process. The two questions below are based on the example. Even though the questions appear very similar, they are different.

- Suppose a CD normally costs $20. How much does it cost on the music store Web site?
- A CD costs $15 on the music store Web site. How much did it cost originally?

The first question is simpler to answer than the second question. You can find the total cost on the music store Web site by doing one calculation at a time. You do not need to keep track of your steps.

The second question is harder to answer, because you cannot easily backtrack the process. You can restate this question by asking how to find x, such that $f(x) = 15$. To build this equation, you need to know how to define the function f.

Here is where a function-machine network can help. While you are calculating $f(20)$, you are also building a network and the rule for $f(x)$. Drawing a network is another tool for keeping track of your steps. It helps you define the function f, so that you can solve an equation.

During a field trip to an art museum, Sasha and Derman overhear their teacher, Ms. Meyer, say, "Isn't it wonderful? We used our budget wisely for this trip. They were going to charge $9 per student, but we talked them down to $6. With the extra money, we were able to bring another busload of students."

Minds in Action   episode 21

After overhearing their teacher, Sasha and Derman discuss cost.

Sasha Now we can figure out what the teachers spent on this trip.

Derman Why would we want to do that?

Sasha I don't know, for experience with high finance? So, we know that a busload is 47 students, but I can't figure out a way to get the answer right away.

Derman Let's just guess.

Sasha You guess how much money they spent. I'll figure out whether that's enough for 47 more students.

Derman Two thousand dollars!

Sasha Well, 2000 isn't divisible by six or nine. Pick a number that's a multiple of nine. Then it will be easier for me.

Derman Okay. Eighteen hundred dollars!

Sasha Good one. Let's see, if they spent $1800, then they could bring $1800 divided by $6, or 300 students. Before they got the lower price, they could only bring $1800 divided by $9, or 200 students. So, now they could bring 100 more students.
That's too many.

$$\frac{1800}{6} - \frac{1800}{9} = 100$$

Derman I'll guess a lower amount. Nine hundred dollars!

Sasha Alright, you figure this one out.

Derman Okay. Using $900 they can bring $900 divided by $6. That's 150 kids. With the higher price they can bring $900 divided by $9, which is 100. So, 50 more kids. Wow, that's close.

$$\frac{900}{6} - \frac{900}{9} = 50$$

Sasha We know the real answer is just a little less than $900.

Derman Eight hundred ninety-nine dollars!

Sasha Enough guessing! Look, we keep doing the same operations.

Sasha draws this network.

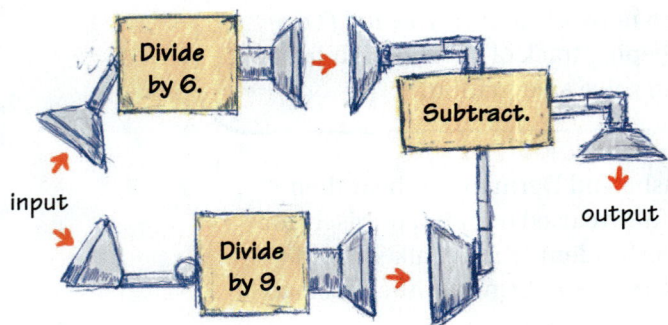

Sasha We can use this machine to build an equation.

Derman Your network says to divide the input by 6, divide the input by 9, and then subtract. The output should be 47. And that's the equation. I'll use the variable b for the input, or budget value.

$$\frac{b}{6} - \frac{b}{9} = 47$$

Sasha We know how to solve that. See, the budget was $846.

Derman Pretty smooth.

For Discussion

2. What steps will you take to solve the equation that Derman finds?

3. Another way to represent this situation is to find the original number of students instead of using the budget. Can you build an equation by guessing, checking, and keeping track of your steps?

Example

Problem The manager of the Texarkana Tube Sox notes that his team has achieved his goal for the year. He says, "Well, right now we're 14 games over .500. We've won 55 percent of our games." What is the Tube Sox's record right now?

> The phrase *14 games over .500* means the team has won 14 more games than it has lost. For example, a team whose record is 22–8 is 14 games over .500.

Solution To solve this problem, build a function-machine network and write an equation. First, choose a variable. Then, ask yourself, "What do I want to find?" You want to solve for the number of wins that the team has now, so that number is the variable. Start by guessing the number of wins. Then check to find whether the percent is correct. Keep track of the steps to build the network.

Guess	**Win-Loss Record**	**Percent Wins**
22 wins: losses: 22–14, or 8 losses	22–8	$\frac{22}{22+8} = 0.733$
50 wins: losses: 50–14, or 36 losses	50–36	$\frac{50}{50+36} = 0.581$

Based on the guesses, the actual number of wins is probably higher than 50. When you keep track of the steps, you can draw this network.

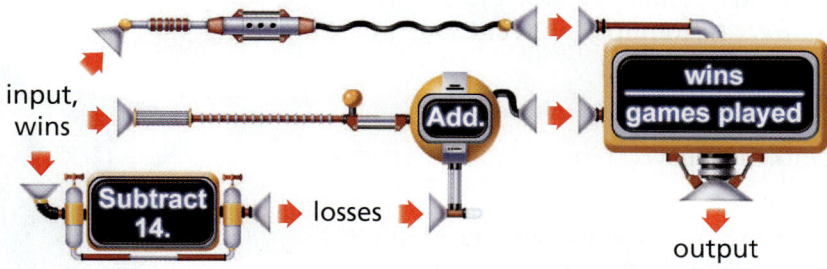

If the input (number of wins) is w, you can find the output from the network by calculating $\frac{w}{2w-14}$.

You want to find the value for w when this expression equals 55 percent. An equation for the problem is $\frac{w}{2w-14} = 0.55$.

> **Remember...**
> The word *percent* means to divide by 100. You can write 55 percent as $\frac{55}{100}$ or 0.55.

You can solve this equation for w by multiplying each side by the quantity $(2w - 14)$. Then use some further basic moves for solving equations.

$$\frac{w}{2w-14} = 0.55$$
$$\frac{w}{2w-14} \cdot (2w-14) = 0.55(2w-14)$$
$$w = 1.1w - 7.7$$
$$w - 1.1w = 1.1w - 7.7 - 1.1w$$
$$-0.1w = -7.7$$
$$w = 77$$

To check your result, find the percent of wins. The record of 77 wins and 63 losses gives a winning percent of exactly 55 percent.

5.11 From Situations to Equations

For Discussion

4. Another way to figure out the record is to guess the number of games the Tube Sox have played. Let g be the total number of games played. Build an equation that g satisfies. Then solve it. You can calculate the number of wins and losses from the total number of games.

> In the example, the total number of games is 140. Make sure that $g = 140$ is a solution to your equation.

Exercises Practicing Habits of Mind

Check Your Understanding

1. In Lesson 2.01, Spiro the Spectacular did this number trick: Choose a number. Add 6. Multiply by 3. Subtract 10. Multiply by 2. Add 50. Divide by 6.
   a. Draw a function-machine network to represent Spiro's steps.
   b. Draw a function-machine network that allows Spiro to undo the steps and find your number.

2. Here is one of Maya's tricks from Lesson 2.01: Choose a number. Multiply by 3. Subtract 4. Multiply by 2. Add 20. Divide by 6. Subtract your starting number.
   a. Draw a function-machine network that represents Maya's trick.
   b. Why can't you draw a function-machine network that undoes Maya's calculation?
   c. Write a function $S(n)$ using the number you chose as the input, and Maya's result as the output. Write the simplest rule possible.

3. At a movie, student tickets cost $5 each and adult tickets cost $8 each. A total of 104 people attended the event.
   a. If 30 students attended, how much ticket money did the theater collect?
   b. Build a function-machine network using the number of student tickets as the input. The output is the amount of ticket money.
   c. If the amount of ticket money was $640, how many students bought tickets?

4. The length of a rectangle is 7 inches longer than the width. The rectangle's area is 1 square foot. What are the dimensions of the rectangle?

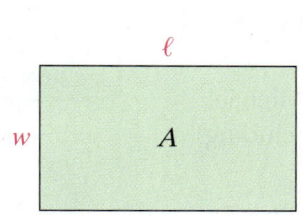
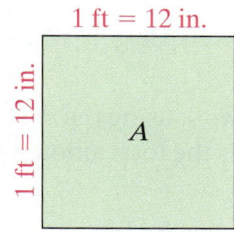

Remember...
To find the area of a rectangle, multiply the length times the width.

Suppose a rectangle has an area of 1 square foot. The rectangle has the same area as a square that is 1 foot on each side. One foot equals 12 inches, so 1 square foot is the same area as a square that is 12 inches by 12 inches.

5. Use graph paper to draw a diagram of your answer to Exercise 4. Show how to cut the rectangle so that you can rearrange its pieces to form a square with sides that are 1 foot in length.

6. A round trip flight from Seattle, Washington, to Orlando, Florida, is one of the longest flights in the continental United States. Due to the jet stream that blows from west to east, a plane flying nonstop from Seattle to Orlando flies at an average speed of 523 miles per hour. The same plane flying from Orlando to Seattle travels at an average speed of 415 miles per hour. The full round trip takes exactly 11 hours. How far is Seattle from Orlando, to the nearest mile?

7. A function $f(n)$ is only defined for positive integers. It operates differently for even and odd integers.

$$f(n) = \begin{cases} 3n + 1 & \text{if } n \text{ is odd} \\ \frac{n}{2} & \text{if } n \text{ is even} \end{cases}$$

In words, this function tells you that if n is an odd number, you triple the number n and add 1. If n is an even number, you divide the number n in half.

a. Find $f(n)$ if $n = 10, 11, 12,$ and 13.

b. The value of $f(3)$ is 10. Find another number k such that $f(k) = 10$.

c. If $n = 5$, find the result of running the number n through this function twice. In other words, find $f(f(5))$.

d. If $n = 5$, find the result of running the number n through this function seven times.

e. **Take It Further** If $n = 5$, find the result of running the number n through this function 100 times.

In other words, take n, find its output f(n), and then find the output when that number is the input.

5.11 From Situations to Equations

On Your Own

8. Michael joins the Old Barn book club. He gets a 10% discount on books and CDs. It costs $15 to join the club.

   a. Build a function-machine network using the cost of the books Michael buys as the input. The output is the total amount he will pay, including the $15 membership fee.

   b. Find a rule for $C(d)$, Michael's cost for buying d dollars worth of books and CDs on the day he joins the club.

   c. How much does Michael need to spend to make joining the club worth the $15 cost?

9. In a 50-50 raffle, half of the collected money goes to prizes and half goes to the charity running the raffle. The charity sells 800 tickets at 75 cents each. The first prize is $150. The second prize is $60. There are three third prizes.

   a. How much money does the charity give in 50-50 raffle prizes?

   b. All three third prizes are worth the same amount. Write an equation that you can use to find the value of each third prize.

   c. Suppose the charity sells only 640 tickets. When the first and second prizes remain the same, what is the total value of the three third prizes?

10. Brent and Jill run the Carolina Cross Country Team competition for two divisions. An entry in the A Division costs $10. An entry in the B Division costs $5. Brent says, "Wow, we had 195 entries. Outstanding."

    a. Brent estimates that 80 entries are for the A Division. If he is correct, how much money did Jill and he collect for entries?

    b. Jill says, "It turns out we collected $1525 for entries. That's not bad." How many A Division entries were there?

11. **Write About It** Adam agrees to new terms on his allowance. He will get 20 cents for the first week. Every week after that, he will get 40 cents more than the week before. Then $A(w) = 0.4w + 0.2$ is a function for his allowance for week w. Explain how to find the total amount of money Adam earns in four months (17 weeks).

> How did Adam find a rule for this function?

12. Adam realizes he has not received as much money in the first four months as his previous $5 allowance per week. He expects that to change quickly. He finds a formula to show the total amount of money he has at the end of w weeks. Adam shows his sister Eva that this function represents his total allowance.

$$T(w) = \begin{cases} 0.2 & \text{if } w = 1 \\ T(w-1) + 0.4w + 0.2 & \text{if } w > 1 \end{cases}$$

> You connect the two statements with the word or. The total allowance is 0.2 if $w = 1$ or the total allowance is $T(w-1) + 0.4w + 0.2$ if $w > 1$.

Eva says, "What, you only speak algebra? Why not just say that your allowance is 20 cents for the first week. Then after that, the new total is whatever amount you had before, plus whatever amount you made that week?"

a. According to the rule, what is the value of $T(1)$?

b. Use the rule to calculate the value of $T(2)$. Remember, you just calculated the value of $T(1)$. The formula uses the previous week's total to calculate the new total.

c. Use the rule to calculate the value of $T(3)$. Remember, you just calculated the value of $T(2)$.

d. Copy the table. Use the rule to complete this table.

e. **Take It Further** Find a pattern in the table. Find a rule that does not require calculating Adam's allowance for each week.

f. Find the amount of money Adam receives in a year (52 weeks). How does that amount compare to the $5 per week he received previously?

Weeks, w	Adam's Earnings, $T(w)$
1	■
2	■
3	■
4	■
5	■
6	■

13. **Standardized Test Prep** Xavier and Telisha live 52.5 miles apart and want to meet for a picnic. A bike path connects their hometowns. Each person starts out at the same time. Xavier walks at 15 minutes per mile. Telisha bikes 1 mile every 6 minutes. How many miles will Xavier walk before he meets Telisha on the bike path?

A. 12 B. 14 C. 15 D. 20

Maintain Your Skills

14. *Consecutive* means following in order. For example, 3, 5, and 7 are consecutive odd numbers.

a. The sum of three consecutive odd numbers is 147. Find the three numbers.

b. The sum of five consecutive odd numbers is 145. Find the average of the five numbers. Use the average to find the five numbers.

5.12 From Situations to Recursive Rules

In Lesson 5.09, you used this recursively defined function.

$$f(n) = \begin{cases} 3 & \text{if } n = 0 \\ f(n-1) + 5 & \text{if } n > 0 \end{cases}$$

When you read this function, use the word *or* to separate the two definitions, or cases, of the function. In words, the function of n equals 3 if n equals zero, or the function of n is given by the formula $f(n-1) + 5$ if n is greater than zero.

A key part of the notation is in the formula on the second line, $f(n-1) + 5$. You find the output for n by taking the previous output, $f(n-1)$, and adding 5. For example, you get $f(13)$ by adding 5 to $f(12)$.

The output values that this recursively defined function generates match the linear function $g(x) = 3 + 5x$, when you input nonnegative integers. Recursively defined functions can also define functions that are not matched by linear functions. A common recursively defined function that computes compound interest does not match a linear function.

> The function $g(x) = 3 + 5x$ is in **closed form,** because you can write $g(x)$ as one expression.

Minds in Action   episode 22

Louis and Andrea talk about their credit card bill.

Louis What's up with this bill? It adds up fast. We owe a thousand dollars.

Andrea We'd better cut up the card right now. At least our interest rate is only 11.99% APR. That's better than a lot of credit cards. We'll pay it down.

Louis The bill tells us that we can pay as little as 2% of what we owe each month. So 2% of $1000 is 20 dollars. That's cheap.

Andrea Yes, but not all of that is going to pay it down. They're basically charging almost 1% interest per month. So 10 dollars of the 20 dollars just goes to interest.

Louis Okay, so after a month we'll owe $990. Then it will even get a little easier, since we won't have to pay as much. Give me a few minutes.

> Why is Andrea correct when she says that the interest is 1% per month? Andrea says that the annual rate is 11.99% and the bank calculates interest monthly. Each month the interest is one twelfth of 11.99%.

Louis builds this table on his computer.

Credit Card Payment: 2% Per Month

Month m	Starting Balance	Payment 2%	Interest 1%	Ending Balance
0	1000.00	(−) 20.00	(+)10.00	990.00
1	990.00	19.80	9.90	980.10
2	980.10	19.60	9.80	970.30
3	970.30	19.41	9.70	960.59
4	960.59	19.21	9.61	950.99
5	950.99	19.02	9.51	941.48
⋮	⋮	⋮	⋮	⋮
100	366.06	7.32	3.66	362.40

Louis Here, I built this payment plan using a spreadsheet. The numbers are rounded to the nearest cent, since they get messy. The spreadsheet shows how many months it will take to pay off the debt on the card. Let's look farther down.

Louis scrolls and scrolls.

Andrea Keep going. How far down are we now, 100 months?

Louis I know! Can you believe that? Even after 100 months we'll still owe more than a third of the money.

Andrea pushes a button to add all the entries in the payment column.

Andrea And we'll already have made over $1250 in payments. Only half of that amount went to pay down the principal. The other half went straight to the bank in interest.

Louis Well, what do we do? We can't just pay it off right now.

Andrea Maybe we can make more than the minimum payment. How does $50 per month sound?

Louis Alright, I guess. I'll change the spreadsheet.

Credit Card Payment: $50 Per Month

Month m	Starting Balance	Payment $50	Interest 1%	Ending Balance
0	1000.00	(−)50.00	(+)10.00	960.00
1	960.00	50.00	9.60	919.60
2	919.60	50.00	9.20	878.80
3	878.80	50.00	8.79	837.59
4	837.59	50.00	8.38	795.97
5	795.97	50.00	7.96	753.93
⋮	⋮	⋮	⋮	⋮
100	(5819.15)	50.00	(58.19)	(5927.34)

Louis So after 100 months, the bank owes us almost 6000 dollars?

Andrea No, no. It just means we've paid the whole thing off in less than 100 months. Get rid of all the rows with negatives. Here, month 22 is the last row.

In spreadsheets, accountants often display negative numbers by using parentheses instead of a negative sign. For example, (58.19) is the same as −58.19.

Credit Card Payment: $50 Per Month

Month m	Starting Balance	Payment $50	Interest 1%	Ending Balance
0	1000.00	(−) 50.00	(+)10.00	960.00
1	960.00	50.00	9.60	919.60
2	919.60	50.00	9.20	878.80
3	878.80	50.00	8.79	837.59
4	837.59	50.00	8.38	795.97
5	795.97	50.00	7.96	753.93
⋮	⋮	⋮	⋮	⋮
21	70.45	50.00	0.70	21.15
22	21.15	21.36	0.21	0.00

You can calculate the last payment by hand or program a computer to do the calculation.

Andrea For that last month, all we do is pay what's left plus the tiny amount of interest for that month. So, the total we pay is $1121.36. That's 22 months at $50, plus the extra. We pay off the whole thing in less time and with much, much less interest.

Louis Wow. Well, let's try to stick to paying $50 per month then. It seems to work out really well.

For Discussion

1. Describe in words the rule that Louis and Andrea use to calculate each month's balance when they make the minimum monthly payments.

   How does the rule change when the credit card charges 15% interest instead of approximately 12%?

Louis follows a rule when he sets up the spreadsheet for minimum payments. You can write the rule in function form. The balance B is a function of the month n.

$$B(n) = \begin{cases} 1000 & \text{if } n = 0 \\ B(n-1) - 0.02 \cdot B(n-1) + 0.01 \cdot B(n-1) & \text{if } n > 0 \end{cases}$$

You can use the Distributive Property to simplify the rule. Remember, $B(n-1)$ is the output of the function B when you input $n - 1$. $B(n-1)$ represents a single value.

When the function notation is confusing, you can think of $B(n-1)$ as a value, such as x. You can replace the expression $B(n-1)$ with x.

$$x - 0.02x + 0.01x$$

In this expression, it is simpler to see that you can combine the like terms to get $0.99x$.

So, a simplified way to write the function is the following.

$$B(n) = \begin{cases} 1000 & \text{if } n = 0 \\ 0.99 \cdot B(n-1) & \text{if } n > 0 \end{cases}$$

Like the function in Lesson 5.10, this function is recursively defined. The difference is that instead of adding a value to the previous output, you multiply the previous output by a value. A function like the one above is not linear. It is an **exponential function.**

> In this situation, what do the three expressions $B(n-1)$, $-0.02 \cdot B(n-1)$, and $+0.01 \cdot B(n-1)$ represent?

> For help defining a function recursively, see the TI-Nspire Handbook, p. 778.

Example 1

Problem Melissa's doctor prescribes amoxicillin for two weeks to cure an ear infection. She starts without any amoxicillin in her body. Melissa takes 1.5 grams of amoxicillin each day. Her body will consume one fourth of the amoxicillin each dose contains each day. Write a recursive function to find how much amoxicillin is present at the end of two weeks of treatment.

Solution To find this function, start by calculating the amount of amoxicillin for a few days.

Amoxicillin Treatment

Day	Amoxicillin (g)	How to Find Amoxicillin Amount
0	0	This is the amount on the day before treatment begins.
1	1.5	This is the amount of the first day's pills.
2	2.625	Add second day's pills (1.5 g). Then subtract $\frac{1}{4}$ of previous total (0.375 g).
3	3.469	Add third day's pills (1.5 g). Then subtract $\frac{1}{4}$ of previous total (0.656 g).
4	4.102	Add fourth day's pills (1.5 g). Then subtract $\frac{1}{4}$ of previous total.
5	4.576	Repeat the process you used for Day 4.

Notice that you are doing the same thing again and again to get from one output to the next. This is exactly what a recursive function does. The amount of amoxicillin A depends on the day d. The function rule is the following.

$$A(d) = \begin{cases} 0 & \text{if } d = 0 \\ A(d-1) + 1.5 - \frac{1}{4}A(d-1) & \text{if } d > 0 \end{cases}$$

You can combine the like terms $A(d-1)$ and $\frac{1}{4}A(d-1)$, which means that you can use the expression $0.75A(d-1) + 1.5$ in a spreadsheet program or calculator.

For help showing this function in a spreadsheet, see the TI-Nspire Handbook, p. 778.

For You to Do

2. Repeat the function in the example for nine more days. How much amoxicillin is in Melissa's body at the end of 14 days?
3. Plot the data for the first 14 days. What does your graph look like?

For Discussion

4. Suppose Melissa continues taking amoxicillin for another two weeks. What will happen to the amount of amoxicillin in her body? Is there an amount of amoxicillin that Melissa could take that would not change the amount in her body from day to day?
5. Suppose Melissa stops taking amoxicillin after 14 days. What happens to the level of amoxicillin in her body after the last day? Extend your graph for the third week.

*This amount of amoxicillin represents a **fixed point**, since its output equals its input.*

Recursively defined functions repeat different operations. In this lesson, you have used recursively defined functions that repeat addition and multiplication. Recursively defined functions can also produce other patterns.

Example 2

Problem The first two outputs for a function are 5 and 8. The recursively defined function is the following. To find an output, take the previous output and subtract the one before it. Find the 100th output.

Solution Since this recursively defined function does not seem to be linear or exponential, use the function to find outputs until a pattern emerges.

Function Outputs

Input	Output	How to Find Output
1	5	The value is given.
2	8	The value is given.
3	3	Take the previous output (8) and subtract the output before the previous output (5).
4	−5	Take the previous output (3) and subtract the output before the previous output (8).
5	−8	Repeat the process. So $-8 = (-5) - 3$.
6	−3	Repeat the process. So $-3 = (-8) - (-5)$.
7	5	Repeat the process. So $5 = (-3) - (-8)$.
8	8	Repeat the process. So $8 = 5 - (-3)$.

The outputs seem to repeat. The eighth output is the same as the second one. When you extend the table, the 14th output is the same as the eighth one. The pattern continues. A function that repeats like this is a **periodic function.** This table shows the inputs that give a certain output value.

Function Inputs and Outputs

Output	Inputs
5	1, 7, 13, 19, 25, . . . , 97, 103, . . . , $6n + 1$
8	2, 8, 14, 20, 26, . . . , 98, 104, . . . , $6n + 2$
3	3, 9, 15, 21, 27, . . . , 99, 105, . . . , $6n + 3$
−5	4, 10, 16, 22, 28, . . . , **100**, 106, . . . , $6n + 4$
−8	5, 11, 17, 23, 29, . . . , 101, 107, . . . , $6n + 5$
−3	6, 12, 18, 24, 30, . . . , 96, 102, . . . , $6n + 6$

You can use fill down in a spreadsheet to model these periodic functions. See the TI-Nspire Handbook, p. 778.

The 100th output is −5. Note that 96 is the largest multiple of 6 that is not more than 100. It takes 4 more steps to go from the 96th output to the 100th.

5.12 From Situations to Recursive Rules

For Discussion

6. What is the 200th output? The 300th output?

In-Class Experiment

In episode 22, Louis and Andrea pay $50 per month on their credit card balance. They pay a total of $1121.36 on a $1000 balance. To find the total that they pay, they use the recursively defined function

$$B(n) = \begin{cases} 1000 & \text{if } n = 0 \\ B(n-1) - 50 + 0.01B(n-1) & \text{if } n > 0 \end{cases}$$

until the balance is below $50. Then they pay off the entire balance (payment plus interest) the next month. This process takes 22 months.

Suppose that instead of paying $50 per month, Louis and Andrea pay a different amount. In this experiment, you will look at different monthly payments. You will see how a different monthly payment affects the total amount they have to pay and the number of months they take to pay off the balance.

7. Use a calculator or computer. Each group in the class chooses a different monthly payment amount in the table. Find how many payments you have to make, what the total payment is, and how much of the total payment each month is interest. Complete the table by collecting the results from each group.

Payment Options: $1000 Balance at 12% Interest

Payment	Months to Pay	Total Payments	Interest
$10	■	■	■
$15	■	■	■
$20	■	■	■
$25	■	■	■
$30	■	■	■
$40	■	■	■
$50	22	$1121.36	$121.36
$60	■	■	■
$75	■	■	■
$100	■	■	■

a. $10 b. $15 c. $20 d. $25 e. $30
f. $40 g. $60 h. $75 i. $100

Exercises Practicing Habits of Mind

Check Your Understanding

1. Describe this function in words. Then use the function to find $F(n)$ for the values of n from 1 to 12.

$$F(n) = \begin{cases} 1 & \text{if } n = 1 \\ 1 & \text{if } n = 2 \\ F(n-1) + F(n-2) & \text{if } n > 2 \end{cases}$$

2. Some banks offer rainy-day savings accounts. You can send part of your paycheck directly to this sort of savings account. The money earns a small amount of interest every month. Kara opens a rainy-day account at Fourth Seventh Bank that offers 1.5% interest annually. The bank splits the interest payments into twelve months.

   a. What percent interest does Kara earn each month from this account? How do you write the percent interest as a decimal? Describe your process in a way that you can use for any interest rate.

   b. Kara deposits $50 into this account every month. How much interest does she earn in the first month? In the second month? In the third month? You can use this table to help you.

   > Assume that the bank does not give interest on money that you deposit this month. The bank pays interest only on the amount already in the account.

   Kara's Account Balance

Month	Starting Balance	Interest	Deposit	Ending Balance
0	$0	$0	$ 0	$0
1	$0	■	$50	■
2	■	■	$50	■
3	■	■	$50	■

   c. Write a recursively defined function to find Kara's account balance after n months.

3. You can apply recursively defined functions to geometric shapes. One such shape is the **Koch snowflake.** The beginning shape in a Koch snowflake is a downward-pointing equilateral triangle. Then the snowflake develops following a recursively defined function.

   > Take every line segment in the shape and replace the middle third with two sides of an equilateral triangle pointing outward.

5.12 From Situations to Recursive Rules 503

For example, using this function once produces the level 1 snowflake.

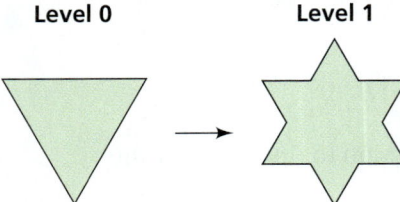

Level 0   Level 1

> The original triangle is the level 0 snowflake, even though it does not look like a snowflake.

In the level 2 snowflake, you transform the twelve line segments in the level 1 snowflake using the same function.

a. Draw a level 2 snowflake.

b. Suppose the original triangle has a side length of 1 and a perimeter of 3. Find the perimeters of the level 1 and level 2 snowflakes.

c. Find a recursively defined function $P(\ell)$ for the perimeter where ℓ is the level number. Is this function linear? Is it exponential?

d. Suppose you change the triangle's size so that the triangle has an area of 1 square unit. Find the areas of the level 1 and level 2 snowflakes.

e. **Take It Further** Find a recursively defined function for the area $A(\ell)$, where ℓ is the level number. Then find the area of the level 6 snowflake. What happens when you apply the function to further levels of the snowflake?

4. The output for a function starts with zero. Then the function rule is "Add 1, add 2, add 3, add 4, and so on." The recursively defined function for this rule is the following.

$$C(n) = \begin{cases} 0 & \text{if } n = 0 \\ C(n-1) + n & \text{if } n > 0 \end{cases}$$

a. Find the value of $C(5)$ by repeating the function.

b. Is this function linear? Explain.

On Your Own

5. Melissa's doctor tells her that, instead of taking three amoxicillin pills per day, she needs to take only two pills.

a. When there is 1.5 grams of amoxicillin in 3 pills, how much amoxicillin is there in 2 pills?

b. It is still true that one fourth of the amoxicillin will not be in her body the next day. How does the change in Melissa's prescription affect the recursively defined function shown below, which you used in Example 1?

$$A(d) = \begin{cases} 0 & \text{if } d = 0 \\ A(d-1) + 1.5 - \frac{1}{4}A(d-1) & \text{if } d > 0 \end{cases}$$

> This exercise is similar to the example in this lesson.

c. Suppose Melissa takes 2 pills of amoxicillin per day. Find the amount of amoxicillin in her body after one week, to the nearest milligram. She starts without any amoxicillin in her body.

6. Each weekday, Cheng travels on the Metro Rail System making a round trip from Greenbelt to Metro Center. The daily fare is $2.85 each way. Cheng purchases a $100 fare card to pay the $2.85 fare for each ride.

   a. Make a table that shows the amount of money Cheng has left on the fare card after n days. Show the values of n from 0 to 5.

   b. Describe a recursively defined function for the situation, using words.

   c. Write the recursively defined function $B(n)$, the amount of money Cheng has left on his fare card after n workdays.

   d. Is this function linear? Is it exponential?

   e. Use the function to find how many days Cheng can ride the Metro to and from work before he needs to add money to the fare card.

7. **Write About It** In Example 2, which asks for the 100th output, the recursively defined function tells you to take the previous output and subtract the output before the previous output. The function gives the values 5 and 8 as the first and second outputs. Explain why this function definition matches the description above.

$$S(n) = \begin{cases} 5 & \text{if } n = 1 \\ 8 & \text{if } n = 2 \\ S(n-1) - S(n-2) & \text{if } n > 2 \end{cases}$$

For Exercises 8 and 9, use Function S from Exercise 7.

8. Find the 374th output.

9. In Function S, the outputs repeat with a period of 6. Suppose the first output is y, the second output is z, and the third output is $z - y$.

   a. Using algebra, find the sequence of the first 6 outputs.

   b. What does using variables to find the sequence of the first 6 outputs tell you about the period and the relationships between numbers in the sequence?

The expression $S(n-1)$ represents the previous output. What does the expression $S(n-2)$ represent?

The **period** is the length of a repeating sequence. The sequence 7, 8, 9, 7, 8, 9, . . . has a period of 3.

10. **Standardized Test Prep** Which of the following is a closed form of the recursive function $T(n)$?

$$T(n) = \begin{cases} 0 & \text{if } n = 0 \\ T(n-1) + \frac{n}{2} & \text{if } n > 0 \end{cases}$$

A. $n - \frac{1}{2}$ **B.** n^2 **C.** $\frac{n^2 + n}{2}$ **D.** $\frac{n^2 + n}{4}$

11. If you have ever been bored, you might have started pressing the same calculator key over and over again. Now try entering the largest number that fits on your calculator screen. Then press the square root key again and again.

    a. Explain why this recursively defined function describes what you are doing. What do the letters b, N, and X represent?
    $$X(b) = \begin{cases} N & \text{if } b = 0 \\ \sqrt{X(b-1)} & \text{if } b > 0 \end{cases}$$

    b. What output do you get eventually? Will you get the same result no matter what number you enter first?

12. Benoit shows you a recursively defined function with some unpredictable behavior. Pick a number N and use this function definition.
    $$Y(b) = \begin{cases} N & \text{if } b = 0 \\ (Y(b-1))^2 + N & \text{if } b > 0 \end{cases}$$

    The function tells you to add N, not $Y(b-1)$.

    a. Describe this function using sentences.

    b. What is the output in the long run when you start with $N = 1$? With $N = 0$? With $N = -1$?

    c. **Take It Further** What starting values for N give outputs that approach infinity? What starting values for N give outputs that do not approach infinity? Prove your results.

    d. **Take It Further** The starting value -1 repeats in a cycle of period 2. This value is the only number with this period. Find a number that repeats in a cycle of period 3.

Maintain Your Skills

Find a closed-form function that gives the same outputs as each recursively defined function.

13. $f(n) = \begin{cases} 3 & \text{if } n = 0 \\ f(n-1) + 4 & \text{if } n > 0 \end{cases}$

14. $g(n) = \begin{cases} 7 & \text{if } n = 0 \\ g(n-1) + 5 & \text{if } n > 0 \end{cases}$

15. $h(n) = \begin{cases} 1 & \text{if } n = 0 \\ h(n-1) - 5 & \text{if } n > 0 \end{cases}$

16. $r(n) = \begin{cases} b & \text{if } n = 0 \\ r(n-1) + a & \text{if } n > 0 \end{cases}$

Mathematical Reflections 5C

In this investigation, you wrote an equation based on a word problem. You used a recursively-defined function to find the monthly payment on a personal loan. These questions will help you summarize what you have learned.

1. A local bank charges 7.5% annual interest on a personal loan of $5000.
   a. What is the amount of interest for the first month of the loan?
   b. When you pay the interest plus an additional $500 for the first month's payment, what is the amount of interest for the second month's payment?
   c. When you continue to pay the interest plus an additional $500 payment, what is the balance on the loan after 6 months?

2. Here is a number trick. Choose a number. Subtract 3. Multiply by 4. Add 8. Divide by 2.
   a. Draw a function-machine network to represent the steps in the number trick.
   b. Draw a function-machine network to undo the steps in the number trick. Find the starting number.
   c. Write a function $T(n)$ that uses the chosen number as the input and the result of the number trick as the output.
   d. Write a function $N(t)$ that uses the result of the number trick as the input and the chosen number as the output.

3. At a community theater, tickets in the orchestra section cost $30.00. Tickets in the balcony cost $20.00. For each performance, the theater sells exactly 100 tickets.
   a. A theater sells 40 orchestra tickets. How much money does it collect?
   b. Build a function-machine network using the number of orchestra tickets sold as the input. The output is the amount of money collected.
   c. If the theater collects $2450, how many orchestra tickets does it sell?

4. How can you use functions to solve problems?
5. When do you use a recursively defined function?
6. What is the monthly payment on a 48-month car loan at 7.9% APR if the car costs $12,000?

The output is a bottle of juice.

Vocabulary

In this investigation, you learned these terms. Make sure you understand what each one means and how to use it.

- closed form
- exponential function
- fixed point
- Koch snowflake
- period
- periodic function

Project Using Mathematical Habits

Managing Money

Do you ever dream of going to college or buying a car? Usually, you save and borrow money for these large expenses. In this project, you will write a recursive rule to use in a spreadsheet and make decisions about managing money.

This project explores three ways to save and invest money: a certificate of deposit (CD), a savings account, and stock. In each case, you earn interest by lending your money. For each type of investment, the Annual Percentage Rate (APR) describes the investment's growth each year.

Materials
Paper, pencil, spreadsheet software

Earning Interest

1. Kara looks at three options for making her annual $600 rainy day investment.
   - savings account at 1.5% APR
   - certificate of deposit at 4.5% APR
   - stock investment at 10% APR

For each option, what is the amount of money that Kara earns if she invests for 3 years? For 10 years? For 30 years? Make a spreadsheet like the one below for each investment period.

2. Research the APR for savings and CD accounts at a local bank. Find the fees charged on minimum balances in various types of accounts. Which type of account is the best for investing a small amount? A large amount?

Comparing Payment Options

Make a spreadsheet showing the payment options for each situation below.

3. The Peña family finances a car for $8000. A car dealership offers a 7.9% APR loan for 4 years. Each month, the dealership charges interest on the balance of the loan. What is the monthly payment rounded to the nearest cent?

4. The Peñas need $32,000 in financing to buy their dream car. The loan is at 7.9% APR for 4 years.
   a. What is the family's monthly payment rounded to the nearest cent?
   b. How does this monthly payment compare to the monthly payment in Exercise 3?

5. The Peñas get a new finance offer for their dream car, a 5-year loan at 8.9% APR.
   a. How much does this reduce the family's monthly payment?
   b. How do the car payments in Exercises 4 and 5 compare?

	A	B	C	D	E
1	Year	Starting Balance	Interest	Deposit	Ending Balance
2	1	0	0	600	600
3					
4					

6. The car dealership makes its final offers on the dream car to the Peñas, a $1000 discount and 7.9% interest for 4 years, or no discount and 4.9% interest for 4 years. Which of these two offers should they take?

7. Nancy buys appliances for $1300 at Adequate Buy. She has two payment options. She can use a credit card that charges 10% APR, or she can use an Adequate Buy credit card that charges no interest for a year. Then she pays 15% APR after the first year.

   Which card should Nancy use if she plans to make monthly payments of $110? Of $40?

8. The United States government offers college student loans that typically carry lower interest rates than car loans. Shannon graduates with a $12,000 student loan. The interest rate on her loan is 5% APR.

   a. If Shannon pays off the loan in 10 years, find her monthly payment rounded to the nearest cent.

   b. What percentage of Shannon's first payment is interest?

   c. Suppose Shannon's student loan is $18,000 at 5% APR for 10 years. Estimate her monthly payment. Then find her monthly payment rounded to the nearest cent.

   d. Suppose Shannon's loan is a bank loan of $12,000 at 8% APR for 10 years instead of a student loan of $12,000 at 5% APR for 10 years. How much more will her total payments be?

Would a $500 discount and 6.4% interest for 4 years be even better?

9. **Take It Further** Julie and Ben owe $215,354 on their existing mortgage. They have already paid for 3 years at 7% APR. A bank advertises a new 30-year loan at 6.5% APR. The bank charges $2500 in fees to issue the loan and adds the fee to the loan amount.

   a. What is the monthly payment on Julie and Ben's existing mortgage?

   b. If they choose to take a new loan, what will be the monthly payment?

   c. How much money will they save, if any, by taking a new loan?

   d. Experiment using a different bank rate or loan amount. Find how the monthly payment changes.

Chapter 5 Review

In **Investigation 5A**, you learned how to
- build a function from a word problem
- determine whether a relationship is a function based on its description or graph
- make input-output tables
- find the domain of a function
- graph a function

The following questions will help you check your understanding.

1. The diagram below shows two linked function machines.

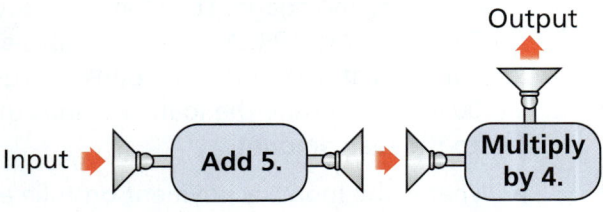

   a. Copy and complete the table for the function network.

Input	Output
0	■
1	■
−4	■
6	■
■	28

   b. Form a new function by reversing the order of the two function machines.

   c. Are the outputs the same for the function networks in parts (a) and (b)? Explain.

2. Use $f(x) = 2(x - 5)$, $x \stackrel{g}{\mapsto} |x^2 - 3|$, and $h(x) = \sqrt{x - 1}$ to calculate the following.

   a. $f(0)$, $f(1)$, and $f(-1)$

   b. $g(0)$, $g(1)$, and $g(-1)$

   c. $h(0)$, $h(1)$, and $h(-1)$

   d. $f(g(3))$ and $g(h(5))$

   e. Find the domains of functions f, g, and h.

3. Determine whether each description is a function. Explain.

   a. input: x, output: x^2

   b. input: x, output: $\pm\sqrt{x}$

In **Investigation 5B**, you learned how to
- determine whether a table represents a linear function
- fit a linear function to a table where possible
- calculate the outputs of a recursive rule
- describe a recursive rule
- find a recursive rule to match a table

The following questions will help you check your understanding.

4. Use Tables A and B for parts (a) and (b).

   Table A

Input	Output
0	4
1	7
2	10
3	13
4	16

   Table B

Input	Output
0	4
1	5
2	8
3	13
4	20

   a. Draw a graph of each table of values. Does each graph appear to be linear?

   b. Add a Δ column to each table and find the differences. Can you match each table with a linear function?

   c. If you can match a table with a linear function, find a closed-form function that agrees with the table.

5. Copy and complete the table for each recursive rule.

Input	Output
1	■
2	■
3	■
4	■
5	■

   a. To get a new output, add 6 to the previous output. When the input is 1, the output is −2.

   b. To get a new output, multiply the previous output by 2 and add 3. When the input is 1, the output is −2.

In **Investigation 5C,** you learned how to

- translate a word problem into an equation
- build and understand a function-machine network
- find a recursive function that models a word problem
- write a rule for a recursive function
- work with recursive functions

The following questions will help you check your understanding.

6. Find the 123rd output for this recursive rule.

$$K(x) = \begin{cases} 2 & \text{if } x = 1 \\ -4 & \text{if } x = 2 \\ K(x-1) - K(x-2) & \text{if } x > 2 \end{cases}$$

7. Kevin opens a savings account. At the end of each month, he will deposit $10 in the account. At the beginning of each month, the bank pays $\frac{1}{4}$% interest on his balance (or 3% interest annually). The table shows Kevin's balance at the end of the first five months.

Kevin's Savings

Month	Balance
1	$10.00
2	$20.03
3	$30.08
4	$40.16
5	$50.26

   a. Explain how the bank calculated the balance at the end of each month.

   b. Write a recursive rule to find the balance for any month m.

   c. What is Kevin's balance at the end of a year?

   d. Set up a spreadsheet to determine Kevin's balance after 5 years. What is the total amount of interest Kevin will earn after 5 years?

8. Melissa's doctor prescribes 2 grams of amoxicillin each day for two weeks. One fourth of the amoxicillin that is in her body on any given day will not be present the next day.

   a. Write a recursive rule to find how much amoxicillin is in her body each day.

   b. How much amoxicillin is in her body on the third day? On the fourteenth day?

Chapter 5 Test

Go Online
pearsonsuccessnet.com

Multiple Choice

For Exercises 1 and 2 use this function-machine network.

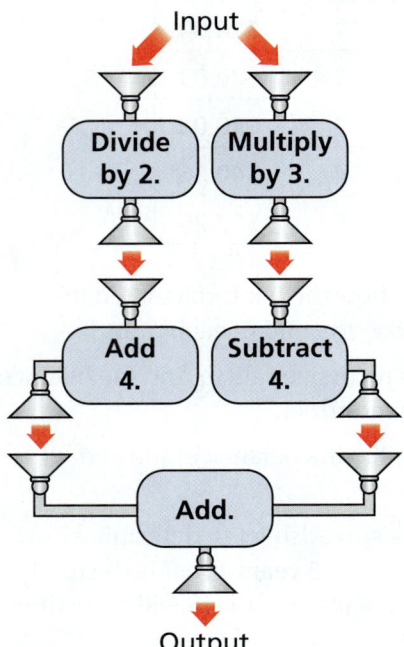

1. If the input value to the network is −6, what is the output value?

A. 21 B. −7
C. −21 D. −30

2. If the output value from the network is 42, what is the input value?

A. 147 B. 21
C. 0 D. 12

3. Which recursive rule makes $f(3)$ equal 35?

A. $f(x) = \begin{cases} 25 & \text{if } x = 0 \\ f(x-1) + x & \text{if } x > 0 \end{cases}$

B. $f(x) = \begin{cases} 29 & \text{if } x = 0 \\ f(x-1) + 3 & \text{if } x > 0 \end{cases}$

C. $f(x) = \begin{cases} 29 & \text{if } x = 0 \\ 2 \cdot f(x-1) & \text{if } x > 0 \end{cases}$

D. $f(x) = \begin{cases} 41 & \text{if } x = 0 \\ f(x-1) - 2 & \text{if } x > 0 \end{cases}$

4. Which table cannot be described by a linear function?

A.
Input	Output
0	10
1	7
2	4
3	1
4	−2

B.
Input	Output
0	13
1	15
2	17
3	20
4	23

C.
Input	Output
0	−4
1	1
2	6
3	11
4	16

D.
Input	Output
0	2
1	1
2	0
3	−1
4	−2

5. What type of function is $h(x)$?

$h(x) = \begin{cases} 11 & \text{if } x = 0 \\ 3 \cdot h(x-1) & \text{if } x > 0 \end{cases}$

A. constant
B. linear
C. exponential
D. none of the above

6. Which rule gives the same outputs as the following recursive rule?

   When the input is 0, the output is 3. To get outputs for integer inputs, add 2 to the previous output.

   A. $x \mapsto 3(2^2)$
   B. $x \mapsto 2x + 3$
   C. $x \mapsto 3x + 2$
   D. $x \mapsto 3x^2 + 3$

Open Response

7. Juliana expects to work overtime this week. She will work 40 hours at her regular pay rate. Then she will work another 15 hours at $5 per hour more than her regular pay rate.

   a. Draw a function-machine network whose input is Juliana's regular pay rate. The output is how much money she will make for the week (including overtime pay).

   b. Juliana will make $735 this week (including overtime pay). What is her regular pay rate?

8. Use the function $g(x) = x^2 - (x - 2)(x - 3)$.

   a. Make a table for the integers x from 0 to 5.
   b. Is this function linear? Explain.

9. Copy and complete the table.

Input	Output	Δ
0		−4
1		−4
2	5	−4
3		−4
4		−4
5		

10. Copy and complete this table for the recursive rule $f(x)$.

    $$f(x) = \begin{cases} 39 & \text{if } x = 0 \\ \frac{2}{3}f(x-1) + 4 & \text{if } x > 0 \end{cases}$$

Input	Output
0	39
1	
2	
3	
4	

11. Describe how to calculate the monthly payment on a 48-month car loan for $12,000 at 7.9% APR.

12. How do you know whether a table represents a linear function? Give at least three examples.

Challenge Problem

13. A recursive rule B is defined as

    $$B(m) = \begin{cases} C & \text{if } m = 0 \\ \frac{3}{4}B(m-1) + 4 & \text{if } m > 0 \end{cases}$$

    where C is an unknown value that you find.

    a. $B(5) = 259$. What is the value of C?
    b. Find the value of $B(1,000,000)$ rounded to three decimal places.

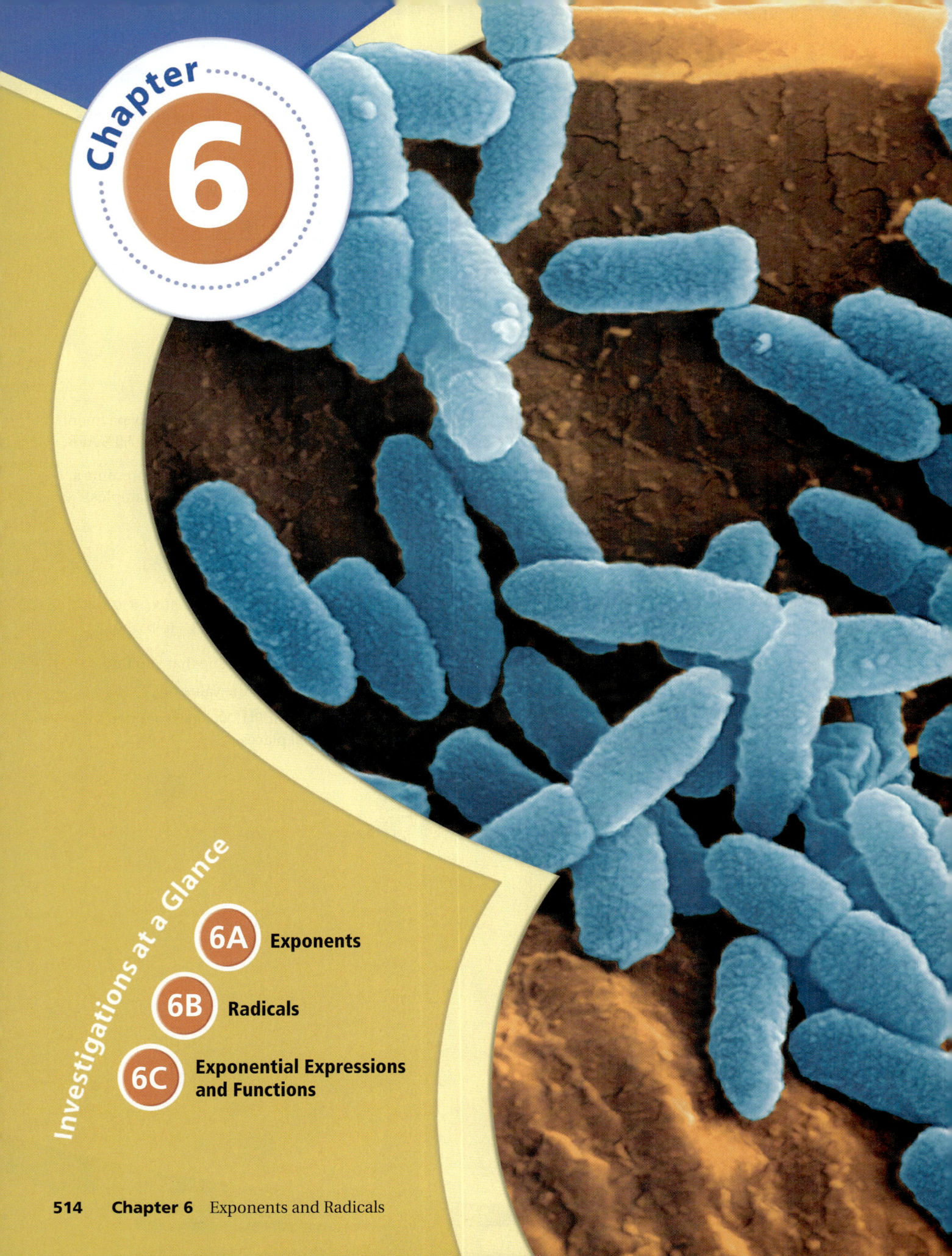

Chapter 6

Investigations at a Glance

- **6A** Exponents
- **6B** Radicals
- **6C** Exponential Expressions and Functions

514 **Chapter 6** Exponents and Radicals

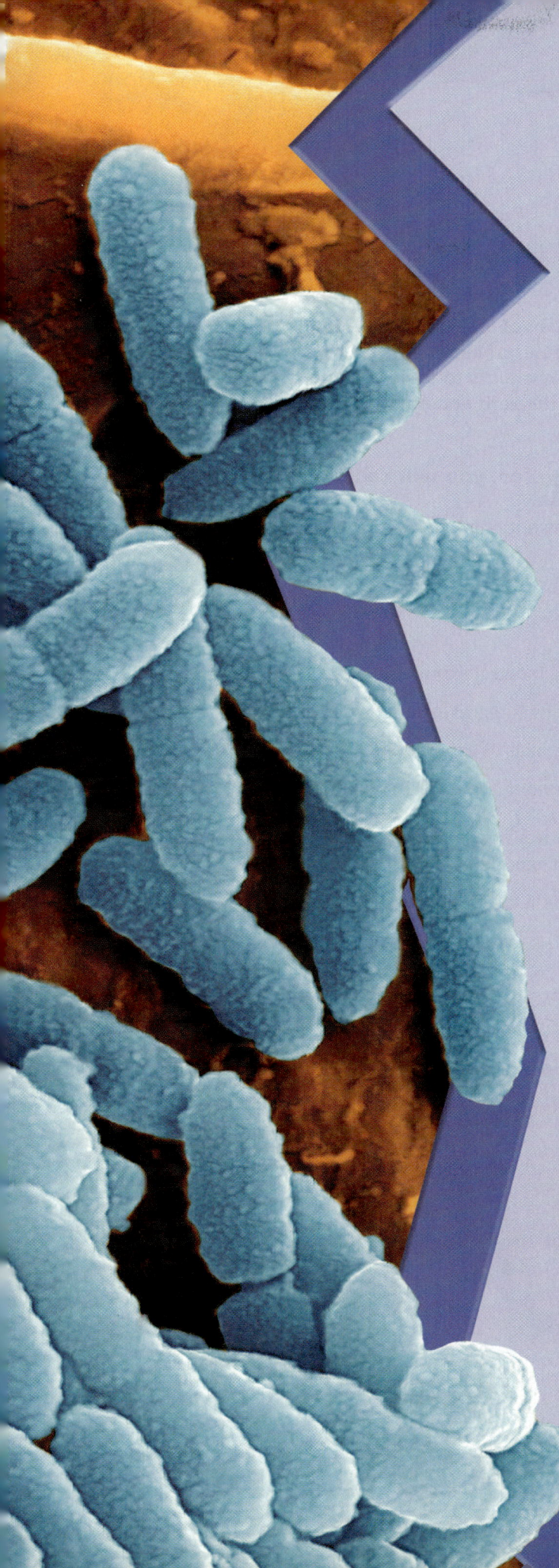

Exponents and Radicals

Perhaps you first used exponents to find areas of squares using the formula $A = s^2$. You read s^2 as "s squared" or "the square of s." The *square of s* means the area of a square built with side s. Likewise, the *cube of s* (or s^3) means the volume of a cube built with side s.

Over time, the idea of exponents grew beyond the integers used for squaring and cubing. Mathematicians worked to keep a set of rules for exponents consistent for other types of exponents. The other types included negative integers and eventually all real numbers.

Exponential functions describe growth. The growth could be in your savings account or in a bacteria population. Computer viruses can also spread exponentially. Each of two infected computers can infect two more, each of which in turn infects two more, and so on. The number infected becomes quite large in a short time—a sign of exponential behavior.

In this chapter, you will learn the rules for exponents. You will learn to "undo" exponents to solve equations. You will also work with exponential functions in which the variable is in the exponent.

Vocabulary and Notation

- base
- compound interest
- constant ratio
- cube of a number
- exponent
- exponential decay
- exponential growth
- irrational number
- negative exponent, a^{-m}
- nth root, $\sqrt[n]{a}$
- radical
- rational number
- scientific notation
- square of a number
- square root, $\sqrt{r}$
- zero exponent, a^0

Investigation 6A

Exponents

In *Exponents*, you will learn about integral (or integer) exponents. You will use the rules of exponents to make calculations. You will undo exponents to solve equations. You also will calculate using the zero exponent and negative exponents.

By the end of this investigation, you will be able to answer questions like these.

1. What are the basic rules of exponents?
2. Why is 2^0 equal to 1?
3. How can you write $\dfrac{2^3 \cdot 2^{-2} \cdot 2^7}{(2^5)^3 \cdot 2^{-2}}$ as a number without exponents?

You will learn how to
- make calculations involving integral exponents
- simplify expressions involving integral exponents
- explain and apply the basic rules of exponents
- calculate with the zero exponent and negative exponents

You will develop these habits and skills:
- Understand the meaning of exponential notation.
- Multiply, add, subtract, and divide with exponents.
- Extend concepts and patterns to build new mathematical knowledge.

A gecko has about 1×10^6 setae on its feet. Each seta branches into about 1×10^3 spatulae.

6.01 Getting Started

You may think of multiplication as repeated addition. The product $4 \cdot 3$ can mean "add 3 copies of 4 together."

$$4 \cdot 3 = \underbrace{4 + 4 + 4}_{\text{3 copies of 4}}$$

You may know that exponents work in a similar way. The expression 4^3 means "multiply 3 copies of 4 together."

$$4^3 = \underbrace{4 \cdot 4 \cdot 4}_{\text{3 copies of 4}}$$

In general, if n is a positive integer, a^n is the product of n factors of a. You read a^n as "a to the n."

$$a^n = \underbrace{a \cdot a \cdot a \cdot \cdots \cdot a}_{n \text{ copies of } a}$$

> You call a the **base** and n the **exponent**.

What does a^1 mean? It may not look like a product, but it means that there is one factor of a.

$$a^1 = \underbrace{a}_{\text{1 copy of } a}$$

Here are some examples of expressions with exponents.

$$a^4 = a \cdot a \cdot a \cdot a$$
$$a^{10} = a \cdot a \cdot a \cdot a \cdot a \cdot a \cdot a \cdot a \cdot a \cdot a$$

Two exponents have special names. To **square** a number means to multiply the number by itself. The expression a^2 ("a squared") means $a \cdot a$. You can square any expression, including expressions with integers, fractions, and variables.

$$a^2 = a \cdot a \qquad\qquad 12^2 = 12 \cdot 12 = 144$$
$$\left(\tfrac{2}{5}\right)^2 = \tfrac{2}{5} \cdot \tfrac{2}{5} = \tfrac{2^2}{5^2} = \tfrac{4}{25} \qquad (4w)^2 = 4w \cdot 4w = 4^2 \cdot w^2 = 16w^2$$
$$(-3)^2 = (-3) \cdot (-3) = 9$$

Similarly, to **cube** a number means to multiply the number times the number times the number. In other words, you find the product of the number's square and the number. The expression a^3 ("a cubed") means $a \cdot a \cdot a$. You can cube any expression.

$$a^3 = a \cdot a \cdot a \qquad\qquad 12^3 = 12 \cdot 12 \cdot 12 = 1728$$
$$\left(\tfrac{2}{5}\right)^3 = \tfrac{2}{5} \cdot \tfrac{2}{5} \cdot \tfrac{2}{5} = \tfrac{2^3}{5^3} = \tfrac{8}{125} \qquad (4w)^3 = 4w \cdot 4w \cdot 4w = 4^3 \cdot w^3$$
$$= 64w^3$$
$$(-3)^3 = (-3) \cdot (-3) \cdot (-3) = -27$$

For You to Explore

1. There are 9 square feet in a square yard. There are 27 cubic feet in a cubic yard. Explain.

2. Here are some additional basic rules, but they are not all true. Substitute numbers for a, b, and c to check whether each equation is true. Decide whether each rule could be a basic rule. Use numerical examples as evidence. Write a convincing argument that summarizes your conclusions.

   Group I
   $a^b \stackrel{?}{=} (-a)^b$
   $a^{b+c} \stackrel{?}{=} a^b + a^c$
   $a^{b+c} \stackrel{?}{=} a^b \cdot a^c$

   Group II
   $a^b \stackrel{?}{=} b^a$
   $a^b \cdot a^c \stackrel{?}{=} a^{bc}$
   $(a^b)^c \stackrel{?}{=} a^{bc}$

   Group III
   $(a^b)^c \stackrel{?}{=} a^{(b^c)}$
   $(a^b)^c \stackrel{?}{=} a^b \cdot b^c$
   $\dfrac{a^b}{a^c} \stackrel{?}{=} a^{b-c}$

   Group IV
   $(ab)^c \stackrel{?}{=} a^c \cdot b^c$
   $a^b \stackrel{?}{=} a(a^{b-1})$
   $(ab)^c \stackrel{?}{=} a(b^c)$

3. Write each expression as a power of 6.

   a. $6^{51}6^{48}$ **b.** $(6^5)^7$ **c.** $6(6^{25}6^{14})$ **d.** $\dfrac{6^{95}}{6^{19}}$

   > You will write each result using a base of 6 and an exponent. For example, 6^{14}.

4. Everyone who is born in the United States is eligible to receive a Social Security number that has nine digits. You can divide the digits into groups of three digits, two digits, and four digits. How many possible Social Security numbers are there?

   Express your answer in two different ways.

   a. Find how many different nine-digit combinations are possible. Express this result as a power of 10.

   b. Think about dividing the nine digits into groups of three digits, two digits, and four digits. How many different combinations are possible for three digits? For two digits? For four digits? Can you use the number of combinations to find the total possible number of Social Security numbers?

Exercises Practicing Habits of Mind

On Your Own

5. Some states make license plates using combinations of three letters followed by three numbers. That is, you can have "ABC 123" on a license plate, but not "123 ABC." Using combinations of three letters followed by three numbers, how many license plates are possible?

6. Many garage door openers use a four-digit code, where each digit can be any number from 0 to 9. What is the total number of possible four-digit codes? Explain.

In Exercises 6 and 7, express your answer as a power of 10.

7. If the code for a garage door opener is only two digits long, how many codes are possible? How many three-digit codes are possible? Explain.

8. Most credit card numbers are 16 digits long.

   a. If each digit can be any number from 0 to 9, how many different credit numbers are possible? Express your result in different ways. (*Hint:* Divide the 16 digits into smaller groups. Then, use your results from Exercises 6 and 7.)

   b. Some credit card numbers have special digits. Suppose a card's number must start with 37 followed by a nonzero digit. Then the 13 following digits can be any number from 0 to 9. How many different credit numbers are possible?

Maintain Your Skills

9. Rewrite each expression using exponents.

   a. $x \cdot x \cdot x \cdot 3 \cdot 3 \cdot y \cdot y$
   b. $a \cdot b \cdot b \cdot b \cdot 3 \cdot b \cdot a \cdot b \cdot a$
   c. $2 \cdot 3 \cdot m \cdot m \cdot m$
   d. $x \cdot x \cdot x \cdot x \cdot \frac{1}{x}$

6.02 Squares, Cubes, and Beyond

In Chapter 1, you explored the any-order, any-grouping properties (AOAG) for both addition and multiplication. In Lesson 6.01, you may have noticed that there is no AOAG property for exponents. For instance,

$$2^{20} = 1{,}048{,}576, \text{ but } 20^2 = 400.$$

In general, changing the order of exponents changes the outcome. This example shows that the any-order part of AOAG does not work.

> Most of the time, $a^b \neq b^a$. What are some examples where they are equal?

For Discussion

1. Check the any-grouping part of AOAG by comparing $(3^2)^4$ and $3^{(2^4)}$. Are they equal? Use a few other examples, such as $(2^3)^4$ and $2^{(3^4)}$. Does the any-grouping part of AOAG work for exponents?

> The convention for a^{b^c} is to consider it as $a^{(b^c)}$.

While there is no AOAG for exponentiation, there are some basic rules for exponents. In Lesson 6.01, you explored a collection of proposed basic rules. Group I explored one of these rules.

$$a^b \cdot a^c = a^{b+c}$$

Why is this rule true? Try it with numbers. For example, $(3^2)(3^5)$.

$$(3^2)(3^5) = \underbrace{(3 \cdot 3)}_{2 \text{ copies}} \cdot \underbrace{(3 \cdot 3 \cdot 3 \cdot 3 \cdot 3)}_{5 \text{ copies}} = \underbrace{(3 \cdot 3 \cdot 3 \cdot 3 \cdot 3 \cdot 3 \cdot 3)}_{2 + 5 = 7 \text{ copies}} = 3^7$$

When you multiply 3^2 and 3^5, there are a total of 7 factors of 3. You use the same process when you find the product $(3^b)(3^c)$.

$$(3^b)(3^c) = \underbrace{(3 \cdot 3 \cdot \ldots \cdot 3)}_{b \text{ copies}} \cdot \underbrace{(3 \cdot 3 \cdot \ldots \cdot 3)}_{c \text{ copies}} = \underbrace{(3 \cdot 3 \cdot \ldots \cdot 3)}_{b + c \text{ copies}} = 3^{b+c}$$

This argument works if the base is 2, -1, $\frac{1}{2}$, or even a variable, such as a. Now that you have an argument, or proof, you can write the theorem. This simple statement, the Law of Exponents, is very important to the discussion of exponents.

Theorem 6.1 The Law of Exponents

For any number a and positive integers b and c, $a^b \cdot a^c = a^{b+c}$.

You can only use Theorem 6.1 if the bases are the same. Consider the following.

$$7^3 \cdot 7^8 = 7^{3+8} = 7^{11} \qquad 6^3 \cdot 7^8 \neq (6 \cdot 7)^{3+8}$$

For You to Do

Simplify each expression.

2. $a^2 \cdot a^5$
3. $k^8 \cdot j^7 \cdot k^{13}$
4. $m^4(m^5)$
5. $r^3(s^7 + r^2)$
6. $4^3 \cdot x^2 \cdot 4 \cdot x^2$
7. $2^3 x^3 (2x)^2$

For Discussion

8. Use Theorem 6.1 and the basic rules for addition and multiplication to prove that $a^b \cdot a^c \cdot a^d = a^{b+c+d}$.

For You to Do

9. **What's Wrong Here?** Matt simplifies the expression $(4m)^3 - 2m - 2m(2m^2 - 1)$ as shown.

$$(4m)^3 - 2m - 2m(2m^2 - 1) = 4m^3 - 2m - 4m^3 + 2m$$
$$= 0$$

Emily simplifies the same expression in another way.

$$(4m)^3 - 2m - 2m(2m^2 - 1) = 64m^3 - 2m - 4m^3 + 2m$$
$$= 60m^3$$

Who is correct? Explain what one of the students did wrong.

Exercises Practicing Habits of Mind

Check Your Understanding

1. Without using a calculator, find which of the following expressions is equal to 2^{12}. Explain.

    a. $2^{10} + 2^2$
    b. $2^6 2^6$
    c. $(2^{10})(2^2)$
    d. $(2^4)(2^3)$
    e. $(2^4)(2^4)(2^4)$
    f. $2^9 + 2^3$
    g. $2^{11} + 2^{11}$
    h. $4(2^{10})$

2. **Write About It** If you write 10^6, 10^9, and 10^n in standard form, how many zeros are in each number? Explain.

3. **Take It Further** Suppose you expand $10^2 \cdot 5^3 \cdot 3^5 \cdot 2 \cdot 10^3 \cdot 8$ and write it as a single integer. Starting on the right, how many zeros are there from the units digit to the first nonzero digit?

4. Explain why the rule $(ab)^n = a^n b^n$ is true. It may help to draw diagrams similar to the diagrams at the beginning of this lesson.

   > In Lesson 6.01, Group IV explored this rule.

5. Use the rule from Exercise 4 to simplify each expression.

   a. $5^3 2^3$
   b. $4^6 25^6$
   c. $9^{10} \left(\frac{1}{9}\right)^{10}$
   d. $20^4 \left(\frac{1}{10}\right)^4$
   e. $20^4 5^4$
   f. $\left(\frac{4}{3}\right)^4 \left(\frac{15}{2}\right)^4$

6. Use the 26 letters in the English alphabet.

   a. How many different combinations of three letters are possible? For example, NEK, KEN, and BBR are combinations.

   b. How many different combinations of n letters are possible?

   c. How many different three-letter combinations use all consonants?

   d. How many different three-letter combinations use all different letters?

   > The vowels are A, E, I, O, and U. Consider the rest of the letters as consonants.

7. In one English dictionary, there are the following numbers of words.

   - 2 one-letter words
   - 96 two-letter words
   - 1238 three-letter words
   - 3391 four-letter words

   Only 2 out of the 26 possible one-letter sets are words.

   a. If you write a letter at random, what is the probability that you form a word? Write your result as a percent. Round to two decimal places.

   b. If you write two letters at random, what is the probability that you form a word? Write your result as a percent. Round to two decimal places.

   c. Which is more likely, forming a word using three random letters, or forming a word using four random letters?

8. A palindrome is a string of letters that is the same whether you read it backwards or forwards.

   a. How many different combinations of three letters are palindromes? An example is EVE.

   b. How many different combinations of four letters are palindromes? An example is OTTO.

   c. **Take It Further** How many different combinations of p letters are palindromes?

On Your Own

9. Rewrite each expression using exponents.

   a. $x \cdot y \cdot x \cdot y \cdot x \cdot y \cdot x$

   b. $m \cdot m^2 \cdot m^3 \cdot 3 \cdot 3 \cdot n \cdot n$

   c. $z \cdot z \cdot z^4 \cdot 5z$

   d. $(2x)^3 \cdot x \cdot x^3$

10. A National Football League field is $53\frac{1}{3}$ yards wide and 120 yards long including both end zones. How many square feet are in a football field?

11. a. If $2^x = 8$, what is the value of x?

    b. If $2^{y-1} = 16$, what is the value of y?

    c. If $2^{5z} = 64$, what is the value of z?

    d. If $(2^w)(2^w) = 64$, what is the value of w?

12. A craftsperson designs Russian nesting dolls so that each doll fits inside of the next larger doll. In a set of nesting dolls, the smallest doll, Doll 0, is 1 inch tall.

0   1   2

Note that these dolls are not drawn to scale.

Suppose each doll is twice as tall as the previous doll. How tall is each of the following dolls?

   a. Doll 1

   b. Doll 3

   c. Doll 8

   d. Doll n

13. In a different set of Russian dolls, Doll 0 is only 0.75 inch tall. Suppose each doll is twice as tall as the previous doll. How tall is each of the following dolls?

    a. Doll 1
    b. Doll 3
    c. Doll 8
    d. Doll n

14. **Standardized Test Prep** What is the value of the expression $2 \cdot 2^2 \cdot 2^3$?

    A. 20
    B. 32
    C. 64
    D. 128

Maintain Your Skills

15. Simplify each expression.

    a. 1
    b. $1 + 10$
    c. $1 + 10 + 10^2$
    d. $1 + 10 + 10^2 + 10^3$
    e. $1 + 10 + 10^2 + 10^3 + 10^4$
    f. $1 + 10 + 10^2 + 10^3 + 10^4 + 10^5$
    g. What is the pattern of the sums?

16. Simplify each expression.

    a. $4 \cdot 1$
    b. $4 \cdot 1 + 9 \cdot 10$
    c. $4 \cdot 1 + 9 \cdot 10 + 5 \cdot 10^2$
    d. $4 \cdot 1 + 9 \cdot 10 + 5 \cdot 10^2 + 2 \cdot 10^3$
    e. $4 \cdot 1 + 9 \cdot 10 + 5 \cdot 10^2 + 2 \cdot 10^3 + 4 \cdot 10^4$
    f. $4 \cdot 1 + 9 \cdot 10 + 5 \cdot 10^2 + 2 \cdot 10^3 + 4 \cdot 10^4 + 7 \cdot 10^5$
    g. $4 \cdot 1 + 9 \cdot 10 + 5 \cdot 10^2 + 2 \cdot 10^3 + 4 \cdot 10^4 + 7 \cdot 10^5 + 2 \cdot 10^6$
    h. What is the pattern of the sums?

17. Which of the following are identities?

a. $(-x)^1 \stackrel{?}{=} -x^1$

b. $(-x)^2 \stackrel{?}{=} -x^2$

c. $(-x)^3 \stackrel{?}{=} -x^3$

d. $(-x)^4 \stackrel{?}{=} -x^4$

e. $(-x)^5 \stackrel{?}{=} -x^5$

f. What is the pattern in the exponents?

An identity is a statement that two expressions are equivalent under the basic rules of algebra.

This sand sculpture contains an estimated 10^{11} grains of sand.

Historical Perspective

A *googol* is a famous large number equal to 10^{100}. The mathematician Edward Kasner used this large number in a book he was writing in 1940. He asked his 9-year-old nephew, Milton Sirotta, for a name for the number. Milton replied, "Googol." The name stuck.

How large is a googol? Here is what it looks like.

10,000,000,000,000,000,000,000,000,000,000,000,000,000,000,
000,000,000,000,000,000,000,000,000,000,000,000,000,000,000,
000,000,000,000

A googol is much greater than the number of grains of sand on Earth or the number of known stars in the sky. In fact, some astronomers estimate that there are between 10^{72} and 10^{87} particles in the entire known universe. That is much less than a googol.

A googolplex is another number that is even greater than a googol. A googolplex looks like this.

$$10^{(10^{100})} \text{ or } 10^{\text{googol}}$$

You can write a googolplex with a 1 followed by a googol zeros. This number is so large that you cannot even write all the zeros. If you tried to write all the zeros of a googolplex in a book, the book would be larger than the entire universe!

6.03 More Basic Rules of Exponents

There is a rule for dividing powers that have the same base.

For You to Do

1. Express $\frac{3^5}{3^3}$ as a power of 3.
2. Express $(2^4)^3$ as a power of 2.
3. Express $(xy)^4$ without using parentheses.

To divide two exponential expressions with the same base, such as 2^7 and 2^3, you can rewrite the exponents as repeated multiplication.

$$\frac{2^7}{2^3} = \frac{\overbrace{2 \cdot 2 \cdot 2 \cdot 2 \cdot 2 \cdot 2 \cdot 2}^{7 \text{ copies}}}{\underbrace{2 \cdot 2 \cdot 2}_{3 \text{ copies}}} = \frac{\overbrace{2 \cdot 2 \cdot 2 \cdot 2 \cdot 2 \cdot 2 \cdot 2}^{7-3 \text{ copies}}}{2 \cdot 2 \cdot 2} = 2^{7-3} = 2^4$$

You can cancel three copies of 2 in the numerator and three copies in the denominator. You are left with $7 - 3$, or 4, copies of 2 in the numerator.

For You to Do

4. Make a diagram like the one above to simplify $\frac{3^5}{3^3}$.

Theorem 6.2

For any number $a \neq 0$ and positive integers b and c where $b > c$,
$$\frac{a^b}{a^c} = a^{b-c}.$$

> In this investigation, you will find a way to remove the restriction $b > c$.

For Discussion

5. Prove Theorem 6.2 by making a diagram like the one above to show that $\frac{a^b}{a^c} = a^{b-c}$. Assume that $b > c$ and $a \neq 0$.
6. How does your diagram change if $b < c$?

For You to Do

Compute each quotient, without a calculator.

7. $\dfrac{10^9}{10^8}$ **8.** $\dfrac{6^3 x^9}{3^3 2^2 x^5}$ **9.** $\dfrac{2^2}{2^5}$

To raise an exponent to another exponent, you can rewrite the exponents as repeated multiplication. For example, how many copies of 7 are in $(7^5)^3$?

$$(7^5)^3 = \underbrace{(7 \cdot 7 \cdot 7 \cdot 7 \cdot 7)}_{5 \text{ copies}} \cdot \underbrace{(7 \cdot 7 \cdot 7 \cdot 7 \cdot 7)}_{5 \text{ copies}} \cdot \underbrace{(7 \cdot 7 \cdot 7 \cdot 7 \cdot 7)}_{5 \text{ copies}} = 7^{5 \cdot 3} = 7^{15}$$

$$\underbrace{\qquad\qquad\qquad\qquad\qquad\qquad}_{3 \text{ copies of } 7^5}$$

Each 7^5 includes five copies of 7. There are three copies of each 7^5, which gives a total of $5 \cdot 3$, or 15, copies of 7.

$$(7^5)^3 = 7^{5 \cdot 3} = 7^{15}$$

For You to Do

10. Make a diagram like the one above to simplify $(2^4)^3$.

These results lead to the third basic rule of exponents.

Theorem 6.3

For any number a and positive integers b and c, $(a^b)^c = a^{bc}$.

For You to Do

Expand each expression.

11. $(2^2)^3$ **12.** $(x^6)^7$

To write an expression, such as $(xy)^4$, without parentheses, multiply the expression by itself.

$$(xy)^4 = \underbrace{xy \cdot xy \cdot xy \cdot xy}_{4 \text{ copies}}$$

Remember that xy means $x \cdot y$. You can use AOAG to rearrange the factors. You can place all the x's together first, and then place all the y's together.

$$(xy)^4 = x \cdot y \cdot x \cdot y \cdot x \cdot y \cdot x \cdot y = \underbrace{x \cdot x \cdot x \cdot x}_{4 \text{ copies}} \cdot \underbrace{y \cdot y \cdot y \cdot y}_{4 \text{ copies}} = x^4 y^4$$

For You to Do

13. Make a diagram like the one above to simplify $(7a^2b)^3$.

Theorem 6.4

For any numbers a and b, and positive integer m, $(ab)^m = a^m b^m$.

Corollary 6.4.1

For any numbers a and b ($b \neq 0$) and positive integer m, $\left(\frac{a}{b}\right)^m = \frac{a^m}{b^m}$.

For Discussion

14. Prove Theorem 6.4 by making a diagram like the one above to show that $(ab)^m = a^m b^m$.

15. Prove Corollary 6.4.1 without making a diagram. (*Hint:* Use Theorem 6.4.)

For You to Do

Expand each expression.

16. $(10x^2)^3$
17. $(a^3 b)^{11}$
18. $\left(\frac{4}{7}\right)^3$
19. $\left(\frac{3x^3 y^2}{wz^4}\right)^3$

Exercises Practicing Habits of Mind

Check Your Understanding

1. Suppose $A = c^3$ and $B = c^2$. Find two ways to write c^8 in terms of A and B.

2. Liz knows that 2^{10} is close to 1000. She estimates the value of 2^{21}. What do you suppose her estimate is?

3. Decide whether each expression equals 3^{15}, without using a calculator. Explain each result.

   a. $(3^6)^9$ b. $(3^{10})(3^5)$
   c. $(3^3)(3^5)$ d. $(3^{15})(3^1)$
   e. $(3^5)(3^5)(3^5)$ f. $3^9 + 3^6$
   g. $(3^5)^3$ h. $3^{14} + 3^{14} + 3^{14}$
   i. $(3^3)^5$ j. $9(3^{13})$
   k. $(3^5)^{10}$ l. $(3^1)^{15}$

4. Decide whether each expression equals 2^3, without using a calculator. Explain each result.

   a. $\dfrac{2^6}{2^2}$ b. $\dfrac{2^6}{2^3}$ c. $(2^2)^1$ d. $\dfrac{(2^2)^5}{2^7}$
   e. $\dfrac{2^9}{2^6}$ f. $\dfrac{2^9}{2^3}$ g. $\dfrac{2^7 2^8}{2^5}$

5. Use the fact that $2^8 = 256$. Find the units digit of 2^{16} and 2^{24}.

6. Find the units digit of $(19^3)^4$.

7. Find the units digit of $(2^5)^2 + (5^2)^2$.

On Your Own

8. In Lesson 6.02, you used a set of Russian nesting dolls. Recall that Doll 0 is 1 inch tall and that each doll is twice as tall as the doll before it. For example, Doll 1 is 2 inches tall, and Doll 2 is 4 inches tall. Now, consider two smaller dolls, Doll −1 and Doll −2.

    −2   −1   0

   a. How tall is Doll −1? How tall is Doll −2?
   b. How tall is Doll −5?

9. **Standardized Test Prep** Simplify the expression $\dfrac{(2x^2 y^3)^3}{4x^4 y}$.

   A. $\dfrac{1}{2}x^6 y^6$ B. $2xy^5$ C. $\dfrac{1}{2}x^2 y^8$ D. $2x^2 y^8$

6.03   More Basic Rules of Exponents   529

10. Decide whether each expression equals 5^6, without using a calculator. Explain each result.

    a. $5 \cdot 5 \cdot 5 \cdot 5 \cdot 5 \cdot 5$
    b. $5^4 5^2$
    c. $(5^3)(3^5)$
    d. $\dfrac{5^{15}}{5^9}$
    e. $\dfrac{(5^2)(5^2)(5^3)}{5}$
    f. $5^5 + 5$
    g. $\dfrac{5^{18}}{5^{12}}$
    h. $(5^2)^3$
    i. $(5^6)^1$
    j. $(5^3)^3$
    k. $\dfrac{(5^3)^3}{5^3}$
    l. $5 + 5 + 5 + 5 + 5 + 5$

11. Use the fact that $4^6 = 4096$. Find the units digit of 4^7 and 4^{12}.

12. Write each expression as a single power of x.

    a. $(x^2)^6$
    b. $(x^2)^5$
    c. $(x^3)^9$
    d. $(x^{10})^{10}$
    e. $\dfrac{x^8}{x^2}$
    f. $\dfrac{x^9}{x^7}$
    g. $\dfrac{1}{x^6}(x^{14})$

13. Simplify each expression.

    a. $(7c)^2$
    b. $(3x^2)^3$
    c. $\left(\dfrac{2a}{3bc}\right)^4$
    d. $\left(\dfrac{m^2 n^3}{p^4 q}\right)^{11}$
    e. $\left(\dfrac{2v^3 w^2}{8v^2 w}\right)^3$
    f. $4a^2\left(\dfrac{a^3}{2a^4}\right)^2$

    A simplified expression has no parentheses and shows each base only once.

14. ZIP Codes in the United States are five-digit combinations of numbers, such as 48104 or 02134. How many possible five-digit ZIP Codes are there?

15. The United States Postal Service uses the ZIP + 4 Code that adds four extra digits at the end of a ZIP Code. If you live in ZIP Code 48104, your ZIP + 4 Code might be 48104-1126. How many possible nine-digit ZIP + 4 Codes are there? Can you find the result in two ways?

Maintain Your Skills

16. For each sequence, find a pattern. Use your pattern to write the next three terms in each sequence.

    a. 256, 128, 64, 32, 16
    b. 625, 125, 25
    c. 27, 9, 3
    d. $\dfrac{1}{8}, \dfrac{1}{4}, \dfrac{1}{2}$
    e. $7^4, 7^3, 7^2$
    f. $3^3, 3^2, 3^1$
    g. $\left(\dfrac{1}{2}\right)^3, \left(\dfrac{1}{2}\right)^2, \left(\dfrac{1}{2}\right)^1$

6.04 Zero and Negative Exponents

In Lessons 6.02 and 6.03, you learned the following three basic rules of exponents. For all numbers a and positive integers b and c,

Rule 1 $a^b \cdot a^c = a^{b+c}$

Rule 2 $\dfrac{a^b}{a^c} = a^{b-c}$, if $a \neq 0$ and $b > c$

Rule 3 $(a^b)^c = a^{bc}$

In each rule, there are annoying restrictions, such as b and c must always be positive integers. Also, for Rule 2, b must be greater than c.

The restrictions exist for the rules because there is no obvious way to describe how to calculate a zero or negative exponent. What does it mean to multiply a number by itself 0 times? What does it mean to multiply a number by itself -4 times?

Recall that in Chapter 1, you defined the meaning of a negative number by expanding an addition table. In episode 23 below, Tony and Sasha explore the definition of a zero exponent. Their goal in developing the definition is to preserve the rules of exponents.

Minds in Action   episode 23

Sasha and Tony are trying to find the value of 2^0.

Sasha $2^0 = 0$ makes sense to me. If 2^5 is five copies of 2, then 2^0 should be zero copies of 2, which is 0.

Tony Yes, that makes some sense. Let's see whether it works with the first basic rule.

$$(a^b)(a^c) = a^{b+c}$$

Sasha Alright. Using our example, we know that $(2^0)(2^5) = 2^{0+5}$.

Tony We can use our definition that $2^0 = 0$ to calculate the value of the left side of the equation.

$$(2^0)(2^5) = (0)(32) = 0$$

Sasha Finding the value of the right side is easy. $0 + 5 = 5$, so $2^{0+5} = 2^5 = 32$. Oh, no.

Tony What?

Sasha Well, now we have found that $0 = 32$, and that's obviously not right. I think we made a bad choice for our definition.

Tony Hmm. We need another definition.

Sasha   We want Theorem 6.1 to hold true, right? So, we want $(2^0)(2^5) = 2^{0+5}$.

2^{0+5} is just 2^5. So, we want $(2^0)(2^5) = (2^5)$.

Tony   We have no choice. Divide each side of this equation by 2^5, and you have $2^0 = \dfrac{2^5}{2^5} = 1$.

Sasha   So, 2^0 has to be 1. Otherwise, the rules we already know won't keep working.

> **Remember...**
> Theorem 6.1 says that if b and c are positive integers, then $a^b \cdot a^c = a^{b+c}$.

For Discussion

1. In the dialog, Sasha and Tony use the basic rule of multiplying exponents to find a definition of 2^0. Another way to find a definition of 2^0 is to use the basic rule for dividing exponents.

$$\frac{a^b}{a^c} = a^{b-c}$$

If you substitute $a = 2$, $b = 7$, and $c = 7$, you get the following equation.

$$\frac{2^7}{2^7} = 2^{7-7}$$

Explain why this approach produces the same definition that Sasha and Tony found, $2^0 = 1$.

Minds in Action   episode 24

Tony and Sasha discuss possible definitions for 2^{-3}.

Tony   Let's try to think this through instead of just guessing what 2^{-3} should be.

Sasha   Alright. Well, we want our favorite rule to keep working.

$$(2^b)(2^c) = 2^{b+c}$$

Tony   Well, what happens if we say $b = -3$ and $c = 3$?

Sasha   I see where you're going. That's genius! Now we can say that $(2^{-3})(2^3) = 2^{-3+3} = 2^0$ since $-3 + 3 = 0$.

Tony   Also, $2^0 = 1$, so we have $(2^{-3})(2^3) = 1$.

Sasha   We can do what we did for 2^0. Solve for 2^{-3} as if it were an unknown.

$$(2^{-3})(2^3) = 1$$
$$2^{-3} = \frac{1}{2^3}$$

So, $2^{-3} = \dfrac{1}{2^3}$.

Tony That surprises me.

Sasha I guess, but if 2^{-3} is going to satisfy the basic rules, that's the only definition that works.

Tony That means $2^{-5} = \frac{1}{2^5}$, $2^{-6} = \frac{1}{2^6}$, and so on.

Sasha So, a negative exponent is like dividing. If you have 2^{-3}, then you divide 1 by 3 factors of 2.

Tony That makes sense. Exponentiation is just repeated multiplication and the opposite of multiplication is division.

For You to Do

2. How can you write $\frac{1}{2^{-3}}$ using only positive exponents?

You can formalize Tony and Sasha's work using these two definitions.

Definition

Zero exponent: If $a \neq 0$, then $a^0 = 1$.

Definition

Negative exponent: If $a \neq 0$, then $a^{-m} = \frac{1}{a^m}$.

> Do you understand why these statements are definitions rather than theorems? Are they the only possible definitions of zero and negative exponents?

For Discussion

3. Is the definition of negative exponents compatible with the definition of zero exponents? In other words, do the definitions satisfy the following equations?
   - $2^0 = 2^{5+(-5)} = 2^5 \cdot 2^{-5}$
   - $a^0 = a^{5+(-5)} = a^5 \cdot a^{-5}$
   - $a^0 = a^{b+(-b)} = a^b \cdot a^{-b}$

For You to Do

Apply the basic rules to find the value of each variable. Check your results.

4. $2^5 \cdot 2^{-3} = 2^a$

5. $2^5 \cdot 2^{-7} = 2^b$

6. $\frac{2^5}{2^7} = 2^c$

7. $\frac{2^5}{2^{-7}} = 2^d$

8. $\frac{2^5}{2^c} = 2^8$

6.04 Zero and Negative Exponents

Exercises Practicing Habits of Mind

Check Your Understanding

A ratio table is similar to a difference table from Investigation 5B, except for the last column. A difference table has a Δ column that shows the difference between two consecutive rows. A ratio table has a ÷ column that shows the ratio between two consecutive rows.

x	f(x)	÷
0	1	2
1	2	3
2	6	5
3	30	

For example, consider this ratio table. The 2 in the first row is the result of dividing the 2 in the second row by the 1 above it. Likewise, the 5 in the third row is the result of dividing 30 by 6. This table does not have constant ratios, since the numbers in the ÷ column are not all the same.

For Exercises 1 and 2, copy and complete each table using the given function. Determine whether each table has a constant ratio.

1. $f(x) = 3^x$

x	3^x	÷
−3		
−2		
−1		
0		
1		
2		
3		

2. $g(x) = \left(\frac{1}{3}\right)^x$

x	$\left(\frac{1}{3}\right)^x$	÷
−3		
−2		
−1		
0		
1		
2		
3		

3. How are the tables in Exercises 1 and 2 related? Explain.

4. Dana says, "You can write any whole number as the sum of powers of 2 without ever repeating any of them."

   Andrew replies, "Maybe. What about 13?"

   Dana answers, "Let's see. 13 is $2^3 + 2^2 + 2^0$."

   Andrew asks, "What about 17?"

   Dana explains, "17 is $2^4 + 2^0$."

   Is Dana correct? Write each number as a sum of the powers of 2.

   a. 14   b. 15   c. 16   d. 31   e. 33

534   Chapter 6   Exponents and Radicals

5. **Take It Further** Prove that Dana is correct for any positive integer n.

6. The multiplication table shows powers of ten, including 10^0, 10^1, 10^2, and so on along the axes. Each square in the table is the product of a number on the horizontal arrow and a number on the vertical arrow. For instance, the upper left corner contains 10^2, since $10^{-3} \cdot 10^5 = 10^{(-3)+5} = 10^2$. Copy and complete the table.

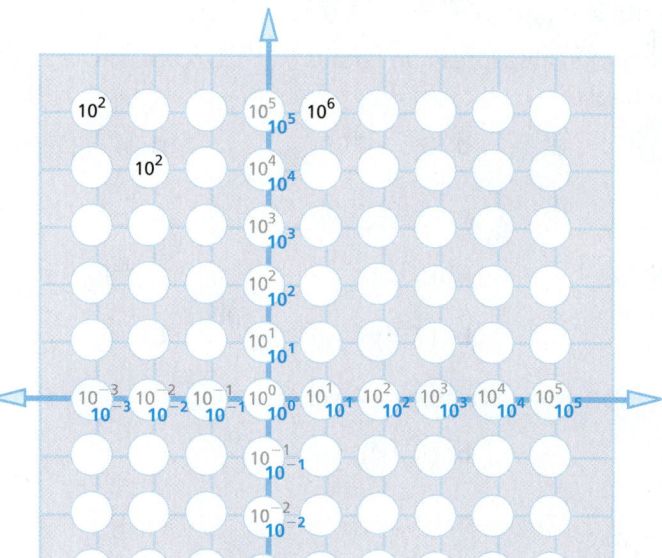

On Your Own

7. **Write About It** Compare your results in Exercise 6 to the following part of an addition table. How are the tables similar? Explain.

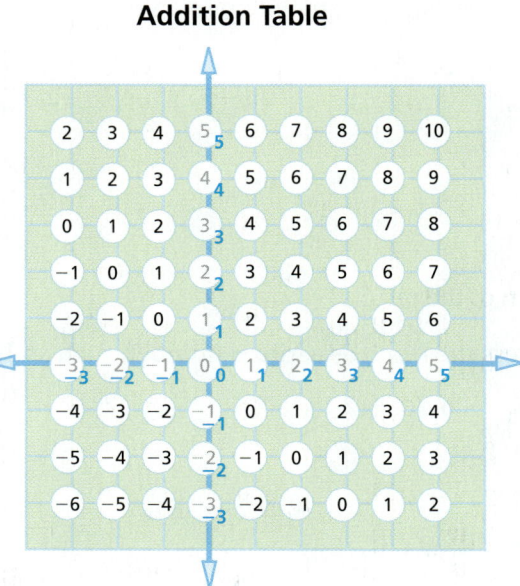

6.04 Zero and Negative Exponents 535

8. Simplify the expression $(4x + 5y - 6z)^0 + (3xy^2 - 5z)^0$. Assume that $4x + 5y - 6z \neq 0$ and $3xy^2 - 5z \neq 0$.

9. Decide whether each expression equals 7^{-10}. Do not use a calculator. Explain each result.

   a. $\left(\frac{1}{7}\right)^{10}$
   b. $7^{-4} \cdot 7^{-3}$
   c. $(7^{13})(7^{-6})$
   d. $\frac{7^3}{7^{13}}$
   e. $\frac{7^2}{7^3 7^4 7^4}$
   f. $\frac{1}{7^{-10}}$
   g. $7^5 \cdot 7^{-2}$
   h. $\left(\frac{1}{7^2}\right)^5$
   i. $(7^5)^{-15}$
   j. $(7^5)^{-2}$
   k. $(7^{-2})^5$
   l. $\frac{1}{7^{10}}$

10. Write each expression as a single power of z.

    a. $(z^{-2})(z^4)$
    b. $((z^3)^3)^{-3}$
    c. $\frac{(z^2)(z^{-4})}{z^2}$
    d. $\frac{(z^0)^4}{z^{10}}$
    e. $\frac{(z^7)^0}{(z^0)(z^{11})}$

11. **Standardized Test Prep** Simplify the expression $\frac{a^5 b^{-3}}{(a^2 b)^0} \cdot \frac{b^2}{a^{-4}}$, where $a \neq 0$ and $b \neq 0$.

    A. ab^{-1}
    B. $a^{-1}b^{-2}$
    C. $a^9 b^{-1}$
    D. $a^3 b$

Maintain Your Skills

12. Find each sum.
    a. 2^0
    b. $2^0 + 2^1$
    c. $2^0 + 2^1 + 2^2$
    d. $2^0 + 2^1 + 2^2 + 2^3$
    e. $2^0 + 2^1 + 2^2 + 2^3 + 2^4$
    f. $2^0 + 2^1 + 2^2 + 2^3 + 2^4 + 2^5$
    g. $2^0 + 2^1 + 2^2 + 2^3 + 2^4 + 2^5 + 2^6$
    h. What is the pattern of the results?

13. Find each sum. Express the result as a mixed number, such as $1\frac{2}{3}$.
    a. 2^0
    b. $2^0 + 2^{-1}$
    c. $2^0 + 2^{-1} + 2^{-2}$
    d. $2^0 + 2^{-1} + 2^{-2} + 2^{-3}$
    e. $2^0 + 2^{-1} + 2^{-2} + 2^{-3} + 2^{-4}$
    f. $2^0 + 2^{-1} + 2^{-2} + 2^{-3} + 2^{-4} + 2^{-5}$
    g. $2^0 + 2^{-1} + 2^{-2} + 2^{-3} + 2^{-4} + 2^{-5} + 2^{-6}$
    h. What is the pattern of the results?

6.05 Scientific Notation

Using large numbers can be difficult and confusing. For example, try comparing the masses of the sun and of Earth.

For Discussion

The mass of the sun is about 1,989,000,000,000,000,000,000,000,000,000 kilograms. The mass of Earth is about 5,973,700,000,000,000,000,000,000 kilograms.

1. Does the sun or Earth have the greater mass?
2. What methods did you use to compare the numbers to find the greater number?

To make this comparison much easier, you can use scientific notation to represent any real number uniquely.

Facts and Notation

A number written in **scientific notation** has the following form.

$$a \times 10^b, \text{ or } -a \times 10^b,$$

where $1 \leq a < 10$ and b is an integer.

The numbers 3.7×10^3 and -2.3×10^1 are written in scientific notation. The numbers -3700, 23, and 15×10^3 are not written in scientific notation.

> In algebra, you use $\cdot$ more often than $\times$ to represent multiplication. For example, $a \cdot b = a \times b$. Scientific notation is the exception. You write $a \times 10^3$, not $a \cdot 10^3$.

For You to Do

3. Why is 15×10^3 not written in scientific notation?

The restrictions on a may seem arbitrary, but they ensure that there is only one way to write any number in scientific notation.

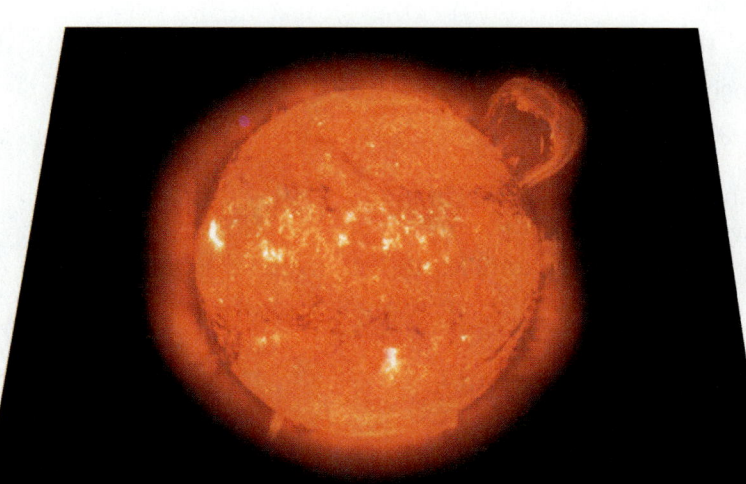

If the sun's circumference is about 2.7×10^6 mi, about how high did this solar flare reach?

Example

Problem Write 47,000 and 0.0037 in scientific notation.

Solution To write a number in scientific notation, you "pull out" multiples of 10 until you are left with a number between 1 and 10.

$$
\begin{aligned}
47{,}000 &= 4700 \times 10 \\
&= 470 \times 10 \times 10 \\
&= 47 \times 10 \times 10 \times 10 \\
&= 4.7 \times 10 \times 10 \times 10 \times 10 \\
&= 4.7 \times 10^4
\end{aligned}
$$

For numbers less than 1, you have to "put in" multiples of 10.

$$
\begin{aligned}
0.0037 &= 0.037 \times \tfrac{1}{10} \\
&= 0.37 \times \tfrac{1}{10} \times \tfrac{1}{10} \\
&= 3.7 \times \tfrac{1}{10} \times \tfrac{1}{10} \times \tfrac{1}{10} \\
&= 3.7 \times \left(\tfrac{1}{10}\right)^3 \\
&= 3.7 \times 10^{-3}
\end{aligned}
$$

Exercises Practicing Habits of Mind

Check Your Understanding

1. Write each number in scientific notation.
   a. 1,340,000
   b. 0.00000609
   c. −3
   d. 0.9×10^5
   e. 379×10^5
   f. 602,000,000,000,000,000,000,000
   g. $(1.3 \times 10^5)(6 \times 10^7)$
   h. $(2.2 \times 10^2)(5 \times 10^4)$

2. Suppose there are approximately 6×10^9 usable telephone numbers in North America that are not assigned. If the government licenses 1×10^8 new telephone numbers each year, how many years will it take until North America runs out of telephone numbers?

538 Chapter 6 Exponents and Radicals

3. Use the data from the beginning of this lesson.

    a. Write the masses of Earth and of the sun in scientific notation. Round each decimal to two decimal places. For example, you would write 1,234,567,890 as 1.23×10^9.

    b. How many times more massive is the sun than Earth?

4. Javan measures the length of his hair at the beginning and end of the month. He finds that his hair grows 1 inch per 30 days. How fast does his hair grow in miles per hour? Express your result in scientific notation.

5. Avogadro's number, 6.02×10^{23}, is an important number in chemistry. It represents the number of atoms (or molecules) in one mole of a substance. One mole of carbon weighs 12 grams. How many atoms of carbon do you have if you have 180 grams of carbon? Write your result in scientific notation.

On Your Own

6. Write each number in scientific notation.

    a. 10,000
    b. 93,000
    c. 42,000,000
    d. −86,500,000,000
    e. 0.073
    f. 0.0000119
    g. $(3.5 \times 10^3)(2 \times 10^6)$
    h. $(13 \times 10^2)(5 \times 10^8)$
    i. $13{,}100 + 2600$
    j. 400^3

7. Write each number in decimal notation.

    a. 1.86×10^6
    b. 9.472×10^{10}
    c. 8.46×10^{-4}
    d. -3.77×10^{-10}
    e. 5.5×10^0
    f. -4.09×10^{13}

8. Find the mean and median of the following numbers: 5×10^4, 5×10^3, 5×10^2, 5×10^1, 5. Which is easier to find, the mean or the median?

9. Write each number in scientific notation.

    a. 900×10^6
    b. 7300
    c. 0.8×10^9
    d. 50
    e. 110×10^2
    f. Find the median of the five numbers.

10. **Standardized Test Prep** Simplify the expression
    $\dfrac{(4.5 \times 10^9)(7.0 \times 10^{-3})}{1.25 \times 10^2}$.

    A. 25,200
    B. 36,000
    C. 252,000
    D. 31,500,000

The Hubble Telescope sends about 120 gigabytes (giga = 10^9) of science data weekly.

In Exercises 11–13, you will find which quantity is greater:
- the number of stars in the universe
- the number of grains of sand on Earth

Which quantity do you think is greater?

11. Based on recent photographs from the Hubble Telescope, scientists estimate that there are 100 billion galaxies. The average galaxy contains 100 billion stars. About how many stars are in the universe? Write your result in scientific notation.

12. Use the following information to estimate the number of grains of sand on Earth.
    - 8000 grains of sand are in 1 cubic centimeter of sand.
    - 1 million cubic centimeters are in 1 cubic meter.
    - 25 billion cubic meters of sand are on Earth.

    About how many grains of sand are on Earth? Write your result in scientific notation.

    There are 100 centimeters in a meter. Why are there 1,000,000 cubic centimeters in a cubic meter?

13. Based on your estimates, which is greater, the number of stars in the universe or the number of grains of sand on Earth? By what factor is it greater?

14. The planets are constantly in motion, so the distance between Earth and other astronomical objects is constantly changing. The table shows the average distance between Earth and a few astronomical objects.

    Average Distance From Earth

Object	Distance (miles)
Moon	2.3×10^4
Mars	1.41×10^8
Neptune	2.7×10^9

    Source: United States National Aeronautics and Space Administration

    A garden snail moves at the rate of about 3×10^{-2} miles per hour. If a garden snail could fly through space at that rate, how many hours would it take to reach the moon? To reach Mars? To reach Neptune?

Maintain Your Skills

15. Express each product in scientific notation.

   a. $(2 \times 10^5)^3$

   b. $(4 \times 10^7)^2$

   c. $(3 \times 10^2)^3$

   d. $(2.5 \times 10^4)^2$

   e. Take It Further How can you express the product $(a \times 10^b)^c$ in scientific notation?

16. Express each quotient in scientific notation.

   a. $\dfrac{9 \times 10^{10}}{3 \times 10^2}$

   b. $\dfrac{8 \times 10^8}{2 \times 10^2}$

   c. $\dfrac{6.4 \times 10^{12}}{4 \times 10^7}$

   d. $\dfrac{3.2 \times 10^{15}}{8 \times 10^5}$

17. Simplify each expression.

   a. 4×10^0

   b. $4 \times 10^0 + 9 \times 10^{-1}$

   c. $4 \times 10^0 + 9 \times 10^{-1} + 5 \times 10^{-2}$

   d. $4 \times 10^0 + 9 \times 10^{-1} + 5 \times 10^{-2} + 2 \times 10^{-3}$

   e. $4 \times 10^0 + 9 \times 10^{-1} + 5 \times 10^{-2} + 2 \times 10^{-3} + 4 \times 10^{-4}$

   f. $4 \times 10^0 + 9 \times 10^{-1} + 5 \times 10^{-2} + 2 \times 10^{-3} + 4 \times 10^{-4} + 7 \times 10^{-5}$

   g. $4 \times 10^0 + 9 \times 10^{-1} + 5 \times 10^{-2} + 2 \times 10^{-3} + 4 \times 10^{-4} + 7 \times 10^{-5} + 2 \times 10^{-6}$

   h. What is the pattern?

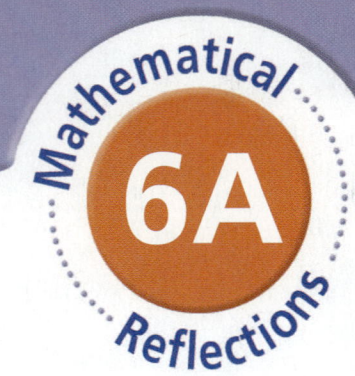

Mathematical Reflections 6A

In this investigation, you used the basic rules of exponents with positive, negative, and zero exponents. These questions will help you summarize what you have learned.

1. Some states in the United States make license plates by using combinations of two numbers, followed by two letters, and then two more numbers. 12AB34 is an example. Using this scheme, how many license plates are possible?

2. Simplify each expression without using a calculator.
   a. $x^2 \cdot x^3$
   b. $(3y)^2 \cdot y^5$
   c. $2^4 \cdot 5^4$
   d. $8^5 \cdot \left(\frac{1}{4}\right)^5$
   e. $a^8 \cdot b^5 \cdot a^{12}$
   f. $r \cdot r^2 \cdot (2t) \cdot r^3 \cdot (2t)^3$

3. Decide whether each expression equals 10^8 without using a calculator. Explain each result.
   a. $(10^2)^4$
   b. $10^5 \cdot 10^3$
   c. $10^5 + 10^3$
   d. $(10^4)^4$
   e. $2^8 \cdot 5^8$
   f. $10 \cdot 10^7$
   g. $\frac{10^{12}}{10^4}$
   h. $\frac{(10^2)^4}{10}$

4. Write each expression as a single power of x.
   a. $(x^{-2})(x^5)$
   b. $\frac{x^4}{x^3}$
   c. $\frac{x^3}{x^4}$
   d. $\frac{(x^2)^{-3}}{x \cdot x^{-1}}$
   e. $\frac{(x^2)^0 \cdot (x^{-3})}{x^{-1}}$

5. Write each number in scientific notation.
   a. 82,000
   b. 0.00039
   c. $-28{,}000{,}000$
   d. 600×10^4
   e. 600×10^{-4}
   f. 0.031×10^5

6. What are the basic rules of exponents?

7. Why is 2^0 equal to 1?

8. How can you write $\frac{2^3 \cdot 2^{-2} \cdot 2^7}{(2^5)^3 \cdot 2^{-2}}$ as a number without exponents?

Vocabulary and Notation

In this investigation, you learned these terms and symbols. Make sure that you understand what each one means and how to use it.

- base
- cube of a number
- exponent
- negative exponent, a^{-m}
- scientific notation
- square of a number
- zero exponent, a^0

The $(1 \times 10^6)(1 \times 10^3)$, or 1×10^9, spatulae on a gecko's feet allow it to climb up surfaces.

Chapter 6 Mid-Chapter Test

Multiple Choice

Solve each exercise without using your calculator. Use a calculator to check your results.

1. Which of the following expressions equals $\frac{a^3}{a^{15}}$?

    A. $\frac{1}{a^{-12}}$ B. $a^{\frac{1}{5}}$

    C. a^{-12} D. a^{-5}

2. If $a^4 = 10{,}000$, then which number is equal to a^{-4}?

    A. $-10{,}000$ B. 0.0001

    C. 10 D. undefined

3. The state of California issues some license plates in the form 2KOZ572. Each plate starts with a digit followed by three letters and then three more digits. Both the letters and digits may repeat, so 0GDD111 is a valid number. Note that the sequence starts with zero, and not the letter O.

    Which expression equals the maximum number of license plates the state of California can issue using this scheme?

    A. $10^3 \cdot 26^4$ B. $10^4 \cdot 26^3$

    C. $10^7 \cdot 26^7$ D. 36^7

4. Which expression is equal to a^9?

    A. $(a^5)^2 \cdot a^0 \cdot \frac{1}{a}$ B. $(a^6)^3$

    C. $(a^4 \cdot a^2 \cdot a^3)^0$ D. $\frac{a^3}{a^{12}}$

5. Given that $3^7 = 2187$, what is the units digit of $3^{14} + 2 \cdot 3^7 + 3^0$?

    A. 0
    B. 2
    C. 4
    D. 7

Open Response

6. Suppose $A = x^2$ and $B = x^3$. Use exponents to write three ways you can use A and B to form x^{14}.

7. Find the value of y that makes the equation $3^{2y+9} = \frac{1}{9}$ true.

8. What is the units digit of $13^5 10^3 + (117 + 921)^0$?

9. Dana says that you can write any integer as the sum of powers of 3 with no repeats.

    Dana explains, "Sure, it works. Here's 10. It's $3^2 + 3^0$ and $9 + 1 = 10$. I can also say that it's $3^1 + 3^1 + 3^1 + 3^0$, but that's no good, since 3^1 repeats. Still, it works. It's $3^2 + 3^0$."

    Is Dana correct? Explain.

10. An atom consists of a combination of protons, electrons, and neutrons.
    - The mass of a proton is 1.67×10^{-27} kilograms.
    - The mass of an electron is 9.11×10^{-31} kilograms.
    - The mass of a neutron is approximately the same as a proton, 1.67×10^{-27} kilograms.

    A single atom of fermium 259 has 100 protons, 100 electrons, and 159 neutrons.

    a. What is the mass of one atom of fermium-259?

    b. What is the mass of one mole of fermium-259? (*Hint:* There are 6.02×10^{23} atoms in one mole of fermium.)

11. **Write About It** Explain why 2^0 is equal to 1.

Challenge Problem

12. Find the last two digits of 3^{42}.

Investigation 6B

Radicals

In *Radicals*, you will learn the difference between rational and irrational numbers. You will represent some irrational numbers as square roots, cube roots, and fourth roots using radicals. You will learn to express results in simplified radical form.

By the end of this investigation, you will be able to answer questions like these.

1. What is an irrational number?

2. What are the basic moves for multiplying and dividing square roots?

3. What does $\sqrt[3]{7}$ mean?

You will learn how to

- distinguish between rational and irrational numbers

- understand the meaning of radicals, such as square roots, cube roots, and fourth roots

- calculate using square roots, cube roots, and other radicals

- express irrational expressions in simplified form

You will develop these habits and skills:

- Understand the difference between rational and irrational numbers.

- Understand the square root function as the inverse of the function $x \mapsto x^2$.

- Understand the basic rules of radicals.

A quilt square has a side length of 8 in. and a diagonal length of $8\sqrt{2}$ in.

544 Chapter 6 Exponents and Radicals

6.06 Getting Started

**Activating Prior Knowledge
Exploring New Ideas**

You will explore the relationship between square roots and squares.

For You to Explore

1. Explain how to locate each point on a number line.
   a. 7
   b. −5
   c. 101
   d. $\frac{3}{7}$
   e. $-\frac{5}{7}$
   f. $\frac{101}{7}$

2. There is only one positive number that satisfies the equation $\phi - 1 = \frac{1}{\phi}$. Based on this definition, find the value of ϕ.

   > You can pronounce the Greek letter ϕ as "fee" or "fy."

3. Follow these steps.
   - Choose an integer a.
   - Square the integer.
   - Find the prime factorization of the squared integer. How many twos are in the prime factorization?

   Repeat this process with at least five integers. Use even and odd integers.

   Is it possible to find an integer a, such that the prime factorization of a^2 contains an odd number of twos? If so, find the integer. If not, explain why.

4. Follow these steps.
   - Choose an integer b.
   - Square the integer.
   - Multiply the squared integer by 2.
   - Find the prime factorization of the result. How many twos are in the prime factorization?

   Repeat this process with at least five integers.

   In general, does the prime factorization of $2b^2$ contain an even or odd number of twos, or does it depend on your choice of integer b? Explain.

5. **Write About It** Can a perfect square ever be twice as great as another perfect square? Use your results from Problems 3 and 4 to explain.

Exercises Practicing Habits of Mind

On Your Own

6. Here is a list of perfect squares: 4, 9, 36, 49, 64, 100, 144, 400, 900. Find the prime factorization of each number. What do you notice about the factors?

7. Which of the prime factorizations represent numbers that are perfect squares? Which represent numbers that are not perfect squares? Try to find each result without calculating the product of the factors.

   a. $a = 2^3 \cdot 3^2$
   b. $b = 2^4 \cdot 3^2$
   c. $c = 3^2 \cdot 5^2 \cdot 7$
   d. $d = 3^2 \cdot 7^2$
   e. $e = 5^2 \cdot 3^6$
   f. $f = 2^5 \cdot 7^2 \cdot 5^2 \cdot 11^2$

8. Use this table to find the first two decimal places of $\sqrt{3}$. What kind of table would help you find the third decimal place of $\sqrt{3}$?

9. **Write About It** Suppose you have a calculator with only the four basic operations of arithmetic: $+$, $-$, $\times$, and $\div$. How can you use your calculator to find an approximation of $\sqrt{2}$?

x	x^2	x	x^2
1.65	2.72	1.73	2.99
1.66	2.76	1.74	3.03
1.67	2.79	1.75	3.06
1.68	2.82	1.76	3.10
1.69	2.86	1.77	3.13
1.70	2.89	1.78	3.17
1.71	2.92	1.79	3.20
1.72	2.96	1.80	3.24

Maintain Your Skills

10. Calculate each sum without using a calculator.

   a. $\frac{1}{2} + \frac{1}{4}$
   b. $\frac{1}{2} + \frac{1}{4} + \frac{1}{8}$
   c. $\frac{1}{2} + \frac{1}{4} + \frac{1}{8} + \frac{1}{16}$
   d. $\frac{1}{2} + \frac{1}{4} + \frac{1}{8} + \frac{1}{16} + \frac{1}{32}$
   e. Describe a pattern in the results.

11. Express each sum as a fraction and as a decimal.

   a. $\left(\frac{1}{1}\right)\left(\frac{1}{2}\right)$
   b. $\left(\frac{1}{1}\right)\left(\frac{1}{2}\right) + \left(\frac{1}{2}\right)\left(\frac{1}{3}\right)$
   c. $\left(\frac{1}{1}\right)\left(\frac{1}{2}\right) + \left(\frac{1}{2}\right)\left(\frac{1}{3}\right) + \left(\frac{1}{3}\right)\left(\frac{1}{4}\right)$
   d. $\left(\frac{1}{1}\right)\left(\frac{1}{2}\right) + \left(\frac{1}{2}\right)\left(\frac{1}{3}\right) + \left(\frac{1}{3}\right)\left(\frac{1}{4}\right) + \left(\frac{1}{4}\right)\left(\frac{1}{5}\right)$
   e. $\left(\frac{1}{1}\right)\left(\frac{1}{2}\right) + \left(\frac{1}{2}\right)\left(\frac{1}{3}\right) + \left(\frac{1}{3}\right)\left(\frac{1}{4}\right) + \left(\frac{1}{4}\right)\left(\frac{1}{5}\right) + \left(\frac{1}{5}\right)\left(\frac{1}{6}\right)$
   f. Describe a pattern in the results.

6.07 Defining Square Roots

In this lesson, you will learn more precisely what the $\sqrt{}$ symbol means by exploring some definitions, facts, and assumptions.

Minds in Action   episode 25

Tony and Sasha puzzle over the rules for square roots.

Tony   Does every real number have a square root?

Sasha I don't think so, because if you take a positive number and square it, you get a positive number. If you take a negative number and square it, you get a positive number. So, I'm pretty sure a negative number can't have a real number as a square root.

Tony   Well, my calculator gives me an error if I try to find $\sqrt{-3}$, so I agree. Do you think all positive numbers have square roots?

Sasha Yes, I think so. Here, show me the graph of $y = x^2$.

Tony produces the graph on his calculator.

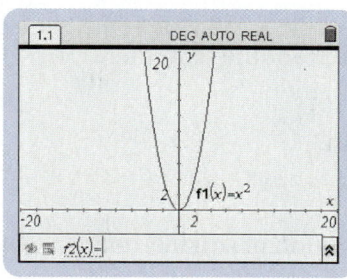

Tony   Can we use the graph to answer my question?

Sasha Sure. The number $\sqrt{7}$ is the number x such that $x^2 = 7$.

Tony   So, I draw a horizontal line 7 units up from the x-axis and find where it crosses the graph.

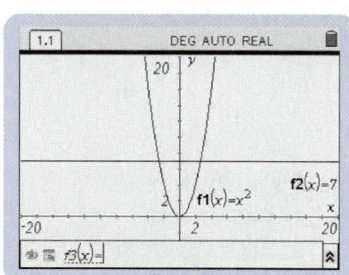

For help graphing an equation on a coordinate plane, see the TI-Nspire™ Handbook, p. 790.

Tony There are two intersections. So, there are two values for x that make $x^2 = 7$. Which one do we choose?

Sasha I think we should choose the one with the positive x-coordinate. Every square root I've seen has been positive.

Tony This might be picky, but how do we know that there isn't a hole in the graph where $y = 7$? Sometimes a calculator just draws over a hole as if it wasn't there.

Sasha I suppose anything is possible, but I don't think there are any holes. Look, I can use the graph and the calculator to get points whose square is very close to 7. It looks like the x-coordinate where $y = 7$ is about 2.6, so I'll start there.

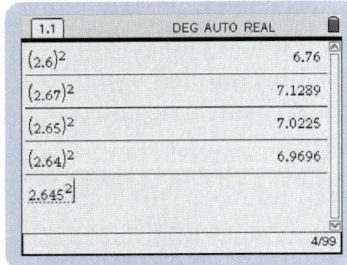

The x-values I'm squaring are getting closer and closer to each other. Also, the squares are getting closer and closer to 7. So, my x-values are getting closer and closer to a number whose square is 7. I can find a number as close to 7 as you want me to. If there were a hole in the graph, I think I could fill it in.

Tony Sasha, someday I want to borrow your brain.

Sasha and Tony's discussion leads to this formal definition of square root.

Definition

If $r \geq 0$, the **square root** $\sqrt{r}$ is a real number s such that $s \geq 0$ and $s^2 = r$.

> If s satisfies both properties, $s = \sqrt{r}$.

Using calculus, you can prove that there are no holes in the graph of $y = x^2$. For now, you can state the idea as an assumption.

Assumption The Square Root Assumption

If $r \geq 0$, there is exactly one nonnegative real number s such that $s^2 = r$. In other words, every nonnegative real number has exactly one square root.

For You to Do

1. Use the graph $y = x^2$, or other methods, to approximate $\sqrt{5}$. Round to three decimal places.

Habits of Mind

Detect the defining properties. You can describe the duck principle in this way: If it walks like a duck and it quacks like a duck, then it is a duck.

Because of the above assumption, you can use the "duck principle" to show when one number is the square root of another number.

Example

Problem Show that $\frac{\sqrt{10}}{\sqrt{2}} = \sqrt{5}$.

Solution To show that a number is equal to $\sqrt{5}$, you need to show that each of the following statements is true.

- The number is not negative.
- The square of the number is 5.

Here is how to show that each statement is true for $\frac{\sqrt{10}}{\sqrt{2}}$.

Step 1 $\sqrt{10}$ and $\sqrt{2}$ are both positive, so their quotient, $\frac{\sqrt{10}}{\sqrt{2}}$, is also positive.

Step 2 $\left(\frac{\sqrt{10}}{\sqrt{2}}\right)^2 = \frac{(\sqrt{10})^2}{(\sqrt{2})^2}$ since $\left(\frac{a}{b}\right)^2 = \frac{a^2}{b^2}$

$= \frac{10}{2}$ since $(\sqrt{10})^2 = 10$ and $(\sqrt{2})^2 = 2$

$= 5$

So, $\frac{\sqrt{10}}{\sqrt{2}}$ is a nonnegative number with a square of 5. There is only one such number, $\sqrt{5}$.

For You to Do

2. Show that $\sqrt{18} \cdot \sqrt{2} = 6$.

To apply the duck principle, use the fact that $6 = \sqrt{36}$.

For Discussion

3. Is the conjecture $\sqrt{x^2} = x$ true for all real numbers x?

Why is $(\sqrt{x})^2 = x$ true for all real numbers $x \geq 0$?

Exercises Practicing Habits of Mind

Check Your Understanding

1. For each equation, approximate x to three decimal places.
   a. $x^2 = 10$
   b. $x^3 = 10$
   c. $x^4 = 10$
   d. $x^2 = \sqrt{10}$

2. Use the duck principle to show that each equation is true.
   a. $\sqrt{2} \cdot \sqrt{3} = \sqrt{6}$
   b. $\dfrac{\sqrt{19}}{\sqrt{5}} = \sqrt{\dfrac{19}{5}}$
   c. $\sqrt{11} \cdot \sqrt{7} = \sqrt{77}$
   d. $\dfrac{\sqrt{12}}{2} = \sqrt{3}$
   e. $\dfrac{10}{\sqrt{10}} = \sqrt{10}$

3. Let $a = \dfrac{1}{\sqrt{2}}$ and $b = \dfrac{\sqrt{2}}{2}$. Find the value of the expression $(a + b)^2$. Simplify your result.

On Your Own

4. Sasha thinks of an integer and gives Tony a few hints. "The square root of my number is between 2 and 3, and my number is prime," Sasha says. Is this enough information to find Sasha's number? Explain.

5. Tony thinks of an integer. Sasha tries to guess this integer. Tony says, "The square root of my number is between 3 and 4, and my number has six factors." Is this enough information to find Tony's number? Explain.

6. Write each expression as the square root of an integer. Let $p = \sqrt{2}$, $r = \sqrt{3}$, and $s = \sqrt{5}$.
   a. pr
   b. ps
   c. rs
   d. Does $p + r = s$?
   e. What is the product of your results for parts (a), (b), and (c)?

7. Find the value of each expression. Let $a = \dfrac{1}{\sqrt{2}}$, $b = \dfrac{1}{2}$, and $c = \dfrac{\sqrt{3}}{2}$.
   a. $2a^2$
   b. $b^2 + c^2$

8. **Standardized Test Prep** For $x > 0$, which expression is equal to $\sqrt{\dfrac{1}{x}}$?

   A. $\dfrac{\sqrt{x}}{x}$
   B. $\dfrac{x}{\sqrt{x}}$
   C. $\dfrac{1}{x}$
   D. $\dfrac{2}{\sqrt{x}}$

pearsonsuccessnet.com

9. The area of a circle is the product of the constant π and the square of the length of the radius of the circle, or $A = \pi r^2$.

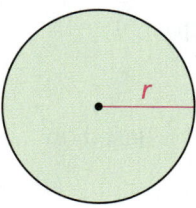

Find the radius of each circle with the given area.

a. 4π b. 2π
c. 3π d. 17π

> The constant π is the ratio of a circle's circumference to its diameter. The value of π is approximately 3.1416.

Maintain Your Skills

10. Determine whether each square root is an integer. For each square root that is *not* an integer, find the two integers it lies between.

    a. $\sqrt{2}$ b. $\sqrt{3}$ c. $\sqrt{4}$
    d. $\sqrt{5}$ e. $\sqrt{6}$ f. $\sqrt{7}$
    g. $\sqrt{8}$ h. $\sqrt{9}$ i. $\sqrt{10}$

    j. What is the least positive integer with a square root greater than 4?

A center-pivot irrigation system with a radius of 1000 ft can water $\pi(1000)^2$, or $1{,}000{,}000\pi$, ft^2 of farmland.

Historical Perspective

In ancient Greece, Pythagoras (namesake of the Pythagorean Theorem) founded a mystical religious group. Its members came to be called the Pythagoreans. They believed that they could describe everything in the world with integers. They looked for mathematical patterns in nature, music, and art. As a part of their religious beliefs, they investigated mathematics and proved a number of important theorems.

A central belief of the Pythagorean school is that you can express all numbers as integers or ratios of integers. In other words, the Pythagoreans believed that all numbers are rational. It came as a great shock when the Pythagorean Hippasus of Metapontum proved that $\sqrt{2}$ was not a rational number. The existence of an irrational number directly contradicted one of the central Pythagorean beliefs.

6.07 Defining Square Roots 551

6.8 Arithmetic with Square Roots

Consider the following calculation. What is the reason for each step?

$$(\sqrt{7} \cdot \sqrt{2})^2 = (\sqrt{7})^2(\sqrt{2})^2$$
$$= 7 \cdot 2$$
$$= 14$$

The product $\sqrt{7} \cdot \sqrt{2}$ is a positive number with a square of 14. Based on the duck principle, the following equation is true.

$$\sqrt{7} \cdot \sqrt{2} = \sqrt{14}$$

This calculation is a specific example of a useful basic rule of square roots.

> **Be careful!**
> $\sqrt{7} + \sqrt{2} \neq \sqrt{7 + 2}$. Explain.

Theorem 6.5

If x and y are nonnegative numbers, then $\sqrt{x} \cdot \sqrt{y} = \sqrt{xy}$.

> You say that the product of the square roots is the square root of the product. Use this basic rule for calculating with square roots.

Proof Use the duck principle as you did in Lesson 6.07. From the definition of a square root, you know that $\sqrt{xy}$ is the unique nonnegative number whose square is xy. To prove that the equation is true, you need to show that the left side of the equation is also a nonnegative number whose square is xy.

Step 1 The product of two nonnegative numbers is nonnegative. Since $\sqrt{x} \geq 0$ and $\sqrt{y} \geq 0$, it follows that $\sqrt{x} \cdot \sqrt{y} \geq 0$.

Step 2 $(\sqrt{x} \cdot \sqrt{y})^2 = (\sqrt{x} \cdot \sqrt{y})(\sqrt{x} \cdot \sqrt{y})$
$$= \sqrt{x}\sqrt{x}\sqrt{y}\sqrt{y}$$
$$= (\sqrt{x})^2(\sqrt{y})^2$$
$$= xy$$

Since the Square Root Assumption in Lesson 6.07 tells you that a square root is unique, both quantities must be equal.

Like all basic rules, this equation is a two-way street. You can use the rule to move from the right side of the equation to the left side of the equation, or from left to right.

For You to Do

Explain how each equation is a consequence of Theorem 6.5.

1. $\sqrt{15} = \sqrt{5} \cdot \sqrt{3}$
2. $\sqrt{2} \cdot \sqrt{\frac{1}{3}} = \sqrt{\frac{2}{3}}$
3. $\sqrt{20} \cdot \sqrt{5} = 10$
4. If $n \geq 0$, then $7n = \sqrt{7} \cdot \sqrt{7n^2}$.

For Discussion

5. Is the square root of the sum of two numbers the same as the sum of the square roots? Explain.

Example

Problem Is the square root of the quotient of two numbers the same as the quotient of the square roots? Explain.

Solution Yes, if the numbers are positive, the square root of the quotient of two numbers is also the quotient of their square roots. In other words, there is another basic rule.

Corollary 6.5.1

If a and b are nonnegative real numbers ($b \neq 0$), then $\dfrac{\sqrt{a}}{\sqrt{b}} = \sqrt{\dfrac{a}{b}}$.

To show that a number is $\sqrt{\dfrac{a}{b}}$, you need to show that each statement is true.

- The number is not negative.
- The number's square is $\dfrac{a}{b}$.

Step 1 If a and b are nonnegative ($b \neq 0$), then $\sqrt{a}$ and $\sqrt{b}$ are both nonnegative. So the quotient $\dfrac{\sqrt{a}}{\sqrt{b}}$ is also nonnegative.

Step 2 Square $\dfrac{\sqrt{a}}{\sqrt{b}}$ and find whether the result is $\dfrac{a}{b}$.

$$\left(\dfrac{\sqrt{a}}{\sqrt{b}}\right)^2 = \dfrac{(\sqrt{a})^2}{(\sqrt{b})^2} \quad \text{because when you square a fraction, you square the numerator and denominator}$$

$$= \dfrac{a}{b} \quad \text{because } (\sqrt{a})^2 = a \text{ and } (\sqrt{b})^2 = b$$

The fraction $\dfrac{\sqrt{a}}{\sqrt{b}}$ is a nonnegative number whose square is $\dfrac{a}{b}$. There is only one such number, $\sqrt{\dfrac{a}{b}}$.

> The duck principle is at work. If the number is nonnegative, and the square is $\dfrac{a}{b}$, then the number must be the square root of $\dfrac{a}{b}$.

The square root of a sum is not, in general, the sum of the square roots. Sometimes you can use the Distributive Property to simplify calculations involving the sum of square roots. Here are some examples.

- $2\sqrt{2} + 5\sqrt{2} = (2 + 5)\sqrt{2} = 7\sqrt{2}$
- $3\sqrt{7} + 19\sqrt{7} = (3 + 19)\sqrt{7} = 22\sqrt{7}$
- $4\sqrt{3} - 2\sqrt{11} - 6\sqrt{3} + 5\sqrt{11} = -2\sqrt{3} + 3\sqrt{11}$

Habits of Mind

Experiment. Try it with numbers! Is $\sqrt{2} + \sqrt{3} = \sqrt{5}$?

6.08 Arithmetic with Square Roots

The rule for finding the sum of square roots is very similar to the rule for combining terms in expressions such as $2x + 4y + 3x + 5y$. You can use the Distributive Property to combine like terms. In the expression above, notice that there is no way to further simplify $-2\sqrt{3} + 3\sqrt{11}$.

Remember...
One version of the Distributive Property states that if a, b, and c are any numbers, then $(a + b)c = ac + bc$.

For You to Do

6. Simplify the expression below by combining like terms.

$$3\sqrt{2} - 6\sqrt{5} - 1.25\sqrt{2} - 2\sqrt{17} + 8\sqrt{5} + 1.25\sqrt{2} + 2\sqrt{6} + \sqrt{6}$$

Exercises Practicing Habits of Mind

Check Your Understanding

1. Find the value of each expression. Let $a = \sqrt{5} + 1$ and $b = \sqrt{5} - 1$.
   a. ab
   b. $a + b$
   c. $a - b$
   d. **Take It Further** $a^2 - b^2$

2. For each equation, find the integer k that satisfies the equation.
   a. $\sqrt{8} = k\sqrt{2}$
   b. $\sqrt{12} = k\sqrt{3}$
   c. $\sqrt{45} = k\sqrt{5}$
   d. $\sqrt{500} = k\sqrt{5}$
   e. $\sqrt{27} = k\sqrt{3}$
   f. Why can you find an integer k in each part above?

3. Use the graph of $y = x^4$ to find approximations of all real numbers x that satisfy each equation.
   a. $x^4 = 15$
   b. $x^4 = 16$
   c. $x^4 = 7$
   d. $x^4 = -7$

4. For each group of numbers,
   - find the products of the possible pairs of numbers
   - find the product of the three products

   a. $\sqrt{2}, \sqrt{3}, \sqrt{11}$
   b. $\sqrt{3}, \sqrt{4}, \sqrt{5}$
   c. $\sqrt{5}, \sqrt{7}, \sqrt{11}$

   d. How does the product of the three products relate to the initial three numbers? Explain.

5. **Standardized Test Prep** Simplify the expression $\sqrt{3} \cdot \sqrt{2} + 5\sqrt{6}$.
   A. $6\sqrt{6}$
   B. $\sqrt{5} + 5\sqrt{6}$
   C. $5\sqrt{11}$
   D. 30

On Your Own

6. For each equation, find the integer k that satisfies the equation.

  a. $\sqrt{8} + \sqrt{2} = k\sqrt{2}$
  b. $\sqrt{12} - \sqrt{3} = k\sqrt{3}$
  c. $\sqrt{500} - 15\sqrt{5} = k\sqrt{5}$
  d. $\sqrt{605} + \sqrt{5} = k\sqrt{5}$
  e. $\sqrt{275} + \sqrt{11} = k\sqrt{11}$

7. Take It Further In general, $\sqrt{x} + \sqrt{y} \neq \sqrt{x+y}$. What statements can you make about the inequality? For example, is the value of one side of the equation always larger than the value of the other side?

Substitute each of the following values for x and y. Calculate the approximate values of each side of the inequality.

  a. $x = 1$ and $y = 1$
  b. $x = 2$ and $y = 7$
  c. $x = 3$ and $y = 3$
  d. $x = 15$ and $y = 10$

8. Use the graph of $y = x^5$ to find approximations of all real numbers x that satisfy each equation.

  a. $x^5 = 15$
  b. $x^5 = 32$
  c. $x^5 = 7$
  d. $x^5 = -7$

9. Sometimes you can simplify square roots by factoring out a perfect square from under the square root symbol. For instance, $\sqrt{12} = \sqrt{4} \cdot \sqrt{3} = 2\sqrt{3}$.

Using a similar method, simplify each expression.

  a. $\sqrt{50}$
  b. $\sqrt{40}$
  c. $\sqrt{2^3 \cdot 5^5}$

10. Order the following expressions from least to greatest.

$\sqrt{39}, \sqrt{7}, \sqrt{9 \cdot 16}, \sqrt{10} + \sqrt{26}, \dfrac{\sqrt{12}}{\sqrt{3}}$

11. In the diagram, there are four squares that share the same lower left corner. The areas of the squares are 100, 200, 300, and 400. Find a, b, c, and $a + b + c$ without using a calculator.

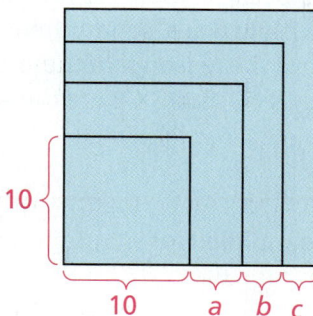

Maintain Your Skills

12. Calculate each difference without using a calculator.

  a. $\dfrac{1}{\sqrt{2}} - \dfrac{\sqrt{2}}{2}$
  b. $\dfrac{1}{\sqrt{3}} - \dfrac{\sqrt{3}}{3}$
  c. $\dfrac{1}{\sqrt{4}} - \dfrac{\sqrt{4}}{4}$
  d. $\dfrac{1}{\sqrt{5}} - \dfrac{\sqrt{5}}{5}$

  e. What is the pattern in the differences?

6.09 Conventions for Roots

You can express the same number in many different ways. Here are some ways to write the number 2.

$$2 = 1 + 1 = \frac{3+1}{2} = \frac{4}{2} = 6 \cdot \frac{1}{3} = 16 \cdot 0.125 = \frac{10}{5}$$

Your result may be equal to someone else's result, but you may have written the result in a different way.

Because there are many ways to write a result, mathematics uses standard forms for writing numbers and expressions. For example, you write variable letters at the end of terms in expressions. You write $3x$ instead of $x3$, even though both expressions could mean the same thing. The standard form for fractions is to write them in lowest terms, without any common factors in the numerator and denominator. You write the fraction $\frac{90}{50}$ in lowest terms as $\frac{9}{5}$.

There is also a set of conventions for writing square roots. The first convention is to have the smallest possible integer inside the radical. For instance, you can write $\sqrt{50}$ with a smaller integer inside the radical.

$$\sqrt{50} = \sqrt{25 \cdot 2}$$
$$= \sqrt{25} \cdot \sqrt{2}$$
$$= \sqrt{5^2} \cdot \sqrt{2}$$
$$= 5\sqrt{2}$$

These moves are legal because of Theorem 6.5.

The form $5\sqrt{2}$ is standard, because there are no perfect squares that divide 2. Numbers such as 2 and 6 are "square-free" because they have no perfect square factors. Recall the reason that these conventions exist is so that you can recognize that $\sqrt{50}$ and $5\sqrt{2}$ are the same result.

For You to Do

Write each square root in simplified form by finding perfect squares in the number under the $\sqrt{}$ symbol.

1. $\sqrt{32}$
2. $\sqrt{92}$
3. $\sqrt{20}$
4. $\sqrt{1800}$

The second convention is to never leave a square root in the denominator of a fraction. You can rewrite the fraction $\frac{1}{\sqrt{2}}$ by multiplying the numerator and denominator by $\sqrt{2}$.

$$\frac{1}{\sqrt{2}} = \frac{1}{\sqrt{2}} \cdot \frac{\sqrt{2}}{\sqrt{2}} = \frac{1 \cdot \sqrt{2}}{\sqrt{2} \cdot \sqrt{2}} = \frac{\sqrt{2}}{2}$$

Conventions have exceptions. Sometimes it is easier to work with expressions by leaving square roots in the denominator.

For example, suppose you find the result $\frac{\sqrt{2}}{2}$ and a friend finds the result $\frac{4}{\sqrt{32}}$. You both have the same result, but it is hard to know that without using the conventions for simplifying square roots.

For You to Do

Write each fraction in simplified form by eliminating the square root in the denominator.

5. $\dfrac{1}{\sqrt{3}}$
6. $\dfrac{\sqrt{2}}{\sqrt{7}}$
7. $\dfrac{3\sqrt{11}}{\sqrt{11}}$
8. $\dfrac{\sqrt{2}}{\sqrt{6}}$

Facts and Notation

The conventions for simplifying square roots are the following:

- **Replace perfect squares inside the square root sign with their square roots outside the square root sign.**
- **Do not leave a square root sign in the denominator.**

Making the number inside the square root sign "square-free" helps identify like terms in square roots. This is useful when you add or subtract radicals. For example, you can simplify the expression $\sqrt{48} - \sqrt{3}$ to a single term.

$$\sqrt{48} - \sqrt{3} = \sqrt{16 \cdot 3} - \sqrt{3}$$
$$= \sqrt{16} \cdot \sqrt{3} - \sqrt{3}$$
$$= 4\sqrt{3} - \sqrt{3}$$
$$= 3\sqrt{3}$$

By factoring out the perfect squares from the number inside the square root sign, you can identify and combine like terms.

Exercises Practicing Habits of Mind

Check Your Understanding

1. The area of a circle is the product of the radius of the circle squared and the constant π. Find the radius of each circle with the given area. Simplify any radicals.

   a. $\dfrac{\pi}{2}$
   b. $\dfrac{\pi}{4}$
   c. $\dfrac{\pi}{31}$

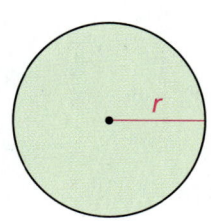

2. Some numbers are larger than their square roots. For instance, $3 > \sqrt{3}$. Other numbers are smaller than their square roots. For instance, $\frac{1}{4} < \sqrt{\frac{1}{4}}$. Find a rule that tells you which values of x satisfy the inequality $x > \sqrt{x}$.

3. In Lesson 6.6, you searched for a number ϕ.
   a. Use the equation $\phi - 1 = \frac{1}{\phi}$ to find the value of $\phi^2 - \phi$.
   b. Use the exact value $\phi = \frac{\sqrt{5} + 1}{2}$ and arithmetic with square roots to confirm the value of $\phi^2 - \phi$.

> Try rewriting the equation without fractions.

4. **Take It Further** There are different ways to express ϕ using square roots. For example, you can write $\phi = \frac{\sqrt{5} + 1}{2}$ and $\phi = \frac{2}{\sqrt{5} - 1}$.
   a. Show that the expressions for ϕ are equal.
   b. Use the first expression for ϕ to calculate a fraction for $\phi - 1$.
   c. Recall that ϕ has the property that $\phi - 1 = \frac{1}{\phi}$. Use your result from part (b) to show that this property is true.

On Your Own

5. Write each radical in simplified form.
   a. $\sqrt{8}$
   b. $\sqrt{27}$
   c. $\sqrt{12}$
   d. $\sqrt{56}$
   e. $\sqrt{26}$
   f. $\sqrt{162}$
   g. $\sqrt{55}$
   h. $\sqrt{121}$
   i. $\sqrt{200}$

6. Annie, Hideki, and Derman rewrite the fraction $\frac{5}{\sqrt{3} + 1}$ in simplified form.

   Annie says, "We need to multiply by $\frac{\sqrt{3}}{\sqrt{3}}$."

   Hideki replies, "No, we need to multiply by $\frac{\sqrt{3} - 1}{\sqrt{3} - 1}$."

   Derman chimes in, "No, we need to multiply by $\frac{\sqrt{3} + 1}{\sqrt{3} + 1}$."

   Which method produces a number in simplified form?

7. For each right triangle, find the length of the third side. Write your result in simplified form.

   a. legs of 4 in. and 6 in.

   b. legs of $\frac{1}{2}$ in. and $\frac{1}{4}$ in.

   c. a leg of $\frac{1}{3}$ in. and a hypotenuse of $\frac{2}{3}$ in.

8. Calculate the area and perimeter of each rectangle given its side lengths.

   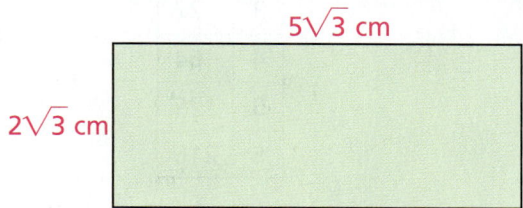

   a. $2\sqrt{3}$ cm and $5\sqrt{3}$ cm

   b. $3\sqrt{5}$ cm and $8\sqrt{2}$ cm

   c. $\frac{\sqrt{7}}{2}$ cm and $4\sqrt{7}$ cm

9. The area of an animal pen is 30 square feet. What are the lengths of the pen's sides if the pen has each given shape? Write your answers in simplified form.

   a. a square

   b. a rectangle with a longer side twice the length of the shorter side

   c. a rectangle with a longer side three times the length of the shorter side

   d. a right triangle with a height five times the length of the base

10. **Standardized Test Prep** What is the height of a triangle with an area of 1 and a base that is six times as long as the height? (*Hint:* The area of a triangle is $\frac{1}{2}$ times the base times the height.)

    A. $\frac{\sqrt{6}}{6}$

    B. $\frac{1}{3}$

    C. $\frac{\sqrt{3}}{3}$

    D. $\sqrt{3}$

Maintain Your Skills

11. Here is an input-output table of the function $f(x) = x^3$. Simplify each square root.

    a. $\sqrt{8}$ **b.** $\sqrt{27}$ **c.** $\sqrt{64}$

    d. $\sqrt{125}$ **e.** $\sqrt{216}$ **f.** What is the pattern?

x	x^3
1	1
2	8
3	27
4	64
5	125
6	216

Historical Perspective

Before people used calculators to compute square roots, they could remember the approximation for a smaller square root, such as $\sqrt{2}$, $\sqrt{3}$, and $\sqrt{5}$. To find $\sqrt{500}$, they could simplify it this way.

$$\sqrt{500} = 10\sqrt{5} \approx 10 \cdot 2.24 = 22.4$$

They used the second convention from page 543 to find the value of $\frac{1}{\sqrt{2}}$ without a calculator. Using long division is a big mess.

```
                    0.7
    1.414213562... )1.00000000000
                  −0.98999494934...
                   ─────────────
```

Since the decimal expansion of $\sqrt{2}$ is a nonrepeating decimal, it is impossible to find the product $0.7 \cdot 1.414213562\ldots$. How do you calculate $1.00000000000 - 0.98999494934\ldots$?

By eliminating the square root in the denominator, you can always divide by an integer. In the example above, instead of dividing 1 by $\sqrt{2}$, you can divide $\sqrt{2}$ by 2.

```
              0.7071...
    2 )1.414213562...
      −1.4
       ─────
       0.014213562...
      −0.014
       ─────
       0.000213562...
      −0.0002
       ─────
       0.000013562...
```

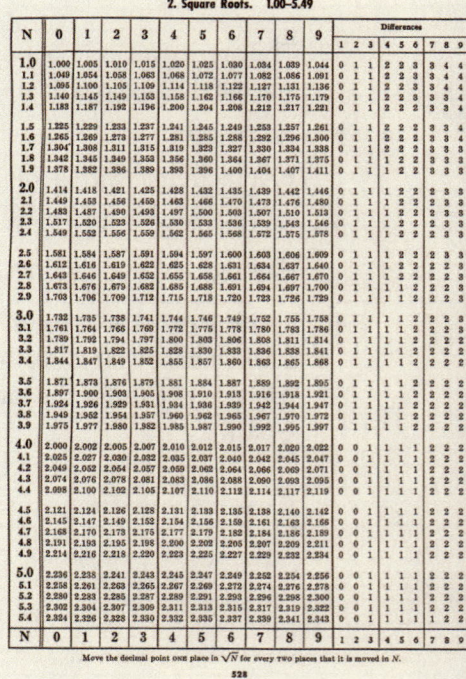

Schoolbooks had tables like this. Can you find the approximate value of $\sqrt{1.34}$ from this table?

560   Chapter 6   Exponents and Radicals

6.10 Rational and Irrational Numbers

You can think of a positive number as a number that measures a distance from 0 on a number line. The set of real numbers ℝ is the set of all positive numbers, their opposites, and 0. The set ℝ includes all integers and fractions.

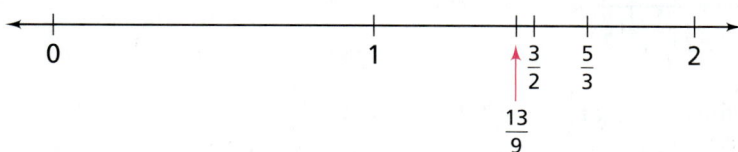

You can write every integer as a fraction. For example, you can write 7 as $\frac{7}{1}$. Positive and negative integers and fractions, along with 0, form the rational number system.

> You use the word *rational* because every rational number is the ratio of two integers.

Definition

A **rational number** is a number that you can express as $\frac{a}{b}$, where a and b are integers and $b \neq 0$. You can denote the set of rational numbers with the symbol ℚ for *quotient*.

For You to Do

Write each number as a fraction with an integer in the numerator and the denominator.

1. 1.341
2. 1.3 + 2.8
3. $5\frac{2}{3}$

> Any decimal that terminates after any number of digits is a rational number. For instance, 17.131 is a rational number, because $17.131 = \frac{17,131}{1000}$. Even some decimals that go on forever are rational numbers. For instance, $\frac{1}{3}$ is a rational number. Its decimal form is 0.333....

The ancient Greeks first believed that every real number was rational. They eventually discovered real numbers that were not rational. Historians believe the first known example of a number that is not rational is $\sqrt{2}$.

In geometry, $\sqrt{2}$ appears as the length of the hypotenuse in a right triangle with legs that both have a length of 1. By the Pythagorean Theorem, where c is the length of the hypotenuse, $1^2 + 1^2 = c^2$. So, $c = \sqrt{1 + 1} = \sqrt{2}$.

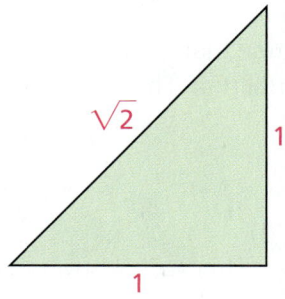

What is the value of $\sqrt{2}$? If you measure $\sqrt{2}$ units on a number line, you find that its value lies between 1 and 2.

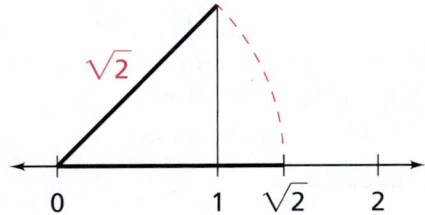

Is $\sqrt{2}$ a rational number? A calculator tells you that $\sqrt{2} \approx 1.414213562$.

The decimal 1.414213562 is a rational number. However, this number is only an approximation of $\sqrt{2}$. No rational number is precisely equal to $\sqrt{2}$. The only way to be sure that this is true is to prove it.

The proof uses contradiction. Assume that $\sqrt{2}$ is rational. Then, work toward developing a false statement. If your assumption results in a statement that is false, you have shown that the initial assumption was false.

Proof Assume that $\sqrt{2}$ is rational.

By the definition of a rational number, you can write $\sqrt{2}$ as a fraction.

$\sqrt{2} = \frac{a}{b}$, where a and b are integers.

Now, square both sides of the equation.

$2 = \frac{a^2}{b^2}$

Multiply both sides of the equation by b^2.

$2b^2 = a^2$

Each step is valid by the basic rules and moves of algebra. If the first equation is true, then the last equation must also be true.

Now, you can apply two facts you verified in Lesson 6.6.

Fact 1 If a is an integer, then the prime factorization of a^2 has an even number of factors of two.

Fact 2 If b is an integer, then the prime factorization of $2b^2$ has an odd number of factors of two.

From the two facts, the expression on the left side of the equation has an odd number of twos, and the expression on the right of the equation has an even number of twos. That cannot happen! You can conclude that the initial assumption, that $\sqrt{2}$ is rational, is false due to this contradiction. Thus, $\sqrt{2}$ is not a rational number.

For Discussion

4. Why can a number not have both an even and an odd number of twos in its prime factorization?

Reflect on this remarkable proof. There are infinitely many fractions that you can make with integers. No amount of computing power can ever find them all. However, if you introduce the variables a and b to form the possible fraction equivalent of $\sqrt{2}$, you deal with all possible cases at once. This reasoning shows the tremendous power and efficiency of algebra.

For You to Do

5. Use a similar argument to show that $\sqrt{5}$ is *not* a rational number.

The proof shows that there are real numbers that are not rational.

Definition

An **irrational number** is a real number that is not a rational number. That is, an irrational number is a real number that you cannot write as a fraction with an integer in both the numerator and denominator.

This diagram shows how the different sets of numbers fit together.

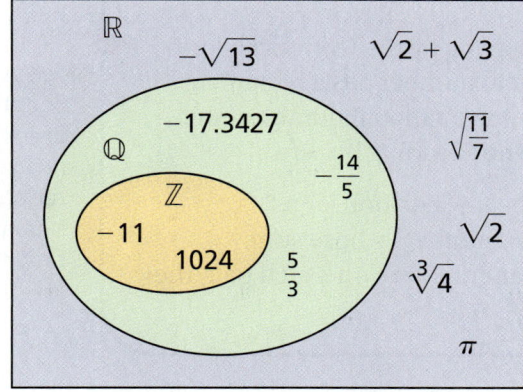

The numbers in $\mathbb{R}$ but not in $\mathbb{Q}$ are the irrational numbers.

According to the diagram, any member of $\mathbb{Z}$ (the integers) is also a member of $\mathbb{Q}$ (the rational numbers). Also, any member of $\mathbb{Q}$ is a member of $\mathbb{R}$ (the real numbers). An irrational number is not a member of $\mathbb{Q}$.

Developing Habits of Mind

Reason about calculations. In Chapter 1, you learned that if you add, subtract, or multiply any two members of $\mathbb{R}$, the real numbers, the result is always a real number. The same is true for any two members of $\mathbb{Z}$: the sum, difference, or product of any two integers is an integer. It makes sense to ask the same questions about rational and irrational numbers.

You can prove that the sum of two rational numbers is rational. By following the process of calculating the sum $\frac{3}{7} + \frac{2}{5}$, you can generalize to calculating $\frac{a}{b} + \frac{c}{d}$. Remember, you can multiply the numerator and denominator of a fraction by the same value to produce an equivalent fraction.

$$\frac{3}{7} + \frac{2}{5} = \qquad\qquad \frac{a}{b} + \frac{c}{d} =$$

$$\frac{3 \cdot 5}{7 \cdot 5} + \frac{2 \cdot 7}{5 \cdot 7} = \qquad\qquad \frac{a \cdot d}{b \cdot d} + \frac{c \cdot b}{d \cdot b} =$$

$$\frac{15}{35} + \frac{14}{35} = \qquad\qquad \frac{ad}{bd} + \frac{bc}{bd} =$$

$$\frac{29}{35} \qquad\qquad \frac{ad + bc}{bd}$$

The numerator $ad + bc$ and the denominator bd must both be integers, so the sum has been written as the ratio of two integers—a rational number! Using variables, this proves that if you add *any* two rational numbers (members of $\mathbb{Q}$), the result must be a rational number. Similar proofs show that if you subtract or multiply any two rational numbers, the result is a rational number.

What about division? You can divide by multiplying by the reciprocal: for example, $\frac{3}{7} \div \frac{2}{5} = \frac{3}{7} \cdot \frac{5}{2} = \frac{15}{14}$. Every nonzero real number has a reciprocal. You can use this to prove that when you divide two rational numbers, the result is a rational number, as long as you are not dividing by zero.

What about irrational numbers? One way to begin is to look for a counterexample: try to find a pair of irrational numbers whose sum, difference, or product isn't irrational. If you can find even one such pair, the general statement can't be true.

> **Habits of Mind**
>
> $\frac{a}{b}$ and $\frac{c}{d}$ are used to represent two general rational numbers. It would be incorrect to write $\frac{a}{b} + \frac{a}{b}$, since that would force both numbers to be the same. All of a, b, c, and d must be integers. To prove the sum is rational, write $\frac{a}{b} + \frac{c}{d}$ as the ratio of two integers.

> You'll be asked to complete these proofs in the exercises.

> See Lesson 1.15 for more about reciprocals. In Exercise 8, you'll prove a necessary detail, that the reciprocal of a nonzero rational number is rational.

For You to Do

6. Find a pair of irrational numbers whose difference is 0.
7. Find a pair of irrational numbers whose sum is 0.
8. Find a pair of irrational numbers whose sum is irrational.
9. Find a pair of irrational numbers whose product is an integer.
10. Find a pair of irrational numbers whose quotient is an integer.

> What is true about x and y if $x - y = 0$?

Now that you know about the sum of two rational or two irrational numbers, what about the sum of one rational and one irrational number? Surprisingly, this sum is always irrational.

Theorem 6.6

The sum of a rational number and an irrational number is irrational.

Proof Let the sum be written as $q + r = x$, where q is rational and r is irrational. Since x is a real number, it is either rational or irrational. Assume that x is rational.

Consider $r = x - q$. If x is rational, and q is rational, then $r = x - q$ must also be rational. Now r is both rational *and* irrational! That cannot happen, so the initial assumption that x is rational must be false. Therefore, x must be irrational.

Habits of Mind
This is the same tactic used to prove that $\sqrt{2}$ is irrational. If you want to prove that a number is irrational, this is one of only a few ways to do so.

For Discussion

11. Prove that the product of a nonzero rational number and an irrational number is irrational, using a similar argument.

Rational numbers have decimal expansions that either stop or contain a finite string of digits that repeats. For example, $\frac{2}{11} = 0.181818\ldots$ is rational. This repeating decimal has two digits that repeat forever. The decimal is periodic.

The decimal expansion of every rational number either terminates or repeats.

Suppose that you calculate $\sqrt{2}$ beyond the nine decimal places that most calculators show. The first hundred digits are:

1.4142135623 7309504880 1688724209 6980785696 7187537694
8073176679 7379907324 7846210703 8850387534 3276415727...

While some sets of digits may repeat for a while, the decimal form never repeats onward forever.

A famous irrational number is ϕ, the number you approximated in Lesson 6.6. An exact value of ϕ is $\phi = \frac{1 + \sqrt{5}}{2}$.

In mathematics, you will see many examples in which a precise value is more useful than an approximate value. In this chapter you will learn to handle precise values, such as $\frac{1 + \sqrt{5}}{2}$, and approximations, such as 1.618.

Square roots are only one kind of irrational number. Another famous irrational number is π. While many people use $\frac{22}{7}$ for π in formulas, π is not precisely equal to a quotient of integers.

Exercises Practicing Habits of Mind

Check Your Understanding

1. Fill in each blank using the word *all*, *some*, or *no*. For help, refer to the diagram showing the sets $\mathbb{Z}$, $\mathbb{Q}$, and $\mathbb{R}$.
   a. __?__ rational numbers are real numbers.
   b. __?__ integers are rational numbers.
   c. __?__ rational numbers are integers.
   d. __?__ integers are irrational numbers.
   e. __?__ real numbers are irrational numbers.
   f. __?__ real numbers are either irrational numbers or rational numbers.

2. Identify each number as rational or not rational. Explain.
   a. $\frac{13}{2}$
   b. -19.13
   c. $\sqrt{17}$
   d. $\sqrt{121}$
   e. $\sqrt{36 - 25}$
   f. $\frac{0.5}{7}$
   g. $\frac{13\pi}{2\pi}$

3. Consider the following unusual definition.
$$f(x) = \begin{cases} 0 & \text{if } x \text{ is rational} \\ 1 & \text{if } x \text{ is irrational} \end{cases}$$
   a. Is f a function? Explain.
   b. **Take It Further** What does the graph of f look like?

4. Is $0.9999\ldots$ a rational number? Explain.

5. **Take It Further** Is $\sqrt{-1}$ a real number? Explain.

6. a. Determine the difference $\frac{3}{7} - \frac{2}{5}$ by finding a common denominator.
   b. Prove that the difference of any two rational numbers must be a rational number.

7. a. Find the solution to the equation $\frac{3}{7} \cdot x = 1$.
   b. Given $a \neq 0$ and $b \neq 0$, solve the equation $\frac{a}{b} \cdot x = 1$ for x.
   c. In the equation $\frac{a}{b} \cdot x = 1$, explain why neither a nor b can equal zero.

8. Use the result from Exercise 7 to prove that the reciprocal of a nonzero rational number must be rational.

Remember...
A function is a machine that returns a single output for each valid input.

If $0.9999\ldots$ is a rational number, how can you write it as a fraction?

On Your Own

9. Plot each number on a number line. Decide whether each number is greater than or less than $\sqrt{2}$.
   a. $\frac{29}{21}$
   b. $\frac{30}{21}$
   c. $\frac{31}{21}$
   d. $\frac{13}{9}$
   e. $\frac{37}{27}$
   f. $\frac{141}{100}$

   Not every real number is rational, but you can approximate every real number using a rational number.

10. Draw a diagram like the diagram of the sets of $\mathbb{Z}$, $\mathbb{Q}$, and $\mathbb{R}$ in this lesson. Then place each number in the diagram.
    a. $\sqrt{6}$
    b. $\frac{17}{9}$
    c. $\sqrt{144}$
    d. 11.55
    e. $\sqrt{13} + \sqrt{3}$
    f. $\sqrt{2.5^2}$
    g. $\frac{91}{7}$
    h. $1 + \sqrt{6}$

11. **Take It Further** Suppose that for two real numbers x and y, both the sum $x + y$ and product xy are integers. Either prove that x and y must be rational numbers, or find a counterexample.

12. a. Determine the product $\frac{3}{7} \cdot \frac{2}{5}$.
    b. Prove that the product of any two rational numbers must be a rational number.

13. **What's Wrong Here** Derman had this to say about the square root of 6:

    Derman: $\sqrt{6}$ is rational because it's the product of two irrational numbers, $\sqrt{2}$ and $\sqrt{3}$.

    Describe what is wrong with Derman's argument.

14. Prove that the quotient of any two nonzero rational numbers must be a rational number.

15. Given that the number π is irrational, show that $\frac{1}{\pi}$ must also be irrational.

    Assume that $\frac{1}{\pi}$ is rational, and then look for a contradiction.

16. **Standardized Test Prep** Which one of these is irrational?
    A. $4 - \sqrt{49}$
    B. π^0
    C. $(5 + \sqrt{2}) + (5 - \sqrt{2})$
    D. $-3 \cdot \sqrt{5}$

For additional practice, go to **Web Code:** bda-0610

Maintain Your Skills

17. Determine whether each square root is an integer. For each square root that is *not* an integer, find the two consecutive integers it lies between.
    a. $\sqrt{11}$
    b. $\sqrt{12}$
    c. $\sqrt{13}$
    d. $\sqrt{14}$
    e. $\sqrt{15}$
    f. $\sqrt{16}$
    g. $\sqrt{17}$
    h. $\sqrt{18}$
    i. $\sqrt{19}$
    j. $\sqrt{20}$
    k. What is the least positive integer with a square root that is greater than 5?

6.11 Roots, Radicals, and the *n*th Root

By definition, the square root of 2 is the nonnegative number x such that $x^2 = 2$.

You can expand this definition. For instance, if y is the number such that $y^3 = 10$, then you can say that y is the "cube root of 10." You can write this as $y = \sqrt[3]{10}$.

You can continue to expand the definition of a root. Consider the number z that satisfies this equation.

$$z^4 = 19$$

So, z is the "fourth root of 19."

$$z = \sqrt[4]{19}$$

The word **radical** refers to roots such as square roots, cube roots, fourth roots, and so on.

There is one slight complication. Recall from Chapter 2 that there are two numbers x that satisfy the equation $x^2 = 3$. From the graph of $y = x^2$, you can see that one of these numbers is positive and one is negative.

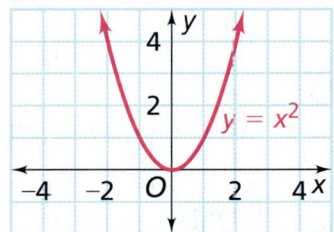

You can define $\sqrt{3}$ as the positive value that satisfies the equation. The number $-\sqrt{3}$ is the negative value.

Notice that while $x^2 = 3$ has two possible real-number results, $x^2 = -3$ has no real-number results. That is because the range is not all real numbers, only nonnegative numbers. Since a horizontal line at $y = -3$ does not intersect the graph of $y = x^2$, there is no real solution to $x^2 = -3$.

This issue does not arise with cube roots. For example, find the value of x that satisfies the equation $x^3 = 7$. Look at the graph of $y = x^3$.

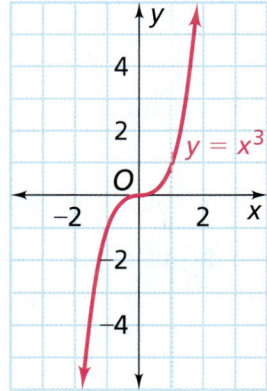

There is only one value of x whose cube equals 7. So, $\sqrt[3]{7}$ is uniquely defined. Also, notice from the graph of $y = x^3$ that the range of the function $f(x) = x^3$ is all real numbers. Any horizontal line will intersect the graph of $y = x^3$ at one point.

When dealing with fourth roots, however, the issue of no real solutions arises again. Look at the graph of $y = x^4$.

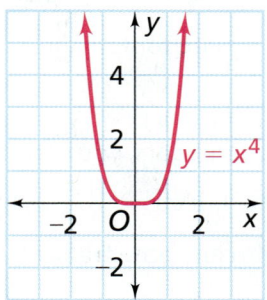

There are two values of x that satisfy the equation $x^4 = 5$. One value is positive and one value is negative. The value $\sqrt[4]{5}$ is defined as the positive of these two values.

Also, notice that the entire graph of $y = x^4$ is in the first two quadrants. So, a horizontal line below the x-axis will not intersect the graph. In other words, $\sqrt[4]{a}$ is not defined if a is negative.

In general, if n is odd, then $\sqrt[n]{a}$ is uniquely defined for any real number a. If n is even, then $\sqrt[n]{a}$ is the positive value of the two possible values if a is nonnegative, and is undefined if a is negative.

Definition

- If n is even, then for $a \geq 0$, the **nth root** $\sqrt[n]{a}$ is the positive value of x that satisfies the equation $x^n = a$.
- If n is odd, then for any real number a, $\sqrt[n]{a}$ is the unique value of x that satisfies the equation $x^n = a$.

For You to Do

Find each value without a calculator.

1. $\sqrt[3]{27}$ 2. $\sqrt[4]{16}$ 3. $\sqrt[6]{1}$ 4. $\sqrt[3]{125}$ 5. $\sqrt[3]{-27}$

In Chapter 5, you found that the function $x \mapsto \sqrt{x}$ cannot take negative inputs. If there was a real number x such that $x = \sqrt{-2}$, then $x^2 = -2$. Since squares of real numbers are never negative, x^2 cannot equal -2.

For Discussion

6. Is there a number w that satisfies the equation $w^3 = -2$?

7. Is there a number y that satisfies the equation $y^4 = -2$?

6.11 Roots, Radicals, and the *n*th Root

In Lesson 6.08, you learned some rules for calculating square roots if $x \geq 0$ and $y \geq 0$.

Rule 1 The product of two square roots is the square root of the product.
$$\sqrt{x} \cdot \sqrt{y} = \sqrt{xy}$$

Rule 2 The quotient of square roots is the square root of the quotient.
$$\frac{\sqrt{x}}{\sqrt{y}} = \sqrt{\frac{x}{y}}$$

Rule 3 When adding square roots, you can combine like terms.
$$a\sqrt{x} + b\sqrt{x} = (a + b)\sqrt{x}$$

The same rules apply with any other radical. For instance, these are the rules for cube roots.

Rule 1 The product of two cube roots is the cube root of the product.
$$\sqrt[3]{x} \cdot \sqrt[3]{y} = \sqrt[3]{xy}$$

Rule 2 The quotient of cube roots is the cube root of the quotient.
$$\frac{\sqrt[3]{x}}{\sqrt[3]{y}} = \sqrt[3]{\frac{x}{y}}$$

Rule 3 When adding cube roots, you can combine like terms.
$$a\sqrt[3]{x} + b\sqrt[3]{x} = (a + b)\sqrt[3]{x}$$

Similar rules hold for fourth roots, fifth roots, and so on.

> Can you simplify expressions with different radicals such as a fifth root and a square root? For the most part, you cannot simplify these expressions.

Exercises Practicing Habits of Mind

Check Your Understanding

1. Graph each equation.
   a. $y = x^2$
   b. $y = x^3$
   c. $y = x^4$
   d. $y = x^5$
   e. $y = x^6$
   f. How can you use the shapes of these graphs to show that $\sqrt[3]{-2}$ exists, but $\sqrt[4]{-2}$ does not exist?

2. The table shows values near 2.2 and the first two digits of the cubes of values near 2.2. Use the table to find the first two decimal places of $\sqrt[3]{11}$.

x	x^3	x	x^3
2.17	10.22	2.24	11.24
2.18	10.36	2.25	11.39
2.19	10.50	2.26	11.54
2.20	10.65	2.27	11.70
2.21	10.79	2.28	11.85
2.22	10.94	2.29	12.01
2.23	11.09	2.30	12.17

3. Is there a way to express radicals using exponents? In other words, can you find a, such that $2^a = \sqrt{2}$? The following questions will help you find a.

   a. Explain why $1 < \sqrt{2} < 2$. Use this fact to show that a cannot be an integer.

   b. Square both sides of the equation $2^a = \sqrt{2}$. Use 2 as the base on the left side of the equation. What is the result?

   c. Both sides of the equation have the same base, so for the expressions to be equal, the exponents must be equal. Write an equation showing that the exponents are equal.

   d. Solve the equation in part (c) for a.

   e. Until now, your definition of exponents only allows for integer exponents. Since a is not an integer, you will have to extend the definition of exponents while making sure that the rules work. The definition of square root lets you say $(\sqrt{2})^2 = 2$. Show that Theorem 6.3 still works by substituting 2^a for $\sqrt{2}$. Replace a with the value you found in part (d).

   f. Use the same process you used in parts (a)–(e) to find b in the equation $2^b = \sqrt[3]{2}$.

   g. Use the same process you used in parts (a)–(e) to find c in the equation $2^c = \sqrt[n]{2}$ in terms of n.

Remember...
Theorem 6.3 states that $(a^b)^c = a^{bc}$.

On Your Own

4. Make input-output tables for the functions $f(x) = \sqrt{x^2}$ and $g(x) = \sqrt[3]{x^3}$. Use inputs that include at least a few negative numbers. How are the two functions similar? How are they different? Have you seen either function before, possibly in a different form?

5. Use the duck principle to show that each equation is true.

   a. $\sqrt[4]{125} \cdot \sqrt[4]{5} = 5$
   b. $\sqrt[3]{18} \cdot \sqrt[3]{12} = 6$
   c. $\dfrac{\sqrt[5]{128}}{\sqrt[5]{16}} = \sqrt[5]{8}$
   d. $\sqrt[4]{100} = \sqrt{10}$
   e. $\sqrt[3]{4} \cdot \sqrt[6]{3} = \sqrt[6]{48}$

Remember...
To show that some number x is $\sqrt[n]{a}$, you need to show that $x^n = a$. If n is even, you have to show that x is not negative.

6. Use the fact that $6561 = 3^8$. Simplify each radical.
   a. $\sqrt{6561}$
   b. $\sqrt[3]{6561}$
   c. $\sqrt[4]{6561}$
   d. $\sqrt[5]{6561}$
   e. $\sqrt[6]{6561}$
   f. $\sqrt[7]{6561}$
   g. $\sqrt[8]{6561}$
   h. $\sqrt[9]{6561}$

   i. Which of the numbers in parts (a)–(h) are integers? Explain.

7. Suppose you need storage space twice the size of your existing storage space that is 10 ft × 10 ft × 10 ft, or 1000 cubic feet

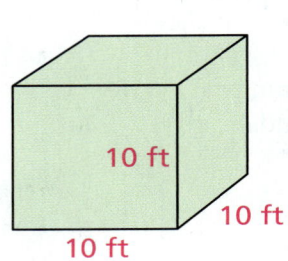
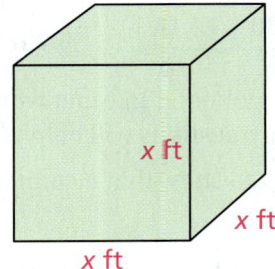

   a. Why can't you double the length of every side of your existing space?
   b. How long does each side of the larger space need to be to make it twice the size of the smaller space?

8. **Standardized Test Prep** Jasper has a cube with a volume of 100 cm³. In which of the following ranges is x, the length of the cube's side, in centimeters?

   A. $4.0 \leq x < 4.5$
   B. $4.5 \leq x < 5.0$
   C. $5.0 \leq x < 5.5$
   D. $5.5 \leq x < 6.0$

Maintain Your Skills

9. Find the median of each set of numbers.
   a. $\sqrt{5}, \sqrt[3]{5}, \sqrt[4]{5}, \sqrt[5]{5}, \sqrt[6]{5}$
   b. $\sqrt{7}, \sqrt[3]{7}, \sqrt[4]{7}, \sqrt[5]{7}, \sqrt[6]{7}$
   c. $\sqrt{31}, \sqrt[3]{31}, \sqrt[4]{31}, \sqrt[5]{31}, \sqrt[6]{31}$
   d. $\sqrt{157}, \sqrt[3]{157}, \sqrt[4]{157}, \sqrt[5]{157}, \sqrt[6]{157}$
   e. What is the pattern?

10. Find the value of k that satisfies each equation.
    a. $\sqrt{7}\sqrt{k} = 7$
    b. $\sqrt[3]{7}\sqrt[3]{k} = 7$
    c. $\sqrt[4]{7}\sqrt[4]{k} = 7$
    d. $\sqrt[5]{7}\sqrt[5]{k} = 7$
    e. $\sqrt[6]{7}\sqrt[6]{k} = 7$
    f. What is the pattern?

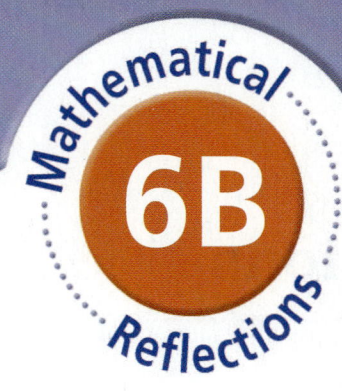

Mathematical Reflections 6B

In this investigation, you distinguished between rational and irrational numbers. You worked with square roots, cube roots, and fourth roots. You also used the basic moves for multiplying and dividing square roots. These questions will help you summarize what you have learned.

1. The prime factorization of a number x is $3^4 \cdot 5^2 \cdot 2^6$.
   a. How do you know that x is a perfect square?
   b. If $x = y^2$, what does y equal?

2. Determine whether each number is rational or irrational.
   a. $\frac{1}{2}$
   b. $\sqrt{3}$
   c. 2π
   d. $\sqrt{9}$
   e. -2.8
   f. $\frac{3\pi}{4\pi}$

3. Find the integer k that satisfies each equation.
   a. $\sqrt{8} = k\sqrt{2}$
   b. $\sqrt{300} = k\sqrt{3}$
   c. $\sqrt{20} + \sqrt{5} = k\sqrt{5}$
   d. $\sqrt{24} + \sqrt{54} = k\sqrt{6}$

4. Use the duck principle to show that each equation is true.
   a. $\sqrt[3]{8} = 2$
   b. $\sqrt{5} \cdot \sqrt{2} = \sqrt{10}$
   c. $\sqrt[4]{2} \cdot \sqrt[4]{8} = 2$
   d. $\sqrt[3]{4} \cdot \sqrt[3]{54} = 6$

5. Write each radical in simplified form.
   a. $\sqrt{32}$
   b. $\sqrt{500}$
   c. $\sqrt{\frac{1}{3}}$
   d. $\sqrt{72}$
   e. $\sqrt{720}$
   f. $\sqrt{\frac{3}{5}}$

6. What is an irrational number?

7. What are the basic moves for multiplying and dividing square roots?

8. What does $\sqrt[3]{7}$ mean?

The length of a quilt is 14 squares. Each quilt square has a diagonal length of $8\sqrt{2}$ in. What is the length of the quilt?

Vocabulary and Notation

In this investigation, you learned these terms and symbols. Make sure that you understand what each one means and how to use it.

- irrational number
- nth root, $\sqrt[n]{r}$
- radical
- rational number
- square root, $\sqrt{r}$

Investigation 6C

Exponential Expressions and Functions

In *Exponential Expressions and Functions,* you will use exponential functions and graphs to find compound interest. You also will represent tables with constant ratios by exponential functions.

By the end of this investigation, you will be able to answer questions like these.

1. How can you find an exponential function that matches a table of outputs?

2. Why is it harder to solve for x in the equation $13 = 2^x$ than in the equation $13 = x^2$?

3. How long will it take your money to double if you invest it at 6% interest?

You will learn how to

- use exponential functions to calculate compound interest
- calculate compound interest in a number of different schemes
- graph exponential functions and recognize important properties of exponential graphs
- match tables with constant ratios to exponential functions

You will develop these habits and skills:

- Understand how and why you can use exponential functions in some specific applications.
- Apply scientific formulas with specific data.
- Use tables to generate graphs of exponential functions.
- Interpret graphs of exponential functions.
- Analyze tables of data to determine whether a linear or exponential function matches it.

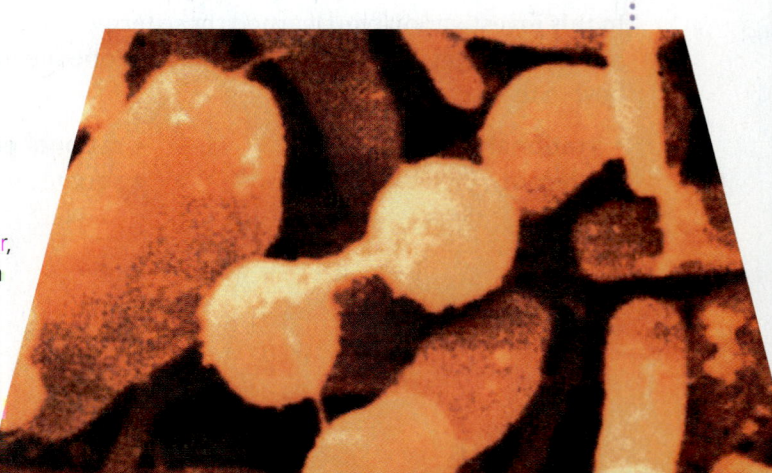

If cells split in two every hour, one cell becomes 2^{24} cells in 24 hours.

6.12 Getting Started

Activating Prior Knowledge
Exploring New Ideas

In the Higher-or-Lower Game, you will explore strategies for finding a given number within a range of numbers. You will learn ways to estimate how long it will take to play the game.

For You to Explore

Higher-or-Lower Game The first player thinks of an integer in a set range of numbers, such as from 1 to 100. The second player tries to guess the number. After each guess, the first player tells the second player whether the chosen number is higher or lower than the guess. The game continues until the second player guesses the number. The goal is to make as few guesses as possible before guessing the correct number.

1. Play the game four times. Use numbers from 1 to 100. Record the number of guesses you make before guessing the correct number.

2. Discuss game strategies. Play the game four more times. Record the number of guesses for each game. Does the average number of guesses decrease?

3. If you play the game using numbers from 1 to 200 instead of from 1 to 100, how much longer do you expect the game to last?

4. What is a good starting number to guess for a game using numbers from 1 to 100? Explain. What number would you start with if your partner tells you that the number is between 500 and 750?

5. Play the game a few times with numbers from 1 to 10. What is the maximum number of guesses you made?

6. **Take It Further** Suppose Holly can make only a specific number of guesses to find a number in a certain range.

    a. Holly finds that if she has only 2 guesses, she can find any number from 1 to 3. What is her strategy?

    b. Holly finds that if she has only 3 guesses, she can find any number from 1 to 7. What is her strategy?

    c. Copy and complete the table, where g is the number of guesses and N is the highest value for which Holly can find any number from 1 to N in g guesses.

    d. Find a rule for $N(g)$.

    e. How many guesses do you need to find a number from 1 to 1000?

    f. If you play the game with numbers from 1 to 200 instead of 1 to 100, how much longer will the game take? Explain.

Guess, g	Number, N
1	1
2	3
3	7
4	▪
5	▪
6	▪

Exercises Practicing Habits of Mind

On Your Own

7. **Write About It** Nikki says that if the Higher-or Lower-Game uses only the numbers 1 through 10, then she can always find the correct number in 4 guesses or fewer. Make a strategy table for this game that always allows you to find the correct number in 4 guesses or fewer. Describe your strategy so that someone who has never played the game knows what number to guess in each situation.

8. Joe says that if he uses the numbers from 1 to 10, he can always find the correct number in 3 guesses or fewer. Use your results from Exercise 7 to decide whether Joe can do what he says.

9. **Write About It** If n is an integer, is -2^n the same as $(-2)^n$? Explain.

10. The pH level of a solution relates to the concentration of hydrogen ions in the solution according to this formula.

    $$\text{concentration of hydrogen ions} = 0.1^{(\text{pH})}$$

    The lower the pH is, the more hydrogen ions there are. Low values of pH indicate acids, while high values indicate bases.

    The letters pH stand for "potential of hydrogen." The pH scale is between 0 and 14.

    a. Pure water is neutral and has a pH of 7. Find the concentration of hydrogen ions for pure water.
    b. How many times more hydrogen ions does a solution with a pH of 6 have than pure water?

11. Industrialization increases the acidity of rain. One way to measure acidity is to look at pH levels. A lower pH corresponds to greater acidity.

    a. Normal rain has an average pH of 5.6. How many times more acidic than pure water is normal rain? Use the formula given in Exercise 10.

    Remember... Recall that pure water has a pH of 7.

    b. Acid rain has a pH of 5 at most. How many times more acidic is acid rain with a pH level of 5 than pure water?
    c. How many times more acidic is acid rain with a pH level of 5 than normal rain?
    d. Rain with a pH of 4.3 was recorded in the United States. How many times more acidic than pure water was this rain?

Maintain Your Skills

12. Copy and complete each table for the given function.

a. $f(a) = 3 \cdot 2^a$

Input, a	Output, f(a)
0	■
1	■
2	■
3	■
4	■

b. $g(a) = 2 \cdot 5^a$

Input, a	Output, g(a)
0	■
1	■
2	■
3	■
4	■

c. $h(a) = 27 \cdot 3^{-a}$

Input, a	Output, h(a)
0	■
1	■
2	■
3	■
4	■

d. $j(a) = 27 \cdot \left(\frac{1}{3}\right)^a$

Input, a	Output, j(a)
0	■
1	■
2	■
3	■
4	■

13. Find a function that agrees with each table.

a.

Input, a	Output, k(a)
0	4
1	12
2	36
3	108
4	324

b.

Input, H	Output, C(H)
0	100
1	50
2	25
3	12.5
4	6.25

c.

Input, x	Output, p(x)
0	2
1	$\frac{1}{2}$
2	$\frac{1}{8}$
3	$\frac{1}{32}$
4	$\frac{1}{128}$

d.

Input, n	Output, Q(n)
0	8
1	12
2	18
3	27
4	40.5

6.13 Compound Interest

Banks set a rate of growth for savings accounts, or the annual percentage rate (APR). They also set rules about how the account grows in value.

> You can also call the APR the growth rate.

Minds in Action episode 26

Tony and Sasha discuss the rules for Tony's savings account.

Tony It says here that I'll make 3% every year on the money in this savings account. The bank pays interest at the end of every year.

Sasha Is 3% a lot? It doesn't seem like much. How much did you put into the account?

Tony I invested $600.

Sasha Okay, so at the end of the year they'll give you 3% of $600, which is $18.

Tony That's not very much, but they say that the longer I leave the money in there, the more interest the account will earn.

Sasha So, you'll make $18 per year. That's not a big deal.

Tony No, I'll make more than $18 from then on. After one year, I won't have $600 anymore. I'll have $618. So, the next time you figure out my interest, you'll have to use $618, instead of $600, as your starting point.

Sasha Alright, at the end of the second year, they'll give you 3% of $618, which is $18.54.

Tony You could keep doing that over and over again. I can think of a recursive rule for this calculation. If I start a year with d dollars, at the end of the year they will pay me $d \cdot (0.03)$ in interest. That's a total of $d \cdot (1.03)$.

Sasha You start a year with d and end it with $d \cdot (1.03)$. That's just multiplying.

Tony Right, that makes the rule exponential. You are multiplying by 1.03 every year.

Sasha That's nice. So, the 1 in 1.03 represents the money you already had?

Tony Right, and the 0.03 is the interest the bank gives me for letting them use my money.

Sasha So, how would you figure out how much you have after 10 years?

> You can write the rule like this.
> $$b(t) = \begin{cases} 600 & \text{if } t = 0 \\ b(t-1) \cdot (1.03) & \text{if } t > 0 \end{cases}$$

Tony I take my $600 and keep multiplying by 1.03. Repeat this ten times using this equation.

$$600(1.03)^{10} = 806.35$$

Sasha That's not bad. Still, it seems like a long time to put your money away for $200.

Tony For every $3 I put in, I get about $1 back in interest after 10 years, no matter how much I put in. I've got $600 to invest now, but maybe I can invest a little more next year.

Sasha I wonder how different the amount would be if the bank doubled the interest rate. If you make $200 at 3% interest, do you make $400 at 6% interest?

Most bank accounts, such as savings accounts and certificates of deposit (CDs), pay interest periodically. At the end of the period, the bank calculates the interest based on the current balance and adds the interest to the account.

For the next period, the bank calculates interest on the current balance, including the previously paid interest. Even interest earns interest! When you calculate interest this way, you earn **compound interest.** The interest grows at an exponential rate.

For Discussion

1. How much will Tony earn on a $600 investment after 10 years at 6% interest per year?

More Frequent Compounding

Generally, banks do not calculate compound interest annually. They may compound the interest every three months, monthly, daily, or even more frequently.

To calculate compound interest, you divide the annual percentage rate of interest into equal parts. The number of parts equals the number of times you calculate interest during the year. You use one of the parts to find the interest.

If two accounts have the same interest rate, the account that is compounded more frequently earns more money. For example, consider Tony's 3% APR account. If you compound it quarterly instead of annually, the growth rate is 0.75% per quarter (3% divided by 4 quarters).

Using Tony and Sasha's reasoning, you multiply the amount in Tony's savings account by 1.0075 each quarter. In 10 years, or 40 quarters, Tony will have $600(1.0075)^{40}$ dollars, or about $809. By choosing an account that is compounded quarterly, Tony will earn slightly more money.

Example 1

Problem Sasha reads an advertisement from BigBank that offers a 2.9% APR savings account compounded monthly. Over 10 years, how does this account compare to Tony's 3% APR account that is compounded annually?

Solution Determine how much money Sasha will have at the end of 10 years at BigBank. You can divide the APR of 2.9% into 12 equal parts, so that you multiply her total by $\frac{0.029}{12}$ each month. At the end of 10 years, her account will be compounded 120 times $(10 \cdot 12)$, so that her total will be the following.

$$600 \cdot \left(1 + \frac{0.029}{12}\right)^{120} \approx 801.58$$

This account earns only a few dollars less than the $806.35 that Tony's 3% APR account earns.

For Discussion

2. Which is better to have, an account at 6% APR compounded annually, or an account at 5.9% APR compounded monthly?

Example 2

Problem Tony invests $600 in a CD that earns 6% APR, compounded annually. How many years will it take for the money in his account to double?

Solution At the end of N years, Tony has $600(1.06)^N$ dollars.

You want to find the value of N, such that

$$1200 = 600 \cdot (1.06)^N$$

For now, you do not know a simple way to solve this equation for an exact value of N. But you can approximate a value for N by guessing, testing, and then refining your guess.

> A CD is a certificate of deposit, which gives higher interest in exchange for a guarantee that you will not withdraw the money before a set date.

$1200 Goal

Guess, N (years)	Account Balance ($)	The actual N is...	The next guess should be...
5	802.94	higher	more than 5
20	1924.28	lower	between 5 and 20
10	1074.51	higher	between 10 and 20 (near 10)
11	1138.98	higher	between 11 and 20 (closing in)
12	1207.32	correct	

The value $N = 12$ is the solution. Even though there is a number N between 11 and 12 that solves the algebra equation, keep in mind that this bank account compounds annually, so there is no increase in the account value between 11 and 12 years. This graph shows the value in Tony's account each year for the first 20 years.

With a calculator you can find that $N \approx 11.896$ solves the equation $1200 = 600 \cdot (1.06)^N$. However, that is not the correct answer for an actual bank account!

For Discussion

3. How long will it take for Tony's account to grow to $2400? To $4800? Explain.

Exercises Practicing Habits of Mind

Check Your Understanding

1. Jesse's savings account earns 2.5% APR compounded annually. His starting balance is $1200.

   a. How much money will Jesse have in the account after 1 year? After 2 years?

   b. Write a formula that gives Jesse's balance after N years.

   c. How much money will Jesse have in the account after 2 years and 9 months? Explain.

2. **Write About It** Tony earns about $200 in interest over 10 years using the savings account in the dialog. Will it take more or less time for Tony to earn the next $200 in interest? Explain.

3. Kevin saves money so that he will have $30,000 in 5 years. If his investment earns 6% interest, compounded annually, how much money does he need to invest today to have $30,000 in 5 years?

4. Suppose a car depreciates in value about 20% each year for the first 5 years.
   a. How much will a new car that costs $20,000 today be worth in 1 year? In 2 years?
   b. Write a rule for the car's value after N years of driving.
   c. Will the car ever be worth less than $1000? Explain.

Most cars actually depreciate more than 20% during the first year, and then less than 20% after that. About 20% is a reasonable average.

On Your Own

5. Use a calculator and sketch the graph of $y = 500(1.08)^x$ using the domain $0 \leq x \leq 20$. Describe a situation that this graph represents.

6. Ariela puts $500 in an investment account at 9% APR, compounded annually. After how many years will she be closest to doubling her starting investment?

7. Ariela wonders how the growth of her investment changes with higher or lower interest rates. Copy and complete the table below. For each interest rate, find the number of years after which Ariela will be closest to doubling her starting $500 investment.

Doubling Time

APR (%)	Number of Years Needed to Double Investment
3	■
4	■
5	■
6	12
7	■
8	■
9	■
10	■
12	■

Some cars eventually appreciate, or gain, in value.

8. Many financial advisors use the Rule of 72 when offering advice about long-term investments.

   The Rule of 72 To find the number of years it takes to double an investment's value, divide 72 by the interest rate. For example, the amount of time it takes to double an investment at 6% interest is about $\frac{72}{6}$, or 12 years.

   a. How does the Rule of 72 compare to the results from Exercise 7?

   b. According to the Rule of 72, how long will it take a credit card balance to double if its interest rate is 18% APR?

   c. If Ariela invests $500 in an account at 9% APR for 40 years, how many times will her money double in value? How much money will she have after 40 years?

9. **Take It Further** Sketch or describe the graph of the following function.

   $$y = (-1)^x$$

   Include noninteger values of x in the domain, such as $\frac{1}{3}$. Notice that some values, such as $\frac{1}{2}$, cannot be in the domain.

10. **Standardized Test Prep** How much is a $100,000 investment worth after 3 years with 2.4% interest compounded annually? Round to the nearest dollar.

    A. $102,400

    B. $107,200

    C. $107,374

    D. $124,000

Maintain Your Skills

11. Suppose you invest $1000. Calculate the total value of each account.

    a. 12 years, 2.5% APR compounded annually

    b. 6 years, 5% APR compounded semiannually

    c. 3 years, 10% APR compounded quarterly

12. Toni enters a contest with a $10,000 first prize. She will invest the winnings for 2 years. How much will she earn in 2 years in an account with each interest rate compounded annually?

    a. 1% APR

    b. 2% APR

    c. 3% APR

    d. 4% APR

    e. 6% APR

    f. 8% APR

6.14 Graphs of Exponential Functions

There are two types of exponential behavior, **exponential growth** and **exponential decay**.

Exponential growth

The amount of money in an interest-bearing bank account increases exponentially over time. In Lesson 6.13, you used a scatter plot for the amount of money in an account bearing 6% interest. If the value of N can be any positive number, you can draw this smooth graph.

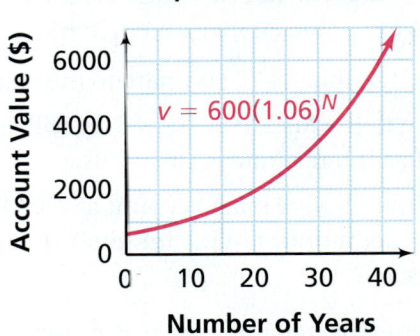

Exponential Growth

$v = 600(1.06)^N$

Exponential decay

Scientists use the carbon dating method to find the age of historic objects. The method uses a form of carbon that you find in plant or animal remains called carbon-14, or C-14. The C-14 decays exponentially by a natural process over time. The graph shows the percent of C-14 remaining after y years.

Notice that you write both exponential growth and exponential decay functions using the same general form $f(x) = a \cdot b^x$, where b is any positive real number. What does the graph of $C = 100 \cdot 2^{\frac{-y}{5700}}$ look like?

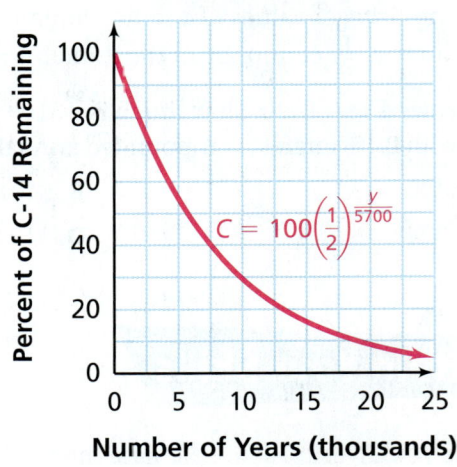

Exponential Decay

$C = 100\left(\frac{1}{2}\right)^{\frac{y}{5700}}$

For Discussion

1. What values of b lead to exponential growth? To exponential decay? Test some positive values of b and make a conjecture.

> For help graphing exponential functions on the coordinate plane, see the TI-Nspire Handbook, p. 790.

You know that exponents can be positive, negative, or zero. In fact, exponential functions can take any real number as input. In some cases, depending on the situation that an exponential function represents, it may not make sense to allow negative numbers as input.

The graph shows the exponential function $f(x) = 3^x$. This function's domain is all real numbers. You may find it difficult to understand what $3^{\frac{1}{4}}$ or $3^{\sqrt{7}}$ means, but they are both real numbers.

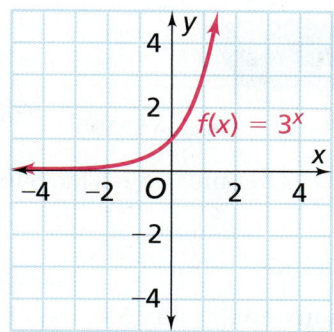

The function increases continuously. As the input increases, the output increases. What is the result when you input negative numbers such as -500 or $-10{,}000{,}000$? Does the function ever cross the x-axis?

Developing Habits of Mind

Detect the key characteristics. According to the graph, $f(x) = 3^x$ appears positive no matter what value you use for x. Looks can be deceiving, but you can prove this fact. For positive values of x, you can develop a convincing argument from the fact that the function $f(x) = 3^x$ is always increasing.

Suppose x is a positive number. If it is an integer, then 3^x is definitely positive, since $3 \times 3 \times 3 \ldots$ must be positive for any number of 3's. If x is not an integer, then you can call r the rounded-down version of x. Then 3^r is definitely positive. Since x is larger than r, 3^x is larger than 3^r. Since 3^x is larger than a positive number, then it must be positive, too.

> For example, if $x = 3\frac{2}{3}$, then $r = 3$.

For negative values of x, the key to the proof is to think about reciprocals. Notice that if a number is positive, then its reciprocal is also positive. For example, both 83 and $\frac{1}{83}$ are positive.

If 3^a is positive, then $\frac{1}{3^a}$ must also be positive. From the definition of negative exponents, $\frac{1}{3^a} = 3^{-a}$. In short, if 3^a is positive, 3^{-a} is also positive. If x is negative, then $-x$ is positive. From the argument above, 3^{-x} must be positive, and then 3^x must be positive for negative values of x.

> Notice that $-x$ is not necessarily a negative number. The negative sign means to take the opposite of x. If x is negative, $-x$ is positive.

For Discussion

2. The argument is the same if the base is 4 or any number greater than 1. If the base is $\frac{1}{4}$, you can flip the argument. Since $\left(\frac{1}{4}\right)^x = 4^{-x}$, you can follow the same argument, replacing x with $-x$. Explain.

Example

Problem Alicia and Berta both save $2500.

Alicia's Plan Alicia saves her money in a jar. She will add $200 every year.

Bertha's Plan Berta saves her money in the bank, earning 6% interest each year compounded annually.

Who will save more money after 5 years? After 15 years?

Solution One way to determine who will save more money is to write a function to represent each savings plan. Then compare the graphs of the two functions. Alicia's plan has a constant difference of $200 per year, so after t years the following equation represents Alicia's savings.

$$a(t) = 2500 + 200t$$

Berta's plan earns interest at a rate of 6% per year. After 1 year, she has $2500(1.06)$. After 2 years, she has $2500(1.06)(1.06)$, or $2500(1.06)^2$. After t years, she has $2500(1.06)^t$. You can write Berta's balance as a function of t.

$$b(t) = 2500(1.06)^t$$

Graph both equations on the same axes.

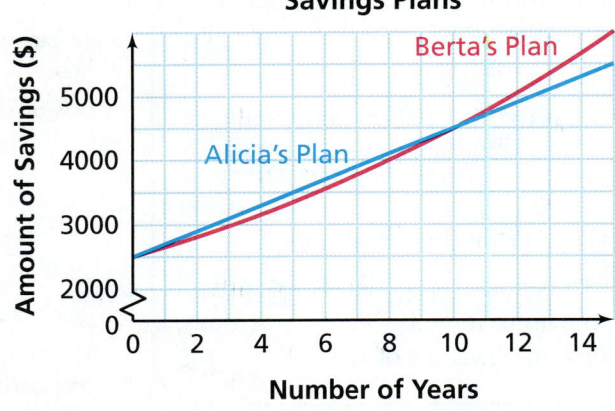

The graphs show that Alicia will have more money after 5 years. Berta will have more money after 15 years. In fact, after about 11 years, Berta will have more money than Alicia.

For Discussion

3. How much more money than Berta does Alicia have after 5 years?
4. How can you find how many years it will take for Alicia's savings to double? For Berta's savings to double?

Exercises Practicing Habits of Mind

Check Your Understanding

Try this experiment with 40 coins, candies, or counters that have two distinguishable sides. Randomly toss them from a cup onto a table. Count the number of heads and return the heads to the cup. Remove the tails. Toss randomly the remaining coins, or "survivors," on the table. Repeat six times.

1. Copy and complete the table. Record the number of survivors.

Toss Number	Number of Survivors
0	40
1	■
2	■
3	■
4	■
5	■
6	■

2. Compare your results with the results from other groups. On average, how many survivors are there for the first toss? For the second toss?

3. **Write About It** Explain why about one fourth of the original number of coins survive the first two tosses.

4. Find a rule to calculate the average number of coins that survive t tosses.

On Your Own

5. Sketch each graph for $-3 \leq x \leq 3$.
   a. $y = 2^x$
   b. $y = 1^x$
   c. $y = 4^x$
   d. $y = \left(\frac{1}{2}\right)^x$
   e. $y = 2^{-x}$
   f. $y = \left(\frac{1}{10}\right)^x$

6. If b is any positive real number, for what values of b is the graph of $y = b^x$ increasing? For what values of b is the graph of $y = b^x$ decreasing?

Increasing means that the value of y becomes greater as the value of x becomes greater.

6.14 Graphs of Exponential Functions

7. A ball drops from 18 feet. On its first bounce, the ball rebounds to 12 feet. On its second bounce, it rebounds to 8 feet.

Bounce Height

Bounce, b	Height, h (ft)
0	18
1	12
2	8
3	■
4	■
5	■

   a. Show that the ratio of the height of bounce 1 to the starting height is equal to the ratio of the height of bounce 2 to the height of bounce 1.
   b. Copy and complete the table to show the height of bounces 3, 4, and 5.
   c. Use the table. If h is the height of a certain bounce, write an expression that represents the height of the next bounce in terms of h.
   d. Use the table. Write an equation that represents the relationship between height h and bounce b.

8. **Standardized Test Prep** What point do the graphs of $y = 2^x$, $y = 3^x$, $y = 5^x$, and $y = (\frac{1}{4})^x$ have in common?

   A. $(-1, 0)$ B. $(0, 0)$ C. $(0, 1)$
   D. The graphs have no common intersection point.

Maintain Your Skills

9. Sketch each graph for $-3 \leq x \leq 3$.
   a. $y = 5 \cdot 2^x$ b. $y = 5 \cdot 1.5^x$ c. $y = 5 \cdot 1.2^x$
   d. $y = 5 \cdot 0.7^x$ e. $y = 5 \cdot 0.5^x$
   f. Where does the graph of $y = 5 \cdot 0.001^x$ cross the y-axis?

10. Sketch each graph for $-3 \leq x \leq 3$ on the same coordinate plane.
    a. $y = 2^x$ b. $(y - 1) = 2^x$ c. $(y + 1) = 2^x$
    d. $(y - 2.5) = 2^x$ e. $(y + 1.5) = 2^x$
    f. Without graphing, describe what the graph of $(y - 99) = 2^x$ looks like.

6.15 Constant Ratios

In Lesson 5.08, you learned that a table of consecutive outputs for a linear function has constant differences. This fact gives you an efficient way to identify tables that you can match with a linear function.

In this lesson, you will learn that consecutive outputs of exponential functions also reveal a pattern that can help you match a function to a function table.

In-Class Experiment

For each exponential function $f(x) = a \cdot b^x$, make an input-output table. Use whole-number inputs from 0 to 5.

1. $f(x) = 10(3)^x$
2. $g(x) = 4(3)^x$
3. $h(x) = 3(3)^x$
4. $j(x) = 10(6)^x$
5. $k(x) = 4(6)^x$
6. $m(x) = 3(6)^x$
7. $n(x) = 10(0.5)^x$
8. $p(x) = 4(0.5)^x$
9. $q(x) = 3(0.5)^x$

Make conjectures about the tables of exponential functions. Think about how to describe each table using a recursive rule. Where in the table do you find a and b?

You may want to use a calculator.

For example, in your first table, where do you find 10? Where do you find 3 in the table?

Minds in Action   episode 27

Sasha and Tony try to match a function to this table.

Table 6

Input, x	Output, y
0	4
1	6
2	9
3	13.5
4	20.25

Tony   First, let's see whether the function could be linear. 6 − 4 is . . .

6.15 Constant Ratios 589

Tony scribbles some calculations on his paper.

Tony Look, this can't be matched with a linear function, because the Δ value isn't a constant.

Tony rewrites the table with the Δ column.

Input, x	Output, y	Δ
0	4	2
1	6	3
2	9	4.5
3	13.5	6.75
4	20.25	

Sasha That's right. Let's try dividing consecutive rows. $\frac{6}{4}$ is 1.5, and $\frac{9}{6}$ is also 1.5.

Tony Oh, yes, and $\frac{13.5}{9} = 1.5$. Also, $\frac{20.25}{13.5} = 1.5$.

Sasha So, the Δ value isn't a constant, but if I divide outputs instead of subtract them, I get a constant value in the division column.

Sasha makes a new table with a ÷ column.

Input, x	Output, y	÷
0	4	1.5
1	6	1.5
2	9	1.5
3	13.5	1.5
4	20.25	

> Recall the up-and-over property from Lesson 5.08. In this table, everything is the product, instead of the sum, of the up-and-over values.

Tony The up-and-over property works here too, except everything is the product of the up-and-over values, instead of the sum.

$$6 = 4 \cdot 1.5$$
$$9 = 6 \cdot 1.5$$
$$13.5 = 9 \cdot 1.5$$
$$\vdots \quad \vdots \quad \vdots$$

Sasha Well, since the up-and-over property works, so does the hockey stick method, except that you start with the number on the blade and multiply by the numbers on the handle.

Input, x	Output, y	÷
0	4	1.5
1	6	1.5
2	9	1.5
3	13.5	1.5
4	20.25	

To get the output for 3 using this method, you start with 4 and then multiply repeatedly by 1.5. The output for 3 is $4 \cdot (1.5)^3$.

Tony The output for 4 is $4 \cdot (1.5)^4$, and . . .

Sasha That's it! The rule $x \mapsto 4 \cdot (1.5)^x$ matches the table.

Tony and Sasha both check a few values of x.

Sasha You know, finding exponential functions is a lot like finding linear functions. When I want to find a linear function, I subtract one output from the next output.

Tony In exponential tables, though, the differences aren't constant, but the consecutive ratios always give the same number.

Sasha Look, the constant ratio is the number that I raise "to the x" in the function.

Tony It's kind of like we change addition to multiplication and multiplication to "power-raising." Instead of "4 plus 1.5 times x," we get something like "4 times 1.5 to the x."

Sasha This needs more thought.

Tony and Sasha wander down the hall and ponder the situation.

> You can write this function recursively.
>
> $f(x) = \begin{cases} 4 & \text{if } x = 0 \\ f(x-1) \cdot 1.5 & \text{if } x > 0 \end{cases}$

> A ratio table shows a **constant ratio** if all the values in the ÷ column are equal.

For Discussion

10. In the dialog, Tony says, "The up-and-over property works here, too, except everything is the product of the up-and-over values, instead of the sum." How could Tony have reached that conclusion?

11. Sasha replies, "Well, since the up-and-over property works, so does the hockey stick method, except that you start with the number on the blade and multiply by the numbers on the handle." Why does the multiplication up-and-over property imply that the multiplication hockey stick method works?

12. Does Sasha's "4 times 1.5 to the x" work when $x = 0$?

For You to Do

13. Make a table for the function $g(x) = 5 \cdot \left(\frac{1}{2}\right)^x$. Use input values between 1 and 5. What is the constant ratio?

Exercises Practicing Habits of Mind

Check Your Understanding

1. Use Sasha's and other methods to determine whether you can match each table with a linear function, exponential function, or neither. Find the linear or exponential function that generates the table, if one exists.

   Model each function using your function modeling language.

   a. Table 1

Input	Output
0	3.12
1	4.52
2	5.92
3	7.32
4	8.72

   b. Table 2

Input	Output
0	19
1	40.09
2	84.59
3	178.48
4	379.6

   c. Table 3

Input	Output
0	1
1	1
2	3
3	7
4	13

2. Find a linear, quadratic, or exponential function that matches each table.

   a. Table 4

Input	Output
0	5
1	4
2	1
3	−4
4	−11

   b. Table 5

Input	Output
0	3
1	6
2	12
3	24
4	48

   c. Table 6

Input	Output
0	2
1	−1
2	−4
3	−7
4	−10

Go Online
pearsonsuccessnet.com

d. **Table 7**

Input	Output
0	0
1	2
2	8
3	26
4	80

e. **Table 8**

Input	Output
0	$\frac{1}{3}$
1	$\frac{5}{6}$
2	$1\frac{1}{3}$
3	$1\frac{5}{6}$
4	$2\frac{1}{3}$

f. **Table 9**

Input	Output
0	1
1	3
2	9
3	19
4	33

3. This exercise is the same as Exercise 2, except that a and b can be any number. Find a function that matches each table.

a. **Table 10**

Input, x	Output, y
0	2
1	$2 + a$
2	$2 + 2a$
3	$2 + 3a$
4	$2 + 4a$

b. **Table 11**

Input, x	Output, y
0	a
1	ab
2	ab^2
3	ab^3
4	ab^4

4. In a TV show, the main character, Ian, had a bank account with a balance of only $.93. Ian was frozen for a thousand years. His balance of $.93 increased by 2.25% every year.

   a. Write a recursive function that describes how much money Ian had after n years.

   b. Use the function in part (a). How can you calculate the amount of money Ian had when he woke up? (*Hint:* Do not actually calculate the value unless you have all day!)

   c. Explain why you can use the function $IAN(x) = 0.93(1.0225)^x$ to calculate how much money was in Ian's account after x years. (*Hint:* It may be useful to compare this function with the function you found in part (a).)

   d. How much money did Ian have when he woke up?

6.15 Constant Ratios

On Your Own

5. Decide whether you can match each table with a linear function, exponential function, or neither. Find a linear or exponential function that generates the table, if one exists.

a. Table D

Input	Output
0	−2
1	1
2	4
3	7
4	10

b. Table E

Input	Output
0	5
1	4
2	1
3	−4
4	−11

c. Table F

Input	Output
0	8
1	5.5
2	3
3	0.5
4	−2

d. Table G

Input	Output
0	0.5
1	1
2	2
3	4
4	8

6. Find a rule that shows the relationship between x and y in the table at the right.

x	y
−4	16
−1	1
0	0
3	9
7	49

7. Write About It Is it possible to have an exponential rule in which every even input gives an even output and every odd input gives an odd output? If it is possible, find the rule. If not, explain.

8. Suppose Jon has 64 mg of caffeine in his bloodstream. After one hour, Jon has 48 mg of caffeine in his bloodstream.

  a. Find a linear relationship for the situation. Then find an exponential relationship for the situation.

  b. Use tables to show the linear and exponential relationships. For inputs, use 0 to 4 hours.

  c. Graph each relationship on the same coordinate plane.

9. A recursive rule defines the first three stages of a sequence of shapes. The first shape is an upward-pointing triangle. To find the next shape, draw a downward-pointing triangle in the middle of every upward-pointing triangle.

Stage 1

Stage 2

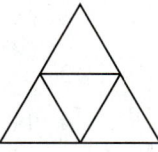

Stage 3

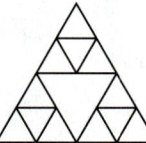

Find a rule that gives the number of upward-pointing triangles at each stage. In Stage 1, there is only one larger triangle, and it is pointing upwards. In Stage 2, there are four smaller triangles, three of which are pointing upwards, and so on.

Only count the smallest triangles at each stage.

a. Draw Stage 4 of this sequence. Using your drawing and the drawings above, copy and complete this table.

Stage	Number of Upward-Pointing Triangles
1	1
2	3
3	■
4	■

b. Find a function that matches the table in part (a).

c. **Take It Further** Find a function that has the number of downward-pointing triangles for each stage as its output.

6.15 Constant Ratios

10. **Standardized Test Prep** What is the first term in this exponential sequence that is an integer greater than 1? ■, ■, ■, 64, 256, 1024, 4096, ...
    A. $\frac{1}{4}$ B. 1 C. 4 D. 16

11. Use these tables from Lesson 5.07 and the methods for finding linear and exponential functions in this lesson. Assume that the grain need per person is 323 kg per year.

World Population

Year	Population (billions)
1975	4.08
1980	4.45
1985	4.86
1990	5.29
1995	5.72
2000	6.12

SOURCE: United Nations Secretariat

World Grain Production

Year	Grain Production (MMT)
1975	1237
1980	1429
1985	1647
1990	1768
1995	1708
2000	1842

SOURCE: United States Department of Agriculture

World Grain Demand

Population (billions)	Grain Demand (MMT)
1	323
2	646
3	969
4	1292
5	1615

a. Are any of these tables linear, or almost linear? Are any of these tables exponential, or almost exponential?

b. If your results from part (a) suggest a linear or exponential pattern, extend the table according to the pattern. Add at least 5 values to each table.

c. Based on your approximations, will there be enough grain for the world in 2010? In 2025? Explain.

d. Do you think there will be more or less grain per person in 2050 than there is today? Explain.

Maintain Your Skills

For Exercises 12 and 13, let $f(x) = 2x + 10$ and $g(x) = 5x + 7$.

12. Find each value.
    a. $f(2)$ b. $g(2)$ c. $f\left(\frac{1}{2}\right)$ d. $f(g(2))$ e. $g(f(2))$ f. $f\left(g\left(\frac{1}{2}\right)\right)$

13. Sketch each graph.
    a. f b. g c. $h(x) = f(g(x))$ d. $j(x) = g(f(x))$

Mathematical Reflections 6C

In this investigation, you used exponential functions to calculate compound interest. You graphed exponential functions. You also found an exponential function to match a table with constant ratios. These questions will help you summarize what you have learned.

1. Find an exponential rule that agrees with each table.

   a.
Input, x	Output, f(x)
0	2
1	6
2	18
3	54

   b.
Input, x	Output, g(x)
0	2
1	$\frac{2}{3}$
2	$\frac{2}{9}$
3	$\frac{2}{27}$

2. Here are several recursive rules. Find an $x \mapsto$ rule that generates the same outputs for all whole number inputs.

   a. If the input is 0, the output is 3. To find the next output, add 9 to the previous output.

   b. If the input is 0, the output is $\frac{1}{16}$. To find the next output, multiply the previous output by 2.

   c. If the input is 0, the output is 10. To find the next output, subtract 4 from the previous output.

   d. If the input is 0, the output is 3. To find the next output, multiply the previous output by 1.5.

3. How can you find an exponential function that matches a table of outputs?

4. Why is it harder to solve for x in the equation $13 = 2^x$ than in the equation $13 = x^2$?

5. How long will it take your money to double if you invest it at 6% interest?

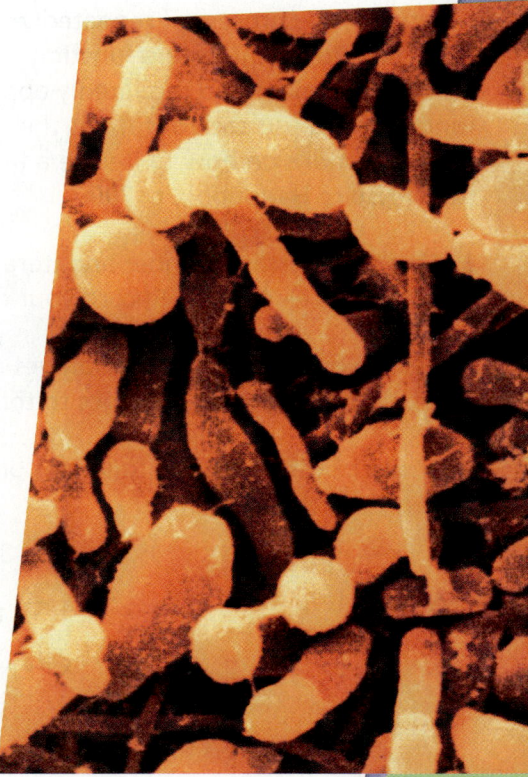

If cells split in two every hour, one cell becomes 16,777,216 cells in 24 hours.

Vocabulary

In this investigation, you learned these terms. Make sure that you understand what each one means and how to use it.

- compound interest
- constant ratio
- exponential decay
- exponential growth

Project: Using Mathematical Habits

Calculating Square Roots

Tony is curious about his calculator. He finds the square root of 12 and the square root of the result. He finds the square root of that result, and so on.

1. Try Tony's experiment using different numbers, such as 123, 14, 0.5, or 1. What is the pattern in your results?

Iteration is the process of repeatedly applying the same function. To iterate a function, you choose a starting number and repeatedly apply the function. You use each output as the next input. For instructions on how to iterate a function, see the TI-Nspire Handbook, p. 790.

2. Choose a starting number and iterate the function $x \mapsto \frac{1}{2}x + 1$. Record your outputs.

When the outputs of an iteration get closer to a number, the iteration converges to that number.

3. Which of the following functions produce iterations that converge?

   a. $x \mapsto \frac{x}{3} + 3$
   b. $x \mapsto 3x - 1$
   c. $x \mapsto 0.7x - 1$
   d. $x \mapsto \frac{x}{10} + 3$
   e. $x \mapsto 3x + 3$
   f. $x \mapsto \frac{x + \frac{16}{x}}{2}$
   g. $x \mapsto \frac{x + \frac{9}{x}}{2}$
   h. $x \mapsto \frac{x + \frac{2}{x}}{2}$

4. Consider the family of functions $x \mapsto ax + 5$, where a is any real number.

   a. For which values of a does the iteration of the function converge?

   b. Suppose a is a value that causes an iteration of the function to converge. Describe the number it converges to in terms of a.

One way to record an iteration is to plot each output against the number of steps completed in the iteration. Suppose you iterate the function in Exercise 3g.

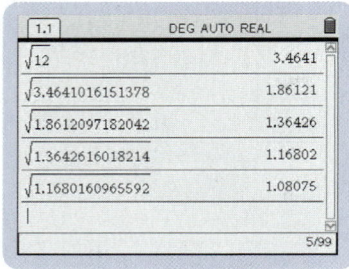

You can make a table that shows the number of steps in an iteration and the output after each step. For example, if the starting number is 12, the table looks like this.

Number of Times Iterated	Output
0	12
1	6.375
2	3.8934
3	3.1025
4	3.0017
5	3.0000
6	3.0000
7	3.0000
8	3.0000

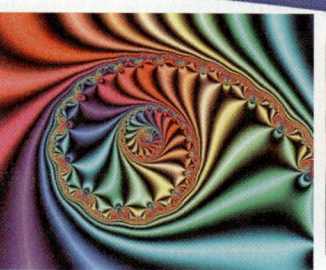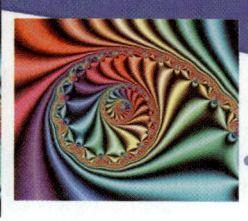

Visual patterns can develop through continuous iterations. This spiral image comes from the famous Julia set.

You also can make a scatter plot of the data. You can graph the outputs against the number of times you iterate the function.

5. From Exercise 3, choose a function that has an iteration that converges and a function that has an iteration that does not converge. Make a scatter plot of the data for each iteration.

6. For each function, choose a starting number. Make a scatter plot of the data for the iteration.

   a. $x \mapsto \frac{x}{6} + 1$ b. $x \mapsto 3x + 1$

   c. $x \mapsto \frac{x + \frac{25}{x}}{2}$ d. $x \mapsto \frac{x + \frac{36}{x}}{2}$

The Babylonian Method A numerical algorithm is a series of computations that produce results that get closer to a desired quantity. The Babylonian method for computing the square root of a positive number is a numerical algorithm. A calculator also uses an algorithm to find a number's square root.

To find $\sqrt{5}$ using the Babylonian method, guess the value of $\sqrt{5}$. You can choose any positive real number. Suppose that your guess is 7. Then divide the number 5 inside the square root sign by your guess, or $5 \div 7$. Note that $\frac{5}{7} < \sqrt{5} < 7$. How do you know that this statement is true?

You can tell that your first guess 7 is not very close to $\sqrt{5}$. Since $\sqrt{5}$ is between $\frac{5}{7}$ and 7, a reasonable second guess is the average of the two numbers, or $\frac{7 + \frac{5}{7}}{2}$, which is approximately 3.85714. In general, if your first guess is x_0, $\sqrt{5}$ lies between x_0 and $\frac{5}{x_0}$.

Your second guess, x_1, is the average of x_0 and $\frac{5}{x_0}$.

$$x_1 = \frac{x_0 + \frac{5}{x_0}}{2}$$

Use your second guess, x_1, and follow the same process to produce your third guess, x_2.

$$x_2 = \frac{x_1 + \frac{5}{x_1}}{2}$$

Your third guess, x_2, is even closer to $\sqrt{5}$ than x_1. Substitute $x_1 \approx 3.85714$ in the equation above to find x_2.

$$x_2 = \frac{3.85714 + \frac{5}{3.85714}}{2} \approx 2.57672$$

Repeat the same process to find x_3.

$$x_3 = \frac{2.57672 + \frac{5}{2.57672}}{2} \approx 2.25859$$

Notice that $(2.25859)^2 \approx 5.10123$. The iteration appears to be converging to $\sqrt{5}$.

7. Compute $\sqrt{5}$ using three different initial guesses. Does each iteration converge to $\sqrt{5}$? What is the result of guessing a smaller initial number, such as 0.01? What is the result of guessing a larger initial number, such as 123?

8. For each iteration in Exercise 7, make a scatter plot of the outputs of your computations.

9. What is the result when you guess a negative number in Exercise 7?

10. Use the Babylonian method to find $\sqrt{4}$.

11. Compute the square roots of at least three positive numbers using the Babylonian method. How many steps of the Babylonian method produce a result accurate to 4 decimal places? To 8 decimal places? Does the number of steps depend on your initial guess?

Chapter 6 Review

In **Investigation 6A,** you learned how to

- make calculations involving integral exponents
- simplify expressions involving integral exponents
- explain and apply the basic rules of exponents
- calculate with positive, zero, and negative exponents

The following questions will help you check your understanding.

1. Simplify each expression.

   a. $x^4 \cdot x^3$
   b. $2^6 \cdot 5^6$
   c. $(x^2)^4$
   d. $\dfrac{x^{11}}{x^5}$
   e. $\dfrac{3^8}{3^6}$
   f. $(12)^5 \cdot \left(\dfrac{1}{6}\right)^5$

2. Without a calculator, decide whether each expression equals 11^{-2}. Explain.

   a. $\dfrac{11^{10}}{11^8}$
   b. $\dfrac{11^8}{11^{10}}$
   c. $\left(\dfrac{1}{11}\right)^2$
   d. $11^0 \cdot 11^{-3} \cdot 11$
   e. $(11^3)^{-5}$
   f. $\dfrac{1}{11^{-2}}$

3. Write each number in scientific notation.

   a. 5,000,000
   b. 0.00045
   c. 850×10^{-5}
   d. $(5.3 \times 10^2)(2 \times 10^{-4})$
   e. 300^2
   f. $\dfrac{4.8 \times 10^6}{6 \times 10^{-2}}$

In **Investigation 6B,** you learned how to

- distinguish between rational and irrational numbers
- understand the meaning of other radicals, such as square roots, cube roots, and fourth roots
- calculate using square roots, cube roots, and other radicals
- express irrational expressions in simplified form

The following questions will help you check your understanding.

4. For each number, state whether it belongs to the set of real numbers ($\mathbb{R}$), rational numbers ($\mathbb{Q}$), or integers ($\mathbb{Z}$). Name all sets that apply.

   a. $\sqrt{2}$
   b. 32
   c. $-\dfrac{1}{2}$
   d. 3π
   e. $\sqrt{9}$
   f. 4.831

5. Find the integer k that satisfies each equation.

   a. $\sqrt{24} = k\sqrt{6}$
   b. $\sqrt{200} = k\sqrt{2}$
   c. $\sqrt{3} + \sqrt{27} = k\sqrt{3}$
   d. $\sqrt{5} \cdot \sqrt{10} = 5\sqrt{k}$
   e. $\sqrt{2} \cdot \sqrt{k} = 2$
   f. $\sqrt{\dfrac{2}{3}} = \dfrac{\sqrt{k}}{3}$

6. Use the duck principle to show that each equation is true.

   a. $\sqrt{3} \cdot \sqrt{3} = 3$
   b. $\sqrt[3]{3} \cdot \sqrt[3]{9} = 3$
   c. $\sqrt[3]{4} \cdot \sqrt[3]{4} = 2\sqrt[3]{2}$
   d. $\sqrt{2} \cdot \sqrt[3]{3} = \sqrt[6]{72}$
   e. $\sqrt[3]{\dfrac{1}{4}} = \dfrac{\sqrt[3]{2}}{2}$

In **Investigation 6C,** you learned how to

- use exponential functions to calculate compound interest
- calculate compound interest in a number of different schemes
- graph exponential functions and recognize important properties of exponential graphs
- match tables with constant ratios to exponential functions

The following questions will help you check your understanding.

7. Tony invests $10,000 in an account that pays 4.5% interest compounded semiannually.

   a. How much money will be in the account after 5 years? After 10 years?

   b. Suppose the interest on the account is compounded monthly. How much money will be in the account after 10 years? If the account is compounded monthly instead of semiannually, how much more interest will Tony's account earn?

8. Use the exponential equation $y = 2 \cdot 5^x$.

   a. Copy and complete the table.

Input, x	Output, y	÷
0	▮	▮
1	10	▮
2	▮	▮
3	▮	▮
4	▮	

   b. If $x = -1$, find the value of y.

   c. Sketch a graph of the function.

   d. If $2 \cdot 5^x = 100$, between what two integers is the value of x?

   e. Find the value of x that solves the equation $2 \cdot 5^x = 100$ to the nearest hundredth.

9. Find an exponential rule $h(x)$ that matches the table below. Use the rule to calculate $h(-2)$ and $h(-5)$.

x	h(x)
0	3
1	12
2	48
3	192
4	768
5	3072

Chapter 6 Test

Multiple Choice

1. How many times greater than $\sqrt{3}$ is $\sqrt{75}$?
   A. between 2 and 3   B. 5
   C. 25   D. 625

2. Which of the following equations could be the equation for this exponential graph?

   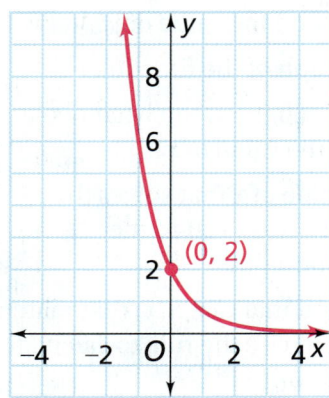

   A. $y = \left(\frac{2}{3}\right)^x$ B. $y = 2 \cdot 3^x$
   C. $y = 2 \cdot \left(\frac{1}{3}\right)^x$ D. $y = \frac{2^x}{3}$

3. Which of the following numbers is irrational?
   A. $\sqrt{3} \cdot \sqrt{3}$ B. $\sqrt{3} \div \sqrt{3}$
   C. $\sqrt{3} - \sqrt{3}$ D. $\sqrt{3} + \sqrt{3}$

4. Which of these statements is true?
   A. All rational numbers are integers.
   B. You can write all real numbers in the form $\frac{p}{q}$, where p and q are integers.
   C. Some irrational numbers are integers.
   D. All integers are rational numbers.

5. Which of these statements about the outputs of the function $f(x) = \left(\frac{1}{3}\right)^x$ is true?
   A. The output must be between 0 and 1.
   B. The output can be any positive number.
   C. The output can be any real number.
   D. The output is only defined when x is an integer.

6. Simplify the expression $\frac{\sqrt{28}}{\sqrt{63}}$.
   A. $\frac{4}{9}$ B. $\frac{2}{3}$
   C. $\frac{2\sqrt{7}}{3}$ D. $\sqrt{7}$

7. Which of the following points is closest to $2\sqrt{11}$ on a number line?

   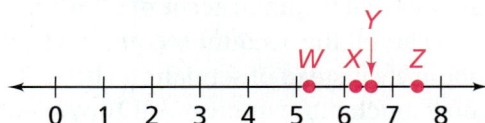

   A. W B. X
   C. Y D. Z

Open Response

8. An exponential rule can generate the following table of values. Copy and complete the table. Then find a rule that you can use to generate the table.

x	y
−2	0.5
−1	■
0	■
1	13.5
2	■
3	121.5

9. Evan invests $500 in an account, compounded annually, for 12 years. At the end of 12 years, Evan has $950.60 in the account. What is the interest rate on the account?

10. Use a calculator to find the value of the variables a, b, and c that make each statement true. Round to two decimal places.

    $2^a = 3$ $\qquad$ $2^b = 5$ $\qquad$ $2^c = 15$

    What is the relationship between a, b, and c? Explain.

11. Explain why $\sqrt[4]{16^3} = 8$.

12. How long will it take your money to double if it is invested at 6% interest?

13. Jesse and Jamie both earn $500 during summer vacation. Jesse invests her $500 in an account that earns 3.5% interest compounded annually. Jamie invests his $500 in an account that earns 3.0% interest compounded quarterly. Whose investment will double first?

14. On the same graph, sketch $y = 2^x$, $y = 4^x$, and $y = \left(\frac{1}{4}\right)^x$.

    a. What point do the graphs have in common?
    b. Which graphs are increasing?
    c. Which graphs are decreasing?

15. Decide whether you can match each table with a linear function, exponential function, or neither. Find a linear or exponential function that generates the table, if one exists.

    a.
Input	Output
0	3
1	12
2	48
3	192

    b.
Input	Output
0	3
1	12
2	21
3	30

    c.
Input	Output
0	3
1	$\frac{3}{4}$
2	$\frac{3}{16}$
3	$\frac{3}{64}$

    d.
Input	Output
0	3
1	5
2	11
3	29

Challenge Problem

16. Find both possible values of x that make the equation $x^{\frac{2}{3}} + x^{\frac{1}{3}} = 12$ true.

Chapter 6 Cumulative Review

These questions will help you summarize what you have learned in previous chapters.

1. Use the functions $f(x) = 3x + 2$, $g(x) = x^2 + 4$, and $h(x) = 2x - 9$.
   a. Calculate $f(0)$, $g(5)$, and $h(3) + g(3)$.
   b. Suppose $p(x) = f(h(x))$. Sketch the graphs of f and p.

2. a. Make an input-output table for the functions $q(x) = \sqrt{x^2}$ and $r(x) = \sqrt[3]{x^3}$. Use input values $-2, -1, 0, 1,$ and 2. Explain how the two functions are similar and how they are different.
   b. Make an input-output table for the function "divide 12 by the input value." Use input values $-4, -3, -2, -1, 0, 1, 2, 3,$ and 4. Explain what happens when the input is 0.

3. Use the recursive function below. Find the value of $P(n)$ for $n = 1$ to $n = 10$.
$$P(x) = \begin{cases} 1 & \text{if } n = 0 \\ 2 \cdot P(n-1) & \text{if } n > 0 \end{cases}$$

4. a. Write each number of weeks as a number of days.

   5 weeks, 8.5 weeks, $10\frac{2}{7}$ weeks

   b. Write each number of days as a number of weeks.

   14 days, 63 days, 100 days, 365 days

   c. Write a rule for converting w weeks into d days. Then write a rule for converting D days into W weeks.

5. Make an input-output table for each rule. Use the integers 0 to 4 as inputs. Explain whether the table represents a function.
   a. The output is the product of the input and 3.
   b. The output is the square root of the input.
   c. The output is 5 less than the input.

6. Simplify each radical expression.
   a. $\sqrt{8^2 + 12^2}$
   b. $\sqrt{\left(\frac{1}{4}\right)^2 + \left(\frac{1}{3}\right)^2}$
   c. $\sqrt{12^2 - 5^2}$

7. An investment account starts with $800 and earns 8% APR compounded annually. After how many years does the account have more than three times its initial value?

8. a. The sum of four consecutive odd numbers is 496. Find the four numbers.
   b. The sum of five consecutive odd numbers is 585. Find the average of the numbers. Then find the numbers.

9. Tell whether each value belongs to the set of real numbers, rational numbers, or integers. Name all sets that apply.
   a. $\sqrt{8}$
   b. $\sqrt{25}$
   c. $\frac{15}{9}$
   d. $\frac{51}{17}$
   e. $\sqrt{1.5^2}$
   f. $2 + \sqrt{3}$
   g. $\sqrt{8} \cdot \sqrt{2}$

10. List the following expressions in order from least to greatest.
$$\sqrt{40},\ \sqrt{5+9},\ \sqrt{5} \cdot \sqrt{9},\ \frac{\sqrt{9}}{\sqrt{5}},\ \frac{\sqrt{5}}{\sqrt{9}}$$

604 Chapter 6 Exponents and Radicals

11. Let $m = \sqrt{5}$, $n = \sqrt{7}$, and $p = \sqrt{12}$.

    a. Find mn, np, mp, and mnp.

    b. Does $m + n = p$? Does $m^2 + n^2 = p^2$? Explain.

12. Write each number in scientific notation.

    a. 100,000

    b. 0.00001

    c. 47,500

    d. 0.052

    e. 200^2

    f. 250×10^3

13. Write each number in decimal notation.

    a. 1.2×10^3

    b. -4.25×10^{-8}

    c. 6.537×10^7

14. Simplify each expression.

    a. $x^5 \cdot x^8$

    b. $(x^3)^7$

    c. $x^{-5} \cdot x^{-7}$

    d. $\dfrac{(x^8)^6}{x^9}$

    e. $\dfrac{x^7 \cdot x^{-5}}{x^{-8}}$

    f. $\dfrac{(x^3)^0}{x^0 \cdot x^5}$

15. Decide whether each expression is equivalent to 3^8. Explain.

    a. $3 \cdot 3 \cdot 3 \cdot 3 \cdot 3 \cdot 3 \cdot 3 \cdot 3$

    b. $3^6 \cdot 3^2$

    c. $(3^2)^6$

    d. $\dfrac{3^{10}}{3^2}$

    e. $3^4 + 3^4$

    f. $3 \cdot 3^8$

16. Find the value of x for each equation.

    a. $3^x = 81$

    b. $2^{x-1} = 64$

    c. $2^{2x} = 16$

17. Consider the graph of $y = b^x$.

    a. For what value(s) of b is the graph a horizontal line?

    b. For what value(s) of b does the graph fall from left to right?

    c. For what value(s) of b does the graph increase from left to right?

18. Start with any number. Add 5. Multiply the result by 3. Then subtract 2.

    a. Find the ending number if you start with -3.

    b. Find the starting number if you end with 13.

For Exercises 19 and 20, use the equation $5x - 2y = 20$.

19. Explain how to transform the equation into each of the following.

    a. $5x = 2y + 20$

    b. $10x - 4y = 40$

    c. $y = \dfrac{5}{2}x - 10$

20. a. Find three points that are on the graph of the equation.

    b. Use two of the three points from part (a). Find the slope of the line through the points.

    c. Use a different pair of points from part (a). Find the slope of the line through the points.

Chapter 6 Cumulative Review

Chapter 7

Investigations at a Glance

- **7A** The Need for Identities
- **7B** Polynomials and Their Arithmetic
- **7C** Factoring to Solve: Quadratics

Polynomials

You can use algebraic expressions, or polynomials, to model smooth, unbroken curves of the natural world. As you model different curves in this chapter, you will extend your basic understanding of expressions.

In Chapter 1, you wrote numbers using place-value parts. For instance, you can write 352 as $3 \times 100 + 5 \times 10 + 2$. Since you know that the places are powers of ten, you can rewrite the above expression as $3 \times 10^2 + 5 \times 10 + 2$. If you replace each 10 with a variable, the result is a polynomial expression, $3x^2 + 5x + 2$.

You can evaluate this polynomial expression for any value of x. In the original expression, if $x = 10$, the expression equals 352. If you substitute -2 for x, the expression equals 4.

In this chapter, you will look closely at the structure of polynomials. You will determine what types of expressions are polynomials and what properties of polynomials they have. You will also explore writing polynomials in different forms. For instance, you can use the fact that $3x^2 + 5x + 2 = (3x + 2)(x + 1)$ to solve the equation $3x^2 + 5x + 2 = 0$.

Vocabulary

- annulus
- binomial
- coefficient
- cubic polynomial
- degree of a monomial
- degree of a polynomial
- expand an expression
- factor an expression
- greatest common factor
- identity
- linear polynomial
- monic
- monomial
- normal form
- parameter
- perfect square trinomial
- polynomial
- polynomial equation
- quadratic polynomial
- quartic polynomial
- quintic polynomial
- trinomial

Investigation 7A

The Need for Identities

In *The Need for Identities*, you will use the basic rules of algebra to transform expressions. Sometimes when you transform an expression into another form, you will notice something about the expression that was not clear in the original form. You can also transform expressions to make your calculations easier.

By the end of this investigation, you will be able to answer questions like these.

1. How do you determine whether two different expressions define the same function?

2. When is it useful to write an expression as a product of expressions?

3. How do you write $3ab - 15a + b - 5$ as a product of two expressions?

You will learn how to
- use basic rules and moves to transform expressions to determine whether different expressions define the same function
- factor expressions by identifying a common factor
- apply the Zero-Product Property to factored expressions
- use algebra to simplify long computations such as computing large sums of consecutive numbers

You will develop these habits and skills:
- Expand powers and products of expressions.
- Identify factors and common factors.
- Divide common factors from an expression.
- Justify arguments using algebraic proof.

You can use either polynomial, $\pi R^2 - \pi r^2$ or $\pi(R - r)(R + r)$, to find the areas of the rings around the bull's-eye.

7.01 Getting Started

Activating Prior Knowledge
Exploring New Ideas

You can write algebraic expressions in many different ways. Using the basic rules of algebra, you can represent a function in another form.

For You to Explore

1. Expand each expression.

   a. $3(x + 4)$

   b. $2x(x - 1)$

   c. $-3x^2(x^2 - 2x + 1)$

   d. $(x - 4)(x + 3)$

   e. $(2x^2 - 1)(3x + 4)$

   f. $(3x - 5)(x^2 - 5x + 6)$

   > You **expand an expression** by multiplying it out. The result will be an expression without parentheses. You can use an expansion box to multiply expressions. Here, the expansion box illustrates the expansion for Exercise 1e.
   >
   > | | $3x$ | 4 |
   > |---|---|---|
   > | $2x^2$ | $6x^3$ | $8x^2$ |
   > | -1 | $-3x$ | -4 |

2. Tony and Sasha plan a student advisory board meeting. They use cafeteria tables that are shaped like hexagons. Each table seats six people.

   They decide to form a row of three tables that will seat 14 people.

   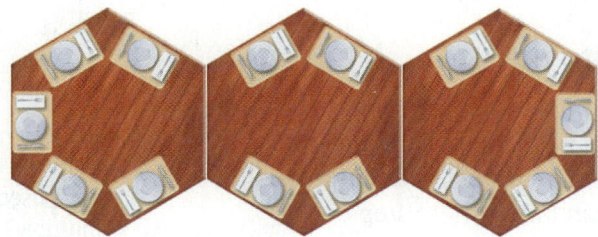

   a. Write at least two formulas for the number of people that you can seat at n tables.

   b. How many tables will be necessary to seat 18 people? To seat 19 people? To seat 67 people?

3. Use this input-output table.

Input	Output
0	0
1	4
2	10
3	18
4	28

   a. Write at least two different functions to describe this table.
   b. Do your functions from part (a) always result in the same output for any input? Explain.

A class wrote 5 different rules that match the table. Can you write more rules than that?

4. Consider the function $f(x) = 3x + 7 + 5x(x - 1)(x - 2)$. Write a simpler function that has the same values when x equals 0, 1, and 2.

Exercises Practicing Habits of Mind

On Your Own

5. Luca has a new method for multiplying numbers.

   Find the sum and difference of the two numbers that you want to multiply. Square each result. Subtract the smaller result from the larger result. Divide the difference by 4. This solution is the product of the numbers. For instance, to multiply 12 times 8, you can follow these steps.

   Is Luca's method easier than the methods you have used in the past to multiply? Explain.

   • The sum is $12 + 8 = 20$. The difference is $12 - 8 = 4$.
   • The square of 20 is $20^2 = 400$. The square of 4 is $4^2 = 16$.
   • Subtract 16 from 400, or $400 - 16 = 384$.
   • Divide the difference by 4, or $384 \div 4 = 96$.

   Use Luca's method to find each product.

   a. $21 \cdot 19$ b. $52 \cdot 48$ c. $107 \cdot 59$

   d. **Take It Further** Prove that Luca's method works for any two numbers a and b.

6. Expand each side to prove that the equation
   $(a^2 + b^2)(c^2 + d^2) = (ac - bd)^2 + (bc + ad)^2$ is true.

610 Chapter 7 Polynomials

7. **a.** Find integers a, b, c, and d such that $a^2 + b^2 = 34$ and $c^2 + d^2 = 13$.

   b. Use the equation from Exercise 6. Show that you can write 34×13 as the sum of the squares of two integers.

   c. Find three numbers that you cannot write as the sum of squares of two integers.

8. The factored expression $(m + 7)(m - 11)$ is equivalent to the expanded form $m^2 - 4m - 77$.

   a. When $m = 6$, the value of $m^2 - 4m - 77$ is a multiple of 13. Explain why.

   b. Name two other positive integers m that make $m^2 - 4m - 77$ a multiple of 13.

   c. Explain why the following is true. If $(m + 7)$ or $(m - 11)$ is a multiple of 13, then $m^2 - 4m - 77$ is a multiple of 13.

   d. Find two values of m that make $m^2 - 4m - 77$ equal to zero.

   e. Explain why the following is true. If $(m + 7)$ or $(m - 11)$ is zero, then $m^2 - 4m - 77$ is zero.

9. Find four pairs of numbers x and y that make the value of the expression $xy^2 + x^2 + y - x - x^2y - y^2$ equal to 0.

10. Prove that $xy^2 + x^2 + y - x - x^2y - y^2 = (x - 1)(y - 1)(y - x)$.

11. If x and y are numbers and $xy^2 + x^2 + y - x - x^2y - y^2 = 0$, explain why either $x = 1$ or $y = 1$, or $x = y$ must be true.

12. **Take It Further** Consider the function below. Write a simpler function that has the same output values for x-values 0, 1, 2, 3, and 4. Does your function always agree with f? Explain.

$$f(x) = \frac{19}{24}x(x-1)(x-2)(x-3) - \frac{8}{3}x(x-1)(x-2)(x-4) +$$
$$\frac{13}{4}x(x-1)(x-3)(x-4) - \frac{5}{3}x(x-2)(x-3)(x-4) +$$
$$\frac{7}{24}(x-1)(x-2)(x-3)(x-4)$$

> **Remember...**
> Two expressions are equivalent if you can get from one expression to the other using the basic rules of algebra.

Maintain Your Skills

13. Expand each expression. Describe a pattern in the results.

    a. $(x + 1)^2$ **b.** $(x + 1)^3$ **c.** $(x + 1)^4$

14. **a.** Expand $(x - 1)(1 + x + x^2 + x^3 + x^4 + x^5 + x^6 + x^7)$.

    b. What is the value of $1 + 2 + 2^2 + 2^3 + 2^4 + 2^5 + 2^6 + 2^7$? Do not use a calculator.

15. Expand each expression. Describe a pattern in the results.

    a. $(x + y)^2$ **b.** $(x + y)^3$ **c.** $(x + y)^4$

7.02 Form and Function

In Lesson 4.15, you found fitting lines for noncollinear data points. Sometimes, you can generate the data exactly with a polynomial function. In this lesson, you will learn how to find quadratic functions that fit a table of data exactly.

Minds in Action episode 28

Sasha, Tony, and Derman want to find a function that describes this table. The domain is all real numbers.

Input, n	Output, $f(n)$
0	0
1	3
2	8
3	15
4	24
5	35

Sasha I have an idea. Let's factor each output. Look, 15 is 3 times 5. 24 is 4 times 6. 35 is 5 times 7. Each output is the input times two more than the input. It even works for the first one. 3 is 1 times 3. So the next number will be 6 times 8. That's 48. In general, if the input is n, the rule is to multiply n and $(n + 2)$.

Sasha writes an equation.

$$f(n) = n(n+2)$$

Input, n	Output, $f(n)$	n^2	$f(n) - n^2$
0	0	0	0
1	3	1	2
2	8	4	4
3	15	9	6
4	24	16	8
5	35	25	10

612 Chapter 7 Polynomials

Tony I actually got something different. The pattern reminded me of n^2, so I made a column for n^2 in the table. Then for each input, I subtracted n^2 from the output. That column showed a simple pattern: 2 times the input. So the rule I got is $f(n) = n^2 + 2n$.

Derman I got something completely different! I noticed that the outputs are 1 less than a perfect square. For example, 35 is 1 less than 6^2, or 36, and 24 is 1 less than 5^2, or 25. The number that you square in each case is 1 more than the input. The next input is 6. If you add 1 to 6, the result is 7. Then find $7^2 - 1$. The result is 48.

Sasha I already said that 48 is the next output!

Derman True, but my rule is different. If the input is n, you square $(n + 1)$ and subtract 1.

Derman writes the following equation.

$$f(n) = (n + 1)^2 - 1$$

Tony If you input 6 in my rule, you get $6^2 + 2(6) = 36 + 12 = 48$. They all seem to work. How did we all get different rules for the same table?

Sasha Tony, I actually think our rules are the same. Even though we came up with the rules differently, I can prove they are identical.

Tony Really? How can you do that?

Sasha Your rule is $f(n) = n^2 + 2n$. If I expand my expression using the Distributive Property, the result is exactly the same. Likewise, if you factor your rule, the result is the same as mine.

Tony That's neat! The equation $n^2 + 2n = n(n + 2)$ is an identity. It remains true if I replace n by any number. Since the expressions are equivalent, the functions are also the same.

Derman Okay, I get it now. I wonder if that's true for my rule.

> An **identity** is a statement that two expressions are equivalent under the basic rules of algebra.

For Discussion

1. Is Derman's rule equivalent to both Sasha's rule and Tony's rule? If so, prove it.

Sasha's argument proves that the two expressions define the same function. You can use tables to provide evidence that two expressions are equivalent. However, tables are not sufficient for proving anything. You can always use the basic rules of algebra to prove that expressions are equivalent. The following principle summarizes these facts.

Principle Form Implies Function

If two expressions are equivalent under the basic rules of algebra, they define functions that produce the same output for any given input.

You learned the basic rules of algebra in Chapter 2.

For Discussion

2. Give an example of the principle above. Two different rules define two functions. Now, prove that the functions are the same.

In this chapter, you will build identities, or pairs of equivalent expressions. Identities are extensions of the basic rules. You can use them in a variety of places. For example, you can use identities to show that two functions are the same.

Example

Problem Prove that $(3x + 1)^2 + (x + 2)^2 - 5$ is a multiple of $10x$, for any integer x.

Solution First, consider a few examples. The table below shows some inputs and outputs for the function $f(x) = (3x + 1)^2 + (x + 2)^2 - 5$.

Input, x	Output, f(x)
0	0
1	20
2	60
3	120
4	200
5	300

You may notice that $f(3)$ is a multiple of 30 and $f(4)$ is a multiple of 40. A similar pattern works no matter what input you use.

As stated earlier in this lesson, you cannot prove that a statement is true using a table. A table only provides evidence that a statement is true. You can start a proof by finding an equivalent expression using the basic rules to expand each part of the expression.

$$(3x + 1)^2 = (3x + 1)(3x + 1)$$
$$= 9x^2 + 3x + 3x + 1$$
$$= 9x^2 + 6x + 1$$
$$(x + 2)^2 = (x + 2)(x + 2)$$
$$= x^2 + 2x + 2x + 4$$
$$= x^2 + 4x + 4$$

So, the expression $(3x + 1)^2 + (x + 2)^2 - 5$ is equivalent to $9x^2 + 6x + 1 + x^2 + 4x + 4 - 5$. Now you can combine like terms to establish the identity.

$$(3x + 1)^2 + (x + 2)^2 - 5 = 10x^2 + 10x$$

The expanded expression is easier to work with because the common factor, $10x$, is in both terms. By the Distributive Property, $10x^2 + 10x = 10x(x + 1)$.

The factored form provides the proof. Since $10x$ is one of the factors, the original expression must be a multiple of $10x$.

> The variable x represents an integer in this case.

Developing Habits of Mind

Experiment. Recall that $(3x + 1)^2$ is not equivalent to $(3x)^2 + 1^2$. Try replacing x with numbers! For example, if $x = 2$, $(3 \cdot 2 + 1)^2 = 49$ and $(3 \cdot 2)^2 + 1^2 = 37$. The expressions are not the same. Note that if $x = 0$, $(3x + 1)^2$ is the same as $(3x)^2 + 1^2$. Experimenting with just one number is not enough.

Are there any other values of x for which $(3x + 1)^2 = (3x)^2 + 1^2$?

> Be careful! You can distribute exponents over multiplication, $(ab)^2 = a^2b^2$. You cannot distribute exponents over addition, $(a + b)^2 \neq a^2 + b^2$.

For You to Do

3. Use the Distributive Property. Factor $8x^2 + 4x$ as completely as possible.

For Discussion

4. One expression below is a multiple of $10x$. How can you identify the expression and prove that it is a multiple of $10x$?

A. $(3x + 1)^2 + (x + 5)^2$ **B.** $(6x + 1)^2 - (4x - 1)^2$
C. $(3x - 1)^2 - (2x + 1)^2$

Exercises Practicing Habits of Mind

Check Your Understanding

1. In a list of consecutive integers, each integer is one greater than the preceding integer. For example, 8, 9, and 10 are three consecutive integers. Also, −7, −6, −5, and −4 are four consecutive integers.

   a. Start with −2. Write a list of four consecutive integers.
   b. Start with n. Write expressions for four consecutive integers.
   c. Write expressions for three consecutive integers if the middle integer is n.
   d. Write and simplify an expression for the sum of two consecutive integers.

   > The second expression is one more than n. The third expression is one more than the second expression.

2. a. Use your expression from Exercise 1d. Show that the sum of two consecutive integers is always odd.
   b. Show that the sum of three consecutive integers is always divisible by 3.
   c. Is the sum of four consecutive integers divisible by 4? Explain.
   d. Is the sum of five consecutive integers divisible by 5? Explain.
   e. **Take It Further** For what whole numbers k is the sum of k consecutive integers always divisible by k?

3. If n is an integer, then the expression $n(n + 1)$ represents the product of two consecutive integers.

   a. Explain how you know that the product of two consecutive integers is an even number.
   b. Is the product of three consecutive integers divisible by 3? Explain.
   c. Is the product of four consecutive integers divisible by 4? Explain.
   d. Is the product of five consecutive integers divisible by 5? Explain.
   e. **Take It Further** Is the product of k consecutive integers divisible by k? Explain.

4. There are two numbers n that make $n(n + 1) = 210$. Find both numbers.

5. Consider the following function.

   $$g(n) = \left(\frac{n(n+1)}{2} + \frac{n(n-1)}{2}\right)\left(\frac{n(n+1)}{2} - \frac{n(n-1)}{2}\right)$$

   Write a simpler expression that can define g.

On Your Own

6. Is the sum of seven consecutive integers always a multiple of 7? Explain.

7. The following function is defined by the messy rule below. Find each value.

    $$s(x) = (x - 3)(x^2 - 3x + 2) - x(x^2 - 6x + 11)$$

    a. $s(0)$ **b.** $s(3)$ **c.** $s(11)$

    d. Expand the expressions in this function to find a simpler rule for $s(x)$.

8. **Write About It** Explain how you know the identity $n^2 + kn = n(n + k)$ is true for any numbers n and k.

   > This identity is an extension of the identity Sasha found for $k = 2$ in Lesson 7.02.

9. A square is 23 inches on each side. You cut a 6-inch square from one corner.

    a. Find the area, in square inches, of the leftover shape. Explain your method.

    b. **Take It Further** Find the prime factors of the area. Relate them to the dimensions of the figure.

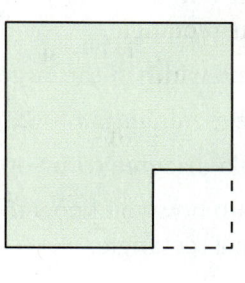

10. A square is x inches on each side. You cut a square, y inches on each side, from one corner. In terms of x and y, find the area, in square inches, of the leftover shape. Explain your method.

11. Tony discusses Exercise 10. "Okay, I can cut up the shape I have into two rectangles. One is larger than the other. Then I can measure the area of each rectangle separately. Last, I add them up." He draws this picture.

    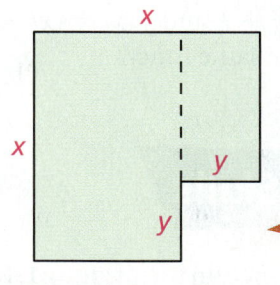

    a. Find the area of each rectangle.

    b. Find the total area of the paper.

    c. If $x = 23$ and $y = 6$, what is the total area according to Tony's formula?

    d. Does Tony's formula disagree with the formula you found in Exercise 10?

    > For each rectangle, express the length and width using x and y.

12. Sasha discusses Exercise 10. "You can cut this shape into two matching shapes if you cut along the diagonal. Then you can flip one of them to make a large rectangle."

    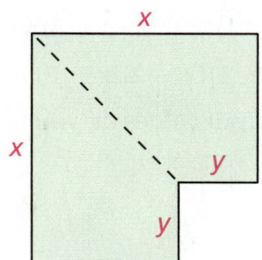

    a. Use your own paper to draw the picture above. Then make the cut. Show how the shape can become one rectangle.

b. What are the length and width of the large rectangle?

c. What is the area of the rectangle if $x = 23$ and $y = 6$?

d. Does Sasha's formula disagree with the formula you found in Exercise 10?

e. Take It Further Explain how you know that this cut-and-paste method works to form a rectangle.

13. Derman discusses Exercise 10. "I can cut a strip off the bottom. I'll move it to the right side to make one large rectangle." He draws this picture to show where to make and move the cut.

    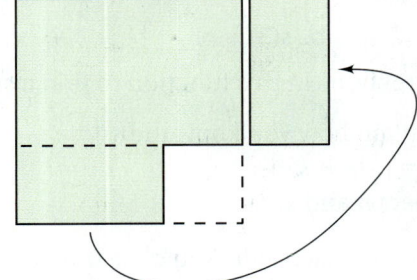

    a. Use your own paper to draw Derman's picture. Then make the cut. Show how the shape can become one rectangle.

    b. What are the length and width of the large rectangle?

    c. What is the area of the rectangle if $x = 23$ and $y = 6$?

    d. Does Derman's formula disagree with your formula in Exercise 10?

    e. Take It Further Explain how you know that Derman's cut-and-paste method works to form a rectangle.

14. **Standardized Test Prep** What is the expanded form of the product $(x + 1)(x^3 - x^2 + x - 1)$?

    A. $x^4 + 1$ **B.** $x^4 - 1$

    C. $x^4 - 2x^3 + 2x^2 - 2x + 1$ **D.** $x^4 + 2x^3 + 2x^2 + 2x + 1$

15. Suppose $g(x) = x^4 + x^2 + 1$ and $f(x) = (x^2 + x + 1)(x^2 - x + 1)$. Prove that g and f are the same function.

Maintain Your Skills

16. Find the value of each function for x values 1, 2, 3, and 4.

    a. $f(x) = 2x + 1$

    b. $g(x) = 2x + 1 + (x - 1)(x - 2)(x - 3)$

    c. $h(x) = 2x + 1 - 5(x - 1)(x - 2)(x - 3)$

    d. $j(x) = 2x + 1 - x^2(x - 1)(x - 2)(x - 3)$

    e. What pattern in the output values do you notice?

7.03 The Zero-Product Property

Look at the row and column at 0 on part of the multiplication table. Notice that all of the products are 0. If either number is zero when you multiply two numbers, the product is zero.

Also, notice that there is never a zero in a multiplication table that is not on the axes. If the product of two numbers is zero, then one or both of the numbers must be zero.

The Zero-Product Property summarizes this result.

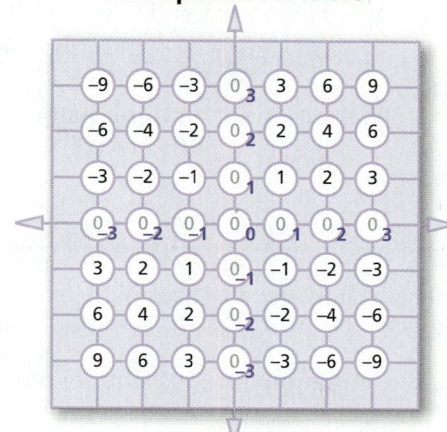

Multiplication Table

Theorem 7.1 The Zero-Product Property

The product of two numbers is zero if and only if one or both of the numbers is zero.

In symbols, if a and b are numbers, then $ab = 0 \Leftrightarrow a = 0$ or $b = 0$.

Remember...
You proved the Zero-Product Property in Lesson 2.05. You also learned in Lesson 4.04 that $\Leftrightarrow$ is a symbol used when either statement implies the other.

For Discussion

The reasons why the Zero-Product Property holds depend on some basic facts about numbers.

1. Why is a product 0 when one of the factors is 0?
2. Use what you know about the multiplication table. Argue that if a and b are both nonzero integers, $ab \neq 0$.

What about numbers that are not integers? If a and b are any real numbers, and $ab = 0$, does either a or b have to be 0? Explain.

Theorem 7.1 is useful in situations if a product is 0. Here are some examples.

- If $(x - 11)(x + 7) = 0$, then $x - 11 = 0$ or $x + 7 = 0$.
- If $(2x - 7)(y - 12) = 0$, then $2x - 7 = 0$ or $y - 12 = 0$.
- If $5(z + 36) = 0$, then $5 = 0$ (which is impossible) or $z + 36 = 0$ (this must be true).

You can use the Zero-Product Property to solve complex equations. For the equation $(x - 11)(x + 7) = 0$, ZPP splits the larger equation into two smaller equations. Use the symbol $\Rightarrow$ for implies.

$$(x - 11)(x + 7) = 0 \Rightarrow x - 11 = 0 \text{ or } x + 7 = 0$$
$$x - 11 = 0 \Rightarrow x = 11$$
$$x + 7 = 0 \Rightarrow x = -7$$

There are no other solutions. The solution set for this equation is $x = -7$ or $x = 11$.

> Use the abbreviation *ZPP* for the Zero-Product Property.

For Discussion

3. **What's Wrong Here?** Mandy and Billy need to find all the solutions to the equation $(x + 7)(x + 11) = 77$.

   Mandy says, "I can break up the equation into two simpler ones.

   $$(x + 7)(x + 11) = 77 \Rightarrow x + 7 = 77 \text{ or } x + 11 = 77.$$

   So, there are two answers, $x = 70$ or $x = 66$."

   Billy replies, "Those answers don't work! Try them in the original equation. I think the solution is $x = 0$. Check it. You'll see it works."

   Mandy answers, "Okay, $x = 0$ works. I'm not convinced it's the only solution. How did I mess up?"

   What is wrong with Mandy's solution? Is it possible to use ZPP to solve this equation? If so, how? Try to find a second solution to the equation.

ZPP works well if an expression is the product of two or more simple expressions. How do you use ZPP if you have an equation such as $2x^3 - 9x^2 - 38x + 21 = 0$?

When you factor an integer, you write it as a product of two or more integers. It is the same for expressions. To **factor an expression** means to write it as the product of two or more expressions. You can factor the expression on the left side of the equation above into three simpler expressions.

> For example, 4×3, 2×6, and $2 \times 3 \times 2$ are all factored forms of the number 12.

$$2x^3 - 9x^2 - 38x + 21 = (x - 7)(x + 3)(2x - 1)$$

Now you can use ZPP to find solutions for x.

When using ZPP, remember the following.

- The expression must be in factored form, since ZPP only applies to products. For instance, you need to find the factored form of $x^3 - 9x$ to solve $x^3 - 9x = 0$.
- The product must be equal to zero.

Example

Problem Find all the values of x that make $x^3 = 25x$ true.

Solution To solve using the ZPP, change the equation. Use a basic move to make one side equal to zero.

$$x^3 = 25x$$
$$x^3 - 25x = 25x - 25x$$
$$x^3 - 25x = 0$$

The ZPP works with products. Factor $x^3 - 25x$ into a product of simpler expressions. Start by finding the factors of each term.

$$x^3 = x \cdot x \cdot x$$
$$25x = 5 \cdot 5 \cdot x$$

The terms have a common factor of x. Use the Distributive Property to "pull out" this factor from each term.

$$x^3 - 25x = x(x^2 - 25)$$

Now the equation is ready for ZPP. Split the equation into simpler equations.

$$x^3 = 25x$$
$$x^3 - 25x = 0$$
$$x(x^2 - 25) = 0$$
$$x = 0, \text{ or } x^2 - 25 = 0$$

So either $x = 0$ or $x^2 - 25 = 0$. If $x^2 - 25 = 0$, then $x^2 = 25$. Therefore, x is either 5 or -5. There are three possible values for x in the solution set.

$$x \in \{-5, 0, 5\}$$

Check these answers.

> The expressions x^3 and $25x$ are different. They cannot be combined into one large term, just as a and b cannot be combined in $3a + 4b$.

> To find $x^3 - 25x$, you multiply x by an expression. Notice that the expression is inside the parentheses.

For You to Do

4. Sketch the graph of $f(x) = x^3 - 25x$. Where does the graph cross the x-axis?

5. Factor $2x^3 + 16xy$. What is a common factor of both terms? What is left when you pull out the common factor?

For Discussion

6. José thinks about the Example. He wonders if he can just divide by x in the beginning. He says, "Well, there's an x on each side, so I can just divide and then solve it from there.

$$x^3 = 25x$$
$$\frac{x^3}{x} = \frac{25x}{x}$$
$$x^2 = 25$$

Why doesn't this give me all the answers? It seems legal. I'm just dividing by x."

How can you help José? Is dividing by x a legal move? Explain.

Developing Habits of Mind

Work backward. What can you do if you do not know how to factor $x^3 - 25x$? You might think about it as follows.

$$x^3 - 25x = x\,(\text{an expression})$$

What goes inside the parentheses? One way to figure it out involves expansion boxes. Write the known factor x in the left column of the expansion box. In each box, write the product. Then find the missing terms in the first row.

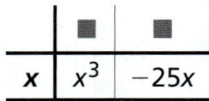

The terms x^2 and -25 are the missing terms, since $x \cdot x^2 = x^3$ and $x \cdot (-25) = -25x$. Now, change the equation.

$$x^3 - 25x = 0$$
$$x(x^2 - 25) = 0$$

For Discussion

Is each statement true or false ? Explain.

7. $abc = 0 \Leftrightarrow a = 0$ or $b = 0$ or $c = 0$

8. $abcd = 0 \Leftrightarrow a = 0$ or $b = 0$ or $c = 0$ or $d = 0$

As you learn more factoring techniques in this chapter, do not forget ZPP! It is the key to solving many equations.

Exercises Practicing Habits of Mind

Check Your Understanding

1. Solve each equation for x.
   - **a.** $x - 8 = 0$
   - **b.** $x + 17 = 0$
   - **c.** $x + b = 0$
   - **d.** $27x + 13 = 0$
   - **e.** $cx - d = 0$
   - **f.** $5x = 0$

2. Find all of the solutions to each equation. Check your answers!
   - **a.** $(x - 7)(x + 5) = 0$
   - **b.** $(x - 3)(y + 7) = 0$
   - **c.** $5x(x + 2) = 0$
   - **d.** $(x + 3)(x + 4)(x + 5) = 0$

3. The equation $6x^2 + 11x - 35 = 0$ has two solutions.
   - **a.** Make a table for $f(x) = 6x^2 + 11x - 35$. Use integer x-values from -5 to 5. Use this table to estimate the two solutions to the equation.
   - **b.** Use an expansion box. Show that $6x^2 + 11x - 35$ is the same as the factored expression $(2x + 7)(3x - 5)$.
   - **c.** What are the two solutions to $6x^2 + 11x - 35 = 0$?

4. **a.** Find the two numbers x that make $(x + 7)(x + 11) = 0$.
   b. Find the two numbers x that make $(x + 7)(x + 11) = 1$. Approximate your result.

5. Ling says, "Factoring is easy. Look at this.
$$x^2 - 4 = 1 \cdot (x^2 - 4) = \tfrac{1}{2}(2x^2 - 8) = 3 \cdot \left(\tfrac{1}{3}x^2 - \tfrac{4}{3}\right) = \ldots$$
I can go on like this all day."

   What would you say to Ling to explain why it is not helpful to factor this way?

6. What are all the solutions to the equation $x^3 = x$?

7. A projectile travels straight up from the ground. Its height from the ground t seconds after it leaves the ground is given by $s(t) = 100t - 16t^2$.
   - **a.** Explain how you could show that the expanded expression $100t - 16t^2$ is equivalent to $t(100 - 16t)$.
   - **b.** Find all solutions to $t(100 - 16t) = 0$. What does each solution represent in the situation?
   - **c.** Use a graphing calculator. Draw a graph to represent $s(t) = 100t - 16t^2$. What two values of t make $s(t)$ zero?
   - **d.** At about what time is the projectile at its highest point? Can you predict this time if you know when $s(t) = 0$?
   - **e.** Draw a picture of the actual path of the projectile.

> Consider another problem. Ling says, "Look, 5 is not a prime number because $5 = \tfrac{1}{2} \times 10$. So 5 factors into two other numbers, neither of which is 1." Is she right? Explain.

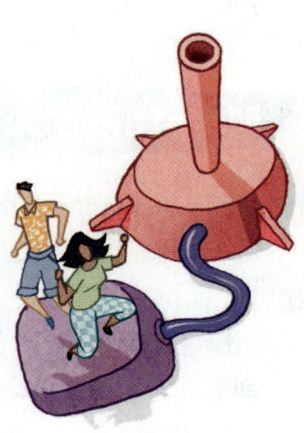

On Your Own

8. Solve each equation for x.

   a. $x - 23 = 0$
   b. $x - a = 0$
   c. $3x - 7 = 0$
   d. $30x - 120 = 0$
   e. $mx + b = 0$

9. Use ZPP. Find all of the solutions to each equation.

   a. $(x - 8)(x - 23) = 0$
   b. $(x + 17)(x + 11) = 0$
   c. $(2x + 5)(x - 10) = 0$
   d. $x(7x - 13) = 0$

10. Is each statement true or false? Explain.

    a. If the product of two integers is divisible by 5, one of the integers is also divisible by 5.
    b. If the product of two integers is divisible by 6, one of the integers is also divisible by 6.
    c. If the product of two real numbers is 5, one of the numbers is 5.
    d. If the product of two expressions is $x^2 - 4$, one of the expressions is $x^2 - 4$.
    e. If the product of two expressions is $x^2 + 4$, one of the expressions is $x^2 + 4$.

11. Consider these two identities. Are they different? Explain.

    A. $(x + a)(x + b) = x^2 + (a + b)x + ab$
    B. $(x - a)(x - b) = x^2 - (a + b)x + ab$

12. Use Exercise 11. Factor $x^2 + 5x + 6$.

13. **Standardized Test Prep** Austin factored the polynomial $15x^2 + x - 28$ into the product $(3x - 4)(5x + 7)$. What are the solutions to the equation $15x^2 + x - 28 = 0$?

    A. $\left\{\frac{4}{3}, -\frac{4}{3}\right\}$
    B. $\left\{-\frac{5}{7}, \frac{4}{3}\right\}$
    C. $\left\{-\frac{4}{3}, \frac{7}{5}\right\}$
    D. $\left\{\frac{4}{3}, -\frac{7}{5}\right\}$

14. **Write About It** Which equation is more difficult to solve? Explain.

    $(2x + 7)(5x - 4) = 0 \qquad (x - 3)(x - 4) = 20$

Maintain Your Skills

15. Find an equation with only the solutions listed.

    a. 3 and 5
    b. −3 and 5
    c. −3 and −5
    d. −3, −5, and 0

16. Find two numbers with a sum that is the first number and a product that is the second number.

    a. 3, 2
    b. 7, 10
    c. 100, 196
    d. 3, $\frac{5}{4}$

7.04 Transforming Expressions

You can use transformations to simplify calculations and show that two expressions are equivalent. For reference, here is a list of some basic rules that you learned in Chapter 2.

The Commutative Property for Addition The order in which you add expressions in a sum does not affect the result.

In symbols, for any two expressions a and b,

$$a + b = b + a.$$

The Associative Property for Addition If you are adding more than two expressions, the order in which you group them does not matter.

For any three expressions a, b, and c,

$$(a + b) + c = a + (b + c).$$

The Commutative Property for Multiplication The order in which you multiply expressions in a product does not affect the result.

For any two expressions a and b,

$$a \cdot b = b \cdot a, \text{ or } ab = ba.$$

The Associative Property for Multiplication If you are multiplying more than two expressions, the order in which you group them does not matter.

For any three expressions a, b, and c,

$$(a \cdot b) \cdot c = a \cdot (b \cdot c), \text{ or } (ab)c = a(bc).$$

The Distributive Property Multiplying an expression by a sum is the same as multiplying the expression by each term in the sum and adding the results.

For any three expressions a, b, and c,

$$a(b + c) = ab + ac.$$

In this chapter, you will often use the Distributive Property "backward." For instance, if you see something that looks like $ab + ac$, you can undistribute the a and write it as $a(b + c)$. Remember, to factor a polynomial means to pull out, or undistribute, a common factor of the terms.

> The expressions ab and ac have a common factor of a.

For example, the terms in the expression $6x^2 + 4ax^2 - 2bx^3$ have a common factor of $2x^2$. By the Distributive Property, this identity is true.

$$6x^2 + 4ax^2 - 2bx^3 = 2x^2(3 + 2a - bx)$$

> They also have a common factor of 2, x, $2x$, or x^2. However, $2x^2$ is the most you can pull out, so $2x^2$ is the **greatest common factor**.

As you learned in Lesson 7.03, it is easier to use the factored form of an expression to solve equations. You can use ZPP after you transform the original expression to the product $2x^2(3 + 2a - bx)$.

You can use an expansion box to factor $6x^2 + 4ax^2 - 2bx^3$. Using the greatest common factor $2x^2$, you can find the other part of the product by working backward.

> Check your work by expanding the result. The expanded expression matches the original expression.

Developing Habits of Mind

Consider more than one strategy. You have used the Distributive Property to make arithmetic calculations easier. Each step is easier because you break one multiplication into two multiplications and an addition.

$$65 \times 103 = 65(100 + 3)$$
$$= 65 \times 100 + 65 \times 3$$
$$= 6500 + 195$$
$$= 6695$$

Similarly, sometimes it is easier to break up a sum of products into one product using the Distributive Property. Multiplication is usually more difficult than addition, unless you multiply by a number such as 10 or 100. You can reduce the number of multiplications in a product to reduce the difficulty of the computations. Which of the following do you prefer to do?

$$57 \times 64 + 57 \times 16 \qquad 57(64 + 16)$$

You can also use the Distributive Property on expressions. One reason to write an expression as a product instead of a sum of products is so you can use ZPP. This allows you to find out when the expression equals 0.

Example

Problem What values of a and b make $6ab^2 = 24a$ true?

Solution To solve, subtract $24a$ from each side. Pull out the common factor $6a$.

$$6ab^2 = 24a$$
$$6ab^2 - 24a = 0$$
$$6a(b^2 - 4) = 0$$
$$6a = 0 \text{ or } b^2 - 4 = 0$$

> You cannot divide by a, because it might be zero! What values of b make $b^2 - 4 = 0$?

If $6a = 0$, then $a = 0$. What property makes this statement true?
If $b^2 - 4 = 0$, b must be either 2 or -2. Why is this statement true?

Go Online
pearsonsuccessnet.com

For You to Do

1. For what values of x and y does $3xy = y^2$?

Exercises Practicing Habits of Mind

Check Your Understanding

1. Find the greatest common factor.

   Sample $9x^3$ and $6x^2$

   Solution $9x^3 = 3 \cdot 3 \cdot x \cdot x \cdot x$
   $6x^2 = 2 \cdot 3 \cdot x \cdot x$

   The expressions $9x^3$ and $6x^2$ have one 3 and two x's in common. The greatest common factor is $3x^2$.

   a. $9x^3$ and $15x^2$
   b. $9x^3$ and $36x$
   c. $15a^2$ and $21b^2$
   d. x^2 and y^2
   e. ab and ac
   f. ab, ac, and bc
   g. p^3q^4 and p^2q^5
   h. p^2q^4 and p^7q
   i. p^3q^4, p^2q^5, and p^7q
   j. $9(x + 3)^3$ and $6(x + 3)^2$

2. Write each expression as a product of two expressions. One expression is the greatest common factor of the terms. If there is no common factor, then the answer is the original expression.

   Sample $9x^3 + 6x^2 = 3x^2(3x + 2)$

   a. $9x^3 - 15x^2$
   b. $9x^3 - 36x$
   c. $15a^2 + 21b^2$
   d. $x^2 + y^2$
   e. $ab - ac$
   f. $ab + ac + bc$
   g. $p^3q^4 + p^2q^5 - p^7q$

   > Do the terms look familiar? Recall Exercise 1.

3. Find all solutions to each equation. Use factoring and ZPP.

   a. $9x^3 + 6x^2 = 0$
   b. $9x^3 = 15x^2$
   c. $9x^3 - 36x = 0$
   d. $ab = ac$
   e. $x^2 = 100x$
   f. $x^2 + y^2 = 0$

4. Write the expression $2x(3x + 7) - 3(3x + 7)$ as a product.

   > Why is the expression $2x(3x + 7) - 3(3x + 7)$ not a product?

7.04 Transforming Expressions

On Your Own

5. Write each expression as a product of expressions.
   a. $3ax + 5bx$
   b. $3ax^2 + 5bx^2$
   c. $3a(x + 7) + 5b(x + 7)$
   d. $3ax + 21a + 5bx + 35b$
   e. $a(x + 1) + b(x + 1)$
   f. $x(a + b) + (a + b)$

6. a. Without using parentheses, write an expression equivalent to $x^2(x + 1) + x + 1$.
   b. Factor $x^3 + x^2 + x + 1$ into a product of two expressions.

7. The region between two circles with the same center is an **annulus**. Use the formula $A = \pi r^2$ for the area of a circle. Show that the area of the annulus is $\pi(R - r)(R + r)$.

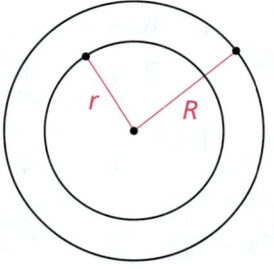

8. You can make a cylinder with a rectangle and two congruent circles. The rectangle's length is the circumference of the end circles. The width of the rectangle is the height of the cylinder.

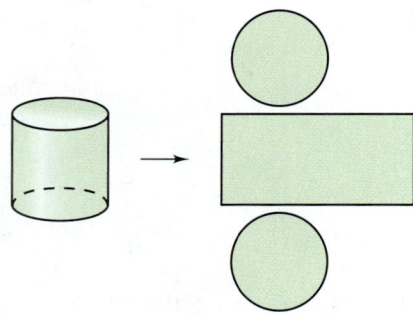

The formula for the circumference of a circle is $C = 2\pi r$. The formula for the area of a circle is $A = \pi r^2$.

   a. Explain how you can calculate the total surface area of the cylinder.
   b. The total surface area is given by the formula below. Use common factors to find another expression for the total surface area.
   $$SA = 2\pi rh + 2\pi r^2$$
   c. **Take It Further** You can describe the total surface area of a cylindrical can as a product. Describe the factors in terms of measurements you can make.

628 Chapter 7 Polynomials

9. **Standardized Test Prep** Factor the expression $3x^3 - 5x^2 + 6x - 10$ into a product of two expressions.

   A. $(x^2 + 2)(3x - 5)$ **B.** $(x + 2)(3x^2 - 5)$

   C. $(x^2 - 2)(3x + 5)$ **D.** $(x - 2)(3x - 5)$

Historical Perspective
Fermat Primes

Pierre de Fermat (1601–1665) was a lawyer in France. Mathematics was only his hobby.

In 1650, Pierre de Fermat conjectured that any number in the form $F(n) = 2^{2^n} + 1$ is prime, where n is a whole number $\{0, 1, 2, 3, \ldots\}$. He proved that the formula always produces primes if n has a value of 0, 1, 2, 3, or 4.

It also seemed to Fermat that the next number in the sequence (5) would produce a prime. Fermat therefore conjectured that all the numbers in the sequence are prime, but he never wrote a complete proof. Today, we call any number in the form $2^{2^n} + 1$ a Fermat number. A Fermat prime is a Fermat number that is prime.

Mathematicians did not disprove his conjecture for many years. In 1732, Leonhard Euler found that

$$F(5) = 2^{32} + 1 = 4{,}294{,}967{,}297 = 641 \cdot 6{,}700{,}417$$

This calculation is easy today using a calculator, but Euler had to make hundreds of calculations without a calculator.

Euler narrowed the possibilities by finding the numbers that are most likely to be factors of $2^{32} + 1$. He discovered that only primes of the form $p = 32k + 1$ divided evenly into $2^{32} + 1$. Using this smaller set of possibilities, Euler used the guess-and-check method until he found the factors $k = 20$ and $p = 641$.

After the inventions of the calculator and the computer, mathematicians found the complete prime factorizations for the Fermat numbers up to $n = 11$. Mathematicians now believe that the only Fermat primes are $F(0)$ to $F(4)$. However, no one has proved this conjecture.

Maintain Your Skills

For Exercises 10 and 11, expand each expression.

10. **a.** $(x - 1)(x^5 + x^4 + x^3 + x^2 + x + 1)$
    b. $(x - 1)(x^7 + x^6 + x^5 + x^4 + x^3 + x^2 + x + 1)$
    c. $(x - 1)(x^9 + x^8 + x^7 + x^6 + x^5 + x^4 + x^3 + x^2 + x + 1)$
    d. $(x - 1)(x^4 + x^3 + x^2 + x + 1)$

11. **a.** $(x - 1)(x^4 + x^2 + 1)(x + 1)$
    b. $(x - 1)(x^6 + x^4 + x^2 + 1)(x + 1)$
    c. $(x - 1)(x^8 + x^6 + x^4 + x^2 + 1)(x + 1)$

12. **Take It Further** Consider the following.
    $$x^3 + x^2 + x + 1 = x^2(x + 1) + (x + 1)$$
    $$= (x + 1)(x^2 + 1)$$

    Factor each expression if possible.
    a. $x^5 + x^4 + x^3 + x^2 + x + 1$
    b. $x^7 + x^6 + x^5 + x^4 + x^3 + x^2 + x + 1$
    c. $x^9 + x^8 + x^7 + x^6 + x^5 + x^4 + x^3 + x^2 + x + 1$
    d. $x^4 + x^3 + x^2 + x + 1$

13. Show that each statement is true.
    a. $x^3 + 1 = (x + 1)(x^2 - x + 1)$
    b. $x^5 + 1 = (x + 1)(x^4 - x^3 + x^2 - x + 1)$
    c. $x^7 + 1 = (x + 1)(x^6 - x^5 + x^4 - x^3 + x^2 - x + 1)$
    d. $x^9 + 1 = (x + 1)(x^8 - x^7 + x^6 - x^5 + x^4 - x^3 + x^2 - x + 1)$

14. Suppose that k is an odd integer greater than 1. Prove that $2^k + 1$ is divisible by 3 and is not a prime number.

15. A source for large primes are the so-called "Mersenne Primes." These prime numbers are in the form $2^n - 1$. For example, $2^3 - 1 = 7$, so 7 is a Mersenne prime. Not all numbers of this form are prime. For example, $2^4 - 1 = 15$, but 15 is not prime.

    Make a table of output values for $2^n - 1$. Is there any pattern to the values of n that produce prime numbers and those that do not? Explain.

Mathematical Reflections 7A

In this investigation, you learned to use basic rules and moves to transform expressions. You also factored expressions and applied the Zero-Product Property to factored expressions. These questions will help you summarize what you have learned.

1. Use the polynomial $x^2 + xy - 6y^2$.
   a. Show that $(x - 2y)(x + 3y) = x^2 + xy - 6y^2$.
   b. If $x = 6$, find a value of y that makes $x^2 + xy - 6y^2 = 0$.
   c. If $y = 3$, find a value of x that makes $x^2 + xy - 6y^2$ a multiple of 11.

2. The following function $t(x)$ is defined by a messy rule. Find each value.
   $$t(x) = (x + 1)(x^2 - 2x + 3) + 2x(x^2 + 5x - 1)$$
   a. $t(0)$
   b. $t(1)$
   c. $t(-2)$
   d. Expand the expressions in this function. Write a simpler rule for $t(x)$.

3. Use ZPP. Find all the solutions to each equation.
   a. $(x - 2)(x + 1) = 0$
   b. $(2x - 3)(x + 5) = 0$
   c. $3x(x + 8) = 0$
   d. $x^2 - 4x = 0$

4. What is the greatest common factor of each set of expressions?
   a. $8x^3$ and $12x$
   b. $24x^2$ and $16x^3$
   c. a^3b^2, a^8b, and a^4b^5c
   d. $10(x + 2)^3$ and $15(x + 2)^4$

5. Solve for x in each equation. Use factoring and ZPP.
   a. $3x^3 + 9x^2 = 0$
   b. $4x^3 = 8x^2$
   c. $x^2 = 49x$
   d. $x^3 = 49x$
   e. $a(x - 2) + b(x - 2) = 0$
   f. $x(a + 2b) + a + 2b = 0$

6. How do you determine whether two different expressions define the same function?

7. When is it useful to write an expression as a product of expressions?

8. How do you write $3ab - 15a + b - 5$ as a product of two expressions?

Vocabulary

In this investigation, you learned these terms. Make sure you understand what each one means and how to use it.

- annulus
- expand an expression
- factor an expression
- greatest common factor
- identity

About how much closer to the target is the skydiver in this photo than the sky diver in the photo on page 608?

Investigation 7B

Polynomials and Their Arithmetic

In *Polynomials and Their Arithmetic*, you will study some details of polynomials. You will be able to define polynomials. You will also add and multiply polynomials, and learn some conventions for writing them.

By the end of this investigation, you will be able to answer questions like these.
1. How can you decide whether two polynomials are equivalent?
2. How is a polynomial useful for describing a rule?
3. Suppose you roll three number cubes numbered 1–6. What is the probability of rolling a total of 12?

You will learn how to
- recognize and provide examples of polynomials
- understand the definitions and importance of the terms *coefficient* and *degree*
- expand polynomials and express them in normal form
- determine whether polynomials in different forms are equivalent
- add, subtract, and multiply polynomials

You will develop these habits and skills:
- Use substitution to make new identities.
- Use the language of polynomials to understand their properties.
- Use the basic rules of algebra to calculate with polynomial expressions.
- Use the Distributive Property to expand polynomials.

If track lanes are 4 ft wide, the polynomial $2\pi(R + 4) - 2\pi R$ tells you the difference in lengths between two lanes that are next to each other.

7.05 Getting Started

You can describe many situations using polynomials. For example, there is a relationship between the probability of rolling a certain sum with number cubes and a polynomial with corresponding exponents. After you learn the properties of polynomials, you can use polynomials to solve problems.

For You to Explore

1. Each face on a standard six-sided number cube has a number from 1 to 6. Suppose you roll two number cubes and want to find the probability of getting a certain sum. You can use a table to determine the number of outcomes. Copy and complete the table.

	1	2	3	4	5	6
1	■	■	■	■	■	■
2	■	■	6	■	■	■
3	■	■	■	■	■	■
4	5	■	■	■	■	■
5	■	■	■	■	■	■
6	■	■	■	■	■	■

   > In this table, the row and column headers indicate the number rolled on each number cube. The numbers in the table are the sums of the numbers rolled.

2. Refer to the table in Problem 1.
   a. What is the most likely sum when rolling two number cubes? How many ways can you roll this sum?
   b. What is the probability of rolling a sum of 8?
   c. What is the probability of rolling a sum of at least 11?

3. Use an expansion box to expand $(x + x^2 + x^3 + x^4 + x^5 + x^6)^2$.

   > Find the product of $(x + x^2 + x^3 + x^4 + x^5 + x^6)$ and $(x + x^2 + x^3 + x^4 + x^5 + x^6)$.

4. Refer to the expansion box in Problem 3.
   a. Which power of x occurs most often?
   b. How many x^8 terms are there?
   c. How many terms have exponents of 11 or higher?

5. **Write About It** Describe the relationship between the table in Problem 1 and the expansion box in Problem 3. How is the expression $(x + x^2 + x^3 + x^4 + x^5 + x^6)$ related to rolling a number cube? Why is the expression squared?

6. **Write About It** Describe how you can use expansion boxes to answer the following question. How many different ways are there to throw three number cubes and roll a total of 10?

Exercises Practicing Habits of Mind

On Your Own

7. George shows you an unusual pair of number cubes. The first cube has faces 1, 3, 4, 5, 6, and 8. The second cube has faces 1, 2, 2, 3, 3, and 4. George says something interesting happens if you look at the sum of two cubes.

   Copy and complete the table. What might George have found surprising?

	1	3	4	5	6	8
1	■	■	■	■	■	■
2	■	■	■	7	■	■
2	■	■	■	■	■	■
3	■	6	■	■	■	■
3	■	■	■	■	■	■
4	■	■	■	■	■	■

8. Find the product using any method.

   $(x + x^3 + x^4 + x^5 + x^6 + x^8)(x + 2x^2 + 2x^3 + x^4)$

9. State whether each equation is an identity.

   a. $16a^2 - 9b^2 \stackrel{?}{=} (4a + 3b)(4a - 3b)$
   b. $8n^2 - 4 \stackrel{?}{=} (4n + 2)(4n - 2)$
   c. $25 - t^6 \stackrel{?}{=} (5 + t^3)(5 - t^3)$
   d. $m^4n^2 - m^2n^4 \stackrel{?}{=} (m^2n + mn^2)(m^2n - mn^2)$
   e. $n^3 - 100 \stackrel{?}{=} (n^2 + 10)(n - 10)$
   f. $a^2 + 2ab + b^2 - 1 \stackrel{?}{=} (a + b - 1)(a + b + 1)$

10. **Take It Further** Show that this statement is true for any choice of a, b, and c.

    $2a^2c^2 + 2a^2b^2 + 2b^2c^2 - (a^4 + b^4 + c^4) =$
    $(a + b - c)(a + b + c)(a + c - b)(b + c - a)$

634 Chapter 7 Polynomials

For Exercises 11 and 12, decide whether the conjecture must be true. If you think it must be true, prove it using the basic rules. If you think it may not be true, explain why.

11. Here are examples of odd numbers added together.

    $1 + 3 = 4$ $5 + 7 = 12$

    $3 + 11 = 14$ $101 + 83 = 184$

    Conjecture: The sum of two odd numbers must be an even number.

12. Here are examples of odd numbers that are the sums of two consecutive integers.

    $3 = 1 + 2$ $11 = 5 + 6$

    $23 = 11 + 12$ $831 = 415 + 416$

    Conjecture: It is always possible to express an odd number as the sum of two consecutive integers.

Remember...
You can write every even number as $2n$ for some integer n. You can write every odd number as $2n + 1$ for some integer n.

Maintain Your Skills

For Exercises 13 and 14, expand each product.

13. **a.** $(1 + x)(1 - x)$ **b.** $(1 + x)(1 - x + x^2)$
    c. $(1 + x)(1 - x + x^2 - x^3)$

14. **a.** $(a - b)(a + b)$ **b.** $(a - b)(a^2 + ab + b^2)$
    c. $(a - b)(a^3 + a^2b + ab^2 + b^3)$

These exercises are similar to those in Lesson 7.01.

7.06 Anatomy of a Polynomial

It can be difficult to understand the definition of a polynomial without first seeing some examples. The following are all polynomials.

$$x^2 - 1 \qquad 3x + 5y + 1 \qquad 2x^3 - 9x - 3x + 2$$
$$\tfrac{6}{7}x^3 - 8x^2 + 1 \qquad \tfrac{3}{7}x + \tfrac{1}{2} \qquad y^2 - x^3 - xy$$
$$x \qquad x^3 - 8x^2 + 1 \qquad 3$$

As you can see from the examples, a polynomial is a sum of one or more terms. Each term is called a monomial.

Definitions

A **monomial** is the product of a number, the **coefficient**, and one or more variables raised to nonnegative integer powers.

> The coefficient can be any real number. Most of the polynomials you will work with in this chapter will have integer or rational coefficients.

The **degree of a monomial** with only one variable is the exponent of the variable. If a monomial has more than one variable, the degree is the sum of the exponents of each variable.

Example 1

Problem Name the coefficient, variable, and degree of each monomial.

a. $3x^2$
b. $-4a^5$
c. b^3
d. $-\tfrac{1}{2}$
e. $7x^3y^5$

Solution

		Coefficient	Variable	Degree
a.	$3x^2$	3	x	2
b.	$-4a^5$	-4	a	5
c.	b^3	1	b	3
d.	$-\tfrac{1}{2}$	$-\tfrac{1}{2}$	none	0
e.	$7x^3y^5$	7	x and y	$3 + 5 = 8$

> Although there is not a variable in the expression, you can write $-\tfrac{1}{2}$ as $-\tfrac{1}{2}x^0$. Remember that any expression raised to the 0 power equals 1. Also, you can use any variable in this expression since there is not any context given.

636 Chapter 7 Polynomials

You can define a polynomial as the sum of any number of monomials like these. Sometimes, a polynomial is made up of only one monomial.

	Coefficient	Variables	Degree
$7x^3y^5$	7	x, y	3 in x 5 in y

Definition

A **polynomial** is a monomial or a sum of two or more monomials.

Facts and Notation

There are many conventions for polynomials—conventions that have to do with the way people prefer to do things rather than with the algebra. You will use the following conventions in this book.

- Coefficients can be any real number. However, most of the polynomials in this book will have integer coefficients. Unless explicitly stated otherwise, assume that all coefficients are integers.

- Polynomials can have any number of variables. However, most polynomials in this book are of one variable. Unless explicitly stated otherwise, assume that *polynomial* means a polynomial of a single variable.

You can think of a polynomial such as $ax^2 + bx + c$ as a polynomial in 4 variables: a, b, c, and x. However, in most cases in this book, the polynomial is in x, with the other letters being unknown coefficients. The text is explicit about which letters are variables and which letters are unknown coefficients.

An unknown coefficient is also known as a **parameter**.

Definition

The **degree of a polynomial** is the greatest degree among all the monomials in the polynomial.

Here are some examples.

- $13x^5 - 9x^3 + \frac{2}{5}x^2 + \frac{1}{7}x - 13$ has degree 5.
- $\frac{13}{2}y - 4y^2 + 9$ has degree 2.
- $2s$ has degree 1.
- 17 has degree 0 $\left(\text{think of } 17x^0\right)$.

There are special names for some polynomials in one variable.

Degree	Type of Polynomial
1	linear
2	quadratic
3	cubic
4	quartic
5	quintic

For Discussion

Find polynomials that satisfy each condition. If it is impossible to satisfy the condition, explain why.

1. a cubic polynomial with three terms, all of different degrees
2. a linear polynomial with two terms, both of different degrees
3. a linear polynomial with three terms, all of different degrees

Polynomials have an arithmetic that is very similar to the arithmetic of numbers. In fact, since each variable is just a placeholder for a number, you might expect that all of the operations of number arithmetic would apply to polynomials. You may also think the basic rules apply the same way.

For You to Do

For Problems 4–7, is each result always a polynomial? Explain.

4. sum of two polynomials
5. product of two polynomials
6. difference of two polynomials
7. quotient of two polynomials

Adding polynomials is like adding any expressions. You combine the like terms to make a simplified expression. Two terms in a polynomial are like terms when they meet the following conditions.

- All variables are the same.
- The exponents of the variables are the same.

Terms	Variable	Exponent	Like Terms
$7x^3$	x	3	
$3x^3$	x	3	yes
$2x^5$	x	5	
$11x$	x	1	no
x^2	x	2	
$3y^2$	y	2	no

The expressions $3x^3$ and $3x^4$ are not like terms even though they have the same coefficient. Explain.

Example 2

Problem Calculate the sum and product of $x^2 - 6x + 5$ and $3x + 7$.

Solution Calculate the sum by combining like terms.

$$(x^2 - 6x + 5) + (3x + 7) = (x^2 - 6x + 5) + (3x + 7)$$
$$= x^2 - 6x + 3x + 5 + 7$$
$$= x^2 + (-6 + 3)x + (5 + 7)$$
$$= x^2 - 3x + 12$$

Calculate the product by expanding. Then collect like terms.

$$(x^2 - 6x + 5)(3x + 7) = 3x(x^2 - 6x + 5) + 7(x^2 - 6x + 5)$$
$$= 3x^3 - 18x^2 + 15x + 7x^2 - 42x + 35$$
$$= 3x^3 + ((-18) + 7)x^2 + (15 - 42)x + 35$$
$$= 3x^3 - 11x^2 - 27x + 35$$

> Expand by multiplying everything in the first polynomial by $3x$. Then multiply by 7 and combine. What is another way to expand?

For Discussion

8. Which basic rules of algebra do you use to combine like terms?

For You to Do

9. **What's Wrong Here?** Jacob and Anna subtracted these polynomials. They got different answers.

$$3x^2 - 7x + 1 \text{ and } 10x^3 - x^2 + 3x$$

Jacob

$$(3x^2 - 7x + 1) - (10x^3 - x^2 + 3x) = 3x^2 - 7x + 1 - 10x^3 - x^2 + 3x$$
$$= -10x^3 + 2x^2 - 4x + 1$$

Anna

$$(3x^2 - 7x + 1) - (10x^3 - x^2 + 3x) = 3x^2 - 7x + 1 - 10x^3 + x^2 - 3x$$
$$= -10x^3 + 4x^2 - 10x + 1$$

Who is correct? What mistake did the other person make?

> **Habits of Mind**
> **Check your work.** Plug any number into the two expressions and subtract the results. Then plug the same number into each of the answers that Jacob and Anna found. If the results are different, you know that the answer is incorrect. If they are the same, you have evidence that they might be correct.

For You to Do

Expand each expression. Combine like terms to get a polynomial answer. Be careful of negative signs!

10. $3x^2 - 7x + 1 - 2(10x^3 - x^2 + 3x)$
11. $(3x - 1)(x^2 + 2x + 5)$

In-Class Experiment

Develop two theorems that answer the following questions.

12. How is the degree of the product of two nonzero polynomials related to the degrees of the polynomials that you are multiplying?

13. How is the degree of the sum of two nonzero polynomials related to the degrees of the polynomials that you are adding?

Why is it important that the polynomials be nonzero?

Here are some polynomials that you can use to develop your theorems.

- $x^2 + 4x + 5$
- $7x^3 - 2x^2 + 1$
- 9
- $-2x^5 + 7x - 1$
- $2x^5 + 5$
- $x^9 + x^3 + 1$
- $3x + 7$
- $14x$
- $4x^3 + 2x + 1$

Exercises Practicing Habits of Mind

Check Your Understanding

1. Find two polynomials with a sum and product that have the following degrees. If you cannot find the polynomials, explain why.

   a. The sum has degree 3 and the product has degree 6.
   b. The sum has degree 4 and the product has degree 2.
   c. The sum has degree 4 and the product has degree 4.
   d. The sum has degree 2 and the product has degree 1.

2. **Take It Further** Find two polynomials with a sum that has degree 1 and a product that has degree 4. If you cannot find the two polynomials, explain why.

3. **a.** Find two polynomials with the same degree that have a sum of $3x^2 + 7x + 4$.

   b. Find two polynomials with different degrees that have a sum of $3x^2 + 7x + 4$.

   c. Find two polynomials that have a sum of 4.

   d. Find two polynomials that have a product of $x^2 - 1$.

4. **Write About It** How does the degree of a polynomial compare to the degree of that polynomial squared? Support your conjecture with at least three examples.

On Your Own

5. Find two polynomials that meet each condition.

   a. The product has degree 6.

   b. The product has degree 1.

   c. The sum has degree 4 and the product has degree 6.

6. **a.** Use $p(x) = x^2 + 4x + 9$. Find a polynomial $r(x)$ such that $p(x) + r(x) = 2x^2 - 6x + 14$.

   b. Find a polynomial $s(x)$ such that $p(x) + s(x) = 2x^2 + 14$.

   c. Find a polynomial $t(x)$ such that $p(x) + t(x)$ has degree 2 and $p(x) \cdot t(x)$ has degree 3.

7. Find the value of a such that $(x + a)(x + 3) = x^2 + 5x + 6$ is an identity. Copying and completing the expansion box at the right may be helpful.

	x	+3
x	■	■
a	■	■

8. **Standardized Test Prep** Use $q(x) = 2x - 3$ and $r(x) = 2x^2 + 3x - 5$. Find $s(x) = q(x) + r(x)$ and $p(x) = q(x) \cdot r(x)$.

   A. $s(x) = 2x^2 + 5x + 8$ and $p(x) = 4x^3 + 12x^2 - 19x + 15$

   B. $s(x) = 2x^2 + 5x + 8$ and $p(x) = 4x^3 - x + 15$

   C. $s(x) = 2x^2 + 5x - 8$ and $p(x) = 4x^3 - 19x + 15$

   D. $s(x) = 2x^2 + 5x - 8$ and $p(x) = 4x^3 - 19x - 15$

9. **Write About It** Suppose you need to explain the phrase *like terms* to a student who has never heard it before. Write a definition of like terms. Explain how you add and subtract them. Be as precise as possible.

10. Suppose you make a frame for a square photo. The frame is 2 inches wide. Find the area of the frame if the photo has the following dimensions.

    a. 3 in. by 3 in.
    b. 9 in. by 9 in.
    c. x in. by x in.

    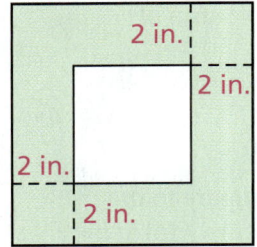

    The area of the border does not include the area of the picture.

    If each side of the photo is 6 inches, the area of the border is $(6 + 4)^2 - 6^2$ square inches.

Maintain Your Skills

For Exercises 11–13, expand and combine like terms.

11. a. $(x + 1)^2 - x^2$ b. $(x + 1)^3 - x^3$
    c. $(x + 1)^4 - x^4$ d. $(x + 1)^5 - x^5$

12. a. $(x + y)^2 - y^2$ b. $(x + y)^3 - y^3$
    c. $(x + y)^4 - y^4$

13. a. $x(x - 1) + x$ b. $x(x - 1)(x - 2) + x(x - 1)$
    c. $x(x - 1)(x - 2)(x - 3) + x(x - 1)(x - 2)$

7.07 Normal Form

Since polynomials are expressions, you can transform them with the basic rules. The reason for transforming polynomials is to find equivalent expressions. For example, if you expand $(x - 1)(x + 1)$, you get $x^2 - 1$. You have derived an identity. Therefore, the expressions are equal for any substitution.

$$(x - 1)(x + 1) = x^2 - 1$$

If you replace x with any number or expression, the resulting statement is true.

Remember...
Sometimes you can transform two expressions into each other using the basic rules of algebra. A statement where the two expressions are equivalent is an identity.

For You to Do

Explain how each fact follows from the above identity.

1. $3 \cdot 5 = 4^2 - 1$

2. Choose a number. Add 1 to it. Subtract 1 from the original number. Multiply your results. The result is one less than the square of the original number.

3. $a(a + 2) = (a + 1)^2 - 1$

4. The only values of x that make $x^2 - 1 = 0$ are 1 and -1.

How can you determine if an equation is an identity? In previous chapters, you transformed one side of an equation to match the other side. When you work with polynomials, it is sometimes easier to expand and collect like terms on each side of the equation. Then you order the terms of each polynomial in the same way. If polynomials are in the same form, or normal form, it is easy to see whether they are equivalent.

Minds in Action   episode 29

Sasha thinks she has found a new identity. She explains it to Tony.

Sasha Look at this identity I found.
$$(x + 1)(x^2 + 2x + 1) = x(3 + 3x + x^2) + 1$$

Tony That can't be true in all cases! What if x is 4?

Sasha The left side equals this.

$$(4 + 1)(4^2 + 2(4) + 1) = (5)(16 + 8 + 1)$$
$$= (5)(25)$$
$$= 125$$

Tony The right side equals this.

$$4(3 + 3(4) + 4^2) + 1 = 4(3 + 12 + 16) + 1$$
$$= 4(31) + 1$$
$$= 124 + 1$$
$$= 125$$

Sasha Both sides are equal. The identity is true.

Tony It might have been a coincidence. How are you sure the two sides will be equal for every number?

Sasha Let's expand and simplify each side. Expand the left side.

$$(x + 1)(x^2 + 2x + 1) = x(x^2 + 2x + 1) + 1(x^2 + 2x + 1)$$
$$= x(x^2) + x(2x) + x(1) + 1(x^2) + 1(2x) + 1(1)$$
$$= x^3 + 2x^2 + x + x^2 + 2x + 1$$
$$= x^3 + 3x^2 + 3x + 1$$

Tony When I expand the right side, I get this.

$$x(3 + 3x + x^2) + 1 = (x(3) + x(3x) + x(x^2)) + 1$$
$$= (3x + 3x^2 + x^3) + 1$$
$$= x^3 + 3x^2 + 3x + 1$$

The two polynomials expand to the same thing. It's an identity!

Sasha Didn't I tell you?

For Discussion

5. Suppose Sasha says "The right side is the same as the left side. They're just in a different order." Can you think of a method for organizing polynomials to make them easier to compare?

6. Show that $(x + 1)^3$ is equivalent to both of Sasha's polynomials.

For You to Do

7. Are the following polynomial expressions equivalent?
$$3x + 7x^4 - 2x^2 - 6 + 3x^2 - x^4 + 2$$
$$\stackrel{?}{=} -10 + 2(3x^4 + 2x^2 + x) - (3x^2 - x) + 6$$

You may have noticed that polynomials often appear with the monomial with the greatest degree at the beginning. For instance, you generally see $7x^3 - 3x^2 + \frac{1}{2}x + 5$ instead of $5 - 3x^2 + \frac{1}{2}x + 7x^3$.

In the first expression, $7x^3 - 3x^2 + \frac{1}{2}x + 5$, the term with the greatest exponent comes first. The term with the second-greatest exponent follows, and so on.

Although $7x^3$ has a greater degree than $\frac{1}{2}x$, $7x^3$ might not have a greater value for every value of x. It depends on what value you substitute for x.

Definition

To write a polynomial in one variable in **normal form**, expand it completely and arrange the monomials by degree from greatest to least.

There are different, acceptable definitions of normal form. Some mathematicians prefer to write the degrees from least to greatest.

Here are a few examples.

- $7x^3 - 3x^2 + \frac{1}{2}x + 5$ normal form
- $5 - 3x^2 + \frac{1}{2}x - 7x^3$ not normal form
- $(y^2 + 1)(y - 1)$ not normal form
- $x^2 - 3x + 9$ normal form

For You to Do

8. Explain why each polynomial in the above list is or is not in normal form. If the polynomial is not in normal form, rewrite it in normal form.

Developing Habits of Mind

Look for a relationship between numbers and polynomials. The normal form of a polynomial is similar to the standard way you write numbers. For instance, it is confusing to say 9378 as three hundred, nine thousand, eight, and seventy. Instead, you say nine thousand, three hundred, seventy-eight.

The same is true of polynomials. You can write 9378 as $9x^3 + 3x^2 + 7x + 8$, where $x = 10$.

Exercises Practicing Habits of Mind

Check Your Understanding

1. Use the polynomial $3 + 4x^2 - 5x + \frac{3}{4}x^5 - 17x^2 + x^4$.

    a. Write the polynomial in normal form.
    b. What is the degree of the polynomial?
    c. What is the coefficient of x?
    d. What is the coefficient of x^2?
    e. What is the coefficient of x^3?
    f. Find a polynomial that when added to this one gives a sum of degree 3.

2. Describe how each polynomial identity is related to the corresponding number fact.

    a. $(x + 5) + (x^2 + 2x + 4) = x^2 + 3x + 9$
    $15 + 124 = 139$

    b. $(x + 1)(x^2 + 2x + 4) = x^3 + 3x^2 + 6x + 4$
    $11 \cdot 124 = 1364$

    c. $(x + 1)^2 = x^2 + 2x + 1$
    $11^2 = 121$

    d. $(x + 1)^3 = x^3 + 3x^2 + 3x + 1$
    $11^3 = 1331$

3. a. What is the prime factorization of 120? Of 168?

    b. How can you use the prime factorizations to find the greatest common factor of 120 and 168?

    c. What is the greatest common factor of $273{,}375 = 3^7 \cdot 5^3$ and $140{,}625 = 3^2 \cdot 5^6$?

    d. Suppose x and y are prime numbers. What is the greatest common factor of $x^7 y^3$ and $x^2 y^6$?

    e. What is the greatest common factor of $120 x^7 y^3$ and $168 x^2 y^6$?

    How do you find the greatest common factor for monomials?

4. Transform the expression below into normal form. For what values of a is the coefficient of x equal to 0?

    $$(x^2 + 3x + a)(x^2 + 3x - 7)$$

For Exercises 5–10, complete each of the following.

- Calculate three numeric examples that follow from each identity by substituting a number for each variable.
- Prove each identity is true. Use the basic rules of algebra.

5. $x^6 - 1 = (x^3 - 1)(x^3 + 1)$
6. $x^6 - 1 = (x - 1)(x + 1)(x^2 + x + 1)(x^2 - x + 1)$
7. $x^6 - 1 = (x^2 - 1)(x^4 + x^2 + 1)$
8. $x^3 - 1 = (x - 1)(x^2 + x + 1)$
9. $(s + t)^2 - (s - t)^2 = 4st$
10. $(n + 1)^2 - n^2 = 2n + 1$
11. **Take It Further** Show that this equation is an identity.
$$(x^3 - 1)(x^3 + 1) = (x^2 - 1)(x^4 + x^2 + 1)$$

On Your Own

12. Use the identity below. Calculate three numeric examples that follow by substituting for x. Then prove that the identity is true, using the basic rules of algebra.
$$(x^2 - x)(x + 1) = (x^2 + x)(x - 1)$$

13. Here are five equations of polynomials. All the expressions are in normal form. A few of the terms are hidden in each expression.

    Three of these cannot be identities. Which three are they? Explain.

    A. $3x^3 + \blacksquare + 2x + 1 \stackrel{?}{=} \blacksquare + 2x + 4$
    B. $\blacksquare + x^2 - 9 \stackrel{?}{=} x^3 + \blacksquare - 9$
    C. $\blacksquare + 3x^2 + \blacksquare + 6 \stackrel{?}{=} x^3 + 3x^2 + \blacksquare$
    D. $x^7 + 7x + \blacksquare \stackrel{?}{=} 3x^7 + \blacksquare + 11$
    E. $x^2 + \blacksquare + 4 \stackrel{?}{=} \blacksquare + x^2 + \blacksquare$

14. Show that each equation is an identity.

    a. $m^2 - n^2 = m(m - n) + n(m - n)$
    b. $m(m - n) + n(m - n) = (m + n)(m - n)$
    c. $(m + 1)(m - n) + (n - 1)(m - n) = (m + n)(m - n)$

15. **Standardized Test Prep** Which polynomial is NOT equivalent to the other three polynomials?

    A. $(3x^3 + 3x^2 + 6x - 1) - 7(x^2 - 1)$

    B. $(x^2 + 2)(3x - 4)$

    C. $(4x^3 - 4x^2 + 6x - 9) - (x^3 - 1)$

    D. $(x - 1)(3x^2 + 5) + (-x^2 + x - 3)$

16. What is the coefficient of the given term in the normal form of $(x + x^2 + x^3 + x^4 + x^5 + x^6)^2$?

    a. x^8 **b.** x^{10}

    What is the coefficient of the given term in the normal form of $(x + x^2 + x^3 + x^4 + x^5 + x^6)^3$?

    c. x^{10} **d.** x^{20}

Maintain Your Skills

17. Find the normal form of each polynomial.

    a. $(1 + x + x^2)(1 + x^3)$

    b. $(1 + x + x^2 + x^3)(1 + x^4)$

    c. $(1 + x + x^2 + x^3 + x^4)(1 + x^5)$

    d. Describe a pattern.

18. Expand each power. Replace x with 1. What is your result?

    a. $(x - 1)^2$ **b.** $(x - 1)^3$ **c.** $(x - 1)^4$

    d. Describe a pattern. Explain why this pattern exists.

19. Write each polynomial in normal form. What is the degree?

    a. $x(x + 1)$ **b.** $x(x + 1)(x + 2)$

    c. $x(x + 1)(x + 2)(x + 3)$ **d.** $x(x + 1)(x + 2)(x + 3)(x + 4)$

    e. Describe a pattern. Explain why this pattern exists.

20. Write each polynomial in normal form. What is the sum of the coefficients of each polynomial?

    a. $x(x + 1)$ **b.** $x(x + 1)(x + 2)$

    c. $x(x + 1)(x + 2)(x + 3)$ **d.** $x(x + 1)(x + 2)(x + 3)(x + 4)$

    e. Describe a pattern.

7.08 Arithmetic With Polynomials

Polynomials are a useful language for describing rules or defining functions. Instead of saying "the function that squares its input and adds 1," you can let the polynomial $x^2 + 1$ describe the rule.

In algebra, it is important to consider polynomials as unique mathematical concepts and to learn to calculate with them. You can transform polynomial expressions using the basic rules. Eventually, you will be able to visualize polynomial calculations. You might even be able to predict results without actually completing the computations.

When you perform repeated calculations, you train your eye to notice patterns. This practice often leads to very useful theorems.

> Just as you calculate with numbers to do arithmetic, you calculate with polynomials to do algebra.

Minds in Action   episode 30

Derman shows Tony and Sasha this problem from his algebra book.

> Find the coefficient of x^6 in the normal form of
> $(3x^2 + 2x + 7)(x^5 + 4x^4 - 2x^3 + 3x + 2)$.

Derman What am I supposed to do with this?

Tony Just multiply everything out. Then look at the coefficient of x^6.

Derman That's a lot of work for such a small question.

Sasha Wait a minute . . . you don't need to multiply it all out. Think about what you'd have to do. Multiply every term in the first polynomial by every term in the second one. Then collect like terms.

Tony Yes, that's exactly what we do with expansion boxes.

Sasha And where would x^6 come from?

Derman If I take $3x^2$ from the first parentheses, I'd have to take $4x^4$ from the second. There's no other way to get a monomial of degree 6.

Sasha So that gives us $(3x^2)(4x^4)$ or $12x^6$. Are there any more combinations?

Derman No, there aren't, if I stick to $3x^2$ from the first polynomial.

Tony We could pick a $2x$ from the first polynomial and match it with x^5 from the second. That would produce another x^6 since $(2x)(x^5) = 2x^6$.

When you perform repeated steps, you train your eye to notice patterns.

Sasha Good work. Any more?

Derman You won't get any more out of $2x$. How about using the 7 from the first polynomial?

Tony You can't get x^6. It doesn't matter what you pick from the second polynomial.

Sasha So, we'll only get two products in the expansion that have degree 6, $12x^6$ from $(3x^2)(4x^4)$, and $2x^6$ from $(2x)(x^5)$. How much do we have in total?

Tony We'll have $12x^6 + 2x^6 = 14x^6$.

Sasha So the coefficient of x^6 in the expansion is 14.

For You to Do

1. Find the coefficient of x^5 in the normal form of $(3x^2 + 2x + 7)(x^5 + 4x^4 - 2x^3 + 3x + 2)$.

For Discussion

2. Find the values of a and b that make the polynomial $(x - a)(x - b)$ equal to $x^2 - 3x + 2$.

Think of *equal* as "the same."

Exercises Practicing Habits of Mind

Check Your Understanding

1. For each equation, find the value of k that makes it true.
   a. $(7x^2 + 2x + k) + (3x + 9) = 7x^2 + 5x + 13$
   b. $(x - 2)(x + k) = x^2 - 4$
   c. $(x^4 - 5x^2 + kx + 2) + (x^2 + 4x - 10) = x^4 - 4x^2 - 6x - 8$
   d. $(x + 2)(x + k) = x^2 + 7x + 10$
   e. $(3x^4 - \frac{1}{3}x^3 + 7x + 5) - (x^4 + kx^3 + 10) = 2x^4 + \frac{1}{6}x^3 + 7x - 5$
   f. $(2x + 1)(kx - 1) = 4x^2 - 1$

2. Without expanding, find the coefficient of x^4 in the normal form of each polynomial.

   a. $(2x^2 + 3x + 5)(x^3 - 1)$
   b. $(x + 1)^5$
   c. $(x - 1)(x^4 + x^3 + x^2 + x + 1)$

3. **Write About It** Explain how you can find the coefficient of x^3 in $(x + 1)^4$ without expanding.

4. Without expanding the left side, explain why the following equation is definitely not an identity.

   $(x^3 - 4x^2 + 5x - 7)(x^2 + 4x + 6) = x^6 - 7x^5 + 5x^3 - 4x^2 - 4x - 42$

5. What is the coefficient of x^3y in $(x + y)^4$?

6. A quadratic polynomial is a polynomial of degree 2. It looks like $ax^2 + bx + c$, where $a \neq 0$. If $a = 1$, $b = 1$, and $c = -6$, the value of this polynomial is 0 when $x = 2$. Find three other possible choices for the numbers a, b, and c that also make the value of the polynomial 0 when $x = 2$.

7. Tony and Derman play a game in the cafeteria. They toss four pennies. If three heads come up, Derman wins. If two heads come up, Tony wins. Otherwise, it is a draw.

   Tony says, "Derman, I think you've got the advantage in this game. You've won 6 times. I've only won twice. There have been 5 draws."

   Derman argues, "You can't tell on the basis of 13 throws. You need about a million throws."

   Tony replies, "Neither of us has time for that. Besides, this is getting tedious."

   Sasha joins them. Tony and Derman fill her in.

   Sasha exclaims, "Algebra to the rescue! Multiply out $(h + t)^4$. You can determine the most likely toss from that."

   Derman agrees, "I guess we could expand $(h + t)^4$ quicker than we could toss a million times."

   Tony asks, "But how does the expansion help us? Why do you want us to use h and t, Sasha?"

   Explain Sasha's method to Tony and Derman.

   Try playing the game. However, experiments are not proof.

8. **Take It Further** Find a quadratic polynomial that defines the function represented in this table.

Input	Output
0	2
1	6
2	12

9. Suppose the sides of a triangle have lengths a, b, and c. A famous formula, proved by Heron of Alexandria in about A.D. 60, states that you can calculate the area of the triangle by this rule.

$$A = \tfrac{1}{4}\sqrt{(a + b + c)(a + b - c)(a + c - b)(b + c - a)}$$

  a. Find the area of a triangle with side lengths 13, 14, and 15.

  b. **Take It Further** Expand this product.
  $(a + b + c)(a + b - c)(c + a - b)(c - a + b)$

  c. Use Heron's formula to derive a formula for the area of a triangle with sides all the same length.

  d. **What's Wrong Here?** What does the formula give for the area of a triangle with side lengths 6, 4, and 10? Explain.

10. **Take It Further** Many geometry books state Heron's formula as follows.

$$A = \sqrt{s(s - a)(s - b)(s - c)}, \text{ where } s = \tfrac{1}{2}(a + b + c)$$

Show that this expression is equivalent to the expression in Exercise 9.

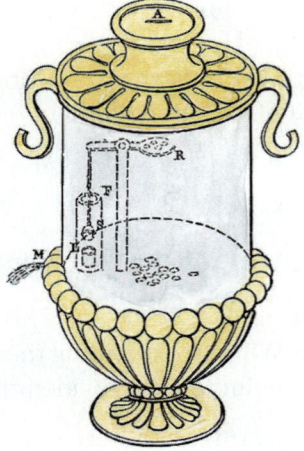

Heron invented the first vending machine. Can you see how inserting a coin would cause the machine to dispense a small amount of water?

On Your Own

11. Without expanding, what is the coefficient of x^4 in the normal form of
$(x^2 + 3x^2 + 1)(2x^4 - x^3 + 5x + 2) + (2x^4 - x^3 + 5x + 2)$?

12. The coefficient of x^3 in the normal form of the polynomial below is 18.

$(x^2 + 3x^2 + 1)(2x^4 - x^3 + 5x + 2) + (2x^4 - x^3 + 5x + 2)$

What is the coefficient of x^3 in the normal form of
$(x^2 + 3x^2 + 1)(2x^4 - x^3 + 5x + 2) - (2x^4 - x^3 + 5x + 2)$?

13. What is the coefficient of x^5 in the normal form of $(x + 1)^5$?

14. **Write About It** Revisit what you explored in Lesson 7.05.

  a. Explain why the coefficient of x^8 in the normal form of this polynomial is 5.
  $(x + x^2 + x^3 + x^4 + x^5 + x^6)^2$

  b. Explain why the coefficient of x^{10} in the normal form of $(x + x^2 + x^3 + x^4 + x^5 + x^6)^2$ is the number of ways you can roll a sum of 10 if you throw two number cubes.

  c. Explain why the coefficient of x^{14} in the normal form of $(x + x^2 + x^3 + x^4 + x^5 + x^6)^3$ is the number of ways you can roll a sum of 14 if you throw three number cubes.

15. Find the coefficient of *xyz* in the expanded form of
    $(x + y + z)(x^2 - xy + y^2 - xz - yz + z^2)$.

16. **Standardized Test Prep** The coefficient of x^5 in the normal form of
    $(x + x^2 + x^3 + x^4 + x^5 + x^6)^2$ is the number of ways you can roll a sum of
    5 with two number cubes. What is the coefficient of x^5 in the normal form?

    A. 4   **B.** 5   **C.** 6   **D.** 7

17. Ed Barbeau, a mathematician from Toronto, writes the following three equations.

    $$1 + 2 = 3$$
    $$4 + 5 + 6 = 7 + 8$$
    $$9 + 10 + 11 + 12 = 13 + 14 + 15$$

    Describe the pattern. What do you notice? What is the next equation in the series? Make some conjectures. What can you prove?

Maintain Your Skills

18. Expand each product.
    a. $(1 - x)(1 + x)$
    b. $(1 - x)(1 + x + x^2)$
    c. $(1 - x)(1 + x + x^2 + x^3)$

19. Find the normal form of each polynomial.
    a. $(1 + x + x^2)(1 + x^3 + x^6)$
    b. $(1 + x + x^2 + x^3)(1 + x^4 + x^8)$
    c. $(1 + x + x^2 + x^3 + x^4)(1 + x^5 + x^{10})$

20. Expand each product.
    a. $(1 + x)(1 + x^2)(1 + x^4)$
    b. $(1 + x)(1 + x^2)(1 + x^4)(1 + x^8)$
    c. $(1 + x)(1 + x^2)(1 + x^4)(1 + x^8)(1 + x^{16})$

21. Expand and simplify each expression.
    a. $(a + b)(a^2 + b^2) - ab(a + b)$
    b. $(a + b)(a^3 + b^3) - ab(a^2 + b^2)$
    c. $(a + b)(a^4 + b^4) - ab(a^3 + b^3)$

Mathematical Reflections 7B

In this investigation, you learned about certain types of polynomials. You also wrote polynomials in normal form and learned methods for adding, subtracting, and multiplying polynomials. These questions will help you summarize what you have learned.

1. Find the product of $(x + x^2 + x^3)$ and $(x^2 + x^3 + x^4 + x^5)$.

2. Let $p(x) = x^2 + 3x + 4$. Find polynomials $r(x)$, and $s(x)$, and $t(x)$ as described.
   a. $r(x)$ such that $p(x) + r(x) = 3x^2 - 8x + 1$
   b. $s(x)$ such that $p(x) - s(x) = 2x - 1$
   c. $t(x)$ such that $p(x) \cdot t(x)$ has degree 4 and $p(x) + t(x)$ has degree 1

3. For each identity, complete the following.
   - Calculate three numeric examples that follow from each identity by substituting a number for x.
   - Prove each identity is true. Use the basic rules.

   a. $x^3 + 1 = (x + 1)(x^2 - x + 1)$
   b. $x^8 - 1 = (x^4 + 1)(x^2 + 1)(x + 1)(x - 1)$
   c. $(x + 1)(x^2 - 5x + 3) = (x^3 + 3) - 2x(2x + 1)$

4. a. Write $p(x) = 3x^7 - 8x + x^6 - 5 + 4x^5 - 2x^4 + x^2 - 8x^3$ in normal form.
   b. What is the degree of the polynomial?
   c. What is the coefficient of x^3?
   d. What is the coefficient of x^2?
   e. Find a polynomial that you can add to $p(x)$ to get a polynomial of degree 5.

5. How can you decide whether two polynomials are equivalent?

6. How is a polynomial useful for describing a rule?

7. Suppose you roll three number cubes numbered 1–6. What is the probability of rolling a total of 12?

If track lanes are 4 ft wide and a race includes a semicircle, the starting blocks are staggered 4π ft apart.

Vocabulary

In this investigation, you learned these terms. Make sure you understand what each one means and how to use it.

- coefficient
- cubic polynomial
- degree of a monomial
- degree of a polynomial
- linear polynomial
- monomial
- normal form
- parameter
- polynomial
- quadratic polynomial
- quartic polynomial
- quintic polynomial

Chapter 7 Mid-Chapter Test

Multiple Choice

1. What is the number of solutions to the equation $(3x - 5)(5x + 7) = 0$?
   A. 0   B. 1
   C. 2   D. 3

2. Expand the following expression. What is the coefficient of x^3?
   $$(x^4 - 3x^3 + 5)(x^2 + 12x + 10)$$
   A. -30 B. 0
   C. 1   D. 30

3. Which expression is NOT a polynomial?
   A. $-2x^4 - 3x^2 + 5$
   B. $x - 13 + \frac{1}{3}x^{10}$
   C. 5
   D. $3x^4 + 5x^3 - 2^x - 3x + 4$

4. Which value of k makes the equation true?
   $$(x^2 + 3x + 4)(x - k) = x^3 - 2x^2 - 11x - 20$$
   A. 2   B. 5
   C. 10   D. 20

5. Which of these four expressions are equivalent?
   I. $x^3 + 27$
   II. $(x + 3)(x^2 + 3x + 9)$
   III. $(x - 3)(x^2 + 3x + 9)$
   IV. $(x + 3)(x^2 - 3x + 9)$

   A. I and II   B. I and III
   C. I and IV   D. III and IV

6. Let $p(x) = 3x^5 - 2x^2 + 4$ and $q(x) = -3x^5 + 3x^2 - 4$. What is the degree of $p(x) \cdot q(x)$?
   A. 2   B. 5
   C. 10   D. 25

Open Response

7. Use the Zero-Product Property. Find both solutions to the equation $(x - 4)(x - 5) = 20$.

8. Function $f(x)$ is defined according to the rule $f(x) = (3x + 5)^2 - 10(3x - 2)$.

   a. Copy and complete this input-output table for $f(x)$.

Input, x	Output, $f(x)$
0	■
1	■
2	■
3	■

   b. All the values in the output column are multiples of 9. Use the rule defined for $f(x)$ to explain why this is true no matter what integer you choose for x.

9. Can two polynomials have degree 3 if neither their sum nor their product has degree 3? If so, give an example. If not, explain.

10. Find three expressions, A, B, and C, that satisfy the following.
    - The greatest common factor of expressions A and B is m^2.
    - The greatest common factor of expressions B and C is 5.
    - Expressions A and C have no common factors.

11. a. Expand the following expression.
    $$(x + x^2 + x^3 + x^6)^2$$

    b. You label the sides of a tetrahedral (four-sided) prism with the numbers 1, 2, 3, and 6. You throw two of these tetrahedrons. What is the most likely sum you will get?

12. How can you tell if two different expressions define the same function?

Investigation 7C

Factoring to Solve: Quadratics

In *Factoring to Solve: Quadratics*, you will learn several techniques for factoring quadratic expressions. You will use factoring and the Zero-Product Property to find all the roots of a quadratic polynomial equation.

By the end of this investigation, you will be able to answer questions like these.

1. Suppose you know the sum and product of two numbers. How can you find the two numbers?

2. How do you determine quickly whether you can factor a monic quadratic expression over $\mathbb{Z}$?

3. How do you solve equations such as $x^2 = 15x + 250$?

You will learn how to
- apply the Difference of Squares Theorem to polynomial expressions and numerical examples
- use difference of squares factoring to solve equations
- factor monic quadratic polynomials
- factor general quadratic polynomials
- use factoring to solve equations

You will develop these habits and skills:
- Find patterns in repeated calculations and make conjectures based on these patterns.
- Use algebraic computation to prove theorems.
- Use geometric diagrams to understand theorems.
- Understand the relationship between the factorization of a quadratic expression and the solutions of a quadratic equation.

$(a + b)^2 = (a - b)^2 + 4ab$

656 Chapter 7 Polynomials

7.09 Getting Started

Activating Prior Knowledge
Exploring New Ideas

In this investigation, you will learn to factor many different types of polynomials, especially quadratic polynomials.

For You to Explore

1. **Write About It** What is the Zero-Product Property (ZPP)? How can you use it?

2. A version of the multiplication table is below. Along the red diagonal, all the numbers are perfect squares.

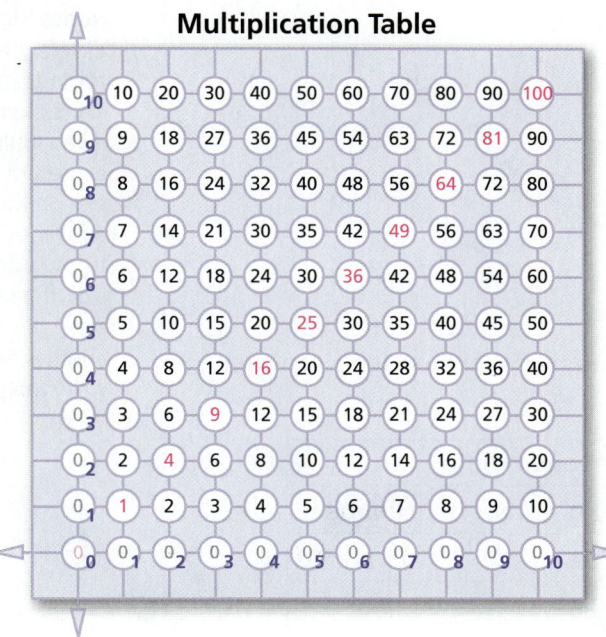
Multiplication Table

Why are the numbers on the diagonal perfect squares?

Start at any number on the perfect-square diagonal. There are eight different directions you can move.

   a. Describe the numerical effect of moving in each direction.

   b. Develop eight rules that explain how to get from any perfect square to its eight neighbors.

   c. Try your rules on one of the perfect squares.

3. Choose a perfect square in the multiplication table in Problem 2. Move up any number of rows. Use that same number and move left that number of columns. How is the number that you land on related to the perfect square that you chose?

Use the pattern that you notice to find the missing expressions represented by gray boxes in a part of the multiplication table. First, write the missing expressions on the axes. Next, multiply an expression on the x-axis times an expression on the y-axis. Finally, write the product in the table. Write each product in terms of x as a difference of two numbers. The expression $x^2 - 4$ appears in the table as an example.

Habits of Mind

Represent a rule. You can find more than one way to describe each of the eight rules. Write each rule as many ways as possible.

7.09 Getting Started 657

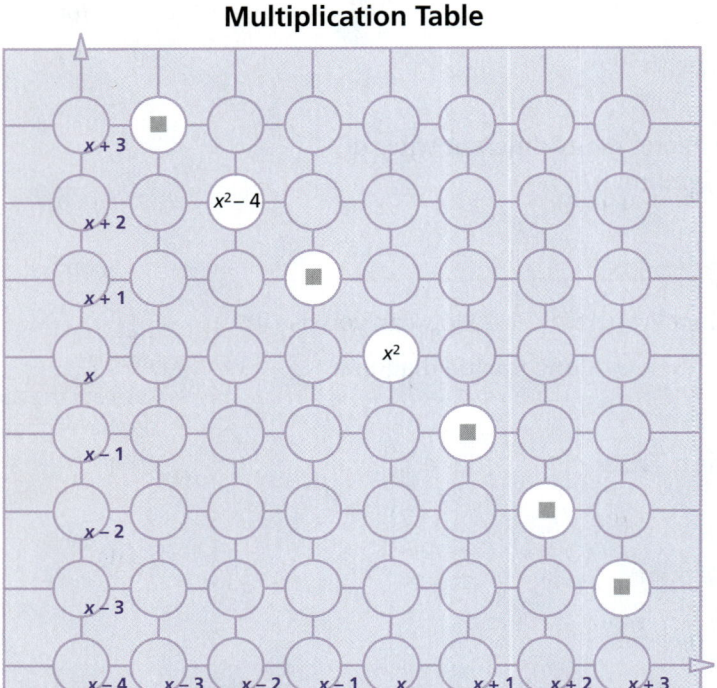

Multiplication Table

4. Copy and complete this table. Find two numbers that have the given sum and product.

Numbers With a Given Sum and Product		
Sum of Two Numbers	Product of Two Numbers	Numbers
20	99	11 and 9
20	96	■
20	75	■
20	36	■
20	−125	■
20	47	■
20	n	■

Notice that you can write different expressions for the same missing expression. For example, if you multiply the expression to the right of x on the horizontal axis times the expression below x on the vertical axis, the result is $(x + 1)(x - 1)$. What is another way that you can write this product?

The last two are much harder! Try to find a pattern in the other results.

658 Chapter 7 Polynomials

Exercises Practicing Habits of Mind

On Your Own

5. This is a portion of a multiplication table surrounding 15^2, or 225.

   a. Copy and complete the table.

   b. Write each number as $15^2 \pm \blacksquare$.

   c. Write each number as $(15 \pm \blacksquare)(15 \pm \blacksquare)$.

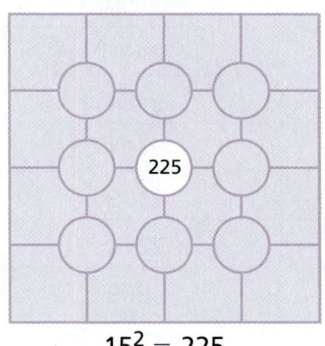

Multiplication Table

$15^2 = 225$

For Exercises 5b and 5c, use your results from Problem 2.

6. Copy and complete the multiplication table.

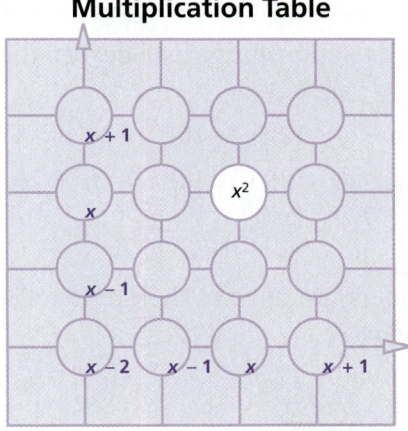

Multiplication Table

7. Find two factors of each number.

   a. $23^2 - 6^2$

   b. $51^2 - 8^2$

   c. $99^2 - 10^2$

   d. $1{,}000{,}000^2 - 13^2$

   e. $a^2 - b^2$

8. a. Sketch the graph of $f(x) = x(100 - x)$. Make sure the graph includes any points where the graph changes direction. Also include any point where the graph crosses an axis.

   b. What are the exact coordinates of the graph's turning point?

Turning point means maximum or minimum.

9. If two numbers add up to 100, can their product ever be the following?

   a. less than 2500
   b. negative
   c. zero
   d. more than 2500
   e. 2436
   f. 1234

Use the graph from Exercise 8. You can also use the TRACE function on a calculator to find the value of $x(100 - x)$ at different points.

10. Copy and complete this table. Find two numbers that have the given sum and product.

Numbers With a Given Sum and Product		
Sum of Two Numbers	Product of Two Numbers	Numbers
100	2500	50 and 50
100	2491	53 and 47
100	2484	■ and ■
100	2451	■ and ■
100	2379	■ and ■
100	2211	■ and ■
100	−309	■ and ■
100	1234	■ and ■
100	n	■ and ■

In the last row, try to find a formula, in terms of n, for the numbers.

11. Expand each product. What relationships exist between the factored form and expanded form?

    a. $(x + 11)(x + 8)$
    b. $(x - 12)(x - 10)$
    c. $(x + 9)(x - 7)$
    d. $\left(x - \frac{2}{3}\right)\left(x - \frac{1}{3}\right)$
    e. $(x - 12)(x - 13)$
    f. $(x + 53)(x + 47)$
    g. $(x + 21)(x - 21)$
    h. $\left(x + \frac{7}{2}\right)\left(x - \frac{7}{2}\right)$

12. **Take It Further** Two numbers add up to b. Their product is c. Find the two numbers, in terms of b and c.

Maintain Your Skills

13. Show that each number fact is true.

    a. $45^2 = 40 \cdot 50 + 5^2$
    b. $35^2 = 30 \cdot 40 + 5^2$
    c. $25^2 = 20 \cdot 30 + 5^2$
    d. Describe the pattern.

For Exercises 14 and 15, prove each identity.

14. a. $x^2 - y^2 = (x + y)(x - y)$
    b. $x^2 - 9 = (x + 3)(x - 3)$
    c. $(x - 3)^2 - 16 = (x + 1)(x - 7)$
    d. $\left(x - \frac{3}{2}\right)^2 - \frac{1}{4} = (x - 2)(x - 1)$
    e. $(x - a)^2 - b^2 = (x - a + b)(x - a - b)$

15. a. $(a + b)^2 - (a - b)^2 = 4ab$
    b. $\left(\frac{a+b}{2}\right)^2 - \left(\frac{a-b}{2}\right)^2 = ab$
    c. $30^2 - 10^2 = 20 \cdot 40$
    d. $18^2 - 7^2 = 25 \cdot 11$

7.10 Factoring a Difference of Squares

You have seen the identity $a^2 - b^2 = (a + b)(a - b)$ several times. Since this result is so important, you can state it as a theorem.

Theorem 7.2 The Difference of Squares

For any numbers a and b, the following is an identity.

$$a^2 - b^2 = (a + b)(a - b)$$

Note that you can replace a and b by any number, variable, or expression.

Proof Like all identities, you can establish this by showing that both sides are equivalent under the basic rules. Expand the right side of the equation and compare to the left side.

$(a + b)(a - b) = a(a - b) + b(a - b)$ Distributive Property
$\qquad\qquad\quad = a^2 - ab + ba - b^2$ Distributive Property
$\qquad\qquad\quad = a^2 - b^2$ $-ab + ba = 0$

Using the basic rules, $(a + b)(a - b)$ became $a^2 - b^2$. This proves the identity.

> Why is $-ab + ba$ equal to 0?

Developing Habits of Mind

Visualize. You can also use a visual explanation to prove Theorem 7.2 above.

Calculate the area of a figure like this figure in two ways.

Let a be the length of the top side. Let b be the length of a side in the missing corner. First, notice that the area of the shaded region is the area of the larger square minus the area of the smaller square.

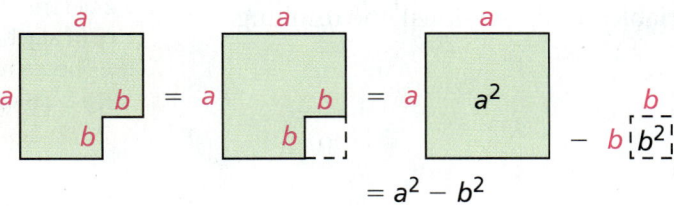

$= a^2 - b^2$

> In this argument, assume that a and b are positive and that $a > b$.

Therefore, the area of the shaded region is $a^2 - b^2$.

Now calculate the area another way. Cut up the shaded region and make another rectangle.

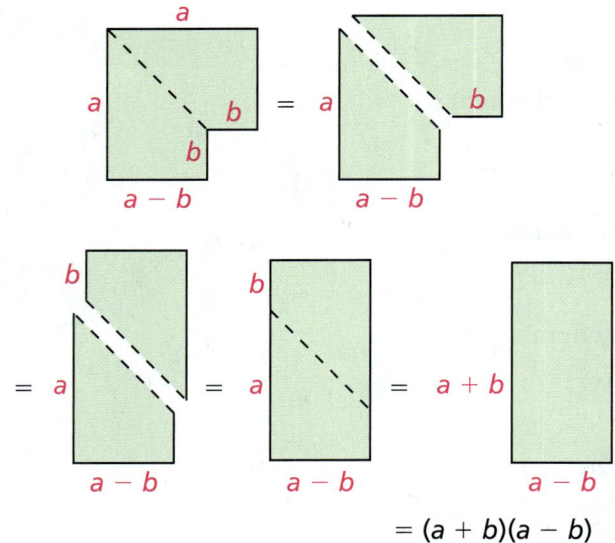

$$= (a + b)(a - b)$$

The area of the shaded region is $(a + b)(a - b)$.

Since $a^2 - b^2$ and $(a + b)(a - b)$ both represent the area of the shaded region, they are equal. Therefore, $a^2 - b^2 = (a + b)(a - b)$.

This is the result of Theorem 7.2.

For Discussion

1. In the first set of diagrams, why is the area of the shaded region $a^2 - b^2$?

2. Look at the final rectangle in the second set of diagrams. Why is the length of the bottom $(a - b)$? Why is the length of the side $(a + b)$?

3. The visual proof assumes that a and b are positive and that $a > b$. Why are these assumptions necessary for this argument?

Why is Theorem 7.2 important? You can use $a^2 - b^2 = (a + b)(a - b)$ to factor a quadratic that is the difference of any two squares. No matter what you substitute for a or b (numbers, variables, or expressions), the resulting statement is always true.

You have seen Theorem 7.2 before. It is not a basic rule of algebra, but you use Theorem 7.2 as if it were a basic rule.

Consider these examples.

If $a = 93$ and $b = 7$, then $93^2 - 7^2 = (93 + 7)(93 - 7)$.

If $a = 5x$ and $b = y^3$, then $25x^2 - y^6 = (5x + y^3)(5x - y^3)$.

This theorem also gives you a basis for factoring any quadratic polynomial.

On the left side, why do you find $-y^6$? $25x^2$?

For You to Do

Each equation below is in the form $a^2 - b^2 = (a + b)(a - b)$. What represents a and b in each equation?

4. $9x^2 - 16 = (3x + 4)(3x - 4)$

5. $10{,}000 - 4 = (100 + 2)(100 - 2)$

6. $16x^6 - 4x^2 = (4x^3 + 2x)(4x^3 - 2x)$

Minds in Action   episode 31

Sasha thinks she has invented a number trick. She tests it on Tony.

Sasha   Tony, give me any two numbers with an average of 100. I'll multiply them quickly in my head.

Tony   All right, 103 and 97.

Sasha   Easy! That's 9991.

Tony scribbles the calculation on paper.

Tony   Wow! That was fast.

Sasha   Give me another.

Tony   Okay, 109 and 91.

Sasha   9919.

Tony   112 and 88.

Sasha   9856.

7.10   Factoring a Difference of Squares

Tony checks the answers on paper.

Tony You're right! How can you do that so quickly?

Sasha You think of a difference of squares. Instead of multiplying 91 by 109, I think of $(100 + 9)(100 - 9)$. That is the same as $100^2 - 9^2$.

Tony Okay. So, it's $10,000 - 81 = 9919$.

Sasha Exactly. Here's the first one.

Sasha scribbles on her piece of paper.

$$103 \cdot 97 = (100 + 3)(100 - 3) = 100^2 - 3^2$$

Tony So, 100^2 is 10,000 and 3^2 is 9. I take 9 from 10,000 and get 9991.

Sasha Exactly!

Tony So, $105 \cdot 95$ is 10,000 minus 5 squared, which is 25. That makes it 9975.

Sasha You got it.

Tony Why do the numbers have to average 100?

Sasha They don't really. It's just that 100^2 is easy to remember. If the two numbers averaged something else, that would just change things a little bit.

Tony How about -9 times 209?

Sasha Well, it's not always easier to do it my way.

For Discussion

7. How would you change Sasha's method if the two numbers average 80?

8. Find two numbers with an average of 100, such that it is easier to multiply them by using Sasha's method than it is to use paper and pencil.

9. Find two numbers with an average of 100, such that it is easier to multiply them by using paper and pencil than it is to use Sasha's method.

For You to Do

Find each product without using a calculator.

10. $89 \cdot 71$

11. $52 \cdot 48$

12. $1007 \cdot 993$

13. $(1000 + x)(1000 - x)$

Exercises Practicing Habits of Mind

Check Your Understanding

1. Theorem 7.2 states that $a^2 - b^2 = (a+b)(a-b)$. Some of the following equations are related identities that result from substituting for a and b.

   Determine whether each equation is an identity. If an equation is an identity, state the substitution that you made for a and b.

   a. $16x^2 - 9y^2 = (4x + 3y)(4x - 3y)$
   b. $8n^2 - 4 = (4n + 2)(4n - 2)$
   c. $25 - t^6 = (5 + t^3)(5 - t^3)$
   d. $(x + 3)^2 - 1 = (x + 4)(x + 2)$
   e. $9 - x^2 = (x + 3)(x - 3)$
   f. $n^3 - 100 = (n^2 + 10)(n - 10)$

2. **a.** What value of x makes the greatest possible product of $(50 + x)$ and $(50 - x)$? Explain.

   b. Consider all pairs of numbers x and y such that $x + y = 100$. Which pair has the greatest possible product?

3. Find all pairs of nonnegative integers x and y that satisfy each equation.

   a. $x^2 - y^2 = 7$
   b. $x^2 - y^2 = 13$
   c. $x^2 - y^2 = 9$

4. Find each difference without using pencil and paper or a calculator.

   a. $80^2 - 20^2$
   b. $75^2 - 25^2$
   c. $87^2 - 13^2$

5. Hideki wants to find an identity for $a^2 + b^2$. He thinks that if you substitute $(-b)$ for b in Theorem 7.2, you get the following.
$$a^2 + b^2 = a^2 - (-b)^2$$
$$= (a + (-b))(a - (-b))$$
$$= (a - b)(a + b)$$

   Is Hideki right? Does $a^2 + b^2 = (a - b)(a + b)$? Explain.

> **Habits of Mind**
> **Visualize.** Sketch the graph of each equation. Where do the graphs intersect the corners of a square on the graph paper?

6. Describe a pattern in this portion of the multiplication table. Explain why the pattern continues.

Multiplication Table

7. What values of k make each equation an identity?
    a. $x^2 - 9 = (x + 3)(x + k)$
    b. $y^2 - k = (y + 10)(y - 10)$
    c. $a^4 - 16 = (a - 2)(a + 2)(a^2 + k)$

8. Use the diagram. Give another visual proof of Theorem 7.2.

9. **Write About It** If a is an integer, can $(a + 1)^2 - a^2$ be even? Explain.

10. Show that each equation is an identity.
    a. $(x + 11)(x + 8) = (x + 9.5)^2 - (1.5)^2$
    b. $(x + 12)(x + 8) = (x + 10)^2 - (2)^2$
    c. $(x + 13)(x + 14) = \left(x + \frac{27}{2}\right)^2 - \left(\frac{1}{2}\right)^2$

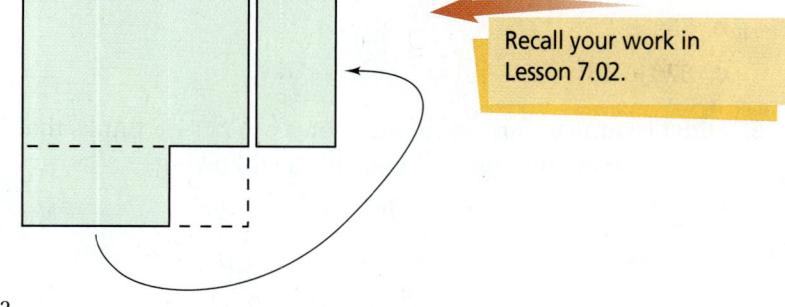

Recall your work in Lesson 7.02.

11. **Take It Further** For the following equation, find r and s in terms of a and b.
$$(x + a)(x + b) = (x + r)^2 - s^2$$

12. A straight metal rail is 2400 cm long. It is firmly fixed at each end. On a warm day, its length increases to 2402 cm. This causes it to buckle. Assume its final shape is closely approximated by an isosceles triangle. Determine how far from the ground its midpoint rises.

Habits of Mind

Experiment. Before you solve this exercise, guess an answer. Then determine how close your guess is.

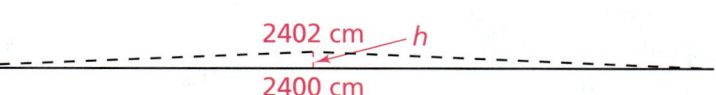

13. Solve each equation.
    a. $x^2 - 9 = 0$
    b. $(x - 3)^2 - 16 = 0$
    c. $\left(x - \frac{3}{2}\right)^2 - \frac{1}{4} = 0$
    d. Express x in terms of a and b if $(x - a)^2 - b^2 = 0$.

On Your Own

14. Find each quotient. Do not use a calculator.
    a. $\frac{13^2 - 4^2}{13 + 4}$
    b. $\frac{9^2 - 4^2}{9 + 4}$
    c. $\frac{27^2 - 4^2}{27 + 4}$
    d. $\frac{x^2 - 4^2}{x + 4}$

15. a. Determine whether $y^6 - 25 = (y^3 + 5)(y^3 - 5)$ is true.
    b. What is the degree of $y^6 - 25$?
    c. What is the degree of $(y^3 + 5)$? Of $(y^3 - 5)$? What is the degree of their product?

16. At the right is a diagram of a 7×7 square with a corner missing.
    a. How many small squares are left in this shape? Explain how you calculated your answer without counting every square.
    b. Suppose you cut off the bottom row of this shape and paste it on the right side. The result is a rectangle. What are the side lengths of this rectangle? Explain.
    c. How is this related to the number fact $7^2 - 1 = (7 + 1)(7 - 1)$?

17. Solve the equation $10{,}000 - k^2 = 9879$. (*Hint:* 9879 is divisible by 89.)

Tree roots can cause a sidewalk to buckle.

18. Find the value of x that results in the least value of each polynomial.
    a. $(x + 3)(x - 3)$
    b. $x^2 + 4$
    c. $(x - 7)^2 - 4$
    d. $x^4 - 16$

19. Determine whether you can express each polynomial as a difference of squares in x with integer coefficients. Explain.
    a. $x^1 - 1$
    b. $x^2 - 1$
    c. $x^3 - 1$
    d. $x^4 - 1$
    e. $x^5 - 1$
    f. $x^6 - 1$
    g. $x^7 - 1$
    h. $x^8 - 1$
    i. $x^9 - 1$

    For Exercises 20 and 21, factor each expression.

20. a. $36x^2 - 64$
    b. $0.36x^2 - 0.64$

21. a. $y^3 - 9y$
    b. $y^4 - 9y^2$

22. **Standardized Test Prep** Without using a calculator, find the product $593 \cdot 607$.
    A. 360,049
    B. 359,991
    C. 359,979
    D. 359,951

If the exercise contains decimal coefficients, your solution can, too.

23. Find all the real numbers that make each equation true.
    a. $x^2 - 4 = 0$
    b. $x^2 - 9 = 0$
    c. $x^2 + 4 = 0$
    d. $x^2 - 5 = 0$
    e. $x^2 - 12 = 0$
    f. $x^4 - 16 = 0$

Maintain Your Skills

24. Expand each product.
    a. $(a - b)(a + b)(a^2 + b^2)$
    b. $(a - b)(a + b)(a^2 + b^2)(a^4 + b^4)$
    c. $(a - b)(a + b)(a^2 + b^2)(a^4 + b^4)(a^8 + b^8)$
    d. What is the pattern? Explain.

25. Factor each polynomial.
    a. $x^2 - z^2$
    b. $x^2 - 25$
    c. $(x - 3)^2 - 36$
    d. $\left(x - \frac{3}{4}\right)^2 - \frac{1}{16}$
    e. $(x - p)^2 - b^2$

If the exercise contains fractions for coefficients, your solution can, too.

26. Find the greatest prime factor of each number.
    a. $16^2 - 1$
    b. $15^2 - 4$
    c. $14^2 - 9$
    d. $13^2 - 16$
    e. $12^2 - 25$
    f. What is the pattern? Explain.

7.11 Factoring Monic Quadratics

You have used expansion boxes to expand products of binomials such as the following.

$$(x + 11)(x + 8) = x^2 + 19x + 88$$
$$(x - 12)(x - 10) = x^2 - 22x + 120$$
$$(x + 9)(x - 7) = x^2 + 2x - 63$$

You can also expand a more general case such as $(x + a)(x + b)$, where a and b are unknown numbers.

$$\begin{aligned}(x + a)(x + b) &= x^2 + ax + xb + ab \\ &= x^2 + ax + bx + ab \\ &= x^2 + (a + b)x + ab\end{aligned}$$

Look back at the examples above. The coefficient of x is the sum of the numbers a and b in the factorization. The constant term is the product of the numbers a and b. Note that both a and b can be either positive or negative. This result is important enough to state as a theorem.

> A **binomial** is a polynomial with two terms.

Theorem 7.3 The Sum and Product Identity

For any numbers a and b, the following is an identity.
$$x^2 + (a + b)x + ab = (x + a)(x + b)$$

> The expansion above proves this theorem.

Notice that the coefficient of x is 1 in both factors. The coefficient of the x^2 term in the expanded quadratic is also 1. Any polynomial with lead coefficient 1 is **monic**. The lead coefficient is the coefficient of the term with the greatest degree. Two examples follow.

- $x^2 + 5x - 1$ is monic.
- $3x^2 + 5x - 1$ is not monic.

Theorem 7.3 gives you a way to factor monic quadratics.

Facts and Notation

If you can factor a polynomial into a product of polynomials with integer coefficients, you can say that the polynomial factors over $\mathbb{Z}$.

For example, you can factor the polynomial $x^2 + 5x + 6$ over $\mathbb{Z}$ since it factors into $(x + 2)(x + 3)$. However, $x^2 + 5x + 3$ does not factor over $\mathbb{Z}$.

> **Remember...**
> In Chapter 6, you identified these number systems.
> - integers ($\mathbb{Z}$)
> - rational numbers ($\mathbb{Q}$)
> - real numbers ($\mathbb{R}$)

Factoring an expression such as $x^2 + 6x - 7$ amounts to answering the following question. What two numbers have a sum 6 and a product -7? The numbers are -1 and 7. You use them in the factorization $(x - 1)(x + 7)$.

Example 1

Problem Factor $x^2 + 12x + 27$.

Solution Find two numbers that add to 12 and multiply to 27. You can make a table of all the possible combinations of numbers that add to 12. Then multiply them and look for a match.

From the table, notice that the two numbers that work are 3 and 9. You use those numbers to write the factored form.

$$(x + 3)(x + 9)$$

Be careful when you make a table of products. This table does not include all possible pairs of integers that add to 12. It does not include pairs with a negative integer, such as -5 and 17.

Sum 12	
Numbers	Product
6 and 6	36
5 and 7	35
4 and 8	32
3 and 9	27
2 and 10	20
1 and 11	11

This table starts with the number that is half of the sum. Why is this a reasonable approach?

For Discussion

1. Refer to the example. Why is it sufficient to look only at positive integers to factor $x^2 + 12x + 27$?

Minds in Action   episode 32

Tony and Sasha discuss their homework.

Tony   So what's the problem?

Sasha reads this problem.

Sasha   Find all values of x that make $x^2 - 21x = 72$.

   The first thing we need to do is move the 72.

Tony   Why's that?

Sasha Factoring doesn't help unless you set the equation equal to zero. So move the 72 by adding −72 to each side.

$$x^2 - 21x - 72 = 0$$

Now we have an equation that we're ready to factor.

> The left side must be equal to zero for you to apply the Zero-Product Property.

Tony Okay, so we want to find two numbers that add to −21 and multiply to −72. That's a tough one.

Sasha Usually, we start the table with two numbers that are equal or close to equal. In this case, we need a positive number and a negative number to get a negative product, −72. Let's start with −21 and 0 and go from there.

Sum −21	
Numbers	Product
−21 and 0	0
−22 and 1	−22
−23 and 2	−46
−24 and 3	−72

Bingo! The factors are $(x + 3)$ and $(x - 24)$.

Habits of Mind

Look for a pattern. Notice the pattern in the sums.

Tony Great! I wonder if we could start by looking at numbers that multiply to −72.

Sasha Good idea! Let's make a table. One number has to be positive and one has to be negative, since the product is −72.

Tony Oh, no, that doubles our work!

Sasha Not really. We know the sum is negative. We only have to look at pairs where the larger factor is negative.

Tony Okay, how about this?

I can stop there, since I found the numbers. They're 3 and −24. So we're almost done.

$$x^2 - 21x - 72 = 0$$
$$(x + 3)(x - 24) = 0$$

Product −72	
Numbers	Sum
1 and −72	−71
2 and −36	−34
3 and −24	−21

Sasha I can take it from here. We can use ZPP to break it up into two smaller equations. So, $x + 3 = 0$ or $x - 24 = 0$.

Tony That means $x = -3$ and $x = 24$ are the two solutions.

Sasha Nice! Okay, I checked the answers and they work. What's the next one?

For You to Do

2. Use Sasha and Tony's method. Factor $x^2 - 14x + 40$ and $x^2 + 14x - 120$.

Not all quadratic expressions factor so easily. Actually, it is pretty rare that you can break a monic quadratic polynomial into two factors using only integers. Take a look at the following example.

Example 2

Problem Factor $x^2 + 18x + 63$.

Solution Look for two numbers that add to 18 and multiply to 63. Since both the sum and the product are positive, both numbers have to be positive. The table to the right shows positive integers that add to 18.

The table could stop at 4 and 14, since the numbers just keep decreasing and you have already passed 63. There are no integers that add to 18 and multiply to 63.

The results are the same if you try the product method. No factors of 63 add to 18.

Can you factor this polynomial? Consider the tables that include the possible integer pairs for factoring this polynomial. You cannot factor the polynomial over $\mathbb{Z}$ using any of these pairs. You may be able to factor the polynomial with rational or irrational numbers.

Sum 18	
Numbers	Product
9 and 9	81
8 and 10	80
7 and 11	77
6 and 12	72
5 and 13	65
4 and 14	56
3 and 15	45
2 and 16	32
1 and 17	17

Product 63	
Numbers	Sum
1 and 63	64
3 and 21	24
7 and 9	16

For Discussion

3. Write down five quadratics that factor over $\mathbb{Z}$ and that start with the following expression.

$$x^2 + 15x + \blacksquare$$

Write five more quadratics that start this way and do not factor over $\mathbb{Z}$.

Can you write a rule to find the missing term? Start by finding pairs of numbers with a sum 15.

If b and c are integers, there are two reasons why you cannot factor the monic quadratic $x^2 + bx + c$ over $\mathbb{Z}$.

- The numbers in the factorization are not integers. A polynomial that does not factor over $\mathbb{Z}$ might factor over $\mathbb{R}$. For example, the table in the example gives factors for $x^2 + 18x + 77$, $x^2 + 18x + 72$, $x^2 + 18x + 32$, and others. The table does not work for $x^2 + 18x + 63$.

  There are two numbers that add to 18 and multiply to 63, but they are not integers. In fact, the two numbers are not even rational. They are $9 + 3\sqrt{2}$ and $9 - 3\sqrt{2}$. As decimals, these numbers are about 13.243 and 4.757.

For You to Do

4. Show that $3 + \sqrt{2}$ and $3 - \sqrt{2}$ add to 6 and multiply to 7.
5. Show that $(x + 3)^2 - 2 = x^2 + 6x + 7$.

- The product is too great for the sum. Recall working with the multiplication tables in Chapter 1. The maximum product for a given sum results when the numbers are equal. You can formalize this idea in a theorem.

Theorem 7.4

For a given number s, if $a + b = s$, the maximum value of the product ab occurs when $a = b$.

> The value s is constant. The variables a and b can change in value, but they must have a sum s.

If the sum of two numbers is 18, their maximum possible product is $9 \times 9 = 81$. This means that you cannot factor the expression $x^2 + 18x + 100$, since two real numbers that have a sum of 18 cannot also have a product of 100.

For Discussion

6. Use the following identity that you proved in Lesson 7.09. Prove Theorem 7.4.
$$\left(\frac{a+b}{2}\right)^2 - \left(\frac{a-b}{2}\right)^2 = ab$$

Exercises Practicing Habits of Mind

Check Your Understanding

1. Determine which equation has integer solutions. Explain.

    A. $x^2 + 14x + 46 = 0$
    B. $x^2 + 14x - 46 = 0$
    C. $x^2 - 14x - 13 = 0$
    D. $x^2 - 14x + 13 = 0$

2. Find integer solutions for each polynomial equation. If the equation does not have integer solutions, explain why.

    a. $x^2 + 13x + 36 = 0$
    b. $x^2 + 13x + 42 = 0$
    c. $x^2 + 13x + 224 = 0$
    d. $x^2 + 13x - 48 = 0$
    e. $x^2 + 13x + 22 = 0$
    f. $x^2 + 13x - 114 = 0$
    g. $x^2 + 13x + 54 = 0$
    h. $x^2 + 13x - 20 = 0$
    i. $x^2 + 13x + 17 = 0$
    j. $x^2 + 13x - 14 = 0$

    A **polynomial equation** is an equation with a polynomial equal to 0.

3. Use the Zero-Product Property and what you know about factoring. Find all integer solutions. To solve some equations, expand the product before using the Zero-Product Property. Equations may have zero, one, or two solutions.

    a. $x^2 = 16x - 60$
    b. $x^2 = 16x - 70$
    c. $x^2 = 16x$
    d. $x^2 - 6x + 9 = 0$
    e. $x^2 = 16$
    f. $x^2 + 8x + 16 = 0$
    g. $(x + 1)(x + 2) = 12$
    h. $x(x + 17) = -70$
    i. $(x + 2)(x + 4) = -4$
    j. $x^2 - 10x = -25$

4. A *perfect square trinomial* is a trinomial with identical factors. For example, $x^2 + 6x + 9$ is a perfect square trinomial. Its factors are $(x + 3)(x + 3)$. The trinomial $x^2 + 6x + 8$ is not a perfect square trinomial. Which of the following are perfect square trinomials?

    A. $x^2 + 10x + 25$
    B. $x^2 + 10x + 26$
    C. $x^2 - 14x + 49$
    D. $x^2 + 12x - 36$
    E. $x^2 + 26x + 169$
    F. $x^2 + 54x + 728$

    A **trinomial** is a polynomial expression with exactly three terms.

5. a. **Write About It** Explain why the expression $x^2 - 6x + 9$ is not negative if x is a real number.

    b. **Take It Further** Show that the expression $x^2 + y^2 + 10x - 8y + 42$ is a positive number, for all values of x and y.

674 Chapter 7 Polynomials

On Your Own

6. Tony factors the quadratic $x^2 - 7x + 12$ by listing all the numbers that add to -7. Then he finds a pair that multiplies to 12. Sasha has another way. She looks at all the numbers that multiply to 12. Then she finds a pair that adds to -7. Which quadratic expressions are easier to factor with Sasha's method? With Tony's method? Explain.

    a. $x^2 - 2x - 35$ b. $x^2 - 13x + 36$
    c. $x^2 + 13x - 36$ d. $x^2 + 32x - 185$
    e. $x^2 + 30x + 189$ f. $x^2 + 19x - 34$

7. Factor each quadratic expression over $\mathbb{Z}$. If an expression is not factorable, explain why.

    a. $x^2 + 6x + 5$ b. $x^2 + 12x + 20$
    c. $x^2 + 18x + 45$ d. $x^2 + 6ax + 5a^2$
    e. $x^2 - 121$ f. $x^2 + 10x + 25$
    g. $x^2 + 10x + 24$ h. $x^2 + 10x + 23$
    i. $x^2 + 10x + 21$ j. $x^2 + 10x + 26$

    In Exercise 7d, think of a as an integer.

8. a. Two numbers add to -16. What is the maximum possible value of their product?

    b. Factor the perfect square trinomial $x^2 - 16x + 64$.

    c. The expression $x^2 + 22x + T$ is a perfect square trinomial. What number is T?

    d. A rectangle has a perimeter of 44 meters. What is the maximum possible area?

    e. Suppose $x^2 + Bx + C$ is a perfect square trinomial and you know B. How can you find C?

9. **Write About It** Suppose that you know the factorization of $x^2 + 30x + 216$. Does knowing the factorization help you find the factorization of each expression given? Explain.

   a. $x^2 - 30x + 216$

   b. $x^2 + 30x - 216$

10. **Standardized Test Prep** What are the integer solutions of $x^2 - 7x = 120$?

    A. −15, −8   **B.** −15, 8   **C.** −8, 15   **D.** 8, 15

11. Use a multiplication table. Draw the line of factors that add to each given number. What is the greatest product on that line?

    a. 10   b. 16   c. even number, n

12. a. Use a multiplication table. Draw the line of factors that add to 9. Are there two numbers that add up to 9 with a product that is *more* than 20? Explain.

    b. Two numbers add to 13. What is their greatest possible product?

    c. Two numbers add to n. What is their greatest possible product?

Look at Lesson 7.10, Exercise 6.

Maintain Your Skills

13. Solve each equation for integer solutions. If no solutions exist, explain why.

    a. $x^2 + 20x + 99 = 0$

    b. $x^2 - 20x + 51 = 0$

    c. $x^2 + 20x = -224$

    d. $x^2 + 20x = 69$

    e. $x^2 + 20x = -104$

    f. $x^2 + 20x - 48 = 0$

    g. $x^2 + 20x + 54 = 0$

    h. $x^2 - 20x = 96$

    i. $x^2 + 20x + 36 = 0$

7.12 Factoring by Completing the Square

To solve quadratic equations, you need to factor all kinds of quadratic polynomials. A polynomial that is the difference of squares is the easiest kind of polynomial to factor. You only need to use Theorem 7.2.

$$a^2 - b^2 = (a + b)(a - b)$$

Not every polynomial is as simple as the one above. However, you can write any quadratic polynomial as a difference of squares by completing the square.

Example 1

Problem Solve the equation $x^2 - 9 = 0$. Then solve $(x + 4)^2 - 9 = 0$.

Solution The left side of the first equation is a difference of squares. Factor this equation using Theorem 7.2. Then set each factor equal to 0 using ZPP.

$$x^2 - 9 = 0$$
$$(x + 3)(x - 3) = 0$$
$$x + 3 = 0 \quad \text{or} \quad x - 3 = 0$$
$$x = -3 \text{ or} \quad x = 3$$

To solve $(x + 4)^2 - 9 = 0$, you could expand the left side and put it in normal form to factor it. However, the form of the expression $(x + 4)^2 - 9$ looks just like the expression $x^2 - 9$. The only difference is that $x + 4$ is squared instead of x. Think of this expression as another difference of squares. Factor it accordingly.

$$(x + 4)^2 - 9 = ((x + 4) + 3)((x + 4) - 3) = (x + 7)(x + 1)$$

From here, you get the two solutions, $x = -7$ and $x = -1$.

Go Online
pearsonsuccessnet.com

Habits of Mind
Visualize. You can cover $x + 4$ with one hand so you can think of it as one thing.

For You to Do

1. Use the method in Example 1 to solve the equation $(x - 4)^2 - 36 = 0$. Try expanding the left side. Factor by the usual method.

For Discussion

2. How does this method work for $(x - 5)^2 - 7 = 0$?

Completing the square is a part of a process that transforms a quadratic polynomial into a difference of squares. To complete the square, you need to build a perfect square trinomial. A **perfect square trinomial** is a trinomial with identical factors. Use this identity to build these trinomials.

Corollary 7.3.1 The Perfect Square Trinomial

For any x and a, the following equation is an identity.

$$(x + a)^2 = x^2 + (2a)x + a^2$$

> Completing the square always works! If there is a factorization, this method finds it. If there is not a factorization, this method tells you why. Some quadratics only factor if you allow noninteger coefficients. This method will even help you find these.

For You to Do

3. Prove Corollary 7.3.1. Use the basic rules.

You can use Corollary 7.3.1 in reverse. Suppose a perfect square trinomial starts with the terms $x^2 + 6x + \blacksquare$. You can find the missing term by recognizing that if $2a = 6$, then $a = 3$. Therefore, the missing term, a^2, is 9. Another way to describe this process is to take half of the coefficient of x and square it. This process completes the perfect square.

Example 2

Problem Factor $x^2 - 66x + 945$.

Solution One way to factor the expression is to find the factors of 945. Another way is to find integers with a sum of -66. Either method can take a long time, especially for a larger number such as 945.

To complete the square on $x^2 - 66x$, add 1089, which is 33^2.

$$x^2 - 66x + 1089 = (x - 33)^2$$

However, you are not trying to factor $x^2 - 66x + 1089$. You have $x^2 - 66x + 945$. So, write what you have in terms of the perfect square, fixing the constant term.

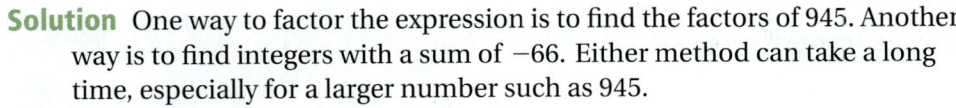

$$= (x - 33)^2 - 144$$

Now it is the difference of two squares. In this form, you can factor $x^2 - 66x + 945$ and solve the equation $x^2 - 66x + 945 = 0$.

For You to Do

4. Factor $x^2 - 66x + 945$. Remember, it is equivalent to $(x - 33)^2 - 144$.

5. Find the two solutions to $x^2 - 66x + 945 = 0$.

For Discussion

For what values of c does $x^2 - 66x + c = 0$ have the following results?

6. two distinct integer solutions

7. only one integer solution

8. no solutions in $\mathbb{Z}$

Minds in Action   episode 33

Tony and Derman try to solve the polynomial equation $x^2 + 120 = 23x$.

Derman First, we subtract $23x$ from each side to get $x^2 - 23x + 120 = 0$. The number 23 is an odd number. That's no fun! That means that the perfect square trinomial will include a fraction.

Tony So what if it's a fraction? They're not that hard.

Derman Okay. To get the perfect square, I divide 23 by 2 and then square it.

$$x^2 - 23x + \left(\frac{23}{2}\right)^2 = x^2 - 23x + \frac{529}{4}$$

Do not forget the Zero-Product Property.

How did Derman calculate $\frac{529}{4}$?

Tony Sounds good to me. Let's find the difference between $\frac{529}{4}$ and 120. I can write 120 as $\frac{480}{4}$.

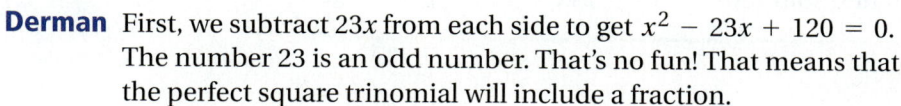

Derman If you factor $x^2 - 23x + \frac{529}{4}$, you get this.

$$\left(x - \frac{23}{2}\right)\left(x - \frac{23}{2}\right) = \left(x - \frac{23}{2}\right)^2$$

So, $x^2 - 23x + 120$ is $\frac{49}{4}$ less than this.

7.12 Factoring by Completing the Square

Derman writes on his paper.
$$x^2 - 23x + 120 = \left(x - \frac{23}{2}\right)^2 - \frac{49}{4}$$

Derman It's the difference of squares.

Tony So, this is what I get.

$$\left(x - \frac{23}{2}\right)^2 - \frac{49}{4} = \left(x - \frac{23}{2} + \frac{7}{2}\right)\left(x - \frac{23}{2} - \frac{7}{2}\right)$$
$$= (x - 8)(x - 15)$$

For You to Do

9. Use completing the square. Solve $x^2 + 19x + 84 = 0$.

For Discussion

10. What happens if you try to complete the square to solve $x^2 - 24x = -200$?

11. For what values of c can you find solutions for $x^2 - 24x = c$?

Minds in Action   episode 34

Shannon and Sasha are sitting at a table next to Tony and Derman. They try to solve the equation $x^2 - 24x + 42 = 0$.

Shannon It looks bad. There are no numbers that add to -24 and multiply to 42.

Sasha Right. So let's start with one that factors. We can see how far off we are. The perfect square trinomial in this case is $x^2 - 24x + 144 = (x - 12)(x - 12) = (x - 12)^2$.

Shannon What we've got is 102 less.

$$\begin{array}{r} x^2 - 24x + 144 \\ (-) x^2 - 24x + 42 \\ \hline 102 \end{array}$$

Sasha If you factor $x^2 - 24x + 144$ you get $(x - 12)^2$. But $x^2 - 24x + 42$ is 102 less than this perfect square. That gives us this.

Sasha writes on her paper.

$$x^2 - 24x + 42 = (x - 12)^2 - 102$$

We made it a difference of squares. We know how to do those.

Shannon Difference of squares? But, Sasha, 102 isn't a square.

680 Chapter 7 Polynomials

Sasha Sure, 102 can be a square. It's just the square of an irrational number.

$$102 = (\sqrt{102})^2$$

Shannon So, $(x - 12)^2 - 102$ factors. It doesn't use integers, but it factors.

$$(x - 12 + \sqrt{102})(x - 12 - \sqrt{102})$$

Sasha And the solutions are $x = 12 - \sqrt{102}$ and $x = 12 + \sqrt{102}$.

Sasha leans towards Tony and Derman's table.

Tony, the one that you and Derman were working on would have factored in the first place.

Tony Sure, but we used a way that always works, whether it factors or not. That makes the process mechanical. I like that.

Sasha I'm impressed. What will you do if there's a number in front of the x^2?

Tony I'm not sure. I'm sure we'll figure it out when we need it.

How did Sasha get these numbers?

Tony and Derman's equation was $x^2 - 23x + 120 = 0$.

For You to Do

12. What is the sum of $12 + \sqrt{102}$ and $12 - \sqrt{102}$?

13. What is the product of $12 + \sqrt{102}$ and $12 - \sqrt{102}$? Explain why both the sum and the product of these two irrational numbers are integers.

Developing Habits of Mind

Use a consistent process. In Lesson 7.11, you learned the sums and products method for finding integer solutions to monic quadratic equations. However, if a quadratic equation has an irrational solution, this method does not work. The sums and products method only works when you can factor a quadratic over $\mathbb{Z}$.

You can complete the square to find any real solution for a quadratic equation. In this lesson, you used this method to find the integer solutions for $x^2 - 66x + 945 = 0$. Also, Shannon and Sasha used this method in episode 34 to find irrational solutions to $x^2 - 24x + 42 = 0$.

Completing the square can also help you determine whether a quadratic equation has no real solutions.

Example 3

Problem Find all real solutions to $x^2 - 12x + 45 = 0$.

Solution Complete the square. First, find half of the coefficient of x, which is -6. Now, make the perfect square trinomial.

$$(x - 6)^2 = x^2 - 12x + 36$$

Rewrite the original equation.

$$x^2 - 12x + 45 = 0$$
$$(x^2 - 12x + 36) + 9 = 0$$
$$(x - 6)^2 + 9 = 0$$

Look at the last equation. The minimum value for $(x - 6)^2$ is 0. So there is no way using real numbers to make the left side equal to 0. The expression $(x - 6)^2 + 9$ is a sum of squares. There is no factoring rule for the sum of squares. The equation $x^2 - 12x + 45 = 0$ has no real solutions.

For Discussion

For what values of c does $x^2 - 35x + c = 0$ have the following results?

14. two distinct solutions

15. only one solution

16. no solutions in $\mathbb{R}$

Exercises Practicing Habits of Mind

Check Your Understanding

1. Solve each equation.

  a. $(x - 3)^2 - 16 = 0$
  b. $(2y + 1)^2 - 100 = 0$
  c. $(n + 5)^2 - 5 = 0$

2. What value of k makes each equation an identity?

  a. $x^2 + 2x = (x + k)^2 - 1$
  b. $x^2 + 4x + 2 = (x + k)^2 - 2$

> Sometimes, there are multiple methods you can use to solve an exercise. Use any factoring method you prefer.

c. $x^2 - 4x + 2 = (x + k)^2 - 2$

d. $x^2 + 12x + 40 = (x + k)^2 + 4$

e. $x^2 + 9x + 10 = (x + k)^2 - 10.25$

f. $x^2 - 25x + 125 = (x + k)^2 - 31.25$

g. $x^2 + 2kx + 72 = (x + k)^2 + k$

3. You can generate this identity by completing the square.
$$x^2 + 8x + 11 = (x + 4)^2 - 5$$

   a. The graph of $y = x^2 + 8x + 11$ is symmetric with respect to a vertical line. What is the equation of the vertical line?

   b. What is the least possible y-value in the graph of $y = x^2 + 8x + 11$?

4. Sasha has a quick way to estimate the square of numbers that are close to 1. Sasha says, "To square 1.01, I add 1 to $2 \times 0.01 = 0.02$ to get 1.02. The right answer is 1.0201. That's pretty close. The closer I am to 1, the better my estimate will be."

   a. Try Sasha's method for 1.03^2.

   b. Try Sasha's method for 1.005^2.

   c. **Take It Further** Find a rule for how close Sasha's method gets you to the exact answer.

5. Solve each polynomial equation. Use completing the square or any other method. Check your answers.

   a. $x^2 - 6x + 10 = 5$

   b. $x^2 + 8x + 2 = 11$

   c. $x^2 + 7 = 6x$

   d. $(2x + 1)(2x - 3) = 5$

   e. $(x + 2) = \dfrac{3}{x + 4}$

6. Expressions for the side lengths of a rectangle and its area are given. Find the value of x and the side lengths of the rectangle.

   a. side lengths: $x + 2$ and $x + 10$

   area: 105

   b. side lengths: $x - 6$ and $x - 10$

   area: 5

   c. side lengths: $x + 3$ and $x + 5$

   area: 30

7. The expression $9a^2 - 24a + 16$ is a perfect square trinomial. It is equivalent to $(3a - 4)^2$.

   a. If $36z^2 + kz + 25$ is a perfect square trinomial, what number is k?

   b. If $49p^2 + 28p + j$ is a perfect square trinomial, what number is j?

8. Derman wants to solve the equation $2x^2 + 4x = 9$. He asks, "How do I solve a nonmonic?" Sasha replies, "Make it a monic by dividing both sides by 2." Tony complains, "That will introduce fractions." Sasha says, "Come on, deal with it!"

   Sasha writes the following.

   $$2x^2 + 4x = 9$$
   $$2x^2 + 4x - 9 = 0$$
   $$x^2 + 2x - \frac{9}{2} = 0$$
   $$x^2 + 2x + 1 - 1 - \frac{9}{2} = 0$$
   $$x^2 + 2x + 1 - \frac{11}{2} = 0$$
   $$(x + 1)^2 - \frac{11}{2} = 0$$
   $$\left(x + 1 + \sqrt{\frac{11}{2}}\right)\left(x + 1 - \sqrt{\frac{11}{2}}\right) = 0$$

   Where did $\frac{11}{2}$ come from?

   Tony says, "I like the way you added and subtracted the thing that completes the square. I can finish it from here."

   a. When Tony says to Sasha, "I like the way you added and subtracted the thing that completes the square," what does he mean?

   b. Finish Derman's problem. Solve $2x^2 + 4x = 9$.

9. Build a polynomial equation of the form $x^2 + bx + c = d$.

   Choose values for b, c, and d (positive or negative). The equation should be different than any of the other equations in this lesson. Solve the equation by completing the square.

   Be careful. Some equations will have no solutions. Also, some values of b can make this exercise easier than others. Which ones are they?

10. Use the equation you built in Exercise 9. Change the value of d so the new equation has no solutions.

On Your Own

11. **Write About It** Suppose you need to teach a robot how to complete the square for any polynomial of the form $x^2 + bx + c$. Write a set of very precise instructions.

12. Solve the equation $x^2 - 6x + 8 = 3$. Use completing the square or any other factoring method. Explain why you chose your method.

13. For each equation, find the value of k that makes it an identity.
    a. $x^2 + 6x = (x + 3)^2 + k$
    b. $x^2 + 4x + 3 = (x + 2)^2 + k$
    c. $x^2 - 6x = (x - 3)^2 + k$
    d. $25x^2 - 30x + 15 = (5x - 3)^2 + k$
    e. $16x^2 + 16x + 72 = (4x + 2)^2 + k$

14. Solve each polynomial equation. Use completing the square or any other method. Check your answers.
    a. $x^2 + 8x = 33$
    b. $x(x + 6) = 160$
    c. $x^2 - 16x + 83 = 20$
    d. $(x + 2)(x - 6) = 240$

15. A number plus 12 times its reciprocal equals 8. What is the number? Is there more than one answer?

16. A number plus 12 times its reciprocal equals 10. What is the number? Is there more than one answer?

17. You can use perfect square trinomials to square some numbers quickly. For example, $1007^2 = 1,014,049$.
    a. **Write About It** Explain how knowing $(x + 7)^2 = x^2 + 14x + 49$ helps you calculate 1007^2 quickly.
    b. Calculate 1009^2, 1013^2, and 997^2 without a calculator.

18. **Standardized Test Prep** You cut a square from each corner of a rectangular piece of sheet metal 10 inches by 6 inches. This forms an open-top rectangular box with a bottom area of 32 square inches. What size squares should you cut from the corners?
    A. $\frac{1}{2}$ in.
    B. 1 in.
    C. $1\frac{1}{2}$ in.
    D. 2 in.

19. Solve each equation. Use any method.
    a. $x^2 + 20 = -12x$
    b. $x(x - 21) = 22$
    c. $x^2 + 8x - 105 = 0$

Maintain Your Skills

20. Complete the square for each polynomial.
    a. $x^2 + 8x$
    b. $x^2 - 8x$
    c. $x^2 + 16x$
    d. $x^2 - 16x$
    e. $x^2 + 5x$
    f. $x^2 - 5x$
    g. $x^2 - bx$
    h. $x^2 + bx$
    i. $x^2 - x$

21. Solve each equation. If no solutions exist, explain why.
    a. $x^2 + 8x - 10 = 0$ b. $x^2 - 8x - 10 = 0$ c. $x^2 + 16x = 17$
    d. $x^2 - 16x = 17$ e. $x^2 + 5x + 10 = 0$ f. $x^2 - 5x + 10 = 0$
    g. $x^2 - x = 0$

22. Solve the equation $10x + x^2 = 39$ by completing the square.

    For Exercises 23 and 24, read the Historical Perspective below.

23. Solve the equation $10x + x^2 = 39$ by following al-Khwarizmi's instructions. (Note that al-Khwarizmi uses "root" to mean x.)

24. You found two solutions to Exercise 23. However, al-Khwarizmi only described one solution. Why do you think he missed the other solution?

Historical Perspective
The Word *Algebra*

The word *algebra* comes from the Arabic language. Abu Ja'far Muhammed ibn Musa al-Khwarizmi was an Arab mathematician and astronomer. In the 800s, he wrote the mathematics book *Al-jabr W'al Muqabala*.

In this book, the phrase *al-jabr* refers to one of the two operations used to solve equations. The usual meaning is to add equal terms to both sides of an equation to eliminate negative terms. The less frequent meaning is to multiply both sides of an equation by one and the same number to eliminate fractions. The word *algebra* became the shorthand way of referring to the techniques in this book.

Al-Khwarizmi's method for completing the square was one of his most powerful techniques. He wrote his problems and solutions using sentences instead of math symbols. One of his most famous problems is this: Add ten roots to one square, and the sum is equal to nine and thirty. You can rewrite this problem as $10x + x^2 = 39$. Here is al-Khwarizmi's solution.

Take half the number of roots, that is, in this case five, and then multiply this by itself and the result is five and twenty. Add this to the nine and thirty, which gives sixty-four; take the square root, or eight, and subtract from it half the number of roots, namely five, and there remains three. This is the root.

This 1983 Union of Soviet Socialist Republics postage stamp with al-Khwarizmi's picture commemorates his birth about 1200 years ago.

Mathematical Reflections 7C

In this investigation, you factored quadratics, using the difference of squares or the sums and products methods. These questions will help you summarize what you have learned.

1. Copy and complete this table. Find two numbers that have the given sum and product.

Sum of Two Numbers	Product of Two Numbers	Numbers
10	25	■, ■
10	24	■, ■
10	21	■, ■
10	16	■, ■
10	9	■, ■

2. Factor each of the following.
   a. $x^2 - 25$
   b. $a^2 - 144$
   c. $49 - y^2$
   d. $4x^2 - 1$

3. Factor each quadratic expression over $\mathbb{Z}$. If you cannot factor an expression, explain why.
   a. $x^2 + 13x + 40$
   b. $x^2 + 14x + 40$
   c. $x^2 - 13x + 40$
   d. $x^2 + 10x + 40$
   e. $x^2 + 3x - 40$
   f. $x^2 - 3x - 40$

4. Factor each quadratic expression over $\mathbb{Z}$ by completing the square.
   a. $x^2 + 32x + 255$
   b. $x^2 - 40x + 396$
   c. $x^2 + 2x - 168$

5. Solve each equation. Use any method.
   a. $x^2 + 5x - 24 = 0$
   b. $x^2 + 2x = 99$
   c. $x(x + 8) = 209$

6. Suppose you know the sum and product of two numbers. How can you find the two numbers?

7. How do you determine quickly whether you can factor a monic quadratic expression over $\mathbb{Z}$?

8. How do you solve equations such as $x^2 = 15x + 250$?

$(a - b)^2 = (a + b)^2 - 4ab$

Vocabulary

In this investigation, you learned these terms. Make sure you understand what each one means and how to use it.

- binomial
- monic
- perfect square trinomial
- polynomial equation
- trinomial

Project: Using Mathematical Habits

Differences of Squares

In number theory, the analysis of what numbers are sums or differences of squares leads to some surprising results. In this chapter, you investigated the question, "Can you write every positive integer as a difference of two squares?" Here are some examples.

$$5 = 9 - 4 = 3^2 - 2^2$$
$$24 = 25 - 1 = 5^2 - 1^2$$
$$28 = 64 - 36 = 8^2 - 6^2$$
$$17 = 81 - 64 = 9^2 - 8^2$$

This project continues the investigation by developing a rule. The rule gives the number of ways you can write a positive integer as a difference of two squares.

For example, you can write 5 as a difference of squares one way, $5 = 9 - 4$. However, you can write 24 as a difference of squares in two ways. Check that there are no other ways.

$$24 = 5^2 - 1^2$$
$$24 = 7^2 - 5^2$$

Finding a Rule

Here are some suggested steps for finding the rule.

Step 1 Make a table. Copy and complete the table in Figure 1. In each cell, write the difference of the squares of the numbers in that row and column.

Difference of Squares

	0^2	1^2	2^2	3^2	4^2	5^2	6^2	7^2	8^2	9^2	10^2
10^2	100		96								
9^2	81								17		
8^2	64										
7^2	49			33							
6^2	36										
5^2	25										
4^2	16										
3^2	9										
2^2	4	3	0								
1^2	1	0									
0^2	0										

Figure 1

Chapter 7 Polynomials

Step 2 Gather data. Use the table below to organize your work. For each integer from 1 to 50, determine all the ways that number can be written as a difference of the squares of two nonnegative integers. The first integer must be positive. For example, the number 49 can be written as $7^2 - 0^2$, which fits the description.

Look for patterns in the data. Make some conjectures.

Number of Ways

Integer	Number of Ways	Difference
1	1	$1 - 0$
2	0	none
⋮	⋮	⋮

Step 3 Analyze special cases. For example, show that 173 can be written as a difference of squares in only one way. Likewise, show that 519 can be written as a difference of squares in two ways.

Analyze the cases without listing every possible case. For example, connect the solution of this system of equations with the analysis of the 173 case.

$$\begin{cases} x + y = 173 \\ x - y = 1 \end{cases}$$

Step 4 Make and test conjectures. If you think something is true, write it down as a conjecture. Then experiment using numbers.

If you find an example for which your conjecture does not work, try to refine your conjecture to plug the hole. If you gain some confidence that your conjecture will always work, try to prove it by replacing the numbers with variables.

Step 5 Write about your work. Explaining a concept in words is the best way to understand it. Let someone read your description for clarity and accuracy.

Chapter 7 Review

In **Investigation 7A,** you learned how to
- use basic rules and moves to transform expressions and determine whether different expressions define the same function
- factor expressions by identifying a common factor
- apply the Zero-Product Property to factored expressions
- use algebra to simplify long computations, such as computing large sums of consecutive numbers

The following questions will help you check your understanding.

1. Consider the following functions.
   $$g(x) = (x + 3)(x^2 - 5x + 4)$$
   $$h(x) = x^3 - 2x^2 - 11x + 12$$
   a. Find the values of each function if x equals 1, 2, or 3.
   b. Show that g and h are the same function.

2. Prove that the following equation is true.
   $$2m^2n - m^3 - mn^2 - 2mn + m^2 + n^2 = (m - 1)(m - n)(n - m)$$

3. Find the sum of the odd numbers from 19 to 101.

4. A square has side length $(k - x)$. A smaller square with side length x is cut from a corner.
   a. In terms of k and x, find the area of the leftover shape.
   b. If k is 12 and x is 5, find the area of the leftover shape by using the formula you found in part (a).

5. Find all solutions to each equation. Use factoring and ZPP.
   a. $(x - 7)(2x + 1) = 0$
   b. $x^3 - 4x^2 = 0$
   c. $x^3 - 4x = 0$
   d. $3a^2 = 12ab$
   e. $a(x + 1) + 3(x + 1) = 0$

6. Write each expression as a product of expressions.
   a. $abc + acx$
   b. $4p(d - 3) + 5q(d - 3)$
   c. $(2 - x)(7) - (2 - x)(y)$
   d. $(a - b)(x) + (a - b)$

In **Investigation 7B,** you learned how to
- recognize and provide examples of polynomials
- understand the definitions and importance of the terms *coefficient* and *degree*
- expand polynomials and express them in normal form
- determine whether polynomials in different forms are equivalent
- add, subtract, and multiply polynomials

The following questions will help you check your understanding.

7. Use the equation $f(x) = x^2 - 4x + 4$.
   a. Find a polynomial $s(x)$ such that $f(x) + s(x) = x^2 - 3x - 6$.
   b. Find the difference $f(x) - s(x)$.
   c. Find the product $f(x) \cdot s(x)$.

8. Consider the following polynomials.
$$2x^3 - 3x^2 + x$$
$$2x^3 + 8x^2 - 1$$

   a. Find their sum. What is the degree of the sum?

   b. Find their difference if $2x^3 + 8x^2 - 1$ is subtracted from $2x^3 - 3x^2 + x$. What is the degree of the difference?

   c. Find their product. What is the degree of the product?

9. Use the polynomial below.
$$2 - 3x^2 + 2x^5 - 4x - x^2 + x^4$$

   a. Write the polynomial in normal form.

   b. What is the degree of the polynomial?

   c. Write the coefficients of each term.

   d. Find a polynomial that, when added to this one, gives a sum of degree 3.

10. Show that each equation is an identity by writing it in normal form.

    a. $a^3 + 8 = a(a^2 - 2a + 4) + 2(a^2 - 2a + 4)$

    b. $(b - 1)^2 + 3(b - 1) = (b + 2)(b - 1)$

11. Without expanding, find the coefficient of x^5 in the normal form of the polynomial below.
$$(x^2 - 8x + 3)(x^4 - 2x^3 + x^2) - (3x^6 + 2x^5 - x^4)$$

12. Find the value of m that makes each equality true.

    a. $(x + 1)(x + m) = x^2 + 5x + 4$

    b. $(2x - 1)(mx + 1) = 6x^2 - x - 1$

    c. $x^4 - x^3 - 6 - (mx^3 - x^2 - 4) = x^4 - 5x^3 + x^2 - 2$

In **Investigation 7C,** you learned how to

- apply the Difference of Squares Theorem to polynomial expressions and numerical examples
- use difference of squares factoring to solve equations
- factor monic quadratic polynomials
- factor general quadratic polynomials
- use factoring to solve equations

The following questions will help you check your understanding.

13. Two numbers add to 16. Their product is as given. Give an example of the numbers. If it is not possible, explain.

    a. less than 64   b. more than 64   c. 0

    d. positive   e. negative   f. 39

    g. −36

14. Factor each pair of expressions.

    a. $49c^2 - 16$ and $0.49c^2 - 0.16$

    b. $121p^3 - 81p$ and $121p^4 - 81p^2$

    c. $9x^2 - 16$ and $\frac{4}{9}x^2 - \frac{9}{16}$

15. Factor each expression.

    a. $x^2 + 12x + 27$

    b. $x^2 - x - 12$

    c. $x^2 - 12x + 27$

16. Factor using the given method.

    a. $4x^2 - 9$ as a difference of two squares

    b. $x^2 + 13x + 42$ using sums and products

    c. $x^2 - 6x - 720$ by completing the square

17. What value of m makes each trinomial a perfect square?

    a. $9x^4 + mx^2 + 16$

    b. $36x^2 - 60x + m$

18. Use ZPP and what you know about factoring. Find the solutions to each equation.

    a. $x^2 - 5x = 14$ b. $x(x + 3) = 40$

    c. $x^2 - 10x + 2 = 0$ d. $x^2 + 4x = 165$

Chapter 7 Test

Multiple Choice

1. If you expand the expression
$$(x^2 + x - 2)(2x - 1)$$
what is the coefficient of x?
   - A. -3
   - B. 3
   - C. 1
   - D. -5

2. How many solutions are there to the equation $x(x^2 - 4) = 0$?
   - A. 0
   - B. 1
   - C. 2
   - D. 3

3. What is the greatest common factor of $12x^2y^3$ and $30xy^5z$?
   - A. $3xy^3z$
   - B. $6xy^3$
   - C. $6x^2y^5$
   - D. $360x^3y^8z$

4. Consider the two functions, p and q.
$$p(x) = 2x^4 - 3x^2 + x - 1$$
$$q(x) = kx^4 + x^3 - x^2 + 4x + 5$$
If $p(x) + q(x)$ has degree 3, what is the value of k?
   - A. 0
   - B. 2
   - C. -2
   - D. -1

5. If the following equation is true
$$x^2 + 5x - 8 = (x + m)(x + n)$$
what is $m + n$?
   - A. 5
   - B. -5
   - C. 8
   - D. -8

6. If the following equation is true
$$x^2 + 10x + 8 = (x + k)^2 - 17$$
what is the value of k?
   - A. 5
   - B. 9
   - C. 25
   - D. 64

7. Which value of k makes the equation $x^2 + 10x = (x + 5)^2 + k$ an identity?
   - A. -25
   - B. 0
   - C. 5
   - D. 25

8. For what value of c does the equation $x^2 - 10x + c = 0$ have only one solution?
   - A. 0
   - B. 4
   - C. 10
   - D. 25

9. What number must you add to $x^2 + \frac{3}{2}x$ to complete the square in $x^2 + \frac{3}{2}x + 2$?
   - A. $\frac{3}{16}$
   - B. $\frac{9}{16}$
   - C. $\frac{3}{4}$
   - D. $\frac{23}{16}$

Open Response

10. Find all the solutions to the equation $x^3 = 9x$.

11. Find two factors of each number.
    a. $25^2 - 2^2$
    b. $1000^2 - 89^2$
    c. $m^2 - n^2$

12. Find each product. Do not use a calculator.
    a. 39×81
    b. 61×42
    c. 105×93
    d. $(200 + x)(200 - x)$

13. Find each quotient. Do not use a calculator.
    a. $\dfrac{11^2 - 9^2}{11 + 9}$
    b. $\dfrac{15^2 - 4^2}{15 + 4}$
    c. $\dfrac{x^2 - 25^2}{x + 25}$

14. Consider these functions.
$$g(x) = x^2 - x + (x + 2)(x + 4)$$
$$h(x) = 2x^2 + 5x + 8$$
Show that g and h are the same function.

692 Chapter 7 Polynomials

15. Suppose $f(x) = (x^2 + 4x - 2)(x^2 - 3x + 1)$.
    a. Write $f(x)$ in normal form.
    b. What is the degree of $f(x)$?
    c. Find a polynomial $g(x)$ so that $f(x) + g(x)$ will have degree 3 and the coefficient of x^2 will be 6.

16. a. Factor $9x^2 - 25y^2$ as the difference of two squares.
    b. Factor $x^2 + 10x + 16$ using sums and products.
    c. Factor $x^2 - 24x + 119$ by completing the square.

17. The sum of a number plus 12 times its reciprocal equals 7. What is the number? Is there more than one answer? Explain.

18. The area of a rectangle is 120. The length of the rectangle is $x - 5$. Its width is $x - 12$. Find x and the side lengths of the rectangle.

19. Two numbers add to -30. What is the greatest possible value of their product?

20. What value of m makes each trinomial a perfect square?
    a. $x^2 - 10x + m$ b. $4x^2 + mx + 9$
    c. $mx^2 - 16x + 1$ d. $81x^4 - mx^2 + 49$

21. Solve the equation $x^2 - 2x - 10 = 0$.

22. Solve the equation $(x - 2)(x + 3) = 36$.

23. A rectangle of width x is 4 times as long as it is wide. A square y units on a side is cut from one corner of the rectangle. In terms of x and y, find the area of the leftover shape.

24. State the Zero-Product Property. Explain how ZPP can help you solve certain equations. Give an example.

25. The equation $(x + 2)(x - 3) = 0$ has two solutions. Find a number that you can add to the left side of the equation that will give a new equation with integer solutions.

26. Suppose $p(x)$ and $q(x)$ are degree 2 polynomials that are impossible to factor over $\mathbb{Z}$. Decide whether each statement is true or false. Explain each answer.
    a. $p(x) + q(x)$ can be a degree 2 polynomial that you can factor over $\mathbb{Z}$.
    b. $p(x) - q(x)$ can be a degree 2 polynomial that you cannot factor over $\mathbb{Z}$.

Challenge Problem

27. For what value(s) of c does $x^2 + 6x + c = 0$ have no real solutions?

Chapter 8

Investigations at a Glance

- **8A** The Quadratic Formula
- **8B** Quadratic Graphs and Applications
- **8C** Working with Quadratics

Quadratics

Mathematicians invented much of algebra to find mechanical methods for working with general problems. Some of these problems relate to the motion of free-falling bodies that are affected solely by the force of gravity. Other problems relate to land and sea populations, environmental issues, and numerous other situations.

One of the most famous mechanical methods is the quadratic formula. It allows you to solve any quadratic equation. In this chapter, you will only solve quadratic equations that have real roots.

You also will look closely at the graphs of quadratic equations. Their shape, a parabola, has some special properties. In addition, you will graph inequalities and make tables for quadratic equations and functions.

In earlier chapters, you developed many tools for working with linear equations and functions. Now you will find that many of these tools apply to quadratic equations and functions.

Vocabulary

- leading coefficient
- line of symmetry
- maximum
- minimum
- monic equation
- nonmonic quadratic
- parabola
- second difference
- vertex
- vertex form

Investigation 8A

The Quadratic Formula

In *The Quadratic Formula*, you will model functions using different forms of quadratic equations. You also will expand upon your work factoring quadratic equations, and you will factor nonmonic equations. Using the quadratic formula, you will find solutions to specific equations.

By the end of this investigation, you will be able to answer questions like these.
1. How can you solve any quadratic equation?
2. How can you factor any quadratic polynomial?
3. How are the roots of a quadratic equation related to its coefficients?

You will learn how to
- use the quadratic formula to solve equations or determine whether an equation has no real solutions
- construct a quadratic equation given the equation's two roots
- factor nonmonic quadratics

You will develop these habits and skills:
- Understand the connection between the quadratic formula and the process of completing the square.
- Calculate comfortably using radicals.
- Successfully apply the quadratic formula to specific examples.
- See the connection between the roots of a quadratic equation and the coefficients of a quadratic equation.

Quadratic functions $f(x) = ax^2 + bx + c$ model the parabolic paths of water spray.

696 Chapter 8 Quadratics

8.01 Getting Started

Activating Prior Knowledge
Exploring New Ideas

A quadratic function is similar to a linear function. There is a pattern that relates the input of the function to its output. You will use a function table and the quadratic formula to analyze a quadratic function.

For You to Explore

1. Suppose $\alpha = 3 + \sqrt{2}$ and $\beta = 3 - \sqrt{2}$. Find the value of each expression.

   a. $\alpha + \beta$ **b.** $\alpha\beta$ **c.** $\alpha^2 - 6\alpha + 7$

   > In this exercise, the Greek letter α (AL fuh) stands for the quantity $3 + \sqrt{2}$. The Greek letter β (BAYT uh) stands for $3 - \sqrt{2}$.

   For Problems 2–11, solve each equation.

   2. $(x - 3)^2 - 2 = 0$
   3. $x^2 - 6x + 7 = 0$
   4. $x^2 - 8x + 11 = 0$
   5. $x^2 - 7x + 7 = 0$
   6. $2x^2 - 14x + 14 = 0$
   7. $2x^2 - 7x + 4 = 0$
   8. $2x^2 + 7x + 4 = 0$
   9. $3x^2 - 28x + 9 = 0$
   10. $4x^2 - 28x + 49 = 0$
   11. $4x^2 - 28x + 50 = 0$

Exercises Practicing Habits of Mind

On Your Own

12. Solve each quadratic equation.

    a. $x^2 - 6x + 4 = 0$
    b. $x^2 + 6x + 4 = 0$
    c. $x^2 - 6x + 2 = 0$
    d. $x^2 + 6x + 2 = 0$
    e. $2x^2 - 12x + 11 = 0$
    f. $2x^2 + 12x + 25 = 0$

13. Complete the following for each equation.
    - Make a table of inputs and outputs. Use at least five different inputs.
    - Sketch each graph on a separate grid using the table.
    - Find the points where each graph crosses the x-axis.

    a. $(x - 3)^2 - 2 = y$
    b. $x^2 - 6x + 7 = y$
    c. $x^2 - 7x + 7 = y$
    d. $2x^2 - 7x + 4 = y$
    e. $2x^2 + 7x + 4 = y$
    f. $4x^2 - 28x + 49 = y$
    g. $3x^2 - 28x + 9 = y$
    h. $4x^2 - 28x + 50 = y$

14. **Write About It** Why does the equation $(x - 4)^2 + 9 = 0$ have no solutions?

15. The graph of an equation can have a *line of symmetry*. Such a line divides a graph into two halves that are mirror images of each other. For example, the y-axis is the line of symmetry for the graph of $y = x^2$.

    Find equations for any lines of symmetry for each graph. Relate the lines of symmetry to the points where the graphs cross the x-axis.

    a. $(x - 3)^2 - 2 = y$
    b. $x^2 - 6x + 7 = y$
    c. $x^2 - 7x + 7 = y$
    d. $2x^2 - 7x + 4 = y$
    e. $2x^2 + 7x + 4 = y$
    f. $4x^2 - 28x + 49 = y$
    g. $3x^2 - 28x + 9 = y$
    h. $4x^2 - 28x + 50 = y$

Maintain Your Skills

16. Find the points of intersection for each pair of graphs.

    a. $(x - 3)^2 - 1 = y$ and $y = 1$
    b. $x^2 - 6x + 10 = y$ and $y = 3$
    c. $x^2 - 7x + 7 = y$ and $y = 0$
    d. $2x^2 - 7x + 6 = y$ and $y = 2$
    e. $2x^2 + 7x + 6 = y$ and $y = 2$
    f. $4x^2 - 28x + 50 = y$ and $y = 1$
    g. $3x^2 - 28x + 12 = y$ and $y = 3$
    h. $4x^2 - 28x + 49 = y$ and $y = -1$

    Review Exercise 13 in this lesson. For help finding the intersection points of two graphs, see the TI-Nspire™ Handbook, p. 790.

17. Find a quadratic equation with integer coefficients that has each of the following solutions.

    a. $x = 3, x = 2$
    b. $x = -3, x = -2$
    c. $x = 6, x = 4$
    d. $x = 3 + \sqrt{2}, x = 3 - \sqrt{2}$
    e. $x = -3 - \sqrt{2}, x = -3 + \sqrt{2}$
    f. $x = 6 + 2\sqrt{2}, x = 6 - 2\sqrt{2}$
    g. $x = 1 + \sqrt{3}, x = 1 - \sqrt{3}$
    h. $x = \frac{1 + \sqrt{3}}{2}, x = \frac{1 - \sqrt{3}}{2}$
    i. $x = \frac{-1 + \sqrt{3}}{2}, x = \frac{-1 - \sqrt{3}}{2}$

8.02 Making It Formal

Mathematicians look for patterns that may help them solve more complex problems. As you solve each equation in the experiment, keep track of the steps that you use to find the solution.

After working through the exercises in Lesson 8.02, you can probably solve any quadratic equation in the world.

In-Class Experiment

Solve $x^2 + rx + s = 0$ given the following conditions. Give precise results that may include radicals.

1. $r = -2$ and $s = -8$
2. $r = -4$ and $s = -1$
3. $r = \frac{5}{2}$ and $s = -\frac{3}{2}$
4. $r = -7$ and $s = 7$
5. in terms of s, $r = -6$
6. in terms of r and s

You have developed a mechanical process that always works. As long as the equation has real-number solutions, the process tells you what they are. The steps in the process are as follows.

> You call this mechanical set of steps an algorithm.

Step 1 Divide through by the coefficient of x^2 so that the equation becomes monic.

> A **monic equation** has a leading coefficient of 1.

Step 2 Complete the square.

Step 3 Factor the result as a difference of squares.

Step 4 Set each factor equal to 0. Solve for x.

For Discussion

7. Explain how this process shows when a quadratic equation has no real roots.

When a process becomes mechanical, you can use algebra to carry it out on a general example. A general example is an example in which you replace the numbers with letters. The result of this process is a formula, or an identity. You can use this formula to handle all of the specific cases by replacing the letters with numbers.

Instead of solving a specific equation in Problem 6, you solved a general equation $x^2 + rx + s = 0$. This result is very important, so it is stated as a theorem.

> The equation $x^2 + rx + s = 0$ is a general monic quadratic.

Theorem 8.1

If the equation $x^2 + rx + s = 0$ has real-number solutions, they are

$$x = \frac{-r + \sqrt{r^2 - 4s}}{2} \text{ and } x = \frac{-r - \sqrt{r^2 - 4s}}{2}$$

Equivalently, you could use the $\pm$ sign to express both solutions in one statement.

$$x = \frac{-r \pm \sqrt{r^2 - 4s}}{2}$$

Proof The proof will be familiar if you did Problem 6 of the previous experiment.

Step 1 The equation is already monic. So you do not have to divide by the coefficient of x^2.

Step 2 Complete the square.

$$x^2 + rx + s = x^2 + rx + \frac{r^2}{4} - \frac{r^2}{4} + s$$
$$= \left(x + \frac{r}{2}\right)^2 - \frac{r^2 - 4s}{4}$$

> Notice that $-\frac{r^2}{4} + s = -\frac{r^2 - 4s}{4}$. Make sure you understand why the equation is true.

Step 3 Factor the result as a difference of squares.

$$\Rightarrow \left(x + \frac{r}{2} + \sqrt{\frac{r^2 - 4s}{4}}\right)\left(x + \frac{r}{2} - \sqrt{\frac{r^2 - 4s}{4}}\right) = 0$$

Step 4 Set each factor equal to 0 and solve for x.

$$\Rightarrow x + \frac{r}{2} + \sqrt{\frac{r^2 - 4s}{4}} = 0 \text{ or } x + \frac{r}{2} - \sqrt{\frac{r^2 - 4s}{4}} = 0$$

$$\Rightarrow x = -\frac{r}{2} - \frac{\sqrt{r^2 - 4s}}{2} \text{ or } x = -\frac{r}{2} + \frac{\sqrt{r^2 - 4s}}{2}$$

$$\Rightarrow x = \frac{-r - \sqrt{r^2 - 4s}}{2} \text{ or } x = \frac{-r + \sqrt{r^2 - 4s}}{2}$$

Developing Habits of Mind

Simplify complicated problems. As equations get more complicated, you will need to do more work to find the solutions. Theorem 8.1 takes all the guesswork out of solving monic quadratic equations. You only need to replace r and s with the correct numbers and simplify.

For example, to solve $x^2 - 6x + 7 = 0$, compare it with the general example.

$$x^2 + r x + s = 0$$
$$\downarrow \qquad \downarrow$$
$$x^2 + (-6) x + 7 = 0$$

Replace r with -6 and s with 7 in the general solutions. Then simplify.

Example 1

Problem Solve the equation $x^2 - 6x + 7 = 0$.

Solution From Lesson 8.01, you already know the solutions are $x = 3 + \sqrt{2}$ and $x = 3 - \sqrt{2}$. This time, you can apply Theorem 8.1 to the equation.

The theorem states that the solutions of the equation $x^2 + rx + s = 0$, in terms of r and s, are as follows.

$$x = \frac{-r + \sqrt{r^2 - 4s}}{2} \text{ or } x = \frac{-r - \sqrt{r^2 - 4s}}{2}$$

Replace r with -6 and s with 7.

$$x = \frac{-(-6) + \sqrt{(-6)^2 - 4(7)}}{2} \text{ or } x = \frac{-(-6) - \sqrt{(-6)^2 - 4(7)}}{2}$$

Simplify the first solution.

$$\begin{aligned} x &= \frac{-(-6) + \sqrt{(-6)^2 - 4(7)}}{2} \\ &= \frac{6 + \sqrt{36 - 28}}{2} \\ &= \frac{6 + \sqrt{8}}{2} \\ &= \frac{6 + 2\sqrt{2}}{2} \\ &= 3 + \sqrt{2} \end{aligned}$$

For You to Do

8. Simplify the second solution from Example 1.

$$\frac{-(-6) - \sqrt{(-6)^2 - 4(7)}}{2}$$

For Discussion

9. The equation $x^2 - 3x + 5 = 0$ has no real roots. What happens if you use the formula in Theorem 8.1 to solve the equation?

Theorem 8.1 only works if the equation is monic. To solve a nonmonic quadratic, divide through by the coefficient of x^2. Then replace r and s with the resulting fractions.

A **nonmonic quadratic** is a quadratic with a leading coefficient that is a number other than 1.

You could work out an example. However, all you will end up doing is running fractions through the formula. Instead, work it through generally. You will find a formula that works for any quadratic.

A general nonmonic equation is $ax^2 + bx + c = 0$. Suppose a is a positive number. Divide both sides by a to obtain the following equation.

$$x^2 + \frac{b}{a}x + \frac{c}{a} = 0$$

> Why can you suppose that a is positive? Can you write any quadratic in this form such that a is positive? Explain.

Now match this equation with the quadratic from Theorem 8.1.

$$x^2 + \underset{\downarrow}{r}\, x + \underset{\downarrow}{s} = 0$$
$$x^2 + \frac{b}{a} x + \frac{c}{a} = 0$$

Replace r with $\frac{b}{a}$ and s with $\frac{c}{a}$ in the general solutions.

$$x = \frac{-\frac{b}{a} + \sqrt{\left(\frac{b}{a}\right)^2 - 4\left(\frac{c}{a}\right)}}{2} \text{ and } x = \frac{-\frac{b}{a} - \sqrt{\left(\frac{b}{a}\right)^2 - 4\left(\frac{c}{a}\right)}}{2}$$

Simplify the first solution.

$$\frac{-\frac{b}{a} + \sqrt{\left(\frac{b}{a}\right)^2 - 4\left(\frac{c}{a}\right)}}{2} = \frac{-\frac{b}{a} + \sqrt{\frac{b^2}{a^2} - 4\left(\frac{c}{a}\right)}}{2} \qquad \text{since } \left(\frac{b}{a}\right)^2 = \frac{b^2}{a^2}$$

$$= \frac{-\frac{b}{a} + \sqrt{\frac{b^2}{a^2} - 4\left(\frac{ac}{a^2}\right)}}{2} \qquad \text{since } \frac{c}{a} = \frac{ac}{a^2}$$

$$= \frac{-\frac{b}{a} + \sqrt{\frac{1}{a^2}(b^2 - 4ac)}}{2} \qquad \text{by the Distributive Property}$$

$$= \frac{-\frac{b}{a} + \frac{1}{a}\sqrt{b^2 - 4ac}}{2} \qquad \text{Because } a > 0 \text{, you can say that } \sqrt{\frac{1}{a^2}} = \frac{1}{a}.$$

$$= \frac{\frac{1}{a}\left(-b + \sqrt{b^2 - 4ac}\right)}{2} \qquad \text{by the Distributive Property}$$

$$= \frac{-b + \sqrt{b^2 - 4ac}}{2a} \qquad \text{since } \frac{\frac{1}{a}}{2} = \frac{1}{2a}$$

For You to Do

10. Show that the other root is $\dfrac{-b - \sqrt{b^2 - 4ac}}{2a}$.

The work you have just done results in one of the most famous theorems in algebra.

Theorem 8.2 The Quadratic Formula

If the equation $ax^2 + bx + c = 0$ has real-number solutions, they are given by the quadratic formula.

$$x = \frac{-b + \sqrt{b^2 - 4ac}}{2a} \text{ and } \frac{-b - \sqrt{b^2 - 4ac}}{2a}$$

Equivalently, you could use the $\pm$ sign to express both solutions in one statement.

$$x = \frac{-b \pm \sqrt{b^2 - 4ac}}{2a}$$

Example 2

Problem Solve the equation $2x^2 + 7x - 15 = 0$.

Solution First match a, b, and c with the appropriate coefficients.

$$ax^2 + bx + c = 0$$
$$\downarrow \quad \downarrow \quad \downarrow$$
$$2x^2 + 7x + (-15) = 0$$

So, $a = 2$, $b = 7$, and $c = -15$. Substitute these values into the quadratic formula.

$$\frac{-b \pm \sqrt{b^2 - 4ac}}{2a} = \frac{-(7) \pm \sqrt{(7)^2 - 4(2)(-15)}}{2(2)}$$

Simplify.

$$\frac{-7 \pm \sqrt{49 - (-120)}}{4} = \frac{-7 \pm \sqrt{169}}{4}$$
$$= \frac{-7 \pm 13}{4}$$
$$= \frac{-7 + 13}{4} \text{ and } \frac{-7 - 13}{4}$$
$$= \frac{6}{4} \text{ and } \frac{-20}{4}$$
$$= \frac{3}{2} \text{ and } -5$$

The two roots of $2x^2 + 7x - 15 = 0$ are $x = \frac{3}{2}$ and $x = -5$.

For Discussion

11. The equation $3x^2 - 5x + 7 = 0$ has no real roots. What happens when you try to solve it using the quadratic formula?

Exercises Practicing Habits of Mind

Check Your Understanding

For Exercises 1–8, solve the equations using any method. If there are no real number solutions, explain why.

1. $3x^2 + 7x + 1 = 0$
2. $3x^2 + 7x = 8$
3. $3x^2 - 7x = 8$
4. $3x^2 - 7x + 8 = 0$
5. $3x^2 - 7x + 2 = 0$
6. $w^2 - \sqrt{5}w = 5$
7. $z^2 - 1 = 2\sqrt{2}z$
8. $x^2 - 6x = k^2 - 9$ (in terms of k)

9. Find all numbers that are 930 less than their squares.

10. Derman poses a problem for Tony: "The square of a number is 29 more than 12 times the number." Help Tony solve Derman's puzzle.

11. **a.** Sasha's father hosts a dinner party. He proposes a toast, and everyone clinks glasses with everyone else, exactly once. There are four couples in all at the dinner party. How many clinks are there?

    b. Derman's mother hosts a dinner party. Derman has no idea how many people are there. He hears 66 clinks for one toast. How many people are at the party?

On Your Own

For Exercises 12–16, solve each equation. If there are no real-number solutions, explain why.

12. $4x^2 - 6x + 1 = 0$
13. $9y^2 - 6y + 1 = 0$
14. $9y^2 + 6y + 1 = 0$
15. $9y^2 + 6y + 2 = 0$
16. $9z^2 + 6z - 2 = 0$

17. If possible, find two numbers with a sum that is 8 and a product that is $\frac{15}{4}$.

18. **Standardized Test Prep** Which quadratic equation has no real solutions?

    A. $-4x^2 - 12x = 0$
    B. $-4x^2 - 12x + 5 = 0$
    C. $-4x^2 - 12x - 9 = 0$
    D. $-4x^2 - 12x - 12 = 0$

19. Find a value of k such that $3x^2 - 12x + k$ has the following solutions.

   a. two real-number solutions
   b. exactly one real-number solution
   c. no real-number solutions

20. **Write About It** Consider the general quadratic equation $ax^2 + bx + c = 0$. Give some conditions of a, b, and c if the equation has the following.

   a. two real roots
   b. two rational roots
   c. exactly one rational root
   d. no real roots

   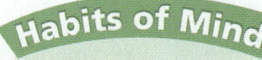
   Assume a, b, and c are integers.

21. For what values of x is $6x^2 - 5x - 4$ negative?

   For Exercises 22 and 23, find the intersection points for the graphs of each pair of equations.

   Habits of Mind
   Visualize. Sketch the graphs.

22. a. $4x - y = 2$ and $y = 3x^2 - 6x - 10$
    b. $4x - y = 13$ and $y = 3x^2 - 6x - 10$

23. **Take It Further**
    a. $3x - y = 1$ and $x^2 + y^2 = 1$
    b. $17x + 11y = 19$ and $x^2 + y^2 = 1$

24. For what values of x is each equation true?
    a. $\left(\frac{x+3}{2}\right)^2 - \left(\frac{x-3}{2}\right)^2 = 3x$
    b. $\left(\frac{x+3}{2}\right)^2 + \left(\frac{x-3}{2}\right)^2 = 3x$

25. a. Find a quadratic equation with roots 5 and 7.
    b. Can you find a second quadratic equation with roots 5 and 7? A third quadratic equation with roots 5 and 7?

26. **Take It Further** Suppose you can take square roots of negative numbers. Find two numbers with a sum of 4 and a product of 7.

Maintain Your Skills

27. Solve each quadratic equation. Find the sum and the product of the roots.

    a. $x^2 - 5x + 3 = 0$
    b. $x^2 - 15x + 3 = 0$
    c. $x^2 + 15x + 56 = 0$
    d. $2x^2 - 15x + 3 = 0$
    e. $x^2 + rx + s = 0$
    f. $x^2 + 15x + 66 = 0$
    g. How do the sum and product of the roots relate to the numbers in each equation?

8.02 Making It Formal

8.03 Going the Other Way

A quadratic equation is like a puzzle. There are numbers that you know, the coefficients, and there are numbers that you do not know, the roots. The object of the puzzle is to find the numbers you do not know in terms of the numbers that you do.

In Lesson 8.02, you found the complete solution to the quadratic puzzle, the quadratic formula. Suppose you know the roots of a quadratic equation. Can you reconstruct the equation?

> Solving quadratic equations is like playing a game such as tic-tac-toe, where you know a foolproof strategy for winning. However, you can still enjoy the game.

Minds in Action episode 35

Tony and Sasha are having lunch after algebra class.

Tony Here's one for you. I had a quadratic equation, solved it, and got roots of 5 and 7. What was my equation?

Sasha thinks for a bit.

Sasha There's no one answer. I can give you a dozen equations that have 5 and 7 as roots.

Tony Give me one.

Sasha $x^2 - 12x + 35 = 0$.

Tony How'd you get that?

Sasha Well, I imagined I was solving it. Since the solutions are integers, it must have factored. Since the roots are 5 and 7, it must have factored like this.

Sasha writes on her napkin.

$$(x - 5)(x - 7) = 0$$

> *It must have factored* means *it must have factored over* $\mathbb{Z}$, the set of integers.

Sasha So, I multiplied this out and got $x^2 - 12x + 35 = 0$.

Tony Do you say that there are others?

Sasha Sure. Multiply both sides of my equation by 2, 3, π, or anything.

For You to Do

1. Find a quadratic equation with roots that are 9 and -5.

Minds in Action episode 36

Tony and Sasha are still talking about equations.

Tony Okay. Suppose I solved an equation and got roots of $3 + 2\sqrt{7}$ and $3 - 2\sqrt{7}$. Would you multiply this mess?

Tony writes on his napkin.

$$(x - (3 + 2\sqrt{7}))(x - (3 - 2\sqrt{7})) = 0$$

Sasha Well, I could. But, there must be a better way.

Silence.

Sasha I know. Let's do it generally, once and for all. Then we'll get a formula where we can plug in numbers.

Tony You've lost me. What do you mean by generally?

Sasha Well, suppose my roots are some numbers m and n. Then my equation must have factored like this.

Sasha pulls out a piece of paper and writes.

$$(x - m)(x - n) = 0$$

Sasha Now multiply it out. See.

$$(x - m)(x - n) = x^2 - mx - nx + mn$$
$$= x^2 - (m + n)x + mn$$

So, I can get the coefficient of x by taking the opposite of the sum of the roots. I can get the constant term by taking the product of the roots.

Tony So, in my example, if the roots are $3 + 2\sqrt{7}$ and $3 - 2\sqrt{7}$, I'd do something like this.

$$3 + 2\sqrt{7} + 3 - 2\sqrt{7} = 6 \text{ and}$$
$$(3 + 2\sqrt{7})(3 - 2\sqrt{7}) = 9 - (2\sqrt{7})^2$$
$$= 9 - 2^2(\sqrt{7})^2$$
$$= 9 - 4 \cdot 7 = -19$$

So, my equation is $x^2 - 6x - 19 = 0$.

Sasha How could you check this?

Tony I can use the quadratic formula, of course.

Tony and Sasha finish lunch and go back to class.

> Any multiple of this equation has the same roots.

For You to Do

2. Solve the equation $x^2 - 6x - 19 = 0$.

The basic result that Sasha and Tony found may seem very different from the Sum and Product Identity in Lesson 7.11. Their work is really just a small step beyond Theorem 7.3. The key is realizing that the solution to the equation $(x + a)(x + b) = 0$ is $x = -a$ or $x = -b$.

Usually, the roots are the key part of the quadratic, so you want to write them without negative signs. You can make a small switch, as Theorem 8.3 shows.

Theorem 8.3 The Sum and Product Theorem

If m and n are real numbers, the quadratic equation $x^2 - (m + n)x + mn = 0$ has m and n as roots.

Some people remember the theorem using this sentence.

$x^2 -$ (the sum of the roots) $\cdot\, x\, +$ (the product of the roots) $= 0$

Proof

$$x^2 - (m + n)x + mn = 0 \Rightarrow (x - m)(x - n) = 0 \quad \text{from Theorem 7.3}$$
$$\Rightarrow x - m = 0 \text{ or } x - n = 0 \quad \text{by ZPP}$$
$$\Rightarrow x = m \text{ or } x = n$$

By definition, if m and n are solutions to the quadratic equation, they are the roots of the equation.

Be careful. If a quadratic equation has roots m and n, then it has factors $(x - m)$ and $(x - n)$. The sign change can sometimes be tricky.

For You to Do

Find the roots of each equation. Then calculate the sum of the roots.

3. $x^2 - 10x + 21 = 0$
4. $x^2 + 10x + 24 = 0$
5. $x^2 - 5x - 1 = 0$
6. $x^2 + rx + s = 0$
7. $11x^2 - 71x + 30 = 0$
8. $15x^2 - 43x + 8 = 0$
9. $ax^2 + bx + c = 0$

In Lesson 8.02, you found a general formula for solving any quadratic equation with real roots. There is also a general solution to a basic linear equation of the form $ax + b = 0$. You can find it by following the basic moves for solving equations.

$$ax + b = 0$$
$$ax = -b$$
$$x = \frac{-b}{a}$$

The basic rules and moves are almost always easier than trying to apply the quadratic formula, but notice the result. How does it compare to your result in Problem 9 on the previous page? Are you surprised that the two results are the same?

This finding becomes very useful when graphing quadratic functions. It is stated here as Theorem 8.4.

Theorem 8.4 The Sum of the Roots Theorem

In a quadratic equation of the form $ax^2 + bx + c = 0$, the sum of the roots of the equation is $\frac{-b}{a}$.

Proof Your work from Problem 9 in For You to Do is the proof to this theorem.

Exercises Practicing Habits of Mind

Check Your Understanding

1. Find a quadratic equation for the given roots.
   a. 3 and 17
   b. -3 and -17
   c. 6 and 34
   d. $2 + \sqrt{3}$ and $2 - \sqrt{3}$
   e. $-2 - \sqrt{3}$ and $-2 + \sqrt{3}$
   f. $10 + 5\sqrt{3}$ and $10 - 5\sqrt{3}$

2. **Take It Further** Suppose the quadratic equation $x^2 - 17x - 78 = 0$ has roots α and β. Without solving the equation, find an equation with the following roots.
   a. $-\alpha$ and $-\beta$
   b. 3α and 3β
   c. $\frac{1}{\alpha}$ and $\frac{1}{\beta}$
   d. α^2 and β^2

3. Suppose a, b, and c are real numbers, and $a \neq 0$. Suppose also that the following equations are true.

   $$\alpha = \frac{-b + \sqrt{b^2 - 4ac}}{2a} \text{ and } \beta = \frac{-b - \sqrt{b^2 - 4ac}}{2a}$$

   Write an expression, in terms of a, b, and c, that is equal to each of the following expressions.
   a. $\alpha + \beta$
   b. $\alpha\beta$
   c. the average of α and β

On Your Own

4. Find a quadratic equation with roots $\sqrt{5} + 3$ and $\sqrt{5} - 3$.

5. **a.** Solve the equation $40x^2 - 131x + 105 = 0$.

   b. Factor over $\mathbb{Z}$ the polynomial $40x^2 - 131x + 105$.

6. **Standardized Test Prep** Which of the following quadratic equations has $4 - \sqrt{3}$ and $4 + \sqrt{3}$ as solutions?

   I. $x^2 - 13x + 8 = 0$ **II.** $x^2 - 8x + 13 = 0$ **III.** $2x^2 - 16x + 26 = 0$

   A. I only   **B.** II only   **C.** I and II   **D.** II and III

7. **Write About It** Explain how to use the quadratic formula to factor quadratic polynomials over $\mathbb{Z}$.

8. Find two numbers with a sum of 1 and a product of -1.

9. Suppose α is one of the numbers you found in Exercise 8. Show each of the following.

   a. $\alpha^2 = \alpha + 1$ **b.** $\alpha^3 = 2\alpha + 1$ **c.** $\alpha^4 = 3\alpha + 2$

   You can choose which number to call α.

   d. Take It Further Express each of the first 10 powers of α in the form $a\alpha + b$ for integers a and b. Describe and explain some patterns.

10. **Take It Further** Suppose you can take square roots of negative numbers. Find an equation with roots that are $1 + \sqrt{-3}$ and $1 - \sqrt{-3}$.

11. **Take It Further** Suppose you have a quadratic equation with rational-number coefficients. The root $1 + \sqrt{5}$ is one root of the equation. What is the other root? Explain.

Maintain Your Skills

12. Suppose α and β are roots of the equation $40x^2 - 81x + 35 = 0$. Find an equation with the following roots.

    a. 2α and 2β **b.** 3α and 3β

    c. 4α and 4β **d.** $-\alpha$ and $-\beta$

    e. What patterns do you find?

13. **Take It Further** Find an equation with roots that are the reciprocals of the roots of each equation.

    a. $x^2 - 5x + 6 = 0$ **b.** $x^2 + 5x + 6 = 0$

    c. $40x^2 - 81x + 35 = 0$ **d.** What patterns do you find?

8.04 Factoring Nonmonic Quadratics

The quadratic formula gives you the solutions to any quadratic equation. With a little work, you can use these solutions to factor any quadratic polynomial.

What can you do if the quadratic is not monic? A good mathematical habit is to make use of something you already know how to do to solve problems you are unsure about.

Minds in Action   episode 37

Tony and Sasha are trying to factor the quadratic $4x^2 + 36x + 45$.

Tony It's not monic. Do we have to play with all the combinations?

Sasha We could. Wait, I see something. $4x^2$ is the same as $(2x)^2$. So we could write the equation using $2x$ chunks.

$$(2x)^2 + 18(2x) + 45$$

Tony Sure, you can do that, but it's still not monic.

Sasha Well, no. But suppose I think of the $2x$ as one thing.

Sasha covers the first $2x$ with her left hand and the second $2x$ with her right hand.

Sasha Do you see? It's something squared plus 18 times that something plus 45. Here, I'll change what's under my hand, the $2x$, to z. Now it looks better.

$$z^2 + 18z + 45$$

Tony Cool! I can factor that by finding numbers that add to 18 and multiply to 45. So, 15 and 3 will work. Look at what I get.

$$z^2 + 18z + 45 = (z + 15)(z + 3)$$

Sasha Remember, we used z as a placeholder for $2x$, so now put the $2x$ back.

$$(z + 15)(z + 3) = (2x + 15)(2x + 3)$$

Tony We should check by multiplying it out, just to be sure.

> What combinations are Tony and Sasha talking about?

You can use what you know about riding a bicycle to help you ride a unicycle.

8.04 Factoring Nonmonic Quadratics   **711**

For You to Do

1. Expand $(2x + 15)(2x + 3)$ and make sure you get the original quadratic from episode 37.

Developing Habits of Mind

Simplify complicated problems. Sasha's idea of lumping a part of an expression into one unit is very useful in mathematics. People often say that $(2x)^2 + 18(2x) + 45$ is a monic quadratic in $2x$. This means that if you think of the variable as $2x$ instead of x, the quadratic looks monic.

Minds in Action   episode 38

Sasha and Tony want to try their method on other quadratics.

Tony Here's one.
$$6x^2 + 11x - 10$$
I know the answer, because I got it by multiplying out two binomials. But I don't think our method will work here.

Sasha We were lucky with $4x^2 + 36x + 45$ because of the leading 4. It's a perfect square. So I could write the first term as $(2x)^2$. And I could write the second term as a multiple of $2x$ to the first power. So it all worked out.

Tony If it were an equation, we could multiply both sides by a number and maybe fix things up. But it's a polynomial, not an equation.

Sasha and Tony sit silently for a while.

Sasha Well, we can still multiply by 6. Just remember that we did it so we can undo it later.

Tony Okay, but let's not forget. It doesn't sound legal.

Sasha Well, like I said, as long as we undo it in end, it should be fine. So, take the quadratic $6x^2 + 11x - 10$ and multiply it by 6.
$$6(6x^2 + 11x - 10) = 36x^2 + 66x - 60 \text{ (6 times)}$$

Tony I see what you're doing. That "6 times" reminds us that we multiplied by 6. Now we can write the polynomial just like we did the last one.
$$(6x)^2 + 11(6x) - 60$$

Now it is monic in $6x$. Let $z = 6x$ and we get this.

$$z^2 + 11z - 60$$

I know how to factor that.

$$(z + 15)(z - 4)$$

Sasha Now unreplace z with $6x$.

$$(6x + 15)(6x - 4)$$

Oh, wait. There are common factors in each binomial, a 3 in the first one and a 2 in the second one. That's the 6 that I multiplied by in the first place! I'll pull the 3 and the 2 out.

$$3(2x + 5) \cdot 2(3x - 2) = 6(2x + 5)(3x - 2)$$

Tony So now I can divide by 6 to undo your multiplying by 6.

$$(2x + 5)(3x - 2)$$

So $6x^2 + 11x - 10 = (2x + 5)(3x - 2)$, and we are done.

Sasha This method will always work, so things just got a lot simpler. All we need to worry about now is factoring monics. We can do that by sums and products.

> Make sure you know how to factor the quadratic.

> Check by multiplying out the right side.

For You to Do

2. Factor $6x^2 - 31x + 35$ using Sasha's method.

3. Factor $6x^2 - 31x + 35$ using the quadratic formula.

4. Which method is easier? Explain.

For Discussion

5. State Sasha and Tony's method as an algorithm, a sequence of steps that describes exactly what to do.

8.04 Factoring Nonmonic Quadratics

Exercises Practicing Habits of Mind

Check Your Understanding

For Exercises 1 and 2, factor each polynomial.

1. a. $9x^2 + 18x - 7$
   b. $6x^2 - 31x + 35$
   c. $15x^2 + 16x - 7$
   d. $9x^2 + 62x - 7$
   e. $9x^4 + 62x^2 - 7$

2. a. $9x^2 + 18xy - 7y^2$
   b. $6x^2 - 31xy + 35y^2$
   c. $15x^2 + 16xa - 7a^2$
   d. $9x^2 + 62xb - 7b^2$

3. When applying the scaling method to $6x^2 - 31x + 35$, you follow these steps.
   - Look at the quadratic expression $6x^2 - 31x + 35$.
   - Multiply by 6.
   - Get a monic quadratic in $6x$.
   - Let $z = 6x$ and work with the resulting quadratic in z.

   Describe how you could get the monic quadratic without the middle steps.

On Your Own

For Exercises 4–6, factor each polynomial.

4. a. $-18x^2 - 65x - 7$
   b. $-18x^2 + 61x + 7$
   c. $25 - 4x^2$
   d. $18x^3 - 61x^2 - 7x$

5. a. $-18x^2 - 65xa - 7a^2$
   b. $-18x^2 + 61xy + 7y^2$
   c. $25y^2 - 4x^2$
   d. $18x^3 - 61x^2y - 7xy^2$

6. a. $4x^2 - 13x + 3$
   b. $4x^2 - 8x + 3$
   c. $4x^2 + 4x - 3$
   d. $4(x + 1)^2 + 4(x + 1) - 3$
   e. $4x^4 - 13x^2 + 3$
   f. $4(x - 1)^4 - 13(x - 1)^2 + 3$
   g. $4(x - 1)^{12} - 13(x - 1)^6 + 3$
   h. $(x^2 + 1)^2 - x^2$

7. **Standardized Test Prep** For what values of x is the equation $2x - \frac{15}{x} = 1$ true?

   A. 3 B. $-3, \frac{5}{2}$ C. $\frac{5}{2}, 3$ D. $-\frac{5}{2}, 3$

8. Solve the equation $2x - \frac{3}{x} = 5$ for x.

9. For the equation $x^2 - 6x + 7 = 0$, let $z = x - 3$.

   a. Express the equation in terms of z.

   b. Solve the equation in z.

   c. Use your result from part (b) to solve the original equation.

   > If $z = x - 3$, $x = z + 3$.

10. For parts (a) and (b), solve the quadratic equation.

    a. $3x^2 + 8x - 35 = 0$

    b. $x^2 + 8x - 105 = 0$

    c. Find a relationship between the solutions to these two equations.

Maintain Your Skills

11. Solve each pair of equations and compare the roots.

    a. $x^2 - 8x + 7 = 0$ and $x^2 - 24x + 63 = 0$

    b. $2x^2 + 11x - 21 = 0$ and $2x^2 + 22x - 84 = 0$

    c. $2x^2 + 11x - 21 = 0$ and $2x^2 + 33x - 189 = 0$

    d. $2x^2 + 11x - 21 = 0$ and $2x^2 + 55x - 525 = 0$

    e. $2x^2 + 11x - 21 = 0$ and $x^2 + 11x - 42 = 0$

    f. $3x^2 + 16x - 35 = 0$ and $x^2 + 16x - 105 = 0$

    g. $3x^2 + 16x - 32 = 0$ and $x^2 + 16x - 96 = 0$

    > How are the equations in each pair related?

12. Find an equation with roots that are as follows.

    a. 7 times the roots of $x^2 - 8x + 7 = 0$

    b. 7 times the roots of $2x^2 + 11x - 21 = 0$

    c. 2 times the roots of $2x^2 + 11x - 21 = 0$

    d. 3 times the roots of $3x^2 + 11x - 21 = 0$

    e. 5 times the roots of $5x^2 + 11x - 21 = 0$

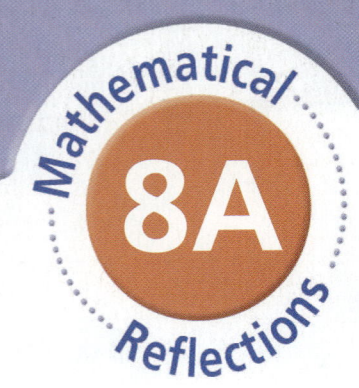

Mathematical Reflections 8A

In this investigation, you learned how to solve quadratic equations using the quadratic formula and to build a quadratic given its roots. These questions will help you summarize what you have learned.

1. Complete the following for each equation.
   - Make a table of inputs and outputs. Use at least five different inputs.
   - Sketch each graph on a separate grid using the table.
   - Find the points where each graph crosses the x-axis.

   a. $x^2 - 2x - 4 = y$
   b. $3x^2 - 2x - 5 = y$
   c. $x^2 - 6x + 9 = y$
   d. $2x^2 + 4x + 3 = y$

2. Find a value of k such that $2x^2 - 3x + k$ has each solution set.

   a. two real-number solutions

   b. one real-number solution

   c. no real-number solutions

3. Find a quadratic equation with the following roots.

   a. 4 and -5
   b. $3 + \sqrt{2}$ and $3 - \sqrt{2}$

4. Factor the following nonmonic polynomials by writing them as monic polynomials in $\mathbb{Z}$.

   a. $2x^2 - 5x - 12$
   b. $6x^2 + 25x + 25$
   c. $4x^2 + 8x - 5$
   d. $9x^2 + 12x + 4$

5. Factor the following quadratic expressions using the quadratic formula.

   a. $4x^2 + 12x + 5$
   b. $6x^2 - 5x - 4$

6. How can you solve any quadratic equation?

7. How can you factor any quadratic polynomial?

8. How are the roots of a quadratic equation related to its coefficients?

Quadratic functions of the form $f(x) = ax^2 + bx + c$ use various a, b, and c values to model different parabolic paths.

Vocabulary

In this investigation, you learned these terms. Make sure you understand what each one means and how to use it.

- monic equation
- nonmonic quadratic

Chapter 8 Mid-Chapter Test

Multiple Choice

1. The equation $5x^2 - 4x + k = 0$ has exactly two real-number solutions. Which of the following could NOT be the value of k?
   A. 0
   B. 1
   C. -1
   D. $\frac{1}{2}$

2. Which quadratic equation has roots $1 + \sqrt{7}$ and $1 - \sqrt{7}$?
   A. $x^2 + 7x - 1 = 0$
   B. $x^2 + 2x + 8 = 0$
   C. $x^2 - 2x - 6 = 0$
   D. $x^2 + 6x - 2 = 0$

3. Which of the following are the solutions of $3x^2 = x + 2$?
   A. $-\frac{2}{3}$ and 1
   B. 2 and 3
   C. 2 and -3
   D. $\frac{2}{3}$ and -1

4. How many times does the graph of $(x - 2)^2 - 1 = y$ cross the x-axis?
   A. 0
   B. 1
   C. 2
   D. 3

5. Factor $4x^2 + 5x - 6$.
   A. $(2x + 3)(2x - 2)$
   B. $(4x + 3)(x - 2)$
   C. $(2x + 1)(2x - 6)$
   D. $(4x - 3)(x + 2)$

6. Two positive integers have a sum of 25. Which of these could be their product?
   A. 10
   B. 26
   C. 46
   D. 25

Open Response

7. Use the quadratic formula to solve $5x^2 - 3x - 1 = 0$.

8. a. Find two numbers with a sum that is 1 and a product that is -1.
   b. Verify that your results have a sum of 1 and a product of -1.

9. Find a quadratic equation with roots $3 + 2\sqrt{2}$ and $3 - 2\sqrt{2}$.

10. Factor $6x^2 + 11x - 10$.

11. Solve $(x + 2)(2x - 7) = -15$.

12. Find the value of k such that $9x^2 - 12x + k = 0$ will have exactly one solution.

Challenge Problem

13. The roots of the quadratic equation $ax^2 + bx + c = 0$ are p and q. The roots of the quadratic equation $cx^2 + bx + a = 0$ are r and s. (a, b, and c are not zero.) Compute $pqrs$, the product of all four roots.

Investigation 8B

Quadratic Graphs and Applications

In *Quadratic Graphs and Applications*, you will optimize quadratic functions. Graphs of quadratic functions have either a maximum or a minimum point. Locating these points helps you graph quadratics.

By the end of this investigation, you will be able to answer questions like these.

1. How can you quickly identify the vertex of the graph of a quadratic equation?

2. How does the symmetry of a parabola help you solve problems that use quadratic functions?

3. Using two different methods, how can you find the vertex of the parabola with the equation $y = x^2 - 4x + 9$?

You will learn how to
- use your knowledge of quadratics to optimize some quadratic functions
- graph quadratic functions and examine the graph to find the vertex
- explore word problems involving quadratic functions

You will develop these habits and skills:
- Use the arithmetic fact that a square is always nonnegative in order to optimize quadratic functions.
- See the connections between the geometry of quadratic graphs and the algebra of quadratic functions.
- Use the graph of a function to find numerical information.

The vertex of a parabola that opens upward is the lowest point on the parabola.

8.05 Getting Started

You can use quadratic functions to model real-world situations. Optimization problems use quadratic functions to determine the greatest area for a rectangular region.

For You to Explore

1. You have 200 feet of fencing to use for building a rectangular dog pen. Find the dimensions of the pen having the greatest possible area.

2. Suppose you build the pen such that it borders an apartment building. You will only need to build three walls. Find the dimensions of the pen having the greatest possible area.

   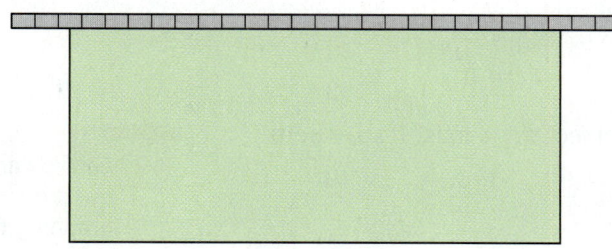

3. Suppose that you have three pets, a dog, a cat, and a monkey. You want to divide the pen into three smaller rectangular sections. There will be one pen for each animal. The pens will be side by side as shown below.

   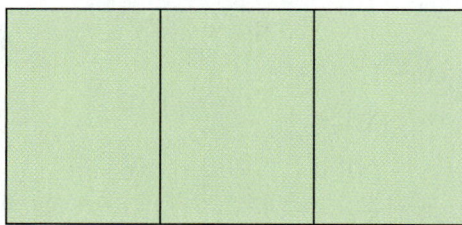

   You still only have 200 feet of fencing. You will have to use some of the fencing to build the dividers between the pens. You want to maximize the area of the entire pen. What should the dimensions be?

> The dimensions are the length and width of the pen.

4. Suppose you build a pen to separate five goats. You have 600 feet of fencing. What dimensions give the maximum area for the entire pen?

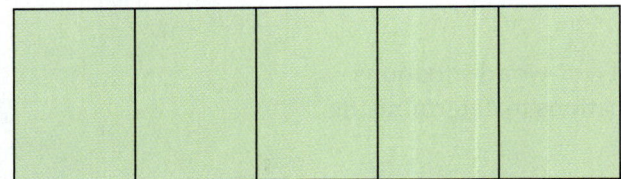

5. **Take It Further** Explain the pattern to the solutions of Problems 1–4 in as much detail as possible.

On Your Own

6. What is the least possible value of the function $f(x) = x^2 - 6x + 8$?

7. Suppose $f(x) = 3 - (x - 2)^2$. Find the value of each expression.
   a. $f(5) - f(-1)$
   b. $f(8) - f(-4)$
   c. $f(3) - f(1)$
   d. $f(2 + \sqrt{17}) - f(2 - \sqrt{17})$

8. Solve these equations using any method. Check each result.
   a. $x^2 + 14x + 40 = 0$
   b. $x^2 - 5x = 24$
   c. $9x^2 = 49$
   d. $x^3 - 4x = 0$

9. Does the graph of $y = (3x + 5)^2 + \frac{1}{3}$ intersect the x-axis? If so, where is the intersection? If not, explain.

> Can you answer this question without graphing the equation?

Maintain Your Skills

For Exercises 10–12, find the least possible value of each function. Find the value of x for which the least value occurs.

10. a. $a(x) = x^2$
    b. $b(x) = (x - 1)^2$
    c. $c(x) = (x + 5)^2$
    d. $d(x) = (x - \sqrt{13})^2$
    e. $e(x) = (x - k)^2$, where k is a constant

11. a. $f(x) = x^2$
    b. $g(x) = x^2 + 5$
    c. $h(x) = x^2 - 17$
    d. $j(x) = x^2 - \sqrt{13}$
    e. $k(x) = x^2 + r$, where r is a constant

12. a. $l(x) = (x - 5)^2$
    b. $m(x) = (x - 3)^2 + 2$
    c. $n(x) = (x + 17)^2 - 11$
    d. $p(x) = \left(x - \frac{5}{3}\right)^2 - \sqrt{13}$
    e. $q(x) = (x - h)^2 + k$, where h and k are constants

720 Chapter 8 Quadratics

8.06 Optimization

Finding a maximum or minimum of a function is a common use of quadratic functions. Linear functions do not have a maximum or a minimum value.

Higher-degree polynomial functions, however, have places on their graphs where the graph "turns around" and heads in the opposite direction, either up or down. These changes occur at the **maximum** or **minimum** of the function.

Businesses try to determine the price to charge for products to maximize their profit. Car designers try to minimize the air resistance of cars. Architects try to maximize the strength of buildings and bridges. Mathematicians try to optimize functions by finding the greatest or least outputs.

> Many of these problems result in optimizing a function.

In Lesson 8.05, you optimized some quadratics. For instance, in Exercise 12 you found that the minimum value of $n(x) = (x + 17)^2 - 11$ is -11. It occurs at $x = -17$, but the minimum value is the least possible output.

Minds in Action   episode 39

Sasha and Tony are working through a similar problem.

Consider the function $f(x) = x^2 - 6x + 8$. What is the least possible value of $f(x)$?

Tony To solve this problem, I started making a table of values. I plugged in the values $x = -2$, $x = -1$, $x = 0$, and so on, up to $x = 6$. I collected all of the values in a table.

Sasha What answer did you find?

Tony Well, look. The values get smaller and smaller until $x = 3$. Then they start getting larger again. So it seems as if the minimum is $f(x) = -1$.

Curves in the car design minimize air resistance.

x	$f(x) = x^2 - 6x + 8$
−2	24
−1	15
0	8
1	3
2	0
3	−1
4	0
5	3
6	8

Sasha I got the same answer. I graphed the function $f(x) = x^2 - 6x + 8$ on a graphing calculator. Here's what it looks like.

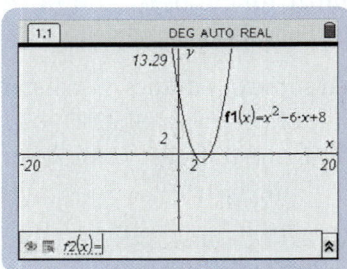

Tony Oh, you can see the minimum right there. $f(x)$ gets smaller and smaller, and then the graph turns around. I think it turns around at $(3, -1)$.

Sasha Yes, it does. This calculator can find the minimum if I command it. I can also trace the graph or zoom in. Here, I'll zoom in around the minimum point.

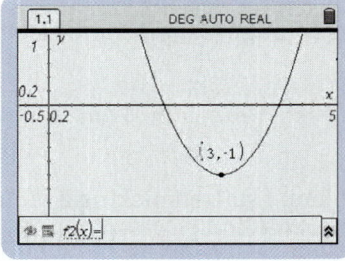

Looks to me like the minimum is where $x = 3$ and $f(x) = -1$.

For help finding the minimum point of the graph, see the TI-Nspire Handbook, p. 790.

For You to Do

By building a table or investigating a graph, find the maximum or minimum of each of the functions in Problems 1 and 2.

1. **a.** $r(x) = x^2 - 4x + 5$ **b.** $s(x) = x^2 - 10x + 15$
   c. $t(x) = (x - 3)^2 - 1$

2. **a.** $u(x) = -x^2 + 4x - 5$ **b.** $v(x) = -x^2 + 100x$
   c. $w(x) = 1 - (x - 3)^2$

3. Without graphing, determine whether the equation $z(x) = -2x^2 + 10x + 45$ has a maximum or a minimum.

Developing Habits of Mind

Prove the conjecture. Sasha and Tony look at a table and graph to determine the minimum of $f(x) = x^2 - 6x + 8$. They find evidence that $f(x) = -1$ is the minimum, but they do not prove that this is true.

You can use completing the square to prove that $f(x) = -1$ is the minimum.

First, complete the square.
$$f(x) = x^2 - 6x + 8$$
$$= (x - 3)^2 - 1$$

Next, look at this form of the function.
$$f(x) = (\text{something})^2 - 1$$

When you square any real number, the result is always positive or zero. So the least value that $(x - 3)^2$ equals is 0. If $(x - 3)^2$ is 0, then the minimum value of $f(x)$ is $f(x) = 0 - 1 = -1$.

The minimum value occurs when $(x - 3)^2$ is zero. So $x = 3$ is the input that gives the minimum, because $3 - 3 = 0$.

For Discussion

Use completing the square to find the minimum or maximum of each function. Then find the value of x that gives the minimum or maximum.

4. $f(x) = x^2 - 8x + 9$ **5.** $g(x) = x^2 - 11x - 2$ **6.** $h(x) = -x^2 - 4x - 1$

Minds in Action episode 40

Derman makes a discovery.

Derman Look, I can find the maximum or minimum much more quickly by calculating the average of the roots of each function.

Sasha What do you mean?

Derman Well, look at the example we already did, $f(x) = x^2 - 6x + 8$. This function has a minimum.

Sasha Yes, the minimum is $f(x) = -1$.

Derman Check this out. If $f(x) = x^2 - 6x + 8$, the sum of the roots is 6 from Theorem 8.4. Since there are two roots, their average is $\frac{6}{2} = 3$. If you plug $x = 3$ into $f(x)$, you get -1, the minimum.

Sasha That might just be a coincidence.

Derman We'll have to try some others to be sure, but I think I'm right.

For Discussion

7. Look at the optimization examples. Try to optimize these functions by using Derman's method of averaging the roots. Does it always work?

If Derman's method always works, you have a quick method for finding the maximum or minimum of a quadratic function. It is useful to state Derman's idea formally.

Conjecture The Average of the Roots

For any quadratic equation, the average of the roots is the x-coordinate of the maximum or minimum of the function.

Example

Problem You have 200 feet of fencing to build a rectangular dog pen. If you want the pen to have the maximum possible area, what should the dimensions of the pen be?

Solution Use the guess-check-generalize method to find the expression that you want to optimize. The perimeter of the rectangle is 200 feet. Suppose one side and its opposite side are both 30 feet. The other two sides equal 140 feet, since $200 - 2(30)$ is 140. Each of these two sides is half of 140 feet, or 70 feet. Multiply 30 by 70. The area of this pen is 2100 square feet.

> In Chapter 2, you can review the guess-check-generalize method for solving word problems.

Try another guess. Suppose one side is 40 feet. Then the opposite side is also 40 feet. The other two sides must total 120 feet, since $200 - 2(40)$ is 120. Each of these two sides is half of 120 feet, or 60 feet. Multiply 40 by 60. The area of this pen is 2400 square feet.

Suppose one side is w feet. The opposite side must also be w feet. The other two sides must total $200 - 2w$. Since the other two sides have equal length, the length of each side is $\frac{200 - 2w}{2}$, or $100 - w$.

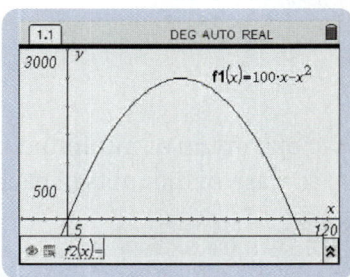

> You can use the perimeter formula to find your equation. The typical area formula is $A = \ell w$. Since the perimeter is 200, you know that $2\ell + 2w = 200$. Solve for either variable. For example, solve for ℓ and find the equation $\ell = 100 - w$. Substitute the expression $100 - w$ into the original area formula to find $A = (100 - w)w$.

The area of that pen would be $w(100 - w)$. The equation for the area is $A = w(100 - w)$.

Expand the right side of the equation to get $A = 100w - w^2$. Graph the equation for w from 0 to 100.

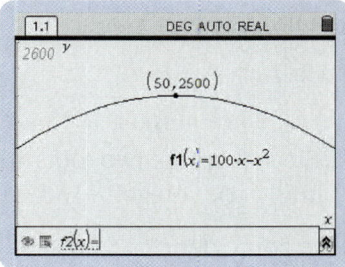

Zoom in to find a good estimate for the maximum. The maximum occurs when $w = 50$ and $A = 2500$, so the maximum area occurs when the pen is a 50-by-50 square.

Habits of Mind

Find relationships. This function equals 0 if $w = 0$ or $w = 100$. Why does this make sense, given that you have 200 feet of fencing?

724 Chapter 8 Quadratics

In Developing Habits of Mind, you used the method of completing the square to minimize $f(x) = x^2 - 6x + 8$. Maximizing $A = 100w - w^2$ will be trickier, since in this case there is a $-w^2$ term.

You can factor out a -1 first to make the quadratic easier to work with.

$$\begin{aligned} 100w - w^2 &= -w^2 + 100w \\ &= -(w^2 - 100w) \\ &= -(w^2 - 100w + 2500 - 2500) \\ &= -((w - 50)^2 - 2500) \\ &= -(w - 50)^2 + 2500 \\ &= 2500 - (w - 50)^2 \end{aligned}$$

The area of the pen with side w is $2500 - (w - 50)^2$. Since $(w - 50)^2$ is never negative, its minimum value is 0. So the expression will be maximized when $(w - 50)^2 = 0$. In this case, $w = 50$ and the maximum area is $2500 - (0) = 2500$.

For Discussion

8. Maximize the function $f(x) = 100x - x^2$ by following Derman's method of averaging the roots.

You need to be careful when choosing to apply Derman's method of averaging the roots. Derman's method only works for quadratic functions. It will not work for polynomial functions of degree 3 or more, such as $f(x) = x^3 + 4x^2 + x - 6$.

Exercises Practicing Habits of Mind

Check Your Understanding

1. Find the minimum value of each function.
    a. $f(x) = (x - 3)^2 - 16$
    b. $g(x) = (x - 3)(x - 7)$
    c. $h(x) = x^2 - 8x - 9$

2. Find a quadratic function that has a minimum value of -12.

3. Of all the pairs of real numbers that sum to 20, which pair has the greatest product?

4. Of all the pairs of real numbers that have a sum 251, which pair has the greatest product?

5. Of all pairs of numbers that add to a constant c, which pair has the maximum product?

On Your Own

6. **Standardized Test Prep** What is the minimum value of the function $g(x) = x^2 + 24x - 18$?

    A. -162 B. -126 C. -18 D. 414

7. What is the minimum value of the function $f(x) = 3x(x - 4)$?

8. You have 180 feet of fence to make a rectangular pen. What are the dimensions of the rectangle with the maximum area?

9. Of all the pairs of real numbers that have sum 90, which pair has the greatest product?

10. You have 180 feet of fence to make a rectangular pen. One side of the pen will be against a 200 foot wall, so it requires no fence. What are the dimensions of the rectangle with the maximum area?

    For help finding the maximum of the function, see the TI-Nspire Handbook, p. 790.

    For Exercises 11 and 12, do the following parts.

    a. Find the minimum value of the function.

    b. Find the value of x that gives the minimum. For parts (c)–(e), refer to this number as m.

    c. Calculate $f(m + 1)$ and $f(m - 1)$.

    d. Calculate $f(m + 2)$ and $f(m - 2)$.

    e. What do you notice about parts (c) and (d)?

11. $f(x) = x^2 + 4x + 10$ 12. $f(x) = 9x^2 - 60x + 80$

Maintain Your Skills

13. Sketch the graph of each equation.

    a. $y = x^2$ b. $y = 2x^2$ c. $y = \frac{1}{2}x^2$

    d. $y = -x^2$ e. $y = -4x^2$

8.07 Graphing Quadratic Equations

In Investigation 3D, you learned about six basic graphs. One of the basic graphs is the graph of $y = x^2$, the most simple quadratic equation. The graph of every quadratic equation is a **parabola**. All parabolas have the same basic shape and properties as the graph of $y = x^2$.

Here are the graphs of $y = ax^2$ for various values of a.

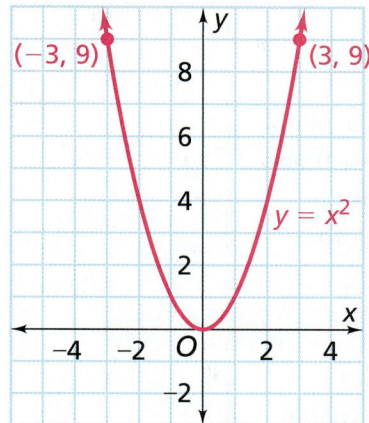

Quadratic functions of the form $f(x) = ax^2 + bx + c$ that model paths of lava ejected from a volcano have negative values of a.

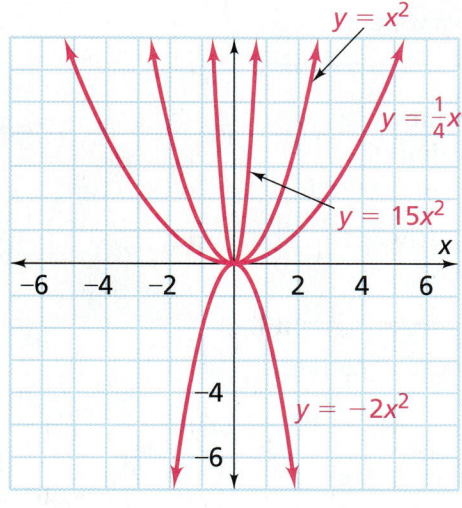

For You to Do

For the values of a, describe how the parabola with equation $y = ax^2$ compares to the graph of $y = x^2$.

1. $a > 1$
2. $a = 1$
3. $0 < a < 1$
4. $-1 < a < 0$
5. $a = -1$
6. $a < -1$

How does the parabola compare to the graph of $y = x^2$ when $a = 0$?

8.07 Graphing Quadratic Equations

Developing Habits of Mind

Find relationships. How do different values of *a* affect the graphs of quadratic equations?

7. Sketch the horizontal line and the three parabolas below on the same coordinate plane.
- $y = x^2$
- $y = 4x^2$
- $y = \frac{1}{4}x^2$
- $y = 9$

Look at the basic graph of $y = x^2$. The *x* values 3 and -3 result in a *y*-value of 9. On the graph of $y = 4x^2$, a *y*-value of 9 results from *x*-values less than 3, specifically 1.5 and -1.5. So the graph of $y = 4x^2$ is narrower than the graph of $y = x^2$.

Look at the graph of $y = \frac{1}{4}x^2$. In this equation, *a* is less than 1. Therefore, you need a greater *x*-value to get a *y*-value of 9. So the graph of $y = \frac{1}{4}x^2$ is wider than the graph of $y = x^2$.

If you examine other equations with different *a* values, you will notice that these two observations are true. The greater the value of *a* is, the narrower the parabola is. Also, as the value of *a* decreases, the parabola widens.

In Chapter 3, you translated a parabola on the coordinate plane by applying simple transformations. Recall that the transformation rule $(x, y) \mapsto (x + 1, y)$ means that you replace each instance of *x* in the original equation with $(x - 1)$.

Remember...
You read $(x, y) \mapsto (x + 1, y)$ as "(x, y) maps to $(x + 1, y)$."

For You to Do

Apply each transformation rule to the graph of $y = x^2$. Write an equation for the parabola. Sketch a graph.

8. $(x, y) \mapsto (x, y + 3)$

9. $(x, y) \mapsto (x, y - 3)$

10. $(x, y) \mapsto (x + 3, y)$

11. $(x, y) \mapsto (x - 3, y)$

12. $(x, y) \mapsto (x + 3, y + 3)$

In For You to Do, you graphed several transformations of $y = x^2$. Notice that the size of the parabola stayed the same, but the parabola moved up, down, left, or right. In fact, the graph of any quadratic function is a translation of the graph of $y = ax^2$.

In Lesson 8.06, every parabola seemed to have exactly one point that was a minimum. The **vertex** is the maximum or minimum point of the parabola. The vertex for the basic parabola with equation $y = x^2$ is $(0, 0)$.

For You to Do

13. Find the vertex for each of the transformed parabolas that you sketched in For You to Do Problems 8–12.

You can summarize the transformation rules described above in a single theorem. Theorem 8.5 will help you relate quadratic equations and their graphs.

Theorem 8.5

The graph of the equation $y - k = a(x - h)^2$ is a parabola with vertex (h, k). It has the same shape as the graph of the equation $y = ax^2$.

You can use the basic rules and moves and the completing-the-square method to transform any quadratic equation from normal form $y = ax^2 + bx + c$ to vertex form.

Developing Habits of Mind

Represent an equation differently. By a simple basic move, you can rewrite the equation in Theorem 8.5 in vertex form. The **vertex form** of a quadratic function is $y = a(x - h)^2 + k$.

Why does it matter which form of an equation you use? Suppose $a > 0$. You know that the square of any number must be nonnegative. So $a(x - h)^2 \geq 0$ no matter what the value of x is. This also means that 0 is the least value of $a(x - h)^2$.

What value of x makes $a(x - h)^2$ equal 0? If you can find the x-value, the equation reduces to $y = k$. Then you know the minimum of the function.

If $x = h$, you can reduce the equation $y = a(x - h)^2 + k$ in the following way.

$$\begin{aligned} y &= a(x - h)^2 + k \\ &= a(h - h)^2 + k \\ &= a(0)^2 + k \\ &= 0 + k \\ &= k \end{aligned}$$

So h is the value of x that gives the minimum y-value, and (h, k) is the minimum point of the function's graph.

By the same argument, if $a < 0$, you can show that k is the greatest value of $a(x - h)^2 + k$. Following the same steps, you can find the maximum of the graph of a quadratic function.

Go Online
pearsonsuccessnet.com

In Lesson 8.06, Tony and Sasha looked for the least possible value of a quadratic function. For the function $f(x) = x^2 - 6x + 8$, they made a table of values similar to this one.

x	$f(x) = x^2 - 6x + 8$
−2	24
−1	15
0	8
1	3
2	0
3	−1
4	0
5	3
6	8
7	15
8	24

Tony and Sasha saw that the outputs decreased in value until $x = 3$. After that, the outputs increased. What they did not mention was that the values repeated in reverse order.

Notice that $f(2) = f(4)$, $f(1) = f(5)$, and so on. Look at the graph. The left side of the parabola is the mirror image of the right side.

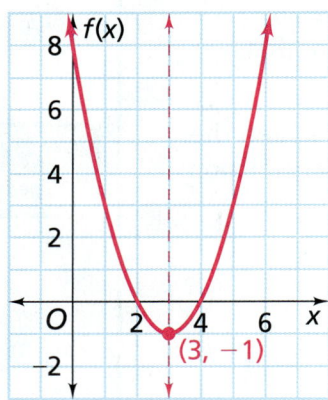

The **line of symmetry** acts as the mirror for the parabola. It will always pass through the vertex of the parabola. Finding the line of symmetry can help you make accurate sketches of the graph of a parabola.

Developing Habits of Mind

Prove the conjecture. How can you be sure that a parabola actually has a line of symmetry? If you fold the graph along the line, both sides match at every point.

Look at the line of symmetry, which has equation $x = 1$. What is the mirror image of $(4, 5)$? Since the line is vertical, the point is at the same height. So its y-coordinate is 5.

For the x-coordinate, $(4, 5)$ is 3 units to the right of the graph of $x = 1$. The reflected point is 3 units to the left. So its x-coordinate is -2. The reflected point is $(-2, 5)$.

Look at the graph of $y = (x - 1)^2 - 4$. The parabola has a line of symmetry at $x = 1$. The points $(4, 5)$ and $(-2, 5)$ are both on the graph. You can see that they are mirror images of each other over the graph of $x = 1$.

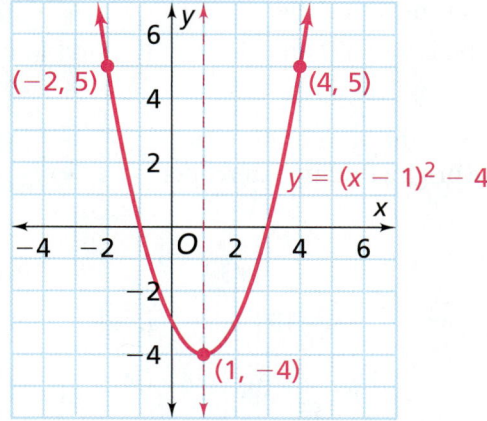

To prove that the line of symmetry reflects the entire parabola, choose a general point on the parabola. The x-coordinate of a point on the right side of the parabola is d units to the right of the line of symmetry. So you can name the point $1 + d$. The x-coordinate of the reflected point is d units to the left of the line of symmetry. So you can name the point $1 - d$.

Remember...
The line of symmetry has equation $x = 1$.

Use the equation of the parabola to find the y-coordinates of these two points. You can substitute the x-coordinate, $d + 1$, to find the y-coordinate of the general point.

You can substitute the x-coordinate, $1 - d$, to find the y-coordinate of the reflected point.

$$y = (x - 1)^2 - 4 \qquad\qquad y = (x - 1)^2 - 4$$
$$= ((1 + d) - 1)^2 - 4 \qquad\qquad = ((1 - d) - 1)^2 - 4$$
$$= (d)^2 - 4 \qquad\qquad\qquad = (-d)^2 - 4$$
$$= d^2 - 4 \qquad\qquad\qquad = d^2 - 4$$

Since both $1 + d$ and $1 - d$ have the same y-coordinate, the parabola is symmetric. This argument works in general. The graph of every equation of the form $y = ax^2 + bx + c$ has a line of symmetry.

Example

Problem A parabola has vertex $(-3, 10)$ and includes the point $(2, 0)$. Find an equation for the parabola. Sketch its graph.

Solution You can use Theorem 8.5 to find the equation. Since the vertex is $(-3, 10)$, the equation is $y - 10 = a(x + 3)^2$. You know the point $(2, 0)$ is on the graph, so it must satisfy the equation. To find a, substitute 2 for x and 0 for y. The result is an equation in one variable. Now you can solve for a.

$$0 - 10 = a(2 + 3)^2$$
$$-10 = a(25)$$
$$\frac{-10}{25} = a$$
$$-\frac{2}{5} = a$$

So the equation is $y - 10 = -\frac{2}{5}(x + 3)^2$. Since a is negative, the graph opens downward. Since $|a| < 1$, the graph is wider than the standard parabola.

To make an accurate graph, it helps to find not only the vertex, but some other points as well. When the vertex is near the origin, finding intercepts is often helpful.

You are already given the point $(2, 0)$, which is an x-intercept. The line of symmetry is $x = -3$. So the other intercept is at $(-8, 0)$. Using these points and the line of symmetry, you can sketch an accurate graph.

Another way to find the graph is to solve the equation for y and enter it into a graphing calculator.

$$y = -\frac{2}{5}(x + 3)^2 + 10$$

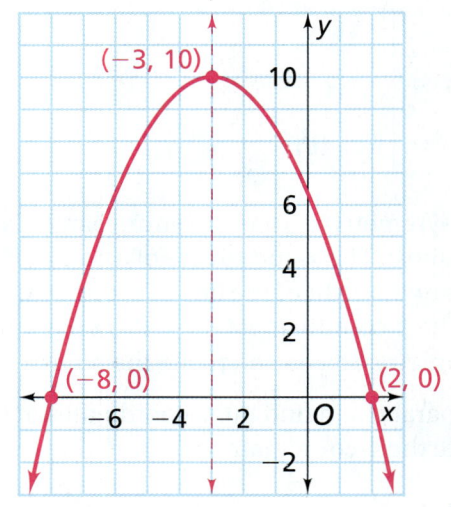

Habits of Mind

Make a connection. A root of the equation $f(x) = 0$ is a zero of the function $f(x)$.

For Discussion

Refer to the Example.

14. Explain why the other x-intercept must be at $(-8, 0)$.

15. Explain why another way to write the equation is $y = -\frac{2}{5}(x - 2)(x + 8)$.

Exercises Practicing Habits of Mind

Check Your Understanding

1. For each of the equations below, sketch a graph. Find each vertex and line of symmetry.

   a. $y - 1 = 4(x - 2)^2$

   b. $y - 3 = -2(x + 1)^2$

   c. $y + 7 = (x - 4)^2$

   d. $y - 5 = -\frac{1}{2}(x + 6)^2$

2. The graph of a quadratic function passes through the origin and has vertex (3, 18).

   a. Use symmetry to identify one other point that must be on the graph of this function.

   b. Find an equation for this function. (*Hint:* There is more than one way to do this.)

   Remember...
   The origin is the point (0, 0), the intersection of the axes in the coordinate plane.

3. Here are two quadratic functions.

   $$f(x) = x^2 - 3x + 4$$
   $$g(x) = 3x^2 + 5x - 8$$

   a. Graph both functions on a calculator. Sketch the graphs of *f* and *g*.

   b. Using the calculator, graph both $h(x) = f(x) + g(x)$ and $j(x) = f(x) - g(x)$. Sketch the graphs of *h* and *j*. What kind of graphs do the functions *h* and *j* produce?

   c. **Write About It** $f(x)$ and $g(x)$ are any two quadratic functions. Will $f(x) + g(x)$ and $f(x) - g(x)$ always be quadratic functions? If so, explain. If not, give some examples and find out what the other possibilities are.

4. If you throw a ball straight up in the air, a quadratic function describes its height in terms of time. Suppose you throw the ball straight up at 96 feet per second. The height of the ball after *t* seconds is given by the formula below.

   $$h(t) = 96t - 16t^2$$

   What is the maximum height the ball will reach?

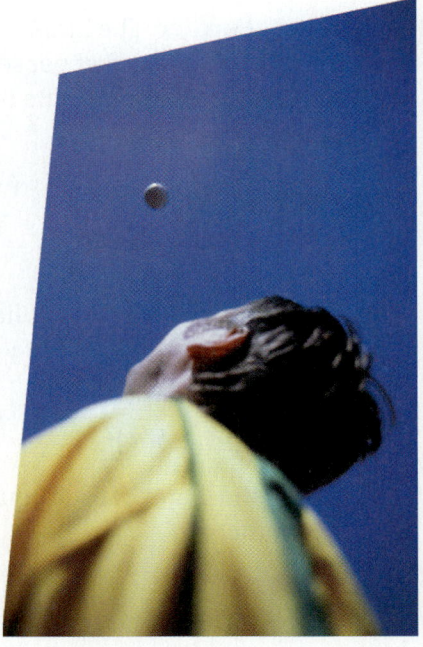

If you throw a ball in the air at 50 ft/s, what quadratic function models the height of the ball?

5. If you throw the ball at a different speed, then you will use a different polynomial to calculate the maximum height. Find the maximum for each function.

   a. You throw a ball at 32 feet per second. The height function is
   $h(t) = 32t - 16t^2$.

   b. You throw a ball at 64 feet per second. The height function is
   $h(t) = 64t - 16t^2$.

   c. You throw a ball at 128 feet per second. The height function is
   $h(t) = 128t - 16t^2$.

6. Curt can throw a ball straight up in the air twice as fast as Ryan can. Ryan can throw a ball straight up in the air three times as fast Taylor can. You may find your work from Exercise 5 useful here.

   a. Curt's throw is how many times as high as Ryan's?

   b. Ryan's throw is how many times as high as Taylor's?

   c. Curt can throw a ball with a speed of 144 feet per second. Curt, Ryan, and Taylor all throw balls straight into the air. Find the maximum height of each throw.

7. **Take It Further** The Empire State Building is approximately 1250 feet tall. About how fast, in feet per second, do you need to throw a ball for it to reach the top of the Empire State Building? How fast is that in miles per hour?

The fastest pitch ever reliably measured was a fastball at 100.9 miles per hour by Nolan Ryan.

An approximate way to convert from feet per second to miles per hour is to multiply by $\frac{2}{3}$.

On Your Own

8. **Standardized Test Prep** What is the vertex form of the equation $y = -x^2 + 8x + 9$? (*Hint:* $y - k = a(x - h)^2$, where (h, k) is the vertex.)

   A. $y - 25 = -1(x - 4)^2$
   B. $y + 25 = (x + 4)^2$
   C. $y - 7 = (x + 4)^2$
   D. $y - 7 = (x + 4)^2$

9. Sketch the graph of each equation below. Find the vertex and line of symmetry.

   a. $(y + 8) = -3(x - 5)^2$
   b. $y = -4(x - 7)^2 - 11$
   c. $(y - 9) = -\frac{3}{4}(x + 1)^2$
   d. $y = 2(x + 6)^2 + 6$

10. **Standardized Test Prep** What are the roots of the quadratic equation $y = 2(x - 5)^2 - 8$?

    A. $x = 0$ and $x = 10$
    B. $x = 1$ and $x = 9$
    C. $x = 2$ and $x = 8$
    D. $x = 3$ and $x = 7$

11. In the equation $x = y^2$, y is not a function of x. You cannot graph the function on a calculator.

    a. Find at least seven points on the graph of $x = y^2$.

    b. Sketch the graph of $x = y^2$. The graph extends into at least one other quadrant in addition to Quadrant I.

    c. **Write About It** How are the graphs of $y = x^2$ and $x = y^2$ related?

    > A point is on the graph of an equation if and only if it makes the equation true under substitution. For example, (4, 2) is a point on the graph of $x = y^2$.

12. Sketch the graph of $(x - 3) = (y + 5)^2$. What is the line of symmetry for this graph? What is the vertex?

13. Two numbers have a sum of 20.

    a. Write an equation for the product of the two numbers.

    b. Use roots to explain why the maximum product must occur when the two numbers are both 10.

    c. Rewrite the equation you wrote in part (a) in vertex form.

14. Consider the quadratic function $y = 4x^2 + 24x - 28$.

    a. Find the vertex of the function's graph.

    b. Write the equation in vertex form.

    c. Find the y-intercept using either form.

15. A quadratic function has zeros -1 and 7. It passes through point (3, 8). What is the vertex of the graph?

    > This means it passes through the points $(-1, 0)$ and $(7, 0)$. The zeros of the function $f(x)$ are the roots of the equation $f(x) = 0$.

Maintain Your Skills

16. What can you say about the vertex of the graph of each function?

    a. a quadratic function with zeros 0 and 1

    b. a quadratic function in the form $f(x) = kx(1 - x)$, where k is a nonzero real number

    c. a quadratic function in the form $f(x) = kx(c - x)$, where k and c are nonzero real numbers

8.08 Jiffy Graphs: Parabolas

In Lesson 8.07, you learned to graph a parabola with an equation in vertex form, $y = a(x - h)^2 + k$. However, as you discovered with lines, you can write the equations of parabolas in many different forms.

You already know that the graph of any quadratic is a parabola. How do you quickly make a sketch of a parabola when you are given its equation in normal form, such as $y = x^2 - 6x + 8$?

Minds in Action   episode 41

Sasha and Tony talk about strategies for sketching parabolas quickly.

Sasha All right, we need to sketch the graph of $y = x^2 - 6x + 8$.

Tony Well, it factors nicely into $y = (x - 4)(x - 2)$.

Sasha Oh, hey! You know, I think we can use the roots to find the line of symmetry.

Tony Okay. Well, the roots are $x = 2$ and $x = 4$.

Sasha Right, so the parabola goes through the points (2, 0) and (4, 0).

Tony Fine. How will you use that to sketch the rest of the graph?

Sasha Here's the thing. Points (2, 0) and (4, 0) have to be symmetric with respect to each other. Here's a picture.

Whatever is halfway between the points is the *x*-value of the line of symmetry. The graph of the parabola starts from there.

Tony Where does it start? That's an entire line.

Sasha Oh, well, take that *x*-value and plug it into the equation to find *y*, and that's the vertex of the graph.

Tony I see, and you're saying it's halfway between the roots.

Sasha Right, as long as I can factor and find the roots, I can do it.

Tony Wait, it might be even easier. You said halfway between the roots. That's the average! There's already a rule for that.

Sasha What is the rule?

Tony You need to pay more attention. We learned that the sum of the roots for $ax^2 + bx + c = 0$ is $-\frac{b}{a}$. So the average of the roots is $\frac{-b}{2a}$.

Since the starting equation is $y = x^2 - 6x + 8$, the average of the roots is $\frac{-(-6)}{2(1)}$. That's 3. It's a good thing, because that's what you got. So the line of symmetry is $x = 3$.

Sasha Oh, I like that.

> Why is it true that the average of the roots equals the x-coordinate of the line of symmetry?

For You to Do

Find the line of symmetry for the graph of each equation. Draw each graph.

1. $y = (x + 7)(x - 3)$
2. $y = -3x^2 - 8x + 4$
3. $y = x(100 - x)$

Sasha and Tony decided that the average of the roots helps find the line of symmetry. In fact, you can use any pair of points on the graph that have the same *y*-value. You find the average of the *x*-coordinates of the points. The average gives you the *x*-coordinate of the vertex. It also gives the axis of symmetry.

In Investigation 8A, you found two points in particular, the roots of the equation, which are also the *x*-intercepts of the graph.

> What is the result when there are no real roots?

Facts and Notation

The following are true for the graph of $y = ax^2 + bx + c$.

- The vertex of the parabola has *x*-coordinate $-\frac{b}{2a}$. You can find its *y*-coordinate by substitution.

- The line of symmetry of the parabola has the equation $x = -\frac{b}{2a}$. The vertex is the only point that lies on both the parabola and its line of symmetry.

- The graph crosses the *y*-axis at the point $(0, c)$. You call this point the *y*-intercept.

- The graph may cross the *x*-axis zero, one, or two times. When *r* is a solution to the quadratic equation $ax^2 + bx + c = 0$, $(r, 0)$ is a point on the graph. You can find this point, called an *x*-intercept, by factoring, completing the square, or using the quadratic formula. You call the values of *x* at these points the roots or zeros.

Minds in Action   episode 42

Tony takes his concerns to Sasha.

Tony Okay, now I'm worried about something.

Sasha What are you worried about?

Tony We just talked about the average of the roots, but there may not even be roots. The equation $y = x^2 - 6x + 8$ had two roots. We could move its graph up 4 units. Then the equation of the new graph doesn't have any roots.

Sasha Oh, do you mean $y = x^2 - 6x + 12$?

Tony Right, that equation has the same graph moved up 4 units. Here, I'll draw it.

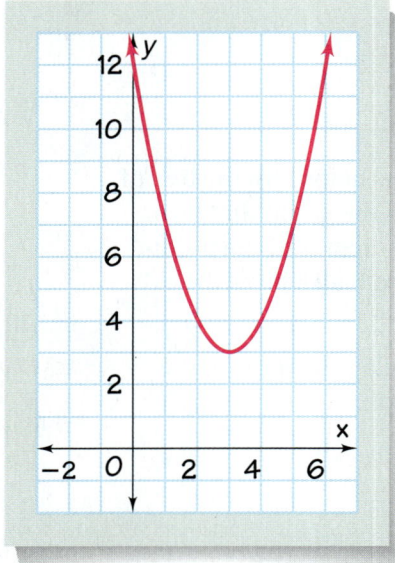

If there aren't any roots, then how can we take their average?

Sasha That's a stumper. Well, normally, I'd get roots from the quadratic formula. Let's see, $a = 1$, $b = -6$, and $c = 12$. The roots are $\frac{6 \pm \sqrt{36 - 48}}{2}$.

If I simplify that, I get $3 + \frac{\sqrt{-12}}{2}$ and $3 - \frac{\sqrt{-12}}{2}$.

Tony Yes, those numbers don't exist. There's no such number as $\sqrt{-12}$.

Sasha Hold on a second. I can still find the average of the roots.

Tony How can you find the average of things that don't exist?

Sasha To take the average of two numbers, I add the numbers and divide by 2. I agree with you that $\sqrt{-12}$ doesn't exist, but I'm going to pretend it does exist for a little while.

Tony Okay. I'm not convinced, but sure.

Sasha So the roots are $3 + \frac{\sqrt{-12}}{2}$ and $3 - \frac{\sqrt{-12}}{2}$. If I add those up, I get $3 + \frac{\sqrt{-12}}{2} + 3 - \frac{\sqrt{-12}}{2}$.

Tony Then you're adding and subtracting that *thing*! So it doesn't matter what it is, since it gets cancelled out. We can still use $-\frac{b}{2a}$.

Sasha I was going to say that. Even when there aren't real-number roots, we can pretend there are. They're just not numbers we can plot on the number line, or on the graph.

Tony Wait a second. So the line of symmetry is still $x = 3$. Of course it is, right? We only moved the parabola *up*, not left or right. So the x-coordinate of the vertex didn't change. Neither did the line of symmetry.

Sasha You're right! And look, the a and b are the same in both equations. Only the c has changed. Of course the average of the roots wouldn't change either. All that work for nothing.

Tony It's not for nothing, Sasha. At least we made sure it always works, whether there are real roots or not.

For You to Do

4. Find the two roots of the quadratic equation $2x^2 - 7x + 8 = 0$. What is the line of symmetry of the graph?

Now you have two ways to graph a parabola. The method you choose depends on the form of the equation you are given. How can you be sure that you can write every quadratic equation in the form $y - k = a(x - h)^2$? Look at an actual example.

The molten-metal sparks follow parabolic paths with different maximum points.

8.08 Jiffy Graphs: Parabolas

Example

Problem Write $y = x^2 - 6x + 8$ in the form $y - k = a(x - h)^2$.

Solution The key is recognizing that the right side of the equation $y - k = a(x - h)^2$ includes a perfect square trinomial. In order to find a perfect square trinomial, you need to complete the square. What you use to complete the square on the right side leads you to the value of k on the left side.

$$y = x^2 - 6x + 8$$
$$= (x^2 - 6x) + 8$$
$$= (x^2 - 6x + 9) - 9 + 8$$
$$= (x - 3)^2 - 1$$
$$y + 1 = (x - 3)^2$$

So $y = x^2 - 6x + 8$ is the same as $y + 1 = (x - 3)^2$.

This equation matches the results that Tony and Sasha found in episode 42. They found that the line of symmetry is at $x = 3$, and you just found that the x-coordinate of the vertex is 3.

The evidence suggests that you can write every quadratic equation in the form $y - k = a(x - h)^2$. You can prove your conclusion for the general form of a quadratic equation by using the same manipulations that you used to derive the quadratic formula.

Proof The normal form of a quadratic equation is $y = ax^2 + bx + c$.

$$y = ax^2 + bx + c$$

$$y = a\left(x^2 + \frac{b}{a}x\right) + c \qquad \text{Distributive Property}$$

$$y = a\left(x^2 + 2\left(\frac{b}{2a}\right)x\right) + c \qquad \text{since } 2\left(\frac{b}{2a}\right) = \frac{b}{a}$$

$$y = a\left(\left(x^2 + 2\left(\frac{b}{2a}\right)x + \left(\frac{b}{2a}\right)^2\right) - \left(\frac{b}{2a}\right)^2\right) + c \qquad \text{Add and subtract } \left(\frac{b}{2a}\right)^2.$$

$$y = a\left(x^2 + 2\left(\frac{b}{2a}\right)x + \left(\frac{b}{2a}\right)^2\right) - a\left(\frac{b^2}{4a^2}\right) + c \qquad \text{Distributive Property}$$

$$y = a\left(x + \frac{b}{2a}\right)^2 + \left(c - \frac{b^2}{4a}\right) \qquad \text{Corollary 7.3.1 and algebra}$$

$$y - \left(c - \frac{b^2}{4a}\right) = a\left(x + \frac{b}{2a}\right)^2 + \left(c - \frac{b^2}{4a}\right) - \left(c - \frac{b^2}{4a}\right) \qquad \text{basic moves of algebra}$$

$$y - \left(c - \frac{b^2}{4a}\right) = a\left(x + \frac{b}{2a}\right)^2$$

So the vertex of the graph of $y = ax^2 + bx + c$ is the point $\left(-\frac{b}{2a}, c - \frac{b^2}{4a}\right)$.

The result itself is not especially useful. The formula for the *y*-coordinate of the vertex is difficult to remember. Most people usually find the *y*-coordinate by substitution once they know the *x*-coordinate.

You have proven that you can write any quadratic in the form $y - k = a(x - h)^2$. You have also shown two other interesting facts.

- As expected, the *x*-coordinate of the vertex is $-\frac{b}{2a}$. So, once again, the line of symmetry is at $x = -\frac{b}{2a}$.
- The value of *a* in the normal form of the quadratic, $y = ax^2 + bx + c$, is also the value of *a* in the vertex form of the quadratic $y - k = a(x - h)^2$. So it is no coincidence that both forms use the letter *a*.

Exercises Practicing Habits of Mind

Check Your Understanding

1. **a.** Use factoring to find the two roots of the quadratic function $y = x^2 + 10x + 24$.

   b. Describe two ways you can show that the vertex of the graph of $y = x^2 + 10x + 24$ is $(-5, -1)$.

2. The quadratic function $y = x^2 + 9x + 30$ does not have real-number roots.

   a. Find the two roots by solving the equation. Express the results as radicals. Do not worry about a negative.

   b. What is the average of the roots?

3. Write the equations of three different quadratics that have $x = 4$ as their line of symmetry. Make sure that each equation has different coefficients of x^2.

4. A quadratic function has zeros at $x = 3$ and at $x = 8$. Its minimum *y*-value is -25. For parts (a) and (b), explain how you can use this information to find each of the following for the graph of the function.

   This means it passes through the points (3, 0) and (8, 0). The zeros are another name for roots or x-intercepts.

   a. the line of symmetry
   b. the vertex
   c. An equation for this function is $f(x) = a(x - 3)(x - 8)$. Find the value of *a*.

8.08 Jiffy Graphs: Parabolas

5. For each function, make a difference table for integers $0 \leq x \leq 6$, similar to the one in Investigation 5B.

   a. $f(x) = x^2$
   b. $g(x) = 2x^2$
   c. $h(x) = 3x^2 - 6x - 1$
   d. $j(x) = 9 - x^2$

Input, x	Output, x^2	Δ
0	0	■
1	1	■
2	4	5
3	9	7
4	16	■
5	■	11
6	36	

   Some of the entries in the table for part (a) are complete.

6. Linda says that she graphs parabolas in the same way that she graphs lines.

   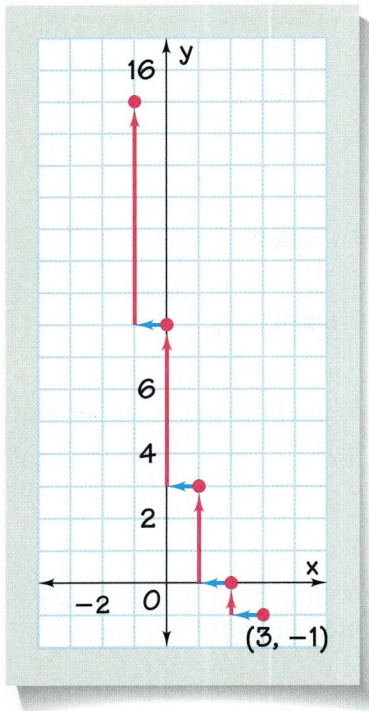

   Linda explains, "For $y = x^2 - 6x + 8$, I start from the vertex. Once I find that, I go left 1 and up 1, and that's another point. Then I go left 1 and up 3, and that's another point. Then left 1 and up 5, left 1 and up 7, and so on.

   It looks a little like I'm finding the slope of a line, but it's different.

   You have to move in both directions to find enough points to make the parabola look good. Oh, and it only works if there's no *a* number. I'm not sure what to do when there is one."

Using Linda's method, sketch a graph of each of the following quadratics.

   a. $y = x^2 + 4x - 5$. Start by finding the vertex.

   b. $y = 2x^2$. Is there any relationship similar to Linda's "left 1 and up 1, then left 1 and up 3, and then left 1 and up 5" for the points on this graph?

   c. $y = 3x^2 - 6x - 1$

   d. $y = 9 - x^2$

7. **Write About It** Describe the connections between Linda's method in Exercise 6 and the difference tables in Exercise 5.

> In part (c), you will need to find how many units to move from one point to the next. Left 1 and up 1 does not work here.

On Your Own

8. **Write About It** Consider the function $y = x^2 - 9$.

   a. Sketch a graph of this function.

   b. Explain why $x = 0$ is the equation of the line of symmetry.

   c. Use the average-of-the-roots concept to explain why $x = 0$ is the equation of the line of symmetry.

   d. What is the value of $-\frac{b}{2a}$ for this quadratic?

9. A quadratic function has roots at $x = 3$ and at $x = 8$. Its maximum y-value is 100. Find the vertex and an equation for the function.

10. Consider the quadratic function $y = -2x^2 - 10x - 12$.

    a. Find the vertex of the graph.

    b. Find all three intercepts for the graph.

    c. Sketch a graph of the function.

11. A quadratic function in the form $y = x^2 - 6x + c$ has the line of symmetry $x = 3$. The location of the vertex depends on the value of c.

    a. If $c = 0$, where is the vertex?

    b. Find a value of c that makes the vertex $(3, 0)$.

    c. If $c = 91$, where is the vertex?

    d. Find the coordinates of the vertex in terms of c.

> You find an intercept by setting variables equal to zero. There are two x-intercepts and one y-intercept.

12. In Exercise 11b, you found the value of c that makes $y = x^2 - 6x + c$ have vertex $(3, 0)$. For parts (a)–(c), find the value of c such that the graph of each function has the given vertex.

    a. $y = x^2 - 10x + c$, vertex $(5, 0)$ **b.** $y = x^2 - 14x + c$, vertex $(7, 0)$

    c. $y = x^2 + 8x + c$, vertex $(-4, 0)$ **d.** Find the vertex of $y = (x - 9)^2$.

    e. Find the vertex of $y = x^2 - 18x + 82$.

13. Here is a table for a quadratic function with only the difference column completed.

Input	Output	Δ
0	■	−3
1	■	−1
2	■	1
3	■	3
4	■	5
5	■	7
6	■	

    a. Find one way to complete the output column.

    b. Find the vertex of the graph of the quadratic you used in part (a).

    c. Is there more than one possible way to complete the table? Explain.

14. **Standardized Test Prep** Which of the following statements about the graph of $y = ax^2 + bx + c$ is NOT true?

    A. The line of symmetry of the graph has the equation $x = -\frac{b}{2a}$.

    B. The graph has a maximum if $a < 0$.

    C. The graph has no x-intercepts if $b^2 - 4ac > 0$.

    D. The y-intercept is equal to c.

15. **Take It Further** $f(x) = ax^2 + bx + c$ is a quadratic function, and $f(m) = f(n)$ for two numbers m and n. Prove the following using algebra.

    If $f(m) = f(n)$, then either $m = n$ or $\frac{m + n}{2} = -\frac{b}{2a}$.

Maintain Your Skills

16. For parts (a)–(d), find the vertex of the graph of each equation. Sketch a graph.

    a. $y = 2x^2$
    b. $y = 2(x - 5)^2$
    c. $(y - 4) = 2(x + 3)^2$
    d. $(y + 3) = 2(x - 1)^2$
    e. What is the vertex of the graph of $(y + 11) = 2(x - 7)^2$?

17. Sketch the graph of each equation.

    a. $y = x^2$
    b. $y = (x - 2)^2$
    c. $y - 3 = x^2$
    d. $y = (2 - x)^2$

Mathematical Reflections 8B

In this investigation, you explored optimization problems using quadratics. You also learned how to identify key components of the graphs of quadratic functions. These questions will help you summarize what you have learned.

1. Consider the function $f(x) = x^2 - 2x - 8$.

   a. Does the graph of $f(x)$ intersect the x-axis? If so, where does it intersect? If not, explain.

   b. What is the least possible value of $f(x)$? What value of x gives the least possible value of $f(x)$?

2. A farmer has 100 feet of fencing to build a corral in the shape of a rectangle. One side of the corral borders a river, so the farmer will only need to fence three sides. The farmer wants the corral to have the largest possible area. What should be the dimensions of the corral? What is the maximum area?

3. Sketch the graph for each of the equations below. Then find the vertex and line of symmetry.

   a. $(y - 3) = 2(x + 1)^2$ b. $(y + 4) = -(x - 2)^2$
   c. $y = \frac{1}{4}(x - 5)^2 + 1$ d. $y = x^2 - 4x + 3$

4. Consider the function $y = x^2 + 2x - 15$.

   a. Use factoring to find the roots of the function.

   b. Use the two roots to find the vertex.

   c. Find the point where the graph intersects the y-axis.

   d. Use the y-intercept and the line of symmetry to find another point.

5. How can you quickly identify the vertex of the graph of a quadratic equation?

6. How does the symmetry of a parabola help you solve problems that use quadratic functions?

7. Using two different methods, how can you find the vertex of the parabola with the equation $y = x^2 - 4x + 9$?

The suspension cables sag in a curve called a catenary until the added weight of the roadway reshapes them into a parabola.

Vocabulary

In this investigation, you learned these terms. Make sure you understand what each one means and how to use it.

- line of symmetry
- maximum
- minimum
- parabola
- vertex
- vertex form

Investigation 8C

Working With Quadratics

In *Working With Quadratics*, you will learn how the concepts you used when you focused on lines extend to higher-degree polynomials. Many of the concepts stay the same, or can easily extend to include these new kinds of functions.

By the end of this investigation, you will be able to answer questions like these.

1. How can you use graphs to solve inequalities that include quadratics?
2. How can you extend difference tables to analyze quadratics?
3. How do you graph the solution set to the inequality $y < 3x^2 - 8x + 5$?

You will learn how to
- use the graphing method to solve or estimate the solutions of complex equations and inequalities
- sketch the solution of inequalities of two variables and systems of inequalities of two variables
- use difference tables to analyze quadratics and other polynomials

You will develop these habits and skills:
- Work with quadratic functions and their graphs.
- Solve quadratic inequalities.
- Extend the idea of difference tables to quadratics.

The Gateway Arch in St. Louis stands 630 ft across as its base. It is an inverted catenary, which is very similar to a parabola. If you think of it as a parabola with vertex (0, 630), what are the values of *a* and *c* in the quadratic function $y = ax^2 + c$?

8.09 Getting Started

**Activating Prior Knowledge
Exploring New Ideas**

In For You to Explore, you will investigate function tables to determine the functions that define them.

For You to Explore

1. Solve each equation.

   a. $x^2 - 5 = x + 1$
   b. $15 - 7x = (x - 3)^2$
   c. $2(2x + 7) = (x + 4)(1 - x)$

2. Solve each inequality. Sketch each solution on a number line.

   a. $x^2 - 5 < x + 1$
   b. $15 - 7x \geq (x - 3)^2$
   c. $2(2x + 7) > (x + 4)(1 - x)$

3. For each table, find a rule that produces these outputs. Express your rule as a closed-form function of n, such as $A(n) = 3n - 7$ or $A(n) = n^2 - 4n + 3$.

Table A

Input, n	Output, $A(n)$
0	0
1	2
2	4
3	6
4	8

Table B

Input, n	Output, $B(n)$
0	0
1	2
2	6
3	12
4	20

Table C

Input, n	Output, $C(n)$
0	2
1	1
2	0
3	−1
4	−2

Table D

Input, n	Output, $D(n)$
0	0
1	3
2	8
3	15
4	24

4. **a. Write About It** Explain how you found a function that generates each table in Problem 3. Are there any other functions that could generate each table?

   b. Take It Further Are there any functions that are not the same as your function that could generate each table?

Exercises Practicing Habits of Mind

On Your Own

5. **a.** Make a sketch of the inequality $x \leq 3$ on a number line.

   b. Describe how you would sketch the inequality $x \leq 3$ on the coordinate plane.

   For parts (c)–(e), use the method that you used in parts (a) and (b) to sketch the inequalities on the coordinate plane.

   c. $y \leq 3$ **d.** $-2 < y \leq 3$ **e.** $x \leq 0$ and $y \leq 0$

6. **a.** Sketch the graph of $y = x$ on the coordinate plane.

   b. Find a point that satisfies the inequality $y > x$.

   c. Where is that point in relation to the graph of $y = x$?

   d. Describe where on the coordinate plane you could find any point that would satisfy the inequality $y > x$.

For Exercises 7–15, find a function for each table. Keep track of the function you find. The solution for one exercise may be useful in a later one.

7. **Table E**

Input	Output
0	3
1	5
2	7
3	9
4	11

8. **Table F**

Input	Output
0	-2
1	$-1\frac{1}{2}$
2	-1
3	$-\frac{1}{2}$
4	0

9. **Table G**

Input	Output
0	-7
1	-4
2	-1
3	2
4	5

10. **Table H**

Input	Output
0	3
1	8
2	13
3	18
4	23

Habits of Mind

Find a process. There are three ways to think about a process.
- You have a table of numbers and want to find a formula, or other simple description, that generates the numbers.
- There is a mystery function generating the table, and you want to find the function. Assume that the table you see is just a piece of a larger table defined by the mystery function.
- You are trying to express some pattern you see in the table. You see a relationship between the columns or within the numbers in the second column.

11. Table I

Input	Output
0	0
1	1
2	4
3	9
4	16

12. Table J

Input	Output
0	0
1	2
2	8
3	18
4	32

13. Table K

Input	Output
0	1
1	2
2	5
3	10
4	17

14. Table L

Input	Output
0	−25
1	−24
2	−21
3	−16
4	−9

15. Table M

Input	Output
0	9
1	15
2	21
3	27
4	33

Maintain Your Skills

16. a. Make a difference table for each table from Exercises 7–15.

   b. Find a pattern for the Δ column of each table.

   c. How does this pattern correspond to the type of function you found for each table?

8.10 Solving by Graphing

In Investigation 4C, you learned several ways to solve systems of two equations and two variables similar to the following.

$$y = 3x - 4$$
$$y = -2x + 5$$

To solve this system using substitution, set the right sides of the two equations equal to each other.

$$3x - 4 = -2x + 5$$

From there, you can use the basic moves to find the value of x. Remember, the x-coordinate of the point of intersection of the two graphs is the same as the solution of the equation you made.

> You finish the exercise by substituting that value into either equation to find the y-coordinate.

In Lesson 8.09, you solved the equation $x^2 - 5 = x + 1$. You probably solved this equation by using the basic moves. You put everything on one side, leaving 0 on the other, and then factored.

Notice that the system of equations below includes the two sides of the original equation.

$$y = x^2 - 5 \qquad y = \text{(left side)}$$
$$y = x + 1 \qquad y = \text{(right side)}$$

The x-coordinate of the points of intersection of these graphs corresponds to a solution to the original equation. This graphing method is simply substitution. It takes two equations with two variables and builds a single equation with one variable.

Sasha and Tony are using the graphing method to solve an equation.

Minds in Action   episode 43

Tony teaches Sasha how to solve equations using a graphing calculator.

Tony   You know, I love this graphing calculator.

Sasha   Why's that?

Tony   I don't have to do algebra anymore! I can solve an equation without algebra.

Sasha   Good luck!

Tony   Say I want to solve $x^3 + 5x = 7x^2 - 5$.

Sasha   I already know how to do that. Move everything to one side and then factor. Oh, do we know how to factor a polynomial with a cubed term in it?

Tony Not really, but watch this. I make two graphs on the same coordinate plane. The first one is $y = x^3 + 5x$ and the second one is $y = 7x^2 - 5$. Here's what it looks like on the calculator. I set the window for x from -2 to 2, and y from -10 to 15.

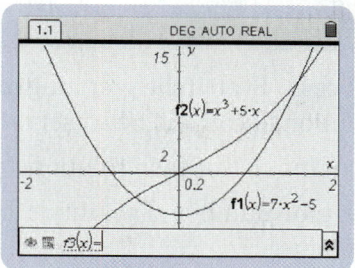

For help graphing the function and adjusting the window settings, see the TI-Nspire Handbook, p. 790.

And there's the answer.

Sasha What do you mean, there's the answer? I just see graphs crossing.

Tony Where they intersect, that x value makes both equations true, so it's the answer. And the y-value is what each side adds up to for that x.

Sasha Okay, but how can I read the answer from the calculator?

Tony You can zoom in on the intersection. You can change the window settings around it. You can trace along the graph. Some calculators can even find the intersection for you.

Sasha That's a nice way to estimate, since I don't know if I can factor polynomials with a degree greater than 2.

Tony This way will even show you how many answers there should be. Just look for how many times the graphs intersect.

Sasha We have to be careful, though. You're never really sure that the calculator is giving you the exact right answer. Plus, the calculator could give some messy decimal when the exact answer is a fraction or something like the square root of 2. And you might have more intersections that aren't in your window.

Tony Yes, you're right, but I think it's good to know many ways to do the same problem. You can check the calculator answer to make sure it's exactly right. And even when it isn't, it'll be really close.

For Discussion

1. Use Tony's method and a graphing calculator to find the solutions to $5x + 3 = 20 - 2x$ and $x^2 = 2x + 15$. What are the advantages and disadvantages of using the calculator to find the solutions?

For You to Do

2. Find an equation where the graphing method is easier than algebra.

3. Find another equation for which algebra is easier than the graphing method.

Developing Habits of Mind

Evaluate the graphing process. Even if the graphing method does not always lead to an exact solution, it can still be a useful tool.

- It gives you an idea about the size of each solution.
- It gives you an idea about the number of solutions, because you can count the intersection points.
- It gives you the ability to approximate each solution to any degree of accuracy, up to the limits of your calculator.
- As you will see in Lesson 8.11, it gives you the ability to decide what numbers make one side greater than the other. So it can be used to solve inequalities.

In Chapter 6, you learned another method for approximating solutions, the Babylonian method.

Exercises Practicing Habits of Mind

Check Your Understanding

1. Use Tony's method to find the number of solutions to the following equations.

   a. $x^2 = 9$ b. $x^2 = 0$ c. $x^2 = -9$

2. Find the number of solutions to each of these equations.

   a. $3x - 7 = 5x + 1$
   b. $3x - \frac{2}{3} = 3x + \frac{5}{4}$
   c. $(x + 1)^3 = \sqrt{x}$
   d. $x^2 = 15$
   e. $x^3 = 15$
   f. $\sqrt{x} = 15$

3. a. Describe the graph of the equation $y = 0$.
   b. Use the graphing method and a graphing calculator to find both solutions to the equation $x^2 + 3x - 10 = 0$.
   c. Find the values of x that make the inequality $x^2 + 3x - 10 < 0$ true.

4. Which of these equations have solutions?

   a. $x^2 - 2x + 3 = 0$
   b. $x^2 - 2x - 3 = 0$
   c. $x^2 + 6x + 11 = 0$
   d. $x^2 + 6x - 11 = 0$
   e. $x^2 + 8x + 12 = 0$
   f. $x^2 + 8x - 12 = 0$

5. **Take It Further** In Exercise 4, some equations in the form $x^2 + Bx + C = 0$ have solutions, and some do not. The solutions depend on the values given for B and C. (Either or both may be positive, negative, or zero.) Find a decision-making rule that shows whether the equation will have solutions.

   > A rule might be that if $B + C$ is greater than 10, then the equation will have solutions. Otherwise, it will not. (This rule does not work.)

On Your Own

You apply basic moves to an equation in order to solve it. This produces other equations with the same solution(s). So, you end up with a string of equations that are all equivalent.

Consider these steps using the basic moves to solve the equation $7(x - 3) = 10x - 42$.

$7(x - 3) = 10x - 42$	Distribute the 7.
$7x - 21 = 10x - 42$	Add 21 to each side.
$7x = 10x - 21$	Subtract $10x$ from each side.
$-3x = -21$	Divide each side by -3.
$x = 7$	

For Exercises 6 and 7, use Tony's graphing method to solve each equation.

6. a. $7(x - 3) = 10x - 42$
   b. $7x = 10x - 21$
   c. $-3x = -21$
   d. $x = 7$
   e. What happens if you apply the graphing method to each of the steps?

7. a. $x^2 = 16$
   b. $x^2 - 16 = 0$
   c. $x^2 - 4x = 21$
   d. $x^2 - 4x - 21 = 0$
   e. $17x - x^2 = 52$
   f. $x^2 - 17x + 52 = 0$

   > Do not use the basic moves on these equations before you use Tony's method. After all, his method means you do not do any algebra, correct?

8.10 Solving by Graphing

8. **Standardized Test Prep** How many solutions are there to the equation $4 = x^3 + 5x^2 + 4$?

   A. 0

   B. 1

   C. 2

   D. 3

9. The figure below shows the graphs of $y = 2x^2 + x - 14$ and $y = 3x - 2$ on a graphing calculator (x and y both range from -10 to 10).

   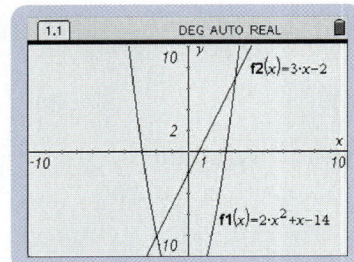

   a. According to the graph, how many solutions are there to the following equation?

   $$2x^2 + x - 14 = 3x - 2$$

   b. Use the graphs to find all values of x that make the equation true.

10. Suppose you know that $x < 4$ is true. Which of these must also be true? Which must be false? Which may be true or false?

    a. $x + 3 < 7$ **b.** $2x > 8$

    c. $4 < x$ **d.** $x \leq 3$

    e. $x < 5$ **f.** $-5x < -20$

    g. $x^2 < 16$ **h.** $|x| > 4$

    i. $-6x > -24$

Habits of Mind

Experiment. If you are not sure, try it with numbers. Do not forget that there are many possibilities for x that make $x < 4$ true.

Maintain Your Skills

11. Use the graphing method to solve each of these equations.

    a. $3x - 2 = -2x + 10$

    b. $3x - 5 = -2x + 7$

    c. $3x + 8 = -2x + 20$

    d. $3(x - 4) - 2 = -2(x - 4) + 10$

8.11 Inequalities With Two Variables

In Lesson 4.14, you looked at strategies for solving inequalities. Those strategies incorporated Tony's method from Lesson 8.10. They also provided a way to solve inequalities of all sorts, even daunting inequalities such as $2x^2 - 21x + 24 > -7\sqrt{2x + 3}$.

Solving such an inequality can be very tricky. You can use the graphing method. You may not find the exact solution, but you will get a good estimate for the solution.

For You to Do

1. Use the graphing method to solve the inequality $2x^2 - 21x + 24 > -7\sqrt{2x + 3}$.

All of the inequalities you have studied so far have had only one variable. You can visualize the solution set of one-variable inequalities by graphing the solution on a number line.

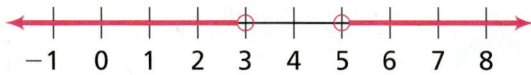

To visualize the solution set of a two-variable inequality, you can graph it on the coordinate plane.

Example 1

Problem Graph the solution set to the inequality $y < 3x + 5$.

Solution First, you graph the corresponding equation, $y = 3x + 5$. Notice that the inequality is $<$, and not $\leq$. So points along the line $y = 3x + 5$ will not be part of the solution set. You can indicate that the line is not in your solution set by drawing a dashed line.

The dashed line in the graph of a two-variable inequality is similar to the open circle in a one-variable inequality.

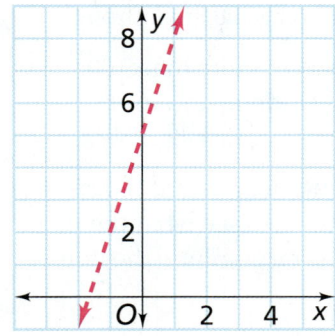

Think of each point that is on the line as having coordinates of the form $(x, 3x + 5)$. You want all the points that satisfy $y < 3x + 5$. So for any x, you want the value of the y-coordinate to be less than $3x + 5$.

Try $x = 0$. The point on the line with x-coordinate 0 would be $(0, 5)$. Any point on the vertical line with equation $x = 0$ with y-coordinate less than 5 is part of the solution set.

Next, try $x = 5$. The point on the line with x-coordinate 5 is $(5, 20)$, and any point with x-coordinate 5 and y-coordinate less than 20 is part of the solution set.

It would take you forever to write out the situation for every possible value of x, but you can see that any point that is below the line is part of the solution set.

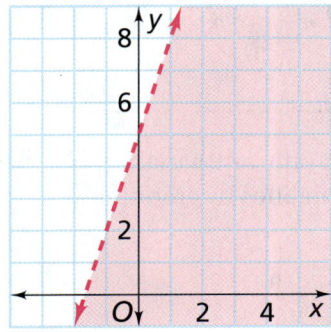

Just as you had systems of equations in Chapter 4, you can also have systems of inequalities. Tony's graphing method helps with these problems, too.

Minds in Action   episode 44

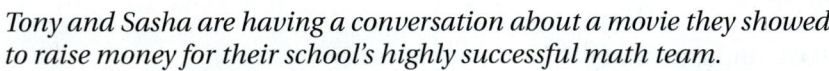

Tony and Sasha are having a conversation about a movie they showed to raise money for their school's highly successful math team.

Tony   What a turnout for the movie. Over 100 people showed up.

Sasha Yes, that was great! We still didn't make it to our $500 goal, though.

Tony   Really? I can't believe that's possible. There were more than 100 people! We charged $8 per adult and $4 per student, and there were some of each.

Sasha Here, make a graph of it. Let's say a is the number of adult tickets, and s is the number of student tickets. We want to see what the graph of $8a + 4s < 500$ looks like. Let's start by graphing the line with equation $8a + 4s = 500$.

756   **Chapter 8**   Quadratics

Tony pulls out some graph paper and quickly sketches this graph.

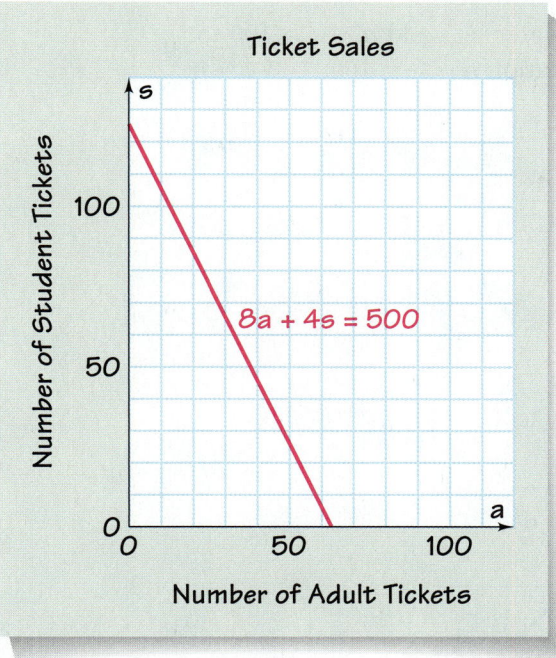

Sasha Since we didn't make $500, we must be below that line.

Tony How do you know that?

Sasha Think about it. If we made $480, the line would have the equation $8a + 4s = 480$. If we made $200, the line would have the equation $8a + 4s = 200$. Here, I'll draw those lines.

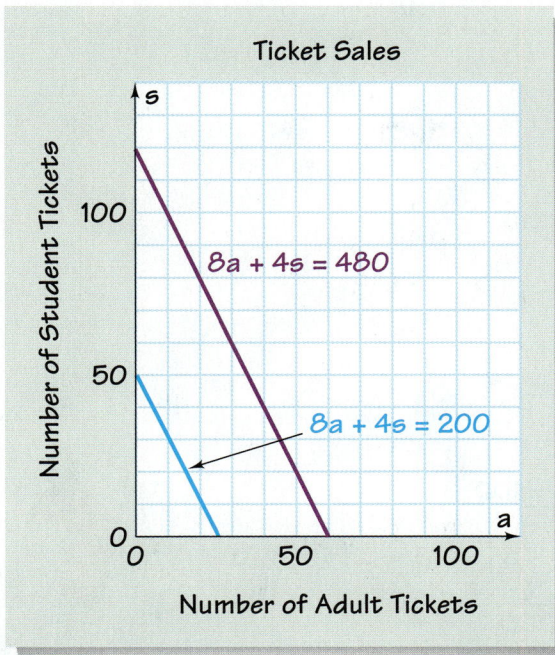

So the graph of $8a + 4s =$ anything less than $500 would be below that line.

8.11 Inequalities With Two Variables

Tony   Okay, I get it. But I still don't think we can be below that first line with over 100 people paying.

Sasha   Look, we had more than 100 people, so let's add $a + s > 100$ to the graph. Here's the line with equation $a + s = 100$.

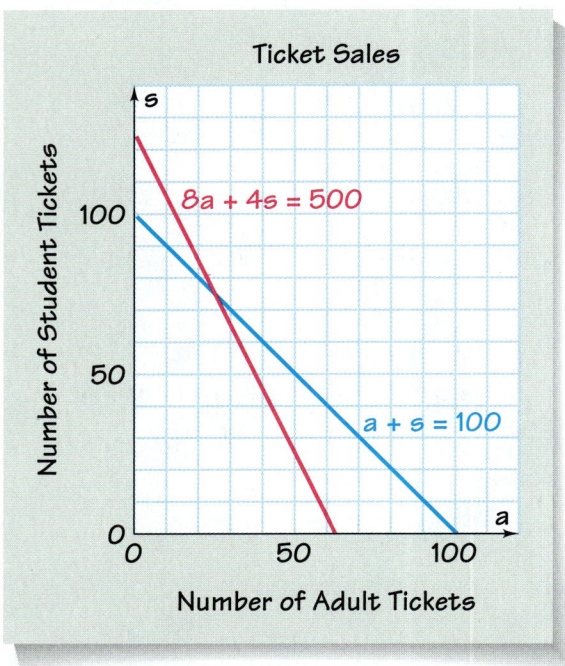

Since we had more than 100 people, we had to be above this line. And we know we're below the graph of $8a + 4s = 500$.

Sasha shades in the graph.

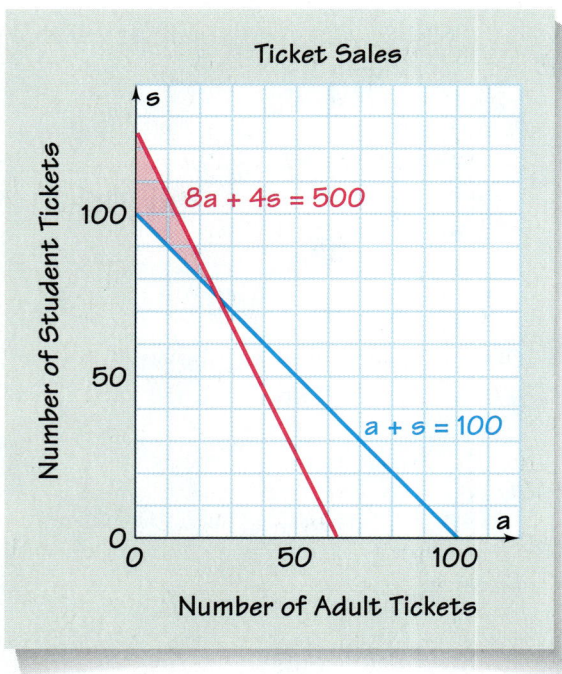

758   **Chapter 8**   Quadratics

Sasha And see that little corner? Our sales must be somewhere in that shaded part. That's what happens when you let students in for half price.

Tony Maybe next year we should charge all of them five dollars.

For Discussion

2. Using algebra, find the intersection of the two lines that Sasha graphed.
3. Are there any other restrictions on the values of a and s?

> What kinds of numbers can a and s be?

As with inequalities of one variable, the solution set for Problem 2 includes more than one number. It is a portion (or portions) of the coordinate plane, instead of a portion of the number line. Graphs describe sets. A shaded region indicates that any point in that region satisfies the inequality. The boundaries of solution regions do not have to be straight lines.

Example 2

Problem Draw a graph with all points that are solutions to both inequalities.

$$y \geq x^2 \quad \text{and} \quad y < 6 - x$$

Solution Start by sketching the graphs of $y = x^2$ and $y = 6 - x$.

The y-coordinate of any point *above* the graph of $y \geq x^2$ is greater than the y-coordinate of the point *on* the graph with the same x-coordinate. So all the points on or above the graph are part of the solution set. Similarly, for $y < 6 - x$, any point *below* the line is part of the solution set.

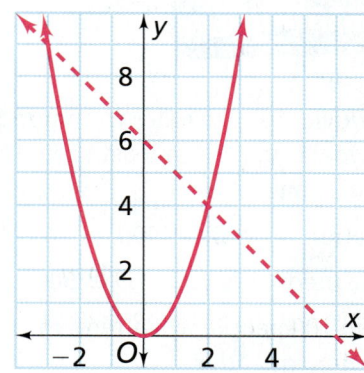

> The graph of $y = x^2$ is solid, because the inequality is $\leq$. A solid boundary indicates that points on the curve are included in the solution set. The graph of $y = 6 - x$ is dashed, because points on the line are not included.

To satisfy both inequalities, a point has to be on or above the graph of $y = x^2$ and below the graph of $y = 6 - x$.

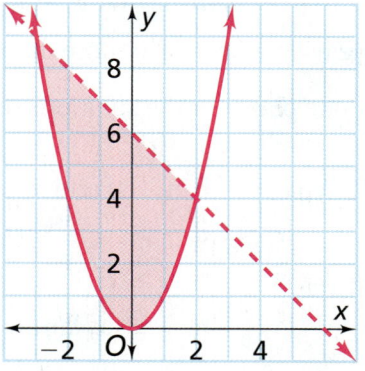

8.11 Inequalities With Two Variables 759

For Discussion

4. What does the solution for this system of inequalities look like?

$$y \geq x^2 \quad \text{and} \quad y < -6 - x$$

For You to Do

5. Using your graphing calculator, sketch the solution set for this system of inequalities.

$$y \geq 2x^2 - 21x + 24 \quad \text{and} \quad y \leq -7\sqrt{2x + 3}$$

For help graphing a system of inequalities, see the TI-Nspire Handbook, p. 790.

Exercises Practicing Habits of Mind

Check Your Understanding

1. For the next showing of a movie, Tony decides to charge $5 per student. Adults will still pay $8. His goal is to raise at least $500. The inequality $8a + 5s \geq 500$ describes this goal.
   a. Graph the line with equation $8a + 5s = 500$.
   b. Graph the solution to the inequality $8a + 5s \geq 500$.

2. Tony expects that more than 100 people will attend the next showing. Graph the solution to the system of inequalities.

$$a + s > 100 \quad \text{and} \quad 8a + 5s \geq 500$$

   Can Tony be sure the movie will make $500 if more than 100 people attend?

3. Draw graphs in the coordinate plane for the solutions of each of these inequalities or systems of inequalities.
   a. $y \leq 5$
   b. $y \geq 0$ and $x \geq 0$
   c. $y > -3$ and $x \geq 4$
   d. $y > 2x - 5$
   e. $2x + 3y < 12$ and $2x + y < 8$
   f. $y \geq x^2$
   g. $y \geq x^2$ and $y \leq 4$
   h. $y \geq |x|$ and $y < -3$

760 Chapter 8 Quadratics

4. **Take It Further** Graphing the inequality $\frac{y-4}{x-3} \geq 2$ is difficult, since x cannot be 3.

   a. Why can't x equal 3 in this inequality?
   b. Draw $\frac{y-4}{x-3} = 2$ and $x = 3$ on a coordinate plane. Use dashed lines for the parts of each graph that should not be in the graph of $\frac{y-4}{x-3} \geq 2$.
   c. Graph the solution set for the inequality.

5. Derman looks at Exercise 4 and says, "Hmm, this is the equation for slope. So it's telling me I want a line through (3, 4) that has a slope of at least 2. There are many lines like that."

   a. Draw a few lines that go through the point (3, 4) and have a slope of at least 2. A slope of at least 2 means that there are no negative slopes!
   b. How steep can these lines be? Is there a boundary?
   c. **Take It Further** What does the set of these lines look like?

Remember...
Use a solid line when the boundary is included in the solution. Use a dashed line when the boundary is not included.

On Your Own

6. a. On the same coordinate plane, graph the two lines $y = x + 1$ and $y = -2x + 11$.
   b. Find the value of x such that $x + 1 = -2x + 11$. What does this value of x represent?
   c. Find two points (x, y) such that $y > x + 1$ and $y < -2x + 11$. Where are these points located on the graph?
   d. Find two points (x, y) such that $y > x + 1$ and $y > -2x + 11$. Where are these points located on the graph?
   e. Shade the entire region where $y < x + 1$ and $y > -2x + 11$ are both true.

Exercises 7 and 8 refer to Exercise 3.

7. In Exercise 3e, you graphed an inequality involving lines with the following equations.

$$2x + 3y = 12$$
$$2x + y = 8$$

Use algebra to find the intersection of the two lines. Then check your result by testing the values of x and y in each equation.

8. a. Sketch the solution set of these inequalities.

   $2(x - 3) + 3y < 12$ and $2(x - 3) + y < 8$

   b. What is the intersection point of the graphs of the corresponding equations?

   c. How is the graph in part (a) related to the graph in Exercise 3e?

   d. Predict the intersection point of the graphs of $2(x - 8) + 3y = 12$ and $2(x - 8) + y = 8$. Then check your prediction.

   e. Predict the intersection point of the graphs of $2(x + 8) + 3y = 12$ and $2(x + 8) + y = 8$. Then check your prediction.

   f. Sketch the solution set of these inequalities.

   $2x + 3(y - 4) < 12$ and $2x + (y - 4) < 8$

   Find the new intersection point.

   g. Predict the intersection point of the graphs of $2(x - 4) + 3(y + 5) = 12$ and $2(x - 4) + (y + 5) = 8$. Then check your prediction.

Use a graphing calculator or computer software to make these graphs.

9. **Standardized Test Prep** Which point is NOT in the intersection of the graphs of $y > x^2 + 5x + 6$ and $y \leq 4$?

   A. (–4, 3)   B. (–3, 4)   C. (–2, 0)   D. (–1, 3)

10. a. Graph $y > |x|$. Where is the shaded area relative to the graph of $y = |x|$?

    b. Use the graph of $y = x^3 - x$ to draw a graph of $y \geq x^3 - x$.

    c. If an inequality has the form $y > f(x)$, do you shade above or below the graph of the equation $y = f(x)$? Explain.

11. **Take It Further** Sketch the graph of each inequality. You might start by finding some points that make the inequality work, or by finding the boundaries.

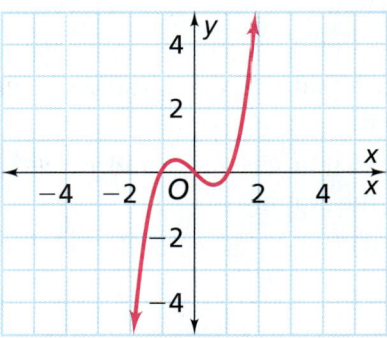

    a. $|x| + |y| \leq 2$ b. $|x + y| \leq 2$

    c. $|x| - |y| \leq 1$ d. $\dfrac{|y|}{|x|} \geq 1$

What makes the graphs for parts (a) and (b) different?

Maintain Your Skills

12. Graph the solution set for each inequality.

    a. $(y - 5) > 3(x + 2)$ b. $(y - 5) \geq 2(x + 2)$

    c. $(y - 5) < \frac{1}{2}(x + 2)$ d. $(y - 5) \leq -\frac{1}{3}(x + 2)$

8.12 Graphing Linear Inequalities

In this lesson, you will explore the connection between equations and inequalities, and learn a technique for sketching the graphs of linear inequalities.

Example

Problem Sketch the graph of the inequality $3x - 2y > 12$.

Solution The graph of the equation $3x - 2y = 12$ is a line. A point that solves $3x - 2y = 12$, such as $(6, 3)$, does *not* make the inequality true. The line is not part of the graph of the inequality. You indicate this by drawing a dashed line.

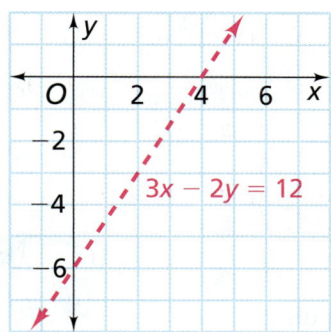

The graph of $3x - 2y \geq 12$ includes the boundary, so that would be drawn with a solid line. Points on the line make $3x - 2y \geq 12$ true.

So which points satisfy the inequality and are in the graph? One way to think about this is to consider a specific value of x. If $x = 6$, the inequality now has one variable and can be written as $18 - 2y > 12$. By comparing this one-variable inequality to the equation $18 - 2y = 12$ and point-testing, the solution is $y < 3$. Any point $(6, y)$ with $y < 3$ satisfies the inequality and is part of the graph. This gives an open ray of solutions below the point $(6, 3)$.

Remember...

A *ray* is a portion of a line that starts at one point and goes in one direction to infinity.

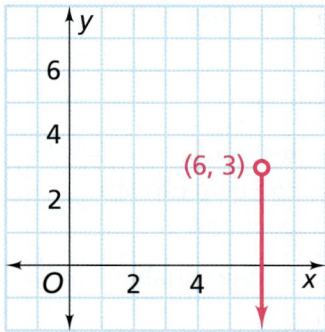

Similar vertical rays will come from any point on the graph of $3x - 2y = 12$. Any point below the line is part of the solution set. The graph of $3x - 2y > 12$ is the half-plane below the graph of $3x - 2y = 12$, shown at the right.

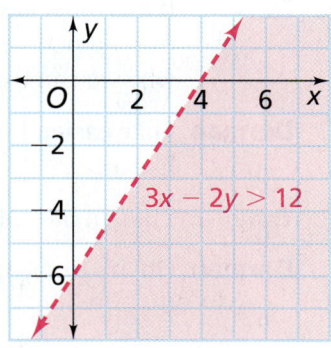

For You to Do

Sketch the graph of each inequality on a coordinate plane.

1. $3x - 2y < 12$
2. $y \leq 1$
3. $x + y > 5$
4. $x + y \leq 5$

In-Class Experiment

In Lesson 3.11 you learned how to graph the equation $2x + 3y = 12$ by using the equation as a point-tester. Use the same coordinate plane and four different colors for the following.

5. In green, plot four points that make the equation $2x + 3y = 12$ true.

6. In black, sketch the graph of $2x + 3y = 12$.

7. In blue, plot four points that make $2x + 3y > 12$ true.

8. In red, plot four points that make $2x + 3y < 12$ true.

Minds in Action

Derman In the experiment, all my blue points were on the same side of the line.

Tony Same for the red points. If that's always true, it gives us an easy way to graph one of these linear inequalities.

Derman Look at the example, $2x + 3y < 12$. I pick $(1, 1)$, and it works. So, does that mean the entire half of the coordinate plane containing $(1, 1)$ is the solution set?

Tony I think so. And I think the solutions to $2x + 3y > 12$ form the other half.

Derman Wow, that would save a lot of work. Is it always true?

Tony It has to be. It works the same way in the example with the rays—they all point to the same side. The ray concept can help explain why we can use half-planes. Using half-planes seems easier.

Derman I like easier. But what about inequalities with only one variable, like $x > 2$?

Tony That's a half-plane, too. Read it: *where is x bigger than 2?*

Derman Oh, it's to the right of the vertical line with equation $x = 2$.

> A linear inequality is one whose corresponding equation is linear. The graph of the equation is a line.

A line divides the coordinate plane into two *half-planes,* and you can test points to decide which half contains the solutions of the linear inequality. As with equations, the *graph of an inequality* is the collection of all points with coordinates that make the inequality true.

> You can also say these points *satisfy* the inequality. The same is true for equations: a value or point *satisfies* an equation whenever it makes the equation true.

Theorem 8.6

The solution to a linear inequality is a half-plane whose boundary is the graph of the corresponding equation. If the inequality uses $<$ or $>$, the solution *does not* include the boundary line. If the inequality uses $\leq$ or $\geq$, the solution *does* include the boundary line.

A system of linear inequalities can be graphed by sketching the graph of each inequality, and then looking for the intersection of the graphs.

Minds in Action

Sasha Let's sketch the graph of this system of inequalities:
$a + s > 100$ and $8a + 4s \geq 400$

Derman This looks familiar. Okay, the first one is a line that goes through (80, 20) and (70, 30) and (60, 40) and…

Sasha Careful, you're talking about $a + s = 100$.

Derman Don't I have to graph the line anyway?

Sasha You do, but those points don't make $a + s > 100$ true. You need to draw a dashed line to make it clear the line isn't in the solution.

Derman Okay, here's my line:

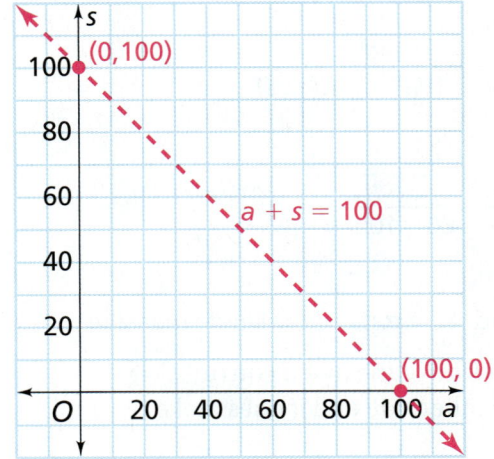

Derman Now what? Do I shade left, right, up, or down?

Sasha Shade one side of the line or the other, whichever makes the inequality true. Pick a point that isn't on the line and we'll test it to decide which way to shade.

Derman I'll pick my favorite point: (0, 0).

Sasha That would be your favorite. Actually, it's a great point to pick when you can. Does $(0, 0)$ make $a + s > 100$ true?

Derman No! And that means we shade the other side of the line!

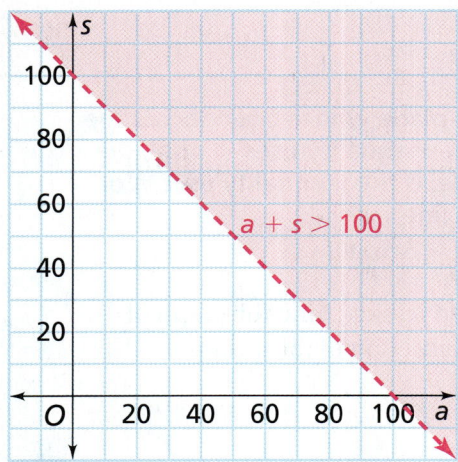

Sasha Now we have to graph $8a + 4s \geq 400$ on the same coordinate plane. We can start by graphing the line $8a + 4s = 400$.

Derman I think this one will be a solid line.

Sasha You're right. It's solid because a point that makes $8a + 4s = 400$ true also makes the inequality true. Let's find the two intercepts…

Sasha and Derman graph the line…

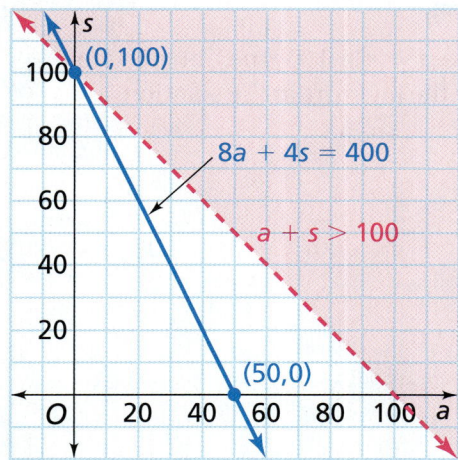

Derman I'll test $(0, 0)$ again. It doesn't work, so we shouldn't shade that side.

Sasha You can test a point on the other side of the line if you're ever unsure. $(100, 100)$ is on the other side and it does make $8a + 4s \geq 400$ true.

Derman Cool. I'll use a different shading so we can find the intersection.

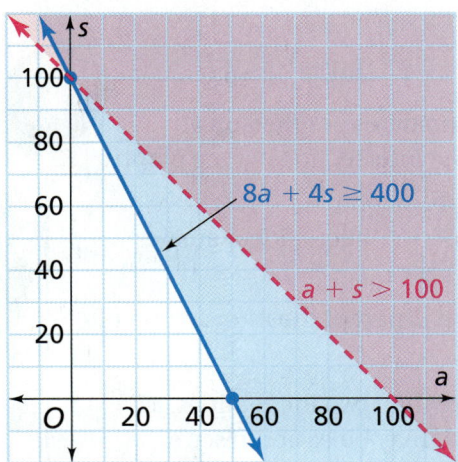

Sasha And see where the red shading and the blue shading combine to make a purple section? That's the intersection. You're right, this does look familiar.

For Discussion

9. Sasha says (0, 0) is a great point to pick "when you can." When might you not be able to pick (0, 0) to test?

10. The point (0, 100) is the intersection of the two lines $a + s = 100$ and $8a + 4s = 400$. Is this point part of the solution to the system of inequalities? Explain.

11. How is the graph of this system of inequalities different from the graph in the Minds in Action from Lesson 8.11?

Developing Habits of Mind

Find a relationship. As with one-variable inequalities graphed on a number line, there is a relationship between the intersections of the graphs of two linear inequalities.

- Any point in the intersection of the graphs of two inequalities satisfies both of the corresponding inequalities.
- If a point makes two inequalities true, then it is part of the intersection of the corresponding graphs.

Systems of inequalities frequently involve more than two inequalities. When more than two inequalities are present, it may be easier to see a complete intersection by "shading out" the half-plane that *doesn't* solve each inequality, instead of "shading in" the half-plane that does. The graph of the system of inequalities then becomes the portion of the plane that is completely unshaded.

For example, here is the graph of the system of inequalities $2x + 3y > 12$ and $2x + 3y < 24$ and $x \geq 0$ and $y \geq 0$:

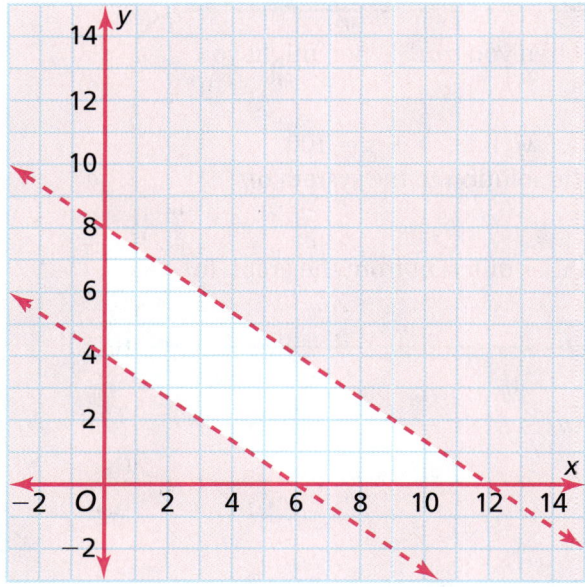

> **Habits of Mind**
> Compare this to Lesson 3.13, in which you learned about the intersections of graphs of equations.

> With normal shading, you have to find the portion of the plane shaded by *all* the inequalities, which may be difficult to determine.

You can check by testing a point from the solution area in all of the inequalities. For example, the point (4, 4) is in the solution area and makes all of the inequalities true.

Exercises Practicing Habits of Mind

Check Your Understanding

1. Graph each inequality.
   a. $x + 2y > 6$
   b. $x + 2y \geq 6$
   c. $x + 2y \leq 6$
   d. $x + 2y < 6$

2. Graph each system of inequalities.
   a. $\begin{cases} x + 2y > 6 \\ x < 4 \end{cases}$
   b. $\begin{cases} x + 2y \leq 6 \\ y > 1 \end{cases}$
   c. $\begin{cases} x + 2y \leq 6 \\ y > 1 \\ x \geq 2 \end{cases}$

3. Write a system of inequalities that is true for all points in Quadrant II but not true for any other points.

4. Graph each system of inequalities. Remember, a point in the intersection of two inequality graphs must make both inequalities true.
   a. $\begin{cases} x + 2y > 6 \\ x + 2y > 12 \end{cases}$
   b. $\begin{cases} x + 2y \leq 6 \\ x + 2y > 12 \end{cases}$
   c. $\begin{cases} x + 2y \geq 6 \\ x + 2y \leq 12 \end{cases}$

Remember... One efficient way to graph a linear equation is to find its two intercepts.

Habits of Mind
Use point-testing. Based on its coordinates, how could you tell if a point is in Quadrant II?

Habits of Mind
Use lumping. What does each inequality say about the quantity $x + 2y$?

5. Three cities are located in the coordinate plane at $A(-8, 0)$, $B(4, 0)$, and $C(0, 8)$. The three lines drawn on the graph below indicate locations that are the same distance from each pair of cities.

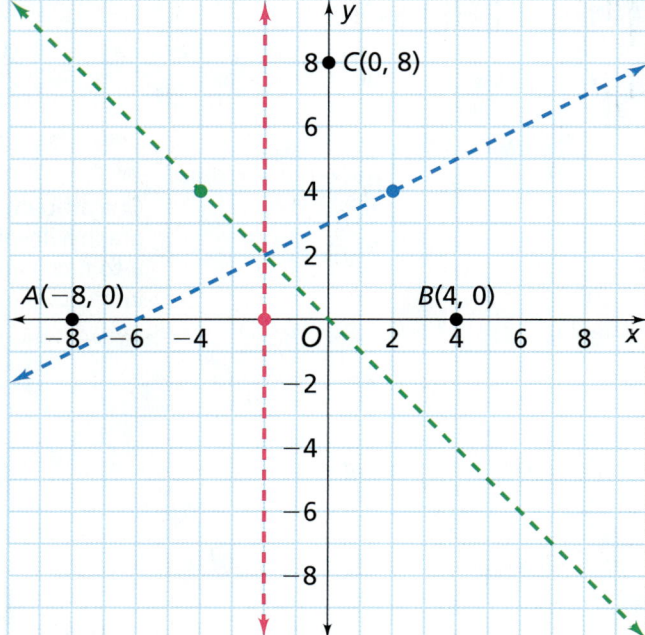

   a. What is true about the point $(-2, 2)$ for the cities?
   b. Using the graph, determine an equation for each of the three lines.
   c. Write a system of inequalities that is true for all points where A is the closest city, and no others.
   d. Write a system of inequalities that is true for all points where B is the closest city, and no others.
   e. Write a system of inequalities that is true for all points where C is the closest city, and no others.

Habits of Mind

Connect equations and graphs. The point $(-2, 2)$ is on all three lines. What does that mean?

6. There are several types of cholesterol. HDL (high-density lipoprotein) is considered "good cholesterol" and LDL (low-density lipoprotein) is considered "bad cholesterol." On a cholesterol test, the ideal results are:

   - HDL: 60 mg/dL and above
   - LDL: less than 100 mg/dL
   - Total cholesterol: less than 200 mg/dL

   Sketch a graph showing the region where all three of these results are true, clearly labeling the axes.

Total cholesterol includes other lipids, but for the purposes of this problem, consider it to be the total of HDL and LDL, which are measured in milligrams per deciliter.

7. **Take It Further** Sketch the graph of $x^2 + y^2 < 25$.

On Your Own

8. Write a system of linear inequalities that has (1, 3) as part of its solution set, but does not have (3, 1) as part of its solution set. Then graph the system.

9. **Standardized Test Prep** This is the graph of which system of inequalities?

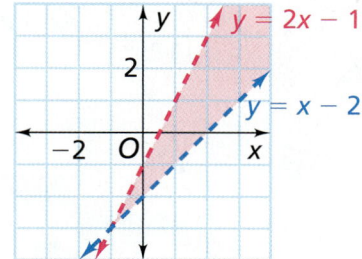

A. $\begin{cases} x - y > 2 \\ y < 2x - 1 \end{cases}$
B. $\begin{cases} x - y > 2 \\ y > 2x - 1 \end{cases}$
C. $\begin{cases} x - y < 2 \\ y > 2x - 1 \end{cases}$
D. $\begin{cases} x - y < 2 \\ y < 2x - 1 \end{cases}$

10. **What's Wrong Here** Jacob drew this graph of $x - 2y > 4$:

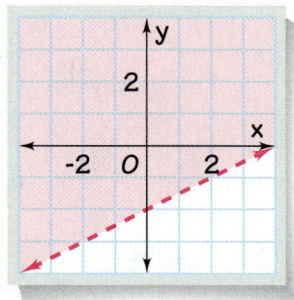

Jacob: I started by drawing the graph of the equation $x - 2y = 4$. It's a dotted line because points on the line don't make the inequality true. Then I shaded up because it's a *greater than* symbol.

Sketch the correct graph of $x - 2y > 4$. How might you convince Jacob that his method is incorrect?

11. **Reflect and Write** Describe the steps you take in graphing the inequality $4x - y < 6$.

12. **Take It Further** Sketch the graph of $|x + y| > 0$.

13. Write a system of three linear inequalities that defines this triangular region:

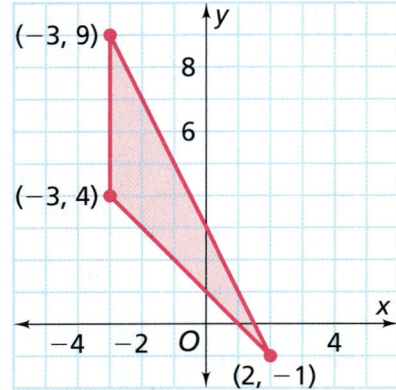

14. Write a system of inequalities you can use to define the rectangle with this boundary:

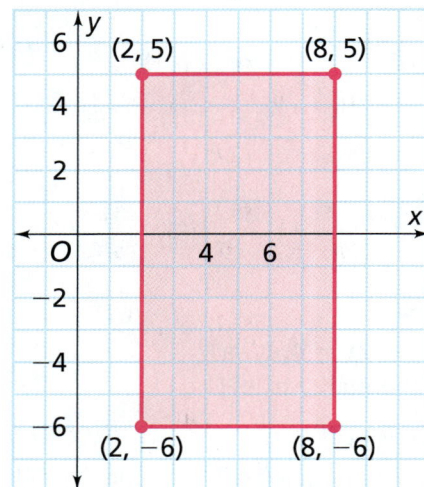

How many inequalities will you need?

Maintain Your Skills

15. Graph each system of inequalities.

    a. $\begin{cases} x + y < 10 \\ x - y > 2 \end{cases}$
    b. $\begin{cases} x + y < 10 \\ x > 2 \end{cases}$
    c. $\begin{cases} x + y < 10 \\ x + y > 2 \end{cases}$
    d. $\begin{cases} x + y < 10 \\ x + 2y > 2 \end{cases}$

772 Chapter 8 Quadratics

8.13 Difference Tables of Quadratics

In Lesson 5.08, you looked at tables generated by linear functions, such as the one below at the left. You added a Δ column to check whether the table could be generated by a linear function.

Input	Output
0	3
1	8
2	13
3	18
4	23

Input	Output	Δ
0	3	5
1	8	5
2	13	5
3	18	5
4	23	

Since the differences are constant, you can find a linear function that generates the table, namely, $f(x) = 5x + 3$.

Then, in Lesson 6.15, you saw that tables generated by exponential functions would show constant ratios in the division column.

In this lesson, you will explore tables generated by polynomials, specifically quadratics. You should not be surprised that there is a way to analyze these tables to determine what kind of polynomial generated them.

Look at this input-output table. The function $f(x) = x^2 + 2x$ generated the data. The difference column is already complete.

Input	Output	Δ
0	0	3
1	3	5
2	8	7
3	15	9
4	24	11
5	35	13
6	48	

For Discussion

1. Describe a pattern in the Δ column of the table above.

One pattern you may have noticed in the Δ column is that the values increase by 2. You can make another difference column. Take the difference between consecutive values in the first-difference column. These "differences of the differences" are called **second differences.**

The table below has the second-difference column added.

Input	Output	Δ	Δ²
0	0	3	2
1	3	5	2
2	8	7	2
3	15	9	2
4	24	11	2
5	35	13	
6	48		

> You indicate second difference by using Δ². This notation means you perform the Δ operation twice. It does not mean to square the differences.

For You to Do

2. Use the function $g(x) = 7x^2 - 5x - 2$ to generate a table with inputs from 0 to 6. Add and complete a difference and a second-difference column.

So far, you have seen two quadratic functions in this lesson. The first, $f(x) = x^2 + 2x$, had constant second differences equal to 2. The second, $g(x) = 7x^2 - 5x - 2$, had constant second differences equal to 14. Notice that 14 is double 7, and 7 is the coefficient of x^2 in $g(x)$. Two is double 1, and 1 is the coefficient of x^2 in $f(x)$.

Try one more example. Below is a difference table for the function $s(t) = -16t^2 + 100t$.

Input, t	Output, s(t)	Δ	Δ²
0	0	84	−32
1	84	52	−32
2	136	20	−32
3	156	−12	
4	144		

> The function $s(t)$ gives the height of an object thrown upward in the air at 100 feet per second. Here, t is the number of seconds.

The second differences are constant, and −32 is twice the coefficient of t^2.

A good conjecture is that the constant second difference for a table generated by a quadratic is twice the leading coefficient. To prove this conjecture, use the quadratic $p(x) = ax^2 + bx + c$. You can make a difference table to show second differences.

The **leading coefficient** is the coefficient of the highest-degree term. For $s(t) = -16t^2 + 100t$, the leading coefficient is -16.

Input	Output	Δ	Δ²
0	c	$a + b$	$2a$
1	$a + b + c$	$3a + b$	$2a$
2	$4a + 2b + c$	$5a + b$	$2a$
3	$9a + 3b + c$	$7a + b$	
4	$16a + 4b + c$		

This table suggests that the second differences for any quadratic function are constant, and always twice the leading coefficient.

Theorem 8.7

For any quadratic function $p(x) = ax^2 + bx + c$, the second differences will be constant. The constant is $2a$, twice the coefficient of the squared term.

Proof To prove the theorem, you want show that the pattern in the above table continues. But you do not have time to make an infinite table. There is a quicker way.

Take any arbitrary input, and call it n. The output would be $p(n) = an^2 + bn + c$.

The next consecutive input must be $n + 1$. Its output would be $p(n + 1) = a(n + 1)^2 + b(n + 1) + c$. Look at how those entries would show up in the table.

Input	Output	Δ
⋮	⋮	⋮
n	$an^2 + bn + c$	
$n + 1$	$a(n + 1)^2 + b(n + 1) + c$	⋮
⋮	⋮	⋮

The value in the difference column at row n is shown below.

$(a(n + 1)^2 + b(n + 1) + c) - (an^2 + bn + c)$

$a((n + 1)^2 - n^2) + b((n + 1) - n) + (c - c)$

$a(2n + 1) + b$

$2an + a + b$

8.13 Difference Tables of Quadratics

You now have a formula for the Δ column. It agrees with each of the tables you have already seen. Also, the formula for the Δ column defines a linear function, just as predicted.

$$n \mapsto 2an + (a + b)$$

Here, *a* and *b* are constants.

As you saw in Lesson 5.08, the first differences of this linear function—that is, the second differences of the original function *p*—are constant.

For You to Do

3. Finish the proof of Theorem 8.7 by showing that the value of the constant second difference is twice the coefficient of x^2.

Minds in Action   episode 45

Tony and Derman are trying to figure out how to get a quadratic function that matches this table with constant second differences.

Input	Output	Δ	Δ²
0	−33	9	2
1	−24	11	2
2	−13	13	2
3	0	15	
4	15		

Derman I think we can figure this out. The second differences are constant. So there must be a quadratic function that fits the table. And since the second difference is 2, the coefficient of x^2 would be 1.

Tony Right. So now let's copy the first two columns of the table, and this time add an extra column with just the value of x^2.

Input	Output	x²
0	−33	0
1	−24	1
2	−13	4
3	0	9
4	15	16

Derman So the real rule is $f(x) = x^2 +$ something. Hey! We can figure out that something by subtracting x^2 from each output of $f(x)$. Let's make a new column for that.

Input	Output	x^2	$f(x) - x^2$
0	−33	0	−33
1	−24	1	−25
2	−13	4	−17
3	0	9	−9
4	15	16	−1

Tony Check it out: −33, −25, −17, −9, and −1. Those numbers can be matched with a linear function. We know how to find those. The linear function is $x \mapsto 8x - 33$. So the whole thing must be $f(x) = x^2 + (8x - 33)$.

How did Tony find the linear function $x \mapsto 8x - 33$?

Derman It works. Wow! It's like knocking down the problem to a simpler one. Once you subtract x^2, the rest of it has to be linear.

For Discussion

4. Use Tony and Derman's method to find a function that fits this table.

Input	Output
0	1
1	10
2	29
3	58
4	97

Tony and Derman suspect that if the second differences are constant, a quadratic function will fit the table. They assume the following theorem.

Theorem 8.8

If a table has constant second differences, there is some quadratic function that agrees with the table.

This theorem is the converse of Theorem 8.7. It is true, and you can use Tony's method to prove it.

Exercises Practicing Habits of Mind

Check Your Understanding

1. Is there a quadratic function that fits this table? If so, find the function. If not, explain.

n	y(n)
0	−2
1	6
2	24
3	52
4	90

2. Find a quadratic function that fits this table.

n	y(n)
0	10
1	22
2	28
3	28
4	22

3. a. Find two values of x that make $(x - 1)(x - 3)(x - 6) = 0$.

   b. Expand the expression $(x - 1)(x - 3)(x - 6)$ so that it has no parentheses.

   What is the degree of $(x - 1)(x - 3)(x - 6)$? What is the constant term? Can you answer without expanding or using a CAS?

4. Copy and complete this difference table for the function $v(x) = (x - 1)(x - 3)(x - 6)$.

x	v(x)	Δ	Δ²
0	−18		
1	0		
2	4		
3	0		
4	−6		
5	−8		
6	0		
7	24		

   If you define $v(x) = (x - 1)(x - 3)(x - 6)$ in your CAS, you can ask for $v(x + 1) - v(x)$. Beware. Make sure that you have not assigned any value to x.

778 Chapter 8 Quadratics

5. Find a quadratic function that fits this table.

Input	Output
0	6
1	−7
2	0
3	27
4	74

On Your Own

6. Does this table match a quadratic function? Explain.

n	$y(n)$
0	−1
1	1
2	9
3	29
4	67

For Exercises 7 and 8, find a function that agrees with the table.

7.
Input, a	Output, b
0	13
1	−1
2	−15
3	−29
4	−43

8.
n	$c(n)$
0	−12
1	−4
2	0
3	0
4	−4

9. Copy and complete the table.

   a. Does this table match a quadratic function?

   b. Describe any patterns you find in the difference table.

n	$D(n)$	Δ
0	1	■
1	2	■
2	4	■
3	8	■
4	16	■
5	32	■
6	64	

10. **Standardized Test Prep** The table at the right defines the quadratic equation $h(x) = ax^2 + bx + c$. What is the coefficient a?

    A. 1
    B. 2
    C. 3
    D. 4

x	h(x)
−4	39
−3	22
−2	9
−1	0
0	−5
1	−6
2	−3
3	4
4	15

For Exercises 11–13, use this input-output table.

11. Show that the table does not match a linear, quadratic, or cubic function.

12. Which of the following rules is the closest fit for the table? Explain.

    Rule 1 $y = 2x - 5$
    Rule 2 $y = 2.8x - 0.6$
    Rule 3 $y = x^2 - x + 1$
    Rule 4 $y = x^3 - 3x^2 + 2x + 1$

Input, x	Output, y
0	1
1	1
2	4
3	7
4	12

13. **Take It Further** Find a polynomial function that fits the table exactly.

Maintain Your Skills

14. Make an input-output table for each function using the inputs 0 through 5.

    a. $f(x) = (x - 1)(x - 4)$
    b. $g(x) = (x - 3)(x - 5)$
    c. $h(x) = x(x - 4)$
    d. $j(x) = 2(x - 1)(x - 2)$
    e. any function $k(x)$ in which $k(2)$ and $k(3)$ both equal zero
    f. **Take It Further** Make an input-output table for any function $\ell(x)$ in which $\ell(0) = 0$, $\ell(1) = 0$, $\ell(2) = 0$, and $\ell(3) = 12$.

15. Make an input-output table using the inputs 0 through 4 for each function.

    a. $f(x) = 2x$
    b. $g(x) = 2x + x$
    c. $h(x) = 2x + x(x - 1)$
    d. $j(x) = 2x + x(x - 1)(x - 2)$
    e. Find a function $k(x)$ that is different from $f(x)$, but that still produces identical outputs for the inputs 0 through 4. For example, the two functions might have different outputs for an input of 5.

Mathematical Reflections 8C

In this investigation, you used graphs to solve or estimate solutions for inequalities and systems of inequalities in two variables. These questions will help you summarize what you have learned.

1. **a.** Sketch the graphs of $y = x^2 + 3x - 4$ and $y = 2x + 2$ on the same coordinate plane.
   b. Using the graphs, find the number of solutions to $x^2 + 3x - 4 = 2x + 2$.
   c. Use the graphs to estimate each value of x that will make the equation true.
   d. Use basic moves and solve the equation for the exact values of x.

2. Graph the solution to each inequality.
   a. $y > 2x - 3$
   b. $y \leq -x + 1$
   c. $y < x^2 - 4$
   d. $y \geq 3x^2 + 9x$

3. Draw a graph such that $y \geq x - 5$ and $y < 4 - x^2$.

4. **a.** Copy and complete the table by finding the first and second differences.
   b. Find a polynomial function that agrees with the table.

Input, x	Output, $f(x)$	Δ	Δ^2
0	1	■	■
1	5	■	■
2	11	■	■
3	19	■	■
4	29	■	
5	41		

5. How can you use graphs to solve inequalities that include quadratics?

6. How can you extend difference tables to analyze quadratics?

7. How do you graph the solution set to the inequality $y < 3x^2 - 8x + 5$?

Vertices of parabolas formed by fireworks are generally no higher than 200 feet above the ground.

Vocabulary

In this investigation, you learned these terms. Make sure you understand what each one means and how to use it.

- leading coefficient
- second difference

Project Using Mathematical Habits

Iteration and Fixed Points

In Investigation 5C, you learned about recursively defined functions, such as

$$B(w) = \begin{cases} 1000 & \text{if } w = 0 \\ 0.99B(w-1) & \text{if } w > 0 \end{cases}$$

You read this function as "Start with 1000. Then multiply by 0.99 w times. That is the output when the input is w."

So, a way to think of it is to keep repeating the function $x \mapsto 0.99x$ as many times as needed. This is the idea of *iteration*. You can write the same function as $B_0 = 1000$, $B_{h+1} = 0.99B_h$.

So $B_0 = 1000$ is the starting value. Then you can calculate B_1. $B_1 = 0.99B_0 = 0.99(1000) = 990$. So $B_1 = 990$. Then you find B_2 by running 990 through the function. $B_2 = 0.99B_1 = 0.99(990) = 980.1$

You can find the value of B_w for any number of iterations by repeating the function w times from the starting value.

Consider the following helpful definitions.

- The value chosen for x_0 when iterating the function $x \mapsto f(x)$ is called the initial value. This is also referred to as the starting value, or the seed value.

- A fixed point for a function is a value with an output that equals its input. Under iteration, fixed points produce the same output repeatedly.

- The end behavior for an iteration is the long-term result of iterating a function on an initial value.

1. **Write About It** What happens during iteration if the initial value is a fixed point for the function? Explain.

2. Find all the fixed points for each function.

   a. $x \mapsto \frac{x}{2} + 5$

   b. $x \mapsto 1.3x + 3$

   c. $x \mapsto x^2$

   d. $x \mapsto x^2 - 12$

   e. $x \mapsto (x-3)(x-4)$

3. Find all the solutions to each equation.

   a. $x = 1.3x + 3$

   b. $x = x^2 - 12$

   c. Use the quadratic formula to find the two fixed points for the function $f(x) = x^2 - 1$.

4. a. Find a function that has $\sqrt{7}$ as one of its fixed points.

   b. Use algebra to find the fixed points for

   $$x \mapsto \frac{x + \frac{n}{x}}{2}$$

   where n is a fixed value.

5. Use algebra to find the values of x that are fixed points for the function.

   $$x \mapsto \frac{x^2 - 40}{2x - 13}$$

782 Chapter 8 Quadratics

6. You can use functions like the one in Exercise 5 to find solutions to quadratic equations without using the quadratic formula.

   a. Show that the function $x \mapsto \dfrac{ax^2 - c}{2ax + b}$ has fixed points whenever $ax^2 + bx + c = 0$.

   b. Give some examples of functions of this type that have 0, 1, or 2 fixed points. Include graphs.

   c. **Take It Further** Investigate Newton's method for finding roots of equations. When solving quadratics, why does using Newton's method lead to functions of the form $x \mapsto \dfrac{ax^2 - c}{2ax + b}$?

7. Iterate each of these functions using initial value x_0. For each, find x_6 (the sixth iteration) and describe the end behavior.

   a. $x_0 = 3$, $x \mapsto \dfrac{x}{2} + 5$

   b. $x_0 = -3$, $x \mapsto \dfrac{x}{2} + 5$

   c. $x_0 = 3$, $x \mapsto \dfrac{x + \frac{2}{x}}{2}$

   d. $x_0 = 10$, $x \mapsto \dfrac{x + \frac{2}{x}}{2}$

   e. $x_0 = -1$, $x \mapsto 2^x$

   f. $x_0 = 3$, $x \mapsto 1 - \dfrac{1}{x}$

8. a. Find the end behavior for $x_0 = 10$ when iterating the function $x \mapsto \dfrac{x + \frac{16}{x}}{2}$.

   b. Find the end behavior for $x_0 = 100$ when iterating the function $x \mapsto \dfrac{x + \frac{3}{x}}{2}$.

9. For each function, find the end behavior for starting values $x_0 = 1, 5,$ and 10.

   a. $f(x) = \dfrac{x^2 - 12}{2x - 7}$

   b. $x \mapsto \dfrac{x^2 - 28}{2x - 11}$

10. a. Different types of functions lead to different end behaviors. What kinds of end behavior are possible? Give examples of each type.

    b. Find some functions that have more than one type of end behavior, depending on the initial value.

Can you describe the iteration in this photo? Is there a fixed point?

Chapter 8 Review

In **Investigation 8A,** you learned how to
- use the quadratic formula to solve equations or determine whether an equation has no real solutions
- construct a quadratic equation given the equation's two roots
- factor nonmonic quadratics

The following questions will help you check your understanding.

1. **a.** Solve the equation $84x^2 - 407x + 155 = 0$.

   b. Factor over $\mathbb{Z}$ the polynomial $84x^2 - 407x + 155$.

2. Solve the following equations. If there are no real-number solutions, explain.

   a. $x^2 - 5x - 14 = 0$

   b. $2x^2 + 5x + 3 = 0$

   c. $2x^2 + 5x = 4$

   d. $x^2 = x - 1$

   e. $(x + 3)(x - 4) = 8$

3. Find a quadratic equation for each of the following pairs of roots.

   a. 3 and -1

   b. $\frac{1}{2}$ and 5

   c. $\sqrt{3}$ and $-\sqrt{3}$

   d. 0 and -5

   e. $1 + \sqrt{2}$ and $1 - \sqrt{2}$

   f. $\sqrt{2} + 1$ and $\sqrt{2} - 1$

4. Factor each quadratic polynomial twice. First, write the quadratic as a monic polynomial. Then use the quadratic formula.

   a. $3x^2 + 11x + 10$

   b. $4x^2 + 4x - 15$

In **Investigation 8B,** you learned how to
- use your knowledge of quadratics to optimize some quadratic functions
- graph quadratic functions and examine the graph to find the vertex
- explore word problems involving quadratic functions

The following questions will help you check your understanding.

5. Each of the following describes a quadratic function. Find the vertex of the graph of each function.

   a. $y + 3 = 2(x - 5)^2$

   b. $y = (x + 1)(x - 3)$

   c. $y = 3x^2 + 18x + 8$

   d.

x	y
-2	9
0	-15
1	-21
2	-23
4	-15
6	9

6. There are many pairs of numbers that sum to 50.

   a. Which pair has the greatest product?

   b. What is that product?

7. A parabola has vertex $(4, -2)$ and includes the point $(3, -5)$.

   a. Use symmetry to identify one other point that must be on the graph of this function.

   b. Find an equation of the parabola.

   c. Sketch the graph of the equation.

   d. How does this graph compare to the graph of $y = x^2$?

8. Consider the quadratic function
   $y = -2x^2 + 4x - 3$.

   a. Find the vertex and line of symmetry of the graph of this equation.
   b. Find all three intercepts for the graph of this equation, if they exist.
   c. Sketch the graph of this equation.
   d. How does the graph of this equation compare to the graph of $y = x^2$?

In **Investigation 8C,** you learned how to

- use the graphing method to solve or estimate the solutions of complex equations and inequalities
- sketch the solutions of inequalities of two variables and systems of inequalities of two variables
- use difference tables to analyze quadratics and other polynomials

The following questions will help you check your understanding.

9. Find a function that agrees with each table.

   a.
Input	Output
0	2
1	5
2	8
3	11
4	14

   b.
Input	Output
0	-2
1	$-1\frac{1}{2}$
2	-1
3	$-\frac{1}{2}$
4	0

10. Use the graphing method to approximate the solutions to each equation. Then solve the equation to find the exact solution(s).

    a. $2(x - 3) + 1 = -3x + 5$
    b. $3(x^2 - 1) = 2(x + 1)$

11. Draw graphs in the coordinate plane for the solutions of each of these inequalities or systems of inequalities.

    a. $y > 1$ and $x \leq 3$
    b. $y \geq -2x + 1$
    c. $x + y > 3$ and $2x - y < 4$
    d. $y > -x^2$
    e. $y \leq 2x^2$ and $y < x + 3$

12. Complete the difference table. Find a quadratic function that fits the table.

Input, x	Output, f(x)	Δ	Δ²
0	3	■	■
1	4	■	■
2	9	■	■
3	18	■	
4	31		

Chapter 8 Test

Multiple Choice

1. How many solutions does the quadratic equation $0 = 3x^2 - 7x - 13$ have?

   A. 0

   B. 1

   C. 2

   D. 3

2. In which quadrant is the vertex of the graph of $y = 3x^2 - 7x - 13$?

   A. I

   B. II

   C. III

   D. IV

3. Which of these points is NOT on the graph of the quadratic function $y = (x - 5)^2 + 10$?

   A. $(0, -15)$

   B. $(5, 10)$

   C. $(10, 35)$

   D. $(15, 110)$

4. For which value of k does the quadratic equation $3x^2 - 24x + k = 0$ have exactly one real-number solution?

   A. -48

   B. -16

   C. 16

   D. 48

5. Which system of inequalities describes the shaded region below?

   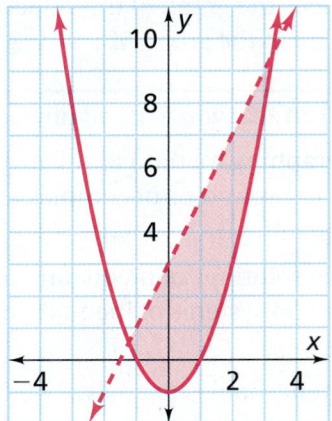

   A. $y \geq x^2 - 1$ and $y < 2x + 3$

   B. $y \leq x^2 - 1$ and $y > 2x + 3$

   C. $y \geq x^2 - 1$ and $y > 2x + 3$

   D. $y \leq x^2 - 1$ and $y < 2x + 3$

6. Two real numbers add up to 50. Which of the following numbers could be their product?

   A. -1000

   B. 1000

   C. 2000

   D. 3000

7. A quadratic function $f(x) = ax^2 + bx + c$ fits this table.

x	f(x)
0	6
1	5
2	12

   What is the value of a?

   A. -1 B. $\frac{1}{2}$ C. 4 D. 8

8. Which equation has solutions $2 + \sqrt{5}$ and $2 - \sqrt{5}$?

    A. $x^2 - 20 = 0$
    B. $x^2 - 4x - 1 = 0$
    C. $x^2 + 4x - 1 = 0$
    D. $x^2 - 4x - 21 = 0$

9. Which is the minimum value of the function $f(x) = x^2 - 12x + 33$?

    A. -12
    B. -3
    C. 3
    D. 33

Open Response

10. You can model the stopping distance of a car with a quadratic function. The stopping distance d, in feet, is related to the speed m, in miles per hour. The equation is $d = \frac{1}{20}m^2 + m$.

    a. According to this rule, what is the stopping distance for a car traveling 30 miles per hour?
    b. If the speed of the car doubles, does the stopping distance double? Give an example.
    c. Use the quadratic formula and the following equation to find the speed m if a car's stopping distance is 300 feet.

    $$300 = \frac{1}{20}m^2 + m$$

11. A parabola has vertex $(2, 27)$ and an x-intercept of -1.

    a. Use the symmetry of the parabola to find the other x-intercept.
    b. Find an equation for this parabola.
    c. Sketch the parabola.

12. Factor $6x^2 + 7x - 20$.

13. Find all the solutions to the equation $(2h + 3)(h - 4) = 13$.

14. Find a quadratic function to fit the table.

x	f(x)
0	-5
1	0
2	11
3	28
4	51

15. How are the roots of a quadratic equation related to its coefficients?

16. Consider the graph of the function $f(x) = x^2 - 8x + c$.

    a. If $c = 0$, find the vertex.
    b. Find a value of c that makes the vertex $(4, 0)$.
    c. If $c = 24$, find the vertex.
    d. Find the coordinates of the vertex in terms of c.

Challenge Problem

17. Use the equation below.
    $$w(x) = (x + 3)(x + 1)(x - 2)(x - 4)$$

    a. What is the degree of $w(x)$?
    b. Add columns to a difference table for $w(x)$ until you reach a column where the differences are constant.
    c. Predict how many difference columns you need to find a constant difference if the equation is quintic (degree 5).

Chapter 8 Cumulative Review

For Exercises 1–3, write each expression as a product.

1. $2ax - 3bx$
2. $2m(y - 2) + 5n(y - 2)$
3. $p(x + y) + (x + y)$

For Exercises 4–9, factor each expression over the set of integers. If an expression is not factorable, explain how you know.

4. $x^2 + 8x + 1$
5. $x^2 + 8x + 7$
6. $x^2 + 8x + 9$
7. $x^2 + 8x + 15$
8. $x^2 + 8x + 12$
9. $x^2 + 8x + 14$

For Exercises 10–12, find the value of k that makes each expression a perfect square trinomial.

10. $64b^2 + 80b + k$
11. $49p^2 + kp + 64$
12. $kr^2 + 36r + 4$

13. Find a value of m so that the number of real solutions of $2x^2 - 8x + m$ is exactly the number given.
    a. 1
    b. 2
    c. 0

For Exercises 14–19, factor each polynomial.

14. $5x^2 + 6x - 8$
15. $5x^2 + 39x - 8$
16. $5x^2 - 3x - 8$
17. $5(x - 5)^2 + 6(x - 5) - 8$
18. $5(x + 1)^2 + 39(x + 1) - 8$
19. $5(x - 5)^4 - 3(x - 5)^2 - 8$

For Exercises 20–22, find an equation whose only solutions are the given numbers.

20. 6 and −7
21. −6 and 7
22. 6, 7, and 0

For Exercises 23–25, find all pairs of nonnegative integers m and n such that the given equation is true.

23. $m^2 - n^2 = 12$
24. $m^2 - n^2 = 48$
25. $m^2 - n^2 = 11$

26. Use the quadratic formula to solve the equation $35x^2 - 108x + 81 = 0$. Then use your results to factor the polynomial $35x^2 - 108x + 81$.

27. Use the quadratic formula to solve the equation $56x^2 - 149x + 99 = 0$. Then use your results to factor the polynomial $56x^2 - 149x + 99$.

28. Explain how you can use the quadratic formula to factor some polynomials over the integers.

29. Use the polynomial $a(x) = 2x^2 - 5x + 7$.
    a. Find a polynomial $b(x)$ such that $a(x) + b(x) = 5x^2 - 2x + 3$.
    b. Find a polynomial $c(x)$ such that $a(x) + c(x) = 10x + 8$.
    c. Find a polynomial $d(x)$ such that $a(x) + d(x)$ has degree 2 and $a(x) \cdot d(x)$ has degree 3.

30. For the function $f(x) = 4x(x + 10)$, explain how to find the minimum value of f.

31. Write the function $y = 3x^2 - 30x + 82$ in vertex form. Then find the vertex and the y-intercept of the graph of the function.

32. Sketch the function $y = x^2 - 16$. What are the roots? Use your results to explain why the line of symmetry in the graph has equation $x = 0$.

33. A quadratic function has roots 2 and 11, and its maximum y-value is 8.
    a. What is the vertex of the graph of the function?
    b. Does the parabola open up or open down?

34. Find a function that agrees with each table.

    a.
Input	0	1	2	3	4
Output	11	2	−7	−16	−25

    b.
Input	0	1	2	3	4	5
Output	14	9	6	5	6	9

35. a. Graph $y = -x + 3$ and $y = \frac{1}{2}x - 6$ on the same coordinate plane.
    b. For what value of x is $-x + 3 = \frac{1}{2}x - 6$? How is that value of x related to the equations in part (a)?
    c. Find a point (x, y) such that $y < -x + 3$ and $y < \frac{1}{2}x - 6$. Shade the region for which every point (x, y) satisfies both inequalities $y < -x + 3$ and $y < \frac{1}{2}x - 6$.

36. Explain why the coefficient of x^5 in the normal form of $(x + x^2 + x^3 + x^4)^2$ is 4.

37. Show that each of the following is an identity.
    a. $a^2 + 2ab + b^2 = a(a + b) + b(a + b)$
    b. $4(a + b)^2 - 9(p + q)^2$
       $= (2a + 2b + 3p + 3q)(2a + 2b - 3p - 3q)$

38. A square with side s is completely inside a circle with radius r.
    a. Write an expression for the area of the circle that is outside the square.
    b. Suppose the radius of the circle is two times the side of the square. Write an expression for the area of the circle that is outside the square.

39. a. A rectangular pen has a perimeter of 440 feet. What size rectangle maximizes the area of the pen?
    b. Of all pairs of real numbers that sum to 220, which two numbers have the greatest product?

40. Make an input-output table using the integers 0 through 4 as the input values for each situation.
    a. The outputs are double the inputs.
    b. The outputs are 5 less than the inputs.
    c. The outputs are the squares of the inputs.

For Exercises 41–43, find the value of y for each equation.

41. $4^{y-2} = 64$

42. $4^{2y} = 16$

43. $y^y = 27$

44. Write an absolute value equation to represent the situation that the distance between a number and 3 is less than 5.

45. Write an equation of the line through $(-1, -7)$ and $(5, 5)$.

46. Evaluate the expression $17 - 3x$ for x-values 10, 5, −2, and −10.

47. If you know that $a \cdot b \cdot c = 100$, find the value of each expression.
    a. $a \cdot b \cdot (-c)$
    b. $a \cdot (-b) \cdot (-c)$
    c. $(-a) \cdot (-b) \cdot (-c)$

TI-Nspire™ Technology Handbook

Recognizing how to use technology to support your mathematics is an important habit of mind. Although the use of technology in this course is independent of any particular hardware or software, this handbook gives examples of how you can apply the TI-Nspire™ handheld technology.

Handbook Contents	Page	Use With Lesson
Iterating a Function	791	Chapter 6 Project
Defining a Function	791	5.04
Defining a Function Recursively	791	5.09, 5.12
Graphing an Equation	792	4.14, 6.07
Graphing a Function	792	5.06, 6.14
Graphing a User-Defined Function by Dragging It Onto the Axes	792	5.06, 8.10
Graphing a User-Defined Function Using the Function Line	793	5.06
Changing the Graphing Window Settings	793	4.14, 8.10
Graphing a System of Inequalities	794	8.11
Finding the Intersection Points(s) of Two Graphs	794	4.14, 8.01
Finding the Maximums, Minimums, and Zeros of a Function	795	8.06
Using Spreadsheets	796	5.02, 5.09, 5.12
Using the Fill-Down Feature on a Spreadsheet	797	5.12
Generating a Scatter Plot	797	3.09
Finding a Linear Regression	798	4.15
Making a Histogram	799	3.07
Making a Box-and-Whisker Plot	799	3.08

Iterating a Function, Chapter 6 Project

1. In the calculator application, type **9** **4** **.** **5** **enter**. Press **ctrl** **x²** and then **ctrl** **(-)**.

   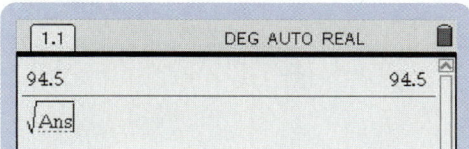

2. Press **enter** repeatedly to iterate the function.

   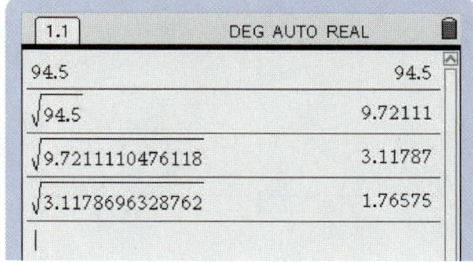

Defining a Function, Lesson 5.04

1. Choose the **Define** option from the **Actions** menu (or type **D** **E** **F** **I** **N** **E**).

   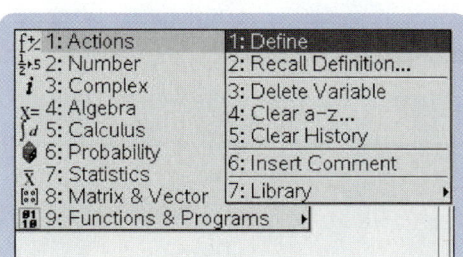

2. Type the function and press **enter**.

   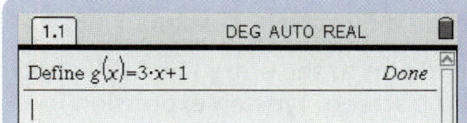

Defining a Function Recursively, Lessons 5.09, 5.12

1. Choose the **Define** option from the **Actions** menu. Name the function by typing **B** **(** **N** **)** **=**. Press **ctrl** **X** to open the **Templates** palette. Choose {ₒ,ₒ} and press **enter**.

   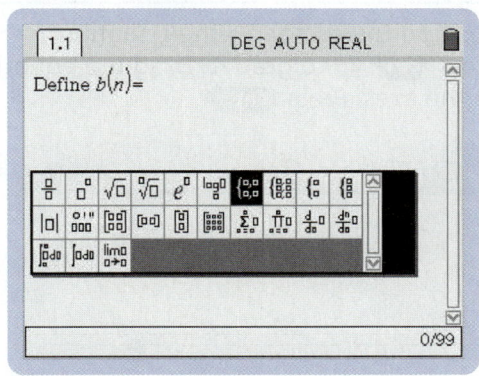

2. Enter the function. Press **tab** to move from box to box. Press **enter** to complete the definition.

   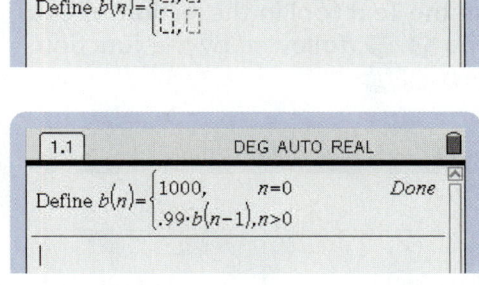

TI-Nspire™ Technology Handbook

Graphing an Equation, Lessons 4.14, 6.07

1. Use the **Text** tool in the **Actions** menu. Write the equation. Press `enter`.

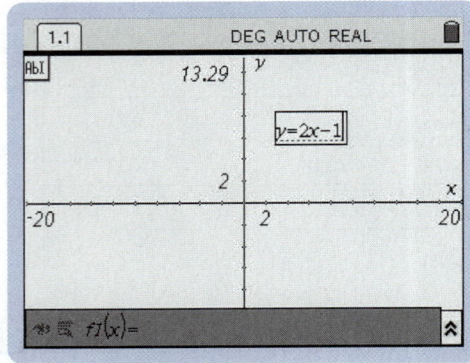

2. Position the cursor on the equation. Press `ctrl` ✶ to grab it. Drag the equation to the axes. Press `enter`.

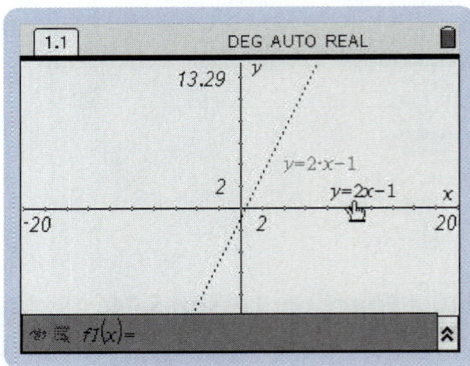

Graphing a Function, Lessons 5.06, 6.14

1. Tab down to the entry line at the bottom of the screen. Type an expression in *x*.

2. Press `enter`.

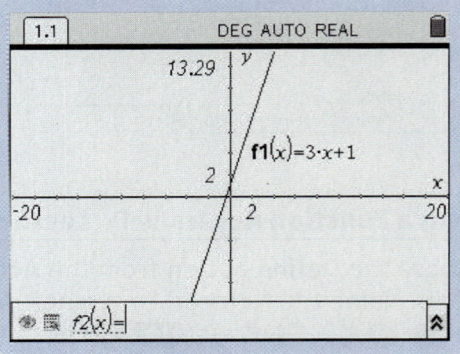

Graphing a User-Defined Function by Dragging It Onto the Axes, Lessons 5.06, 8.10

1. Use the **Text** tool in the **Actions** menu. Type **Y** **=**, followed by the function. Press `enter`.

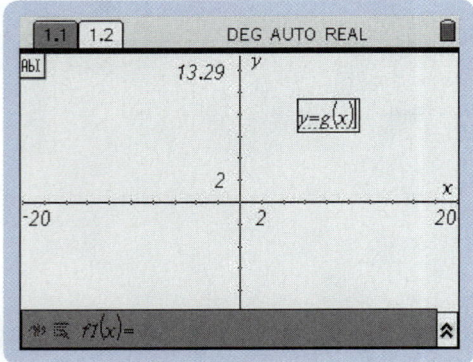

2. Position the cursor on the equation. Press `ctrl` ✶ to grab it. Drag the equation to the axes. Press `enter`.

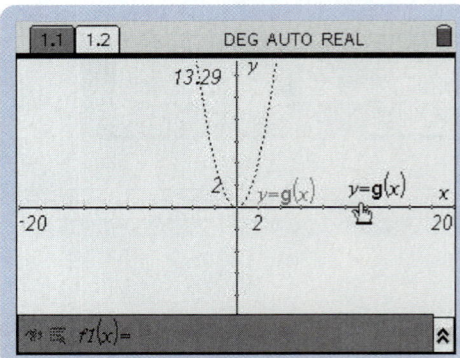

Graphing a User-Defined Function Using the Function Line, Lesson 5.06

1. Type the function into the function line. Press `enter` to graph it.

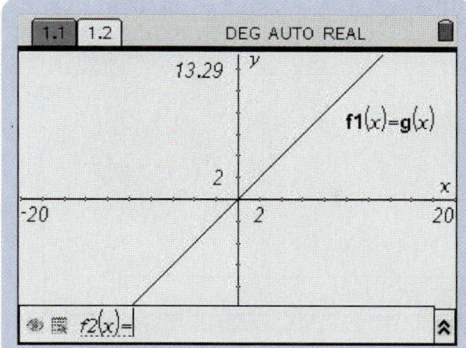

2. Redefine the function in the Calculator application.

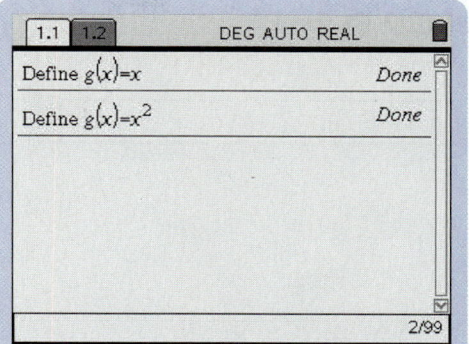

3. Switch to the Graphs & Geometry screen to see the updated graph.

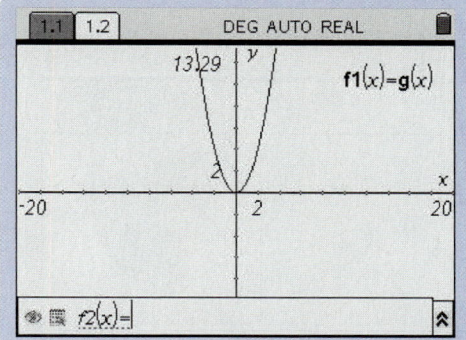

Changing the Graphing Window Settings, Lessons 4.14, 8.10

1. Choose the **Window Settings** option in the **Window** menu.

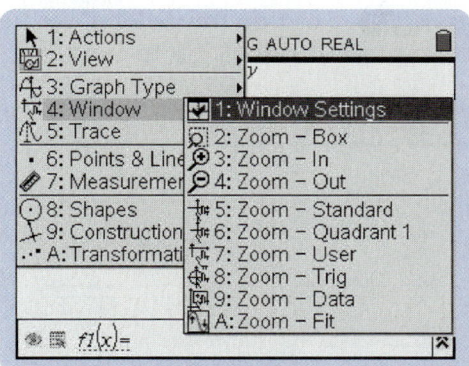

2. Press `tab` to navigate from field to field. Change the window settings as desired. Press `enter` to confirm.

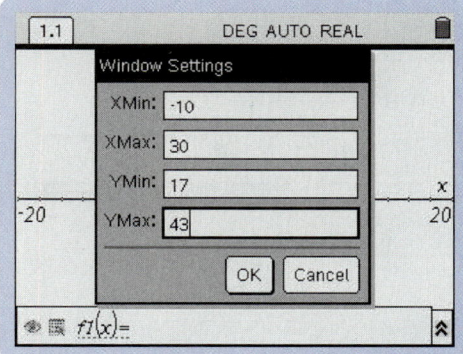

TI-Nspire™ Technology Handbook

Graphing a System of Inequalities, Lesson 8.11

1. Navigate to the function line using the **tab** key. Press ⇐ to delete the =. Type the inequality. (Use **ctrl** < for ≤ and **ctrl** > for ≥.)

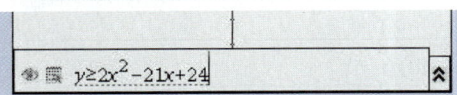

2. Press **enter** to graph the inequality.

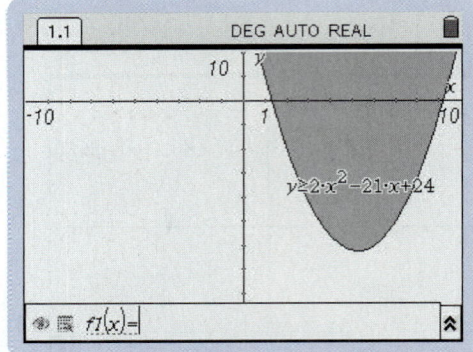

3. Enter the second inequality.

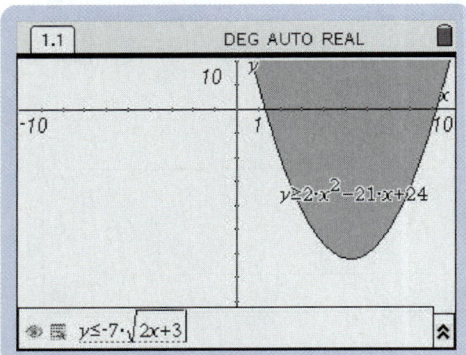

4. Press **enter** to graph the inequality.

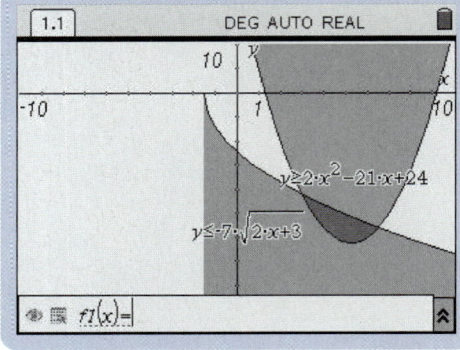

Finding the Intersection Point(s) of Two Graphs, Lessons 4.14, 8.01

1. Choose the **Intersection Point(s)** option from the **Points & Lines** menu.

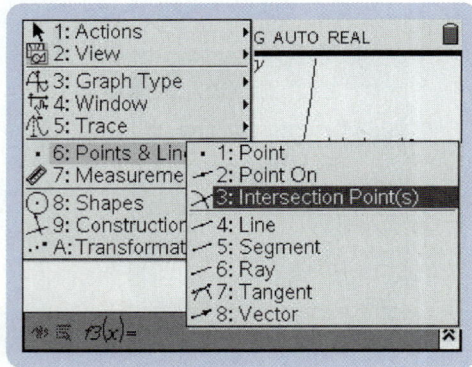

2. Position the pointer on the first graph. Press **enter**. Position the pointer on the second graph. Press **enter** to confirm.

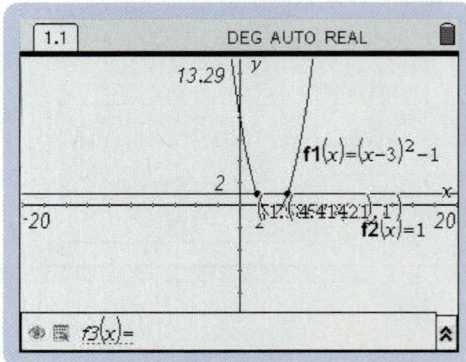

TI-Nspire™ Technology Handbook

3. Position the pointer on one set of coordinates. Press **ctrl** 🖱 to grab it. Drag the coordinates to the desired location and press **enter**.

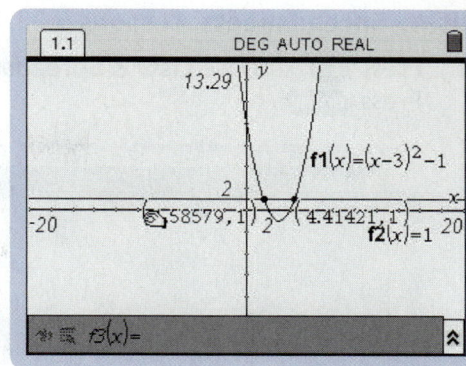

Finding the Maximums, Minimums, and Zeros of a Function, Lesson 8.06

1. Choose the **Graph Trace** option in the **Trace** menu.

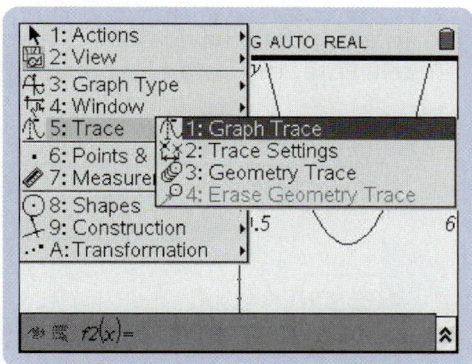

2. Use the ◀ and ▶ keys to move the trace cursor along the graph. Zeros are indicated by the letter z. Press **enter** to set the coordinates.

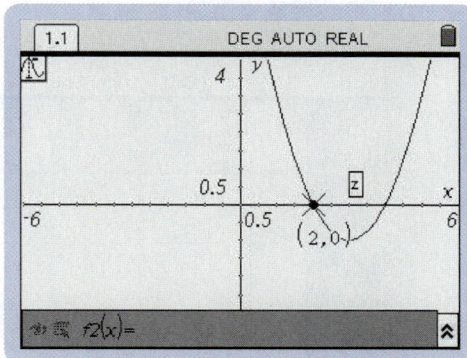

3. Minimums and maximums are indicated by the letters m and M, respectively. Press **enter** to get the coordinates.

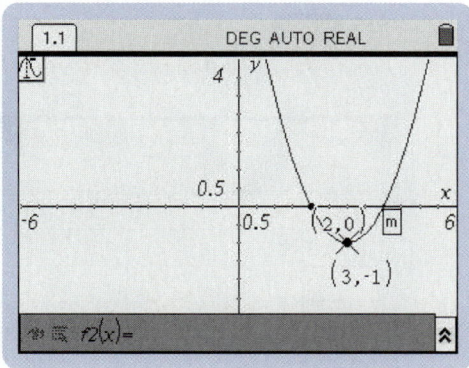

Using Spreadsheets, Lessons 5.02, 5.09, 5.12

1. Press **(home)**. Choose **Lists & Spreadsheets**. Press **enter**.

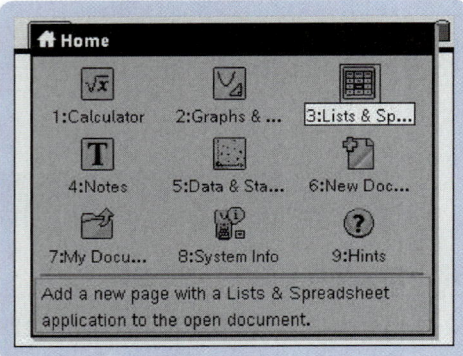

2. To label columns, navigate to the header cell. Type the column name. Press **enter**. Choose **Resize** from the **Actions** menu.

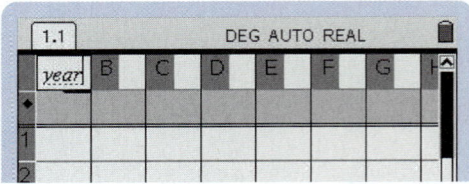

3. Press ◁ or ▷ until the column is the desired width. Press **enter**.

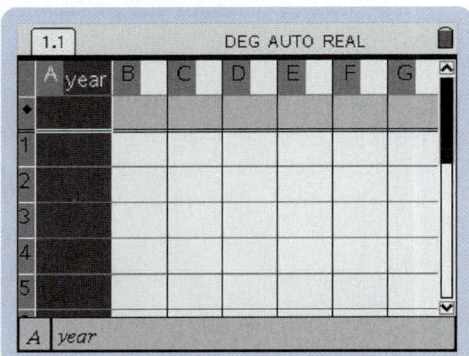

4. To enter data, navigate to the appropriate cell. Enter the data and press **enter**.

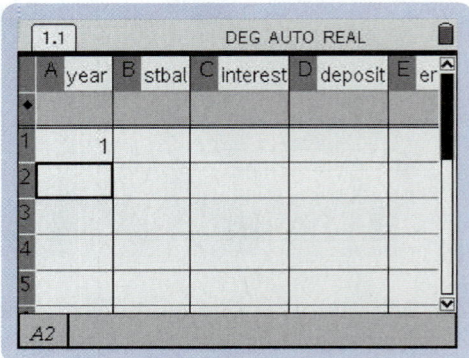

5. Type = A 1 + 1 in cell A2.

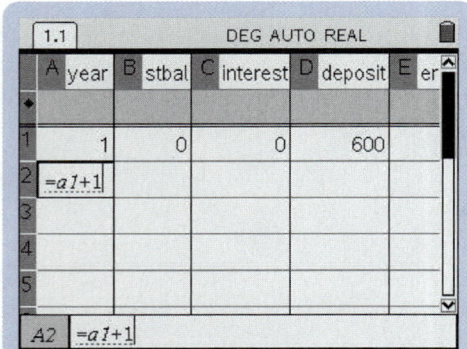

6. Press **enter**.

Using the Fill-Down Feature in a Spreadsheet, Lesson 5.12

1. Navigate to the cell you wish to fill down. Choose **Fill Down** from the **Data** menu.

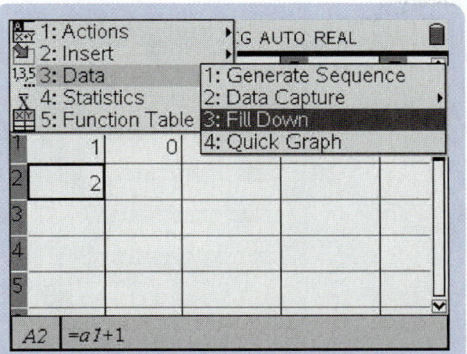

2. Press ▼ to highlight the desired range of cells. Press **enter**.

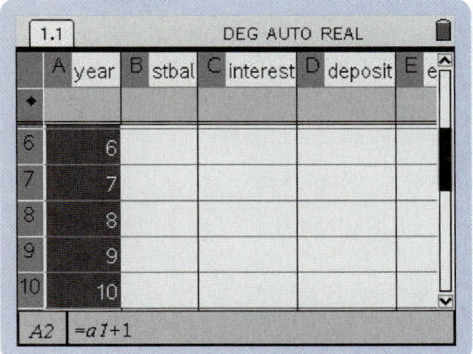

Generating a Scatter Plot, Lesson 3.09

1. Use existing data in a spreadsheet. Choose the **Scatter Plot** option in the **Graph Type** menu.

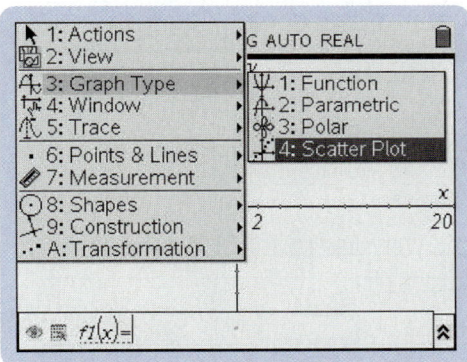

2. Select the desired variable from the *x*-value box. Press **enter**. Press **tab**. Do the same for the *y*-value box.

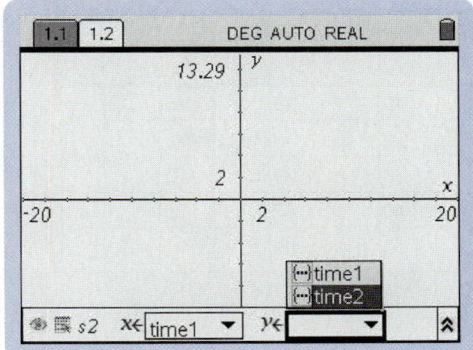

3. Choose **Zoom—Data** from the **Window** menu.

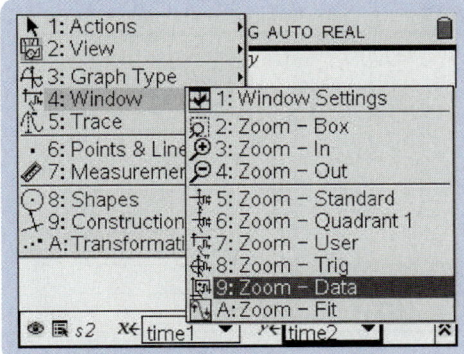

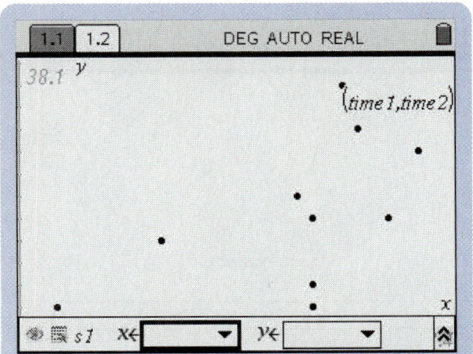

TI-Nspire™ Technology Handbook

Finding a Linear Regression, Lesson 4.15

1. Use existing data in a spreadsheet. Choose **Stat Calculations** in the **Statistics** menu. Choose **Linear Regression (mx+b)**.

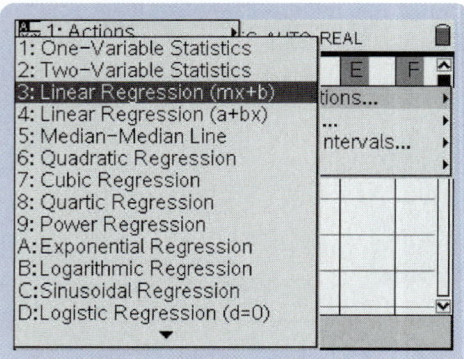

2. Select the desired spreadsheet columns in the **X List** and **Y List** fields.

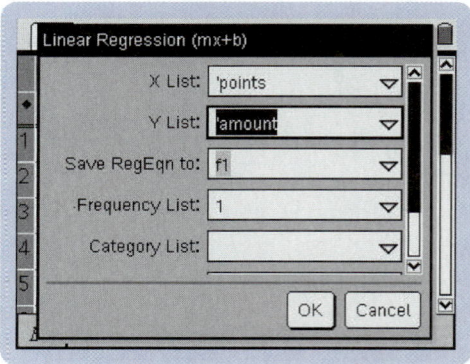

3. Press **enter** to store the linear regression in the spreadsheet.

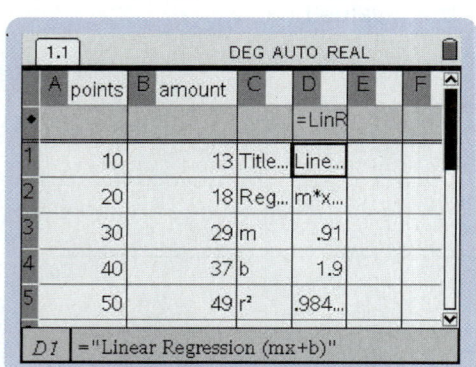

4. To graph the linear regression, navigate to the Graphs & Geometry screen. Choose **Function** from the **Graph Type** menu.

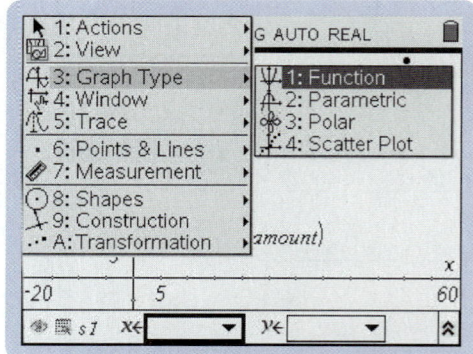

5. Tab down to the function entry line. Press ▲ to scroll up to **f1**.

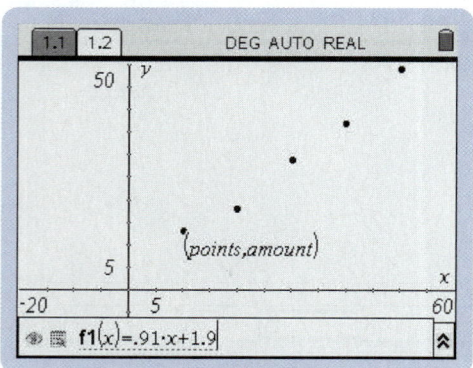

6. Press **enter** to graph the line.

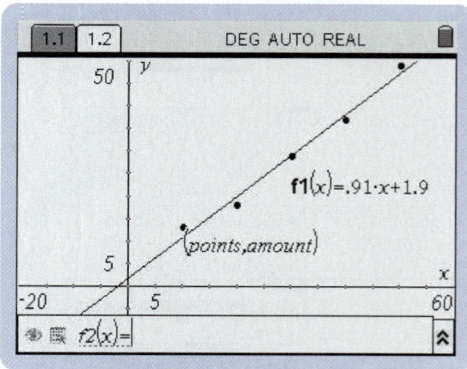

Making a Histogram, Lesson 3.07

1. Navigate to the column with the data you wish to graph. Choose the **Quick Graph** option from the **Data** menu.

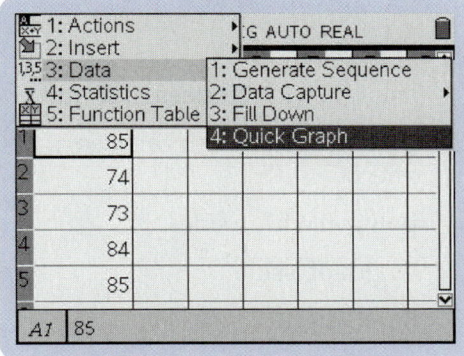

2. Choose the **Histogram** option from the **Plot Type** menu.

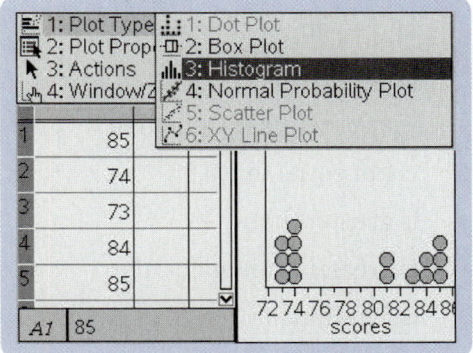

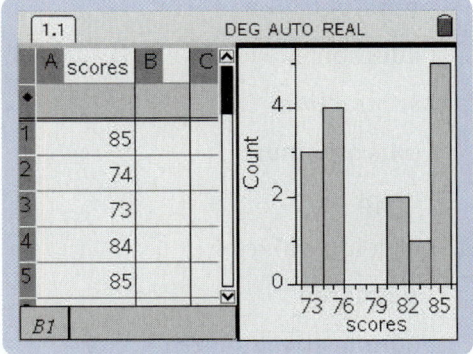

Making a Box-and-Whisker Plot, Lesson 3.08

1. Navigate to the column with the data you wish to graph. Choose the **Quick Graph** option from the **Data** menu. Choose **Box Plot** from the **Plot Type** menu.

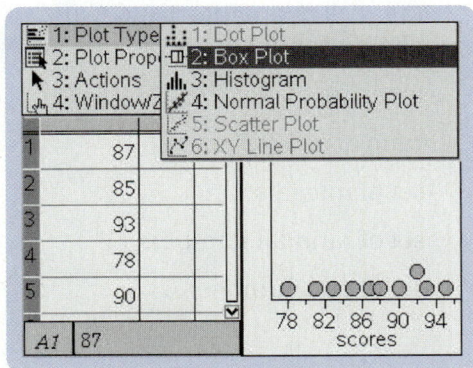

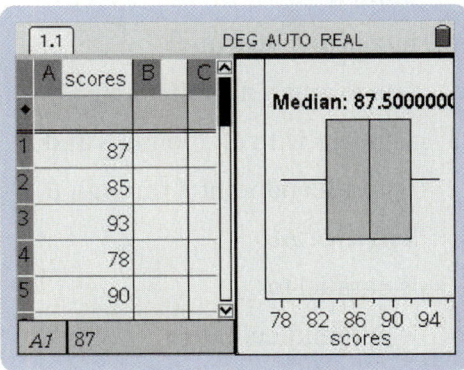

TI-Nspire™ Technology Handbook

Tables

Table 1 Math Symbols

Symbol	Meaning
...	and so on
=	is equal to
≈	is approximately equal to
≠	is not equal to
>	is greater than
≥	is greater than or equal to
<	is less than
≤	is less than or equal to
·, ×	multiplication
+	addition
−	subtraction
±	plus or minus
↦	maps to
$\mid x - y \mid$	absolute value of $(x - y)$
n^2	n squared
$\sqrt{x}$	nonnegative square root of x
Δ	difference (delta)
⇔	if and only if
{ }, ∅	empty set
∈	is an element of
A	point A
A'	image of A, A prime
$\overleftrightarrow{AB}$	line through A and B
$\overline{AB}$	segment with endpoints A and B
$\overrightarrow{AB}$	ray with endpoint A through B
AB	length of $\overline{AB}$
∥	is parallel to
⊥	is perpendicular to
≅	is congruent to
~	is similar to
∠A	angle A
∠ABC	angle with sides $\overrightarrow{BA}$ and $\overrightarrow{BC}$
$m\angle A$	measure of angle A
°	degree(s)
△ABC	triangle with vertices A, B, and C
▱$ABCD$	parallelogram with vertices A, B, C, and D
n-gon	polygon with n sides
s	length of a side
b	base length
h	height, length of an altitude
a	apothem
P	perimeter
A	area
B	area of a base
V	volume
d	diameter
r	radius
C	circumference
π	pi, the ratio of the circumference of a circle to its diameter
⊙A	circle with center A
$\overset{\frown}{AB}$	arc with endpoints A and B
$\overset{\frown}{ABC}$	arc with endpoints A and C and containing B
$m\overset{\frown}{AB}$	measure of $\overset{\frown}{AB}$
$a : b, \frac{a}{b}$	ratio of a to b
ℤ	set of integers
ℚ	set of rational numbers
ℝ	set of real numbers

Table 2 Measures

United States Customary	Metric

Length

12 inches (in.) = 1 foot (ft)	10 millimeters (mm) = 1 centimeter (cm)
36 in. = 1 yard (yd)	100 cm = 1 meter (m)
3 ft = 1 yard	1000 mm = 1 meter
5280 ft = 1 mile (mi)	1000 m = 1 kilometer (km)
1760 yd = 1 mile	

Area

144 square inches (in.^{2}) = 1 square foot (ft^2)	100 square millimeters (mm^2) = 1 square centimeter (cm^2)
9 ft^2 = 1 square yard (yd^2)	10,000 cm^2 = 1 square meter (m^2)
43,560 ft^2 = 1 acre (a)	10,000 m^2 = 1 hectare (ha)
4840 yd^2 = 1 acre	

Volume

1728 cubic inches (in.^{3}) = 1 cubic foot (ft^3)	1000 cubic millimeters (mm^3) = 1 cubic centimeter (cm^3)
27 ft^3 = 1 cubic yard (yd^3)	1,000,000 cm^3 = 1 cubic meter (m^3)

Liquid Capacity

8 fluid ounces (fl oz) = 1 cup (c)	1000 milliliters (mL) = 1 liter (L)
2 c = 1 pint (pt)	1000 L = 1 kiloliter (kL)
2 pt = 1 quart (qt)	
4 qt = 1 gallon (gal)	

Weight and Mass

16 ounces (oz) = 1 pound (lb)	1000 milligrams (mg) = 1 gram (g)
2000 pounds = 1 ton (t)	1000 g = 1 kilogram (kg)
	1000 kg = 1 metric ton

Temperature

32°F = freezing point of water	0°C = freezing point of water
98.6°F = normal body temperature	37°C = normal body temperature
212°F = boiling point of water	100°C = boiling point of water

Time

60 seconds (s) = 1 minute (min)	365 days = 1 year (yr)
60 minutes = 1 hour (h)	52 weeks (approx.) = 1 year
24 hours = 1 day (d)	12 months = 1 year
7 days = 1 week (wk)	10 years = 1 decade
4 weeks (approx.) = 1 month (mo)	100 years = 1 century

Table 3 Formulas From Geometry

You may need geometric formulas as you work through your algebra book. Here are some perimeter, area, and volume formulas.

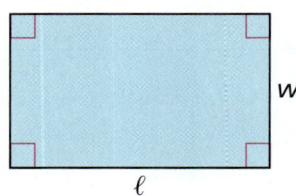

$P = 2\ell + 2w$
$A = \ell w$

Rectangle

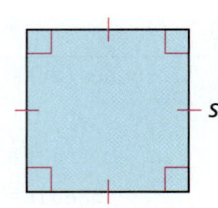

$P = 4s$
$A = s^2$

Square

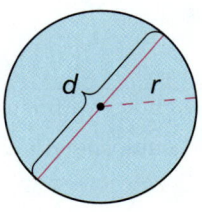

$C = 2\pi r$ or $C = \pi d$
$A = \pi r^2$

Circle

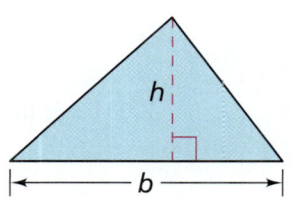

$A = \tfrac{1}{2}bh$

Triangle

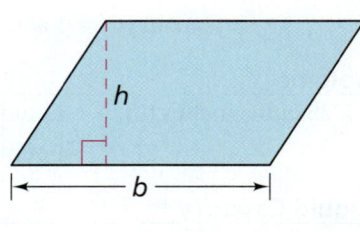

$A = bh$

Parallelogram

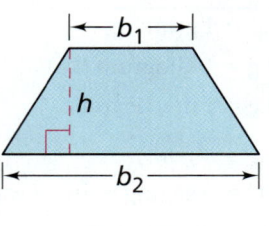

$A = \tfrac{1}{2}(b_1 + b_2)h$

Trapezoid

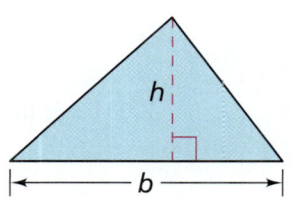

$V = Bh$
$V = \ell w h$

Rectangular Prism

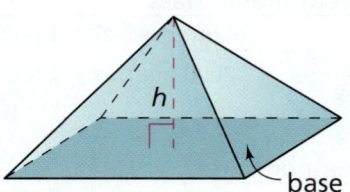

$V = \tfrac{1}{3}Bh$

Regular Pyramid

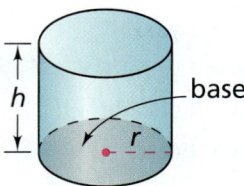

$V = Bh$
$V = \pi r^2 h$

Right Cylinder

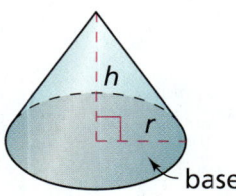

$V = \tfrac{1}{3}Bh$
$V = \tfrac{1}{3}\pi r^2 h$

Right Cone

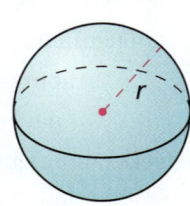

$V = \tfrac{4}{3}\pi r^3$

Sphere

Properties and Theorems

Chapter 1

Any-Order Addition Property in $\mathbb{Z}$, p. 28

The order in which you add two numbers in a sum does not affect the result.
$$5 + 3 = 8 \quad \text{and} \quad 3 + 5 = 8$$

Any-Grouping Addition Property in $\mathbb{Z}$, p. 28

When you add more than two numbers, the way you group them does not matter.
$$5 + (3 + 7) = 15 \quad \text{and} \quad (5 + 3) + 7 = 15$$

Any-Order Multiplication Property in $\mathbb{Z}$, p. 28

The order in which you multiply two numbers in a product does not affect the result.
$$5 \cdot (-3) = -15 \quad \text{and} \quad -3 \cdot (5) = -15$$

Any-Grouping Multiplication Property in $\mathbb{Z}$, p. 28

When you multiply more than two numbers, the way you group them does not matter.
$$4 \cdot (3 \cdot 5) = 60 \quad \text{and} \quad (4 \cdot 3) \cdot 5 = 60$$

Additive Identity Property in $\mathbb{Z}$, p. 30

When you add 0 to any number, the result is the number itself. The number 0 is the additive identity.
$$4 + 0 = 4 \quad \text{and} \quad 0 + 4 = 4$$

Multiplicative Identity Property in $\mathbb{Z}$, p. 30

When you multiply 1 by any number, the result is the number itself. The number 1 is the multiplicative identity.
$$3 \cdot 1 = 3 \quad \text{and} \quad 1 \cdot 3 = 3$$

Additive Inverse Property in $\mathbb{Z}$, p. 30

When you add any number to its opposite, the result is 0. If the sum of two numbers is 0, each number is the opposite of the other. Every integer has a unique additive inverse, or opposite.
$$5 + (-5) = 0 \quad -2 + (2) = 0$$

Distributive Property, p. 30

Multiplying a number by a sum is the same as multiplying the number by each term in the sum and then adding the results.
$$3 \cdot (4 + 5) = 3 \cdot 4 + 3 \cdot 5$$
$$3 \cdot (9) = 12 + 15$$
$$27 = 27$$

Chapter 2

Commutative Property of Addition, p. 111

For any numbers a and b, $a + b = b + a$.

Associative Property of Addition, p. 111

For any numbers a, b, and c,
$a + (b + c) = (a + b) + c$.

Commutative Property of Multiplication, p. 111

For any numbers a and b, $ab = ba$.

Associative Property of Multiplication, p. 111

For any numbers a, b, and c, $a(bc) = (ab)c$.

Additive Identity, p. 111

For any number a, $a + 0 = a$.

Additive Inverse, p. 111

For any number a, $a + (-a) = 0$
If $a + b = 0$, then $b = -a$.

Multiplicative Identity, p. 111

For any number a, $a \cdot 1 = a$.

Multiplicative Inverse, p. 111

For any nonzero number a, $a \cdot \frac{1}{a} = 1$.
If $ab = 1$, then $b = \frac{1}{a}$.

Distributive Property, p. 111

For any numbers a, b, and c,
$a(b + c) = ab + ac$.

Basic Moves for Solving Equations, p. 144
- For any three numbers a, b, and c, $a = b$ if and only if $a + c = b + c$.
- For any three numbers a, b, and c, where $c \neq 0$, $a = b$ if and only if $ac = bc$.

Theorem 2.1, p. 148

If a is any real number, then $a \cdot 0 = 0 \cdot a = 0$.

Theorem 2.2, p. 148

The number 0 does not have a reciprocal.

Theorem 2.3, p. 148

For all real numbers a and b, $a - b = a + (-b)$.

Chapter 3

Theorem 3.1, p. 203

The absolute value of a number x is its distance from 0 on the number line.

Theorem 3.2 Pythagorean Theorem, p. 206

In a right triangle in which the lengths of the legs are a and b, and the length of the hypotenuse is c, the side lengths have the relationship $a^2 + b^2 = c^2$.

Chapter 4

Slope, p. 329

In the Cartesian plane, the slope between two points with different x-coordinates is the change in their y-coordinates divided by the change in their x-coordinates.

For any two points $A(x_1, y_1)$ and $B(x_2, y_2)$,

$$m(A, B) = \frac{\text{rise}}{\text{run}} = \frac{\text{change in the } y\text{-coordinates}}{\text{change in the } x\text{-coordinates}}$$
$$= \frac{\Delta y}{\Delta x} = \frac{y_2 - y_1}{x_2 - x_1}$$

Average Speed, p. 334

$$\text{average speed} = \frac{\Delta \text{distance}}{\Delta \text{time}}$$

Theorem 4.1, p. 335

The slope between two points on a distance-time graph is the average speed of travel between those points.

Collinearity and Slope, p. 343

Three points A, B, and C, are collinear if and only if the slope between A and B is the same as the slope between B and C.

A, B, and C are collinear $\Leftrightarrow m(A, B) = m(B, C)$.

Theorem 4.2, p. 353

The slope between any two points on a line is constant.

Theorem 4.3, p. 382

If two distinct lines have the same slope, then they are parallel.

Theorem 4.4, p. 383

If two lines have different slopes, then they must intersect in exactly one point.

Theorem 4.5
Additive Property of Equality, p. 387

If $X = A$ and $Y = B$, then $X + Y = A + B$, where A, B, X, and Y can be any mathematical expressions.

Theorem 4.6, p. 391

Given the system $ax + by = e$ and $cx + dy = f$, where a, b, c, d, e, and f are known constants, the unique solution is
$(x, y) = \left(\frac{de - bf}{ad - bc}, \frac{af - ce}{ad - bc} \right)$ when $ad - bc \neq 0$.
If $ad - bc = 0$, the graphs of the two equations have the same slope, so they are either parallel (the system has no solutions) or the same (the system has infinitely many solutions).

Chapter 5

Theorem 5.1, p. 468

When the differences between consecutive outputs in a table are the same, and the differences between consecutive inputs are the same, you can write a linear function for the table.

Chapter 6

Theorem 6.1 The Law of Exponents, p. 520

For any number a and positive integers b and c, $a^b \cdot a^c = a^{b+c}$.

Theorem 6.2, p. 526

For any number $a \neq 0$ and positive integers b and c, where $b > c$, $\frac{a^b}{a^c} = a^{b-c}$.

Theorem 6.3, p. 527

For any number a and positive integers b and c, $(a^b)^c = a^{bc}$.

Theorem 6.4, p. 528

For any numbers a and b, and positive integer m, $(ab)^m = a^m b^m$.

Corollary 6.4.1, p. 528

For any numbers a and b ($b \neq 0$), and positive integer m, $\left(\frac{a}{b}\right)^m = \frac{a^m}{b^m}$.

Zero Exponent, p. 533

If $a \neq 0$, then $a^0 = 1$.

Negative Exponent, p. 533

If $a \neq 0$, then $a^{-m} = \frac{1}{a^m}$.

Scientific Notation, p. 537

A number written in scientific notation has the form $a \times 10^b$, or $-a \times 10^b$, where $1 \leq a < 10$ and b is an integer.

Square Root, p. 548

If $r \geq 0$, the square root of r, $\sqrt{r}$, is a real number s such that $s \geq 0$ and $s^2 = r$.

Theorem 6.5, p. 552

If x and y are any nonnegative numbers, then $\sqrt{x} \cdot \sqrt{y} = \sqrt{xy}$.

Theorem 6.6, p. 565

The sum of a rational number and an irrational number is irrational.

Corollary 6.5.1, p. 553

If a and b are nonnegative real numbers ($b \neq 0$), then $\frac{\sqrt{a}}{\sqrt{b}} = \sqrt{\frac{a}{b}}$.

nth root, p. 569

- If n is even, and if $a \geq 0$, then $\sqrt[n]{a}$ is the positive value of x that satisfies the equation $x^n = a$.
- If n is odd, then for any real number a, $\sqrt[n]{a}$ is the unique value of x that satisfies the equation $x^n = a$.

Exponential Growth and Decay, p. 584

An exponential function has the form $f(x) = a \cdot b^x$, where b is any positive real number.

Chapter 7

Form Implies Function Principle, p. 614

If two expressions are equivalent under the basic rules of algebra, they define functions that produce the same output for any given input.

Theorem 7.1 The Zero-Product Property, p. 619

The product of two numbers is zero if and only if one or both of the numbers is zero. If a and b are numbers, then

$$ab = 0 \Leftrightarrow a = 0 \text{ or } b = 0$$

Types of Polynomials, p. 637

- linear polynomial (degree 1)
- quadratic polynomial (degree 2)
- cubic polynomial (degree 3)
- quartic polynomial (degree 4)
- quintic polynomial (degree 5)

Theorem 7.2 The Difference of Squares, p. 661

For any numbers a and b,
$a^2 - b^2 = (a + b)(a - b)$.

Theorem 7.3
The Sum and Product Identity, p. 669

For any numbers a and b,
$x^2 + (a + b)x + ab = (x + a)(x + b)$.

Theorem 7.4, p. 673

For a given number s, if $a + b = s$, the maximum value of the product ab occurs when $a = b$.

Corollary 7.3.1
The Perfect Square Trinomial, p. 678

For any number a, $(x + a)^2 = x^2 + (2a)x + a^2$.

Chapter 8

Theorem 8.1, p. 700

If the equation $x^2 + rx + s = 0$ has real-number solutions, they are

$$x = \frac{-r + \sqrt{r^2 - 4s}}{2} \text{ and } x = \frac{-r - \sqrt{r^2 - 4s}}{2}$$

Theorem 8.2 The Quadratic Formula, p. 703

If the equation $ax^2 + bx + c = 0$ has real-number solutions, then

$$x = \frac{-b + \sqrt{b^2 - 4ac}}{2a} \text{ and } x = \frac{-b - \sqrt{b^2 - 4ac}}{2a}$$

Theorem 8.3
The Sum and Product Theorem, p. 708

If m and n are real numbers, the quadratic equation $x^2 - (m + n)x + mn = 0$ has m and n as roots.

Theorem 8.4
The Sum and Product of the Roots Theorem, p. 709

In a quadratic equation of the form $ax^2 + bx + c = 0$, the sum of the roots of the equation is $\frac{-b}{a}$.

The Average of the Roots, p. 724

For any quadratic, the average of the roots is the x-coordinate of the maximum or minimum of the function.

Theorem 8.5, p. 729

The graph of the equation $y - k = a(x - h)^2$ is a parabola with vertex (h, k). It has the same shape as the graph of the equation $y = ax^2$.

Theorem 8.6, p. 765

The solution to a linear inequality is a half-plane whose boundary is the graph of the corresponding equation. If the inequality uses < or >, the solution *does not* include the boundary line. If the inequality uses ≤ or ≥ the solution *does* include the boundary line.

Theorem 8.7, p. 775

For any quadratic function $p(x) = ax^2 + bx + c$, the second differences will be constant. The constant is $2a$, twice the coefficient of the squared term.

Theorem 8.8, p. 777

If a table has constant second differences, there is some quadratic function that agrees with the table.

Glossary

A

absolute value (p. 202) If x and y are two numbers, then the absolute value of $(x - y)$, written $|x - y|$, is the distance between the numbers x and y on a number line.

absolute zero (p. 132) Absolute zero is the temperature 0 kelvins.

additive identity (p. 30) The number 0 is the additive identity because when you add 0 to any number the result is the number itself.

additive inverse (p. 30) The additive inverse of a number is the number's opposite. The sum of a number and its additive inverse is 0.

algebraic expression See **expression**.

algorithm (p. 61) An algorithm is a set of ordered steps for solving a problem.

annual percentage rate (APR) (p. 562) The annual percentage rate is the yearly rate of growth.

annulus (p. 628) The annulus is the region between two circles with the same center.

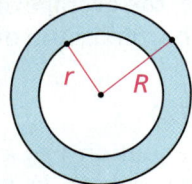

area (p. 100) Area is the number of square units contained within a two-dimensional figure.

association (p. 247) An association is a dependent relationship between two variables.

average (p. 223) Three types of averages used to describe data sets are the mean, the median, and the mode.

axiom (p. 29) An axiom is a basic fact that does not require justification.

axis See **coordinate plane**.

B

backtracking (p. 121) Backtracking is the process of solving an equation using, in reverse order, steps that undo the operations.

balance point (p. 408) The balance point is the point that represents the mean of data values.

base (p. 517) A base is a number that is multiplied repeatedly.

base case (p. 474) The base case is the starting output in a table for a recursively defined function.

basic moves for solving equations (p. 144) The two basic moves for solving equations state that you can add the same number to each side of an equation or multiply each side of an equation by the same number without changing the solutions of the equation.

basic rules of arithmetic (p. 28) The basic rules of arithmetic govern how addition and multiplication work for the set of integers.

binary operation (p. 112) A binary operation takes two numbers and produces one number.

binomial (p. 669) A binomial is a polynomial expression with exactly two terms.

box-and-whisker plot (p. 237) A box-and-whisker plot is a data display that uses quartiles to form the center box and the maximum and minimum values to form the whiskers.

Players' Heights

66 67 68 69 70 71 72 73 74 75
Height (in.)

C

Celsius (p. 131) The Celsius scale is a temperature scale based on 100 equal parts between the boiling point and the freezing point of water.

closed form (p. 496) You can write a function $g(x)$ in closed form as one expression. A closed form uses direct calculation to find an output for any input.

coefficient (p. 636) A coefficient is the number factor in a monomial.

collinear (p. 342) Collinear points are points that lie on the same line.

combining like terms (p. 104) Combining like terms is the process of grouping like terms to simplify an expression.

composition of functions (p. 441) A composition of functions is a combination of two or more functions, in which you apply one function to an input and then apply the second function to the output of the first.

compound interest (p. 579) Compound interest is interest calculated on the current balance, including the previously paid interest.

conjecture (p. 27) A conjecture is a statement that you believe to be true based on specific examples.

consecutive integers (p. 616) Consecutive integers are integers that differ by 1.

constant (p. 294) A constant is a numerical invariant.

constant ratio (p. 591) A ratio table shows a constant ratio if all the values in the division column are equal.

converges (p. 598) When the outputs of an iteration get closer and closer to a number, the iteration converges to that number.

coordinate (p. 189) A coordinate is the unique number that describes the location of a point on the number line.

The point on the line corresponds to the number 2.5.

coordinate plane (p. 189) The coordinate plane, also called the Cartesian plane, is a two-dimensional system for describing location. The most common system assigns coordinates to points in the plane using two number lines that are perpendicular to each other. The horizontal number line is the *x-axis* and the vertical number line is the *y-axis*. The intersection of the axes is the *origin*.

Coordinate Plane

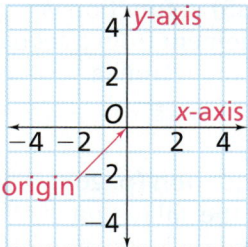

counterexample (p. 120) A counterexample is an example that proves a statement is false.

correlation coefficient (p. 256) The correlation coefficient is a numerical calculation that measures the strength of associations.

cube (p. 517) To cube a number, you multiply the number times the number times the number.

cubic polynomial (p. 637) A cubic polynomial is a polynomial of degree 3.

cutoff point (p. 401) A cutoff point is an intersection point of two graphs used to help find the solution of an inequality in one variable. The *x*-coordinates of all the cutoff points divide the number line into regions to check.

D

decimal expansion (p. 41) The decimal expansion of a number gives the address of the number on a number line. The number is written as a sum of units, tenths, hundredths, and so on.

decimal representation (p. 42) The decimal representation of a number is the decimal form of the number. The decimal representation of a number can be used to approximate the value of, for example, a fraction or a square root.

degree of a monomial (p. 636) The degree of a monomial is the sum of the exponents of each variable within the monomial.

degree of a polynomial (p. 637) The degree of a polynomial is the greatest degree among all the monomials in the polynomial.

difference (p. 465) In a function table, the difference is the change between two consecutive outputs in the table.

direct variation (p. 289) A direct variation is the relation of two variables that are in a constant ratio.

domain (p. 445) The domain of a function is the set of inputs of the function.

dot plot (p. 230) A dot plot is a graphical representation of a data set that shows data points on a simple scale.

E

elimination method (p. 388) The elimination method for solving a system of equations is adding or subtracting two equations to produce a new equation in which one of the variables is eliminated.

ellipse (p. 281) An ellipse is an oval shape that has some unique properties, including both vertical and horizontal symmetry.

empty set (p. 127) The empty set (or null set) is a set with no elements. The solution set to an equation with no solutions is the empty set, also called the null set. In symbols, it is { } or ∅.

end behavior (p. 782) The end behavior for an iteration is the long-term result of iterating a function of an initial value.

equation (p. 126) An equation is a mathematical sentence that states that two quantities are equal.

equivalent fractions (p. 37) Equivalent fractions are two or more fractions that refer to the same location on a number line.

evaluate (p. 98) To evaluate an expression, replace the variable(s) with the given value(s) of the variable(s) and simplify.

expand an expression (p. 609) To expand an expression, multiply where parentheses indicate multiplication.

expansion box (p. 72) An expansion box is a table in which numbers being multiplied are written in place-value parts along the top and down the side of the table. Each pair of place-value parts is multiplied and the products are added to give the final product.

exponent (p. 517) An exponent is a superscript number that indicates how many times to use the base as a factor.

exponential decay (p. 584) A situation modeled with a function of the form $y = ab^x$, where $a > 0$ and $0 < b < 1$.

exponential function (p. 499) An exponential function is a function in which each output is found by multiplying the previous output by some value.

exponential growth (p. 584) A situation modeled with a function of the form $y = ab^x$, where $a > 0$ and $b > 1$.

expression (p. 93) An expression is a mathematical phrase that uses operations to combine numbers and variables.

extension of a rule (p. 20) The extension of a rule extends a process from one group to a larger group. For example, you can extend the basic rules of arithmetic for whole numbers to integers.

F

factor an expression (p. 620) To factor an expression, write an expression as a product of two or more expressions.

Fahrenheit (p. 131) Fahrenheit is a temperature scale in which the freezing point of water is 32° and the boiling point of water is 212°.

false position (p. 164) The false position method is a process for equation solving in which you choose a convenient answer and adjust it until the you find the correct answer.

family (p. 357) A family is a collection or a set in which all the elements share a common form.

Fermat number (p. 629) A Fermat number is any number in the form $2^{2^n} + 1$. A *Fermat prime* is a Fermat number that is also a prime number.

first quartile See **five-number summary**.

fitting line (p. 406) A fitting line is a line that comes close to the data points in a scatter plot.

five-number summary (p. 237) A five-number summary is an overview of a sorted set of data that uses five key values.

- The *minimum* is the least value in the set.
- The *first quartile* is the data value that is greater than or equal to the lowest 25% of the data values.
- The *median* is the middle value of the set.
- The *third quartile* is the data value that is greater than or equal to the lowest 75% of the data.
- The *maximum* is the greatest value in the set.

fixed point (p. 500) A fixed point is an input that remains unchanged by a function.

frequency table (p. 223) A frequency table for a data set is a list of categories that classifies the number of data that occur in each category.

What Do You Call Carbonated Drinks?

State	"Pop"	"Soda"	"Coke"	Other
Minnesota	4265	630	39	92
New York	3321	7364	262	200
Georgia	49	346	2196	149
Washington	2678	714	105	98

SOURCE: Alan McConchie's Survey

function (p. 435) A function is a rule that assigns each element from a set of inputs to exactly one element from a set of outputs.

G

graph of an equation (p. 268) The graph of an equation is the collection of all points with coordinates that make the equation true.

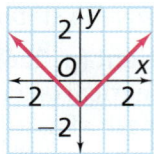

The coordinates of the points on the graph make $y = |x| - 1$ true.

graph of a function (p. 450) The graph of a function g is the graph of the equation $y = g(x)$.

graph of a number (p. 189) A graph is the point that represents a number on the number line.

greatest common factor (p. 625) The greatest common factor of an expression is the factor common to all terms that has the greatest coefficient and the greatest exponent.

growth rate See **annual percentage rate.**

guess-check-generalize method (p. 162) The guess-check-generalize method is a problem-solving method used to find the equation for a word problem. You guess the answer to the problem and keep track of the steps you use to check the guess. You repeat this process until you are able to generalize the steps with a variable and write the appropriate equation.

H

hexagon (p. 609) A hexagon is a polygon with exactly six sides.

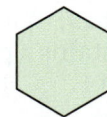

histogram (p. 231) A histogram is a graphical representation of a data set that shows frequencies of data as bars.

I

identity (p. 613) An identity is a statement that two expressions are equivalent under the basic rules of algebra.

image (p. 201) The image of a point is the matching point after a transformation.

in terms of (p. 166) To solve an equation for one variable in terms of another, isolate the variable you want to solve for on one side of the equation and the expression containing the other variable on the other side of the equation.

independent (p. 247) Independent describes a relationship between two variables that are not associated.

inequality (p. 398) An inequality is a statement that compares two expressions using an inequality symbol.

initial value (p. 782) The initial value is the value chosen for x_0 when iterating the function $x \mapsto f(x)$.

input (p. 425) The input of a function is a value to which you apply the function.

integer (p. 28) An integer is a number in the set $\mathbb{Z} = \{\cdots, -3, -2, -1, 0, 1, 2, 3, \cdots\}$

interquartile range (p. 239) The interquartile range of a data set is the difference between the third quartile and the first quartile.

intersection point (p. 279) An intersection point is a point where two or more graphs intersect.

inverse variation (p. 291) An inverse variation is the relation between two variables that have a constant product.

irrational number (p. 563) An irrational number is a real number that is not a rational number. An irrational number is a real number that you cannot write as a fraction with integers in both the numerator and denominator.

iterate a function (p. 598) To iterate a function, you choose a starting number and repeatedly apply the function.

K

kelvin (p. 132) A kelvin is the unit of measure in the Kelvin temperature scale.

Koch snowflake (p. 503) A Koch snowflake begins with a downward-pointing equilateral triangle. The middle third of each line segment is replaced with two sides of an equilateral triangle pointing outward. The pattern repeats for each new level of the Koch snowflake.

L

lattice point (p. 319) The lattice point is a point that has integers for both coordinates.

leading coefficient (p. 775) The leading coefficient of a polynomial is the coefficient of the highest degree term of the polynomial.

least common denominator (p. 68) The least common denominator of two or more fractions is the least common multiple of their denominators.

like terms (p. 104) Like terms are terms in which the variable factors are exactly the same.

line of best fit (p. 409) A line of best fit is the graph of the linear equation that most accurately shows the relationship between two sets of data.

line of symmetry (p. 730) The line of symmetry of a parabola acts as a mirror for a parabola and passes through the vertex.

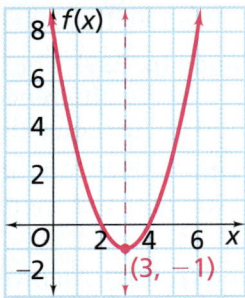

line segment (p. 192) A line segment is a part of a line consisting of two endpoints and all of the points between the two endpoints.

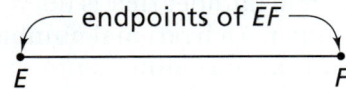

linear equation (p. 149) A linear equation is an equation in which the variable terms are not raised to a power. The graph of a linear equation is a line.

linear function (p. 461) A linear function is a function with a graph that is a line. For a linear function, the differences between consecutive outputs are the same, and the differences between consecutive inputs are the same.

linear polynomial (p. 637) A linear polynomial is a polynomial of degree 1.

linear regression (p. 410) Linear regression is the method for finding a line of best fit.

lowest terms (p. 38) A fraction is in lowest terms when the numerator and denominator have no common factor other than 1.

#

maximum of a data set *See* **five-number summary.**

maximum of a function (p. 721) The maximum of a function is the greatest output of the function. The maximum occurs at the point on the graph of the function where the graph "turns around" and heads downward. This point is the *vertex* of the parabola.

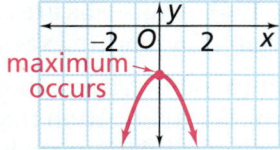

mean (p. 223) To find the mean of a set of numbers, divide the sum of the numbers by the number of values in the set.

median (p. 223) The median is the middle value in an ordered set of values. If there is an even number of values, the median is the mean of the two middle values. *See also* **five-number summary.**

minimum of a data set *See* **five-number summary.**

minimum of a function (p. 721) The minimum of a function is the least output of the function. The minimum occurs at the point on the graph of the function where the graph "turns around" and heads upward. This point is the *vertex* of the parabola.

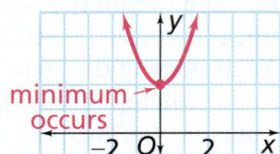

mode (p. 223) The mode is the data value that occurs most often in a data set.

monic (p. 669) A monic polynomial is a polynomial with a leading coefficient of 1.

monic equation (p. 699) A monic equation is an equation that contains a polynomial with a leading coefficient of 1.

monomial (p. 636) A monomial is the product of a number, the *coefficient*, and one or more variables raised to nonnegative integer powers.

multiplicative identity (p. 30) The number 1 is the multiplicative identity because when you multiply any number by 1 the result is the number itself.

multiplicative inverse (p. 111) The multiplicative inverse of a nonzero number is the number's reciprocal. The product of a nonzero number and its multiplicative inverse is 1.

N

negatively associated (p. 255) Two variables are negatively associated when large values of the first variable tend to occur with small values of the second, and small values of the first variable tend to occur with large values of the second.

negative exponent (a^{-m}) (p. 533) If $a \neq 0$, then $a^{-m} = \frac{1}{a^m}$.

negative number (p. 12) Negative numbers are the numbers less than zero.

noncollinear points (p. 612) Noncollinear points are three or more points that are not on the same line.

nonmonic quadratic (p. 701) A nonmonic quadratic is a quadratic with a leading coefficient that is a number other than 1.

normal form (p. 645) A polynomial is in normal form if it has been expanded and the monomial terms are arranged in order from greatest degree to least degree.

nth root (p. 569) The nth root is the value of x that satisfies the equation $x^n = a$. If n is even, the nth root is the positive value of x that satisfies the equation.

null set See **empty set**.

number line (p. 12) A number line is a line that represents real numbers and continues forever in two directions.

O

opposites (p. 13) Two numbers are opposites if they are equidistant from zero and on opposite sides of zero on a number line. The sum of opposites is zero.

ordered pair (p. 189) An ordered pair describes the location of a point, or the point's graph, in the coordinate plane. The first number in the ordered pair, the *x-coordinate*, tells how far the point is to the right or left of the origin, measuring along the *x*-axis. The second number, the *y-coordinate*, tells how far the point is above or below the origin, measuring along the *y*-axis.

The point in the plane corresponds to two numbers, 2 and 4.

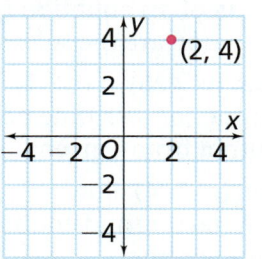

origin (p. 189) The origin is the intersection of the *x*-axis and the *y*-axis. See also **coordinate plane**.

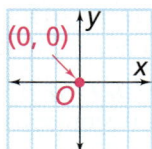

outlier (p. 253) An outlier of a data set is a data point that is clearly separated from the rest of the data.

output (p. 425) The output of a function is the resulting value after a function is evaluated for a specific input.

P

parabola (p. 727) A parabola is the graph of a quadratic equation.

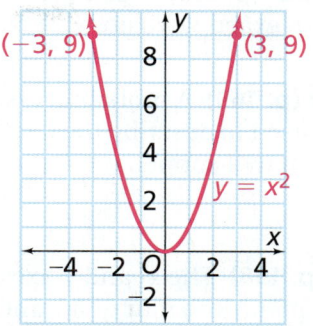

parallel lines (p. 355) Parallel lines are lines in the same plane that do not intersect.

parameter (p. 637) A parameter is an unknown coefficient.

perfect square (p. 179) A perfect square is an integer that is the square of another integer.

perfect square trinomial (p. 678) A perfect square trinomial is a trinomial with identical factors.

perimeter (p. 107) The perimeter of a polygon is the sum of the lengths of the polygon's sides.

period (p. 505) A period is the length of a repeating sequence.

periodic function (p. 501) A periodic function is a function in which the outputs repeat in a pattern.

place-value part (p. 61) A place-value part is a number that has a single leading digit followed by some number of zeros.

point-tester (p. 268) A point-tester is an equation used to determine whether particular points are on a graph.

polynomial (p. 637) A polynomial is a monomial or a sum of two or more monomials.

polynomial equation (p. 674) A polynomial equation is an equation in which a polynomial is equal to 0.

positively associated (p. 255) Two variables are positively associated when large values of the first variable tend to occur with large values of the second, and small values of the first variable tend to occur with small values of the second.

positive number (p. 12) A positive number is a number greater than 0.

prime factorization (p. 545) A prime factorization is a number written as a product of its prime factors.

prime notation (p. 197) Prime notation uses a superscript tick mark next to a point's letter name to indicate a transformed point.

prime number (p. 233) A prime number is a number with exactly two positive factors, 1 and itself.

probability (p. 169) A probability is a fraction or decimal used to describe the likelihood that a specific event will happen.

Q

quadrant (p. 198) The x- and y-axes divide the coordinate plane into four quadrants.

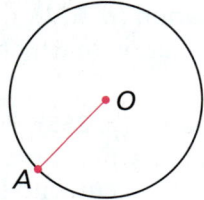

quadratic expression (p. 672) A quadratic expression is a polynomial expression in one variable in which the degree is 2.

quadratic polynomial (p. 637) A quadratic polynomial is a polynomial of degree 2.

quartic polynomial (p. 637) A quartic polynomial is a polynomial of degree 4.

quintic polynomial (p. 637) A quintic polynomial is a polynomial of degree 5.

R

radical (p. 568) A radical is a number such as a square root, a cube root, a fourth root, and so on.

radius (p. 286) A radius of a circle is a segment with endpoints at the center of the circle and on the circle. The radius is also the length of a segment from the center of the circle to the circle.

range of a data set (p. 239) The range of a data set is the difference between the maximum and minimum values of the data.

range of a function (p. 445) The range of a function is the set of outputs produced by the function.

rational number p. 561 A rational number is a number that you can express as $\frac{a}{b}$, where a and b are integers and b is not equal to 0. The symbol $\mathbb{Q}$ denotes the set of rational numbers.

real number (p. 561) The set of real numbers $\mathbb{R}$ is the set of all positive numbers, their opposites, and 0.

recipe (p. 14) A recipe is a set of steps to a desired result.

reciprocal (p. 77) The reciprocal of a fraction is the result you get by exchanging the numerator and the denominator. When you multiply a number by its reciprocal, the product is 1.

recursive rule (p. 474) A recursive rule is a description that tells how to get an output from previous outputs.

repeating decimal (p. 43) A repeating decimal is a decimal that has a set of digits that repeats infinitely many times.

reversible operation (p. 120) An operation is reversible if there is a second operation that always brings you back to the situation before the first operation.

rise (p. 324) Rise is the difference between the starting and ending points on a vertical number line.

roots of an equation (p. 706) The roots of an equation are the solutions of the equation.

rule (p. 425) A rule is the set of operations that a function machine performs to produce an output from a given input.

run (p. 324) Run is the difference between the starting and ending points on a horizontal number line.

S

scatter plot (p. 253) A scatter plot is a graph that shows each pair of related data as a point in the coordinate plane.

scientific notation (p. 537) A number in scientific notation is in the form $a \times 10^b$ or $-a \times 10^b$, where $1 \leq a < 10$ and b is an integer.

second difference (p. 774) A second difference is the difference between consecutive values in the first difference column in a difference table.

seed value See **initial value**.

slope (p. 329) The slope between two points with different x-coordinates is the change in the y-coordinates divided by the change in the x-coordinates of the points.

slope of a line (p. 353) The slope of a line is the slope between any two points on the line.

solution (p. 126) A solution is a value of a variable that makes an equation true.

solution set (p. 127) A solution set is the collection of all solutions of an equation or inequality.

solve (p. 162) To solve an equation, find all the numbers that make the equation true.

speed (p. 333) Speed is the rate at which distance traveled changes.

square (p. 517) To square a number, you multiply the number times itself.

square root (p. 548) A square root of a number n is a positive number that you multiply by itself to get the product n.

starting value See **initial value**.

stem-and-leaf display (p. 232) A stem-and-leaf display is a graph that organizes the leading digits of data as stems. The remaining digits become leaves. In an ordered stem-and-leaf display, the leaves are sorted and written in ascending order.

Ages of Winners of Best Actor in a Leading Role

2	9
3	2 7 8 1 6 7 8
4	3 2 5 6 0 7 3 5
5	1 4 2
6	1 0

Key: 2 | 9 means 29 years

subscript (p. 329) The subscripts "1" and "2" indicate that x_1 and x_2 represent different variables.

substitution method (p. 375) The substitution method for solving a system of equations is solving one equation for one of its variables and then replacing that variable in the other equation with the resulting expression.

system of equations (p. 378) A system of equations is a group of equations with the same variables. A solution of the system is a set of values of the variables that make all the equations true.

T

tetrahedron (p. 655) A tetrahedron is a four-sided solid.

theorem (p. 148) A theorem is a fact that follows logically from other known facts.

third quartile See **five-number summary**.

transformation (p. 196) A transformation is a rule that takes a set of points and produces another set of points.

trinomial (p. 674) A trinomial is a polynomial expression with exactly three terms.

two-way frequency table (p. 246) A two-way frequency table displays the distribution for two categorical variables.

V

value (p. 387) A value is a variable, a number, or any mathematical expression.

variable (p. 93) A variable is a placeholder for an unknown number.

vertex (p. 728) A vertex is the maximum or minimum point of a parabola.

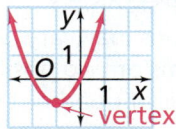

vertex form (p. 729) The vertex form of a quadratic function is $y = a(x - h)^2 + k$.

X

x-axis See **coordinate plane**.

x-coordinate See **ordered pair**.

x-intercept (p. 358) An x-intercept is a point where a graph crosses the x-axis.

Y

y-axis See **coordinate plane**.

y-coordinate See **ordered pair**.

y-intercept (p. 358) A y-intercept is a point where a graph crosses the y-axis.

Z

ℤ (p. 28) ℤ is the set of integers.

zero exponent (a^0) (p. 533) If $a \neq 0$, then $a^0 = 1$.

Zero-Product Property (p. 619) If a and b are numbers, then $ab = 0 \Leftrightarrow a = 0$ or $b = 0$.

zero (p. 732) A zero of a function $f(x)$ is a root of the equation $f(x) = 0$. The zeros correspond to the x-intercepts of the graph of the function.

Selected Answers

Chapter 1
Lesson 1.01
On Your Own
6. It increases by 2; moving up is the same as adding 1, and moving right is the same as adding 1.

Lesson 1.02
Check Your Understanding
1. a. on 6/18, with check number 003 **b.** More than $160 **c.** Answers may vary. Sample: He could deposit more money into his account. **2. a.** 36°F **b.** −11°F **3. a.** 3 **b.** 14 **c.** −3 **d.** −1 **e.** Subtract 9. **f.** 5

On Your Own
4. a. 3 **c.** 15 **e.** Subtract 7.

Lesson 1.03
Check Your Understanding
1. a–d. Explanations may vary. Samples are given. **a.** True; sums of two positive integers are in the upper right quadrant of the extended addition table, where all entries are positive numbers. **b.** True; sums of two negative integers are in the lower left quadrant of the extended addition table, where all entries are negative numbers. **c.** False; for example, $-5 + 7 = 2$. **d.** False; for example, $-7 + 5 = -2$. **2.** $3 + (-11) = (-4) + (-4)$ $(-23) + 13 = 1 + (-11)$ $20 + (-10) = 2 + 8$ $32 + (-18) = 16 + (-2)$ **3.** Answers may vary. Sample: Find the answer to the addition problem $11 + (-5)$. **4.** Answers may vary. Sample: To evaluate $a - b$, locate a in the addition table, and move down b entries.
5. a, c, e **6.** 143 will show up in every column. The 143's form a diagonal, down and to the right.

On Your Own
7. a. 6 **c.** −7 **e.** 0 **9. a.** 0 **11.** The positive numbers are located above the "0 diagonal" from Exercise 10; a large triangle in the upper right part of the table.

Lesson 1.04
Check Your Understanding
1. a. 1444 **b.** −1444 **c.** −1444 **d.** 1444 **e.** −1444 **f.** 1444 **2. a.** 4 **b.** 4 **c.** −4 **d.** −4 **e.** $\frac{1}{4}$ **f.** $-\frac{1}{4}$
3. 9 and 9 **4. a.** Answers may vary. Sample: $4 \cdot (3) = 12$. Moving down 1 entry subtracts 4, so moving down 6 entries to −3 subtracts 24. Therefore $4 \cdot (-3) = -12$. **b.** Answers may vary. Sample: $4 \cdot (-3) = -12$. Moving left 1 entry adds 3, so moving left 8 entries adds 24. Therefore $-4 \cdot (-3) = 12$. **5.** 8 times; $10 \cdot 1 = 10$, $5 \cdot 2 = 10$, $2 \cdot 5 = 10$, $1 \cdot 10 = 10$, $(-10) \cdot (-1) = 10$, $(-5) \cdot (-2) = 10$, $(-2) \cdot (-5) = 10$, $(-1) \cdot (-10) = 10$ **6.** 72 **7. a.** 0 **b.** 1

On Your Own
8. b, d. Examples may vary. Samples are given. **b.** False; for example, $(-2)(-3) = 6$ and $(-2)(-5) = 10$. **d.** True; for example, $(-2)(3) = -6$ and $(2)(-5) = -10$. **9.** 4 and 4 **12.** in the upper right quadrant and the lower left quadrant; large squares in the upper right and lower left quadrants

14. Answers may vary. Sample: As you move up the diagonal, the differences between each entry and the previous one are successive even numbers, starting with 4.

Lesson 1.05
Check Your Understanding
1. Answers may vary. Sample: The table is symmetric about the diagonal along the perfect squares; therefore, the order of the multiplication does not matter. **2.** Answers may vary. Sample: The numbers in the 1 column of the multiplication table are identical to the numbers directly to the right in the vertical axis, and the numbers in the 1 row of the multiplication table are identical to the numbers directly below in the vertical axis.
3. 5; $5 + (-5) = 0$ **4.** all but inverses of addition

On Your Own
5. Answers may vary. Samples are given. **a.** $10 \cdot 473$ **c.** $42 \cdot (200 + 3)$ **6. a.** 39 **e.** −18

Lesson 1.06
On Your Own
5. a–d.

[number line showing: 2, d. $2\frac{1}{4}$, c. $2\frac{1}{2}$, b. 3, a. $3\frac{1}{2}$, 4]

6. a.

[number line from 0 to 72, with marks at 24, 48, 72]

Lesson 1.07
Check Your Understanding
1. $\frac{1}{7}, \frac{3}{7}, \frac{4}{7}, \frac{6}{7}, \frac{9}{7}, \frac{10}{7}$ **2.** $\frac{0}{6}$ or 0, $\frac{1}{6}, \frac{4}{6}$ or $\frac{2}{3}, \frac{5}{6}, \frac{6}{6}$ or 1 **3.** $\frac{0}{3}$ or 0, $\frac{1}{3}, \frac{2}{3}, \frac{4}{3}$ or $1\frac{1}{3}, \frac{5}{3}, \frac{5}{3}$ or $1\frac{2}{3}$
4. a. 8 **b.** 25 **c.** 9 **d.** 14 **e.** 51 **f.** 6 **g.** $2\frac{1}{2}$ **h.** 6

i. 33 **5.** The numbers are not in order.
6.

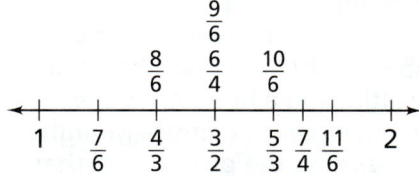

a. $\frac{8}{6} = \frac{4}{3}, \frac{9}{6} = \frac{6}{4} = \frac{3}{2}, \frac{10}{6} = \frac{5}{3}$ **b.** $\frac{7}{6}$
7. Answers may vary.
Sample: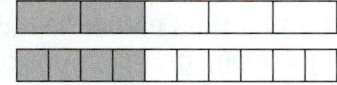

On Your Own
8. Answers may vary. Sample: $\frac{7}{3}, \frac{-7}{-3}, \frac{14}{6}, \frac{-42}{-24}$
11. a. Q **e.** R   **14. a.** 2 **c.** 5

Lesson 1.08
Check Your Understanding
1. a. 0.4 **b.** 0.66666 . . . , repeating decimal
c. 0.875 **d.** 2.25 **e.** 0.55555 . . . , repeating decimal **f.** 0.63636 . . . , repeating decimal
2. a. $\frac{12}{25}$ **b.** $\frac{247}{100}$ **c.** $\frac{1}{5}$ **d.** $\frac{3333}{1000}$ **e.** $\frac{19}{5}$ **f.** $-\frac{1369}{1000}$
g. $\frac{8}{9}$ **h.** $\frac{41}{99}$ **3.** Yes, and yes; explanations may vary. Sample: The mean of two numbers always exists and is always between the two numbers.   **4. a–c.** Answers may vary. Samples are given. **a.** 0.991, 0.992 **b.** 0.99991, 0.99992
c. 0.9999991, 0.9999992 **d.** Yes; explanations may vary. Sample: You can divide the segment between the two points on a number line into thirds. The points of division are two numbers between the original two.
5.

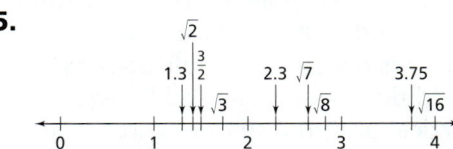

6. a. The scale is way off. **b.** Either 3 will be indistinguishable from 0, or the number line will be extremely long.

On Your Own
7. 0.06, 0.09, 0.12, 0.18, 0.21, 0.24, 0.27
9. a. $\frac{163}{100}$ **e.** $-\frac{1}{8}$ **12.** 3.009, 3.08, 3.18, 3.5999, 3.7

Lesson 1.09
Check Your Understanding
1. a.

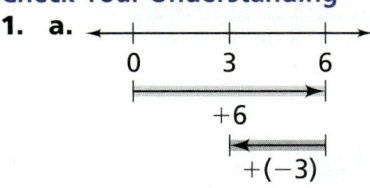

b.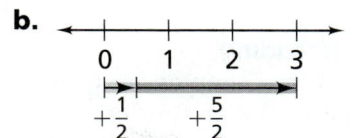

c.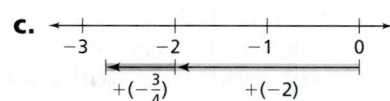

d.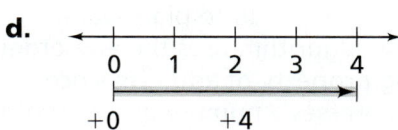

2. Answers may vary. Sample:

3. a. Q **b.** S **c.** P **d.** R   **4.** Tony lined up the tips of the arrows.   **5. a.** $\frac{8}{3}$ **b.** $\frac{1}{2}$ **c.** $\frac{1}{3}$ **d.** $\frac{5}{77}$ **e.** 0
6. a. 1, $\frac{3}{2}$, 2, $\frac{5}{2}$, 3 **b.** $\frac{1}{4}, \frac{3}{4}, 1, \frac{5}{4}, \frac{3}{2}$ **c.** $\frac{1}{8}, \frac{3}{8}, \frac{1}{2}, \frac{5}{8}, \frac{3}{4}$
d. $\frac{1}{9}, \frac{2}{9}, \frac{1}{3}, \frac{4}{9}, \frac{5}{9}$

On Your Own
9. a. 0.4, 0.6, 0.8, 1, 1.2
c. 1.1, 3.3, 4.4, 5.5, 6.6   **10. a.** 0 **d.** 8

Lesson 1.10
Check Your Understanding
1. a. 8 **b.** 7 **c.** 12 **d.** 5   **2.** Moving the negative sign rotates the rectangle, but the area remains the same.   **3.** If 0 had an inverse, the product of the inverse and zero would be 1. But the product of any number and 0 is always 0.   **4. a.** V **b.** Y **c.** U **d.** X   **5. a.** $\frac{1}{4}$ **b.** 2 **c.** 4
d. $\frac{1}{2}$ **e.** $-\frac{1}{9}$ **f.** $-\frac{1}{3}$ **g.** Answers may vary. Sample: First find the number that must equal the quantity in the parentheses in order to make the equation true. Then find the number to fill in the blank that would make the sum inside the parentheses equal the number you got in the first step.

On Your Own
6. a. 6 **d.** $\frac{8}{15}$ **8. a.** V **c.** Y

Lesson 1.11
On Your Own
3. $A = 2, B = 3, C = 9$ **5. a.** $94.97

Lesson 1.12
Check Your Understanding
1–7. Answers may vary. Samples are given.
1. This algorithm uses the any-order, any-grouping property of addition. It works best with summands that are close to round numbers. **2.** This algorithm uses the any-order property of addition. It works best with a sum featuring several summands, where certain pairs of them add to place-value parts. **3.** This algorithm uses the any-order, any-grouping property of addition since borrowing expresses a number as a sum of two summands, one of which you then add to a neighboring number in the subtraction problem. This algorithm will work well in nearly any situation, though others may work better in some cases. **4.** This algorithm relies on the any-grouping property of addition along with the property that subtraction is the same as adding the opposite. It works best when the difference between the two numbers is less than either of them.
5. This algorithm uses the any-order property of addition, since it does not matter which place values you add first. This algorithm is convenient for adding numbers in your head.
6. This operation works because addition and subtraction are inverse operations. This algorithm is convenient for adding numbers in your head. **7.** This algorithm uses the any-order property of addition. It only works with consecutive integers.

On Your Own
10. 8795 **13.** $98\frac{1}{3}$ yd or 295 ft **14. a.** No; the units are not the same. **c.** $5333\frac{1}{3}$ yd^2

Lesson 1.13
Check Your Understanding
1. 1 **2. a.** 15; 15 **b.** 16; 56; 60 **c.** when they have no common factor **d.** No; the product of two denominators is always a common denominator, and therefore a greater common denominator cannot be the *least* common denominator. **3. a.** $\frac{23}{44}$ **b.** $\frac{4}{5}$ **c.** Answers may vary. Sample: Jill's method works because each summand is being multiplied by 1, and therefore does not change. **d.** yes

On Your Own
4. 21 **5. a.** $\frac{1}{11}$ **c.** $\frac{1}{4}$ **9. a.** $\frac{5}{3}$ **c.** $\frac{3}{4}$

Lesson 1.14
Check Your Understanding
1. a. Multiply each of the place-value parts of one number by the other number. Add the results. **b.** Multiplying a number by the sum of the place-value parts of another number is the same as adding the products of that number and each place-value part of the other number. **c.** This algorithm is almost always useful, though it can sometimes be hard to do in your head. **2. a.** Multiplying by $\frac{1}{2}$ and then multiplying by 10 is the same as multiplying by $\frac{10}{2}$, or 5, by the any-grouping principle of multiplication. **b.** This algorithm is most useful when it is easy to calculate half of a number. **c.** Take a quarter of a number and then multiply by 100. **3. a.** This algorithm is based on the Distributive Property since $8 \cdot 99 = 8 \cdot (100 - 1) = 800 - 8 = 792$ **b.** This algorithm works only when multiplying by 99, and works best when the resulting subtraction is easy to calculate. **c.** Multiply by 100 and then subtract twice the starting number. **4. a.** To see how this algorithm works, consider an example. To multiply 29 and 24, you can write 29 as a sum of 1 and powers of 2. So 29×24
$= (16 + 8 + 4 + 1) \times 24$
$= (2^4 + 2^3 + 2^2 + 1)$
$= (2^4 \times 24) + (2^3 \times 24)$
$\quad + (2^2 \times 24) + (1 \times 24)$
Notice that this process exactly mimics the way you find the sum of the starred entries in the double column in the table. **b.** This algorithm is not useful in most cases. **5. a.** This algorithm works because multiplication is repeated addition. As the slanted line goes up each vertical unit, it also goes across the number of units given by the product of the factor that comes from the dashed horizontal line and the factor that comes from the intersection of the slanted line and the bold horizontal line. **b.** This algorithm is mainly useful as a visualization tool.
c.
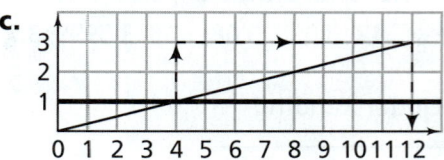

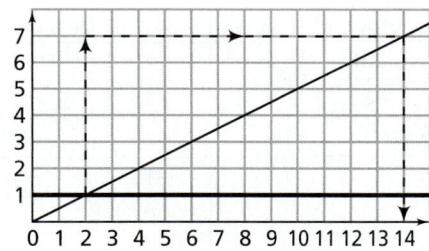

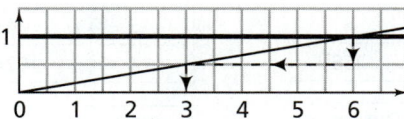

d. To divide a number by 2, for instance, draw a slanted multiplication line that crosses the horizontal line at 2. Start at the number you want to divide by 2 and move up until you reach the multiplication line. Then move to the left until you reach the vertical line. The number you reach is the quotient.

On Your Own
6. c. 12 days **8. a.** 3738 **c.** 73,593 **9.** $A = 4$, $B = 2$, $C = 8$, $D = 5$, $E = 7$

Lesson 1.15
Check Your Understanding
1. Answers may vary. Sample: To transport 17 people in cars that seat 4 per car, you need 5 cars. **2.** Answers may vary. Sample: If a restaurant bill is $17 for four people, the cost per person is $4.25. **3. a.** $\frac{7}{10}$ **b.** 3 **c.** 1 **d.** $\frac{3}{2}$ **e.** because of the any-order, any-grouping properties **4. a.** $\frac{5}{6}$ **b.** 2 **c.** Answers may vary. Sample: Multiplying by the denominator is the same as multiplying by the numerator of the reciprocal, and vice versa. **5. a.** 21 **b.** 46 **c.** 22 **d.** 25 **e.** $\frac{7}{4}$

On Your Own
8. a. 80 **c.** 75 **10. a.** $\frac{1}{5}$

Chapter 2
Lesson 2.01
On Your Own
4. Yes, it will always work. **5.** You get twice your number every time. **7.** 10

Lesson 2.02
Check Your Understanding
1. a. 10 **b.** 6 **c.** 52 **d.** 64 **e.** $m - 1$ **f.** $n + 1$
2. a. doctors **b.** gallons of water **c.** medical kits **d.** pillows **e.** blankets **3. a.** II **b.** IV **c.** I **d.** III **e.** V **4. a.** Choose a number. Multiply by 2 and then add 1. **b.** Choose a number, subtract 1, and then multiply by -2. **c.** Choose a number, add 2, multiply by 5, and then subtract 2. **d.** Choose a number, add 1, multiply by 3, subtract 2, multiply by 7, and then subtract 9. **5.** $2 \cdot ((x + 5) - 11) + 3$

On Your Own
6. b. 16 **7. b.** III **10. a.** ℓw **b.** $2\ell + 2w$
11. a. $\frac{x}{2}$

Lesson 2.03
Check Your Understanding
1. 610 beds, 2700 pounds of food, 5000 gallons of water; 1310 beds, 5600 pounds of food, 10,500 gallons of water **2. a.** 10 **b.** 10 **c.** 10 **d.** 10 **3. a.** $3(n - 1) + 5$ **b.** 35 **c.** 5
4. a. $5(3n - 2)$ **b.** 50 **c.** 10 **5. a.** 24 **b.** $\frac{35}{2}$
c. $\frac{7}{4}$ **d.** $\frac{7}{4}$ **6. a.** $3 \cdot (7 + 3) = 30$
b. $(-3 + 3) \cdot 5 + 11 = 11$
c. $-3 + 3 \cdot (5 + 11) = 45$
d. $25 - (5 + 4 \cdot 5) = 0$
e. $25 - (5 + 4) \cdot 5 = -20$

On Your Own
7. a. 2 cubic meters **9. a.** 14 **e.** -28 **10. a.** 32 **e.** 60 **11. a.** 2.5 meters per second

Lesson 2.04
Check Your Understanding
1. The trick results in 6 every time; yes; $\frac{(2x + 7) \cdot 5 + 25}{10} - x = 6$ **2.** Add 35.
3. a. Subtract 3. **b.** Subtract your starting number. **4. a.** 15 **b.** 15 **c.** 15 **d.** 15 **e.** 15 **f.** 15 **g.** 15
h. $\frac{x + 2x + 3x + 4x + 5x}{x} =$
$\frac{1}{x}(x + 2x + 3x + 4x + 5x) =$
$\frac{x}{x} + \frac{2x}{x} + \frac{3x}{x} + \frac{4x}{x} + \frac{5x}{x} =$
$1 + 2 + 3 + 4 + 5 = 15$
5. a. $12x + 6$; $8x + 10$ **b.** $7x - 28$; $2x + 6$
c. $3x - 4$; $12x - 15$ **d.** $90 - 18x$; $38 - 4x$

On Your Own
6. a. yes **c.** No; by way of a counterexample, let $x = 1$ and $y = 0$. Then $6xy = 0$, but $4x + 2y = 4$. **7. a.** $10x + 18$; $10x + 22$
9. e. $\frac{4}{3}$ **12. b.** 35

Lesson 2.05
Check Your Understanding
1. a. $\frac{a}{b} = a \cdot \frac{1}{b}$ **b.** $c - d = c + (-d)$
c. $ab = (-a) \cdot (-b)$ **d.** If $a \cdot b = 1$, then $a = \frac{1}{b}$ and $b = \frac{1}{a}$. **2. a.** If "$a = 0$" is true, then "$a = 0$ or $b = 0$" is true **b.** Every nonzero number has a reciprocal. **c.** The left side becomes b and the right side becomes 0.
d. It shows that either a or b has to be 0. That is, if $a \neq 0$, then $b = 0$.

On Your Own
3. a. 4♥6 = 3(4) + 6 = 18 **b.** 22 **c.** no
5. a. $x + 2$ **d.** $4x + 8$ **6. a.** $4x + 19$
7. c. $6x - 23$ **8. a.** $x \to x + 6 \to 3x + 18 \to 3x + 8 \to 6x + 16 \to 6x + 66 \to x + 11$

Lesson 2.06
On Your Own
8. a. 9 **d.** Impossible; any number other than 0 divided by itself equals 1. **9. a.** 5 times **f.** unable to determine

Lesson 2.07
Check Your Understanding
1. Unbuckle the seat belt, open the door, stand up, and close the door. The steps are reversed and then performed in the opposite order.
2. Answers may vary. Sample: $2 \to 2 + 6 = 8 \to 8 \div 4 = 2 \to 2 \times 8 = 16 \to 16 + 7 = 23 \to 23 \times 10 = 230$ Undo by dividing by 10, subtracting 7, dividing by 8, multiplying by 4, and subtracting 6. **3. a.** Add 13; subtract 13.
b. Divide by -2; multiply by -2. **c.** Multiply by 5, subtract 12 and then multiply by 3; Divide by 3, add 12, and then divide by 5. **d.** Multiply by 15 and then subtract 36; add 36 and then divide by 15. **4.** 10 **5.** $\frac{1}{3}$
6. a.

Input, x	Output, x^2
-4	16
-3	9
-2	4
-1	1
0	0
1	1
2	4
3	9
4	16

b. There is more than one input for certain outputs.

c.

Input, x	Output, x^3
-4	-64
-3	-27
-2	-8
-1	-1
0	0
1	1
2	8
3	27
4	64

yes

d.

Input, x	Output, x^4
-4	256
-3	81
-2	16
-1	1
0	0
1	1
2	16
3	81
4	256

Input, x	Output, x^5
-4	-1024
-3	-243
-2	-32
-1	-1
0	0
1	1
2	32
3	243
4	1024

Input, x	Output, x^6
-4	4096
-3	729
-2	64
-1	1
0	0
1	1
2	64
3	729
4	4096

Input, x	Output, x^7
-4	$-16,384$
-3	-2187
-2	-128
-1	-1
0	0
1	1
2	128
3	2187
4	16,384

All odd powers are reversible.

e. The product of an even number of negative numbers is positive. All odd powers of -3 are negative.

On Your Own
7. a. Square a number and then add 6; not reversible. **b.** Multiply by 3 and then subtract 28; add 28 and then divide by 3.
8. -2 **11.** Tables B and D **14. a.** 5 **d.** -6

Lesson 2.08
Check Your Understanding
1. -4 **2.** $\frac{117}{2}$ **3.** 120 **4.** -8 **5.** 55
6. $\frac{39}{5}$ **7. a.** 7 **b.** 1 **c.**

a	b
0	$\frac{25}{2}$
1	12
2	$\frac{23}{2}$
3	11
4	$\frac{21}{2}$
5	10

d. $b = \frac{75 - 3a}{6}$ **8. a.** $1^3 + 26(1) = 27 = 11(1)^2 + 16$; $8^3 + 26(8) = 720 = 11(8)^2 + 16$
b. Answers may vary. Sample: 0 and 3 (any number other than 1, 2, or 8 is not a solution).
c. 2

On Your Own
10. a. Add 2, multiply by 3, and then subtract 1.   **11. a.** 4   **d.** $-\frac{5}{3}$

Lesson 2.09
On Your Own
10. a. 6   **13. a.** no   **b.** yes   **14. a.** yes   **c.** no
15. a. 42

Lesson 2.10
Check Your Understanding
1. $\ell = 15$ **2.** $j = 5$ **3.** $n = \frac{3}{2}$ **4.** $x = \frac{8}{5}$
5. $x = -5$ **6.** $y = 8$ **7.** $a = 3$ **8.** $u = 7$
9. $m = 9$ **10. a–e.** Answers may vary. Samples are given. **a.** $x + 5$ **b.** $11 - x$
c. $5x + 15$ **d.** $6x - 12$ **e.** the value of the expression when $x = 3$ **11. a.** $r = 14$
b. $x = -2$ **c.** $a = -\frac{3}{20}$ **d.** $s = 50$

On Your Own
12. $r = 2$ **14.** $p = 12$ **15.** $x = 4$
16. a. $x = 7$ **e.** $x = 3$ **17. b.** $x + 2$
19. a. $x = 3$ **c.** $b = \frac{9}{5}$

Lesson 2.11
Check Your Understanding
1. a. $x = 9$ **b.** $x = -\frac{1}{6}$ **c.** $x = -\frac{1}{6}$
d. $a = 9$ **e.** $z = 9$ **f.** True for all values of n.   **2.** Answers may vary. Sample: Subtract $48x$ from each side. Add 15 to each side. Divide by the coefficient of x, which is 25.   **3.** The ending number will be 11.   **4. a.** Subtract 6 from each side.   **b.** Subtract t from each side. **c.** Add 100 to each side.   **d.** Subtract $3t$ from each side.   **e.** Subtract $5t$ from each side.
f. Multiply each side by 5.   **5.** $x = \frac{7}{2}$ for all the equations in Exercise 4; since all the equations came about by applying the basic moves to the same equation, they all have the same solution.   **6. a.** Subtract 13 from 27 to get 14. Divide 14 by 4 to get $\frac{7}{2}$. Add 7 to get $\frac{21}{2}$.   **b.** $4(x - 7) + 13 = 27$
$4(x - 7) + 13 - 13 = 27 - 13$ $4(x - 7) = 14$
$\frac{4(x-7)}{4} = \frac{14}{4}$ $x - 7 = \frac{7}{2}$ $x - 7 + 7 = \frac{7}{2} + 7$ $x = \frac{21}{2}$ **c.** Answers may vary. Sample: The two processes are similar in that the backtracking steps in part (a) are exactly the operations performed in part (b). They are different in that, when you use backtracking, you are only performing the operations on the number on the right side of the equation. When you use basic moves to solve, you must always perform the operation on each side of the equation.   **7. a.** $4z + 2 = z - 4$; by the basic moves, $z = -2$.   **b.** $2x + 2 = 2x + 7$; after subtracting $2x$ from each side, you get $2 = 7$, which is false.   **c.** $3s + 12 = 3(s + 3) + 3$; by the Distributive Property, $3(s + 3) + 3 = 3s + 9 + 3 = 3s + 12$.

On Your Own
8. $f = 20$ **11. a.** Subtract 4 from each side.
e. Divide each side by 2.
13. a. $x \to 3x \to 3x + 5 \to 12x + 20 \to 12x + 36 \to x + 3 \to 3$ **b.** Yes; the ending number is always 3.   **16. a.** all numbers

Lesson 2.12
Check Your Understanding
1. $r = 4$ **2.** $w = \frac{3}{4}$ **3.** no solution
4. $u = \frac{32}{7}$ **5.** $r = 4$ **6.** all real numbers
7. a–e. Answers may vary. Samples are given.
a. $2x + 1 = 7$ **b.** $3x + 4 = 2x + 9$
c. $7x - 10 = 4x - 5$ **d.** $14x + 21 = 8x - 45$
e. $x = x + 1$ **8. a.** Subtract 15 from each side.
b. Subtract $(6x + 2y)$ from each side.
c. Subtract $6x$ from each side.   **d.** Subtract $6x$ from each side and then divide each side by 2.   **9.** 19   **10. a.** 72   **b.** -15 **c.** 100
11. a. false   **b.** true   **c.** false   **d.** may be true or false   **e.** true   **f.** true   **g.** may be true or false
h. true   **i.** may be true or false

On Your Own
12. $a = -\frac{5}{2}$ **13.** all real numbers
15. a. $x = \frac{20}{3}$ **16. a.** true   **b.** false

Lesson 2.13
Check Your Understanding
1. $x = \frac{9}{2}$ **2.** $j = 1$ **3.** $k = \frac{8}{3}$
4. $x = -10$ **5.** $s = -\frac{6}{5}$ **6.** $w = -4$
7. $q = \frac{5}{2}$ **8.** $e = \frac{9}{4}$ **9.** $x = 1$ **10.** $z = -\frac{1}{3}$
11. Answers may vary. Sample: If $a = b = 1$, then $(a + b)^2 = (1 + 1)^2 = 2^2 = 4$, but $a^2 + b^2 = 1 + 1 = 2$.

12. $\boxed{\begin{array}{c}a\\b\end{array}}\boxed{\begin{array}{c}a\\b\end{array}}\boxed{\begin{array}{c}a\\b\end{array}}\boxed{\begin{array}{c}a\\b\end{array}} = \boxed{\begin{array}{c}a\ a\ a\ a\\b\ b\ b\ b\end{array}}$

13. $\boxed{\begin{array}{c}a\\b\\c\end{array}}\boxed{\begin{array}{c}a\\b\\c\end{array}}\boxed{\begin{array}{c}a\\b\\c\end{array}}\boxed{\begin{array}{c}a\\b\\c\end{array}} = \boxed{\begin{array}{c}a\ a\ a\ a\\b\ b\ b\ b\\c\ c\ c\ c\end{array}}$

14. $\boxed{\begin{array}{c}x\\y\\z\end{array}}\boxed{\begin{array}{c}x\\y\\z\end{array}}\boxed{\begin{array}{c}x\\y\\z\end{array}}\boxed{\begin{array}{c}x\\y\\z\end{array}}\boxed{\begin{array}{c}x\\y\\z\end{array}}\boxed{\begin{array}{c}x\\y\\z\end{array}}\boxed{\begin{array}{c}x\\y\\z\end{array}} = \boxed{\begin{array}{c}x\ x\ x\ x\ x\ x\ x\\y\ y\ y\ y\ y\ y\ y\\z\ z\ z\ z\ z\ z\ z\end{array}}$

On Your Own
15. $a = \frac{13}{2}$ **19.** $x = -\frac{1}{2}$ **22. a.** $24x - 84$
f. $-12x + 24$

Lesson 2.14
On Your Own
5. a. sometimes true **c.** never true; $-3 \neq 3$
f. always true; $6 = 6$ **6.** $15 per hour **7. a.** 3

Lesson 2.15
Check Your Understanding
1. a. Answers may vary. Sample: because one fourth of 4 is 1, which is an easy number to work with **b.** 5 **c.** 15; 12 is $4 \cdot 3$, and 15 is $5 \cdot 3$.
d. 168 **2. a.** no **b.** yes **c.** no
d. $8(35 + n) = 360$ **e.** $n = 10$ **3.** 5 **4. a.** yes
b. no **c.** yes **d.** $103.53 **5.** 9 years old

On Your Own
6. 504 pages **7.** 51 years old **9. a.** not join
11. 98 **12.** $12

Lesson 2.16
Check Your Understanding
1. a. The equation states that the ratio between price with discount and original price is 80%. **b.** Division by zero is undefined.
c. $d - 12 = \frac{8}{10}d$ **d.** $10d - 120 = 8d$
e. $d = 60$ **2. a.** $\frac{3}{10}$ **b.** $\frac{7}{10}$ **c.** 0.9 **d.** $1 - p$
3. 0.75 **4.** no **5. a.** 7.44; 8.0 **b.** no;
$\frac{6.4 + 8.0 + 8.1 + 6.5 + 8.2 + 7.6}{6} \approx 7.467$
c. Answers may vary. Sample:
8.0, $\frac{6.4 + 8.0 + 8.1 + 6.5 + 8.2 + 8.0}{6} \approx 7.533$
d. $\frac{37.2 + x}{6} = 7.5$ **e.** $x = 7.8$ **6. a.** 7.4
b. 7.7; 7.25

On Your Own
7. 141 **9.** 16 years old **10.** about 2545 miles

Lesson 2.17
Check Your Understanding
1. $y = -x - 13$ **2. a.** $y = \frac{13}{4}$ **b.** $y = \frac{33}{4}$
c. $x = -\frac{13}{2}$ **d.** No; replacing x with 20 and y with 13 yields $79 = 78$, which is false. **e.** No; since the equation in part (e) is equivalent to the equation in part (d), (20,13) is not a solution. **3. a.** $w = \frac{4}{3}h$ **b.** $h = \frac{3}{4}w$ **c.** $\frac{45}{4}$ in.
d. 28 in. **e.** 35 in. **4. a.** No; if you substitute 10 for x and 6 for y, you get $86 = 90$, which is false.
b. $y = \frac{15}{2}$; any other value for y makes the equation false. **c.** Answers may vary. Samples: (0, 15), (18, 0), (6, 10), (12, 5) **d.** The points fall on a straight line. **5. a.** between $2524 and $2674 **b.** $4524 to $4674
c. $p - 75 \leq g \leq p + 75$ **6. a.** Once you remove the border, the remaining space should have the proportions of the photograph. So if you take away 4 from the width and 4 from the height, then these should be in a 4-to-3 ratio.

b. $w = \frac{4(h-4)}{3} + 4$, or $\frac{4h-4}{3}$ **c.** $\frac{44}{3}$ in.
d. $\frac{56}{3}$ in. **e.** $\frac{76}{3}$ in. **7. a.** No; 4 nickels and 8 dimes are $1. **b.** No; 6 nickels and 4 dimes are $.70. **c.** $0.05n + 0.1d = 0.9$ **d.** $d = 9 - 0.5n$
e. No; if Chi had an odd number of nickels, $9 - 0.5n$ would not be an integer.

On Your Own
8. a. not true; $5y = 10x + 20$ **d.** true
9. a. $2\ell + 2w$ **c.** $\ell = -5 + 3w$ **11. a.** no
12. a. $p = \frac{210 - 41\ell}{26}$

Chapter 3
Lesson 3.01
On Your Own
10. a five-pointed star **12. a.** Answers may vary. Sample: Connect in order the points (2, 1), (2, 4), (4, 1), and (4, 4). **14. a.** Answers may vary. Sample: (3, 3), (6.5, −4), (5, −5), (7, 0) **15. a.** Answers may vary. Samples: (0, 0), (27, 3), (π, π), (−7, −0.5), (−1, −1), (−77, 2.7) **16.** Answers may vary. Sample: (−2, 3), (−1, 3), and (−1, −2); (3, −2), (−2, 10), and (3, 10)

Lesson 3.02
Check Your Understanding
1. a. The point moves to the right. **b.** The point moves up. **c.** The point moves to the left. **2.**
a. The points, and the square, move 1 unit to the right. **b.** The points, and the square, move 5 units to the right and 2 units up. **c.** The points, and the square, move 2 units to the left and 1 unit up. **3. a.** Yes; answers may vary. Sample: $(x, y) \mapsto (x + 5, y + 4)$ **b.** Yes; answers may vary. Sample: $(x, y) \mapsto (x + 5, y - 2)$
4. a. The points move vertically to twice their original distance from the x-axis. The square is transformed into a rectangle twice as tall as it is wide, with twice the area. **b.** The points move horizontally to twice their original distance from the y-axis. The square is transformed into a rectangle twice as wide as it is tall, with twice the area. **c.** The points move horizontally and vertically to twice their original distances from both the x-axis and y-axis. The square remains a square, but with side lengths twice as long. **d.** Each point moves counterclockwise to the position of an adjacent corner of the square. The square remains unchanged. **5.** Answers may vary. Samples: $(x, y) \mapsto (-x, y)$, $(x, y) \mapsto (y, x)$

6. a.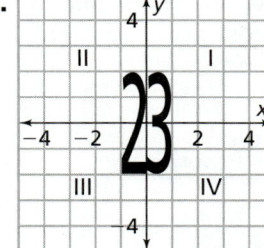

b.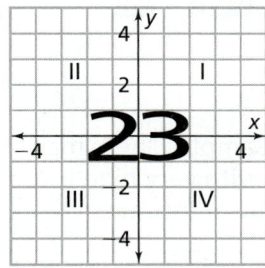

c.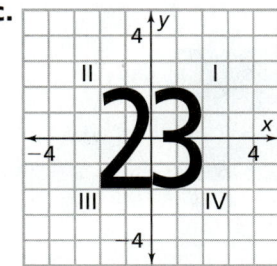

7. Answers may vary. Sample: Any two quadrants must be either adjacent or opposite. If a line passes through only two opposite quadrants (and no other quadrants), it must also pass through the only point that the borders of the two quadrants have in common, namely the origin. For a line to pass through two adjacent quadrants, but not a third quadrant, it must be entirely on one side of one of the axes. This is possible only if the line is parallel to that axis—that is, vertical or horizontal. Therefore it is not possible for a slanted line to pass through only two quadrants and not pass through the origin as well.

On Your Own
8. a. The new point is the same distance away from, but on the other side of, the y-axis.
10. c. yes; a rectangle; 27 square units
13. a cube

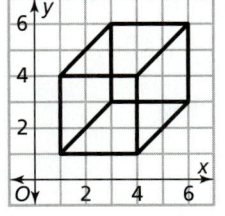

Lesson 3.03
Check Your Understanding
1. a. 6 **b.** 100 **c.** $\sqrt{2}$ **d.** 5 **e.** $|b|$ **2.** The quantity $\pm a + b$ is equal to $a + b$ or $-a + b$, whereas $\pm(a + b)$ is equal to $a + b$ or $-a - b$.
3. a. Answers may vary. Sample: Find the two numbers that are 7 units away from 5; 12 and -2. **b.** $x = -3$ or $x = -11$ **4. a.** $x = 8$ or $x = 2$ **b.** $x = \frac{23}{3}$ or $x = -3$ **c.** $\frac{5}{2}$ **d.** no solution
e. $x = 6$ or $x = -1$ **f.** $x = 2$ $x = \frac{10}{3}$
5. a. 381,500 km $\pm$ 25,000 km; 406,500 km, 356,500 km **b.** 29 $\pm$ 4; 33, 25
c. $4500 \pm (0.05)(\$4500)$; \$4725, \$4275
6. a–f. Answers may vary. Samples are given. **a.** $|x| = 11$ **b.** $|x - 17| = 12$
c. $|x + 6| = 9$ **d.** $|x| = -5$ **e.** $|x - 4| = 0$
f. $|2x - 17| = 5$

On Your Own
8. b. $\sqrt{41}$ **10. a.** Examples may vary. Samples are given. some values:
$|1 + 1| = |1| + |1|$,
$|1 + (-1)| \neq |1| + |-1|$,
$|2 + (-1)| \neq |2| + |-1|$
11. a. $x = -61$ or $x = -223$ **c.** no solution
14. no solution

Lesson 3.04
Check Your Understanding
1. a–c. Answers may vary. Samples are given. **a.** Fred starts 8000 feet from home and then walks home at a steady rate. **b.** The number of people willing to buy a movie ticket decreases as the price of the ticket increases. **c.** Julie starts with 8 gallons of gas in her tank. She runs out after 200 miles. **2. a–b.** Answers may vary. Samples are given. **a.** George starts out slowly, then speeds up for 4.5 hours, then slows down for 0.5 hour, and then stops, 25 miles from home. **b.** Martha starts out faster than George, and travels at varying speeds for about 3.5 hours, at which time she is 30 miles from home. Then she turns around and takes another 5.5 hours driving home. **c.** Assuming they are taking the same route, George and Martha pass each other, going in opposite directions. **d.** George is not moving. **e.** 60 miles
f. 25 miles **3.** The graph starts at the origin because, at time 0, the height of the water is 0. The height increases at a constant rate, which means that for every additional unit of time, the height increases by the same amount. **4.** (I)–B; (II)–A; (III)–D; (IV)–F; (V)–E; (VI)–C; buckets I and II have straight sides, so the water level rises at a constant rate. But since II

is narrower than I, the graph for II is steeper. The water level in bucket III rises at a constant rate until the bucket becomes narrower, and then it rises at a faster constant rate. Bucket IV starts narrow, so it starts to fill quickly. It slows down, so the graph becomes less steep over time. When it is halfway filled, it begins to fill more quickly again, and the graph becomes steeper. Bucket V begins filling slowly since it has a wide base, so the graph starts relatively flat. Bucket V gets narrower, so the water level rises more quickly, and the graph gets steeper. Bucket VI is the opposite of bucket V, so its graph starts steep and becomes less steep over time.

On Your Own
5. b. He turns around and starts back home.
6. Answers may vary. Sample:

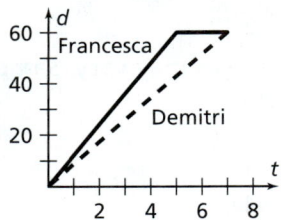

8. d. 5

Lesson 3.05
On Your Own
3. a. Add the test scores and divide by 7. *Mean* is what people most often think of as the average. **b.** Put the test scores in numerical order. The median is the fourth test score. The median tells the middle point of a data set. **c.** Find the test score that occurs most often. The mode tells the value or values that occur most often in a data set. **4. b.** 1.64 **6. b.** There are five modes for this data set. **7. b.** There are a few very high salaries that skew the mean.

Lesson 3.06
Check Your Understanding
1. a. Answers may vary. Sample: Add 20 points to five different test scores. **b.** Answers may vary. Sample: Change the top 11 scores to 100. **2.** B **3.** 3×10^4 **4. a.** Subtract 1 from every element in the set. The mean and the median will also be 1 less. **b.** Add 10 to every element in the set. The mean and the median will also be 10 more.

On Your Own
5. b.

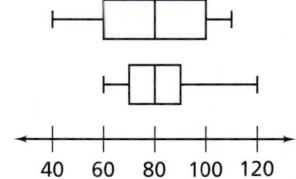

7. a. Yes; the average winning per play is 18.25 coins, while the cost per play is only 4 coins. **8. a.** 21 **10.** no

Lesson 3.07
Check Your Understanding
1.

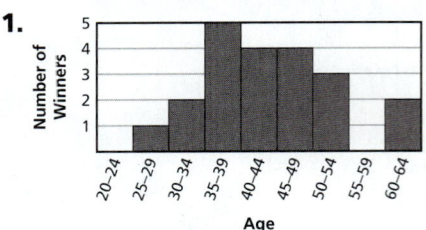

2. Answers may vary. Sample: There may be relatively few families with very high incomes, and many more with lower incomes.

3. a.

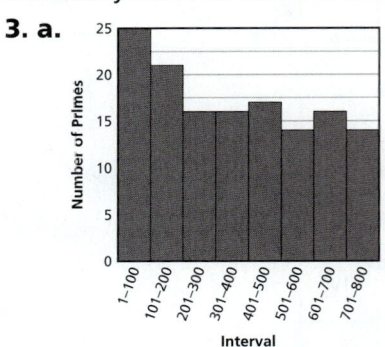

b. They decrease.

On Your Own
6.

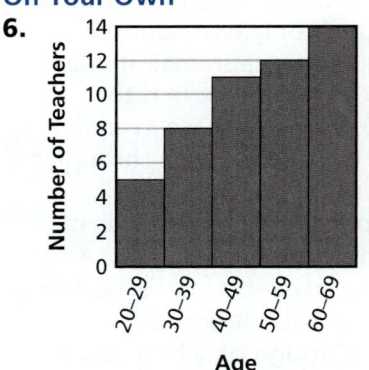

7. b. 10–19 and 20–29 **d.** no

Lesson 3.08
Check Your Understanding
1. C **2.** Answers may vary. **3.** Answers may vary. **4. a.** Answers may vary. Sample:

b. Yes; see the sample answer for part (a) as an example.   **5.** Answers may vary. Sample: Subtract 40 from each data point and then multiply each data point by 2.

On Your Own
6. a. No. The plot does not tell you how the data are distributed within each quartile.
c. No. The plot does not tell you how the data are distributed within each quartile.

9.

Life Expectancy

(Box plot showing Male and Female life expectancy, with x-axis "Years" from 30 to 90)

Answers may vary. Sample: The life expectancies of women are in general higher than those of men.

Lesson 3.09
Check Your Understanding
1. a. $\frac{54}{117}$ is the ratio of students who agree that school should end one hour later to all students. **b.** $\frac{42}{117}$ is the ratio of non-athletes who participated in the survey to all students who participated in the survey. **c.** $\frac{23}{42}$ is the ratio of those who agree that school should end one hour later to non-athletes. **d.** $\frac{23}{54}$ is the ratio of non-athletes to those who agree that school should end one hour later. **e.** $\frac{23}{117}$ is the ration of students surveyed who are non-athletes and agree that school should end one hour later to all students surveyed.
2. Non, athletes are not more likely to agree than non-athletes. Tess is paying attention only to the numbers of athletes and non-athletes who agree with the idea of extending the school day. She should be looking at the percentage of athletes and non-athletes that agree. $\frac{31}{75}$, or about 41.3% of non-athletes agree, but $\frac{23}{42}$, or about 54.7% of non-athletes agree.   **3.** Males; About 22.8% of males surveyed were wearing a watch, and about 20.9% of females surveyed were wearing a watch.

On Your Own
11. a. Non-athletes; about 48.4% of non-athletes $\left(\frac{16}{33}\right)$ are left-eye dominant, but only 21.1% $\left(\frac{11}{52}\right)$ of athletes are left-eye dominant.
b. Yes; The variables of eye dominance and athletic status are associated, since the difference in percentages is significant.

12. a. $\frac{1}{3}$, or about 33.3%

b. $\frac{2}{15}$, or about 13.3% **c.** Answers may vary. Sample: These percentages seem significantly different, so it appears there is an association between these variables. To investigate further, find more people from Connecticut and L.A. and see if they are left-handed.

13. Answers may vary. Sample: Whether a family owns a minivan or not and whether the family has three or more children or one or two children. Larger families would usually need larger vehicles, and so are more likely to own a minivan.

Lesson 3.10
Check Your Understanding
1. Answers may vary.   **2.** Answers may vary.
3.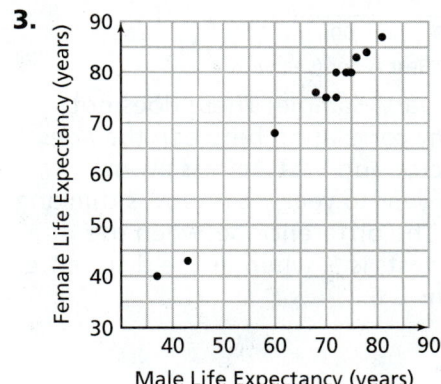

4. Answers may vary. Sample: If you draw the graph of $y = x$, almost all the points are above the line.

5. a.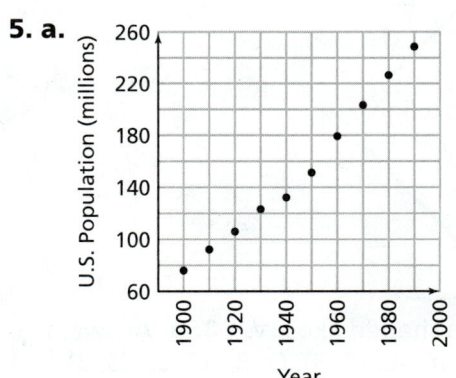

b. Answers may vary. Actual populations: 62.9 million in 1890, 281.4 million in 2000

6.

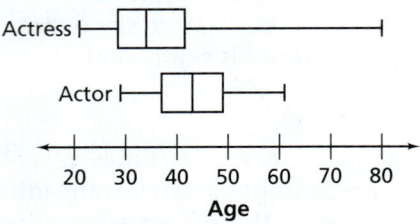

Answers may vary. Sample: The median age of the Best Actress winner is less than the first quartile of the Best Actor winner.

7.

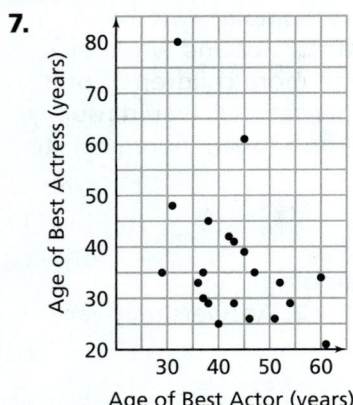

Answers may vary. Sample: There does not seem to be any correlation between the ages of the Best Actor and Best Actress award winners from year to year. **9.** Abby is thinking of the mean. The difference between the means of the tests is 9, whereas the difference of the medians is 6.

Lesson 3.11
On Your Own

6.

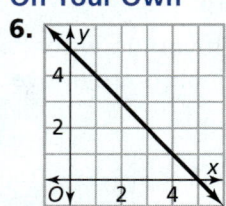

The graph is a line.

7.

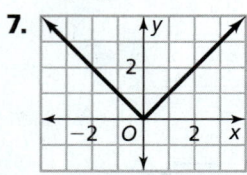

The graph is shaped like a V. **8. a.** Answers may vary. Sample: (0, 3), (1, 3), (2, 3), (3, 3), (4, 3), (5, 3) **b.** Answers may vary. Sample: (3, 0), (3, 1), (3, 2), (3, 4), (3, 5), (3, 6) **c.** The y-coordinate is 3.

9. b. 6 and 7; $(6)^2 - 13(6) + 42 = 36 - 78 + 42 = 0$, $(7)^2 - 13(7) + 42 = 49 - 91 + 42 = 0$

c.

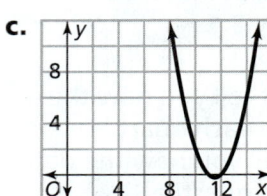

$y = (x - 5)^2 - 13(x - 5) + 42$, or $y = x^2 - 23x + 132$, or $y = (x - 11)(x - 12)$

Lesson 3.12
Check Your Understanding

1. a. Answers may vary. Sample: (0, 4), (1, 4), (2, 4), (−1, 4), (−2, 4), (1.2, 4)

b. The graph is a horizontal line passing through the point (0, 4).

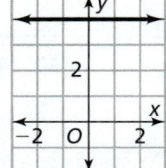

2. a.

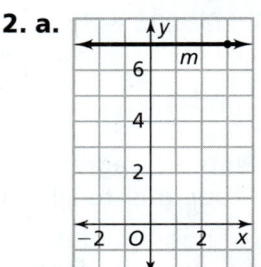

b. Answers may vary. Sample: (0, 7), (1, 7), (−1, 7), (900, 7), (0.01, 7), (−7, 7)
c. Answers may vary. Sample: (0, 0), (1, −7), (−1, 1), (90, 1), (1, 90), (−7, 5)
d. A point is on m if its y-coordinate is 7.
e. $y = 7$

3. a.

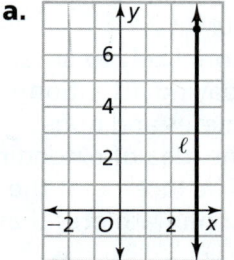

b. Answers may vary. Sample: (3, 0), (3, 1), (3, −1), (3, 900), (3, 0.01), (3, −3) **c.** Answers may vary. Sample: (0, 0), (−3, 1), (1, −1), (0.01, 900), (900, 0.01), (5, −3) **d.** A point is on ℓ if its x-coordinate is 3. **e.** $x = 3$
4. a. (5, 0) and (−3, 4) are on the graph. (−3, 0) is not on the graph. **b.** Answers may vary. Sample: (−5, 0), (0, 5), (3, 4), (3, −4)

5. a. Answers may vary. Sample: (0, 0), (1, 1), (17, 17), (−1, −1), (π, π) **b.** Answers may vary. Sample: (0, 1), (1, 0), (3, 4), (−1, 1), (π, −π) **c.** The graph is a line that passes through the origin.

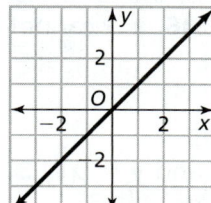

The x- and y-coordinates for each point on the line are equal.

6. a. Answers may vary. Sample:

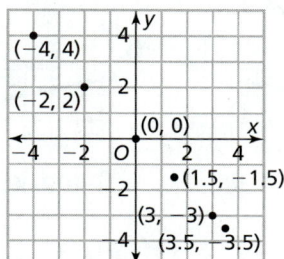

b. The graph is a line. **c.** D; the x- and y-coordinates for each point on the line are opposites.

On Your Own
7. a. $y = 4$ **8. a.** on neither **d.** on r
10. b. $y = 2$ **11. b.** $x = -4$
c.

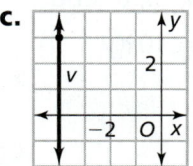

Lesson 3.13
Check Your Understanding
1. The equation $2y + 3x = 4$ has a different graph from the other three. You can change the other three into each other using basic moves. **2. a.** 5 **b.** $\frac{5}{2}$ **c.** $\frac{25}{2}$ **d.** $\frac{9}{2}$ **e.** $-\frac{5}{2}$ **f.** 15
a–f.

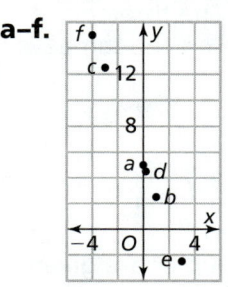

g.

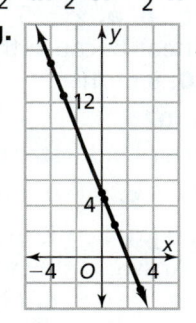

3. The first graph is the graph of $y - 3 = |x|$ and the second graph is the graph of $y = |x - 3|$. You can tell which graph is which by testing points from the graph in each equation. **4.** From left to right and top to bottom, the graphs correspond to equations b, a, d, and c. You can tell which graph corresponds to which equation by plotting several points that satisfy each equation.

5. a. $h = 160 - 16t^2$ **b.** 160 ft **c.** 144 ft, 96 ft, 16 ft **d.** 3.2 s

e. 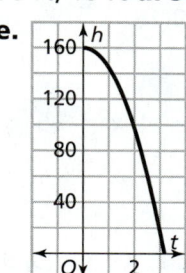   **f.**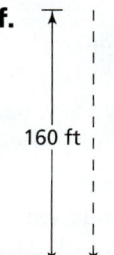

6. a. $h = 320 - 16t^2$ **b.** 320 ft **c.** 304 ft, 256 ft, 176 ft, 64 ft **d.** No; the grape takes about 4.5 seconds to fall 320 feet.

e.

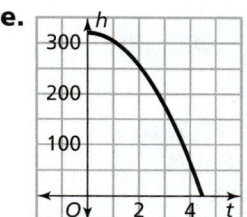

On Your Own
8. a. II; the graph of $y = -2$ is a horizontal line that passes through $(0, -2)$.

9.

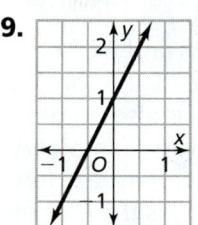

Lesson 3.14
Check Your Understanding
1. a. (100, 25) satisfies neither equation. **b.** (−25, −25) does not satisfy the second equation. **c.** (1000, 1000) does not satisfy the second equation. **d.** (1000, 500) satisfies neither equation. **e.** (500, 500) satisfies both equations. **2.** Answers may vary. Sample: $x = 3$, $y = -1$ **3. a.** No; if the graphs intersect at a point (a, b), then $b = 3a - 2 = 3a + 2$. But $3a - 2 = 3a + 2$ implies $-2 = 2$, which is false. Therefore, the two graphs do not intersect. **b.** You get a false statement. **4. a–b.** Answers may vary. Samples are given. **a.** $y = 0$, $y = 1$

b. The graphs never intersect because they are both horizontal lines. **5. a.** The equation $x^2 + y^2 = 25$ corresponds to the circle. The equation $16x^2 + 9y^2 = 288$ corresponds to the ellipse. **b.** The four intersection points are $(3, 4)$, $(-3, 4)$, $(-3, -4)$ and $(3, -4)$. The square of any number, positive or negative, is always positive.
$(\pm 3)^2 + (\pm 4)^2 = 9 + 16 = 25$
$16(\pm 3)^2 + 9(\pm 4)^2 = 16(9) + 9(16) = 144 + 144 = 288$

On Your Own
7. Answers may vary. Sample: $y = 4$; $x = -5$

Lesson 3.14
On Your Own
4. a. Answers may vary. Sample: $(-3, 9), (-2, 4), (-1, 1), (0, 0), (1, 1), (2, 4), (3, 9)$
5. a.

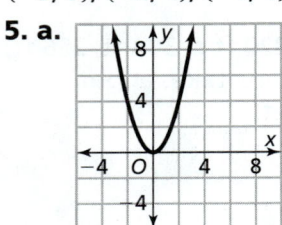

6. c. shifted 3 units to the left   **7. a.** yes
9. b. 39.2 m/s; 78.4 m/s; 156.8 m/s
c. v doubles   **10. a.** 250 lawns

Lesson 3.15
Check Your Understanding
1. a. $200,000 **b.** 21 **c.** It is an inverse variation. If the number of winners doubles, then the prize for each winner is halved. **d.** $p = \frac{1,000,000}{w}$, where w is the number of winners and p is the prize per winner. **2. a.** Yes; since $(8, 2)$ is on the graph, $(2 \cdot 8, 2 \cdot 2) = (16, 4)$ is also on the graph. **b.** $c = \frac{1}{4}$ **c.** Answers may vary. Sample: A campground shower costs $.25 per minute. Here x is the length of the shower, and y is the cost of the shower in dollars. **3. a.** no **b.** no **c.** yes **d.** yes **e.** no **f.** yes **4. a.** no **b.** no **c.** yes **d.** yes **e.** yes **f.** no **5.** The value of y decreases; y cannot equal 0.   **6.** The graph is symmetrical about the lines $y = x$ and $y = -x$ and symmetrical about the origin.   **7. a.** Answers may vary. Samples: $(12, -1), (6, -2), (4, -3), (3, -4), (2, -6), (1, -12)$ **b.** Quadrants II and IV; for $xy = -12$ to be true, either x or y must be negative, while the other is positive.

c.

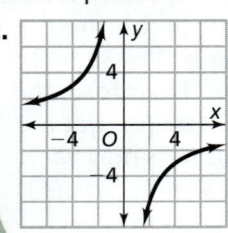

8. 0   **9. a.** $(-a)(-b) = (-1)(-1)(ab) = ab = 100$; $ba = ab = 100$ **b.** $(-b, -a)$

On Your Own
10. a. $25 **d.** Direct variation; when the number of cartons doubles, the total cost also doubles.   **12. a.** $y = 7x$ **16. a.** x cannot be 0. Division by 0 is undefined.

Lesson 3.16
Check Your Understanding
1. all of them   **2.** $y = x^2$ and $y = |x|$ **3.** none of them   **4. a.** I: $y = |x|$; II: $y = x^3$; III: $y = \frac{1}{x}$ **b.** I: $y = x^2$; II: $y = x$; III: $y = x^3$
5. a. $y = \sqrt{x}$ **b.** $y = x^3$ **c.** $y = |x|$ **d.** $y = x$
e. $y = x^2$ **f.** $y = \frac{1}{x}$ **g.** $y = x^3$ **h.** $y = \sqrt{x}$
6. $\frac{1}{x}, \sqrt{x}, |x|, x^2, x^3$
7. a.

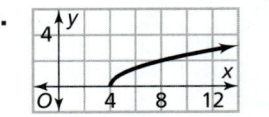

b.

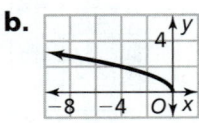

$x \geq 4$ and $y \geq 0$ $x \leq 0$ and $y \geq 0$

On Your Own
9. $\frac{1}{x}, x, x^3, x^2, |x|$ **12. a.** 2   **14. c.** The value of d quadruples.

Lesson 3.17
Check Your Understanding
1. Answers may vary. Sample: $(y - 7) = \frac{1}{2}(x - 3)$ **2.** Sasha did not replace each instance of x with $(x - 3)$.   **3. a.** $(0, 0)$ and $(5, 5)$ **b.** 1   **4.** I: $x^3 + (y + 4)^3 = 10x(y + 4)$
II: $x^3 + (y - 4)^3 = 10x(y - 4)$
III: $(x + 4)^3 + y^3 = 10(x + 4)y$

On Your Own
7. a. $x^2 + (y + 5)^2 = 6x + 8(y + 5) - 24$
10. $N = -6$ **11. a.** no **d.** yes

Chapter 4
Lesson 4.01
On Your Own
7. a. 3 ft   **8. a.** $x = 5$ **9. a.** The three points are collinear because they are on the same line.   **10.** 8 mi/h

Lesson 4.02
Check Your Understanding
1. a. $\frac{7}{4}$ **b.** $\frac{7}{4}$ **c.** $-\frac{8}{9}$ **d.** $-\frac{8}{9}$ **e.** $-\frac{8}{9}$ **f.** $-\frac{5}{4}$ **g.** $\frac{4}{5}$
h. $-\frac{5}{4}$ **i.** 0 **j.** 0 **k.** 1 **l.** undefined
2. a–d. Answers may vary. Samples are given.
a. $(0, 6)$ **b.** $(1, 4.5)$ **c.** $(2, -6)$ **d.** $(3, -1)$ **e.** The points are collinear.   **3. a–b.** Answers may vary. Samples are given. **a.** $A(0, 0), B(2, 2)$

b. C(0, 0), D(−2, 2) **c.** F(2, 3), G(−2, 3)
d. K(7, 2), L(7, −2) **4.** Answers may vary. Sample: The graphs that have constant slope involve only x and y multiplied by constant coefficients, with no exponentiation.

4. a.

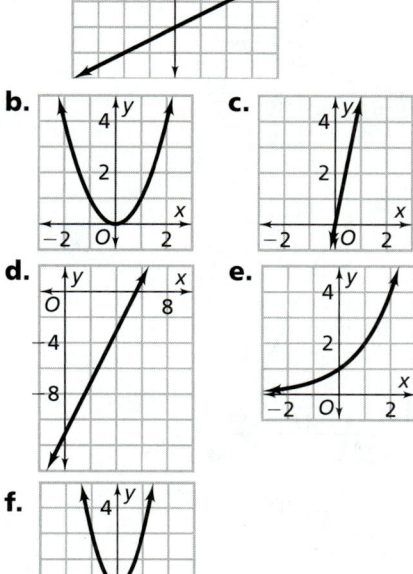

5. Answers may vary. Sample: Ski slopes, hiking trails, and roller coaster tracks all vary in steepness. **6.** r = 2

On Your Own
7. a. $-\frac{2}{3}$ **d.** undefined **8. a.** Answers may vary. Sample: (4, 0) **9. a.** One point is above and to the right of the other point. **10. a.** $-\frac{4}{3}$

Lesson 4.03
Check Your Understanding
1. a. 75 mi/h **b.** 0 mi/h **c.** Answers may vary. Sample: If you have points D(0.5, 37.5) and E(1.25, 75), then m(D,E) = 50. **2. a.** $6 **b.** About 57 mi/h; no, he will not get fined.
3. a. $6 **b.** about 67 mi/h; yes **c.** about 3 hours, 5 minutes **4. a.** at most $59\frac{1}{11}$ mi/h
b.

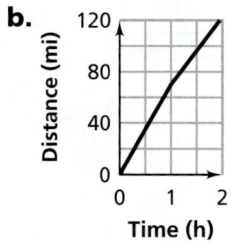

5. a. 280 mi; 4 h **b.** Answers may vary. Sample:

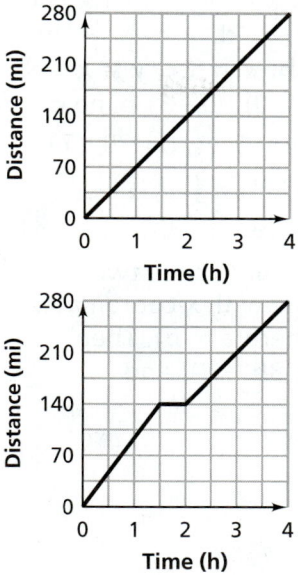

On Your Own
6. a. Car A: Hybrid car; Car B: Sedan; Car C: SUV **7. a.** About 41 s **8. a.** miles per hour **10. a.** 1,150 yd **b.** about 26 s
13. a. between O and P, Q and S, and S and U **b.** between Q and S

Lesson 4.04
Check Your Understanding
1. a. yes **b.** yes **c.** yes **d.** no **2.** points A, B, and D; m(A, B) = m(B, D) = 1 **3.** Answers may vary. Sample: It is sufficient to compare just two of the slopes to test collinearity. If you know two of the slopes are equal, then the third must be equal to the other two.
4. a–c. Answers may vary. Samples are given.
a. (1, −4) **b.** (−4, 0) **c.** (2, 4) **5.** Answers may vary. Sample: $\frac{y-3}{x-2} = -\frac{7}{10}$

On Your Own
6. a. Answers may vary. Sample: (0, −3), (2, 5), (4, 13); yes **8. a.** Not on ℓ; the slope between R(−2, 4) and (1, 3) is $-\frac{1}{3}$. **9. a.** $a = \frac{11}{4}$

Lesson 4.05
On Your Own
7. a. 9000 ft **8. c.** 42,000 ft; yes
11. a. $\frac{y}{x-5} = \frac{1}{2}$ **12. e.** y = 2x − 5

Lesson 4.06
Check Your Understanding
1. $y - 2 = -\frac{1}{4}(x - 6)$; yes; both equations simplify to $y = -\frac{1}{4}x + \frac{7}{2}$.
2. Answers may vary. Sample: An equation of the line through the points (5, 6) and (3, 2) is y − 2 = 2(x − 3); (1, −2) is on the line because −2 − 2 = 2(1 − 3) simplifies to the true statement −4 = −4, and (6, 6) is not on the

line because $6 - 2 = 2(6 - 3)$ simplifies to the false statement $4 = 6$. **3. a.** $y - 7 = -1(x - 6)$ **b.** $y - 4 = x - 5$ **c.** $y = \frac{1}{3}x$ **d.** $y = \frac{1}{3}x + 10$ **e.** $y = -x$ **4. a.** $y = 7$ **b.** $x = 5$ **c.** $y = x$ **d.** $y = 0$ **5. a.** yes; $\frac{3}{4}$, $(4, 0)$, $(0, -3)$ **b.** no **c.** yes; $\frac{3}{4}$, $(4, 0)$, $(0, -3)$ **d.** yes; 5, $\left(\frac{7}{5}, 0\right)$, $(0, -7)$ **e.** yes; $\frac{3}{4}$, $(4, 0)$, $(0, -3)$ **f.** yes; $-\frac{5}{3}$, $\left(-\frac{27}{5}, 0\right)$, $(0, -9)$ **g.** no **h.** yes; $\frac{3}{4}$, $(3, 0)$, $\left(0, -\frac{9}{4}\right)$ **i.** yes; $-\frac{5}{3}$, $\left(\frac{24}{5}, 0\right)$, $(0, 8)$ **6.** Choose two points A and B on the line with x-coordinates a and b, respectively (where $a \neq b$). Then $A = (a, 3a - 7)$, $B = (b, 3b - 7)$, and $m(A, B) = \frac{(3b - 7) - (3a - 7)}{b - a} = \frac{3b - 3a}{b - a} = \frac{3(b - a)}{b - a} = 3$.

On Your Own
9. a. -5 **11. b.** $42.50

Lesson 4.07
Check Your Understanding
1. a. $y - 3 = -1(x - 4)$ **b.** $y - 5 = \frac{1}{3}(x + 2)$ **c.** $y + 3 = \frac{4}{5}(x - 7)$ **d.** $y + 5 = -\frac{11}{7}(x + 1)$ **e.** $y + \frac{1}{2} = 2\left(x + \frac{3}{2}\right)$ **f.** $y + 9.8 = -4.38(x - 14.6)$ **g.** $y = \frac{5}{6}x + 12$ **h.** $y = -\frac{2}{3}x - 3$ **i.** $y = \frac{5}{16}x - \frac{8}{5}$ **j.** $y = \frac{21}{13}x + 5$ **k.** $y = 9$ **l.** $x = -8$

2. a. 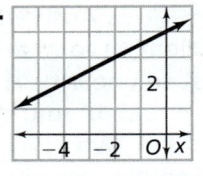 **b.**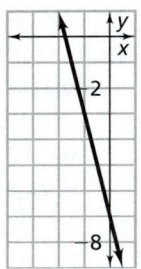

c. 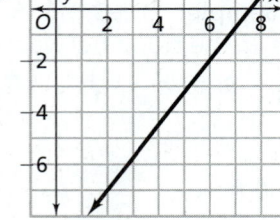 **d.**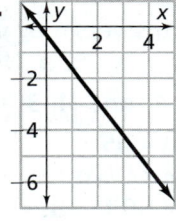

e. 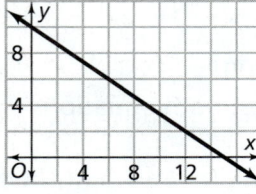 **f.**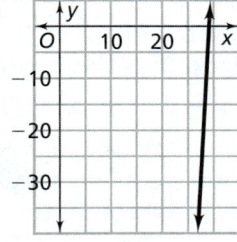

g.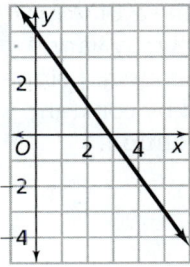

h.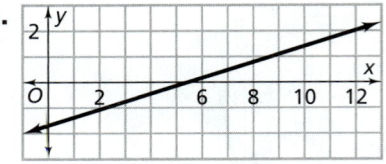

3. a. 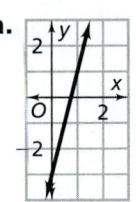 **b.**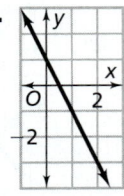

c. 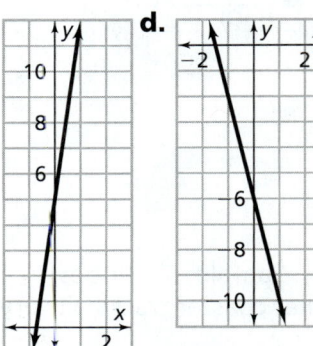 **d.**

e. 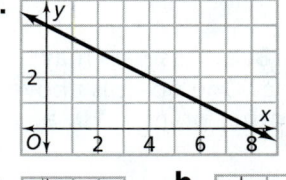 **f.**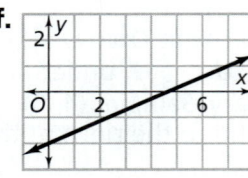

g. 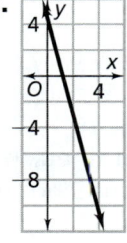 **h.**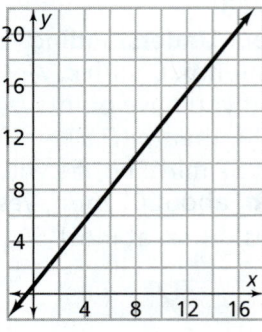

On Your Own
4. $\frac{389}{3}$ **8.** $y + 5 = 4(x + 3)$ **19.** $y = \frac{5}{4}x - \frac{1}{2}$ **40.** $y = 6x - 1$

Lesson 4.08
Check Your Understanding
1. a. Yakov **b.** at 2 s **c.** 20 ft **d.** Yakov's speed is 20 ft/s; Demitri's speed is 10 ft/s. **e.** $y = 20x$ **f.** $y = 10x + 20$ **g.** $20x = 10x + 20$; $x = 2$

2. a. They run at the same speed. **b.** Yakov does not overtake Demitri. **c.** Both speeds are 10 ft/s. **d.** $y = 20x$ **e.** $y = 20x + 20$ **f.** Yakov does not overtake Demitri. **3. a.** Yakov is ahead of and stays ahead of Demitri.
b. No; the graphs keep getting farther and farther apart. **c.** $(-2, -20)$ **d.** no

On Your Own
5. Derman **7.** yes; in about 45 seconds

Lesson 4.09
On Your Own
7. a. A and C are on neither; B is on both.
8. b. Answers may vary. Sample: $(0, 0)$; $(5, 5)$ is on p but not on q; $(0, 2)$. **9.** Answers may vary. Sample: $x + y = -2$ and $2x + y = 0$

Lesson 4.10
Check Your Understanding
1. $1.29 **2.** $v = 1.29$; $a = 0.89$ **3. a.** BigPhone costs $.57; LittlePhone costs $.67.
b. 3.5 min **c.** BigPhone **4. a.** $\left(-\frac{1}{4}, -8\frac{1}{2}\right)$
b. $\left(3, \frac{3}{4}\right)$ **c.** $(-4, -12)$ **d.** $(-2, 5)$ **e.** no solution
f. $\left(\frac{1}{2}, 2\right)$ **5. a.** Walton: $2.82; Newtham: $2.25 **b.** Walton: $4.15; Newtham: $4.00
c. Walton: $t = 2.25 + 0.19m$; Newtham: $t = 1.50 + 0.25m$

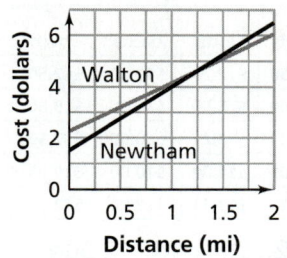

d. 1.25 mi **e.** Walton **f.** when the distance is greater than 1.25 mi **6. a.** $\left(\frac{1}{8}, \frac{15}{8}\right)$ **b.** $\left(\frac{14}{3}, 3\right)$
c. $\left(\frac{100}{19}, \frac{100}{19}\right)$ **7.** Answers may vary. Sample: comparing the costs of two phone service plans based on the number of minutes used
8. Answers may vary. Sample: comparing the costs of three phone service plans based on the number of minutes used

On Your Own
9. a. Just Plumbing **13. a.** $(84, 1482)$ **b.** No solution; the slopes are the same.

Lesson 4.11
Check Your Understanding
1. a. parallel **b.** intersecting **c.** parallel **d.** identical
e. intersecting **f.** intersecting **2.** Tony is right.
3. Answers may vary. Sample: BiggerPhone plan costs $.39 for a connection and $.04 per minute. The line $y = 0.04x + 0.39$ is parallel to and above the line $y = 0.03x + 0.39$ for all values of x.
4. The two equations are equivalent.

On Your Own
5. $y - 15 = -\frac{1}{5}(x - 10)$ **8.** $y = ax$
9. a. $y = -3$

Lesson 4.12
Check Your Understanding
1. a. $x = 18$, $y = 12$ **b.** $a = \frac{1}{2}$, $b = 5$ **c.** $x = 2$, $y = 0$ **d.** no solution **e.** $w = -3$, $z = 0$
f. $x = 2$, $y = 15$ **2.** The cost of one granola bar is $.50. The cost of one drink is $1.25.
3. Multiply each side of the second equation by -2. Add the equations. Solve for y. Substitute 8 for y in one of the original equations. Solve for x. Check the solution by substituting both values into each equation. **4. a.** $y = 1$
b. $x = 6$ **c.** The line $5x + 3y = 33$ also passes through $(6, 1)$. **5.** $x = 6$, $y = 3$, $z = -2$
6. Answers may vary. Sample: Multiply each side of the second equation by $-\frac{a}{c}$. This yields $-ax - \frac{ady}{c} = -\frac{af}{c}$. Add this equation to the first equation in the system. The resulting equation is $by - \frac{ady}{c} = e - \frac{af}{c}$, or $\frac{bcy - ady}{c} = \frac{ce - af}{c}$. Solve for y to get $y = \frac{ec - af}{bc - ad} = \frac{af - ec}{ad - bc}$. To find x, multiply each side of the second equation by $-\frac{b}{d}$ and follow a similar line of reasoning.

On Your Own
7. a. Answers may vary. Sample: $y = 3x + 3$, $y = 3x - 7$
8. c. $8.25 **10. a.** $(7, -5)$ **11. d.** no solution

Lesson 4.13
On Your Own
10. a. 3 **b.** $(0, 0)$, $(2, 2)$, $(-2, -2)$ **c.** $x = 0$, $x = -2$, or $x = 2$ **d.** $x < -2$ or $0 < x < 2$
11. a. $a > 13$

Lesson 4.14
Check Your Understanding
1. a. [number line: open circle at 5, shaded left toward 0]
b. [number line: closed circle at 4, shaded right]
c. [number line: open circle at 6, shaded right]
d. [number line: closed circle at $\frac{11}{2}$, shaded left]

2. a. $x > \frac{73}{7}$ **b.** $1 < x < 7$ **c.** $x < -11$ or $x > 5$
d. $2.9 \leq x \leq 3.1$ **e.** No solution. The inequality is never true. **f.** $x > \frac{73}{7}$ **g.** $x \leq -1$ or $x = 0$ or $x \geq 1$ **3. a.** $x < 5$ **b.** Answers may vary. Sample: The image on the graphing calculator does not give any useful information

about the intersection of the lines, since the two lines are so close together. You could adjust the graphing calculator's window to find the intersection, but it is easier to solve the inequality with algebra. **4. a.** $x > \frac{11}{3}$ **b.** Subtract $2x$ from each side, add 17 to each side, and divide each side by 3. **c.** $x > \frac{20}{3}$

d.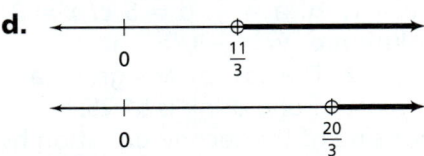

The solution to part (c) is the solution to part (a) translated 3 units to the right. **e.** $x > \frac{44}{3}$ **f.** $x > -\frac{13}{3}$ **5.** $x \neq 4$ **6a.** $x = -3$ **b.** $x = -11$ **c.**

d. $x \leq -11$ or $x > -3$ **e.** Answers may vary. Sample: Graph the equation $y = 2$. The solution to the inequality is the set of all x-coordinates for which the graph of $y = \frac{x-5}{x+3}$ is below the graph of $y = 2$.

On Your Own
9. $-1 < x < 0$ or $x > 1$

10. b. true

11. a.

14. a. always true

Lesson 4.15
Check Your Understanding
1. a. x is the temperature in °F and y is the number of attendees in thousands.
b. yes, $47.1 \approx 0.678(80) - 7.1$ **2. a.** at the center of the ruler **b.** at the center of the coin **c.** Yes; answers may vary. Sample: A boomerang has its balance point between its arms. **3.** A

4. a. no **b.** The scatterplot shows that there is a linear trend to the data and that the balance point is along this linear trend. **c.** yes

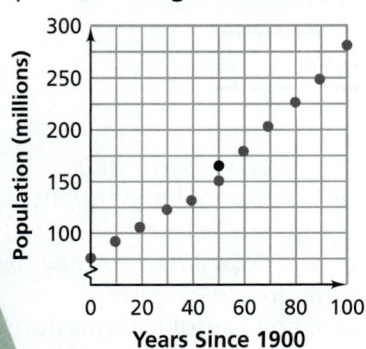

On Your Own
5. a. yes

9. a. The predicted values are too high.

Chapter 5
Lesson 5.01
On Your Own
6. Sasha's rule is "x returns $x + 3$," or "Add 3 to the input," or anything equivalent. **7. a.** Yes, you can fill in the second line with 2 or -2 and the fourth line with 1 or -1. **9.** any number greater than 3, because these inputs will give different outputs

Lesson 5.02
Check Your Understanding
1. a. 540 s **b.** 210 s **c.** 246 s **d.** 81 s **e.** 145.8 s **f.** $S = 60M$ **2. a.** 0.15 h **b.** 0.583 h **c.** 0.683 h **d.** 2.25 h **e.** 4.05 h **f.** $H = \frac{M}{60}$ **3. a.** Alan: $7.31, Lou: $12.18, Katie: $8.91 **b.** $c + 0.05c + 0.18c = 1.23c$
4. a.

Charity Run Donations

Number of Miles	Mom	Uncle	Teacher	Coach	Agustina	Total
1	$ 3.50	$ 2.75	$10.00	$ 2.50	$5.00	$23.75
2	$ 7.00	$ 5.50	$10.00	$ 5.00	$5.00	$32.50
3	$10.50	$ 8.25	$10.00	$ 7.50	$5.00	$41.25
4	$14.00	$11.00	$10.00	$10.00	$5.00	$50.00
5	$17.50	$13.75	$10.00	$12.50	$5.00	$58.75

b. $3.50d + 2.75d + 10 + 2.50d + 5 = 15 + 8.75d$, where d is the distance Antonio runs in miles. **c.** $76.25 **d.** 4 mi; 10 mi **5.** The new rule would be that if Antonio runs d miles, he will raise $22.75 + 10.25d$ dollars.

On Your Own
6. a. 180 min **8. c.** 21,600 ft **10.** $1.95\left(\frac{M}{24}\right)$; 246.2 mi

Lesson 5.03
Check Your Understanding
1. a. a function; Output column: $-13, -8, -3, 2, 7, 12, 17$ **b.** a function; Output column: 9, 4, 1, 0, 1, 4, 9 **c.** Not a function; for input -3, there are many outputs, $\frac{1}{2}$, $\frac{1}{4}$, etc. **d.** a function; Output column: $-4, -5, -6, -7, -6, -5, -4$ **e.** Not a function; for input -3, there are two outputs, -3 and 3.
2. a. $x \mapsto 5x + 2$ **b.** $x \mapsto x^2$ **d.** $X \mapsto |x| - 7$

3. a. The missing output values are −5, 1, −17, 25; the missing input value is 7. **b.** $6x - 5$ **4. a.** The missing output values are −30, −24, −42, 0; the missing input value is $\frac{37}{6}$. **b.** $6(x - 5)$ **c.** no

On Your Own
5. a. a function; Output column: 2, 1, 0, −1, −2 **6. a.** A function; for each day, there is one average temperature. **7. a.** Not a function; for some average temperatures, there is not exactly one day of the year with that average temperature.

Lesson 5.04
Check Your Understanding
1. Output column: 5, 3, 1, −1, −3, −5 **2. a.** 8; $\frac{1}{2}$
b. $1 \to \boxed{x^2 + 4} \to 5 \to \boxed{\frac{1}{x}} \to \frac{1}{5}; \frac{1}{5}.$
c. $x \to \boxed{x^2 + 4} \to x^2 + 4 \to \boxed{\frac{1}{x}} \to \frac{1}{x^2 + 4}; \frac{1}{29}$
d. $x \to \boxed{\frac{1}{x}} \to \frac{1}{x} \to \boxed{x^2 + 4} \to \left(\frac{1}{x}\right)^2 + 4;$
$h(\text{REC}(1)) = 5; h(\text{REC}(5)) = 4\frac{1}{25};$ no
e. Division by 0 is undefined. **3.** Answers may vary. Sample: Choose f and g to be the same function. **4.** $f(x) = x$ and $f(x) = -x$
5. a. 2; 6 **b.** yes **c.** 0 **d.** yes **e.** 0

On Your Own
6. a. Yes; only g maps 5 to 14. **e.** There are none. **7.** $d = 30t$, where t is time in hours and d is distance in miles. **9. c.** 9

Lesson 5.05
Check Your Understanding
1. a. all negative real numbers **b.** no invalid inputs **2. a.** all real numbers ≥ 2 **b.** all real numbers **c.** all real numbers except 2 **d.** all real numbers **3. a.** all real numbers except 0 **b.** all real numbers **4. a.** No; Tables I and II both define functions; Table III does not, as input −1 has two outputs. **b.** Table I: domain—$-3, -1, \frac{1}{2}, 2, 9, 100$; range—3, 4, 7, 8, 12; Table II: domain—$-2, 4, 7, 11, 13$; range—$-4, 0, 3, 9, 16$ **5.** Answers may vary. Sample: $f(x) = x$, $a = 3$, and $f(3x) = 3 \cdot f(x)$ **6. a.** 1 **b.** 11 **c.** 21

On Your Own
7. all real numbers except 5 and −5 **8. b.** Yes; yes; if the remainder is defined so that it must be 0, 1, or 2, then you can divide 0 and negative numbers by 3 and get a remainder.

Lesson 5.06
Check Your Understanding
1. $A(n) = -2n + 9; B(s) = s^2 - 1;$
$C(n) = n + \frac{1}{n}; D(x) = 0.125x + 12.875$

2. no; no; yes; yes **3.** the first and fourth graphs **4. a.** yes **b.** Answers may vary. Sample: yes

x	2 − 5x		x	−5(x + 1) + 7
0	2		0	2
1	−3		1	−3
2	−8		2	−8
3	−13		3	−13
4	−18		4	−18

c. The graphs are the same. **d.** yes **5.** No; answers may vary. Sample: $s(1) = 0$ and $t(1) = 0.01$ **6.** Rule C: Output column: 5, 10, 20, 40, 80, 160 Rule D: The tables are the same for identical inputs. Rule C inputs are nonnegative integers. Rule D inputs are all real numbers. **7.** Output column: 4, 2, 6, 2, 4, 4, 5, 2, 6, 2, 6, 4, 4, 2, 8; conjectures may vary. Sample: Square numbers have an odd number of factors, and all numbers except for 1 have at least two factors; explanations may vary. Sample: Prime numbers only have two factors.

On Your Own
8. a. $4x + 9$

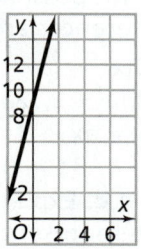

12. a. Answers may vary. Sample:

x	p(x)		x	g(x)
−2	−4		−2	undef.
−1	−3		−1	−3
0	−2		0	−2
1	−1		1	−1
2	0		2	0

no

13. a. yes **c.** no **14. a.** not the same function

Lesson 5.07
On Your Own
11. a.

Table A

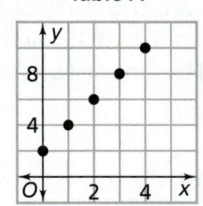

Table B

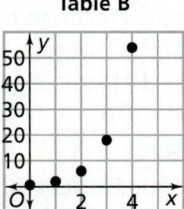

b. yes; no **12. b.** Answers may vary. Sample: 32 is twice 16, so support length must be twice

5, or 10. 48 is 3 times 16, so support length must be three times 5, or 15.

Lesson 5.08
Check Your Understanding

1. a.

Input	Output	Δ
0	1	7
1	8	7
2	15	7
3	22	7
4	29	7
5	36	

b.

Input	Output	Δ
0	−4	0
1	−4	2
2	−2	4
3	2	6
4	8	8
5	16	

c.

Input	Output	Δ
0	1	−3
1	−2	−3
2	−5	−3
3	−8	−3
4	−11	−3
5	−14	

d.

Input	Output	Δ
0	4	6
1	10	6
2	16	6
3	22	6
4	28	6
5	34	

2. a. $L(x) = 2x + 1$ **b.** Not possible; consecutive output differences are not the same. **c.** $N(x) = 3$ **d.** $O(x) = \frac{1}{3}x - \frac{1}{3}$
3. a. Output column: 3, $a + 3$, $2a + 3$, $3a + 3$, $4a + 3$, $5a + 3$ **b.** $f(x) = ax + 3$ **4. a.** Output column: b, $a + b$, $2a + b$, $3a + b$, $4a + b$, $5a + b$ **b.** $f(x) = ax + b$ **c.** Explanations may vary. Sample: This table represents any table that has constant differences a and an output b for input 0. It shows that any input x has output $ax + b$, which is a linear function.
5. a. No; the differences in the Δ column are not constant. Instead, they alternate between −2 and 2. **b.** Output for 0 is 1. Subsequent values alternate between 1 and −1. $x \mapsto (-1)^x$

On Your Own
6. a. Matt has not noticed that the differences between consecutive inputs are not the same. **8. f. a.** $f(x) = 6x - 11$ **b.** $f(x) = 3^x$ **c.** $f(x) = \frac{4}{5}x - 2$ **d.** $f(x) = -2x + 9$ **9.** Yes; for input 2, output is 3. For input 4, output is 11. For consecutive inputs 2, 3, and 4 to have constant-difference outputs, the output for 3 has to be halfway between 3 and 11, or 7. The constant difference is 4. The linear function is $E(x) = 4x - 5$.

Lesson 5.09
Check Your Understanding
1. a. Output column: 2, 6, 10, 14, 18, 22
b. Output column: 2, 6, 18, 54, 162, 486
c. Output column: 2, 6, 14, 30, 62, 126

d. Output column: 2, 6, 10, 14, 18, 22
2. a. no linear function **b.** $x \mapsto 2x + 5$
c. $x \mapsto 2x - 3$ **d.** no linear function

3. a. $f(n) = \begin{cases} 8 & \text{if } n = 0 \\ \frac{f(n-1)}{2} & \text{if } n > 0 \end{cases}$

b. $f(n) = \begin{cases} 5 & \text{if } n = 0 \\ f(n-1) + 2 & \text{if } n > 0 \end{cases}$

c. $f(n) = \begin{cases} -3 & \text{if } n = 0 \\ f(n-1) + 2 & \text{if } n > 0 \end{cases}$

d. $f(n) = \begin{cases} 3.4 & \text{if } n = 0 \\ 10f(n-1) & \text{if } n > 0 \end{cases}$

4. a. $.32 **b.** $10.24; $327.68

5. a.

Week	Allowance
1	$ .16
2	$1.12
3	$1.84
4	$2.38
5	$2.79

b. $3.72; $3.93 **c.** no

6. a.

Week	Allowance
1	$10.00
2	$8.50
3	$7.38
4	$6.54
5	$5.91

b. $4.45; $4.11 **c.** yes; no **7.** Input column: 0, 1, 2, 3, 4, 5, Output column: 1, 2, 6, 24, 120; Rule: g maps 0 to 1, 1 to 1, and any other positive integer n to the product of all positive integers less than or equal to n; $g(n) = 1 \cdot 2 \cdot 3 \cdot \ldots \cdot (n-1) \cdot n$.

On Your Own
9. For input 0, the output is $5000; for other inputs, multiply the previous output by 1.1; $6655. **11. c.** 13 lawns

Lesson 5.10
On Your Own
7. a. $1980 **b.** $49.50; $29.70 **c.** $1772.77
d. 69 months **9. a.** $d + 0.045d$ represents your investment plus the interest on the investment. **10. a.** 4.66; 4.6

c. Last score → [Add 23.3] → [Divide by 6.] → 6-event average

Lesson 5.11
Check Your Understanding
1. a.

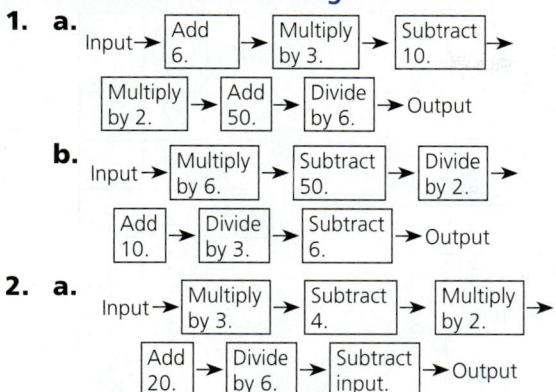

b.

2. a.

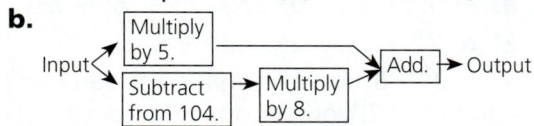

b. Answers may vary. Sample: You cannot backtrack through the part of the machine that uses two inputs. **c.** $S(n) = 2$ **3. a.** $742
b.

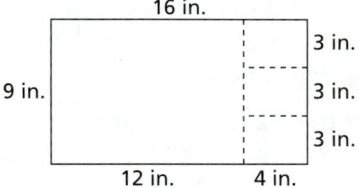

c. 64 students **4.** 16 in. by 9 in. **5.** Answers may vary. Sample:

```
         16 in.
   ┌─────────────┬──────┐
   │             │ 3 in.│
9 in.│             ├──────┤
   │             │ 3 in.│
   │             ├──────┤
   │             │ 3 in.│
   └─────────────┴──────┘
       12 in.     4 in.
```

6. 2545 miles **7. a.** 5, 34, 6, 40 **b.** 20 **c.** 8 **d.** 2 **e.** 2

On Your Own
8. c. $150 **9. b.** $210 + 3p = 300$ **12. a.** 0.20

Lesson 5.12
Check Your Understanding
1. For inputs 1 and 2, outputs are 1. For any other input, the output is the sum of the two previous outputs. 1, 1, 2, 3, 5, 8, 13, 21, 34, 55, 89, 144 **2. a.** 0.125% each month; 0.00125; divide the annual interest rate by 12.
b. $0; $.06; $.13
c.
$$S(n) = \begin{cases} 0 & \text{if } n = 0 \\ S(n-1) + 0.00125 S(n-1) + 50 & \text{if } n > 0 \end{cases}$$

3. a.

b. 4, $\frac{16}{3}$ **c.** $P(\ell) = \begin{cases} 3 & \text{if } \ell = 0 \\ \frac{4}{3}P(\ell-1) & \text{if } \ell > 0 \end{cases}$

exponential **d.** $\frac{4}{3}, \frac{40}{27}$

e. $A(\ell) = \begin{cases} 1 & \text{if } \ell = 0 \\ A(\ell-1) + \frac{3}{4}\left(\frac{4}{9}\right)^\ell & \text{if } \ell > 0 \end{cases}$

about 1.5954; the area seems to get closer and closer to 1.6. **4. a.** 15 **b.** not linear because the differences are not constant

On Your Own
5. a. 1 g **6. b.** Sample: value at day 0 is $100. The value at the end of each day is $5.70 less than the value at the end of the previous day. **8.** 8 **11. b.** 1; you get the same result no matter what positive number N you begin with.

Chapter 6
Lesson 6.01
On Your Own
5. $26^3 \cdot 10^3 = 17{,}576{,}000$ **6.** 10^4; there are ten choices for each digit, and four digits. **8. a.** 10^{16}

Lesson 6.02
Check Your Understanding
1. a. $2^{10} + 2^2 \neq 2^{12}$; $2^{10} + 2^2 = 2^2(2^8 + 1)$ This number is divisible by an odd number $(2^8 + 1)$, but 2^{12} is divisible only by even powers of 2, which are all even.
b. $2^6 \cdot 2^6 = 2^{12}$; this follows from Theorem 6.1.
c. $(2^{10})(2^2) = 2^{12}$; this follows from Theorem 6.1. **d.** $(2^4)(2^3) \neq 2^{12}$; by Theorem 6.1, $(2^4)(2^3) = 2^7$.
e. $(2^4)(2^4)(2^4) = 2^{12}$; this follows from For Discussion Problem 8.
f. $2^9 + 2^3 \neq 2^{12}$; $2^9 + 2^3 = 2^3(2^6 + 1)$. This number is divisible by an odd number $(2^6 + 1)$, but 2^{12} is divisible only by even powers of 2, which are all even. **g.** $2^{11} + 2^{11} = 2^{12}$; $2^{11} + 2^{11} = 2 \cdot 2^{11} = 2^1 \cdot 2^{11} = 2^{1+11} = 2^{12}$ **h.** $4(2^{10}) = 2^{12}$; $4(2^{10}) = 2^2(2^{10}) = 2^{2+10} = 2^{12}$

2. 10^6, 10^9, and 10^n have 6 zeros, 9 zeros, and n zeros respectively; when you multiply a number by 10, it has the effect of adding one zero to the end of the number. **3.** 8
4. Answers may vary. Sample: in the product $(ab)(ab)(ab)\ldots$ (where (ab) is multiplied n times), there are n instances of a, and n instances of b. By AOAG, the product equals $(aaa\ldots)(bbb\ldots) = a^n b^n$. **5. a.** 10^3 **b.** 100^6
c. 1 **d.** 2^4 **e.** 100^4 **f.** 10^4 **6. a.** 26^3 **b.** 26^n
c. 21^3 **d.** $26 \cdot 25 \cdot 24 = 15{,}600$ **7. a.** 7.69%
b. 14.20% **c.** The three-letter word is more likely. **8. a.** 26^2 **b.** 26^2 **c.** If p is even, there are $26^{\frac{p}{2}}$. If p is odd, there are $26^{\frac{(p+1)}{2}}$.

On Your Own
9. a. $x^4 y^3$ **11. a.** 3 **12. c.** 256 in.
13. c. 192 in.

Lesson 6.03
Check Your Understanding
1. Answers may vary. Sample: $A^2 B$; B^4
2. 2,000,000 **3a.** No; $(3^6)^9 = 3^{6 \cdot 9} = 3^{54}$
b. Yes; the result holds due to Theorem 6.1. **c.** no; $(3^3)(3^5) = 3^{3+5} = 3^8$ **d.** no; $(3^{15})(3^1) = 3^{15+1} = 3^{16}$ **e.** Yes; the result holds due to For Discussion Problem 8.
f. no; $3^9 + 3^6 = (3^6)(3^3 + 1) = (3^6)(28)$ This product is even while 3^{15} is odd. **g.** Yes; the result holds due to Theorem 6.4. **h.** yes; $3^{14} + 3^{14} + 3^{14} = 3 \cdot 3^{14} = 3^1 \cdot 3^{14} = 3^{1+14} = 3^{15}$ **i.** Yes; the result holds due to Theorem 6.4. **j.** yes; $9(3^{13}) = (3^2)(3^{13}) = 3^{2+13} = 3^{15}$ **k.** no; $(3^5)^{10} = 3^{5 \cdot 10} = 3^{50}$
l. Yes; the result holds due to Theorem 6.4. **4a.** no; $\frac{2^6}{2^2} = 2^{6-2} = 2^4$ **b.** yes; $\frac{2^6}{2^3} = 2^{6-3} = 2^3$ **c.** no; $(2^2)^1 = 2^{2 \cdot 1} = 2^2$ **d.** yes; $\frac{(2^2)^5}{2^7} = \frac{2^{10}}{2^7} = 2^{10-7} = 2^3$ **e.** yes; $\frac{2^9}{2^6} = 2^{9-6} = 2^3$
f. no; $\frac{2^9}{2^3} = 2^{9-3} = 2^6$ **g.** no; $\frac{2^7 2^8}{2^5} = \frac{2^{15}}{2^5} = 2^{15-5} = 2^{10}$ **5.** 6; 6 **6.** 1 **7.** 9

On Your Own
8. a. $\frac{1}{2}$ in.; $\frac{1}{4}$ in. **10. a.** Yes; this is the definition of 5^6, five multiplied by itself six times. **11.** 4; 6 **12. a.** x^{12} **13. a.** $49c^2$

Lesson 6.04
Check Your Understanding

1.

x	3^x	÷
−3	$\frac{1}{27}$	3
−2	$\frac{1}{9}$	3
−1	$\frac{1}{3}$	3
0	1	3
1	3	3
2	9	3
3	27	

2.

x	$\left(\frac{1}{3}\right)^x$	÷
−3	27	$\frac{1}{3}$
−2	9	$\frac{1}{3}$
−1	3	$\frac{1}{3}$
0	1	$\frac{1}{3}$
1	$\frac{1}{3}$	$\frac{1}{3}$
2	$\frac{1}{9}$	$\frac{1}{3}$
3	$\frac{1}{27}$	

3. The outputs are reciprocals.
4. a. $2^3 + 2^2 + 2^1$ **b.** $2^3 + 2^2 + 2^1 + 2^0$
c. 2^4 **d.** $2^4 + 2^3 + 2^2 + 2^1 + 2^0$
e. $2^5 + 2^0$ **5.** Answers may vary. Sample: if n is a power of 2, you are done. Suppose n is not a power of 2. Then $2^a < n < 2^{a+1}$ for some integer a. Therefore $n = 2^a + k$ for some integer k less than 2^a. If k is a power of 2, you are done. If not, then $2^b < k < 2^{b+1}$ for some integer $b < a$. Therefore $k = 2^b + m$ for some integer m less than 2^b. Continue with this process. Eventually it will end, because you started with a finite positive integer.

6.

			10^2	10^3	10^4	10^5	10^6	10^7	10^8	10^9	10^{10}
			10^1	10^2	10^3	10^4	10^5	10^6	10^7	10^8	10^9
			10^0	10^1	10^2	10^3	10^4	10^5	10^6	10^7	10^8
			10^{-1}	10^0	10^1	10^2	10^3	10^4	10^5	10^6	10^7
			10^{-2}	10^{-1}	10^0	10^1	10^2	10^3	10^4	10^5	10^6
10^{-3}	10^{-2}	10^{-1}	10^0	10^1	10^2	10^3	10^4	10^5			
10^{-4}	10^{-3}	10^{-2}	10^{-1}	10^0	10^1	10^2	10^3	10^4			
10^{-5}	10^{-4}	10^{-3}	10^{-2}	10^{-1}	10^0	10^1	10^2	10^3			
10^{-6}	10^{-5}	10^{-4}	10^{-3}	10^{-2}	10^{-1}	10^0	10^1	10^2			

On Your Own
8. 2 **10. a.** z^2

Lesson 6.05
Check Your Understanding
1. a. 1.34×10^6 **b.** 6.09×10^{-6} **c.** -3×10^0
d. 9×10^4 **e.** 3.79×10^7 **f.** 6.02×10^7

g. 7.8×10^{12} **h.** 1.1×10^7 **2.** 60 years
3. a. 1.99×10^{30}; 5.97×10^{24} **b.** about 330,000 **4.** 2.192×10^{-8} mi/h
5. 9.03×10^{24}

On Your Own
6. b. 9.3×10^4 **7. b.** 94,720,000,000
d. -0.000000000377 **11.** 1×10^{22}

Lesson 6.06
On Your Own
7. a. not a perfect square **b.** perfect square
8. 1.73; to get more accuracy, you would need a table that breaks the interval between 1.730 and 1.830 into thousandths.

Lesson 6.07
Check Your Understanding
1. a. $x \approx 3.162$ **b.** $x \approx 2.154$ **c.** $x \approx 1.778$
d. $x \approx 1.778$ **2. a.** Since the product of two positive numbers is positive, $\sqrt{2} \cdot \sqrt{3}$ is positive. Square the product to get $(\sqrt{2} \cdot \sqrt{3})^2 = (\sqrt{2})^2 \cdot (\sqrt{3})^2 = 2 \cdot 3 = 6$. So $\sqrt{2} \cdot \sqrt{3}$ is a nonnegative number with a square of 6. There is only one such number, $\sqrt{6}$.
b. Since the quotient of two positive numbers is positive, $\frac{\sqrt{19}}{\sqrt{5}}$ is positive. Square the quotient to get $\left(\frac{\sqrt{19}}{\sqrt{5}}\right)^2 = \frac{(\sqrt{19})^2}{(\sqrt{5})^2} = \frac{19}{5}$. So $\frac{\sqrt{19}}{\sqrt{5}}$ is a nonnegative number with a square of $\frac{19}{5}$. There is only one such number, $\sqrt{\frac{19}{5}}$.
c. Since the product of two positive numbers is positive, $\sqrt{11} \cdot \sqrt{7}$ is positive. Square the product to get $(\sqrt{11} \cdot \sqrt{7})^2 = (\sqrt{11})^2 \cdot (\sqrt{7})^2 = 11 \cdot 7 = 77$. So $\sqrt{11} \cdot \sqrt{7}$ is a nonnegative number with a square of 77. There is only one such number, $\sqrt{77}$. **d.** Since the quotient of two positive numbers is positive, $\frac{\sqrt{12}}{2}$ is positive. Square the quotient to get $\left(\frac{\sqrt{12}}{2}\right)^2 = \frac{(\sqrt{12})^2}{2^2} = \frac{12}{4} = 3$. So $\frac{\sqrt{12}}{2}$ is a nonnegative number with a square of 3. There is only one such number, $\sqrt{3}$.
e. Since the quotient of two positive numbers is positive, $\frac{10}{\sqrt{10}}$ is positive. Square the quotient to get $\left(\frac{10}{\sqrt{10}}\right)^2 = \frac{10^2}{(\sqrt{10})^2} = \frac{100}{10} = 10$. So $\frac{10}{\sqrt{10}}$ is a nonnegative number with a square of 10. There is only one such number, $\sqrt{10}$. **3.** 2

On Your Own
5. Yes, Tony's number is 12. **6. c.** $\sqrt{15}$
7. a. 1 **9. b.** $\sqrt{2}$

Lesson 6.08
Check Your Understanding
1. a. 4 **b.** $2\sqrt{5}$ **c.** 2 **d.** $4\sqrt{5}$ **2. a.** 2 **b.** 2 **c.** 3
d. 10 **e.** 3 **f.** In each equation, the number under the radical on the left side of the equation is divisible by a perfect square.
3. a. ± 1.968 **b.** ± 2 **c.** ± 1.627 **d.** no solution **4. a.** $\sqrt{6}, \sqrt{22}, \sqrt{33}$; 66 **b.** $\sqrt{12}, \sqrt{15}, \sqrt{20}$; 60 **c.** $\sqrt{35}, \sqrt{77}, \sqrt{55}$; 385 **d.** The final product is the product of the original numbers under the square root signs. **5.** A

On Your Own
6. a. 3 **8. a.** 1.72 **9. a.** $5\sqrt{2}$
11. $a = 10\sqrt{2} - 10$; $b = 10\sqrt{3} - 10\sqrt{2}$; $c = 20 - 10\sqrt{3}$; 10

Lesson 6.09
Check Your Understanding
1. a. $\frac{\sqrt{2}}{2}$ **b.** $\frac{1}{2}$ **c.** $\frac{\sqrt{31}}{31}$ **2.** If $x > 1$, then $x > \sqrt{x}$. If $0 < x < 1$, then $x < \sqrt{x}$. If $x = 0$ or $x = 1$, then $x = \sqrt{x}$. **3. a.** $\phi^2 - \phi = 1$
b. $\left(\frac{\sqrt{5}+1}{2}\right)^2 - \frac{\sqrt{5}+1}{2} =$
$\frac{5 + 2\sqrt{5} + 1}{4} - \frac{\sqrt{5}+1}{2} =$
$\frac{5 + 2\sqrt{5} + 1}{4} - \frac{2\sqrt{5}+2}{4} =$
$\frac{5 + 2\sqrt{5} + 1 - 2\sqrt{5} + 2}{4} = \frac{4}{4} = 1$
4. a. $\frac{2}{\sqrt{5}-1} = \frac{2}{\sqrt{5}-1} \cdot \frac{\sqrt{5}+1}{\sqrt{5}+1} = \frac{2\sqrt{5}+2}{5-1} = \frac{\sqrt{5}+1}{2}$ **b.** $\phi - 1 = \frac{\sqrt{5}+1}{2} - 1 = \frac{\sqrt{5}+1}{2} - \frac{2}{2} = \frac{\sqrt{5}-1}{2}$ **c.** $\frac{1}{\phi} = \frac{2}{\sqrt{5}+1} = \frac{2}{\sqrt{5}+1} \cdot \frac{\sqrt{5}-1}{\sqrt{5}-1} = \frac{2\sqrt{5}-2}{5-1} = \frac{\sqrt{5}-1}{2} = \phi - 1$

On Your Own
5. a. $2\sqrt{2}$ **6.** Hideki's method
7. a. $2\sqrt{13}$ in. **8. a.** perimeter = $14\sqrt{3}$ cm; area = 30 cm^2

Lesson 6.10
Check Your Understanding
1. a. all **b.** all **c.** some **d.** no **e.** some **f.** all
2. a. Rational; $\frac{13}{2}$ is the ratio of two integers.
b. rational; $-19.13 = -\frac{1913}{100}$ **c.** Irrational; you can use the same argument that shows that $\sqrt{2}$ is irrational for any prime number.
d. rational; $\sqrt{121} = 11$ **e.** Irrational; $\sqrt{36 - 25} = \sqrt{11}$, and the square root of a prime number is irrational. **f.** rational; $\frac{0.5}{7} = \frac{5}{70}$
g. rational; $\frac{13\pi}{2\pi} = \frac{13}{2}$ **3. a.** Yes; there is only one output for each input. **b.** The graph would

look like two broken number lines, one at $f(x) = 0$ for all rational numbers, and one at $f(x) = 1$ for all irrational numbers. On each "line" there would be a gap between any two points you choose, no matter how close they are. In fact, there would be infinitely many gaps. **4.** yes; $0.9999\ldots = 1$
5. No; if $a = \sqrt{-1}$, then $a^2 = -1$. But if $a > 0$, then $a^2 > 0$. If $a < 0$, then $a^2 > 0$. And if $a = 0$, then $a^2 = 0$. Therefore there is no real number a such that $a^2 = -1$, and $\sqrt{-1}$ is not a real number.

Lesson 6.11
Check Your Understanding
1. a. 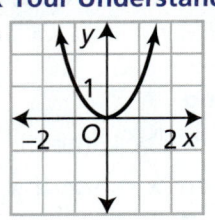 **b.**

c. 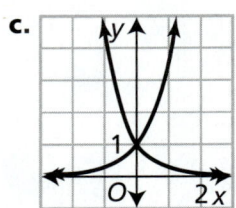 **d.**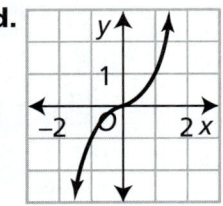

e.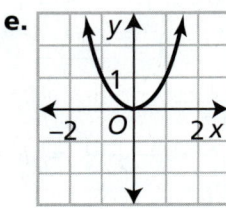

f. Since the graph of $y = x^3$ passes through the graph of $y = -2$, you know that there is a number with cube -2. This number is $\sqrt[3]{-2}$. Since the graph of $y = x^4$ does not pass through the graph of $y = -2$, there is no real number with fourth power -2. Therefore $\sqrt[4]{-2}$ does not exist. **2.** 2.22
3. a. You know that $1 < 2$. Take the square root of each side to get $1 < \sqrt{2}$. You also know that $2 < 4$. Take the square root of both sides to get $\sqrt{2} < 2$. Since the function $f(x) = 2^x$ is continually increasing, and since $2^0 = 1$ and $2^1 = 2$, you know that $0 < a < 1$.
b. $2^{2a} = 2$ **c.** $2a = 1$ **d.** $a = \frac{1}{2}$
e. $(2^{\frac{1}{2}})^2 = 2^{\frac{2}{2}} = 2$ **f.** $b = \frac{1}{3}$ **g.** $c = \frac{1}{n}$

On Your Own
5. a. $\sqrt[4]{125}$ and $\sqrt[4]{5}$ are both positive, so their product is positive.
$(\sqrt[4]{125} \cdot \sqrt[4]{5})^4 = (\sqrt[4]{125})^4 \cdot (\sqrt[4]{5})^4$
$= 125 \cdot 5 = 625 = 5^4$. Since $\sqrt[4]{125} \cdot \sqrt[4]{5}$ is a nonnegative number with a fourth power equal to 5^4, the number is 5. **6. a.** 81
7. a. Doubling the length of each side yields 8 times the volume.

Lesson 6.12
On Your Own
8. Joe cannot always find the number in three guesses or fewer. **10. a.** 0.0000001 **b.** 10 times as many

Lesson 6.13
Check Your Understanding
1. a. \$1230; \$1260.75 **b.** $J = 1200(1.025)^N$, where J is the amount of money Jesse has.
c. \$1260.75; the interest is paid annually, only at the end of the year. **2.** Less time; at the end of the first year, Tony's balance is greater than at the beginning of the first year. As a result, he earns more interest in the second year than in the first. **3.** \$22,417.75
4. a. \$16,000; \$12,800 **b.** $V = 20,000(1 - 0.2)^N$
c. Yes; the value of the car will be less than \$1000 after 14 years.

On Your Own
6. 8 years **8. a.** The rule of 72 is very close to the results in Exercise 7.

Lesson 6.14
Check Your Understanding
1. Answers may vary. **2.** Answers may vary. Sample: about 20; about 10 **3.** Half of $\frac{1}{2}$ is $\frac{1}{4}$.
4. $C(t) = 40\left(\frac{1}{2}\right)^t$

On Your Own
6. $b > 1$; $0 < b < 1$ **7. c.** $\frac{2}{3}h$

Lesson 6.15
Check Your Understanding
1. a. $f(x) = 1.4x + 3.12$ **b.** None exists.
c. None exists. **2. a.** $f(x) = 5 - x^2$
b. $f(x) = 3(2)^x$ **c.** $f(x) = 2 - 3x$
d. $f(x) = 3^x - 1$ **e.** $k(x) = \frac{1}{3} + \frac{x}{2}$
f. $f(x) = 2x^2 + 1$ **3. a.** $y = 2 + ax$
b. $y = a(b)^x$
4. a. $m(n) = \begin{cases} 0.93 & \text{if } n = 0 \\ m(n-1) \cdot 1.0225 & \text{if } n > 0 \end{cases}$
b. Multiply 0.93 by 1.0225 once for the first year, then again for the second year, then again for the third year, and so on, 1000 times.
c. Multiplying 0.93 by 1.0225 n times is the same as evaluating $0.93 \cdot 1.0225^n$.
d. \$4,283,508,450

On Your Own
5. a. $D(x) = -2 + 3x$ **6.** Answers may vary. Sample: $y = x^2$ **8. a.** $y = 64 - 16x$; $y = 64\left(\frac{3}{4}\right)^x$ **9. b.** $f(n) = 3^{n-1}$

Chapter 7
Lesson 7.01
On Your Own
5. a. 399 **b.** 2496 **c.** 6313
d. $ab = \frac{(a+b)^2 - (a-b)^2}{4} = \frac{a^2 + 2ab + b^2 - (a^2 - 2ab + b^2)}{4} = \frac{a^2 + 2ab + b^2 - a^2 + 2ab - b^2}{4} = \frac{4ab}{4} = ab$
6. Both sides are equal to $a^2c^2 + a^2d^2 + b^2c^2 + b^2d^2$. **8. a.** The factor $(m + 7)$ is 13 when $m = 6$ since $6 + 7 = 13$, so $m^2 - 4m - 77$ is a multiple of 13. **d.** -7 and 11

Lesson 7.02
Check Your Understanding
1. a. $-2, -1, 0, 1$ **b.** $n, (n + 1), (n + 2), (n + 3)$ **c.** $(n - 1), n, (n + 1)$ **d.** $2n + 1$
2. a. If n is an integer, $2n$ is even, so $2n + 1$ is odd. **b.** $n + (n + 1) + (n + 2) = 3n + 3 = 3(n + 1)$, which is divisible by 3. **c.** No; $n + (n + 1) + (n + 2) + (n + 3) = 4n + 6$. The sum of four consecutive integers is not divisible by 4. **d.** Yes; $n + (n + 1) + (n + 2) + (n + 3) + (n + 4) = 5n + 10 = 5(n + 2)$. The sum of five consecutive integers is divisible by 5. **e.** When k is odd, the sum of k numbers will be divisible by k. **3. a.** Answers may vary. Sample: The product of an even number and an odd number is always even. n must be either even or odd. If n is odd, then $n + 1$ will be even. **b.** Yes; when one of the factors is a multiple of 3, the entire product will be a multiple of 3 as well. **c.** Yes; when one of the factors is a multiple of 4, the entire product will be a multiple of 4 as well. **d.** Yes; when one of the factors is a multiple of 5, the entire product is a multiple of 5. **e.** Yes; when one of the factors is a multiple of k, the entire product is a multiple of k. **4.** $n = 14$ or $n = -15$ **5.** n^3

On Your Own
7. a. -6 **11. a.** $x(x - y); y(x - y)$
b. $x(x - y) \cdot y(x - y) = x^2 - y^2$ in.^{2}
c. 493 in.^{2} **d.** no **12. b.** $(x + y)$ and $(x - y)$
13. c. 493 in.^{2}

Lesson 7.03
Check Your Understanding
1. a. 8 **b.** -17 **c.** $-b$ **d.** $-\frac{13}{27}$ **e.** $\frac{d}{c}$ **f.** 0
2. a. $x = 7$ or $x = -5$ **b.** $x = 3$ or $y = -7$
c. $x = 0$ or $x = -2$ **d.** $x = -3, x = -4$, or $x = -5$
3. a. Estimates may vary. Sample: $\frac{5}{3}, -\frac{7}{2}$

x	f(x)
-5	60
-4	17
-3	-14
-2	-33
-1	-40
0	-35
1	-18
2	11
3	52
4	105
5	170

b. $(2x + 7)(3x - 5) = 6x^2 + 11x - 35$

	3x	-5
2x	$6x^2$	$-10x$
+7	$21x$	-35

c. $x = \frac{5}{3}$ or $-\frac{7}{2}$ **4. a.** $x = -7, x = -11$
b. $x \approx -6.8$ or $x \approx -11.2$ **5.** Answers may vary. Sample: Ling is just finding numeric factors, and they do not give her helpful information. **6.** $x = 0, x = 1$, or $x = -1$
7. a. Answers may vary. Sample: Apply the Distributive Property to $t(100 - 16t)$.
b. $t = 0$ s or $t = 6.25$ s; $t = 0$ is when the projectile is initially fired and $t = 6.25$ s is when the projectile lands. **c.** $t = 0$ s; $t = 6.25$ s

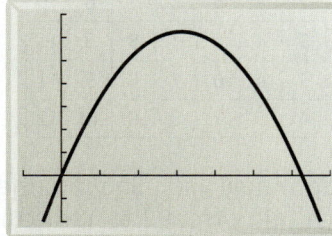

d. At about 3.125 s; you can predict this time because it's halfway between the two values where $s(t) = 0$. **e.** The projectile goes straight up to its maximum height and then back down again.

maximum height: 156.25 ft

Projectile rises to 156 ft, 3 in. and falls straight back down.

On Your Own
8. a. $x = 23$ **9. a.** $x = 8$ or $x = 23$ **10. a.** True; 5 is a prime number. **12.** $(x + 3)(x + 2)$

Lesson 7.04
Check Your Understanding
1. a. $3x^2$ **b.** $9x$ **c.** 3 **d.** 1 **e.** a **f.** 1 **g.** p^2q^4
h. p^2q **i.** p^2q **j.** $3(x + 3)^2$ **2. a.** $3x^2(3x - 5)$
b. $9x(x^2 - 4)$ or $9x(x - 2)(x + 2)$
c. $3(5a^2 + 7b^2)$ **d.** $x^2 + y^2$ **e.** $a(b - c)$
f. $ab + ac + bc$ **g.** $p^2q(pq^3 + q^4 - p^5)$
3. a. $x = 0$ or $x = -\frac{2}{3}$ **b.** $x = 0$ or $x = \frac{5}{3}$
c. $x = 0$, $x = 2$, or $x = -2$ **d.** $a = 0$ or $b = c$
e. $x = 0$ or $x = 100$ **f.** $x = 0$ and $y = 0$
4. $(2x - 3)(3x + 7)$

On Your Own
5. a. $x(3a + 5b)$ **6. a.** $x^3 + x^2 + x + 1$
8. a. Find the area of the two circular bases and add the area of the rectangle.

Lesson 7.05
On Your Own

	1	3	4	5	6	8
1	2	4	5	6	7	9
2	3	5	6	7	8	10
2	3	5	6	7	8	10
3	4	6	7	8	9	11
3	4	6	7	8	9	11
4	5	7	8	9	10	12

7. Observations may vary. Sample: the number of times each value from 2 to 12 occurs is the same as for two standard number cubes. So with these two number cubes, you have the same probability of getting any particular total as you would with standard number cubes.
8. $x^2 + 2x^3 + 3x^4 + 4x^5 + 5x^6 + 6x^7 + 5x^8 + 4x^9 + 3x^{10} + 2x^{11} + x^{12}$ **9. a.** yes
b. no

Lesson 7.06
Check Your Understanding
1. a. Answers may vary. Sample: $x^3 - 2x + 4$, $2x^3 + x^2 + x - 5$ **b.** Not possible; if the sum has degree 4, the product must have degree 4 or greater. **c.** Answers may vary. Sample: x^4, 1
d. Not possible; if the sum has degree 2, the product must have degree 2 or greater.
2. Answers may vary. Sample: x^2, $-x^2 + x$
3. a–d. Answers may vary. Samples are given.
a. $2x^2 + 4x + 2$, $x^2 + 3x + 2$
b. $3x^2 + 6x + 1$, $x + 3$ **c.** $x + 5$, $-x - 1$
d. $x + 1$, $x - 1$ **4.** The degree of the squared polynomial is twice the degree of the original; answers may vary. Sample:
$(x + 1)^2 = x^2 + 2x + 1$,
$(x^2 + 2)^2 = x^4 + 4x^2 + 4$,
$(2x^3 + 1)^2 = 4x^6 + 4x^3 + 1$

On Your Own
5. Answers may vary. Samples are given.
a. x, x^5 **6. b.** $s(x) = x^2 - 4x + 5$ **7.** $a = 2$

Lesson 7.07
Check Your Understanding
1. a. $\frac{3}{4}x^5 + x^4 - 13x^2 - 5x + 3$ **b.** 5 **c.** -5
d. -13 **e.** 0 **f.** Answers may vary. Sample: $-\frac{3}{4}x^5 - x^4 + x^3$ **2. a–d.** Replace x with 10 in each identity to derive the number fact.
3. a. $120 = 2^3 \cdot 3 \cdot 5$; $168 = 2^3 \cdot 3 \cdot 7$ **b.** 24 is the greatest common factor since both have $2^3 \cdot 3$ as factors. **c.** $3^2 \cdot 5^3 = 1125$ **d.** x^2y^3
e. $24x^2y^3$ **4.** $x^4 + 6x^3 + (a + 2)x^2 + (3a - 21)x - 7a$; $a = 7$ **5–8.** Answers may vary. Samples are given.
5. $(1^3 - 1)(1^3 + 1) = 1^6 - 1$
$0 = 0$
$(x^3 - 1)(x^3 + 1) =$
$x^6 + x^3 - x^3 - 1 = x^6 - 1$
6. $2^6 - 1 = (2 - 1)(2 + 1)$
$(2^2 + 2 + 1)(2^2 - 2 + 1)$
$64 - 1 = (1)(3)(4 + 2 + 1)(4 - 2 + 1)$
$63 = 3 \cdot 7 \cdot 3$
$(x - 1)(x + 1)(x^2 + x + 1) \cdot (x^2 - x + 1) =$
$(x - 1)(x^2 + x + 1)(x + 1) \cdot (x^2 - x + 1) =$
$(x^3 - x^2 + x^2 - x + x - 1) \cdot$
$(x^3 + x^2 - x^2 - x + x + 1) =$
$(x^3 - 1)(x^3 + 1) = x^6 - 1$

7. $(2^6 - 1) = (2^2 - 1)(2^4 + 2^2 + 1)$
$64 - 1 = (4 - 1)(16 + 4 + 1); 63 = (3)(21)$
$(x^2 - 1)(x^4 + x^2 + 1) =$
$x^6 + x^4 + x^2 - (x^4 + x^2 + 1) =$
$x^6 + x^4 + x^2 - x^4 - x^2 - 1 =$
$x^6 - 1$
8. $1^3 - 1 = (1 - 1)(1^3 + 1 + 1)$
$1 - 1 = (0)(1 + 1 + 1)$
$0 = 0$
$(x - 1)(x^2 + x + 1) =$
$x^3 + x^2 + x - (x^2 + x + 1) =$
$x^3 + x^2 + x - x^2 - x - 1 =$
$x^3 - 1$ **9.** Answers may vary;
$(s + t)^2 - (s - t)^2 =$
$s^2 + 2st + t^2 - (s^2 - 2st + t^2) =$
$s^2 + 2st + t^2 - s^2 + 2st - t^2 = 4st$
10. Answers may vary; $(n + 1)^2 - (n)^2 =$
$n^2 + 2n + 1 - n^2 = 2n + 1$
11. $(x^3 - 1)(x^3 + 1) = x^6 - 1 =$
$(x^2 - 1)(x^4 + x^2 + 1)$

On Your Own
14. a. $m^2 - n^2 = (m + n)(m - n) =$
$m(m - n) + n(m - n)$ **16. a.** 5

Lesson 7.08
Check Your Understanding
1. a. $k = 4$ **b.** $k = 2$ **c.** $k = -10$ **d.** $k = 5$
e. $k = -\frac{1}{2}$ **f.** $k = 2$ **2. a.** 3 **b.** 5 **c.** 0
3. To get x^3, you must multiply x by itself three times and then multiply the result by 1. There are four ways to do this among the four terms of the product, so the coefficient is 4. **4.** The degrees of the two polynomials are different. **5.** 4 **6.** Answers may vary. Sample: $a = 2$, $b = 2$, and $c = -12$; $a = 1$, $b = -\frac{5}{2}$, and $c = 1$; $a = -\frac{3}{4}$, $b = 1$, and $c = 1$ **7.** When you expand $(h + t)^4$, where h represents heads and t represents tails, you get $h^4 + 4h^3t + 6h^2t^2 + 4ht^3 + t^4$. It shows 6 ways to get two heads and two tails, 4 ways to get 3 heads and one tail, and 6 other tosses that result in a draw. **8.** $x^2 + 3x + 2$
9. a. 84 **b.** $2a^2c^2 + 2a^2b^2 + 2b^2c^2 - a^4 - b^4 - c^4$ **c.** $A = \frac{\sqrt{3}}{4}s^2$ **d.** 0; the sum of the lengths of any 2 sides of a triangle must be greater than the length of the third side.
10. See Figure 1.

On Your Own
12. 20 **15.** −3

Lesson 7.09
On Your Own
6.

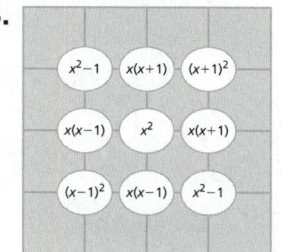

7. b. 43 and 59 **9. a.** yes
11. b. $x^2 - 22x + 120$ **d.** $x^2 - x + \frac{2}{9}$

Lesson 7.10
Check Your Understanding
1. a. True; substitute $4x$ for a and $3y$ for b.
b. false **c.** True; substitute 5 for a and t^3 for b. **d.** True: substitute $(x + 3)$ for x and 1 for b. **e.** false **f.** false **2. a.** 0; since $(50 + x)(50 - x) = 50^2 - x^2$, and because $x^2 \geq 0$, the product is greatest when x^2 is least. **b.** $x = 50$, $y = 50$ **3. a.** $x = 4$, $y = 3$
b. $x = 7$, $y = 6$ **c.** $x = 5$, $y = 4$; or $x = 3$, $y = 0$
4. a. 6000 **b.** 5000 **c.** 7400 **5.** no; $(-b)^2 = b^2$
6. The entry that is k away from a^2 is $a^2 - k^2$; moving along the diagonal is the same as moving down k and to the right k, or up k and to the left k. In either case, the product is $(a + k)(a - k)$, or $a^2 - k^2$. **7. a.** $k = -3$
b. $k = 100$ **c.** $k = 4$

Figure 1 $A = \sqrt{\frac{1}{2}(a + b + c)\left(\frac{1}{2}(a + b + c) - a\right)\left(\frac{1}{2}(a + b + c) - b\right)\left(\frac{1}{2}(a + b + c) - c\right)}$
$= \sqrt{\frac{1}{2}(a + b + c)\left(\frac{a}{2} + \frac{b}{2} + \frac{c}{2} - a\right)\left(\frac{a}{2} + \frac{b}{2} + \frac{c}{2} - b\right)\left(\frac{a}{2} + \frac{b}{2} + \frac{c}{2} - c\right)}$
$= \sqrt{\frac{1}{2}(a + b + c)\left(-\frac{a}{2} + \frac{b}{2} + \frac{c}{2}\right)\left(\frac{a}{2} - \frac{b}{2} + \frac{c}{2}\right)\left(\frac{a}{2} + \frac{b}{2} - \frac{c}{2}\right)}$
$= \sqrt{\frac{1}{2}(a + b + c)\frac{1}{2}(-a + b + c)\frac{1}{2}(a - b + c)\frac{1}{2}(a + b - c)}$
$= \sqrt{\frac{1}{16}(a + b + c)(b + c - a)(a + c - b)(a + b - c)}$
$= \frac{1}{4}\sqrt{(a + b + c)(a + b - c)(a + c - b)(b + c - a)}$

8.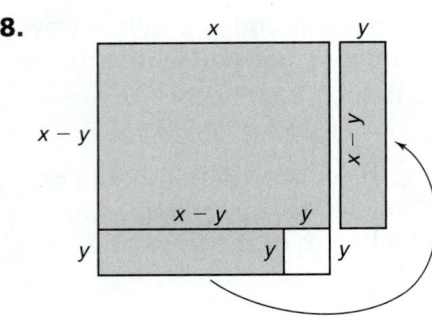

9. No; $(a + 1)^2 - a^2 = a^2 + 2a + 1 - a^2 = 2a + 1$, which is odd for all a.
10. a. $(x + 9.5)^2 - (1.5)^2 = ((x + 9.5) + 1.5)((x + 9.5) - 1.5) = (x + 11)(x - 8)$ **b.** $(x + 10)^2 - (2)^2 = ((x + 10) + 2)((x + 10) - 2) = (x + 12)(x + 8)$
c. $\left(x + \frac{27}{2}\right)^2 - \left(\frac{1}{2}\right)^2 = \left(\left(x + \frac{27}{2}\right) - \left(\frac{1}{2}\right)\right) \cdot \left(\left(x + \frac{27}{2}\right) + \left(\frac{1}{2}\right)\right) = (x + 13)(x + 14)$
11. $r = \frac{a + b}{2}$, $s = \pm\frac{a - b}{2}$ **12.** 49 cm
13. a. $x = 3$ or $x = -3$ **b.** $x = 7$ or $x = -1$
c. $x = 2$ or $x = 1$ **d.** $x = a + b$ or $x = a - b$

On Your Own
14. a. 9   **15. a.** yes   **16. a.** 48; this is a 7-by-7 square (49 squares) with one missing.
17. $k = 11$ or $k = -11$ **18. a.** 0
21. a. $y(y + 3)(y - 3)$

Lesson 7.11
Check Your Understanding
1. D; D is of the form $x^2 + bx + c = 0$, where the roots sum to $-b$ and have a product of c.
2. a. $x = -9$ and $x = -4$ **b.** $x = -6$ and $x = -7$ **c.** No integer solution; the maximum product of integers that have a sum of 13 is 42, which is less than 224. **d.** $x = 3$ and $x = -16$
e. $x = -2$ and $x = -11$ **f.** $x = -19$ and $x = 6$
g. No integer solution; the maximum product of integers that have a sum of 13 is 42, which is less than 54. **h.** No integer solution; there are no integers that have a sum of 13 and a product of -20. **i.** No integer solution; there are no integers that have a sum of 13 and a product of 17. **j.** $x = 1$ and $x = -14$
3. a. $x = 10$ and $x = 6$ **b.** no solutions
c. $x = 0$ and $x = 16$ **d.** $x = 3$ **e.** $x = 4$ and $x = -4$ **f.** $x = -4$ **g.** $x = -5$ and $x = 2$
h. $x = -7$ and $x = -10$ **i.** no solutions
j. $x = 5$ **4.** A, C, and E   **5. a.** The expression $x^2 - 6x + 9$ factors to $(x - 3)^2$, and a square can never be negative.
b. $x^2 + y^2 + 10x - 8y + 42 = (x^2 + 10x + 25) + (y^2 - 8y + 16) + 1 = (x + 5)^2 + (y - 4)^2 + 1$, which is always positive.

On Your Own
8. a. 64 **b.** $(x - 8)(x - 8)$ **11. a.** 25

Lesson 7.12
Check Your Understanding
1. a. $x = 7$ and $x = -1$ **b.** $y = \frac{9}{2}$ and $y = -\frac{11}{2}$
c. $n = -5 + \sqrt{5}$ and $n = -5 - \sqrt{5}$
2. a. $k = 1$ **b.** $k = 2$ **c.** $k = -2$ **d.** $k = 6$
e. $k = 4.5$ **f.** $k = -12.5$ **g.** $k = 8$ and $k = -9$
3. a. $x = -4$ **b.** $y = -5$ **4. a.** 1.06 **b.** 1.01
c. The error is $|1 - x|^2$.   **5. a.** $x = 5$ or $x = 1$
b. $x = -9$ or $x = 1$ **c.** $x = 3 - \sqrt{2}$ or $x = 3 + \sqrt{2}$ **d.** $x = -1$ or $x = 2$
e. $x = -1$ or $x = -5$ **6. a.** 5; 7-by-15
b. 11; 1-by-5 **c.** $-4 + \sqrt{31}$; $(-1 + \sqrt{31})$ by $(1 + \sqrt{31})$ **7. a.** 60 or -60 **b.** 4   **8. a.** Tony is referring to adding 1 and subtracting 1, which have a sum of zero. **b.** $x = -1 - \sqrt{\frac{11}{2}}$ and $x = -1 + \sqrt{\frac{11}{2}}$ **9.** Answers may vary. Sample:
$x^2 + 2x + 3 = 5$; $x^2 + 2x - 2 = 0$
$x^2 + 2x + 1 - 1 - 2 = 0$
$(x + 1)^2 - 3 = 0$
$(x + 1 + \sqrt{3})(x + 1 - \sqrt{3}) = 0$
The solutions are $x = -1 - \sqrt{3}$ and $x = -1 + \sqrt{3}$.   **10.** Answers may vary. Sample: $x^2 + 2x + 3 = -15$

On Your Own
13. a. $k = -9$ **14. a.** $x = -11$ or $x = 3$
15. $x = 2$ or $x = 6$ **19. a.** $x = -10$ or $x = -2$

Chapter 8
Lesson 8.01
On Your Own
12. a. $x = 3 \pm \sqrt{5}$ **15. a.** $x = 3$

Lesson 8.02
Check Your Understanding
1. $x = \frac{-7 \pm \sqrt{37}}{6}$ **2.** $x = \frac{-7 \pm \sqrt{145}}{6}$
3. $x = \frac{7 \pm \sqrt{145}}{6}$ **4.** No real solutions; you get a negative number under the square root sign.   **5.** $x = 2$ or $x = \frac{1}{3}$ **6.** $w = \frac{\sqrt{5} \pm 5}{2}$
7. $z = \sqrt{2} \pm \sqrt{3}$ **8.** $x = 3 \pm k$ **9.** $x = 31$ or $x = -30$ **10.** $x = 6 \pm \sqrt{65}$ **11. a.** 28 clinks
b. 12 people

On Your Own
12. $x = \frac{3 \pm 2\sqrt{5}}{4}$ **19. a.** $k < 12$ **b.** $k = 12$
c. $k > 12$ **21.** $-\frac{1}{2} < x < \frac{4}{3}$ **24. a.** all real numbers   **25. a.** $x^2 - 12x + 35 = 0$

Lesson 8.03
Check Your Understanding
1. Answers may vary. Samples are given.
a. $x^2 - 20x + 51 = 0$ **b.** $x^2 + 20x + 51 = 0$
c. $x^2 - 40x + 204 = 0$ **d.** $x^2 - 4x + 1 = 0$
e. $x^2 + 4x + 1 = 0$ **f.** $x^2 - 20x + 25 = 0$
2. a. $x^2 + 17x - 78 = 0$
b. $x^2 - 51x - 702 = 0$ **c.** $x^2 + \frac{17}{78}x - \frac{1}{78} = 0$
or $78x^2 + 17x - 1 = 0$
d. $x^2 - 445x + 6084 = 0$ **3. a.** $\frac{-b}{a}$ **b.** $\frac{c}{a}$ **c.** $\frac{-b}{2a}$

On Your Own
4. Answers may vary. Sample:
$x^2 - 2\sqrt{5}x - 4 = 0$ **8.** $\frac{1 \pm \sqrt{5}}{2}$

Lesson 8.04
Check Your Understanding
1. a. $(3x + 7)(3x - 1)$ **b.** $(3x - 5)(2x - 7)$
c. $(5x + 7)(3x - 1)$ **d.** $(9x - 1)(x + 7)$
e. $(9x^2 - 1)(x^2 + 7)$ or
$(3x + 1)(3x - 1)(x^2 + 7)$
2. a. $(3x + 7y)(3x - y)$ **b.** $(2x - 7y)(3x - 5y)$
c. $(3x - a)(5x + 7a)$ **d.** $(9x - b)(x + 7b)$
3. Answers will vary. Sample: Multiply the constant term by the coefficient of the x^2-term and change the coefficient of the x^2-term to 1.

On Your Own
4. a. $-(9x + 1)(2x + 7)$ **8.** $x = 3$ or $x = -\frac{1}{2}$ **10. a.** $x = -5$ or $x = \frac{7}{3}$

Lesson 8.05
On Your Own
6. -1 **8. a.** $x = -10$ or $x = -4$ **b.** $x = 8$ or $x = -3$ **9.** No; explanations may vary. Sample: There are no real solutions.

Lesson 8.06
Check Your Understanding
1. a. -16 **b.** -4 **c.** -25 **2.** Answers may vary. Sample: $f(x) = (x + 5)^2 - 12$ **3.** 10 and 10
4. $\frac{251}{2}$ and $\frac{251}{2}$ **5.** $\frac{c}{2}$ and $\frac{c}{2}$

On Your Own
7. -12 **8.** 45 ft by 45 ft **9.** 45 and 45

Lesson 8.07
Check Your Understanding
1. a. 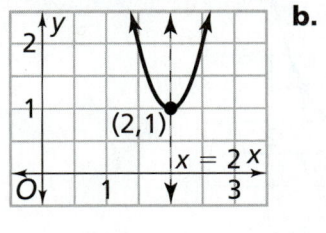 **b.**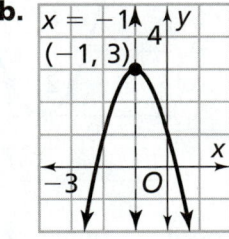

c.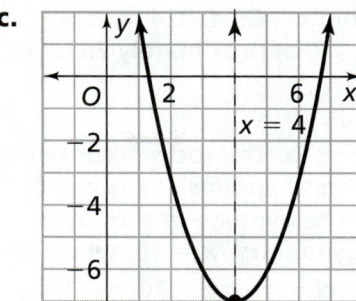

d.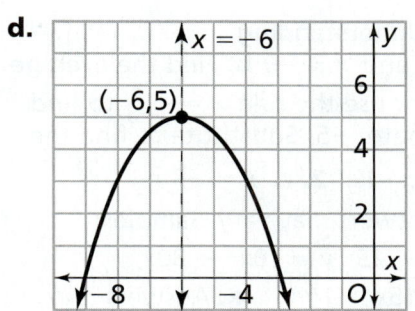

2. a. $(6, 0)$ **b.** $y = -2(x - 3)^2 + 18$

3. a.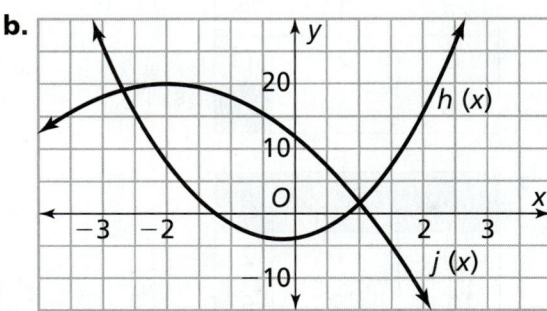

b.

The graphs are also parabolas. **c.** h and j will usually be quadratic. j will be linear if $f(x)$ and $g(x)$ have the same x^2 coefficient and constant if $f(x)$ and $g(x)$ have the same x and x^2 are coefficients. h will be linear if $f(x)$ and $g(x)$ have opposite x^2 coefficients and constant if $f(x)$ and $g(x)$ have opposite x and x^2 coefficients.   **4.** 144 ft **5. a.** 16 ft **b.** 64 ft **c.** 256 ft **6. a.** four times as high

b. nine times as high **c.** Curt: 324 ft; Ryan: 81 ft; Taylor: 9 ft **7.** approximately 282.8 ft/s or about 189 m/h

On Your Own
13. a. $y = x(20 - x)$ **b.** The roots occur when the product is 0. This happens when $x = 0$ or when $x = 20$. The average of the roots gives the line of symmetry, $x = 10$, where the maximum occurs. **c.** $y = -(x - 10)^2 + 100$
15. (3, 8)

Lesson 8.08
Check Your Understanding
1. a. $x = -4$ and $x = -6$ **b.** Find the average of the roots or use the rule $x = -\frac{b}{2a}$ to find the x-coordinate, -5. Substitute to find the y-coordinate, -1. **2. a.** $x = \frac{-9 \pm \sqrt{-39}}{2}$ **b.** $\frac{-9}{2}$ **3.** Answers may vary. Samples: $y = x^2 - 8x + 15$; $y = 10x^2 - 80x$; $y = -2x^2 + 16x + 14$ **4. a.** Answers may vary. Sample: The line of symmetry is found by averaging the roots. $x = 5.5$ **b.** Answers may vary. Sample: The minimum y-value is at the vertex, so the vertex is $(5.5, -25)$. **c.** 4

5. a.

Input	Output	Δ
0	0	1
1	1	3
2	4	5
3	9	7
4	16	9
5	25	11
6	36	

b.

Input	Output	Δ
0	0	2
1	2	6
2	8	10
3	18	14
4	32	18
5	50	22
6	72	

c.

Input	Output	Δ
0	-1	-3
1	-4	3
2	-1	9
3	8	15
4	23	21
5	44	27
6	71	

d.

Input	Output	Δ
0	9	-1
1	8	-3
2	5	-5
3	0	-7
4	-7	-9
5	-16	-11
6	-27	

6. a.

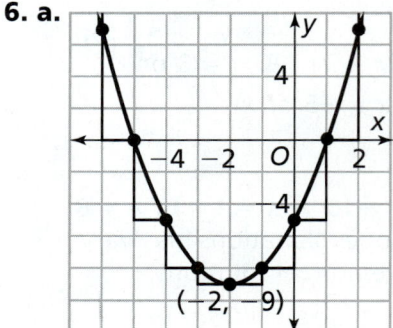

b.

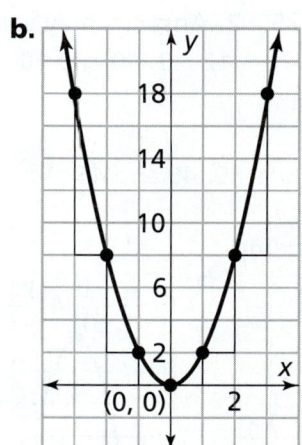

There is a relationship. Starting from the vertex, the next point is across 1 and up 2, then across 1 and up 6, then across 1 and up 10, and so on. Each of the numbers here is twice what it would be for $y = x^2$.

c.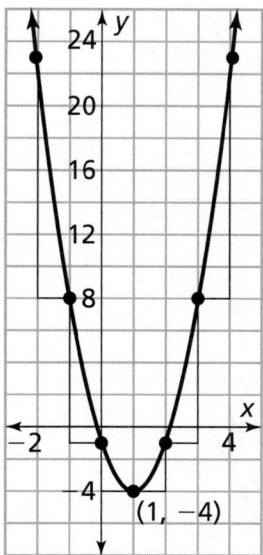

d.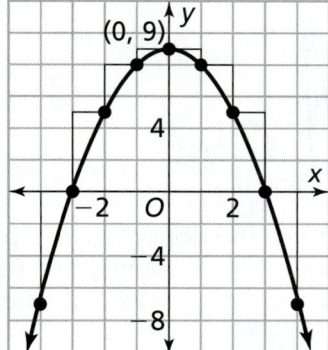

7. Answers may vary. Sample: The numbers in the Δ column of the difference tables are the numbers to go up or down with Linda's method.

On Your Own
9. vertex (5.5, 100); $y = -16(x - 3)(x - 8)$
11. a. (0, −9) **c.** (3, 82)

Lesson 8.09
On Your Own
7. Answers may vary. Sample: $E(n) = 2n + 3$
10. Answers may vary. Sample: $H(n) = 5n + 3$

Lesson 8.10
Check Your Understanding
1. a. 2 **b.** 1 **c.** 0 **2. a.** 1 **b.** 0 **c.** 0 **d.** 2 **e.** 1 **f.** 1
3. a. horizontal line containing (0, 0); the x-axis **b.** −5 and 2 **c.** $-5 < x < 2$ **4.** b, d, e, f **5.** $x^2 + Bx + C$ has solutions if $B^2 \geq 4C$.

On Your Own
7. a. $x = \pm 4$ **10. a.** true **b.** false

Lesson 8.11
Check Your Understanding
1. a.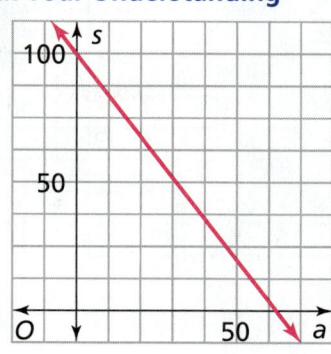

b.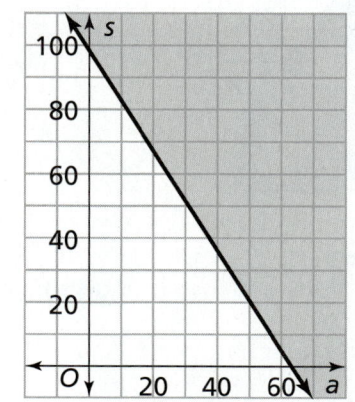

2.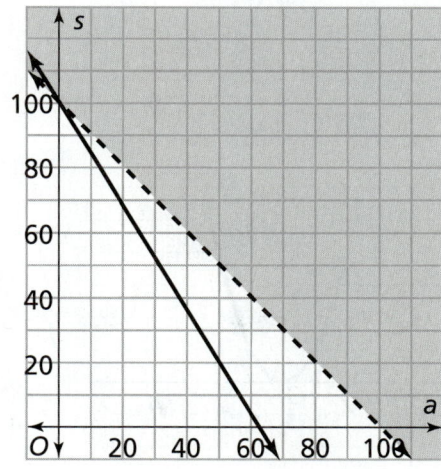

yes

3. a.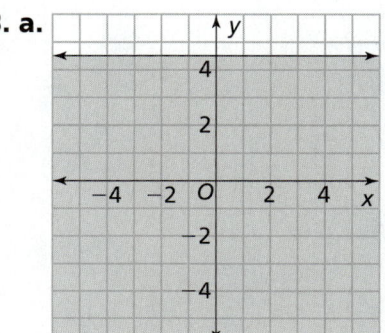

b. 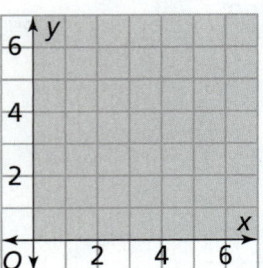 **c.**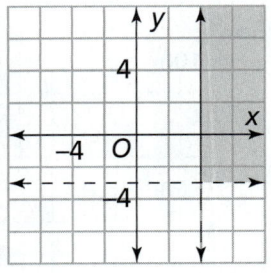

d.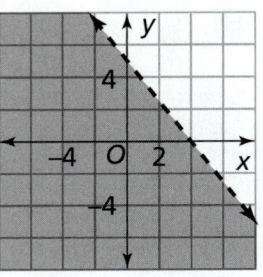

e.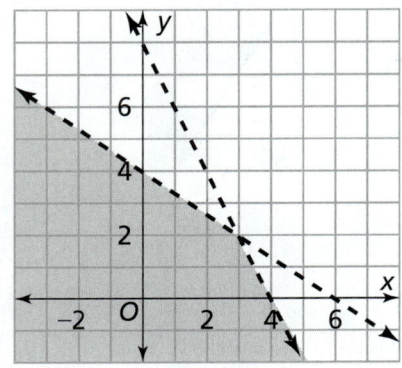

f.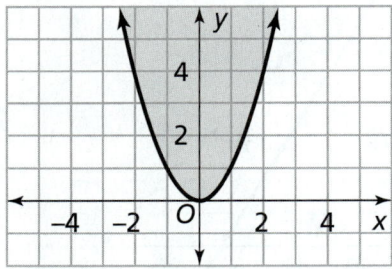

g.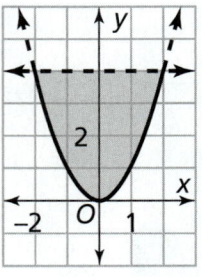

h. no solution

4. a. If $x = 3$, the denominator $= 0$ and division by 0 is undefined.

b–c.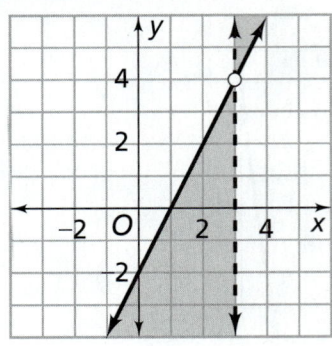

5. a. Answers may vary. Sample:

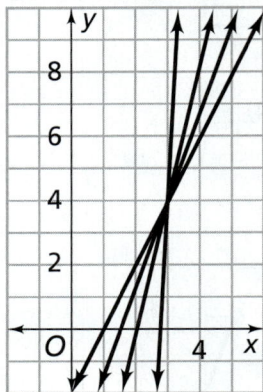

b. There is no limit to the slope. Yes. See part (c). **c.** This is the set of lines bounded by the line $(y - 4) = 2(x - 3)$, or $y = 2x - 2$, and the vertical line $x = 3$.

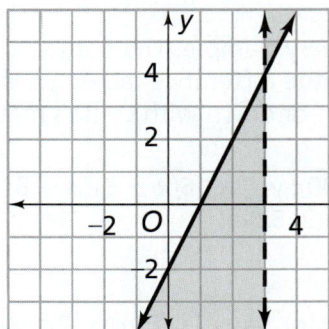

On Your Own
7. (3, 2) **8. b.** (6, 2) **d.** (11, 2)

Lesson 8.12
Check Your Understanding
1. a.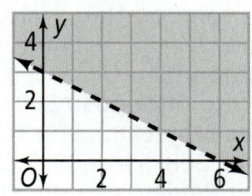

b.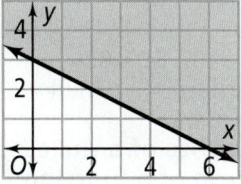

c.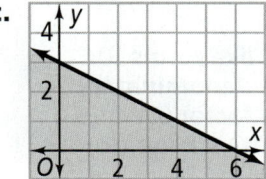

d.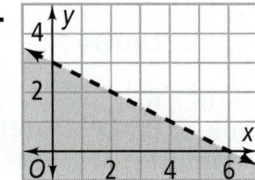

2. a.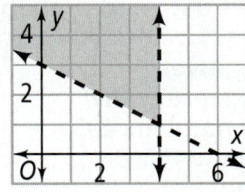

b.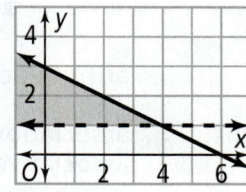

c.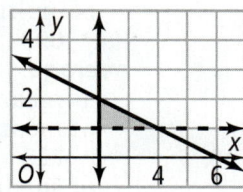

3. $\begin{cases} x < 0 \\ y > 0 \end{cases}$

On Your Own
8. Check students' work.

9. D

10.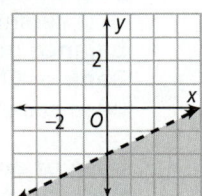

Answers may vary. Sample: Points that Jacob has shaded should not be shaded, since they do not make the inequality true. For example, Jacob has shaded (0, 0), but substituting (0, 0) into the inequality gives $0 > 4$, which is false.

Index

A

absolute value 202, 203, 204, 280
    graph of absolute value equation 302
absolute zero 132
Academy Awards 220
addition
    algorithms 61, 63, 64, 65
    associative property of 28, 111, 625
    commutative property of 28
    crisscross table 69
    of fractions 67
    of like terms 638
    of negative numbers 17
    on the number line 46
    of polynomials 638
    of positive numbers 17
    property of equality 144, 387
    table 9, 17
addition algorithms
    consecutive integers 65
    from left to right 64
    using columns 61
addition property of equality 144, 387
addition table 9
    extending 17
additive identity 30, 104, 111
additive inverse 30, 111, 112
ages of U.S. Presidents 318
algebra, the word 686
algorithm(s) 61, 699
    addition 61, 63, 64, 65
    of arithmetic 58
    division 82
    expansion box 72, 75
    multiplication 71
    Russian method for multiplication 73
    subtraction 61, 64
al-Khwarizmi 686
analytic geometry 195
annual percentage rate (APR) 562
annulus 628
any-order, any-grouping (AOAG) properties 28, 47, 52, 104, 111, 520
AOAG property. *See* any-order, any-grouping properties.
area
    of circle 551, 557, 628
    of rectangle 493
    of trapezoid 100
arithmetic of polynomials 637, 633
association 247
associative property
    of addition 28, 111, 625
    of multiplication 28, 111, 609
average
    as mean 170
    as mean, median, or mode 223
    of quadratic roots 724, 737
    speed between two points 320, 335, 336
Avogadro's number 539
axiom 29

B

backing-up method 475
backtracking 117, 121
    reversing the operations 121
balance point 226, 408
Bank of China Tower 71
base case for recursive rule 460, 475
base of an exponent 517
basic graphs 289, 298
    direct variation 289, 290
    family of 307
    inverse variation 294
basic rules of arithmetic. *See* rules of arithmetic.
best fit
    line of 406, 408, 409, 410
    quadratic function 612
binary operation 112
binomial 669
boiling temperature of water 131
box-and-whisker plot 237, 239, 241
    five-number summary 237
    first quartile 237
    interquartile range 239
    maximum 237
    median 237
    minimum 237
    paired comparison 241
    range 239
    third quartile 237
Boyle's Law 101
Bush, George W. 208

C

Cartesian coordinates 195
Cartesian plane 189, 195, 328
categorical data 245
Celsius, Anders 131
Celsius temperature scale 12, 131
centigrade 131
certificate of deposit 580
Chapter Project 82, 179, 315, 415, 508, 598, 688, 782
Chapter Review 84, 180, 316, 416, 510, 600, 690, 784
Chapter Test 86, 182, 318, 418, 512, 602, 692, 786
circle
    area of 551, 557, 628
    circumference of 628
    graph of 286
circumference of a circle 628
closed form of a function 496
coefficient 636, 637
collinear points 324, 325, 342, 353
    test for 343
combine like terms 104
common denominator 67
common factor 626
commutative property
    of addition 28, 111, 625
    of multiplication 28, 111, 625
completing the square 723, 740
    factor by 677, 678
composition of functions 441
compound interest 578, 579
conjecture 27
connect data and probability 247
consecutive
    integers 616, 617
    odd numbers 495
    outputs 465
constant 294
    differences 589
    ratio 591
    slope 330
convert
    decimal to fraction 42
    fraction to decimal 42
coordinate(s) 189
coordinate geometry 195
coordinate plane 189
    distance in 205
    ordered pair 189
    origin 189, 193
    quadrants of 198
    x-axis 189
    x-coordinate 189
    y-axis 189
    y-coordinate 189
correlation 247
correlation coefficient 256

credit card payoff 502
cross-sums game 6
cube a number 124, 517
cube root 568
cubic
   growth 299
   polynomial 637
Cumulative Review 184, 420, 604, 788
cutoff points for solving inequalities 401

D

data displays 230
decimal 41
   convert to fraction 42
   expansion 41
   form of a rational number 561
   notation 41
   representation 42
degree
   of a monomial 636
   of a polynomial 637
delta 329
denominator of fraction 38
dependent variable 439
depreciation 582
Descartes, René 195
   folium of 311
Developing Habits of Mind, 20, 29, 38, 42, 47, 52, 72, 77, 105, 120, 122, 153, 173, 203, 204, 223, 225, 237, 247, 256, 269, 274, 280, 290, 294, 300, 307, 310, 328, 335, 378, 401, 409, 429, 441, 466, 475, 489, 564, 585, 615, 622, 626, 645, 661, 681, 700, 712, 723, 728, 729, 731, 752, 768
difference of squares 688, 689
   factor 661
difference table 465–467, 534
   for quadratic function 773
Diophantus 159, 484
direct variation 289, 290
   standard equation for 290
distance
   in the coordinate plane 205
   between Earth and moon 207
   on a number line 202
distance-time graph 324, 333, 334, 335, 336, 364, 366, 371
distinct lines 382
Distributive Property 30, 52, 104, 111, 154, 155, 554, 625, 626
division 82
   algorithms 82
   of fractions 77

division algorithms
   ladder 82
   traditional 82
   using lines 74
   using subtraction 82
Dodgeball Game 6
domain 445, 446
dot plot 230
drawing with graphs 315
duck principle 549, 552, 553

E

Eisenhower, Dwight D. 97
elimination method to solve systems of equations 387, 388
ellipse 281
Empire State Building 734
empty set 127
end behavior of recursive function 782
equation(s) 126, 160
   absolute value 302
   check by substitution 289
   equivalent 753
   family of 357
   graphing 298, 299
   graph of 268, 450
   of a line 353, 355, 356, 358
   linear 149, 353
   modeling 139
   monic 699, 700
   nonmonic 702
   plug into 272
   as point tester 267, 268, 300, 353
   representing 139
   satisfy 265, 266, 268, 280
   solution of 126, 269
   solution set 127
   solve 138, 144
   square root 301
   standard form of parabola 729
   substitution 272
   system of 378, 387, 750
   vertex form of parabola 729
equivalent
   equations 753
   expressions 611, 613
   fractions 37, 38, 67
   statements 384
Euler 629
evaluate an expression 98
even number 10, 635
expand an expression 609
expansion
   box 72, 75, 153, 154
   boxes to factor 622, 626
   of an expression 609

exponent 517
   base of 517
   negative 532, 533
   zero 531, 533
exponential
   growth 584
   decay 584
   function 499, 584, 585, 589
expression(s) 93, 126
   equivalent 611, 613
   evaluate 98
   factored form of 620
   scientific formula 98
   simplify 103, 352
   transformation of 625
extension of a rule 20

F

factor
   by completing the square 677, 678
   a difference of squares 661
   an expression 620
   nonmonic quadratics 711
   over $\mathbb{Z}$ 669
   sums and products 669
factored form of an expression 620
Fahrenheit temperature scale 12, 131
Fahrenheit, Daniel 131
false position 164, 485
family
   of equations 357
   of graphs 307
Fermat
   number 629
   primes 629
Fermat, Pierre de 195, 629
fingerprinting 208
first quartile 237
fitting line 406
five-number summary 237, 239
   first quartile 237
   maximum 237
   median 237
   minimum 237
   third quartile 237
fixed point 782
   of a function 500
floor function 455
folium of Descartes 311
For Discussion, 19, 24, 31, 38, 47, 53, 63, 68, 93, 94, 99, 103, 105, 121, 122, 126, 127, 128, 139 (2), 144, 145, 148, 149 (2), 168, 173, 198, 211, 223, 231, 239, 241, 247, 255, 274, 279, 291, 293, 299, 302, 306, 307,

309, 328, 342, 353, 359 (2), 377, 383, 384, 388, 389, 430, 436 (2), 441, 445, 446, 450, 452, 475, 476, 488, 490, 492, 499, 500, 501, 520, 521, 526, 528, 532, 533, 537, 549, 553, 563, 565, 579, 580, 581, 584, 585, 586, 591, 614, 615, 616, 619, 620, 622 (2), 638, 639, 644, 650, 662, 664, 670, 672, 673, 677, 679, 680, 682, 699, 701, 703, 713, 723, 724, 725, 732, 751, 759, 760, 767, 773, 777

For You to Do 12 (3), 13 (2), 19, 23, 24, 30, 31, 37 (2), 38, 42 (2), 53, 61, 68, 78, 98, 105, 138, 145, 149 (2), 153, 154, 163, 167, 196, 198 (2), 202, 203, 204, 206, 212, 224, 230, 232 (2), 247, 248, 255, 256, 267, 274, 289 (2), 291, 293, 300, 301, 309, 328, 329, 334, 335, 337, 343, 354, 358, 359, 364, 365, 375, 377, 382, 388, 399, 401, 408, 428, 429, 430, 446, 450, 465, 467, 474, 500, 521 (2), 526 (2), 527 (3), 528 (2), 533 (2), 537, 549 (2), 554, 556, 557, 561, 563, 564, 592, 615, 621, 626, 638, 639, 640, 643, 644, 645, 650, 663, 664, 672, 673, 677, 678, 679, 680, 681, 701, 702, 706, 707, 708, 712, 713, 722, 727, 728, 729, 737, 739, 751, 755, 760, 764, 774, 776

For You to Explore 9, 35, 59, 91, 117, 135, 159, 190, 219, 285, 323, 349, 371, 395, 425, 461, 483, 518, 545, 575, 609, 633, 657, 697, 719, 747

fourth root 568
fraction(s)
 addition 67
 common denominator 68
 convert to decimal 42
 denominator 38
 division 77
 equivalent 37, 38, 67
 from percent 80
 least (lowest) common denominator 67, 68
 in lowest terms 38, 68
 modeling 38
 multiplication 77
 on number line 35, 37
 numerator 38
 reciprocal 77
 subtraction 67
 visualizing 38
free fall 276, 287, 304
freezing temperature of water 131
frequency table 223
fuel efficiency 339
function 425, 434, 435, 436, 440, 445, 446, 496, 500
 backing up 475
 base case 474, 475
 closed form 496
 composition of 441
 domain 445, 446
 exponential 499
 graph of 449, 450
 image of 201, 445
 input 425, 430
 Koch snowflake 503
 linear 468
 machine 429, 430, 434, 436, 483
 multiple inputs 442, 443
 naming 440
 notation 440, 441
 output 425, 430
 periodic 501
 range 445
 recursive 782
 recursive rule 474, 475
 rule 425, 483
 table 461, 465
 transformation notation 441

G

googol 525
googolplex 525
Gore, Al 208
graph(s)
 absolute value 302
 basic 298
 of a circle 286
 in the coordinate plane 265
 cubic growth 299
 cutoff points 401
 of distance-time 324, 333, 334, 335, 336, 364, 366, 371
 drawing with 315
 of an equation 268, 450
 equation of a 298, 299
 of an exponential function 585
 family of 307
 of a function 449, 450
 of inequalities with one variable 395
 intersection of 279, 365, 374
 jiffy 358, 736
 of a line 358
 line of symmetry 737
 of a number 189
 origin 733
 of a parabola 727, 729
 by plotting points 272, 274
 of a quadratic equation 727, 729, 736, 737
 quadratic growth 298
 related quantities 210
 sketch of 313
 of speed-time 336
 square root 301
 of systems of inequalities 756–760
 translation of 305, 728
 turning point 659
 vertex 728, 737
 x-intercept 358, 737
 y-intercept 358, 737
gravity 287
greatest common factor 625, 626, 646
guess-check-generalize method 162, 167
Guess My Rule game 425, 426, 427, 436, 449, 450, 451, 453

H

Habits of Mind 4–7, 246, 253, 564, 565, 768, 769, 770. *See also* Developing Habits of Mind.
Heron of Alexandria 652
Heron's rule 652
high definition television (HDTV) 172
Higher or Lower game 575
histogram 231
Historical Perspective 131, 195, 525, 551, 560, 629, 686
hockey-stick method 467, 474, 591
Hubble Telescope 540

I

identity
 additive 30, 104, 111
 equation 613, 614, 643
 multiplicative 30, 104, 111
if and only if 343, 384
image
 of function 445
 after transformation 201

In-Class Experiment 5 (2), 6 (2), 7 (2), 110, 245, 441, 502, 589, 640, 699, 764
independent 247
independent variable 439
inequality(ies) with one variable 398
   graph 395
   solve 395, 399, 400, 401
input 425, 430, 434, 435, 440
integer(s) 28
   on a number line 37
   $\mathbb{Z}$ 669
interest 476, 578
   earned 476
   owed 476, 484
interquartile range 239
intersection
   of graphs 279, 365, 374
   point 279
inverse
   additive 30, 111, 112
   multiplicative 111
inverse variation 291, 294
   standard equation for 294
irrational number 563–565
iterate a function 598
iteration 782

J

jiffy graphs 358, 736

K

Kasner, Edward 525
Kelvin temperature scale 132
Koch snowflake 503

L

ladder division 82
lattice point 319
law of exponents 520, 521, 526, 527, 528
leading coefficient 775
Leaning Tower of Pisa 276
least (lowest) common denominator 68
life expectancy 238
lightning and thunder 296
like terms 104, 638
   combining 104
line(s)
   of best fit 406, 408, 409, 410
   distinct 382
   equation of 353, 354, 355, 356, 358
   graph of 358
   intersecting 383
   intersection point 365
   parallel 355, 382
   segment 192
   slope of 353, 382
   of symmetry 698, 730, 737
linear equation 149, 355
   solution of 148, 149
linear inequality 763, 764, 765, 768
linear function 461, 468, 589
linear polynomial 637
linear regression 410
linear trend 406, 407
look-and-say sequence 7
lowest terms 38, 68

M

magnitude of a number.
   See absolute value.
managing money 508
maps to 196, 436, 440, 728
margin of error 208
Mathematical Reflections 33, 56, 81, 115, 132, 157, 178, 217, 262, 283, 314, 347, 368, 393, 414, 458, 481, 507, 542, 573, 597, 631, 654, 687, 716, 745, 781
maximum
   in a box-and-whisker plot 237
   of a quadratic function 721
mean 170, 219, 223, 226, 408, 409
median 219, 223, 226, 237
Mersenne prime 630
Mid-Chapter Test 57, 133, 263, 369, 459, 543, 655, 717
Minds in Action 17, 67, 99, 103, 121, 143, 197, 206, 240, 253, 272, 292, 305, 353, 363, 364, 398, 428, 449, 451, 489, 496, 531, 532, 547, 578, 589, 612, 643, 649, 663, 670, 679, 680, 706, 707, 711, 712, 721, 723, 736, 738, 750, 756, 764, 765, 776
minimum
   in a box-and-whisker plot 237
   of a quadratic functions 721
mobile phone service plans 457
mode 219, 223
modeling 93, 438
mole of an element 539
monic
   equation 699, 700
   polynomial 669
monomial 636, 637
multiplication
   algorithm 71
   area model 51
   expansion box 72, 75
   of fractions 77
   rules 51
   symbol 24
   table 9, 23, 26
   vertical number line 51
multiplication algorithms
   expansion box 72, 75
   multiply by closest place value 73
   multiply by five 73
   Russian method 73
   traditional 72
   using lines 74
multiplication table 9, 23, 26
   extending 23
multiplication
   by zero 148
multiplicative
   identity 30, 104, 111
   inverse 111
   property of equality 144, 389

N

naming a function 440, 441
negative exponent 532, 533
negatively associated 255
negative of a number 13
negative number(s) 12
   adding 17
   subtracting 17
Newton's method for finding roots 783
normal form of a polynomial 627, 645
*n*th **root** 569
null set 127
number line 12, 189
   addition 46
   decimals 41
   distance on 202
   fractions on 35, 37
   integers on 35
   multiplication 51
   use to help solve equation 138
number puzzle 159
numbers
   consecutive odd 495
   integers 28
   whole 12
number tricks 91, 92, 99, 103, 106, 108, 113, 135, 136, 147, 444, 492
numerator of fraction 38

O

O'Neill, Thomas P. 117
odd number(s) 635
   consecutive 495
opposite of a number 13, 112
optimization 719, 721
ordered pair 174, 189
origin 189, 193, 733
output 425, 430, 434, 435, 440
   consecutive 465

P

paired comparison in a box-and-whisker plot 241
palindrome 522
parabola 727
   graph of 729
   line of symmetry 730
   maximum 728
   minimum 728
   normal form 729
   vertex 728, 737
   vertex form 729
parallel lines 355, 382
parameter 637
Pythagoreans 551
pedometer 212
percent 333, 491
   as a fraction 80
perfect square 179, 546
perfect square trinomial 674, 678, 740
period 505
periodic function 501
pH, potential of hydrogen 576
pi (π) 551
pitch of a roof 327, 332, 345
place-value part 61
points, collinear 325
point-testers 267, 268
polynomial(s) 636, 637
   addition of 638
   arithmetic of 638, 649
   cubic 637
   degree of 637
   equation 674
   leading coefficient 775
   like terms 638
   linear 637
   monic 669
   normal form of 643, 645
   parameter of 637
   quadratic 637
   quartic 637
   quintic 637
positively associated 255
positive numbers
   adding 17
   subtracting 17

prime
   factorization 545, 646
   notation 197
prime number 233
probability 169
   connect data and 247
property(ies)
   any-order, any-grouping (AOAG) 28, 47, 52, 104, 111
   associative 28, 104, 111
   commutative 28, 104, 111
   distributive 30, 52, 104, 111
   identity 30, 104, 111
   inverse 30, 111
   up-and-over 465, 590
   Zero-Product 112, 148
property of equality
   addition 144, 387
   multiplication 144, 389
Ptolemy 195, 198
Pythagoras 551
Pythagorean theorem 206

Q

quadrant 198
quadratic
   expression 672
   formula 700–703, 711
   growth 298
   polynomial 637, 651
quadratic equation 699.
   See also quadratic function.
   coefficients 780
   general form 700
   graph of 727, 729, 736
   line of symmetry 737
   monic 699, 700
   nonmonic 701
   normal form 729
   parabola 727
   roots of 706, 738
   solve 699
   solve nonmonic 702
   vertex form 729
quadratic function. *See also*
   quadratic equation.
   average of roots 724
   best fit 612
   difference table 773
   maximum 721
   minimum 721
   optimization 719, 721
   roots of 738
   second difference 775
   zeros of 741
quartic polynomial 637
quintic polynomial 637

R

radical 557
   symbol 568
radius of circle 286
range
   of data set 239
   of function 445
   interquartile 239
ray 763
rate
   of change 333, 336
   of data transfer 339
ratio table 534
rational number(s) 551, 561–565
   $\mathbb{Q}$ 669
real number(s)
   $\mathbb{R}$ 669
recipe 14
reciprocal 77
rectangle
   area of 493
recursive function
   end behavior 782
   fixed points 782
   initial value 782
   iteration 782
   seed value 782
recursive rule 474, 475
   base case 474, 475
   backing up 475
Reflect and Write 251, 772
repeating decimal 43
representing data
   linear trend 406, 407
   scatter plot 406
reversible operation 120
reversing the operation 121
   backtracking 117, 121
rise 324
rise-to-run ratio 323
roots of a quadratic 706, 732, 737, 738
rule of 72 583
rule(s)
   of algebra 613
   of exponents 526, 527, 528
   extension of a 20
   for a function 435
   for radicals 570
   for square roots 570
rules of arithmetic 28, 104, 110
   any-order, any-grouping (AOAG) 28
   associative property, addition 28
   associative property, multiplication 28

commutative property, addition 28
commutative property, multiplication 28
distributive 30, 52
identity 30
inverse 30
using words 110
using symbols 110
run 324
Russian method for multiplying 73
Ryan, Nolan 734

S

San Francisco, California 294
earthquake 294
satisfy an equation 265, 268, 280
savings account 476
scatter plot 253
scientific
formula 98
notation 537
second differences 774–777
of quadratic functions 775
simplify
an expression 103, 352, 530
square root 560
sketch of a graph 313
sky diving 124
slope(s) 327, 329
between points 327, 328, 335, 343, 353
constant 330
of intersecting lines 383
of a line 353, 382
of parallel lines 382
rise 327
rise over run 329
run 327
undefined 329
Social Security number 518
solution(s)
of an equation 126, 269
of an inequality 399, 400
of linear equations 148, 149
ordered pairs as solutions 174
solution set 127
solve equation(s) 143, 162
additive property of equality 387
basic moves 144, 404
by false position method 164, 485
by graphing 750
by guess, check, generalize 162, 167
multiplicative property of equality 389

nonmonic quadratic 702
for one variable in terms of another 166, 172, 173, 352
quadratic 699
solve inequality(ies)
with one variable 395
with two variables 755–760
solve system of equations 391, 750
by elimination 387
by substitution 374, 375, 376
solve system of inequalities 755
speed-time graph 336
speed 74, 333
spreadsheet 497, 498
square a number 124, 155, 517
square root 42, 547, 548, 565, 568
approximate 560
Babylonian method of finding 599
calculate 598
conventions 556
graph of square root equation 301
simplify 560
square root sign. *See* radical.
standard equation
for direct variation 290
for inverse variation 294
standard form of a polynomial. *See* normal form.
Standardized Test Prep 15, 22, 25, 32, 40, 44, 50, 54, 66, 69, 75, 80, 96, 102, 108, 114, 125, 130, 142, 147, 152, 155, 165, 171, 176, 201 (2), 209, 216, 226, 227, 229, 234, 235, 241, 242, 243, 260, 271, 278, 281, 297, 304, 332, 340, 344, 345, 357, 361, 367, 380, 385, 391, 405, 413, 433, 439, 444, 448, 457, 464, 472, 479, 495, 505, 524, 529, 540, 554, 567, 588, 596, 618, 624, 629, 641, 648, 653, 668, 676, 685, 704, 710, 715, 726, 734 (2), 744, 754, 762, 771, 780
stem-and-leaf display 232
subscripts 329
substitution
in an equation 272
to solve systems of equations 374, 375, 376
subtraction 13
algorithms 61, 64, 65
definition of 148

of fractions 67
of negative numbers 17
of positive numbers 17
subtraction algorithms
by counting up 65
subtract some more 64
using columns 64
Sudoku 5
Sum and Product
Identity 669, 708
Theorem 708
Sum of the Roots Theorem 709
summand 11
symmetry, line of 698, 730
system of equations 378, 387
infinitely many solutions of 391
no solution 391
solve 391, 750
solve by elimination 387
solve by substitution 374, 375, 376
system of inequalities
solve by graphing 756–760

T

Take It Further 11, 25, 31, 32, 36, 43 (2), 44, 54, 69 (3), 74, 75, 79, 114, 125 (2), 129, 137, 142, 148 (2), 166, 170, 174, 175 (2), 177, 199 (3), 209, 228 (2), 229 (2), 242, 249, 261, 278, 280, 296, 303, 304 (2), 313 (2), 332, 340, 341, 346, 357 (2), 362, 381, 391 (2), 396, 402, 404, 432, 447 (2), 448, 455, 485, 486, 495, 504, 506 (2), 509, 522 (2), 554, 555, 558, 566 (2), 567, 583, 611, 616, 617, 618 (2), 628, 634, 641, 647, 651, 652 (2), 660, 666, 674, 683, 705 (2), 709, 710 (4), 720, 734, 744, 747, 753, 761 (2), 762, 770, 772, 780 (2), 783
television
high definition 172
standard width, height 174
temperature conversion formula 131
temperature scale 131
Celsius 12
Fahrenheit 12
term 104
tetrahedron 655
theorem 148
thermometer 12, 131
third quartile 237
thunder and lightning 296

TI-Nspire™ Technology Handbook 239, 398, 400, 402, 410, 431, 443, 453, 455, 475, 476, 499, 500, 501, 547, 584, 598, 698, 722, 726, 751, 760
toothpick puzzles 5
transformation 196
　image for 201
　notation 440, 441
transforming expressions 625
translation of a graph 305, 728
trapezoid 100
　area of 100
trinomial 674
turning point of a graph 659
two-variable data 253–261
two-way frequency table 246, 247, 248

U

United States
　census 411
　debt 413
　population 411
　presidents' ages 318
up-and-over property 465, 590

V

variable 93, 100
variation
　direct 289, 290
　inverse 291, 294
vertex form of quadratic function 729
vertex of a parabola 728, 737

W

What's Wrong Here? 39, 44, 48, 49, 96, 101, 153, 155, 156, 166, 167, 171, 208, 212, 221, 310, 351, 377, 404, 471, 567, 652, 771
whole numbers 12
wireless phone plans 415
Write About It 15, 16, 40, 60, 65, 70, 83, 119, 124, 137, 161, 200, 201, 207, 208, 213, 221, 243, 244, 258, 261, 271, 288, 295, 304, 312, 326, 341, 357, 360, 367 (3), 380, 385 (2), 386, 403, 410, 439, 494, 505, 522, 535, 546, 576 (2), 581, 587, 594, 617, 641, 642, 651, 652, 666, 674, 676, 684, 685, 698, 705, 733, 735, 743 (2), 747

X

x-**axis** 189
x-**coordinate** 189
x-**intercept** 358, 737

Y

y-**axis** 189
y-**coordinate** 189
y-**intercept** 358, 737

Z

zero 10, 26, 77
　as an exponent 531, 533
　multiply by 148
　of a quadratic function 732
Zero-Product Property 112, 619, 620, 657
ZIP Codes 530

Acknowledgments

Staff Credits
The Pearson people on the CME Project team—representing design, editorial, editorial services, digital product development, publishing services, and technical operations—are listed below. Bold type denotes the core team members.

Ernest Albanese, Scott Andrews, Carolyn Artin, Michael Avidon, Margaret Banker, Suzanne Biron, Beth Blumberg, Stacie Cartwright, Carolyn Chappo, Casey Clark, Bob Craton, Jason Cuoco, Sheila DeFazio, Patty Fagan, **Frederick Fellows**, **Patti Fromkin**, Paul J. Gagnon, Cynthia Harvey, Gillian Kahn, Jonathan Kier, Jennifer King, Elizabeth Krieble, Sara Levendusky, Lisa Lin, Carolyn Lock, Clay Martin, **Carolyn McGuire**, Rich McMahon, Eve Melnechuk, Cynthia Metallides, **Hope Morley**, **Jen Paley**, Linda Punskovsky, Mairead Reddin, Marcy Rose, Rashid Ross, Carol Roy, Jewel Simmons, Ted Smykal, Laura Smyth, Kara Stokes, Richard Sullivan, Tiffany Taylor-Sullivan, Catherine Terwilliger, Mark Tricca, Lauren Van Wart, Paula Vergith, **Joe Will**, **Kristin Winters**, Allison Wyss

Additional Credits
Niki Birbilis, Gina Choe, Christine Nevola, Jill A. Ort, Lillian Pelaggi, Deborah Savona

Cover Design and Illustration
9 Surf Studios

Cover Photography
Mike Chew/Corbis; Ajosch/AFP/Getty Images

Illustration
Kerry Cashman, Rich McMahon, Jen Paley, Ted Smykal

Photography
Chapter 1: Pages 2–3, Randy Faris/Corbis; **8**, Jason Hawkes/Corbis; **12**, Thom Lang/Corbis; **25**, Kyodo News; **29**, Javier Pierini/Digital Vision/GettyImages; **33**, Atlanpic/Alamy; **34**, Clement McCarthy/Alamy; **39**, Robert Estall photo agency/Alamy; **56 Inset**, Rubberball/Royalty Free; **56 BR**, Clement McCarthy/Alamy; **71 BR**, Pablo San Juan/Corbis; **71 inset**, Mike McQueen/Corbis; **74**, AP Photo/Charlie Riedel; **83**, AP Photo/Austin Daily Herald, Eric Johnson.

Chapter 2: Pages 88–89, Darrin Zammit Lupi /Reuters/Corbis; **90l**, JUPITERIMAGE/Brand X/Alamy; **90r**, JUPITERIMAGE/Brand X/Alamy; **98**, Larry Williams/Corbis; **101**, Beth Perkins/Getty Images; **108**, Robert Fried Photography; **115**, Ariel Skelley/Corbis; **116**, Anthony West/Corbis; **124**, Handout/Reuters/Corbis; **129**, Design Pics Inc./Alamy; **131**, Mary Evans Picture Library/Alamy; **132**, Stefan Schuetz/zefa/Corbis; **134**, Bob Elsdale/Getty Images; **136**, William Manning/Corbis; **155**, Paul A. Souders/Corbis; **157**, Bob Elsdale/Getty Images; **158**, Jim McIsaac/Getty Images; **160**, David Young-Wolff/Photo Edit; **170**, John Eder/Getty Images; **172**, Gene Blevins/LA Daily News/Corbis; **178**, VALDRIN XHEMAJ/epa/Corbis.

Chapter 3: Pages 186–187, Lester Lefkowitz/Getty Images; **188**, Richard T. Nowitz/Corbis; **192**, Farrell Grehan/Corbis; **195**, Erich Lessing/Art Resource, NY; **196**, Kelly-Mooney Photography/Corbis; **198**, Bibliothèque Nationale, Paris, France, Lauros / Giraudon / The Bridgeman Art Library; **206**, Joseph Sohm/Visions of America/Corbis; **208**, Digital Art/Corbis; **212**, Mark Harmel/Getty Images; **217**, Richard T. Nowitz/Corbis; **218–219**, Edgar Mueller; **228**, Paul Wood/Alamy; **240**, Matthias Kulka/zefa/Corbis; **243**, Elsa/Getty Images; **262**, Edgar Mueller; **364**, Ausloeser/zefa/Corbis; **271**, Sam Jordash/Getty Images; **276**, Ken Welsh/Alamy; **279**, TIMLI/Photonica/Getty Images, Inc.; **281**, Victor Habbick Visions/Photo Researchers, Inc.; **283**, Varie/Alt/Corbis; **284**, James L. Amos/Corbis; **287**, PhotoAlto/SuperStock; **294**, Hulton Archive/Getty Images; **296**, Ralph H. Wetmore II/Getty Images, Inc.; **298**, Jim West/Alamy; **303**, Jeff Greenberg/Photo Edit; **311**, Jamie Squire/Getty Images, Inc.; **314**, James L. Amos/Corbis.

Chapter 4: Pages 320–321, Team Russell/ImageState/International Stock Photography Ltd.; **320–321 background**, Craig Tuttle/Corbis; **322**, David R. Frazier Photolibrary, Inc./Alamy; **323tl**, Dennis Hallinan/Alamy; **323tr**, JG Photography/Alamy; **323bl**, Wes Thompson/Corbis; **323br**, Reino Hanninen/Alamy; **329**, Craig Lovell/Corbis; **340**, Michael Steele/Getty Images; **346**, Kara Stokes; **347**, David R. Frazier Photolibrary, Inc./Alamy; **348**, Kay Nietfeld/epa/Corbis; **350**, Jeff Greenberg/Photo Edit **368**, John Kelly/Getty Images; **370**, Brian Bahr/Getty Images, Inc.; **379**, Grant Faint/The Image Bank/Getty Images, Inc.; **382**, tom viggars/Alamy; **391**, Simon Marcus/Corbis; **393**, AP Photo/Sue Ogrocki; **394**, Gunter Marx Photography/Corbis; **406**, Ted Horowitz/Corbis; **410**, AP Photo/Glodow Nead Communications, George Nikitin; **414**, Gunter Marx Photography/Corbis; **415**, Charles Gullung/zefa/Corbis.

Chapter 5: Pages 422–423 Charles O'Rear/Corbis; **422 inset**, Hulton Archive/Getty Images, Inc.; **424**, Digital Vision Ltd; **433**, Ingram Publishing/Alamy; **458**, Digital Vision Ltd; **460**, Kara Stokes; **462tr**, Getty Images, Inc.; **462bl**, Joe McDonald/Corbis; **471**, Buzz Pictures/Alamy; **481**, Kara Stokes; **482**, Kara Stokes; **507**, Kara Stokes; **509**, Gabe Palmer/Corbis.

Chapter 6: Pages 514–515, Juergen Berger/Science Photo Library; **516**, Dr. Dennis Kunkel/Visuals Unlimited/Getty Images; **525**, Roger Bamber/Alamy; **530**, Rudy Sulgan/Corbis; **537**, Planetary Photojournal; **540 tr**, Editorial/Getty Images; **540 inset**, AP Images/NASA; **542**, Peter Weber/Getty Images; **544**, Gary Conner/Photo Edit, Inc.; **551**, George Steinmetz/Corbis; **560 both**, Carolyn Chappo; **573**, Gary Conner/Photo Edit, Inc.; **574**, Custom Medical Stock Photo; **582**, Car Culture/Corbis; **597**, Custom Medical Stock Photo; **599**, Alfred Pasieka/Science Photo Library.

Chapter 7: Pages 606–607, Cliff Leight/Getty Images; **608b**, Skyscan/Corbis; **608 inset**, Comstock/Veer; **630**, Bridgeman-Giraudon/Art Resource, NY; **631**, Skyscan/Corbis; **631 inset**, Comstock/Veer; **632**, Bertrand Collet/Alamy; **642 frame**, Photodisc/SuperStock; **642**, Rob Lewine/Corbis; **649**, Digital Vision Ltd./SuperStock; **654**, ImageDJ/Alamy; **656**, Hope Morley; **667**, EuroStyle Graphics/Alamy; **686**, public domain; **687**, Hope Morley;

Chapter 8: Pages 694–695, Martin Rugner/Age Fotostock; **696,** DAJ/Getty Images, Inc.; **711,** Design Pics, Inc./Alamy; **716,** DAJ/Getty Images, Inc.; **718,** Atlantide Phototravel/Corbis; **721,** Car Culture/Getty Images, Inc.; **727,** R. Ian Lloyd/Masterfile; **733,** Frank Bodenmueller/zefa/Corbis; **739,** Lester Lefkowitz/Getty Images, Inc.; **745,** Robert Glusic/Corbis; **756,** Panoramic Images/Getty Images, Inc.; **781,** Robert E. Daemmrich/Getty Images, Inc.; **783,** Kara Stokes.

Text Acknowledgments

6, "Dodge Ball" excerpted from *The Heart of Mathematics,* 2nd Edition by Edward Burger and Michael Starbird. Copyright © 2005 by Key College Publishing, Emeryville, California. Used by permission; **208,** 2000 Presidential Election Poll Results. Copyright © International Communications Research. Used by permission; **223,** Pop vs. Soda Poll Results. popvssoda.com. Copyright © Alan McConchie. Used by permission; **593,** Adapted *Futurama* storyline from "A Fishful of Dollars" by Patrick M. Verrone. Copyright © 1999 20th Century Fox/FOX Broadcasting Company; **596,** "United Nations Population Estimates" from www.un.org. Copyright © 2000–2007 by The United Nations; Page **653,** Math problem written by Ed Barbeau. Reprinted by permission of Ed Barbeau, Professor Emeritus of Mathematics, University of Toronto.

Note: Every effort has been made to locate the copyright owner of the material reprinted in this book. Omissions brought to our attention will be corrected in subsequent editions.

Additional Credits

Chapter 1: Whole chapter taken from Chapter 1 of *CME Project: Algebra 1.*

Chapter 2: Whole chapter taken from Chapter 2 of *CME Project: Algebra 1.*

Chapter 3: Lessons 3.01 through 3.06, 3.08, and 3.11 through 3.18 taken from Chapter 3 of *CME Project: Algebra 1.* Lessons 3.07, 3.09, and 3.10 taken from *CME Project: Algebra 1 Common Core Additional Lessons.*

Chapter 4: Whole chapter taken from Chapter 4 of *CME Project: Algebra 1.*

Chapter 5: Whole chapter taken from Chapter 5 of *CME Project: Algebra 1.*

Chapter 6: Lessons 6.01 through 6.09 and 6.11 through 6.15 taken from Chapter 6 of *CME Project: Algebra 1.* Lesson 6.10 taken from *CME Project: Algebra 1 Common Core Additional Lessons.*

Chapter 7: Whole chapter taken from Chapter 7 of *CME Project: Algebra 1.*

Chapter 8: Lessons 8.01 through 8.11 and 8.13 taken from Chapter 8 of *CME Project: Algebra 1.* Lesson 8.12 taken from *CME Project: Algebra 1 Common Core Additional Lessons.*